University Casebook Series

December, 1980

ACCOUNTING AND THE LAW, Fourth Edition (1978), with Problems Pamphlet (Successor to Dohr, Phillips, Thompson & Warren)

George C. Thompson, Professor, Columbia University Graduate School of Business.
Robert Whitman, Professor of Law, University of Connecticut.
Ellis L. Phillips, Jr., Member of the New York Bar.
William C. Warren, Professor of Law Emeritus, Columbia University.

ACCOUNTING FOR LAWYERS, MATERIALS ON (1980)

David R. Herwitz, Professor of Law, Harvard University.

ADMINISTRATIVE LAW, Seventh Edition (1979), with 1979 Problems Supplement (Supplement edited in association with Paul R. Verkuil, Dean and Professor of Law, Tulane University)

Walter Gellhorn, University Professor Emeritus, Columbia University.
Clark Byse, Professor of Law, Harvard University.
Peter L. Strauss, Professor of Law, Columbia University.

ADMIRALTY, Second Edition (1978), with Statute and Rule Supplement

Jo Desha Lucas, Professor of Law, University of Chicago.

ADVOCACY, see also Lawyering Process

ADVOCACY, INTRODUCTION TO, Third Edition (1981)

Board of Student Advisers, Harvard Law School.

AGENCY, see also Enterprise Organization

AGENCY–ASSOCIATIONS–EMPLOYMENT–PARTNERSHIPS, Second Edition (1977)

Abridgement from Conard, Knauss & Siegel's Enterprise Organization.

ANTITRUST AND REGULATORY ALTERNATIVES (1977), Fifth Edition

Louis B. Schwartz, Professor of Law, University of Pennsylvania.
John J. Flynn, Professor of Law, University of Utah.

ANTITRUST SUPPLEMENT—SELECTED STATUTES AND RELATED MATERIALS (1977)

John J. Flynn, Professor of Law, University of Utah.

BIOGRAPHY OF A LEGAL DISPUTE, THE: An Introduction to American Civil Procedure (1968)

Marc A. Franklin, Professor of Law, Stanford University.

BUSINESS ORGANIZATION, see also Enterprise Organization

BUSINESS PLANNING (1966), with 1980 Supplement

David R. Herwitz, Professor of Law, Harvard University.

BUSINESS TORTS (1972)

Milton Handler, Professor of Law Emeritus, Columbia University.

CIVIL PROCEDURE, see Procedure

CLINIC, see also Lawyering Process

COMMERCIAL AND CONSUMER TRANSACTIONS, Second Edition (1978)

William D. Warren, Dean of the School of Law, University of California, Los Angeles.
William E. Hogan, Professor of Law, Cornell University.
Robert L. Jordan, Professor of Law, University of California, Los Angeles.

COMMERCIAL LAW, CASES & MATERIALS ON, Third Edition (1976)

E. Allan Farnsworth, Professor of Law, Cornell University.
John Honnold, Professor of Law, University of Pennsylvania.

COMMERCIAL PAPER, Second Edition (1976)

E. Allan Farnsworth, Professor of Law, Columbia University.

COMMERCIAL PAPER AND BANK DEPOSITS AND COLLECTIONS (1967), with Statutory Supplement.

William D. Hawkland, Professor of Law, University of Illinois.

COMMERCIAL TRANSACTIONS—Text, Cases and Problems, Fourth Edition (1968)

Robert Braucher, Professor of Law Emeritus, Harvard University, and
The late Arthur E. Sutherland, Jr., Professor of Law, Harvard University.

COMPARATIVE LAW, Fourth Edition (1980)

Rudolf B. Schlesinger, Professor of Law, Hastings College of the Law.

COMPETITIVE PROCESS, LEGAL REGULATION OF THE, Second Edition (1979), with Statutory Supplement

Edmund W. Kitch, Professor of Law, University of Chicago.
Harvey S. Perlman, Professor of Law, University of Virginia.

CONFLICT OF LAWS, Seventh Edition (1978), with 1980 Supplement

Willis L. M. Reese, Professor of Law, Columbia University, and
Maurice Rosenberg, Professor of Law, Columbia University.

CONSTITUTIONAL LAW, Fifth Edition (1977), with 1980 Supplement

Edward L. Barrett, Jr., Professor of Law, University of California, Davis.

CONSTITUTIONAL LAW, Tenth Edition (1980)

Gerald Gunther, Professor of Law, Stanford University.

CONSTITUTIONAL LAW, INDIVIDUAL RIGHTS IN, Third Edition (1981)

Gerald Gunther, Professor of Law, Stanford University.

CONTRACT LAW AND ITS APPLICATION, Second Edition (1977)

Addison Mueller, Professor of Law Emeritus, University of California, Los Angeles.
Arthur I. Rosett, Professor of Law, University of California, Los Angeles.

UNIVERSITY CASEBOOK SERIES—Continued

CONTRACT LAW, STUDIES IN, Second Edition (1977)

Edward J. Murphy, Professor of Law, University of Notre Dame.
Richard E. Speidel, Professor of Law, University of Virginia.

CONTRACTS, Third Edition (1977)

John P. Dawson, Professor of Law Emeritus, Harvard University, and
William Burnett Harvey, Professor of Law and Political Science, Boston University.

CONTRACTS, Third Edition (1980), with Statutory Supplement

E. Allan Farnsworth, Professor of Law, Columbia University.
William F. Young, Professor of Law, Columbia University.

CONTRACTS, Second Edition (1978), with Statutory and Administrative Law Supplement (1978)

Ian R. Macneil, Professor of Law, Cornell University.

COPYRIGHT, Unfair Competition, and Other Topics Bearing on the Protection of Literary, Musical, and Artistic Works, Third Edition (1978)

Benjamin Kaplan, Professor of Law Emeritus, Harvard University, and
Ralph S. Brown, Jr., Professor of Law, Yale University.

CORPORATE FINANCE, Second Edition (1979), with 1980 New Developments Supplement

Victor Brudney, Professor of Law, Harvard University.
Marvin A. Chirelstein, Professor of Law, Yale University.

CORPORATE READJUSTMENTS AND REORGANIZATIONS (1976)

Walter J. Blum, Professor of Law, University of Chicago.
Stanley A. Kaplan, Professor of Law, University of Chicago.

CORPORATION LAW, BASIC, Second Edition (1979), with Documentary Supplement

Detlev F. Vagts, Professor of Law, Harvard University.

CORPORATIONS, see also Enterprise Organization

CORPORATIONS, Fifth Edition—Unabridged (1980)

William L. Cary, Professor of Law, Columbia University.
Melvin Aron Eisenberg, Professor of Law, University of California, Berkeley.

CORPORATIONS, Fifth Edition—Abridged (1980)

William L. Cary, Professor of Law, Columbia University.
Melvin Aron Eisenberg, Professor of Law, University of California, Berkeley.

CORPORATIONS, THE LAW OF: WHAT CORPORATE LAWYERS DO (1976)

Jan G. Deutsch, Professor of Law, Yale University.
Joseph J. Bianco, Professor of Law, Yeshiva University.

CORPORATIONS COURSE GAME PLAN (1975)

David R. Herwitz, Professor of Law, Harvard University.

CREDIT TRANSACTIONS AND CONSUMER PROTECTION (1976)

John Honnold, Professor of Law, University of Pennsylvania.

CREDITORS' RIGHTS, see also Debtor-Creditor Law

UNIVERSITY CASEBOOK SERIES—Continued

CRIMINAL JUSTICE, THE ADMINISTRATION OF, Second Edition (1969)

Francis C. Sullivan, Professor of Law, Louisiana State University.
Paul Hardin III, Professor of Law, Duke University.
John Huston, Professor of Law, University of Washington.
Frank R. Lacy, Professor of Law, University of Oregon.
Daniel E. Murray, Professor of Law, University of Miami.
George W. Pugh, Professor of Law, Louisiana State University.

CRIMINAL JUSTICE ADMINISTRATION AND RELATED PROCESSES, Successor Edition (1976), with 1980 Supplement

Frank W. Miller, Professor of Law, Washington University.
Robert O. Dawson, Professor of Law, University of Texas.
George E. Dix, Professor of Law, University of Texas.
Raymond I. Parnas, Professor of Law, University of California, Davis.

CRIMINAL JUSTICE, LEADING CONSTITUTIONAL CASES ON (1980)

Lloyd L. Weinreb, Professor of Law, Harvard University.

CRIMINAL LAW, Second Edition (1979)

Fred E. Inbau, Professor of Law Emeritus, Northwestern University.
James R. Thompson, Professor of Law Emeritus, Northwestern University.
Andre A. Moenssens, Professor of Law, University of Richmond.

CRIMINAL LAW, Third Edition (1980)

Lloyd L. Weinreb, Professor of Law, Harvard University.

CRIMINAL LAW AND ITS ADMINISTRATION (1940), with 1956 Supplement

Jerome Michael, late Professor of Law, Columbia University, and
Herbert Wechsler, Professor of Law, Columbia University.

CRIMINAL LAW AND PROCEDURE, Fifth Edition (1977)

Rollin M. Perkins, Professor of Law Emeritus, University of California, Hastings College of the Law.
Ronald N. Boyce, Professor of Law, University of Utah.

CRIMINAL PROCEDURE, Second Edition (1980)

Fred E. Inbau, Professor of Law Emeritus, Northwestern University.
James R. Thompson, Professor of Law Emeritus, Northwestern University.
James B. Haddad, Professor of Law, Northwestern University.
James B. Zagel, Chief, Criminal Justice Division, Office of Attorney General of Illinois.
Gary L. Starkman, Assistant U. S. Attorney, Northern District of Illinois.

CRIMINAL PROCEDURE, CONSTITUTIONAL (1977), with 1980 Supplement

James E. Scarboro, Professor of Law, University of Colorado.
James B. White, Professor of Law, University of Chicago.

CRIMINAL PROCESS, Third Edition (1978), with 1979 Supplement

Lloyd L. Weinreb, Professor of Law, Harvard University.

DAMAGES, Second Edition (1952)

Charles T. McCormick, late Professor of Law, University of Texas, and
William F. Fritz, late Professor of Law, University of Texas.

DEBTOR–CREDITOR LAW (1974), with 1978 Case-Statutory Supplement

William D. Warren, Dean of the School of Law, University of California, Los Angeles.
William E. Hogan, Professor of Law, Cornell University.

DECEDENTS' ESTATES (1971)

Max Rheinstein, late Professor of Law Emeritus, University of Chicago.
Mary Ann Glendon, Professor of Law, Boston College.

DECEDENTS' ESTATES AND TRUSTS, Fifth Edition (1977)

John Ritchie, Professor of Law Emeritus, University of Virginia.
Neill H. Alford, Jr., Professor of Law, University of Virginia.
Richard W. Effland, Professor of Law, Arizona State University.

DECEDENTS' ESTATES AND TRUSTS (1968)

Howard R. Williams, Professor of Law, Stanford University.

DOMESTIC RELATIONS, see also Family Law

DOMESTIC RELATIONS, Third Edition (1978) with 1980 Supplement

Walter Wadlington, Professor of Law, University of Virginia.
Monrad G. Paulsen, Dean of the Law School, Yeshiva University.

DYNAMICS OF AMERICAN LAW, THE: Courts, the Legal Process and Freedom of Expression (1968)

Marc A. Franklin, Professor of Law, Stanford University.

ELECTRONIC MASS MEDIA, Second Edition (1979)

William K. Jones, Professor of Law, Columbia University.

ENTERPRISE ORGANIZATION, Second Edition (1977), with 1979 Statutory and Formulary Supplement

Alfred F. Conard, Professor of Law, University of Michigan.
Robert L. Knauss, Dean of the School of Law, Vanderbilt University.
Stanley Siegel, Professor of Law, University of California, Los Angeles.

EQUITY AND EQUITABLE REMEDIES (1975)

Edward D. Re, Adjunct Professor of Law, St. John's University.

EQUITY, RESTITUTION AND DAMAGES, Second Edition (1974)

Robert Childres, late Professor of Law, Northwestern University.
William F. Johnson, Jr., Professor of Law, New York University.

ESTATE PLANNING PROBLEMS (1973), with 1977 Supplement

David Westfall, Professor of Law, Harvard University.

ETHICS, see Legal Profession, and Professional Responsibility

EVIDENCE, Fourth Edition (1981)

David W. Louisell, late Professor of Law, University of California, Berkeley.
John Kaplan, Professor of Law, Stanford University.
Jon R. Waltz, Professor of Law, Northwestern University.

EVIDENCE, Sixth Edition (1973), with 1980 Supplement

John M. Maguire, late Professor of Law Emeritus, Harvard University.
Jack B. Weinstein, Professor of Law, Columbia University.
James H. Chadbourn, Professor of Law, Harvard University.
John H. Mansfield, Professor of Law, Harvard University.

UNIVERSITY CASEBOOK SERIES—Continued

EVIDENCE (1968)

Francis C. Sullivan, Professor of Law, Louisiana State University.
Paul Hardin, III, Professor of Law, Duke University.

FAMILY LAW, see also Domestic Relations

FAMILY LAW (1978), with 1981 Supplement

Judith C. Areen, Professor of Law, Georgetown University.

FAMILY LAW: STATUTORY MATERIALS, Second Edition (1974)

Monrad G. Paulsen, Dean of the Law School, Yeshiva University.
Walter Wadlington, Professor of Law, University of Virginia.

FEDERAL COURTS, Sixth Edition (1976), with 1980 Supplement

Charles T. McCormick, late Professor of Law, University of Texas.
James H. Chadbourn, Professor of Law, Harvard University, and
Charles Alan Wright, Professor of Law, University of Texas.

FEDERAL COURTS AND THE FEDERAL SYSTEM, Hart and Wechsler's Second Edition (1973), with 1981 Supplement

Paul M. Bator, Professor of Law, Harvard University.
Paul J. Mishkin, Professor of Law, University of California, Berkeley.
David L. Shapiro, Professor of Law, Harvard University.
Herbert Wechsler, Professor of Law, Columbia University.

FEDERAL PUBLIC LAND AND RESOURCES LAW (1981)

George C. Coggins, Professor of Law, University of Kansas.
Charles F. Wilkinson, Professor of Law, University of Oregon.

FEDERAL RULES OF CIVIL PROCEDURE, 1980 Edition

FEDERAL TAXATION, see Taxation

FOOD AND DRUG LAW (1980)

Richard A. Merrill, Dean of the School of Law, University of Virginia.
Peter Barton Hutt, Esq.

FUTURE INTERESTS (1958)

Philip Mechem, late Professor of Law Emeritus, University of Pennsylvania.

FUTURE INTERESTS (1970)

Howard R. Williams, Professor of Law, Stanford University.

FUTURE INTERESTS AND ESTATE PLANNING (1961), with 1962 Supplement

W. Barton Leach, late Professor of Law, Harvard University.
James K. Logan, formerly Dean of the Law School, University of Kansas.

GOVERNMENT CONTRACTS, FEDERAL (1975), with 1980 Supplement

John W. Whelan, Professor of Law, Hastings College of the Law.
Robert S. Pasley, Professor of Law Emeritus, Cornell University.

HOUSING—THE ILL-HOUSED (1971)

Peter W. Martin, Professor of Law, Cornell University.

INJUNCTIONS (1972)

Owen M. Fiss, Professor of Law, Yale University.

UNIVERSITY CASEBOOK SERIES—Continued

INSTITUTIONAL INVESTORS, 1978

David L. Ratner, Professor of Law, Cornell University.

INSURANCE (1971)

William F. Young, Professor of Law, Columbia University.

INTERNATIONAL LAW, see also Transnational Legal Problems and United Nations Law

INTERNATIONAL LEGAL SYSTEM (1973), with Documentary Supplement

Noyes E. Leech, Professor of Law, University of Pennsylvania.
Covey T. Oliver, Professor of Law, University of Pennsylvania.
Joseph Modeste Sweeney, Professor of Law, Tulane University.

INTERNATIONAL TRADE AND INVESTMENT, REGULATION OF (1970)

Carl H. Fulda, late Professor of Law, University of Texas.
Warren F. Schwartz, Professor of Law, University of Virginia.

INTERNATIONAL TRANSACTIONS AND RELATIONS (1960)

Milton Katz, Professor of Law, Harvard University, and
Kingman Brewster, Jr., Professor of Law, Harvard University.

INTRODUCTION TO LAW, see also Legal Method, On Law in Courts, and Dynamics of American Law

INTRODUCTION TO THE STUDY OF LAW (1970)

E. Wayne Thode, late Professor of Law, University of Utah.
Leon Lebowitz, Professor of Law, University of Texas.
Lester J. Mazor, Professor of Law, University of Utah.

JUDICIAL CODE and Rules of Procedure in the Federal Courts with Excerpts from the Criminal Code, 1981 Edition

Henry M. Hart, Jr., late Professor of Law, Harvard University.
Herbert Wechsler, Professor of Law, Columbia University.

JURISPRUDENCE (Temporary Edition Hardbound) (1949)

Lon L. Fuller, Professor of Law Emeritus, Harvard University.

JUVENILE COURTS (1967)

Hon. Orman W. Ketcham, Juvenile Court of the District of Columbia.
Monrad G. Paulsen, Dean of the Law School, Yeshiva University.

JUVENILE JUSTICE PROCESS, Second Edition (1976), with 1980 Supplement

Frank W. Miller, Professor of Law, Washington University.
Robert O. Dawson, Professor of Law, University of Texas.
George E. Dix, Professor of Law, University of Texas.
Raymond I. Parnas, Professor of Law, University of California, Davis.

LABOR LAW, Eighth Edition (1977), with Statutory Supplement, and 1979 Case Supplement

Archibald Cox, Professor of Law, Harvard University, and
Derek C. Bok, President, Harvard University.
Robert A. Gorman, Professor of Law, University of Pennsylvania.

LABOR LAW (1968), with Statutory Supplement and 1974 Case Supplement

Clyde W. Summers, Professor of Law, University of Pennsylvania.
Harry H. Wellington, Dean of the Law School, Yale University.

UNIVERSITY CASEBOOK SERIES—Continued

LAND FINANCING, Second Edition (1977)

Norman Penney, Professor of Law, Cornell University.
Richard F. Broude, of the California Bar.

LAW AND MEDICINE (1980)

Walter Wadlington, Professor of Law and Professor of Legal Medicine, University of Virginia.
Jon R. Waltz, Professor of Law, Northwestern University.
Roger B. Dworkin, Professor of Law, Indiana University, and Professor of Biomedical History, University of Washington.

LAW, LANGUAGE AND ETHICS (1972)

William R. Bishin, Professor of Law, University of Southern California.
Christopher D. Stone, Professor of Law, University of Southern California.

LAWYERING PROCESS (1978), with Civil Problem Supplement and Criminal Problem Supplement

Gary Bellow, Professor of Law, Harvard University.
Bea Moulton, Professor of Law, Arizona State University.

LEGAL METHOD

Harry W. Jones, Professor of Law Emeritus, Columbia University.
John M. Kernochan, Professor of Law, Columbia University.
Arthur W. Murphy, Professor of Law, Columbia University.

LEGAL METHODS (1969)

Robert N. Covington, Professor of Law, Vanderbilt University.
E. Blythe Stason, late Professor of Law, Vanderbilt University.
John W. Wade, Professor of Law, Vanderbilt University.
Elliott E. Cheatham, late Professor of Law, Vanderbilt University.
Theodore A. Smedley, Professor of Law, Vanderbilt University.

LEGAL PROFESSION (1970)

Samuel D. Thurman, Dean of the College of Law, University of Utah.
Ellis L. Phillips, Jr., Professor of Law, Columbia University.
Elliott E. Cheatham, late Professor of Law, Vanderbilt University.

LEGISLATION, Third Edition (1973)

Horace E. Read, late Vice President, Dalhousie University.
John W. MacDonald, Professor of Law Emeritus, Cornell Law School.
Jefferson B. Fordham, Professor of Law, University of Utah, and
William J. Pierce, Professor of Law, University of Michigan.

LEGISLATIVE AND ADMINISTRATIVE PROCESSES (1976)

Hans A. Linde, Professor of Law, University of Oregon.
George Bunn, Professor of Law, University of Wisconsin.

LOCAL GOVERNMENT LAW, Revised Edition (1975)

Jefferson B. Fordham, Professor of Law, University of Utah.

MASS MEDIA LAW (1976), with 1979 Supplement

Marc A. Franklin, Professor of Law, Stanford University.

MENTAL HEALTH PROCESS, Second Edition (1976)

Frank W. Miller, Professor of Law, Washington University.
Robert O. Dawson, Professor of Law, University of Texas.
George E. Dix, Professor of Law, University of Texas.
Raymond I. Parnas, Professor of Law, University of California, Davis.

UNIVERSITY CASEBOOK SERIES—Continued

MUNICIPAL CORPORATIONS, see Local Government Law

NEGOTIABLE INSTRUMENTS, see Commercial Paper

NEW YORK PRACTICE, Fourth Edition (1978)

Herbert Peterfreund, Professor of Law, New York University.
Joseph M. McLaughlin, Dean of the Law School, Fordham University.

OIL AND GAS, Fourth Edition (1979)

Howard R. Williams, Professor of Law, Stanford University
Richard C. Maxwell, Professor of Law, University of California, Los Angeles.
Charles J. Meyers, Dean of the Law School, Stanford University.

ON LAW IN COURTS (1965)

Paul J. Mishkin, Professor of Law, University of California, Berkeley.
Clarence Morris, Professor of Law Emeritus, University of Pennsylvania.

OWNERSHIP AND DEVELOPMENT OF LAND (1965)

Jan Krasnowiecki, Professor of Law, University of Pennsylvania.

PARTNERSHIP PLANNING (1970) (Pamphlet)

William L. Cary, Professor of Law, Columbia University.

PERSPECTIVES ON THE LAWYER AS PLANNER (Reprint of Chapters One
through Five of Planning by Lawyers) (1978)

Louis M. Brown, Professor of Law, University of Southern California.
Edward A. Dauer, Professor of Law, Yale University.

PLANNING BY LAWYERS, MATERIALS ON A NONADVERSARIAL LEGAL
PROCESS (1978)

Louis M. Brown, Professor of Law, University of Southern California.
Edward A. Dauer, Professor of Law, Yale University.

PLEADING AND PROCEDURE, see Procedure, Civil

POLICE FUNCTION (1976) (Pamphlet)

Chapters 1–11 of Miller, Dawson, Dix & Parnas' Criminal Justice Administration, Second Edition.

PREVENTIVE LAW, see also Planning by Lawyers

PROCEDURE—Biography of a Legal Dispute (1968)

Marc A. Franklin, Professor of Law, Stanford University.

PROCEDURE—CIVIL PROCEDURE, Second Edition (1974), with 1979 Supplement

James H. Chadbourn, Professor of Law, Harvard University.
A. Leo Levin, Professor of Law, University of Pennsylvania.
Philip Shuchman, Professor of Law, University of Connecticut.

PROCEDURE—CIVIL PROCEDURE, Fourth Edition (1978), with 1980 Supplement

Richard H. Field, late Professor of Law, Harvard University.
Benjamin Kaplan, Professor of Law Emeritus, Harvard University.
Kevin M. Clermont, Professor of Law, Cornell University.

PROCEDURE—CIVIL PROCEDURE, Third Edition (1976), with 1978 Supplement

Maurice Rosenberg, Professor of Law, Columbia University.
Jack B. Weinstein, Professor, of Law, Columbia University.
Hans Smit, Professor of Law, Columbia University.
Harold L. Korn, Professor of Law, Columbia University.

UNIVERSITY CASEBOOK SERIES—Continued

PROCEDURE—PLEADING AND PROCEDURE: State and Federal, Fourth Edition (1979)

David W. Louisell, late Professor of Law, University of California, Berkeley.
Geoffrey C. Hazard, Jr., Professor of Law, Yale University.

PROCEDURE—FEDERAL RULES OF CIVIL PROCEDURE, 1980 Edition

PROCEDURE PORTFOLIO (1962)

James H. Chadbourn, Professor of Law, Harvard University, and
A. Leo Levin, Professor of Law, University of Pennsylvania.

PRODUCTS LIABILITY (1980)

Marshall S. Shapo, Professor of Law, Northwestern University.

PRODUCTS LIABILITY AND SAFETY (1980), with Statutory Supplement

W. Page Keeton, Professor of Law, University of Texas.
David G. Owen, Professor of Law, University of South Carolina.
John E. Montgomery, Professor of Law, University of South Carolina.

PROFESSIONAL RESPONSIBILITY (1976), with 1979 Problems, Cases and Readings, Supplement, 1980 Statutory (National) Supplement, and 1980 Statutory (California) Supplement

Thomas D. Morgan, Professor of Law, University of Illinois.
Ronald D. Rotunda, Professor of Law, University of Illinois.

PROPERTY, Fourth Edition (1978)

John E. Cribbet, Dean of the Law School, University of Illinois.
Corwin W. Johnson, Professor of Law, University of Texas.

PROPERTY—PERSONAL (1953)

S. Kenneth Skolfield, late Professor of Law Emeritus, Boston University.

PROPERTY—PERSONAL, Third Edition (1954)

Everett Fraser, late Dean of the Law School Emeritus, University of Minnesota.
Third Edition by Charles W. Taintor, late Professor of Law, University of Pittsburgh.

PROPERTY—INTRODUCTION, TO REAL PROPERTY, Third Edition (1954)

Everett Fraser, late Dean of the Law School Emeritus, University of Minnesota.

PROPERTY—REAL PROPERTY AND CONVEYANCING (1954)

Edward E. Bade, late Professor of Law, University of Minnesota.

PROPERTY—FUNDAMENTALS OF MODERN REAL PROPERTY (1974), with 1980 Supplement

Edward H. Rabin, Professor of Law, University of California, Davis.

PROPERTY—PROBLEMS IN REAL PROPERTY (Pamphlet) (1969)

Edward H. Rabin, Professor of Law, University of California, Davis.

PROSECUTION AND ADJUDICATION (1976) (Pamphlet)

Chapters 12–16 of Miller, Dawson, Dix & Parnas' Criminal Justice Administration, Successor Edition.

PUBLIC REGULATION OF DANGEROUS PRODUCTS (paperback) (1980)

Marshall S. Shapo, Professor of Law, Northwestern University.

UNIVERSITY CASEBOOK SERIES—Continued

PUBLIC UTILITY LAW, see Free Enterprise, also Regulated Industries

REAL ESTATE PLANNING (1980), with 1980 Problems, Statutes and New Materials Supplement

Norton L. Steuben, Professor of Law, University of Colorado.

RECEIVERSHIP AND CORPORATE REORGANIZATION, see Creditors' Rights

REGULATED INDUSTRIES, Second Edition, 1976

William K. Jones, Professor of Law, Columbia University.

RESTITUTION, Second Edition (1966)

John W. Wade, Professor of Law, Vanderbilt University.

SALES (1980)

Marion W. Benfield, Jr., Professor of Law, University of Illinois.
William D. Hawkland, Chancellor, Louisiana State University Law Center.

SALES AND SALES FINANCING, Fourth Edition (1976)

John Honnold, Professor of Law, University of Pennsylvania.

SECURITY, Third Edition (1959)

John Hanna, late Professor of Law Emeritus, Columbia University.

SECURITIES REGULATION, Fourth Edition (1977), with 1980 Selected Statutes Supplement and 1980 Cases and Releases Supplement

Richard W. Jennings, Professor of Law, University of California, Berkeley.
Harold Marsh, Jr., Member of the California Bar.

SENTENCING AND THE CORRECTIONAL PROCESS, Second Edition (1976)

Frank W. Miller, Professor of Law, Washington University.
Robert O. Dawson, Professor of Law, University of Texas.
George E. Dix, Professor of Law, University of Texas.
Raymond I. Parnas, Professor of Law, University of California, Davis.

SOCIAL WELFARE AND THE INDIVIDUAL (1971)

Robert J. Levy, Professor of Law, University of Minnesota.
Thomas P. Lewis, Dean of the College of Law, University of Kentucky.
Peter W. Martin, Professor of Law, Cornell University.

TAX, POLICY ANALYSIS OF THE FEDERAL INCOME (1976)

William A. Klein, Professor of Law, University of California, Los Angeles.

TAXATION, FEDERAL INCOME (1976), with 1980 Supplement

Erwin N. Griswold, Dean Emeritus, Harvard Law School.
Michael J. Graetz, Professor of Law, University of Virginia.

TAXATION, FEDERAL INCOME, Second Edition (1977), with 1979 Supplement

James J. Freeland, Professor of Law, University of Florida.
Stephen A. Lind, Professor of Law, University of Florida.
Richard B. Stephens, Professor of Law Emeritus, University of Florida.

TAXATION, FEDERAL INCOME, Volume I, Personal Income Taxation (1972), with 1979 Supplement; Volume II, Taxation of Partnerships and Corporations, Second Edition (1980)

Stanley S. Surrey, Professor of Law, Harvard University.
William C. Warren, Professor of Law Emeritus, Columbia University.
Paul R. McDaniel, Professor of Law, Boston College Law School.
Hugh J. Ault, Professor of Law, Boston College Law School.

UNIVERSITY CASEBOOK SERIES—Continued

TAXATION, FEDERAL WEALTH TRANSFER (1977)

Stanley S. Surrey, Professor of Law, Harvard University.
William C. Warren, Professor of Law Emeritus, Columbia University, and
Paul R. McDaniel, Professor of Law, Boston College Law School.
Harry L. Gutman, Instructor, Harvard Law School and Boston College Law School.

TAXATION OF INDIVIDUALS, PARTNERSHIPS AND CORPORATIONS, PROBLEMS in the (1978)

Norton L. Steuben, Professor of Law, University of Colorado.
William J. Turnier, Professor of Law, University of North Carolina.

TAXES AND FINANCE—STATE AND LOCAL (1974)

Oliver Oldman, Professor of Law, Harvard University.
Ferdinand P. Schoettle, Professor of Law, University of Minnesota.

TORT LAW AND ALTERNATIVES: INJURIES AND REMEDIES, Second Edition (1979)

Marc A. Franklin, Professor of Law, Stanford University.

TORTS, Sixth Edition (1976)

William L. Prosser, late Professor of Law, University of California, Hastings College.
John W. Wade, Professor of Law, Vanderbilt University.
Victor E. Schwartz, Professor of Law, American University.

TORTS, Third Edition (1976)

Harry Shulman, late Dean of the Law School, Yale University.
Fleming James, Jr., Professor of Law Emeritus, Yale University.
Oscar S. Gray, Professor of Law, University of Maryland.

TRADE REGULATION (1975), with 1979 Supplement

Milton Handler, Professor of Law Emeritus, Columbia University.
Harlan M. Blake, Professor of Law, Columbia University.
Robert Pitofsky, Professor of Law, Georgetown University.
Harvey J. Goldschmid, Professor of Law, Columbia University.

TRADE REGULATION, see Antitrust

TRANSNATIONAL LEGAL PROBLEMS, Second Edition (1976), with Documentary Supplement

Henry J. Steiner, Professor of Law, Harvard University.
Detlev F. Vagts, Professor of Law, Harvard University.

TRIAL, see also Lawyering Process

TRIAL ADVOCACY (1968)

A. Leo Levin, Professor of Law, University of Pennsylvania.
Harold Cramer, of the Pennsylvania Bar.
Maurice Rosenberg, Professor of Law, Columbia University, Consultant.

TRUSTS, Fifth Edition (1978)

George G. Bogert, late Professor of Law Emeritus, University of Chicago.
Dallin H. Oaks, President, Brigham Young University.

TRUSTS AND SUCCESSION (Palmer's), Third Edition (1978)

Richard V. Wellman, Professor of Law, University of Georgia.
Lawrence W. Waggoner, Professor of Law, University of Michigan.
Olin L. Browder, Jr., Professor of Law, University of Michigan.

UNIVERSITY CASEBOOK SERIES—Continued

UNFAIR COMPETITION, see Competitive Process and Business Torts

UNITED NATIONS IN ACTION (1968)
Louis B. Sohn, Professor of Law, Harvard University.

UNITED NATIONS LAW, Second Edition (1967), with Documentary Supplement (1968)
Louis B. Sohn, Professor of Law, Harvard University.

WATER RESOURCE MANAGEMENT, Second Edition (1980)
Charles J. Meyers, Dean of the Law School, Stanford University.
A. Dan Tarlock, Professor of Law, Indiana University.

WILLS AND ADMINISTRATION, 5th Edition (1961)
Philip Mechem, late Professor of Law, University of Pennsylvania.
Thomas E. Atkinson, late Professor of Law, New York University.

WORLD LAW, see United Nations Law

University Casebook Series

CASES AND MATERIALS

ON

LABOR LAW

By

ARCHIBALD COX
Carl M. Loeb University Professor
Harvard Law School

DEREK CURTIS BOK
President, Harvard University

ROBERT A. GORMAN
Professor of Law
University of Pennsylvania

NINTH EDITION

Mineola, New York
THE FOUNDATION PRESS, INC.
1981

Library of Congress Cataloging in Publication Data

Cox, Archibald, 1912—
    Cases and materials on labor law.

    (University casebook series)
    Bibliography: p.
    Includes indexes.
    1. Labor laws and legislation—United States—Cases.

I. Bok, Derek Curtis.   II. Gorman,
Robert A., 1937—   III. Series.
KF3318.C6   1981   344.73'01   81–9731
                  347.3041   AACR2

ISBN 0–88277–027–6

Cox et al., Cs Labor Law 9th Ed. U.C.B.

FOR

MARK, ANDREW

and JEFFREY

*

PREFACE

As was observed in the Preface to the eighth edition of this casebook, "The law governing unionization and collective bargaining has not changed dramatically in the years since the last edition." The major decisions of the courts and of the National Labor Relations Board in the past five years have marked no significant departure from earlier doctrine but have on the whole generated further refinements in that doctrine.

There have, however, been recent decisions of which the informed student of Labor Law should be aware, particularly Supreme Court decisions on such matters as NLRB jurisdiction, protected concerted activity, secondary boycott pressures, the duty to bargain in good faith, the enforcement of no-strike and arbitration provisions in labor contracts, the duty of fair representation, and the preemption of state labor law. NLRB decisions, reflecting frequent changes in membership over the past five years, have modified the applicable rules governing election-campaign communications and Board deference to contractual arbitration procedures. These decisions not only elaborate substantive provisions of the Labor Act; more significantly for the law student, they also explore the scope and objectives of the Act, the institutional competence of the judiciary and of the administrative agency, and the extent to which government should regulate private conduct—fundamental issues in the Labor Law course.

For this reason, a revision of this casebook is in order. Revision has brought with it the opportunity not only to incorporate new cases but also to re-edit old ones, to prepare new text notes discussing current developments, and to devise new Problems for Discussion to reflect emerging issues. As stated in the Preface to the prior edition, the Problems for Discussion "are designed to test the students' understanding of the principal cases, to have them extend the rationale of those cases to new factual situations and to become acquainted with a wider range of factual situations and major legal problems; in short, this edition continues to afford the option to teach the course through the 'problem method' rather than direct consideration of cases already decided." The issues explored and the overall organization and approach of the casebook remain basically unchanged from prior editions.

A special effort was made in this edition, with only modest success, to reduce the size of the casebook. Although some instructors manage to cover almost the entire book, most instructors must decide whether to cover certain material especially briskly or to omit it altogether. Responses to a questionnaire recently distributed to teachers of Labor Law suggest that most believe it rather important to cover (in addition to the basic material on Sections 8(a)(1), (3) and (5) and labor-contract enforcement) the materials on secondary boycotts and recognitional picketing, election proceedings (especially the appropriate bargaining unit), and the duty of fair representation: somewhat fewer think it important to cover union security and preemption of state law; and fewer yet emphasize such subjects as the historical introduction, employer domination of unions, featherbedding and work-assignment disputes, labor and antitrust, discipline of union members, and arbitrator's decisions (e. g., just cause and management rights). Obviously, each instructor must make his or her own informed decision about the purposes of the Labor Law course and the subjects within it that best achieve those purposes.

* * * *

In the editing of cases, brackets will usually indicate material rewritten by the authors, and omissions are shown by ellipses. The omission of footnotes is generally not indicated, and where footnotes are retained they have been renumbered. No attempt has been made to take account of cases decided subsequent to June 1981; a decision of the United States Supreme Court, rendered in late June, has been edited and is set forth in an Appendix at the end of this book, and appropriate references thereto have been made in the body of the book.

The basic labor legislation and illustrative collective bargaining agreement have been compiled separately and are published by Foundation Press in a separate Statutory Supplement.

Two students at the University of Pennsylvania Law School deserve special mention for their very capable assistance in the preparation of this edition; they are Jay Levin '81 and Matthew Quilter '82. We are also grateful to Kathleen McClendon for her cheerful and flawless secretarial assistance.

ARCHIBALD COX
DEREK C. BOK
ROBERT A. GORMAN

July, 1981

BIBLIOGRAPHY

Although the text, cases and problems in this volume, coupled with classroom discussion, ought to be sufficient for study of the course in Labor Law, it is important for a law student to become familiar with the books and other publications in the field. They may be useful in filling up omissions, clarifying problems and organizing notes. Much more important, knowledge of the leading Labor Law books and an ability to use them will be valuable in practicing law. One who has taken a course in Labor Law ought at the very least to be thoroughly familiar not only with the publications of the National Labor Relations Board but also with at least one of the principal Labor Law services. Most research begins with these sources instead of the general digests more commonly used in other fields.

The following references give a brief description of standard works in the field of labor relations law:

A. General Texts.

1. Cox, *Law and the National Labor Policy* (1960). A series of lectures covering several broad topics such as the role of law in the administration of collective bargaining, the public interest in internal union affairs and public policy toward union organization.

2. Gorman, *Basic Text on Labor Law: Unionization and Collective Bargaining* (1976); C. Morris, ed., *The Developing Labor Law* (1970, with annual supplements). Both of these works are comprehensive treatments of almost all of the topics considered in this casebook. The bibliographies provided are full, and the substantive discussion is exhaustive. New editions of both books are forthcoming.

3. Gregory & Katz, *Labor and the Law* (3d ed. 1979). A short history of the development of labor law, written for the layman, which discusses the leading cases and statutes and the questions of policy involved.

4. Wellington, *Labor and the Legal Process* (1968). A comprehensive book containing analysis and policy recommendations for many of the major topics considered in this casebook.

B. Texts Covering Particular Aspects of Labor Law.

1. The Labor Injunction.

   (a) Frankfurter & Greene, *The Labor Injunction* (1930). An exhaustive analysis of the use of federal court injunctions in labor disputes prior to the Norris-LaGuardia Act of 1932.

2. The National Labor Relations Act.
    (a) Rosenfarb, *The National Labor Policy* (1940). An early discussion of the NLRA, its interpretation and administration.
    (b) *NLRB Annual Reports.* These reports, prepared by the NLRB staff, are the most up-to-date sources of information and statistics concerning the workload and decisions of the NLRB (and to a lesser extent, the courts), under the Labor Act.
    (c) Millis and Brown, *From the Wagner Act to Taft-Hartley* (1950). Dr. Millis was Chairman of the NLRB from 1941 to 1945. This useful volume is sympathetic towards the Wagner Act and very critical of the Taft-Hartley amendments. The extensive treatment of NLRB decisions gives it some of the characteristics of a lawyer's book even though its authors are economists.
3. Arbitration.
A number of books deal with the subject of labor arbitration.
    (a) Elkouri & Elkouri, *How Arbitration Works* (3d ed. 1973), and Updegraff, *Arbitration and Labor Relations* (3d ed. 1970), deal with the scope and nature of the arbitration and grievance procedure, substantive subjects of arbitration (such as seniority and discipline, and procedural questions (such as arbitrability, standards of evidence and the use of precedent).
    (b) Fairweather, *Practice & Procedure in Labor Arbitration* (1973), and Fleming, *The Labor Arbitration Process* (1965), focus in somewhat greater detail upon arbitration procedures. The latter work has particularly useful discussions of problems of "due process" for the individual grievant.
    (c) Hays, *Labor Arbitration: A Dissenting View* (1966), is by an eminent federal judge, arbitrator and teacher of Labor Law, who offers a highly critical view of labor arbitrators and of judicial involvement in the arbitration process.
    (d) National Academy of Arbitrators, *Proceedings of the Annual Meeting.* This series of annual volumes published by the Bureau of National Affairs, contains excellent papers and addresses on the theory, practice and legal aspects of labor arbitration.
    (e) Arbitration Journal. This quarterly journal, which deals with commercial and other forms of arbitration as well as labor arbitration, frequently carries useful articles on current issues in the labor field.

C. Articles.

The best writing in the field of Labor Law is found in articles published in various law reviews. The articles which seem most helpful are cited at pertinent points throughout this volume.

D. Labor Services.

The two principal Labor Law services are published by Bureau of National Affairs and Commerce Clearing House. Both services, published weekly, provide current decisions of the courts and of the NLRB, generally prior to their publication in official form or in the reporter system. (Court decisions are in full text; NLRB decisions are generally abstracted, with full text provided for the more important cases.) These decisions, supplied initially in looseleaf form for insertion in binders, are periodically bound up into permanent volumes. Each of the services has a looseleaf volume containing case tables, as well as a detailed subject matter index which leads the user into synopses of cases organized by subject matter. The organization is more specific than that available in the general digests, and the immediate incorporation of current cases makes these services the preferred method of research in the Labor Law field. The services also publish (and ultimately bind) current decisions in areas closely allied to federal and state labor relations law, such as arbitration decisions and cases dealing with employment discrimination on the basis of race, religion, sex, national origin and age.

E. General Books.

The average law student would be well advised to do supplementary reading in books which increase one's knowledge of the labor movement and one's understanding of labor economics and industrial relations. There are many books which fill this need, ranging from college textbooks through the good biographies of labor leaders to discussions of public labor policy. The volumes listed below are a few among many of equal merit.

1. *Industrial Relations.*

    (a) Golden & Ruttenberg, The Dynamics of Industrial Democracy (1942).

    (b) Kerr, Dunlop, Harbison & Myers, Industrialism and Industrial Man (1964).

    (c) Slichter, Union Policies and Industrial Management (1941).

    (d) Slichter, Healy & Livernash, The Impact of Collective Bargaining on Management (1960).

2. *Labor Economics.*

    (a) Freeman, Labor Economics (1972) (paperback).

    (b) Rees, The Economics of Trade Unions (2d ed. 1977).

    (c) Rees, The Economics of Work and Pay (2d ed. 1979).

    (d) Reynolds, Labor Economics and Labor Relations (7th ed. 1978).

3. *Labor History.*

    (a) I. Bernstein, The Lean Years (1960), and Turbulent Years (1969) (a history of the American worker 1920–1933, and 1933–1941; both available in paperback).

    (b) Blum, A History of the American Labor Movement (1972).

    (c) Millis & Montgomery, Organized Labor (1945).

    (d) Perlman, History of Trade Unionism in the United States (1922).

    (e) Perlman & Taft, History of Labor in the United States, 1896–1932 (1935).

    (f) P. Taft, Organized Labor in American History (1964).

4. *Labor Negotiations.*

    (a) Peters, Strategy and Tactics in Labor Negotiations (1955).

    (b) Stevens, Strategy and Collective Bargaining Negotiations (1963).

    (c) Walton & McKersie, A Behavioral Theory of Labor Negotiations (1965).

5. *Labor Unions.*

    (a) Bok & Dunlop, Labor and the American Community (1969) (available in paperback).

    (b) Leiserson, American Trade Union Democracy (1959).

    (c) P. Taft, The Structure and Government of Labor Unions (1954).

    (d) Ulman, The Rise of the National Trade Union (2d ed. 1966).

SUMMARY OF CONTENTS

ANALYTICAL TABLE OF CONTENTS

Abstracted cases are distinguished from the principal cases by being enclosed in parentheses.

INTRODUCTION

PART ONE

THE EVOLUTION OF LABOR RELATIONS LAWS

ANALYTICAL TABLE OF CONTENTS

ANALYTICAL TABLE OF CONTENTS

PART FOUR

STRIKES, BOYCOTTS AND PICKETING

xxxiii

PART FIVE

LABOR AND THE ANTI-TRUST LAWS

PART SIX

FEDERALISM AND LABOR RELATIONS

PART SEVEN

THE INDIVIDUAL AND THE UNION

TABLE OF CASES

The principal cases are in italic type. Cases cited or discussed are in roman type. References are to Pages.

TABLE OF CASES

xliv

*

CASES AND MATERIALS

ON

LABOR LAW

INTRODUCTION

SCOPE OF THE COURSE

Modern labor laws regulate nearly all aspects of the relation between employer and employee. When an employer prepares forms to be filled out by applicants for employment, it must consider not only the National Labor Relations Act but also state fair employment practices acts, which regulate hiring on the basis of race, national origin and sex, and Title VII of the 1964 Civil Rights Act, which deals with the same matter at the federal level. Working conditions in factories and mines are controlled by safety laws and sanitary regulations; again, these have been promulgated not only by the states but also by the federal government (most conspicuously and recently in the form of the Occupational Safety and Health Act). State statutes limit the employment of and the kind of work that can be assigned to women; these laws must in turn be tested against the often conflicting federal laws and regulations on the same subject. At one end of the spectrum, state and federal laws prohibit oppressive child labor, and at the other federal law (and a few states) bars discrimination in hiring and firing directed against the older worker. Hours of work are regulated directly by state legislation and indirectly by the Fair Labor Standards Act.

Minimum wages are fixed by the FLSA, under the Walsh-Healey Act and by state legislation. The form in which wages are to be paid, the frequency of payment and kinds of deductions which may be made are controlled by law. If an employee is taken sick, he may be entitled to benefits under a state insurance plan or a collective bargaining agreement to which the law gives sanctions. If an employee is injured during the course of his employment, the entire workmen's compensation system as well as the law of torts is drawn into question. If he is laid off, the unemployment compensation laws are applicable, and, even though there is no unemployment, the employer must concern himself with the taxes imposed by this legislation. When the employee retires or dies, payments may fall due under a pension plan raising a host of legal questions whether the plan has been established unilaterally or through collective bargaining; perhaps the most comprehensive regulation is embraced within the federal Pension Reform Act of 1974, known as ERISA (Employee Retirement Income Security Act) and administered by both the Department of Labor and the Internal Revenue Service. Indeed, the United States Department of Labor is charged with administering more than 160 federal statutes governing the employment relationship.

A collective bargaining agreement may provide not only the law of the plant but also an elaborate quasi-judicial system for its administration and enforcement. In the case of a breakdown of relations between employer and organized employees, their respective rights and remedies are governed by the common law of strikes and picketing developed through the labor injunction, by state strike-control laws or the Taft-Hartley Act. Still other statutes regulate advertising for and transporting replacements or strikebreakers.

This is not all. Wise attorneys who represent some of our best-known corporations have expressed the view that a lawyer has a responsibility to advise his clients with respect to all aspects of the employer's moral as well as legal obligations to employees, obligations which run from the cradle to the grave. Even on a more mundane level it is obvious that any attorney advising a sizable corporation on the law applicable to employment relations must deal with a still wider range of topics than those suggested above.

These circumstances make very pointed the question, why is the conventional law school course in Labor Law confined to questions centering about union organization and collective bargaining. Perhaps the answer lies partly in history and partly in habit, but there are sound reasons which would persuade us thus to define the subject matter even as an original question.

In the first place Labor Law is concerned with the governance of workers in industrial establishments, and collective bargaining is the heart of that subject. Despite all the detailed regulations mentioned above, the rules which most vitally affect workers in their daily lives are made in each industrial establishment either by the employer unilaterally or by the negotiation and administration of collective agreements. We place "floors" under wages and "ceilings" over hours, leaving the wage rates paid to the overwhelming proportion of our workers and the hours actually worked to be determined by private adjustment. In parts of continental Europe remedies against unfair discharges are provided by law. In the United States they are provided by collective bargaining agreements and grievance arbitration. Many of the guarantees of social security enjoyed by American workers have their roots in contracts rather than legislation. Since a single course of not more than 60 classroom hours cannot cover the entire field, it seems proper to concentrate on this institution of industrial self-government. Its constitution is the National Labor Relations Act, the Railway Labor Act and similar basic statutes and court decisions. Its statutory law is written in collective bargaining agreements. In the grievance and arbitration procedures are found its administrative and judicial tribunals.

A second reason for concentrating on this branch of Labor Law is that it emphasizes those aspects of the subject which contrast with other law school courses. The law of unionization, collective bargaining, strikes and picketing deals with groups of people rather than individuals. While a corporation is, in some senses, an aggregation of many individuals, it is to be distinguished from a labor organization partly on the ground that the law has always treated corporations as entities in their dealings with outsiders and partly on the ground that a corporation is primarily an aggregation of property rather than a combination of people. The law of strikes and picketing and the problems of administering and enforcing collective bargaining agreements are profoundly influenced by the special problems of controlling group conduct detached from property interests. The law must also deal with the relationship between the collectivity and its individual members; the governmentally sanctioned control that a labor organization has over the economic wellbeing of the individual worker makes imperative a thoughtful comparison of the internal relationships within the union and those within other "voluntary" membership groups within our society, such as the church, the political party, the professional organization or the social club.

Third, Labor Law as here conceived is a course which should lead to an appreciation of the interplay between law and life, which is less obvious in fields where both legal and social and economic developments have proceeded at a slower pace. Modern unions and collective bargaining have emerged as significant institutions during the short period since 1877. The response of the law to these social and economic developments, the law's effect upon the institutions, the changes in legal doctrine to correct actual or supposed blunders, all give a sense of growth which is not so easily achieved in other contexts. This sense of immediacy is highlighted further by the fact that many of the principles of Labor Law have been incorporated over the past decade in the legal rules regulating group conflict between students and universities, tenants and landlords, and community organizations and their governors.

Fourth, building the course about problems of organization and collective bargaining focuses attention upon the limitations of law. The average law student is likely to have an exaggerated sense of the extent to which human relationships can be organized by legislation, administrative order and judicial decision. Labor Law raises a number of sharp questions. In regulating the relationship between workers and their employers, what should be handled by governmental pronouncement and what should be left by the law to private adjustment? On those matters left to private adjustment, to what extent should government regulate the kinds of peaceful economic pressures that either party may bring to bear upon the other? On those matters meet for governmental regulation, how much should be addressed by legislation, and in what detail? What should be left to the administrative agency charged with implementing the basic legislation? What role should the courts play? In each instance, one must carefully examine the respective competences and limitations of each of these institutions, private and governmental.

Fifth, much of a lawyer's practice involves making private rules which are to govern the relationship between individuals, corporations, labor unions and other groups over a continuing period of time. The importance of negotiation and drafting has been increasingly recognized by law teachers. Because a collective bargaining agreement governs a complicated relationship having many aspects, the study of such agreements and their operation together with the statutory and judicial framework should afford an excellent vehicle for gaining an insight into this kind of professional activity.

Sixth, the study of unionization and collective bargaining provides an opportunity to consider the procedures, and the strengths and weaknesses, of different kinds of dispute-resolution mechanisms. The normal law school course focuses upon the public judicial system as the preeminent mechanism for resolving conflicts between private parties. Against that context, it may be somewhat strange to deal with a body of law which had its source in a distrust of the judiciary, judges being perceived as both biased against the working class and institutionally incapable of managing disputes between labor and management. In the Labor Law course, one can study the National Labor Relations Board, can compare the Board's functions with those of a judge and jury, and can assess the two different modes of operation which can be utilized by an administrative agency—adjudication and rulemaking. One can also study the contractual grievance procedure—culminating in grievance arbitration—as an alternative, privately created mechanism for resolving labor-management disputes; and one can then appraise the relationship between the arbitration process and the judicial process, and between the arbitrator and the NLRB.

Needless to say, it is difficult to keep these characteristics of Labor Law constantly before a class. The specific, substantive problems are much too fascinating. But the possibility is always present, and the hope that students will gain an appreciation of these ideas, if only by osmosis, seems sufficiently well founded to justify choosing this focus.

One final point may be mentioned. Obviously the hours allotted to a single course are too few to cover the whole field of Labor Law. But if the student is well trained in reading and interpreting statutes—with emphasis on *reading*—and has acquired a feeling for the attitude with which judges and agencies approach social and economic legislation, he or she will be better equipped to handle legislation dealing with wages and hours, factory conditions, employment discrimination based on race or sex, and the like. The ground covered by the casebook should make a considerable contribution to a student's ability to deal with statutes and he can also acquire here a feeling for judicial attitudes toward labor laws.

*

Part One

THE EVOLUTION OF LABOR RELATIONS LAWS

I. THE RISE OF THE LABOR MOVEMENT [1]

ECONOMIC CONDITIONS

The years between the Civil War and World War I were the time of building industrial empires. In 1865 the technological developments of the industrial revolution invited large scale enterprise. Textiles had been on a factory basis since the 1820's and in 1855 the Bessemer process had become commercially feasible. Vast natural resources—timber, coal, oil, iron ore, copper and precious metals—awaited exploitation. The expansion of transportation facilities opened wider markets. The profits of the wartime years supplied ample capital while quantities of workers stood waiting in Europe and Asia to be carried at bargain rates to the railroad camps, mines and mills. Gould, Vanderbilt, Harriman and James J. Hill built their railway empires; Rockefeller organized the Standard Oil Company; Armour & Company was formed; and under the guiding hand of Andrew Carnegie the billion dollar United States Steel Corporation came into existence.

The statistics document what the names recall. Between 1860 and 1910 the amount of capital invested in manufacturing increased twelvefold; the annual value of manufactured products increased fifteenfold; and 5,500,000 wage earners came to be employed in industry instead of 1,500,000. The statistics also reveal the rising importance of large scale industrial establishments and the increasing concentration of economic power, which seem scarcely to have been slowed by the passage of the Sherman Act and the "trust-busting" campaigns of Theodore Roosevelt. Between 1899 and 1909 the number of manufacturing establishments increased approximately 30 per cent; the number of wage earners increased 40 per cent in the same period. Not only were more workers becoming employed in each industrial establishment but the very large establishments were coming to occupy an increasingly important position and were employing a larger proportion of the workers. In 1904 establishments whose an-

---

1. Convenient histories of the labor movement are found in Perlman, History of Trade Unionism in the United States (1922); Perlman and Taft, History of Labor in the United States, 1896–1932 (1935); Millis and Montgomery, Organized Labor ch. I–V, XI–XII (1945); F. R. Dulles, Labor in America (1966); A. Blum, A History of the American Labor Movement (1972).

nual product was valued in excess of $1,000,000, already employed 25 per cent of the wage earners and produced 38 per cent of the total annual products. A decade later the percentages had risen to 35 per cent of the wage earners and 48 per cent of the total annual product.

The growth of the large corporation had many significant consequences for workers, two of which require mention here. First, it put an end to the personal relationship between employer and employee which was possible in small establishments. Second, the bargaining power of the individual worker dwindled until individual bargaining became an empty slogan. "A single employee was helpless in dealing with an employer. He was dependent ordinarily on his daily wage for the maintenance of himself and family. If the employer refused to pay him the wages that he thought fair, he was nevertheless unable to leave the employ and to resist arbitrary and unfair treatment. Union was essential to give laborers an opportunity to deal on equality with their employer." American Steel Foundries v. Tri-City Council, 257 U.S. 184 (1921).

Concurrently with the growing industrialization of the country other conditions developed which stimulated the rise of a strong labor movement and profoundly influenced its form. Labor unions, whether formed along craft or industrial lines, depend upon group action, and group action is impossible unless the members of the group have a keen enough awareness of their common interest to give them internal solidarity. Before the Civil War there was no class consciousness on the part of American wage earners. Under the social and economic conditions then prevailing a wage earner one day might be a property owner or entrepreneur a few months later. To the West the abundance of free land offered proprietorship to anyone willing to undergo the hardships of frontier life. Everywhere the extraordinarily rapid growth of industry and commerce held out opportunities for personal advancement. Workers tended to identify themselves with the propertied classes and when times were bad, to join with farmers and other debtors in support of political movements seeking to restore freedom of opportunity instead of forming economic organizations concerned with the interests of employees. Since the tide of immigration brought workers of many different nationalities to America, it gave the labor force a heterogeneity which also helps to explain the absence of class feeling before the Civil War. In the post-war period, however, conditions became more favorable to unionization.

Second, the increase in the population and the disappearance of the frontier hastened the growth of cities. As urban dwellers, workers became completely dependent on their wages whereas earlier they were able to lessen the impact of wage cuts or layoffs by keeping small gardens and perhaps a few cows. City life also increased social intercourse; more and more workers learned the strength of their economic ties with other employees in the same occupation. Thus, urbanization proved conducive to the growth of labor unions.

Third, the changed character of the immigrants who began to arrive after 1880 stimulated organization of the skilled workers. The immigrants formed a growing reservoir of unskilled labor which was a threat to the craftsmen both because it increased the competition for existing jobs and because it offered constant encouragement to employers to adapt jobs to the capacities of the semi-skilled or un-skilled. In self-protection the skilled employees sought to secure "job ownership" and control over access to their trades. But although immigration encouraged organization of the skilled workers it discouraged unionization on a wider basis. Racial antagonisms, language difficulties, and differences in custom and point of view continued to separate the unskilled workers. "The fact that many of the newer immigrants, arriving in the United States with backgrounds of racial or class oppression, had developed habits of docility rendered easier the introduction of employer policies in which there was little place for collective dealing and labor organization and at the same time sincerely convinced many of the trade-union leaders that to attempt to organize the unskilled was, save in exceptional cases, a task of insurmountable difficulty."[2]

Fourth, the nucleus of a strong trade union movement already existed. There had been periods of great trade union activity before the Civil War, but they were followed in the main by depression, disappointment and collapse. When organization took place, it was confined to the skilled trades, in which the necessary group consciousness most naturally developed. Two carpenters, two machinists or two electricians could find a bond in their common calling, which would be strengthened, no doubt, by common pride in their craftsmanship. The discovery of similar problems would soon focus attention on their identity of interest. Thus the bootmakers, carpenters, painters, iron molders and other skilled workers formed their local trade (i. e., craft) organizations. At the end of the 1860's more than thirty national trade unions were in existence and total union membership was not much below 300,000. Nine new national trade unions appeared during the three years 1870–1873. These unions, despite their inability to survive depressions, created a tradition of trade union activity to be quickened by the economic changes and turmoil of the post war decades.

The "triumph of business enterprise" and the conditions just mentioned not only explain the emergence of a strong labor movement during the period 1870–1914, but they shaped the philosophy and structure of the American Federation of Labor, which gave the movement leadership. For the most part the unionism of this period was organized along craft lines. It foreswore reform and political action in order to seek the immediate improvement of the wage earner's status by economic methods. Yet before the American work-

2. Millis and Montgomery, Organized
Labor (1945), 88–89.

ers were ready to embrace "business unionism", they flocked once more in the 1880's to the banner of panacea and reform.

THE KNIGHTS OF LABOR

Through the depression of the mid-seventies and its violent unsuccessful strikes, a secret society of workingmen grew steadily. Founded in 1869 by Uriah S. Stephens and six other Philadelphia tailors, the Noble Order of the Knights of Labor dropped its secrecy in 1879 when its membership was 20,000. For another two years the membership remained constant, but during the next six years the Knights enjoyed spectacular success. Its 20,000 members in 1881 had more than doubled a year later only to redouble themselves in the ensuing two-year period. In the summer of 1885 the paid up membership had become 104,000. During the next fourteen months it increased to roughly 700,000. Then the bubble burst. By 1888 the membership in good standing dropped to 222,000, in 1890 to 100,000; in 1893 the number was only 75,000.

A number of circumstances contributed to the success of the Knights of Labor. The time was ripe for an upheaval. People were shocked by political corruption and financial scandals. As prices and freight rates mounted, an outcry swelled against the trusts and railroad monopolies that was later to lead to the Interstate Commerce Act, the Sherman Act and the "trust-busting" campaigns of Theodore Roosevelt. But although its constitution decried, and its national leaders sought to discourage, the use of strikes and boycotts, the greatest appeal of the Knights lay in the spectacular successes which they scored with these weapons. In 1884 direct strike action failed to halt the wage cuts brought on by a minor depression and labor turned to the boycott as a weapon. In 1885 there were seven times as many boycotts as in 1884, most of which were instituted or taken up by the Knights of Labor. Many were successful, but the most spectacular victory was won in 1885 when Jay Gould, the most powerful capitalist in the country, met the Executive Board in conference and satisfied its demands. For the first time in American history a labor organization had forced a business and financial magnate to meet and deal with it on an equal footing.

Despite the Knights' success in conducting strikes and boycotts, it cannot be sufficiently emphasized that the movement was reformist and broadly humanitarian, seeking panaceas which would restore equality of opportunity and lift the wage earners out of their class. The Knights saw no conflict between employers and workers as such; the conflict was between the producing and non-producing classes. The Knights clung to the premise that no man need remain a wage earner, an ideal real enough while there were cheap lands to the west and ample opportunities to establish a small business in some rapidly growing community. The 1884 platform reveals the Knights' preoccupation with political measures and reform. In addition to listing such labor objectives as the eight hour day and the abolition of child labor, the platform laid great stress on direct representation and legislation, taxation of the unearned increment in land, abrogation of all laws not resting equally upon employers and employees, compulsory arbitration, compulsory education and free textbooks, income and inheritance taxes, government ownership of railroads and telegraph lines and a cooperative industrial system. The ultimate goal was "the abolishment of the wage system." Thus in the Knights of Labor the American worker had a final fling at what Professors Millis and Montgomery have called "the more romantic, reformist type of unionism. The arousing of a great hope, accompanied by a proportionately great disappointment, was perhaps necessary before he was willing to abandon the type of unionism for which he had manifested profound affection for almost a century." [3] Many of the dominant characteristics of the American Federation of Labor are attributable to the reflections of trade union leaders on the causes of the Knights' collapse.

THE AMERICAN FEDERATION OF LABOR

Trade union membership grew slowly but steadily during the years in which workers were flocking to the Knights. Many individuals belonged both to the Knights and to the trade union organization of their craft. In other instances trade union locals were accepted into the Knights as complete assemblies, in which their separate identity was maintained. All told the trade unions could count 250,000 members in 1886 when a committee of five issued a call to a convention in Columbus, Ohio, "for the purpose of forming an American Federation or alliance of all national and international trades unions." At this convention the American Federation of Labor was formed. Samuel Gompers became the first president and remained in office, with one brief interruption, until his death in 1924.

The dominant characteristics of the New American Federation of Labor were the reverse of the Knights'. Where the Knights was a humanitarian, reformist movement, the AFL developed what Selig Perlman termed "a philosophy of pure wage consciousness" in order to signify "a labor movement reduced to an opportunistic basis, accepting the existence of capitalism and having for its object the enlarging of the bargaining power of the wage earner in the sale of his labor." The term also implied "an attitude of aloofness from all those movements which aspire to replace the wage system by cooperation, whether voluntary or subsidized by government, whether greenbackism, socialism or anarchism." [4]

Where the Knights had looked ultimately to political action, the AFL unions relied on economic power. This is not to imply that the AFL did not support social and labor legislation; it did so repeatedly,

3. Millis and Montgomery, Organized Labor (1945), 59.

4. Perlman, History of Trade Unionism in the United States (1922), 78.

but it concentrated on short-run objectives, steered clear of political entanglements and refused to allow its energies to be diverted from the task of improving the immediate economic position of its members.

This effort to improve the position of the wage earner "here and now", within the existing economic system, led the AFL unions under Gompers' leadership to put chief reliance on collective bargaining. They realized that the individual employee was usually helpless in dealing with his employer and sought to increase the workers' bargaining power by substituting collective strength for individual weakness. This approach also had a strong theoretical foundation. Gompers, Strasser, and other leaders who guided AFL in its formative years had too much background in Marxist and socialist doctrine to deny that there were points of conflict between employers and employees. Their early experience in the Cigar Workers Union convinced them, however, that regardless of the theoretical merits or demerits of the Marxist conception of the class struggle, immediate improvements in wages, hours and working conditions would have to be achieved within the existing form of society. Thus they saw each collective bargaining agreement as one of a series of treaties negotiated between the employers and the organized employees through which, for the time being, they would adjust their differences.

During the 1880's collective agreements became fairly common in the building trades, and during the 1890's national agreements were signed in the stove and glass container industries. In 1898 the United Mine Workers negotiated a contract covering the important bituminous coal fields and shortly later obtained a similar agreement applicable to anthracite. The form and content of collective bargaining agreements has always varied so widely that generalization is dangerous but it seems fair to say that the AFL collective bargaining agreements were usually conceived as contracts under which the employer would hire workers and the unions would man the jobs. After union recognition, wages, hours and job security were most important. The prevailing conception seems to have been one of a bargain and sale of labor, and it was not until the 1930's when union organization spread into the mass production industries that a philosophy of collective bargaining developed which speaks of "industrial democracy" and sees in the collective agreement and grievance procedures the substantive and procedural rules for the government of industrial workers. Even today there is a marked difference in this respect between many craft agreements and the industrial union contracts in basic industries.

In 1886 the principle of craft organization fitted comfortably into the new philosophy of business unionism. If the bargaining power of the workers was to be increased by substituting collective strength for individual weakness, it was imperative to organize into one group all the workers in the same occupation; they were the ones, and the only ones, who would destroy labor standards by underbidding each other. In addition, by establishing "job ownership" or "job control", the organized workers could achieve a fair degree of security, which must have appealed to many of them not only as a form of insurance against unemployment during hard times but also as a defense against the threatening competition of unskilled labor.

In the AFL philosophy craft autonomy was closely allied to the principle of craft organization. In 1886 and for years thereafter the chief problem of American unionism seemed to be to stay organized. Trade union leaders concluded that the internal solidarity of the craft group should not be risked by the loss of its identity in larger units— the industry, the AFL, the world labor movement—where solidarity would grow less as the size of the unit increased. Nor was a close knit organization required. A national organization of the whole trade union movement was useful chiefly to formulate broad policies, to unite the crafts in spreading organization into new fields, and to act as spokesman, especially on political issues affecting labor. In securing immediate economic objectives experience seemed to show that reliance should be placed on the independent action of the craft unions which had their own solidarity and knew their own needs.

The problem of staying organized also gave rise to the ruthless opposition to dual unionism which has played so important a role in American trade union history. The concurrent existence of the Knights and the trade unions, both in the same field, had resulted in dual authority and divided loyalty, which sapped the trade unions' strength. Thus the AFL became devoted to the principle that in each recognized field of activity there should be but one union, chartered by the AFL, which would have exclusive jurisdiction.

The organizational structure of the American Federation of Labor paralleled its philosophy. As the name implied, it was a federation of trade unions. The dominant units were autonomous International Unions which were "affiliated" with the American Federation of Labor. Under each International were the local unions it had chartered. It was in the locals that individual workers held their membership.

With this philosophy and internal structure, the trade union movement experienced a period of solid, and sometimes spectacular, growth. For ten years after it was founded in 1886, the AFL's membership remained virtually constant. This was a truly remarkable success, for a depression occurred in 1893, and in every previous depression, as Gompers noted in 1899, the trade unions had been "literally mowed down and swept out of existence. Here for the first time the unions manifested their stability and permanence."[5] In 1897 AFL

---

5. American Federation of Labor, Convention Proceedings, 1899, quoted in Perlman, History of Trade Unionism in the United States (1922), 135–136.

entered a period of rapid growth. Between 1897 and 1900 membership rose from something less than 275,000 to 548,000. By 1903 the number of members was 1,465,000, five and one half times the membership only a decade before. AFL membership then remained fairly constant until 1910 when it again began to rise. By 1914 there were more than 2,000,000 AFL members.

The increase in membership was concentrated in the skilled trades and a few industries. More than half was attributable to the phenomenal growth of unions among coal miners, railroad workers and building trades employees. The great mass of semi-skilled and unskilled workers remained unorganized. Yet despite this limitation, union membership in 1914 was perhaps nine times greater than in 1869. The post-Civil War era was marked—in Charles A. Beard's phrase—by the "Triumph of Business Enterprise." But the years are no less significant for the rise of a permanent labor movement.

REASONS FOR ORGANIZING

The basic urge which leads workers to organize, the spark which gave unions life and the power of growth under favorable conditions, is the human drive toward self-advancement. In the United States this has meant advancement through self-help in relation to one's job, partly because this seemed to be the teaching of experience and partly, perhaps, because self-reliance is the heritage of a people only a few generations from life on the frontier.

Self-help through economic action necessarily requires increasing the bargaining power of employees; hence one of the basic purposes of a labor union is to eliminate competition among employees in the labor market. The labor union seeks to exercise the power of a monopolist. The growth of the large corporation diminished the bargaining power of the individual worker to such an extent that talk of freedom of individual contract became an empty slogan. Thus, the near-monopoly which the union obtains is often opposed by the near-monopsony of the large corporation which is the only buyer of labor in a local market.

Three other human desires should be noted among the forces that led workers to organize. (1) One is the desire for job security. Skilled craftsmen organized in order to secure control over available jobs so as to hold them against the competition of unskilled immigrants. (2) Employees wished to substitute what we should term "the rule of law" for the arbitrary and often capricious exercise of power by the boss. Forty years ago a foreman could discharge an employee for any reason or no reason. Labor unions have subordinated this absolute power to the rules set forth in collective agreements, and administration of the rules is usually subject to impartial review. The illustration afforded by the regularization of discipline is typical of what has occurred throughout life in industrial establishments. (3) Finally, unions helped to give employees a sense of participation in the business enterprises of which they are part—a function of labor unions which became important as organization spread into mass production industries.

Experience quickly taught union supporters that an effective union could not exist in a competitive industry unless its wage scale covered all the important firms. By the mid-1920's, for example, the Amalgamated Clothing Workers had negotiated collective bargaining agreements covering nearly all the New York shops. Amalgamated had not organized the firms located in the Philadelphia area although their goods were sold in the same competitive market. New York firms began to move to the low wage Philadelphia area. Also, production in the New York market decreased $15,000,000 from 1925 to 1927, while the production of Philadelphia increased $3,000,000. Amalgamated faced three choices: (a) to keep up its wage scale in New York despite the loss of sales and declining employment; (b) to accept wage cuts putting its employers' labor costs on a parity with Philadelphia; and (c) to organize Philadelphia and establish the union scale in that branch of the industry.

In spreading organization unions relied on three kinds of weapons:

(1) Their chief reliance was on a wide variety of arguments, persuasion and social pressures aimed directly at converting workers to ardent union membership.

(2) When this was not enough—or when enough employees had been organized, but an employer refused to recognize the union—unions resorted to strikes, boycotts and picketing. Some were peaceful. Violence crept into others simply because emotions ran high and working men do not observe the niceties of the parlor. Sometimes violence was deliberately planned even to the point of pitched battles.

(3) Labor unions also sought the support of public opinion. Their appeal was to intellectuals and reformers of all kinds. Such support has recently declined but at least until the mid-1950's most "liberals" and "progressives" were sympathetic to the cause of organized labor.

EMPLOYER OPPOSITION

Probably it was inevitable that employers would oppose the rise of labor organizations, some bitterly. Unions not only increased the power of employees to demand and secure higher wages, shorter hours and other benefits increasing labor costs, and so seemed to threaten the company's profits; they also curtailed the power of corporate management to make unilateral decisions. Few persons like to surrender power, and the more absolute their authority has been, the more reluctant they are to let it go. Perhaps it is for this reason that in later years disputes over the functions or prerogatives of management, which arose when unions pressed collective bargaining into new fields, began to stir more heated emotions than controversies over wage rates. In any event employers did fight unionization. They resorted to three kinds of measures:

(1) Employers, like unions, used the weapons of self-help. Threats of reprisals were often enough to discourage an incipient union. Labor spies were hired to report on any movement toward organization and to give the names of active leaders. Union leaders were discharged and often they were put on black lists circulated by trade associations. Many of the top union officials today are men whose attitudes were molded by years of working under assumed names, moving on from town to town as their identity was discovered. During World War I and again early in the 1930's some employers sought to prevent the growth of bona fide labor organizations by setting up works councils and company unions that would give employees the forms of union organization without the substance. Perhaps it is unnecessary also to recall the professional strikebreakers supplied by Pinkerton's and other detective agencies.

(2) The second group of weapons used by employers were various methods of appealing to and organizing public opinion. Since the techniques are as much a part of the mores of our times as of yesterday, it is unnecessary to say more than that unionization ran counter to the American tradition of individualism, and this more than anything else led distinguished citizens, including President Eliot of Harvard, to glorify the strikebreaker as a modern American hero.

(3) Employers sought and obtained government aid through the courts. Their requests gave rise to the first major phase in the development of labor law—the rise and decline of the labor injunction.

Later, organized labor also turned to the government not so much for direct social and economic legislation, as in continental Europe, but to clear the way for self-help through collective bargaining. Labor's first political objective, in point of emphasis as well as time, was to persuade the legislative branch of the government to stop the judicial intervention into labor disputes which was impeding unionization. Second, organized labor gradually turned to the government for affirmative assistance through legal recognition of the rights to self-organization and collective bargaining.

These two threads—the rise and decline of the labor injunction and the emergence of the legally protected rights to organize and bargain collectively—run through the development of the law of labor management relations from 1880 until 1947.

II.　JUDICIAL INTERVENTION

A.　THE LABOR INJUNCTION IN PRIVATE DISPUTES

Scholars have traced the roots of the basic common law of strikes and picketing far back into the 18th century.[1] The earliest reported American labor case was tried in 1806 when the Philadelphia cordewainers (shoemakers) were indicted for striking for higher wages. Recorder Levy charged the jury that "a combination of workmen to raise their wages may be considered from a two-fold point of view; one is to benefit themselves, the other to injure those who do not join their society. The rule of law condemns both."[2] Later, criminal prosecutions fell into disuse partly as the result of the adverse decision in *Commonwealth* v. *Hunt*[3] and partly because of public opinion. On the civil side, however, the volume of labor litigation sharply increased, and although it is impossible to reconstruct the legal atmosphere of the post Civil War period, it seems fair to say that when the labor disputes engendered by the conflict over union organization were taken to the courts, the judges were substantially free, despite the scattered precedents, to create new law appropriate to the new occasion, guided only by the vague "principles" which emerged from rulings upon more familiar situations. The problem which confronted attorneys and judges may be illuminated, therefore, by considering how a court sitting in 1909 should have decided the following case.

Problem for Discussion

Dainty Garment Company was a manufacturer of ladies' underwear in New York City. By 1908 its employees and the employees of other New York shops had been organized by the International Ladies Garment Workers. Wage rates were standardized. Average hourly earnings were 50 cents. In 1909 Dainty Garment shut down. Three weeks later a new shop was opened 40 miles up the Hudson in Beacon, New York, by a concern known as Super-Dainty Garments, Inc. All but the qualifying shares of its stock are owned by the brother-in-law of Dainty's owner. Dainty's owner is general manager of the new shop. Super-Dainty is paying 20 cents an hour to inexperienced help and 30 cents is the average hourly earnings of an experienced operator. Labor costs are more than 50 per cent of the total cost of manufacturing.

1. See e. g., Sayre, Criminal Conspiracy, 35 Harv.L.Rev. 393 (1922); Landis, Cases on Labor Law (1st ed.), 1–37. The common law of strikes and picketing is summarized in 4 Restatement, Torts, ch. 38. The summary is far more favorable to the cause of organized labor than the bulk of the court decisions.

2. The Philadelphia Cordewainers' Case, 3 Commons & Gilmore, Doc.Hist.Am. Soc. 59–248.

3. 4 Metc. (Mass.) 111 (1842).

ILG sent organizers to Beacon. A number of employees became members. Super-Dainty countered by discharging the employees who joined the union and threatening to leave town if the shop was unionized. ILG picketed the shop. There were five instances of name calling and violence during the past week, but the picketing was otherwise peaceful. Nevertheless, the picketing is discouraging many employees from working and interferes with the pick-up and delivery of goods because unionized teamsters refuse to cross the picket lines.

(a) Assume that careful legal research produces neither an applicable statute nor a judicial precedent in a labor controversy. As lawyer for Super-Dainty, would you think that you had a reasonable chance of securing any form of legal relief? What remedies would you seek? What arguments would you present in support of them?

(b) What would be your answering arguments as attorney for ILG?

(c) As judge, how would you go about reaching a decision? What considerations would you deem relevant? What would be your decision?

VEGELAHN v GUNTNER

Supreme Judicial Court of Massachusetts, 1896.
167 Mass. 92, 44 N.E. 1077.

[After a preliminary hearing upon the bill of complaint an injunction issued *pendente lite* restraining the respondents "from interfering with the plaintiff's business by patrolling the sidewalk or street in front or in the vicinity of the premises occupied by him, for the purpose of preventing any person or persons who now are or may hereafter be in his employment, or desirous of entering the same, from entering it, or continuing in it; or by obstructing or interfering with such persons, or any others, in entering or leaving the plaintiff's said premises; or by intimidating, by threats or otherwise, any person or persons who now are or may hereafter be in the employment of the plaintiff, or desirous of entering the same, from entering it, or continuing in it; or by any scheme or conspiracy among themselves or with others, organized for the purpose of annoying, hindering, interfering with, or preventing any person or persons who now are or may hereafter be in the employment of the plaintiff, or desirous of entering it, or from continuing therein."]

The hearing on the merits was before HOLMES, J., who reported the case for the consideration of the full court, as follows:

"The facts admitted or proved are that, following upon a strike of the plaintiff's workmen, the defendants have conspired to prevent the plaintiff from getting workmen, and thereby to prevent him from carrying on his business unless and until he will adopt a schedule of prices which has been exhibited to him, and for the purpose of compelling him to accede to that schedule, but for no other purpose. If

he adopts that schedule he will not be interfered with further. The
means adopted for preventing the plaintiff from getting workmen are,
(1) in the first place, persuasion and social pressure. And these
means are sufficient to affect the plaintiff disadvantageously, although
it does not appear, if that be material, that they are sufficient to crush
him. I ruled that the employment of these means for the said purpose was lawful, and for that reason refused an injunction against
the employment of them. If the ruling was wrong, I find that an injunction ought to be granted.

"(2) I find also, that, as a further means for accomplishing the
desired end, threats of personal injury or unlawful harm were conveyed to persons seeking employment or employed, although no actual violence was used beyond a technical battery, and although the
threats were a good deal disguised, and express words were avoided.
It appeared to me that there was danger of similar acts in the future.
I ruled that conduct of this kind should be enjoined.

"The defendants established a patrol of two men in front of
the plaintiff's factory, as one of the instrumentalities of their plan.
The patrol was changed every hour, and continued from half-past six
in the morning until half-past five in the afternoon, on one of the
busy streets of Boston. The number of men was greater at times, and
at times showed some little inclination to stop the plaintiff's door,
which was not serious, but seemed to me proper to be enjoined. The
patrol proper at times went further than simple advice, not obtruded
beyond the point where the other person was willing to listen, and conduct of that sort is covered by (2) above, but its main purpose was in
aid of the plan held lawful in (1) above. I was satisfied that there
was probability of the patrol being continued if not enjoined. I ruled
that the patrol, so far as it confined itself to persuasion and giving notice of the strike, was not unlawful, and limited the injunction accordingly.

"There was some evidence of persuasion to break existing contracts. I ruled that this was unlawful, and should be enjoined.
* * *"

[The final decree was as follows: " * * * that the defendants, and each and every [sic] of them, their agents and servants,
be restrained and enjoined from interfering with the plaintiff's business by obstructing or physically interfering with any persons in
entering or leaving the plaintiff's premises * * * or by intimidating, by threats, express or implied, of violence or physical harm
to body or property, any person or persons who now are or hereafter
may be in the employment of the plaintiff, or desirous of entering the same, from entering or continuing in it, or by in any way
hindering, interfering with, or preventing any person or persons
who now are in the employment of the plaintiff from continuing
therein, so long as they may be bound so to do by lawful contract."]

ALLEN, J.   *   *   *   The patrol was maintained as one of the means of carrying out the defendants' plan, and it was used in combination with social pressure, threats of personal injury or unlawful harm and persuasion to break existing contracts. It was thus one means of intimidation, indirectly to the plaintiff, and directly to persons actually employed, or seeking to be employed, by the plaintiff, and of rendering such employment unpleasant or intolerable to such persons. Such an act is an unlawful interference with the rights both of employer and of employed. An employer has a right to engage all persons who are willing to work for him, at such prices as may be mutually agreed upon, and persons employed or seeking employment have a corresponding right to enter into or remain in the employment of any person or corporation willing to employ them. These rights are secured by the constitution itself. [Citations omitted.] No one can lawfully interfere by force or intimidation to prevent employers or persons employed or wishing to be employed from the exercise of these rights. It is in Massachusetts, as in some other states, even made a criminal offense for one, by intimidation or force, to prevent, or seek to prevent, a person from entering into or continuing in the employment of a person or corporation. Pub.St. c. 74, § 2. Intimidation is not limited to threats of violence or of physical injury to person or property. It has a broader signification, and there also may be a moral intimidation which is illegal. * * * The patrol was unlawful interference both with the plaintiff and with the workmen, within the principle of many cases; and, when instituted for the purpose of interfering with his business, it became a private nuisance. [Citations omitted.]

The defendants contend that these acts were justifiable, because they were only seeking to secure better wages for themselves, by compelling the plaintiff to accept their schedule of wages. This motive or purpose does not justify maintaining a patrol in front of the plaintiff's premises, as a means of carrying out their conspiracy. A combination among persons merely to regulate their own conduct is within allowable competition, and is lawful, although others may be indirectly affected thereby. But a combination to do injurious acts expressly directed to another, by way of intimidation or constraint, either of himself or of persons employed or seeking to be employed by him, is outside of allowable competition, and is unlawful. * * *

A question is also presented whether the court should enjoin such interference with persons in the employment of the plaintiff who are not bound by contract to remain with him, or with persons who are not under any existing contract, but who are seeking or intending to enter into his employment. A conspiracy to interfere with the plaintiff's business by means of threats and intimidation, and by maintaining a patrol in front of his premises, in order to prevent persons from entering his employment, or in order to prevent persons who are in his employment from continuing therein, is unlawful, even though such persons are not bound by contract to enter into or to continue in his employment; and the injunction should not be so limited as to relate only to persons who are bound by existing contracts. * * * We therefore think that the injunction should be in the form as originally issued. So ordered.

FIELD, C. J. (dissenting).   *   *   *

HOLMES, J. (dissenting). * * * In the first place, a word or two should be said as to the meaning of the report. I assume that my brethren construe it as I meant it to be construed, and that, if they were not prepared to do so, they would give an opportunity to the defendants to have it amended in accordance with what I state my meaning to have been. There was no proof of any threat or danger of a patrol exceeding two men, and as, of course, an injunction is not granted except with reference to what there is reason to expect in its absence, the question on that point is whether a patrol of two men should be enjoined. Again, the defendants are enjoined by the final decree from intimidating by threats, express or implied, of physical harm to body or property, any person who may be desirous of entering into the employment of the plaintiff, so far as to prevent him from entering the same. In order to test the correctness of the refusal to go further, it must be assumed that the defendants obey the express prohibition of the decree. If they do not, they fall within the injunction as it now stands, and are liable to summary punishment. The important difference between the preliminary and the final injunction is that the former goes further, and forbids the defendants to interfere with the plaintiff's business "by any scheme * * * organized for the purpose of * * * preventing any person or persons who now are or may hereafter be * * * desirous of entering the [plaintiff's employment] from entering it." I quote only a part, and the part which seems to me most objectionable. This includes refusal of social intercourse, and even organized persuasion or argument, although free from any threat of violence, either express or implied. And this is with reference to persons who have a legal right to contract or not to contract with the plaintiff, as they may see fit. Interference with existing contracts is forbidden by the final decree. I wish to insist a little that the only point of difference which involves a difference of principle between the final decree and the preliminary injunction, which it is proposed to restore, is what I have mentioned, in order that it may be seen exactly what we are to discuss. It appears to me that the opinion of the majority turns in part on the assumption that the patrol necessarily carries with it a threat of bodily harm. That assumption I think unwarranted, for the reasons which I have given. Furthermore, it cannot be said, I think, that two men, walking together up and down a sidewalk, and speaking to those who enter a certain shop, do necessarily and always thereby convey a threat of force. I do not think it possible to discriminate, and to say that two workmen, or even two representatives of an organization of workmen, do; especially when they are, and are known to be, under the injunction of this court not to do so. See Stimson, Labor Law, § 60, especially pages 290, 298–300; Reg. v. Shepherd, 11 Cox.Cr. Cas. 325. I may add that I think the more intelligent workingmen believe as fully as I do that they no more can be permitted to usurp the state's prerogative of force than can their opponents in their controversies. But, if I am wrong, then the decree as it stands reaches the patrol, since it applies to all threats of force. With this I pass to the real difference between the interlocutory and the final decree.

I agree, whatever may be the law in the case of a single defendant (Rice v. Albee, 164 Mass. 88, 41 N.E. 122), that when a plaintiff proves that several persons have combined and conspired to injure his business, and have done acts producing that effect, he shows temporal damage and a cause of action, unless the facts disclose or the defendants prove some ground of excuse or justification; and I take it to be settled, and rightly settled, that doing that damage by combined persuasion is actionable, as well as doing it by falsehood or by force. [Citations omitted.]

Nevertheless, in numberless instances the law warrants the intentional infliction of temporal damage, because it regards it as justified. It is on the question of what shall amount to a justification, and more especially on the nature of the considerations which really determine or ought to determine the answer to that question, that judicial reasoning seems to me often to be inadequate. The true grounds of decision are considerations of policy and of social advantage, and it is vain to suppose that solutions can be attained merely by logic and general propositions of law which nobody disputes. Propositions as to public policy rarely are unanimously accepted, and still more rarely, if ever, are capable of unanswerable proof. They require a special training to enable any one even to form an intelligent opinion about them.

In the early stages of law, at least, they generally are acted on rather as inarticulate instincts than as definite ideas, for which a rational defense is ready.

To illustrate what I have said in the last paragraph: It has been the law for centuries that a man may set up a business in a small country town, too small to support more than one, although thereby he expects and intends to ruin some one already there, and succeeds in his intent. In such a case he is not held to act "unlawfully and without justifiable cause," as was alleged in Walker v. Cronin and Rice v. Albee. The reason, of course, is that the doctrine generally has been accepted that free competition is worth more to society than it costs, and that on this ground the infliction of the damage is privileged. Com. v. Hunt, 4 Metc. (Mass.) 111, 134. Yet even this proposition nowadays is disputed by a considerable body of persons, including many whose intelligence is not to be denied, little as we may agree with them.

I have chosen this illustration partly with reference to what I have to say next. It shows without the need of further authority that the policy of allowing free competition justifies the intentional inflicting of temporal damage, including the damage of interference with a man's business by some means, when the damage is done, not for its own sake, but as an instrumentality in reaching the end of victory in the battle of trade. In such a case it cannot matter whether the plaintiff is the only rival of the defendant, and so is aimed at specially, or is one of a class all of whom are hit. The only debatable ground is the nature of the means by which such damage may be inflicted. We all agree that it cannot be done by force or threats of force. We all agree, I presume, that it may be done by persuasion to leave a rival's shop, and come to the defendant's. It may be done by the refusal or withdrawal of various pecuniary advantages, which, apart from this consequence, are within the defendant's lawful control. It may be done by the withdrawal of, or threat to withdraw, such advantages from third persons who have a right to deal or not to deal with the plaintiff, as a means of inducing them not to deal with him either as customers or servants. Com. v. Hunt, 4 Metc. (Mass.) 111, 112, 133; Bowen v. Matheson, 14 Allen, 499; Heywood v. Tillson, 75 Me. 225; Steamship Co. v. McGregor [1892] App.Cas. 25. I have seen the suggestion made that the conflict between employers and employed was not competition, but I venture to assume that none of my brethren would rely on that suggestion. If the policy on which our law is founded is too narrowly expressed in the term "free competition," we may substitute "free struggle for life." Certainly, the policy is not limited to struggles between persons of the same class, competing for the same end. It applies to all conflicts of temporal interests.

I pause here to remark that the word "threats" often is used as if, when it appeared that threats had been made, it appeared that unlawful conduct had begun. But it depends on what you threaten. As a general rule, even if subject to some exceptions, what you may do in a certain event you may threaten to do—that is, give warning of your intention to do—in that event, and thus allow the other person the chance of avoiding the consequence. So, as to "compulsion," it depends on how you "compel." Com. v. Hunt, 4 Metc. (Mass.) 111, 133. So as to "annoyance" or "intimidation." Connor v. Kent, Curran v. Treleaven, 17 Cox, Cr.Cas. 354, 367, 368, 370. In Sherry v. Perkins, 147 Mass. 212, 17 N.E. 307, it was found as a fact that the display of banners which was enjoined was part of a scheme to prevent workmen from entering or remaining in the plaintiff's employment, "by threats and intimidation." The context showed that the words as there used meant threats of personal violence and intimidation by causing fear of it.

So far, I suppose, we are agreed. But there is a notion, which latterly has been insisted on a good deal, that a combination of persons to do what any one of them lawfully might do by himself will make the otherwise lawful conduct unlawful. It would be rash to say that some as yet unformulated truth may not be hidden under this proposition. But, in the general form in which it has been presented and accepted by many courts, I think it plainly untrue, both on authority and principle. Com. v. Hunt, 4 Metc. (Mass.) 111; Randall v. Hazelton, 12 Allen, 412, 414. There was combination of the most flagrant and dominant kind in Bowen v. Matheson, and in the Steamship Co. Case, and combination was essential to the success achieved.[4] But it is not necessary to cite cases. It is plain from the slightest consideration of practical affairs, or the most superficial reading of industrial history, that free competition means combination, and that the organization of the world, now going on so fast, means an ever-increasing might and scope of combination. It seems to me futile to set our faces against this tendency. Whether beneficial on the whole, as I think it, or detrimental, it is inevitable, unless the fundamental axioms of society, and even the fundamental conditions of life, are to be changed.

One of the eternal conflicts out of which life is made up is that between the effort of every man to get the most he can for his services, and that of society, disguised under the name of capital, to get his services for the least possible return. Combination on the one side is patent and powerful. Combination on the other is the necessary and desirable counterpart, if the battle is to be carried on in a fair and equal way. * * *

If it be true that workingmen may combine with a view, among other things, to getting as much as they can for their labor, just as capital may combine with a view to getting the greatest possible return, it must be true that, when combined, they have the same liberty that combined capital has, to support their interests by argument, persuasion, and the bestowal or refusal of those advantages which they otherwise lawfully control. I can remember when many people thought that, apart from violence or breach of contract, strikes were wicked, as organized refusals to work. I suppose that intelligent economists and legislators have given up that notion today. I feel pretty confident that they equally will abandon the idea that an organized refusal by workmen of social intercourse with a man who

4. These cases are summarized, pp. 30–31, infra.

shall enter their antagonist's employ is unlawful, if it is dissociated from any threat of violence, and is made for the sole object of prevailing, if possible, in a contest with their employer about the rate of wages. The fact that the immediate object of the act by which the benefit to themselves is to be gained is to injure their antagonist does not necessarily make it unlawful, any more than when a great house lowers the price of goods for the purpose and with the effect of driving a smaller antagonist from the business. * * *

Problems for Discussion

1. In *Vegelahn* v. *Guntner*, how would you characterize: (a) the interest of the plaintiff with which the defendants were interfering? (b) the objective of the defendants? (c) the method or conduct utilized by the defendants? Which of these was at the core of the court's finding that a tort had been committed?

2. What was the essential point of difference between Mr. Justice Holmes and the court majority? Was the difference one of fact, or of law, or of social policy? What criteria can judges (particularly appellate judges) use to detemine how to choose between the Holmes formulation and that of the court?

3. Why did the employer in *Vegelahn* seek relief through an injunctive action? What other forms of relief were available? Regarding each possible form of relief, consider whether there are significant differences in: (a) the substantive rules of law applied; (b) the method of proof; (c) the procedural safeguards for the defendants; (d) the mode of enforcement of the remedy. As counsel for the plaintiff, which would you seek? Could you successfully seek more than one?

PLANT v. WOODS

Supreme Judicial Court of Massachusetts, 1900.
176 Mass. 492, 57 N.E. 1011.

Bill in equity, filed in the Superior Court, * * * to restrain the defendants from any acts or the use of any methods tending to prevent the members of the plaintiff association from securing employment or continuing in their employment. * * *

HAMMOND, J. This case arises out of a contest for supremacy between two labor unions of the same craft, having substantially the same constitution and by-laws. The chief difference between them is that the plaintiff union is affiliated with a national organization having its headquarters in Lafayette, in the state of Indiana, while the defendant union is affiliated with a similar organization having its headquarters in Baltimore, in the state of Maryland. The plaintiff union was composed of workmen who, in 1897, withdrew from the defendant union. * * *

The contest became active early in the fall of 1898.   In September of that year the members of the defendant union declared "all painters not affiliated with the Baltimore headquarters to be nonunion men," and voted "to notify bosses" of that declaration. * * *

A duly authorized agent of the defendants would visit a shop where one or more of the plaintiffs were at work, and inform the employer of the action of the defendant union with reference to the plaintiffs, and ask him to induce such of the plaintiffs as were in his employ to sign applications for reinstatement in the defendant union. As to the general nature of these interviews the master finds that the defendants have been courteous in manner, have made no threats of personal violence, have referred to the plaintiffs as nonunion men, but have not otherwise represented them as men lacking good standing in their craft; that they have not asked that the Lafayette men be discharged, and in some cases have expressly stated that they did not wish to have them discharged, but only that they sign the blanks for reinstatement in the defendant union. The master, however, further finds, from all the circumstances under which those requests were made, that the defendants intended that employers of Lafayette men should fear trouble in their business if they continued to employ such men, * * * and as a means to this end they caused strikes to be instituted in the shops where strikes would seriously interfere with the business of the shops, and in all other shops they made such representations as would lead the proprietors thereof to expect trouble in their business. * * * It is well to see what is the meaning of this threat to strike, when taken in connection with the intimation that the employer may "expect trouble in his business." It means more than that the strikers will cease to work. That is only the preliminary skirmish. It means that those who have ceased to work will by strong, persistent, and organized persuasion and social pressure of every description do all they can to prevent the employer from procuring workmen to take their places. It means much more. It means that, if these peaceful measures fail, the employer may reasonably expect that unlawful physical injury may be done to his property; that attempts in all the ways practiced by organized labor will be made to injure him in his business, even to his ruin, if possible; and that by the use of vile and opprobrious epithets and other annoying conduct, and actual and threatened personal violence, attempts will be made to intimidate those who enter or desire to enter his employ; and that whether or not all this be done by the strikers or only by their sympathizers, or with the open sanction and approval of the former, he will have no help from them in his efforts to protect himself. However mild the language or suave the manner in which the threat to strike is made under such circumstances as are disclosed in this case, the employer knows that he is in danger of passing through such an ordeal as that above described, and those who make the threat know that as well as he does. Even if the intent of the strikers, so far as respects their own conduct and influence, be to discountenance all actual or threatened injury to person or property or business except that which is the direct necessary result of the interruption of the work, and even if their connection with the injurious and violent conduct of the turbulent among them or of their sympathizers be not such as to make them liable criminally, or even answerable civilly in damages to those who suffer, still, with full knowledge of what is to be expected, they give the signal, and in so doing must be held to avail themselves of the degree of fear and dread which the knowledge of such consequences will cause in the mind of those—whether their employer or fellow workmen—against whom the strike is directed; and the measure of coercion and intimidation imposed upon those against whom the strike is threatened or directed is not fully realized until all those probable consequences are considered. Such is the nature of the threat, and such the degree of coercion and intimidation involved in it. If the defendants can lawfully perform the acts complained of in the city of Springfield, they can pursue the plaintiffs all over the state in the same manner, and compel them to abandon their trade, or bow to the behests of their pursuers. It is to be observed that this is not a case between the employer and employed, or, to use a hackneyed expression, between capital and labor, but between laborers all of the same craft, and each having the same right as any one of the others to pursue his calling. In this as in every other case of equal rights the right of each individual is to be exercised with due regard to the similar right of all others, and the right of one be said to end where that of another begins. The right involved is the right to dispose of one's labor with full freedom. This is a legal right, and it is entitled to legal protection. * * * The same rule is stated with care and discrimination by Wells, J., in Walker v. Cronin, 107 Mass. 555: "Every one has a right to enjoy the fruits and advantages of his own enterprise, industry, skill and credit. He has no right to be protected against competition, but he has a right to be free from malicious and wanton interference, disturbance, or annoyance. If disturbance or loss come as the result of competition, or the exercise of like rights by others, it is damnum absque injuria, unless some superior right by contract, or otherwise, is interfered with. But if it come from the merely wanton or malicious acts of others, without the justification of competition, or the service of any interest or lawful purpose, it then stands upon a different footing." In this case the acts complained of were calculated to cause damage to the plaintiffs, and did actually cause such damage; and they were intentionally done for that purpose. Unless, therefore, there was justifiable cause, the acts were malicious and unlawful. Walker v. Cronin, ubi supra; Carew v. Rutherford, 106 Mass. 1, and cases cited therein.

* * * In cases somewhat akin to the one at bar this court has had occasion to consider the question how far acts manifestly coercive and intimidating in their nature, which cause damage and injury to the business or property of another, and are done with intent to cause such injury, and partly in reliance upon such coercion, are justifiable. [The court then discussed *Bowen v. Matheson*, 14 Allen 499 (Mass.1867), which is abstracted p. 30, infra.] On the other hand, it was held in Carew v. Rutherford, 106 Mass. 1, that a conspiracy against a mechanic—who is under the necessity of employing workmen in order to carry on his business— to obtain a sum of money from him, which he is under no legal obligation to pay, by inducing his workmen to leave him, or by deterring others from entering into his employ, or by threatening to do this, so that he is induced to pay the money demanded under a reasonable apprehension that he cannot carry on his business without yielding to the demands, is illegal, if not criminal, conspiracy; that the acts done under it are illegal, and that the money thus obtained may be recovered back. Chapman, C. J., speaking for the court, says that "there is no doubt that, if the parties under such circumstances succeed in injuring the business of the mechanic, they are liable to pay all the damages done to him." That case bears a close analogy to the one at bar. The acts there threatened were like those in this case, and the purpose was, in substance, to force the plaintiff to give his work to the defendants, and to extort from him a fine because he had given some of his work to other persons. Without now indicating to what extent workmen may combine, and in pursuance of an agreement may act by means of strikes and boycotts to get the hours of labor reduced, or their wages increased, or to procure from their employers any other concession directly and immediately affecting their own interests, or to help themselves in competition with their fellow workmen, we think this case must be governed by the principles laid down in Carew v. Rutherford, ubi supra. The purpose of these defendants was to force the plaintiffs to join the defendant association, and to that end they injured the plaintiffs in their business, and molested and disturbed them in their efforts to work at their trade. It is true they committed no acts of personal violence, or of physical injury to property, although they threatened to do something which might reasonably be expected to lead to such results. In their threat, however, there was plainly that which was coercive in its effect upon the will. It is not necessary that the liberty of the body should be restrained. Restraint of the mind, provided it would be such as would be likely to force a man against his will to grant the thing demanded, and actually has that effect, is sufficient in cases like this. * * * The necessity that the plaintiffs should join this association is not so great, nor is its relation to the rights of the defendants, as compared with the right of the plaintiffs to be free from molestation, such as to bring the acts of the defendant under the shelter of the principles of trade competition. Such acts are without justification, and therefore are malicious and unlawful, and the conspiracy thus to force the plaintiffs was unlawful. Such conduct is intolerable, and inconsistent with the spirit of our laws. * * *

HOLMES, C. J. (dissenting). * * * If the decision in the present case simply had relied upon Vegelahn v. Guntner, I should have hesitated to say anything, although I might have stated that my personal opinion had not been weakened by the substantial agreement with my views to be found in the judgments of the majority of the house of lords in Allen v. Flood. But, much to my satisfaction, if I may say so, the court has seen fit to adopt the mode of approaching the question which I believe to be the correct one, and to open an issue which otherwise I might have thought closed. The difference between my Brethren and me now seems to be a difference of degree, and the line of reasoning followed makes it proper for me to explain where the difference lies.

I agree that the conduct of the defendants is actionable unless justified. May v. Wood, 172 Mass. 11, 14, 51 N.E. 191, and cases cited. I agree that the presence or absence of justification may depend upon the object of their conduct; that is, upon the motive with which they acted. Vegelahn v. Guntner, 167 Mass. 92, 105, 106, 44 N. E. 1077, 35 L.R.A. 722. I agree, for instance, that, if a boycott or a strike is intended to override the jurisdiction of the courts by the action of a private association, it may be illegal. Weston v. Barnicoat, 175 Mass. 454, 56 N.E. 619, 49 L.R.A. 612. On the other hand, I infer that a majority of my Brethren would admit that a boycott or strike intended to raise wages directly might be lawful, if it did not embrace in its scheme or intent violence, breach of contract, or other conduct unlawful on grounds independent of the mere fact that the action of the defendants was combined. A sensible workingman would not contend that the courts should sanction a combination for the purpose of inflicting or threatening violence, or the infraction of admitted rights. To come directly to the point, the issue is narrowed to the question whether, assuming that some purposes would be a justification, the purpose in this case of the threatened boycotts and strikes was such as to justify the threats. That purpose was not directly concerned with wages. It was one degree more remote. The immediate object and motive was to strengthen the defendants' society as a preliminary and means to enable it to make a better fight on questions of wages or other matters of clashing interests.

I differ from my Brethren in thinking that the threats were as lawful for this preliminary purpose as for the final one to which strengthening the union was a means. I think that unity of organization is necessary to make the contest of labor effectual, and that societies of laborers lawfully may employ in their preparation the means which they might use in the final contest. * * *

BOWEN v. MATHESON, 14 Allen 499 (Mass.1867). Plaintiff and defendants were competitors engaged in the business of furnishing seamen to vessels sailing from the Port of Boston. The defendants entered into a combination for the purpose of controlling the entire business and destroying competitors who did not comply with their terms (among which was a prohibition upon furnishing seamen for wages below a stipulated amount); they agreed, among other things, not to furnish seamen to any vessel which shipped men furnished by the plaintiff. On demurrer to these allegations *held*, for defendants. "If the effect is to destroy the business of shipping masters who are not members of the association, it is such a result as in the competition of business often follows from a course of proceeding that the law permits. New inventions and new methods of transacting business often destroy the business of those who adhere to old methods. Sometimes associations break down the business of individuals * * *. As the declaration sets forth no illegal acts on the part of defendants, the demurrer must be sustained."

MOGUL STEAMSHIP COMPANY v. MCGREGOR, GOW & CO., 23 Q.B. Div. 598 (1889). Defendants, a number of shipowners, formed themselves into a combination for the purpose of driving the plaintiffs and other competitors from the field and thereby securing control of the carriage of tea from certain Chinese ports. In order to accomplish this object defendants during the tea harvest of 1885 combined to offer very low freight rates with a view to "smashing" the rates and thereby rendering it unprofitable for the plaintiffs to send their ships to those ports. Defendants offered a five per cent rebate to all shippers and agents who would deal exclusively with defendants' vessels, and any agent who broke the condition forfeited his entire rebate on all shipments made on behalf of all his principals during the whole year. Plaintiffs brought this action for damages and an injunction against the continuance of the conspiracy. *Held*, for defendants. Acts which intentionally damage another's trade are actionable if done without just cause or excuse. Here, just cause or excuse is to be found in the defendants' right "to carry on their own trade freely in the mode and manner that best suits them, and which they think best calculated to secure their advantage. * * * It is urged, however, on the part of plaintiffs, that even if the acts complained of would not be wrongful had they been committed by a single individual, they became actionable when they are the result of concerted action among several. * * * [It is impossible] to acquiesce in the view that the English law places any such restriction on the combination of capital as would be involved in the recognition of such a distinction. * * * The truth is, that the combination of capital for purposes of trade and competition is a very different thing from such a combination of several persons against one, with a view to harm him, as falls under the head of an indictable conspiracy. There is no just cause or excuse in the latter class of cases. There is just cause or excuse in the former. There are cases in which the very fact of a combination is evidence of a design to do that which is hurtful without just cause—is evidence—to use a technical expression—of malice. But it is perfectly legitimate, as it seems to me, to combine capital for all the mere purposes of trade for which capital may, apart from combination, be legitimately used in trade. To limit combinations of capital, when used for purposes of competition, in the manner proposed by the argument of the plaintiffs, would in the present day, be impossible—would be only another method of attempting to set boundaries to the tides."

Problems for Discussion

1. In *Plant* v. *Woods*, how would you characterize: (a) the interest of the plaintiffs with which the defendants were interfering? (b) the objective of the defendants? (c) the method or conduct utilized by the defendants? Which of these was at the core of the court's finding that a tort had been committed?

2. What was the essential point of difference between Mr. Justice Holmes and the court majority? Was the difference one of fact, or of law, or of social policy? Is there a narrowing of differences in the four-year period between the *Vegelahn* and *Plant* decisions?

3. Does the court in *Plant* help the reader understand why picketing or striking with an object of forcing the plaintiffs to change their union affiliation is tortious and enjoinable? Does Mr. Justice Holmes help the reader to understand why such activity is legal? Does he see certain affirmative values to be served by these forms of pressure? Does he not also concede that there are certain limits to their use? How does he formulate those limits? Can judges formulate those limits?

4. Assume that in 1904 a case reaches the Supreme Judicial Court of Massachusetts in which the Stone Masons Union seeks to enjoin the Bricklayers Union from combining and conspiring to interfere with the employment of stone masons in the work of cleaning and pointing brick walls by threatening building contractors with strikes by the bricklayers unless the bricklayers are given not only the work of laying brick but also the cleaning and pointing of brick walls. Assuming *Plant* v. *Woods* to be binding precedent, what judgment should the court render? (Are the respective interests of the employer, the plaintiff employees, the defendant employees, the public any different? Does that matter in deciding the case?)

5. Can *Plant* v. *Woods* be reconciled with *Bowen* v. *Matheson* and *Mogul S.S. Co.* v. *McGregor, Gow & Co.*?

Development of the "objectives" test.—As the division of opinion in *Plant* v. *Woods* suggests, wide divergences can be found in judicial rulings upon the lawfulness of various labor objectives. Although the cases noted immediately below could probably be opposed by contrary rulings from other jurisdictions, they do illustrate the dominant trend in judicial opinions at the time and also the present state of the common law in many jurisdictions (except as modified by constitutional and statutory developments to be discussed later).

In UNITED SHOE MACHINERY CORP. v. FITZGERALD, 237 Mass. 537, 130 N.E. 86 (1921), the plaintiff employer, which had individual contracts with its machinists binding them to work for a year at specified rates, was struck and picketed in support of union demands for collective bargaining. The court held this to be an unlawful objective, and issued an injunction. In HOPKINS v. OXLEY STAVE CO., 83 F. 912 (10th Cir. 1897), the plaintiff installed certain machines for hooping barrels, previously done by hand (more expensively and utilizing more workers). When the company resisted union demands to discontinue the use of these machines, the union notified the plaintiff's customers (suppliers of meat, flour and other commodities) that they must cease purchasing machine-hooped barrels in which to pack their wares, and induced the Trades Assembly of Kansas City to declare a boycott of all products packed in machine-hooped barrels. The district court enjoined any hindering or interfering with the plaintiff's business and customers. The two objects of the defendants—to deprive the plaintiff and its customers of their right freely to conduct their business, and "to deprive the public at large of the advantages to be derived from the use of an invention which was not only designed to diminish the cost of making certain necessary articles, but to lessen the labor of human hands"—were held unlawful. In CENTRAL METAL PRODUCTS CORP. v. O'BRIEN, 278 F. 827 (6th Cir. 1922), the plaintiff company hired members of the Carpenters Union to install on a construction site the metal doors, frames, transoms and sash that it manufactured, but the Amalgamated Sheet Metal Workers called a strike of its members employed by other contractors at the site when the plaintiff refused to assign the installation work to sheet metal workers instead of to carpenters. The court enjoined the strike and threats to strike.

B. THE SHERMAN ACT

In 1890, Congress in the Sherman Act declared unlawful "every contract, combination in the form of trust or otherwise, or conspiracy, in restraint of trade or commerce among the several States, or with foreign nations * * * " Violations were made punishable as federal crimes, the Attorney General of the United States was authorized to institute injunction proceedings in federal courts, and persons injured in their business as a result of such unlawful conduct were given the right to sue civilly for treble damages. Although the obvious objective of the legislation was the elimination of agreements between manufacturers or suppliers to fix the price or regulate the supply of goods, or allocate customers or exclude competitors, the Sherman Act was soon applied more often to labor unions than to business corporations. When in 1894 the American Railway Union, organized by Eugene V. Debs, instituted a strike against the Pullman Company to protest a wage cut—a strike which spread over a wide area and generated robbery, violence and property damage— the United States Circuit Court issued an injunction at the request of the Attorney General, invoking the Sherman Antitrust Act. United States v. Debs, 64 Fed. 724 (N.D.Ill.1894). The Supreme Court affirmed, but did not rely on the specific congressional authorization to enjoin given by the Sherman Act. In re Debs, 158 U.S. 564 (1895). It was not until Loewe v. Lawlor, popularly known as the *Danbury Hatters* case, that the Court squarely considered whether the Sherman Act applied to combinations of workers.

Before reading the following case, read carefully the text of Sections 1 and 2 of the Sherman Act in the Statutory Supplement. Consider whether that language could reasonably be construed to prohibit: (a) the forming and joining of labor unions; (b) collective bargaining between a union and an employer; (c) peaceful strikes, picketing and boycotts in aid of employee demands. What standards could a court use to determine the proper reach of the statutory ban, a most important question in view of the powerful remedies afforded under the Act?

LOEWE v. LAWLOR

Supreme Court of the United States, 1908.
208 U.S. 274, 28 S.Ct. 301, 52 L.Ed. 488.

MR. CHIEF JUSTICE FULLER delivered the opinion of the court:

This was an action brought in the circuit court for the district of Connecticut under § 7 of the antitrust act of July 2, 1890 [26 Stat. at L. 210, chap. 647, U.S.Comp.Stat.1901, p. 3202], claiming threefold damages for injuries inflicted on plaintiffs by combination or conspiracy declared to be unlawful by the act.

[The complaint alleged that the plaintiffs were hat manufacturers located in Danbury, Connecticut, the bulk of whose business was through wholesalers and retailers in other states. The defendants were members of the United Hatters of North America, which was alleged to have 9000 members in a large number of locals and to be combined with 1,400,000 others in the American Federation of Labor. The objective of the defendants was to unionize the workers employed by all American hat manufacturers and to achieve this by "restraining and destroying" their interstate trade, by "intimidation and threats" made to these manufacturers and their customers, and by boycotting them and their customers by appeals to union members throughout the United States. It was further alleged that of the eighty-two hat manufacturers in the nation, seventy had already been organized, and that a boycott was instituted against the plaintiffs when they refused to recognize the union. The defendants were said to have conspired intentionally and maliciously to interfere with the plaintiffs' production of hats and their distribution in interstate commerce, by inducing a strike at their factories and a boycott of the hats when sold elsewhere, as well as a boycott of the wholesalers selling them and of those who purchased (even hats made by others than the plaintiffs) from those wholesalers. The boycott of the wholesalers and dealers was effected by direct pressure and by distributing circulars, as well as by publicizing the boycott in local newspapers and union publications. The plaintiffs alleged actual damage to their business and property in the amount of $80,000.]

Defendants filed a demurrer to the complaint, assigning general and special grounds. The demurrer was sustained as to the first six paragraphs, which rested on the ground that the combination stated was not within the Sherman act, and this rendered it unnecessary to pass upon any other questions in the case; and, upon plaintiffs declining to amend their complaint, the court dismissed it with costs. 148 Fed. 924; and see 142 Fed. 216, 130 Fed. 633.

The case was then carried by writ of error to the circuit court of appeals for the second circuit, and that court, desiring the instruction of this court upon a question arising on the writ of error, certified that question to this court. The certificate consisted of a brief statement of facts, and put the question thus: "Upon this state of facts can plaintiffs maintain an action against defendants under § 7 of the anti-trust act of July 2, 1890?" * * *

In our opinion, the combination described in the declaration is a combination "in restraint of trade or commerce among the several states," in the sense in which those words are used in the act, and the action can be maintained accordingly.

And that conclusion rests on many judgments of this court, to the effect that the act prohibits any combination whatever to secure action which essentially obstructs the free flow of commerce between the states, or restricts, in that regard, the liberty of a trader to engage in business.

The combination charged falls within the class of restraints of trade aimed at compelling third parties and strangers involuntarily not to engage in the course of trade except on conditions that the combination imposes; and there is no doubt that (to quote from the well-known work of Chief Justice Erle on Trade Unions) "at common law every person has individually, and the public also has collectively, a right to require that the course of trade should be kept free from unreasonable obstruction." But the objection here is to the jurisdiction, because, even conceding that the declaration states a case good at common law, it is contended that it does not state one within the statute. Thus, it is said that the restraint alleged would operate to entirely destroy plaintiffs' business and thereby include intrastate trade as well; that physical obstruction is not alleged as contemplated; and that defendants are not themselves engaged in interstate trade.

We think none of these objections are tenable, and that they are disposed of by previous decisions of this court. * * *

In W. W. Montague & Co. v. Lowry, 193 U.S. 38, 48 L.Ed. 608, 24 Sup.Ct.Rep. 307, which was an action brought by a private citizen under § 7 against a combination engaged in the manufacture of tiles, defendants were wholesale dealers in tiles in California, and combined with manufacturers in other states to restrain the interstate traffic in tiles by refusing to sell any tiles to any wholesale dealer in California who was not a member of the association, except at a prohibitive rate. The case was a commercial boycott against such dealers in California as would not or could not obtain membership in the association. The restraint did not consist in a physical obstruction of interstate commerce, but in the fact that the plaintiff and other independent dealers could not purchase their tiles from manufacturers in other states because such manufacturers had combined to boycott them. This court held that this obstruction to the purchase of tiles, a fact antecedent to physical transportation, was within the prohibition of the act. Mr. Justice Peckham, speaking for the court, said, concerning the agreement, that it "restrained trade, for it narrowed the market for the sale of tiles in California from the manufacturers and dealers therein in other states, so that they could only be sold to the members of the association, and it enhanced prices to the nonmember."

The averments here are that there was an existing interstate traffic between plaintiffs and citizens of other states, and that, for the direct purpose of destroying such interstate traffic, defendants combined not merely to prevent plaintiffs from manufacturing articles then and there intended for transportation beyond the state, but also to prevent the vendees from reselling the hats which they had imported from Connecticut, or from further negotiating with plaintiffs for the purchase and intertransportation of such hats from Connecticut to the various places of destination. So that, although some of the means whereby the interstate traffic was to be destroyed were acts within a state, and some of them were, in themselves, as a part of their obvious purpose and effect, beyond the scope of Federal authority, still, as we have seen, the acts must be considered as a whole, and the plan is open to condemnation, notwithstanding a negligible amount of intrastate business might be affected in carrying it out. If the purposes of the combination were, as alleged, to prevent any interstate transportation at all, the fact that the means operated at one end before physical transportation commenced, and, at the other end, after the physical transportation ended, was immaterial.

Nor can the act in question be held inapplicable because defendants were not themselves engaged in interstate commerce. The act made no distinction between classes. It provided that "every" contract, combination, or conspiracy in restraint of trade was illegal. The records of Congress show that several efforts were made to exempt, by legislation, organizations of farmers and laborers from the operation of the act, and that all these efforts failed, so that the act remained as we have it before us.

In an early case (United States v. Workingmen's Amalgamated Council, 26 L.R.A. 158, 4 Inters.Com.Rep. 831, 54 Fed. 994) the United States filed a bill under the Sherman act in the circuit court for the eastern district of Louisiana, averring the existence of "a gigantic and widespread combination of the members of a multitude of separate organizations for the purpose of restraining the commerce among the several states and with foreign countries," and it was contended that the statute did not refer to combinations of laborers. But the court, granting the injunction, said:

"I think the congressional debates show that the statute had its origin in the evils of massed capital; but, when the Congress came to formulating the prohibition, which is the yardstick for measuring the complainant's right to the injunction, it expressed it in these words: 'Every contract or combination in the form of trust, or otherwise in restraint of trade or commerce among the several states or with foreign nations, is hereby declared to be illegal.' The subject had so broadened in the minds of the legislators that the source of the evil was not regarded as material, and the evil in its entirety is dealt with. They made the interdiction include combinations of labor as well as of capital; in fact, all combinations in restraint of commerce, without reference to the character of the persons who entered into them. It is true this statute has not been much expounded by judges, but, as it seems to me, its meaning, as far as relates to the sort of combinations to which it is to apply, is manifest, and that it includes combinations which are composed of laborers acting in the interest of laborers. * * *

We think a case within the statute was set up and that the demurrer should have been overruled.

Judgment reversed and cause remanded with a direction to proceed accordingly.

———

Problems for Discussion

1. If the strike at the hat factories in Danbury had been successful in shutting them down, so that no boycott of wholesalers and their customers had been necessary, would the strikers have violated the Sherman Act?

2. Is there a material difference between the boycott effected by the manufacturers and wholesalers of tile described in the *Montague* case (discussed in the principal case) and the boycott effected by the laborers in *Loewe* v. *Lawlor*, such that antitrust liability in the former case would not be controlling in the latter?

3. Assume that Super-Dainty Garment Co. (p. 17, supra) was a Philadelphia firm selling in the New York and Chicago markets in competition with New York manufacturers. If the Pennsylvania courts were unwilling to issue injunctions in labor disputes, would there be any basis for suit in a federal court? (Consider this question again after reading the following Note.)

———

CORONADO COAL CO. v. UNITED MINE WORKERS, 268 U.S. 295, 45 S.Ct. 551, 69 L.Ed. 963 (1925). The plaintiffs were a number of coal companies, interrelated in organization and physical location, controlled by the Bache-Denman Coal Company. They brought an action under the Sherman Act for treble damages against the International of the Mine Workers, its District No. 21 and other locals, for damage to business and property stemming from a violent strike at the plaintiffs' Sebastian County mines in Arkansas. Bache, the manager of the mines—which had been unionized by District 21, a regional mineworkers organization—announced his intention to close them down and then reopen them on a nonunion basis. When the mines were reopened, union members attacked guards there and committed serious injury to persons and property. In a later episode, union sympathizers armed with guns attacked workers, equipment and other property; two persons were killed, and dynamite was used to destroy the mine premises. After a trial resulted in a verdict of $200,000 which was then trebled, the case was remanded by the Supreme Court, since the evidence failed to support a claim under the Sherman Act; the Court found only a "local motive" for the defendants' actions, a protest against the use of nonunion workers at the mines and against the mineowners' breach of contract with the union. In the Court's words, "it was in fact a local strike, local in its origin and motive, local in its waging, and local in its felonious and murderous ending," and although reprehensible such a strike would fall outside the ban of the Sherman Act.

On remand, new evidence was introduced, which demonstrated to the Court that the objective of District 21 was not simply "local" but was directed at so crippling the plaintiffs' nonunion mines as to prevent their competition with unionized mines in adjacent states. Pertinent passages of the Court's opinion follow.

"Part of the new evidence was an extract from the convention proceedings of District No. 21 at Ft. Smith, Ark., in February, 1914, in which the delegates discussed the difficulties presented in their maintenance of the union scale in Arkansas, Oklahoma, and Texas because of the keen competition from the nonunion fields of Southern Colorado and the nonunion fields of the South in Alabama and Tennessee. Stewart, the president, called attention to a new field in Oklahoma which he said would be a great competitor of union coal fields, and that District No. 21 would be forced to call a strike to bring in to line certain operators in that section, and in the event that they did so the District would fight such a conflict to the bitter end regardless of cost. * * *

"A new witness was one Hanraty, who was for seven years president of District No. 21 * * * He said that he made speeches all through District No. 21 and did not remember a speech in which he did not mention the danger from nonunion coal in taking the markets of union coal and forcing a nonunion scale, and that it was a constant subject of discussion among the officers and members.

"In addition to this, the testimony of McNamara, already discussed, while ineffective to establish the complicity of the International Union with this conspiracy, contains much, if credited, from which the jury could reasonably infer that the purpose of the union miners in District No. 21 and the local unions engaged in the plan was to destroy the power of the owners and lessees of the Bache-Denman mines to send their output into interstate commerce 1:

compete with that of union mines in Oklahoma, in Kansas, in Louisiana markets, and elsewhere. It appeared that 80 per cent. of all the product of the mines in Sebastian county went into other states.

" * * * The mere reduction in the supply of an article to be shipped in interstate commerce by the illegal or tortious prevention of its manufacture or production is ordinarily an indirect and remote obstruction to that commerce. But when the intent of those unlawfully preventing the manufacture or production is shown to be to restrain or control the supply entering and moving in interstate commerce, or the price of it in interstate markets, their action is a direct violation of the Anti-Trust Act. * * * We think there was substantial evidence at the second trial in this case tending to show that the purpose of the destruction of the mines was to stop the production of non-union coal and prevent its shipment to markets of other states than Arkansas, where it would by competition tend to reduce the price of the commodity and affect injuriously the maintenance of wages for union labor in competing mines, and that the direction by the District Judge to return a verdict for the defendants other than the International Union was erroneous."

III. THE CLAYTON ACT AND THE DEVELOPMENT OF THE UNIONS, 1890–1930 [1]

Throughout the years 1886–1914 there gradually developed, despite the hostile attitude of the courts and the organized opposition of employers, a strong body of opinion which held that workers should be granted the right to organize unions without employer interference, and that the employers should be required to recognize and deal with their employees' unions. As early as 1894, the United States Strike Commission, which had been investigating the causes of the Pullman strike, criticized the attitude of some of the courts and urged employers to recognize and bargain with labor organizations. In 1902 a report made by the Industrial Commission to Congress ridiculed the suggestion that individual freedom was lost under a system of collective agreements and stressed their effectiveness in promoting industrial peace. It declared—

"The chief advantage which comes from the practice of periodically determining the conditions of labor by collective bargaining directly

1. See Jones, The Enigma of the Clayton Act, 10 Ind. & Lab.Rel.Rev. 201 (1957).

between employers and employees is, that thereby each side obtains a better understanding of the actual state of the industry, of the conditions which confront the other side, and of the motives which influence it. Most strikes and lockouts would not occur if each party understood exactly the position of the other. Where representatives of employers and employees can meet personally together and discuss all the considerations on which the wage scale and the conditions of labor would be based, a satisfactory agreement can, in the great majority of instances, be reached. * * *

"It is not to be supposed that the introduction of joint conferences and arbitration committees in a trade will render strikes and lockouts thereafter impossible. * * * Nevertheless experience both in England and in our own country shows that where these practices have once become fairly well established they greatly reduce the number of strikes and lockouts, and in many trades do away with them altogether for long periods of time. Even when a cessation of employment does intervene, the experience of the beneficial effects of peaceful methods usually leads to their reestablishment." [2]

Another federal commission found the Anthracite Coal strike in 1902 was caused partly by the question of union recognition, and called attention to a truth demonstrated by experience which is still too often ignored:

"Experience shows that the more full the recognition given to a trades union, the more businesslike and responsible it becomes. Through dealing with business men in business matters, its more intelligent, conservative, and responsible members come to the front and gain general control and direction of its affairs. If the energy of the employer is directed to discouragement and repression of the union, he need not be surprised if the more radically inclined members are the ones most frequently heard." [3]

When Woodrow Wilson was elected in 1912, urging that there be a "New Freedom," the tariff was reduced, the banking and currency system was reformed, and the anti-trust laws were strengthened by the enactment of the Federal Trade Commission and Clayton Anti-trust Acts. The Clayton Act also contained two sections inserted at the request of organized labor, which Samuel Gompers hailed as "labor's charter of freedom". Many supposed that they swept out of the federal courts the precedents at common law and under the Sherman Act which had proved so detrimental to the labor movement. It was not until some years later that the hope proved false.

2. H.R.Doc. No. 380, 57th Cong., 1st   3. Anthracite Coal Strike Comm. Rep.,
   Sess. 844–845.   S.Doc. 6, 58th Cong., Spec.Sess., 63.

The gains of organized labor under the new spirit of the Wilson Administration were soon strengthened by the emotional fervor of a war to make the world safe for democracy. Widened profit margins and the wartime scarcity of labor also made employers less reluctant to grant wage increases, and the AFL affiliates enhanced their prestige and secured new members by successful strikes. Both employers and the government made important concessions to the labor unions in order to secure their cooperation in increasing industrial output. Possibly the most important factor, however, was the encouragement given to unionization by the federal government's wartime labor policies.

In the autumn of 1917 it became apparent that governmental intervention would be necessary to prevent labor disputes from impeding the production of war materials, and in January 1918, President Wilson set up a War Labor Conference Board under the joint chairmanship of former President William H. Taft and Frank P. Walsh. The War Labor Conference Board recommended the establishment of a National War Labor Board which was promptly organized and adopted the following principle as one of the policies which would guide its action:

"The right of workers to organize in trade unions and to bargain collectively, through chosen representatives, is recognized and affirmed. This right shall not be denied, abridged, or interfered with by the employers in any manner whatsoever."

This policy was followed by other government agencies and was vigorously enforced by the National War Labor Board. In several cases the government seized and operated the plants of companies which persisted in anti-union tactics in defiance of the Board's orders.

Thus the ideas expressed in the series of official reports quoted above became the foundation of the national labor policy. For the first time the right to organize and bargain collectively received effective government protection. Although the concept was soon abandoned, it was kept alive in the transportation industry and reinvigorated in 1933 when it was embodied in the National Industrial Recovery Act. Two years later with the enactment of the National Labor Relations Act it became the foundation of present labor law.

As a result of the favorable economic conditions and government policies which prevailed during the six year period 1914–1920, trade union memberships increased almost 2,500,000. In 1920 the average annual membership of all unions exceeded 5,000,000, nearly double their membership in 1914. The AFL experienced its proportionate share of the growth for its membership increased from 2,000,000 to 4,000,000. Despite the large total increase, however, the increase was concentrated in a few trades. In 1920 two-thirds of all union members were to be found in four groups: 17.6% in building construction; 17% in metals, machinery and shipbuilding; 7.4% in clothing; and 24.9% in transportation and commerce. The trade union movement had not reached the unskilled workers in mass production industry.

In 1918 and 1919, the AFL made its greatest attempt to enter this untouched field. The drive began with an effort to organize the basic steel industry, which was dominated by the giant United States Steel Corporation. An intensive organizing campaign, spearheaded by the Amalgamated Association of Iron, Steel and Tin Workers, began in August 1918. The corporations countered by improving working conditions, but also by mass discharges of union members, the prohibition of union meetings, espionage and violence. When Judge Gary of United States Steel persisted in refusing to recognize the union as spokesman for the workers, a strike vote was overwhelmingly approved, but the union, fearful of the consequences of a strike, made every effort to delay it and to initiate bargaining. When repressive action became more severe—the expulsion of union organizers, the terrorizing of employees by deputy sheriffs, and further mass discharges—343,000 steel workers went on strike on September 23, 1919. The strike, marked by violence between the strikers and privately hired guards and deputies, lasted nearly three months, but in the end it was broken and union organization in the industry was utterly obliterated.

The breaking of the steel strike both reflected and encouraged the stiffened attitude of employers toward labor unions. When the war ended, President Wilson attempted to put the policies of the National War Labor Board on a more permanent footing by appointing representatives of the public, employers and labor to a National Industrial Conference; but the effort failed when employer members refused to join in a resolution, requiring unanimity, supporting the right of workers to organize without discrimination and to bargain collectively on wages, hours and conditions of employment through representatives of their own choosing.

It was not long before another open shop campaign was organized to restore the right of every American "to enter any trade or business he chose and to work on conditions satisfactory to himself without interference from a union." The campaign was strengthened by the psychological desire for a return to normalcy, post war reaction, and anti-Red hysteria.

Throughout the 1920's economic conditions were also unfavorable to a labor movement. Trade unions have usually grown strong during a rise in the business cycle when prices were outrunning wages; real wages rose considerably during the 1920's. Large mass production establishments became increasingly dominant especially in such growing industries as iron and steel, automobile, rubber and petroleum. In 1914 establishments with an annual production of over one million dollars employed 35 per cent of the wage earners. By 1929 the percentage had risen to 58. Employment in small shops rapidly declined. In 1914 shops whose annual production was valued at less than $20,000, employed approximately 8 per cent of the nation's wage earners. In 1929 the proportion had dwindled to 3 per cent. In this adjustment many jobs became routine and employment in the established trades declined. The new unskilled laborers lacked any union tradition. Many of them were immigrants inclined to follow the employers' wishes and when strikes occurred, replacements were easy to find. Some industries, notably cotton textiles, moved south to find cheaper labor which had not been influenced by the unionism.

The large corporations were strongholds of anti-unionism, with both the impersonality and resources to use every kind of weapon. While many of the old practices continued, the industrial giants also developed new and more benevolent personnel policies. "Welfare capitalism" was in the ascendancy. Profit-sharing plans had a rapid birth rate, and died as rapidly. The science of personnel management was growing. Jobs were rationalized. New bonus systems were installed; they yielded the individual greater compensation for increased production. Hiring and firing became a function of the personnel manager, and the foreman lost many of the dictatorial powers which had been a constant source of irritation to his subordinates. Employee welfare plans and similar activities were encouraged to build morale; the worker acquired "company consciousness" instead of a sense of loyalty to his craft.

In this development the Employee Representation Plan, Works Council or "company union" bulked large. The National War Labor Board had declared and enforced the right of workers to bargain through representatives of their own choosing, but apparently neither the Board nor other government agencies looked too closely to see whether the representative was a bona fide union or an organization financed and controlled by the employer. Company unions became popular during the war, and between 1919 and 1928 their memberships rose from 403,000 to 1,500,000; in roughly the same period the American Federation of Labor lost 400,000 members. Most company unions were utterly dependent on the employer for support. Not only did they lack financial strength but they could not change their constitutions or take other action without the approval of the employer. They built up a company *esprit de corps*, however, and were thought to furnish a bulwark against penetration by an "outside union."

Judicial decisions during the early 1920's were also extremely unfavorable to labor unions. In all but a few liberal courts, notably the New York Court of Appeals, continued reliance was placed on the restrictive tests of "unlawful objectives" and "unlawful means." The Clayton Act, which Samuel Gompers had hailed as labor's "charter of freedom," was rendered impotent by a series of Supreme Court decisions of which *Duplex Printing Press Co. v. Deering* is the leading illustration.

DUPLEX PRINTING PRESS CO. v. DEERING

Supreme Court of the United States, 1921.
254 U.S. 443, 41 S.Ct. 172, 65 L.Ed. 349, 16 A.L.R. 196.

MR. JUSTICE PITNEY delivered the opinion of the Court.

This was a suit in equity brought by appellant in the District Court for the Southern District of New York for an injunction to restrain a course of conduct carried on by defendants in that district and vicinity in maintaining a boycott against the products of complainant's factory, in furtherance of a conspiracy to injure and destroy its good will, trade, and business—especially to obstruct and destroy its interstate trade. * * * Complainant is a Michigan corporation, and manufactures printing presses at a factory in Battle Creek, in that state, employing about 200 machinists in the factory, in addition to 50 office employees, traveling salesmen, and expert machinists or road men, who supervise the erection of the presses for complainant's customers at their various places of business. * * * [It] conducts its business on the "open shop" policy, without discrimination against either union or non-union men. The individual defendants and the local organizations of which they are the representatives are affiliated with the International Association of Machinists, an unincorporated association having a membership of more than 60,000, and are united in a combination, to which the International Association also is a party, having the object of compelling complainant to unionize its factory and enforce the "closed shop," the eight-hour day, and the union scale of wages, by means of interfering with and restraining its interstate trade in the products of the factory. Complainant's principal manufacture is newspaper presses of large size and complicated mechanism, varying in weight from 10,000 to 100,000 pounds, and requiring a considerable force of labor and a considerable expenditure of time—a week or more—to handle, haul, and erect them at the point of delivery. These presses are sold throughout the United States and in foreign countries; and, as they are especially designed for the production of daily papers, there is a large market for them in and about the city of New York. They are delivered there in the ordinary course of interstate commerce; the handling, hauling, and installation work at destination being done by employees of the purchaser under the supervision of a specially skilled machinist supplied by complainant. The acts complained of and sought to be restrained have nothing to do with the conduct or management of the factory in Michigan, but solely with the installation and operation of the presses by complainant's customers. None of the defendants is or ever was an employee of complainant, and complainant at no time has had relations with either of the organizations that they represent. In August, 1913 (eight months before the filing of the bill), the International Association called a strike at complainant's factory in Battle Creek, as a result of which union machinists to the number of about 11 in the factory and 3 who supervised the erection of presses in the field left complainant's employ. But the defection of so small a number did not materially interfere with the operation of the factory, and sales and shipments in interstate commerce continued.

The acts complained of made up the details of an elaborate programme adopted and carried out by defendants and their organizations in and about the city of New York as part of a country-wide programme adopted by the International Association, for the purpose of enforcing a boycott of complainant's product. The acts embraced the following, with others: Warning customers that it would be better for them not to purchase, or having purchased, not to install, presses made by complainant, and threatening them with loss should they do so; threatening customers with sympathetic strikes in other trades; notifying a trucking company, usually employed by customers to haul the presses, not to do so, and threatening it with trouble if it should; inciting employees of the trucking company, and other men employed by customers of complainant, to strike against their respective employers in order to interfere with the hauling and installation of presses, and thus bring pressure to bear upon the customers; notifying repair shops not to do repair work on Duplex presses; coercing union men, by threatening them with loss of union cards and with being blacklisted as "scabs" if they assisted in installing the presses; threatening an exposition company with a strike if it permitted complainant's presses to be exhibited; and resorting to a variety of other modes of preventing the sale of presses of complainant's manufacture in or about New York City, and delivery of them in interstate commerce, such as injuring and threatening to injure complainant's customers and prospective customers, and persons concerned in hauling, handling, or installing the presses. In some cases the threats were undisguised; in other cases polite in form, but none the less sinister in purpose and effect.   *   *   *

All the judges of the Circuit Court of Appeals concurred in the view that defendants' conduct consisted essentially of efforts to render it impossible for complainant to carry on any commerce in printing presses between Michigan and New York and that defendants had agreed to do and were endeavoring to accomplish the very thing pronounced unlawful by this court in Loewe v. Lawlor, 208 U.S. 274, 28 S.Ct. 301, 52 L.Ed. 488, 13 Ann.Cas. 815, and Lawlor v. Loewe, 235 U.S. 522, 35 S.Ct. 170, 59 L.Ed. 341. The judges also agreed that the interference with interstate commerce was such as ought to be enjoined, unless the Clayton Act of October 15, 1914, forbade such injunction.

* * * [The Court held that the Clayton Act applied to injunction actions which were pending at the time of the Act's passage.]

Looking first to the [Sherman Act] the thing declared illegal by its first section (26 Stat. 209 [Comp.St. § 8820]) is:

"Every contract, combination in the form of trust or otherwise, or conspiracy, in restraint of trade or commerce among the several states, or with foreign nations." * * *

In Loewe v. Lawlor, 208 U.S. 274, 28 S.Ct. 301, 52 L.Ed. 488, 13 Ann.Cas. 815, where there was an effort to compel plaintiffs to unionize their factory by preventing them from manufacturing articles intended for transportation beyond the state, and also by preventing vendees from reselling articles purchased from plaintiffs and negotiating with plaintiffs for further purchases, by means of a boycott of plaintiffs' products and of dealers who handled them, this court held that there was a conspiracy in restraint of trade actionable under section 7 of the Sherman Act (section 8829), * * *. And when the case came before the court a second time, 235 U.S. 522, 534, 35 S.Ct. 170, 59 L.Ed. 341, it was held that the use of the primary and secondary boycott and the circulation of a list of "unfair dealers," intended to influence customers of plaintiffs and thus subdue the latter to the demands of the defendants, and having the effect of interfering with plaintiffs' interstate trade, was actionable. * * *

Upon the question whether the provisions of the Clayton Act forbade the grant of an injunction under the circumstances of the present case, the Circuit Court of Appeals was divided; the majority holding that under section 20, "perhaps in conjunction with section 6," there could be no injunction. * * *

As to section 6, it seems to us its principal importance in this discussion is for what it does not authorize, and for the limit it sets to the immunity conferred. The section assumes the normal objects of a labor organization to be legitimate, and declares that nothing in the anti-trust laws shall be construed to forbid the existence and operation of such organizations or to forbid their members from *lawfully* carrying out their *legitimate* objects. * * *

The principal reliance is upon section 20. * * * The first paragraph merely puts into statutory form familiar restrictions upon the granting of injunctions already established and of general application in the equity practice of the courts of the United States. It is but declaratory of the law as it stood before. The second paragraph declares that "no such restraining order or injunction" shall prohibit certain conduct specified—manifestly still referring to a "case between an employer and employees, * * * involving, or growing out of, a dispute concerning terms or conditions of employment," as designated in the first paragraph. It is very clear that the restriction upon the use of the injunction is in favor only of those concerned as parties to such a dispute as is described. The words defining the permitted conduct include particular qualifications consistent with the general one respecting the nature of the case and dispute intended; and the concluding words, "nor shall any of the acts specified in this paragraph be considered or held to be violations of any law of the United States," are to be read in the light of the context, and mean only that those acts are not to be so held when committed by parties concerned in "a dispute concerning terms or conditions of employment." If the qualifying words are to have any effect, they must operate to confine the restriction upon the granting of injunctions, and also the relaxation of the provisions of the anti-trust and other laws of the United States, to parties standing in proximate relation to a controversy such as is particularly described.

The majority of the Circuit Court of Appeals appears to have entertained the view that the words "employers and employees," as used in section 20, should be treated as referring to "the business class or clan to which the parties litigant respectively belong," and that, as there had been a dispute at complainant's factory in Michigan concerning the conditions of employment there—a dispute created, it is said, if it did not exist before, by the act of the Machinists' Union in calling a strike at the factory—section 20 operated to permit members of the Machinists' Union elsewhere, some 60,000 in number, although standing in no relation of employment under complainant, past, present, or prospective, to make that dispute their own and proceed to instigate sympathetic strikes, picketing, and boycotting against employers wholly unconnected with complainant's factory and having relations with complainant only in the way of purchasing its product in the ordinary course of interstate commerce, and this where there was no dispute between such employers and their employees respecting terms or conditions of employment.

We deem this construction altogether inadmissible. Section 20 must be given full effect according to its terms as an expression of the purpose of Congress; but it must be borne in mind that the section imposes an exceptional and extraordinary restriction upon the equity powers of the courts of the United States and upon the general operation of the anti-trust laws, a restriction in the nature of a special privilege or immunity to a particular class, with corresponding detriment to the general public; and it would violate rules of statutory construction having general application and far-reaching importance to enlarge that special privilege by resorting to a loose construction of the section, not to speak of ignoring or slighting the qualifying

words that are found in it. Full and fair effect will be given to every word if the exceptional privilege be confined—as the natural meaning of the words confines it—to those who are proximately and substantially concerned as parties to an actual dispute respecting the terms or conditions of their own employment, past, present, or prospective.
* * *

The qualifying effect of the words descriptive of the nature of the dispute and the parties concerned is further borne out by the phrases defining the conduct that is not to be subjected to injunction or treated as a violation of the laws of the United States, that is to say:

(a) "Terminating any relation of employment, * * * or persuading others by peaceful means so to do;" (b) "attending at any place where any such person or persons may lawfully be, for the purpose of peacefully obtaining or communicating information, or from peacefully persuading any person to work or to abstain from working;" (c) "ceasing to patronize or to employ any party to such dispute, or * * * recommending, advising, or persuading others by peaceful and lawful means so to do;" (d) "paying or giving to, or withholding from, any person engaged in such dispute, any strike benefits; * * *" (e) "doing any act or thing which might lawfully be done in the absence of such dispute by any party thereto."

The emphasis placed on the words "lawful" and "lawfully," "peaceful" and "peacefully," and the references to the dispute and the parties to it, strongly rebut a legislative intent to confer a general immunity for conduct violative of the anti-trust laws, or otherwise unlawful. The subject of the boycott is dealt with specifically in the "ceasing to patronize" provision, and by the clear force of the language employed the exemption is limited to pressure exerted upon a "party to such dispute" by means of "peaceful and *lawful*" influence upon neutrals. There is nothing here to justify defendants or the organizations they represent in using either threats or persuasion to bring about strikes or a cessation of work on the part of employees of complainant's customers or prospective customers, or of the trucking company employed by the customers, with the object of compelling such customers to withdraw or refrain from commercial relations with complainant, and of thereby constraining complainant to yield the matter in dispute. To instigate a sympathetic strike in aid of a secondary boycott cannot be deemed "peaceful and lawful" persuasion. In essence it is a threat to inflict damage upon the immediate employer, between whom and his employees no dispute exists, in order to bring him against his will into a concerted plan to inflict damage upon another employer who is in dispute with his employees.

The majority of the Circuit Court of Appeals, very properly treating the case as involving a secondary boycott, based the decision upon the view that it was the purpose of section 20 to legalize the secondary boycott "at least in so far as it rests on or consists of refusing to work for any one who deals with the principal offender." Characterizing the section as "blindly drawn," and conceding that the meaning attributed to it was broad, the court referred to the legislative history of the enactment as a warrant for the construction adopted. Let us consider this.

By repeated decisions of this court it has come to be well established that the debates in Congress expressive of the views and motives of individual members are not a safe guide, and hence may not be resorted to, in ascertaining the meaning and purpose of the lawmaking body. * * * But reports of committees of House or Senate stand upon a more solid footing, and may be regarded as an exposition of the legislative intent in a case where otherwise the meaning of a statute is obscure. * * * And this has been extended to include explanatory statements in the nature of a supplemental report made by the committee member in charge of a bill in course of passage.

In the case of the Clayton Act, the printed committee reports are not explicit with respect to the meaning of the "ceasing to patronize" clause of what is now section 20. See House Rept. No. 627, 63d Cong., 2d Sess., pp. 30, 33–36; Senate Rept. No. 698, 63d Cong., 2d Sess., pp. 29–31; the latter being a reproduction of the former. But they contain extracts from judicial opinions and a then recent text-book sustaining the "primary boycott," and expressing an adverse view as to the secondary or coercive boycott, and, on the whole, are far from manifesting a purpose to relax the prohibition against restraints of trade in favor of the secondary boycott.

Moreover, the report was supplemented in this regard by the spokesman of the House committee (Mr. Webb) who had the bill in charge when it was under consideration by the House. The question whether the bill legalized the secondary boycott having been raised, it was emphatically and unequivocally answered by him in the negative.
* * *

The extreme and harmful consequences of the construction adopted in the court below are not to be ignored. The present case furnishes an apt and convincing example. An ordinary controversy in a manufacturing establishment, said to concern the terms or conditions of employment there, has been held a sufficient occasion for imposing a general embargo upon the products of the establishment and a nationwide blockade of the channels of interstate commerce against them, carried out by inciting sympathetic strikes and a secondary boycott against complainant's customers, to the great and incalculable damage of many innocent people far remote from any connection with or control over the original and actual dispute—people constituting, indeed, the general public upon whom the cost must ultimately fall, and whose vital interest in unobstructed commerce constituted the prime and paramount concern of Congress in enacting the anti-trust laws, of which the section under consideration forms after all a part.

Reaching the conclusion, as we do, that complainant has a clear right to an injunction under the Sherman Act as amended by the Clayton Act, it becomes unnecessary to consider whether a like result would follow under the common law or local statutes; there being no suggestion that relief thereunder could be broader than that to which complainant is entitled under the acts of Congress.   *   *   *

MR. JUSTICE BRANDEIS, dissenting, with whom MR. JUSTICE HOLMES and MR. JUSTICE CLARKE, concur.

The Duplex Company, a manufacturer of newspaper printing presses, seeks to enjoin officials of the machinists' and affiliated unions from interfering with its business by inducing their members not to work for plaintiff or its customers in connection with the setting up of presses made by it.   Unlike Hitchman Coal & Coke Co. v. Mitchell, 245 U.S. 229, 38 S.Ct. 65, 62 L.Ed. 260, L.R.A.1918C, 497, Ann.Cas. 1918B, 461, there is here no charge that defendants are inducing employees to break their contracts.   Nor is it now urged that defendants threaten acts of violence.   But plaintiff insists that the acts complained of violate both the common law of New York and the Sherman Act, and that, accordingly, it is entitled to relief by injunction under the state law and under section sixteen of the Clayton Act, October 15, 1914, c. 323, 38 Stat. 730, 737.

The defendants admit interference with plaintiff's business but justify on the following ground: There are in the United States only four manufacturers of such presses; and they are in active competition.   Between 1909 and 1913 the machinists' union induced three of them to recognize and deal with the union, to grant the eight-hour day, to establish a minimum wage scale, and to comply with other union requirements.   The fourth, the Duplex Company, refused to recognize the union; insisted upon conducting its factory on the open shop principle; refused to introduce the eight-hour day and operated, for the most part, ten hours a day; refused to establish a minimum wage scale; and disregarded other union standards.   Thereupon two of the three manufacturers, who had assented to union conditions, notified the union that they should be obliged to terminate their agreements with it unless their competitor, the Duplex Company, also entered into the agreement with the union, which, in giving more favorable terms to labor, imposed correspondingly greater burdens upon the employer.   Because the Duplex Company refused to enter into such an agreement, and in order to induce it to do so, the machinists' union declared a strike at its factory, and in aid of that strike instructed its members and the members of affiliated unions not to work on the installation of presses which plaintiff had delivered in New York.   Defendants insisted that by the common law of New

York, where the acts complained of were done, and where this suit was brought, and also by section 20 of the Clayton Act, 38 Stat. 730, 738, the facts constitute a justification for this interference with plaintiff's business.

First. As to the rights at common law: Defendants' justification is that of self-interest. They have supported the strike at the employer's factory by a strike elsewhere against its product. They have injured the plaintiff, not maliciously, but in self-defense. They contend that the Duplex Company's refusal to deal with the machinists' union and to observe its standards threatened the interest, not only of such union members as were its factory employees, but even more of all members of the several affiliated unions employed by plaintiff's competitors and by others whose more advanced standards the plaintiff was, in reality, attacking; and that none of the defendants and no person whom they are endeavoring to induce to refrain from working in connection with the setting up of presses made by the plaintiff is an outsider, an interloper. In other words, that the contest between the company and the machinists' union involves vitally the interest of every person whose co-operation is sought. May not all with a common interest join in refusing to expend their labor upon articles whose very production constitutes an attack upon their standard of living and the institution which they are convinced supports it? Applying common law principles the answer should, in my opinion, be: Yes, if as a matter of fact those who so co-operate have a common interest.

The change in the law by which strikes once illegal and even criminal are now recognized as lawful was effected in America largely without the intervention of legislation. This reversal of a common-law rule was not due to the rejection by the courts of one principle and the adoption in its stead of another, but to a better realization of the facts of industrial life. It is conceded that, although the strike of the workmen in plaintiff's factory injured its business, the strike was not an actionable wrong; because the obvious self-interest of the strikers constituted a justification. See Pickett v. Walsh, 192 Mass. 572, 78 N.E. 753, 6 L.R.A.,N.S., 1067, 116 Am.St.Rep. 272, 7 Ann. Cas. 638. Formerly courts held that self-interests could not be so served. Commons, History of Labor in the United States, vol. 2, c. 5. But even after strikes to raise wages or reduce hours were held to be legal because of the self-interest, some courts held that there was not sufficient causal relationship between a strike to unionize a shop and the self-interest of the strikers to justify injuries inflicted. Plant v. Woods, 176 Mass. 492, 57 N.E. 1011 * * *. But other courts, repeating the same legal formula, found that there was justification, because they viewed the facts differently. National Protective Ass'n v. Cumming, 170 N.Y. 315, 63 N.E. 369 * * *.

When centralization in the control of business brought its corresponding centralization in the organization of workingmen, new facts had to be appraised. A single employer might, as in this case, threaten the standing of the whole organization and the standards of all its members; and when he did so the union, in order to protect itself, would naturally refuse to work on his materials wherever found. When such a situation was first presented to the courts, judges concluded that the intervention of the purchaser of the materials established an insulation through which the direct relationship of the employer and the workingmen did not penetrate; and the strike against the material was considered a strike against the purchaser by unaffected third parties. Burnham v. Dowd, 217 Mass. 351, 104 N.E. 841 * * *. But other courts, with better appreciation of the facts of industry, recognized the unity of interest throughout the union, and that, in refusing to work on materials which threatened it, the union was only refusing to aid in destroying itself. Bossert v. Dhuy, 221 N.Y. 342, 117 N.E. 582 * * *.

So, in the case at bar, deciding a question of fact upon the evidence introduced and matters of common knowledge, I should say, as the two lower courts apparently have said, that the defendants and those from whom they sought cooperation have a common interest which the plaintiff threatened. This view is in harmony with the views of the Court of Appeals of New York. For in New York, although boycotts like that in Loewe v. Lawlor, 208 U.S. 274, 28 S.Ct. 301, 52 L.Ed. 488 are illegal because they are conducted not against a product but against those who deal in it and are carried out by a combination of persons not united by common interest but only by sympathy, * * * it is lawful for all members of a union by whomever employed to refuse to handle materials whose production weakens the union. * * * "The voluntary adoption of a rule not to work on non-union made material and its enforcement * * * differs entirely from a general boycott of a particular dealer or manufacturer with a malicious intent and purpose to destroy the good will or business of such dealer or manufacturer." Bossert v. Dhuy * * *. In my opinion, therefore, plaintiff had no cause of action by the common law of New York.

Second. As to the anti-trust laws of the United States: [The Clayton Act] was the fruit of unceasing agitation, which extended over more than 20 years and was designed to equalize before the law the position of workingmen and employer as industrial combatants. Aside from the use of the injunction, the chief source of dissatisfaction with the existing law lay in the doctrine of malicious combination, and, in many parts of the country, in the judicial declarations of the illegality at common law of picketing and persuading others to leave work. The grounds for objection to the latter are obvious. The objection to the doctrine of malicious combinations requires some explanation. By virtue of that doctrine, damage resulting from conduct such as striking or withholding patronage or persuading others to do either, which without more might be damnum absque injuria because the result of trade competition, became actionable when done for a purpose which a judge considered socially or economically harmful and therefore branded as malicious and unlawful. It was objected that, due largely to environment, the social and economic ideas of judges, which thus became translated into law, were prejudicial to a position of equality, between workingman and employer; that due to this dependence upon the individual opinion of judges great confusion existed as to what purposes were lawful and what unlawful; and that in any event Congress, not the judges, was the body which should declare what public policy in regard to the industrial struggle demands.

By 1914 the ideas of the advocates of legislation had fairly crystalized upon the manner in which the inequality and uncertainty of the law should be removed. It was to be done by expressly legalizing certain acts regardless of the effects produced by them upon other persons. As to them Congress was to extract the element of injuria from the damages thereby inflicted, instead of leaving judges to determine according to their own economic and social views whether the damage inflicted on an employer in an industrial struggle was damnum absque injuria, because an incident of trade competition, or a legal injury, because in their opinion, economically and socially objectionable. This idea was presented to the committees which reported the Clayton Act. The resulting law set out certain acts which had previously been held unlawful, whenever courts had disapproved of the ends for which they were performed; it then declared that, when these acts were committed in the course of an industrial dispute, they should not be held to violate any law of the United States. In other words the Clayton Act substituted the opinion of Congress as to the propriety of the purpose for that of differing judges; and thereby it declared that the relations between employers of labor and workingmen were competitive relations, that organized competition was not harmful and that it justified injuries necessarily inflicted in its course. Both the majority and the minority report of the House committee indicate that such was its purpose. If, therefore, the act applies to the case at bar, the acts here complained of cannot "be considered or held to be violations of any law of the United States," and hence do not violate the Sherman Act.

The Duplex Company contends that section 20 of the Clayton Act does not apply to the case at bar, because it is restricted to cases "between an employer and employees, or between employers and employees, or between employees, or between persons employed and persons seeking employment, involving, or growing out of, a dispute concerning terms or conditions of employment"; whereas the case at bar arises between an employer in Michigan and workingmen in New York not in its employ, and does not involve their conditions of employment. But Congress did not restrict the provision to employers and workingmen in their employ. By including "employers and employees" and "persons employed and persons seeking employment" it showed that it was not aiming merely at a legal relationship between a specific employer and his employees. Furthermore, the plaintiff's contention proves too much. If the words are to receive a strict technical construction, the statute will have no application to disputes between employers of labor and workingmen, since the very acts to which it applies sever the continuity of the legal relationship. Iron Moulders' Union v. Allis-Chalmers Co., 166 F. 45, 52–53, 91 C.C.A. 631, 20 L.R.A.,N.S., 315. Louisville etc. Ry. Co. v. Wilson, 138 U.S. 501, 505, 11 S.Ct. 405, 34 L.Ed. 1023; Cf. Rex v. Neilson, 44 N.S. 488, 491. The further contention that this case is not one arising out of a dispute concerning the conditions of work of one of the parties is, in my opinion, founded upon a misconception of the facts.

Because I have come to the conclusion that both the common law of a state and a statute of the United States declare the right of industrial combatants to push their struggle to the limits of the justification of self-interest, I do not wish to be understood as attaching any constitutional or moral sanction to that right. All rights are derived from the purposes of the society in which they exist; above all rights rises duty to the community. The conditions developed in industry may be such that those engaged in it cannot continue their struggle without danger to the community. But it is not for judges to determine whether such conditions exist, nor is it their function to set the limits of permissible contest and to declare the duties which the new situation demands. This is the function of the legislature which, while limiting individual and group rights of aggression and defense, may substitute processes of justice for the more primitive method of trial by combat.

Problems for Discussion

1. Was the strike at the Duplex plant in Michigan a violation of the Sherman Act? What exactly was done by the defendant Machinists employed by the New York newspapers? Is there any difference in the treatment of this factual issue by Mr. Justice Pitney and Mr. Justice Brandeis?

2. What were the critical phrases on the interpretation of which the *Duplex* case turned? As a matter of textual reading which party had the stronger case? What light, if any, did other parts of Section 20 throw upon the issue?

3. What justification was there for resorting to legislative history? Is there ever any justification for the practice? How did Mr. Justice Pitney use legislative history? Mr. Justice Brandeis? Is either use more reliable?

4. How likely is it that Congressmen voting on the Clayton Act "intended" not to shelter the "secondary boycott" and that they knew what that term meant? Did they "intend" to exclude from the protection of the Clayton Act the refusal simply to work on "hot goods" as described by Mr. Justice Brandeis? If so, why?

5. Would Mr. Justice Brandeis have joined in the endorsement of an injunction had the New York machinists gone beyond refusing to work on the "hot" printing presses and had instead refused altogether to work for their newspaper employers? Or had they gone yet further and sought to pressure teamsters to refuse to truck the hot presses or to refuse to work altogether for *their* trucker employers?

IV. THE NORRIS-LAGUARDIA ACT

A. LEGISLATIVE BACKGROUND

The narrow interpretation put upon Section 20 of the Clayton Act in the *Duplex* case marked, at least for the time being, the failure of the first legislative attempt to curtail the use of the injunction in labor disputes. Throughout the 1920's injunctions were quickly sought and readily obtained under the "means" and "objectives" tests. Nevertheless there were constant additions to the body of opinion which opposed the intervention of the courts into labor disputes and regarded judicial interpretations of the Clayton Act as a frustration of sound legislative policy. In 1932 this policy was adopted by Congress in the Norris-LaGuardia Act, which also served as a model for a number of state anti-injunction statutes.

The classic exposition of what were believed to be the evils of the labor injunction is Frankfurter and Greene, The Labor Injunction (1930). A shorter discussion may be found in Gregory, Labor and the Law (2d rev. ed. 1958) ch. I–VII. The uses and abuses of the labor injunction are more appropriately a matter for classroom discussion than textual exposition, but it seems appropriate to summarize here the main points made by its critics in advocating legislative curtailment of the power of the courts.

1. *Substantive Considerations of Labor Policy*

Many of the criticisms of judicial intervention into labor disputes stemmed from the premise that the courts could neither adjudicate the underlying labor controversy nor adopt measures to remedy the causes of strikes and industrial unrest. Regardless of whether the employees were provoked to strike by the action of their employer, the "means test" applied, and if violence broke out on the picket line, the picketing might be enjoined and the leaders cited for contempt without any inquiry into the occasion which gave rise to their conduct. Much the same was true of the "objectives test." Although in some cases objectives which were held unlawful were objectives which an inquiry into the merits might condemn, there are others in which the courts applied abstract concepts without real consideration of the underlying economic and human problems. In enjoining strikes for the closed shop, the courts did not inquire into the employees' need or lack of need for strengthening their organization; into the union's need or lack of need for security against employer attacks; or into the use to which the union might be expected to put the power which the closed shop gave. In *Duplex Printing Press Co. v. Deering* (p. 44 supra) the courts found no occasion to inquire either into the wages or working conditions prevailing at the Duplex plant or into their effect upon the standards which the defendants were seeking to establish in the plants of the three competitors.

It is not intended to suggest by these illustrations that critics of the labor injunction believed the courts should make such inquiries. Probably the courts were quite unsuited to adjudicating disputes "on their merits"—no one suggested that they should. The point is simply that the grant or denial of an injunction bore no relation to the merits of the underlying social and economic dispute, and that the courts could do nothing about the basic industrial problems stemming from the workers' difficulties in finding a place in the new industrial world.

The solution proposed was union organization and collective bargaining. But the pressure often needed on employees to join unions and on employers to recognize those unions (or simply not to destroy them through coercion and discrimination) took the form of strikes, picketing and boycotts. Judicial intervention which curtailed concerted activities on the part of organized employees tended to thwart the spread of collective bargaining. Organized labor and its supporters also singled out certain specific legal doctrines as especially objectionable.

"Yellow dog contracts." Prior to the decision in *Hitchman Coal & Coke Co. v. Mitchell,* 245 U.S. 229 (1918) the "yellow dog" contract had been chiefly a psychological weapon. That decision put into the hands of employers a new and powerful instru-

ment, which could not be used under the government's wartime labor policies but which after the war became virtually a method of fastening a closed, non-union shop on workers by judicial decree. In 1927 Circuit Judge Parker interpreted the *Hitchman* case as holding that the right of union members to use lawful propaganda to increase their membership was subordinate to the contractual rights of any employer which had exacted from some of its employees promises not to join a union; Judge Parker therefore concluded that it was unlawful for union organizers to approach employees working under such contracts for the purpose of inducing them to join the union and go on strike in order to compel the company to recognize the union. UMW v. Red Jacket Consol. Coal & Coke Co., 18 F.2d 839 (4th Cir. 1927).

As a result of such decisions "yellow dog contracts" enjoyed wide popularity. But in the end the decisions enforcing "yellow dog" contracts proved self-defeating. They became the focus for aroused opposition to judicial intervention in labor disputes. The reaction reached a peak on May 7, 1930, when the Senate voted to reject Judge Parker's nomination to a vacancy on the United States Supreme Court. The same sentiment was largely responsible for the enactment of the Norris-LaGuardia Act by a coalition of Democrats and insurgent Republicans in 1932.

The objectives test. The second point on which criticism of the labor injunction tended to focus was the so-called "objectives test," under which the courts decided according to their views of social and economic policy the question whether the employees' demands justified their combining to inflict injury on an employer. The application of this doctrine under decisions like *Plant v. Woods* (p. 25, supra); and *Duplex Printing Press Co. v. Deering* (p. 44, supra) was so severely narrow as to handicap many organizational activities; but perhaps the sharpest accusation was that the courts were applying a "double standard": one law of combination and competition for corporate enterprises, another for labor unions. In explanation some judges were said to lack understanding of elementary labor economics. The majority opinion in the *Hitchman* case, for example, completely ignored the effect that the failure to maintain union standards in the unorganized "panhandle" of West Virginia would have upon union wage scales in Pennsylvania, Ohio, Indiana and Illinois. Other judges were charged with a calculated bias against labor unions, and there is evidence that employers selected with considerable care the judge to whom an application for a labor injunction would be made. Some insight into the justice of the accusation that the courts had one rule for combinations of capital and another for the group activities of employees may be gained by comparing the decision in *Plant v. Woods* (p. 25, supra), and the abstracts on p. 32, supra, with the abstracts of *Bowen v. Matheson* (p. 30, supra) and *Mogul S. S. Co. v. McGregor, Gow & Co.* (p. 30, supra).

Vicarious responsibility. An unfortunate characteristic of many American strikes has been the accompanying violence. Labor unions attributed much of it to the strike-breakers, plug-uglies and agents provocateur supplied by private detective agencies; they also blamed the courts for failing to make allowances for the emotional tensions of a strike which give rise to threats, assaults, fights and other violence. History also demonstrates that labor unions did not hesitate to use force where peaceful methods failed—sòmetimes violence was planned in the detail of a military assault—but probably few unions would have contended that the law should overlook such misconduct. Their first criticism was that the courts sought to deal with violence in connection with labor disputes by injunctions and citations for contempt instead of leaving the protection of persons and property to the normal processes of the criminal law. They also complained of the doctrines under which the misconduct of a few individuals was attributed to the labor organization which sponsored a strike or picket line.

Under the law of conspiracy as developed in labor cases, unions "were held responsible not for acts of agents who had authority to act, but for every act committed by any member of a union merely because he was a member, or because he had some relation to the union although not authorized by virtue of his position to act for the union in what he did." [1] Under the rule enunciated in the *Debs* case, see United States v. Debs, 64 Fed. 724, 764 (7th Cir. 1894), aff'd on other grounds, 158 U.S. 564 (1895), a union which called a strike might be held responsible for violations of the criminal law even though the violations were not shown to have been permitted by union members and the union did everything possible to prevent them. Under either line of reasoning an injunction might be issued and union leaders cited for contempt in such a way as to break a strike merely because of unlawful acts which the union had not authorized and for which it would not be responsible under the normal rules of agency.

2. *Procedural Objections*

In equity, proceedings for an injunction are usually commenced by presenting to the chancellor a sworn bill of complaint, accompanied by affidavits, on the basis of which the complainant asks for an *ex parte* restraining order binding until both sides can be heard upon the complainant's request for an injunction *pendente lite* (more often known as a "temporary injunction"). In the case of a labor dispute a restraining order would be requested to forbid the picketing and other concerted activities which accompany a strike. Since the chancellor made his decision *ex parte*, he heard only the employer's side of

---

1. Mr. Justice Frankfurter dissenting in United Brotherhood of Carpenters and Joiners v. United States, 330 U. S. 395 (1947).

the case.   And in the highly emotional atmosphere of a labor dispute it was all too easy for the complainant to make allegations which would justify the issuance of a restraining order and to support them with affidavits of misconduct on the part of the defendant union officers and employees.

The *ex parte* restraining order was often the decisive step in the labor dispute, for the strike was likely to be the climax of an organizational drive, and once the strike was halted, it could not be revived. The effect of *ex parte* restraining orders was frequently enhanced by protracted delays before the hearing on the merits.   A thirty-day delay was not uncommon before the application for a temporary injunction came on to be heard.   Even this application might be determined on the papers alone without an opportunity to cross-examine witnesses.   The trial came still later—unless the case had been rendered moot by the collapse of the strike and the defeat of the union.   The appellate process was even slower.

Severe criticism was also levelled at the obscurity of injunctions written by lawyers but addressed to workingmen.   In *Great Northern Ry. Co. v. Brosseau*, 286 F. 414 (D.C.N.D.1923), Judge Amidon commented—

"During the 30 years that courts have been dealing with strikes by means of injunctions, these orders have steadily grown in length, complexity, and the vehemence of their rhetoric.   They are full of the rich vocabulary of synonyms which is a part of our English language. They are also replete with superlative words and the superlative phrases of which the legal mind is fond.   The result has been that such writs have steadily become more and more complex and prolix."

The enforcement of labor injunctions also raised cries of abuse. Large corporations imported strike breakers into the community and surrounded them with armed guards furnished by private detective agencies.   It was often their affidavits that furnished the basis for injunctive relief.   When the decree issued, the guards were sworn in as deputy sheriffs or deputy marshals.   The class of plug-uglies from whom the "private detectives" on the rolls of strike-breaking agencies were recruited was not adept at preserving order; perhaps it was only natural that they should be more concerned with breaking the strike.

Under these conditions it seems unlikely that the labor injunction was as useful in maintaining order and protecting property as the ordinary police.   But what seemed particularly unfair to the workers was the practice of citing those engaged in violence for contempt of court instead of prosecuting them for breaches of peace or other violations of the criminal law.   The respondent was tried by the same judge who issued the injunction and was not entitled to the benefit of a jury of his peers. Consequently, not only did one person seem to be acting as prosecutor and judge, but the strikers lost the protection of a trial before a body which might have been more sympathetic towards their cause and more understanding of the emotional tensions of a labor dispute.

3. Considerations of Judicial Administration

In the eyes of many students of the labor injunction the merits of the contending arguments of management and labor were far less important than its effect on the prestige of the courts. It was plain to anyone that labor cases turned on questions of social and economic policy more suitable for legislative than judicial determination. Since judicial doctrines favored employers and were regarded as highly unfair by union men, workers acquired a distrust of the courts which shook their confidence in law and which even today must be taken into account in shaping labor policies.

"The history of the labor injunction in action puts some matters beyond question. In large part, dissatisfaction and resentment are caused, first, by the refusal of courts to recognize that breaches of the peace may be redressed through criminal prosecution and civil action for damages, and, second, by the expansion of a simple, judicial device to an enveloping code of prohibited conduct, absorbing, *en masse*, executive and police functions and affecting the livelihood, and even lives, of multitudes. Especially those zealous for the unimpaired prestige of our courts have observed how the administration of law by decrees which through vast and vague phrases surmount law, undermines the esteem of courts upon which our reign of law depends. Not government, but 'government by injunction', characterized by the consequences of a criminal prosecution without its safeguards, has been challenged." [2]

B. INTERPRETATION OF THE NORRIS-LAGUARDIA ACT

The following questions, requiring close analysis of its text, are designed to raise some of the major problems in the application of the Norris-LaGuardia Act.

Problems for Discussion

1. How does the Norris-LaGuardia Act apply to the *Duplex* case? Could Duplex circumvent the Act by suing in the New York courts?

2. A Delaware corporation operating a supermarket at a location in Baltimore, Md., where 90 percent of its patrons were black, brought an

2. Frankfurter and Greene, The Labor
Injunction (1930) at p. 200.

action in the United States District Court to enjoin the local chapter of NAACP from picketing the store with signs demanding the immediate employment of a black manager and 90 percent black clerks. The plaintiffs' current employment practices are not discriminatory. May the complaint be dismissed for want of jurisdiction? See *New Negro Alliance* v. *Sanitary Grocery Co.*, 303 U.S. 552 (1938).

3. Members of the Fishermen's Union work for vessel owners who pay them a minimum wage plus a specified percentage of the proceeds of the sale of the catch of each vessel upon each voyage. The owners of the vessels sell the catch to dealers who resell the fresh fish in local and interstate commerce. The Union has called a strike and its members are picketing the docks of the fish dealers in support of a demand that the dealers raise the price at which they sell fish and agree not to sell below a minimum scale fixed by the Union. Would the Norris-LaGuardia Act bar equitable relief in a state or federal court? See Hawaiian Tuna Packers v. International Longshoremen's and Warenousemen's Union, 72 F.Supp. 562 (D. Hawaii 1947); Commonwealth v. McHugh, 326 Mass. 249, 93 N.E.2d 751 (1950).

4. The leadership of the AFL–CIO has over a long period of time taken a public position in opposition to United States dealings with Communist nations. When the United States Government recently authorized the sale of huge quantities of grain to the Soviet Union, the AFL–CIO adopted a resolution condemning such trade. It announced that Soviet Russia should not be aided by the United States in overcoming its own economic woes, and it coupled its objection with a claim that any grain which was in fact shipped to the Soviet Union should be transported not on Communist vessels but on ships manned by American seamen. When a Yugoslav vessel had docked in New York and was preparing to take on a cargo of several tons of grain bound for the Soviet Union, some locals of the Longshoremen's Union began to picket the vessel, their picket signs protesting any trade with Communist countries. Other longshoremen have refused to cross the picket line in order to load the ship. Would the Norris-LaGuardia Act bar an action for an injunction in a federal district court? Compare New Orleans S.S. Ass'n v. General Longshore Workers, ILA Local 1418, 626 F.2d 455 (5th Cir. 1980), with NLRB v. International Longeshoremen's Ass'n, 332 F.2d 992 (4th Cir. 1964).

5. A railroad obtained permission from public utility commissions in four states to discontinue various small stations where the traffic was not sufficient to warrant the expense of maintaining personnel. The union, invoking section 6 of the Railway Labor Act, asked the railroad to agree that no existing jobs would be eliminated by management without the agreement of the union. The railroad refused to bargain upon this matter, and following unsuccessful negotiation on related matters the union struck. The railroad then sought to have the strike enjoined in the district court. The court of appeals sustained the granting of an injunction by the district court. Upon certiorari, what judgment should the Supreme Court enter? See *Order of R.R. Telegraphers* v. *Chicago & N.W. Ry.*, 362 U.S. 330, 80 S.Ct. 761, 4 L.Ed.2d 774 (1960). Would the railroad be entitled to relief against violence interfering with its opera-

tion during the strike? See *Brotherhood of R.R. Trainmen* v. *Toledo, P. & W. R.R.*, 321 U.S. 50, 64 S.Ct. 413, 88 L.Ed. 534 (1944).

C. EFFECT ON THE ANTITRUST LAWS

It will be recalled that in Loewe v. Lawlor, supra p. 36, the Supreme Court held that the Sherman Act applied to combinations of workers. That case was an action for damages, but with the introduction in the Clayton Act of 1914 of the private injunctive action, the federal courts became available to private parties for equity relief against antitrust violations. The Supreme Court affirmed the grant of such relief, at least against the secondary boycott—in the face of the other more labor-protective provisions of the Clayton Act—in the *Duplex* case, at p. 44 supra. In the course of time, however, the usefulness of the Sherman Act as a strike-breaking weapon was curtailed by decisions holding that certain strikes at manufacturing establishments did not have the necessary relationship to interstate commerce to come under federal authority. Apparently coverage depended upon the strikers' purpose. If a union made up of employees at a manufacturing establishment called a strike for the purpose of raising their wages or improving their working conditions, the combination did not violate the Sherman Act even though shipments in interstate commerce were halted or reduced. E. g., United Leather Workers v. Herkert & Meisel Trunk Co., 265 U.S. 457, 44 S.Ct. 623, 68 L.Ed. 1104 (1924). However, if a union which had organized some establishments in an industry were to call an organizational strike or institute a boycott in order to organize non-union factories and protect its members against the competition of cheap, non-union goods, then the strike would be unlawful. Coronado Coal Co. v. United Mine Workers, 268 U.S. 295 (1925); Alco-Zander Co. v. Amalgamated Clothing Workers, 35 F.2d 203 (E.D.Pa.1929).

Whether this distinction would have survived the expanded concept of interstate commerce which developed after 1937 is uncertain. The Court wrestled with the problem in Apex Hosiery Co. v. Leader, 310 U.S. 469, 60 S.Ct. 982, 81 L.Ed. 1311 (1940) (see p. 993, infra), and concluded that labor unions would not violate the Sherman Act unless they acted with the purpose of restraining competition in the market in which the products of their employer were sold. Before this doctrine had an opportunity to develop, however, the *Hutcheson* case placed drastic restrictions upon the application of the Sherman Act to labor unions.

UNITED STATES v. HUTCHESON

Supreme Court of the United States, 1940.
312 U.S. 219, 61 S.Ct. 463, 85 L.Ed. 788.

MR. JUSTICE FRANKFURTER delivered the opinion of the Court.

* * * Anheuser-Busch, Inc., operating a large plant in St. Louis, contracted with Borsari Tank Corporation for the erection of an additional facility. The Gaylord Container Corporation, a lessee of adjacent property from Anheuser-Busch, made a similar contract for a new building with the Stocker Company. Anheuser-Busch obtained the materials for its brewing and other operations and sold its finished products largely through interstate shipments. The Gaylord Corporation was equally dependent on interstate commerce for marketing its goods, as were the construction companies for their building materials. Among the employees of Anheuser-Busch were members of the United Brotherhood of Carpenters and Joiners of America and of the International Association of Machinists. The conflicting claims of these two organizations, affiliated with the American Federation of Labor, in regard to the erection and dismantling of machinery had long been a source of controversy between them. Anheuser-Busch had had agreements with both organizations whereby the Machinists were given the disputed jobs and the Carpenters agreed to submit all disputes to arbitration. But in 1939 the president of the Carpenters, their general representative, and two officials of the Carpenters' local organization, the four men under indictment, stood on the claims of the Carpenters for the jobs. Rejection by the employer of the Carpenters' demand and the refusal of the latter to submit to arbitration were followed by a strike of the Carpenters, called by the defendants against Anheuser-Busch and the construction companies, a picketing of Anheuser-Busch and its tenant, and a request through circular letters and the official publication of the Carpenters that union members and their friends refrain from buying Anheuser-Busch beer.

These activities on behalf of the Carpenters formed the charge of the indictment as a criminal combination and conspiracy in violation of the Sherman Law. Demurrers denying that what was charged constituted a violation of the laws of the United States were sustained (D.C., 32 F.Supp. 600) and the case came here under the Criminal Appeals Act.

Section 1 of the Sherman Law on which the indictment rested is as follows: "Every contract, combination in the form of trust or otherwise, or conspiracy, in restraint of trade or commerce among the several States, or with foreign nations, is hereby declared to be illegal." The controversies engendered by its application to trade union activities and the efforts to secure legislative relief from its consequences are familiar history. The Clayton Act of 1914 was the result. Act of October 15, 1914, 38 Stat. 730. "This statute was the fruit of unceasing agitation, which extended over more than 20 years and was designed to equalize before the law the position of work-ingmen and employer as industrial combatants." Duplex Printing Press Co. v. Deering, 254 U.S. 443, 484, 41 S.Ct. 172, 182, 65 L.Ed. 349, 16 A.L.R. 196. Section 20 of that Act * * * withdrew from the general interdict of the Sherman Law specifically enumerated practices of labor unions by prohibiting injunctions against them—since the use of the injunction had been the major source of dissatis-faction—and also relieved such practices of all illegal taint by the catch-all provision, "nor shall any of the acts specified in this para-graph be considered or held to be violations of any law of the United States". The Clayton Act gave rise to new litigation and to re-newed controversy in and out of Congress regarding the status of trade unions. By the generality of its terms the Sherman Law had necessarily compelled the courts to work out its meaning from case to case. It was widely believed that into the Clayton Act courts read the very beliefs which that Act was designed to remove. Spe-cifically the courts restricted the scope of § 20 to trade union activities directed against an employer by his own employees. Duplex Printing Press Co. v. Deering, supra. Such a view it was urged, both by powerful judicial dissents and informed lay opinion, misconceived the area of economic conflict that had best be left to economic forces and the pressure of public opinion and not subjected to the judgment of courts. Id., 254 U.S. at pages 485, 486, 41 S.Ct. at page 183, 65 L.Ed. 349, 16 A.L.R. 196. Agitation again led to legislation and in 1932 Congress wrote the Norris-LaGuardia Act. Act of March 23, 1932, 47 Stat. 70, 29 U.S.C. §§ 101–115, 29 U.S.C.A. §§ 101–115.

The Norris-LaGuardia Act removed the fetters upon trade union activities, which according to judicial construction § 20 of the Clayton Act had left untouched, by still further narrowing the circumstances under which the federal courts could grant injunctions in labor dis-putes. More especially, the Act explicitly formulated the "public pol-icy of the United States" in regard to the industrial conflict and by its light established that the allowable area of union activity was not to be restricted, as it had been in the Duplex case, to an immediate employer-employee relation. Therefore, whether trade union conduct constitutes a violation of the Sherman Law is to be determined only by reading the Sherman Law and § 20 of the Clayton Act and the Norris-LaGuardia Act as a harmonizing text of outlawry of labor conduct.

Were then the acts charged against the defendants prohibited or permitted by these three interlacing statutes? If the facts laid in the indictment come within the conduct enumerated in § 20 of the Clayton Act they do not constitute a crime within the general terms of the Sherman Law because of the explicit command of that section that such conduct shall not be "considered or held to be violations of any law of the United States". So long as a union acts in its self-interest and does not combine with non-labor groups, the licit and the illicit under § 20 are not to be distinguished by any judgment regarding the wisdom or unwisdom, the rightness or wrongness, the selfishness or unselfishness of the end of which the particular union activities are the means. There is nothing remotely within the terms of § 20 that differentiates between trade union conduct directed against an employer because of a controversy arising in the relation between employer and employee, as such, and conduct similarly directed but ultimately due to an internecine struggle between two unions seeking the favor of the same employer. Such strike between competing unions has been an obdurate conflict in the evolution of so-called craft unionism and has undoubtedly been one of the potent forces in the modern development of industrial unions. These conflicts have intensified industrial tension but there is not the slightest warrant for saying that Congress has made § 20 inapplicable to trade union conduct resulting from them.

In so far as the Clayton Act is concerned, we must therefore dispose of this case as though we had before us precisely the same conduct on the part of the defendants in pressing claims against Anheuser-Busch for increased wages, or shorter hours, or other elements of what are called working conditions. The fact that what was done was done in a competition for jobs against the Machinists rather than against, let us say, a company union is a differentiation which Congress has not put into the federal legislation and which therefore we cannot write into it.

It is at once apparent that the acts with which the defendants are charged are the kind of acts protected by § 20 of the Clayton Act. The refusal of the Carpenters to work for Anheuser-Busch or on construction work being done for it and its adjoining tenant, and the peaceful attempt to get members of other unions similarly to refuse to work, are plainly within the free scope accorded to workers by § 20 for "terminating any relation of employment", or "ceasing to perform any work or labor", or "recommending, advising or persuading others by peaceful means so to do". The picketing of Anheuser-Busch premises with signs to indicate that Anheuser-Busch was unfair to organized labor, a familiar practice in these situations, comes within the language "attending at any place where any such person or persons may lawfully be, for the purpose of peacefully obtaining or communicating information, or from peacefully persuading any person to work or to abstain from working". Finally, the recommendation to union members and their friends not to buy or use the product of Anheuser-Busch is explicitly covered by "ceasing to patronize * * * any party to such dispute, or from recommending, advising, or persuading others by peaceful and lawful means so to do."

Clearly, then, the facts here charged constitute lawful conduct under the Clayton Act unless the defendants cannot invoke that Act because outsiders to the immediate dispute also shared in the conduct. But we need not determine whether the conduct is legal within the restrictions which Duplex Printing Press Co. v. Deering gave to the immunities of § 20 of the Clayton Act. Congress in the Norris-LaGuardia Act has expressed the public policy of the United States and defined its conception of a "labor dispute" in terms that no longer leave room for doubt. * * * Such a dispute, § 13(c), 29 U.S.C.A. § 113(c), provides, "includes any controversy concerning terms or conditions of employment, or concerning the association or representation of persons in negotiating, fixing, maintaining, changing, or seeking to arrange terms or conditions of employment, regardless of whether or not the disputants stand in the proximate relation of employer and employee". And under § 13(b) a person is "participating or interested in a labor dispute" if he "is engaged in the same industry, trade, craft, or occupation in which such dispute occurs, or has a direct or indirect interest therein, or is a member, officer, or agent of any association composed in whole or in part of employers or employees engaged in such industry, trade, craft, or occupation".

To be sure, Congress expressed this national policy and determined the bounds of a labor dispute in an act explicitly dealing with the further withdrawal of injunctions in labor controversies. But to argue, as it was urged before us, that the Duplex case still governs for purposes of a criminal prosecution is to say that that which on the equity side of the court is allowable conduct may in a criminal proceeding become the road to prison. It would be strange indeed that although neither the Government nor Anheuser-Busch could have sought an injunction against the acts here challenged, the elaborate efforts to permit such conduct failed to prevent criminal liability punishable with imprisonment and heavy fines. That is not the way to read the will of Congress, particularly when expressed by a statute which, as we have already indicated, is practically and historically one of a series of enactments touching one of the most sensitive national problems. Such legislation must not be read in a spirit of mutilating narrowness. * * * The appropriate way to read legislation in a situation like the one before us, was indicated by Mr. Justice Holmes on circuit: "A statute may indicate or require as its justification a change in the policy of the law, although it expresses that change only in the specific cases most likely to occur in the mind. The Legislature has the power to decide what the policy of the law shall be, and if it has intimated its will, however indirectly, that will should be recognized and obeyed. The major premise of the conclusion expressed in a statute, the change of policy that induces the enactment, may not be set out in terms, but it is not an adequate discharge of duty for the courts to say: We see what you are driving at, but you have not said it, and therefore we shall go on as before." Johnson v. United States, 163 Fed. 30, 32.

The relation of the Norris-LaGuardia Act to the Clayton Act is not that of a tightly drawn amendment to a technically phrased tax provision. The underlying aim of the Norris-LaGuardia Act was to restore the broad purpose which Congress thought it had formulated in the Clayton Act but which was frustrated, so Congress believed, by unduly restrictive judicial construction. This was authoritatively stated by the House Committee on the Judiciary. "The purpose of the bill is to protect the rights of labor in the same manner the Congress intended when it enacted the Clayton Act, October 15, 1914, 38 Stat.L. 738, which act, by reason of its construction and application by the Federal courts, is ineffectual to accomplish the congressional intent." H.Rep.No.669, 72d Congress, 1st Session, p. 3. The Norris-LaGuardia Act was a disapproval of Duplex Printing Press Co. v. Deering, supra, and Bedford Cut Stone Co. v. Journeyman Stone Cutters' Association, 274 U.S. 37, 47 S.Ct. 522, 71 L.Ed. 916, 54 A.L.R. 791, as the authoritative interpretation of § 20 of the Clayton Act, for Congress now placed its own meaning upon that section. The Norris-LaGuardia Act reasserted the original purpose of the Clayton Act by infusing into it the immunized trade union activities as redefined by the later Act. In this light § 20 removes all such allowable conduct from the taint of being "violations of any law of the United States", including the Sherman Law.   *   *   *

MR. JUSTICE MURPHY took no part in the disposition of this case.

MR. JUSTICE STONE (concurring).

As I think it clear that the indictment fails to charge an offense under the Sherman Act, as it has been interpreted and applied by this Court, I find no occasion to consider the impact of the Norris-LaGuardia Act on the definition of participants in a labor dispute in the Clayton Act, as construed by this Court in Duplex Printing Press Co. v. Deering, 254 U.S. 443, 41 S.Ct. 172, 65 L.Ed. 349, 16 A.L.R. 196 —an application of the Norris-LaGuardia Act which is not free from doubt and which some of my brethren sharply challenge.   *   *   *

MR. JUSTICE ROBERTS. I am of opinion that the judgment should be reversed. [Justice Roberts concluded that there was an illegal secondary boycott which interfered with the interstate shipment of materials to Anheuser-Busch, Borsari and Stocker.]   *   *   *

By a process of construction never, as I think, heretofore indulged by this court, it is now found that, because Congress forbade the issuing of injunctions to restrain certain conduct, it intended to repeal the provisions of the Sherman Act authorizing actions at law and criminal prosecutions for the commission of torts and crimes defined by the anti-trust laws.   *   *   *   [T]o attribute to Congress an intent to repeal legislation which has had a definite and well understood scope and effect for decades past, by resurrecting a rejected construction of the Clayton Act and extending a policy strictly limited by the Congress itself in the Norris-LaGuardia Act, seems to me a usurpation by the courts of the function of the Congress not only novel but fraught, as well, with the most serious dangers to our constitutional system of division of powers.

THE CHIEF JUSTICE joins in this opinion.[3]

Problems for Discussion

1. If you were counsel for the Government, how would you have sought to convince the Court that the Clayton Act was irrelevant? How did Mr. Justice Frankfurter meet this argument? On what principle of statutory interpretation is this part of the opinion predicated? Compare Landis, Statutes and The Sources of Law (1934), pp. 214 *et seq.*

2. In considering the foregoing questions note the following excerpts from arguments presented in support of the Norris-LaGuardia Act while its proposed enactment was a public issue:

(a) "But the immunity accorded is circumscribed: It is not immunity from legal as distinguished from equitable remedies,—hitherto unlawful conduct remains unlawful * * *. Section 9 of the proposed bill [which became Section 13] settles all of these questions so far as application for equitable relief is concerned. Immunity from injunctions extends to all the categories that we have described, save alone as to persons who are not engaged in the same industry with the complainant."—Frankfurter and Greene, The Labor Injunction (1930), pp. 215–216.

(b) *"Is the denial of all adequate judicial remedies in case of an illegal strike a denial of due process of law?* This question is not pertinent for the bill only withdraws the remedy of injunction. Civil action for damages and criminal prosecution remain available instruments. Illegal strikes are not made legal."—Frankfurter and Greene, Congressional Power Over the Labor Injunction, 31 Col.L.Rev. 385, 408 (1931).

3. The *Hutcheson* case grew out of a program developed in the late 1930's by Assistant Attorney General Thurman Arnold to utilize criminal prosecutions under the Sherman Act to combat certain labor union abuses. He assured that there was no intention to prosecute unions for using strikes, boycotts, and other coercion having a reasonable connection to wages, hours, health or safety, or the establishment and maintenance of collective bargaining. The primary targets, rather, were these: (a) union attempts to prevent the use of cheaper material, improved equipment or more efficient methods; (b) union attempts to compel the hiring of useless and unnecessary labor (as distinguished from "reasonable requirements that a minimum amount of labor be hired in the interests of

------

3. Among the best of the multitude of comments on the *Hutcheson* case are Nathanson and Wirtz, The Hutcheson   Case: Another View, 36 Ill.L.Rev. 41 (1941); Note, 29 Calif.L.Rev. 399 (1941).

safety and health or of avoidance of undue speeding of the work"); (c) union extortion of businesses; (d) union cooperation with businesses in enforcing price-fixing schemes; and (e) union attempts to wrest work from other unions already in established collective bargaining relationships (jurisdictional disputes). Was this program of antitrust enforcement against unions sound policy? Do you perceive any clash between it and the then recently enacted Wagner Act? If there was such a conflict between the nation's antitrust policy and its labor-relations policy, how ought it be resolved?

V. THE WAGNER ACT[1]

1935

NLRB created to administer it

A. Origins and Constitutionality[2]

Railway Labor Act

The passage of the National Labor Relations Act was the culmination of a long period of development, in which one of the more significant events was the enactment in 1926 of the Railway Labor Act. The provisions of that Act were agreed upon in advance through private negotiations between the railroads and the interested unions, and little change was made by the Congress. In general, the emphasis of the Act was on the peaceful settlement of labor disputes, thus reflecting the strategic importance of the transportation industry in the national economy. Adjustment boards were to be established by agreement of the carriers and the workers to settle differences over the interpretation of contracts and to decide minor disputes over working conditions. More elaborate provisions were included to assist in resolving disputes over the negotiation of wages and working conditions. Section 2 of the Act imposed a duty on both sides to make "every reasonable effort to make and maintain agreements concerning rates of pay, rules, and working conditions * * *" In addition, a mediation board was established consisting of five members appointed by the President. In the event of a break-down in the contract negotiations between unions and carriers, the dispute could be referred to this board, or the board could proffer its services on its own motion. The Board could then seek to mediate or otherwise assist the negotiations between the parties. While no solution was to be imposed upon the parties by the government, the mediation board was empowered to encourage the parties to arbi-

---

1. The National Labor Relations Act is the subject of an exhaustive literature. Millis & Brown, From the Wagner Act to Taft-Hartley (1950), is a particularly helpful volume.

2. See Magruder, A Half Century of Legal Influence Upon the Development of Collective Bargaining. 50 Harv.L.Rev. 1071 (1937).

trate their differences and procedures were established whereby both sides might easily agree to submit to final and binding arbitration. If the controversy could not be settled by these techniques, the mediation board was empowered to notify the President if the dispute threatened to disrupt interstate commerce to such a point that any section of the country would be deprived of essential transport services. The President could then appoint a board to investigate and report on the dispute within thirty days. Neither party was allowed to change the conditions out of which the dispute arose for another thirty days following the making of the report. Thereafter, the parties were free to resort to economic warfare to settle their differences.

The provisions requiring that the status quo be maintained for as much as sixty days represented a substantial concession on the part of the unions. In return, labor obtained a guarantee against interference by the railroads in the process of union organization. Hence, the Act declared that the representatives or parties to railway disputes should be designated "by the respective parties in such manner as may be provided in their corporate organization or unincorporated association, or by other means of collective action, without interference, influence or coercion exercised by either party over the self-organization or designation of representatives by the other." After the enactment of this statute the Texas & N. O. R. Co. resorted to inducement and coercion, including discriminatory discharges, to set up on its lines a company union in lieu of the Brotherhood of Railway and Steamship Clerks. The resulting litigation ended in a landmark decision of the United States Supreme Court. TEXAS & N. O. R. Co. v. BROTHERHOOD OF RAILWAY & S. S. CLERKS, 281 U.S. 548, 50 S.Ct. 427, 74 L.Ed. 1034 (1930). The Court, in the following passage, upheld the power of Congress to prohibit interference with self-organization, or with the selection of representatives, for the amicable adjustment of disputes.

"We entertain no doubt of the constitutional authority of Congress to enact the prohibition. The power to regulate commerce is the power to enact "all appropriate legislation" for its "protection or advancement" (The Daniel Ball, 10 Wall. 557, 564, 19 L.Ed. 999); to adopt measures "to promote its growth and insure its safety" (County of Mobile v. Kimball, 102 U.S. 691, 696, 697, 26 L.Ed. 238); to "foster, protect, control, and restrain" (Second Employers' Liability Cases, 223 U.S. 1, 47, 32 S.Ct. 169, 174, 56 L.Ed. 327, 38 L.R. A.,N.S., 44). Exercising this authority, Congress may facilitate the amicable settlements of disputes which threaten the service of the necessary agencies of interstate transportation. In shaping its legislation to this end, Congress was entitled to take cognizance of actual conditions and to address itself to practicable measures. The legality of collective action on the part of employees in order to safeguard their proper interests is not to be disputed. It has long been recognized that employees are entitled to organize for the purpose of securing the redress of grievances and to promote agreements with employers relating to rates of pay and conditions of work. American Steel Foundries v. Tri-City Central Trade Council, 257 U.S. 184, 209, 42 S.Ct. 72, 66 L.Ed. 189, 27 A.L. R. 360. Congress was not required to ignore this right of the employees but could safeguard it and seek to make their appropriate collective action an instrument of peace rather than of strife. Such collective action would be a mockery if representation were made futile by interferences with freedom of choice. Thus the prohibition by Congress of interference with the selection of representatives for the purpose of negotiation and conference between employers and employees, instead of being an invasion of the constitutional right of either, was based on the recognition of the rights of both. * * * The Railway Labor Act of 1926 does not interfere with the normal exercise of the right of the carrier to select its employees or to discharge them. The statute is not aimed at this right of the employers but at the interference with the right of employees to have representatives of their own choosing. As the carriers subject to the act have no constitutional right to interfere with the freedom of the employees in making their selections, they cannot complain of the statute on constitutional grounds. * * * "

As time went on, certain defects in the Railway Labor Act became increasingly apparent to labor. In 1934, therefore, substantial amendments were enacted to meet these objections. First, in an effort to eliminate the device of the "company union" controlled by the employer, the 1934 amendments declared it unlawful (and subject to criminal penalties) for carriers to use their funds to assist company unions or to induce their employees to join such unions. Second, in order to resolve employer challenges to the capacity of union representatives seeking to negotiate, the National Mediation Board was given the added task of conducting elections or using other appropriate methods to determine which union was desired by the employees. Third, in order to eliminate the disparities that developed among different grievance-adjustment boards across the nation, Congress in 1934 created the National Railroad Adjustment Board. The purpose of the Board was (and is) to resolve grievances over the meaning of collective bargaining agreements. It was to be composed of eighteen representatives selected by the carriers and

an equal number chosen by the employees, and it was to be divided
into four separate divisions, each having jurisdiction over different
occupations. Decisions of the Board were made enforceable by the
winning party in the federal district courts. With the passage of
these amendments—and the extension in 1936 of the Act's coverage
to air carriers as well as railroads—the Railway Labor Act assumed
the form which has endured, with only minor modifications, until the
present day.

The Philosophy of the Wagner Act

In every respect American trade union history after 1933 stood
in contrast with the twenties. A few facts epitomize what occurred.
In 1933 less than 3,000,000 workers were members of trade unions.
Early in the 1940's 12,000,000 workers were organized. Between
1937 and 1940 the great industrial giants of the steel, automobile,
rubber and electrical manufacturing industries were forced to begin
adapting themselves to the ways of collective bargaining.

These events were part of the New Deal revolution. Their explanation lies in the conditions which gave it birth. The stock market
panic of 1929 and the deep depression of the early and middle thirties
stirred intellectual, social and economic ferment. During the first
third of the century the mass of the American people were not ready
to listen to those who criticized existing institutions. The collapse
of the economic system after 1929 dispelled the worker's faith in welfare capitalism and made the middle classes more sympathetic towards the objectives of organized labor. The challenge which the
unions presented to corporate employers was strengthened by the
attack of the Roosevelt administration upon "entrenched greed."
The new Keynesian economics with its emphasis on mass purchasing
power and consumption was favorable to any movement which would
increase the bargaining power of the workers. Political power shifted
away from business to farm and labor groups. Outside the labor
field there was written such far-reaching legislation as the Securities
Act, the Securities and Exchange Commission Act, the Public Utilities
Holding Company Act, the Federal Deposit Insurance Corporation
Act, the Agricultural Adjustment Acts, the Agricultural Marketing
Agreement Act of 1937 and the Bituminous Coal Act. In the field of
labor legislation, the National Labor Relations Act and federal wage
and hour, child labor and social security laws were enacted. Labor
leaders were regularly consulted by the President upon important issues and were often given representation on government commissions
concerned with labor policy and social welfare. More important
than all these factors, however, were two others: (1) the federal
government's policy of giving active encouragement to unionization
and collective bargaining and (2) the formation of the Congress of
Industrial Organizations.

The impetus for general legislation aiding unionization came from the search for measures to halt the deepening depression which followed the stock market panic of 1929. Keynesian economics pointed toward increasing mass purchasing power as a way of speeding up economic activity. One method Congress could have used was to fix minimum wages and maximum hours (to spread employment), and another was to encourage unionization. Measures of the second type offered several advantages: unions might raise wages above the minimum, they could police their contracts without direct governmental regulation of terms of employment, and there was reason to hope that such legislation would not be as vulnerable to constitutional attack as wage and hour laws.

In the National Industrial Recovery Act of 1934, Congress adopted both approaches. Fair labor standards were to be established by raising wages, shortening hours and eliminating industrial homework, child labor and other sweatshop practices. Section 7 of the NIRA declared that "employees shall have the right to organize and bargain collectively through representatives of their own choosing," and shall be free from "interference, restraint, or coercion" by employers in unionizing "or in other mutual aid or protection," and also that no employee or person seeking employment could be required to join a company union or to refrain from joining a union of his own choosing. The NIRA also attempted to organize industry through trade associations and codes of fair competition that would eliminate cut-throat competition and so stabilize prices.

In 1935, the National Industrial Recovery Act collapsed partly as a result of its own weight although the immediate occasion was a Supreme Court decision holding the basic statute unconstitutional. The administration's policy toward business turned away from the philosophy of cartelization to the older tradition of enforced competition, but it scarcely slackened its interest in building up the bargaining power of employees. The Wagner Act of 1935 [3] established on a permanent foundation the legally protected right of employees to organize and bargain collectively through representatives of their own choosing. The basic idea reaches back before 1900 but much of its elaboration was the work of the NIRA period.

3. The official title of the act was the National Labor Relations Act. The colloquial name is used here to distinguish the act in its original form from the present National Labor Relations Act which contains provisions derived from the original act and others added by the Taft-Hartley Act in 1947 and the Landrum-Griffin Act in 1959.

The text of the National Labor Relations Act is printed in the statutory supplement. Students should follow the text in studying these pages.

The heart of the Wagner Act was Section 7, which originally provided—

"Employees shall have the right to self-organization, to form, join or assist labor organizations, to bargain collectively through representatives of their own choosing, and to engage in concerted activities for the purpose of collective bargaining or other mutual aid or protection."

These three rights—to organize, to bargain collectively and to engage in peaceful strikes and picketing—were to be implemented and enforced through the other provisions of the Act. Section 8(1) of the Wagner Act (now Section 8(a)(1)), outlawing employer coercion of employees in the exercise of their Section 7 rights, covers such antiunion tactics as beating up labor organizers, locking out employees to destroy incipient unions, industrial espionage, threats of economic reprisal and the more subtle techniques of promising or granting economic benefits in order to show that the union has little to offer the employees. Section 8(2) was designed to outlaw company-formed "representation plans" or "work councils" which were carefully controlled so as to give employees the forms of organization without the substance and which were known as "company unions." Section 8(3) forbade discrimination in hiring or firing, and Section 8(4) outlawed such discrimination in the specific case of an employee asserting rights before the NLRB.

While those four subsections have their most common application at the stage when the employees are taking steps to form a union (or when an outside union is seeking to persuade them to organize), Section 8(5) relates primarily to the period after the employees have organized and are seeking to engage in collective bargaining. It imposes upon the employer an affirmative duty to bargain with the union which (under Section 9(a)) has been selected "by the majority of the employees in a unit appropriate for such purposes"; moreover, this union is to be the "exclusive" representative, and the employer may deal with no other employee representative. To determine which group of employees should have a say in the selection of a bargaining representative, and to determine formally whether a labor organization (and which) has majority support, the National Labor Relations Board is given authority by Section 9 of the Act to conduct representation proceedings, culminating in a secret-ballot election and a certification of the results (and of any union receiving a majority of the valid votes cast).

To administer both the unfair labor practice and representation provisions of the Act, Congress established the kind of administrative agency which was becoming an increasingly common method of implementing New Deal legislation. The NLRB was created under

Sections 3 and 4, and under Section 10 (which regulates NLRB procedure in unfair labor practice cases) the Board assumed the functions of both prosecutor and judge by issuing complaints of violation, having its staff prosecute the complaints and then passing upon the merits of the case. Judicial enforcement and review were authorized under Section 10(e) and (f) upon petition to an appropriate federal court of appeals. While the courts were authorized to review most questions of law, their power with respect to findings of fact was restricted to determining whether the findings were "supported by evidence." These provisions gave rise to bitter controversy and the Taft-Hartley amendments later made significant changes in both NLRB organization and the scope of judicial review.

Although the Wagner Act was partly an economic measure designed to enable industrial workers to raise their wages and improve their standard of living, it also embodied a conscious, carefully articulated program for minimizing labor disputes. Its sponsors held, and its supporters still believe, that enforcement of the guarantees of the rights to organize and bargain collectively is the best method of achieving industrial peace without undue sacrifice of personal and economic freedom.

The Act has reduced strikes and other forms of industrial unrest for a number of reasons. Most obviously, the prohibition of employer unfair labor practices and the legal compulsion to recognize and bargain with the union designated by a majority of employees in an appropriate unit will tend to eliminate strikes for those purposes. Moreover, collective bargaining itself tends to reduce the number of strikes and lockouts. Four points may be made in support of this proposition. (1) Collective bargaining enables employers and employees to dig behind their prejudices and exchange their views to such an extent that on many points they reach agreement while on others they discover that the area of disagreement is so narrow that it is cheaper to compromise than to do battle. (2) Recognition, experience in bargaining, and the resulting maturity bring a sense of responsibility to labor unions. (3) Because collective bargaining replaces the weakness of the individual in bargaining and better enables employees to raise wages and improve labor standards, strikes to secure these objectives tend to be eliminated. (4) Collective bargaining substitutes what may be called industrial democracy—joint consensual determination of wages and other conditions of employment—for the unilateral and sometimes arbitrary power of the employer. Moreover, the collective agreement establishes a rule of law; it is the measure of both the employer's and employees' rights and obligations.

Although the Wagner Act was intended to provide a foundation for a comprehensive system of industrial relations, it was not a complete labor code. The sponsors dealt only with the labor problems which seemed most urgent in 1935, leaving others to state law or to the future. Three limitations are especially significant.

First. The Wagner Act was primarily concerned with the organizational phases of labor relations. The aim was to prevent practices which interfered with the growth of labor unions and the development of collective bargaining. Once the union was organized and the employer accorded it recognition as the representative of its employees, the function of the statute, as originally conceived, was completed. Even the duty to bargain with the majority representatives was imposed by Section 8(5) chiefly because the refusal to bargain was a method of destroying the union. (In this respect the development of the law has departed significantly from the original conception.)

Second. The Wagner Act was concerned exclusively with the activities of employers which were thought to violate the rights guaranteed by Section 7. Unions were not beyond reproach, but most of them were so weak that their misconduct raised no serious national problems until the 1940's. Hence the original statute did not deal with their activities.

Third. The Wagner Act left substantive terms and conditions of employment entirely to private negotiation. The Act did not fix wages, hours or other conditions of employment. It did not authorize any administrative tribunal to fix them. When a dispute arose concerning substantive terms and conditions of employment, the Act provided no governmental machinery for its adjustment. The basic theory of the law in its original form, as today, was that the arrangement of substantive terms and conditions of employment was a private responsibility from which the government should stand apart. It was hoped that the processes of collective bargaining would result in a lessening of industrial strife, but no one supposed that strikes would not occur. In the end the force which makes management and labor agree is often an awareness of the costs of disagreement. The strike is the motive power which makes collective bargaining operate. Freedom to strike, the threat of a strike and possibly a number of actual strikes are, therefore, indispensable parts of a national labor policy based upon the establishment of wages, hours and other terms and conditions of employment by private collective bargaining.

Constitutionality

The enactment of the Wagner Act was followed by an immediate constitutional challenge from major industries. The chief argument was that the Act, when applied to manufacturing establishments, went beyond the power of Congress under the commerce clause and invaded the powers reserved to the states by the Tenth Amendment. The NLRA gives the NLRB jurisdiction over unfair labor practices and questions of representation "affecting commerce." In the test cases which came before the Supreme Court the NLRB had applied the statute to an interstate bus line, the Associated Press, an integrated producer of basic steel, and a small clothing manufacturer who shipped and sold suits in interstate commerce.

The government was successful in all four cases. Portions of the lead opinion follow.

NLRB v. JONES & LAUGHLIN STEEL CORP.

Supreme Court of the United States, 1937.
301 U.S. 1, 57 S.Ct. 615, 81 L.Ed. 893 (1937).

MR. CHIEF JUSTICE HUGHES delivered the opinion of the Court.

 * * * Although activities may be intrastate in character when separately considered, if they have such a close and substantial relation to interstate commerce that their control is essential or appropriate to protect that commerce from burdens and obstructions, Congress cannot be denied the power to exercise that control. Schechter Corporation v. United States, supra. Undoubtedly the scope of this power must be considered in the light of our dual system of government and may not be extended so as to embrace effects upon interstate commerce so indirect and remote that to embrace them, in view of our complex society, would effectually obliterate the distinction between what is national and what is local and create a completely centralized government. Id. The question is necessarily one of degree. * * *

That intrastate activities, by reason of close and intimate relation to interstate commerce, may fall within federal control is demonstrated in the case of carriers who are engaged in both interstate and intrastate transportation. There federal control has been found essential to secure the freedom of interstate traffic from interference or unjust discrimination and to promote the efficiency of the interstate service. The Shreveport Case (Houston, E. & W. T. R. Co. v. United States), 234 U.S. 342, 351, 352, 34 S.Ct. 833, 58 L.Ed. 1341; Railroad Commission of Wisconsin v. Chicago, B. & Q. R. Co., 257 U.S. 563, 588, 42 S.Ct. 232, 237, 66 L.Ed. 371, 22 A.L.R. 1086. It is manifest that intrastate rates deal *primarily* with a local activity. But in rate making they bear such a close relation to interstate rates that effective control of the one must embrace some control over the other. * * *

Upon the same principle, the Anti-Trust Act has been applied to the conduct of employees engaged in production. * * *

It is thus apparent that the fact that the employees here concerned were engaged in production is not determinative. The question remains as to the effect upon interstate commerce of the labor practice involved. *   *   *

Fourth. Effects of the Unfair Labor Practice in Respondent's Enterprise. Giving full weight to respondent's contention with respect to a break in the complete continuity of the "stream of commerce" by reason of respondent's manufacturing operations, the fact remains that the stoppage of those operations by industrial strife would have a most serious effect upon interstate commerce. In view of respondent's far-flung activities, it is idle to say that the effect would be indirect or remote. It is obvious that it would be immediate and might be catastrophic. We are asked to shut our eyes to the plainest facts of our national life and to deal with the question of direct and indirect effects in an intellectual vacuum. Because there may be but indirect and remote effects upon interstate commerce in connection with a host of local enterprises throughout the country, it does not follow that other industrial activities do not have such a close and intimate relation to interstate commerce as to make the presence of industrial strife a matter of the most urgent national concern. When industries organize themselves on a national scale, making their relation to interstate commerce the dominant factor in their activities, how can it be maintained that their industrial labor relations constitute a forbidden field into which Congress may not enter when it is necessary to protect interstate commerce from the paralyzing consequences of industrial war? We have often said that interstate commerce itself is a practical conception. It is equally true that interferences with that commerce must be appraised by a judgment that does not ignore actual experience.

Experience has abundantly demonstrated that the recognition of the right of employees to self-organization and to have representatives of their own choosing for the purpose of collective bargaining is often an essential condition of industrial peace. Refusal to confer and negotiate has been one of the most prolific causes of strife. This is such an outstanding fact in the history of labor disturbances that it is a proper subject of judicial notice and requires no citation of instances. *   *   *

It is not necessary again to detail the facts as to respondent's enterprise. Instead of being beyond the pale, we think that it presents in a most striking way the close and intimate relation which a manufacturing industry may have to interstate commerce and we have no doubt that Congress had constitutional authority to safeguard the right of respondent's employees to self-organization and freedom in the choice of representatives for collective bargaining.

The Congress of Industrial Organizations

The second major development in labor union history during the 1930's was the rise of the great industrial unions associated in the Congress of Industrial Organizations. The industrial unions organized the great mass production industries which had theretofore been scarcely touched by labor unions. Their power and the spread of unionism into these new areas brought about fundamental changes not only in the labor movement but also in the nature and processes of collective bargaining.

Early in the 1930's it became apparent to John L. Lewis, Sidney Hillman, David Dubinsky and a number of others that the workers in the mass production industries could not be brought into the labor movement unless substantial changes were made in the structure and thinking of the American Federation of Labor. The principle of craft unionism was unsuited to industries, such as rubber and automobiles, where production engineering had broken skilled jobs down into simple repetitive movements which workers could easily learn to perform. Not only was it difficult, if not impossible, to fit these jobs into the structure of the established craft unions, but the workers lacked any feeling of craft solidarity which might furnish a basis for group action. A second difficulty was the adherence of many AFL leaders to the principle that organization must be voluntary and should not be imposed from outside. Since there was neither an active union movement nor any tradition of unionism in the mass production industries, and since they were the strongholds of anti-unionism, it seemed manifest to Lewis and his associates that organizers must be sent into the field without awaiting a spontaneous movement which could never arise. The AFL was not equipped for this task since it had never had the primary responsibility for spearheading an organizing campaign.

When these considerations and others like them were placed before the AFL by Lewis, Hillman and their associates, they encountered strong opposition. The crafts were unwilling to surrender jurisdiction to industrial organizations. Their motives were doubtless compounded of a desire to retain their power, reluctance to abandon a traditional and successful principle, and perhaps the recollection of the conflicts of interest between skilled craftsmen and unskilled workers competing for the same jobs. The matter was hotly debated at a number of annual conventions and meetings of the Executive Board and ultimately came to a head in the 1935 annual convention. The industrial unionists lost a sharp battle in the resolutions committee and were defeated again on the floor. Immediately they summoned an informal gathering to discuss methods of keeping industrial unionism alive, and shortly thereafter the officers of eight AFL international unions formed the Committee for Industrial Organization. Although they professed their desire to work within the AFL, their action challenged the principle of exclusive jurisdiction, which was deeply embedded in trade union philosophy. In the eyes of the old line AFL leaders the members of the Committee were plainly guilty of "dual unionism"—treason in the labor movement—and they ordered the committee to disband. When it refused, the unions which joined it were suspended from the AFL. In 1937 the Congress of Industrial Organizations was formally organized.

The organizational structure of the CIO closely followed the established AFL pattern. The CIO philosophy, however, contrasted sharply with the trade unions' historic ideals. As their names imply, the CIO International Unions embraced the workers in entire industries or groups of industries—United Automobile Workers of America, United Steelworkers of America, Textile Workers Union of America, etc. While the aims of AFL were influenced by its tendency to favor the skilled workers, the CIO was primarily a movement of the unskilled workers; in negotiating wage increases, for example, the CIO more often pressed for flat increases "across the board", thus raising the real wages of the unskilled workers more rapidly than those of the skilled. On the whole the CIO unions were probably less attached to existing institutions than the AFL and quicker to espouse political action. Thus, the CIO displayed an intense interest not only in traditional labor objectives, but in price control, low cost housing, improved educational opportunities, public health and foreign policy.

The emergence of the CIO had a profound influence on the administration of the Wagner Act. In particular, it vastly complicated the task of the National Labor Relations Board in determining the appropriate unit in which to conduct representation elections pursuant to Section 9 of the Act. The CIO, of course, was generally committed to the concept of industrial unionism and sought to represent all workers within the plants and companies of given industries. On the other hand, the AFL was founded on the principle of craft unionism with the result that AFL unions sought to represent particular groups of skilled workers within plants and companies. As a result, CIO and AFL unions vigorously pressed their respective claims before the NLRB, particularly in industries already organized by the CIO, where AFL unions sought to split off groups of craftsmen into separate units.

During the early 1950's, there was increased pressure within the AFL and CIO to reunite. With changes in leadership of both organizations, the prospects for unification improved, and a special subcommittee was appointed in 1952 to eliminate raiding of membership between member unions of the two confederations.   In 1953, a no-raiding pact was drawn up and approved by sixty-five AFL affiliates and twenty-nine CIO affiliates, representing a total of ten million workers.   Under its terms, the signatory unions agreed not to attempt to displace another union and raid its membership in any plant where an "established bargaining relationship" existed.   Disputes involving the application of the agreement were referred to arbitration if the parties could not agree among themselves.

Following the adoption of the no-raiding agreement, plans for total unification developed rapidly, and a draft constitution to this effect was prepared and ratified by the AFL and CIO in 1955.

VI. THE TAFT-HARTLEY ACT [1]
1947

From 1935 until 1947 the national labor policy was founded upon the Norris-LaGuardia and Wagner Acts supplemented by wartime emergency measures.   The Norris-LaGuardia Act established the predicate that peaceful, concerted activities—strikes, boycotts, or picketing—should not be enjoinable by law.   "So long as a union acts in its self-interest and does not combine with non-labor groups, the licit and the illicit * * * are not to be distinguished by any judgment regarding the wisdom or unwisdom, the rightness or unrightness, the selfishness or unselfishness, of the end of which the particular union activities are the means."   United States v. Hutcheson, 312 U.S. 219, 232, 61 S.Ct. 463, 85 L.Ed. 788 (1941). The Wagner Act established the twin rights to organize and bargain collectively and made it government policy to encourage unionization and collective bargaining.

Both statutes made permanent contributions to our national labor policy, but their fundamental assumptions were modified by the enactment of the Taft-Hartley Act in 1947.   The Taft-Hartley bill was bitterly opposed by organized labor and most so-called "liberals."   It was vetoed by President Truman and passed over his veto. The student will have a chance to form his own opinion of the merits

1. For comments on the Taft-Hartley amendments, see Cox, Some Aspects of the Labor Management Relations Act, 1947, 61 Harv.L.Rev. 1, 274 (1947–48); Perkins, Basic Labor Law Issues Under the Taft-Hartley Act, 27 B.U. L.Rev. 371 (1947); Wollett, Collective Bargaining, Public Policy and the NLRA of 1947, 23 Wash.L.Rev. 205 (1948).   See generally H. Millis & E. Brown, From the Wagner Act to Taft-Hartley (1950).

of this legislation as specific problems are raised in later portions of this book. It may be helpful, however, to say a few words about the background of the act and the new trends which it introduced into labor law.

The Spread of Unions and Collective Bargaining

Between 1935 and 1947 labor unions grew and collective bargaining spread rapidly with the aid and encouragement of the federal government. In 1935 only three million workers belonged to labor unions. In 1947 there were nearly fifteen million union members—roughly five times as many. Two thirds of the workers in manufacturing were covered by union agreements and about one third in non-manufacturing industries outside of agriculture and the professions. In some industries, such as coal mining, construction, railroading, and trucking, over four fifths of the employees worked under collective bargaining agreements.

Although government policies scarcely explain this phenomenal development, they exerted important influence. One factor was the Wagner Act and the work of the NLRB. The bare legal protection curbed anti-union tactics. For the government to prosecute an employer for unfair labor practices gave psychological impetus to unionization. Furthermore the NLRB in both Washington and the regional offices was staffed by enthusiasts burning with zeal for organized labor.

A second factor was the federal government's wartime labor policy. The United States could not become the arsenal of democracy without the whole-hearted cooperation of organized labor, and the surest method of obtaining cooperation was to give unions a permanent role in directing the mobilization and allocation of our national resources. Prominent labor figures were given positions of leadership in major federal agencies, such as the Office of Defense Mobilization and the War Production Board, and President Roosevelt made it plain that high officials in the labor movement had quick access to the White House. Labor's role in government reached a peak in the organization of the War Labor Board, which was tripartite; the public, industry and organized labor were equally represented. After Pearl Harbor the country could not safely tolerate any interruption in the production and distribution of goods. Organized labor gave a pledge not to resort to strikes provided that all labor management controversies not resolved in collective bargaining were submitted to a War Labor Board for final decision.

The psychological impact of these measures was tremendous. The union organizer could plausibly argue "It is patriotic to join a union. The President wants you to become a union member." The role of unions in government and the high praise regularly heaped upon organized labor by government officials seemed to prove his point.

The third important factor was the policies of the War Labor Board. The public members of the War Labor Board and many of the employer members were staunch believers in strong unions and collective bargaining. Their policies and decisions gave it encouragement. Still more important, once a union had organized a plant War Labor Board policies encouraged the development of procedures confirming and strengthening the union's role in the plant—use of company bulletin boards, preferential seniority for shop stewards, strong grievance machinery controlled by the union, and arbitration of unsettled grievances.

Reasons for the Enactment of the Taft-Hartley Act

By 1947 the labor movement had achieved great power. Sumner Slichter wrote, "The trade unions are the most powerful economic organizations in the community—in fact, they are the most powerful economic organizations which the community has ever seen." [2] Yet it would be a mistake to suppose that power of labor unions was evenly distributed. In the South and in many agricultural states organized labor was weak indeed. Unions were much stronger, by and large, in manufacturing and mining than in wholesale and retail distribution or among office and clerical workers. The United Mine Workers could defy public opinion but most unions were still vulnerable to shifts in the wind of public sentiment.

The public was worried about the power of unions. Its worry was partly an irrational but widespread fear of "the labor bosses." John L. Lewis and the United Mine Workers had carried on two long strikes during wartime in defiance of the government ending only when the government granted substantial concessions. In 1946 there was a great wave of strikes which shut down the steel mills, automobile assembly plants, packing-houses, electrical products industry, the East and West Coast seaports and a few public utilities. Today it seems plain that this wave of strikes simply marked release from wartime restrictions. In 1947 there were many who saw the danger of nationwide stoppages as a threat to the social system.

But if some of the fear was irrational, there were also careful observers sympathetic to organized labor who perceived the need for measures halting the abuse of power. Their bill of particulars might have included seven specific criticisms.

2.   Slichter, The Challenge of Industrial
       Relations (1947).

(1) Too many strikes were called under circumstances threatening serious injury to the public health or safety—in the coal mines and in public utilities for example.

(2) Although corruption had not been uncovered as high in the union movement as during the Senate investigation of 1957, it was all too plain that some so-called "labor unions" were primarily rackets.

(3) Strikes and picketing were too often marked by violence organized and promoted by union leaders when peaceful measures failed to achieve their objective.

(4) During the war many building trades unions refused to admit new members and charged exorbitant fees for issuing working permits to the new employees attracted to the industry by defense construction. This practice generated ill will among workers who might otherwise have remained sympathetic to organized labor.

(5) The construction industry was also hampered by strikes resulting from jurisdictional disputes. Should the forms into which concrete was poured be taken down by carpenters or laborers? Should riggers move furnaces and air conditioning units off the trucks or freight cars and set them in place in the construction of a new building or should this work be done by plumbers? Large projects were often tied up for days while labor unions disputed each other's right to job assignments.

(6) The secondary boycott had become an exceedingly powerful weapon in the hands of certain unions. The International Brotherhood of Teamsters could tie up any business dependent upon trucking for supplies and outgoing shipments. The United Brotherhood of Carpenters through its control of construction projects could boycott materials produced by any firm on which it desired to impose economic pressure. The *Allen Bradley Case* (p. 878, infra) involved a particularly offensive boycott and was highly publicized.

(7) The emphasis which organized labor in the United States places upon closed and union shop contracts has engendered controversy almost as long as there have been labor unions. In 1947 exponents of the open shop collected many instances of the unions' abuse of the power which the closed and union shop confer upon them. In a few unions the membership rolls were closed and the resulting monopoly of jobs was passed from father to son. Individual employees were expelled for such improper reasons as refusing to take part in political activities, criticizing union officials, refusing to join in an organized slowdown, and testifying adversely to the union in an arbitration proceeding. No doubt the cases cited were extraordinary, but the publicity given them lent force to the attack upon all union security contracts and even those who saw the merit in closed and union shop agreements felt the need for safeguards against abuse.

In analyzing the background of the Taft-Hartley Act one must also give a prominent place to anti-unionism. Many business concerns continued to make war on all unions despite the National Labor Relations Act. Others accepted the forms of collective bargaining under legal and economic compulsion hoping that the tide would turn and they might some day be free from "the union."

The irreconcilables were strengthened by the changing frontiers of union organization. By the end of the war most of the big industrial concerns in the Northeast and Midlands had been organized as well as on the Pacific Coast. Union organizers were now seeking to enlist distributive and clerical workers many of whom were employed in small enterprises where they worked in close contact with the boss. People who genuinely sympathized with the plight of unorganized workers in mines, mills and factories doubted the need for unions in wholesale and retail trades or office buildings where the business itself was smaller and economically weaker than the union.

By the mid-forties organized labor was also ready to invade the South where unionization had lagged far behind older industrial areas but where rapid industrialism presented an increasing competitive threat to union labor standards. Operation Dixie encountered an entire social and political system quite unlike the older milieu and one which sometimes seemed impenetrable by ordinary organizing methods.

In sum, the Taft-Hartley Act was the product of diverse forces— the off-spring, a critic might say, of an unhappy union between the opponents of all collective bargaining and the critics of the unions' abuses of power. The former group was probably the more influential of the two in writing the Taft-Hartley amendments, for organized labor's unfortunate decision to oppose all legislation left its sympathetic critics in a dilemma.

Contributions of the Taft-Hartley Act to the National Labor Policy

In reflecting on the thirty-five years since its enactment, one might say that the Taft-Hartley Act has left these marks upon our labor laws.

First, the Taft-Hartley Act abandoned the notion that law has no role to play in the handling of labor disputes. The philosophy of the Norris-LaGuardia Act was qualified, if not rejected, and the labor injunction was revived in a modified and restricted form which eliminated many abuses. Section 8(b) outlaws the following concerted activities:

(1) violence and intimidation;

(2) secondary boycotts; i. e. the refusal to work for employer *A* unless he ceases to do business with employer *B*, with whom the union has its real dispute;

(3) strikes to compel an employer to commit some unfair labor practice, such as discharging an employee for belonging (or not belonging) to a particular union, or bargaining with the striking union after the NLRB has certified a different representative;

(4) jurisdictional strikes over work assignments.

The weapons thus withheld, especially the secondary boycott, have been important to certain unions in the past. Nevertheless, the points at which the Taft-Hartley Act revives legal intervention into everyday disputes are trivial in comparison to those it leaves untouched. Also, the law intrudes only in areas where the overwhelming consensus of opinion condemns the unlawful conduct.

Second, the Taft-Hartley Act carried forward the fundamental rights to organize and bargain collectively, but it also ushered in a period of marked change in the government's attitude towards unionization. The amendments represent an abandonment of the policy of affirmatively encouraging the spread of union organization and collective bargaining. This appears most strikingly in Section 7, which now places the right to refrain from such activities on equal footing with the rights originally guaranteed, and in the provisions subjecting the organizational activities of labor unions to restrictions similar to those imposed on the activities of employers. The government, instead of aiding one side, now stands in the center. The change of policy appears to have been based on the belief that labor unions had become so strong that legislative action was required to redress the balance of power in the collective bargaining process. But it is not the unions with crushing economic power that feel the change; it is the unorganized employees and the weak, newly-organized locals.

Third, the Taft-Hartley Act ratified previous NLRB regulation of collective bargaining and even extended governmental regulation of the negotiation of collective bargaining agreements. Prior to 1947 the NLRB had gone a considerable distance in regulating both the subject matter of collective bargaining and the way in which negotiations should be conducted. Congress accepted this approach. By imposing a duty to bargain collectively upon labor unions it espoused the view that the public has an interest not only in the employers dealing with the employees as a group but also in the way in which collective negotiations are carried on. This was underscored by the detail in which Section 8(d) regulates the renewal or reopening of collective bargaining agreements. In the Taft-Hartley Act Congress also undertook to regulate for the first time the substantive terms which might be included in a labor contract. Section 8(a) (3) outlaws the closed shop and permits only a limited form of union shop. Section 302 prescribes and limits the terms of pension and health and welfare trust funds.

Fourth, the Taft-Hartley Act marks a turning point at which law began to play a larger role in the administration of collective bargaining agreements. NLRA Section 301 provides that suits for violation of collective bargaining agreements in industries affecting commerce may be brought by or against a labor organization as an entity in any appropriate federal court. Although it seems probable that collective bargaining agreements would have been treated as enforceable contracts without Section 301, its enactment committed the federal courts to that view and encouraged both unions and employers to seek legal sanctions in situations in which they might otherwise have relied upon persuasion or economic power. Since 1947 there has been rapid growth in the law pertaining to the interpretation and enforcement of labor contracts.

VII. THE LANDRUM-GRIFFIN ACT [6]

Twelve years after the passage of the Taft-Hartley Act, Congress once again undertook to enact basic changes in the body of national labor legislation. At the outset, Congress sought to draft provisions to regulate the internal affairs of unions. Nevertheless, this effort was soon coupled with a quite separate undertaking designed to introduce amendments to the National Labor Relations Act governing the relations between unions and employers.

In general, the amendments to the NLRA were in keeping with the basic purposes that had underlain the Taft-Hartley amendments of 1947. Various loopholes in the secondary boycott provisions were closed; in particular, the exertion of secondary pressures through the use of "hot cargo" agreements was prohibited. Substantial limitations were also placed upon the power of unions to picket for the purpose of organizing workers or obtaining recognition from an employer. These restrictions, however, simply represented an extension of the policy which Congress had adopted in 1947 to limit union activities which tended to coerce employees in deciding whether or not to join a union. As a "sweetener" for the labor unions, workers who had been replaced in the course of an economic strike were expressly given the right to vote in union elections. In this way, employers would be discouraged from provoking a strike in order to hire non-union replacements and thereby oust the incumbent labor organization.

Far more novel were the provisions regulating the internal affairs of labor organizations, for earlier legislation had scarcely touched upon this subject. For several years there had been growing concern about the relationship between the union and its members. The

6. See J. Bellace & A. Berkowitz, The Landrum-Griffin Act: Twenty Years of Federal Protection of Union Members' Rights (1979).

problem became prominent during the 1950's when hearings by a Select Committee of the Senate (the McClellan Committee) produced evidence of misconduct by the officials of a few unions ranging from embezzlement to the making of "sweetheart" contracts with employers. To cope with abuses of this sort, a wide variety of provisions were enacted by the Congress. Certain provisions required that elections be held periodically for local and national union officers and that union members be assured a right to vote, to run for union office, and to comment upon and nominate candidates. Every union member was given an equal right to attend membership meetings and to participate in the voting and deliberations at such meetings. Other provisions required the filing of extensive information bearing upon the financial affairs of unions and their officials. Still other sections of the Act flatly prohibited certain types of conduct such as the embezzlement of union funds or property and the making of loans by a union to its officials in excess of a stipulated amount.

A more detailed consideration of the Labor Management Reporting and Disclosure Act is reserved until Part Seven of the casebook.

VIII. JURISDICTION, ORGANIZATION AND PROCEDURE OF THE NLRB

A. NLRB JURISDICTION

The two most significant statutes which accord the rights of unionization and collective bargaining to American workers are the National Labor Relations Act of 1935, as amended in 1947 and 1959, and the Railway Labor Act of 1926, as amended in 1934, which covers employees of railroad and airline carriers. As broad as is the coverage of these statutes, it is important to note that large segments of the workforce are not covered by either; indeed, it is probable that not much more than half of the total labor force in the United States is covered by the NLRA or RLA.

The coverage of the National Labor Relations Act, while far broader than that of the Railway Labor Act, is by no means all-embracing in its coverage of American workers. Large numbers of "employees" fall into special categories which are specifically excluded by Section 2(3) of the NLRA, and many others work for "employers" who are excluded under Section 2(2). Still other workers are employed in enterprises which have too tenuous a connection with interstate commerce to be subject to the Labor Act.

In expressly wording the NLRA to cover enterprises "affecting commerce," Congress appeared to extend the Act to the full limit of its constitutional power. In *Wickard* v. *Filburn*, 317 U.S. 111 63 S.Ct. 82, 87 L.Ed. 122 (1942), Congress was held to have authority under the commerce clause to regulate even the production of wheat consumed entirely at the farm on which it was grown because changes in the volume of such wheat could affect the supply and demand for grain sold across State boundaries. Since the *Wickard* case, the commerce power has been held to extend to used car dealers,[1] grocery stores,[2] newspapers selling but 1½% of their copies in other States,[3] maintenance firms,[4] and a host of other activities having but a slender relationship to interstate commerce. There would seem to be very few, if any, business enterprises whose activities have no discernible effect upon the commerce between the States.[5]

As a practical matter, it has not been necessary under the Act to determine the exact boundaries of the commerce power, for the National Labor Relations Board has not been given sufficient funds to enforce the law even with respect to all of the myriad enterprises that are plainly subject to the commerce clause. As a result, the Board has voluntarily refused to take cognizance of a great number of employers who, though technically within reach of the commerce power, are not considered to have a significant impact on commerce. The Board has declared that employers must engage directly or indirectly in interstate commerce to an extent exceeding certain prescribed dollar minima in order to be subject to its jurisdiction. The following is a list of some of the standards which the Board has established:

1. *Non-retail Firms:* All such firms with an annual outflow or inflow, direct or indirect, in excess of $50,000.

2. *Office Buildings:* All such buildings with a gross annual revenue of $100,000 provided that at least $25,000 is derived from organizations which would fall under NLRB jurisdiction under any of the new standards.

3. *Retail Concerns:* All such concerns doing $500,000 or more gross volume of business.

1. Liddon White Truck Co., 76 N.L.R.B. 1181 (1948).

2. Providence Public Market Co., 79 N.L.R.B. 1482 (1948).

3. Mabee v. White Plains Publishing Co., 327 U.S. 178 (1946).

4. D. A. Schulte v. Gangi, 328 U.S. 193 (1946).

5. Cf. NLRB v. Reliance Fuel Oil Corp., 297 F.2d 94 (2d Cir. 1962), reversed, 371 U.S. 224 (1963).

4. *Instrumentalities, Links and Channels of Interstate Commerce* (trucking companies, etc.): All such entities which derive $50,000 or more annually from the interstate (or linkage) portion of their operations, or from services performed for employers in commerce.

5. *Public Utilities:* All utilities which have at least $250,000 gross annual volume or qualify under the jurisdictional standard applicable to non-retail firms.

6. *Transit Systems* (other than taxicabs, which are governed by the standard for retail concerns): All such systems with an annual gross volume of $250,000 or more.

7. *Newspapers and Communications Systems:* Radio, television, telegraph and telephone systems: $100,000 gross volume. Newspapers: $200,000 gross volume.

8. *National Defense:* All firms having a "substantial impact on national defense."

9. *Business in the Territories and District of Columbia:* District of Columbia: Plenary. Territories: The normal jurisdictional standards will apply.

10. *Associations:* Associations will be regarded as a single employer for jurisdictional purposes.

11. *Colleges and Universities:* All private, nonprofit colleges and universities having a gross annual revenue of at least $1,000,000 for operating expenses.

12. *Symphony Orchestras:* All symphony orchestras which have a gross annual revenue of at least $1,000,000.

Through the cumulative effect of the limits on the commerce power itself and the self-imposed restrictions of the Board, several million employees have been left outside the scope of the National Labor Relations Act.

Section 2(2) of the NLRA excludes several important categories of employers—the United States Government, wholly owned government corporations, Federal Reserve Banks, states and their political subdivisions, and railroads and airlines subject to the Railway Labor Act. To the excluded categories of employers specifically listed in the Act, the Supreme Court, in a 5–to–4 decision, recently added secondary schools operated by the Roman Catholic Church. In NLRB v. CATHOLIC BISHOP OF CHICAGO, 440 U.S. 490, 99 S.Ct. 1313, 59 L.Ed.2d 533 (1979), the Court was confronted with the question whether the NLRB could properly assert jurisdiction to order bargaining between two groups of Catholic high schools and their lay teachers. The Court found that a construction of the

NLRA so as to permit Board jurisdiction would raise a serious constitutional question under the First Amendment regarding the entanglement of the federal government in the operations of private religious schools. It therefore held that there was no clear congressional purpose to permit such jurisdiction and affirmed an order of the court of appeals denying enforcement of the Board order.

No doubt the most significant group of excluded employers are public employers—federal, state, county and municipal governments. Their exclusion results in the lack of protection under the Labor Act for some three million employees working for federal agencies (in Washington, D.C. and throughout the country), and for some 13.5 million state and local government employees working for police and fire departments, school boards, court systems, highway and sanitation departments, and the like. The rights of employees in the federal service to organize and to bargain collectively are set forth in a presidential Executive Order having its origins in an order issued by President Kennedy in 1962. Comparable rights of state employees were for many years governed either by skeletal legislation (often limited to a ban upon work stoppages, coupled with severe civil and criminal penalties) or by judicial decision. The period since the mid-1960's has witnessed the proliferation of comprehensive state statutes, commonly modeled upon the federal Labor Act, extending to public employees the right to form and bargain collectively through labor organizations and creating new agencies (or reviving old ones from the private sector) to conduct elections and hear unfair labor practice cases (but also, with only very few exceptions, retaining a ban upon public-employee strikes). In the same period, there has been a dramatic increase in membership of public-sector unions: by January 1, 1979, 25 percent (6,094,000) of all union members in this country worked in the public sector—1.4 million in the federal service, 980,000 state employees, and 3.7 million in local government.

Section 2(3) adds to these employer exclusions a number of classes of excluded *employees*. Perhaps the most significant excluded employee class is the agricultural laborer. The Board has interpreted this exclusion rather narrowly, holding that no worker can be considered agricultural unless his duties form an integral part of ordinary farming operations. Moreover, his work must ordinarily be of a sort performed before the products can be marketed through normal channels. Hence, employees primarily engaged in duties which merely serve to increase the value of already-marketable products do not fall within the exclusion unless their duties are merely an incident to the employer's normal farming operations. Under this interpretation, workers employed in slaughtering, packing, processing and refining and the like have been found to be subject to the

NLRA. The Supreme Court has generally deferred to the Board's decisions on these jurisdictional matters. See Bayside Enterprises, Inc. v. NLRB, 429 U.S. 298, 97 S.Ct. 576, 50 L.Ed.2d 494 (1977). Nevertheless, as a result of the agricultural exemption, more than three million workers are removed from the Act's coverage. The labor-management relations of agricultural workers are governed by the laws of the individual states, most of which continue to develop their rules through common law decisions, with judges using the same uncertain criteria observed in judicial decisions at the turn of the century. See pp. 17–32 supra. There are, however, four states—Arizona, California, Idaho, and Kansas—which in the early 1970s enacted legislation patterned for the most part after the NLRA; Agricultural Labor Relations Boards are created, organizing and bargaining rights are accorded to agricultural workers within the state, and provision is made for elections and unfair labor practice proceedings. See Babbitt v. United Farm Workers Nat'l Union, 442 U.S. 289, 99 S.Ct. 2301, 60 L.Ed.2d 895 (1979); Agricultural Labor Relations Bd. v. Superior Court, 16 Cal.3d 392, 128 Cal.Rptr. 183, 546 P.2d 687, appeal dismissed, 429 U.S. 802, 97 S.Ct. 33, 50 L.Ed.2d 63 (1976).

Another important excluded employee category consists of "supervisors." That term is defined in Section 2(11) to mean

> "any individual having authority, in the interest of the employer, to hire, transfer, suspend, lay off, recall, promote, discharge, assign, reward, or discipline other employees, or responsibly to direct them, or to adjust their grievances, or effectively to recommend such action, if in connection with the foregoing the exercise of such authority is not of a merely routine or clerical nature, but requires the use of independent judgment."

Section 14(a) of the Labor Act makes it clear that there is no intention actually to prohibit supervisors from unionizing; it merely frees the employer from any obligation to deal with such supervisors "as employees for the purpose of any law, either national or local, relating to collective bargaining." Congress sought to guarantee the single-minded loyalty of supervisors and not, by giving them any right to organize and the employer a correlative duty to bargain, to encourage a conflict of economic interest between the employer and its own representatives. Moreover, any active participation in union affairs on the part of supervisors is likely to be construed as an interference by the employer in union activities, which constitutes a violation of Sections 8(a)(1) and (2) of the Labor Act; the effect of these provisions is to permit supervisors to enjoy only a nominal membership in a union which also represents rank-and-file employees.

Although there is no express exclusion in the Labor Act for "managerial employees," such as company vice-presidents, they have been excluded by the "common law" of the Board. In spite of the fact that they are technically "employees" and that they may not directly "supervise" the work of others (but instead make company policy on sales, purchases or product lines), the Board has concluded that Congress would not have intended to invite the conflict of interest that would flow were such managerial employees to organize and bargain with the employer; indeed, on a broader rationale, such managerial employees *are* "the employer." This Board-made exclusion for managerial employees (and the broader rationale) has been approved by the Supreme Court, in NLRB v. BELL AEROSPACE Co., 416 U.S. 267, 94 S.Ct. 1757, 40 L.Ed.2d 134 (1974). The Board on remand, at 219 N.L.R.B. 384 (1975), formulated the definition of "managerial employee" as follows:

"[T]hose who formulate and effectuate management policies by expressing and making operative the decisions of their employer, and those who have discretion in the performance of their jobs independent of their employer's established policy * * *. [M]anagerial status is not conferred upon rank-and file workers, or upon those who perform routinely, but rather it is reserved for those in executive-type positions, those who are closely aligned with management as true representatives of management."

In a controversial decision, the Supreme Court divided five-to-four and held that the full-time faculty members at a large private university were all "managerial employees" and thus outside of the protections of the NLRA. In NLRB v. YESHIVA UNIV., 444 U.S. 672, 100 S.Ct. 856, 63 L.Ed.2d 115 (1980), the University administration refused to bargain with a faculty association which had been certified by the NLRB, and thus challenged the Board's policy, announced in 1970, of asserting jurisdiction over college and university faculty in the private sector. The Court majority, after examining the extent to which the faculty played a role on such matters as faculty appointments, curriculum, degree requirements and the like, concluded that they were in effect managers of the enterprise who were beyond the jurisdiction of the Board. The dissenting Justices stated that management of the institution was actually in the hands of the University administration, whose interests and decisions were sometimes in conflict with those of the faculty, and who commonly endorsed faculty decisions not because they were made in the interests of management but rather because the faculty were experienced professionals (and professional employees are clearly not excluded from the coverage of the NLRA). Attempts are being made by bargaining representatives for faculty in higher education to have the NLRB construe the *Yeshiva* decision so as not to embrace faculty at many private colleges and universities, and to have Congress amend the Labor Act so as expressly to include all faculty members regardless of their decisionmaking authority within their institutions.

The Labor Act—by giving organizing and bargaining rights only to "employees"—gives rise to a problem of great difficulty and significance, common to other social, economic, or labor legislation (as well as tax laws) : the drawing of a line between an employment relation, on the one hand, and, on the other hand, a contractual undertaking by one independent businessman to do a job for another.

Generally speaking, the courts have developed two somewhat inconsistent approaches for separating independent contractors from "employees" within the meaning of particular pieces of social or labor legislation.

One school looks to the familiar law of master and servant developed for the purposes of determining when to impose vicarious liability for personal injuries under the doctrine of *respondeat superior*. This approach directs attention, predominantly and sometimes even exclusively, to the question whether the alleged master has the contractual right to control the manner in which the alleged servant performs the work, in contrast to receiving a final product without controlling the way in which the job is done.

The other school minimizes the element of control and, looking to what it calls the economic realities of the situation, asks whether the putative employees are subject to the evils which the statute is intended to remedy, and, if so, whether the statutory remedy fits their situation. Under the latter view, but not the former, the definition of "employee" may vary from statute to statute depending upon the purposes of the particular legislation.

The meaning given to the term "employee" under the National Labor Relations Act has changed over time, and has generated what might charitably be termed a "dialogue" between Congress and the Board (with the Supreme Court serving as interlocutor). The original Wagner Act defined the term "employee" in Section 2(3) simply to "include any employee," and provided no exemption for independent contractors. The Board considered the common law test of control but chose instead to apply the term "employee" more expansively to various classes of persons who would have been held to be independent contractors under that test. This reading of the Act was challenged before the Supreme Court in the case that follows, and then reexamined by Congress in enacting the Taft-Hartley amendments of 1947.

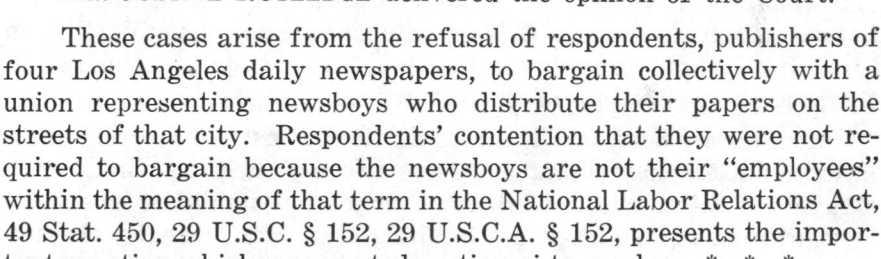

NLRB v. HEARST PUBLICATIONS, INC.

Supreme Court of the United States, 1944.
332 U.S. 111, 64 S.Ct. 851, 88 L.Ed. 1170.

MR. JUSTICE RUTLEDGE delivered the opinion of the Court.

These cases arise from the refusal of respondents, publishers of four Los Angeles daily newspapers, to bargain collectively with a union representing newsboys who distribute their papers on the streets of that city. Respondents' contention that they were not required to bargain because the newsboys are not their "employees" within the meaning of that term in the National Labor Relations Act, 49 Stat. 450, 29 U.S.C. § 152, 29 U.S.C.A. § 152, presents the important question which we granted certiorari to resolve. * * *

The newsboys work under varying terms and conditions. They may be "bootjackers," selling to the general public at places other than established corners, or they may sell at fixed "spots." They may sell only casually or part-time, or full-time; and they may be employed regularly and continuously or only temporarily. The units which the Board determined to be appropriate are composed of those who sell full-time at established spots. Those vendors, misnamed boys, are generally mature men, dependent upon the proceeds of their sales for their sustenance, and frequently supporters of families. Working thus as news vendors on a regular basis, often for a number of years, they form a stable group with relatively little turnover, in contrast to schoolboys and others who sell as bootjackers, temporary and casual distributors. * * *

I.

The principal question is whether the newsboys are "employees." Because Congress did not explicitly define the term, respondents say its meaning must be determined by reference to common-law standards. In their view "common-law standards" are those the courts have applied in distinguishing between "employees" and "independent contractors" when working out various problems unrelated to the Wagner Act's purposes and provisions.

The argument assumes that there is some simple, uniform and easily applicable test which the courts have used, in dealing with such problems, to determine whether persons doing work for others fall in one class or the other. Unfortunately this is not true. Only by a long and tortuous history was the simple formulation worked out which has been stated most frequently as "the test" for deciding whether one who hires another is responsible in tort for his wrong-doing. But this formula has been by no means exclusively controlling in the solution of other problems. And its simplicity has been illusory because it is more largely simplicity of formulation than of application. Few problems in the law have given greater variety of application and conflict in results than the cases arising in the borderland between what is clearly an employer-employee relationship and what is clearly one of independent entrepreneurial dealing. This is true within the limited field of determining vicarious liability in tort. It becomes more so when the field is expanded to include all of the possible applications of the distinction.

It is hardly necessary to stress particular instances of these variations or to emphasize that they have arisen principally, first, in the struggle of the courts to work out common-law liabilities where the legislature has given no guides for judgment, more recently also under statutes which have posed the same problem for solution in the light of the enactment's particular terms and purposes. It is enough to point out that, with reference to an identical problem, results may be contrary over a very considerable region of doubt in applying the distinction, depending upon the state or jurisdiction where the determination is made; and that within a single jurisdiction a person who, for instance, is held to be an "independent contractor" for the purpose of imposing vicarious liability in tort may be an "employee" for the purposes of particular legislation, such as unemployment compensation. See, e. g., Globe Grain & Milling Co. v. Industrial Commn., 98 Utah 36, 91 P.2d 512. In short, the assumed simplicity and uniformity, resulting from application of "common-law standards," does not exist.

Mere reference to these possible variations as characterizing the application of the Wagner Act in the treatment of persons identically situated in the facts surrounding their employment and in the influences tending to disrupt it, would be enough to require pause before accepting a thesis which would introduce them into its administration. This would be true, even if the statute itself had indicated less clearly than it does the intent they should not apply.

Two possible consequences could follow. One would be to refer the decision of who are employees to local state law. The alternative would be to make it turn on a sort of pervading general essence distilled from state law. Congress obviously did not intend the former result. It would introduce variations into the statute's operation as wide as the differences the forty-eight states and other local jurisdictions make in applying the distinction for wholly different purposes. Persons who might be "employees" in one state would be "independent contractors" in another. * * *

Both the terms and the purposes of the statute, as well as the legislative history, show that Congress had in mind no such patchwork plan for securing freedom of employees' organization and of collective bargaining. The Wagner Act is federal legislation, administered by a national agency, intended to solve a national problem on a national scale. * * *

II.

Whether, given the intended national uniformity, the term "employee" includes such workers as these newsboys must be answered primarily from the history, terms and purposes of the legislation. The word "is not treated by Congress as a word of art having a definite meaning * * *." Rather "it takes color from its surroundings * * * [in] the statute where it appears," United States v. American Trucking Associations, Inc., 310 U.S. 534, 545, 60 S.Ct. 1059, 1065, 84 L.Ed. 1345, and derives meaning from the context of that statute, which "must be read in the light of the mischief to be corrected and the end to be attained." * * * Congress had in mind a wider field than the narrow technical legal relation of "master and servant," as the common law had worked this out in all its variations, and at the same time a narrower one than the entire area of rendering service to others. The question comes down therefore to how much was included of the intermediate region between what is clearly and unequivocally "employment," by any appropriate test, and what is as clearly entrepreneurial enterprise and not employment.

It will not do, for deciding this question as one of uniform national application, to import wholesale the traditional commonlaw conceptions or some distilled essence of their local variations as exclusively controlling limitations upon the scope of the statute's effectiveness. To do this would be merely to select some of the local, hairline variations for nation-wide application and thus to reject others for coverage under the Act. That result hardly would be consistent with the statute's broad terms and purposes. * * *

The mischief at which the Act is aimed and the remedies it offers are not confined exclusively to "employees" within the traditional legal distinctions separating them from "independent contractors." * * *

Unless the common-law tests are to be imported and made exclusively controlling, without regard to the statute's purposes, it cannot be irrelevant that the particular workers in these cases are subject, as a matter of economic fact, to the evils the statute was designed to eradicate and that the remedies it affords are appropriate for preventing them or curing their harmful effects in the special situation.   Interruption of commerce through strikes and unrest may stem as well from labor disputes between some who, for other purposes, are technically "independent contractors" and their employers as from disputes between persons who, for those purposes, are "employees" and their employers.   Cf. Milk Wagon Drivers' Union Local No. 753 v. Lake Valley Farm Products, Inc., 311 U.S. 91, 61 S.Ct. 122, 85 L.Ed. 63.   Inequality of bargaining power in controversies over wages, hours and working conditions may as well characterize the status of the one group as of the other.   The former, when acting alone, may be as "helpless in dealing with an employer," as "dependent * * * on his daily wage" and as "unable to leave the employ and to resist arbitrary and unfair treatment" as the latter.   For each, "union * * * [may be] essential to give * * * opportunity to deal on equality with their employer."   And for each, collective bargaining may be appropriate and effective for the "friendly adjustment of industrial disputes arising out of differences as to wages, hours, or other working conditions."   49 Stat. 449, 29 U.S.C.A. § 151.   In short, when the particular situation of employment combines these characteristics, so that the economic facts of the relation make it more nearly one of employment than of independent business enterprise with respect to the ends sought to be accomplished by the legislation, those characteristics may outweigh technical legal classification for purposes unrelated to the statute's objectives and bring the relation within its protections.

* * * In this light, the broad language of the Act's definitions, which in terms reject conventional limitations on such conceptions as "employee," "employer," and "labor dispute," leaves no doubt that its applicability is to be determined broadly, in doubtful situations, by underlying economic facts rather than technically and exclusively by previously established legal classifications. * * *

It is not necessary in this case to make a completely definitive limitation around the term "employee."   That task has been assigned primarily to the agency created by Congress to administer the Act. Determination of "where all the conditions of the relation require protection" involves inquiries for the Board charged with this duty. Everyday experience in the administration of the statute gives it familiarity with the circumstances and backgrounds of employment relationships in various industries, with the abilities and needs of the workers for self organization and collective action, and with the adaptability of collective bargaining for the peaceful settlement of their disputes with their employers.   The experience thus acquired must be brought frequently to bear on the question who is an employee under the Act. Resolving that question, like determining whether unfair labor practices have been committed, "belongs to the usual administrative routine" of the Board.   *   *   *

In making that body's determinations as to the facts in these matters conclusive, if supported by evidence, Congress entrusted to it primarily the decision whether the evidence establishes the material facts. Hence in reviewing the Board's ultimate conclusions, it is not the court's function to substitute its own inferences of fact for the Board's, when the latter have support in the record. National Labor Relations Board v. Nevada Consolidated Copper Corp., 316 U.S. 105, 62 S.Ct. 960, 86 L.Ed. 1305; cf. Walker v. Altmeyer, 2 Cir., 137 F.2d 531. Undoubtedly questions of statutory interpretation, especially when arising in the first instance in judicial proceedings, are for the courts to resolve, giving appropriate weight to the judgment of those whose special duty is to administer the questioned statute. Norwegian Nitrogen Products Co. v. United States, 288 U.S. 294, 53 S.Ct. 350, 77 L.Ed. 796; United States v. American Trucking Associations, Inc., 310 U.S. 534, 60 S.Ct. 1059, 84 L.Ed. 1345. But where the question is one of specific application of a broad statutory term in a proceeding in which the agency administering the statute must determine it initially, the reviewing court's function is limited. Like the commissioner's determination under the Longshoremen's & Harbor Workers' Act, that a man is not a "member of a crew" (South Chicago Coal & Dock Co. v. Bassett, 309 U.S. 251, 60 S.Ct. 544, 547, 84 L.Ed. 732) or that he was injured "in the course of his employment" (Parker v. Motor Boat Sales, Inc., 314 U.S. 244, 62 S.Ct. 221, 222, 86 L.Ed. 184) and the Federal Communications Commission's determination that one company is under the "control" of another (Rochester Telephone Corp. v. United States, 307 U.S. 125, 59 S.Ct. 754, 83 L.Ed. 1147), the Board's determination that specified persons are "employees" under this Act is to be accepted if it has "warrant in the record" and a reasonable basis in law.

In this case the Board found that the designated newsboys work continuously and regularly, rely upon their earnings for the support of themselves and their families, and have their total wages influenced in large measure by the publishers who dictate their buying and selling prices, fix their markets and control their supply of papers. Their hours of work and their efforts on the job are supervised and to some extent prescribed by the publishers or their agents. Much of their sales equipment and advertising materials is furnished by the publishers with the intention that it be used for the publisher's benefit. Stating that "the primary consideration in the determination of the applicability of the statutory definition is whether effectuation of the declared policy and purposes of the Act comprehend securing to the individual the rights guaranteed and protection afforded by the Act," the Board concluded that the newsboys are employees. The record sustains the Board's findings and there is ample basis in the law for its conclusion.

*   *   *

[The concurring opinion of MR. JUSTICE REED and the dissenting opinion of MR. JUSTICE ROBERTS have been omitted.]

In the Taft-Hartley Act of 1947, Congress amended Section 2(3) expressly to exclude independent contractors. As the following passage from the legislative reports[7] indicates, Congress intended by the amendment not only to narrow the scope of the Board's jurisdiction and the reach of the Labor Act but also to reprimand the Board for assumed indifference to the terms of the statute and the Court for assumed undue deference to the administrative agency. Indeed, by the very act of giving this new (or clearer) definition to the term "employee" Congress also expressed its will to curb the power of the Board in relation to that of the judiciary.

"An 'employee,' according to all standard dictionaries, according to the law as the courts have stated it, and according to the understanding of almost everyone, with the exception of members of the National Labor Relations Board, means someone who works for another for hire. But in the case of National Labor Relations Board v. Hearst Publications, Inc. (322 U.S. 111, 64 S.Ct. 851, 88 L.Ed. 1170 (1944)), the Board expanded the definition of the term 'employee' beyond anything that it ever had included before, and the Supreme Court, relying upon the theoretic 'expertness' of the Board, upheld the Board. In this case the Board held independent merchants who bought newspapers from the publisher and hired people to sell them to be 'employees'. The people the merchants hired to sell the papers were 'employees' of the merchants, but holding the merchants to be 'employees' of the publisher of the papers was most far reaching. It must be presumed that when Congress passed the Labor Act, it intended words it used to have the meanings that they had when Congress passed the act, not new meanings that, 9 years later, the Labor Board might think up. In the law, there always has been a difference, and a big difference, between 'employees' and 'independent contractors'. 'Employees' work for wages or salaries under

7. H.R.Rep. No. 245, 80th Cong., 1st Sess. at 18 (1947).

direct supervision. 'Independent contractors' undertake to
do a job for a price, decide how the work will be done, usually hire others to do the work, and depend for their income
not upon wages, but upon the difference between what they
pay for goods, materials, and labor and what they receive
for the end result, that is, upon profits. It is inconceivable
that Congress, when it passed the act, authorized the Board
to give to every word in the act whatever meaning it wished.
On the contrary, Congress intended then, and it intends
now, that the Board give to words not far-fetched meanings
but ordinary meanings. To correct what the Board has
done, and what the Supreme Court, putting misplaced reliance upon the Board's expertness, has approved, the bill
excludes 'independent contractors' from the definition of
'employee'."

Problems for Discussion

1. Was Congress correct in charging that the Supreme Court in
Hearst was "relying upon the theoretic 'expertness' of the Board" to
justify its rejection of the common law agency test in construing the term
"employee" in the Wagner Act? Can you sketch out what the Supreme
Court opinion would have been had the Board decided to adopt the common
law test?

2. If another case involving "newsboys" came before the Board in
1948, and the Board found them to be "employees" within the coverage
of the Act, using the then new definition in Section 2(3), what should
be the proper scope of judicial review of that finding? Should the court
of appeals affirm if the finding is reasonable and has support in the record
(even though the court might not have made the same decision in the
first instance)? Or should the court affirm only if it believes the Board
decision is "correct" (i. e., one that the court would itself have made)?
After reflecting on this problem, consider whether your conclusion is
consistent with the decision of the Supreme Court which follows.

NLRB v. UNITED INSURANCE CO.

Supreme Court of the United States, 1969.
390 U.S. 254, 88 S.Ct. 988, 19 L.Ed.2d 1083.

MR. JUSTICE BLACK delivered the opinion of the Court.

In its insurance operations respondent United Insurance Company uses "debit agents" whose primary functions are collecting
premiums from policyholders, preventing the lapsing of policies, and
selling such new insurance as time allows. The Insurance Workers
International Union, having won a certification election, seeks to

represent the debit agents, and the question before us is whether these agents are "employees" who are protected by the National Labor Relations Act or "independent contractors" who are expressly exempted from the Act. Respondent company refused to recognize the Union, claiming that its debit agents were independent contractors rather than employees. In the ensuing unfair labor practice proceeding the National Labor Relations Board held that these agents were employees and ordered the company to bargain collectively with the Union. 154 N.L.R.B. 38. On appeal the Court of Appeals found that the debit agents were independent contractors and refused to enforce the Board's order. 371 F.2d 316 (C.A.7th Cir.). The importance of the question in the context involved to the administration of the National Labor Relations Act prompted us to grant the petitions of the Board and the Union for certiorari. 389 U.S. 815, 88 S.Ct. 49, 19 L.Ed.2d 66.

At the outset the critical issue is what standard or standards should be applied in differentiating "employee" from "independent contractor" as those terms are used in the Act. Initially this Court held in N. L. R. B. v. Hearst Publications, 322 U.S. 111, 64 S.Ct. 851, 88 L.Ed. 1170, that "Whether * * * the term 'employee' includes [particular] workers * * * must be answered primarily from the history, terms and purposes of the legislation." 322 U.S., at 124, 64 S.Ct. at 857. Thus the standard was one of economic and policy considerations within the labor field. Congressional reaction to this construction of the Act was adverse and Congress passed an amendment specifically excluding "any individual having the status of an independent contractor" from the definition of "employee" contained in § 2(3) of the Act. The obvious purpose of this amendment was to have the Board and the courts apply general agency principles in distinguishing between employees and independent contractors under the Act. And both petitioners and respondents agree that the proper standard here is the law of agency. Thus there is no doubt that we should apply the common-law agency test here in distinguishing an employee from an independent contractor. * * *

There are innumerable situations which arise in the common law where it is difficult to say whether a particular individual is an employee or an independent contractor, and these cases present such a situation. On the one hand these debit agents perform their work primarily away from the company's offices and fix their own hours of work and work days; and clearly they are not as obviously employees as are production workers in a factory. On the other hand, however, they do not have the independence, nor are they allowed the initiative and decision-making authority, normally associated with an independent contractor. In such a situation as this there is no shorthand formula or magic phrase that can be applied to find the answer, but all of the incidents of the relationship must be assessed and weighed with no one factor being decisive. <u>What is important is that the total factual context is assessed in light of the pertinent common-law agency principles.</u> When this is done, the decisive factors in these cases become the following: the agents do not operate their own independent businesses, but perform functions that are an essential part of the company's normal operations; they need not have any prior training or experience, but are trained by company supervisory personnel; they do business in the company's name with considerable assistance and guidance from the company and its managerial personnel and ordinarily sell only the company's policies; the "Agent's Commission Plan" that contains the terms and conditions under which they operate is promulgated and changed unilaterally by the company; the agents account to the company for the funds they collect under an elaborate and regular reporting procedure; the agents receive the benefits of the company's vacation plan and group insurance and pension fund; and the agents have a permanent working arrangement with the company under which they may continue as long as their performance is satisfactory. [The Court quoted from a letter written to the debit agents by the company's chairman of the board: "If any agent believes he has the power to make his own rules and plan of handling the company's business, then that agent should hand in his resignation at once * * * * The company is going to have its business managed in your district the same as all other company districts in the many states where said offices are located. * * *"]

The Board examined all of these facts and found that they showed the debit agents to be employees. This was not a purely factual finding by the Board, but involved the application of law to facts— what do the facts establish under the common law of agency: employee or independent contractor? It should also be pointed out that such a determination of pure agency law involved no special administrative expertise that a court does not possess. On the other hand, the Board's determination was a judgment made after a hearing with witnesses and oral argument had been held and on the basis of written briefs. <u>Such a determination should not be set aside just because a court would, as an original matter, decide the case the other way.</u> As we said in Universal Camera Corp. v. N.L.R.B., 340 U.S. 474, 71 S.Ct. 456, 95 L.Ed. 456, "Nor does it [the requirement for canvassing the whole record] mean that even as to matters not requiring expertise a court may displace the Board's choice between two fairly conflicting views, even though the court would justifiably have made a different choice had the matter been before it *de novo.*" 340 U.S., at 488, 71 S.Ct. at 465. <u>Here the least that can be said for the Board's decision is that it made a choice between two fairly conflicting views,</u>

and under these circumstances the Court of Appeals should have enforced the Board's order. It was error to refuse to do so.

Reversed.

MR. JUSTICE BRENNAN and MR. JUSTICE MARSHALL took no part in the consideration or decision of these cases.

Problems for Discussion

1. Are you persuaded by the Court's reasons for requiring the court of appeals to give substantial deference to the Board's finding?

2. Is it consistent for the Court to state that the determination whether the insurance agents are "employees" involves no special administrative expertise that a court does not possess and then to hold that the court ought not make an independent determination of the issue? (Is the Court's first assumption soundly based?)

B. NLRB ORGANIZATION AND PROCEDURE [8]

Although it is customary to speak of "the Board" as if the National Labor Relations Board and its large staff of employees thought and acted as a single person, this usage is highly misleading. In reality, the NLRB is composed of various categories of persons exercising quite different responsibilities. The adjudicative responsibilities of the agency are ultimately entrusted to the five members of the Board, appointed by the President of the United States for five-year terms by and with the consent of the Senate. In the course of the Taft-Hartley amendments of 1947, the Congress also established the office of General Counsel, appointed to a four-year term by the President by and with the consent of the Senate. The General Counsel has authority to investigate charges of unfair labor practices, to decide whether complaints should be issued on the basis of these charges and to direct the prosecution of such complaints. The General Counsel also represents the Board in court proceedings to enforce or review Board decisions.

To assist the Board members and the General Counsel in discharging their responsibilities, a large staff has been created. Or-

---

8. See J. Feerick, H. Baer & J. Arfa, NLRB Representation Elections—Law, Practice & Procedure (1980); F. McCulloch & T. Bornstein, The National Labor Relations Board (1974); K. McGuiness, How to Take a Case Before the National Labor Relations Board (4th ed. 1975); Murphy, The National Labor Relations Board—An Appraisal, 52 Minn.L.Rev. 819 (1968).

ganizationally, the staff is divided between the Washington office and over thirty Regional Offices. The Regional Offices are under the general supervision of the General Counsel. Each Regional Office is under the direction of a Regional Director aided by a Regional Attorney. Their staff consists principally of Field Examiners, who investigate charges and conduct elections, and attorneys, who prosecute complaints at hearings before Administrative Law Judges (called Trial Examiners prior to August 1972) and act as legal counsel to the Regional Director.

---

1. Unfair Labor Practice Cases.

The General Counsel may issue a complaint only upon a formal charge that the employer or the union has engaged in an unfair labor practice. Such a charge may be filed by any person or employer or qualified labor organization in the office for the region in which the alleged unfair labor practice occurred. Section 10(b) of the Act requires that a charge be filed and served upon the charged party within six months of the alleged unfair labor practice. When a charge is filed, the Regional Director normally requires the person making the charge to submit the supporting evidence in the form of affidavits, lists of witnesses, etc. The charged party (respondent) may or may not be asked to submit a reply. In either case, a Field Examiner then makes a thorough investigation of the facts and surrounding circumstances. For example, if a charge is filed against the employer, the Field Examiner interviews the union officials and employees concerned, locates other witnesses, goes to the plant and may discuss the case with company officials.

If this preliminary investigation discloses that the charge is without foundation, the case is likely to be dropped forthwith. Otherwise, further investigation may ensue and there will commonly be an informal conference at the local office of the Board, attended by both the respondent and the charging party, at which the alleged unfair practices are thoroughly discussed and possible settlements considered. The nature of any particular settlement depends, of course, on the circumstances of the case. Where the charge is that the company has violated Section 8(a) (1) by unlawful activities of foremen and other supervisors—threatening those who join the union with reprisals, circulating anti-union petitions, threatening the closing of the plant if it is organized, etc.—the normal remedy after a complaint and hearing would be an order to cease and desist from such interference and to post appropriate notices informing the employees that the company will not interfere with, restrain or coerce them in the exercise of their right of self-organization. Consequently, if informal conferences convince the officials of a company that acts of interference have occurred, or if the company is doubtful whether there has been interference but sincerely desires its employees to have the freedom guaranteed by the Act, then it is usually possible to convince the Regional Offices and the union of the company's good faith and to work out in the informal conferences a satisfactory form of announcement to be posted in the plant. Sometimes cases are settled in this manner even though the employer is convinced that there have been no unfair labor practices, for making the desired announcement may be far less burdensome than litigation before the Board. On the other hand, when a case involves an allegation that an employee was discharged for engaging in union activities, the employer may have strong reasons for refusing to accede to the Board's normal demand that it reinstate the discharged employee with back pay. It is important, for example, for an employer who has not violated the Act to maintain the authority of its supervisory staff and show that union membership is no protection against punishment for breaches of plant discipline. Even this kind of case, however, is often settled without a hearing. The investigation of the Field Examiner may convince the company officials that some inferior supervisor has in fact acted unfairly, and in that event it is as sound industrial relations promptly to correct the error as it is to maintain the supervisor's prestige by backing him up when he is right. Conversely, the investigation of the Field Examiner or the explanation made by the company may convince the Regional Director that the discharge was justified. In that event, the Regional Director may persuade the union to withdraw its charge or else, if the union refuses, he may decline to issue a complaint.

It is important to emphasize the informality of these investigations, conferences and settlements. Except for such steps as are required by sound administration, including the reduction to writing of any settlement agreement, the entire procedure up to this point is conducted with all possible informality and an eye to amicable adjustments. In the past, most unfair labor practice cases were disposed of in one way or another in the Regional Offices by these informal personal negotiations. In the fiscal year ending June 30, 1979, for example, of the 41,500 unfair labor practice charges that were "closed," 95 percent were closed by the NLRB Regional Offices prior to a formal hearing. (Approximately 35 percent were disposed of by dismissing the charge involved, more than 30 percent by voluntary withdrawal of the charge, and 28 percent by settlement.) Of the cases that year in which Regional Office investigations indicated that the unfair labor practice charges were meritorious, their settlement rate of 84.5 percent was the highest in NLRB history, involving some 11,572 cases.

If it is impossible to dispose of an unfair labor practice case in the Regional Office, formal proceedings are commenced by the filing of a complaint. The General Counsel has delegated to the Regional Directors authority to issue complaints except in cases "involving novel and complex issues." Should the Regional Director refuse to issue a complaint, the matter may be appealed to the General Counsel. If the General Counsel declines to issue a complaint, it is generally understood that the charging party has no further recourse. Vaca v. Sipes, 386 U.S. 171, 87 S.Ct. 903, 17 L.Ed.2d 842 (1967). However, once a complaint has issued, the charging party may be entitled to an evidentiary hearing on his objections to a negotiated settlement. Leeds & Northrup Co. v. NLRB, 357 F.2d 527 (3d Cir. 1966).

Upon the issuance of a complaint the Board may petition the district court, under Section 10(j) of the Act, for appropriate interlocutory relief preventing continuance of the unfair labor practice. Although infrequently sought (62 in fiscal year 1979) and rarely issued (20 granted and 10 denied), Section 10(j) injunctions have been issued against unions as well as employers, the more common employer violations being discriminatory discharges, recognition of minority unions and bad faith or "surface" bargaining, and the more common union violations involving strike violence and hiring-hall discrimination.

The complaint, which is drafted by the Regional Attorney or a member of his staff, specifies the violations of the Act which the company is alleged to have committed and contains a notice of the time and place of hearing. The Act and the Board's rules give the respondent the right to answer a complaint. The answer is filed with the Regional Director, as are all motions made prior to the hearing. Normally, the answer is to be filed within ten days from service of the complaint, but extensions may be granted on the Regional Director's own motion or for good cause shown by any party.

The hearing is usually held in the city or town where the alleged violation occurred before an Administrative Law Judge appointed from the Division of Administrative Law Judges in Washington (or from one of the geographically decentralized divisions which the Board has recently established). The case is prosecuted for the Board by an attorney from the Regional Office. The charging party is permitted to intervene, and its attorneys may take part in the proceedings. The respondent, of course, may and usually does appear by an attorney as in the normal court proceeding. Section 10(b) of the Act provides that unfair labor practice proceedings "shall, so far as practicable, be conducted in accordance with the rules of evidence applicable in the district courts" under the rules of civil procedure adopted by the Supreme Court. Evidence is introduced through witnesses and documents, just as in an ordinary civil trial.

At the conclusion of the hearing both parties are entitled as a matter of right to argue orally before the Administrative Law Judge and file a written brief. In practice, however, it has not been customary for either party to make an oral argument.

After the hearing is completed, the Administrative Law Judge prepares a decision containing proposed findings of fact and recommendations for the disposition of the case. The Administrative Law Judge's decision is then filed with the Board, and a copy is served on the respondent and any other parties. Within twenty days after service of the Administrative Law Judge's decision, counsel for any party or for the Board may file exceptions together with a brief in support thereof. Cross exceptions may then be filed within the succeeding ten days by any party who has not previously filed exceptions. Permission to argue orally before the Board itself must be specially requested in writing, and it is granted only in unusual cases. If no exceptions are filed, the Board normally adopts the decision of the Administrative Law Judge.

Although minor changes are made from time to time, the Board's procedure after the filing of exceptions, briefs and oral argument, if permitted, has recently been as follows. When the record is complete, the Executive Secretary assigns cases among the five Board members in rotation. A case assigned to Member A is transmitted to his Chief Legal Assistant who thereupon assigns it to some junior legal assistant on Member A's staff. The latter examines the record and decides whether the case is one which the full Board should consider or is sufficiently routine for decision by a three-member panel. Thereafter one of A's legal assistants prepares a draft decision—or in doubtful and very important cases a memorandum—which is reviewed by his superiors and then transmitted to the Board members who will participate. Under the panel system copies also go to the two members who were not on the panel so that they or one of their legal assistants can check the draft and decide whether the case is sufficiently important to ask for consideration by the full Board. Any member may ask to have a case referred to the full Board.

In routine cases the members of the three-member panel go over the draft opinion and approve it—or suggest changes—without the need for a formal conference. Member A may read it either before it is sent to his colleagues or while they have it under consideration. Where there is a difference of opinion or important issues are at stake, a conference is held. In cases sufficiently important for decision by the full Board there is always a conference. Thereafter the opinion is prepared, approved by the members and issued by the Board.

The five members of the Board decide in this fashion more than one hundred unfair labor practice cases a month. It is obvious that in most of them the basic responsibility rested on the administrative law judge and the legal assistants who prepared draft decisions for the Board. Only a relatively small number of really important cases could receive full consideration from the members themselves, however conscientiously they attended to their duties.

The Rules and Regulations issued by the Board provide for handling a charge that a labor organization has violated Section 8(b) in the same manner that the Board handles charges against employers. In the case of strikes and other concerted activities alleged to violate Sections 8(b) (4), 8(b) (7), or 8(e), however, the Regional Office must give its investigation precedence over all other cases not of the same character. If there is reason to believe that the charge is true, the Regional Director files a petition for "appropriate injunctive relief pending the final adjudication of the Board" (Section 10(*l*)). The proceeding before the Board is then expedited and upon the Board's final decision, any order of the district court expires.

Board orders carry no sanctions, although every Regional Office includes a compliance officer who determines whether Board orders are being complied with and endeavors to secure voluntary compliance. If the respondent does not comply with a Board order, the Board must secure enforcement by filing a petition in a federal court of appeals; this action is taken on behalf of the Board by its Enforcement Division (which is a part of the Office of the General Counsel), and the enforcement petition is uniformly filed in the circuit in which the unfair labor practice was committed. The Board may in fact secure such an enforcement order even when there has been no refusal to comply. Similarly, if the respondent desires to have the Board's order reviewed and set aside, it may file a petition for that purpose since under Section 10(f) it is a "person aggrieved." That section gives such a person a choice of courts of appeals, for review may be sought where the unfair labor practice was committed, or where the person does business or in the Court of Appeals for the District of Columbia. Respondents frequently avail themselves of the right to seek review without waiting for the Board to file a petition for enforcement, particularly since this will give the respondent the power to select the circuit for review, a choice sometimes thought to be significant in the ultimate outcome of the case. If the decision of the Board denies relief in whole or in part to the charging party, that party becomes a "person aggrieved" who may also seek appellate review. The Supreme Court has also held that a party who is not aggrieved by the Board's decision, and whose position is sustained by the Board, may nonetheless intervene to protect its interests in the event another party petitions for review or for enforcement. UAW Local 283 v. Scofield, 382 U.S. 205, 86 S.Ct. 373, 15 L.Ed.2d 272 (1965).

Upon the filing of a petition for enforcement or for review by a court of appeals, the pleadings, testimony and transcript of proceedings before the Board are certified to the court, and the case is put on its ordinary appellate docket. No objection that has not been urged before the Board may be considered by the court, save in exceptional cases. In such proceedings, the court is authorized to enter a decree setting aside, enforcing, or modifying the order and enforcing it as so modified. Review of the decree of a court of appeals may be had in the Supreme Court upon the granting of a petition for a writ of certiorari in the same manner as other cases.

In reviewing an order issued by the NLRB, courts must accept the Board's findings of fact "if supported by substantial evidence on the record considered as a whole" (Section 10(f)). This general standard of review eludes precise definition. "Substantial evidence" requires more than a scintilla; taking account of the facts and inferences on both sides of the issue, there must be enough evidence to support the agency's conclusion in a reasonable and reasoning mind. In other words, the court must not freely substitute its judgment for the Board's, yet it need not approve findings that the judges consider unreasonable or unfair. The deference given to the Board's findings is based in part on the fact that the administrative law judge is in a position to observe the witnesses at first hand. It is also partly due to the fact that the Board is "one of those agencies presumably equipped or informed by experience to deal with a specialized field of knowledge, whose findings within that field carry the authority of an expertness which courts do not possess and therefore must respect." Universal Camera Corp. v. NLRB, 340 U.S. 474, 71 S.Ct. 456, 95 L. Ed. 456 (1951). The degree of deference which the courts will pay to the "expertness" of the Board tends to vary according to the nature of the question involved. In particular, if the issue is a highly technical one, far removed from the ordinary experience of the judge, the court will be less likely to disturb the Board's findings, particularly if the Board has set forth the basis for its findings with reasonable clarity and if its reasoning and conclusions do not appear inconsistent with its decisions in related cases.

In defining the scope and nature of judicial review, courts have traditionally distinguished between questions of law and questions of fact. In practice, this distinction is often difficult to draw with precision. Certain decisions, for example, involve "mixed questions of law and fact," as in NLRB v. Hearst Publications, 322 U.S. 111, 64 S.Ct. 851, 88 L.Ed. 1170 (1944), where the Board was interpreting the statutory term "employee" but in so doing considered various factual questions, such as the business relationship of newsboys to the newspaper and the economic power of the former in dealing with the latter. Other decisions which appear to involve pure questions of fact, may actually contain principles of law. For example, if the Board should conclude that employers who grant a wage increase during a representation campaign interfere with the free choice of the employees in voting for or against the union, the Board is not merely deciding the factual question of the effect of the increase upon the minds of the employees; the Board is also laying down a principle of law that the risk of interference in the generality of cases is sufficiently large that such increases should be prohibited entirely without requiring the burdensome and perhaps impractical task of investigating the effects of the employer's action in each case.

One may question how much actually turns on formal distinctions between questions of law, questions of fact, and mixed questions of law and fact. Where elements of law are involved in the issues under review, the Supreme Court has at times freely substituted its own judgment for that of the administrative agency while at other times it has declared that "the judicial function is exhausted when there is found to be a rational basis for the conclusions approved by the administrative body." Rochester Tel. Corp. v. United States, 307 U.S. 125, 59 S.Ct. 754, 83 L.Ed. 1147 (1939). The degree of deference accorded by the courts has not seemed to turn necessarily on any formal definition regarding the nature of the question involved. Instead, though it is difficult to generalize on the question, courts have tended to assume greater responsibility in passing upon issues of law where (1) they require a weighing of other statutes or policies not confided to the special jurisdiction of the Board; (2) they involve common-law or constitutional considerations rather than "technical" matters requiring administrative expertise; (3) they involve controversial questions which demand the prestige of judicial resolution; or (4) they require the interpretation of statutory language in the light of legislative history rather than specialized judgments of a kind which the agency is peculiarly qualified to make.

The principles which guide appellate courts in reviewing questions of law and fact are plainly of a very general nature leaving much to the discretion of the judges involved. In exercising this discretion, courts will presumably be influenced to some degree by such other factors as the respect they hold for the capabilities and impartiality of the Board and the cogency and comprehensiveness of the arguments made by that agency in support of its conclusions. These factors are unavoidably subjective and may therefore cause considerable variation from one court to another concerning the nature of review. It is for this reason, perhaps, that there is often a significant disparity among circuit courts in their rates of affirmance of NLRB decisions. For example, in the Board's 1979 fiscal year, 84.6 percent of its decisions reaching the Third Circuit court were affirmed in full there, while the Second Circuit court affirmed in full only 44.8 percent of the Board decisions it reviewed. (Examining the five-year period 1974–78, however, one finds the disparities muted, varying from a 62.5 percent affirmance rate in the Eighth Circuit to 76.4 percent in the Fifth Circuit.)   Statistics such as these suggest that the principles governing the scope and nature of judicial review should be taken as providing only the most general indication of the nature of review to be accorded by any given court in a particular case.

Since the order made by the federal court of appeals in a proceeding under the Act is an equity decree, it may be enforced by proceedings for contempt.   The Board has been held to have exclusive authority to prosecute civil contempts with the result that neither unions nor employers may petition the court for this purpose.

2.   *Representation Cases.*

In addition to the work that the Regional Office does in unfair labor practice cases, it also plays the most important day-to-day role in processing representation cases.   Election petitions are filed in the Regional Office, and the bulk of these seek the holding of a representation election in order to determine the desires of the employees concerning the selection of a union for collective bargaining. (Other elections may be held to decertify a union already representing employees in bargaining.)   Such representation petitions may be filed either by an employer upon whom a demand for recognition and bargaining has been made by a union, or by a union seeking to represent employees (and demonstrating that it has what is known as a "showing of interest" from thirty percent of the employees within the bargaining unit, generally evidenced by signed cards authorizing that union to be bargaining agent).

The regional staff investigates the petition, in order to determine such questions as whether the employer and the union are covered by the National Labor Relations Act and whether the group of employees within which the election is sought constitute "an appropriate bargaining unit."   In most cases, these issues are resolved through the consent of the parties, either on their own initiative or after an investigation and conference in the Regional Office.   If these matters are contested, they will be made the subject of a hearing conducted by a hearing officer from the Regional Office.   The transcript of the hearing is then transferred to the Regional Director, who makes decisions on issues such as the Board's jurisdiction and the appropriate bargaining unit, and (eventually, after an election is conducted) the eligibility of voters and objections to the validity of the election. His decisions on such matters, both those which are made prior to the election and those which are made after the election, are subject to appeal in a limited set of circumstances to the National Labor Relations Board—not, as in complaint cases, to the General Counsel. The Regional Director has the power to issue an order setting the time and place of the election, to rule on objections and to certify the election results. All of the election issues discussed above were, until 1961, determined in the first instance by the Board itself; in that year Section 3(b) of the Labor Act was amended to authorize their delegation to the Regional Directors.

Decisions made by the NLRB in representation proceedings can normally not be challenged directly by judicial review. The Labor Act in its terms provides for judicial review, in the courts of appeals, only of final orders in unfair labor practice cases. If a person is aggrieved by a Board decision in a representation case, the appropriate manner for precipitating court action is for that person to commit an unfair labor practice, challenge within the unfair labor practice proceeding the decision made by the Board in the representation case (which the Board will normally reaffirm in the unfair labor practice case), and only then seek review in a court of appeals. Most commonly, this is done by an employer—seeking review, for example, of a Board appropriate-unit decision—by refusing to bargain with a union recently certified after a Board election. The purpose of this seemingly circuitous review mechanism, contemplated under Section 9(d) of the Act, is to prevent obstructive recourse to the courts at various stages of the representation proceeding and long delay in the determination of employee preferences on the matter of unionization. In certain extraordinary cases, however—to be explored further in the materials below (pp. 311–19)—a federal district court may have jurisdiction directly to enjoin the Board or a Regional Director from implementing a decision in the context of a representation proceeding.

Part Two

THE ESTABLISHMENT OF THE COLLECTIVE BARGAINING RELATIONSHIP

I. PROTECTION OF THE RIGHT OF SELF–ORGANIZATION

A. INTERFERENCE, RESTRAINT AND COERCION [1]

Section 8(a) (1) of the Act declares it to be an unfair labor practice to interfere with, restrain or coerce employees in the exercise of the right to self-organization, to form, join or assist labor organizations, to bargain collectively and to engage in concerted activities for the purpose of collective bargaining or other mutual aid or protection. Accordingly, it has been held that violations of sub-sections (2), (3), (4) and (5) are also violations of Section 8(a) (1). Nevertheless, it is convenient for purposes of analysis to distinguish the acts of interference, coercion and restraint which merely violate Section 8(a) (1) from those acts which also constitute violations of the other sections. Interference with employees' exercise of the right of self-organization may also be treated separately from the rather different problems raised by allegations of interference with other concerted activities.

In giving effect to Section 8(a) (1) to protect the right to join a union, the National Labor Relations Board has emphasized the need to preserve the employees' "free choice." The precise meaning of this term, however, is not immediately clear. To be sure, one can readily deduce that employees must not be physically intimidated in deciding whether to support a union, for no choice made under these circumstances can be considered "free" in the ordinary sense of the word. But once one passes beyond a few obvious cases of this kind, further analysis is required to determine from what influences the employee is to be "free."

We may assume that having allowed the employees to decide for themselves whether or not to be represented by a union, Congress contemplated that they should be permitted to make a reasoned choice concerning this issue. Such a choice implies that employees should have access to relevant information, that they should use this data to estimate the probable consequences if the union is selected or rejected,

---

1. See generally Bok, The Regulation of Campaign Tactics in Representation Elections Under the National Labor Relations Act, 78 Harv.L.Rev. 38 (1964); J. Getman, S. Goldberg & J. Herman, Union Representation Elections: Law and Reality (1976); R. Williams, P. Janus & K. Huhn, NLRB Regulation of Election Conduct (1974).

and that they should appraise these consequences in the light of their own preferences and desires to determine whether a vote for the union promises to promote or impair their self-interest.   This definition provides a key to the meaning of a free and unrestrained choice under the statute.   Ideally, at least, the employees should be free from restrictions which unduly obstruct the flow of relevant information, from misrepresentations and threats which tend to distort their assessment of the consequences of unionization, and from acts of retribution which would penalize them for having exercised the choice guaranteed them under the Act.

The preceding discussion provides a framework for the materials which follow.   The first group of cases takes up various rules imposed by the employer which limit employees or union organizers from communicating with one another on company property.   The next series of cases has to do with the limitations which the Board may impose on the content of speeches and literature disseminated by the union and employer prior to an election under Section 9 of the NLRA.   In particular, attention will be devoted to such problems as threats made by employers to discourage voting for the union; inflammatory speeches relating to racial policies of the union, violence and the like; and misrepresentations of material facts made by either side.   The final group of cases will take up various forms of interference, other than speech, which may impair the employees' freedom of choice.

---

1.   *Restrictions on Solicitation and Distribution*

REPUBLIC AVIATION CORP. v. NLRB

Supreme Court of the United States, 1945.
324 U.S. 793, 65 S.Ct. 982, 89 L.Ed. 1372, 157 A.L.R. 1081.

MR. JUSTICE REED delivered the opinion of the Court.

In the Republic Aviation Corporation case, the employer, a large and rapidly growing military aircraft manufacturer, adopted, well before any union activity at the plant, a general rule against soliciting which read as follows:

"Soliciting of any type cannot be permitted in the factory or offices."

The Republic plant was located in a built-up section of Suffolk County, New York.   An employee persisted after being warned of the rule in soliciting union membership in the plant by passing out application cards to employees on his own time during lunch periods.   The employee was discharged for infraction of the rule and, as the National Labor Relations Board found, without discrimination on the part of the employer toward union activity.

Three other employees were discharged for wearing UAW-CIO union steward buttons in the plant after being requested to remove the insignia. The union was at that time active in seeking to organize the plant. The reason which the employer gave for the request was that as the union was not then the duly designated representative of the employees, the wearing of the steward buttons in the plant indicated an acknowledgment by the management of the authority of the stewards to represent the employees in dealing with the management and might impinge upon the employer's policy of strict neutrality in union matters and might interfere with the existing grievance system of the corporation.

The Board was of the view that wearing union steward buttons by employees did not carry any implication of recognition of that union by the employer where, as here, there was no competing labor organization in the plant. The discharges of the stewards, however, were found not to be motivated by opposition to the particular union, or we deduce, to unionism.

The Board determined that the promulgation and enforcement of the "no solicitation" rule violated Section 8(1) of the National Labor Relations Act as it interfered with, restrained and coerced employees in their rights under Section 7 and discriminated against the discharged employee under Section 8(3). It determined also that the discharge of the stewards violated Sections 8(1) and 8(3). As a consequence of its conclusions as to the solicitation and the wearing of the insignia, the Board entered the usual cease and desist order and directed the reinstatement of the discharged employee with back pay and also the rescission of "the rule against solicitation in so far as it prohibits union activity and solicitation on company property during the employees' own time." 51 NLRB 1186, 1189. The Circuit Court of Appeals for the Second Circuit affirmed, 142 F.2d 193, and we granted certiorari, 323 U.S. 688, 65 S.Ct. 55, 89 L.Ed. 557, because of conflict with the decisions of other circuits. * * * [We also granted certiorari in Le Tourneau Co. v. National Labor Relations Board, which raises the same issue.]

These cases bring here for review the action of the National Labor Relations Board in working out an adjustment between the undisputed right of self-organization assured to employees under the Wagner Act and the equally undisputed right of employers to maintain discipline in their establishments. Like so many others, these rights are not unlimited in the sense that they can be exercised without regard to any duty which the existence of rights in others may place upon employer or employee. Opportunity to organize and proper discipline are both essential elements in a balanced society.

The Wagner Act did not undertake the impossible task of specifying in precise and unmistakable language each incident which would constitute an unfair labor practice. On the contrary that Act left to the Board the work of applying the Act's general prohibitory language in the light of the infinite combinations of events which might be charged as violative of its terms.   *   *   *

The gravamen of the objection of both Republic and Le Tourneau to the Board's orders is that they rest on a policy formulated without due administrative procedure. To be more specific it is that the Board cannot substitute its knowledge of industrial relations for substantive evidence. The contention is that there must be evidence before the Board to show that the rules and orders of the employers interfered with and discouraged union organization in the circumstances and situation of each company. Neither in the Republic nor the Le Tourneau cases can it properly be said that there was evidence or a finding that the plant's physical location made solicitation away from company property ineffective to reach prospective union members. Neither of these is like a mining or lumber camp where the employees pass their rest as well as their work time on the employer's premises, so that union organization must proceed upon the employer's premises or be seriously handicapped.   *   *   *

[The Court then summarized the provisions of section 10(a), (b) and (c) which prescribe the procedure to be followed in unfair labor practice cases.]

Plainly this statutory plan for an adversary proceeding requires that the Board's orders on complaints of unfair labor practices be based upon evidence which is placed before the Board by witnesses who are subject to cross-examination by opposing parties. Such procedure strengthens assurance of fairness by requiring findings on known evidence. Ohio Bell Tel. Co. v. Public Utilities Comm. of Ohio, 301 U.S. 292, 302, 57 S.Ct. 724, 729, 81 L.Ed. 1093; United States v. Abilene & S. Ry. Co., 265 U.S. 274, 288, 44 S.Ct. 565, 569, 68 L.Ed. 1016. Such a requirement does not go beyond the necessity for the production of evidential facts, however, and compel evidence as to the results which may flow from such facts. Market St. R. Co. v. Railroad Comm. of California et al., 324 U.S. 548, 65 S.Ct. 770, 89 L.Ed. 1171. An administrative agency with power after hearings to determine on the evidence in adversary proceedings whether violations of statutory commands have occurred may infer within the limits of the inquiry from the proven facts such conclusions as reasonably may be based upon the facts proven. One of the purposes which lead to the creation of such boards is to have decisions based upon evidential facts under the particular statute made by experienced officials with an adequate appreciation of the complexities of the subject which is entrusted to their administration. National Labor Relations Board v. Virginia Power Co., 314 U.S. 469, 479, 62 S.Ct. 344, 349, 86 L.Ed. 348; National Labor Relations Board v. Hearst Publications, 322 U.S. 111, 130, 64 S.Ct. 851, 860, 88 L.Ed. 1170.

In the Republic Aviation Corporation case the evidence showed that the petitioner was in early 1943 a non-urban manufacturing establishment for military production which employed thousands. It was growing rapidly. Trains and automobiles gathered daily many employees for the plant from an area on Long Island, certainly larger than walking distance. The rule against solicitation was introduced in evidence and the circumstances of its violation by the dismissed employee after warning was detailed.

As to the employees who were discharged for wearing the buttons of a union steward, the evidence showed in addition the discussion in regard to their right to wear the insignia when the union had not been recognized by the petitioner as the representative of the employees. * * *

No evidence was offered that any unusual conditions existed in labor relations, the plant location or otherwise to support any contention that conditions at this plant differed from those occurring normally at any other large establishment. * * *

These were the facts upon which the Board reached its conclusions as to unfair labor practices. The Intermediate Report in the Republic Aviation case, 51 NLRB at 1195, set out the reason why the rule against solicitation was considered inimical to the right of organization.[2] This was approved by the Board. Id., 1186. The Board's reasons for concluding that the petitioner's insistence that its employees refrain from wearing steward buttons appear at page 1187 of the report.[3] In the Le Tourneau Company case the discussion of the reasons underlying the findings was much more extended. 54 NLRB 1253, 1258 et seq. We insert in the note below a quotation which shows the character of the Board's opinion.[4] Furthermore, in

2. 51 NLRB 1195: "Thus under the conditions obtaining in January 1943, the respondent's employees, working long hours in a plant engaged entirely in war production and expanding with extreme rapidity, were entirely deprived of their normal right to 'full freedom of association' in the plant on their own time, the very time and place uniquely appropriate and almost solely available to them therefor. The respondent's rule is therefore in clear derogation of the rights of its employees guaranteed by the Act."

labor organization in the plant. Furthermore, there is no evidence in the record herein that the respondent's employees so understood the steward buttons or that the appearance of union stewards in the plant affected the normal operation of the respondent's grievance procedure. On the other hand, the right of employees to wear union insignia at work has long been recognized as a reasonable and legitimate form of union activity, and the respondent's curtailment of that right is clearly violative of the Act."

3. We quote an illustrative portion. 51 NLRB 1187, 1188: "We do not believe that the wearing of a steward button is a representation that the employer either approves or recognizes the union in question as the representative of the employees, especially when, as here, there is no competing

4. 54 NLRB at 1259, 1260: "As the Circuit Court of Appeals for the Second Circuit has held, 'It is not every interference with property rights that is within the Fifth Amendment and * * * Inconvenience or even some dislocation of property rights, may be necessary in order to safeguard the

both opinions of the Board full citation of authorities was given including Matter of Peyton Packing Company, 49 NLRB 828, 50 NLRB 355, hereinafter referred to.

The Board has fairly, we think, explicated in these cases the theory which moved it to its conclusions in these cases. The excerpts from its opinions just quoted show this. The reasons why it has decided as it has are sufficiently set forth. We cannot agree, as Republic urges, that in these present cases reviewing courts are left to "sheer acceptance" of the Board's conclusions or that its formulation of policy is "cryptic." See Eastern-Central Motor Carriers Ass'n v. United States, 321 U.S. 194, 209, 64 S.Ct. 499, 506, 88 L.Ed. 668.

appellent

Not only has the Board in these cases sufficiently expressed the theory upon which it concludes that rules against solicitation or prohibitions against the wearing of insignia must fall as interferences with union organization but in so far as rules against solicitation are concerned, it had theretofore succinctly expressed the requirements of proof which it considered appropriate to outweigh or overcome the presumption as to rules against solicitation. In the Peyton Packing Company case, 49 NLRB 828, at 843, hereinbefore referred to, the presumption adopted by the Board is set forth.[5]

Although this definite ruling appeared in the Board's decisions, no motion was made in the court by Republic or Le Tourneau after the Board's decisions for leave to introduce additional evidence to show unusual circumstances involving their plants or for other purposes. * * * We perceive no error in the Board's adoption of this presumption. The Board had previously considered similar rules in industrial establishments and the definitive form which the Peyton

right to collective bargaining.' The Board has frequently applied this principle in decisions involving varying sets of circumstances, where it has held that the employer's right to control his property does not permit him to deny access to his property to persons whose presence is necessary there to enable the employees effectively to exercise their right to self-organization and collective bargaining, and in those decisions which have reached the courts, the Board's position has been sustained. * * *

5. 49 NLRB at 843, 844: "The Act, of course, does not prevent an employer from making and enforcing reasonable rules covering the conduct of employees on company time. Working time is for work. It is therefore within the province of an employer to promulgate and enforce a rule prohibiting union solicitation during working hours. Such a rule must be presumed to be valid in the absence of evidence that it was adopted for a discriminatory purpose. It is no less true that time outside working hours, whether before or after work, or during luncheon or rest periods, is an employee's time to use as he wishes without unreasonable restraint, although the employee is on company property. It is therefore not within the province of an employer to promulgate and enforce a rule prohibiting union solicitation by an employee outside of working hours, although on company property. Such a rule must be presumed to be an unreasonable impediment to self-organization and therefore discriminatory in the absence of evidence that special circumstances make the rule necessary in order to maintain production or discipline."

Packing Company decision gave to the presumption was the product of the Board's appraisal of normal conditions about industrial establishments. Like a statutory presumption or one established by regulation, the validity, perhaps in a varying degree, depends upon the rationality between what is proved and what is inferred.

In the Republic Aviation case, petitioner urges that irrespective of the validity of the rule against solicitation, its application in this instance did not violate Section 8(3), because the rule was not discriminatorily applied against union solicitation but was impartially enforced against all solicitors. It seems clear, however, that if a rule against solicitation is invalid as to union solicitation on the employer's premises during the employee's own time, a discharge because of violation of that rule discriminates within the meaning of Section 8(3) in that it discourages membership in a labor organization.

MR. JUSTICE ROBERTS, dissents in each case.

BETH ISRAEL HOSP. v. NLRB, 437 U.S. 483, 98 S.Ct. 2463, 57 L.Ed.2d 370 (1978). The Hospital had an explicit rule barring solicitation or distribution of literature by employees "in patient-care and all other work areas, and areas open to the public such as lobbies, cafeteria and coffee shop, corridors, elevators, gift shop, etc." When the Hospital's general director observed an employee distributing the union newsletter in the Hospital cafeteria to other employees, he ordered her to stop; the employee was also given a written notice threatening dismissal for further violation of the Hospital rule. (The newsletter, among other things, disparaged the Hospital's ability to provide adequate patient care, primarily because of understaffing.) The Board's finding of violations of Sections 8(a)(1) (for the no-solicitation rule) and 8(a)(3) (for the written notice), and its order requiring rescission of the rule as regards the cafeteria and coffee shop, were affirmed by the Supreme Court.

Although the Board generally requires employers to permit employee solicitation on union matters during nonworking time, it has tolerated hospital bans on such solicitation in working areas devoted strictly to patient care; but such solicitation must be permitted in other areas such as lounges and cafeterias open to visitors and even to patients "absent a showing that disruption to patient care would necessarily result if solicitation and distribution were permitted in those areas." Since Beth Israel Hospital produced no such evidence, the Board properly concluded that the possibility of disruption to patient care resulting from solicitation in the cafeteria (where a three-day survey revealed that 77% of the patrons were employees, 9% were visitors and 1.56% were patients) was remote.

The Court rejected the Hospital's argument that, because the potential disruption to patient care flowing from solicitation in a patient-access cafeteria was a medical judgment, the Board was inexpert on this matter and should not on judicial review be accorded the deference contemplated by *Republic Aviation.* "It is true that the Board is not expert in the delivery of health-care services, but neither is it in pharmacology, chemical manufacturing, lumbering, shipping or any of a host of varied and specialized business enterprises over which the Act confers its jurisdiction. But the Board is expert in federal national labor relations policy, and it is in the Board, not [the Hospital], that the 1974 amendments vested responsibility for developing that policy in the health-care industry. * * * The judicial role is narrow: The rule which the Board adopts is judicially reviewable for consistency with the Act, and for rationality," both of which requirements are satisfied in this case. The Court found that the Board's conclusion regarding lack of impact on patient care was supported by the record. Patient use of the cafeteria was voluntary, random and infrequent (and could be avoided by unusually sensitive patients), and the Hospital had itself permitted charitable solicitations there in the past. Even if the importance of the Hospital's mission was such as to warrant considering whether the union could effectively communicate with employees elsewhere on the premises, there was no such place at Beth Israel (the employee lockerrooms, where the Hospital did permit solicitation, being scattered, sex-segregated and available to only one-quarter of the workforce).

Two separate concurring opinions (speaking for a total of four Justices) emphasized that the cafeteria at Beth Israel was substantially comparable to an all-employee cafeteria, and that a different result might be warranted in other cases where the cafeteria was used principally by patients and their visitors.

NLRB v. MAGNAVOX CO., 415 U.S. 322, 94 S.Ct. 1099, 39 L.Ed.2d 358 (1974). The IUE had been bargaining representative of the Magnavox employees for nearly twenty years, during which time the labor contracts had authorized the company to issue rules for the "maintenance of orderly conditions on plant property" and had provided for bulletin boards for union notices. During that period, the company had prohibited employees from distributing literature on company property, including parking lots and other nonworking areas, even during nonworking time. When the company rejected a union proposal to change this no-solicitation rule, charges were filed with the NLRB under Section 8(a)(1). The Board held that, since the workplace was the natural and typically the only place where all employees could gather to discuss work matters including unionization, the employer's ban was unlawful, with respect to both solicitation against the incumbent union and solicitation in support of that union. Although the court of appeals disagreed and found the contract provision to constitute a waiver of on-premises distribution, the Supreme Court reversed and gave its approval to the Board's decision.

The Court, in an opinion by Justice Douglas, endorsed *Republic Aviation* and the *Peyton Packing* presumptions, and noted that the employer had made no contention that its rule was necessary to promote production or discipline. It also held that the union did not have the power to waive the normally applicable solicitation and distribution rights of the employees. It is true that unions may waive the Section 7 right to strike, as a quid pro quo for grievance and arbitration provisions or other employer concessions; but such a waiver assumes that the union has been freely selected and is fairly representing employees in the bargaining unit. However, when the Section 7 right at stake is the exercise of a choice regarding unionization or a change in representative, "it is difficult to assume that the incumbent union has no self-interest of its own to serve by perpetuating itself as the bargaining representative." The union's access to a bulletin board is not a fair substitute, since it may be adequate to preserve the status quo but not to give the union's adversaries adequate access to co-workers. Although these arguments most clearly dictate the non-waiver of the distribution rights of employees opposed to the union, "employees supporting the union have as secure § 7 rights as those in opposition."

In a separate opinion, Justice Stewart (for himself and two other Justices) agreed that "the clear policy of federal labor law forbids either the union or the employer to freeze out another union or to entrench the incumbent union by infringing the § 7 rights of dissident employees." He saw no reason, however, why the incumbent union could not waive the literature-distribution rights of its own supporters, since the union was free to communicate through the bulletin board, union meetings and the force of its status as bargaining representative; for the Board now to restore these rights of union supporters would upset the "delicate balance achieved in the give and take of negotiations" and would give the union an undeserved windfall.

On the disputed issue, do you agree with Justice Douglas or with Justice Stewart?

Problems for Discussion

1. Until last June, the employer had never had a formal shop rule barring solicitation during working time. Late that month, an organizing

campaign was begun by the Machinists Union. The employer soon posted a notice, informing employees that the significant increase in solicitation and discussion regarding the union during working time had demonstrably interfered with production and safety, and that as a result no solicitation of employees would be permitted during working time. In spite of that rule, supervisors authorized two working-time solicitations in July, one for contributions for flowers to be sent to a widow of a deceased co-worker and another for contributions to the Red Cross to aid earthquake victims in Italy and Mexico. When two employees sought to use part of their working time one day to distribute authorization cards on behalf of the union, their supervisor warned them not to do so on pain of discharge. Has an unfair labor practice been committed? See *Permian Corp.*, 189 N.L.R.B. 860 (1971), aff'd mem., 457 F.2d 512 (5th Cir. 1972), and compare *Serv-Air, Inc. v. NLRB*, 395 F.2d 557 (10th Cir.), cert. denied 393 U.S. 840, 89 S.Ct. 121, 21 L.Ed.2d 112 (1968), with *Wm. L. Bonnell Co. v. NLRB*, 405 F.2d 593 (5th Cir. 1969).

2. In June, some of the employees at the Restful Nursing Home began wearing blue union buttons about the size of a half-dollar with white print reading "Local 1199" in the middle and "Hospital Division AFL–CIO" around the border. The employer ordered the employees to remove the buttons, calling their attention to a longstanding rule barring the wearing of any buttons or insignia on uniforms. When one of the employees refused to remove the union button, he was given a formal disciplinary warning for insubordination and violation of working rules. Does the warning violate Section 8(a)(1)? See *Ohio Masonic Home*, 205 N.L.R.B. 357 (1973).

3. May Department Store had a rule prohibiting solicitation of any kind on its selling floor, on escalators, in elevators, on stairways used by its customers, or in its public cafeteria when the store is open to the public. A union began a campaign to organize May's employees, and employee Stein began handing out union literature to, and discussing the union with, her fellow employees on the selling floor and in the customer cafeteria, at a time when both Stein and the other employees were on their break. When Stein declined to adhere to her supervisor's request that she obey the company no-solicitation rule, she was suspended indefinitely. The union has filed a charge against the employer under Section 8(a)(1). Should the charge be sustained? See *NLRB v. May Dep't Stores*, 59 N.L.R.B. 976 (1944), enf'd as mdf'd 154 F.2d 533 (8th Cir.), cert. denied 329 U.S. 725 (1946).

4. The employer has a shop rule prohibiting "unauthorized distribution of literature of any description in working areas of company property at any time." The employees are accorded a small facility for eating their lunch, which they either take with them to work, buy from a vending machine located near the shop floor, or buy from a sandwich truck parked outside the front entrance. Several employees have traditionally eaten their lunch at their machine, on the working floor. One day, employee Lloyd during his lunch period distributed to each employee—both in the lunchroom facility and on the working floor—a single-page flyer giving

facts about the Machinists Union and encouraging employees to apply for membership. Some of the flyers were left alongside the employees' machines or found their way to the floor. When Lloyd the next week began to distribute a similar union flyer, supervisor Wallace threatened him with a one-week suspension for violation of company rules. Has Section 8(a)(1) been violated? See *Stoddard-Quirk Mfg. Co.*, 138 N.L.R.B. 615 (1962).

5. In 1980, the company and the union executed a collective bargaining agreement which provided, among other things, that employees may not distribute any literature on company property. During the term of the contract, company supervisors orally prohibited the distribution by employees at plant gates of literature pertaining to their candidacy for office in the union while permitting the distribution of campaign literature by other employees, other institutional union and company literature, and the sale and distribution of newspapers, cookies, and candy in furtherance of charitable causes. The individual employees who were prohibited from distributing their literature filed a charge with the Board, alleging that they are being discriminated against by the employer and that the contract provision is unlawful as applied to the right to distribute literature pertaining to candidacy for union office. Does the charge have merit? See *General Motors Corp. v. NLRB*, 512 F.2d 447 (6th Cir. 1975).

Would your analysis be different if the attempted distribution had been by an incumbent union officer and the literature had pertained to the union's campaign to recruit new members and its program of meetings and social activities in the coming months?

NLRB v. BABCOCK & WILCOX CO.

Supreme Court of the United States, 1956.
351 U.S. 105, 76 S.Ct. 679, 100 L.Ed. 975.

MR. JUSTICE REED delivered the opinion of the Court.

In each of these cases the employer refused to permit distribution of union literature by nonemployee union organizers on company-owned parking lots. The National Labor Relations Board, in separate and unrelated proceedings, found in each case that it was unreasonably difficult for the union organizer to reach the employees off company property and held that, in refusing the unions access to parking lots, the employers had unreasonably impeded their employees' right to self-organization in violation of § 8(a)(1) of the National Labor Relations Act. Babcock & Wilcox Co., 109 N.L.R.B. 485, 494; Ranco, Inc., id., 998, 1007, and Seamprufe, Inc., id., 24, 32.

The plant involved in No. 250, Labor Board v. Babcock & Wilcox Co., is a company engaged in the manufacture of tubular products such as boilers and accessories, located on a 100-acre tract about

one mile from a community of 21,000 people. Approximately 40%
of the 500 employees live in that town and the remainder live within
a 30-mile radius. More than 90% of them drive to work in private
automobiles and park on a company lot that adjoins the fenced in
plant area. The parking lot is reached only by a driveway 100 yards
long which is entirely on company property excepting for a public
right-of-way that extends 31 feet from the metal of the highway to
the plant's property. Thus, the only public place in the immediate
vicinity of the plant area at which leaflets can be effectively distributed to employees is that place where this driveway crosses the
public right-of-way. Because of the traffic conditions at that place
the Board found it practically impossible for union organizers to
distribute leaflets safely to employees in motors as they enter or leave
the lot. The Board noted that the company's policy on such distribution had not discriminated against labor organizations and that other
means of communication, such as the mail and telephones, as well as
the homes of the workers, were open to the union.[6] The employer
justified its refusal to allow distribution of literature on company
property on the ground that it had maintained a consistent policy
of refusing access to all kinds of pamphleteering and that such distribution of leaflets would litter its property.

The Board found that the parking lot and the walkway from it
to the gatehouse, where employees punched in for work, were the
only "safe and practicable" places for distribution of union literature.
The Board viewed the place of work as so much more effective a
place for communication of information that it held the employer
guilty of an unfair labor practice for refusing limited access to company property to union organizers. It therefore ordered the employer to rescind its no-distribution order for the parking lot and
walkway, subject to reasonable and nondiscriminating regulations
"in the interest of plant efficiency and discipline, but not as to deny
access to union representatives for the purpose of effecting such
distribution." 109 N.L.R.B., at 486.

The Board petitioned the Court of Appeals for the Fifth Circuit for enforcement. That court refused enforcement on the
ground the statute did not authorize the Board to impose a servi-

---

6. *"Other union contacts with em-*
ployees: In addition to distributing
literature to some of the employees,
as shown above, during the period of
concern herein the Union has had other contacts with some of the employees. It has communicated with
over 100 employees of Respondent on
3 different occasions by sending literature to them through the mails.
Union representatives have communicated with many of Respondent's employees by talking with them on the
streets of Paris, by driving to their
homes and talking with them there,
and by talking with them over the
telephone. All of these contacts have
been for the purpose of soliciting the
adherence and membership of the employees in the Union." 109 N.L.R.B.,
at 492–493.

tude on the employer's property where no employee was involved. Labor Board v. Babcock & Wilcox Co., 222 F.2d 316.

* * *

[The Court considered as well two other cases with facts similar to those in *Babcock & Wilcox*. In both, the Board required that the employer give the nonemployee organizers access to company property; one court of appeals granted enforcement while the other denied enforcement. The Court granted certiorari "because of the conflicting decisions on a recurring phase of enforcement of the National Labor Relations Act."]

In these present cases the Board has set out the facts that support its conclusions as to the necessity for allowing nonemployee union organizers to distribute union literature on the company's property. In essence they are that nonemployee union representatives, if barred, would have to use personal contacts on streets or at home, telephones, letters or advertised meetings to get in touch with the employees. The force of this position in respect to employees isolated from normal contacts has been recognized by this Court and by others. See Republic Aviation Corporation v. Labor Board, supra, at 799, note 3; Labor Board v. Lake Superior Lumber Corp., supra, at 150. We recognize, too, that the Board has the responsibility of "applying the Act's general prohibitory language in the light of the infinite combinations of events which might be charged as violative of its terms." Labor Board v. Stowe Spinning Co., 336 U.S. 226, 231. We are slow to overturn an administrative decision.

 It is our judgment, however, that an employer may validly post his property against nonemployee distribution of union literature if reasonable efforts by the union through other available channels of communication will enable it to reach the employees with its message and if the employer's notice or order does not discriminate against the union by allowing other distribution. In these circumstances the employer may not be compelled to allow distribution even under such reasonable regulations as the orders in these cases permit.

This is not a problem of always open or always closed doors for union organization on company property. Organization rights are granted to workers by the same authority, the National Government, that preserves property rights. Accommodation between the two must be obtained with as little destruction of one as is consistent with the maintenance of the other. The employer may not affirmatively interfere with organization; the union may not always insist that the employer aid organization. But when the inaccessibility of employees makes ineffective the reasonable attempts by nonemployees to communicate with them through the usual channels, the right to exclude from property has been required to yield to the extent needed to permit communication of information on the right to organize.

The determination of the proper adjustments rests with the Board. Its rulings, when reached on findings of fact supported by substantial evidence on the record as a whole, should be sustained by the courts unless its conclusions rest on erroneous legal foundations. Here the Board failed to make a distinction between rules of law applicable to employees and those applicable to nonemployees.

The distinction is one of substance. No restriction may be placed on the employees' right to discuss self-organization among themselves, unless the employer can demonstrate that a restriction is necessary to maintain production or discipline. Republic Aviation Corp. v. Labor Board, 324 U.S. 793, 803. But no such obligation is owed nonemployee organizers. Their access to company property is governed by a different consideration. The right of self-organization depends in some measure on the ability of employees to learn the advantages of self-organization from others. Consequently, if the location of a plant and the living quarters of the employees place the employees beyond the reach of reasonable union efforts to communicate with them, the employer must allow the union to approach his employees on his property. No such conditions are shown in these records.

The plants are close to small well-settled communities where a large percentage of the employees live. The usual methods of imparting information are available. See, e. g., note 7, supra. The various instruments of publicity are at hand. Though the quarters of the employees are scattered they are in reasonable reach. The Act requires only that the employer refrain from interference, discrimination, restraint or coercion in the employees' exercise of their own rights. It does not require that the employer permit the use of its facilities for organization when other means are readily available.

Labor Board v. Babcock & Wilcox Co., No. 250, is

Affirmed.

MR. JUSTICE HARLAN took no part in the consideration or decision of these cases.

Problems for Discussion

1. Grossinger's is an elaborately appointed resort hotel located on a 468-acre tract in the Catskill Mountains near Liberty, N.Y., a village of 5,000 people. There are guest rooms. The staff varies from 565 to 786 employees depending upon the season. About 60 percent live on the premises,

where 300 rooms, meals, shops, and many recreational facilities are available. Other employees go to and from work by automobile. Hotel and Restaurant Employees and Bartenders International Union is seeking to organize Grossinger's employees. Has Grossinger's a duty to admit professional organizers to the premises? See *NLRB* v. *S. & H. Grossinger's Inc.*, 372 F.2d 26 (2d Cir. 1967).

Would the result be different if the employees all lived in quarters that were physically remote from those of the guests and separated from the guest quarters by a lightly travelled public road? See *NLRB* v. *Kutsher's Hotel & Country Club, Inc.*, 427 F.2d 200 (2d Cir. 1970).

2. Under Section 6 of the Labor Act, the NLRB has the power, after notice and hearings pursuant to the Administrative Procedure Act, to promulgate as would a legislature substantive rules of labor law. The notice, given to the public generally, sets forth the text of the proposed rule, and an opportunity is given to all interested parties to communicate with the Board in writing and orally in the hearings. There are generally no limitations upon the kinds of evidence that the Board may receive in such rulemaking proceedings.

The Board is considering the adoption of a rule which would provide: "If the company which the union is attempting to organize is situated in a city with more than 50,000 residents, the employer is obligated to provide access to its premises for union distribution of literature at such points as may, consistent with safety and orderly ingress and egress, provide the union with ready and easy access to the employees as they enter and leave the employer's premises unless the employer proves, by clear and convincing evidence, that the union is able through the exercise of reasonable efforts to utilize available channels of communication to reach the employees."

Evaluate the wisdom of the rule substantively. Evaluate the propriety of using the rulemaking process, rather than an unfair labor practice proceeding, to announce such a rule. What evidence do you believe would be relevant to the Board in its adoption of such a rule? See *Monogram Models, Inc.*, 192 N.L.R.B. 705 (1973); *Agricultural Labor Relations Bd.* v. *Superior Court*, 16 Cal.3d 392, 128 Cal.Rptr. 183, 546 P.2d 687 (1976).

3. American Cotton Company operates a mill employing 1,000 workers in a community of 3,500 people. American holds title to the streets and sidewalks, and owns not only the mill but also most of the stores and houses. The only public buildings are the churches, the schools and a motion picture theatre (all of which are unavailable for private meetings). Although there is space in the plant for large employee gatherings (and some have been convened on such matters as job safety), it has never been made available for non-company uses. The Textile Workers Union, which is seeking to organize American's employees, has asked American to make the space available for a union meeting some evening next week. Assuming that this would not interfere with production or endanger the premises, must the company accede?

Would your advice be any different if American owned a social hall, two miles from the mill, which it commonly rents to others for social functions, and it is that hall which the union has asked American to make available one evening for the purposes of a union meeting? See *NLRB* v. *Stowe Spinning Co.*, 336 U.S. 226, 69 S.Ct. 541, 93 L.Ed. 638 (1949). **¶/o**

4. Shamrock Refining Company operates a large chemical plant on three shifts. The Oil, Chemical and Atomic Workers (OCAW) seek to organize the employees there. One of the employees on the day shift (8 a.m. to 4 p.m.), Tom Williams, is one of the leaders in the unionization movement; he is bright, likeable, aggressive and articulate. His work exposes him to volatile chemicals, he works under arduous conditions, and his lunchtime is brief; he and his fellow workers must shower at the end of the work day, and most promptly head thereafter for their cars in the company parking lot, a short trip home, and a drink or two before dinner. The shift that works from 4 p.m. until midnight takes a dinner break from 7:30 until 8 p.m. Williams, anxious to gain entry to the company cafeteria at that time to engage in conversation and solicitation with the employees on the later shift, has driven his car into the company parking lot on three occasions and headed through the main entrance to the plant, but has each time been stopped by a guard. Williams has been told that, while he is free to solicit on his own mealtime on his own shift, he is not free to come onto company property when he is not at work there, and that continued attempts to do so may lead to discipline for insubordination.

You are counsel to the OCAW local which is seeking to organize Shamrock Refining. Inform the union whether there is any way that Williams can gain access on company property to the employees on the night shift. The union would prefer to have Williams meet with those employees inside the plant (in nonworking areas), but it also wants to know whether he can station himself on the company's parking lot and other privately owned approaches to the plant. See *Diamond Shamrock Co. v. NLRB*, 443 F.2d 52 (3d Cir. 1971); *Tri-County Med. Center, Inc.*, 222 N.L.R.B. 1089 (1976).

NOTE

The Union's Right to Equal Access; the Captive-Audience Doctrine. An employer with a valid no-solicitation or no-distribution rule may frequently wish to "violate" that rule, for example, by assembling its employees on company property during working hours for purposes of delivering an antiunion address. The rule may be concededly valid and the address concededly noncoercive and within the shelter of Section 8(c) of the Labor Act ("The expressing of any views, argument, or opinion, or the dissemination thereof, whether in written, printed, graphic, or visual form, shall not constitute or be evidence of an unfair labor practice under any of the provisions of this Act, if such expression contains no threat of reprisal or force or promise of benefit."). Yet the union may believe that it is put at a substantial disadvantage in the absence of a similar opportunity to address a "captive audience" for the purpose of communicating the union message. In BONWIT TELLER, INC. v. NLRB, 96 N.L.R.B. 608 (1951), remanded on other grounds 197 F.2d 640 (2d Cir. 1952), cert. denied 345 U.S. 905 (1953), the Board held the employer's denial of such a request to constitute an unfair labor practice. The employer was held to have interfered with the section 7 right of the employees "to hear both sides of the story under circumstances which reasonably approximate equality." Section 8(c) was thought no obstacle to such a conclusion since it was not the employer's speech that was treated as unlawful but rather its conduct in denying the union equal time. Two years later, in LIVINGSTON SHIRT CO., 107 N.L. R.B. 400 (1953), the Board, with newly appointed members, departed from the *Bonwit Teller* rationale and concluded that Section 8(c) forbade the conditioning of the exercise of the employer's right to speak noncoercively upon its willingness to afford the union comparable time and setting. It stated that as a general matter there was a rough equality between the employer's use of its property to address its employees and the union's use of its property (the union hall) and of other solicitation methods (e. g., by employees on non-working time and by home visits). The Board held:

> We rule therefore that, in the absence of either an unlawful broad no-solicitation rule (prohibiting union access to company premises on other than working time) or a privileged no-solicitation rule (broad, but not unlawful because of the character of the business), an employer does not commit an unfair labor practice if he makes a preelection speech on company time and premises to his employees and denies the union's request for an opportunity to reply.

In effect, the Board declared that it would require the employer to grant a union's request for equal time in, most typically, the retail and department-store trade (where employers could validly adopt a "broad but not unlawful" rule barring solicitation even during nonworking time on the selling floor) ; but that there would be no such requirement for manufacturing and wholesale enterprises where valid no-solicitation rules obtained.

The United States Supreme Court was presented, in NLRB v. UNITED STEELWORKERS (NUTONE AND AVONDALE), 357 U.S. 357, 78 S.Ct. 1268, 2 L.Ed.2d 1383 (1958), with employer denials of union requests to depart from concededly valid no-solicitation rules subsequent to the employers' antiunion solicitation. The Court held that an employer's denial of such a request does not in itself constitute an unfair labor practice, stating that:

> [T]he Taft Hartley Act does not command that labor organizations as a matter of abstract law, under all circum-

stances, be protected in the use of every possible means of reaching the minds of individual workers, nor that they are entitled to use a medium of communication simply because the employer is using it.

The Court went on to state in dictum, however, that the result could be different if the no-solicitation rules "truly diminished the ability of the labor organizations involved to carry their message to the employees."

> If, by virtue of the location of the plant and of the facilities and resources available to the union, the opportunities for effectively reaching the employees with a pro-union message, in spite of a no-solicitation rule, are at least as great as the employer's ability to promote the legally authorized expression of his anti-union views, there is no basis for invalidating these "otherwise valid" rules.

The denial of "equal time" will thus ordinarily be presumed lawful (even, as in the *Avondale* case before the Court, when the employer's solicitation is in itself coercive and unlawful), and the burden will be upon the General Counsel to demonstrate that the union is seriously incapacitated from communicating with the employees by other means. (It is unclear, however, whether this burden is discharged simply upon a showing of "inequality" between the employer's "captive audience" speech and the union's alternative means, or by the more rigorous showing that objectively considered the union has no practicable means of communicating effectively with the employees.) The lack of alternative means will thus become an issue in these "equal time" cases, just as they are in cases of employer denials to nonemployees of access to its property for purposes of solicitation, but as they are not in cases of solicitation restrictions upon employees. The Court ignored the argument, although implicitly rejecting it, that apart from "alternative means" the employer's conduct should be held unlawful because, by "discriminatorily" applying the no-solicitation rule to the union but not to itself, the employer was conclusively demonstrating that the rule was designed to hamper the union rather than to effectuate any legitimate employer interest in plant safety, efficiency or discipline. See James Hotel Co., 142 N.L.R.B. 761 (1963) (employer's disregarding its own no-solicitation rule does not invalidate it, citing *Nutone*).

In recent years the Board has, in cases involving aggravated employer unfair labor practices under Sections 8(a)(1) and (3), ordered that the charging union be given access by the employer to company property, either to solicit employees during nonworking

time or to deliver a "captive audience" speech. TEAMSTERS LOCAL 115
v. NLRB (Haddon House Food Prods., Inc.), 640 F.2d 392 (D.C.Cir.
1981). While some courts consider the union's communicational alternatives as relevant to the issuance of such an order, the better view
is that such alternatives bear only on the question whether the employer commits an unfair labor practice when it bars the union from
its property and not on the question of remedies after the Board has
already found serious employer violations of Sections 8(a)(1) and
(3). UNITED STEELWORKERS v. NLRB (Florida Steel Corp.), 646 F.
2d 616 (D.C.Cir. 1981) (an exhaustive treatment of the Board's "union access" remedies).

Election-Eve Captive Audience Speeches. The Board has announced a firm rule outlawing "captive audience" speeches on company time within the 24-hour period prior to an election. PEERLESS
PLYWOOD CO., 107 N.L.R.B. 427 (1953). The rule proscribes such
addresses whether by company or union, in view of their "unwhole-
some and unsettling effect" so shortly before the election, and their
tendency to "interfere with that sober and thoughtful choice which
a free election is designed to reflect." To redress both the "mass
psychology" created by the address and the unfair advantage it
gives to the last speaker, violation of the *Peerless Plywood* rule
will result in the setting aside of an election victory by the speaker
and the ordering of a new election. By its terms, the decision does
not impede noncoercive employer (or union) speeches before the
24-hour period, the dissemination of other forms of propaganda
even during the 24-hour period, or the delivery during that period
of campaign speeches on or off company property if employee attendance is voluntary and on the employee's own time.

EXCELSIOR UNDERWEAR INC.

National Labor Relations Board, 1966.
156 N.L.R.B. 1236.

[During an election campaign in which the employer had written to the employees, the union asked for a list of employee names
and addresses in order to make a response, but the employer refused.
The union lost the election, 206 to 35, and objected to the election
for a number of reasons, one of which was the employer's refusal
to furnish the list. When the regional director overruled these objections, the NLRB agreed to review the decision upon the union's
petition, and consolidated another case raising similar issues. The
Board determined that the cases presented questions of substantial
importance and ordered oral argument, which is rarely done, and invited certain groups to file briefs amicus curiae and to participate

in oral argument, among them the Chamber of Commerce of the United States, the AFL–CIO, the International Union of Electrical Workers, the United Auto Workers, the National Association of Manufacturers, the Retail Clerks Union, the Textile Workers Union, and the Teamsters.]

We are persuaded, for the reasons set out below, that higher standards of disclosure than we have heretofore imposed are necessary, and that prompt disclosure of the information here sought by the Petitioners should be required in all representation elections. Accordingly, we now establish a requirement that will be applied in all election cases.   That is, within 7 days after the Regional Director has approved a consent-election agreement entered into by the parties pursuant to Section 102.62 of the National Labor Relations Board Rules and Regulations or after the Regional Director or the Board has directed an election pursuant to Section 102.62 of the National Labor Relations Board Rules and Regulations or after the Regional Director or the Board has directed an election pursuant to Sections 102.67, 102.69, or Section 102.85 thereof, the employer must file with the Regional Director an election eligibility list, containing the names and addresses of all the eligible voters. The Regional Director, in turn, shall make this information available to all parties in the case.   Failure to comply with this requirement shall be grounds for setting aside the election whenever proper objections are filed.[7]

The considerations that impel us to adopt the foregoing rule are these: "The control of the election proceeding, and the determination of the steps necessary to conduct that election fairly [are] matters which Congress entrusted to the Board alone."   In discharging that trust, we regard it as the Board's function to conduct elections in which employees have the opportunity to cast their ballots for or against representation under circumstances that are free not only from interference, restraint, or coercion violative of Act, but also from other elements that prevent or impede a free and reasoned choice.   Among the factors that undoubtedly tend to impede such a choice is a lack of information with respect to one of the choices available.   In other words, an employee who has had an effective opportunity to hear the arguments concerning representation is in a better position to make a more fully informed and reasoned choice.   Accordingly, we think that it is appropriate for us

---

7. * * * However, the rule we have here announced is to be applied prospectively only. It will not apply in the instant cases but only in those elections that are directed, or consented to, subsequent to 30 days from the date of this Decision. We impose this brief period of delay to insure that all parties to forthcoming representation elections are fully aware of their rights and obligations as here stated.

to remove the impediment to communication to which our new rule is directed.

As a practical matter, an employer, through his possession of employee names and home addresses as well as his ability to communicate with employees on plant premises, is assured of the continuing opportunity to inform the entire electorate of his views with respect to union representation. On the other hand, without a list of employee names and addresses, a labor organization, whose organizers normally have no right of access to plant premises, has no method by which it can be certain of reaching all the employees with its arguments in favor of representation, and, as a result, employees are often completely unaware of that point of view. This is not, of course, to deny the existence of various means by which a party might be able to communicate with a substantial portion of the electorate even without possessing their names and addresses. It is rather to say what seems to us obvious—that the access of all employees to such communications can be insured if all parties have the names and addresses of all the voters.[8] In other words, by providing all parties with employees' names and addresses, we maximize the likelihood that all the voters will be exposed to the arguments for, as well as against, union representation.   *   *   *

While the rule we here announce is primarily predicated upon our belief that prompt disclosure of employee names and addresses is necessary to insure an informed electorate, there is yet another basis upon which we rest our decision. As noted [previously], an employer is presently under no obligation to supply an election eligibility list until shortly before the election.   *   *   *   With little time (and no home addresses) with which to satisfy itself as to eligibility of the "unknowns", the union is forced either to challenge all those who appear at the polls whom it does not know or risk having ineligible employees vote. The effect of putting the union to this choice, we have found, is to increase the number of challenges, as well as the likelihood that the challenges will be determinative of the election, thus requiring investigation and resolution by the Regional

---

8. A union that does not know the names or addresses of some of the voters may seek to communicate with them by distributing literature on sidewalks or street corners adjoining the employer's premises or by utilizing the mass media of communication. The likelihood that *all* employees will be reached by these methods is, however, problematical at best. See NLRB v. United Aircraft Corp., et al., 324 F.2d 128, 130 (C.A. 2), cert. denied 376 U.S. 951. Personal solicitation on plant premises by employee supporters of the union, while vastly more satisfactory than the above methods, suffers from the limited periods of nonworking time available for solicitation '(generally and legally forbidden during working time, Peyton Packing Company, Inc., 49 N.L.R.B. 828, 843) and, in a large plant, the sheer physical problems involved in communicating with fellow employees.

Director or the Board. <u>Prompt disclosure of employee names as well</u> <u>as addresses will, we are convinced, eliminate the necessity for chal-</u> <u>lenges based solely on lack of knowledge as to the voter's identity.</u> * * *

The arguments against imposing a requirement of disclosure are of little force, especially when weighed against the benefits resulting therefrom. Initially, we are able to perceive no substantial infringement of employer interests that would flow from such a requirement. A list of employee names and addresses is not like a customer list, and an employer would appear to have no significant interest in keeping the names and addresses of his employees secret (other than a desire to prevent the union from communicating with his employees—an interest we see no reason to protect). Such legitimate interest in secrecy as an employer may have is, in any event, plainly outweighed by the substantial public interest in favor of disclosure where, as here, disclosure is a key factor in insuring a fair and free election. * * *

The argument is also made (by the Employer in the *Excelsior* case) that under the decisions of the Supreme Court in *NLRB* v. *Babcock & Wilcox*, and *NLRB* v. *United Steelworkers* (Nutone, Inc.), the Board may not require employer disclosure of employee names and addresses unless, in the particular case involved, the union would otherwise be unable to reach the employees with its message. * * *

Initially, as we read *Babcock* and *Nutone*, the existence of alternative channels of communication is relevant only when the opportunity to communicate made available by the Board would interfere with a significant employer interest—such as the employer's interest in controlling the use of property owned by him. Here, <u>as we have shown, the employer has no significant interest in the</u> <u>secrecy of employee names and addresses.</u> Hence, <u>there is no ne-</u> <u>cessity for the Board to consider the existence of alternative chan-</u> <u>nels of communication before requiring disclosure of that informa-</u> <u>tion.</u> Moreover, even assuming that there is some legitimate employer interest in non-disclosure, we think it relevant that the subordination of that interest which we here require is limited to a situation in which employee interests in self-organization are shown to be substantial. For, whenever an election is directed (the pre-condition to disclosure) the Regional Director has found that a real question concerning representation exists; when the employer consents to an election, he has impliedly admitted this fact. <u>The opportunity to communicate on company premises</u> sought in *Babcock* and *Nutone* <u>was not limited to the situation in</u> <u>which employee organizational interests were substantial, i. e., in</u>

which an election had been directed; we think that on this ground also the cases are distinguishable. Finally, both *Babcock* and *Nu-tone* dealt with the circumstances under which the Board might find an employer to have committed an unfair labor practice in violation of Section 8 of the Act, whereas, the instant cases pose the substantially distinguishable issue of the circumstances under which the Board may set aside an election.   * * *

* * * We do not limit the disclosure requirement to the situation in which the employer has mailed anti-union literature to employees' homes   * * *   because we believe that access to employee names and addresses is fundamental to a fair and free election regardless of whether the employer has sent campaign propaganda to employees' homes. We do not limit the requirement of disclosure to furnishing employee names and addresses to a mailing service   * * *   because this would create difficult practical problems and because we do not believe that the union should be limited to the use of the mails in its efforts to communicate with the entire electorate.

Problems for Discussion

1. The employers in *Excelsior* and the supporting amici curiae argued that the involuntary disclosure of employee names and addresses violated the employees' right under Section 7 to refrain from forming and joining labor organizations and also their right to have their privacy protected against harassment and coercion by the union in employee homes. The NLRB rejected these arguments. What do you suppose were the Board's reasons? Do you agree with them?

2. A union, anxious to organize a company employing some fifty workers, has with the cooperation of two of those workers secured the names and addresses of eight others. It has had difficulty in contacting any other employees and has written to the company requesting that the company use its payroll records to furnish a complete list of employee names and addresses. The company, although conceding that the list would not take long to prepare, has refused to prepare one or turn it over to the union; it claims that the files are company property and that the union will have to use its own resources to compile such a list. The union has filed a charge of violation of Section 8(a)(1). Should the Regional Director issue an unfair labor practice complaint? no. maybe

-----

NLRB v. Wyman–Gordon Co., 394 U.S. 759, 89 S.Ct. 1426, 22 L.Ed.2d 709 (1969). After the Board had ordered a representation election involving two competing unions, the employer refused to produce an "Excelsior list" when ordered to do so by the Board. After the election was held and the unions were defeated, the election was set aside on their objections and a new election ordered. When the company once again refused to obey a Board order to supply a list of employees, the Board issued a subpoena for the list, which was enforced in the the federal district court. The court of appeals, however, reversed, holding that the Board's directive to the company was invalid, since it was based on the rule in the *Excelsior* case which the Board had announced without complying with the rulemaking procedures set forth in the Administrative Procedure Act, 5 U.S.C.A. § 553 et seq. The Supreme Court therefore had to decide whether the requirement to furnish the Excelsior list was validly promulgated in the *Excelsior* case itself or was in any event validly applied to the Wyman-Gordon Company.

The APA defines a "rule" as "an agency statement of general or particular applicability and future effect," and requires that the promulgation of a rule be preceded, *inter alia,* by publication in the Federal Register of notice of proposed rulemaking, a public hearing, and publication of the rule as adopted. An agency "adjudication" is defined as the "formulation of an order," and an "order" is defined to include "the whole or a part of a final disposition * * * of an agency in a matter other than rule making." Procedure for an "adjudication" under the APA includes notice, opportunity for pleadings, a hearing and a decision. Through a somewhat curious configuration of Justices, the position of the Board and the district court was endorsed, so that the Wyman-Gordon Company had to turn over the list of employee names and addresses.

Four Justices (speaking through Justice Fortas) concluded that the Board in *Excelsior* had purported to announce a "rule" of general applicability (but not applicable to the parties before it) without complying with the formalities or the substance of rulemaking (e. g., the rule was not published in the Federal Register and only selected organizations were notified of the "hearing"). Adjudications do generate announcements of general agency policies, which through *stare decisis* furnish a guide to agency action in future cases. "But this is far from saying * * * that commands, decisions, or policies announced in adjudication are 'rules' in the sense that they must, without more, be obeyed by the affected public." In spite of the defective procedure in the *Excelsior* case, however, the "Fortas group" concluded that the order to the Wyman-Gordon Company was valid, since the company was specifically directed to disclose the list as part of the Board's election order, which *was* the product of a valid procedure. Proceeding then to an analysis of the substantive validity of the *Excelsior* requirement, the Fortas group held that the Board acted within its discretion in requiring disclosure of names and addresses in order to promote an informed employee electorate and to balance the employer's access to employees; and that the list was "evidence" within Section 11(1) of the Labor Act which the Board was empowered to subpoena in the course of a representation proceeding.

Three other Justices (speaking through Justice Black) stated that if the *Excelsior* requirement had been invalidly promulgated without conformity to rulemaking procedures, this surely cannot be cured by subsequently making it part of an order against Wyman-Gordon. But the Black group concluded that the *Excelsior* requirement was a valid component of the adjudication of a specific case in which the Board followed proper procedures (i. e., notice, pleadings, hearing, and decision). Justice Black pointed out that it is quite appropriate for agencies to announce new doctrines in adjudicatory proceedings and to have agency decisional precedents guide future conduct in much the same way as a new "rule" promulgated under the rulemaking power. The NLRB is authorized to articulate policy either through rulemaking (in Section 6 of the NLRA) or adjudication, and "so long as the matter involved can be dealt with in a way satisfying the definition of either 'rule making' or 'adjudication' under the Administrative Procedure Act, that Act, along with the Labor Relations Act, should be read as conferring upon the Board the authority to decide, within its informed discretion, whether to proceed by rule making or adjudication." The Board's articulation of the list-requirement in *Excelsior* and of its reasons for applying that requirement only prospectively were part of a valid adjudication resulting in an order not to overturn a certification election.

In a dissenting opinion, Justice Douglas pointed out the values of the rulemaking procedure: notification to the public of future regimentation, and an opportunity for all affected persons to be heard; a curb upon the arbitrary exercise of power by agencies increasingly remote from the individuals affected; assurance that legal principles will be clearly articulated and not easily circumvented by the agency. Pointing out that the Board in *Excelsior* knew that the problem before it affected employers and unions generally, and that it chose to invite various amici curiae and to apply the requirement prospectively only, Justice Douglas stated: "[A]n agency is not adjudicating when it is making a rule to fit future cases. A rule like the one in *Excelsior* is designed to fit all cases at all times. It is not particularized to special facts. It is a statement of far-reaching policy covering all future representation elections." He admonished the Board for failing to use its rulemaking authority, and concluded that the court of appeals should be affirmed.

Justice Harlan also dissented, believing that by announcing a requirement which was to be effective only thirty days thereafter, the Board in *Excelsior* had clearly made a rule ("an agency statement * * * of future effect") without complying with rule-

making procedures.   "An agency chooses to apply a rule prospectively only because it represents such a departure from pre-existing understandings that it would be unfair to impose the rule upon the
parties in pending matters.   But it is precisely in these situations,
in which established patterns of conduct are revolutionized, that
rule-making procedures perform the vital functions that my brother
DOUGLAS describes so well   *   *   *."   The requirements of the
APA would be "completely trivialized" if such an invalid rule could
then be enforced in subsequent adjudications.

Problems for Discussion

1.   Did the Board carry a majority of the Court on the question of
the validity of the procedure in *Excelsior*?   Did the Board carry a majority
of the Court on the legality, assuming the invalidity of the *Excelsior*
procedure, of applying the *Excelsior* requirement to the Wyman-Gordon
Company?   If the answer is "no" to each of these questions, then who
"won" the case?

2.   How unfair would it have been to apply "the *Excelsior* requirement" to the Excelsior Company itself, so as to overturn its election victory?
Had the Board done so, could there have been a plausible claim that its
"order" was procedurally defective?   If not, then (as Justice Black suggests) why does the procedure lose its status as a valid "adjudication"
when the Board's sense of fairness dictates a thirty-day delay in the application of its newly announced requirement?

3.   If the *Excelsior* question—Should an employer, as a condition of
a valid election, be required to turn over to the Board and to the union a
list of employee names and addresses?—had been presented to you (as a
member of the NLRB) initially, how would you go about assessing whether
rulemaking or adjudication would be a more appropriate procedure for
finding an answer?

4.   What would you predict to be the likely effect of *Wyman-Gordon*
upon the conduct of the Board?   Will the Board use rulemaking more
often, even for principles which could be applied directly to the parties
before the Board in an adjudicatory proceeding?   Or will the Board, even
in cases in which it would prefer to make the ruling apply only prospectively, continue to use adjudication and (instead of what was done in
Excelsior) announce new policy retroactively?   Apart from its own "rules"
of procedure, the Board has used the rulemaking procedure in only two rather narrow "substantive" areas—to consider the extent of its jurisdiction
over colleges and universities, symphony orchestras and race-tracks and to
require the employer to re-offer reinstatement to former employee-discrimi-
natees currently in the armed services.

2. Election Propaganda [9]

(a) Threats of Reprisal

One of the most difficult and controversial problems in the protection of freedom of self-organization is the degree of freedom of expression to be allowed employers. Company officials often wish to make speeches or distribute leaflets, bulletins and other publications in an effort to dissuade their employees from joining labor organizations. The character of these communications varies widely, running the gamut from a dignified letter to propaganda campaigns based essentially on base appeals to prejudice against the foreign-born and racial intolerance.

The problem is difficult because it involves the pursuit of two inconsistent goals. We value freedom of expression so highly as to look askance at any restriction and forbid restraints not justified by the clearest necessity. Most of us also value full freedom for employees in forming, joining and assisting labor organizations of their own choosing—at least this is the national labor policy. To pursue either goal to its logical extreme necessarily causes some sacrifice of the other. Any argument which discloses the speaker's strong wishes is not wholly an appeal to reason if the listener is in the speaker's power. In a southern mill town where a textile concern is the only large employer and its owners dominate the whole community, even a dispassionate expression of the company's opinion will make the ordinary employee think twice about openly supporting a labor union distasteful to the employer. Judge Learned Hand described the situation very clearly in NLRB v. Federbush Co., 121 F.2d 954, 957 (2d Cir. 1941):

> "Words are not pebbles in alien juxtaposition; they have only a communal existence; and not only does the meaning of each interpenetrate the other, but all in their aggregate take their purport from the setting in which they are used of which the relation between the speaker and the hearer is perhaps the most important part. What to an outsider will be no more than the vigorous presentation of a conviction, to an employee may be the manifestation of a determination which it is not safe to thwart."

9. See, in addition to the references at page 114, n. 1: Aaron, Employer Free Speech: The Search for a Policy, in Public Policy and Collective Bargaining 28 (Shister et al., eds. 1962); Christensen, Free Speech, Propaganda and the National Labor Relations Act, 38 N.Y.U.L.Rev. 243 (1963); Goldberg, Getman & Brett, *Union Representation Elections*: The Authors Respond to the Critics, 79 Mich.L.Rev. — (1981); Pollitt, The National Labor Relations Board and Race Hate Propaganda in Union Organization Drives, 17 Stanford L.Rev. 373 (1965); Roomkin & Abrams, Using Behavioral Evidence in NLRB Regulation: A Proposal, 90 Harv.L.Rev. 1441 (1977); Symposium (Miller, Raskin, Eames, Flanagan), Four Perspectives on Union Representation Elections, 28 Stan.L.Rev. 1163 (1976).

It is difficult to announce in general terms any principle that will in all cases fairly adjust the competing interests of free speech and uncoerced employee choice.   The task of making that adjustment in particular cases is generally performed by the National Labor Relations Board subject to a review in the courts of appeals which is nominally rather circumscribed but which in fact can be rather vigorous.   Where the line is to be drawn must unquestionably depend upon the values of the decisionmaker (particularly as to such matters as governmental regulation of private conduct and governmental fostering of unionization) and upon that person's appreciation of the dynamics of personal relations in an industrial setting. The Board presumably has a greater appreciation of these dynamics than do the courts.   But there is a continuing debate concerning the extent to which the Board—which although it acts much like a court is also a lawmaking agency the composition of which is responsive to political currents—should interpose its "values" and, in any event, concerning whether on such matters the courts are any less competent than is the Board.

Under the Wagner Act the NLRB severely limited the employer's freedom of expression.   The NLRB policy was to insist upon employers' observing rigid neutrality.   The Board reasoned that the choice of a bargaining representative was the workers' exclusive concern, in which the employer had no more interest than the employees would have in participating in the choice of the company's board of directors.   The rationale was never accepted by the courts without some qualification, and during the 1940's the Supreme Court decisions expanding the scope of the constitutional guaranty cast grave doubt upon its validity.   The issue eventually reached the Court in NLRB v. Virginia Elec. & Power Co., 314 U.S. 469, 62 S.Ct. 344, 86 L.Ed. 348 (1941) (discussed by the court of appeals in NLRB v. Golub Corp., infra pp. 146, 149), in which the Court in substance rejected the contention that all employer speeches or literature—whether criticizing a union or praising it—necessarily interfere with free employee choice and violate Section 8(a)(1).   The Court did, however, authorize the Board to find coercion when the record in a particular case so justifies "under all of the circumstances."   The Board still continued to regulate employer speech rather sharply, and Congress in 1947 enacted Section 8(c) of the Labor Act, which provides:

> "The expressing of any views, argument, or opinion, or the dissemination thereof, whether in written, printed, graphic, or visual form, shall not constitute or be evidence of an unfair labor practice under any of the provisions of this Act, if such expression contains no threat of reprisal or force or promise of benefit."

As will be seen in the cases that follow, Section 8(c) has by no means resolved all problems in the accommodation of free speech and uncoerced employee choice or in the relationship between the Board and the appellate courts.

In 1948, in the noted case of GENERAL SHOE CORP., 77 N.L.R.B. 124, the Board—observing that Section 8(c) spoke only to the Board's use of speech and literature in unfair labor practice proceedings leading to a court-enforceable remedial order—held that that provision did not limit the Board's power in election cases. It therefore held that it had the power, as to elections that were won through communications or conduct which could not be held an unfair labor practice, to set aside the election results and order a new election. The Board majority reasoned as follows:

> "It is true that for 2 months before the election of July 31, 1946, the respondent engaged in a course of conduct consisting of publication, through its supervisors, in letters, in pamphlets, in leaflets, and in speeches, of vigorously disparaging statements concerning the Union, which undeniably were calculated to influence the rank-and-file employees in their choice of a bargaining representative. However, these statements contained no threat of reprisal or promise of benefit and appear to be only such expressions of opinion as are excluded from our consideration in an unfair labor practice case by reason of Section 8(c) of the amended Act. * * *
>
> "When we are asked to invalidate elections held under our auspices, our only consideration derives from the Act which calls for freedom of choice by employees as to a collective bargaining representative. Conduct that creates an atmosphere which renders improbable a free choice will sometimes warrant invalidating an election, even though that conduct may not constitute an unfair labor practice. An election can serve its true purpose only if the surrounding conditions enable employees to register a free and untrammelled choice for or against a bargaining representative. * * *
>
> "We do not subscribe to the view, apparently held by our two dissenting colleagues, that the criteria applied by the Board in a representation proceeding to determine whether certain alleged misconduct interfered with an election need necessarily be identical to those employed in testing whether an unfair labor practice was committed, although the result will ordinarily be the same. In election proceedings, it is the Board's function to provide a laboratory in which an experiment may be conducted, under conditions as nearly ideal as possible, to determine the uninhibited desires of the employees. It is our duty to establish

those conditions; it is also our duty to determine whether they have been fulfilled. When, in the rare extreme case, the standard drops too low, because of our fault or that of others, the requisite laboratory conditions are not present and the experiment must be conducted over again. That is the situation here."

After 1952, the Board began to give greater latitude to employer speech even in cases involving petitions to set aside elections. In "close cases," the Board tended to characterize the employer's remarks not as coercive but rather as the expression of the employer's legal position or its opinion or prediction. For example, in Esquire, Inc., 107 N.L.R.B. 1238 (1954), the employer, prior to an election, sent several letters to his employees pointing out, *inter alia,* that he disagreed with the determination by the Board as to the appropriate unit of employees and that he would refuse to bargain if the union won the election in order to contest the Board's determination and that a year or two of litigation would elapse before a court could review and enforce a Board order to bargain. The Board held that the statement was "merely an expression of the Employer's legal position" and therefore not unlawful. In Southwestern Co., 111 N.L.R.B. 807 (1955), the employer, prior to an election, stated to certain of his employees, many of whom were immigrants from Estonia, that they might be deported by the Immigration Department if they joined the "Communist" union, and that the union, if it won the election, would control hiring and would replace existing employees with persons possessing greater union seniority and with blacks. The Board held that the statements contained no threats of reprisal but merely reflected opinions concerning actions which persons wholly independent of the employer might take if the union won the election. In Silver Knit Hosiery Mills, Inc., 99 N.L.R.B. 422 (1952), the plant manager read a speech to the employees on company time and property the day before the election in which he said that the union might resort to a strike in order to enforce its demands if it were to win the election; that the "company has no intention of yielding to such pressure"; that everybody "knows that strikes mean trouble, misery, lost work and lost pay"; that the company "is not required to grant requests but is only required by the law to bargain in good faith"; that if everybody's wages were raised, the cost of production would be so high that the company could not obtain orders and the "mill would be forced to close." The manager added that he was not saying that this would necessarily happen and that he hoped it would not. The Board held that the speech constituted privileged electioneering "in the nature of a prophecy that labor trouble might bring financial difficulties which would in turn prevent the Employer from continuing to operate."

In 1961, with the advent of a new administration in the White House and the appointment of new members to the NLRB, the Board began to assert a greater role in regulating speech and literature in election campaigns. Not only did the Board become more attentive to employee interests in determining whether speech was coercive and thus an unfair labor practice, but it also scrutinized campaign propaganda more vigorously for abuses short of coercion but sufficient to warrant setting aside a representation election.

A significant case in this development was DAL–TEX OPTICAL CO., 137 N.L.R.B. 1782 (1962). There, a 1959 election victory for the employer was set aside and Section 8(a)(1) violations found, based on the employer's threats and promises of benefit; subsequently the employer unlawfully discharged or demoted certain supervisors and employees because of their adverse testimony in the Board proceeding. Just before the re-run election was to take place (in September 1961), the employer's president delivered several speeches to employees in the plant. On September 18, he stated his belief that the first election was valid and his intention to litigate that matter through the courts if necessary, in which case "the election to be held on September 22nd will not mean a thing if the Union wins it. My guess is that it will be another couple of years before this matter is settled. In the meantime, we will go on just as we are without any Union. * * * I believe in law and order. When the Courts decide the matter I will abide by the decisions of the Courts." He then proceeded to recount employee benefits such as recent merit raises, and the profit-sharing and pension plans, and continued: "Do you want to gamble all of these things? If I am required by the Court to bargain with this Union, whenever that may be, I will bargain in good faith, but I will have to bargain on a cold-blooded business basis. You may come out with a lot less than you have now. * * * If I am required to bargain and I cannot agree there is no power on earth that can make me sign a contract with this Union, so what will probably happen is the Union will call a strike. I will go right along running this business and replace the strikers. * * * They will lose all of their benefits. Strikers will draw no wages, no unemployment compensation and be out of a job."

The following day the employer made another speech in which he pointed out that the employees at his company had the highest wages in the industry, that it was he and not the Union who paid their wages, and that no Union would make him change his policy of giving merit raises to deserving employees (and none to undeserving employees). The president's speech on September 21 reiterated the comments made in the two earlier speeches.

The union lost the second election, 101–96, and filed objections which were sustained by the Board. It found that the employer's speeches contained illegal threats: the comments about bargaining "from scratch" were reasonably read as threats that the employees would suffer economic loss and reprisal if they selected a union, and the comments about their replacement in the event of a strike were "calculated to create a fear that there would necessarily be a loss of employment and financial security if the Union won" (especially in the context of contemporaneous company unfair labor practices). Other employer comments were calculated to convey the futility of designating the union as bargaining representive: the employer went beyond merely stating an intention to litigate the validity of the prior election, and his statements about not being required by law to sign a contract and not intending to change his wage policy constituted in context a clear message that the company was determined not to bargain.

The Board found these statements coercive, not protected by Section 8(c), and an unfair labor practice. A fortiori, they warranted setting aside an election, where the test for allowable conduct (i. e., the *General Shoe* "laboratory conditions" test) is stricter yet. Earlier decisions, in which the Board condoned implied threats couched in the guise of statements of legal position, were repudiated, and "we shall look to the economic realities of the employer-employee relationship and shall set aside an election where we find that the employer's conduct has resulted in substantial interference with the election, regardless of the form in which the statement was made."

[In considering *Dal-Tex* and the cases that follow, among the issues you should bear in mind are: (a) Would the very same speeches have been allowed by the Board had the employer not already committed several serious unfair labor practices? (b) Could the employer have gotten across the same message, lawfully, merely by careful re-drafting of the text of his speeches? (and what are the responsibilities of the attorney in this context?) (c) How does the Board know that employees will be "coerced" by such remarks, or even that they pay any attention to them at all? and (d) Might such remarks be more readily tolerated if the union is afforded an opportunity to respond?]

Although the Board's approach has for the most part secured judicial endorsement (or at least acquiescence), some federal courts of appeals have thought the Board too zealous in restraining communications in the course of a certification-election campaign. The following case is an example.

NLRB v. GOLUB CORP.

United States Court of Appeals, Second Circuit, 1967.
388 F.2d 921.

FRIENDLY, CIRCUIT JUDGE:

[After proffering authorization cards from a majority of the 31 employees in Golub's Mechanicville food store, the Meat Cutters Union petitioned for a certification election, which was set for February 17, 1965. Within two weeks of the election, the employer sent three letters and made an election-eve speech to employees at a dinner meeting. The union lost the election 24–4, but the election was set aside; and the Board found that the employer had unlawfully refused to bargain in violation of Section 8(a)(5), and that certain passages in the letters of February 2 and 8 and the speech of February 16 violated Section 8(a)(1). The court of appeals denied enforcement.]

In contrast to many § 8(a)(1) proceedings, the violations here found consisted solely of writings and a speech addressed to the employees as a group—there was no finding of interrogation or surveillance, of discriminatory discharge, or of the grant of benefits. The case thus sharply raises the issue how far the Board may go in curbing speech consistently with § 8(c) and the First Amendment.

· The Board had no criticism of the company's letters of February 11 and 12, and only faulted portions of the letters of February 2 and 8 and a rather small part of Golub's speech of February 16. To quote simply the contested passages would create a false impression; it is necessary to place them in their setting by summarizing the entire communications.

The February 2 letter began by telling the employees of the forthcoming election. It accused the union of making false promises which "you can easily find out about * * * from others" and of picking on a single store to avoid a vote for all the chain's employees. It assured employees that the ballot would be absolutely secret, that they were "protected by law from anyone who attempts to interfere with your making a free choice," and that they were not bound by having signed a union card. It then went on to say "To get you to vote for them, the Union has been making many promises— promises to make demands which could be excessive. Companies that have been forced to meet excessive Union demands have been known to be forced out of business. The employees at the other local chain (Saveway) were not fooled by Union promises and flatly rejected them just a short time ago." [10] After arguing that union member-

---

10. The last two sentences were found to have violated § 8(a)(1).

ship would mean dues, assessments, other financial burdens, and possibly sympathy strikes, the letter continued:

> "The retail food business is the most competitive business in the world. Customers, not Unions, help pay your wages. We bring customers into our stores if we attract them with competitive prices. Even the large chains cannot meet these Union demands without making drastic adjustments because they also have to remain competitive. Large chains which have been forced to sign up with the Unions have been known to increase the work load of all their individual employees by reducing the number of employees in order to offset the higher costs. They find that they have to get the same amount of work done by fewer people to remain competitive." [11]

In conclusion the company promised to write again and asked the employees to keep an open mind.

The February 8 letter began by asking the employees to "look at the true facts of what outside interference would mean to you." The first set of facts consisted of the payment of dues and other union obligations, much as the earlier letter had depicted. Then came a paragraph found to have violated § 8(a)(1) which we quote in the margin.[12] The letter went on to challenge "two false arguments"—that employees who did not sign up or vote for the union would be fired if the union won and that Central's owners really wanted a union. It urged employees not to put their future in the hands of union representatives with little interest in their need or problems, and warned that a union might cook up a dispute "just to 'keep the pot boiling' or perhaps to help one of their favorites in your store," and that choice of a union "possibly could mean long drawn

---

11. The last two sentences were found to have violated § 8(a)(1).

12. "2. What does the choice of a union do to personal relationships? It means the end of a close relationship between you and your manager—or other management personnel. You certainly must recall that from time to time you may have asked the manager for some special personal arrangement or privilege which he probably gladly granted, such as time off when your children were sick, weddings, for haircuts, a school prom, emergencies at home, and to catch up on studies. If there were a union contract, such personal privileges most likely could not be granted. Special privileges could be forbidden under a contract and be in violation of the contract. In such cases, we could not deal directly with you, but only through your union representative. You will not be able to solve problems directly as we have been doing. Do not be fooled by those who tell you otherwise—especially those fellow employees who might try to *frighten* you into thinking that they can control your job."

out strikes." It told the employees who planned to make their careers with the company that they did not need a union "to get the greatest benefits which this company can give and which it gives without unions" and appealed to those employees who were working their way through school or college not to foist a burden on their fellows. The letter concluded by asking how a union can "truthfully promise job security," arguing that "their exorbitant, excessive and outlandish demands often result in layoffs and even force companies out of business," and that job security really rested in sales and service to customers. Golub promised to write again, and requested the employees to "keep an open mind until the election."

Golub's February 16 speech was a long one, stretching over 10½ printed pages of the joint appendix. Only two excerpts were found to have violated § 8(a)(1). The first we quote in the margin.[13] In the second Golub dealt with the small 1% profit margin characteristic of grocery chains and the correspondingly narrow leeway for "many additional unrealistic demands which add to your overhead and expenses." He then told of a large chain which had raised prices after negotiating a union contract and as a result had been required to discharge around 25% of its help and make the remaining staff "do a tougher job because they have got to do the work those who were let out have to do," and of another market, and also a discount store, that were being forced out of business due to a union contract.

While we have considered it necessary to set out the communications at some length, the basic issue is whether an employer coerces his employees in the exercise of § 7 rights, as forbidden by § 8(a)(1), when he prophesies that unionization will decrease or wholly eliminate work opportunities, increase work loads, or create greater rigidity in personnel relationships, or whether such predictions come within the protection § 8(c) affords to the expression "of any views, argument or opinion, or the dissemination thereof * * * if such expression contains no threat of reprisal or force or promise of benefit." While the answer would seem easy enough, the trend of Board decisions toward ever increasing restrictions on employer speech makes it desirable to attain perspective by a brief historical survey.

13. "We have never had tensions or misunderstanding. We have always been able to talk them out, and they are here. They bring in these tensions and these difficulties which you would be subject to under their regime. Now, don't forget also that if they were to come in that many of the human things that we are now doing as a matter of course would no longer be possible if they were here under contract. Many of the little human things like we do, like giving you privileges where you want to go out to dances or if you have to play in a basketball game, or a child is sick, or of a dozen reasons. We will always give you reasonable consideration. Under a contract we would be subject to the rules of that contract. If we did these things, we could be charged with favoritism, we would be violating our contract. These things could well go by the board as a result * * *."

Under the Wagner Act, 49 Stat. 449 (1935), which contained § 8(a)(1) but nothing like § 8(c), the Board condemned almost any anti-union expression by an employer. It was sustained against First Amendment attack by some courts including this one, on the basis that employer arguments have "an ambivalent character." Since "what to an outsider will be no more than the vigorous presentation of a conviction, to an employee may be the manifestation of a determination which it is not safe to thwart," we held that "the Board must decide how far the second aspect obliterates the first," with the substantial evidence rule available to support its decision. NLRB v. Federbush Co., 121 F.2d 954, 957 (2 Cir. 1941). The Supreme Court evidently thought otherwise. NLRB v. Virginia Electric & Power Co., 314 U.S. 469, 62 S.Ct. 344, 86 L.Ed. 348 (1941), dealt with employer notices pointing out that in the fifteen years since an organization strike had failed, confidence and understanding had reigned without the existence of a labor organization in any department. It went on to state that the company would freely entertain employee grievances and that it believed the mutual interest of all could "best be promoted through confidence and cooperation." The Board found the communications a violation of § 8(1). The Court interpreted the words of the Wagner Act to avoid constitutional doubts arising from the First Amendment. It held that speech, which by its own terms was not coercive, did not violate the Act unless part of a course of conduct that was coercive.[14] As the Board appeared to have found that the employer's words had violated the Act in and of themselves, the Court remanded to the Board so that it could determine whether the totality of the employer's conduct, of which his communications were a part, coerced its employees in violation of the statute. The Board later held that it did. See Virginia Electric & Power Co. v. NLRB, 319 U.S. 533, 63 S.Ct. 1214, 87 L.Ed. 1568 (1943).

This decision and the Board's rather halting response to it, see, e. g., A. J. Shawalter Co., 64 N.L.R.B. 573 (1945); Clark Bros., 70 N.L.R.B. 802 (1946), enforced on a limited basis in 163 F.2d 373 (2 Cir. 1947), constituted the background for § 8(c) of the Taft-Hartley Act, 61 Stat. 142 (1947). The Hartley bill as passed by the House provided that "Expressing any views, argument, or opinion, or the dissemination thereof, whether in written, printed, graphic or visual form, if it does not by its own terms threaten force or economic reprisal," shall not constitute or be evidence of an unfair labor

---

14. The Court, in a dictum in Thomas v. Collins, 323 U.S. 516, 537, 65 S.Ct. 315, 326, 89 L.Ed. 430 (1945), interpreted *Virginia Electric* as deciding that an employer's attempts to persuade employees to join or not to join a union are "within the First Amendment's guaranty" and can be restricted only when "other things are added which bring about coercion, or give it that character."

practice. H.R. 3020, 80th Cong. 1st Sess., § 8(d)(1)(1947). The reference in the bill as passed by the Senate was less clear, reading:

> The Board shall not base any finding of unfair labor practice upon any statement of views or arguments, either written or oral, if such statement contains under all the circumstances no threat, express or implied, of reprisal or force, or offer, express or implied, of benefit; Provided, That no language or provision of this section is intended to nor shall it be construed or administered so as to abridge or interfere with the right of either employers or employees to freedom of speech as guaranteed by the first amendment to the Constitution of the United States, H.R. 3020, as passed Senate, § 8(c).

The Conference Committee eliminated both the "by its own terms" of the House bill and the "under all the circumstances" and the unnecessary proviso of the Senate bill. While the Act thus went less far than the House bill, the detailed analysis of the compromise which Senator Taft submitted makes clear that, at the very least, the final form limits the extent to which context can be used to impart sinister meanings to innocuous words:

> The House conferees were of the opinion that the phrase "under all the circumstances" in the Senate amendment was ambiguous and might be susceptible of being construed as approving certain Board decisions which have attempted to circumscribe the right of free speech where there were also findings of unfair labor practices. Since this was certainly contrary to the intent of the Senate, * * * the Senate conferees acceded to the wish of the House group that the intent of this section be clarified. 93 Cong.Rec. 601 (1947).

In its Annual Report for 1948 the Board announced that § 8(c)

> "appears to enlarge somewhat the protection accorded by the original statute and to grant immunity beyond that contemplated by the free speech guarantees of the Constitution. For example, the Clark Bros. 'compulsory audience' doctrine has been held to be invalidated by this section of the act. Nor can a noncoercive speech any longer be held to violate the act because at other times, and on other occasions, the employer has committed other unfair labor practices. *However, words and conduct may be so intertwined as to be considered a single coercive act.* Thus where an employer delivered a speech to his employees impressing them with the fact that a union was an unnecessary

outside influence which he preferred not to have in his plant, and immediately thereafter polled the employees on whether he should 'step out completely and let the business go on its own power,' the Board found that the speech and the poll together constituted a threat that, if the employees voted for the union, the employer might discontinue operations. The speech and poll jointly were therefore found to violate section 8(a)(1) of the act." 13 N.L.R.B. Ann. Rep. 49–50 (1948). (Emphasis supplied.)

The Board can draw no comfort here from the sentence we have italicized since the company is not claimed to have indulged in any conduct violative of § 8(a)(1) other than its communications to employees.

In the light of this history and the Supreme Court's more recent warning of the dangers of ever finding an unfair labor practice in employer argument alone, see NLRB v. Exchange Parts Co., 375 U.S. 405, 409 n. 3, 84 S.Ct. 457, 11 L.Ed.2d 435 (1964), we find the approach here taken unacceptable. In holding the passages we have cited to be violations, the Trial Examiner stated simply that "the letters and speech * * * were calculated to create and instill in the minds of employees a fear of loss of privileges and economic suffering as a result of their adherence to the Union, and constituted interferences, restraint, and coercion within the meaning of Section 8(a)(1) of the Act." This is reading the Act as if § 8(c) did not exist; while there is a risk that an employer's prediction of adverse consequences from unionization may be taken as a threat to produce them, to hold that this danger alone suffices to convert a prediction into a threat of reprisal would go back to the very position of the early 1940's which § 8(c) was adopted to change. The Examiner did not advance matters by a conclusory statement that the company "exceeded the bounds of lawful expression within the meaning of Section 8(c) of the Act." Only if respondent's words contained a "threat of reprisal" did they go beyond the bounds of § 8(c). But, as the dictionaries tell us, a "threat of reprisal" means a "threat of retaliation" and this in turn means not a prediction that adverse consequences will develop but a threat that they will be deliberately inflicted in return for an injury—"to return evil for evil." Whatever vitality decisions such as NLRB v. Hearst Publications, 322 U.S. 111, 130, 64 S.Ct. 851, 88 L.Ed. 1170 (1944), and Gray v. Powell, 314 U.S. 402, 412, 62 S.Ct. 326, 86 L.Ed. 301 (1941), giving weight to an agency's construction of statutory language may have generally, cf. Social Security Board v. Nierotko, 327 U.S. 358, 368–370, 66 S.Ct. 637, 90 L.Ed. 718 (1946), and NLRB v. Highland Park Mfg. Co., 341 U.S. 322, 71 S.Ct. 758, 95 L.Ed. 969 (1951), such considerations have little weight when the statute being enforced approaches the limits of constitutional power. In such a case we encounter the overriding principle of construction requiring that statutes be read so as to avoid serious constitutional doubt, for which it here suffices to cite Int'l Ass'n of Machinists v. Street, 367 U.S. 740, 749–750, 81 S.Ct. 1784, 6 L.Ed.2d 1141 (1961).

The error of the Board in finding violations of the Act in the two passages from the letter of February 2 and the second set of remarks in the speech of February 16·predicting loss of work, harder work, or even a close-down as a result of unionization is apparent. Nothing in these communications could reasonably be interpreted as a threat to make the employees' lot harder in retaliation for their voting for the union, as in NLRB v. Cousins Associates, Inc., 283 F.2d 242, 243 (2 Cir. 1960), and Edward Fields, Inc. v. NLRB, 325 F.2d 754, 760 (2 Cir. 1963), see 141 N.L.R.B. 1182 for a fuller statement of the facts. The only fair reading is that the employer would take these steps solely from economic necessity and with regret. * *

Although the case as to the prediction of the effect of unionization on the grant of special privileges is a shade closer, we reach the same conclusion. Golub's speech made it clear enough that he would not aim to withdraw special privileges if a union contract were signed, and certainly not to withdraw them in retaliation for the union contract, but that he feared that the rules of the contract or the union's administration of it might forbid giving such benefits to one employee unless they were uniformly given to all. The same is true of the letter of February 8 when this is read as a whole. While these fears may have been unwarranted, they were not shown to have so far transcended the bounds of reason as to justify the Board in finding them to be disguised threats of reprisal. * * *

Enforcement denied.

HAYS, CIRCUIT JUDGE (dissenting):

The majority opinion demonstrates once more the inescapable truth that United States Circuit Judges safely ensconced in their chambers do not feel threatened by what employers tell their employees. An employer can dress up his threats in the language of prediction ("You will lose your job" rather than "I will fire you") and fool judges. He doesn't fool his employees; they know perfectly clearly what he means.

Virginia Electric & Power authorized employers to announce their opposition to unions; it did not legalize threatening language. And Section 8(c) expressly excepts threats.

The error into which the majority falls is to believe that one can identify threatening language regardless of the circumstances in which the language is used and regardless of the ears to which it is directed. A dictionary definition will suffice because it makes no difference whether the words are addressed to a judge or to a machine hand, they must mean the same thing.

* * *

The extent to which the majority will go in defending the employer's rights is indicated by their treatment of the employer's threats to discontinue making "special personal arrangement[s]" and granting privileges "such as time off when your children [are] sick, weddings, for haircuts, a school prom, emergencies at home, and to catch up on studies." These "fears" (of the employer!) may have been "unwarranted" says the majority, but "they were not shown" to be unreasonable. If it is not obvious on its face that no employee would believe that the *union* would interfere with his taking time off for a haircut, and that the employees undoubtedly (and correctly) understood that it was the *employer* who was going to withdraw these privileges, then certainly such a matter ought to be left to the Board's expertise, without requiring a "showing" that the Board was right.

NLRB v. GISSEL PACKING CO.

Supreme Court of the United States, 1969.
395 U.S. 575, 89 S.Ct. 1918, 23 L.Ed.2d 547.

[The Court considered four cases, all raising common issues of employer coercion during organizing campaigns and the authority of the Board to order the employer, as a remedy for such coercion, to bargain with a union which had demonstrated majority support through means other than a Board-supervised representation election. In one of the cases, the petitioner Sinclair Company operated two plants at which the Teamsters in 1965 had begun an organizing campaign, had obtained from 11 of 14 employees engaged in wire weaving signed cards authorizing the Teamsters to act as bargaining representative, and had made a request for recognition by the company, which the company refused. The Teamsters then petitioned for an election. In company communications to the employees, several references were made to a three-month strike in 1952, when the employees were represented by a different union; the strike had led to the union's loss of support among company employees. (Other portions of the Court's opinion are set forth at pages 322–36 infra.)]

When petitioner's president first learned of the Union's drive in July, he talked with all of his employees in an effort to dissuade them from joining a union. He particularly emphasized the results of the long 1952 strike, which he claimed "almost put our company out of business," and expressed worry that the employees were forgetting the "lessons of the past." He emphasized, secondly, that the Company was still on "thin ice" financially, that the Union's "only weapon is to strike," and that a strike "could lead to the closing of the plant," since the parent company had ample manufacturing facilities elsewhere. He noted, thirdly, that because of their age and the limited usefulness of their skills outside their craft, the employees might not be able to find re-employment if they lost their jobs as a result of a strike. Finally, he warned those who did not believe that the plant could go out of business to "look around Holyoke and see a lot of them out of business." The president sent letters to the same effect to the employees in early November, emphasizing that the parent company had no reason to stay in Massachusetts if profits went down.

During the two or three weeks immediately prior to the election on December 9, the president sent the employees a pamphlet captioned: "Do you want another 13-week strike?" stating, *inter alia,* that: "We have no doubt that the Teamsters Union can again close the Wire Weaving Department and the entire plant by a strike. We have no hopes that the Teamsters Union Bosses will not call a strike. * * * The Teamsters Union is a strike happy outfit." Similar communications followed in late November, including one stressing the Teamsters' "hoodlum control." Two days before the election, the Company sent out another pamphlet that was entitled: "Let's Look at the Record," and that purported to be an obituary of companies in the Holyoke-Springfield, Massachusetts, area that had allegedly gone out of business because of union demands, eliminating some 3,500 jobs; the first page carried a large cartoon showing the preparation of a grave for the Sinclair Company and other headstones containing the names of other plants allegedly victimized by the unions. Finally, on the day before the election, the president made another personal appeal to his employees to reject the Union. He repeated that the Company's financial condition was precarious; that a possible strike would jeopardize the continued operation of the plant; and that age and lack of education would make re-employment difficult. The Union lost the election 7–6, and then filed both objections to the election and unfair labor practice charges which were consolidated for hearing before the trial examiner.

* * *

[The Board, finding that the president's communications were reasonably read by the employees in the circumstances to threaten loss of jobs if the union were to win the election, held that the employer had violated Section 8(a)(1) and that the election should be set aside. It also held that the employer violated Section 8(a)(5) by refusing to bargain in good faith with the Teamsters Union which at the time of its request for recognition demonstrated majority support through its authorization cards. The court of appeals sustained the conclusions of the Board, as well as its order that the employer bargain with the union on request. The Supreme Court, affirming the judgment of the court of appeals, considered Sinclair's claim that the Board and court had acted in violation of the First Amendment to the federal Constitution and Section 8(c) of the Labor Act.]

Any assessment of the precise scope of employer expression, of course, must be made in the context of its labor relations setting. Thus, an employer's rights cannot outweigh the equal rights of the employees to associate freely, as those rights are embodied in § 7 and protected by § 8(a)(1) and the proviso to § 8(c). And any balancing of those rights must take into account the economic dependence of the employees on their employers, and the necessary tendency of the former, because of that relationship, to pick up intended implications of the latter that might be more readily dismissed by a more disinterested ear. Stating these obvious principles is but another way of recognizing that what is basically at stake is the establishment of a nonpermanent, limited relationship between the employer, his economically dependent employee and his union agent, not the election of legislators or the enactment of legislation whereby that relationship is ultimately defined and where the independent voter may be freer to listen more objectively and employers as a class freer to talk. Cf. New York Times Co. v. Sullivan, 376 U.S. 254 (1964).

Within this framework, we must reject the Company's challenge to the decision below and the findings of the Board on which it was based. The standards used below for evaluating the impact of an employer's statements are not seriously questioned by petitioner and we see no need to tamper with them here. Thus, an employer is free to communicate to his employees any of his general views about unionism or any of his specific views about a particular union, so long as the communications do not contain a "threat of reprisal or force or promise of benefit." He may even make a prediction as to the precise effects he believes unionization will have on his company. In such a case, however, the prediction must be carefully phrased on the basis of objective fact to convey an employer's belief as to demonstrably probable consequences beyond his control or to convey a management decision already arrived at to close the plant in case of unionization. See Textile Workers v. Darlington Mfg. Co., 380 U.S. 263, 274, n. 20 (1965). If there is any implication that an employer may or may not take action solely on his own initiative for reasons unrelated to economic necessities and known only to him, the statement is no longer a reasonable prediction based on available facts but a threat of retaliation based on misrepresentation and coercion, and as such without the protection of the First Amendment. We therefore agree with the court below that "[c]onveyance of the employer's belief, even though sincere, that unionization will or may result in the closing of the plant is not a statement of fact unless, which is most improbable, the eventuality of closing is capable of proof." 397 F.2d 157, 160. As stated elsewhere, an employer is free only to tell "what he reasonably believes will be the likely economic consequences of unionization that are outside his control," and not "threats of economic reprisal to be taken solely on his own volition." NLRB v. River Togs, Inc., 382 F.2d 198, 202 (C.A.2d Cir. 1967).

Equally valid was the finding by the court and the Board that petitioner's statements and communications were not cast as a prediction of "demonstrable 'economic consequences,'" 397 F.2d, at 160, but rather as a threat of retaliatory action. The Board found that petitioner's speeches, pamphlets, leaflets, and letters conveyed the following message: that the company was in a precarious financial condition; that the "strike-happy" union would in all likelihood have to obtain its potentially unreasonable demands by striking, the probable result of which would be a plant shutdown, as the past history of labor relations in the area indicated; and that the employees in such a case would have great difficulty finding employment elsewhere. In carrying out its duty to focus on the question: "[W]hat did the speaker intend and the listener understand?" (A. Cox, Law and the National Labor Policy 44 (1960)), the Board could reasonably conclude that the intended and understood import of that message was not to predict that unionization would inevitably cause the plant to close but to threaten to throw employees out of work regardless of the economic realities. In this connection, we need go no further than to point out (1) that petitioner had no support for its basic assumption that the union, which had not yet even presented any demands, would have to strike to be heard, and that it admitted at the hearing that it had no basis for attributing other plant closings in the area to unionism; and (2) that the Board has often found that employees, who are particularly sensitive to rumors of plant closings, take such hints as coercive threats rather than honest forecasts.

Petitioner argues that the line between so-called permitted predictions and proscribed threats is too vague to stand up under traditional First Amendment analysis and that the Board's discretion to curtail free speech rights is correspondingly too uncontrolled. It is true that a reviewing court must recognize the Board's competence in the first instance to judge the impact of utterances made in the context of the employer-employee relationship, see NLRB v. Virginia Electric & Power Co., 314 U.S. 469, 479 (1941). But an employer, who has control over that relationship and therefore knows it best, cannot be heard to complain that he is without an adequate guide for his behavior. He can easily make his views known without engaging in " 'brinkmanship' " when it becomes all too easy to "overstep and

tumble [over] the brink." Wausau Steel Corp. v. NLRB, 377 F.2d
369, 372 (C.A. 7th Cir. 1967). At the least he can avoid coercive
speech simply by avoiding conscious overstatements he has reason to
believe will mislead his employees. * * *

Problems for Discussion

1. During a vigorous campaign prior to a representation election, the
president of the Ace Manufacturing Company makes a speech along the
following lines: "I do not like unions, and I don't think you need one.
I have always treated you well, and will continue to do so even without
a union. Unions bring high initiation fees and monthly dues, which will
come out of your pocket and reduce your earnings. Unions also bring
hoodlumism, high prices and strikes, which neither you nor the Company
can afford. Vote against the union, for the Company's benefit and for
your own benefit." Has the Company violated Section 8(a)(1)?

2. Assume that the President of the Ace Manufacturing Company
makes the speech set forth in Problem 1, and that three days later he
discharges employee Smith, who has a poor work record and a leadership
position in the Union. The Union has filed charges under Section 8(a)(3),
alleging that the discharge was because of his union activities. At the
unfair labor practice hearing, the General Counsel seeks to introduce evidence of the text of the President's speech, to prove anti-union animus.
Counsel for the Company objects. How should the Administrative Law
Judge rule?

3. Assume, instead, that two days before the Company's President
made the speech set forth in Problem 1, he interrogated several employees
about their union sympathies, warned employees of serious discipline if
they discussed the union during their break time, and discharged an employee "because you are mixed up in this union business." Would the
President's speech then be unlawful? (Consider the House bill, the Senate
bill, and Section 8(c) as enacted.) If so, how should the Board word its
cease-and-desist order?

4. Able Tool & Die Company, located in Westfield, Massachusetts,
manufactures components of industrial machinery pursuant to orders from
buyers in the New England states. It employs 42 workers engaged in
production and maintenance work. The International Association of Machinists petitioned for an election among these employees, and the Regional
Director of the NLRB set the election for January 30. On January 22,
the Company President distributed to all employees, over his signature, the
following leaflet:

VOTE NO-UNION

The NLRB election will be held here at the plant on January
30. You will be asked to vote for the IAM or to vote for No-Union.
I will abide by the results of the election, but it is important for you
to know that while the Union has vigorously campaigned and said

critical things about management, you stand to lose if you vote for the Union. A Union victory can result in SERIOUS HARM.

(1) Competing companies organized by the IAM in this region uniformly have a wage scale BELOW that which exists here at Able. If the Union wins the election, the Company will bargain with the Union as required by law, but the law gives the Company the right to bargain hard and to insist on the reduction of certain economic benefits which you now have.

(2) If tough bargaining takes place, the Union can extract concessions only by calling a strike. If you join the strike—and just you try not to!—you and your family will lose your earnings (which will not be replaced by unemployment benefits because you have chosen to leave work) and the law permits me to hire another worker to replace you permanently. You will lose all of the benefits that come with length of service with this Company.

(3) Should the Union insist that the Company take action which will adversely affect quality or result in higher prices, our customers may choose not to buy from us any more. If they did this, just think how many jobs would be discontinued!

(4) Another way a union can harm our business is by striking. If we were struck, every account of any substance would desert us like a sinking ship. There would be a cutback in production, and perhaps a closing of our doors.

The choice on January 30 is yours and yours alone. Your future may depend on it. Vote to continue our happy working relationship. Vote NO-UNION.

On January 29, employees at Able received at their homes a mailing from the Westfield Chamber of Commerce which detailed the severe economic impact on the general business of Westfield in the event the Able plant were to close down. It also referred to prison terms served by two of the organizers sent to Westfield by the international office of the Machinists.

The election resulted in a 22-to-20 defeat for the Machinists.

A representative of the IAM has consulted you, and has asked what can be done to protect the interests of the Union. What is your response? See *Oak Mfg. Co.*, 141 N.L.R.B. 1323 (1963); *Greensboro Hosiery Mills, Inc.*, 162 N.L.R.B. 1275 (1967), enf't denied 398 F.2d 414 (4th Cir. 1968); and compare *Freeman Mfg. Co.*, 148 N.L.R.B. 577 (1964), with *Blaser Tool & Mold Co.*, 196 N.L.R.B. 374 (1972).

5. You are counsel to Southern Textile Company, which has been alerted by the Textile Workers Union to an organizing campaign recently begun in one of your mills. The president of the company has expressed to you her deep concern about unionization, both as a matter of principle and as a matter of hard economics. She believes that Southern's capacity to compete in the market will be severely undermined by wage increases and by any serious interference with the right of management to direct the workforce. She has asked you to prepare a series of leaflets, to be

distributed weekly to the employees and "to push my right to speak out against the union to the fullest extent the law allows, indeed maybe somewhat beyond, if that is likely to work."

(a) In dealing with the president's request, could you with confidence lift passages out of speeches or leaflets which the Board has ruled in past cases not to constitute unfair labor practices? *only if - - - - -*

(b) Are you obliged to refuse your client's request, or to discourage her from taking such action, or to impose conditions on your willingness to honor her request? What is the appropriate response of the attorney in such a case?

6. Evaluate the following proposition: Because of (a) the possible infringement of First Amendment rights when Government bans arguably coercive speech; (b) the desirability of informing employees of the consequences of unionization; (c) the vagueness of any test requiring the finding of a coercive impact "under all of the circumstances" and the difficulties of administering such a standard (for the Regional Director, the Administrative Law Judge, the NLRB, the courts of appeals and, most important, the speakers at the plant level); (d) uncertainty regarding the validity of the Board's psychological assumptions; (e) the disrespect for law that is encouraged when "artful" draftsmanship is rewarded and post-election litigation is invited; (f) the frequent lack of an effective administrative remedy after the fact; and (g) the frequent possibility that opportunities for response by the other party to the election campaign will rectify any wrongdoing—the Board should not find speech coercive (either as an unfair labor practice or to set aside an election) unless it explicitly threatens conduct which would itself be unlawful.

(b) Factual Misrepresentations

In addition to regulating campaign speeches and literature which contain threats of reprisal, the National Labor Relations Board has also been concerned about factual misrepresentations circulated shortly before an election. In the same year that the Board decided the *Dal-Tex* case, page 144 supra, it also announced a more aggressive policy in screening communications "where a party has misrepresented some material fact, within its special knowledge, so shortly before the election that the other party or parties do not have time to correct it, and the employees are not in a position to know the truth of the fact asserted." In HOLLYWOOD CERAMICS CO., 140 N.L.R.B. 221 (1962), the Board—in an effort to preserve the "laboratory conditions" in which there is "full and complete freedom of choice in selecting a bargaining representative"—set aside an election won by a union which had shortly before distributed a handbill purporting to compare wage rates at the company's plant with rates at other companies; the Board found the handbill to understate seriously the rates at the plant at which the election was being held. The Board acknowledged the impracticability of monitoring the vast amount of vague, ambiguous and inartistically drawn messages, and minor distortions of fact; to warrant setting aside an election under *Hollywood Ceramics*, the misrepresentation—whether intentional or not—must be a "substantial departure from the truth" and must be such as "may reasonably be expected to have a significant impact on the election."

Although the courts of appeals generally agreed that such regulation of non-coercive campaign misrepresentations was within the discretion of the Board, there were a not insignificant number of judicial reversals of Board decisions in this area, with some courts being yet more critical of campaign representations than was the Board; and some courts even suggested that the Board improperly displayed a greater tolerance of union misstatements than of comparable employer statements. *E. g.,* Peerless of America, Inc. v. NLRB, 576 F.2d 119 (7th Cir. 1978); Cross Baking Co. v. NLRB, 453 F.2d 1346 (1st Cir. 1971). Even within the Board, the *Hollywood Ceramics* principle came in for heavy criticism. One member, in dissent, stated that he saw no reason why representations made in a Board election campaign should be any more rigorously scrutinized than representations made in the more significant context of a political election; he charged the Board majority with "treating employees not like mature individuals capable of facing the realities of industrial life and making their own choices but as retarded children who need to be protected at all costs." Medical Ancillary Services, 212 N.L.R.B. 582, 585 (1974) (Member Penello). The Board, while recognizing the increasing sophistication of the workers participating in labor elections, nonetheless concluded "we are not yet ready to say that we will leave all our voters in all of our elections and in all circumstances to sort out, with no protection from us, from among a barrage of flagrant deceptive misrepresentations." Modine Mfg. Co., 203 N.L.R.B. 527 (1973).

With a change in membership of the Board, the majority attitude toward campaign misrepresentations changed as well, and *Hollywood Ceramics* was overruled (over two dissents) in Shopping Kart Food Market, Inc., 228 N.L.R.B. 1311 (1977). The *Shopping Kart* majority stated that the "ill effects" of the *Hollywood* rule "include extensive analysis of campaign propaganda, restriction of free speech, variance in application as between the Board and the courts, increasing litigation, and a resulting decrease in the finality of election results." Board rules "must be based on a view of employees as mature individuals who are capable of recognizing campaign propaganda for what it is and discounting it." Reliance was also placed upon a major empirical study of NLRB elections, which had concluded essentially that employees are affected only negligibly if at all by campaign representations and that the NLRB should therefore sharply curtail their regulation.   Henceforth, the NLRB majority concluded, "Board intervention will continue to occur in instances where a party has engaged in such deceptive campaign practices as improperly involving the Board and its processes, or the use of forged documents which render the voters unable to recognize the propaganda for what it is."

In little more than a year, with one of the members of the *Shopping Kart* majority resigning, that case was itself overruled by a new 3-to-2 Board majority, in the following case, which once again endorsed the principles of *Hollywood Ceramics.*   Although only a part of the disagreement within the Board turns upon the findings set forth in Getman, Goldberg & Herman, *Union Representation Elections: Law and Reality* (1976), that book represents a major empirical study which repays careful reading by all students of labor law and of administrative law generally.   In reflecting upon the sequence of events just recounted, and the opinions which follow, the student should attempt to assess the influence of intuition, legal scholarship and the membership of the Board in the decisionmaking process.   (One should also assess the wisdom of so soon overruling a major Board decision which had itself made a dramatic change in the law.)

overruled

GENERAL KNIT OF CALIFORNIA, INC.
239 N.L.R.B. 619 (1978).

[After a certification election was won, 134 to 104, by the petitioner United Steelworkers of America, the employer filed objections, claiming that after midnight on the day of the election and when the polls opened in the morning, the Union distributed a leaflet which materially misrepresented the financial condition of the company.   The leaflet allegedly suggested that General Knit had had 1976 profits of $19.3 million when in fact it had sustained a loss in excess of $5 million.   The Acting Regional Director recommended that the objections be overruled, and the company sought review by the Board.]

As found by the Acting Regional Director, the sole issue raised by these objections concerns the propriety of the aforesaid leaflet. Petitioner admits that it distributed a leaflet on the morning of the election which stated, in relevant part:

WHO IS FOOLING WHO???
GENERAL KNIT CAN CRY POOR MOUTH IF THEY
WANT, BUT LET'S LOOK AT THE FACTS.

IN 1976, GENERAL KNIT HAD SALES OF $25 MILLION.

GENERAL KNIT IS OWNED BY ITOH WHO HAS A NET WORTH IN EXCESS OF $200 MILLION.

THIS COMPANY HAD AN INCREASE OF 12.5% IN SALES FOR PERIOD ENDING MARCH 31, 1977.

DURING THIS PERIOD THIS COMPANY HAD A *PROFIT OF $19.3 MILLION*.

DON'T BE FOOLED BY GENERAL KNIT AND THEIR HIGH PRICE LAWYERS.

ITOH WHO OWNS GENERAL KNIT IS MAKING IT BIG AND CAN AFFORD DECENT WAGES FOR ITS EM-PLOYEES.

VOTE YES, TODAY, AND MAKE THE COMPANY SHARE SOME OF THEIR HIGH PROFITS WITH YOU —THE WORKER.

Petitioner asserts that the leaflet is accurate, and that it states unambiguously that General Knit's parent company—ITOH, not General Knit—had profits of $19.3 million. Further, Petitioner claims that the Employer adequately responded with its own leaflet by 8 a. m. on the morning of the election. The Employer claims, however, that it was not until about 10:15 a. m. on election day—after the first voting session was over—that it was able to respond.

The Acting Regional Director found that if the quoted profit figures in the leaflet referred to ITOH, then the leaflet was substantially correct and could not form the basis of objectionable conduct. He made no other factual findings in recommending that the objection be overruled. Rather, he concluded:

> Assuming *arguendo*, the words, "This Company," refer to General Knit, I conclude, under all the circumstances herein, that the alleged material misrepresentation does not constitute an egregious mistake of fact warranting the setting aside of an election, and does not otherwise violate the standards of conduct set forth in *Shopping Kart Food Market*, 228 NLRB 1311 (1977).

And, indeed, were the Board to continue to adhere to the principle of *Shopping Kart*, the Acting Regional Director's conclusion would appear to be correct. After much deliberation, however, we have decided that the principle expressed in the majority and concurring opinions in *Shopping Kart* is inconsistent with our responsibility to insure fair elections.   Accordingly, we hereby overrule *Shopping Kart Food Market, Inc.*, and return to the standard of review for alleged misrepresentations most cogently articulated in *Hollywood Ceramics Company, Inc.*   That standard indicates that

> [A]n election should be set aside only where there has been a misrepresentation or other similar campaign trickery, which involves a substantial departure from the truth, at a time which prevents the other party or parties from making an effective reply, so that the misrepresentation, whether deliberate or not, may reasonably be expected to have a significant impact on the election.

[handwritten margin note: Standard]

In *Shopping Kart,* which itself overruled *Hollywood Ceramics*, a Board majority determined that elections would no longer be set aside solely because of misleading campaign statements, whether oral or written, unless a party had engaged in deceptive practices which improperly involved the Board and its processes or the use of forged documents.   * * *   [T]hen-Chairman Murphy joined in overruling *Hollywood Ceramics* because she believed that the decision had been expanded greatly beyond its original intent and because she agreed with Members Penello and Walther that "the Board's rules concerning preelection statements must recognize employees as mature adults capable of recognizing and evaluating campaign rhetoric for what it is."   The *Shopping Kart* majority clearly thought the *Hollywood Ceramics* rule failed to take this into account.   In this, they were in error.   Rather, the principles of *Hollywood Ceramics* clearly recognize employee ability to assess the bulk of campaign propaganda. As can be discerned from the general principle in that decision, noted above, the area of the Board's concern involving alleged misrepresentations is truly a circumscribed one.   The parties are left to campaign vigorously and aggressively.   But, as was also noted in the principal dissent in *Shopping Kart,* the *Hollywood Ceramics* rule was also meant to embody the

> * * *   firm belief that employees should be afforded a degree of protection from overzealous campaigners who distort the issues by substantial misstatements of relevant and material facts *within the special knowledge of the campaigner,* so shortly before the election that there is no effective time for reply.

Such a view has nothing to do with an assumption that employees are "naive and unworldly," as the *Shopping Kart* majority charged. Such a view does have something to do, however, with a conviction that no matter what the ultimate sophistication of a particular electorate, there are certain circumstances where a particular misrepresentation or misrepresentations may materially affect an election. In such circumstances, that election should be set aside in order to maintain the integrity of Board elections and thereby protect employee free choice. This is what the *Hollywood Ceramics* rule was meant to insure.

In the past, under *Hollywood Ceramics,* the Board has successfully established and preserved the integrity of its electoral processes, thus assuring employees of the free exercise of their Section 7 rights. Thus, for example, in 1976, the Board conducted 8,899 elections. In 7,982 of these, or nearly 90 percent, neither side challenged the validity of the result through objections. Rather, both sides were satisfied with the integrity of the result. We believe that the direction of a new election, where, under *Hollywood Ceramics,* the Board finds that a substantial and material misrepresentation of fact had a reasonable tendency to affect the results of the election, has been a significant factor in the Board's electoral success, since the parties, knowing the serious consequences of their acts, have been deterred from engaging in conduct which would tend to interfere improperly with a free election.

In addition to acting as a deterrent to deceitful campaign trickery, the existence of the *Hollywood Ceramics* standard has provided a means of redress for a party who doubts the validity of the election results because of prejudicial campaigning by the prevailing side. The parties' access to the Board for review further legitimizes the integrity of the electoral process.[15] And, because of its deterrent effect, the *Hollywood Ceramics* standard has been well accepted by the courts and by the parties who have used our election

15. The need for such a review process is reflected, to an extent, by the degree to which the parties have continued to bring alleged misrepresentations to the Board even after the issuance of *Shopping Kart.* Thus, in the 12 months after *Shopping Kart* issued, the Board received 180 cases raising objections based on alleged misrepresentations, as contrasted with 307 in 1976. It appears that, despite our clear statement that we would no longer consider mere misrepresentations as grounds for setting aside an election, the parties have nevertheless perceived a need for Board review in this area.

Our dissenting colleagues argue that the decline in the number of objections based on alleged misrepresentations demonstrates *Shopping Kart's* success. In our view, however, a rule which merely eliminates a certain classification of cases, at the expense of an important principle, is not a success. Moreover, under their approach, one criterion in ruling on cases is its effect on the caseload. Yet, such a consideration has no place in the administration of the Act. If the Board is overburdened, the solution is more efficient procedures and/or increased staff, not a voluntary abnegation of our statutory responsibility.

procedure.[16]   Indeed, if anything, the courts in certain circumstances have applied *Hollywood Ceramics* more strictly than the Board has done.

Finally, enforcement of the *Hollywood Ceramics* rule has not been administratively burdensome in the past.   For example, in 1976, the Board processed 13,184 representation cases and 32,406 unfair labor practice cases.   Of the representation cases, only 307 involved *Hollywood Ceramics* allegations.   Thus, the administrative burden is slight in comparison with the substantial benefit to the Board's electoral procedure.

In disagreeing with the principles of *Hollywood Ceramics*, the *Shopping Kart* majority, in essence, disagreed with the general proposition that misrepresentations may, in fact, affect the way employees vote and thereby undermine the integrity of our electoral processes.   As support for its view, the *Shopping Kart* majority relied on certain findings of one empirical study and what that study purported to prove.[17]   In that study, its authors attempted to verify empirically certain assumptions which they believed underlay the Board's regulation of election conduct—most importantly, the Board's assumption that electioneering by the employer and union affects the employee's decision as to how to cast his or her ballot. They concluded that this assumption was not supported by voter behavior in the 31 elections they studied.   Rather, the authors found, on the basis of interviews with voters both before and after the elections involved, that the parties' electioneering had not affected the decision of 81 percent of the voters.   Thus, 81 percent voted in accordance with the intent they expressed to interviewers prior to the bulk of the union-management campaign.   From this finding, the authors concluded that the voters' decisions seemed to be determined by their attitudes toward unions and toward their jobs, both of

16.   See, e.g., Abbott Laboratories v. N. L.R.B., 540 F.2d 662 (4th Cir. 1976); N.L.R.B. v. Modine Manufacturing Co., 500 F.2d 914 (8th Cir. 1974); Metco, Incorporated v. N.L.R.B., 496 F.2d 1342 (5th Cir. 1974); Coronet-Western, a division of Coronet Industries, Inc. v. N.L.R.B., 518 F.2d 31 (9th Cir. 1975).   Member Penello lists the cases in which the courts have denied enforcement of Board Orders in *Hollywood Ceramics* situations—47 cases in a period of 12 years. While this list is visually impressive, we are more impressed by the number of elections during this same period—nearly 100,-000 up to the date *Shopping Kart* issued—in which no objections alleging misrepresentations were filed.   In our view, the *Hollywood Ceramics* rule, by acting as a deterrent, made such a statistic possible.

17.   Getman and Goldberg, "The Behavioral Assumptions Underlying NLRB Regulation of Campaign Misrepresentations: An Empirical Evaluation," 28 Stanford L.Rev. 263 (1976); see also Getman, Goldberg, and Herman, "Union Representation Elections: Law and Reality" (1976), for the authors' final report on the study.

which had been established prior to the campaign, and which for 81 percent of the voters remained unchanged during the campaign. Of the remaining 19 percent, 6 percent were undecided at the first interview, while 13 percent voted contrary to the intent they had expressed to interviewers immediately after the filing of a petition for an election. Interestingly, in attempting to determine how voters in these two groups made their voting decisions, the authors found that the votes of the undecided 6 percent correlated with their "familiarity" with the unions' campaigns. Thus, those employees who voted for a union recalled significantly more issues raised by the union than did those who voted against the union. A similar pattern existed for the 13 percent who switched their votes. Finally, the authors found that the votes of the undecided and switchers were determinative in 9 of the 31 elections; that is, in 29 percent of the elections they studied.

In evaluating the findings summarized above, the authors speculated that the campaign itself had had little effect on voting decisions, but that the extent of familiarity with and reaction to each side's campaign was determined by a voter's initial attitude toward unions in general. However, the study was not designed to investigate the actual reasons for the reaction of voters to the campaigns, and theirs is by no means the only possible conclusion to be drawn from the data. The results of 43 years of conducting elections, investigating objections, and holding hearings at which employees testify concerning their recollection of campaign tactics convince us that employees are influenced by certain union and employer campaign statements. Even the authors acknowledged that, of the 19 percent, those who ultimately voted against the union may have been influenced by the employer's campaign, even though they did not recall specific issues.

The authors' final recommendations, including the suggested deregulation of misrepresentations, were based on their findings *vis-a-vis* the 81 percent of voters rather than the 19 percent. Such a narrow focus might have been warranted if the authors had concluded either that the votes of the 19 percent had not affected the results of a significant number of elections or that the 19 percent, in deciding how to vote, had not based that decision on information provided during the campaign.[18] But where, as this study indicates,

18. Our dissenting colleague, Member Penello, accuses us of erring and of a "fourfold misrepresentation" in our discussion of the undecided and switchers in the study. We object to this characterization, when it is apparent that he is merely challenging our interpretation of the study, not the factual data that we cite. He asserts that the study's findings did not

not only are a substantial minority of employees influenced by the campaign, but their votes also affected the outcome of over a quarter of the elections, we find this persuasive evidence for maintaining reasonable procedures to insure that the employees exercise their franchise in an atmosphere free from substantial and material misrepresentations.

Even if this particular study were clearly supportive of all of the authors' conclusions, however, we would still not find it an adequate ground for rejecting a rule which had been well established for 15 years.   While we welcome research from the behavioral sciences, 1 study of only 31 elections in 1 area of the country—although it may provide food for thought—is simply not sufficient to disprove the assumptions upon which the Board has regulated election conduct, especially since, in our experience, statements made by either side can significantly affect voter preference.

Nevertheless, as the Board recognized in *Modine Manufacturing Company*, the *Hollywood Ceramics* rule has not been free from criticism.   In this regard, we note in particular the following criticisms which have been heard more frequently than others.   These are (1) the lack of predictability as to how the *Hollywood Ceramics* factors will be weighed in determining whether an election will or will not be set aside; and (2) the complaint that the *Hollywood Ceramics* standard is administratively objectionable because it provides a vehicle for delay of the ultimate result through appeals to the Board and the courts, which delay collective bargaining and thereby undermine the employees' chosen bargaining representative.

The first criticism is an outgrowth of our application of our standard to a myriad of factual patterns such that the result is, naturally, not the same in each instance.   If there have been any inconsistencies in the results in the cases we have considered, these

support a conclusion that 19 percent of the voters were affected by the campaign information, but rather that, at most, the 5 percent who ultimately voted for the union were affected.   His position, in contrast to our view, gives little weight to the study's observation that those who voted for the union had greater exposure to the union's campaign information than did those who voted against the union—a finding which suggests that if the others had had similar exposure, they, too, might have voted for the union.   Moreover, in contrast to the majority, he discounts the study's recognition that the mere existence of an employer campaign may have influenced employees, on the grounds that the influence was not from any factual assertions.   Yet how could the employer's campaign have been free of factual assertions?   In light of these matters, we view our interpretation as more consistent with the study's findings in regard to the 19 percent who either were undecided or did switch.

have stemmed from judgmental differences as to the reasonable effect of a misrepresentation on the electorate, not from any fundamental difference in standards or from any desire to regulate the conduct of one party more closely than that of another. In any event, our primary focus is on the future application of this standard and not on the past. It is our goal to adhere strictly to the standard articulated in *Hollywood Ceramics* and to apply that standard equally to both sides, while still allowing the parties the opportunity to campaign vigorously for their particular positions. In *Hollywood Ceramics*, we said that we would not set aside an election merely because a misrepresentation occurred at sometime during the campaign. In *Modine Manufacturing, supra,* we reiterated:

> We do not wish to have unrealistic standards, or insist upon such improbable purity of word and deed that we will obstruct or delay our administrative task of conducting elections in so high a number of cases that any hard-fought campaign will almost inevitably result in our elections being invalidated.

> Nor do we believe it wise to direct hearings as a matter of course in any case in which misrepresentations are alleged to have been made, and thus regularly delay the intended effect of our elections and substantially divert the resources of this Agency from the host of other pressing matters demanding our attention.

This will also be the standard which we shall use in evaluating campaign statements hereafter. In this way, we can act expeditiously on objections involving alleged misrepresentations and thereby decrease substantially the delay between the election and either the certification of result, the certification of representative, or the direction of a new election. This procedure partially negates the second criticism of opponents to *Hollywood Ceramics,* discussed above, by making delays less likely. In general, however, it seems that the problem of delay has been greatly exaggerated since in all but a minute number of cases the parties have ceased litigation following the Board's review of the Regional Director's decision with regard to objections. Thus, in 1976, only 9 cases raising *Hollywood Ceramics* issues were appealed to the circuit courts, while, since 1947, the highest number of such cases to be appealed in any single year was 11, in 1968 and 1975. In any event, we would not—as our dissenting colleagues seem to do—place a greater value on expediency of case processing than on maintaining standards to preserve the integrity of the electoral process.   *   *   *

Inasmuch as there has been no investigation of the Employer's objections to the election in the instant case under *Hollywood Ceramics* standards, the Board, having duly considered the matter, is of the opinion that the Employer's objections raise an issue which requires further investigation at the regional level. Accordingly, we shall remand this case to the Regional Director for a Supplemental Report on Objections which may, at his discretion, be based on a further investigation or a hearing.   *   *   *

MEMBER PENELLO, dissenting:

I adhere to the sound principles of *Shopping Kart Food Market, Inc.*, 228 NLRB 1311 (1977). I dissent from the majority's hasty reversal of that decision. I would overrule the Employer's objections and certify the Union so that it could get on with the business of collective bargaining without further delay.

I.

*   *   * The postponement of collective bargaining pending Board and court perusal of campaign puffery is part and parcel of the *Hollywood Ceramics* approach. If an additional illustration be deemed necessary, it is provided by *J. I. Case Co. v. N. L. R. B.*, 555 F.2d 202 (8th Cir. 1977). In that proceeding, employees in two voting groups chose the union as their bargaining representative on December 18, 1974. Nine months later, the Board adopted the Hearing Officer's report overruling the employer's *Hollywood Ceramics* objections, and certified the union. Six more months elapsed before the Board issued its decision in the summary judgment case. On May 18, 1977, 2½ years after the election, the Eighth Circuit denied the Board's petition for enforcement of its bargaining order.

The court concluded that two statements made by the union concerning benefits it had negotiated for the production and maintenance employees at the plant constituted material misrepresentations. First, the union stated that "the yearly wage of skilled workers exceeds $19,000 and goes up to $20,000 and more." In fact, this statement was literally true because 8 of the 51 skilled workers at the plant were earning at least $19,000 and 1 was earning in excess of $20,000. The court, however, noted that the average wage of such workers was only $16,570.12 and added:

> We do not think this significant disparity can be excused as mere exaggeration or explained away as a vague or ambiguous statement. [555 F.2d at 205.]

The second misrepresentation concerned the claim that union workers had won such benefits "as 95% of wages plus paid insurance in the event of lay-off." Again, this statement was literally true, but the union failed to specify that employees were entitled only to 95 percent of *net* wages, rather than *gross* wages, in the event of layoff. The court held that the union's statement was objectionable because the difference between a percentage based on gross wages and one based on net wages "may be substantial." 555 F.2d at 206.

[These court decisions] cannot be faulted on legal grounds, for they turned on an application of the Board's own *Hollywood Ceramics* criteria. Why did the Board and the courts reach opposite results if they were applying the same test? To a large degree, the explanation lies in the very nature of the standards formulated by the Board. Thus, the *Hollywood Ceramics* rule requires the decisionmaker to answer such questions as: When does a departure from the "truth" become "substantial"? What issues in an election campaign are "material"? How much time is necessary for an "effective reply"? With standards as vague and flexible as these to apply, it is not surprising that the Board and the courts often disagree on the treatment of misrepresentation objections, or that the election loser frequently chooses to litigate rather than negotiate.

For an employer, the possibility of success before the courts is a real one. In stark contrast to the Board's overall "set aside" rate of only 15 percent, in misrepresentation cases the Board loses before the courts approximately 50 percent of the time. Under the *Hollywood Ceramics* approach, courts have denied enforcement of Board bargaining orders in the following cases during the past dozen or so years: [47 court cases were cited, decided between 1966 and 1978].

In all these cases, collective bargaining was effectively frustrated by the Board's *Hollywood Ceramics* rule. Under the *Hollywood Ceramics* approach, however, an employer determined to defeat the desires of its employees for collective representation need not prevail before a court of appeals in order to attain its goal. In fact, it need only file an objection, alleging that some union statement or document was misleading. By doing so, an employer can set into motion the Board's postelection machinery and demand a painstaking analysis of all that was said during the campaign.

The period of delay afforded employers under *Hollywood Ceramics* is very substantial indeed. The median time from the date of election to the date of issuance of a decision by the Regional Director on objections is approximately 2 months. After the Regional Director's decision issues, an employer can still appeal to the Board, either by way of exceptions or by a request for review, a procedure which would guarantee an additional 3 months, and then rest assured that 9½ more months would elapse while a refusal-to-bargain charge is initiated and processed to Board decision. The time lag during the final period, which begins with the issuance of the Board's bargaining order and ends with a decision by a court of appeals, is 7½ months. To summarize, these statistics reveal that the entire process—from Board election to circuit court opinion—takes 22 months or almost 2 years. * * *

Shopping Kart sought to eliminate obstructionist tactics and promote the prompt commencement of meaningful collective bargaining. * * *

In *Shopping Kart*, the Board, after reviewing the adverse consequences of the *Hollywood Ceramics* rule and the dubious assumptions on which it is based,[19] overruled the case, and returned to the

19. The primary assumption underlying the *Hollywood Ceramics* rule is that employees cast their ballots in reliance upon the factual assertions made by the parties during an election campaign. Prior to *Shopping Kart*, the courts recognized that this assumption was totally unverified and that reexamination of it would be warranted in light of a then pending voting study. Getman v. N.L.R.B., 450 F.2d 670, 675–676 (D.C.Cir.1971); Harlan #4 Coal Company v. N.L.R.B., 490 F.2d 117, 122–123, fn. 5 (6th Cir. 1974). In the latter case, the court said that the Board, in deciding to set aside an election,

> * * * base[s] its findings concerning the impact of various campaign tactics largely on its own speculation * * *. Recently however, some empirical research has been conducted. The preliminary results of this research indicate that campaigns have little impact on voting behavior and that the impact they may have is often just the opposite of that which the Board has assumed they would have. [Citing Getman, Goldberg, and Herman, "The National Labor Relations Board Voting Study: A Preliminary Report," I. J. Legal Studies 233 (1972).]

In Shopping Kart, the results of the voting study were analyzed as offering some support for the view that employees are "mature individuals who are capable of recognizing campaign propoganda for what it is and discounting it." 228 N.L.R.B. at 1313.

My colleagues correctly report the study's finding that 81 percent of the employees voted in accord with their precampaign intent and thus were unaffected by the parties' electioneering. However, the majority errs in asserting that the study found that the votes of the remaining 19 percent (13 percent who voted contrary to their precampaign intent (switchers) and 6 percent who were undecided) were based on information provided by the campaign. The study made no such finding. What the study found was that only the 5 percent of the total sample who either switched to the union or were originally undecided and ultimately voted for the union could be said to have been influenced by the content of the campaign of the party for which they voted. Getman and Goldberg, "The Behavioral Assumptions Underlying NLRB Regulation of Campaign Misrepresentations: An Empirical Evaluation," 28 Stanford L.Rev. 263, 282 (1976). Thus, in contrast, "there was * * * no evidence that familiarity with the content of the company campaign was associated wtih switching to the company" or voting for the company after

policy that was in effect during the first 20 years of the Act's administration of not inquiring into the truth or falsity of campaign material. Specifically, the Board stated that intervention would be limited to "instances where a party has engaged in such deceptive campaign practices as * * * the use of forged documents which render the voters unable to recognize the propaganda for what it is." 228 NLRB at 1313.

Unlike the *Hollywood Ceramics* rule, the *Shopping Kart* standard draws a clear line between what is and what is not objectionable. Under *Shopping Kart*, elections will be set aside "not on the basis of the *substance* of the representation, but the deceptive *manner* in which it was made." 228 NLRB at 1314. As long as the campaign material is what it purports to be, i. e., mere propaganda of a particular party, the Board would leave the task of evaluating its contents solely to the employees. In contrast, no voter could recognize a forged document "for what it is" because the deception goes to its very essence.

Since the application of *Shopping Kart* yields highly predictable results, it greatly reduces the incentive for protracted litigation and the possibility of disagreements between the Board and the courts. The opportunity for delay under *Shopping Kart* is virtually nonexistent, as objections merely alleging false or inaccurate statements can be summarily overruled. *Shopping Kart* also furthers the goal of consistent and equitable adjudications. In subsequent cases, *Shopping Kart* has been applied with an even hand to overrule both union and employer misrepresentation objections.

The majority cites certain statistics in footnote [15] of their opinion which indicate that "in the 12 months after *Shopping Kart* is-

initially being undecided. *Id.* at 281, 282. To summarize, the majority has made a fourfold misrepresentation of the number of employees who were found to have been affected by campaign literature in casting their ballots.

In their subsequent book on the voting study, the authors reiterated that the undecided and the switchers who voted against the union did not rely on information provided by the company. Getman, Goldberg, and Herman, "Union Representation Elections: Law and Reality" (1976) at pp. 103–104, 107–108. The authors hypothesized that the vote of these employees may be a product not of the content of the company campaign, but of the mere existence of the campaign itself, which may lead employees to believe that the employer is now aware of the dissatisfaction that caused the organizing effort and therefore should be given an opportunity to improve working conditions without the presence of the union. It is in this sense only that the authors suggested that these voters may be "influenced by the employer's campaign." *Id.* at 108. Inasmuch as this suspected influence does not result from factual assertions made by the company, it lends no support for the assumption which forms the basis of the *Hollywood Ceramics* rule.

sued, the Board received 180 cases raising objections based on alleged misrepresentations, as contrasted with 307 in 1976." In my opinion, a 41-percent decline in the number of misrepresentation cases after just 1 year of *Shopping Kart* is a stunning tribute to the effectiveness of that decision. According to my colleagues, the filing of the 180 misrepresentation cases justified reinstating the *Hollywood Ceramics* rule because, despite the issuance of *Shopping Kart,* "the parties have nevertheless perceived a need for Board review in this area." That argument is simply astonishing. As discussed above, it is the parties who wish to delay collective bargaining that "perceive a need for Board review in this area." I submit that they are the ones responsible for filing most of the 180 objection cases. * * *

III.

My colleagues themselves highlight the extent to which the *Hollywood Ceramics* standards are capable of varying interpretations when they state that their "goal" is "to adhere strictly" to them. More importantly, that statement marks a radical departure from the most recent Board interpretation of the *Hollywood Ceramics* decision.

Four years before *Shopping Kart* was decided, the Board reconsidered the *Hollywood Ceramics* rule in *Modine Manufacturing Company* and concluded that it should be applied in a *less* restrictive fashion. * * * Today, my colleagues depart from the thrust of [such] Board cases, apparently adopt the approach of the courts, and implicitly find, for the first time in 14 years, that a union statement of company profitability constitutes a material misrepresentation which would justify setting aside the election if the employer did not have an adequate opportunity to reply.

The restrictive interpretation that my colleagues place upon the *Hollywood Ceramics* rule is further illustrated by an examination of the precise statement that is regarded as objectionable. It will be recalled that the union leaflet referred to the $19.3 million profits of "this company" without specifying whether the profits were those of ITOH or General Knit. Inasmuch as the immediate antecedent in the leaflet of the phrase "this company" is ITOH, and as ITOH did report profits of $19.3 million, the Union's statement is technically correct. By refusing to overrule the Employer's objections, the majority must be holding that parties have not only a duty under *Hollywood Ceramics* to refrain from an outright falsification, but also a duty to avoid statements which, when read in isolation, are ambiguous.   *   *   *

Notwithstanding their intention to police the *Hollywood Ceramics* rule "strictly," my colleagues state that parties will be allowed "to campaign vigorously for their particular positions." Precisely how these dual objectives will be simultaneously realized is left unsaid. Even more perplexing is the majority's quotation of the liberalized *Modine* standard immediately after saying that the *Hollywood Ceramics* rule will be applied "strictly." Finally, the majority concludes this baffling paragraph with the following pronouncement: "In this way, we can act expeditiously on objections involving alleged misrepresentations and thereby decrease substantially the delay between the election and either the certification of result, the certification of representative, or the direction of a new election." Exactly what "way" are my colleagues referring to? Is there some new avenue or boulevard of review in these cases which will obviate the delay inherent in the *Hollywood Ceramics* approach?

Contrary to my colleagues, I fear that their decision will result in delays in the processing of objections cases far beyond those experienced under prior interpretations of the *Hollywood Ceramics* rule. From today forward, our Regional Directors and the Board itself must "strictly" scrutinize campaign literature, attempting to track down half-truths and ferret out latent ambiguities. As Professor Bok has observed, a standard such as the majority's which proscribes ambiguous statements "transform[s] the task of separating truth from falsehood into an effort to decide how much each side will be required to disclose affirmatively in order to make its declarations sufficiently accurate and clear. This is hardly an easy task, for almost every partisan speech in an election campaign bristles with assertions that require qualifications and additions in order to present a fully accurate picture of the facts." [20] Not only have my colleagues made the job of the decisionmaker exceedingly more difficult, but also they have increased the "opportunities for legal maneuvering to post-pone bargaining rights," as the election loser now need only discover "some litigable ambiguity" in the opposing party's literature.   *   *   *

MEMBER MURPHY, dissenting:

In *Shopping Kart Food Market, Inc.*, a Board majority, with me concurring, overruled *Hollywood Ceramics Company, Inc.*, and

---

20. "The Regulation of Campaign Tactics in Representation Elections Un- der the National Labor Relations Act," 78 Harv.L.Rev. 38, 86 (1964).

held that the Board would no "longer probe into the truth or falsity of the parties' campaign statements." My colleagues in a new majority have today overruled *Shopping Kart* and thus have restored a proven delaying tactic to the arsenal of those who would forestall the certification of election results.   *   *   *

Since the Board has neither the qualifications, the practical experience, nor the resources to make valid psychological assessments of the actual effects of a given statement on the behavior of a given set (or group of subsets) of employees, our criteria in such cases are based on assumptions about the likely effect on employees of various kinds of statements. Assumptions regarding reasonably predictable effects necessarily imply assumptions regarding the susceptibilities of the employees who are the "targets" of the statement in issue. At the outset, it is reasonably predictable that certain kinds of statements made to employees (*e. g.*, threats of violence, discharge, reprisal, etc.) are likely to have much more impact and effect on the employees and their exercise of free choice than other kinds of statements (*e. g.*, misrepresentations regarding financial issues). In other words, it is reasonable to assume that an employee who has been threatened is likely to act (or at least consider acting) in a way which will avoid the perceived consequences of the threat. This is especially true if the employee considers the person making the threat to be capable of carrying it out. Coercion is the antithesis of freedom, and this is nowhere more than in the "political" milieu of an organizational campaign.

On the other hand, most "misrepresentation" in the preelection period takes the form of what may be termed campaign propaganda. And while it may be that employees have not always been able to determine the truth or falsity of such statements, it is also apparent that campaign misrepresentations do not in themselves create an atmosphere of fear and coercion, as do threats. Rather, they merely require (if anything) an evaluation by the employees to whom they are addressed. Accordingly, it may be said that such statements do not inspire the kind of "behavioral imperative" that threats engender. Moreover, it is, I think, reasonable to assume that most employees view statements made by either party in a campaign as inevitably tinged with self-interest; regard such rhetoric therefore with a degree of cynicism; and then vote primarily on the basis of their own desires, prejudices, or expectations.

It is worth examining, in this light, the rule of *Hollywood Ceramics*, to which my colleagues in the new majority assert they are now returning. In *Hollywood Ceramics*, the Board   *   *   *   went on to say that it would not set aside an election if "consideration of all the circumstances" indicated that "the statement would not be likely to have a real impact on the election." The Board cited, as examples of such circumstances: (1) a misrepresentation regarding "an unimportant matter so that it could only have had a *de minimis* effect; (2) a statement "so extreme as to put employees on notice of its lack of truth"; (3) where "the employees possessed independent knowledge with which to evaluate the statements"; and (4) where "the party making the statement possesses intimate knowledge of the subject matter so that the employees * * * may be expected to attach added significance to its assertion."

If the above-quoted language of *Hollywood Ceramics* is any guidance, the Board would expect employees to discount a misrepresentation if, *inter alia*, the statement were sufficiently "extreme" or if the party making the statement did *not* have "intimate knowledge of the subject matter." In other words, where one party grossly distorts some aspect of the other party's assets, profits, likely behavior, pay rates, dues structure, etc., employees in the view of the *Hollywood Ceramics* Board may be expected to see such statements for what they are: campaign rhetoric by a party not necessarily possessed of the relevant information.

However, in spite of this implicit assumption that employees can be expected to evaluate campaign claptrap, *Hollywood Ceramics* has been applied in what could only be termed a condescending manner: the Board has repeatedly stepped in to protect employees from their—presumed—inability to place in perspective a party's exaggeration, rhetoric, or misrepresentations. If presidential elections were supervised by the Board's new majority here, democracy in the United States would be long dead or at least long denied. * * *

Problems for Discussion

1. Review Problem 4 on page 157 supra—the Able Tool & Die problem. Assume that the representative of the IAM has informed you that the allegation in the Company leaflet about union wages elsewhere is false (although he believes the Company President probably thought it to be true); and that the Chamber of Commerce assertion concerning the prison record of Union officials is also false. (No steps were taken by the Union to challenge these assertions prior to the election.) Should the Board order a new election? See *Lipman Motors, Inc. v. NLRB*, 451 F.2d 823 (2d Cir. 1972).

2. In the Able Tool & Die problem, should Board action be affected had the Union loss been by a margin not of 22-to-20 but rather 36-to-6? Should the NLRB treat this wide disparity in votes as indicating a severe impact of the coercive or false statements, or rather as indicating that even a new and fully fair election would still result in an election victory for the Company? Can the Board answer such a question by resort to *a priori* reasoning?

Consider the results of a systematic empirical study in Getman, Goldberg & Herman, Union Representation Election: Law and Reality 150 n. 21 (1976): "The data indicate that no matter what type of speech employees are exposed to, the votes of approximately 80 percent are predictable on the basis of pre-campaign attitudes. Indeed, the data suggest that the actual number of employees influenced by the campaign is far less. Since no more than 20 percent, and probably far fewer, are subject to campaign influence, the Board would be on exceedingly safe ground if it were to refuse to entertain objections based on speech unless the margin of victory was less than 20 percent. By this rather simple change in its practice, the Board could eliminate a portion of its caseload of objections with little risk that employee rights of free choice were being injured."

3. Are there any obstacles under the federal Constitution to reversing the union's election victory, in cases like *Hollywood Ceramics* and *General Knit*, because of its communications regarding wage-rate comparisons or company profits? See *Bausch & Lomb, Inc. v. NLRB*, 451 F.2d 873 (2d Cir. 1972).

Consider this passage from the concurring opinion of Mr. Justice Jackson in Thomas v. Collins, 323 U.S. 516, 65 S.Ct. 315, 89 L.Ed. 430 (1945): "[I]t cannot be the duty, because it is not the right, of the state to protect the public against false doctrine. The very purpose of the First Amendment is to foreclose public authority from assuming a guardianship of the public mind through regulating the press, speech and religion. In this field every person must be his own watchman for truth, because the forefathers did not trust any government to separate the true from the false for us."

Consider too the decision of a three-judge district court in Vanasco v. Schwartz, 401 F.Supp. 87 (E.D.N.Y.1975), aff'd by an equally divided Court, 423 U.S. 1041, 96 S.Ct. 763, 46 L.Ed.2d 630 (1976). There, the State of New York enacted legislation concerning state elections and election campaigns, and established a Board of Elections whose regulations prohibited "misrepresentations of any candidate's qualifications," "misrepresentation of any candidate's position including, but not limited to, misrepresentation as to political issues or his voting record, [or] use of false or misleading quotations," and "misrepresentation of any candidate's party affiliation." Violations of the regulations were punishable by fines and cease-and-desist orders, enforceable in state courts. The federal court, observing that these provisions were not limited to the banning of intentional or reckless falsehoods, held that they were "overbroad" and would unduly "chill" campaign speech protected by the Fourteenth Amendment.

(c) Inflammatory Appeals

SEWELL MFG. CO., 138 N.L.R.B. 66 (1962). An election was
held at the company's plants in two small Georgia towns, near the
Alabama border. The Amalgamated Clothing Workers lost the election, 985–331, but the Board set it aside. During the preceding four
months, the employer had circulated copies of Militant Truth, a
four-page monthly which regularly had articles linking unions,
blacks, racial integration, Communism and anti-Christianity. Two
weeks before the election, the employer mailed to its employees a
large picture of an unidentified black man dancing with an unidentified white woman and a newspaper article (from four years before, relating to a representation election in another state involving a different company and a different international union) with
headlines referring to "race mixing" and with a photograph of a
white man, identified as the president of the International Union
of Electrical Workers, dancing with a black woman. Later, an article in a local newspaper cited financial contributions made by
organized labor to the Congress of Racial Equality, and two days
before the election the employer sent a letter to all employees in
which he mentioned the fact that the union uses membership funds
to support various civil rights groups.

The Board stated that, unlike a political election in which "the
law permits wide latitude in the way of propaganda—truth and un-
truth, promises, threats, appeals to prejudice," the Board has the
responsibility "to insure that the voters have the opportunity of
exercising a reasoned, untrammeled choice" regarding unionization,
and to conduct elections in which employees "cast their ballots for
or against a labor organization in an atmosphere conducive to the
sober and informed exercise of the franchise, free not only from
interference, restraint, or coercion violative of the Act, but also from
other elements which prevent or impede a reasoned choice." Although minor or isolated references to race might have to be tolerated, "prejudice based on color is a powerful emotional force" and
"a deliberate appeal to such prejudice is not intended or calculated
to encourage the reasoning faculty. * * * The Board does not
intend to tolerate as 'electoral propaganda' appeals or arguments
which can have no purpose except to inflame the racial feelings of
voters in the election."

Some statements with racial overtones—such as the union's
position on segregation or union financial contributions to civil
rights groups—will be appropriate, but only if "temperate in tone,
germane, and correct factually," because employees are entitled to
have knowledge about these matters. But "the burden will be on
the party making use of a racial message to establish that it was
truthful and germane, and where there is doubt [it] will be resolved
against him." In this case, the employer "calculatedly embarked on

a campaign so to inflame racial prejudice of its employees that they would reject the [union] out of hand on racial grounds alone." The atmosphere was so inflamed that a reasoned decision by the employees was an impossibility. The "photographs and the news articles were not germane to any legitimate issue involved in the election and reinforce our conclusion that their purpose was to exacerbate racial prejudice and to create an emotional atmosphere of hostility" to the union.

Problems for Discussion

1. Do you believe that the justification for NLRB regulation in cases such as *Sewell* is more or less persuasive than the justification for regulation in cases such as *Dal-Tex*, *Golub* and *Gissel* on the one hand and *General Knit* on the other? Stated another way, what is the order of priority for governmental regulation to assure dispassion, freedom from economic coercion, and accurate facts, in a labor election?

2. In 1974, the State of New York, as part of comprehensive legislation regulating state elections and campaigns, prohibited the use of literature or of the media to make "attacks on a candidate based on race, sex, religion or ethnic background." The legislation established a Board of Elections which promulgated a Fair Campaign Code (containing the same proscription) to be enforceable by fines and cease-and-desist orders. This legislative and administrative provision was held unconstitutional by a three-judge district court in Vanasco v. Schwartz, 401 F.Supp. 87 (E.D. N.Y.1975), aff'd by an equally divided Court 423 U.S. 1041, 96 S.Ct. 763, 46 L.Ed.2d 630 (1976). The court stated that in political elections the First Amendment protects all speech except "fighting words" (whose very utterance inflicts injury or tends to incite an immediate breach of the peace) and "malicious" untruths (statements known to be false or with a reckless disregard of the truth). Neither exception applied here, where the state attempted to justify regulation simply on the grounds that attacks based on a candidate's race, sex, religion or ethnic background are unrelated to fitness for office. The court held: "Such an assumption is an exercise in self-delusion. The Supreme Court has recognized that [g]iven the realities of our political life, it is by no means easy to see what statements about a candidate might be altogether without relevance to his fitness for the office he seeks. * * * It would be a retreat from reality to hold that voters do not consider race, religion, sex or ethnic background when choosing political candidates. * * * New York's attempt to eliminate an entire segment of protected speech from the arena of public debate is clearly unconstitutional."

Earlier, in Thomas v. Collins, 323 U.S. 516, 65 S.Ct. 315, 89 L.Ed. 430 (1945), the Supreme Court had said: "[E]mployers' attempts to persuade to action with respect to joining or not joining unions are within the First Amendment's guaranty. * * * When to this persuasion other things are added which bring about coercion, or give it that character, the limit of the right has been passed. * * * But short of that limit the employer's freedom cannot be impaired."

Is the Board's decision, order and doctrine in *Sewell* constitutional?

3.   During the course of an organizing drive involving a laundry, the union distributed numerous leaflets to the employees, who were predominantly Negro.   While several leaflets made familiar claims concerning the economic benefits to be derived from collective bargaining, some dwelt heavily on racial themes.   For example, one leaflet was headed "FREEDOM IS EVERYBODY'S FIGHT."   Beside a picture of a dog with bared fangs was the caption: "Dogs couldn't stop us."   Next to a picture of a policeman clubbing a prostrate form was the caption: "Police brutality couldn't stop us."   Following a picture of a fire hydrant and hose were the words: "Fire hoses couldn't stop us."   And beside the picture of a fat, bald-headed man (labelled BOSS) carrying a bag of money in one hand and a barbed club in the other were the words: "Are you going to let [the boss] stop you?"   The leaflet concluded with the statement: "A yes vote for the union is a yes vote for freedom."   Another leaflet contained an appeal to vote for the union coupled with the exhortation: "Be a free person—not a 'Handkerchief head Uncle Tom!'"   Still another leaflet quoted Martin Luther King on the subject of labor unions and then ended with a statement that "the labor hater is almost always a twin-headed creature spewing anti-Negro talk from one mouth, and anti-union talk from the other."

The representation election resulted in a victory for the union by a vote of 68–59.   Should the Board set aside the election?   See *Archer Laundry Co.*, 150 N.L.R.B. 1427 (1965); *N.L.R.B. v. Sumter Plywood Corp.*, 535 F.2d 917 (5th Cir. 1976), cert. denied 429 U.S. 1092, 97 S.Ct. 1105, 51 L.Ed.2d 538 (1977).

4.   Shortly before an election at its plant, the management of Mid-America Machinery, Inc. exhibited to its employees—on company time near the end of the workday—a color motion picture, roughly one-half hour in length, entitled "And Women Must Weep."   (The film is distributed by the National Right-to-Work Committee, and is designed to point out the evils of compulsory unionism.)   The motion picture, made principally with professional actors, purports to depict accurately a strike in a "middle American" community.   It shows the strike to have been sparked by an arrogant and irresponsible clique of union officers, to have split the community and alienated neighbors, and to have provoked excesses of violence, both on the picket line and throughout the community; the climax of the film is the shooting of an infant child of a worker who has been unsympathetic to the union cause.

The union lost the election and promptly filed objections.   It claims that the film inflamed the emotions, contained implied employer threats and contained a number of factual misrepresentations relating to the actual circumstances of the strike depicted.   (The latter claim is true. Indeed, the International Association of Machinists, the union depicted in "And Women Must Weep," has prepared a short film by way of rebuttal, entitled "Anatomy of a Lie.")   Should the Board set aside the election?   See *Luxuray of New York v. NLRB*, 447 F.2d 112 (2d Cir. 1971);

Litho Press, 211 N.L.R.B. 1014 (1974), enf'd 512 F.2d 73 (5th Cir. 1975). [Is it relevant whether the union showed "Anatomy of a Lie" at the union hall, after the employer's showing? Is it relevant whether the union had time to do so but did not?]

---

3.   *Other Forms of Interference, Restraint or Coercion*

NLRB v. LORBEN CORP.

United States Court of Appeals, Second Circuit, 1965.
345 F.2d 346.

MARSHALL, CIRCUIT JUDGE. * * * The basic facts are simple and undisputed. On April 1, 1963, Local 1922, International Brotherhood of Electrical Workers, AFL–CIO, began organizing respondent's plant and secured the adherence of four of the 25 or 26 employees. On April 4 the union held a meeting to decide what to do about the discharge of one of the employees believed to have been discharged for union activities. A strike was decided upon and picketing began the next day with placards reading: "Employees of Lorben Electronics Corporation on Strike—Please help us maintain decent working conditions." About two days later the discharged employee asked respondent's president whether he wanted to have any discussions with the union's officials and the president said he did not want to do so. Subsequently, respondent's president, on advice of counsel, prepared a paper with a question: "Do you wish Local 1922 of the Electrical Workers to represent you?" Under this were two columns, "yes" and "no." The plant superintendent handed the sheet to each employee explaining to each that each was free to sign or not sign. This was done throughout the plant. All of the employees signed in the "no" column. There is no evidence of any employee [sic] hostility to the union and the Trial Examiner found an absence of any "other unfair labor practices." However, the Examiner found that the respondent had violated the Act. While the Examiner mentioned the failure of respondent to advise the employees of the purpose of the interrogation and to assure them that no reprisals would follow, he based his decision primarily on his finding that the respondent had no legitimate purpose for the interrogation. The Board based its decision on the first two reasons and refused to rely on the third. We deny enforcement of the Board's order.

Employer interrogation of employees as to their desire to be represented by a particular union is not coercive or intimidating on its face. It is extremely difficult to determine how often and under what circumstances threats will be inferred by the employees. The resulting confusion from efforts to set up basic ground rules in this field is carefully explored by Prof. Derek C. Bok, The Regulation of Campaign Tactics in Representation Elections Under the National Labor Relations Act, 78 Harv.L.Rev. 38, 106 (1964).

The problem of delineating what is coercion by interrogation has resisted any set rules or specific limitations. The Board's original determination that interrogation by the employer was unlawful per se, Standard-Coosa-Thatcher Co., 85 N.L.R.B. 1358 (1949), was disapproved by the courts and the Board retreated to the position that interrogation would only be unlawful where it was found to be coercive in the light of all surrounding circumstances. As the Board stated in Blue Flash Express, Inc., 109 N.L.R.B. 591, 594 (1954): "We agree with and adopt the test laid down by the Court of Appeals for the Second Circuit in the Syracuse Color Press case [209 F.2d 596, cert. denied, 347 U.S. 966, 74 S.Ct. 777, 98 L.Ed. 1108 (1954)] which we construe to be that the answer to whether particular interrogation interferes with, restrains, and coerces employees must be found in the record as a whole." In Bourne v. NLRB, 332 F.2d 47, 48 (2 Cir. 1964), this Circuit reaffirmed this comprehensive approach and we attempted to suggest some of the many factors that must be considered anew in each case to determine whether a particular interrogation is coercive:

"(1) The background, i. e., is there a history of employer hostility and discrimination?

"(2) The nature of the information sought, e. g., did the interrogator appear to be seeking information on which to base taking action against individual employees?

"(3) The identity of the questioner, i. e., how high was he in the company hierarchy?

"(4) Place and method of interrogation, e. g., was employee called from work to the boss's office? Was there an atmosphere of 'unnatural formality'?

* * *

To enforce the Board's order which rests on this narrow ground alone, would be to depart from the line of decisions of this Circuit cited above, once approved by the Board, and we are not so inclined. While it is true that questioning can very well have a coercive effect where the purpose is not explained and there are no assurances against retaliation, cf. NLRB v. Camco, Inc., 340 F.2d 803 (5 Cir. 1965), we hold that the absence of these two factors, without more and in the face of the undisputed facts in the record of this case, fails to show coercion within the meaning of section 8(a)(1).

* * *

FRIENDLY, CIRCUIT JUDGE (dissenting):

The Board supported its conclusion that Lorben "violated 8(a) (1) of the Act in polling the employees" by saying that it relied "principally on the manner in which the poll was conducted, particularly the fact that Respondent did not explain the purpose of the poll to all of the employees, and did not offer or provide any assurances to the employees that their rights under the Act would not be infringed."

I fail to understand on what basis, in a case like this, we may properly reject the conditions to permissible interrogation which the Board has developed and here enforced. The Board's adoption, in Blue Flash Express, Inc., 109 N.L.R.B. 591, 594 (1954), of language used by this court in granting enforcement in NLRB v. Syracuse Color Press, Inc., 209 F.2d 596, 599 (2 Cir.), cert. denied 347 U.S. 966, 74 S.Ct. 777, 98 L.Ed. 1108 (1954), did not prevent it from later concluding, in the light of experience, that proper administration demanded working rules for reconciling the employer's desire to know what was afoot and the employees' need to be free from harassment, which would provide a test more definite, and more readily applicable, than "whether, under all the circumstances, the interrogation reasonably tends to restrain or interfere with the employees in the exercise of rights guaranteed by the Act," 109 N.L.R.B. at 593. See NLRB v. A. P. W. Prods., Inc., 316 F.2d 899, 905–906 (2 Cir.1963); Dickinson, Administrative Justice and the Supremacy of Law in the United States 143, 205 (1927). An agency receiving over 14,000 unfair labor practice charges a year, see 28 NLRB Ann.Rep. 161 (1963), ought not be denied the right to establish standards, appropriate to the statutory purpose, that are readily understandable by employers, regional directors and trial examiners, and be forced to determine every instance of alleged unlawful interrogation by an inquiry covering an employer's entire union history and his behavior during the particular crisis and to render decisions having little or no precedential value since "the number of distinct fact situations is almost infinite." See Bok, [The Regulation of Campaign Tactics Under the National Labor Relations Act, 78 Harv.L.Rev. 38 (1964)] at 111, and also at 64–65. The Board's power to rule that certain types of conduct constitute unfair labor practices without further proof of motivation or effect has been sustained in cases too numerous for anything more than illustrative citation. Republic Aviation Corp. v. NLRB, 324 U.S. 793, 65 S.Ct. 982, 89 L.Ed. 1372 (1945) (prohibition of union solicitation on company premises outside of working hours); Brooks v. NLRB, 348 U.S. 96, 75 S.Ct. 176, 99 L.Ed. 125 (1954) (one-year rule on duty to bargain); NLRB v. Katz, 369 U.S. 736, 82 S.Ct. 1107, 8 L.Ed.2d 230 (1962) (*per se* violations of duty to bargain); NLRB v. Marcus Trucking Co., 286 F.2d 583 (2 Cir. 1961) (contract bar rule). * * *

* * * Strict rules may not suit the casual question privately put to a few employees. But when the employer sets in motion a formal tabulation of this sort, it is not too much to ask that he provide some explanation and assure his employees against reprisal. Although my brothers condemn the Board's requirements, they do not explain why these rules are inappropriate or, more relevantly, why the Board may not reasonably think them so. * * *

* * * [O]ne need not hold a doctoral degree in psychology to realize that the method of polling here utilized, in contrast to other methods of testing employee sentiment that were readily available, entailed serious risk that some employees would indicate a position quite different from that really held and would then feel obliged to adhere to it. Whether by design or by accident, the first workers to be questioned might be preponderantly against the union; the display of such votes would inevitably affect later voters who would be inclined to "follow the leader" and would see little use in bucking a trend; and all this could have a snowballing effect. I cannot believe that if the Board had utilized its rule-making power, under § 6 of the Act, see Peck, The Atrophied Rule-Making Powers of the National Labor Relations Board, 70 Yale L.J. 729 (1961), to prohibit such a means of ascertaining employee views as tending to "interfere with" rights guaranteed by § 7, and insisted on methods whereby each employee would indicate his sentiments without knowing those of others, any court would strike that down. I see no justification for a different result when the Board has followed the equally valid course of reaching its conclusion by the decision of a particular case. See NLRB v. A. P. W. Prods., Inc., supra, 316 F.2d at 905.

I would grant enforcement.

OPERATING ENGINEERS LOCAL 49 v. NLRB
(STRUKSNES CONSTRUCTION CO.)

United States Court of Appeals, District of Columbia Circuit, 1965.
353 F.2d 852.

National Labor Relations Board, 1967.
165 N.L.R.B. 1062.

[The respondent, Struksnes Construction Co., performed highway construction work in North Dakota. The union began to organize at one job site, and its representative, McPherson, requested recognition as bargaining agent; he asserted, in a letter of August 12, 1963, that the union represented twenty employees in what was a unit of twenty-six employees. Mr. Struksnes denied that the union had such support. He then proceeded to circulate among all of his employees a petition which was inscribed: "Do you want me to bargain with and sign a contract with Operating Engineers Local 49? Please sign your name and answer Yes or No." Struksnes personally solicited the signatures of employees at the end of one shift, and his two foremen secured signatures from the others. "I told them what was up here, and I asked them to sign yes or no, and it wouldn't make any difference." He did not, however, call a general meeting to explain his purpose for ascertaining the workers' desires regarding a union contract or to assure them of no reprisals. Twenty-four men signed the statement, nine voting yes, and fifteen voting no; the identity and the vote of each employee was known to Mr. Struksnes and his foremen. Apart from this incident there was no bias shown against union supporters and no interference with organizing efforts. The Board found the poll not to violate Section 8(a)(1), but the court of appeals set aside the Board's order.]

OPINION OF THE COURT OF APPEALS

* * * We are by no means satisfied with the Board's ad hoc acquiescence in, if not approval of, the manner in which the Employer polled his men. * * * The Board here simply dismisses, *sub silentio*, the development of a permanent record of the votes of each employee set against his signature after interrogation had been conducted in personal approach by the employer and his foremen, and otherwise under the circumstances we outlined. Although a majority of the employees were members of the union, had they succumbed to coercion when they voted in the negative upon being queried as to whether or not they desired their employer to enter into a contract with their union? The Board's Decision and Order discloses no treatment of the possibly inherent restraint resulting from such contacts. * * *

In respect of the conclusion here reached by the Board, its reasoning seems to have applied and found satisfied the criteria suggested in *Blue Flash Express, Inc.* In our judgment, that is not enough * * *.

We think the Board should come to grips with this constantly recurring problem for the protection of the employees as to their section 7 rights and for that of an employer acting in good faith. It would seem that the Board could, in the exercise of its expertise, develop appropriate policy considerations [21] and outline at least min-

---

21. We agree with the views set forth in Judge Friendly's dissenting opinion in N.L.R.B. v. Lorben Corporation, * * *; and see Peck, The Atrophied Rule-Making Powers of the National Labor Relations Board, 70 Yale L.J. 729 (1961).

imal standards to govern the ascertainment of union status, or even in given permissible situations, the desire of the employees respecting a contract with the Union.[22]

We will set aside the Board's order and remand this case for further consideration not inconsistent with this opinion.

Reversed and remanded.

[The dissenting opinion of EDGERTON, C. J., has been omitted.]

NLRB SUPPLEMENTAL DECISION AND ORDER

* * *

A.   *Standards Applicable to Determining the Legality of Polls*

We have, in accord with the court's directive, reviewed Board and court decisions, as well as articles by scholars in this field, in order to establish standards which may be used as guidelines to determine whether a poll is lawful.

In our view any attempt by an employer to ascertain employee views and sympathies regarding unionism generally tends to cause fear of reprisal in the mind of the employee if he replies in favor of unionism and, therefore, tends to impinge on his Section 7 rights. As we have pointed out, "An employer cannot discriminate against union adherents without first determining who they are." That such employee fear is not without foundation is demonstrated by the innumerable cases in which the prelude to discrimination was the employer's inquiries as to the union sympathies of his employees.

It was the Board's original view that an employer's poll of his employees was in and of itself coercive and therefore a *per se* violation of Section 8(a)(1).[23] Some courts disagreed with that view, and the Board in *Blue Flash* established the rule that whether a poll interferes with, restrains, or coerces employees "must be found in the record as a whole," and that the time, place, personnel involved, information sought, and the employer's known preference must be

---

22. * * *
   Rule-making in this area, it would seem, might have obviated the difficulty here as in many of the cases with which the Board says it has been "continually confronted." Certainly the Board has rule-making authority as the Act expressly provides. 29 U.S.C. § 156 (1964).

23. See cases to that effect cited in *Blue Flash Express, Inc.*, supra. It

is well established that an employer, in questioning his employees as to their union sympathies, is not expressing views, argument, or opinion within the meaning of Section 8(c) of the Act, as the purpose of an inquiry is not to express views but to ascertain those of the person questioned. Martin Sprocket & Gear Co., Inc. v. N.L.R.B., 329 F.2d 417 (C.A.5); N.L.R.B. v. Minnesota Mining & Mfg. Co., 179 F.2d 323 (C.A.8).

considered. The Board found the poll in *Blue Flash* lawful on the ground that (1) the employer's sole purpose was to ascertain whether the union demanding recognition actually represented a majority of the employees, (2) the employees were so informed, (3) assurances against reprisal were given, and (4) the questioning occurred in a background free from employer hostility to union organization.

Although the courts have not disapproved of the Board's *Blue Flash* rule, some of the courts have disagreed with the Board on the application of the rule in specific cases, and a few courts have adopted their own tests for determining whether a poll was lawful under *Blue Flash*. The result has been to create considerable uncertainty in this area of labor-management relations. Furthermore, our experience since *Blue Flash* indicates that that rule has not operated to discourage intimidation of employees by employer polls.

As recent Board decisions have emphasized, there are clearly uncoercive methods for an employer to verify a union's majority status. An employer faced with a union demand for recognition may normally refrain from according recognition; he may also request proof of majority status; or he may file a petition, or suggest that the union do so, and await the outcome of a Board election.

We have therefore determined, in the light of all the foregoing considerations, and in accord with the court's remand, to adopt the following revision of the *Blue Flash* criteria:

> Absent unusual circumstances, the polling of employees by an employer will be violative of Section 8(a)(1) of the Act unless the following safeguards are observed: (1) the purpose of the poll is to determine the truth of a union's claim of majority, (2) this purpose is communicated to the employees, (3) assurances against reprisal are given, (4) the employees are polled by secret ballot, and (5) the employer has not engaged in unfair labor practices or otherwise created a coercive atmosphere.

The purpose of the polling in these circumstances is clearly relevant to an issue raised by a union's claim for recognition and is therefore lawful. The requirement that the lawful purpose be communicated to the employees, along with assurances against reprisal, is designed to allay any fear of discrimination which might otherwise arise from the polling, and any tendency to interfere with employees' Section 7 rights. Secrecy of the ballot will give further assurance that reprisals cannot be taken against employees because the views of each individual will not be known. And the absence of employer unfair labor practices or other conduct creating a coercive atmosphere will serve as a further warranty to the employees that the poll does not have some unlawful object, contrary to the lawful purpose stated by the employer. In accord with presumptive rules applied by the Board with court approval in other situations, this rule is designed to effectuate the purposes of the Act by maintaining a reasonable balance between the protection of employee rights and legitimate interests of employers.

On the other hand, a poll taken while a petition for a Board election is pending does not, in our view, serve any legitimate interest of the employer that would not be better served by the forthcoming Board election. In accord with long-established Board policy, therefore, such polls will continue to be found violative of Section 8(a)(1) of the Act. - only if forthcoming Board election

B. *The Polling Issue in the Instant Case*

* * *

We have reviewed the circumstances of this poll in the light of the court's opinion and remand order and also of the rule established herein. In view of the failure of the Respondent to inform its employees of the purpose of the poll and the nonsecret manner in which the employees were polled, the Respondent's conduct would probably be found unlawful if this case were now before us for an initial determination under the new rule. We are satisfied, however, that in the special circumstances of this case no remedial order is warranted. Thus the poll previously was found lawful by the Board under the *Blue Flash* rule, which was in effect at the time the events herein occurred. Moreover, as the court noted in its opinion, the work at the jobsite where the poll was taken apparently was scheduled to be concluded within 3 months after these events took place, which was more than 3 years ago. All things considered, we find in these circumstances that effectuation of the purposes of the Act does not require a remedial order. Accordingly, we shall reaffirm the Board's original Decision and Order dismissing the complaint in its entirety.

Problems for Discussion

1. What are the respective merits and disadvantages of the rather firm guidelines developed by the Board on remand in *Struksnes* and the more flexible guidelines mandated by the court of appeals in *Lorben*? In making that appraisal, you should consider such matters as the impact of these different guidelines upon the parties engaging in an organizing or election campaign, the Regional Director in issuing a complaint, the Administrative Law Judge and the Board in making their decision and the courts of appeals in reviewing that decision. You should also consider the validity of the Board's underlying assumption that systematic ques-

tioning of employees about their support for the union does in fact have a coercive impact. See p. 201 (item 7), infra.

2.   Were a case to arise now before the Board involving an employer poll regarding employee support for the union, and the employer were situated in the second federal circuit, which guidelines should the Board employ in deciding the case? (You should consult sections 10(e) and (f) of the Labor Act.)

3.   Considering the nature of the guidelines articulated by the Board on remand in the *Struksnes* case, can it be argued that the Board's action violated the mandate of the Supreme Court in NLRB v. Wyman-Gordon Co., p. 136 supra? Is the order ultimately entered by the Board in *Struksnes* of relevance to this question?

4.   Assume that in each of the following hypothetical situations, the employer's poll is conducted under the following circumstances: employees are told the purpose of the inquiry, they are informed that their jobs are not endangered and that they are free not to answer, and the employee responses are tabulated by a three-employee committee without any matching of names with votes. In each instance, has the employer acted lawfully?

(a) The employer learns that a union organizer is making home visits to employees, and the employer conducts a poll to determine how many employees would like to bargain collectively.

(b) The union files a petition for an election, and the employer polls the employees to determine how many have signed authorization cards, acting upon information from some employees that the union was unable to secure valid cards from thirty percent of the workers so as to make a "showing of interest" before the NLRB. See *S. H. Kress & Co. v. NLRB*, 317 F.2d 225 (9th Cir. 1963).

(c) The Regional Director has ordered that a certification election is to be held, and two weeks before the election date the employer conducts a poll to determine how many employees favor the union.

[Why, by the way, doesn't the union violate the Labor Act by making the home visits and gathering the authorization cards?]

5.   The company employed an undercover operative to report on the incipient organizational activities of the union at one of its plants. The operative posed as an ardent supporter of organized labor, worked his way into a strategic position to uncover any movement to organize the company's employees and on one occasion openly supported a strike by addressing the strikers at a union-sponsored rally. He was accepted by union officials as a sympathizer with organized labor. Eventually the union uncovered the employer operative and filed a Section 8(a)(1) charge against the company. The employer defends on the ground that it was impossible for the employees to be coerced by the operative's surveillance since they were totally unaware of it. How should the Board rule? See *Virginia Elec. & Power Co.* v. *NLRB*, 44 N.L.R.B. 404 (1942), enf'd 132 F.

2d 390 (4th Cir. 1942), aff'd 319 U.S. 533 (1943); *Cannon Electric Co.,*
151 N.L.R.B. 1465 (1965).

NLRB v. EXCHANGE PARTS CO.

Supreme Court of the United States, 1964.
375 U.S. 405, 84 S.Ct. 457, 11 L.Ed.2d 435.

MR. JUSTICE HARLAN delivered the opinion of the Court.

This case presents a question concerning the limitations which
§ 8(a) (1) of the National Labor Relations Act, 49 Stat. 452 (1935),
as amended, 29 U.S.C. § 158(a) (1), places on the right of an employer to confer economic benefits on his employees shortly before a
representation election.   The precise issue is whether that section
prohibits the conferral of such benefits, without more, where the
employer's purpose is to affect the outcome of the election. * * *

[On November 9, 1959, the Company was advised by the Boilermakers Union that a majority of employees had designated it as
their bargaining representative.   On November 16, the Union filed
an election petition with the NLRB, and an election was ultimately
ordered to be held on March 18, 1960.   On March 4, the Company
sent its employees a letter, accompanied by a detailed statement of
the benefits granted by the Company since 1949; the letter made
such statements as "The Union can't put any of those things in your
envelope—*only the Company can do that.* * * *   [I]t didn't
take a Union to get any of those things and * * * it won't take a
Union to get additional improvements in the future."   Included in
the statement of benefits for 1960 were a new system for computing overtime during holiday weeks which had the effect of increasing wages for those weeks, and a new vacation schedule which enabled employees to extend their vacations by sandwiching them
between two weekends.   This was the first general announcement of
these changes to the employees.   The Union lost the election.

The Board found that the announcement and grant of the overtime and vacation benefits were arranged with the intention of inducing the employees to vote against the union, and held this to
violate Section 8(a)(1).   The court of appeals accepted the finding
regarding the Company's intention but reversed the Board, noting
that "the benefits were put into effect unconditionally on a permanent basis, and no one has suggested that there was any implication the benefits would be withdrawn, if the workers voted for the
union."   The Supreme Court reversed.]

The broad purpose of § 8(a) (1) is to establish "the right of
employes to organize for mutual aid without employer interference."

Republic Aviation Corp. v. N. L. R. B., 324 U.S. 793, 798, 65 S.Ct. 982, 985, 89 L.Ed. 1372. We have no doubt that it prohibits not only intrusive threats and promises but also conduct immediately favorable to employees which is undertaken with the express purpose of impinging upon their freedom of choice for or against unionization and is reasonably calculated to have that effect. In Medo Photo Supply Corp. v. N. L. R. B., 321 U.S. 678, 686, 64 S.Ct. 830, 834, 88 L.Ed. 1007, this Court said: "The action of employees with respect to the choice of their bargaining agents may be induced by favors bestowed by the employer as well as by his threats or domination." Although in that case there was already a designated bargaining agent and the offer of "favors" was in response to a suggestion of the employees that they would leave the union if favors were bestowed, the principles which dictated the result there are fully applicable here. The danger inherent in well-timed increases in benefits is the suggestion of a fist inside the velvet glove. Employees are not likely to miss the inference that the source of benefits now conferred is also the source from which future benefits must flow and which may dry up if it is not obliged.[24] The danger may be diminished if, as in this case, the benefits are conferred permanently and unconditionally. But the absence of conditions or threats pertaining to the particular benefits conferred would be of controlling significance only if it could be presumed that no question of additional benefits or renegotiation of existing benefits would arise in the future; and, of course, no such presumption is tenable.

Other Courts of Appeals have found a violation of § 8(a) (1) in the kind of conduct involved here. * * * It is true, as the court below pointed out, that in most cases of this kind the increase in benefits could be regarded as "one part of an overall program of interference and restraint by the employer," 304 F.2d, at 372, and that in this case the questioned conduct stood in isolation. Other unlawful conduct may often be an indication of the motive behind a grant of benefits while an election is pending, and to that extent it is relevant to the legality of the grant; but when as here the motive is otherwise established, an employer is not free to violate § 8(a) (1) by conferring benefits simply because it refrains

---

24. The inference was made almost explicit in Exchange Parts' letter to its employees of March 4, already quoted, which said: "The Union can't put any of those * * * [benefits] in your envelope—*only the Company can do that.*" (Original italics.) We place no reliance, however, on these or other words of the respondent dissociated from its conduct. Section 8(c) of the Act, 61 Stat. 142 (1947), 29 U.S.C. § 158 (c), provides that the expression or dissemination of "any views, argument, or opinion" "shall not constitute or be evidence of an unfair labor practice under any of the provisions of this Act, if such expression contains no threat of reprisal or force or promise of benefit."

from other, more obvious violations. We cannot agree with the Court of Appeals that enforcement of the Board's order will have the "ironic" result of "discouraging benefits for labor." 304 F.2d, at 376. The beneficence of an employer is likely to be ephemeral if prompted by a threat of unionization which is subsequently removed. Insulating the right of collective organization from calculated good will of this sort deprives employees of little that has lasting value.

Problems for Discussion

1. Why is a promise of benefit linked in Section 8(c) with a threat of reprisal, both being excluded from the protection of that section of the Act? When a union promises benefits contingent upon being elected bargaining representative, is there a violation of Section 8(b)(1) (or an exclusion from the protection of Section 8(c))?

2. When Justice Harlan in *Exchange Parts* considers an outright grant of a benefit, as distinguished from a promise to grant it if the union loses, how does he (and the other Justices) know that such a grant will be understood by employees to be an intrusive threat? If you were an employee and witnessed your employer granting an unprecedented benefit on the eve of a representation election, would you be intimidated? *NO.*

3. During a representation campaign at its Fort Lee, New Jersey plant, the Rosow Textile Company raised wages at its eighty-five plants across the country, including its Fort Lee plant. The union immediately filed an unfair labor practice charge. Should the General Counsel issue a complaint? See *Delchamps, Inc. v. NLRB*, 588 F.2d 476 (5th Cir. 1979).

4. Fashionfair Department Store is the only large unorganized department store in the city, all the others having been organized in a large drive four years ago. Several months ago, the union initiated an organizing campaign at Fashionfair. During the campaign, the union negotiated new agreements with the other large stores in which a ten cent wage increase was included. Immediately thereafter, Fashionfair raised its wages by ten cents in accordance with its policy of several years standing to maintain a five cent premium over the wage rates at other stores. Would the wage increase be lawful under *Exchange Parts*? Would it be relevant that the company's policy is based on a determination

    (a) simply to maintain the five cent premium in order to enhance the company's prestige and public image? or

    (b) to prevent its own employees from leaving and going to work for competitors? (See *NLRB v. Gotham Indus., Inc.*, 406 F.2d 1306 (1st Cir. 1969).) or

    (c) to keep out incipient union organizing pursuant to an announced company policy made four years ago?

5. The management of Acme Manufacturing Co. called ten meetings with employees in the one-month period prior to the date set for a Board-supervised representation election. Although attendance was voluntary, almost all of the employees attended these meetings. Meetings of this

kind had not been held in the past and, with the exception of the plant manager, the management representatives at the meetings were not previously known to the employees. The president of Acme told the employees that the union organizing campaign had brought home to her the fact that employees might have some legitimate complaints. She refrained from specifically soliciting such complaints at these meetings, and in fact stated that while she had an open mind she was making no promises that action would be taken on any or all complaints. When the president opened up the meetings for questions and discussion, the employees inevitably began to air certain of their grievances, which led to further discourse (sometimes quite vigorous) between employees and management representatives. The union narrowly lost the election and, arguing that the meetings unlawfully interfered with employee rights, has sought a rerun election. How should the Board rule? Compare Raley's, Inc., 236 N.L.R.B. 971 (1978), enf'd mem., 105 L.R.R.M. 2304, 89 CCH Lab. Cas. ¶ 12157 (9th Cir. 1979), with Uarco, Inc., 216 N.L.R.B. 1 (1975).

6. The Newberry Company has had a long-established policy of periodic performance reviews of every employee at six-month intervals. Wage increases were based on merit and were therefore neither automatic nor uniform. However, an employee who performed satisfactorily could reasonably expect a wage increase; if no increase was granted, an explanation would be given. In May 1976, just before the company was to begin its performance reviews, Local 554 of the General Drivers Union informed Newberry by letter that it was about to undertake an organizing campaign among the company's employees.

Upon advice of counsel, the company posted a copy of the union's letter on the employee bulletin board and announced that it was temporarily suspending the wage review system. In several instances, management informed employees that they deserved wage increases but that the company could not grant them until the union issue was settled. The Board, in a proceeding under Section 8(a)(1), finds that the company's action has coerced employees, and orders that employees be made whole for any loss suffered by suspension of the wage review. Should the court of appeals enforce the Board's order? See *J. J. Newberry Co.* v. *NLRB*, 442 F.2d 897 (2d Cir. 1971).

---

4. *Union Misconduct Affecting Self-Organization*

Most important of all the Taft-Hartley amendments affecting the establishment of collective bargaining relationships was the creation of a list of unfair labor practices by labor organizations. The heart of the original Wagner Act was contained in Section 7—

"Employees shall have the right to self-organization, to form, join, or assist labor organizations, to bargain collectively through representatives of their own choosing, and to engage in concerted activities, for the purpose of collective bargaining or other mutual aid or protection."

In passing the original act Congress rejected the argument that mutuality required a grant of protection against interference, coercion and restraint by labor organizations as well as by employers; and although this decision was often defended on the ground that it would bring about federal intervention in matters better regulated by local police authorities, the true ground of objection was that such a measure would be inconsistent with the policy of encouraging union organization and collective bargaining.

The Taft-Hartley amendments remade Section 7 by guaranteeing employees, in addition to the right to form, join or assist labor organizations, "the right to refrain from any or all such activities". Moreover, Section 8(b) (1) declares it to be an unfair labor practice for a labor organization or its agents to restrain or coerce employees in the exercise of rights guaranteed by Section 7. Section 8(b) (4) prohibits various concerted activities to bring about unionization.

The psychological effect of this reversal of policy cut wide and deep into industrial relations. Since these amendments seem to declare the indifference of the government to the spread of organization, they remove one of the most effective arguments of the union organizer, who had theretofore been in a position to appeal to unorganized workers on the ground that in joining a labor union they would follow their government's desires. The practical impact of this group of amendments on techniques of organization is also important. For example, Section 8(b)(4) forbids the use of the secondary boycott to achieve recognition and also (as expanded in 1959 in Section 8(b)(7)) prohibits certain primary strikes and picketing by unions seeking immediate recognition and bargaining rights. These and related union violations in aid of organization are considered in detail in Part Four of this casebook.

Still other union organizational tactics are proscribed by Section 8(b)(1), also enacted in 1947. Its position and language, except for the omission of the words "interfere with," roughly parallel those of Section 8(a)(1), and its sponsors repeatedly explained that it would make it unfair for unions to engage in activities which were unfair when engaged in by employers.[25] But the scope of Section

25. 93 Cong.Rec. 4136, 4500. In its original form the amendment, following the exact words of Section 8(a) (1), made it an unfair labor practice for a labor organization "to interfere with, restrain or coerce" employees in the exercise of the rights guaranteed by Section 7, Supplemental Views of Senator Taft and Others, S.Rep. 105, 80th Cong., 1st Sess., p. 50; 93 Cong. Rec. 4136. Senator Ives opposed this amendment as "definitely anti-labor". 93 Cong.Rec. 4139–4140. Five days later he stated that it would be acceptable if the words "interfere with" were struck out. 93 Cong.Rec. 4399. The deletion was made without objection on the basis of Senator Taft's statement that "elimination of the words 'Interfere with' would not, so far as they ['the attorneys'] know, have any effect on the court decisions. Elimination of those words would not make any substantial change in the meaning". 93 Cong.Rec. 4399. Moreover, as Senator Morse pointed out on the floor, the National Labor Relations Board appears never to have distinguished between interference and coercion or restraint. 93 Cong.Rec. 4557.

8(b)(1) is very much narrower than that of Section 8(a)(1). One great difference is this: although an employer is forbidden to express the hope that he may be able to raise wages and improve working conditions if the union is defeated, an important argument made by labor organizations to secure union members, the legitimacy of which cannot be questioned, is that if enough employees join the union it will be able to obtain additional advantages whereas if they do not, it may be unable to prevent a reduction in wages. Many unions offer mutual insurance and similar benefits to their members in addition to what is obtained by collective bargaining. It cannot be the intent of Section 8(b) (1) to prohibit them from pointing out these advantages in seeking to enlist new members. Much the same is true of social pressures. While an employer may not segregate a union employee in order to hold him up to the ridicule of his fellows, it will scarcely be asserted that labor organizations are forbidden to ostracize nonmembers or to impose other social pressures upon them.

In many cases, however, especially those involving fraud or intimidation, the two sections operate alike. The NLRB Annual Report for the year ending June 30, 1950, gives a summary of typical cases under Section 8(b) (1) (A):

"Union conduct not connected with strikes was held violative of section 8(b) (1) (A) where it was found to have been reasonably calculated to coerce employees in maintaining or refraining from acquiring union membership. Thus, the Board * * * held coercive: a speech in front of an employer's store informing the audience that the union intended to organize the store and 'that wives and children of employees had better stay out of the way if they didn't want to get hurt'; a union president's warning to rival union supporters not to come to work, accompanied by such threats as that there would be 'trouble out there, guns, knives, and blackjacks'; assaults and batteries on nonunion employees during an organizational campaign; and a union official's remark to an employee, in the course of an organizational drive, that 'there may be trouble later' if the employees refused to sign a dues checkoff authorization."

It should be noted at this point that Section 8(b)(1)(A) serves two other important functions, typically outside the context of organizing activities. It protects workers who are already union members against disciplinary action taken by the union—such as expulsion, suspension or fines—for certain classes of protected employee activities. (See pp. 1097–123, infra.) It also provides a remedy before the NLRB for some forms of discrimination or oppression by a union representative against unpopular individuals or minority groups. (See pp. 1002–09, infra.)

The Labor Act also imposes some limits upon the extent to which a union may induce discrimination by the employer in aid of organization (see Section 8(b)(2) and pp. 1082–90, infra), and upon the extent to which a union may use promises of benefit. Compare the *Exchange Parts* case, p. 190, supra. The latter issue is the subject of the following case.

NLRB v. SAVAIR MFG. CO.

Supreme Court of the United States, 1974.
414 U.S. 270, 94 S.Ct. 495, 38 L.Ed.2d 495.

MR. JUSTICE DOUGLAS delivered the opinion of the Court.

The National Labor Relations Board, acting pursuant to § 9(c) of the National Labor Relations Act, as amended, 61 Stat. 144, 29 U.S.C. § 159(c), conducted an election by secret ballot among the production and maintenance employees of respondent at the request of the Mechanics Educational Society of America (hereafter Union). Under the Act the Union, if it wins the election, becomes "the exclusive representative of all the employees" in that particular unit for purposes of collective bargaining. The Union won the election by a vote of 22–20. [The employer refused to bargain with the certified union, and the Board found a violation of Section 8(a)(5) and issued a bargaining order. The court of appeals reversed, and the Supreme Court affirmed the order to dismiss the complaint.]

It appeared that prior to the election, "recognition slips" were circulated among employees. An employee who signed the slip before the election [26] became a member of the Union and would not have to pay what at times was called an "initiation fee" and at times a "fine." If the Union was voted in, those who had not signed a recognition slip would have to pay. * * *

The Board originally took the position that pre-election solicitation of memberships by a union with a promise to waive the initiation fee of the union was not consistent with a fair and free choice

---

26. * * *
The Court of Appeals read the Hearing Officer's Report to state that the waiver was limited to those signing up before the election, as do we. * * * The Board argues that unions have a valid interest in waiving the initiation fee when the union has not yet been chosen as a bargaining representative, because " '[e]mployees otherwise sympathetic to the union might well have been reluctant to pay out money before the union had done anything for them. Waiver of the [initiation fees] would remove this artificial obstacle to their endorsement of the union.' " See Amalgamated Clothing Workers v. NLRB, 345 F.2d 264, 268. While this union interest is legitimate, the Board's argument ignores the fact that this interest can be preserved as well by waiver of initiation fees available not only to those who have signed up with the union before an election but also to those who join after the election. The limitation imposed by the Union in this case—to those joining before the election—is necessary only because it serves the additional purpose of affecting the Union organizational campaign and the election.

of bargaining representatives.   Lobue Bros., 109 N.L.R.B. 1182. Later in DIT–MCO, Inc., 163 N.L.R.B. 1019, the Board explained its changed position as follows:

> "We shall assume, *arguendo*, that employees who sign cards when offered a waiver of initiation fees do so solely because no cost is thus involved; that they in fact do not at that point really want the union to be their bargaining representative.   The error of the *Lobue* premise can be readily seen upon a review of the consequences of such employees casting votes for or against union representation.   Initially, it is obvious that employees who have received or been promised free memberships will not be required to pay an initiation fee, *whatever the outcome of the vote*.   If the union wins the election, there is by postulate no obligation; and if the union loses, *there is still no obligation*, because compulsion to pay an initiation fee arises under the Act only when a union becomes the employees' representative and negotiates a valid union-security agreement.   Thus, whatever kindly feeling toward the union may be generated by the cost-reduction offer, when consideration is given only to the question of initiation fees, it is completely illogical to characterize as improper inducement or coercion to vote 'Yes' a waiver of something that can be avoided simply by voting 'No.'

> "The illogic of *Lobue* does not become any more logical when other consequences of a vote for representation are considered.   Thus, employees know that if a majority vote for the union, it will be their exclusive representative, and, provided a valid union-security provision is negotiated, they will be obliged to pay dues as a condition of employment.   Thus, viewed solely as a financial matter, a 'no' vote will help to avoid any subsequent obligations, a 'yes' may well help to incur such obligations.   In these circumstances, an employee who did not want the union to represent him would hardly be likely to vote for the union just because there would be no initial cost involved in obtaining membership.   Since an election resulting in the union's defeat would entail not only no initial cost, but also insure that no dues would have to be paid as a condition of employment, the financial inducement, if a factor at all, would be in the direction of a vote against the union, rather than for it."
Id., at 1021–1022.

We are asked to respect the expertise of the Board on this issue, giving it leeway to alter or modify its policy in light of its ongoing experience with the problem. The difficulty is not in that principle but with the standards to govern the conduct of elections under § 9(c)(1)(A). * * *

[T]he Board's analysis ignores the realities of the situation.

Whatever his true intentions, an employee who signs a recognition slip prior to an election is indicating to other workers that he supports the union. His outward manifestation of support must often serve as a useful campaign tool in the union's hands to convince other employees to vote for the union, if only because many employees respect their coworkers' views on the unionization issue. By permitting the union to offer to waive an initiation fee for those employees signing a recognition slip prior to the election, the Board allows the union to buy endorsements and paint a false portrait of employee support during its election campaign.

That influence may well have been felt here for, as noted, there were 28 who signed up with the Union before the election petition was filed with the Board and either seven or eight more who signed up before the election. We do not believe that the statutory policy of fair elections * * * permits endorsements, whether for or against the union, to be bought and sold in this fashion.

In addition, while it is correct that the employee who signs a recognition slip is not legally bound to vote for the union and has not promised to do so in any formal sense, certainly there may be some employees who would feel obliged to carry through on their stated intention to support the union. And on the facts of this case, the change of just one vote would have resulted in a 21–21 election rather than a 22–20 election.

Any procedure requiring a "fair" election must honor the right of those who oppose a union as well as those who favor it. The Act is wholly neutral when it comes to that basic choice. * * *

Whether it would be an "unfair" labor practice for a union to promise a special benefit to those who sign up for a union seems not to have been squarely resolved. The right of a free choice is, however, inherent in the principles reflected in § 9(c)(1)(A). * * *

In the *Exchange Parts* case we said that, although the benefits granted by the employer were permanent and unconditional, employees were "not likely to miss the inference that the source of benefits now conferred is also the source from which future benefits must flow and which may dry up if it is not obliged." 375 U.S., at 409. If we respect, as we must, the statutory right of employees to resist efforts to unionize a plant, we cannot assume that unions exercising powers are wholly benign towards their antagonists whether they be nonunion protagonists or the employer. The failure to sign a recognition slip may well seem ominous to nonunionists who fear that if they do not sign they will face a wrathful union regime, should the union win. That influence may well have had a decisive impact in this case where a change of one vote would have changed the result.

Affirmed.

[The dissenting opinion of MR. JUSTICE WHITE has been omitted.]

Problems for Discussion

1.   Does the union's conduct in the *Savair* case violate Section 8(b) (1)? What would be the advantages to the employer of attacking that conduct through unfair labor practice procedures rather than the procedures actually utilized in that case?

2.   The union promised to waive payment of dues and initiation fees until after a certification election and until it had negotiated an agreement with the employer. The union won the election 50–43. The employer refused to bargain, claiming that the union was able to "buy" employee-members before the election and portray a false picture of its employee support in violation of *Savair* and that therefore the election should be set aside. The Board, in a proceeding under Section 8(a)(5) for refusal to bargain, has rejected the employer's argument and issued a bargaining order. Should the Board's order be enforced on review? See *NLRB* v. *Wabash Transformer Corp.*, 509 F.2d 647 (8th Cir. 1975).

AN EMPIRICAL POSTSCRIPT

As has already been mentioned, many of the Board's assumptions relating to the impact of election campaigns have been challenged, as the result of a major empirical study, in Getman, Goldberg & Herman, Union Representation Elections: Law and Reality (1976). An attempt will be made here to summarize the findings and conclusions of those authors, although a full appreciation of their work will depend upon the student's examination of the complete book.

1.   Most workers are not unsophisticated about union organizing campaigns; a very substantial number have been union members elsewhere and a large number have voted in previous NLRB elections.

2.   Most workers have firm opinions about whether or not they want a union, even before the campaign has begun; these opinions are based on general attitudes about working conditions and unions. The votes of 81 percent of the employees could be predicted from their pre-campaign attitudes and intent.

3. The amount of authorization cards signed by employees is a reasonably accurate predictor of their vote in a subsequent NLRB election. 72 percent of the employees who signed cards later voted for union representation. 79 percent of the employees who did not sign cards later voted against union representation.

4. Employees are not generally attentive to the campaign. The average employee in the study remembered fewer than 10 percent of the company campaign themes and 7 percent of the union themes. There is no evidence that specific issues of the employer's campaign were related to employee vote; initial union supporters who switched to the company were no more familiar with the company campaign than those who did not switch. Such a switch is not caused by greater information supplied by the company during the campaign or by employer coercion; rather, the employee's dissatisfaction with working conditions apparently lessens. Only the small percentage of employees who started as company supporters but ultimately vote for the union appear to fit the NLRB stereotype of the employee who is convinced by the campaign issues; such employees are significantly more familiar with the union campaign than company supporters who did not switch.

5. Although some 20 percent of the employees questioned reported employer threats of reprisals, or actual reprisals, against union supporters, this perception was unrelated to actual employer threats and reprisals. Even when employees are not reminded by the employer of its economic power and the ability to use it against union supporters, employees are aware of those facts. Lawful employer speech can just as effectively generate fears of reprisal, so that it is not surprising that employer campaigning viewed by the Board as potentially coercive and unlawful is not any more associated with a loss of union support than is "clean" campaigning. Indeed, persons starting out as union supporters are unaffected by threats or reprisals, as they have in effect anticipated these in making their initial decision to support the union; such employer action is regarded as confirmation of the need for protection by a union. Unions do not lose significantly more of their initial supporters in elections marked by very serious employer coercion than in elections in which there is no unlawful campaigning.

6. The promise or grant of benefits—even in conjunction with employer reprisals—does not increase the perception or fear of reprisals, in comparison to "clean" employer campaigns. Such promises or grants are regarded as untrustworthy or as inadequate compared to the expected benefits of unionization. Employees who reported promises and grants of benefit were actually more likely to vote for union representation than were other employees.

7.   Any discharge of a union supporter during an organizing campaign is likely to be viewed by other union supporters as having been motivated by the employer's anti-union sentiments, whether or not that was in fact the case.   That view does not, however, coerce such workers into voting against the union.   In fact, employees reporting such a discriminatory discharge were more likely to vote for the union than employees not reporting such action.

8.   Although illegal interrogation took place in some sixteen of the elections studied (involving more than 400 employees), and general interrogation was widespread in those elections, only 29 employees reported that interrogation had taken place.   Employees appear not to be sensitive to interrogation—indeed, some 43 percent of the union voters believed that the employer was fully aware of their position on unionization anyway—and it seems unlikely that interrogation is a substantial deterrent to union support.

9.   In spite of the assumption in *Savair* that employees who are inclined to vote against the union will submerge that inclination once it is known that they have signed an authorization card, there is no empirical support for such an assumption.   Nor does there appear to be any significant relationship between the proportion of authorization cards initially signed and a subsequent gain in union strength by the time of the election.

10.   These and other conclusions induced the authors to make the following recommendations: (a) NLRB campaign regulations should not be based on Board assumptions about the impact of particular campaign practices.   (b) As in a political campaign, labor elections should not be set aside (or unfair labor practices found) on account of written or oral campaign communications by employers or unions; the right of rebuttal, and voter intelligence, should be relied upon, rather than the government, to uncover invalid and irrelevant communications.   (c) Express or implied threats and promises should not be unlawful and should not be a basis for invalidating an election; even discriminatory discharges should not justify invalidating an election, although there should of course be unfair labor practice redress for the discriminatee. (d) If an employer holds campaign meetings, or permits individual campaigning by supervisors, on company premises, it should be required to afford the union an equal opportunity.   (e) Since flagrant retaliatory *acts* by an employer (as distinguished from speech) may have the effect of seriously chilling incipient union support, NLRB unfair labor practice remedies should be strengthened so as to include preliminary injunctive relief to obtain reinstatement of discharged employees, treble damages for lost earnings, and loss of government contracts.

What flaws, if any, do you find in these recommendations? If you were an NLRB member would you adopt them? If so, would you promulgate them in an adjudicatory proceeding (are you free to do so in the absence of "record evidence"?) or only after rulemaking proceedings?

B.   COMPANY DOMINATION OR ASSISTANCE [27]

REPORT OF THE SENATE COMMITTEE ON EDUCATION AND LABOR ON THE WAGNER ACT

S.Rep. 573, 74th Cong., 1st Sess., pp. 9–11.

The second unfair labor practice deals with the so-called "company-union problem." It forbids an employer to dominate or interfere with the formation or administration of any labor organization or contribute financial or other support to it. * * *

This bill does nothing to outlaw free and independent organizations of workers who by their own choice limit their cooperative activities to the limits of one company. Nor does anything in the bill interfere with the freedom of employers to establish pension benefits, outing clubs, recreational societies, and the like, so long as such organizations do not extend their functions to the field of collective bargaining, and so long as they are not used as a covert means of discriminating against or in favor of membership in any labor organization. Such agencies, confined to their proper sphere, have promoted amicable relationships between employers and employees and the committee earnestly hopes that they will continue to function.

The so-called "company-union" features of the bill are designed to prevent interference by employers with organizations of their workers that serve or might serve as collective bargaining agencies. Such interferences exist when employers actively participate in framing the constitution or bylaws of labor organizations; or when, by provisions in the constitution or bylaws, changes in the structure of the organization cannot be made without the consent of the employer. It exists when they participate in the internal management or elections of a labor organization or when they supervise the agenda or procedure of meetings. It is impossible to catalog all the practices that might constitute interference, which may rest upon subtle but conscious economic pressure exerted by virtue of the employment relationship. The question is one of fact in each case. And where several of these interferences exist in combination, the employer may be said to dominate the labor organization by overriding the will of employees.

---

27. See Getman, The *Midwest Piping* Doctrine, 31 U.Chi.L.Rev. 292 (1964); Note, New Standards for Domination and Support Under Section 8(a)(2), 82 Yale L.J. 510 (1973); Note, Section 8(a) (2): Employer Assistance to Plant Unions and Committees, 9 Stan.L.Rev. 351 (1957).

The committee feels justified, particularly in view of statutory precedents, in outlawing financial or other support as a form of unfair pressure. It seems clear that an organization or a representative or agent paid by the employer for representing employees cannot command, even if deserving it, the full confidence of such employees. And friendly labor relations depend upon absolute confidence on the part of each side in those who represent it. * * *

NATIONAL LABOR RELATIONS BOARD SIXTEENTH ANNUAL REPORT

Fiscal year ended June 30, 1951. Pages 155–159.

The Board customarily finds a labor organization to be dominated by the employer when its organization is directly instigated and encouraged, or directly participated in, by supervisors or other managerial employees and the employer provides financial or other direct support to the organization.

Thus, the Board found illegal domination in a case where the employer's manager directed employees to participate in an "Employee Management Policy Committee," under threat of closing the plant if a committee was not formed. The plant manager then personally solicited and ordered employees to "elect" representatives from lists prepared by the employer, and acted as chairman of the first meetings of the committee. The Board cited as additional factors indicating domination the fact that the meetings were held on company time and property and were attended by supervisors and other representatives of the employer. In another such case, the vice president of the employer and most of its managerial and supervisory employees were members of the association found dominated. Also, the employer extended substantial assistance to the organization including loans totaling $1,000 and the profits of plant vending machines. In addition, the employer granted the dominated organization free rent and utilities, free use of plant space for candy concessions and two cafeterias, besides permitting the organization to hold meetings, elections and organizing campaigns on company time and premises. * * *

Employer interference with the formation and administration of a labor organization or the contribution of financial or other support which violates 8(a) (2), but falls short of actual domination, is held to be illegal assistance.

In one case, * * * the employer's president, in a speech made soon after a union started organizing its employees, suggested that the employees organize an "inside union" and that, if they did, certain "adjustments" would be made. When an "Employees Committee" was organized thereafter, the employer (1) promptly recognized it without proof of majority; (2) offered, negotiated, and granted a 25 percent wage increase, freely permitting the committee to use company time and property in the process; (3) had the committee, in return for the wage increase, circulate petitions among employees to withdraw from the union; and (4) contributed company time and property as well as money and management assistance in the drafting and circulation of the petitions. The Board held this to be illegal assistance falling short of domination, and ordered the employer to withhold recognition from the committee until it should be certified by the Board as a bona fide representative of a majority of employees.

Illegal assistance more often takes less flagrant forms. Thus, the Board found illegal assistance in a number of cases where an employer agreed to, or enforced, an unauthorized or illegal union-security clause, thereby assisting the union in recruiting or maintaining membership. The Board also held in another case that the employer violated 8(a) (2) by including, through error an illegal discriminatory contract clause and then delaying publication of a correction until 5 months after the error was discovered.

Various types of favoritism by the employer toward one union, or other encouragement of membership in one union in preference to another, were also held to be illegal assistance in a number of cases.
* * *

The conduct of the employer which the Board found to be illegal assistance in [one] case included: A threat to one employee of disciplinary action if she did sign a petition for the favored union; a threat to another employee of loss of job security if she did not vote for the favored union; denial to the other union's adherents of the right, previously granted the favored union, to circulate petitions in the plant; recall of a laid-off employee for the purpose of assisting the favored union, and the granting of recognition to the favored union despite the Board's refusal to certify it while unfair labor practice charges were pending.

NOTE:—Prior to 1947, the Board drew a distinction—when fashioning remedies under Section 8(a)(2)—between a dominated or supported union that was affiliated with the AFL or CIO and one that was an independent union. The dominated or supported union that was unaffiliated was ordered disestablished, that is, the company was ordered forever to refrain from recognizing such a union (or any successor) as bargaining representative, even if thereafter that union and its members and officers were to purge themselves of employer influence. The sanction for dominating or illegally supporting a union affiliated with the AFL or CIO was, however, much less harsh. The offending employer was ordered to break off relations with that union until such time as it was certified by the Board after a fair election. The Board justified this remedial distinction by the assumption that an employer could not so dominate or interfere with an affiliated union as likely for long to cripple its independence in representing employees. Congress in 1947 rejected such an assumption and sought to have the Board make case-by-case determinations as to the capacity of a dominated union—whether or not affiliated—ultimately to free itself of employer control. This was done by adding Section 9(c)(2) to the representation-election provisions of the Act and by amending Section 10(c) dealing with Board remedies. The Board considered these changes in CARPENTER STEEL CO., 76 N.L.R.B. 670 (1948), and announced its future policy:

"In all cases in which we find that an employer has dominated, or interfered with, or contributed support to a labor organization, or has committed any of these proscribed acts, we will find such conduct a violation of Section 8(a) (2) of the Act, as amended in 1947, regardless of whether the organization involved is affiliated. Where we find that an employer's unfair labor practices have been so extensive as to constitute domination of the organization, we shall order its disestablishment, whether or not it be affiliated. Identical standards must also be applied to affiliated and unaffiliated local unions in these situations in which, following disestablishment, a new labor organization appears on the scene, and a question arises as to whether it is the 'successor' of the old.

"The Board believes that disestablishment is still necessary as a remedy, in order effectively to remove the consequences of an employer's unfair labor practices and to make possible a free choice of representatives, in those cases, perhaps few in number, in which an employer's control of any labor organization has extended to the point of actual domination.

"But when the Board finds that an employer's unfair labor practices were limited to interference and support and never reached the point of domination, we shall only order that recognition be withheld until certification, again without regard to whether or not the organization happens to be affiliated. Subsequent representation proceedings in such situations will be governed, of course, by the provisions of Section 9(c) (2)."

HERTZKA & KNOWLES v. NLRB

United States Court of Appeals, Ninth Circuit, 1974.
503 F.2d 625.

CHOY, CIRCUIT JUDGE:

[Hertzka & Knowles is a medium-sized architectural firm in San Francisco. In September 1971 its professional employees voted for the Architectural Employees (OAE) as bargaining representative, but after months of fruitless negotiations an employee petitioned the NLRB for a decertification election, which was held in December 1972 and lost by the OAE. The Board, on charges filed by the OAE, found that employer remarks shortly before the decertification election violated Section 8(a)(1). The Board found that the employer improperly threatened to close the business and to blacklist union supporters, and that it also warned without basis in fact that business would decline were the firm unionized. It ordered the employer to cease and desist from threatening reprisals, and set aside the decertification and called for a new election. These Section 8(a)(1) findings and order were affirmed by the court of appeals. The Board also found that the employer violated Section 8(a)(2) because of conduct immediately after the election. At that time, at a meeting of the partners and the employees, five in-house committees were established, to deal with "professional stature within the firm, remuneration for professional services, minimum standards, efficiency and physical environment." Each committee was composed of five employees and one management representative. The Board ordered the employer to withdraw recognition and support from and to disestablish the committees. The court of appeals declined, however, to enforce the Board's order under Section 8(a)(2). Its discussion of the issue follows.]

When the results of the decertification election became clear on December 6, Hanna, a partner in the firm, called a meeting of both partners and professional personnel for the next morning. The meeting was opened by Hanna who commented that the eleven pro-union votes indicated a degree of dissatisfaction which had to be taken into account. He then asked for suggestions from the floor on how to accomplish a management-employee dialogue.

Employee Smith suggested the committee system previously described. The source of the idea, he later testified, was a proposal put forth by OAE during their unsuccessful negotiations with Hertzka & Knowles prior to decertification. The idea of adding a management representative to the committees was Smith's; he felt it would lessen what he termed the "long, tedious process" of negotiating with management that had been experienced with OAE as the

bargaining agent.   Smith's motion to adopt this system was second-
ed by two other employees and was approved by the employees, in
the examiner's words, "overwhelmingly."   An employee then suggested that the partners vote on the proposal.   The suggestion was
enthusiastically embraced, and the proposal passed unanimously.

The committees, though at the time of the Board hearing still
in a nascent state, operate in a not unusual fashion.   Their purpose
is to discuss and formulate proposals for changes in employment
terms and conditions; in some cases, it was contemplated that proposals would have to be passed on to management.   Meetings are
sometimes held on company time without loss of pay.   On some committees the management member votes but apparently not on others.
The firm representative, like other committee members, is consulted
on meeting times and participates fully in the proceedings.

The issue for our consideration is whether the employer's participation in the system's approval and operation represents an illicit degree of interference, under § 8(a)(2), with its formation and
administration.

Central to the National Labor Relations Act is the facilitation
of employee free choice and employee self-organization.   Indeed, §
8(a)(2) is, in part, a means to that end, for it seeks to permit employees to freely assert their demands for improvements in working
conditions.   Literally, however, almost any form of employer cooperation, however innocuous, could be deemed "support" or "interference."   Yet such a myopic view of § 8(a)(2) would undermine its
very purpose and the purpose of the Act as a whole—fostering free
choice—because it might prevent the establishment of a system the
employees desired.   Thus the literal prohibition of § 8(a)(2) must
be tempered by recognition of the objectives of the NLRA.

In saying this, we are merely repeating what Senator Wagner
said of § 8(a)(2) when he introduced his bill to the Senate:

> The erroneous impression that the bill expresses a bias for
> some particular form of union organization probably arises
> because it outlaws the company-dominated union.   Let me
> emphasize that nothing in the measure discourages em-
> ployees from uniting on an independent—or company-union
> basis, if by these terms we mean simply an organization
> confined to the limits of one plant or one employer.   Noth-
> ing in the bill prevents employers from maintaining free
> and direct relations with their workers.   *   *   *   The only
> prohibition is against the sham or dummy union which is
> dominated by the employer, which is supported by the em-
> ployer, which cannot change its rules and regulations with-

out his consent, and which cannot live except by the grace of the employer's whims.

Statutory History of the United States: Labor Organization 278–79 (R. Koretz, ed. 1970) (remarks of Feb. 21, 1935).

For this same reason courts have emphasized that there is a line between cooperation, which the Act encourages, and actual interference or domination considered from the standpoint of the employees, which the Act condemns. See, e. g., Federal-Mogul Corp. v. NLRB, 394 F.2d 915, 918 (6th Cir. 1968); NLRB v. Prince Macaroni Manufacturing Co., 329 F.2d 803, 809–812 (1st Cir. 1964); Chicago Rawhide Manufacturing Co. v. NLRB, 221 F.2d 165, 167–168 (7th Cir. 1955). In NLRB v. Wemyss, 212 F.2d 465 (9th Cir. 1954), we declined to approve a Board finding that an employer interfered with and dominated the administration of an in-house committee system. Judging the § 8(a)(2) issue from the subjective standpoint of the employees, we said:

> [T]he question is whether the organization exists as the result of a choice freely made by the employees, in their own interests, and without regard to the desires of their employer or whether the employees formed and supported the organization, rather than some other, because they knew their employer desired it and feared the consequences if they did not.

Id. at 471. We indicated that the employer must be shown to have interfered with the "freedom of choice" of the employees. Id. at 472. The sum of this is that a § 8(a)(2) finding must rest on a showing that the employees' free choice, either in type of organization or in the assertion of demands, is stifled by the degree of employer involvement at issue. Cf. NLRB v. Keller Ladders Southern, Inc., 405 F.2d 663, 667 (5th Cir. 1968); Note, New Standards for Domination and Support Under Section 8(a)(2), 82 Yale L.J. 510, 519–32 (1973).

Judged by this standard, we do not think there is substantial evidence, in the totality of circumstances, that Hertzka & Knowles violated § 8(a)(2). Unlawful support is not shown by the fact the committees meet at the firm and on firm time. E. g., Coppus Engineering Corp. v. NLRB, 240 F.2d 564, 573 (1st Cir. 1957). Nor is it a weighty circumstance that Hanna called and opened the meeting at which the committee system was adopted. The idea was still that of an employee, and it was approved by the employees. There was no evidence produced at the hearing, that the employees' preference was affected by this fact. Finally, that the partners voted on the proposal is relatively meaningless; it was the result of a suggestion made by an employee and its enthusiastic acceptance by the body of employees.

The question essentially comes down to the significance of having management partners on the committees. True, this may mean bargaining is "weaker" than if there were a formally organized union. Yet this feature too was chosen by the employees, and it is one with which, for all the record shows, they are not dissatisfied. This is perhaps not unreasonable given the close contact that must exist between partners and professional associates in an architectural firm. There is no evidence, furthermore, of actual interference with the assertion of employee demands through the committees. At most, there is the management vote on some committees, and even where the partner votes, the employees can easily outvote him.

For us to condemn this organization would mark approval of a purely adversial [sic] model of labor relations. Where a cooperative arrangement reflects a choice freely arrived at and where the organization is capable of being a meaningful avenue for the expression of employee wishes, we find it unobjectionable under the Act.

The Board will prepare a revised proposed order complying with this opinion.

Enforced in part and not enforced in part.

Problems for Discussion

1. The Nassau Contractors' Association negotiates on behalf of numerous construction companies with area construction unions. During negotiations between the Association and the Union of Operating Engineers, Clifford Smith and William Dean were members of the Union negotiating team and Milton Hendrickson, president of Hendrickson Brothers, one of the companies represented by the Association, was a member of the Association negotiating team. Both Smith and Dean are master mechanics and were employed by members of the Association at the time of the negotiations. The duties of a master mechanic are to make recommendations for the hiring of mechanics and to supervise the other mechanics to make sure that heavy equipment is kept in good working order. Smith is employed by Hendrickson, is responsible for the maintenance of over one million dollars worth of equipment, maintains a desk in the general offices of Hendrickson Bros., and has access to a company car at all times. Has the Association and/or Hendrickson Bros. violated Section 8(a)(2)? See *Nassau and Suffolk Contractors' Ass'n*, 118 N.L. R.B. 174 (1957).

Assume that employees Smith and Dean are not members of the union's negotiating team but are: (a) union vice-president and secretary-treasurer; or (b) representatives of the local union to the International's annual meeting; or (c) simply members of the local. Does their status in any of these cases raise a serious issue of violation under Section 8(a)(2)?

2. The IBEW began an organizing campaign at the various plants of the Virginia Power Company. The president of the Company posted in all plants a bulletin, over his signature, which was highly critical of national and international unions. The bulletin stated that the Company would not interfere with the right of employees to join any union. It went on to state that Company officials were ready and willing to listen to any complaints or requests from individual employees, that the Company had always done so in the past, but that if the IBEW were brought in, the Company would be forbidden to bargain with individual employees. The bulletin described a history of harmonious relations between the Company and its employees and described strikes and unrest at companies organized by international unions. It closed by emphasizing that the employees had the right to refrain from joining the IBEW.

When the IBEW filed an election petition, the Company president called a meeting of employee representatives, freely chosen by the employees, at the Company's main office in Norfolk. At the Norfolk meeting, the president made a speech reiterating much of what was stated in the bulletin. He went on to urge the employees to organize their own union, write their own by-laws, and select representatives without interference from any contentious international. An Independent Union was subsequently organized without any financial support or participation by management. The Independent was voted in at the Board-conducted election by the employees of every plant. The IBEW then filed a Section 8(a)(2) charge and a complaint issued. What should be the ruling on the complaint? See NLRB v. Virginia Elec. and Power Co., 314 U.S. 469, 62 S.Ct. 344, 86 L.Ed. 348 (1942).

Would your answer be affected if it could be shown that the Company allowed the Independent Union to use the Company's photocopy machine for union purposes, to use the Company cafeteria for union meetings, and to retain the profits from a coffee vending machine which the Company permitted the Union to install in the cafeteria? See NLRB v. Post Pub. Co., 311 F.2d 565 (7th Cir. 1963).

INTERNATIONAL LADIES GARMENT WORKERS v. NLRB (BERNHARD–ALTMANN TEXAS CORP.)

Supreme Court of the United States, 1961.
366 U.S. 731, 81 S.Ct. 1603, 6 L.Ed.2d 762.

MR. JUSTICE CLARK delivered the opinion of the Court.

* * *

In October 1956 the petitioner union initiated an organizational campaign at Bernhard-Altmann Texas Corporation's knitwear manufacturing plant in San Antonio, Texas. No other labor organization was similarly engaged at that time. During the course of that campaign, on July 29, 1957, certain of the Company's Topping Department employees went on strike in protest against a wage reduction. That dispute was in no way related to the union campaign, however, and the organizational efforts were continued during the strike. Some of the striking employees had signed authorization cards solicited by the union during its drive, and, while the strike was in progress, the union entered upon a course of negotiations with the employer. As a result of those negotiations, held in New, York City where the home offices of both were located, on August 30, 1957, the employer and union signed a "memorandum of understanding." In that memorandum the company recognized the union as exclusive bargaining representative of "all production and shipping employees." The union representative asserted that the union's comparison of the employee authorization cards in its possession with the number of eligible employees representatives of the company furnished it indicated that the union had in fact secured such cards from a majority of employees in the unit. Neither employer nor union made any effort at that time to check the cards in the union's possession against the employee roll, or otherwise, to ascertain with any degree of certainty that the union's assertion, later found by the Board to be erroneous, was founded on fact rather than upon good-faith assumption. The agreement, containing no union security provisions, called for the ending of the strike and for certain improved wages and conditions of employment. It also provided that a "formal agreement containing these terms" would "be promptly drafted * * * and signed by both parties within the next two weeks."

Thereafter, on October 10, 1957, a formal collective bargaining agreement, embodying the terms of the August 30 memorandum, was signed by the parties. The bargaining unit description set out in the formal contract, although more specific, conformed to that contained in the prior memorandum. It is not disputed that as of execution of the formal contract the union in fact represented a clear majority of employees in the appropriate unit.

* * *

At the outset, we reject as without relevance to our decision the fact that, as of the execution date of the formal agreement on October 10, petitioner represented a majority of the employees. As the Court of Appeals indicated, the recognition of the minority union on August 30, 1957, was "a *fait accompli* depriving the majority of the employees of their guaranteed right to choose their own representative." 280 F.2d at page 621. It is, therefore, of no consequence that petitioner may have acquired by October 10 the necessary majority if, during the interim, it was acting unlawfully. Indeed, such acquisition of majority status itself might indicate that the recognition secured by the August 30 agreement afforded petitioner a deceptive cloak of authority with which to persuasively elicit additional employee support.

*   *   *

In their selection of a bargaining representative, § 9(a) of the Wagner Act guarantees employees freedom of choice and majority rule. J. I. Case Co. v. National Labor Relations Board, 321 U.S. 332, 339, 64 S.Ct. 576, 581, 88 L.Ed. 762. In short, as we said in Brooks v. National Labor Relations Board, 348 U.S. 96, 103, 75 S.Ct. 176, 181, 99 L.Ed. 125, the Act placed "a nonconsenting minority under the bargaining responsibility of an agency selected by a majority of the workers." Here, however, the reverse has been shown to be the case. Bernhard-Altmann granted exclusive bargaining status to an agency selected by a minority of its employees, thereby impressing that agent upon the nonconsenting majority. There could be no clearer abridgment of § 7 of the Act, assuring employees the right "to bargain collectively through representatives of their own choosing" or "to refrain from" such activity. It follows, without need of further demonstration, that the employer activity found present here violated § 8(a) (1) of the Act which prohibits employer interference with, and restraint of, employee exercise of § 7 rights. Section 8(a) (2) of the Act makes it an unfair labor practice for an employer to "contribute * * * support" to a labor organization. The law has long been settled that a grant of exclusive recognition to a minority union constitutes unlawful support in violation of that section, because the union so favored is given "a marked advantage over any other in securing the adherence of employees." * * *

The petitioner, while taking no issue with the fact of its minority status on the critical date, maintains that both Bernhard-Altmann's and its own good-faith beliefs in petitioner's majority status are a complete defense. To countenance such an excuse would place in permissibly careless employer and union hands the power to completely frustrate employee realization of the premise of the Act—that its prohibitions will go far to assure freedom of choice and majority rule in employee selection of representatives. We find nothing in the statutory language prescribing scienter as an element of the unfair labor practices are involved. The act made unlawful by § 8(a) (2) is employer support of an accomplished fact. More need not be shown, for, even if mistakenly, the employees' rights have been invaded. It follows that prohibited conduct cannot be excused by a showing of good faith.

This conclusion, while giving the employee only the protection assured him by the Act, places no particular hardship on the employer or the union. It merely requires that recognition be withheld until the Board-conducted election results in majority selection of a representative. The Board's order here, as we might infer from the employer's failure to resist its enforcement, would apparently result in similarly slight hardship upon it. We do not share petitioner's apprehension that holding such conduct únlawful will somehow induce a breakdown, or seriously impede the progress of collective bargaining. If an employer takes reasonable steps to verify union claims, themselves advanced only after careful estimate—precisely what Bernhard-Altmann and petitioner failed to do here—he can readily ascertain their validity and obviate a Board election. We fail to see any onerous burden involved in requiring responsible negotiators to be careful, by cross-checking, for example, well-analyzed employer records with union listings or authorization cards. Individual and collective employee rights may not be trampled upon merely because it is inconvenient to avoid doing so. Moreover, no penalty is attached to the violation. Assuming that an employer in good faith accepts or rejects a union claim of majority status, the validity of his decision may be tested in an unfair labor practice proceeding. If he is found to have erred in extending or withholding recognition, he is subject only to a remedial order requiring him to conform his conduct to the norms set out in the Act, as was the case here. No further penalty results.   *   *   *

   [The partial dissent of Mr. Justice Douglas has been omitted.]

   Note: It is ordinarily a violation of Section 8(a)(2) for a company to enter into a collective agreement with any union before that company has hired a substantial proportion of its full workforce. In 1959, Congress enacted Section 8(f) as part of the Landrum-Griffin Act. The Section authorizes, in the construction industry only, the execution of an agreement with a minority union (not otherwise illegally dominated or assisted) which requires membership in that union within seven days (instead of the usual thirty days under the proviso to Section 8(a)(3)) as a condition of employment. Such "pre-hire agreements" were authorized in the construction industry because of the short duration of many jobs in that industry and because of the common practice and need of employers to rely on union hiring halls to supply a pool of skilled labor. (See 1959 U.S. Code Cong. and Admin. News p. 2344). Section 8(f) expressly provides, however, that such pre-hire agreements will not serve as a contract bar to a representation or decertification election under Section 9.

MIDWEST PIPING AND SUPPLY CO., INC.

National Labor Relations Board, 1945.
63 NLRB 1060.

[From and after January 1943, the Steelworkers, CIO, and the Steamfitters, AFL, were seeking to organize respondent's plant. The Steelworkers filed a complaint alleging that respondent had encouraged his employees to join the Steamfitters and threatened them with discharge if they joined the Steelworkers. On January 9, 1945, the Trial Examiner issued an Intermediate Report finding that respondent had violated Sections 8(a) (1) and 8(a) (3) of the Act. Thereafter, the record was reopened on the motion of the Steelworkers and new evidence was taken to the effect that respondent had entered into a closed shop agreement with the Steamfitters in December of 1944 even though Steelworkers had notified respondent on October 9, 1944 that it represented a majority of workers in the plant in question and had filed a representation petition with the Board covering the same workers. The evidence also established that just prior to signing the contract, respondent had been presented with membership cards by the Steamfitters indicating that the latter represented a majority of the employees involved. On April 26, 1945, the Trial Examiner issued a Supplemental Intermediate Report wherein he found that by executing the contract with the Steamfitters, respondent had engaged in an unfair labor practice within the meaning of Sections 8(a) (1) and 8(a) (2) of the Act.]

* * * We agree, however, with the Trial Examiner that after the close of the original hearing herein, the respondent violated the Act by entering into a "union shop" agreement with the Steamfitters. The respondent knew, at the time that the contract was executed, that there existed a real question concerning the representation of the employees in question. The record shows that both the Steamfitters and the Steelworkers had vigorously campaigned in the plant, had apprised the respondent of their conflicting petitions, which are still pending, alleging the existence of a question concerning the representation of the employees covered by the agreement. Under such circumstances, the Congress has clothed the Board with the exclusive power to investigate and determine representatives for the purposes of collective bargaining. In the exercise of this power, the Board usually makes such determination, after a proper hearing, and at a proper time, by permitting employees freely to select their bargaining representatives by secret ballot. In this case, however, the respondent elected to disregard the orderly representative procedure set up by the Board under the Act, for which both unions had theretofore petitioned the Board, and to arrogate to itself the resolution of the representation dispute against the Steelworkers and in favor of the Steamfitters.[28] In our opinion such conduct by the respondent contravenes the letter and the spirit of the Act, and leads to those very labor disputes affecting commerce which the Board's administrative procedure is designed to prevent.

We further find that the respondent's afore-mentioned conduct also constitutes a breach of its obligation of neutrality. As we have previously held, a neutral employer, on being confronted with conflicting representation claims by two rival unions, "would not negotiate a contract with one of them until its right to be recognized as the collective bargaining representative had been finally determined under the procedures set up under the Act." Here, the respondent knew that the Board already had jurisdiction over the existing question concerning the representation of the employees covered by the contract, and that in accordance with its usual practice, the Board would not proceed to a resolution of that question until it had passed upon the then pending original complaint herein, hearing on which had already been concluded. That no unfair labor practices are found herein on the original complaint does not alter the effect of the respondent's later breach of its neutrality obligation.

We are of the opinion and find that the respondent, by executing a "union shop" agreement with the Steamfitters in the face of the representation proceedings pending before the Board, indicated its approval of the Steamfitters, accorded it unwarranted prestige, encouraged membership therein, discouraged membership in the Steelworkers, and thereby rendered unlawful assistance to the Steamfitters, which interfered with, restrained, and coerced its employees in the exercise of rights guaranteed in Section 7 of the Act.

The Board has tended to apply broadly the *Midwest Piping* doctrine by readily finding that a "real question involving representation" exists. The courts of appeals, however, have been less ready to find that such a question exists. For example, in NLRB v. Swift & Co., 294 F.2d 285 (3d Cir. 1961), the court refused to enforce a Board order finding a Section 8(a)(2) violation. The Board had concluded that a question involving representation existed when

---

28. Respondent relied on signed membership cards as proof of the Steamfitters' claim of majority status. Under the circumstances, we do not regard such proof as conclusive. Among other things, it is well known that membership cards obtained during the heat of rival organizing campaigns like those of the respondent's plants, do not necessarily reflect the ultimate choice of a bargaining representative; indeed, the extent of dual membership among the employees during periods of intense organizing activity is an important unknown factor affecting a determination of majority status, which can best be resolved by a secret ballot among the employees.

an insurgent union filed an election petition. Swift thus had violated Section 8(a)(2) when it signed a contract with the incumbent union. The court found that no "real question" existed since 95% of the employees in the bargaining unit were submitting dues to the incumbent union under a voluntary checkoff provision of the contract and no administrative determination had been made that an election should be held. *Accord*, St. Louis Independent Packing Co. v. NLRB, 291 F.2d 700 (7th Cir. 1961) (court enforced a Board order finding a Section 8(a)(2) violation solely because a Board order of election had issued).

What appears to be the prevailing judicial approach has been capsulized:

> "To recognize one of two competing unions while the employees' choice between them is demonstrably in doubt, is an unfair labor practice under what the courts have accepted as the normal and proper application of the Midwest Piping doctrine. * * * And in principle the same result follows when majority support for the recognized union exists, but has been achieved by coercion or some other unfair labor practice. * * * But where a clear majority of the employees, without subjection to coercion or other unlawful influence, have made manifest their desire to be represented by a particular union, there is no factual basis for a contention that the employer's action thereafter in recognizing the union or contracting with it is an interference with their freedom of choice."

NLRB v. AIR MASTER CORP., 339 F.2d 553, 557 (3d Cir. 1965).

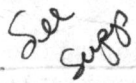

Problems for Discussion

1. Brown Company operates a wholesale and warehouse business with sufficient effect on commerce for the NLRB to exercise its jurisdiction. Brown has never recognized a union as the bargaining representative of its 70 non-supervisory employees. On October 20th the CIO claimed to have been designated as bargaining representative by 45 employees and requested immediate recognition. Brown replied that he would have to consult his lawyer and promised a prompt reply. On October 23 AFL claimed 50 employees as members and threatened to post pickets outside the warehouse unless Brown immediately granted it recognition. When Brown refused, AFL picketing commenced. It tied up the business completely because no truck driver would cross the picket line. Brown will lose $1,000 each day the picketing continues. He thinks that the AFL claim of a majority may be supportable but regards the issue as doubtful because employee sentiment is sharply divided. He has no objection to signing an AFL contract if he can lawfully do so. What course

would you advise Brown to follow? Should it make any difference whether CIO has filed a petition for investigation and certification of representatives? See *Novak Logging Company*, 119 N.L.R.B. 1573 (1958).

2. Ace Machine Works is a machine shop employing 80 production and maintenance workers. IAM has been the bargaining representative since 1950. The current contract expires on December 31. On October 25 IUE demands recognition as exclusive bargaining representative, and files a petition under Section 9 accompanied by authorization cards from 26 employees. IAM shows Ace that 54 employees paid dues on October 15. Is Ace guilty of an unfair labor practice if it bargains a new contract with IAM as exclusive representative? Can and should *Midwest Piping* be distinguished? If Ace declines to bargain a new agreement pending the outcome of the representation proceeding but allows IAM to continue to process grievances as exclusive representative, does Ace violate Section 8(a)(1) or 8(a)(2)? See *Shea Chemical Corp.*, 121 N.L.R.B. 1027 (1958).

C. DISCRIMINATION [29]

EDWARD G. BUDD MFG. CO. v. NLRB

United States Court of Appeals, Third Circuit, 1943.
138 F.2d 86.

[In 1933, the employees of the company formed an association and elected representatives to confer with management on various matters of mutual concern. The association was initially suggested by management and was established pursuant to a plan drawn up by company officials. After its formation, management cooperated fully with the organization and treated its representatives with "extraordinary leniency." In 1941, however, the UAW sought unsuccessfully to organize the employees. Thereafter, the union filed charges alleging that the company had unlawfully supported and dominated the association and had discharged two employees, Milton Davis and Walter Weigand (a representative of the association), for supporting the union. Following a complaint, the Board issued a decision and order requiring the disestablishment of the association and the reinstatement of the two employees. On petition to review the Board's order, the court of appeals found sufficient evidence to uphold the conclusion that the association was employer-dominated and that Milton Davis had been discriminatorily discharged. The court then considered the discharge of Walter Weigand.]

29. See Christensen & Svanoe, Motive and Intent in the Commission of Unfair Labor Practices: The Supreme Court and the Fictive Formality, 77 Yale L.J. 1269 (1968); Getman, Section 8(a)(3) of the NLRA and the Effort to Insulate Free Employee Choice, 32 U. Chi.L.Rev. 735 (1965); Note, Intent, Effect, Purpose, and Motive as Applicable Elements to § 8(a)(1) and § 8 (a)(3) violations of the National Labor Relations Act, 7 Wake Forest L.Rev. 616 (1971); Oberer, The Scienter Factor in Sections 8(a)(1) and (3) of the Labor Act: of Balancing, Hostile Motive, Dogs and Tails, 52 Cornell L.Q. 491 (1967).

The case of Walter Weigand is extraordinary. If ever a workman deserved summary discharge it was he. He was under the influence of liquor while on duty. He came to work when he chose and he left the plant and his shift as he pleased. In fact, a foreman on one occasion was agreeably surprised to find Weigand at work and commented upon it. Weigand amiably stated that he was enjoying it.[30] He brought a woman (apparently generally known as the "Duchess") to the rear of the plant yard and introduced some of the employees to her. He took another employee to visit her and when this man got too drunk to be able to go home, punched his time-card for him and put him on the table in the representatives' meeting room in the plant in order to sleep off his intoxication. Weigand's immediate superiors demanded again and again that he be discharged, but each time higher officials intervened on Weigand's behalf because as was naively stated he was "a representative" [of the association]. In return for not working at the job for which he was hired, the petitioner gave him full pay and on five separate occasions raised his wages. One of these raises was general; that is to say, Weigand profited by a general wage increase throughout the plant, but the other four raises were given Weigand at times when other employees in the plant did not receive wage increases.

The petitioner contends that Weigand was discharged because of cumulative grievances against him. But about the time of the discharge it was suspected by some of the representatives that Weigand had joined the complaining CIO union. One of the representatives taxed him with this fact and Weigand offered to bet a hundred dollars that it could not be proved. On July 22, 1941 Weigand did disclose his union membership to the vice-chairman (Rattigan) of the Association and to another representative (Mullen) and apparently tried to persuade them to support the union. Weigand asserts that the next day he with Rattigan and Mullen, were seen talking to CIO organizer Reichwein on a street corner. The following day, according to Weigand's testimony, Mullen came to Weigand at the plant and stated that Weigand, Rattigan and himself had been seen talking to Reichwein and that he, Mullen, had just had an interview with Personnel Director McIlvain and Plant Manager Mahan. According to Weigand, Mullen said to him, "Maybe you didn't get me in a jam." And, "We were seen down there." The following day Weigand was discharged.

As this court stated in National Labor Relations Board v. Condenser Corp., supra, 3 Cir., 128 F.2d at page 75, an employer may discharge an employee for a good reason, a poor reason or no reason at all so long as the provisions of the National Labor Relations Act are not violated. It is, of course, a violation to discharge an employee because he has engaged in activities on behalf of a union. Conversely an

30. Weigand stated that he was carried on the payroll as a "rigger". He was asked what was a rigger. He replied: "I don't know; I am not a rigger."

employer may retain an employee for a good reason, a bad reason or no reason at all and the reason is not a concern of the Board. But it is certainly too great a strain on our credulity to assert, as does the petitioner, that Weigand was discharged for an accumulation of offenses. We think that he was discharged because his work on behalf of the CIO had become known to the plant manager. That ended his sinecure at the Budd plant. The Board found that he was discharged because of his activities on behalf of the union. The record shows that the Board's finding was based on sufficient evidence.

The order of the Board will be enforced.

Problems for Discussion

1. In the *Budd* case, was there not "just cause" for Weigand's discharge, solely on the basis of his work record? If the Board had found that the discharge was for work-related reasons, would its conclusion have been supported "by evidence," as was the standard for impregnability of Board fact-findings on judicial review under the Wagner Act of 1935? Would its conclusion have been supported "by substantial evidence on the record considered as a whole," the standard as amended by the Taft-Hartley Act in 1947?

2. If the Board had held that Weigand's discharge was in part attributable to his union activities and in part attributable to his wretched work record, should this conclusion be set aside on judicial review? If the accuracy of such a factual determination were to be assumed, i. e., the discharge was attributable to "mixed motives," has a violation of Section 8(a)(3) been made out?

3. What is the purpose of the remedy in the Section 8(a)(3) case? Was it proper, for example, for the Board to order that Weigand be reinstated? What was the purpose of the reinstatement order? A deterrent or punishment as to the Budd Company? Protection for Weigand and restoration for the wrong done him? A demonstration to other employees that the Government will not permit unionization to be jeopardized by employer reprisal?

4. In an action in a civil court for breach of an employment contract on the part of the employer, to what remedies will the wronged employee normally be entitled? Should any conventional limitations upon the remedial power of a court of law or equity similarly apply to the National Labor Relations Board? Does Section 10(c) offer any illumination?

5. Assume that, upon his reinstatement, Weigand continues to live a life of leisure and debauchery while on the job. What is the Company's recourse?

NOTE:—During the Taft-Hartley debates considerable dissatisfaction was expressed concerning the narrow scope of judicial review of NLRB findings. There were wide differences in this respect between the House and Senate bills, and the Conference Report, which made relevant changes in sections 10(b), (c) and (e), was a compromise. The Statement of the House Managers explained that:

"(14) Under the language of section 10(e) of the present act, findings of the Board, upon court review of Board orders, are conclusive 'if supported by evidence'. By reason of this language, the courts have, as one has put it, in effect 'abdicated' to the Board. *N. L. R. B.* v. *Standard Oil Co.*, 138 F.2d 885 (1943). See also: *Wilson & Co.* v. *N. L. R. B.*, 126 F.2d 114 (1942), *N. L. R. B.* v. *Columbia Products Corp.*, 141 F.2d 687 (1944), *N. L. R. B.* v. *Union Pacific Stages, Inc.*, 99 F.2d 153. In many instances deference on the part of the courts to specialized knowledge that is supposed to inhere in administrative agencies has led the courts to acquiesce in decisions of the Board, even when the findings concerned mixed issues of law and of fact (*N. L. R. B.* v. *Hearst Publications, Inc.*, 322 U.S. 111, 64 S.Ct. 851, 88 L.Ed. 1170; *Packard Motor Car Co.* v. *N. L. R. B.*, 330 U.S. 485, 67 S.Ct. 789, 91 L.Ed. 615, decided March 10, 1947), or when they rested only on inferences that were not, in turn, supported by facts in the record (*Republic Aviation* v. *N. L. R. B.*, 324 U.S. 793, 65 S.Ct. 982, 89 L.Ed. 1372, 157 A.L.R. 1081; *Le Tourneau Co.* v. *N. L. R. B.*, 324 U.S. 793, 65 S.Ct. 982, 89 L.Ed. 1372, 157 A.L.R. 1081).

"As previously stated in the discussion of amendments to section 10(b) and section 10(c), by reason of the new language concerning the rules of evidence and the preponderance of the evidence, presumed expertness on the part of the Board in its field can no longer be a factor in the Board's decisions. * * *

"The Senate amendment provided that the Board's findings with respect to questions of fact should be conclusive if supported by substantial evidence on the record considered as a whole. The provisions of section 10(b) of the conference agreement insure the Board's receiving only legal evidence, and section 10(c) insures its deciding in accordance with the preponderance of the evidence. These two statutory requirements in and of themselves give rise to questions of law which the courts will hereafter be called upon to determine—whether the requirements have been met. This, in conjunction with the language of the Senate amendment with respect to the Board's findings of fact—language which the conference agreement adopts—will very materially broaden the scope of the courts' reviewing power. This is not to say that the courts will be required to decide any case de novo, themselves weighing the evidence, but they will be under a duty to see that the Board observes the provisions of the earlier sections, that it does not infer facts that are not supported by evidence or that are not consistent with evidence in the record, and that it does not concentrate on one element of proof to the exclusion of others without adequate explanation of its reasons for disregarding or discrediting the evidence that is in conflict with its findings. The language also precludes the substitution of expertness for evidence in making decisions. It is believed that the provisions of the conference agreement relating to the courts' reviewing power will be adequate to preclude such decisions as those in *N. L. R. B.* v. *Nevada Consol. Copper Corp.* (316 U.S. 105, 62 S.Ct. 960, 86 L.Ed. 1305) and in the *Wilson, Columbia Products, Union Pacific Stages, Hearst, Republic Aviation,* and *Le Tourneau,* etc., cases, supra, without unduly burdening the courts. The conference agreement therefore carries the language of the Senate amendment into section 10(e) of the amended act."

In Universal Camera Corp. v. NLRB, 340 U.S. 474, 490, 71 S. Ct. 456, 466, 95 L.Ed. 456, the Court held that under the amendment to Section 10(e) "courts must now assume more responsibility for the reasonableness and fairness of Labor Board decisions than some courts have shown in the past." On the other hand, the Court pointed out that Section 10(e) was not intended "to negative the function of the Labor Board as one of these agencies presumably equipped or informed by experience to deal with a specialized field of knowledge, whose findings within that field carry the authority of an expertness which courts do not possess and therefore must respect. Nor does it mean that even as to matters not requiring expertise a court may displace the Board's choice between two fairly conflicting views, even though the court would justifiably have made a different choice had the matter been before it *de novo.* Congress has merely made it clear that a reviewing court is not barred from setting aside a Board decision when it cannot conscientiously find that the evidence supporting that decision is substantial, when viewed in the light that the record in its entirety furnishes, including that body of evidence opposed to the Board's view." 340 U.S. 474, 488, 71 S.Ct. 456, 464–65.

MUELLER BRASS CO. v. NLRB

United States Court of Appeals, Fifth Circuit, 1977.
544 F.2d 815.

James C. Hill, Circuit Judge:

This case is before the court upon the petition of Mueller Brass Co. (the "Company") for review of, and upon cross-application for enforcement of, an order of the National Labor Relations Board (the "Board"). The issues presented are whether substantial evidence on the record as a whole supports the Board's findings that the Company violated Sections 8(a)(1) and (3) of the National Labor Relations Act (the "Act"), 29 U.S.C.A. §§ 158(a)(1) and (3), by discharging employees Hansford Stone and James Roy Rogers * * *.

The appropriate standard of review in this case is clear. We are to sustain the Board's determinations if they are supported by substantial evidence on the record considered as a whole. 29 U.S. C.A. § 160(e); *NLRB v. Brown*, 380 U.S. 278, 85 S.Ct. 980, 13 L.Ed.2d 839 (1965); *Universal Camera Corp. v. NLRB*, 340 U.S. 474, 71 S.Ct. 456, 95 L.Ed. 456 (1951); *International Organization of Masters, Mates and Pilots v. NLRB*, 539 F.2d 554 (5th Cir. 1976). It is not our function to overturn the Board's choice between two equally plausible inferences from the facts if the choice is reasonable, even though we might reach a contrary result if deciding the case *de novo*. *NLRB v. United Insurance Co.*, 390 U.S. 254, 88 S.Ct. 988, 19 L.Ed.2d 1083 (1968); *NLRB v. Mueller Brass Co.*, 501 F.2d 680, 683–684 (5th Cir. 1974); *NLRB v. Standard Forge & Axle Co.*, 420 F.2d 508 (5th Cir. 1969), *cert. denied*, 400 U.S. 903, 91 S.Ct. 140, 27 L.Ed.2d 140 (1970). However, even though our scope of review is thus limited, we should deny enforcement if, after a full review of the record, we are unable *conscientiously* to conclude that the evidence supporting the Board's determinations is substantial.[31] *Universal Camera Corp. v. NLRB, supra; NLRB v. Mueller Brass Co.*, 509 F.2d 704, 707 (5th Cir. 1975); *NLRB v. O. A. Fuller Super Markets, Inc.*, 374 F.2d 197, 200 (5th Cir. 1967).

The Company began production in 1971 in Fulton, Mississippi. The union conducted unsuccessful organizing campaigns in 1971 and 1973, and began its third campaign in early 1974. In *NLRB v. Mueller Brass Co.*, 501 F.2d 680 (5th Cir. 1974), this Court upheld the Board's findings that the Company violated §§ 8(a)(1) and (3) of the Act by discharging an employee, and by making threats and suggesting that union organizers were being blacklisted by employees [sic] in the area. Significantly, this court found that "[t]here is no question from the record that the Company was strongly anti-union." *Id.* at 685.

Later, in *NLRB v. Mueller Brass Co.*, 509 F.2d 704 (5th Cir. 1975), this court refused to enforce orders of the Board. This

---

31. It is important to bear in mind that "[t]he substantiality of evidence must take into account whatever in the record fairly detracts from its weight." *Universal Camera Corp. v. NLRB*, 340 U.S. at 488, 71 S.Ct. at 464. *See also Bowman Transportation, Inc. v. Arkansas-Best Freight System, Inc.*, 419 U.S. 281, 234 n. 2, 95 S.Ct. 438, 42 L. Ed.2d 447 (1974).

court found that "even considered against the Company's prior anti-union sentiment," the unrefuted testimony did not constitute substantial evidence that the Company had created an impression of surveillance. In addition, this Court upheld the suspension of an employee involved in the case *sub judice*, finding no substantial evidence to indicate that the Company had treated him differently from other employees who falsified a report in violation of Company rules. With this background, we proceed to the case at bar.

Hansford Stone, Jr. went to work for the Company in March, 1972. Stone was given a verbal warning about absenteeism in February, 1974, and he received a written warning in April, 1974. Stone was specifically informed and warned about an automatic termination under Plant Rule 40.[32]

On April 25, 1974, Stone went to see his physician, Dr. Collum, who advised him that he should go to the hospital. Stone reported this to the Company and Glenn Grissom, the personnel representative, placed him on sick leave. Grissom advised Stone that he should contact the Company when he was able to return to work and that he should present his doctor's release at that time.

Stone was hospitalized from April 25 until May 4, but he did not return to work until May 14. He did not contact the Company between the date of his hospital release and the date of his return to work. Charles Henson, the Company's general foreman, received a report that Stone had been seen around town and, upon inquiry, the Company received a note on May 9 from Dr. Collum stating that Stone should have been able to return to work on May 6, 1974. Thus, on May 9, 1974, Stone was terminated pursuant to Plant Rule 40. Subsequently, the Company received an insurance report indicating that Stone had been discharged from the hospital and that no home confinement was required.

Stone presented himself for work on May 14, 1974. He presented a May 13th note from Dr. Collum stating that he should be able to return to work on May 14. Stone was shown Dr. Collum's May 9th note and asked why he did not report to work on May 6. Stone stated that he had contracted a sore throat. He then left and returned the same day with a third note from Dr. Collum attempting to void the preceding two notes. The Company refused to reinstate him.

---

32. Company Rule 40 of the 1974 rules provided: An employee who is absent for three consecutive working days without permission will be considered a voluntary quit.

The Administrative Law Judge (ALJ) found that Stone's unexcused absence from work in combination with his previous record of absenteeism and the report that he had been seen visiting around town were a sufficient basis for the Company's belief that he had deliberately overstayed his excused absence and then prevailed upon his doctor to contradict his earlier reports. Despite the Company's admitted opposition to the union and its knowledge of Stone's sympathies,[33] the ALJ concluded that Stone was terminated for violating the rule about unexcused absences. The Board disagreed and from its review of the record concluded that the discharge of Stone was motivated by the Company's opposition to the union and its desire to rid itself of a known union adherent.

The conduct of Stone *pales* in comparison to the actions which formed the basis for the discharge of James Roy Rogers. Rogers began his employment with the Company in February, 1972. Prior to his discharge in February, 1974, he worked the 11:00 p. m. to 7:00 a. m. shift at the plant. Rogers had been active in union organization for approximately one and one-half years and was well known as a union activist by Company officials. He was discharged for conduct which was characterized by the Administrative Law Judge as "vulgar and offensive" by "any standard of acceptable conduct."

In summary, on January 31, 1974, during the 5:00 a. m. break Rogers displayed a mechanized artificial male sex organ to a female employee at the plant. The female employee was embarrassed and turned away. The very next night Rogers, on a dare from a fellow employee, approached another female employee and made her an indecent and offensive proposition. She, too, was embarrassed and upset by the remark.

A few days later Frank Robinson, the Company's Industrial Relations Manager, received a report that there had been an incident in the plant the previous week which had upset the female employees. The person responsible for the incident was not identified. The next day Robinson began an inquiry into the matter and after an extensive investigation, Rogers was interviewed and admitted the incidents involved. Rogers was then discharged by the Company for violation of Plant Rule 22.[34]

With regard to the discharge of Rogers, the ALJ felt that, in light of the Company's opposition to the union, its knowledge of

33. In fact, the ALJ had previously concluded that remarks made to Stone by Company officials violated Section 8(a)(1) of the Act. *See infra.*

34. Company Rule 22 provides: An employee shall not engage in disorderly, immoral, indecent or illegal conduct.

Rogers' union sympathies, its prior discrimination against him,[35] and its protracted investigation into his offenses, despite the absence of employee complaints, compared to its investigations into prior offenses toward female employees, the discharge of Rogers for his improper conduct was a pretext for finally getting rid of him. The Board agreed with the ALJ that the discharge of Rogers was pretextual.

In controversies involving employee discharges or suspensions, the motive of the employer is the controlling factor. *NLRB v. Brown*, 380 U.S. at 287, 85 S.Ct. 980. Absent a showing of antiunion motivation, an employer may discharge an employee without running afoul of the fair labor laws for a good reason, a bad reason or no reason at all. *NLRB v. O. A. Fuller Super Markets, Inc.*, *supra*. The mere fact that a specific employee not only breaks a Company rule but also evinces a pro-union sentiment is alone not sufficient to destroy the just cause for his discharge. *NLRB v. Mueller Brass Co.*, 509 F.2d at 711; *see NLRB v. Soft Water Laundry, Inc.*, 346 F.2d 930 (5th Cir. 1965). The essence of discrimination in violation of Section 8(a)(3) of the Act is in treating like cases differently. Finally, the Board must sustain the burden of showing evidence on the record which establishes a reasonable inference of causal connection between the Company's antiunion animus and the employee's discharge.

In the case *sub judice*, the ALJ concluded that the Company's antiunion sentiment played no part in its decision to terminate Hansford Stone. In reversing, the Board overstepped its bounds. As we observed in *NLRB v. McGahey*, 233 F.2d 406, 412–13 (5th Cir. 1956):

> The Board's error is the frequent one in which the existence of the reasons stated by the employer as the basis for the discharge is evaluated in terms of its reasonableness. If the discharge was excessively harsh, if lesser forms of discipline would have been adequate, if the discharged employee was more, or just as, capable as the one left to do the job, or the like then, the argument runs, the employer must not actually have been motivated by managerial considerations, and (here a full 180 degree swing is made) the stated reason thus dissipated as pretense, nought remains but antiunion purpose as the explanation. But as we have so often said: management is for management. Neither Board nor Court can second-guess it or give it gentle guidance by over-the-shoulder supervision. Manage-

---

35. Rogers' name was prominent in 204 N.L.R.B. 617 (1973), *enforcement granted*, 501 F.2d 680 (5th Cir. 1974), and he was suspended in 208 N.L.R.B. 534 (1974), *enforcement denied*, 509 F. 2d 704 (5th Cir. 1975).

ment can discharge for good cause, or bad cause, or no cause at all. It has, as the master of its own business affairs, complete freedom with but one specific, definite qualification: it may not discharge when the real motivating purpose is to do that which Section 8(a)(3) forbids.

The Board cites two reasons for its decision to reverse the conclusion of the ALJ: the fact that the Company made no effort to contact Stone prior to discharging him and the Company's failure to credit the doctor's final note which attempted to void all previous notes. However unreasonable the Board may consider these actions on the part of the Company, there is no evidence in the record to indicate that the Company had ever conducted its business otherwise. We know of no requirement that it do so. We conclude that there is no substantial evidentiary basis in the record for the finding that the discharge of Stone was discriminatory and in violation of Section 8(a)(3) of the Act.

We are literally shocked by the conclusion of the Board that Rogers was discharged in violation of the Act and that he is entitled to be reinstated. Rogers' admitted conduct and statements were vulgar and offensive by any standard of decency. The Board was of the opinion that, in light of the prevailing mores in the plant and the treatment afforded to prior transgressors of decent moral standards, the termination of Rogers was pretextual. The answer to such an argument lies in *Frosty Morn Meats, Inc. v. NLRB*, 296 F.2d 617, 621 (5th Cir. 1961):

> * * * If, however, the misdeeds of the employee are so flagrant that he would almost certainly be fired anyway there is no room for discrimination to play a part. The employee will not have been harmed by the employer's union animus, and neither he nor any others will be discouraged from membership in a union, since all will understand that the employee would have been fired anyway. It must be remembered that the statute prohibits discrimination, and that the focus on dominant motivation is only a test to reveal whether discrimination has occurred. Discrimination consists in treating like cases differently. If an employer fires a union sympathizer or organizer, a finding of discrimination rests on the assumption that in the absence of the union activities he would have treated the employee differently.

When an employee gives his employer as much reason to fire him as Judkins did, by refusing to follow instructions and by giving not only his supervisors but also his fellow employees the impression that he was uncooperative, there is no basis for the conclusion that the employer has treated him differently than he would have treated a non-union employee. As a speculative matter, it may or may not be true that union animus loomed larger in the employer's motivation than Judkins' shortcomings as a worker. But when the evidence of just cause for discharge is as great as it is here, the record as a whole does not support the conclusion that the discharged employee was deprived of any right because of union activities. The power of reinstatement is remedial. It is not punitive. It is not to penalize an employer for anti-unionism by forcing on the pay-roll an employee unfit to stay on the job.

Rogers was discharged for good and sufficient cause. Insofar as the Board's order requires reinstatement and back pay for him, enforcement is denied. * * *

GODBOLD, CIRCUIT JUDGE (dissenting):

The majority opinion departs from our proper role in reviewing NLRB orders and from the standards that guide us in this role.

(1) The discharge of Stone

The majority opinion is neither more nor less than a retrial of this aspect of the case.

Stone has a prior record of absenteeism and was warned about it. From April 25 to May 4 he was hospitalized. He did not report for work, and the company was told that he was being seen around town. Thereafter it received three notes from Stone's doctor. The first note, received May 9, stated that Stone should have been able to return to work May 6. That same day the company terminated him without discussion or notice, pursuant to a plant rule that one absent for three consecutive working days without permission would be considered a voluntary quit.

Stone showed up for work May 14 bringing the second note from his doctor, dated May 13. It said that he should be able to return to work May 14. Stone was not permitted to go to work, and he left the plant. The company then called the doctor and asked him what the May 13 note meant, and the doctor said that it referred to a sore throat that Stone had contracted. An hour later the doctor called back and asked the company to accept the May 13 note as a release for Stone's return to work and to destroy the May 9 note. Later the same day, May 14, Stone came back with the third note, in which the doctor said that he probably told Stone to take a week off after leaving the hospital on May 4, because of his back problems, but that he was well enough to work as of

May 14, that all previous statements made by the doctor were "null and void" and no other notes would be forthcoming.

The ALJ drew from these events an inference that Stone had used his excused absence for sickness as an excuse to stay out after May 6 and had prevailed on the doctor to contradict his earlier reports. That was a permissible inference. The Board, however, drew a different inference. It noted the following elements of proof: (1) The company was hostile to the union and previously had been before the NLRB for commission of unfair labor practices. (2) The company knew of Stone's union sentiment and had actively sought to dissuade him from his union adherence. (3) The company made no effort to contact Stone to determine his condition. (4) On May 9, after determining Stone's release date from the hospital, the company summarily terminated him and gave him no notice that he had been terminated. (5) The company admitted it had no reason to doubt the authenticity of the third note from the doctor. From all of the evidence the Board drew inferences that the third note dissipated the suspicion that Stone had been malingering, and that the discharge was pretextual. Certainly it was entitled to draw these inferences from the evidence before it.

Language quoted by Judge Hill from *NLRB v. McGahey*, 233 F.2d 406 (C.A.5, 1956), does not change the standard of review that this court has followed in innumerable cases. Further on in the opinion the court specifically noted that:

> In the choice between lawful and unlawful motives, the record taken as a whole must present a substantial basis of believable evidence pointing toward the unlawful one.

Id. at 413. *McGahey* teaches us that reasonableness, or lack of it, may be circumstantial evidence of the employer's motive in a discharge case, but the Board's view of employer action is not to be treated as talismanic. In the present case the Board did not consider the employer's action in the context of reasonableness or unreasonableness. It accepted the third note as credible, found it was sufficient to dissipate the charge of malingering, and pointed out that the company admitted there was no reason to doubt the authenticity of the note. On this evidence the Board concluded that the discharge was pretextual. Similarly, if introduced, evidence that the company was not acting in accordance with its usual practices would have been part of the overall evidence to be considered. But it is quite different to hold that evidence of motive is insubstantial unless it includes evidence of behavior inconsistent with usual practices.

This is a substantial evidence case. The record fully supports the Board's inference of improper motive.

(2) The discharge of Rogers

This is a plain, everyday substantial evidence case except for two factors. First, the status of Rogers as a target for company action is recorded in two previous decisions of this court. Second, Rogers' conduct, which the Board found was the asserted basis for a pretextual discharge, was sexually oriented.[36]

In *Mueller I, NLRB v. Mueller Brass Co.*, 501 F.2d 680 (C.A.5, 1974), we enforced a Board order finding Mueller guilty of § 8(a) (3) discharges and § 8(a)(1) coercion. One of the targets of the coercive company statements was Rogers. 501 F.2d at 686. In that same case the ALJ made this finding with respect to Rogers:

> * * * respondent's industrial relations manager, Gregory, told an employee in September 1972, that Rogers' name was on the desk of every employer in the area as a "union pusher" and that, if he lost his job with respondent, he would be unable to get another in that area.

This was quoted and relied upon in *Mueller II*, discussed below. See 509 F.2d at 708 n. 5.[37] In *Mueller II, NLRB v. Mueller Brass Co.*, 509 F.2d 704 (C.A.5, 1975), we declined to enforce a Board order making Rogers whole for a three-day suspension for falsifying excuses for absenteeism because there was no substantial evidence that he was treated differently than others committing like offenses. In the present case, *Mueller III*, the Board properly considered this background in reaching its conclusions that the discharge was pretextual.

I turn now to the factor strongly emphasized by the majority, the sexual content of Rogers' actions. The Board found that what Rogers did was not out of keeping with the general level of conduct in the plant, where bawdy sexual horseplay was commonplace, accepted, and not the subject of discipline. The evidence fully supports the Board's finding. Pornographic pictures were passed around by employees and pornographic books left in accessible places for employees and supervisors to examine. The use of strong language, including four-letter words, dirty jokes and suggestive

---

36. "In view of Respondent's opposition to the Union, its knowledge of Rogers' union sympathies, its prior discrimination against him, and the protracted investigation into Rogers' two offenses, despite the absence of any employee complaints, as compared with its complacency over complaints by women employees in similar situations, I am satisfied that Respondent relied on Rogers' improper conduct as a pretext for finally getting rid of him. I therefore find that Respondent violated Section 8(a)(3) in discharging Rogers."

Appendix p. 359.

37. Additionally, in *Mueller I*, this court found that there was "no question from the record that the Company was strongly antiunion." 501 F.2d at 685.

remarks was common among employees and supervisors. One witness told of means in the plant to order films, plainly referring to
pornographic films. The general foreman on Rogers' 11 p. m. to 7
a. m. shift freely exchanged sex jokes with female employees and
joined in the general appreciation of pornographic material which
turned up around the plant. There is testimony that in one incident
he invited two women to examine a book with pictures of men and
women having intercourse and approved their suggestion that they
take it into the ladies' room to look at it even though neither was
scheduled for a break. This foreman was present when Rogers had
the artificial sex organ, saw it and laughed at it, and did not say
or do anything about its presence. The industrial relations manager
of the plant was present, saw the organ and laughed at it. Another
foreman saw it later the same evening and "just died laughing."
Rogers displayed the device to a group of male and female employees.
Only one gave any indication of offense. The rest laughed at it.

Of equal, if not greater significance, is the evidence of other
specific incidents of sexually oriented evidence that did not subject
the participants to discipline. Rule 22 was given as the basis for
Rogers' discharge: "An employee shall not engage in disorderly,
immoral, indecent or illegal conduct." No one other than Rogers has
ever been discharged for violation of this rule. I have already described the conduct of Rogers' foreman and the industrial relations
manager with respect to the very circumstances which cost Rogers
his job. Also there is evidence of three specific incidents of sexually
oriented conduct by male employees toward female employees. With
respect to one incident, the husband and the father of the female victim complained to the plant manager and he promised to take action. There is no evidence that any action was ever taken, and the
supervisor who was the alleged culprit was later promoted. More
than a year later the female employee asked about the matter and
was told that she ought to drop it since her complaint was so old.

In two other incidents female employees complained of of-
fensive, sexually oriented remarks made to them by male employees.
One of these occurred just a week before the hearing in this case.
The male employees were not disciplined.

*   *   *   [T]he discipline inflicted was the harshest available.
This uncontroverted evidence of disparate treatment acquires even
greater force when laid against the strong antiunion bias specifically
manifested in the past by threats directed at Rogers. 509 F.2d at
708 n. 5.

I turn to some of the cases concerning coarse, abusive and pro-
fane conduct. In *Mueller I* we enforced an order reinstating employee Blanton who verbally abused a supervisor, accused him of
being a "damn liar," and invited him to fight. We relied on the

grounds that the incident was provoked by the employer and that "[e]xpression of his [Blanton's] anger in the language of the mill" was "not nearly as shocking" as the employer suggested. * * * This court, in *NLRB v. Georgia Rug Mill*, 308 F.2d 89 (C.A.5, 1962), enforced the Board order directing reinstatement by an antiunion employer of a union adherent who had replied with obscenities to a supervisor's questioning him concerning unauthorized absence.   In *NLRB v. Princeton Inn Co.*, 424 F.2d 264 (C.A.3, 1970), the Board found that a union adherent's foul and abusive language toward a female employee was pretext for discharge, considered against his prior usage of similar language without warning, and the employer's background of antiunion bias, and the fact that a supervisor present did not admonish the employee. The court enforced. The union adherent in *NLRB v. Reynolds Wire Co.*, 121 F.2d 627 (C.A.7, 1941), was fired on the alleged ground that he had scribbled on the newly painted door of the toilet an obscene remark describing the paint job. It was characteristic for employees to scribble indecent remarks on toilet walls and doors. The company had requested that employees refrain from doing this, but it had never fired anyone for doing it or indicated that it would be grounds for discharge. The Board's reinstatement order was enforced.

There are, of course, many cases in which employees have been fired for obscene language or conduct, and the discharges have been held not to violate the Act. The key to understanding is that the drawing of permissible inferences from consideration of what the employee did and said, the mores of the work place, the employee's union adherence, and the antiunion bias of the employer, is the province of the Board, not to be undone by judges. In this instance, the Board was entitled to conclude that, although Rogers' conduct was "bad" in the sense that it was coarse and vulgar, he would not have been discharged in the absence of antiunion bias. It then becomes our duty to enforce. We do not sit as monitors of the level of sexual horseplay permitted in industrial plants or as censors of conduct by a worker which from an Olympian level we think distasteful. Nor do we have any business substituting our judgments of good taste for the experience and expertise of the Board in day-to-day matters of industrial life. * * *

Problems for Discussion

1. Consider the discharge of Stone for unexcused absenteeism. What evidence was likely before the Administrative Law Judge on the issue of Stone's ailments between May 4 and May 14? How free was the NLRB to disagree with the ALJ on this issue? How much weight should be given by the appeals court to the fact that the NLRB and the ALJ disagreed, when the court applies the test of "substantial evidence on the record

considered as a whole"? Was the court correct in concluding that, at worst, the record sustained the inference that the company was merely acting "unreasonably" and not discriminatorily?

2. Consider the discharge of Rogers for indecent conduct. Given the facts set forth in the majority and dissenting opinions, is the only reasonable conclusion that Rogers was discharged "for cause"? (Consider the prevailing mores within the plant, and the apparent supervisory condonation.) If it is plausible to conclude that the indecent-conduct accusation was merely a pretext, must not the Board's order be enforced? What are the relative capabilities of the ALJ, the NLRB, and the appellate court in assessing the gravity of the employee's misdeeds and therefore the likely motive of the employer?

3. Had the Board's conclusions regarding the company's motive in both discharges been reached by a federal trial judge, could a court of appeals have reversed them as "clearly erroneous"? Had they been made by a civil jury, could a trial court have properly overturned them on a motion for a judgment n. o. v. or for a new trial? Is the NLRB entitled to a greater or lesser measure of deference on appellate review of fact-findings than the trial judge or the jury?

4. Does it make sense to have a single standard of review of fact-findings without regard to the kind of fact in dispute? Consider the questions: (a) was Stone lying when he claimed he was ill between May 4 and May 14? (b) was Rogers' conduct disruptive or offensive within the context of his plant? (c) had the company "condoned" this conduct in the past? (d) was the company aware of Stone's and Rogers' union activities at the time of their discharges? (e) even assuming some wrongdoing by Stone and Rogers, was discharge an unusually harsh discipline? (f) what really motivated the company in discharging them? Are findings by the ALJ on each of these issues entitled to the same degree of deference by the NLRB? Are findings by the NLRB on each of these issues entitled to the same degree of deference by the court of appeals?

5. Is it fair to say that the NLRB's decision reflects a belief that the policies of the NLRB might be too readily subverted if an anti-union employer could point to a minor contemporaneous delinquency by a union supporter as a justification for severe discipline? Is it fair to say that the opinion of the court majority reflects a belief that sound economic judgments by employers might be too readily subverted if a delinquent employee could point to contemporaneous union activity as a shield protecting incompetence or substandard behavior on the job? If this is an accurate statement of the conflict between the NLRB and the court of appeals, whose view should prevail?

6. How does the court majority know that in the case of a discharged union supporter who has committed "flagrant misdeeds", onlooking employees will understand that their own jobs are not jeopardized by their union activities? Compare the findings in the Getman, Goldberg & Herman study, at pp. 200–01 supra.

Cases like *Wellington Mill* and *Mueller Brass* are often characterized as "pretext" cases, in which the General Counsel claims that the business justification asserted by the employer was in fact nonexistent and is no more than an after-the-fact cover-up for discipline which is discriminatorily motivated. It is also possible to analyze such cases as involving "mixed motives," in which the factfinder can reasonably conclude that the employer's motivation was in part anti-union and in part job-related. The NLRB has through the years tended to conclude that if anti-union animus plays any part in the discipline Section 8(a)(3) is violated, while many courts have required that it be the "substantial" or "predominant" cause, or that it be the "but for" cause. In *Mueller Brass*, both the majority and the dissent appear to endorse the principle that the employer does not violate the NLRA if it would have discharged the employee anyway, even apart from his union activity; this would require the General Counsel to prove that "but for" the union activity the employee would not have been discharged. The Board has concluded in WRIGHT LINE, INC., 251 N.L.R.B. No. 150 (1980), that this is the proper test in both "pretext" cases and "mixed motive" cases under Section 8(a)(3). On November 4, 1980, General Counsel Lubbers sent the following memorandum to all Regional Directors, explaining the impact of *Wright Line.*

MEMORANDUM 80–58

I. Introduction

The Board has recently set forth a uniform test and method of analysis to be applied in Section 8(a)(3) cases involving motive. In Wright Line, A Division of Wright Line, Inc., 251 NLRB No. 150, the Board recognized the "intolerable confusion" that existed in this area of the law, and adopted the test of causality applied by the Supreme Court in Mt. Healthy City School District Board of Education v. Doyle, 429 U.S. 274, a case involving a discharge motivated in part by constitutionally protected activity.

II. The Wright Line Test

This test involves a two-part analysis. Initially, the General Counsel must establish a prima facie case that protected conduct was "a motivating factor" in the employer's decision. The burden then shifts to the employer to demonstrate, as an affirmative defense, that the decision would have been the same even in the absence of protected conduct. If the employer fails to establish the affirmative defense, the General Counsel will prevail, regardless of the quantum of unlawful motivation involved. If the employer does establish this defense, it would appear that the General Counsel would have the opportunity to rebut it. Absent such rebuttal, the employer would prevail.

Although the Board emphasizes that Wright Line represents a clarification, rather than a reformulation, of the traditional Board analysis in dual motivation cases, several changes in past practice should be noted. Most importantly, Wright Line substitutes a more precise analytical framework for the previously used "in part" test, which was susceptible of a looser application which often created enforcement problems in the courts. Thus, in the past, the Board's inquiry, at times, appeared to go no further than an initial determination that the employer's actions were motivated at least "in part" by an employee's protected activity. In contrast, future Board decisions will go further and determine whether, if the employer's action was in fact based in part on legitimate business reasons, the action would have been the same even in the absence of protected activity.

Secondly, the Wright Line test will be applied to both pretext and mixed motive cases. Although the Board notes that these two types of Section 8(a)(3) cases are analytically different, it is clear, that the Mt. Healthy-Wright Line test is readily applicable to both. In both pretext and dual motive cases, the General Counsel must establish a *prima facie* case of discrimination. The employer will then present the affirmative defense, and the General Counsel may offer rebuttal. Based on the entire record, the Board will determine that: (a) the General Counsel's *prima facie* case was successfully rebutted by a showing that union activities played no role in the employer's action, or that unprotected activities, standing alone, would have caused the employer's action (no violation); (b) the employer's reason for the action was not, in fact, relied upon (*i. e.*, a pretext case); or (c) the asserted reason was relied upon in part, but the employer cannot show that such reason alone would have caused the employer's action (*i. e.*, a mixed-motive case). Thus, as stated by the Board, a pretext case is one in which the employer's affirmative defense is "wholly without merit," whereas in a dual motive case, the affirmative defense "has at least some merit."

A third change in Board practice signaled by Wright Line is basically a semantic one. In order to avoid further confusion, the Board intends to eliminate some words used previously; that is: "in part," "dominant or primary motive," "motivating or substantial cause," *etc.* * * *

IV. Applicability of Wright Line to Regional Office Investigations

It is recognized that, even prior to Wright Line, Regional offices investigated the employer's asserted justification for an action alleged as unlawful. Such evidence was, and is, relevant to the issue of whether there is a *prima facie* case. In addition, such evidence is now relevant to an affirmative defense in Wright Line cases.

After all of the evidence has been gathered from all parties and independent sources, the Region will have to evaluate the evidence in light of Wright Line. Of course, if a *prima facie* case is not established, the charge would be dismissed, absent withdrawal, on traditional grounds. If a *prima facie* case is established, and it is *reasonably debatable* as to whether the employer has established its Wright Line defense, the Region should issue complaint, absent settlement. If a *prima facie* case is established, but the employer has *clearly established* its Wright Line defense, the charge should be dismissed, absent withdrawal.

———

Discrimination on the Basis of Race or Sex. In UNITED PACK-INGHOUSE WORKERS v. NLRB, 416 F.2d 1126 (D.C.Cir. 1969), cert. denied, 396 U.S. 903 (1969), the court on its own initiative held that employer discrimination in working conditions among white, black and latin employees was without more a violation of Section 8(a)(1) of the Labor Act. The court found that "invidious discrimination on account of race or national origin" deters the exercise of section 7 employee rights.

  This effect is twofold: (1) racial discrimination sets up an unjustified clash of interests between groups of workers which tends to reduce the likelihood and the effectiveness of their working in concert to achieve their legitimate goals under the Act; and (2) racial discrimination creates in its victims an apathy or docility which inhibits them from asserting their rights against the perpetrator of the discrimination.

The court found these effects to be evidenced in the record and to have been recognized by "union leaders, businessmen, government officials and psychologists," and remanded to the Board to consider the full record in light of the court's theory. The Board found insufficient evidence of racial discrimination and dismissed the claim under Section 8(a)(1), without addressing whether it agreed with the court's analysis of that section.

  Shortly after, however, the Board did address the issue and held (one member dissenting and one member finding no discrimination in fact and thus avoiding the legal issue) that "discrimination on the basis of race, color, religion, sex, or national origin is not *per se* a violation of the Act." JUBILEE MFG. CO., 202 N.L.R.B. 272 (1973), enf'd per curiam, 87 L.R.R.M. 3168, 75 CCH Lab.Cas. ¶ 10405 (D.C. Cir. 1974) (alleged discrimination in pay rates between men and women employees). Such discrimination standing alone was held not to be "inherently destructive" of employee Section 7 rights and therefore not violative of Section 8(a)(1) or (3). "There must be actual evidence, as opposed to speculation, of a nexus between the alleged discriminatory conduct and the interference with, or restraint of, employees in the exercise of those rights protected by the Act." The Board distinguished its decisions holding that the employer's race discrimination might warrant setting aside an election, or finding a refusal to bargain or finding interference with employees taking con-

certed action on hiring policies; in all those instances, unlike race or sex discrimination pure and simple, there was "the necessary direct relationship between the alleged discrimination and our traditional and primary functions of fostering collective bargaining, protecting employees' rights to act concertedly" and conducting free and sober elections. The Board has in effect relegated such job-discrimination claims to the court-enforcement machinery of Title VII of the Civil Rights Act of 1964 and the Equal Employment Opportunity Commission, rejecting the conclusion of the court of appeals in *United Packinghouse* that the powers of the Board and the EEOC were intended by Congress to be concurrent.

NLRB v. ADKINS TRANSFER CO.

United States Court of Appeals, Sixth Circuit, 1955.
226 F.2d 324.

McALLISTER, CIRCUIT JUDGE.

The National Labor Relations Board filed a petition for enforcement of its order issued against respondent, Adkins Transfer Company, finding it guilty of violation of Section 8(a)(3) and (1) of the National Labor Relations Act * * *

Respondent is a small truck line operator, carrying on its business between Chicago and Nashville, with the latter as the extreme southern point served. Its Nashville terminal utilized approximately eight trucks per day in transporting shipments to other cities, and four pick-up trucks for local work in Nashville. There is no evidence of any anti-union attitude on the part of the respondent, but, on the contrary, it has been on good terms with the local Teamsters Union, which is the charging party in the case. In fact, all of its road drivers are members of the Teamsters Union, and all of its local pick-up men and dock men are also members of the union. In addition, all extra employees engaged by respondent are procured by calling the local Teamsters union hall, whereupon the union sends such extra employees to respondent's place of business. This practice is followed in spite of the fact that there is in effect in the State of Tennessee the type of statute known as an open shop statute.

In November, 1953, respondent employed a mechanic and a helper whose duties were exclusively the maintenance and servicing of respondent's trucks. These are the employees involved in this case. In the same month that their employment commenced, the two employees joined the local Teamsters Union. Thereafter, the union demanded that respondent bargain with it for the purpose of entering into two contracts—one, a mechanic's contract for one of the employees, and the other, a service contract, for the other employee.

At that time, one of the employees was paid at the rate of $1.25 per hour, and the other, 75 cents per hour. The union representative met with respondent's president and showed him copies of the union's uniform contracts covering mechanics and service men which were currently in effect between the union and other Nashville motor carriers. The various job classifications and the applicable wage rates specified in the contracts were discussed. As the union representative pointed out, under the contracts which he proposed that respondent adopt, one of the employees would receive $1.75 an hour, an increase of 50 cents over his current rate, and the other would receive between $1.25 and $1.40 per hour, an increase of between 50 and 65 cents over his current rate. There was no discussion as to whether a compromise could be reached on wage scales.

The first meeting between the union representative and respondent's president took place November 16. A second meeting occurred November 20. On the next day, the foreman came into the shop where the two employees were working, and stated that he had bad news for them—that the president was going to close the shop because he was not going to pay the union scale. At the direction of respondent's president, the foreman thereafter discharged the two employees. Respondent's president testified with regard to this incident, without contradiction or challenge, that it was "purely and simply a question of costs." Respondent's mechanical work since the discharge of the employees has been done on a job-by-job basis by local truck and automobile dealers, and the servicing has been done partly by its own operating employees and partly by independent business concerns. Respondent's president testified that he found this method of having the mechanical work done had resulted in even lower labor costs than those entailed by its former method of operation, under which respondent had paid $2.00 an hour for ·the combined services of the two employees. Respondent never replaced the two men, and its president testified on the hearing that it did not intend to.

A hearing was held before the trial examiner who, after listening to the witnesses, filed findings of fact, conclusions of law, and a recommendation. He set forth in his findings that respondent's president testified, credibly, that, based upon his experience in dealing with the union, he believed that if respondent had continued its maintenance department at Nashville without raising the wages of the two employees to meet the union scale, a strike would have ensued which would have effectively closed down respondent's entire business operations. The examiner stated that the accuracy of such opinion was substantiated by the statement of the union representative who testified, on the hearing, that he knew of no instance when the union permitted a contracting employer to pay union members different wage rates than were provided in the union's uniform industry agreement for the particular employee classification. He found that respondent's president, rather than capitulating to the union demands and increasing the wages of the two employees, which he considered economically disadvantageous to respondent, had discontinued the maintenance department and discharged the two maintenance employees. He further found that respondent's president testified that the fact that the two employees joined the union did not motivate their discharge. The trial examiner concluded his findings with the following statement: "This is not a case where an employer who is generally hostile towards unions and opposes employee organization seeks to defeat his employees' efforts to engage in collective bargaining by discontinuing a department in which a majority of the employees have selected a collective bargaining representative. * * * In this regard, it is significant that the complaint does not charge that the Respondent has refused to bargain in good faith with the Union. Here, the Respondent had only two practical choices, either to pay its maintenance employees the wage rates demanded by the Union, or discontinue its maintenance department. No area for bargaining with the Union existed." The examiner then went on to point out that the union representative had testified that, if respondent had kept the maintenance department open but had declined to sign the union contract, the union procedure would have been to call a strike, and that a strike in which the Teamsters Union controlled the over-the-road men and the dock men—as in this case—usually resulted in a 100% shutdown of the company. The examiner, therefore, found that respondent had committed no unfair labor practice by choosing to discontinue its maintenance department and to discharge the two maintenance employees, especially in the absence of evidence of other unfair labor practices or animus toward the union; and that, accordingly, respondent did not discharge the employees to encourage or discourage membership in the labor organization, in violation of Section 8(a)(1) and (3) of the Act. He concluded by recommending that the complaint be dismissed.

The Board, however, rejected the recommendations of the trial examiner and his conclusions as to the alleged unfair labor practices. It held that the discharges established a prima facie case that the dismissal was violative of Section 8(a)(3) and (1) of the Act for the reason that the employees would not have been so summarily dismissed if they had not joined the union, and had not sought, through the union, to exercise the rights incident to union membership. The Board further said that respondent had not sustained its burden of dispelling the inferences fairly to be drawn, and that its claim that the dismissals represented an attempt to resolve a difficult economic position was supported "by nothing more than its subjective anticipation of what the Union might do, rather than upon what the Union actually did do in its representation of these employees." It, therefore, held that the dismissal was violative of the Act and out-lined the remedies already mentioned.   *   *   *

We are of the view that the trial examiner was right and the Board was wrong in its decision and order. Only such discrimination as encourages or discourages membership in a labor organization is proscribed by the Act. Radio Officers' Union of Commercial Telegraphers Union, A. F. L. v. National Labor Relations Board, 347 U.S. 17, 74 S.Ct. 323, 98 L.Ed. 455. In order to establish an 8(a)(3) violation, there must be evidence that the employer's act encouraged or discouraged union membership. The section requires that the discrimination in regard to tenure of employment have both the purpose and effect of discouraging union membership, and to make out a case, it must appear that the employer has, by discrimination, encouraged or discouraged membership in a labor organization. There was no such discrimination in the instant case. A company may suspend its operations or change its business methods so long as its change in operations is not motivated by the illegal intention to avoid its obligations under the Act. National Labor Relations Board v. Houston Chronicle Pub. Co., 5 Cir., 211 F.2d 848. An employer may discharge or refuse to reemploy one of his employees for any reason, just or unjust, except discrimination because of union activities and relationships, and the controlling and ultimate fact which determines an issue of the kind here presented is, what was the true reason back of the discharge.   *   *   *

It is true that what might be termed the secondary reason for the discharge of the two employees was because they were members of the union, but the fact that they were members of the union was only incidental, and was not the real reason behind their discharge. The real reason was because the union wage scales were too high for respondent to operate profitably the department in question; and, since the employees were members of the union, respondent would be obliged to pay those rates, or close the department, or suffer a strike. It is plain that there was no interference or restraint or coercion of the employees in their rights to self-organization or collective bargaining, and there was no discrimination to encourage or discourage membership in a labor organization. Consequently, there was no violation of Section 8(a)(3) and (1) of the Act.

Respondent had no feeling against the labor union. All of his employees were already members of the union, and his relations with them and the union were friendly and cooperative. The only consideration that actuated respondent in dismissing the employees was, not that they were members of the union, but that the union wage scales were too high for this particular employment and that such services could be more cheaply performed by outside business concerns. All of these facts are indubitable from the evidence before us. It is our view that the trial examiner's finding and recommended disposition are both factually and legally correct, and that the Board's findings of fact to the contrary are not supported by substantial evidence on the record as a whole.

In accordance with the foregoing, a decree will be entered denying enforcement of the order of the Board.

Problems for Discussion

1. Is the court correct in concluding that the employer did not "discriminate" in a manner which "discourages" union membership? Would the mechanic and helper not have retained their jobs had they not sought union membership and representation? Does not their discharge for this reason clearly discriminate and discourage? *Who* is discouraged from union membership and activities?

2. Would the court's decision have been different if the following facts were true, in isolation or combination? (a) The wage increase requested by the union was not such as to make it "unprofitable" to continue the two employees but simply less profitable than before. (b) The union had not represented any of the company's other employees but simply sought to represent the two employees ultimately discharged. (c) The union's wage demand was "isolated" and was not part of an area pattern, and was stated to be subject to further negotiation.

An analogous problem to that presented in the principal case arises when an employer "because of the union" decides to close its plant and relocate elsewhere. There is general agreement that if the employer's move is motivated by hostility toward and a desire to escape the union, the action violates Section 8(a)(3). "It is * * * well settled that [the employer] may not transfer its situs to deprive his employees of rights protected by Section 7." Local 57, ILGWU v. NLRB (Garwin Corp.), 374 F.2d 295 (D.C. Cir.), cert. denied 387 U.S. 942 (1967) (BURGER, J.). The relocation is said to be for "anti-union animus" and is labelled a "runaway shop." Over the years, however, there has been disagreement between the Board and the courts of appeals as to the legality of a relocation which is precipitated by wage increases, actual or impending, effected through unionization. As in *Adkins Transfer*, the courts have been generally more willing than the Board to countenance employer relocation triggered by a worsening economic picture to which the union substantially contributes. For example, in NLRB v. RAPID BINDERY, INC., 293 F.2d 170 (2d Cir. 1961), the employer moved its bindery operation from cramped and outmoded quarters very shortly after a union was certified; the employer impressed the employees while the election was pending with the likelihood of such a move, and it failed to bargain with the union concerning the relocation after the union was certified. Although the Board found a violation of Section 8(a)(3), the court of appeals reversed, holding:

> "All of the evidence points to motivation for sound business reasons. Though there may have been animosity between Union and Rapid, animosity furnishes no basis for the inference that this was the preponderant motive for the move when convincing evidence was received demonstrating business necessity. The decided cases do not condemn an employer who considers his relationship with his plant's union as only one part of the broad economic picture he must survey when he is faced with determining the desirability of making changes in his operations."

In another case, NLRB v. Lassing, 284 F.2d 781 (6th Cir. 1960), cert. den. 366 U.S. 909 (1961), the court stated:

> "The advent of the Union was a new economic factor which necessarily had to be evaluated by the respondent as a part of the overall picture pertaining to costs of operation. It is completely unrealistic in the field of business to say that management is acting arbitrarily or unreasonably in changing its method of operations based on reasonably anticipated increased costs, instead of waiting until such increased costs actually materialize.
>
> " * * * Fundamentally, the change was made because of reasonably anticipated increased costs, regardless of whether this increased cost was caused by the advent of the Union or by some other factor entering into the picture."

Is it practical, or even possible, to authorize relocations or plant removals motivated by the anticipation of increased costs which a union will bring, but to hold illegal such action when motivated by "anti-union animus"? What is anti-union animus, if not a resistance to the union because of the economic burdens it will impose—in the form not only of increased financial benefits for the workers but also of restrictions upon the employer in governing the enterprise, which presumably can also be translated into economic burdens? Are not these added labor-related costs exactly what engenders employer antipathy toward the union? How often is it that the employer nurtures "anti-union animus" which is not economically based? If such is rare indeed, then what is left of Section 8 (a)(3) in these kinds of cases?

These issues arise not only in cases of layoff and subcontracting, as in *Adkins Transfer*, and of plant relocation, but also in cases of the closing and termination of the business of a single plant of a multi-plant concern, or of the complete termination and liquidation of an enterprise. That is the scenario of the following case.

TEXTILE WORKERS UNION v. DARLINGTON MFG. CO.

Supreme Court of the United States, 1965.
380 U.S. 263, 85 S.Ct. 994, 13 L.Ed.2d 827.

MR. JUSTICE HARLAN delivered the opinion of the Court.

*   *   *   *   *   *   *   *   *   *

Darlington Manufacturing Company was a South Carolina corporation operating one textile mill. A majority of Darlington's stock was held by Deering Milliken & Co., a New York "selling house" marketing textiles produced by others. Deering Milliken in turn was controlled by Roger Milliken, president of Darlington, and by other members of the Milliken family. The National Labor Relations Board found that the Milliken family, through Deering Milliken, operated 17 textile manufacturers, including Darlington, whose products, manufactured in 27 different mills, were marketed through Deering Milliken.

In March 1956 petitioner Textile Workers Union initiated an organizational campaign at Darlington which the company resisted vigorously in various ways, including threats to close the mill if the union won a representation election. On September 6, 1956, the union won an election by a narrow margin. When Roger Milliken was advised of the union victory, he decided to call a meeting of the Darlington board of directors to consider closing the mill. Mr. Milliken testified before the Labor Board:

> "I felt that as a result of the campaign that had been conducted and the promises and statements made in these letters that had been distributed [favoring unionization], that if before we had had some hope, possible hope of achieving competitive [costs] * * * by taking advantage of new machinery that was being put in, that this hope had diminished as a result of the election because a majority of the employees had voted in favor of the union * * *." (R. 457.)

The board of directors met on September 12 and voted to liquidate the corporation, action which was approved by the stockholders on October 17. The plant ceased operations entirely in November, and all plant machinery and equipment was sold piecemeal at auction in December.

The union filed charges with the Labor Board claiming that Darlington had violated §§ 8(a) (1) and 8(a) (3) of the National Labor Relations Act by closing its plant, and § 8(a) (5) by refusing to bargain with the union after the election. The Board, by a divided vote, found that Darlington had been closed because of the anti-union animus of Roger Milliken, and held that to be a violation of § 8(a) (3). The Board also found Darlington to be part of a single integrated employer group controlled by the Milliken family through Deering Milliken; therefore Deering Milliken could be held liable for the unfair labor practices of Darlington. Alternatively, since Darlington was a part of the Deering Milliken enterprise, Deering Milliken had violated the Act by closing part of its business for a discriminatory purpose. The Board ordered back pay for all Darlington employees until they obtained substantially equivalent work or were put on preferential hiring lists at the other Deering Milliken mills. Respondent Deering Milliken was ordered to bargain with the union in regard to details of compliance with the Board order. 139 N.L.R.B. 241.

On review, the Court of Appeals, sitting *en banc*, denied enforcement by a divided vote. 325 F.2d 682. The Court of Appeals held that even accepting *arguendo* the Board's determination that Deering Milliken had the status of a single employer, a company has the absolute right to close out a part or all of its business regardless of anti-union motives. The court therefore did not review the Board's finding that Deering Milliken was a single integrated employer. We granted certiorari * * * to consider the important questions involved. We hold that so far as the Labor Act is concerned, an employer has the absolute right to terminate his entire business for any reason he pleases, but disagree with the Court of Appeals that such right includes the ability to close part of a business no matter what the reason. We conclude that the case must be remanded to the Board for further proceedings.

Preliminarily it should be observed that both petitioners argue that the Darlington closing violated § 8(a) (1) as well as § 8(a) (3) of the Act. We think, however, that the Board was correct in treating the closing only under § 8(a) (3). Section 8(a) (1) provides that it is an unfair labor practice for an employer "to interfere with, restrain, or coerce employees in the exercise of" § 7 rights. Naturally, certain business decisions will, to some degree, interfere with concerted activities by employees. But it is only when the interference with § 7 rights outweighs the business justification for the employer's action that § 8(a) (1) is violated. See, *e.g.*, Labor Board v. Steelworkers, 357 U.S. 357, 78 S.Ct. 1268; Republic Aviation Corp. v. Labor Board, 324 U.S. 793, 65 S.Ct. 982. A violation of § 8(a) (1) alone therefore presupposes an act which is unlawful even absent a discriminatory motive. Whatever may be the limits of § 8(a) (1), some employer decisions are so peculiarly matters of management prerogative that they would never constitute violations of § 8(a) (1), whether or not they involved sound business judgment, unless they also violated § 8(a) (3). Thus it is not questioned in this case that an employer has the right to terminate his business, whatever the impact of such action on concerted activities, if the decision to close is motivated by other than discriminatory reasons. But such action, if discriminatorily motivated, is encompassed within the literal language of § 8(a) (3). We therefore deal with the Darlington closing under that section.

We consider first the argument, advanced by the petitioner union but not by the Board, and rejected by the Court of Appeals, that an employer may not go completely out of business without running afoul of the Labor Act if such action is prompted by a desire to avoid unionization. Given the Board's findings on the issue of motive, acceptance of this contention would carry the day for the Board's conclusion that the closing of this plant was an unfair labor practice, even on the assumption that Darlington is to be regarded as an independent unrelated employer. A proposition that a single businessman cannot choose to go out of business if he wants to would represent such a startling innovation that it should not be entertained without the clearest manifestation of legislative intent or unequivocal judicial precedent so construing the Labor Act. We find neither.

So far as legislative manifestation is concerned, it is sufficient to say that there is not the slightest indication in the history of the Wagner Act or of the Taft-Hartley Act that Congress envisaged any such result under either statute.

As for judicial precedent * * * the courts of appeals have generally assumed that a complete cessation of business will remove an employer from future coverage by the Act. Thus the Court of Appeals said in this case: The Act "does not compel a person to become or remain an employee. It does not compel one to become or remain an employer. Either may withdraw from that status with immunity, so long as the obligations of an employment contract have been met." 325 F.2d, at 685. * * *

The AFL–CIO suggests in its *amicus* brief that Darlington's action was similar to a discriminatory lockout, which is prohibited "because designed to frustrate organizational efforts, to destroy or undermine bargaining representation, or to evade the duty to bargain." One of the purposes of the Labor Act is to prohibit the discriminatory use of economic weapons in an effort to obtain future benefits. The discriminatory lockout designed to destroy a union, like a "runaway shop," is a lever which has been used to discourage collective employee activities in the future. But a complete liquidation of a business yields no such future benefit for the employer, if the termination is bona fide. It may be motivated more by spite against the union than by business reasons, but it is not the type of discrimination which is prohibited by the Act. The personal satisfaction that such an employer may derive from standing on his beliefs or the mere possibility that other employers will follow his example are surely too remote to be considered dangers at which the labor statutes were aimed. Although employees may be prohibited from engaging in a strike under certain conditions, no one would consider it a violation of the Act for the same employees to quit their employment *en masse*, even if motivated by a desire to ruin the employer. The very permanence of such action would negate any future economic benefit to the employees. The employer's right to go out of business is no different.

We are not presented here with the case of a "runaway shop," whereby Darlington would transfer its work to another plant or open a new plant in another locality to replace its closed plant. Nor are we concerned with a shutdown where the employees, by renouncing the union, could cause the plant to reopen. Such cases would involve discriminatory employer action for the purpose of obtaining some benefit in the future from the new employees. We hold here only that when an employer closes his entire business, even if the liquidation is motivated by vindictiveness towards the union, such action is not an unfair labor practice.[38]

While we thus agree with the Court of Appeals that viewing Darlington as an independent employer the liquidation of its business was not an unfair labor practice, we cannot accept the lower court's view that the same conclusion necessarily follows if Darlington is regarded as an integral part of the Deering Milliken enterprise.

The closing of an entire business, even though discriminatory, ends the employer-employee relationship; the force of such a closing is entirely spent as to that business when termination of the enterprise takes place. On the other hand, a discriminatory partial closing may have repercussions on what remains of the business, affording employer leverage for discouraging the free exercise of § 7 rights among remaining employees of much the same kind as that found to exist in the "runaway shop" and "temporary closing" cases. More-

38. Nothing we have said in this opinion would justify an employer interfering with employee organizational activities by threatening to close his plant, as distinguished from announcing a decision to close already reached by the board of directors or other management authority empowered to make such a decision. We recognize that this safeguard does not wholly remove the possibility that our holding may result in some deterrent effect on organizational activities independent of that arising from the closing itself. An employer may be encouraged to make a definitive decision to close on the theory that its mere announcement before a representation election will discourage the employees from voting for the union, and thus his decision may not have to be implemented. Such a possibility is not likely to occur, however, except in a marginal business; a solidly successful employer is not apt to hazard the possibility that the employees will call his bluff by voting to organize. We see no practical way of eliminating this possible consequence of our holding short of allowing the Board to order an employer who chooses so to gamble with his employees not to carry out his announced intention to close. We do not consider the matter of sufficient significance in the overall labor-management relations picture to require or justify a decision different from the one we have made.

over, a possible remedy open to the Board in such a case, like the remedies available in the "runaway shop" and "temporary closing" cases, is to order reinstatement of the discharged employees in the other parts of the business. No such remedy is available when an entire business has been terminated. By analogy to those cases involving a continuing enterprise we are constrained to hold, in disagreement with the Court of Appeals, that a partial closing is an unfair labor practice under § 8(a) (3) if motivated by a purpose to chill unionism in any of the remaining plants of the single employer and if the employer may reasonably have foreseen that such closing will likely have that effect.

While we have spoken in terms of a "partial closing" in the context of the Board's finding that Darlington was part of a larger single enterprise controlled by the Milliken family, we do not mean to suggest that an organizational integration of plants or corporations is a necessary prerequisite to the establishment of such a violation of § 8 (a) (3). If the persons exercising control over a plant that is being closed for anti-union reasons (1) have an interest in another business, whether or not affiliated with or engaged in the same line of commercial activity as the closed plant, of sufficient substantiality to give promise of their reaping a benefit from the discouragement of unionization in that business; (2) act to close their plant with the purpose of producing such a result; and (3) occupy a relationship to the other business which makes it realistically foreseeable that its employees will fear that such business will also be closed down if they persist in organizational activities, we think that an unfair labor practice has been made out.

Although the Board's single employer finding necessarily embraced findings as to Roger Milliken and the Milliken family which, if sustained by the Court of Appeals, would satisfy the elements of "interest" and "relationship" with respect to other parts of the Deering Milliken enterprise, that and the other Board findings fall short of establishing the factors of "purpose" and "effect" which are vital requisites of the general principles that govern a case of this kind.

Thus, the Board's findings as to the purpose and foreseeable effect of the Darlington closing pertained *only* to its impact on the Darlington employees. No findings were made as to the purpose and effect of the closing with respect to the employees in the other plants comprising the Deering Milliken group. It does not suffice to establish the unfair labor practice charged here to argue that the Darlington closing necessarily had an adverse impact upon unionization in such other plants. We have heretofore observed that employer action which has a foreseeable consequence of discouraging concerted activities generally does not amount to a violation of § 8(a) (3) in the absence of a showing of motivation which is aimed at achieving the prohibited effect. * * *

In these circumstances, we think the proper disposition of this case is to require that it be remanded to the Board so as to afford the Board the opportunity to make further findings on the issue of purpose and effect. * * *

MR. JUSTICE STEWART took no part in the decision of this case.

MR. JUSTICE GOLDBERG took no part in the consideration or decision of this case.

On remand, the Board reversed the Trial Examiner and found that the Millikens had closed the Darlington plant with the purpose of deterring union organization at other establishments in which they had dominant interests. The United States Court of Appeals for the Fourth Circuit enforced the ensuing order by a 5–2 vote. Darlington Mfg. Co. v. NLRB, 397 F.2d 760 (4th Cir. 1968) cert. den. 393 U.S. 1023 (1969). In response to the claim of Roger Milliken that the record demonstrated that the purpose of the Darlington closing was (if not for legitimate business reasons) to exact retribution against only the employees at that site, the court concluded: "[I]t was sufficient for the Board to find that the election of the union was a substantial cause of Darlington's closing and that the employer was actually motivated, at least in part, by a purpose to chill unionism in other Deering Milliken mills. The coexistence of this chilling purpose with an antiunion purpose directed against Darlington does not impair the Board's decision."

Problems for Discussion

1. After observing that Section 8(a)(1) may be violated without proof of anti-union animus while such animus must be shown to violate Section 8(a)(3), Justice Harlan states that cases of plant closings must be treated under Section 8(a)(3). Why? Might not the problem illustrated by such cases as *Adkins Transfer* and *Darlington* be better analyzed in terms of Section 8(a)(1)?

2. Does the analysis of Justice Harlan also apply to the discharge of an individual employee for reasons other than anti-union animus? That is, is Section 8(a)(3) "preemptive" in such cases and anti-union animus necessary to a violation, or can the Board hold that even in the absence of anti-union animus the employer's asserted business reason is so flimsy as to be outweighed by the harm to the Section 7 rights of the employee?

(a) Was there anti-union animus behind the discharge of the employee who was soliciting for the union on his lunchtime in violation of the company rule in *Republic Aviation Corp. v. NLRB*, p. 115 supra? Why was the discharge held to violate Section 8(a)(3)?

(b) Does an employer commit an unfair labor practice when it acts on reliable (but in fact false) information that union organizer Jones has threatened to dynamite the union's way into the plant, and discharges Jones? See *NLRB* v. *Burnup & Sims*, 379 U.S. 21, 85 S.Ct. 171, 13 L.Ed. 2d 1 (1964).

3. Why should the fairness or unfairness of a business closing depend upon its effect upon the organizational freedom of other employees not directly affected by the closing? Why is the effect upon employees whose jobs are eliminated unimportant? Can they demonstrate that there has been "discrimination" which "discourages" union membership? Is the Court's requirement that there be an intention to discourage, and discouragement of, employees *other* than the dischargees also a requirement in the case of a discharge of a single employee?

4. Was Justice Harlan correct in asserting that there is no effective remedy for the discriminatory shutdown of an entire business?

5. George Lithograph Company until recently ran a complete printing operation, but it closed down its mailing department (which was being profitably operated) when the employees there were organized by the Lithographers and Photoengravers Union. That union, which intends to attempt to organize employees elsewhere within the George plant, filed a charge alleging that the closing of the department constituted a violation of Sections 8(a)(1) and (3) of the Labor Act. The Administrative Law Judge found that there was "not a scintilla of evidence from which it could be reasonably inferred that the closing of the mailing department had a chilling effect on the union activities of Respondent's remaining employees." The Union has filed exceptions with the Board to the report of the Administrative Law Judge. What arguments should the Union make? Should the Board reverse its Judge? See *George Lithograph Co.*, 204 N.L.R.B. 431 (1973).

6. Assume that a New York manufacturer of women's clothing, recently organized, closes down its plant—avowedly to escape the union and to "show" the employees that unionization was unwise—and moves its equipment to a newly purchased plant building in Florida. Assume also that the cost of labor in Florida is somewhat cheaper than in New York, and that attempts at unionization in the relevant area in Florida have been over the years met with worker indifference if not hostility. Can the "runaway" employer successfully argue that, on such a record, *Darlington* compels the dismissal of a Section 8(a)(3) complaint? (The hypothetical is inspired by the *Garwin* case, at p. 254 infra.)

D.   REMEDIES FOR UNFAIR LABOR PRACTICES

PHELPS DODGE CORP. v. NLRB

Supreme Court of the United States, 1941.
313 U.S. 177, 61 S.Ct. 845, 85 L.Ed. 1271.

MR. JUSTICE FRANKFURTER delivered the opinion of the Court.

The dominating question which this litigation brings here for the first time is whether an employer subject to the National Labor Relations Act may refuse to hire employees solely because of their affiliations with a labor union. Subsidiary questions grow out of this central issue relating to the means open to the Board to "effectuate the policies of this Act [chapter]," if it finds such discrimination in hiring an "unfair labor practice". Other questions touching the remedial powers of the Board are also involved.   *   *   *

It is no longer disputed that workers cannot be dismissed from employment because of their union affiliations. Is the national interest in industrial peace less affected by discrimination against union activity when men are hired? The contrary is overwhelmingly attested by the long history of industrial conflicts, the diagnosis of their causes by official investigations, the conviction of public men, industrialists and scholars.   *   *   *   Such a policy is an inevitable corollary of the principle of freedom of organization. Discrimination against union labor in the hiring of men is a dam to self organization at the source of supply. The effect of such discrimination is not confined to the actual denial of employment; it inevitably operates against the whole idea of the legitimacy of organization. In a word, it undermines the principle which, as we have seen, is recognized as basic to the attainment of industrial peace.

*   *   *   [A]n embargo against employment of union labor was notoriously one of the chief obstructions to collective bargaining through self-organization. Indisputably the removal of such obstructions was the driving force behind the enactment of the National Labor Relations Act. The prohibition against "discrimination in regard to hire" must be applied as a means towards the accomplishment of the main object of the legislation. We are asked to read "hire" as meaning the wages paid to an employee so as to make the statute merely forbid discrimination in one of the terms of men who have secured employment. So to read the statute would do violence to a spontaneous textual reading of § 8(3) in that "hire" would serve no function because, in the sense which is urged upon us, it is included in the prohibition against "discrimination in regard to   *   *   *   any term or condition of employment". Contemporaneous legislative history, and, above all, the background of industrial experience forbid such textual mutilation.   *   *   *

Since the refusal to hire Curtis and Daugherty solely because of their affiliation with the Union was an unfair labor practice under § 8(3), the remedial authority of the Board under § 10(c) became operative. Of course it could issue, as it did, an order "to cease and desist from such unfair labor practice" in the future. Did Congress also empower the Board to order the employer to undo the wrong by offering the men discriminated against the opportunity for employment which should not have been denied them?

Reinstatement is the conventional correction for discriminatory discharges. Experience having demonstrated that discrimination in hiring is twin to discrimination in firing, it would indeed be surprising if Congress gave a remedy for the one which it denied for the other. * * * [I]f § 10(c), had empowered the Board to "take such affirmative action * * * as will effectuate the policies of this Act [chapter]", the right to restore to a man employment which was wrongfully denied him could hardly be doubted. * * * Attainment of a great national policy through expert administration in collaboration with limited judicial review must not be confined within narrow canons for equitable relief deemed suitable by chancellors in ordinary private controversies. Compare Virginian R. Co. v. System Federation, 300 U.S. 515, 552, 57 S.Ct. 592, 601, 81 L.Ed. 789. To differentiate between discrimination in denying employment and in terminating it, would be a differentiation not only without substance but in defiance of that against which the prohibition of discrimination is directed. * * * To attribute such a function to the participial phrase [in section 10(c)] introduced by "including" is to shrivel a versatile principle to an illustrative application. We find no justification whatever for attributing to Congress such a casuistic withdrawal of the authority which, but for the illustration, it clearly has given the Board. The word "including" does not lend itself to such destructive significance. * * *

* * * There remain for consideration the limitations upon the Board's power to undo the effects of discrimination. Specifically, we have the question of the Board's power to order employment in cases where the men discriminated against had obtained "substantially equivalent employment." * * *

Denial of the Board's power to order opportunities of employment in this situation derives wholly from an infiltration of a portion of § 2 (3) into § 10(c). The argument runs thus: § 10(c) specifically refers to "reinstatement of employees"; the latter portion of § 2(3) refers to an "employee" as a person "who has not obtained any other regular and substantially equivalent employment"; therefore, there can be no reinstatement of an employee who has obtained such employment. The syllogism is perfect. But this is a bit of verbal logic from which the meaning of things has evaporated. * * *

To deny the Board power to neutralize discrimination merely because workers have obtained compensatory employment would confine the "policies of this Act" to the correction of private injuries. The Board was not devised for such a limited function. * * * To be sure, reinstatement is not needed to repair the economic loss of a worker who, after discrimination, has obtained an equally profitable job. But to limit the significance of discrimination merely to questions of monetary loss to workers would thwart the central purpose of the Act, directed as that is toward the achievement and maintenance of workers' self-organization. That there are factors other than loss of wages to a particular worker to be considered is suggested even by a meager knowledge of industrial affairs. Thus, to give only one illustration, if men were discharged who were leading efforts at organization in a plant having a low wage scale, they would not unnaturally be compelled by their economic circumstances to seek and obtain employment elsewhere at equivalent wages. In such a situation, to deny the Board power to wipe out the prior discrimination by ordering the employment of such workers would sanction a most effective way of defeating the right of self-organization.

Therefore, the mere fact that the victim of discrimination has obtained equivalent employment does not itself preclude the Board from undoing the discrimination and requiring employment. But neither does this remedy automatically flow from the Act itself when discrimination has been found. A statute expressive of such large public policy as that on which the National Labor Relations Board is based must be broadly phrased and necessarily carries with it the task of administrative application. There is an area plainly covered by the language of the Act and an area no less plainly without it. But in the nature of things Congress could not catalogue all the devices and stratagems for circumventing the policies of the Act. Nor could it define the whole gamut of remedies to effectuate these policies in an infinite variety of specific situations. Congress met these difficulties by leaving the adaptation of means to end to the empiric process of administration. The exercise of the process was committed to the Board, subject to limited judicial review. Because the relation of remedy to policy is peculiarly a matter for administrative competence, courts must not enter the allowable area of the Board's discretion and must guard against the danger of sliding unconsciously from the narrow confines of law into the more spacious domain of policy. On the other hand, the power with which Congress invested the Board implies responsibility— the responsibility of exercising its judgment in employing the statutory powers. * * *

[The Board had also ordered that the workers wrongfully denied employment should be compensated with backpay from the date of the discrimination to the date of their employment by the

Company, less actual earnings. The Supreme Court, over Board assertions of burden and inadministrability, held that the Board ought in appropriate cases to deduct as well moneys which the worker could have earned during the backpay period but which he unjustifiably refused to earn.]

Note on Remedies

In recent years various critics have urged the NLRB to utilize more stringent remedies to counteract the mounting number of discriminatory discharges and other unfair labor practices affecting organizational rights of employees. The Board has indeed become somewhat more aggressive in formulating effective remedies, not however without some resistance from the courts of appeals. The courts have paid lip-service to the formula of the *Phelps Dodge* case—wide discretion for the Board in formulating remedies, subject to limited judicial review—while at the same time carefully testing the Board's remedies against the policies of the Labor Act. The student should consider not only how the Board might best remedy and deter the commission of unfair labor practices but also how vigorous judicial review should be. (For a comprehensive treatment of the Board's remedies for all unfair labor practices, see D. McDowell & K. Huhn, NLRB Remedies for Unfair Labor Practices (1976).)

The Board's remedial inventiveness was tested in a sequence of cases beginning in the 1960s involving J. P. Stevens & Co., a multi-plant textile concern in the South, which embarked upon a campaign of vigorous (and pervasively illegal) resistance to unionization. This resistance was marked by threats of discharge and of plant closings, actual discharges and other discipline, coercive interrogation, surveillance, restrictions upon solicitation for the union, and the use of Company bulletin boards to publicize the names of union supporters. In a number of instances, the Board issued the following remedial orders (some of which were thought by some courts of appeals to go beyond the policies of the NLRA, but do you agree?): (1) to post the usual notice not only in the individual Company plants in which the unfair labor practices had been committed but in all of its forty-three plants in North and South Carolina; (2) to mail a copy of the notice to each employee at the forty-three plants; (3) to convene all employees during working time and have a responsible Company official read them the notice; (4) to give the Union access to those plants for one year to use the Company bulletin boards where employee notices are posted; (5) to allow union organizers to have access to parking lots and other nonwork areas, including areas within the company's plants (such as cafeterias or canteens); (6) to afford an opportunity to a union representative to address groups of workers on the shop floor whenever company representatives make anti-union speeches; (7)

to furnish the Union upon request a list of employee names and addresses in all of the Company's plants; and (8) to reimburse the NLRB for its litigation expenses, including the salary of its attorneys. (For a very thorough treatment of Board remedies granting union access to the property of a repeated offender, see UNITED STEELWORKERS v. NLRB (Florida Steel Corp.), 646 F.2d 616 (D.C. Cir. 1981). See also TEAMSTERS LOCAL 115 v. NLRB (Haddon House Food Prods., Inc.), 640 F.2d 392 (D.C.Cir. 1981) (public reading of NLRB notice).)

In spite of these orders, J. P. Stevens in a number of instances continued to commit violations that were characterized in contempt proceedings as "massive, cynical and flagrantly contemptuous." The Company and several of its supervisors were adjudged in civil contempt and ordered to purge themselves by taking a number of stipulated steps; in one case, the court assessed "a compliance fine against the Company of $100,000 for such non-compliance and if the violation is of a continuing nature, an additional fine of $5,000 per day for each day of continued violation, and upon any of the individual respondents responsible for non-compliance a fine of $1,000 for such non-compliance and an additional fine of $100 per day for each day of continued violation"; and also directed the company to establish, in consultation with a representative of the NLRB, a continuing program "for the proper education of Company supervisory and management personnel in all its plants in North and South Carolina in the area of the rights of union organizers and plant employees who wish to organize or who wish to join a union." [39]

On October 19, 1980, J. P. Stevens employees voted overwhelmingly to approve a labor contract of potentially historic significance for the unionization of the textile industry in the South. The company agreed to pay $3,000,000 in backpay for its unionized employees in Roanoke Rapids, North Carolina; agreed to a grievance and arbitration procedure there, as well as to provide certain safeguards for employee seniority, health and safety; granted a wage increase; and, most pertinently, agreed to abide in all its plants by applicable judicial and NLRB orders and precedents in resisting future unionization efforts. In return, the union—the Amalga-

39. See J. P. Stevens & Co. v. NLRB, 380 F.2d 292 (2d Cir.), cert. denied 389 U.S. 1005, 88 S.Ct. 564, 19 L.Ed.2d 600 (1967); Textile Workers Union v. NLRB, 388 F.2d 896 (2d Cir. 1968); J. P. Stevens & Co. v. NLRB, 417 F.2d 533 (5th Cir. 1970); NLRB v. J. P. Stevens & Co., 563 F.2d 8 (2d Cir.), cert. denied 434 U.S. 1064, 98 S.Ct. 1240, 55 L.Ed.2d 765 (1978), and 96 L.

R.R.M. 2748, 82 CCH Lab.Cas. ¶ 10,- 212 (2d Cir. 1977) ("J. P. Stevens XVIII"; contempt); J. P. Stevens & Co. v. NLRB, 612 F.2d 881 (4th Cir.), cert. denied, 446 U.S. 956, 101 S.Ct. 315, 66 L.Ed.2d 145 (1980); J. P. Stevens & Co. v. NLRB, 623 F.2d 322 (4th Cir. 1980), cert. denied, — U.S. —, 101 S.Ct. 856, 66 L.Ed.2d 800 (1981).

mated Clothing and Textile Workers Union—agreed to end its world-wide boycott of J. P. Stevens products as well as its "propaganda campaign" to discredit company officials. See N. Y. Times, October 20, 1980.

Since the early 1960s, the Board has remedied serious acts of employer coercion and discrimination by issuing an order requir-ing the employer to bargain with the union seeking to organize the employees there (at least when the union can show that it had the preexisting support of a majority of the employees, generally through signed authorization cards), even though the union may not have been able to win a formal NLRB certification election. The Board's theory in support of such a bargaining order is that the em-ployer's actions have eroded majority support for the union, the re-sults of an NLRB election would be unreliable because of the co-ercion, and a period of bargaining is necessary to restore the Sec-tion 7 rights of the employees. See NLRB v. Gissel Packing Co., at p. 322 infra.

A particularly interesting case in which a bargaining order was issued by the Board is LOCAL 57, LADIES' GARMENT WORKERS v. NLRB (GARWIN CORP.), 374 F.2d 295 (D.C.Cir. 1967). There, an employer had been bargaining with the union in New York, and was party to a collective bargaining agreement. It closed its plant, discharged its employees, and moved its operations to Miami, Flori-da. The Board found the "runaway shop" to violate Section 8 (a)(1) and (3) because the purpose was to deprive the New York employees of their Section 7 rights and to avoid dealing with the union, and also to violate Section 8(a)(5) because of failure to consult the union about the move to Miami. The court of appeals agreed that "the record amply supports the Trial Examiner's find-ing that there was no genuine economic motivation independent of the hostility toward the union." The Trial Examiner had found the traditional Board remedies—backpay until comparable employ-ment was found, and an offer of reinstatement at the Florida plant along with moving expenses—to be inadequate, since the employees (mostly married women) could not readily move and since the tight labor market in New York resulted in a negligible backpay liabil-ity. The Board, agreeing that there was greater need to fashion a remedy which would "remove any consequences of the unfair labor practices which enable the [company] to benefit from [its] unlawful course of conduct," was reluctant to order a return to New York City and instead ordered the Florida company to bar-gain with the same union there, irrespective of whether it had ma-jority status. The Board concluded that the Section 7 right of the Florida employees to choose their own bargaining representative (or to have none at all) "must yield to the statutory objective of fashioning a meaningful remedy for the unfair labor practices found."

A divided court of appeals overturned the bargaining order, concluding that "the remedy does not effectuate a policy of the Act and indeed violates one of the Act's most basic policies, i. e., employee freedom to select a bargaining agent." The majority opinion, written by then Circuit Judge Burger, contained the following passages:

"Underlying Board compulsory bargaining orders is an eminently reasonable principle: those workers who have voted for a representative should not have their choice cancelled out by an employer's unfair labor practice. If a union loses its majority because some workers were coerced or because the company wrongfully refused to bargain with it, restoration of the status quo calls for Board recognition of the Union. A compulsory bargaining order in such circumstances is merely a recognition of the earlier vote of the workers, which is reasonably presumed to represent a more accurate reflection of their sentiments than the later vote, colored if not distorted by the company's illegal conduct. If the union majority is lost after an unfair labor practice because of a normal labor turnover during the period of the subsequent litigation, only slightly different considerations are involved. The Board may reasonably conclude that the employer's prior illegal act could similarly discourage union membership of new workers entering the bargaining unit.

"The crucial element in all these cases is that the interest being protected is the freedom of choice of the workers in a bargaining unit. The compulsory bargaining order is intended to put into effect what these workers had voted. Even when the majority of the plant vote against the union after an unfair labor practice and the swing votes are cast by new workers, a substantial number of the workers still in the unit had opted for the union when free to do so; there is, moreover, the additional factor that the later vote may have been tainted by the company's unfair labor practices. The suggestion in [Franks Bros. v. NLRB, 321 U.S. 702, 64 S.Ct. 817, 88 L.Ed. 1020 (1944)], that the Board could remove from the employer the benefit of its illegal act was merely the other side of the coin of making the injured employees whole.

"The right to choose a union and have that union operate in a climate free of coercion, which is the goal of Board compulsory bargaining orders, is a cornerstone of the National Labor Relations

Act; equally protected by the Act with the right of the workers to choose that representative is the right to have none. Yet the remedy fashioned by the Board in this case imposes on the Florida workers a bargaining representative without reference to their choice. Such an infringement of the Florida employees' Section 7 rights might be justified if some rights of the New York workers depended on that balancing or if for some other valid reason the Board considered it necessary to promote industrial peace.

"The Board, however, justified its order only as being necessary to remove from the Employer the benefits of its wrongdoing. The hard question presented to us is whether this, standing alone and without relationship to redressing grievances of the New York workers, who suffered the violation of their statutory rights, is enough to justify infringing fundamental rights of comparable magnitude vested by law in the Florida workers.

"The Board does not claim the bargaining order will restore to the New York workers their lost rights but, on the contrary, premised its remedial order on the assumption that few if any New York workers would accept reinstatement in Florida and, refusing to order the company to return to New York, decided that the New York workers would have to find their redress in back pay. The Board did not predicate its remedy on any finding that the unfair labor practices in New York precluded a free and untainted vote by the Florida workers. * * * Even assuming the latter was intended, the remedy could not stand, for there is nothing in the record suggesting that the Florida workers were aware of what had occurred in New York. This is a different situation from that presented by new workers entering a bargaining unit at the original site—or near it—which still contains discriminatees. * * *

The remedy at issue is not entirely new; the Board has applied it to "runaways" where the move was of such a short distance that the Board could assume that, absent the unfair labor practices, workers would have followed the employer to the new site. In these cases, the Board has required the company to bargain even if a substantial number does not follow the Employer. However, even though the Board has thus limited its application, this remedy has met with divided judicial response. The Ninth Circuit has upheld the Board's order that a company which had failed to bargain about a twelve-mile move must deal with the union as the workers' representative even if the union does not have a majority at the new location. NLRB v. Lewis, 246 F.2d 886 (9th Cir. 1957). But the Second Circuit refused, more recently, to enforce this remedy since the "Union does not appear to represent any of the employees in the [new] plant." NLRB v. Rapid Bindery, Inc., 293 F.2d 170, 177 (2d Cir. 1961). We consider this the sound view, at least as applied to the facts of this case. * * *

"As final argument, the Board urges here that the remedy is necessary to deter other employers from fleeing union relationships and thus to protect statutory rights of employees generally, although this rationale was not suggested prior to filing the Board brief here. It has been established, however, that the purpose of Board remedies is to rectify the harm done the injured workers, not to provide punitive measures against errant employers. '[T]he power to command affirmative action is remedial, not punitive.' Republic Steel Corp. v. NLRB, 311 U.S. 7, 12, 61 S.Ct. 77, 79, 85 L.Ed. 6 (1940). Deterrence alone is not a proper basis for a remedy. * * * "

[handwritten margin note: remedial not punitive]

Judge McGowan in dissent stated that "We must decide whether the particular accommodation [of two conflicting policies of the Act] made by the Board in response to the particular circumstances of this case fairly falls within the range of the Board's primary authority to effectuate the purposes of the Act. * * * [I]t cannot be said that the Board's present action is unrelated to the purpose of the Act. The order prevents petitioners from successfully evading their duty to bargain with the union. I cannot agree with the majority that that conclusion was so misplaced as to warrant the substitution of judicial judgment."

On remand, 169 N.L.R.B. 1030 (1968), the Board concluded that the possibility existed that employees at the Florida location, in formulating their desires with regard to representation, would be influenced by fears generated by their employer's illegal conduct in New York. It therefore ordered the company upon request to furnish to the union the names and addresses of all of its Florida employees for one year; to grant the union reasonable access to company bulletin boards for one year; to afford union organizers access to plant parking lots and plant approaches during nonworking hours; and to bargain with the union upon proof that a majority of the Florida employees designated it their representative.

Problems for Discussion

1. Does the Board have the power to order the "runaway" company to return from Florida to New York? Even if the Board has that power, should it ever exercise it? Should it ever, for example, issue such an order in a case in which the plant removal was based in part on valid economic considerations but primarily on anti-union animus? See *Frito-Lay, Inc.*, 232 N.L.R.B. 753 (1977), enf't denied 585 F.2d 62 (3d Cir. 1978).

2. Is the Board's order on remand any less objectionable than its order in the initial proceeding? Does the Board's opinion address the concern of the court of appeals that the rights of Florida employees are being impaired without any restorative effect for the New York employees? Does the fact that the board order runs in favor of this single union,

rather than all unions, demonstrate what the rationale of the Board must have been in fashioning this remedy? Should that feature of the remedy be sustained on judicial review?

———

No matter how creative the NLRB may be in fashioning remedies, it is almost inevitable that there will be a high degree of ineffectiveness for Board orders issued at the end of an unfair labor practice proceeding, many months after the critical events. Employees entitled to reinstatement may have moved away, or may have secured another job with which they are satisfied, or may be disinclined to return to work with the company which had unlawfully discharged them. Backpay awards often come too late to make employees truly whole; and when they follow upon illegal plant closings or runaway shops, they cannot fully substitute for the job benefits formerly deriving from seniority with the malefactor employer. The union which is the beneficiary of orders such as those involving employee names and addresses, access to bulletin boards and the like often cannot develop the momentum it had at the time of the unfair labor practices. For these reasons, charging parties would often prefer to have interim relief while an unfair labor practice proceeding makes its way through the Administrative Law Judge, the NLRB and the courts of appeals.

Such relief is in fact available under Section 10(j) of the Act, which authorizes the Board to seek a temporary injunction in a federal district court to restrain either the union or the employer from engaging in unfair labor practices. The injunction may be sought after a complaint has been issued by the Regional Director and while an unfair labor practice hearing is pending before an Administrative Law Judge. The legislative history of Section 10(j) indicates that the purpose of this section was to prevent parties from "violating the Act to accomplish their unlawful objective before being placed under any legal restraint [thereby making it] impossible or not feasible to restore or preserve the status quo pending litigation." In light of this purpose, the section seems plainly suited to certain forms of unlawful behavior relating to organizational activity, as well as to various other types of unfair labor practices. For example, it seems well within the intendment of Section 10(j) to seek a temporary injunction to restrain violence occurring during an organizing campaign or to prevent an employer from frustrating the union's organizational efforts through flagrant unfair practices which would otherwise have to be contested during many months of litigation.

Despite its apparent applicability, the Section 10(j) injunction has been used only infrequently by the Board. In each of the years between 1964 and 1974, the Board typically sought only some fifteen to twenty 10(j) injunctions; and even a more assertive resort to the courts by fiscal year 1979 generated the filing of only sixty-two petitions in that year, almost all of them against employers. Of the thirty cases actually decided in 1979, the injunction was granted in twenty and denied in ten.

Although the Act authorizes the Board to seek Section 10(j) relief whenever there is reasonable cause to believe the Act has been violated, the courts generally require more than that in order to warrant the issuance of equitable relief. The court of appeals in MINNESOTA MINING & MFG. CO. v. METER, 385 F.2d 265 (8th Cir. 1968), announced the prevailing rule:

> " * * * Section 10(j) is reserved for a more serious and extraordinary set of circumstances where the unfair labor practices, unless contained, would have an adverse and deleterious effect on the rights of the aggrieved party which could not be remedied through the normal Board channels. In determining the propriety of injunctive relief the district court should be able to conclude with reasonable probability from the circumstances of the case that the remedial purpose of the Act would be frustrated unless immediate action is taken. To hold otherwise and condition the granting of temporary relief solely on a determination of 'reasonable cause' would effectively circumvent the normal N.L.R.B. processes established by the Act and muddle the proper allocation of administrative and judicial functions."

Most charges of antiunion discrimination, interference, coercion or restraint arise upon controverted facts. The courts are not only reluctant to substitute judicial hearings for the administrative procedure established by Congress but they question the appropriateness of seeking to remedy delays in NLRB relief by conducting the necessary hearings in already overburdened courts. See, e. g., McLeod v. General Elec. Co., 366 F.2d 847, 850 (2d Cir. 1966). Other courts are reluctant to grant a temporary order requiring reinstatement and backpay, believing that the final order ultimately issued by the Board will sufficiently recompense the unlawfully discharged employee. Do you agree?

II. SELECTION OF THE REPRESENTATIVE FOR THE PURPOSES OF COLLECTIVE BARGAINING [1]

To a great extent, the conduct of collective bargaining in American industry is initiated through voluntary employer recognition of unions as the freely chosen representative of a majority of employees, without the need for governmental intervention. When, however, an employer declines to extend such recognition voluntarily, a union may resort to the procedures of the National Labor Relations Board. As has just been noted, the Board may order an employer to bargain as a remedy for seriously coercive or discriminatory unfair labor practices, even though the union has not won a formal Board-supervised certification election; the Board's authority is explored in greater detail at pp. 320–46 infra. But in the far greater number of cases, in which the employer has not acted illegally and its dispute with the union centers about such matters as a doubt about the union's claim of majority support, or disagreement about the unit of employees which the union is to represent, or where there is a conflict between two competing unions each claiming to be the majority choice, collective bargaining does not begin until the Board makes an authoritative determination as to such issues. It does so in its certification proceedings under Section 9 of the NLRA, in accordance with procedures outlined at pp. 112–13 supra.

Typically a proceeding under Section 9 is commenced by a union petition for investigation and certification filed in the appropriate regional office of the NLRB. Such a petition takes the form shown in the Statutory Supplement to this casebook, and sets forth the names of the employer and the petitioning union, the size and composition of the unit claimed to be appropriate, the name of any competing union and other relevant information. Through the years, the NLRA has announced an evolving policy toward petitions filed by *employers*. At first, no provision was made for an employer petition, for fear that an employer might too readily interfere with employee self-organization by filing for an election at opportune moments. Then the statute was amended to permit an employer petition as a shield against the crossfire of two competing unions presenting conflicting representation claims. In the Taft-Hartley amendments of 1947, Congress went further and authorized an employer to file whenever any person or labor organization presents a claim for recognition as the bargaining representative.

The Taft-Hartley Act also made a highly significant change in representation proceedings by introducing the petition for "decerti-

---

1. See J. Feerick, H. Baier & J. Arfa,
    NLRB   Representation   Elections—
    Law, Practice & Procedure (1980).

fication". Under Section 9(c)(1)(A)(ii) any employee or group of employees may file a petition alleging that a substantial number of employees assert that a majority of the employees in the bargaining unit do not wish to be represented by the collective bargaining representative currently certified (or informally recognized) by the employer. If the Board "finds that a question of representation exists", it is to conduct an election to determine the desires of the employees. Generally speaking the same rules govern proceedings on petitions for decertification as govern other proceedings under Section 9.

When a petition is filed under Section 9, regardless of who files it, three broad questions may arise: (A) whether to proceed with an investigation and certification; (B) what is the unit appropriate for the purposes of collective bargaining; and (C) what union, if any, is the choice of the majority of the employees in the appropriate unit. These questions are discussed in Sections A, B, and C of this chapter. Section D deals with judicial review of representation proceedings.

A. Grounds for Not Proceeding to an Investigation and Certification

The most important grounds on which the Board may decline to proceed to an investigation or certification have been (1) the want of a substantial interest on the part of the petitioning union, (2) the commission of unremedied unfair labor practices, (3) a prior certification or the elapse of less than a year since the last previous election, and (4) the subsistence of a valid collective bargaining agreement.

A petitioning union, while it need not show a majority, must nevertheless make a preliminary showing of real strength among the employees before the Board will proceed to investigation and certification. The showing is usually made by submitting to the Regional Office either the union's membership rolls and applications, or else cards signed by individual employees authorizing the union to act as their representative. A Field Examiner checks the cards against the company payroll and when there is doubt may inquire into the currency and authenticity of the signatures. A showing of authorizations from 30 per cent of the employees in the appropriate bargaining unit is usually sufficient, but in exceptional instances the test has been varied. (A second union wishing to intervene in the representation proceeding, for example to block an election agreement or to introduce evidence bearing on the eligibility of voters or on the appropriate bargaining unit, may do so upon a showing of only 10 percent support; while all that is needed to secure a place on the ballot is a single authorization card.) The employer has never been given the right, however, to challenge the evidence of the union's strength or to urge dismissal on the ground that a sufficient showing had not been made. The rule is an administrative expedient for avoiding expenditure of money and personnel in cases in which no certification is likely to result and the question is therefore regarded as one with which the employer has no legitimate concern. It has in fact been held that the Regional Director is not obligated to disclose authorization cards upon demand made under the Freedom of Information Act. Pacific Molasses Co. v. NLRB, 577 F.2d 1172 (5th Cir. 1978).

no duty to disclose under F.I. Act.

For many years, it has been the Board's policy not to proceed with an election while substantial unfair labor practice charges are pending; a union will sometimes file a so-called blocking charge, which the Board will resolve before proceeding with the processing of an earlier-filed election petition. Whether or not an unfair labor practice charge has been filed, however, a union which believes that the employer has acted unlawfully during the organizing campaign may choose to proceed to an election and, if it loses, to seek a bargaining order on the basis of the prior events. If the election is set aside and the union shows that it had majority support prior to the unfair practices, the Board may order the employer to bargain with the union.

will not proceed during pendency of unfair labor practice charge

In order to impart as much stability to a collective bargaining relationship once established as is consistent with full freedom of choice, the Board has had a rule of long standing that the certification of a collective bargaining representative is a bar to another investigation within one year. It applies a correlative principle in its unfair labor practice cases: an employer must honor the Board's certification for a year and continue to bargain with the certified union despite changes in employee sentiment. (See pages 347–351 infra.) Congress extended this certification-bar principle to any case in which there has been a prior NLRB election, regardless whether a union is or is not certified as the winner. Section 9(c) (3), added to the Act in 1947, forbids holding an election within twelve months of a preceding valid election.

must exist 1 year.

old law

One of the most difficult problems in representation controversies has been to determine the effect to be given to a valid subsisting collective bargaining agreement when it is alleged that a majority of the employees in an appropriate bargaining unit wish to be represented by a different union than the union which negotiated the agreement with the employer.[2] The problem may be illustrated by the following example.

2. This general subject is discussed in Willcox, The Triboro Case—Mountain or Molehill, 56 Harv.L.Rev. 576 (1943); Lenhoff, The Present Status of Collective Contracts in the American Legal System, 39 Mich.L.Rev. 1109, 1126–1133 (1941); Rice, The Legal Significance of Labor Contracts Under the National Labor Relations Act, 37 Mich. L.Rev. 693, 711–724 (1939); Change

Assume that on December 15, 1977, the National Labor Relations Board certified the United Steelworkers as the representative of all the production and maintenance workers of Smith Tool Company for the purposes of collective bargaining. On January 31, 1978, Smith Tool Company and the Steelworkers executed a collective bargaining agreement applicable to all production and maintenance workers for a period of five years. It contained the usual terms, including a union shop clause, and provided for adjusting wages semi-annually to reflect any increase or decrease in the cost of living as shown by the Bureau of Labor Statistics index for the area in which Smith Tool had its plant. In January, 1981, International Association of Machinists files a petition for investigation and certification alleging that a majority of the production and maintenance workers had designated IAM as their collective bargaining representative. Is the collective bargaining agreement a bar to holding an election in 1981 or to the certification of IAM in the event that it proves to be the majority choice? If not, and if IAM is certified, must the employer bargain about changes demanded by IAM in wages and other terms of employment fixed by the agreement? What becomes of the agreement? If it contains a no-strike clause, may the employees lawfully strike to secure IAM's demands?

One solution to the problem would be to hold that a collective bargaining agreement bars a new certification throughout its existence; but this would permit the contracting parties to insulate the union's position for an unreasonably long time, inconsistent with the statutory policy of assuring workers full freedom of choice as to union representation. But to exalt the latter policy would lead to a too frequent reassessment of employee preferences, at the expense of the kind of industrial stability which flows from a freely negotiated collective bargaining agreement. The Board's solution—one which attempts to balance the conflicting policies of stability and self-determination—has been its so-called contract bar rules, which in their original incarnation forbade proceeding to a new election within one year of a contract's coming into existence. Today, the contract may bar (with some exceptions) an election for up to three years of its term.

If a collective agreement is to serve as a bar, it must be reduced to writing and be executed by all the contracting parties. The agreement must apply to the employees covered in the rival union's petition. It must encompass employees in an appropriate unit and it must grant recognition to the union as exclusive representative of

of Bargaining Representative During the Life of a Collective Agreement Under the Wagner Act, 51 Yale L.J. 465 (1942). The "contract bar" rule is considered in Freidin, The Board, the "Bar" and the Bargain, 59 Colum.L. Rev. 61 (1959).

all workers in that unit, union members and nonmembers alike. In addition, the contract must embody substantial terms and conditions of employment and not merely concern itself with wages alone or with provisions of an insubstantial or peripheral nature.[3] A collective bargaining agreement containing "a clearly unlawful union-security provision" is no bar to an election, but "contracts containing ambiguous though not clearly unlawful union-security provisions will bar representation proceedings in the absence of a determination of illegality as to the particular provision involved by this Board or a Federal court pursuant to an unfair labor practice proceeding."[4] In 1962, the Board took the further step of declaring that contracts would act as a bar even though they contain provisions in violation of Section 8(e);[5] but also ruled that contracts discriminating amongst employees on grounds of race would not bar an election.[6]

Once a contract is executed satisfying all the preceding requirements, it will immediately be deemed to operate as a bar (unless the agreement clearly specifies some condition precedent to its becoming binding in effect).[7] On the other hand, the agreement may later cease to be a bar for any one of several reasons. In the first place, a contract for a fixed term will bar a petition filed by a rival union for only the first three years of its life, even if the specified term is for a longer period and even though contracts of a greater duration are commonly used in the industry or area in question.[8] (A contract which fails to provide any fixed duration will not serve as a bar for any period whatsoever.)[9]

Second, if the bargaining representative has become "defunct," the contract will not act as a bar to an election. A union is held to be defunct if it is unable or unwilling to represent the employees in the bargaining unit.[10] Inability or unwillingness may be evidenced, for example, by a failure for more than a brief period to hold meetings, elect officers or process grievances. It is the status of the

---

3. All of these requirements were set forth by the Board in Appalachian Shale Products Co., 121 N.L.R.B. 1160, (1962).

4. Paragon Products Corp., 134 NLRB 662 (1961).

5. Food Haulers, Inc., 136 NLRB 394 (1962).

6. Pioneer Bus Co., Inc., 140 NLRB 54 (1962).

7. Appalachian Shale Products Co., 121 NLRB 1160, 1162 (1958).

8. General Cable Corp., 139 N.L.R.B. 1123 (1962). If the agreement is for a longer term, it will still serve as a bar to the filing of an election petition by the signatory employer or union (unless the union was recognized without certification, in which case it can even during the contract term seek an election and certification).

9. Ibid.

10. Hershey Chocolate Corp., 121 N.L.R.B. 901 (1958).

union which is signatory to the contract which is relevant in determining "defunctness"; thus, if the signatory Local becomes defunct,
it is irrelevant that the nonsignatory International is willing and
able to assume the functions of representation. A major case announcing the reasons behind the "defunctness" exception to the contract-bar rule is CONTAINER CORP., 61 N.L.R.B. 823 (1945), where
the Board stated:

exception to K-bar rule

"The issue is whether the purposes and policies of the Act will
best be effectuated by directing an immediate election, or by requiring
the Company's employees to forego the selection of a bargaining representative until the terminal date of the contract is at hand. Here,
as in all representation proceedings where a current collective bargaining contract is urged as a bar to an election, we decide that issue
by weighing two basic interests of employees and society which the
Act was designed to foster and protect, namely, the interest in stability of industrial relations achieved and maintained through collective
bargaining, and the sometimes conflicting interest in employees' full
freedom to choose their bargaining representatives. Normally, a current agreement between an employer and a labor organization acting
as the exclusive bargaining representative of employees in an appropriate unit is both means and proof of the achievement of that stability which is an objective of the statute, for such an agreement identifies the employees' recognized bargaining representative, settles
questions pertaining to wages, hours, and working conditions, and be-
tokens the successful operation of the collective bargaining process. * * * But where it appears that the contract either in its
form or provisions, or in its operation, does not serve to stabilize
industrial relations in the manner contemplated by the statute, the
Board holds that it presents no obstacle to the employees' present
exercise of their right to choose a bargaining representative. The
instant case in our opinion clearly falls within the category of cases
where the collective bargaining agreement fails to fulfill its statutory function. The labor organization which negotiated the contract is defunct. The contract is not being administered on behalf
of the employees; it cannot be interpreted and enforced through
the application of its grievance procedure, or altered to meet changing circumstances by the process of collective bargaining. To treat
the instrument in these circumstances as a bar to an immediate determination of representatives would in no real sense stabilize industrial relations, but would, rather, negate the purposes of the Act.

"We find, for the foregoing reasons, that the contract in question
is not a bar to this proceeding. We do not, of course, *ipso facto* set
aside the contract, or necessarily affect whatever legal rights may
have survived the destruction of the union which negotiated and
signed it."

K not set aside

3.

schism

Third, an existing labor contract will not bar a representation election if the bargaining representative is involved in a "schism." A schism exists when a local union votes in open meeting to disaffiliate from its parent because of a basic intra-union conflict over policy existing at the highest level of the parent union. Such a policy split becomes so serious as to disrupt intra-union relationships and so fractures the bargaining representative as to generate confusion and instability. The confusion can be eliminated and stability restored only by holding a new election. HERSHEY CHOCOLATE CORP., 121 N.L.R.B. 901 (1958).

4.

change of circ.

Finally, a contract may cease to operate as a bar when changes in circumstances have occurred due to expansion or changes in the employer's operations. Thus, if less than 30% of the existing staff were working for the employer when the contract in question was executed or if less than 50% of the present job classifications existed on the date of execution, the contract will have no barring effect. The same result will obtain following relocation of facilities or a merger of two or more operations provided that these changes either involve the hiring of substantially all new employees or create an entirely new operation with major changes in personnel. These principles were announced by the Board in GENERAL EXTRUSION CO., 121 N.L.R.B. 1165 (1958).

Ordinarily, contracts which meet the various requirements set forth above will cease to be a bar upon their termination.[11] Nevertheless, a rival union must bear certain other requirements in mind in order for its petition to be considered by the Board. In particular, the rival union must file its petition not more than 90 days nor less than 60 days before the termination of the contract.[12] The purpose of these rules is to discourage election activity too far in advance of termination and to provide during the last 60 days an insulated period during which the parties to the old agreement can work out a new contract without being distracted by claims from rival unions. If a new contract is agreed upon and executed during this period, it too will serve as a bar provided that it satisfies the various requirements previously discussed, and provided, of course, that no petition was timely filed in the preceding "open" period of thirty days.

---

11. As mentioned above, a contract for a fixed term will not be considered to bar a rival petition after the elapse of three years. For the purpose of the following discussion, therefore, "termination" refers to the termination date specified in the contract *or* a date three years subsequent to the execution of the contract, whichever occurs sooner.

12. Leonard Wholesale Meats, Inc., 136 N.L.R.B. 1000 (1962). In health care institutions, brought within the Labor Act in 1974, the analogous "open" period is 90 to 120 days prior to contract termination. Trinity Lutheran Hosp., 218 N.L.R.B. No. 34 (1975).

If no such contract has been executed when the 60 days expire, however, a petition can be filed at any time prior to the execution of a new agreement. The principal case announcing these rules is DE LUXE METAL FURNITURE CO., 121 N.L.R.B. 995 (1958).

AMERICAN SEATING CO.

National Labor Relations Board, 1953.
106 NLRB 250.

The facts in the case are undisputed. On September 20, 1949, following an election, the Board certified International Union, United Automobile, Aircraft and Agricultural Implement Workers of America, (UAW-CIO), and its Local No. 135, herein called the UAW-CIO, as bargaining representative of the Respondent's production and maintenance employees. On July 1, 1950, the Respondent and the UAW-CIO entered into a three year collective bargaining contract covering all employees in the certified unit. Shortly before the expiration of two years from the date of signing of the contract, Pattern Makers' Association of Grand Rapids, Pattern Makers' League of North America, AFL, herein called the Union, filed a representation petition seeking to sever a craft unit of pattern makers from the existing production and maintenance unit. Both the Respondent and the UAW-CIO opposed the petition, contending that their three year contract which would not expire until July 1, 1953 was a bar. In a decision issued on September 4, 1952, the Board rejected this contention. It held that, as the contract had already been in existence for two years, and as the contracting parties had failed to establish that contracts for three year terms were customary in the seating industry, the contract was not a bar during the third year of its term. Accordingly, the Board directed an election in a unit of pattern makers which the Union won.

On October 6, 1952, the Board certified the Union as bargaining representative of the Respondent's pattern makers. Approximately 10 days later, the Union submitted to the Respondent a proposed collective bargaining agreement covering terms and conditions of employment for pattern makers to be effective immediately. The Respondent replied that it recognized the Union as bargaining representative of the pattern makers and that it was willing to negotiate or discuss subjects properly open for discussion, but that the existing contract with the UAW-CIO was still in full force and effect and remained binding upon all employees, including pattern makers, until its July 1, 1953 expiration date. * * * In support of this position, the Respondent argues that the UAW-CIO was the agent of the pattern makers when it entered into the 1950 agreement with that organization, and that the pattern makers, as principals, are bound by that contract to the expiration date thereof, notwithstanding that they have changed their agent. The General Counsel, on the other hand, contends that the certification of the Pattern Makers resulted in making the existing contract with the UAW-CIO inoperative as to the employees in the unit of pattern makers.

The Respondent's principal-agent argument assumes that common law principles of agency control the relationship of exclusive bargaining representative to employees in an appropriate unit. We think that this assumption is unwarranted and overlooks the unique character of that relationship under the National Labor Relations Act. * * * A duly selected statutory representative is the representative of a shifting group of employees in an appropriate unit—which includes not only those employees who approve such relationship, but also those who disapprove and those who have never had an opportunity to express their choice. Under agency principles, a principal has the power to terminate the authority of his agent at any time. Not so in the case of a statutory bargaining representative. Thus, in its most important aspects the relationship of statutory bargaining representative to employees in an appropriate unit resembles a political rather than a private law relationship. In any event, because of the unique character of the statutory representative, a solution for the problem presented in this case must be sought in the light of that special relationship rather than by the device of pinning labels on the various parties involved and applying without change principles of law evolved to govern entirely different situations. * * *

The purpose of the Board's rule holding a contract of unreasonable duration not a bar to a new determination of representatives is the democratic one of insuring to employees the right at reasonable intervals of reappraising and changing, if they so desire, their union representation. Bargaining representatives are thereby kept responsive to the needs and desires of their constituents; and employees dissatisfied with their representatives know that they will have the opportunity of changing them by peaceful means at an election conducted by an impartial government agency. Strikes for a change of representatives are thereby reduced and the effects of employee dissatisfaction with their representatives are mitigated. But, if a newly chosen representative is to be hobbled in the way proposed by the Respondent, a great part of the benefit to be derived from the no-bar rule will be dissipated. There is little point in selecting a new bargaining representative which is unable to negotiate new terms and conditions of employment for an extended period of time.

We hold that, for the reason which led the Board to adopt the rule that a contract of unreasonable duration is not a bar to a new determination of representatives, such a contract may not bar full statutory collective bargaining, including the reduction to writing of any agreement reached, as to any group of employees in an appropriate unit covered by such contract, upon the certification of a new collective bargaining representative for them. Accordingly, we find that by refusing on and after October 16, 1952, to bargain with the Pattern Makers concerning wages, hours and other working conditions for employees in the unit of pattern makers, the Respondent violated Section 8(a) (5) and (1) of the Act.

Problems for Discussion

1. Suppose that the employer in the *American Seating* case had reduced the pattern makers' wages immediately after the NLRB certification to a rate lower than that fixed in the UAW contract. Would it be liable for breach of contract? If so, who should bring the action? Could UAW maintain an action? Compare *U. S. Gypsum Co. v. United Steelworkers*, 384 F.2d 38 (5th Cir. 1967). Alternatively, would you support the argument that the labor contract merely serves as the status quo which the employer may change after bargaining to impasse, so that its conduct is regulated only by Section 8(a)(5) and not by the entire contract?

2. Assume that the UAW contract contained a clause providing that there should be no strikes during the term of the agreement. Assume further that American Seating Co. and Pattern Makers' League were unable to agree upon the terms of a new contract after good faith negotiations. Would it be a breach of contract for the pattern makers to strike?

3. Suppose that Pattern Makers negotiated a substantial wage increase, that other skilled employees began to talk of seeking craft representation and that UAW, before the expiration of its contract, demanded immediate wage increases for all employees. Would American have a duty to bargain?

B. THE APPROPRIATE BARGAINING UNIT [13]

1. *Significance*

Section 9(a) of the federal Labor Act provides that a representative chosen by "the majority of the employees in a unit appropriate for such purposes" is to be the "exclusive" representative of all employees in that unit. As an incident to conducting a representation election, the Board must determine which group of jobs shall serve as the election constituency. That group of jobs is denoted the appropriate bargaining unit, and the persons employed

13. See J. Abodeely, R. Hammer & A. Sandler, The NLRB and the Appropriate Bargaining Unit (1981); A. Weber, The Structure of Collective Bargaining (1961).

in those jobs at the time of the election are entitled to vote whether they wish to continue to settle terms and conditions of employment on an individual basis—or, as some would have it, by "unilateral" act of the employer—or whether they wish to have one or another employee representative. Any such majority representative, the "exclusive" spokesman in dealing with the employer on these matters, is empowered and obliged to bargain not only for the employees who voted for it or who are its members, but for *all* employees in the bargaining unit. The model of majority rule within discretely bounded election units is obviously borrowed from the American political tradition.

Several important and sometimes misunderstood features of this statutory design should be noted. First, the unit is comprised of jobs or job classifications and not of the particular persons working at those jobs at any given time. The bargaining unit does not change simply because Machinist Jones retires and is replaced by Machinist Williams. Second, what is commonly known as the "appropriate bargaining unit" might more accurately be denoted the appropriate *election* unit since employees represented in different election units may choose to "re-group" as a single larger entity for purposes of conducting actual negotiations. The composition of the *negotiating* unit will thus frequently depend less upon the Board's unit determination than upon the structure of the employer and the union and upon alliances among employers or unions. Third, a determination of the appropriate bargaining unit by the National Labor Relations Board is not a prerequisite to bargaining; an employer and a union are in most instances free to agree informally upon an appropriate unit and upon the commencement of bargaining for the employees in that unit. Fourth, it is the task of the Board to delineate only "an" appropriate bargaining unit; it is not obliged to select only one which is the most appropriate or the optimal unit. The Board thus theoretically has a wide variety of choices. The employees in a single plant might be grouped as one unit or divided according to craft or department, or into larger classifications. If a single company has several plants they may constitute one unit or several units. Bargaining also takes place in multiemployer units on a city-wide, regional or even industry-wide basis. The relevant facts vary from locality to locality and industry to industry, and the unit may be different for different companies in the same locality and industry.

While the Labor Act empowers the Board to make unit determinations, it gives the Board only the most modest guidance in doing so. Section 9(b) begins:

> The Board shall decide in each case whether, in order
> to assure to employees the fullest freedom in exercising the

> rights guaranteed by this Act, the unit appropriate for the
> purposes of collective bargaining shall be the employer unit,
> craft unit, plant unit, or subdivision thereof

and proceeds to add explicit limitations upon the Board's powers in
three rather narrowly circumscribed situations. One of the limitations protects the right of craft employees to be represented separately, in spite of an earlier certification within a more all-en-
compassing bargaining unit. Another forbids the Board to group
professional and nonprofessional employees within a single bargaining unit "unless a majority of the professional employees vote
for inclusion in such unit." Section 2(12) defines a professional employee as one whose work is predominantly intellectual, requiring the constant exercise of discretion and judgment and knowledge of an advanced type acquired through prolonged, specialized and intellectual instruction (as opposed to the routine or physical work of a nonprofessional). Section 9(b) also unqualifiedly
forbids the Board to include within a single unit both guards and
non-guards, regardless of the preferences of the guards. Congress was primarily concerned with the conflict of loyalties which
would confront the guards if they were expected to enforce the
employer's security rules and protect its property against fellow
unit members, especially during periods of economic confrontation. For these reasons, the statute goes beyond forbidding the
grouping of guards and non-guards in the same bargaining unit
and forbids the Board as well to certify any employee organization as a representative for a separate unit of guards if that organization "admits to membership, or is affiliated directly or indirectly with an organization which admits to membership, employees other than guards."

These limitations in Section 9(b), and several other pertinent
restrictions upon the Board's authority in election cases (such as
the election-bar rule) were not incorporated in the original Wagner Act of 1935 but were added in the Taft-Hartley Act of 1947
in the context of a Congressional call for greater legislative and
judicial limitation of agency discretion. In spite of that, Board
decisions on unit-determination matters typically invite a judgmental assessment of a number of relevant criteria and are typically shielded rather well against extensive judicial review. Judicial review is limited both because of the presumed expertise of the
agency, stemming from its familiarity with the industrial context
and, as noted above, the possible appropriateness of a number of different bargaining units in the same case. Moreover, as a matter
of procedure, a unit determination can, except in the most extraordinary circumstances, be challenged only by the rather circuitous method of committing an unfair labor practice; this meth-

od is sufficiently exhausting and frequently technically obscure so as to serve as an additional obstacle to effective judicial supervision.

Although the jurisdiction of the Board to adjudicate unfair labor practice cases is perhaps the more dramatic, its jurisdiction to make unit determinations is at the heart of our system of collective bargaining and has a most pervasive impact upon industrial relations.

. (1) A large unit, commonly favored by the employer, will typically be much more difficult for the union to organize than a small one. The size of the unit may thus determine whether there will be an election at all (since the union must first make a "showing of interest") and if so, whether collective bargaining will be instituted.

(2) A large unit may engross within it employees of differing skills, attitudes and interests. The more diversified the constituency, the more likely there will be conflicts of interest and strains upon the union's ability to represent all unit employees fairly in negotiating and administering the collective bargaining agreement.

(3) The size and composition of the unit will directly affect the structure and composition of the union representative, which not only must represent all in the unit but must also court all unit employees as a source of financial and bargaining power.

(4) The smaller and the more homogeneous the unit, the more likely it is that the individual worker will be effectively represented and will have his voice heard in a democratic manner within union councils; the larger the unit, the more diluted the impact of any single employee on the shaping of union policy.

(5) The size of the unit will also shape the kinds of issues that will be addressed in collective bargaining and dealt with in the labor agreement.

(6) Fragmented units tend to bring economic headaches to the employer. Not only are they typically easier to organize, but they also involve the greater cost and disruption that come with frequent bargaining cycles and meetings; moreover, they expose the employer to "whipsaw" strikes by employees in one unit which inure, cumulatively, to the benefit of employees in other units.

(7) Fragmented units, represented by different unions, often bring with them disputes between those unions about the right to represent employees of uncertain representational status (e. g., in newly created job titles) or the right of members of one union to oust from their jobs members of another (a work-assignment dispute).

(8) Larger units bring the danger of a more massive work-stoppage in the event of a bargaining dispute; smaller units may permit the employer to transfer work from one unit, shut down by a strike, to some other unit which is still in operation and subject to an existing labor contract (or which is not organized at all).

As can be noted, different unions and different employers may have differing preferences regarding the size of the bargaining unit, depending upon the nature of the industry and the structure and composition of the workforce. On the whole, however, it is likely that unions will favor the smaller unit, since it can be more readily organized. Since 1960, the Board has tended to echo this preference, since the smaller unit assures greater homogeneity of employee interest and maximizes employee self-determination.

In a very large proportion of the cases in which representation petitions are filed, the problem of defining the collective bargaining unit can be resolved without the necessity for formal proceedings. If one union claims to represent all the employees in the only plant of a shoe box company and no other union asserts an interest, plainly the plant-wide unit would be appropriate. The case would be no harder if each of two unions asserted the same claim. In other instances either the pattern of organization in the industry or else Board precedents will set at rest any possible question. For example, absent some extraordinary circumstance, no one would suggest that pattern makers in steel-related industries are not entitled to a separate unit if they so desire; they are highly skilled workers who have long bargained as a craft. In most cases, therefore, the Regional Director and the parties work out a stipulation defining the unit and there remains only the task of determining which union, if any, is the majority choice.

But where voluntary agreement on the unit cannot be achieved, formal proceedings are required. At any time after the petition for investigation and certification has been filed, the Regional Director may issue a notice of hearing and serve it on all interested parties. The hearing is held before a hearing officer who is generally, though not invariably, the field examiner to whom the petition was originally assigned for investigation. It differs from the hearing held in a complaint case in one important respect: The Board is not in a position of prosecutor; the unions concerned and occasionally the employer take a leading part, and the hearing officer may himself play an affirmative role in eliciting needed information. The evidence covers a wide range for there are few facts concerning the history and organization of an industrial establishment which are not relevant in a close case.

Until 1961, the evidence gathered in the preliminary hearing went directly to the Board and the Board itself determined the appropriate bargaining unit. Since 1961, however, power to make this determination, at least in the first instance, has been delegated to the Regional Director. The determinations of the Regional Director are then subject to review, but only on limited grounds, by the Board.

2. *Criteria for Unit Determinations*

The Labor Act tells the Board very little about the criteria or standards which should be employed in making unit determinations. Section 9(b) enjoins the Board "to assure to employees the fullest freedom in exercising the rights guaranteed by this Act." Those rights, enumerated in Section 7, are the right to form and join a union, to bargain collectively and to engage in concerted activities to those ends—and the right to refrain from doing so. If the Board holds "appropriate" a very large unit covering, for example, many geographically dispersed plants staffed by employees of differing skills and working conditions, the exercise of Section 7 rights may be frustrated: effective communication by the union in organizing and in formulating and administering contract terms may be hampered, intensive interest in collective bargaining within one group of employees may be "cancelled out" by the votes of those elsewhere who oppose it, and negotiation and administration of the labor contract may be crippled by the conflicting interests of employees within the unit. Conversely, a unit which is "too small," and which excludes some employees with common skills, working conditions and economic interests, may curtail the bargaining power of the union representing only the unit employees, may generate (perhaps with the aid of the employer) divisions and in-fighting among employees in the plant or conversely may generate pressures to settle terms of employment for the non-unit employees along the lines negotiated for the unit employees (in spite of the possible desire of the non-unit employees to "refrain from" unionization and collective bargaining). For these reasons, the Board in making its unit determinations seeks an employee group which is united by *community of interest*, and which neither embraces employees having a substantial conflict of economic interest nor omits employees sharing a unity of economic interest with other employees in the election or bargaining constituency.

The Board draws upon this criterion of community of interest in order to determine whether, for example, employees with special craft skills and training should be separated out for purposes of voting and bargaining or whether they should be grouped along with semi-skilled and unskilled employees in an "industrial" unit; whether "production and maintenance" employees should be grouped in a single unit with "white-collar employees" doing technical or clerical work; whether the unit should comprise only employees working in a single plant, store or office of the employer or whether there should be a grouping of employees in several—or indeed all —of the employer's plants, stores or offices; and whether it is sound to go even beyond the employees of a single employer and to group those employees with persons employed by other employers in the same industry in the same competitive market. In making judgments about "community of interest" in these different settings, the Board will look to such factors as: (1) similarity in the scale and manner of determining earnings; (2) similarity in employment benefits, hours of work and other terms and conditions of employment; (3) similarity in the kind of work performed; (4) similarity in the qualifications, skills and training of the employees; (5) frequency of contact or interchange among the employees; (6) geographic proximity; (7) continuity or integration of production processes; (8) common supervision and determination of labor-relations policy; (9) history of collective bargaining; (10) desires of the affected employees; (11) extent of union organization. See NLRB v. Purnell's Pride, Inc., 609 F.2d 1153 (5th Cir. 1980).

It can readily be seen that community of interest is a vague standard which does not lend itself to mechanical application. It is a multi-factor criterion, and it is rare in any given case that all of the factors point conveniently in the direction of the same size unit. As already noted, it is indeed possible that on the basis of community of interest, the Board may conclude that there are several units any one of which may be, in the language of the statute, "a unit appropriate" for collective bargaining.

3. *Single-Location versus Multi-Location Unit* [14]

Many companies carry on their operations in a variety of geographical locations. Manufacturing concerns may have several plants; retail enterprises may have a network of individual stores; insurance companies may have many separate offices. Where a union seeks to organize a company of this kind, it is possible to conceive of a unit comprising all the employees in the company, or all of the firm's employees within a given geographical region (state, municipality, etc.), or all the employees within a single plant, office or store, or, conceivably, only a particular class of employees within a single plant or branch, such as the cafeteria employees at a downtown department store.

14. Comment, Appropriate Bargaining Unit Determinations in the Retail Chain Industry, 14 B.C.Ind. & Comm. L.Rev. 94 (1972); Note, The Board and Section 9(c)(5): Multilocation and Single-Location Bargaining Units in the Insurance and Retail Industries, 79 Harv.L.Rev. 811 (1966).

The determinations of the Board in cases of this kind will often touch upon strong interests of the parties concerned. From the union's standpoint, a narrowly defined unit may markedly influence the success of an organizing drive, for it may be much easier to win elections in a few separate stores than to mount a successful campaign simultaneously in a number of plants or stores spread out over a substantial geographical area. Conversely, the employer may favor a broader unit not only because it will make the job of the union organizer more difficult but also because it may be simpler administratively to deal with a single bargaining agent representing all of its places of business in a given area.

Faced with these conflicting interests the NLRB tended at one time to favor the union's claim for a smaller unit in order to encourage collective bargaining. MAY DEPARTMENT STORES, 50 N.L. R.B. 669 (1943), is a fair example. After failing to make a sufficient showing of membership in support of its petition for certification as representative of a store-wide unit of several thousand employees, a CIO union sought certification as the representative of the 28 workers in the men's busheling department. Both the company and AFL opposed the establishment of such a unit on the ground that the appropriate unit was store-wide, and pointed to the admitted purpose of CIO to organize the employees on that basis. Nevertheless, the Board set up the unit sought by CIO.

"Assuming, without deciding, that a store-wide unit will best effectuate the purposes of the Act, we note that no labor organization claims to represent the employees in such a unit. We believe that collective bargaining should be made an immediate possibility for the employees in the busheling rooms without requiring them to await the uncertain date when the employees may be organized in a larger unit. We find accordingly that the employees in the busheling rooms constitute an appropriate unit. However, our finding in this respect does not preclude a later determination at another stage of self-organization that a larger unit is appropriate."

Section 9(c) (5) was added by the Taft-Hartley Act as a result of the criticism of these decisions. In view of this Section, the Board has conceded that "extent of organization" (as exemplified by the *May Department Stores* decision) cannot be used as the *sole* reason for establishing a given unit. But the Board has maintained that extent of organization remains as a relevant factor to be considered, and this position has been upheld by the Supreme Court, in NLRB v. METROPOLITAN LIFE INS. CO., 380 U.S. 438, 85 S.Ct. 1061, 13 L.Ed. 2d 951 (1965).

The weight given by the NLRB to the extent of organization has varied over the years. During the 1950's, the NLRB frequently required multi-store and multi-plant units, particularly where wages and personnel policies were centrally administered for the plants and stores in question. Commencing in 1962, however, the Board seemed more willing once again to establish smaller units of employees in order to facilitate collective bargaining. In SAV-ON DRUGS, INC., 138 N.L.R.B. 1032 (1962), the Board reversed its policy of grouping together a company's retail stores in a metropolitan or similar area and held that a single store might constitute an appropriate unit. It recognized that several factors, such as the geographical separation of each store, favored a single store unit, and that its former policy frequently "operated to impede the exercise by employees in retail chain operations of their rights to self-organization." Two years later, the Board went yet further and held, in NLRB v. Frisch's Big Boy Ill-Mar, Inc., 147 N.L.R.B. 551 (1964), enf't denied 356 F.2d 895 (7th Cir. 1966), that a single store in a chain-store operation is "presumptively appropriate." Indeed, over a dissenting opinion charging that the majority was making arbitrary unit determinations consistent only with extent of organization, it was held in F. W. Woolworth Co., 144 N.L.R.B. 307 (1963), that even the kitchen staff in a single store could be considered an appropriate unit. Although the kitchen workers were processed along with all other workers in the store with respect to hiring, pay, vacations, sick time, discount privileges, pension rights and the like, the majority reasoned that the kitchen staff had its own special duties and separate supervision within the store.

Unit determinations for multi-plant operations proceeded along a line parallel to the retail chain-store determinations. In DIXIE BELLE MILLS, INC., 139 N.L.R.B. 629 (1962), the Board announced what was in substance a presumption that one plant of a multi-plant industrial operation is an appropriate unit. In that case, in which the union petitioned for an election at a single textile plant, the Board found the employees at that plant to constitute an appropriate unit in spite of the fact that the same employer operated other mills and warehouses twenty miles away, and in spite of the finding of the Regional Director that the company's operations at the different locations were integrated. The Board emphasized the low degree of employee interchange and the autonomy of supervision at the individual-plant level on day-to-day business and labor relations decisions. The Board announced the following guidelines:

"A single plant unit, being one of the unit types listed in the statute as appropriate for bargaining purposes, is presumptively appropriate. * * * Moreover, even assuming that the unit urged by the Employer and found by the Regional Director here may be the most appropriate unit, this does not establish it as the only appropriate one.

* * * [T]he crucial question in each case is whether the unit requested is appropriate."

This single-location presumption has been widely followed by the NLRB in multi-location industries. See, e. g., Metropolitan Life Ins. Co., 156 N.L.R.B. 1408 (1966); Wyandotte Savings Bank, 245 N.L.R.B. No. 120 (1979).

NLRB v. CHICAGO HEALTH & TENNIS CLUBS, INC.

United States Court of Appeals, Seventh Circuit, 1977.
567 F.2d 331, cert. denied, 437 U.S. 904, 98 S.Ct. 3089, 57 L.Ed.2d 1133 (1978).

SWYGERT, CIRCUIT JUDGE.

In the two cases before us, the National Labor Relations Board ("the Board") petitions for enforcement of its orders directing each of the respondents to cease and desist from refusing to bargain collectively with the union which had been certified as the exclusive bargaining representative. These two cases have been consolidated for this opinion because they present the identical legal issue: whether the Board abused its discretion in certifying a single retail store as an appropriate unit for collective bargaining where such store constitutes only one of a chain of stores owned and operated by the company in the Chicago metropolitan area. For the reasons set forth, we grant the petition in *Chicago Health Clubs* and deny enforcement in *Saxon Paint*.

I

(A) *Parties*

No. 77–1227. Chicago Health & Tennis Clubs is an Illinois corporation engaged in the sale of club memberships and providing services of exercise training and weight loss counseling for its members. It operates sixteen clubs in the Chicago metropolitan area (Chicago and suburbs). Its central office is located in Chicago's central business district and all clubs are within a 28-mile radius of this office.

No. 77–1504. Saxon Paint & Home Care Centers is an Illinois corporation engaged in the retail sale of paint, wallpaper, and home decorating supplies. It owns and operates twenty-one stores in the Chicago metropolitan area (Cook County). In addition, Saxon has seven other stores in Illinois, Indiana, and Wisconsin. Although these seven stores are operated by separate corporate entities, they are owned in part by the same stockholders and are operated through a single managerial hierarchy. All of the Chicago metropolitan area stores are within a 30-mile radius of each other.

(B) *Procedural History*

[In each of the two cases, a local of the Retail Clerks Union petitioned for a representation election in a unit limited to the employees of a single store in the company's chain. The Regional Director found the single-store unit appropriate, and the Board denied review. The union won the election in both instances, but the employer refused to bargain, claiming the inappropriateness of the unit. The Board found refusals to bargain in violation of Sections 8(a)(1) and (5), and has petitioned for enforcement of its bargaining orders.]

II

The primary responsibility for determining the appropriateness of a unit for collective bargaining rests with the Board. It is given broad discretion in determining bargaining units "to assure to employees the fullest freedom in exercising the rights guaranteed by [the Act]." 29 U.S.C. § 159(b). The Board is not required to select the most appropriate bargaining unit in a given factual situation; it need choose only an appropriate unit within the range of appropriate units. *Wil-Kil Pest Control Co. v. NLRB*, 440 F.2d 371, 375 (7th Cir. 1971). It follows that Board unit determinations are rarely to be disturbed. *South Prairie Construction Co. v. Local No. 627, International Union*, 425 U.S. 800, 805, 96 S.Ct. 842, 48 L.Ed.2d 382 (1976); *Packard Motor Co. v. NLRB*, 330 U.S. 485, 491, 67 S.Ct. 789, 91 L.Ed.2d 1040 (1947).

Although Board determinations are subject to limited review, they are not immune from judicial scrutiny. We must bear in mind that section 10(e) of the Act clothes the courts of appeals with authority to enter decrees "enforcing, modifying, and enforcing as so modified, or setting aside in whole or in part the order of the Board." 29 U.S.C. § 160(e). Indeed, the Supreme Court has held that we are not " 'to stand aside and rubber-stamp' Board determinations that run contrary to the language or tenor of the Act." * * * Accordingly, we have the responsibility of determining whether the Board's unit determinations were unreasonable, * * * arbitrarily or capriciously made, * * * or unsupported by substantial evidence. * * *

In making unit determinations, the Board must effect the policy of the Act to assure employees the fullest freedom in exercising their rights, yet at the same time "respect the interest of an integrated multi-unit employer in maintaining enterprise-wide labor relations." *NLRB v. Solis Theatre Corp.*, 403 F.2d 381, 382 (2d Cir. 1968). * * * In reaching its decision, the Board considers several criteria, no single factor alone being determinative. * * * These factors include: (a) geographic proximity of the stores in relation to each other * * *; (b) history of collective bargaining or unionization * * *; (c) extent of employee interchange between various stores * * *; (d) functional integration of operations * * *; and (e) centralization of management, particularly in regard to central control of personnel and labor relations. * * * As the geographic proximity of the stores in the two cases before us is almost identical, our decision whether to grant the petitions for enforcement must rest on an analysis of the other factors.

One further item deserves note before proceeding to a discussion of the individual cases. Although the Board has vascillated in deciding the proper scope of a bargaining unit in the retail chain industry,[15] it has apparently now adopted the administrative policy that a single store is "presumptively an appropriate unit for bargaining." *Haag Drug Corp.*, 169 N.L.R.B. 877–78 (1968).[16] That presumption, however, is not conclusive and "may be overcome

---

15. The Board's unit determinations in regard to multistore retail operations has fluctuated from one extreme to another. Before enactment of the Taft-Hartley Act in 1947, the Board regularly approved single retail chain-store bargaining units. *See, e. g., Koppers Stores*, 73 N.L.R.B. 504 (1947). Sometime after the Taft-Hartley Act, however, the Board developed a virtual presumption against the appropriateness of single-store units. For example, in *Safeway Stores, Inc.*, 96 N.L.R.B. 998, 1000 (1951), the Board stated:

[A]bsent unusual circumstances, the appropriate collective bargaining unit in the retail . . . trade should embrace all employees within the categories sought who perform their work within the Employer's administrative division or [geographic] area.

See also Weis Markets, Inc., 142 N.L.R.B. 708, 710 (1963); *Daw Drug Co.*, 127 N.L.R.B. 1316 (1960); *Crown Drug Co.*, 108 N.L.R.B. 1126 (1954).

The presumption encompassing all retail stores within a geographic or administrative area was discarded in 1962 when the Board announced that thereafter it would "apply to retail chain operations the same unit policy which we apply to multiplant enterprises in general." *Sav-On Drugs, Inc.*, 138 N. L.R.B. 1032, 1033 (1962). Two years

later, in a complete reversal of its policy articulated in *Safeway*, the Board held that the single unit is "presumptively appropriate unless it be established that the single plant has been effectively merged into a more comprehensive unit so as to have lost its individual identity." *Frisch's Big Boy Ill-Mar, Inc.*, 147 N.L.R.B. 551 n. 1 (1964), *enforcement denied*, 356 F.2d 895 (7th Cir. 1966). *See Haag Drug Co.*, 169 N.L.R.B. 877 (1968).

16. Several Board decisions since 1968 suggest, however, a weakening of the presumptive appropriateness of single store units. *See, e. g., Kirlin's Inc. of Central Illinois*, 227 N.L.R.B. No. 174 (1977); *Twenty-First Century Restaurant Corp.*, 192 N.L.R.B. 881 (1971); *Waiakamilo Corp. d/b/a McDonald's*, 192 N.L.R.B. 878 (1971); *The Pep Boys —Manny, Moe & Jack*, 172 N.L.R.B. 246 (1968). Some decisions seem impossible to reconcile. For example, in two cases decided within two months of each other, the Board came down with completely different results even though both cases arose from the same geographic area and both cases involved retail drugstore chains having highly centralized operations. *Compare Walgreen Co.*, 198 N.L.R.B. 1138 (Aug. 30, 1972) (single store appropriate), with *Gray Drug Stores, Inc.*, 197 N.L.R.B. 924 (June 26, 1972) (single store inappropriate).

where factors are present in a particular case which would counter the appropriateness of a single store unit.   .   .   . " *Id.* at 878.

[margin handwritten note: presumption is that single store is appropriate - but not conclusive]

We turn now to the two cases before us.

(A) *Saxon Paint, No. 77–1504*

Although the Board recognized that the Chicago area Saxon stores exhibited "a high degree of centralized administration," it nevertheless found a single store unit appropriate. In large part, the Board based its unit determination on the role of the local store manager, adopting the Regional Director's finding that "substantial responsibility is invested in the Employer's store managers." We believe that the Board exaggerated the control exercised by the store manager over labor and administrative matters and hold that the Board's finding that the store manager possesses autonomy and authority is not supported by substantial evidence.

The evidence in the record clearly establishes that Saxon is a highly integrated operation. Each Saxon store is similar in all respects to each of the other Saxon stores in Cook County. All of the stores are open on the same days and at the same times. They sell the same merchandise at the same price and the physical layout of each store is similar. Special sales and promotions are held at the same time in each store with the same sale prices being charged. Advertising covers the entire metropolitan area and is prepared by headquarters as are store signs and window displays. The stores are "as much alike in this respect as peas in a pod." *NLRB v. Frisch's Big Boy Ill-Mar, Inc.*, 356 F.2d 895, 896 (7th Cir. 1966).

Personnel and labor relations policies for the Saxon stores are also centrally administered, being formulated by the personnel director who maintains his office at corporate headquarters. Payrolls, accounts, personnel files, and other records are maintained at the general office. Employee job classifications are the same at each store, and employees within a particular classification perform the same duties and are required to have the same skills and experience. Employees within the same classification, experience, and seniority receive the same wages. A uniform fringe benefit program is maintained at each store, and store employees enjoy company-wide seniority.

The actual operations of the Cook County stores are also highly centralized. Under the vice president of operations are three district managers who are responsible for assuring that all stores within their respective districts are being operated in full compliance with the policies and procedures formulated at headquarters, including personnel and labor relations policies. These district managers visit the stores within their district on the average of every two days and maintain further contact with the individual stores through frequent telephone calls and written memoranda. In addition, the company maintains a messenger service which visits each metropolitan area store daily.

At the store level and below the district managers, the company employs fourteen store managers in all three districts. Seven of these managers are assigned to single stores, the remaining seven managers are each assigned to two stores. The evidence establishes that, contrary to the Board's conclusion, these store managers have limited involvement in the store's non-labor business activities. The individual store managers have no authority to commit the employer's credit, purchase or order merchandise and supplies, arrange for repair or maintenance work, change prices, or resolve customer complaints. At best it can be said that it is the responsibility of the store managers to implement the company's policies and procedures within the individual stores.

The store managers' involvement in labor relations and personnel matters is also severely limited. They have no authority to do any of the following: (a) hire new employees; (b) grant promotions, wage increases or changes in job classifications; (c) discharge or suspend employees for disciplinary reasons; (d) lay-off employees; (e) handle employee grievances; (f) grant requests for vacations or leaves of absence; (g) permanently or temporarily transfer employees between any of the stores; and (h) post the weekly work schedule without prior approval by the district manager. While the store manager may offer recommendations in certain of these areas, the record shows that these recommendations, even in such key areas as employee discharge, may not be followed. Furthermore, in certain areas such as promotion and wage increases, the store manager may not even be consulted before a decision is made. As the Second Circuit noted in *NLRB v. Solis Theatre Corp.*, 403 F.2d 381, 383 (2d Cir. 1968):

> It appears, therefore, that instead of being in a decision making position, the "manager" has little or no authority on labor policy but is subject to detailed instructions from the central office.

That Saxon is completely integrated functionally is best illustrated by its hiring and training practices. Hiring is done almost exclusively through the corporate offices. Job applications are taken and interviews are held at the personnel office. The store manager may interview an applicant only after the applicant has first interviewed with the personnel director and then the district manager. Applicants may be rejected and new employees hired, however, without prior consultation with or participation by the store manager.

Similarly, the training of new employees comes under the primary jurisdiction of the central personnel department. The company issues manuals to all new employees and provides them with formal training, lasting from one to two weeks, at its corporate headquarters. In sum, it is apparent that there is no local autonomy among the individual stores and that the store managers lack the authority to resolve issues which would be subject to collective bargaining. *See Frisch's Big Boy,* 356 F.2d at 897.

That Saxon's business is both centralized and integrated and that the individual stores lack meaningful identity as a self-contained unit is further supported by the numbers of employee transfers, both temporary and permanent, among the metropolitan area stores. During a thirteen month period and discounting employees not covered in the unit, eighteen percent of all employees were transferred permanently among the Chicago stores. Additional testimony showed that temporary transfers frequently occur, almost on a daily basis. While this alone may be insufficient to negate a single store unit, we cannot agree with the Board's finding that "the degree of employee interchange [was] too inconsequential and insubstantial to rebut the appropriateness of a single store unit," particularly when this factor is considered in light of all of the other factors.

That a single store is inappropriate here is further shown by the history of collective bargaining. The pattern of unionization both at stores in other regions and at stores within the Chicago metropolitan area has always been district wide. * * * The record also reveals that the Retail Clerks Union once petitioned the Board for a representation election among all of the company's Chicago metropolitan area stores. An election was conducted in 1965 among the then existing five Saxon stores. A second election, held in 1967, also included a sixth Saxon store which was opened during the intervening period of time. We agree that this bargaining history is not controlling because the elections were conducted pursuant to an agreement between the union and the company. But we cannot agree that this history is entitled to little or no weight for, at a minimum, it shows that the union previously considered and treated all of the company's stores in the Chicago metropolitan area as a single unit.

The Board argues that the instant case is controlled by this court's recent decision in *Walgreen Co. v. NLRB,* 564 F.2d 751 (7th Cir. 1977), which held that a single store in a chain of drug stores within the Chicago metropolitan area was an appropriate unit. We are not persuaded the Board's order should be enforced on the basis of *Walgreen* for it is distinguishable both in the absence of bargaining history and in the amount of autonomy exercised by the store manager. In *Walgreen*, the district managers supervised a larger number of stores and visited each store far less frequently than in the case at bar. Furthermore, most of the personnel and labor related decisions such as hiring, firing, and promotions "were based on" the recommendations of the store manager. Thus the court found that much of the employment activities were supervised directly by the local store manager "without significant interference" by the central organization. We cannot say, with the particular facts before us, that the local store manager here operates "without significant interference" by the central office.

The factual situation involved in this case is rather more analogous to that found in *NLRB v. Frisch's Big Boy Ill-Mar, Inc.*, 356 F.2d 895 (7th Cir. 1966). In *Frisch's*, this court refused to enforce a Board order finding a single store unit appropriate among ten restaurants in Indianapolis, Indiana. After reviewing the record, we found that the restaurants were a single, integrated enterprise and that each restaurant lacked sufficient autonomy, even though the individual restaurant manager could order supplies and merchandise and could independently hire employees within centrally prescribed wage rates. In finding a single store unit inappropriate, this court said:

> It is evident to us that the decisions left to the managers do not involve any significant elements of judgment as to employment relations.
>
> * * *
>
> It is obvious to us that none of the store managers will be deciding questions affecting the employees in the context of collective bargaining. 356 F.2d at 897.

It would be an anomaly indeed to find a single store appropriate here when the store managers in this case have considerably less autonomy than the store managers in *Frisch's*.

For the reasons herein stated, we conclude that the Board's determination that a single Saxon store was an appropriate bargaining unit is not supported by substantial evidence and therefore is arbitrary and unreasonable. Accordingly, the Board's order is set aside and enforcement is denied.

(B) *Chicago Health Clubs, No. 77–1227*

Chicago Health Clubs is, at first sight, quite similar factually to *Saxon Paint*. The company's sixteen stores (clubs) are in a similar geographic proximity to each other. Many of its operations and procedures are centralized.

Other similarities are readily apparent. Chicago Health Clubs has two area supervisors (similar to Saxon's district managers) who oversee its sixteen clubs.   These supervisors visit their respective clubs two or three times a week and maintain frequent telephone contact.   Despite these similarities, we conclude that substantial evidence supports the Board's finding that a single club is an appropriate bargaining unit.

Notably absent in this case is any prior history of collective bargaining.   In addition, the extent of employee interchange among the various clubs is minimal.   Furthermore, there are significant differences in the functional integration of the clubs, the extent to which the company is centralized, and the degree of autonomy of the local club managers.

Unlike the Saxon stores which are virtually identical with each other, Chicago Health Clubs operates at least three types of clubs. Some clubs exclusively serve women, others serve men on one day and women on another.   Still others serve men and women on the same day.   The clubs also differ in the type of facilities available. Some have handball courts, others have swimming pools.   One has a tennis court.

Although many aspects of the company's operations and procedures are centralized, they are not as highly centralized as in *Saxon Paint*.   For example, even though official personnel and payroll records are maintained at the central office, each club manager also maintains records detailing needed information about the club employees.   Similarly, the central office controls the advertising for all sixteen clubs, but the advertising may be directed at only one geographical area or may be on behalf of only one of the clubs.

Also unlike the store managers in *Saxon Paint*, the club managers exercise a marked degree of control over personnel and labor relations matters.   Applicants apply at the individual clubs and are interviewed by the club manager without further interview by the area supervisor.   Part-time employees, a large number if not a majority of all employees, are hired and fired by the club manager without consultation with the area supervisor.   Although full-time employees are hired with the approval of the area supervisor, the decision is based on the applicant's interview with the club manager. In hiring, the club manager sets the wage rate for new employees within the perimeters determined by the area supervisor.

Additionally, unlike the store managers in *Saxon Paint*, the club managers here exercise considerable disciplinary authority over rank-and-file employees.   A club manager may reprimand employees without prior approval.   Moreover, in extreme cases, the club manager has the authority to discharge or suspend employees without prior consultation with the area supervisor.

The club manager exercises control over the working conditions of employees in many other respects. For example, the club manager handles employee complaints and grievances about wages and hours, schedules vacations, grants or denies overtime, decides whether employees may take their lunch break on or off the premises, administers the local payroll system, and trains employees in exercise instruction and sales. Thus, unlike *Saxon Paint* and like *Walgreen,* much of the day-to-day employment activities are supervised directly by the local club manager "without significant interference" by the central corporate organization.

Based on the autonomy of the club manager, the insubstantial amount of employee interchange among the metropolitan clubs, and the absence of any collective bargaining history, we conclude that the Board's determination that a single store was an appropriate bargaining unit is reasonable in light of all the facts presented in this case. Since Chicago Health Clubs has admitted its refusal to bargain with the union representing this single club, we accordingly enforce the Board's order.

In summary, the Board's order in No. 77–1227 shall be enforced. Enforcement of the Board's order in No. 77–1504 is denied.

Problems for Discussion

1. How pertinent is it, in deciding the appropriate bargaining unit, that the store manager does or does not have significant decisionmaking authority on such non-personnel matters as pricing and advertising of merchandise, repairs to the store, or resolution of customer complaints? How pertinent is the centralization of such personnel matters as payroll records and personnel files?

2. Had the court of appeals agreed that the single Saxon Paint store was an appropriate unit, to what extent if at all would this have unduly interfered with or complicated the company's decisions on personnel and non-personnel matters?

3. Does the fact that prior labor elections and contracts in the Saxon Paint chain were structured on a multi-store basis necessarily suggest that a single-store unit is inappropriate? Does the fact that the union previously lost an election in a multi-store unit in *Saxon Paint* suggest perhaps that it was principally motivated by "extent of organization" when it petitioned for the single-store unit? Assuming that to be true, is that a factor which should reinforce the Board's single-store finding, or undermine it?

---

4. Craft Unit v. Plantwide Unit

The question whether to allow particular groups of skilled employees to bargain separately through their own union was for some twenty years the most controversial problem confronting the Board in the area of unit determinations. Board decisions frequently determined the success or failure of rival AFL and CIO organizing campaigns, for one of the commonest situations to arise was the case in which AFL organized the skilled or semi-skilled workers in a plant into craft unions while CIO induced a majority of all the employees to join an industrial organization. In such a situation a ruling that a plant-wide unit was appropriate deprived AFL of any voice in the plant and cost it many dues-paying members, while the setting up of craft units would enable AFL to maintain a salient from which to engage in further raids upon the CIO. More recently, the influence of the Board in this respect has been reduced by operation of various plans—notably the AFL–CIO no-raiding agreement—whereby organized labor has sought to limit union rivalry. Nonetheless, the issue of the craft unit versus the plantwide unit is by no means moribund.

Once again, there are no easy premises from which decisions may be logically derived. A broader unit may serve to enhance the bargaining power of all the employees in the plant. And if a single bargaining agent represents all the employees in a given plant, the employer will be freed from the administrative burdens and multiple crises that can result where he must bargain separately with several different unions, each of which may possess the power to disrupt operations in the event of a strike. On the other hand, skilled employees may have particular needs and problems resulting from the distinct nature of the services they perform; they will also feel entitled to higher rates of pay in recognition of their greater skills. Hence, such employees may justifiably fear that their special interests will be slighted if they are merged into a larger unit. Faced with these conflicting considerations, the NLRB has taken a variety of approaches through the years to the problem of craft severance. In a general way, however, it is possible to suggest several factors which have been given weight by the Board in making these determinations.

History of Collective Bargaining in the Plant and Industry. Often the most persuasive factors can be found in the history of the labor relations of the company involved. If voluntary alignments had previously developed and if the employer negotiated in the past with defined groups of employees, an extremely strong showing would be necessary to warrant setting up new units, for such a record would indicate not only which employees had mutual interests but also a pattern in which collective bargaining could succeed. For example, to create an industrial unit in the building construction industry could only create an absurd anomaly; for many years it has been organized exclusively on a craft basis. In other cases there may be evidence that although there has never been any previous organization of the respondent's employees, a particular grouping has developed naturally at other plants in the same industry and may therefore be assumed to be appropriate throughout.

Integration of Processes and Management. The employer's organizational structure, both in terms of the production processes and management activities, is given considerable weight in determining the appropriate unit. Where processes are highly integrated and goods flow in a continuous process from department to department it is better to establish a single unit, other things being equal, than to set up a number of groups to engage in separate bargaining. Closely related to this factor is the company's method of dealing with problems of personnel policy. Centralization of authority in a Director of Personnel or Vice-President in charge of Industrial Relations points strongly in the direction of an inclusive unit while the delegation of wide authority to foremen or to department heads may suggest that collective bargaining in smaller units is more likely to succeed.

Skills. As previously mentioned, workers who have special skills and follow a single trade have mutual problems and mutual interests often peculiar to their craft, which gives them a solidarity not felt by workers who perform routine operations on the assembly line. This circumstance, tradition and habit, and often simply the strength of a craft union in the field, may make it appropriate for skilled workers to bargain in groups separate even from other employees in the same plant. The influence of these factors on the Board's determinations is revealed in a great number of decisions but seldom more strikingly than by its rulings that the patternmakers, a few of whom are employed in many large mass production establishments, are almost always entitled despite all other circumstances to bargain as a separate unit through the Patternmakers' League.

Desires of Employees. Collective bargaining is group action. Its effectiveness depends in good part upon the coherence of the group. Hence the Board in making its unit determinations has considered the wishes of employees. When only one union asserts an interest and there is no dispute as to the appropriate unit the Board's decision will usually correspond with the union's wishes. But when more than one union asserts an interest or there exist two or more appropriate units, the desires of the employees take on great significance.

The Board determines the desires of the employees in a special election known as a "Globe election," under a doctrine first announced in GLOBE MACHINE & STAMPING CO., 3 N.L.R.B. 294

(1937). In that case, the factors pointing to a single plantwide unit were equal to those favoring separate craft units. With the balance so even the Board decided to leave to the workers themselves the question whether they preferred to be established as a separate craft unit, apart from a broader industrial unit, or to be included in the more comprehensive unit. Thus, at the Globe Machine plant, three separate elections were ordered, one among the polishers, one among the punch press operators, and one for the rest of the plant. If the polishers and punch press operators voted for their craft unions, they would have separate units; but if they voted for the United Auto Workers-CIO, they would be included under the Board's certification of UAW-CIO as representative of the employees in an industrial unit embracing all employees at the plant.[17]

The practice of ordering Globe elections was immediately criticized. By freely allowing minority groups to vote for separate representation, it was argued, the Board was disregarding the interests of the majority and magnifying the risk of strikes by powerful craft units which could bring entire factories to a standstill. In response to criticism of this kind, the Board shifted its ground in the AMERICAN CAN CO. case, 13 N.L.R.B. 1252 (1939), and held that a minority could not be severed when a larger unit had been established by a previous Board determination and where bargaining had been successfully carried on by the larger unit.

The AFL bitterly protested against the *American Can* doctrine from its inception, and despite the exceptions to the rule that developed over time, the craft unions strongly urged remedial action by the Congress. The result of these efforts was Section 9(b) (2) of the NLRA which forbade the Board deciding "that any craft unit is inappropriate for such purposes on the ground that a different unit has been established by a prior Board determination." This provision was far weaker than the AFL proposal which would have made the creation of a craft unit mandatory whenever a majority of the employees in that unit so desired.

The full import of this weakness became apparent in 1948 with the decision of the Board in NATIONAL TUBE CO., 76 N.L.R.B. 1199 (1948). In that proceeding, the petitioner sought to sever a group of bricklayers from a long-established industrial unit in the basic steel industry. Petitioner contended that Section 9(b)(2) barred the NLRB from taking any account of a prior unit determination or of previous bargaining history in deciding whether or not to allow the minority to vote for severance. The Board, however,

17. A Globe election may also be used when only one union is seeking representation but the Board finds more than one unit appropriate. Under-

wood Machinery Co., 79 N.L.R.B. 1287 (1948), enf'd 179 F.2d 118 (1st Cir. 1949).

National Tube [handwritten margin note]

flatly disagreed, stating that Section 9(b)(2) permitted prior history to be considered so long as it was not the *sole* ground for preventing the creation of a craft unit. Accordingly, the Board took into account the traditional bargaining pattern in basic steel, together with the highly integrated nature of the production process in that industry, and concluded that a craft unit would be inappropriate. The reasoning of the Board in this case became known as the *National Tube* doctrine and was subsequently extended so as to deny craft severance in the basic aluminum, lumber and wet milling industries.

By 1954 President Eisenhower's appointees had replaced most of the NLRB members who had participated in *National Tube*. In AMERICAN POTASH CO., 107 N.L.R.B. 1418 (1954) the Board then swung over to a position far more favorable to craft unions. Their conclusions appear in the following excerpts:

Am Potash [handwritten margin note]

"[W]e find that the intent of Congress will best be effectuated by a finding, and we so find, that a craft group will be appropriate for severance purposes in cases where a true craft group is sought and where, in addition, the union seeking to represent it is one which traditionally represents that craft. * * *

"In adopting this new rule, we have given grave consideration to the argument of employer and union groups that fragmentation of bargaining units in highly integrated industries which are characteristic of our modern industrial system can result in loss of maximum efficiency and sometimes afford an opportunity for jurisdictional disputes as to work assignments. We are cognizant of the disruptive economic and social conditions that can and sometimes do occur as the result of craft existence in industrial plants, as where, for example, a small cohesive craft group, by striking, closes down a large industrial plant employing thousands of workers. The alternative, however, is to deny crafts separate representation, and experience has shown that this approach, which was predominant under the *American Can* decision, was no less productive of labor unrest.

"The lesson which we draw is that, consistent with the clear intent of Congress, it is not the province of this Board to dictate the course and pattern of labor organization in our vast industrial complex. If millions of employees today feel that their interests are better served by craft unionism, it is not for us to say that they can only be represented on an industrial basis or for that matter that they must bargain on strict craft lines. All that we are considering here is whether true craft groups should have an opportunity to decide the issue for themselves. * * * *"

The Board in *American Potash* thus concluded that the extension of the *National Tube* doctrine and its "so-called integration of operations theory" to other industries would "result in the emasculation of the principle of craft independence"; it stated, however, that in order not to upset bargaining patterns in the industries in which *National Tube* had already been applied, it would continue to decline to entertain petitions for craft or departmental severance in those industries.   Despite some judicial criticism,[18] the Board adhered to its position until 1966, when it decided the following case.

MALLINCKRODT CHEMICAL WORKS

National Labor Relations Board, 1966.
162 NLRB 387.

[After formal recitals the majority opinion said:]

Petitioner seeks a unit composed of: All instrument mechanics, their apprentices and helpers in the Employer's instrument department at the Weldon Spring, Missouri, location.   Although the Petitioner has asserted at the hearing and in its brief that it seeks severance of the instrument mechanics as a "functionally distinct and homogeneous traditional departmental group" and not as a craft—a contention upon which it based its motion for reconsideration of the Board's order granting review—it has also, on the record and in its brief, asserted its willingness to "go along with any other unit that the Board may determine to be appropriate."

The Employer's Operations.   The Employer is engaged at Weldon Spring in the purification of uranium ore and the manufacture of uranium metal under a cost plus fixed fee contract with the Atomic Energy Commission.   It is the single facility contracting with AEC whose production process fully embraces the step by step extraction of uranium from its adulterated ores and converting it into a finished product in the form of solid metals, ultimately to be used by AEC and the Department of Defense.

The Employer's uranium division occupies a 200 acre tract consisting of between 40 and 50 buildings, staffed by about 560 employees.   Of these, fully half are guards, supervisors, professional, technical, and clerical employees.   The remaining production and maintenance unit is comprised of 130 production operators and ap-

---

18.   Perhaps most noteworthy was the decision in NLRB v. Pittsburgh Plate Glass Co., 270 F.2d 167 (4th Cir. 1959), cert. denied 361 U.S. 943, 80 S.Ct. 407, 4 L.Ed.2d 363 (1960).   There, the court condemned *American Potash* as disregardful of the interests of the industrial union, as an abdication to the craft employees of the Board's responsibility to make unit determinations, and as arbitrary in its retention of the *National Tube* doctrine in four industries but in no others (even though equally functionally integrated) and thus also plainly in violation of Section 9(b)(2).   See also Royal McBee Corp. v. NLRB, 302 F.2d 330 (4th Cir. 1962).

proximately 150 maintenance employees of which 12 are instrument mechanics, the classification which Petitioner seeks to sever. * * *

Coordination of the Instrument Mechanics in the Production Process. It is the principal function of the instrument mechanic to make adjustments and alterations on improperly operating instruments so that the production process may continue unimpeded. Close to three-fourths of the repairs performed by the instrument mechanics occur at the place of the breakdown, that is, on the production line. While the job requirements of operator and instrument mechanic are clearly defined and do not overlap, the operator is required to work with and does assist the mechanic in order to permit a speedy repair and the continuation of production. It is also necessary that the activities between the two be coordinated so that the operator may read the panel and relay the reading to the instrument mechanic. The operator also manually operates the instrument in order to see that it is functioning properly. We conclude from the foregoing that the instrument mechanics' role in the Employer's production process is uniquely and integrally a part upon which the production flow is dependent. * * *

It is clear * * * that the instrument mechanics are skilled workmen who work under separate supervision, and we find that the instrument mechanics constitute an identifiable group of skilled employees similar to groups we have previously found to be journeymen or craft instrument mechanics.

Whether Petitioner Qualifies as a Traditional Representative of Instrument Mechanics. * * * although Petitioner did not as of the time of the hearing represent any instrument mechanics in separate craft units, it did number, among its members, employees performing duties similar to those regularly assigned to the instrument mechanics in this case. Petitioner is also a party to collective-bargaining agreements which assign the exclusive performance of instrumentation work to employees classified as electricians. Petitioner is a party to one collective-bargaining agreement which provides for the maintenance of an apprenticeship program for training electricians in certain functions which, in this case, are performed by the Employer's instrument mechanics. Twelve members of Petitioner have taken courses in instrumentation work presented at a St. Louis high school; the course, however, was not confined solely to instruction in all the various types of instrument work, but appears to have placed primary emphasis on work of the electrician craft. In addition to the foregoing, Petitioner relies upon the fact that its parent organization, International Brotherhood of Electrical Workers, AFL–CIO, has often participated in proceedings and been granted representation rights for separate units of instrument mechanics.

The foregoing, in our view, falls short of establishing that Petitioner qualifies as a traditional representative of instrument mechanics of the kind involved in this case. However, for reasons stated below, we do not now view the Petitioner's failure to satisfy the traditional representative test as it has developed since the American Potash decision as in itself a decisive ground for dismissal.

Reconsideration of the American Potash Doctrine. * * *
[T]he Employer urges that to the extent the American Potash decision forbids realistic consideration of bargaining history and integration of the craft employees' functions in the production process unless the case involves one of the so-called National Tube industries, it is plainly discriminatory in application and requires reversal.

We believe there is much force to the Employer's arguments and contentions, and we have undertaken in this and other cases a review of our present policies regarding severance elections.

At the outset, it is appropriate to set forth the nature of the issue confronting the Board in making unit determinations in severance cases. Underlying such determinations is the need to balance the interest of the employer and the total employee complement in maintaining the industrial stability and resulting benefits of an historical plant-wide bargaining unit as against the interest of a portion of such complement in having an opportunity to break away from the historical unit by a vote for separate representation. The Board does not exercise its judgment lightly in these difficult areas. Each such case involves a resolution of "what would best serve the working man in his effort to bargain collectively with his employer, and what would best serve the interest of the country as a whole."
* * *

The cohesiveness and special interest of a craft or departmental group seeking severance may indicate the appropriateness of a bargaining unit limited to that group. However, the interests of all employees in continuing to bargain together in order to maintain their collective strength, as well as the public interest and the interests of the employer and the plant union in maintaining overall plant stability in labor relations and uninterrupted operation of integrated industrial or commercial facilities, may favor adherence to the established patterns of bargaining.

The problem of striking a balance has been the subject of Board and Congressional concern since the early days in the administration of the Wagner Act. [The Board then reviewed the *National Tube* and *American Potash* opinions.] On the basis of what has already been indicated herein respecting the legislative history of the Section, we believe the revised construction of the statute adopted in American Potash was erroneous * * * American Potash established two basic tests: (1) the employees involved must constitute a true craft or departmental group, and (2) the union seeking to carve out a craft or departmental unit must be one which has traditionally devoted itself to the special problems of the group involved. * * * Thus, by confining consideration solely to the interests favoring severance, the American Potash tests preclude the Board from discharging its statutory responsibility to make its unit determinations on the basis of all relevant factors, including those which weigh against severance. In short, application of these mechanistic tests leads always to the conclusion that the interests of craft employees always prevail. It does this, moreover, without affording a voice in the decision to the other employees, whose unity of association is broken and whose collective strength is weakened by the success of the craft or departmental group in pressing its own special interests.

Furthermore, the American Potash decision makes arbitrary distinctions between industries by forbidding the application of the National Tube doctrine to other industries whose operations are as highly integrated, and whose plantwide bargaining patterns are as well established, as is the case in the so-called "National Tube" industries. In fact, the American Potash decision is inherently inconsistent in asserting that "* * * it is not the province of this Board to dictate the course and pattern of labor organization in our vast industrial complex," while, at the same time, establishing rules which have that very effect. Thus, American Potash clearly "dictate[s] the course and pattern of labor organization" by establishing rigid qualifications for unions seeking craft units and by automatically precluding severance of all such units in National Tube industries.

It is patent from the foregoing that the American Potash tests do not effectuate the policies of the Act. * * * We shall, therefore, no longer allow our inquiry to be limited by them. Rather, we shall, as the Board did prior to *American Potash*, broaden our inquiry to permit evaluation of all considerations relevant to an informed decision in this area. The following areas of inquiry are illustrative of those we deem relevant:

1. Whether or not the proposed unit consists of a distinct and homogeneous group of skilled journeymen craftsmen performing the functions of their craft on a nonrepetitive basis, or of employees constituting a functionally distinct department, working in trades or occupations for which a tradition of separate representation exists.

2.   The history of collective bargaining of the employees sought and at the plant involved, and at other plants of the employer, with emphasis on whether the existing patterns of bargaining are productive of stability in labor relations, and whether such stability will be unduly disrupted by the destruction of the existing patterns of representation.

3.   The extent to which the employees in the proposed unit have established and maintained their separate identity during the period of inclusion in a broader unit, and the extent of their participation or lack of participation in the establishment and maintenance of the existing pattern of representation and the prior opportunities, if any, afforded them to obtain separate representation.

4.   The history and pattern of collective bargaining in the industry involved.

5.   The degree of integration of the employer's production processes, including the extent to which the continued normal operation of the production processes is dependent upon the performance of the assigned functions of the employees in the proposed unit.

6.   The qualifications of the union seeking to "carve out" a separate unit, including that union's experience in representing employees like those involved in the severance action.

In view of the nature of the issue posed by a petition for severance, the foregoing should not be taken as a hard and fast definition or an inclusive or exclusive listing of the various considerations involved in making unit determinations in this area.   No doubt other factors worthy of consideration will appear in the course of litigation. * * *

Turning to the facts of this case, we conclude that it will not effectuate the policies of the Act to permit the disruption of the production and maintenance unit by permitting Petitioner to "carve out" a unit of instrument mechanics.   Our conclusion is predicated on the following considerations.

The Employer is engaged in the production of uranium metal. It is the only enterprise in the country which is engaged in all phases of such production. All of its finished product is sold to the Atomic Energy Commission. Continued stability in labor relations at such facilities is vital to our national defense.

The Employer produces uranium metal by means of a highly integrated continuous flow production system which the record herein shows is beyond doubt as highly integrated as are the production processes of the basic steel, basic aluminum, wet milling, and lumbering industries. The process itself is largely dependent upon the proper functioning of a wide variety of instrument controls which channel the raw materials through the closed pipe system and regulate the speed of flow of the materials as well as the temperatures within different parts of the system. These controls are an integral part of the production system. The instrument mechanics' work on such controls is therefore intimately related to the production process itself. Indeed, in performing such work, they must do so in tandem with the operators of the controls to insure that the system continues to function while new controls are installed, and existing controls are calibrated, maintained, and repaired.

The instrument mechanics have been represented as part of a production and maintenance unit for the last 25 years. The record does not demonstrate that their interests have been neglected by their bargaining representative. In fact, the record shows that their pay rates are comparable to those received by the skilled electricians who are currently represented by the Petitioner, and that such rates are among the highest in the plant. The instrument mechanics have their own seniority system for purposes of transfer, layoff, and recall. Viewing this long lack of concern for maintaining and preserving a separate group identity for bargaining purposes, together with the fact that Petitioner has not traditionally represented the instrument mechanic craft, we find that the interests served by maintenance of stability in the existing bargaining unit of approximately 280 production and maintenance employees outweigh the interests served by affording the 12 instrument mechanics an opportunity to change their mode of representation.

* * * [I]t appears that the separate community of interests which these employees enjoy by reason of their skills and training has been largely submerged in the broader community of interests which they share with other employees by reason of long and uninterrupted association in the existing bargaining unit, the high degree of integration of the employer's production processes, and the intimate connection of the work of these employees with the actual uranium metal-making process itself. * * *

FANNING, Member, dissenting: * * *

I think it manifest from the language of 9(b) and the proviso under consideration that Congress did not enact into law the requirement that craft employees always be given an opportunity to vote for separate representation. It is also apparent, however, that the wording of the proviso did not in any way dilute the strength of the presumption running in favor of the appropriateness of craft units, whether that issue is presented in a severance case or in one involving the initial organization of the employees involved. * * *

I believe that the effectuation of Congressional intention in this area can best be achieved by placing upon the parties who would deny separate representation to craft employees, the burden of demonstrating that the separate community of interests normally possessed by craftsmen has become submerged in the larger community of interests of the employees in the broader unit.

For my part, I do not believe that such burden is met merely by a showing of a bargaining history on a broader basis, no matter how long it has endured. I believe there must be a showing that the bargaining history has, because of the nature and quality of the representation afforded craft employees, contributed to a strengthening of their ties and interests with those of the other employees, or that the history and pattern of representation in the industry involved is one of plant-wide, rather than craft or departmental representation. Although I believe that this latter factor may militate against craft representation in the industry, I shall, nevertheless, permit such separate representation where it is necessary to free a small group of skilled craftsmen from a bargaining structure in which, because of their minority position, their legitimate special interests have been subordinated to the interests of the majority of unskilled employees.

Similarly, I am not persuaded that the fact that craft employees work in close association with other employees in operating and maintaining a highly integrated production system necessarily destroys their right to seek representation in a separate unit. I recognize, however, that the separate identity of craft employees may be destroyed, or their separate community of interests submerged in the broader community of interests shared by all employees in the plant, in particular circumstances. For example, where the exigencies of a particular integrated production system are such as to require of craft employees: direct participation in the production process itself; the repetitive performance of routine tasks at more or less fixed work stations along the assembly line or channel of flow; or the acquisition of special skills in addition to those acquired in the course of normal training and experience in their craft, in order to enable them to work on their employer's specialized equipment; I believe it fair to conclude that the equities weigh in favor of maintaining the existing pattern of representation. * * *

Finally, I do not view the 25-year bargaining history for the production and maintenance unit as supporting the finding that a separate unit of instrument mechanics is inappropriate. Examination of that history reveals, as already noted, that other units have been severed therefrom without noticeable loss in the collective strength of the production and maintenance employees, and I venture the opinion that the severance of these 12 instrument mechanics would not weaken the capability of the 280 production and maintenance employees to bargain effectively in the future. Moreover, there is no indication in this record that the inclusion of the instrument mechanics in the larger unit has resulted in a loss of separate identity; indeed, the very factors cited by the majority for their conclusion that the needs of the instrument mechanics have not been neglected by the Intervenor also indicate that the Employer and the Intervenor continue to recognize their separate identity and special interests. Accordingly, I believe that, in the absence of evidence compelling the conclusion that the instrument mechanics do not, as craftsmen, share a community of interests separate and distinct from the community of interests they share with other employees in the existing production and maintenance unit, I believe this is a situation in which Section 9(b) (2) contemplates that a craft unit cannot be found to be inappropriate unless the employees in the proposed unit vote against separate representation. I therefore, dissent from my colleagues' refusal to direct the election as requested by the Petitioner.[19]

Problems for Discussion

1. Is the Board's analysis in *Mallinckrodt*, which retreats from a policy more favorable to craft severance, consistent with the congressional directive in Section 9(b) that unit determinations are to be shaped by the objective of assuring the "fullest freedom in exercising" statutory rights? For example, can one harmonize this statutory directive with the Board's balancing of the interests of the larger unit against those of the craft unit? What is the justification for the Board's considering such factors as integration of production processes, and the public interest in this defense industry?

2. What is the meaning and significance of the following key words employed by the NLRB in enunciating the relevant areas of inquiry for deciding cases such as *Mallinckrodt*? (a) "stability" (b) "separate identity" (c) "participation" (d) "history and pattern of collective bargaining."

3. As between the standards and criteria of *Mallinckrodt* and those of *American Potash*, which provide greater predictability? Which are likely to yield results most sensitive to all of the interests involved and to the concerns of Congress? All things considered, which decision do you feel provides the better solution to the underlying problem?

4. The standards established by the Board in *Mallinckrodt* involving the issue of craft severance are also applicable to the initial formation of units. Is this appropriate?

5. In *American Potash*, the Board had defined a "true craft unit" as consisting of a "distinct and homogeneous group of skilled journeymen craftsmen, working as such, together with the apprentices and/or helpers. To be a 'journeyman craftsman,' an individual must have a kind and

19. The *Mallinckrodt* case, and its progeny, are discussed in a Note, Craft Severance: NLRB's New Approach, 42   Ind.L.J. 554 (1967); Sharp, Craft Certification: New Expansion of an Old Concept, 33 Ohio St.L.J. 102 (1972).

degree of skill which is normally acquired only by undergoing a substantial period of apprenticeship or comparable training." Having this definition in mind, along with the principles of *Mallinckrodt*, how should the Board decide the following case:

At one of the plants of a Michigan corporation engaged in the manufacture of reclining chairs and other furniture, a unit of 540 production and maintenance employees has been represented by the United Furniture Workers since 1956. In 1981, the International Society of Skilled Trades seeks to sever nine tool-and-die employees. These workers are skilled specialists, and although there is no formal apprenticeship program for them the employer requires two years of experience. They personally own their own tools, and spend 95 percent of their time at workbenches within a separate, enclosed toolroom; they go into the production area only to install or test a newly made die, and when their work is slack they are on occasion loaned to other tooling departments. They share the same supervisors as production employees, as well as a common lunchroom, restrooms and parking facilities; but they have a separate timeclock and lockerroom. They are the highest paid employees in the plant. There has been one tool-and-die employee on the plant collective bargaining committee for some time. Should this group of nine employees be severed for *yes* purposes of a certification election? See *Rohr Corp.*, 157 N.L.R.B. 1351 (1966), and compare *LA–Z Boy Chair Co.*, 235 N.L.R.B. 77 (1978), with *Buddy L. Corp.*, 167 N.L.R.B. 808 (1967).

5. *Multi-Employer and Coalition Bargaining.*[20]

The growth of industrial unions under the auspices of the CIO gave impetus to a tendency toward collective negotiations on a multi-employer or even industry-wide basis. A second factor is the growing realization of many employers that they have greater bargaining power as a group than where the union bargains with competing companies one at a time, threatening each with a strike while the others are filling the needs of their customers. Finally, competing enterprises may desire to bargain on a multi-employer basis in order to make certain that their rivals do not enjoy more favorable terms.

Where multi-employer bargaining prevails, negotiations are usually carried on between the international union and an association of employers selling in the same market. A single master agreement is usually signed and thereafter subsidiary agreements dealing with the problems of individual companies may be worked out between the employers and the local unions concerned.

Many who have had wide experience in labor relations are convinced that the spread of industry-wide bargaining in the United

---

20. See Benetar, Coalition Bargaining Under the NLRA, and Abramson, Co-ordinated Bargaining by Unions, N.Y. U. 20th Annual Conf. on Labor 219, 231 (1968); Goldberg, Coordinated Bargaining Tactics of Unions, 54 Cornell L.Rev. 897 (1969); C. Rehmus, Multi-employer Bargaining (1965).

States would put labor relations on a sounder basis. The wider the basis of discussion, the more likely it is that the negotiations will be in the hands of experienced leaders and that they will bring to their aid staffs of experts with pertinent data revealing the long range implications of the proposals discussed. In a word, better organization for bargaining means more intelligent and responsible negotiation on the part of management and labor alike. Much can be achieved, moreover, by an industry acting as a unit: it becomes possible to think of such problems as technological displacement on an industry basis and so to achieve social and economic gains that no company could undertake alone. Labor desires industry-wide bargaining, partly because it avoids wasting manpower in successive negotiations with a number of employers, partly because it may secure gains which no one employer can grant for fear of competitive disadvantage. It is doubtless also a factor that centralization strengthens the leaders' control. Many businessmen have come to the same conclusion for similar reasons: competitive disadvantages based on disparities in labor cost are reduced if not abolished; the industry as a whole can face strike threats which might be disastrous to a single employer through the loss of its market; the national officers of a union are likely to have a better understanding of management problems than local leaders and in industry-wide bargaining can keep extremists under some measure of control.

But for all these advantages there may be offsetting costs. Most serious perhaps is the scope of any strike resulting from a breakdown in industry-wide negotiations. The public importance of negotiations rises in rapid progression as proportionately larger segments of an industry become involved. It is also argued that multi-employer bargaining results in undue restraints upon competition. If all the companies selling in a single market are to grant identical wage increases, they may conclude that their selfish interests are served better by granting whatever increase is necessary to buy labor peace and then passing the cost on to the public than by attempting to hold down costs. The very existence of high labor costs in an industry may discourage the entrance of new competitors or the migration of industry to different geographic areas; and this may be aggravated when a union uses multi-employer bargaining (with or without the consent of the employers) to establish embargoes on goods produced in other geographic areas, or to refuse to supply labor to any company not a member of the employers' association, or to escalate its wage demands to employers outside of the association in order to make it uneconomical for them to remain in business. Such agreements raise serious problems of legality under the federal antitrust laws, a subject considered in greater detail at pages 878–99, infra.

Although the existence of multi-employer bargaining therefore raises very broad questions of economic and social policy, the National Labor Relations Board has refrained from addressing those questions in determining whether a multi-employer unit is appropriate for the purposes of collective bargaining. The NLRA does not specifically authorize the Board to find multi-employer units appropriate, yet even in the early years of that Act bargaining on a multi-employer or industry-wide basis was not unusual and the Board interpreted the term "employer" in Section 2(2) to reflect this industrial fact. Shipowner's Ass'n of the Pacific Coast, 7 N.L.R.B. 1002 (1938). The term "employer" included any person acting in an employer's interest and that person, the Board reasoned, might be an association, so that the "employer" unit referred to in Section 9 of the NLRA could be a multi-employer association. (The Taft-Hartley amendments to Section 2(2) did not change the Board's reasoning. Associated Shoe Industries of Southeastern Mass., Inc., 81 N.L. R.B. 224 (1949)).

In determining whether such a unit is in fact appropriate, the Board looks for an employer's participation for a substantial period of time in joint bargaining negotiations and its consistent adoption of the agreements resulting from such negotiations; such a controlling bargaining history indicates a desire on the part of the participating employers to be bound by joint, rather than individual, action and warrants the establishment of the multi-employer unit. Neither the lack of a formal association of employers nor the fact that the results of joint negotiations have been incorporated in separate uniform contracts will be determinative. Conversely, the mere adoption by an employer of contracts negotiated by an employer group will not be held to require the inclusion of its employees in the multi-employer unit. Consistent with its principle that the multi-employer unit is a consensual unit, the Board will look also for the consent of the union having representative status.

Prior to 1952, once a multi-employer unit had been established it would control the structure of bargaining for all categories of workers employed by a participating company. Concern arose, however, that this policy impeded union organization because it forced all subsequent organization within a company to be on a multi-employer basis. In Joseph E. Seagram & Sons, 101 N.L.R.B. 101 (1952), the Board reversed its policy, so that an employer may be part of a multi-employer unit for one category of its employees but may function as a single-employer unit with regard to other groups of employees.

An employer decision to participate in multi-employer bargaining is not irrevocable. Changes in economic conditions may convince a company or a union that it would be wise to withdraw from multi-employer bargaining and to bargain on an individual basis. But to permit a party to withdraw at any time—particularly once bargain-

ing has begun and the terms of a contract begin to take shape—
would invite disruptive maneuvering and could unfairly upset the
assumptions on which all parties have been relying in their dealings.
Accordingly, the Board has imposed limitations, through the unfair
labor practice provisions dealing with good-faitn bargaining, upon
the power of the parties to withdraw from multi-employer bargaining. A company [21] or a union [22] is permitted to withdraw, without
regard to reason or motive, provided it announces its intention to do
so unequivocally and before bargaining commences.[23] Even after
bargaining begins, a party may withdraw under limited circumstances. One such circumstance is the consent, either express or
implied, of the other party.[24] In the case of the withdrawal of an
employer-member of a multi-employer group, the consent of the
multi-employer group is also necessary.[25] Any untimely attempt by
the employer-member to withdraw without the consent of both the
union and the employer association constitutes a violation of Section
8(a)(5).[26]

The presence of "unusual circumstances" has also been held to
justify an otherwise untimely withdrawal. The exception is a narrow one and has been limited to such dire economic pressures as
imminent bankruptcy or forced closing,[27] as well as cases of severe
shrinkage of the bargaining unit through the allowed withdrawal of
most of the employer-members.[28] Whether an impasse in multi-employer bargaining constitutes an "unusual circumstance" justifying
an otherwise untimely withdrawal is an issue that divides the courts
of appeals. Several circuit courts have held that an impasse does
constitute such an unusual circumstance; the rationale appears in
part to be that employer rights should be similar to those of the
union, which can in the midst of negotiations deal with and settle (at

21. Retail Associates, Inc., 120 N.L.
R.B. 388 (1958).

22. Evening News Ass'n, 154 N.L.R.B.
1494 (1965); Publishers' Ass'n v.
NLRB, 364 F.2d 293 (2d Cir.) cert.
denied, 385 U.S. 971 (1966).

23. NLRB v. Sheridan Creations, Inc.,
357 F.2d 245 (2d Cir.) cert. denied
385 U.S 1005 (1966).

24. See N. L. R. B. v. John J. Cor-
bett Press, Inc., 163 N.L.R.B. 154
(1967), enf'd 401 F.2d 673 (2d Cir.
1968).

25. Teamsters Local 378 (Olympia Automobile Dealers Ass'n), 243 N.L.R.B.
No. 138 (1979).

26. *Ibid.* That case also holds that a
union which executes a separate, final
agreement with an employer-member
who withdrew from the multi-employer group without its consent violates Section 8(b)(3).

27. Hi-Way Billboards, Inc., 206 N.L.
R.B. 22 (1973), enf't denied on other
grounds 500 F.2d 181 (5th Cir. 1974).

28. Connell Typesetting Co., 212 N.L.
R.B. 918 (1974) (out of the original 36
employers, only 13 remained—the union being unwilling to consent to their
withdrawal—and these employers had
a total employee complement of only
36 workers); NLRB v. Southwestern
Colorado Contractors Ass'n, 447 F.2d
968 (10th Cir. 1971).

least on an interim basis) with individual employers within the group, and in part to be that the impasse indicates that no real progress can be made through continued bargaining within the multi-employer framework.[29] Other courts, however, have endorsed the Board's view that "an impasse is but one thread in the complex tapestry of collective bargaining," is an ordinary and expectable event in labor negotiations, and does not justify late withdrawal from the multi-employer unit.[30]

The Board has also held that a union may engage in a "partial withdrawal," that is it may abandon multi-employer bargaining with respect to one or more employers while continuing such bargaining with those remaining in the unit.[31] This power of the union to shape the scope of the bargaining unit is thought simply to be the correlative of the right of any employer or group of employers timely to withdraw from the unit as well.

In many of the industries in which multiemployer bargaining has developed, the employers are small and numerous and the union represents workers on an area-wide basis at a number of different companies. More recently, the converse structure has developed, with a single large company being confronted at the bargaining table by representatives of a number of different unions representing employees in different bargaining units within that company. The grouping of forces by the various unions has been called "coordinated" or "coalition" bargaining. As will be developed in greater detail below, see pages 454–55 infra, it is unlawful for a single union or groups of unions to insist upon, or to strike in support of demands for, the expansion of bargaining to units larger than those certified by the NLRB. At base, the rationale appears to be that bargaining about wages and other fundamental working conditions should not be frustrated by the use of economic weapons to modify the scope of bargaining units, when that issue has been (or can be) peacefully and expeditiously resolved by the Board. But union coordination in bargaining need not be directed at an improper expansion of the unit for bargaining. The function of coordinated or coalition bargaining has been considered in cases in which an employer has refused to bargain with a properly recognized

29. NLRB v. Independent Ass'n of Steel Fabricators, Inc., 582 F.2d 135 (2d Cir. 1978), cert. denied, 439 U.S. 1130, 99 S.Ct. 1049, 59 L.Ed.2d 91 (1979); NLRB v. Beck Engraving Co., 522 F.2d 475 (3d Cir. 1975). See Murphy, Impasse and the Duty to Bargain in Good Faith, 39 U. of Pitt.L.Rev. 1, 50–60 (1977); Comment, Effect of Negotiating Impasse on Employer's Right to Withdraw from a Multi-Employer Bargaining Association, 17 B.C.Ind. & Comm.L.Rev. 525 (1976).

30. NLRB v. Marine Mach. Works, Inc., 635 F.2d 522 (5th Cir. 1981); NLRB v. Charles D. Bonanno Linen Serv., Inc., 630 F.2d 25 (1st Cir. 1980), cert. granted — U.S. —, 101 S.Ct. 1512, 67 L.Ed.2d 813 (1981).

31. Pacific Coast Ass'n of Pulp & Paper Mfrs., 163 N.L.R.B. 892 (1967).

or certified union which brings to the bargaining table representatives of other unions from other company bargaining units. The following case contains a full discussion of the dynamics of coalition or coordinated bargaining so that, although it arises in the context of what may be (at this point in the course) unfamiliar principles of law, it constitutes a useful introduction to this recent development in bargaining structure.

GENERAL ELECTRIC CO. v. NLRB

United States Court of Appeals, Second Circuit, 1969.
412 F.2d 512.

FEINBERG, CIRCUIT JUDGE: * * *

[General Electric, a manufacturer and seller of electrical equipment and related products, employs about 290,000 workers in over 60 plants and 400 other installations, such as service shops and warehouses. About half of its employees are represented by more than 80 unions in roughly 150 bargaining units; approximately 80,000 workers in some 90 of those units are represented by the International Union of Electrical, Radio and Machine Workers (IUE). The company, which does business in all 50 states, has traditionally bargained with the IUE International for a single national agreement covering all employees represented by the IUE and its locals; local issues are addressed in supplementary local contracts. During the term of the 1963–66 national agreement, the IUE and seven other international unions whose locals also had agreements with General Electric formed a Committee on Collective Bargaining (CCB). This was an outgrowth of the unions' dissatisfaction with the traditional separate negotiations between the company and the different unions, in which the unions believed that General Electric was playing off each union against the other. The avowed purposes of the members of the CCB were to coordinate bargaining in 1966 with GE and its chief competitor, Westinghouse, to formulate national goals and otherwise support one another.

When the CCB attempted to persuade company representatives to meet for preliminary discussions prior to the October 1966 contract termination date, GE responded in March 1966 that it would meet with the IUE but would not participate in any "eight-union coalition discussions or in any other steps in the direction of industry-wide bargaining." When company representatives appeared for a meeting in early May, after receiving assurances of individual bargaining from IUE, they noted that the IUE negotiating committee had added seven members—one from each of the other seven unions comprising the CCB—and promptly refused to confer. This refusal persisted even after GE was informed that the seven new members were not voting members of the IUE committee and were present solely to aid in IUE negotiations, not to represent their own unions. The IUE filed refusal-to-bargain charges under Section 8(a)(5) of the Labor Act, and an action was initiated by the Board for a preliminary injunction under Section 10(j) to compel GE to bargain with the "mixed" committee; amidst injunctions, reversals and stays, the company bargained in August 1966, sometime with the IUE alone and sometime with the "mixed" committee. It was not until October 1968 that the NLRB issued a decision finding GE to have violated Section 8(a)(5). The company petitioned for review of the Board's order, which required bargaining with the IUE through its committee, and the Board cross-petitioned for enforcement.]

The basic question before us is whether a union's inclusion of members of other unions on its bargaining committee justifies an employer's refusal to bargain. The Company contends that there is more to the case than that, claiming that the IUE was engaged in an illegal attempt to obliterate bargaining unit lines and was, as the Board put it, " 'locked in' to a conspiratorial understanding." We discuss that phase of the case below, but turn first to the crucial issue before us.

Section 7 of the National Labor Relations Act, 29 U.S.C. § 157, guarantees certain rights to employees, including the right to join together in labor organizations and "to bargain collectively through representatives of their own choosing." This right of employees and the corresponding right of employers, see section 8(b)(1)(B) of the Act, 29 U.S.C. § 158(b)(1)(B), to choose whomever they wish to represent them in formal labor negotiations is fundamental to the statutory scheme. In general, either side can choose as it sees fit and neither can control the other's selection, a proposition confirmed in a number of opinions, some of fairly ancient vintage. For example, the following asserted objections to bargaining representatives have all been rejected as defenses to charges of refusal to bargain: that a local union president could not act for the international union in grievance handling, see Prudential Insurance Co. of America v. NLRB, 278 F.2d 181, 182–183 (3d Cir. 1960); that an AFL "general organizer," not a member or officer of the union, could not bargain for the latter, see NLRB v. Deena Artware, Inc., 198 F.2d 645, 650–651 (6th Cir. 1952), cert. denied, 345 U.S. 906, 73 S.Ct. 644, 97 L.Ed. 1342 (1953); that employees could not be represented by a local union, a majority of whose members were employed by a rival industry and which the employees were not eligible to join, see Pueblo Gas & Fuel Co. v. NLRB, 118 F.2d 304, 307–308 (10th Cir. 1941); and that an international union representative could not negotiate for a local, see Oliver Corp., 74 N.L.R.B. 483 (1947).

There have been exceptions to the general rule that either side can choose its bargaining representatives freely, but they have been rare and confined to situations so infected with ill-will, usually personal, or conflict of interest as to make good-faith bargaining impractical. See, e. g., NLRB v. ILGWU, 274 F.2d 376, 379 (3d Cir. 1960) (ex-union official added to employer committee to "put one over on the union"); Bausch & Lomb Optical Co., 108 N.L.R.B. 1555 (1954) (union established company in direct competition with employer); NLRB v. Kentucky Utilities Co., 182 F.2d 810 (6th Cir. 1950) (union negotiator had expressed great personal animosity towards employer). But cf. NLRB v. Signal Manufacturing Co., 351 F.2d 471 (1st Cir. 1965) (*per curiam*), cert. denied 382 U.S. 985, 86 S.Ct. 562, 15 L.Ed.2d 474 (1966) (similar claim of animosity rejected). Thus, the freedom to select representatives is not absolute, but that does not detract from its significance. Rather the narrowness and infrequency of approved exceptions to the general rule emphasizes its importance. Thus, in arguing that employees may not select members of other unions as "representatives of their own choosing" on a negotiating committee, the Company clearly undertakes a considerable burden, characterized in an analogous situation in NLRB v. David Buttrick Co., 399 F.2d 505, 507 (1st Cir. 1968), as the showing of a "clear and present" danger to the collective bargaining process. * * *

Turning to specific policy reasons for inclusion of members of other unions on a negotiating committee, we are told that a union has an interest in using experts to bargain, whether the expertise be on technical, substantive matters or on the general art of negotiating. In filling that need, no good reason appears why it may not look to "outsiders," just as an employer is free to do. See Detroit Newspaper Publishers Ass'n v. NLRB, 372 F.2d 569, 572 (6th Cir. 1967); NLRB v. Local 294, International Brotherhood of Teamsters, 284 F.2d 893 (2d Cir. 1960). However, the heat generated by this controversy does not arise from that bland consideration. The Company has in the past made effective use of its own ability to plan centralized bargaining strategy in dealing with the various unions representing its employees while keeping the actual bargaining with each union separate. * * * IUE claims that having members of the other unions on its committee increases communications between all of them and to that extent reduces the ability of the Company to play one off against the other. In any event, the plain facts are that the IUE proposed negotiating technique is a response to the Company's past bargaining practices, that it is designed to strengthen the IUE's bargaining position, and that both sides know it.

The Board held that a mixed-union negotiating committee is not per se improper and that absent a showing of "substantial evidence of ulterior motive or bad faith" an employer commits an unfair labor practice unless it bargains with such a group. The Company and *amicus* attack the Board rule on a number of grounds. They claim that the rule will inevitably allow the injection of conflicting interests and "outside and extraneous influences" into the bargaining process, will make the always difficult task of determining the motives of the other side an impossibility, is an improper effort by the Board to adjust economic power, and finally is unworkable because an employer confronted with bad faith or ulterior motives can only break off negotiations with the mixed group and file unfair labor practices charges with the Board, an option disruptive of collective bargaining at best and in actuality no remedy at all.

The claim that outside influences and alleged conflicts require an outright ban on mixed-union committees is not weighty in view of the cases discussed above * * *. Equally unpersuasive is the assertion that the Board made an improper effort to adjust economic power. The Board gave no such rationale for its decision. Of course, it would be nonsense to pretend that IUE's purpose was not to increase its bargaining strength, but that goal is a normal one for unions or employers. That Board application of an old policy to a new situation may have such an effect does not vitiate a rule if it is otherwise justified. The possibility that there will be improper attempts to ignore unit boundaries is, of course, real. The Company argues that different unions certified for separate units may not force an employer to bargain with them jointly as to all units on any subject, despite the implications of United States Pipe & Foundry Co. v. NLRB, 298 F.2d 873 (5th Cir.), cert. denied, 370 U.S. 919, 82 S.Ct. 1557, 8 L.Ed.2d 499 (1962), which approved an arrangement whereby three unions conditioned their agreements in separate but substantially simultaneous negotiations upon a joint demand for common contract expiration dates. The Board did not come to grips with this problem, and we similarly do not now consider the extent to which the law permits cooperation in bargaining among unions or employers. Compare Wagner, Multi-Union Bargaining: A Legal Analysis, 19 Lab.L.J. 731 (1968), and Note, Is Coalition Bargaining Legal?, 18 W.Res.L.Rev. 575 (1967), with Anker, Pattern Bargaining, Antitrust Laws and the National Labor Relations Act, 19 N.Y.U. Ann.Conf. on Labor 81 (1967). The point is that the chance that negotiators may improperly press impermissible subjects is inherent in the bargaining process, and therefore must be taken. As to the increased difficulty in determining motives of the other side, we agree that this may occur. However, although evidence that bargaining for other employees is being attempted may be difficult to obtain, the Board is certainly capable of making such a determination when a case comes before it. * * * In view of the overall policy of encouraging free selection of representatives, we agree with the Board's rejection of a per se rule which bans mixed-union committees.

In sum, we do not think that the Company has demonstrated the type of clear and present danger to the bargaining process that is required to overcome the burden on one who objects to the representatives selected by the other party. We hold that the IUE did have the right to include members of other unions on its negotiating committee, and the Company was not lawfully entitled to refuse to bargain with that committee so long as it sought to bargain solely on behalf of those employees represented by the IUE, a question we discuss further below.

[The court then went on to hold that, since General Electric was not obligated by its contract to commence formal bargaining until August 1966, its refusal to bargain with the mixed committee became unlawful only at that time and not as early as the informal and preliminary discussions sought by the IUE in May. The court also found that there was evidence to support the conclusion of the Board that the IUE was not "locked in" to joint bargaining with the other seven unions so as to relinquish its freedom of independent decisionmaking and that the IUE had no "ulterior motive" or bad faith in negotiating through its mixed committee; the committee at no time tried to bargain for any employees other than those represented by the IUE, and the court concluded that the company thus had an obligation at least to confer with the committee to put to the test the claim of the IUE that it was negotiating for itself alone.]

C. REPRESENTATION ELECTION PROCEDURES

Seventy or seventy-five per cent of the controversies concerning the representation of employees involve neither a dispute as to the propriety of a present determination of representatives nor real doubt concerning the bargaining unit. Such cases are almost invariably handled informally in the Regional Office by what are known as "consent elections". With the help of the Regional Director's staff, the company and the union or unions concerned enter into a consent election agreement, the principal provisions of which specify the bargaining unit, the eligibility of voters and the date of the election. Normally the agreement vests in the Regional Director final authority to rule on any disputes that may arise concerning the conduct of the election and to issue his or her determination as to the result. An alternative form of agreement, referred to as a stipulation for consent, provides that the parties will reserve their normal rights of review with respect to these questions.

In contested cases the Regional Director conducts formal proceedings, decides whether a present determination of representatives is appropriate and defines the unit appropriate for the purposes of collective bargaining. A formal Direction of Election is then issued ordering an election in the designated bargaining unit within a specified period (usually between 25 and 30 days).

The details of the election are arranged in the Regional Office. In general the procedure resembles any local election. A voting list is prepared, polling places and voting hours are designated, and notices are published in advance. The Board's agents supervise the election but the interested parties are entitled to have watchers at the polls and to challenge any ballot. The ballots are secret and in the first instance offer each employee an opportunity to vote for any union claiming the right to represent them or for "no union". At the close of the voting, the ballots are counted. Certain votes may be challenged, and if the challenges cannot be resolved informally the ballots will be set aside. If there are enough challenged votes to affect the outcome of the election, a ruling on the disputed ballots will be made by the Regional Director who will also pass upon any other objections which the parties may have taken to the election.

The decisions of the Regional Director—both before the election (e. g., appropriate bargaining unit) and after (e. g., objections)— are subject to review by the National Labor Relations Board, but the Board grants review only on the following grounds:

(1) Where a substantial question of law or policy is involved.

(2) Where the Regional Director's decision on a substantial factual issue is clearly and prejudicially erroneous.

(3) Where the conduct of the hearing in an election case or any ruling made in connection with the proceeding has resulted in prejudicial error.

(4) Where there are compelling reasons for reconsidering an important Board rule or policy.

Although most of the problems that arise in determining the eligibility of employees to vote are matters of detail, significant problems of eligibility may arise if an election takes place during the course of a strike. Many employers will attempt to keep their plant in operation during a strike by hiring new employees, or replacements, where qualified and willing persons are available for this purpose. In such cases, a determination must be made whether the strikers and/or their replacements are entitled to vote. If the strike has been precipitated or prolonged by the employer's unfair labor practice, it is well settled that the striking employees have the right to return to their jobs and to displace any replacements hired by the company subsequent to the commission of the unfair labor practice. Hence, in these situations, the strikers, and not the replacements, are eligible to vote. Conversely, if the strike is unlawful or if it is conducted for certain improper objectives, or if the strikers have engaged in certain types of misconduct, they may be discharged by the employer whereupon they will lose their eligibility to vote. If an ordinary economic strike takes place, however, without unfair labor practices or misconduct on either side, the employer may not penalize its employees for striking by discharging them, but it may seek to keep the business operating by hiring permanent replacements with the result that the replaced strikers have no immediate claim to their jobs. (All these rules are taken up in detail at pp. 832–36, 864–66, infra). The most troublesome problems of eligibility have arisen in deciding the respective voting rights of such economic strikers, on the one hand, and the permanent replacements, on the other.

The guiding legal rules have shifted. At first, the Board ruled that economic strikers should vote and their replacements should not, but it later decided that both groups should vote. Congress in 1947 declared that striking employees not entitled to reinstatement were not eligible to vote but this controversial provision was modified in 1959 by the present language of Section 9(c)(3): "Employees engaged in an economic strike who are not entitled to reinstatement shall be eligible to vote under such regulations as the Board shall find are consistent with the purposes and provisions of this Act in any election conducted within twelve months after the commencement of the strike."

The NLRB has formulated the following principles to determine eligibility. Strikers are presumed to be "economic" unless they are found by the Board to be on strike over employer unfair labor practices. Likewise, replacements for economic strikers are presumed to be permanent employees and eligible to vote. An economic striker loses this status, and thus his or her eligibility to vote, if before the election the striker obtains permanent employment elsewhere, or is discharged or refused reinstatement for misconduct rendering him or her unsuitable for reemployment, or the employer eliminates the striker's job for economic reasons. The burden is on the party challenging the vote of an economic striker or a replacement to prove, respectively, that the economic striker has abandoned the struck job or that the replacement was not permanent; in the former case, a mere showing that the striker has accepted another job (which is often done to tide an employee through the strike) will not be sufficient. All issues as to voting eligibility of strikers and replacements are to be deferred until after the election for disposition by way of challenges.

It is a well settled rule that a representative will be certified even though less than a majority of all the employees in the unit cast ballots in favor of the union. It is enough that the union be designated by a majority of the valid ballots, and this is so even though only a small proportion of the eligible voters participates. There has been more difficulty with respect to elections in which none of the choices received a majority of the ballots. It is clear that where only one union is involved, a tie vote will be treated as if the union had lost the election. But what disposition should be made where two or more unions are involved, and there is no majority on the first ballot for any single union although the unions collectively have received a majority of the votes cast? Congress answered this question in 1947 when it enacted Section 9(c)(3), which provides that a run-off election shall be conducted in which the two highest choices on the first ballot (which may include "no union") shall appear on the run-off ballot.

Requests to set aside an election may be made on allegations of interference with the employees' freedom of choice. In a few cases the Board has set aside an election in the absence of improper conduct by the employer or the union—e. g., upon finding that a wave of hysteria or terrorism sweeping the community made it impossible for the employees to exercise full freedom of choice. P. D. Gwaltney, Jr., 74 N.L.R.B. 371 (1947). But in the majority of cases, elections have been set aside because of conduct by the union or the employer. As previously discussed, the Board has taken such action even in cases where no unfair labor practices have occurred. (See pp. 141–43, supra.)

D. REVIEW OF REPRESENTATION PROCEEDINGS

The National Labor Relations Act has no provision for direct judicial review of Board determinations, such as the appropriate bargaining unit, made in the course of representation proceedings. While Section 10(f) does provide that a party may have judicial review if "aggrieved by a final order" of the Board, decisions in representation proceedings are not "final orders." AFL v. NLRB, 308 U.S. 401, 60 S.Ct. 300, 84 L.Ed. 347 (1940). Since such orders issue only in unfair labor practice cases, an aggrieved party must commit an unfair labor practice in order to obtain judicial review. Section 9(d) provides that the record in the representation case is to become a part of the record which is certified to the federal court of appeals in the unfair labor practice case. Perhaps the most common example of this rather elaborate review machinery in action is the employer's refusal to bargain with a union certified by the Board as bargaining representative, when that certification is based upon a determination of a bargaining unit or of the validity of the union's election victory which the employer wishes to challenge on review. The reasons why Congress was reluctant to provide for direct judicial review of representation decisions are explored in the opinions in Leedom v. Kyne, immediately following.

Even when review can finally be secured in a court of appeals, it is difficult to secure a reversal on the merits of a Board representation decision. Such matters as the appropriateness of the bargaining unit and the impact of a party's speech or conduct upon the outcome of a labor election often raise complex or subtle issues meet for the exercise of an expert and experienced judgment by the administrative agency. Since Congress has provided so little guidance on these representation issues in the terms of the Labor Act, courts are loathe to overrule a Board decision in which the agency has taken care to scrutinize the record, to state its standards for decision and to articulate the reasons for its conclusion—even if the court might have been inclined to reach a different result had it decided the case in the first instance. While most courts of appeals accord a substantial measure of deference in representation cases, the decision in cases such as *Chicago Health Clubs*, at pages 278–86 supra, demonstrate that there are courts which seek vigorously to be assured that the Board is not masking arbitrary action with stock formulae and reliance on dubious precedents.

LEEDOM v. KYNE

Supreme Court of the United States, 1958.
358 U.S. 184, 79 S.Ct. 180, 3 L.Ed.2d 210.

MR. JUSTICE WHITTAKER delivered the opinion of the Court.

* * * Buffalo Section, Westinghouse Engineers Association, Engineers and Scientists of America, a voluntary unincorporated labor organization, hereafter called the Association, was created for the purpose of promoting the economic and professional status of the nonsupervisory professional employees of Westinghouse Electric Corporation at its plant in Cheektowaga, New York, through collective bargaining with their employer. In October 1955, the Association petitioned the National Labor Relations Board for certification as the exclusive collective bargaining agent of all nonsupervisory professional employees, being then 233 in number, of the Westinghouse Company at its Cheektowaga plant, pursuant to the provisions of § 9 of the Act, 29 U.S.C. § 159, 29 U.S.C.A. § 159. A hearing was held by the Board upon the petition. A competing labor organization was permitted by the Board to intervene. It asked the Board to expand the unit to include employees in five other categories who performed technical work and were thought by it to be "professional employees" within the meaning of § 2(12) of the Act, 29 U.S.C. § 152(12), 29 U.S.C.A. § 152(12). The Board found that they were not professional employees within the meaning of the Act. However, it found that nine employees in three of those categories should nevertheless be included in the unit because they "share a close community of employment interests with [the professional employees, and their inclusion would not] destroy the predominantly professional character of such a unit." The Board, after denying the Association's request to take a vote among the professional employees to determine whether a majority of them favored "inclusion in such unit," included the 233 professional employees and the nine nonprofessional employees in the unit and directed an election to determine whether they desired to be represented by the Association, by the other labor organization, or by neither. The Association moved the Board to stay the election and to amend its decision by excluding the nonprofessional employees from the unit. The Board denied that motion and went ahead with the election at which the Association received a majority of the valid votes cast and was thereafter certified by the Board as the collective bargaining agent for the unit.

Thereafter respondent, individually, and as president of the Association, brought this suit in the District Court against the members of the Board. * * * [The trial court] denied the Board's motion [for summary judgment] and granted the plaintiff's motion and entered judgment setting aside the Board's determination of the bargaining unit and also the election and the Board's certification. 148 F.Supp. 597.

On the Board's appeal it did not contest the trial court's conclusion that the Board, in commingling professional with nonprofessional employees in the unit, had acted in excess of its powers and had thereby worked injury to the statutory rights of the professional employees. Instead, it contended only that the District Court lacked jurisdiction to entertain the suit. The Court of Appeals held that the District Court did have jurisdiction and affirmed its judgment. 101 App.D.C. 398, 249 F.2d 490. Because of the importance of the question and the fact that it has been left open in our previous decisions, we granted certiorari, 355 U.S. 922, 78 S.Ct. 366, 2 L.Ed.2d 353.

Petitioners, members of the Board, concede here that the District Court had jurisdiction of the suit under § 24(8) of the Judicial Code, 28 U.S.C. § 1337, 28 U.S.C.A. § 1337, unless the review provisions of the National Labor Relations Act destroyed it. In American Federation of Labor v. National Labor Relations Board, 308 U.S. 401, 60 S.Ct. 300, 303, 84 L.Ed. 347, this Court held that a Board

Not a final order

order in certification proceedings under § 9 is not "a final order" and therefore is not subject to judicial review except as it may be drawn in question by a petition for enforcement or review of an order, made under § 10(c) of the Act, restraining an unfair labor practice. But the court was at pains to point out in that case that "[t]he question [there presented was] distinct from * * * whether petitioners are precluded by the provisions of the Wagner Act from maintaining an independent suit in a district court to set aside the Board's action because contrary to the statute * * *." Id., 308 U.S. at page 404, 60 S.Ct. at page 302. * * *

The record in this case squarely presents the question found not to have been presented by the record in American Federation of Labor v. National Labor Relations Board, supra. This case, in its posture before us, involves "unlawful action of the Board [which] has inflicted an injury on the [respondent]." Does the law, "apart from the review provisions of the * * * Act," afford a remedy? We think the answer surely must be yes. This suit is not one to "review," in the sense of that term as used in the Act, a decision of the Board made within its jurisdiction. Rather it is one to strike down an order of the Board made in excess of its delegated powers and contrary to a specific prohibition in the Act. Section 9 (b) (1) is clear and mandatory. It says that in determining the unit appropriate for the purposes of collective bargaining, "the Board *shall not* (1) decide that any unit is appropriate for such purposes if such unit includes both professional employees and employees who are not professional employees unless a majority of such professional employees vote for inclusion in such unit." (Emphasis added.) Yet the Board included in the unit employees whom it found were not professional employees, after refusing to determine whether a majority of the professional employees would "vote for inclusion in such unit." Plainly, this was an attempted exercise of power that had been specifically withheld. It deprived the professional employees of a "right" assured to them by Congress. Surely, in these circumstances, a Federal District Court has jurisdiction of an original suit to prevent deprivation of a right so given. * * *

In Switchmen's Union of North America v. National Mediation Board, 320 U.S. 297, 64 S.Ct. 95, 88 L.Ed. 61, this Court held that the District Court did not have jurisdiction of an original suit to review an order of the National Mediation Board determining that all yardmen of the rail lines operated by the New York Central system constituted an appropriate bargaining unit, because the Railway Labor Board had acted within its delegated powers. But in the course of that opinion the Court announced principles that are controlling here. "If the absence of jurisdiction of the federal courts meant a sacrifice or obliteration of a right which Congress had created, the inference would be strong that Congress intended the statutory provisions governing the general jurisdiction of those courts to control." * * *

Here, differently from the Switchmen's case, "absence of jurisdiction of the federal courts" would mean "a sacrifice or obliteration of a right which Congress" has given professional employees, for there is no other means, within their control (American Federation of Labor v. National Labor Relations Board, supra), to protect and enforce that right. And "the inference [is] strong that Congress intended the statutory provisions governing the general jurisdiction of those courts to control." 320 U.S. at page 300, 64 S.Ct. at page 97. This Court cannot lightly infer that Congress does not intend judicial protection of rights it confers against agency action taken in excess of delegated powers. * * *

The Court of Appeals was right in holding, in the circumstances of this case, that the District Court had jurisdiction of this suit, and its judgment is affirmed.

Affirmed.

MR. JUSTICE BRENNAN, whom MR. JUSTICE FRANKFURTER joins, dissenting.

The legislative history of the Wagner Act, and the Taft-Hartley amendments, shows a considered congressional purpose to restrict judicial review of National Labor Relations Board representation certifications to review in the Courts of Appeals in the circumstances specified in § 9(d), 29 U.S.C. § 159(d), 29 U.S.C.A. § 159(d). The question was extensively debated when both Acts were being considered, and on both occasions Congress concluded that, unless drastically limited, time-consuming court procedures would seriously threaten to frustrate the basic national policy of preventing industrial strife and achieving industrial peace by promoting collective bargaining.

The Congress had before it when considering the Wagner Act the concrete evidence that delays pending time-consuming judicial review could be a serious hindrance to the primary objective of the Act— bringing employers and employees together to resolve their differences through discussion. Congress was acutely aware of the experience of the predecessor of the present Labor Board under the National Industrial Recovery Act, which provided that investigations and certifications by the Board could be brought directly to the courts for review. Such direct review was determined by the Congress to be "productive of a large measure of industrial strife * * *," and was specifically eliminated in the Wagner Act. Although Congress recognized that it was necessary to determine employee representatives before collective bargaining could begin, Congress concluded that the chance for industrial peace increased correlatively to how quickly collective bargaining commenced. For this reason Congress ordained that the courts should not interfere with the prompt holding of representation elections or the commencement of collective bargaining once an employee representative has been chosen. Congress knew that if direct judicial review of the Board's investigation and certification of representatives was not barred, "the Government can be delayed indefinitely before it takes the first step toward industrial peace." Therefore, § 9(d) was written to provide "for review in the courts only after the election has been held and the Board has ordered the employer to do something predicated upon the results of the election." [32] After the Wagner Act was passed, a proposed amendment to allow judicial review after an election but before an unfair labor practice order was specifically rejected. In short, Congress set itself firmly against direct judicial review of the investigation and certification of representatives, and required the prompt initiation of the collective-bargaining process after the Board's certification, because of the risk that time-consuming review might defeat the objectives of the national labor policy. See American Federation of Labor v. National Labor Relations Board, 308 U.S. 401, 409–411, 60 S.Ct. 300, 304–305, 84 L.Ed. 347; Madden v. Brotherhood and Union of Transit Employees, 4 Cir., 147 F.2d 439, 158 A.L.R. 1330.

When the Taft-Hartley amendments were under consideration, employers complained that because § 9(d) allowed judicial review to an employer only when unfair labor practice charges were based in whole or in part upon facts certified following an investigation of representatives, these "cumbersome proceedings" meant that the employer could have review only by committing an unfair labor practice "no matter how much in good faith he doubted the validity of the certification." A House amendment therefore provided for direct review in the Courts of Appeals of Board certifications on appeal of any person interested, as from a final order of the Board. Opponents revived the same arguments successfully employed in the Wagner Act debates: "Delay would be piled upon delay, during which time collective bargaining would be suspended pending determination of the status of the bargaining agent. Such delays can only result in industrial strife." Both sides recognized that the House amendment would produce a fundamental change in the law. The Senate rejected the House amendment; the amendments proposed by that body continued only the indirect and limited review provided in original § 9(d). In conference, the Senate view prevailed. Senator Taft reported:

> "Subsection 9(d) of the conference agreement conforms to the Senate amendment. The House bill contained a provision which would have permitted judicial review of certifica-

---

32. 79 Cong.Rec. 7658.

tions even before the entry of an unfair labor practice order. In receding on their insistence on this portion, the House yielded to the view of the Senate conferees that such provision would permit dilatory tactics in representation proceedings."

The Court today opens a gaping hole in this congressional wall against direct resort to the courts.   *   *   *

There is nothing in the legislative history to indicate that the Congress intended any exception from the requirement that collective bargaining begin without awaiting judicial review of a Board certification or the investigation preceding it.   Certainly nothing appears that an exception was intended where the attack upon the Board's action is based upon an alleged misinterpretation of the statute.   The policy behind the limitation of judicial review applies just as clearly when the challenge is made on this ground.   Plainly direct judicial review of a Board's interpretation of the statute is as likely to be as drawn out, and thus as frustrative of the national policy, as is review of any other type of Board decision.   *   *   *   I daresay that the ingenuity of counsel will, after today's decision, be entirely adequate to the task of finding some alleged "unlawful action," whether in statutory interpretation or otherwise, sufficient to get a foot in a District Court door under 28 U.S.C. § 1337, 28 U.S.C.A. § 1337. *   *   *

It is no support for the Court's decision that the respondent union may suffer hardship if review under 28 U.S.C. § 1337, 28 U.S.C.A. § 1337 is not open to it.   The Congress was fully aware of the disadvantages and possible unfairness which could result from the limitation on judicial review enacted in § 9(d).   The House proposal for direct review of Board certifications in the Taft-Hartley amendments was based in part upon the fact that, under the Wagner Act, the operation of § 9(d) was "unfair to   *   *   *   the union that loses, which has no appeal at all no matter how wrong the certification may be; [and to] the employees, who also have no appeal   *   *   *."   Congress nevertheless continued the limited judicial review provided by § 9(d) because Congress believed the disadvantages of broader review to be more serious than the difficulties which limited review posed for the parties.   Furthermore, Congress felt that the Board procedures and the limited review provided in § 9(d) were adequate to protect the parties.

   *   *   *   The Board, in making the certification in dispute, has interpreted [§ 9(b)] as requiring the approval of the professional employees of a mixed bargaining unit of professionals and nonprofessionals only when the professionals are a minority in the unit, since only in such a case would they need this protection against the ignoring of their particular interests.   This interpreta-

tion is the basis of respondent union's complaint in its action under 28 U.S.C.A. § 1337 in the District Court. But an alleged error in statutory construction was also the basis of the District Court action in the *Switchmen's* case. Thus the two cases are perfectly parallel. And just as surely as in the case of the Mediation Board under the Railway Labor Act, the Congress has barred District Court review of National Labor Relations Board certifications under the Labor Management Relations Act. * * *

The Court seizes upon the language in Switchmen's, "If the absence of jurisdiction of the federal courts meant a sacrifice or obliteration of a right which Congress had created, the inference would be strong that Congress intended the statutory provisions governing the general jurisdiction of those courts to control." 320 U.S. at page 300, 64 S.Ct. at page 97. * * * The Court used the "sacrifice or obliteration" language solely to distinguish the situation where Congress created a "right" but no tribunal for its enforcement. * * *

But here, as the Congress provided the Mediation Board under the Railway Labor Act, the Congress has provided an agency, the NLRB, to protect the "right" it created under the National Labor Relations Act. Congress has in addition enacted "an appropriate safeguard and opportunity to be heard" in procedures to be followed by the Board. It has indeed gone further than in the Railway Labor Act. Whereas no judicial review of any kind was there provided, some, although limited, judicial review is provided under § 9(d). This was considered by Congress as "a complete guarantee against arbitrary action by the Board." Plainly we have here a situation where it may be said precisely as in Switchmen's that "Congress for reasons of its own decided upon the method for protection of the 'right' it created. It selected the precise machinery and fashioned the tool which it deemed suited to that end." * * *

I would reverse and remand the case to the District Court with instructions to dismiss the complaint for lack of jurisdiction of the subject matter.[33]

BOIRE v. GREYHOUND CORP., 376 U.S. 473, 84 S.Ct. 894, 11 L.Ed.2d 849 (1964). A union filed a petition for an election among the porters, janitors and maids working at four Florida bus terminals operated by Greyhound. The petition designated Greyhound and Floors, Inc. as employers, Floors being a corporation engaged by Greyhound

33. Leedom v. Kyne is discussed in Cox, The Major Labor Decisions of the Supreme Court October Term 1958, Proceedings of the ABA Section of Labor Relations Law 23, 31–37 (1959). See also Goldberg, District Court Review of NLRB Representation Proceedings, 42 Ind.L.J. 455 (1967).

to provide cleaning, maintenance and related services for the four terminals. At the Board hearing on the petition, Greyhound claimed that Floors was the sole employer of the employees in question. But the Board found that although Floors hired, paid, disciplined, transferred, promoted and discharged the employees, Greyhound was also an employer since it took part in setting up work schedules, determined the number of employees needed, and helped direct the work performed. Greyhound then filed suit in a federal district court to enjoin the forthcoming election. The district court concluded that it had jurisdiction on the basis of Leedom v. Kyne and further found that the Board's findings were insufficient as a matter of law to establish a joint employer relationship. The court of appeals affirmed. On certiorari, *held, the judgment should be reversed.* "[W]hether Greyhound possessed sufficient indication of control to be an 'employer' is essentially a factual issue, unlike the question in Kyne, which depended solely upon construction of the statute. The Kyne exception is a narrow one, not to be extended to permit plenary District Court review of Board orders in certification proceedings whenever it can be said than an erroneous assessment of the particular facts before the Board has led it to a conclusion which does not comport with the law."

[margin handwriting: factual v statutory interpretation]

Problems for Discussion

1. After the filing of an election petition by the Ridgewood College Faculty Association, representatives of the College administration moved to dismiss on two grounds: first, that the College is an instrumentality of the state government and is therefore excluded from the definition of "employer" in the Labor Act; and second, that the College faculty have a substantial voice in making decisions on educational and personnel matters, so that they are properly to be treated as "managerial employees" who are not covered by the NLRA. The College, although privately founded, has in recent years financed almost one-third of its annual budget with grants from the state legislature, and it has been agreed that one-third of its trustees are to be appointed by the state Board of Regents.

After a hearing, the Regional Director concludes that the College is to be treated as a private rather than a public institution, and that the Ridgewood faculty are not given effective decisionmaking responsibility on many College matters but are frequently ignored by department chairmen, deans, and the trustees. The Regional Director has ordered that an election be held in thirty days, and the Board has refused to review this order.

Can the College secure a district court injunction against the holding of a representation election? Given the parties, the Board's action, and the timing of the injunction request, is the case more or less appropriate for injunctive relief than was Leedom v. Kyne? Cf. *Physicians Nat'l House Staff Ass'n v. Fanning*, 642 F.2d 492 (D.C.Cir. 1980), cert. denied —— U.S. ——, —— S.Ct. ——, —— L.Ed.2d —— (1981).

[margin handwriting: more]

2. If *Leedom* had been decided differently and the union had been denied injunctive relief, what action could it have taken—if any—to secure judicial review of the bargaining unit found appropriate by the Board? If the union in *Leedom* had lost the representation election and desired to secure judicial review of the Board's unit determination, how might it have done so in a manner consistent with Justice Brennan's dissenting opinion?

III. SECURING BARGAINING RIGHTS THROUGH UNFAIR LABOR PRACTICE PROCEEDINGS

Although it is generally agreed that the Board-conducted election is the fairest way to determine the collective bargaining preference of employees, proceedings under Section 9 of the Labor Act are not the only way for a union to secure representative status. Many unions are voluntarily recognized without formal certification. The union must, however, have majority support in an appropriate unit for such recognition to be lawful, and the recognition of a minority union—even in the good-faith belief that it represents a majority— can render both the employer and union liable to unfair labor practice charges. See pp. 210–13, supra. It is also possible for a union to secure bargaining status through unfair labor practice proceedings brought against the employer. For many years, the Board held that an employer violated Section 8(a)(5) if, without a good-faith doubt of the union's claim, it refused to bargain with a union which made a convincing showing without an election that it had the support of a majority of employees in an appropriate unit; such a showing was commonly made through "authorization cards" which were solicited by the union, signed by employees, and designated the union as bargaining representative for wages, hours and other terms and conditions of employment. In contrast to the election, which is by secret ballot and which tests employee sentiment as of the date of the election, the unfair labor practice proceeding tests employee sentiment as of a date in the past when the union made its demand for recognition and often through a method of "balloting" which is public and characterized by peer-group (and union) pressures. Moreover, a contested election proceeding will normally lead to the certification of results within a month or two of the petition, while demonstration of employee sentiment in a contested unfair labor practice proceeding against the employer may take more than a year from the filing of the charge.

In spite of the apparent advantages of the Board-supervised representation election, the question remains whether Congress actually did contemplate that a union could secure or maintain bargaining rights through other methods.   This issue generally arises in one of four situations.

(1) The employer rejects the union's showing of majority support through authorization cards and then engages in coercive unfair labor practices designed to undermine that support.   Under what circumstances may the Board, as a remedy for the employer unfair labor practices, order the employer to bargain with the union?

(2) The employer rejects the union's showing of majority support through authorization cards and, while engaging in no coercive conduct, insists that the union be certified after a Board-conducted election before it will recognize it as bargaining representative. May the Board order the employer to bargain with the union?

(3) A union has at some time in the past been extended bargaining rights, either after Board certification or after informal recognition, but the employer claims that it believes the union no longer has majority support and that it will therefore withdraw recognition.   Under what circumstances will the Board find this withdrawal to be unlawful and therefore order the employer to continue bargaining with the union?

(4) A union has been representing employees of a company which is "acquired" by another company (e. g., through merger or through purchase of assets) and the union insists that the successor company continue to honor the predecessor's obligation to bargain. Under what circumstances will the Board find that the successor must bargain with the union which represented the employees of the predecessor company?

These are the four issues to be treated in the materials immediately following.   All raise in common the question whether in particular circumstances a union should be required to demonstrate its representative status through a secret-ballot election rather than through unfair labor practice proceedings in which there is reliance upon authorization cards or earlier designations which now may be "stale" and inaccurate.   Those who are generally sympathetic to the election procedures argue that a Board bargaining order, after a lengthy proceeding based on events long in the past, runs the serious risk of imposing an unwanted and unrepresentative union upon the employees in the bargaining unit.   Those who are sympathetic to the bargaining order urge either that in many instances it will more accurately reflect employee wishes than will an election or that it will foster industrial stability in the face of disruptive and unnecessary demands for an election.

NLRB v. GISSEL PACKING CO.[1]

Supreme Court of the United States, 1969.
395 U.S. 575, 89 S.Ct. 1918, 23 L.Ed.2d 542.

MR. CHIEF JUSTICE WARREN delivered the opinion of the Court.

These cases involve the extent of an employer's duty under the National Labor Relations Act to recognize a union that bases its claim to representative status solely on the possession of union authorization cards, and the steps an employer may take, particularly with regard to the scope and content of statements he may make, in legitimately resisting such card-based recognition. The specific questions facing us here are whether the duty to bargain can arise without a Board election under the Act; whether union authorization cards, if obtained from a majority of employees without misrepresentation or coercion, are reliable enough generally to provide a valid, alternate route to majority status; whether a bargaining order is an appropriate and authorized remedy where an employer rejects a card majority while at the same time committing unfair practices that tend to undermine the union's majority and make a fair election an unlikely possibility; and whether certain specific statements made by an employer to his employees constituted such an election-voiding unfair labor practice and thus fell outside the protection of the First Amendment and § 8(c) of the Act, 49 Stat. 452, as amended, 29 U.S.C. § 158(c). For reasons given below, we answer each of these questions in the affirmative.

* * *

Nos. 573 and 691.

In each of the cases from the Fourth Circuit, the course of action followed by the Union and the employer and the Board's response were similar. In each case, the union waged an organizational campaign, obtained authorization cards from a majority of employees in the appropriate bargaining unit, and then on the basis of the cards, demanded recognition by the employer. All three employers refused to bargain on the ground that authorization cards were inherently unreliable indicators of employee desires; and they either embarked on, or continued, vigorous antiunion campaigns that gave rise to numerous unfair labor practice charges. In *Gissel*, where the employer's campaign began almost at the outset of the Union's or-

1. See Christensen & Christensen, Gissel Packing and "Good Faith Doubt": The Gestalt of Required Recognition of Unions Under the NLRA, 37 U.Chi. L.Rev. 411 (1970); Note, NLRB v. Gissel Packing Co.: Bargaining Orders and Employee Free Choice, 45 N.Y.U. L.Rev. 318 (1970); Note, "After All, Tomorrow is Another Day": Should   Subsequent Events Affect the Validity of Bargaining Orders?, 31 Stanford L. Rev. 505 (1979); Pettibone, Section 10 (j) Bargaining Orders in Gissel-Type Cases, 27 Lab.L.J. 648 (1976); Pogrebin, NLRB Bargaining Orders Since Gissel: Wandering from a Landmark, 46 St. John's L.Rev. 193 (1971).

ganizational drive, the Union (petitioner in No. 691), did not seek an election, but instead filed three unfair labor practice charges against the employer, for refusing to bargain in violation of § 8(a) (5), for coercion and intimidation of employees in violation of § 8(a) (1), and for discharge of union adherents in violation of § 8(a) (3). In *Heck's* an election sought by the Union was never held because of nearly identical unfair labor practice charges later filed by the Union as a result of the employer's antiunion campaign, initiated after the Union's recognition demand. And in *General Steel*, an election petitioned for by the Union and won by the employer was set aside by the Board because of the unfair labor practices committed by the employer in the pre-election period.

In each case, the Board's primary response was an order to bargain directed at the employers, despite the absence of an election in *Gissel* and *Heck's* and the employer's victory in *General Steel*. More specifically, the Board found in each case that (1) the union had obtained valid authorization cards [2] from a majority of the employees in the bargaining unit and was thus entitled to represent the employees for collective bargaining purposes; and (2) that the employers' refusal to bargain with the unions in violation of § 8(a) (5) was motivated not by a "good faith" doubt of the unions' majority status, but by a desire to gain time to dissipate that status. The Board based its conclusion as to the lack of good faith doubt on the fact that the employers had committed substantial unfair labor practices during their antiunion campaign efforts to resist recognition. Thus, the Board found that all three employers had engaged in restraint and coercion of employees in violation of § 8(a) (1)—in *Gissel*, for coercively interrogating employees about union activities, threatening them with discharge and promising them benefits; in *Heck's*, for coercively interrogating employees, threatening reprisals, creating the appearance of surveillance, and offering benefits for opposing the Union; and in *General Steel*, for coercive interrogation and threats of reprisals, including discharge. In addition, the Board found that the employers in *Gissel* and *Heck's* had wrongfully discharged employees for engaging in union activities in violation of § 8(a) (3). And, because the employers had rejected the card-based

---

2. The cards used in all four campaigns in Nos. 573 and 691 and in the one drive in No. 585 unambiguously authorized the Union to represent the signing employee for collective bargaining purposes; there was no reference to elections. Typical of the cards was the one used in the Charleston campaign in *Heck's*, and it stated in relevant part:

"Desiring to become a member of the above Union of the International Brotherhood of Teamsters, Chauffeurs, Warehousemen and Helpers of America, I hereby make application for admission to membership. I hereby authorize you, or your agents or representatives to act for me as collective bargaining agent on all matters pertaining to rates of pay, hours or any other condition of employment."

bargaining demand in bad faith, the Board found that all three had refused to recognize the unions in violation of § 8(a) (5).

Only in *General Steel* was there any objection by an employer to the validity of the cards and the manner in which they had been solicited, and the doubt raised by the evidence was resolved in the following manner. The customary approach of the Board in dealing with allegations of misrepresentation by the union and misunderstanding by the employees of the purpose for which the cards were being solicited has been set out in Cumberland Shoe Corp., 144 N. L. R. B. 1268 (1964), and reaffirmed in Levi Strauss & Co., 172 N. L. R. B. No. 57, 68 L. R. R. M. 1338 (1968). Under the *Cumberland Shoe* doctrine, if the card itself is unambiguous (i. e., states on its face that the signer authorizes the union to represent the employee for collective bargaining purposes and not to seek an election), it will be counted unless it is proved that the employee was told that the card was to be used *solely* for the purpose of obtaining an election. In *General Steel*, the trial examiner considered the allegations of misrepresentation at length and, applying the Board's customary analysis, rejected the claims with findings that were adopted by the Board and are reprinted in the margin. [3]

Consequently, the Board ordered the companies to cease and desist from their unfair labor practices, to offer reinstatement and back pay to the employees who had been discriminatorily discharged, to bargain with the Union on request, and to post the appropriate notices.

[The Court of Appeals for the Fourth Circuit rejected the Board's findings that the employers' refusal to bargain violated § 8 (a)(5) and declined to enforce those portions of the Board's orders directing the respondent companies to bargain in good faith, holding that the 1947 Taft-Hartley amendments to the Act withdrew from the Board the authority to order an employer to bargain under § 8(a) (5) on the basis of cards, in the absence of NLRB certification, unless the employer knows independently of the cards that there is in

---

3. "Accordingly, I reject respondent's contention that if a man is told that his card will be secret, or will be shown only to the Labor Board for the purpose of obtaining an election, that this is the absolute equivalent of telling him that it will be used 'only' for the purpose of obtaining an election.

*   *   *   *   *   *

"With respect to the 97 employees named in the attached Appendix B Respondent in its brief contends, in substance, that their cards should be rejected because each of these employees was told *one or more* of the following: (1) that the card would be used to get an election (2) that he had the right to vote either way, even though he signed the card (3) that the card would be kept secret and not shown to anybody except to the Board in order to get an election. For reasons heretofore explicated, I conclude that these statements, singly or jointly, do not foreclose use of the cards for the purpose designated on their face."

fact no representation dispute. Thus, under these rulings a company could not be ordered to bargain unless (1) there was no question about a union's majority status (either because the employer agreed the cards were valid or had conducted its own poll so indicating), or (2) the employer's § 8(a)(1) and (3) unfair labor practices committed during the representation campaign were so extensive and pervasive that a bargaining order was the only available Board remedy irrespective of a card majority.

In case 585, the Sinclair Company refused to recognize the Teamsters Union, which had obtained authorization cards from 11 of the Company's 14 employees. The Company did not assert any irregularities in the solicitation of the cards, but claimed that cards are inherently unreliable. The Union petitioned for a representation election, and the Company embarked upon a vigorous campaign of speeches, pamphlets, leaflets and letters attacking the Teamsters and unions in general. The Company stated that it was in an unsound financial state; that the Teamsters were a "strike-happy" union, run by hoodlums, which would make unreasonable demands; that a strike would probably cause the Company to close the plant; that many unionized plants in the area had closed and that a plant closing because of the Teamsters would lead to the workers' unemployment because of their age and limited skills. The Union lost the election 7 to 6 and filed both objections to the election and unfair labor practice charges. The Board found that the Company's statements violated Section 8(a)(1) and that its refusal to bargain was designed to gain time to dissipate the Teamsters' majority and thus violated Section 8(a)(5); it set aside the election, issued a cease-and-desist order, and ordered the Company to bargain, finding that its conduct had been so inherently coercive and pervasive that a bargaining order would be proper even in the absence of a card majority. The Court of Appeals for the First Circuit sustained the Board's findings and conclusions and enforced its order in full.]

II.

In urging us to reverse the Fourth Circuit and to affirm the First Circuit, the National Labor Relations Board * * * asks us to approve its current practice, which is briefly as follows. When confronted by a recognition demand based on possession of cards allegedly signed by a majority of his employees, an employer need not grant recognition immediately, but may, unless he has knowledge independently of the cards that the union has a majority, decline the union's request and insist on an election, either by requesting the union to file an election petition or by filing such a petition himself under § 9(c)(1)(B). If, however, the employer commits independent and substantial unfair labor practices disruptive of election conditions, the Board may withhold the election or set it aside, and issue instead a bargaining order as a remedy for the various violations. * * *

* * * [T]he Union, petitioner in No. 691, argues that we should accord a far greater role to cards in the bargaining area than the Board itself seeks in this litigation. In order to understand the differences between the Union and the Board, it is necessary to trace the evolution of the Board's approach to authorization cards from its early practice to the position it takes on oral argument before this Court. Such an analysis requires viewing the Board's treatment of authorization cards in three separate phases: (1) under the *Joy Silk* doctrine, (2) under the rules of the *Aaron Brothers* case, and (3) under the approach announced at oral argument before this Court.

The traditional approach utilized by the Board for many years has been known as the *Joy Silk* doctrine. Joy Silk Mills, Inc. v. NLRB, 85 N.L.R.B. 1263 (1949), enforced 87 U.S.App.D.C. 360, 185 F.2d 732 (1950). Under that rule, an employer could lawfully refuse to bargain with a union claiming representative status through possession of authorization cards if he had a "good faith doubt" as to the union's majority status; instead of bargaining, he could insist that the union seek an election in order to test out his doubts. The Board, then, could find a lack of good faith doubt and enter a bargaining order in one of two ways. It could find (1) that the employer's independent unfair labor practices were evidence of bad faith, showing that the employer was seeking time to dissipate the union's majority. Or the Board could find (2) that the employer had come forward with no reasons for entertaining any doubt and therefore that he must have rejected the bargaining demand in bad faith. An example of the second category was Snow & Sons, 134 N.L.R.B. 709 (1961), enforced 308 F.2d 687 (C.A. 9th Cir. 1962), where the employer reneged on his agreement to bargain after a third party checked the validity of the card signatures and insisted on an election because he doubted that the employees truly desired representation. The Board entered a bargaining order with very broad language to the effect that an employer could not refuse a bargaining demand and seek an election instead "without valid ground therefor," 134 N.L.R.B. at 710–711. * * *

The leading case codifying modifications to the *Joy Silk* doctrine was Aaron Brothers, 158 N.L.R.B. 1077 (1966). There the Board made it clear that it had shifted the burden to the General Counsel to show bad faith and that an employer "will not be held to have violated his bargaining obligation * * * simply because

he refuses to rely on cards, rather than an election, as the method
for determining the union's majority." 158 N.L.R.B., at 1078. Two
significant consequences were emphasized. The Board noted (1)
that not every unfair labor practice would automatically result in
a finding of bad faith and therefore a bargaining order; the Board
implied that it would find bad faith only if the unfair labor practice was serious enough to have the tendency to dissipate the union's
majority. The Board noted (2) that an employer no longer needed
to come forward with reasons for rejecting a bargaining demand.
The Board pointed out, however, that a bargaining order would
issue if it could prove that an employer's "course of conduct" gave
indications as to the employer's bad faith. * * *

[margin note: when bargaining ord will issue]

Although the Board's brief before this Court generally followed
the approach as set out in *Aaron Brothers*, supra, the Board announced at oral argument that it had virtually abandoned the *Joy
Silk* doctrine altogether. Under the Board's current practice, an
employer's good faith doubt is largely irrelevant, and the key to the
issuance of a bargaining order is the commission of serious unfair
labor practices that interfere with the election processes and tend
to preclude the holding of a fair election. Thus, an employer can
insist that a union go to an election, regardless of his subjective
motivation, so long as he is not guilty of misconduct; he need give
no affirmative reasons for rejecting a recognition request, and he
can demand an election with a simple "no comment" to the union.
The Board pointed out, however, (1) that an employer could not
refuse to bargain if he *knew*, through a personal poll for instance,
that a majority of his employees supported the union, and (2) that
an employer could not refuse recognition initially because of questions as to the appropriateness of the unit and then later claim, as
an afterthought, that he doubted the union's strength. * * *

[margin note: new policy; key to order is commission of serious unfair lbr practic; exceptions]

III.

A.

The first issue facing us is whether a union can establish a
bargaining obligation by means other than a Board election and
whether the validity of alternate routes to majority status, such as
cards, was affected by the 1947 Taft-Hartley amendments. The
most commonly traveled route for a union to obtain recognition
as the exclusive bargaining representative of an unorganized group
of employees is through the Board's election and certification procedures under § 9(c) of the Act (29 U.S.C. § 159(c) (1964 ed.)');
it is also, from the Board's point of view, the preferred route. A
union is not limited to a Board election, however, for, in addition

[margin note: issue; two routes: election & cards]

to § 9, the present Act provides in § 8(a) (5) (29 U.S.C. § 158(a) (5) (1964 ed.)), as did the Wagner Act in § 8(5), that "it shall be an unfair labor practice for an employer * * * to refuse to bargain collectively with the representatives of his employees, subject to the provisions of section 9(a)." Since § 9(a), in both the Wagner Act and the present Act, refers to the representative as the one "designated or selected" by a majority of the employees without specifying precisely how that representative is to be chosen, it was early recognized that an employer had a duty to bargain whenever the union representative presented "convincing evidence of majority support." Almost from the inception of the Act, then, it was recognized that a union did not have to be certified as the winner of a Board election to invoke a bargaining obligation; it could establish majority status by other means under the unfair labor practice provision of § 8(a)(5)—by showing convincing support, for instance, by a union-called strike or strike vote, or, as here, by possession of cards signed by a majority of the employees authorizing the union to represent them for collective bargaining purposes.

We have consistently accepted this interpretation of the Wagner Act and the present Act, particularly as to the use of authorization cards. See, *e. g.*, NLRB v. Bradford Dyeing Assn., 310 U.S. 318, 339–340, 60 S.Ct. 918, 929 (1940); Franks Bros. Co. v. NLRB, 321 U.S. 702, 64 S.Ct. 817 (1943); United Mine Workers v. Arkansas Flooring Co., 351 U.S. 62, 76 S.Ct. 559 (1956). * * * we find unpersuasive the Fourth Circuit's view that the 1947 Taft-Hartley amendments, enacted some nine years before our decision in *United Mine Workers*, supra, require us to disregard that case. * * * An early version of the bill in the House would have amended § 8(5) of the Wagner Act to permit the Board to find a refusal to bargain violation only where an employer had failed to bargain with a union "currently recognized by the employer or certified as such [through an election] under section 9." Section 8(a) (5) of H.R. 3020, 80th Cong., 1st Sess. (1947). The proposed change, which would have eliminated the use of cards, was rejected in Conference (H.R.Conf. Rep.No. 510, 80th Cong., 1st Sess., 41 (1947)), however, and we cannot make a similar change in the Act simply because, as the employers assert, Congress did not expressly approve the use of cards in rejecting the House amendment. Nor can we accept the Fourth Circuit's conclusion that the change was wrought when Congress amended § 9(c) to make election the sole basis for *certification* by eliminating the phrase "any other suitable method to ascertain such representatives," under which the Board had occasionally used cards as a certification basis. A certified union has the benefit of numerous special privileges which are not accorded unions recognized voluntarily or under a bargaining order [4] and which, Congress could determine, should not be dispensed unless a union has survived the crucible of a secret ballot election.

The employers rely finally on the addition to § 9(c) of subparagraph, (B), which allows an employer to petition for an election whenever "one or more individuals or labor organizations have presented to him a claim to be recognized as the representative defined in section 9(a)." That provision was not added, as the employers assert, to give them an absolute right to an election at any time; rather, it was intended, as the legislative history indicates, to allow them, after being asked to bargain, to test out their doubts as to a union's majority in a secret election which they would then presumably not cause to be set aside by illegal antiunion activity.[5] We agree with the Board's assertion here that there is no suggestion that Congress intended § 9(c) (1) (B) to relieve any employer of his § 8(a) (5) bargaining obligation where, without good faith, he engaged in unfair labor practices disruptive of the Board's election machinery. And we agree that the policies reflected in § 9(c) (1) (B) fully support the Board's present administration of the Act; for an employer can insist on a secret ballot election, unless, in the words of the Board, he engages "in contemporaneous unfair labor practices likely to destroy the union's majority and seriously impede the election." Brief for Petitioner 36.

*   *   *

B.

We next consider whether authorization cards are such inherently unreliable indicators of employee desires that whatever

---

4. E. g., protection against the filing of new election petitions by rival unions or employees seeking decertification for 12 months (§ 9(c)(3)), protection for a reasonable period, usually one year, against any disruption of the bargaining relationship because of claims that the union no longer represents a majority (see Brooks v. NLRB, 348 U.S. 96, 75 S.Ct. 176, 90 L.Ed. 125 (1954)), protection against recognitional picketing by rival unions (§ 8(b)(4) (C)), and freedom from the restrictions placed in work assignments disputes by § 8(b)(4)(D), and on recognitional and organizational picketing by § 8(b)(7).

5. The Senate report stated that the "present Board rules * * * discriminate against employers who have reasonable grounds for believing that labor organizations claiming to represent the employees are really not the choice of the majority." S.Rep. No. 105, 80th Cong., 1st Sess., 10–11 (1947). Senator Taft stated during the debates:

"Today an employer is faced with this situation. A man comes into his office and says, 'I represent your employees. Sign this agreement or we strike tomorrow.' * * * The employer has no way in which to determine whether this man really does represent his employees or does not. The bill gives him the right to go to the Board * * and say, 'I want an election. I want to know who is the bargaining agent for my employees.' " 93 Cong.Rec. 3954 (1947).

[handwritten margin note: all cards sufficiently unreliable to substantiate refusal to bargain]

the validity of other alternate routes to representative status, the cards themselves may never be used to determine a union's majority and to support an order to bargain. In this context, the employers urge us to take the step the 1947 amendments and their legislative history indicate Congress did not take, namely, to rule out completely the use of cards in the bargaining arena. Even if we do not unhesitatingly accept the Fourth Circuit's view in the matter, the employers argue, at the very least we should overrule the *Cumberland Shoe* doctrine and establish stricter controls over the solicitation of the cards by union representatives.

[handwritten margin note: arguments for overruling Cumberland Shoe]

The objections to the use of cards voiced by the employers and the Fourth Circuit boil down to two contentions: (1) that, as contrasted with the election procedure, the cards cannot accurately reflect an employee's wishes, either because an employer has not had a chance to present his views and thus a chance to insure that the employee choice was an informed one, or because the choice was the result of group pressures and not individual decision made in the privacy of a voting booth; and (2) that quite apart from the election comparison, the cards are too often obtained through misrepresentation and coercion which compound the cards' inherent inferiority to the election process. Neither contention is persuasive, and each proves too much. The Board itself has recognized, and continues to do so here, that secret elections are generally the most satisfactory—indeed the preferred—method of ascertaining whether a union has majority support. The acknowledged superiority of the election process, however, does not mean that cards are thereby rendered totally invalid, for where an employer engages in conduct disruptive of the election process, cards may be the most effective—perhaps the only—way of assuring employee choice. As for misrepresentation, in any specific case of alleged irregularity in the solicitation of the cards, the proper course is to apply the Board's customary standards (to be discussed more fully below) and rule there was no majority if the standards were not satisfied. It does not follow that because there are some instances of irregularity, the cards can never be used; otherwise, an employer could put off his bargaining obligation indefinitely through continuing interference with elections.

That the cards, though admittedly inferior to the election process, can adequately reflect employee sentiment when that process has been impeded, needs no extended discussion, for the employers' contentions cannot withstand close examination. The employers argue that their employees cannot make an informed choice because the card drive will be over before the employer has had a chance to present his side of the unionization issues. Normally, however, the union will inform the employer of its organization

drive early in order to subject the employer to the unfair labor practice provisions of the Act; the union must be able to show the employer's awareness of the drive in order to prove that his contemporaneous conduct constituted unfair labor practices on which a bargaining order can be based if the drive is ultimately successful.
* * *

Further, the employers argue that without a secret ballot an employee may, in a card drive, succumb to group pressures or sign simply to get the union "off his back" and then be unable to change his mind as he would be free to do once inside a voting booth. But the same pressures are likely to be equally present in an election, for election cases arise most often with small bargaining units where virtually every voter's sentiments can be carefully and individually canvassed. And no voter, of course, can change his mind after casting a ballot in an election even though he may think better of his choice shortly thereafter.

The employers' second complaint, that the cards are too often obtained through misrepresentation and coercion, must be rejected also in view of the Board's present rules for controlling card solicitation, which we view as adequate to the task where the cards involved state their purpose clearly and unambiguously on their face. We would be closing our eyes to obvious difficulties, of course, if we did not recognize that there have been abuses, primarily arising out of misrepresentations by union organizers as to whether the effect of signing a card was to designate the union to represent the employee for collective bargaining purposes or merely to authorize it to seek an election to determine that issue. And we would be equally blind if we did not recognize that various courts of appeals and commentators have differed significantly as to the effectiveness of the Board's *Cumberland Shoe* doctrine to cure such abuses.

* * *

We need make no decision as to the conflicting approaches used with regard to dual-purpose cards, for in each of the five organization campaigns in the four cases before us the cards used were single-purpose cards, stating clearly and unambiguously on their face that the signer designated the union as his representative.
* * *

In resolving the conflict among the circuits in favor of approving the Board's *Cumberland* rule, we think it sufficient to point out that employees should be bound by the clear language of what they sign unless that language is deliberately and clearly canceled by a union adherent with words calculated to direct the signer to disregard and forget the language above his signature. There is nothing inconsistent in handing an employee a card that says the signer authorizes the union to represent him and then telling him that the card will probably be used first to get an election. * * *

We agree, however, with the Board's own warnings in Levi Strauss, 172 N.L.R.B.No. 57, 68 L.R.R.M. 1338, 1341, and n. 7 (1968), that in hearing testimony concerning a card challenge, trial examiners should not neglect their obligation to ensure employee free choice by a too easy mechanical application of the *Cumberland* rule.[6] We also accept the observation that employees are more likely than not, many months after a card drive and in response to questions by company counsel, to give testimony damaging to the union, particularly where company officials have previously threatened reprisals for union activity in violation of § 8(a)(1). We therefore reject any rule that requires a probe of an employee's subjective motivations as involving an endless and unreliable inquiry. We nevertheless feel that the trial examiner's findings in *General Steel* (see n. 3, supra) represent the limits of the *Cumberland* rule's application. We emphasize that the Board should be careful to guard against an approach any more rigid than that in *General Steel*. And we reiterate that nothing we say here indicates our approval of the *Cumberland Shoe* rule when applied to ambiguous, dual-purpose cards. * * *

C.

Remaining before us is the propriety of a bargaining order as a remedy for a § 8(a)(5) refusal to bargain where an employer has committed independent unfair labor practices which have made

6.   In explaining and reaffirming the *Cumberland Shoe* doctrine in the context of unambiguous cards, the Board stated:

"Thus the fact that employees are told in the course of solicitation that an election is contemplated, or that a purpose of the card is to make an election possible, provides in our view *insufficient* basis in itself for vitiating unambiguously worded authorization cards on the theory of misrepresentation. A different situation is presented, of course, where union organizers solicit cards on the explicit or indirectly expressed representation that they will use such cards *only* for an election and subsequently seek to use them for a different purpose . . .."

The Board stated further in a footnote:

"The foregoing does not of course imply that a finding of misrepresentation is confined to situations where employees are expressly told in *haec verba* that the 'sole' or 'only' purpose of the cards is to obtain an election. The Board has never suggested such a mechanistic application of the foregoing principles, as some have contended. The Board looks to substance rather than to form. It is not the use or nonuse of certain key or 'magic' words that is controlling but, whether or not the totality of circumstances surrounding the card solicitation is such, as to add up to an assurance to the card signer that his card will be used for no purpose other than to help get an election." 172 N.L.R.B. No. 57, 68 L.R.R.M. 1338, 1341, and n. 7.

the holding of a fair election unlikely or which have in fact undermined a union's majority and caused an election to be set aside. We have long held that the Board is not limited to a cease-and-desist order in such cases, but has the authority to issue a bargaining order without first requiring the union to show that it has been able to maintain its majority status. See NLRB v. Katz, 369 U.S. 736, 748, n. 16, 82 S.Ct. 1107, 1114 (1962); NLRB v. P. Lorillard Co., 314 U.S. 512, 62 S.Ct. 397 (1942). And we have held that the Board has the same authority even where it is clear that the union, which once had possession of cards from a majority of the employees, represents only a minority when the bargaining order is entered. Franks Bros. Co. v. NLRB, 321 U.S. 702, 64 S.Ct. 817 (1943). We see no reason now to withdraw this authority from the Board. If the Board could enter only a cease-and-desist order and direct an election or a rerun, it would in effect be rewarding the employer and allowing him "to profit from [his] own wrongful refusal to bargain," Franks Bros., supra, at 704, while at the same time severely curtailing the employees' right freely to determine whether they desire a representative. The employer could continue to delay or disrupt the election processes and put off indefinitely his obligation to bargain; and any election held under these circumstances would not be likely to demonstrate the employees' true, undistorted desires.[7]

The employers argue that the Board has ample remedies, over and above the cease-and-desist order, to control employer misconduct. The Board can, they assert, direct the companies to mail notices to employees, to read notices to employees during plant time and to give the union access to employees during working time at the plant, or it can seek a court injunctive order under § 10(j) (29 U.S.C. § 160

---

[7]. A study of 20,153 elections held between 1960 and 1962 shows that in over two-thirds of the cases, the party who caused the election to be set aside [i. e., the "wrongdoer" who won the first election] won in the rerun election. See D. Pollitt, NLRB Re-Run Elections: A Study, 41 N.C.L. Rev. 209, 212 (1963). The study shows further that certain unfair labor practices are more effective to destroy election conditions for a longer period of time than others. For instance, in cases involving threats to close or transfer plant operations, the union won the rerun only 29% of the time, while threats to eliminate benefits or refuse to deal with the union if elected seemed less irremediable with the union winning the rerun 75% of the time. Id., at 215–216. Finally, time appears to be a factor. The figures suggest that if a rerun is held too soon after the election before the effects of the unfair labor practices have worn off, or too long after the election when interest in the union may have waned, the chances for a changed result occurring are not as good as they are if the rerun is held sometime in between those periods. Thus, the study showed that if the rerun is held within 30 days of the election or over nine months after, the chances that a different result will occur are only one in five; when the rerun is held within 30–60 days after the election, the chances for a changed result are two in five. Id., at 221.

(j)) as a last resort. In view of the Board's power, they conclude, the bargaining order is an unnecessarily harsh remedy that needlessly prejudices employees' § 7 rights solely for the purpose of punishing or restraining an employer. Such an argument ignores that a bargaining order is designed as much to remedy past election damage [8] as it is to deter future misconduct. If an employer has succeeded in undermining a union's strength and destroying the laboratory conditions necessary for a fair election, he may see no need to violate a cease-and-desist order by further unlawful activity. The damage will have been done, and perhaps the only fair way to effectuate employee rights is to re-establish the conditions as they existed before the employer's unlawful campaign. There is, after all, nothing permanent in a bargaining order, and if, after the effects of the employer's acts have worn off, the employees clearly desire to disavow the union, they can do so by filing a representation petition.   * * *

* * * While refusing to validate the general use of a bargaining order in reliance on cards, the Fourth Circuit nevertheless left open the possibility of imposing a bargaining order, without need of inquiry into majority status on the basis of cards or otherwise, in "exceptional" cases marked by "outrageous" and "pervasive" unfair labor practices. Such an order would be an appropriate remedy for those practices, the court noted, if they are of "such a nature that their coercive effects cannot be eliminated by the application of traditional remedies, with the result that a fair and reliable election cannot be had." NLRB v. Logan Packing Co., 386 F.2d 562, 570 (C.A. 4th Cir. 1967); see also NLRB v. Heck's, supra, 398 F.2d at 338. The Board itself, we should add, has long had a similar policy of issuing a bargaining order, in the absence of a § 8(a)(5) violation or even a bargaining demand, when that was the only available, effective remedy for substantial unfair labor practices. See, e. g., United Steelworkers of America v. NLRB, 376 F.2d 770 (C.A.D.C. Cir. 1967); J. C. Penney Co., Inc. v. NLRB, 384 F.2d 479, 485–486 (C.A.10th Cir. 1967).

---

8. The employers argue that the Fourth Circuit correctly observed that, "in the great majority of cases, a cease and desist order with the posting of appropriate notices will eliminate any undue influences upon employees voting in the security of anonymity." NLRB v. S. S. Logan Packing Co., 386 F.2d, at 570. It is for the Board and not the courts, however, to make that determination, based on its expert estimate as to the effects on the election process of unfair labor practices of varying intensity. In fashioning its remedies under the broad provisions of § 10(c) of the Act (29 U.S.C.A. 160(c)), the Board draws on a fund of knowledge and expertise all its own, and its choice of remedy must therefore be given special respect by reviewing courts. See Fibreboard Paper Products Corp. v. NLRB, 379 U.S. 203, 85 S.Ct. 398, 13 L.Ed. 2d 233 (1964). "[I]t is usually better to minimize the opportunity for reviewing courts to substitute their discretion for that of the agency." Consolo v. FMC, 383 U.S. 607, 621, 86 S.Ct. 1018, 1027, 16 L.Ed.2d 131 (1966).

The only effect of our holding here is to approve the Board's use of the bargaining order in less extraordinary cases marked by less pervasive practices which nonetheless still have the tendency to undermine majority strength and impede the election processes. The Board's authority to issue such an order on a lesser showing of employer misconduct is appropriate, we should reemphasize, where there is also a showing that at one point the union had a majority; in such a case, of course, effectuating ascertainable employee free choice becomes as important a goal as deterring employer misbehaviour. In fashioning a remedy in the exercise of its discretion, then, the Board can properly take into consideration the extensiveness of an employer's unfair practices in terms of their past effect on election conditions and the likelihood of their recurrence in the future. If the Board finds that the possibility of erasing the effects of past practices and of ensuring a fair election (or a fair rerun) by the use of traditional remedies, though present, is slight and that employee sentiment once expressed through cards would, on balance, be better protected by a bargaining order, then such an order should issue.

We emphasize that under the Board's remedial power there is still a third category of minor or less extensive unfair labor practices, which, because of their minimal impact on the election machinery, will not sustain a bargaining order. There is, the Board says, no *per se* rule that the commission of any unfair practice will automatically result in a § 8(a) (5) violation and the issuance of an order to bargain. See Aaron Brothers, supra.

With these considerations in mind, we turn to an examination of the orders in these cases. In *Sinclair*, No. 585, the Board made a finding, left undisturbed by the First Circuit, that the employer's threats of reprisal were so coercive that, even in the absence of a § 8(a) (5) violation, a bargaining order would have been necessary to repair the unlawful effect of those threats. The Board therefore did not have to make the determination called for in the intermediate situation above that the risks that a fair rerun election might not be possible were too great to disregard the desires of the employees already expressed through the cards. The employer argues, however, that his communications to his employees were protected by the First Amendment and § 8(c) of the Act (29 U.S.C. § 158(c) (1964 ed.)), whatever the effect of those communications on the union's majority or the Board's ability to ensure a fair election; it is to that contention that we shall direct our final attention in the next section.

In the three cases in Nos. 573 and 691 from the Fourth Circuit, on the other hand, the Board did not make a similar finding that a bargaining order would have been necessary in the absence of an unlawful refusal to bargain. Nor did it make a finding that, even though traditional remedies might be able to ensure a fair election, there was insufficient indication that an election (or a rerun in *General Steel*) would definitely be a more reliable test of the employees' desires than the card count taken before the unfair labor practices occurred. * * * [W]e therefore remand these cases to the Board for proper findings.

* * *

***

Problems for Discussion

1. Under the *Joy Silk Mills* doctrine, what did the Board infer from the fact that the employer had engaged in coercive and discriminatory conduct after its refusal to bargain? For what violation of the Act was the bargaining order a remedy? What are the answers to these two questions after the Supreme Court's decision in *Gissel*? Although the *Gissel* Court states, at the outset of part IIIC of its opinion, that the bargaining order is designed to cure the employer's refusal to bargain in violation of Section 8(a)(5), is that consistent with the Court's own analysis, or with the position taken by the Board on oral argument, or with the Court's decision five years later in *Linden Lumber* (immediately below)?

These rather abstract questions should be reconsidered in the context of the questions which follow.

2. Assume that a union gathers a majority of cards, but never shows them to the employer or demands recognition. The employer thereafter commits serious violations of Sections 8(a)(1) and (3). May the Board order the employer to bargain with the union? See *NLRB v. Marsellus Vault & Sales, Inc.*, 431 F.2d 933 (2d Cir. 1969).

3. Assume that a union secures authorization cards from 40 percent of the employees in the plant, and petitions the NLRB for a certification election. The employer immediately institutes a blatant and relentless effort to block further unionization efforts: it threatens on several occasions to close down the plant if the employees vote for the union; it coercively interrogates the employees about their support for the union; it subcontracts work being performed by the most active union supporters and threatens others with discharge and physical violence; it grants an unprecedented bonus; and without reason or investigation, it discharges a number of union activists. The union loses the election, 42 to 40. The NLRB finds that in all respects the employer has violated the Labor Act, and the General Counsel seeks a bargaining order, in spite of the fact that the union never demonstrated majority support either through authorization cards or in the election. May the Board order the employer to bargain? Compare United Dairy Farmers Coop. Ass'n v. NLRB, 633 F.2d 1054 (3d Cir. 1980), with Teamsters Local 115 v. NLRB (Haddon House Food Prods., Inc.), 640 F.2d 392 (D.C.Cir. 1981).

4. Union presents evidence of a card majority on February 1, 1980, but the employer refuses to recognize Union as bargaining representative,

and thereafter embarks upon a campaign of unlawful promises and discharges. On March 1, 1980, Union files charges under Sections 8(a)(1), (3), and (5), and while the case is pending before the Administrative Law Judge, the employer on August 1, 1980 without bargaining with Union reduces the pay rate of a group of employees (claiming, as is true, that business losses demand either such a reduction or the contracting out of that work to be done less expensively). The Administrative Law Judge finds on February 1, 1981, that the employer's violations of Sections 8(a)(1) and (3) were sufficiently serious as to warrant not only cease-and-desist and reinstatement orders but also an order to begin bargaining with Union. Union also contends that it is entitled to an order requiring the employer to restore the pay of the employees whose pay rate was unilaterally reduced by the employer in August 1980, on the theory that the employer violated Section 8(a)(5) when it refused to bargain and that it therefore was obligated to bargain with Union at all times thereafter regarding rates of pay (as required by Sections 8(a)(5) and 9(a)). Are the employees entitled thus to reimbursement, and does this depend upon a union demand for recognition and a finding of a Section 8(a)(5) violation? See Trading Port, Inc., 219 N.L.R.B. 298 (1975); Beasley Energy, Inc., 228 N.L.R.B. 93 (1977).

5. The Warehousemen's Union obtained twenty unambiguous authorization cards from an appropriate unit of twenty-five in the shipping department of Watson Shirts, Inc. These cards were presented to Mr. Watson, president of the company, who refused to bargain with the Warehousemen. The Union then filed an election petition, a hearing was held, and an election was ordered. One week before the election was scheduled, Mr. Watson called a meeting of shipping department employees, informed them that wages would be raised from $2.00 to $2.50 per hour and that two weeks paid vacation would be instituted. He further told them that if the union were voted in, these increased benefits would be rescinded and the plant might be closed. The Union lost the election by a vote of 15 to 5.

The Union filed charges and the Company was held to have violated Sections 8(a)(1) and (5). The Administrative Law Judge ordered the Company to bargain with the Union. Before the Board, the Company introduced evidence that in the six months between the election and the Administrative Law Judge's decision, fifteen employees had quit and been replaced, and that of the remaining ten, only six had signed authorization cards. (The Company conceded, however, that the facts and events surrounding the organizing campaign and election were then still well known by the employees.) The Company also demonstrated that in the year between the Administrative Law Judge's decision and the Board hearing, there had been a complete turnover in personnel and that no one in the shipping department now knew very much about the Union campaign. The Board nevertheless issued the bargaining order.

The Board then petitioned for enforcement. At oral argument before the court, it was stipulated that, during the two-year period between the Board's decision and argument before the court, Watson had died and been replaced by his son, who had previously worked in the shipping department, had joined the Warehousemen's Union, and was known by all to be a friend of the labor movement. Attorneys for Watson argued that the employees should not be forced to submit to representation by the Warehousemen because a fair election was now a clear possibility.

Should the bargaining order be enforced? See *NLRB v. Western Drug*, 600 F.2d 1324 (9th Cir. 1979); *NLRB v. American Cable Systems, Inc.*, 427 F.2d 446 (5th Cir.), cert. denied 400 U.S. 957 (1970).

6. A union seeking to organize company truckdrivers secured a majority of authorization cards and asked the employer to recognize and bargain with it. Within a week, however, the majority was dissipated by the employer's threats of business closure, coercive interrogation, threats of discharge, threats to sell its trucks and the sale of trucks, direct dealing with the employees, and the formation and domination of an employee committee to supplant the union. Charges having been filed under Sections 8(a)(1), (2), and (3), the Regional Director issues a complaint and commences an injunctive action in the federal district court under Section 10(j), seeking an order preventing the employer from advertising for sale and selling its trucks and also requiring the employer to bargain with the union pending the completion of the unfair labor practice hearing. Should the court issue such an order? Compare *Seeler v. Trading Port, Inc.*, 517 F.2d 33 (2d Cir. 1975), with *Boire v. Pilot Freight Carriers, Inc.*, 515 F.2d 1185 (5th Cir. 1975).

In most cases decided since *Gissel*, the Board has simply recounted the employer violations and made a conclusory finding on the question whether they were severe enough to preclude a fair election. For example, in General Stencils, Inc., 178 N.L.R.B. 108 (1969), the Board issued a bargaining order in a case in which a union, which had demonstrated a majority by authorization cards, had not petitioned for an election. A bargaining order was found necessary because the employer's threats of plant closings and loss of jobs were "widespread," "tended to destroy the employees' free choice," and "were of such a nature as to have a lingering effect and make a fair * * * election quite dubious if not impossible."

The Court of Appeals upheld most—but not all—of the Board's findings of specific violations. NLRB v. GENERAL STENCILS, INC., 438 F.2d 894 (2d Cir. 1971). The court then found itself unsure whether a bargaining order was still warranted. The court noted widespread inconsistencies in past Board decisions and criticized the Board for failing to establish any criteria defining when employer violations were serious enough to warrant a bargaining order. The Board was urged to employ one of three methods (in descending order of desirability) to articulate its position on bargaining orders. The best course would be for the Board to use the rulemaking procedure to hold hearings and formulate general principles defining the kinds of employer coercion most likely to lead to bargaining orders and those curable by milder remedies. Alternatively, the full Board could announce such general principles in a particular case. Third, the Board could explain fully in each case "just what it considers to have precluded a fair election and why, and in what respects the case differs from others where it has reached an opposite conclusion." The court remanded the case to the Board for a new determination whether a bargaining order was warranted.

On remand, a three-member panel declined to formulate any general principles. General Stencils, Inc., 195 N.L.R.B. 1109 (1972). Rather, it affirmed the bargaining order on the ground that threats of job closings and job loss were "serious" threats which would interfere with employee freedom and would not otherwise be curable. Chairman Miller, in a dissenting opinion, did attempt to formulate a rough set of principles. He agreed with his colleagues that the great variety of situations faced by the Board made it extremely difficult to arrive at such a formulation. But he found at least two situations in which a bargaining order would be warranted in nearly all cases.

> "Initially, our decisions suggest two categories of employer misconduct which may usefully be regarded as sufficient *per se* to justify imposition of an order to bargain: (1) the grant of significant benefits and (2) repeated violations of Section 8(a)(3). In *United Packing Company* and several other recent cases respondent employers have reacted to a union organizing campaign by promptly identifying and remedying a source of employee dissatisfaction. In *United Packing*, a wage increase was promised during the campaign and delivered after the employees voted against the union in a Board-conducted election. It was clear the wage increase was offered and granted to thwart the union. It was clear to us in assessing the employer's conduct that our traditional remedy for that violation, which does not include rescission of the wage increase, would not eradicate the impact of the employer's action. There, clearly, the establishment of a bargaining relationship was the only means by which the employees' rights to an untrammeled choice could be protected. * * *

> "Similarly, the reassignment, demotion, or discharge of union adherents will carry a message which cannot be lost on employees in the voting group. While there is some slight chance that a single 8(a)(3) violation will not be perceived as employer retribution, repeated violation will rarely if every be misinterpreted. The impact on employees

might be erased if our standard make-whole remedy could be swiftly obtained. But unfortunately, in the usual litigated case, restoration to employment comes months or years later, if at all, and thus the coercive effect of the discrimination is unlikely ever to be undone. The Board, therefore, since *Gissel*, has regularly issued a bargaining order where a union majority was dissipated by such tactics. * * *

"These, I believe, are the only two categories of conduct where we can, with confidence, suggest a *per se* rule. Manifestly, the case before us is not within either category, and the feature which removes it from either is the absence of employer *action*. The employer who identifies the sources of employee discontent and remedies them, or identifies the principal union adherents and removes them, demonstrates *by his actions* that he will oppose the union by unlawful means and that employees who support it do so at their grave peril. The message is communicated to all by means which will be clear to all. In the matter of employer resistance to employee rights, actions do indeed speak louder than words. * * *

"This distinction between action and speech requires that in each case where a *Gissel* remedy is sought exclusively on the basis of threats, we must attempt to answer three specific, but closely related, questions:

"1.   What actions were threatened?

"2.   Were the threats under all circumstances, likely to be seriously regarded?

"3.   How widely were the threats disseminated among the employee group?"

Chairman Miller agreed with his colleagues that the threat of a plant closing and threats of loss of jobs were the most serious of threats. He found it appropriate to deal with three sub-issues in answering the second question: the source of the threat (low-level or high-level supervisor), its deliberateness (printed literature or informal discussions), and its specificity. Although concluding that the threats there were likely to be taken quite seriously, Chairman Miller would not have issued a bargaining order, because the threats were not widely disseminated and appeared to be known only to one or a few employees.

The Court of Appeals, commending Chairman Miller's attempt to establish general rules, again refused to enforce the bargaining order on the ground that the Board's conclusion was not "supported by substantial evidence on the record considered as a whole." NLRB v. General Stencils, Inc., 472 F.2d 170 (2d Cir. 1972). The court did not agree that the record supported the conclusion that the employer's violations were serious. Dissenting Judge Hays urged enforcement, pointing to language in *Gissel* which indicated that the Board has almost total discretion, because of its expertise, to decide when a bargaining order is appropriate. The same Court of Appeals has recently reiterated its disaffection with the Board in bargaining-order cases, and has explicitly adopted and elaborated upon Chairman Miller's guidelines. NLRB v. Jamaica Towing, Inc., 632 F.2d 208 (2d Cir. 1980). Almost every other circuit has joined in the criticism. E. g., NLRB v. Appletree Chevrolet, Inc., 608 F.2d 988 (4th Cir. 1979); Peerless of America, Inc. v. NLRB, 484 F.2d 1108 (7th Cir. 1973).

Is it not illusory for the courts to expect the Board to differentiate between the impact of "egregious" unfair labor practices and the impact of "technical" unfair labor practices, when there is significant empirical evidence that employee preferences for the union are not really affected differentially by lawful employer conduct and unlawful employer conduct? See pages 200–01, supra.

LINDEN LUMBER DIV., SUMMER & CO. v. NLRB

Supreme Court of the United States, 1974.
419 U.S. 301, 95 S.Ct. 429, 42 L.Ed.2d 465.

MR. JUSTICE DOUGLAS delivered the opinion of the Court.

These cases present a question expressly reserved in National Labor Relations Board v. Gissel Packing Co., 395 U.S. 575, 595, 601, n. 18, 89 S.Ct. 1918, 1930, 1933, 23 L.Ed.2d 547 (1969).

In *Linden* respondent union obtained authorization cards from a majority of petitioner's employees and demanded that it be recognized as the collective-bargaining representative of those employees. Linden said it doubted the union's claimed majority status and suggested the union petition the Board for an election. The union filed such a petition with the Board but later withdrew it when Linden declined to enter a consent election agreement or abide by an election on the ground that respondent union's organizational campaign had been improperly assisted by company supervisors. Respondent union thereupon renewed its demand for collective bargaining; and again Linden declined, saying that the union's claimed membership had been improperly influenced by supervisors. Thereupon respondent union struck for recognition as the bargaining representative and shortly filed a charge of unfair labor practice against Linden based on its refusal to bargain.

There is no charge that Linden engaged in an unfair labor practice apart from its refusal to bargain. The Board held that Linden should not be guilty of an unfair labor practice solely on the basis "of

342 ESTABLISHMENT OF COLLECTIVE BARGAINING   Pt. 2

its refusal to accept evidence of majority status other than the results of a Board election." 190 N.L.R.B. 718, 721 (1971).

In *Wilder* there apparently were 30 employees in the plant and the union with 11 signed and two unsigned authorization cards requested recognition as the bargaining agent for the company's production and maintenance employees. Of the 30 employees 18 were in the production and maintenance unit which the Board found to be appropriate for collective bargaining. No answer was given by Wilder, and recognitional picketing began. The request was renewed when the two unsigned cards were signed, but Wilder denied recognition. Thereupon the union filed unfair labor practice charges against Wilder. A series of Board decisions and judicial decisions, not necessary to recapitulate here, consumed about seven years until the present decision by the Court of Appeals. The Board made the same ruling as respects Wilder as it did in Linden's case. See 198 N.L.R.B. No. 123 (1972). On petitions for review the Court of Appeals reversed 159 U.S.App.D.C. 228, 487 F.2d 1099 (1973). We reverse the Court of Appeals.

In *Gissel* we held that an employer who engages in "unfair" labor practices "likely to destroy the union's majority and seriously impede the election" may not insist that before it bargains the union get a secret ballot election. 395 U.S., at 600, 89 S.Ct. at 1933. There were no such unfair labor practices here, nor had the employer in either case agreed to a voluntary settlement of the dispute and then reneged. As noted, we reserved in *Gissel* the questions "whether, absent election interference by an employer's unfair labor practices, he may obtain an election only if he petitions for one himself; whether, if he does not, he must bargain with a card majority if the Union chooses not to seek an election; and whether, in the latter situation, he is bound by the Board's ultimate determination of the card results regardless of his earlier good faith doubts, or whether he can still insist on a Union-sought election if he makes an affirmative showing of his positive reasons for believing there is a representation dispute." Id., at 601, n. 18, 89 S.Ct. at 1933. * * *

In the present cases the Board found that the employers "should not be found guilty of a violation of Section 8(a)(5) solely upon the basis of [their] refusal to accept evidence of majority status other than the results of a Board election." 190 N.L.R.B., at 721; see 198 N.L.R.B., at ——. The question whether the employers had good reasons or poor reasons was not deemed relevant to the inquiry. The Court of Appeals concluded that if the employer had doubts as to a union's majority status, it could and should test out its doubts by petitioning for an election. * * *

To take the Board's position is not to say that authorization cards are wholly unreliable as an indication of employee support of the union. An employer concededly may have valid objections to recognizing a union on that basis. His objection to cards may, of course, mask his opposition to unions. On the other hand he may have rational, good-faith grounds for distrusting authorization cards in a given situation. He may be convinced that the fact that a majority of the employees strike and picket does not necessarily establish that they desire the particular union as their representative. Fear may indeed prevent some from crossing a picket line; or sympathy for strikers, not the desire to have the particular union in the saddle, may influence others. These factors make difficult an examination of the employer's motive to ascertain whether it was in good faith. To enter that domain is to reject the approval by *Gissel* of the retreat which the Board took from its "good faith" inquiries.

The union which is faced with an unwilling employer has two alternative remedies under the Board's decision in the instant case. It can file for an election; or it can press unfair labor practices against the employer under *Gissel*. The latter alternative promises to consume much time. In *Linden* the time between filing the charge and the Board's ruling was about 4½ years; in *Wilder,* about 6½ years. The Board's experience indicates that the median time in a contested case is 388 days. *Gissel*, 395 U.S., at 611, n. 30, 89 S.Ct. 1918, 1938. On the other hand the median time between the filing of the petition for an election and the decision of the regional director is about 45 days. In terms of getting on with the problems of inaugurating regimes of industrial peace, the policy of encouraging secret elections under the Act is favored. The question remains—should the burden be on the union to ask for an election or should it be the responsibility of the employer?

The Court of Appeals concluded that since Congress in 1947 authorized employers to file their own representation petitions by enacting § 9(c)(1)(B) the burden was on them. But the history of that provision indicates it was aimed at eliminating the discrimination against employers which had previously existed under the Board's prior rules, permitting employers to petition for an election only when confronted with claims by two or more unions. There is no suggestion that Congress wanted to place the burden of getting a secret election on the employer. * * *

The Board has at least some expertise in these matters and its judgment is that an employer's petition for an election, though permissible, is not the required course. It points out in its brief here that an employer wanting to gain delay can draw a petition to elicit protests by the union, and the thought that an employer petition would obviate litigation over the sufficiency of the union's showing of interest is in its purview apparently not well taken. A union petition to be sure must be backed by a 30% showing of employee interest. But the sufficiency of such a showing is not litigable by the parties.

In light of the statutory scheme and the practical administrative procedural questions involved, we cannot say that the Board's decision that the union should go forward and ask for an election on the employer's refusal to recognize the authorization cards was arbitrary and capricious or an abuse of discretion.

In sum, we sustain the Board in holding that, unless an employer has engaged in an unfair labor practice that impairs the electoral process,[9] a union with authorization cards purporting to represent a majority of the employees, which is refused recognition, has the burden of taking the next step in invoking the Board's election procedure.

Reversed.

MR. JUSTICE STEWART, with whom MR. JUSTICE WHITE, MR. JUSTICE MARSHALL, and MR. JUSTICE POWELL join, dissenting.

* * *

Section 9(a) expressly provides that the employees' exclusive bargaining representative shall be the union "designated or selected" by a majority of the employees in an appropriate unit. Neither § 9 (a) nor § 8(a)(5), which makes it an unfair labor practice for an employer to refuse to bargain with the representative of his employees, specifies how that representative is to be chosen. The language of the Act thus seems purposefully designed to impose a duty upon an employer to bargain whenever the union representative presents convincing evidence of majority support, regardless of the method by which that support is demonstrated. And both the Board and this Court have in the past consistently interpreted §§ 8(a)(5) and 9(a) to mean exactly that. * * *

As the Court recognized in *Gissel,* the 1947 Taft-Hartley amendments strengthen this interpretation of the Act. One early version of the House bill would have amended the Act to permit the Board to find an employer unfair labor practice for refusing to bargain with a union only if the union was "currently recognized by the employer or certified as such [through an election] under section 9." Section 8(a)(5) of H.R. 3020, 80th Cong., 1st Sess. The proposed change, which would have eliminated any method of requiring employer recognition of a union other than a Board-supervised election, was rejected in Conference. H.R.Conf.Rep. No. 510, 80th Cong., 1st Sess., 41. After rejection of the proposed House amendment, the House Conference Report explicity stated that § 8(a)(5) was intended to follow the provisions of "existing law." Ibid. And "ex-

---

9. We do not reach the question whether the same result obtains if the employer breaches its agreement to permit majority status to be deter- mined by means other than a Board election. See Snow & Sons, 134 N.L. R.B. 709 (1961), enf'd, 308 F.2d 687 (CA9 1962). * * *

isting law" unequivocally recognized that a union could establish majority status and thereby impose a bargaining obligation on an unwilling employer by means other than petitioning for and winning a Board-supervised election.   NLRB v. Gissel Packing Co., supra, at 596–598, 89 S.Ct. 1918, 1930–1932.

[The NLRB] may define "convincing evidence of majority support" solely by reference to objective criteria—for example, by reference to "a union-called strike or strike vote, or, as here, by possession of cards signed by a majority of the employees * * *."   Id., at 597, 89 S.Ct. at 1931.

Even with adoption of such an objective standard for measuring "convincing evidence of majority support," the employer's "subjective" doubts would be adequately safeguarded by § 9(c)(1)(B)'s assurance of the right to file his own petition for an election. * * *

* * * When an employer is confronted with "convincing evidence of majority support," he has the *option* of petitioning for an election or consenting to an expedited union-petitioned election. As the Court explains, § 9(c)(1)(B) does not require the employer to exercise this option. If he does not, however, and if he does not voluntarily recognize the union, he must take the risk that his conduct will be found by the Board to constitute a violation of his § 8 (a)(5) duty to bargain. In short, petitioning for an election is not an employer obligation; it is a device created by Congress for the employer's self-protection, much as Congress gave unions the right to petition for elections to establish their majority status but deliberately chose not to require a union to seek an election before it could impose a bargaining obligation on an unwilling employer. NLRB v. Gissel Packing Co., 395 U.S., at 598–599, 89 S.Ct. 1918, 1932–1933. * * *

Problems for Discussion

1. What are the reasons given by Justice Douglas for preferring a certification election to an unfair labor practice proceeding for demonstrating a union's majority status? Can you think of others?

2. In making such a judgment, was the Court engaged in a legislative rather than a judicial act? Were not the dissenters correct in stating that Congress had already resolved this question, at least in 1947? If the issue before the Court does reduce itself to one of statutory construction, was the Court majority correct in endorsing the Board's conclusion simply because it was not "arbitrary and capricious or an abuse of discretion"?

3. In its *Gissel* decision, the Court conjectured that most employers know when a union is organizing and gathering authorization cards, so

that employees are generally as likely to learn of the employer's arguments against unionization then as they are when there is a full campaign leading to a certification election. (This proposition also bears upon the issue in *Linden Lumber*, does it not?) Are you in agreement with the Court's methodology or its conclusion? Consider the following passages from Getman, Goldberg & Herman, Union Representation Elections: Law and Reality 134–35 (1976):

> "In eighteen elections we were able to determine the proportion of authorization cards signed before the employer knew about the card-signing drive. In ten of these elections, all cards were signed before the employer was aware of the card-signing drive; in four, 50–75 percent were signed before the employer found out; and in four others nearly all cards were signed after employer knowledge.

> "It appears, then, that in most elections the employer does not know about the card-signing drive in time to respond before a majority of the cards have been signed. It does not follow, however, that cards do not represent reasonably firm union sentiments. * * * [In all of the elections studied,] 72 percent of all card-signers voted for union representation, even though few of them had heard the employer's side of the unionization issue at the time they signed a card. Furthermore, * * * campaign familiarity was generally low. Those card-signers who did switch to the company were no more familiar with the company campaign than those who voted union.

> "In sum, the voting decision, made after hearing the employer's arguments, is not substantially more informed than the card-signing decision. Nor, for most employees, are the two choices different. For those few employees for whom the card-sign choice and the election choice are different, that difference is not associated with greater familiarity with the company campaign. Accordingly, the fact that most employees sign cards before having heard the employer's arguments ought not prevent the issuance of a bargaining order based on cards."

[The authors nonetheless endorse the *Linden Lumber* decision. Ibid. at 153.]

4. On June 1, the IBEW tendered authorization cards from 13 of the company's 16 employees and asked for recognition as bargaining representative. The owner to whom the cards were shown declined recognition, saying he would have to take up the matter with his partners. On June 2, pursuant to an agreement among the partners, all of the employees were questioned and 13 acknowledged that they had in fact signed cards designating the IBEW as their representative. On June 3, the partners come to you, their attorney, and ask whether they must or should recognize and bargain with the IBEW. What is your answer? See *Sullivan Elec. Co. v. NLRB*, 479 F.2d 1270 (6th Cir. 1973).

BROOKS v. NLRB

Supreme Court of the United States, 1954.
348 U.S. 96, 75 S.Ct. 176, 99 L.Ed. 125.

MR. JUSTICE FRANKFURTER delivered the opinion of the Court.

The National Labor Relations Board conducted a representation election in petitioner's Chrysler-Plymouth agency on April 12, 1951. District Lodge No. 727, International Association of Machinists, won by a vote of eight to five, and the Labor Board certified it as the exclusive bargaining representative on April 20. A week after the election and the day before the certification, petitioner received a handwritten letter signed by 9 of the 13 employees in the bargaining unit stating: "We, the undersigned majority of the employees * * * are not in favor of being represented by Union Local No. 727 as a bargaining agent."

Relying on this letter and the decision of the Court of Appeals for the Sixth Circuit in National Labor Relations Board v. Vulcan Forging Co., 188 F.2d 927, petitioner refused to bargain with the union. The Labor Board found, 98 N.L.R.B. 976, that petitioner had thereby committed an unfair labor practice in violation of §§ 8(a)(1) and 8(a)(5) of the amended National Labor Relations Act, 61 Stat. 140–141, 29 U.S.C. § 158(a)(1), (a)(5), 29 U.S.C.A. § 158(a)(1, 5), and the Court of Appeals for the Ninth Circuit enforced the Board's order to bargain, 204 F.2d 899. In view of the conflict between the Circuits, we granted certiorari, 347 U.S. 916, 74 S.Ct. 517.

The issue before us is the duty of an employer toward a duly certified bargaining agent if, shortly after the election which resulted in the certification, the union has lost, without the employer's fault, a majority of the employees from its membership.

Under the original Wagner Act, the Labor Board was given the power to certify a union as the exclusive representative of the employees in a bargaining unit when it had determined by election or "any other suitable method", that the union commanded majority support. § 9(c), 49 Stat. 453. In exercising this authority the Board evolved a number of working rules, of which the following are relevant to our purpose:

(a) A certification, if based on a Board-conducted election, must be honored for a "reasonable" period, ordinarily "one year," in the absence of "unusual circumstances."

(b) "Unusual circumstances" were found in at least three situations: (1) the certified union dissolved or became defunct; (2) as a result of a schism, substantially all the members and officers of the certified union transferred their affiliation to a new local or international; (3) the size of the bargaining unit fluctuated radically within a short time.

(c) Loss of majority support after the "reasonable" period could be questioned in two ways: (1) employer's refusal to bargain, or (2) petition by a rival union for a new election.

(d) If the initial election resulted in a majority for "no union," the election—unlike a certification—did not bar a second election within a year.

The Board uniformly found an unfair labor practice where, during the so-called "certification year," an employer refused to bargain on the ground that the certified union no longer possessed a majority. While the courts in the main enforced the Board's decisions, they did not commit themselves to one year as the determinate content of reasonableness. The Board and the courts proceeded along this line of reasoning:

(a) In the political and business spheres, the choice of the voters in an election binds them for a fixed time. This promotes a sense of responsibility in the electorate and needed coherence in administration. These considerations are equally relevant to healthy labor relations.

(b) Since an election is a solemn and costly occasion, conducted under safeguards to voluntary choice, revocation of authority should occur by a procedure no less solemn than that of the initial designation. A petition or a public meeting—in which those voting for and against unionism are disclosed to management, and in which the influences of mass psychology are present—is not comparable to the privacy and independence of the voting booth.

(c) A union should be given ample time for carrying out its mandate on behalf of its members, and should not be under exigent pressure to produce hothouse results or be turned out.

(d) It is scarcely conducive to bargaining in good faith for an employer to know that, if he dillydallies or subtly undermines, union strength may erode and thereby relieve him of his statutory duties at any time, while if he works conscientiously toward agreement, the rank and file may, at the last moment, repudiate their agent.

(e) In situations, not wholly rare, where unions are competing, raiding and strife will be minimized if elections are not at the hazard of informal and short-term recall.

Certain aspects of the Labor Board's representation procedures came under scrutiny in the Congress that enacted the Taft-Hartley Act in 1947, 61 Stat. 136. Congress was mindful that, once employees had chosen a union, they could not vote to revoke its authority and refrain from union activities, while if they voted against having a union in the first place, the union could begin at once to agitate for a new election. The National Labor Relations Act was amended to provide that (a) employees could petition the Board for a decertification election, at which they would have an opportunity to choose no longer to be represented by a union, 61 Stat. 144, 29 U.S.C. § 159(c) (1) (A) (ii), 29 U.S.C.A. § 159(c) (1) (A) (ii) ; (b) an employer, if in doubt as to the majority claimed by a union without formal election or beset by the conflicting claims of rival unions, could likewise petition the Board for an election, 61 Stat. 144, 29 U.S.C. § 159(c)(1)(B), 29 U.S.C.A. § 159(c)(1)(B) ; (c) after a valid certification or de-certification election had been conducted, the Board could not hold a second election in the same bargaining unit until a year had elapsed, 61 Stat. 144, 29 U.S.C. § 159(c)(3), 29 U.S.C.A. § 159(c)(3) ; (d) Board certification could only be granted as the result of an election, 61 Stat. 144, 29 U.S.C. § 159(c)(1), 29 U.S.C.A. § 159(c)(1), though an employer would presumably still be under a duty to bargain with an uncertified union that had a clear majority, see National Labor Relations Board v. Kobritz, 1 Cir., 193 F.2d 8.

The Board continued to apply its "one-year certification" rule after the Taft-Hartley Act came into force, except that even "unusual circumstances" no longer left the Board free to order an election where one had taken place within the preceding 12 months. * * * The issue is open here. * * *

Petitioner contends that whenever an employer is presented with evidence that his employees have deserted their certified union, he may forthwith refuse to bargain. In effect, he seeks to vindicate the rights of his employees to select their bargaining representative. * * * The underlying purpose of this statute is industrial peace. To allow employers to rely on employees' rights in refusing to bargain with the formally designated union is not conducive to that end, it is inimical to it. Congress has devised a formal mode for selection and rejection of bargaining agents and has fixed the spacing of elections, with a view of furthering industrial stability and with due regard to administrative prudence.

We find wanting the arguments against these controlling considerations. * * *

To be sure, what we have said has special pertinence only to the period during which a second election is impossible. * * * [T]he Board has ruled that one year after certification the employer can ask for an election or, if he has fair doubts about the union's continuing majority, he may refuse to bargain further with it. This, too, is a matter appropriately determined by the Board's administrative authority.

We conclude that the judgment of the Court of Appeals enforcing the Board's order must be affirmed.

Upon the expiration of the "certification year," the presumption of majority status continues, but it becomes rebuttable. There is also a presumption of continued majority status following the expiration of a collective bargaining agreement. The applicable principles were recently reviewed by the Board in BARTENDERS ASS'N, 213 N.L.R.B. No. 74 (1974). There, the union and the employers' association had a long history of collective bargaining. Following the expiration of a labor contract in June 1973, the union and the association continued to negotiate. In August, the employers notified the union that they doubted the union's continued majority and would not bargain until the union demonstrated that it had majority support. The Board endorsed the following statement:

> "It is well settled that a certified union, upon expiration of the first year following its certification, enjoys a rebuttable presumption that its majority representative status continues. This presumption is designed to promote stability in collective-bargaining relationships, without impairing the free choice of employees. Accordingly, once the presumption is shown to be operative, a *prima facie* case is established that an employer is obligated to bargain and that its refusal to do so would be unlawful. The *prima facie* case may be rebutted if the employer affirmatively establishes either (1) that at the time of the refusal the union in fact no longer enjoyed majority representative status; or (2) that the employer's refusal was predicated on a good-faith and reasonably grounded doubt of the union's continued majority status. As to the second of these, i. e., 'good faith doubt,' two prerequisites for sustaining the defense are that the asserted doubt must be based on objective considerations and it must not have been advanced for the purpose of gaining time in which to undermine the union. [This second point means, in effect, the assertion of doubt must be raised 'in a context free of unfair labor practices.']"

The Board held that the rebuttable presumption favoring the incumbent union operates in the same manner if the union's majority status was initially established without the benefit of Board certification. The employer association attempted to establish an objective basis for a good faith doubt by pointing out that only about one-third of the employees in the appropriate unit had authorized dues checkoffs under the expired contract and that fewer than half were union members. The Board, however, observed that employees could be union supporters without wishing to incur the obligations of union membership; moreover, the number of employees authorizing dues checkoffs was a particularly unreliable indication of union support, since some employees might pay dues directly to the union. The employer association was therefore ordered to bargain.

The principles of presumptive majority for the incumbent union can on occasion place the employer in a most difficult legal position, for pointing in the other direction are the principles embraced in the so-called *Midwest Piping* doctrine, which require an employer to refrain from recognizing either union when there are competing claims to recognition by more than one; the employer is even forbidden to bargain for a new contract with an incumbent union when a rival union has filed an election petition backed by a showing of interest from thirty percent of the employees in the bargaining unit. Shea Chem. Corp., 121 N.L.R.B. 1027 (1958). The courts of appeals have been somewhat more willing than the Board to permit the employer to continue bargaining with an incumbent union in these cases. See pp. 215–16, supra.

An employer is generally free to test a union's continuing majority upon the expiration of a contract either by refraining from recognizing and bargaining with the union, thus precipitating an unfair labor practice charge under Section 8(a)(5), or by petitioning for a representation election. At one time the Board held that the employer had to demonstrate in the refusal-to-bargain case that it had a good faith doubt of the union's continuing majority, in order to make out a defense, but that no such showing had to be made to warrant the employer's securing an election. Recognizing the anomaly, the Board changed this rule in United States Gypsum Co., 157 N.L.R.B. 652 (1966), and now requires that an employer, in order to secure a representation election to test the status of an incumbent union, must also demonstrate objective grounds for doubting the union's majority support.

Problems for Discussion

1. Watson Shoes, Inc., conducted negotiations with the Warehousemen's Union, representing shipping department employees, for two months following the expiration of a three-year contract. When negotiations reached an impasse, the Union struck and 20 of 25 employees in the department joined the strike. When the following events occurred, Mr. Watson informed the Union that it was terminating negotiations and declining to recognize the Union as bargaining representative any further: (a) After a week, ten of the strikers returned to work; (b) Watson hired ten applicants to serve as permanent replacements for those continuing on strike; (c) Three of the nonstrikers formed an independent employee representative and filed a decertification petition with the NLRB; (d) Fifteen of the workers came to Mr. Watson, individually and in small groups, to complain that for the last half-year of the contract the Union was not processing various grievances, and some stated that

the department would run more smoothly if they could handle individual grievances on their own. Has the company violated Section 8(a)(5)? See NLRB v. Maywood Plant of Grede Plastics, 628 F.2d 1 (D.C.Cir. 1980); National Cash Register Co. v. NLRB, 494 F.2d 189 (8th Cir. 1974); Arkay Packaging Corp., 227 N.L.R.B. 397 (1976).

Would your answer be affected if, after the company introduced such evidence in the Section 8(a)(5) proceeding, the General Counsel came forward with evidence that eighteen employees in the unit were in fact dues-paying Union members throughout the pertinent period (a fact of which Mr. Watson was unaware)? See Orion Corp. v. NLRB, 515 F.2d 81 (7th Cir. 1975).

2. When United Shoe Workers presented evidence that 390 of 560 employees had become members, Sof'-Shoe, Inc. granted recognition and commenced collective bargaining. Negotiations have gone on for four months. Some points of agreement have been reached but not on such major issues as wages, seniority, union security, and arbitration. Sof'-Shoe is convinced (1) that all except 60 or 70 employees have already lost interest in United Shoe Workers and (2) that, if it were to withdraw recognition and grant an immediate, long-overdue wage increase, union sentiment would disappear entirely. What would be your advice? See NLRB v. San Clemente Pub. Corp., 408 F.2d 367 (9th Cir. 1969); Brennan's Cadillac, Inc., 231 N.L.R.B. 225 (1977).

3. Massachusetts Machine Shop, until July 3, 1981, located its one plant in Roxbury, Massachusetts. The production and maintenance employees there were represented by the United Electrical Workers. As the contract-termination date of June 30, 1981, approached, the company informed the union of its intention to close the plant and move the machinery and equipment forty miles away to Nashua, New Hampshire, where business would continue, the same supervisors would be employed, and the same job structure would be retained. Negotiations between the company and the UEW resulted in an agreement providing for a travel allowance for employees who decided to commute to Nashua and for severance pay for those who did not. Although the union requested that the company recognize it as bargaining representative in Nashua, the company stated that it could not make a commitment to do so until it knew the makeup of the workforce at the new plant.

On July 3 the Roxbury plant closed and on July 21, the Nashua plant opened. Only about half of the machinery was installed by that date; of the 19 employees at the new site, 11 had previously worked in Roxbury (where there had been a total workforce of 44). By July 28, 15 additional employees had been hired from the Nashua area. The UEW then repeated its request for recognition (without an election and without proffering any authorization cards), and again the company refused.

Has the company violated Section 8(a)(5)? See Mass. Mach. & Stamping, Inc., 231 N.L.R.B. 801 (1977).

4. At the conclusion of a three-year labor agreement, during which time the union has been actively processing grievances and has been collect-

ing dues pursuant to a lawful union shop provision, the employer declines to negotiate with the union for a new agreement. The union's attorney writes to the company president, stating in effect: "We are a certified union which has continued to have employee support throughout the contract term. NLRB law is clear that when the contract terminates, we are presumed to continue to have such support and the company must bargain with the union absent objective facts suggesting that such support has been lost. You rely on no such facts, and you are therefore in violation of Section 8(a)(5)." The company's attorney responds: "We have engaged in no acts of coercion or discrimination toward the union or its members. The *Gissel* and *Linden Lumber* decisions of the Supreme Court make it clear that in such circumstances a representation election is the preferred mode for demonstrating union majority support and that lesser showings—such as presumptions anchored in an employee referendum years before—run the risk of imposing an unwanted union on a majority of the workers. Those two decisions base the duty to bargain on a secret ballot and not on an employer's subjective beliefs about union support. We will bargain for a new agreement, but only if you petition for and win an NLRB election." Which is the sounder position? Compare Daisy's Originals, Inc. v. NLRB, 468 F.2d 493 (5th Cir. 1972), with NLRB v. Frick Co., 423 F.2d 1327 (3d Cir. 1970). See also NLRB v. Tahoe Nugget, Inc., 584 F.2d 293 (9th Cir. 1978).

Assume that the union in the above hypothetical case responds to the employer's refusal to bargain by petitioning for a certification election and filing a Section 8(a)(5) charge. Assume too that the union loses the election, the NLRB certifies the results, and the union raises no objections; and that the Board subsequently concludes that the employer's position outlined above was in violation of Section 8(a)(5). Should the Board, as a remedy in the unfair labor practice case, order the company to bargain with the union? See Peoples Gas System, Inc. v. NLRB, 629 F.2d 35 (D.C. Cir. 1980).

NLRB v. BURNS INTERNATIONAL SECURITY SERVICES, INC.[10]

Supreme Court of the United States, 1972.
406 U.S. 272, 92 S.Ct. 1571, 32 L.Ed.2d 61.

MR. JUSTICE WHITE delivered the opinion of the Court.

Burns International Security Services, Inc. (Burns), replaced another employer, the Wackenhut Corp. (Wackenhut), which had

---

10. See Goldberg, The Labor Law Obligations of a Successor Employer, 63 Nw.U.L.Rev. 735 (1969); Morris & Gaus, Successorship and the Collective Bargaining Agreement: Accommodating *Wiley* and *Burns*, 59 Va.L.Rev. 1359 (1973); Note, Contractual Successorship: The Impact of *Burns*, 40 U.Chi.L.Rev. 617 (1973); Slicker, A Reconsideration of the Doctrine of Employer Successorship—A Step Toward a Rational Approach, 57 Minn.L.Rev. 1051 (1973).

previously provided plant protection services for the Lockheed Aircraft Service Co. (Lockheed) located at the Ontario International Airport in California. When Burns began providing security service, it employed 42 guards; 27 of them had been employed by Wackenhut. Burns refused, however, to bargain with the United Plant Guard Workers of America (UPG) which had been certified after a National Labor Relations Board (Board) election as the exclusive bargaining representative of Wackenhut's employees less than four months earlier. The issues presented in this case are whether Burns refused to bargain with a union representing a majority of employees in an appropriate unit and whether the National Labor Relations Board could order Burns to observe the terms of a collective-bargaining contract signed by the union and Wackenhut that Burns had not voluntarily assumed. Resolution turns to a great extent on the precise facts involved here.

I

The Wackenhut Corp. provided protection services at the Lockheed plant for five years before Burns took over this task. On February 28, 1967, a few months before the changeover of guard employers, a majority of the Wackenhut guards selected the union as their exclusive bargaining representative in a Board election after Wackenhut and the union had agreed that the Lockheed plant was the appropriate bargaining unit. On March 8, the Regional Director certified the union as the exclusive bargaining representative for these employees, and, on April 29, Wackenhut and the union entered into a three-year collective-bargaining contract.

Meanwhile, since Wackenhut's one-year service agreement to provided security protection was due to expire on June 30, Lockheed had called for bids from various companies supplying these services, and both Burns and Wackenhut submitted estimates. At a pre-bid conference attended by Burns on May 15, a representative of Lockheed informed the bidders that Wackenhut's guards were represented by the union, that the union had recently won a Board election and been certified, and that there was in existence a collective-bargaining contract between Wackenhut and the union. App. 4–5, 126. Lockheed then accepted Burns' bid, and on May 31 Wackenhut was notified that Burns would assume responsibility for protection services on July 1. Burns chose to retain 27 of the Wackenhut guards, and it brought in 15 of its own guards from other Burns locations.

During June, when Burns hired the 27 Wackenhut guards, it supplied them with membership cards of the American Federation of Guards (AFG), another union with which Burns had collective-bargaining contracts at other locations, and informed them that they had to become AFG members to work for Burns, that they would not receive uniforms otherwise, and that Burns "could not live with" the existing contract between Wackenhut and the union. On June 29, Burns recognized the AFG on the theory that it had obtained a card majority. On July 12, however, the UPG demanded that Burns recognize it as the bargaining representative of Burns' employees at Lockheed and that Burns honor the collective-bargaining agreement between it and Wackenhut. When Burns refused, the UPG filed unfair labor practice charges, and Burns responded by challenging the appropriateness of the unit and by denying its obligation to bargain. * * *

[The Board found the Lockheed plant an appropriate unit and held that Burns violated Sections 8(a)(1) and (2) by unlawfully recognizing and assisting the AFG, and that it violated Sections 8(a)(1) and (5) by failing to recognize and bargain with the UPG and by refusing to honor the labor contract between UPG and Wackenhut. Burns did not challenge the finding of unlawful assistance, and the court of appeals sustained the finding of refusal to bargain but not the Board's order to honor the Wackenhut contract. The Supreme Court granted certiorari but declined to review the propriety of the Board's determination that the Lockheed plant was an appropriate bargaining unit.]

II

We address first Burns' alleged duty to bargain with the union * * * Because the Act itself imposes a duty to bargain with the representative of a majority of the employees in an appropriate unit, the initial issue before the Board was whether the charging union was such a bargaining representative. * * * In an election held but a few months before, the union had been designated bargaining agent for the employees in the unit and a majority of these employees had been hired by Burns for work in the identical unit. It is undisputed that Burns knew all the relevant facts in this regard and was aware of the certification and of the existence of a collective-bargaining contract. In these circumstances, it was not unreasonable for the Board to conclude that the union certified to represent all employees in the unit still represented a majority of the employees and that Burns could not reasonably have entertained a good-faith doubt about that fact. Burns' obligation to bargain with the union over terms and conditions of employment stemmed from its hiring of Wackenhut's employees and from the recent election and Board certification. It has been consistently held that a mere change of employers or of ownership in the employing industry is not such an "unusual circumstance" as to affect the force of the Board's certification within the normal operative period if a majority of employees after the change of ownership or management were employed by the preceding employer. * * * 11

It would be a wholly different case if the Board had determined that because Burns' operational structure and practices differed from those of Wackenhut, the Lockheed bargaining unit was no longer an appropriate one.[12]   Likewise, it would be different if Burns had not hired employees already represented by a union certified as a bargaining agent,[13] and the Board recognized as much at oral argument. But where the bargaining unit remains unchanged and a majority of the employees hired by the new employer are represented by a recently certified bargaining agent there is little basis for faulting the Board's implementation of the express mandates of § 8(a)(5) and § 9(a) by ordering the employer to bargain with the incumbent union. This is the view of several courts of appeals, and we agree with those courts. * * *

11. * * * Where an employer remains the same, a Board certification carries with it an almost conclusive presumption that the majority representative status of the union continues for a reasonable time, usually a year. See Brooks v. NLRB, 348 U.S. 96, 98–99, 75 S.Ct. 176, 178–179, 99 L.Ed. 125 (1954). After this period, there is a rebuttable presumption of majority representation. Celanese Corp. of America, 95 N.L.R.B. 664, 672 (1951). If there is a change of employers, however, and an almost complete turnover of employees, the certification may not bar a challenge if the successor employer is not bound by the collective-bargaining contract, particularly if the new employees are represented by another union or if the old unit is ruled an accretion to another unit. Cf. McGuire v. Humble Oil & Refining Co., 355 F.2d 352 (CA2), cert. denied 384 U.S. 988, 86 S.Ct. 1889, 16 L.Ed.2d 1004 (1966). * *

12. The Court of Appeals was unimpressed with the asserted differences between Burns' and Wackenhut's operations: "All of the important factors which the Board has used and the courts have approved are present in the instant case: 'continuation of the same types of product lines, departmental organization, employee identity and job functions.' * * * Both Burns and Wackenhut are na-

tionwide organizations; both performed the identical services at the same facility; although Burns used its own supervisors, their functions and responsibilities were similar to those performed by their predecessors; and finally, and perhaps most significantly, Burns commenced performance of the contract with 27 former Wackenhut employees out of its total complement of 42." 441 F.2d 911, 915 (1971) (citation omitted). Although the labor policies of the two companies differed somewhat, the Board's determination that the bargaining unit remained appropriate after the changeover meant that Burns would face essentially the same labor relations environment as Wackenhut: it would confront the same union representing most of the same employees in the same unit.

13. The Board has never held that the National Labor Relations Act itself requires that an employer who submits the winning bid for a service contract or who purchases the assets of a business be obligated to hire all of the employees of the predecessor though it is possible that such an obligation might be assumed by the employer. But cf. Chemrock Corp., 151 N.L.R.B. 1074 (1965). However, an employer who declines to hire employees solely because they are members of a union commits a § 8(a)(3) unfair labor practice. * * *

III

[In Part III of its opinion, the Court held that the duty of Burns to bargain with the union which formerly represented the Wackenhut employees did not carry with it the duty to observe the substantive terms of the labor contract between the union and Wackenhut, to which Burns had in no way agreed. The Board had held that the obligation to honor the contract flowed from the same statutory policies as warranted continued bargaining by the successor, and that honoring the contract would foster the federal policies, noted in John Wiley & Sons v. Livingston, 376 U.S. 543, 84 S.Ct. 909, 11 L.Ed.2d 898 (1964), p. 577 infra, of peacefully settling industrial disputes and protecting employees in business changes. The Court distinguished *Wiley*, which had been an action under Section 301 of the Labor Act to compel arbitration of the question whether any substantive contract terms would bind the successor employer. Unlike the merger in the *Wiley* case, there were no dealings whatever between Wackenhut and Burns and thus no reason to infer in law or in fact that Burns assumed the Wackenhut labor contract or that the employees would have reasonably expected it. Moreover, there is no national policy comparable to that in *Wiley* strongly favoring arbitration of disputes which would outweigh the strong national policy favoring freedom of contract and the settlement of contract terms not by government dictation but rather by free collective bargaining. Excerpts from Part III of the Court's opinion are set forth at pp. 590–91, infra.]

IV

[T]he Board's opinion stated that "[t]he obligation to bargain imposed on a successor-employer includes the negative injunction to refrain from unilaterally changing wages and other benefits established by a prior collective-bargaining agreement even though that agreement had expired. In this respect, the successor-employer's obligations are the same as those imposed upon employers generally during the period between collective-bargaining agreements." App. 8–9. This statement by the Board is consistent with its prior and subsequent cases that hold that whether or not a successor employer is bound by its predecessor's contract, it must not institute terms and conditions of employment different from those provided in its predecessor's contract, at least without first bargaining with the employees' representative. * * * Thus, if Burns, without bargaining to impasse with the union, had paid its employees on and after July 1 at a rate lower than Wackenhut had paid under its contract, or otherwise provided terms and conditions of employment different from those provided in the Wackenhut collective-bargaining agreement, under the Board's view, Burns would have committed a § 8(a)(5) unfair labor practice and would have been subject to an order to restore to employees what they had lost by this so-called unilateral change. * * *

Although Burns had an obligation to bargain with the union concerning wages and other conditions of employment when the union requested it to do so, this case is not like a § 8(a)(5) violation where an employer unilaterally changes a condition of employment without consulting a bargaining representative. It is difficult to understand how Burns could be said to have *changed* unilaterally any pre-existing term or condition of employment without bargaining when it had no previous relationship whatsoever to the bargaining unit and, prior to July 1, no outstanding terms and conditions of employment from which a change could be inferred. The terms on which Burns hired employees for service after July 1 may have differed from the terms extended by Wackenhut and required by the collective-bargaining contract, but it does not follow that Burns changed *its* terms and conditions of employment when it specified the initial basis on which employees were hired on July 1.

Although a successor employer is ordinarily free to set initial terms on which it will hire the employees of a predecessor, there will be instances in which it is perfectly clear that the new employer plans to retain all of the employees in the unit and in which it will be appropriate to have him initially consult with the employees' bargaining representative before he fixes terms. In other situations, however, it may not be clear until the successor employer has hired his full complement of employees that he has a duty to bargain with a union, since it will not be evident until then that the bargaining representative represents a majority of the employees in the unit as required by § 9(a) of the Act, 29 U.S.C. § 159(a). Here, for example, Burns' obligation to bargain with the union did not mature until it had selected its force of guards late in June. The Board quite properly found that Burns refused to bargain on July 12 when it rejected the overtures of the union. It is true that the wages it paid when it began protecting the Lockheed plant on July 1 differed from those specified in the Wackenhut collective-bargaining agreement, but there is no evidence that Burns ever unilaterally changed the terms and conditions of employment it had offered to potential employees in June after its obligation to bargain with the union became apparent. * * * The Board's order requiring Burns to make whole its employees for any losses suffered by reason of Burns' refusal to honor and enforce the contract, cannot therefore be sustained on the ground that Burns unilaterally changed existing terms and conditions of employment, thereby committing an unfair labor practice which required monetary restitution in these circumstances.

Affirmed.

MR. JUSTICE REHNQUIST, with whom THE CHIEF JUSTICE, MR. JUSTICE BRENNAN, and MR. JUSTICE POWELL join [concurring and dissenting] * * *

Although the Court studiously avoids using the term "successorship" in concluding that Burns did have a statutory obligation to bargain with the union, it affirms the conclusions of the Board and the Court of Appeals to that effect which were based entirely on the successorship doctrine. Because I believe that the Board and the Court of Appeals stretched that concept beyond the limits of its proper application, I would enforce neither the Board's bargaining order nor its order imposing upon Burns the terms of the contract between the union and Wackenhut. I therefore concur in No. 71–123 and dissent in No. 71–198. * * *

The Court concludes that because the trial examiner and the Board found the Lockheed facility to be an appropriate bargaining unit for Burns' employees, and because Burns hired a majority of Wackenhut's previous employees who had worked at that facility, Burns should have bargained with the union, even though the union never made any showing to Burns of majority representation. There is more than one difficulty with this analysis.

First, it is by no means mathematically demonstrable that the union was the choice of a majority of the 42 employees with which Burns began the performance of its contract with Lockheed. True, 27 of the 42 had been represented by the union when they were employees of Wackenhut, but there is nothing in the record before us to indicate that all 27 of these employees chose the union as their bargaining agent even at the time of negotiations with Wackenhut. There is obviously no evidence whatever that the remaining 15 employees of Burns, who had never been employed by Wackenhut, had ever expressed their views one way or the other about the union as a bargaining representative. It may be that, if asked, all would have designated the union. But they were never asked. Instead, the trial examiner concluded that because Burns was a "successor" employer to Wackenhut, it was obligated by that fact alone to bargain with the union.

* * * The imposition of successorship in this case is unusual because the successor instead of purchasing business or assets from or merging with Wackenhut was in direct competition with Wackenhut for the Lockheed contract. I believe that a careful analysis of the admittedly imprecise concept of successorship indicates that important rights of both the employee and the employer to in-

dependently order their own affairs are sacrificed needlessly by the application of that doctrine to this case.   *   *   *

[Implications in the Court's opinion in John Wiley & Sons v. Livingston] suggest that employees are indeed entitled to a measure of protection against change in the employing entity where the new employer continues to make use of tangible or intangible assets used in carrying on the business of the first employer. They also make clear that the successorship doctrine, carried to its ultimate limits, runs counter to other equally well-established principles of labor law. Industrial peace is an important goal of the Labor Management Relations Act. But Congress has time and again refused to sacrifice free collective bargaining between representatives of the employees and the employer for a system of compulsory arbitration. *   *   *

Wiley, supra, speaks in terms of a change in the "ownership or corporate structure of an enterprise" as bringing into play the obligation of the successor employer to perform an obligation voluntarily undertaken by the predecessor employer. But while the principle enunciated in *Wiley* is by no means limited to the corporate merger situation present there, it cannot logically be extended to a mere naked shifting of a group of employees from one employer to another without totally disregarding the basis for the doctrine. The notion of a change in the "ownership or corporate structure of an enterprise" connotes at the very least that there is continuity in the enterprise, as well as change; and that that continuity be at least in part on the employer's side of the equation, rather than only on that of the employees. If we deal with the legitimate expectations of employees that the employer who agreed to the collective-bargaining contract perform it, we can require another employing entity to perform the contract only when he has succeeded to some of the tangible or intangible assets by the use of which the employees might have expected the first employer to have performed his contract with them.   *   *   *

The rigid imposition of a prior-existing labor relations environment on a new employer whose only connection with the old employer is the hiring of some of the latter's employees and the performance of some of the work which was previously performed by the latter, might well tend to produce industrial peace of a sort. But industrial peace in such a case would be produced at a sacrifice of the determination by the Board of the appropriateness of bargaining agents and of the wishes of the majority of the employees which the Act was designed to preserve.   *   *   *

Problems for Discussion

1. From March of 1980 until March of 1981, the Spruce Up Corp. operated nineteen of the twenty-seven barber shops at the Fort Bragg military base. The other eight shops were operated by two other persons. In August 1980, the Barbers Union was certified as bargaining agent for the Spruce Up barbers. Later in 1980, bidding was opened for the operation of all barber shops in the fort. Early in 1981, Cicero Fowler, a barber employed in one of the shops in the fort, was notified that he was low bidder and that he would take over all the shops on March 1. The Union demanded that Fowler bargain with it, and Fowler refused. The Union filed a Section 8(a)(5) charge and a complaint issued.

At the hearing, the Administrative Law Judge finds that on March 17, the date of the initial refusal to bargain, Fowler employed 22 former Spruce Up barbers and 26 other barbers; that on March 31, he employed 21 former Spruce Up barbers and 26 other barbers; and that on April 14, he employed 32 former Spruce Up barbers and 23 other barbers. The General Counsel argues that, since Fowler intended at all times to make the Spruce Up barbers the "nucleus" of his workforce, he was obligated to bargain as of March 17 because the Spruce Up barbers constituted a "legally significant portion" of Fowler's workforce. The Administrative Law Judge finds that Fowler did not discriminate in hiring on the basis of union membership and that at all times Fowler intended to hire as many Spruce Up barbers as possible.

Has Fowler violated Section 8(a)(5), and if so, as of what date? See *Spruce Up Corp.*, 209 N.L.R.B. 194 (1974), enf'd mem. 529 F.2d 516 (4th Cir. 1975).

2. In April 1979, Charmfit, Inc., executed a three-year contract with the ILGWU covering Charmfit's Los Angeles employees. In April 1981, Harry Froehlich, director of the Los Angeles plant, received instructions from the company's central office to begin phasing out operations because production of the company's product, lingerie, was being shifted to other plants. By July, production had been ended, and all fifty-five employees had been terminated and awarded severance pay according to the terms of the contract. In August, Froehlich purchased the Los Angeles plant from Charmfit and signed a covenant not to compete, wherein he promised not to manufacture lingerie.

In late October, Froehlich reopened the plant as a sewing subcontractor under the name of Radiant Fashions. He employed thirty workers, all of whom had been Charmfit employees represented by the ILGWU. The Union demanded that Radiant recognize and bargain with it and Froehlich has refused. Has Radiant violated Section 8(a)(5)? See *Radiant Fashions, Inc.*, 202 N.L.R.B. 938 (1973). Would your analysis be affected if only twenty of the thirty Radiant employees had formerly worked for Charmfit?

3. In November 1980, the Kroger Company executed a contract with the Retail Clerks Union covering employees in all fifty-three of its retail

supermarkets. In 1981, Lowell Zimmer purchased one of these super-markets. The store was closed for two days and reopened as Zim's Foodliner with the same employees as were employed when the store was owned by Kroger. The employees are paid the same wages by Zim's as by Kroger. Zimmer refused to bargain with the Retail Clerks, who filed a Section 8(a)(5) charge. At a hearing before the Administrative Law Judge, Zimmer has argued that Zim's should not be considered to be a successor because the size of the bargaining unit has been drastically reduced and because employer-employee relations are significantly different in chain-store and single-store operations. Should Zim's be held to have violated Section 8(a)(5) and ordered to bargain with the Retail Clerks? See NLRB v. Fabsteel Co., 587 F.2d 689 (5th Cir.), cert. denied 442 U.S. 943, 99 S.Ct. 2887, 61 L.Ed.2d 313 (1979); Zim's Foodliner, Inc. v. NLRB, 495 F.2d 1131 (7th Cir. 1974).

4. Suppose that Zimmer, instead of immediately reopening the store, had first written a letter to each of the store's employees, offering them their jobs at greatly reduced wages, and that the employees agreed to return to work at these low wages. When the Retail Clerks demanded to meet with Zimmer, he agreed. The Union nevertheless filed a Section 8(a)(5) charge, claiming that Zimmer violated the Act by bargaining directly with the employees and unilaterally reducing wages without consulting with the union. Has Zimmer violated Section 8(a)(5)? See International Ass'n of Machinists v. NLRB (Boeing Co.), 595 F.2d 664 (D.C. Cir. 1978).

Part Three

COLLECTIVE BARGAINING

I. NEGOTIATION OF THE COLLECTIVE BARGAINING AGREEMENT

Once a union has achieved majority status both the employer and the union come under a duty "to bargain collectively." Sections 8 (a) (5) and 8(b) (3). In normal course they negotiate a collective bargaining agreement establishing, for a specified term, the wages, hours, and other terms and conditions of employment in the bargaining unit. Shortly before the expiration or upon the reopening of the existing agreement there will be new contract negotiations looking towards carrying forward many provisions of the existing contract but changing others. Between these periodic negotiations the relationship between management and union is likely to be rather more formally structured by grievance procedures, arbitration, and other institutions of contract administration.

This section of the casebook is focussed upon the legal rights and duties of employer and union during the period when there is no agreement or a new agreement is being negotiated. The chief questions can be conveniently grouped under four main headings:

(1) How far does the designation of a union as the "exclusive representative of all the employees in such unit for the purposes of collective bargaining" exclude other methods of dealing with wages and conditions of employment, such as discussions with individual employees or another union, unilateral employer action or concerted action by independent groups of employees within the bargaining unit?

(2) What does the duty to bargain collectively about clearly-bargainable subjects require of the employer and the union in their relations with each other? Section 8(d) provides that the duty includes "to meet at reasonable times and confer in good faith." What is the meaning of "good faith"? How may the absence of good faith be demonstrated?

(3) Over what topics must the employer and the union bargain collectively? In other words, what content should be given to the statutory phrase "wages, hours, and other terms and conditions of employment" contained in Section 8(d)?

363

(4) What is the role of the strike in the collective bargaining process and what steps have been taken, by Government and by private parties, to minimize recourse to the strike? How are the rights and obligations of the parties affected during the period of a strike?

A. EXCLUSIVE REPRESENTATION AND MAJORITY RULE [1]

J. I. CASE CO. v. NATIONAL LABOR RELATIONS BOARD

Supreme Court of the United States, 1944.
321 U.S. 332, 64 S.Ct. 576, 88 L.Ed. 762.

MR. JUSTICE JACKSON delivered the opinion of the Court.

This cause was heard by the National Labor Relations Board on stipulated facts which so far as concern present issues are as follows:

The petitioner, J. I. Case Company, at its Rock Island, Illinois, plant, from 1937 offered each employee an individual contract of employment. The contracts were uniform and for a term of one year. The Company agreed to furnish employment as steadily as conditions permitted, to pay a specified rate, which the Company might redetermine if the job changed, and to maintain certain hospital facilities. The employee agreed to accept the provisions, to serve faithfully and honestly for the term, to comply with factory rules, and that defective work should not be paid for. About 75% of the employees accepted and worked under these agreements.

According to the Board's stipulation and finding, the execution of the contracts was not a condition of employment, nor was the status of individual employees affected by reason of signing or failing to sign the contracts. It is not found or contended that the agreements were coerced, obtained by any unfair labor practice, or that they were not valid under the circumstances in which they were made.

While the individual contracts executed August 1, 1941 were in effect, a C.I.O. union petitioned the Board for certification as the exclusive bargaining representative of the production and maintenance employees. On December 17, 1941 a hearing was held, at which the Company urged the individual contracts as a bar to representation proceedings. The Board, however, directed an election, which was won by the union. The union was thereupon certified as the exclusive

1. See Schatzki, Majority Rule, Exclusive Representation, and the Interests of Individual Workers: Should Exclusivity be Abolished?, 123 U.Pa.L. Rev. 897 (1975); Smith, Evolution of the "Duty to Bargain" Concept in American Law, 39 Mich.L.Rev. 1065 (1941); Weyand, Majority Rule in Collective Bargaining, 45 Col.L.Rev. 556 (1945). For an examination of similar issues from the perspective of comparative law, see Bok, Reflections on the Distinctive Character of American Labor Laws, 84 Harv.L. Rev. 1394 (1971).

bargaining representative of the employees in question in respect to wages, hours, and other conditions of employment.

The union then asked the Company to bargain. It refused, declaring that it could not deal with the union in any manner affecting rights and obligations under the individual contracts while they remained in effect. It offered to negotiate on matters which did not affect rights under the individual contracts, and said that upon the expiration of the contracts it would bargain as to all matters. Twice the Company sent circulars to its employees asserting the validity of the individual contracts and stating the position that it took before the Board in reference to them.

The Board held that the Company had refused to bargain collectively, in violation of § 8(5) of the National Labor Relations Act, 29 U.S.C.A. § 158(5); and that the contracts had been utilized, by means of the circulars, to impede employees in the exercise of rights guaranteed by § 7 of the Act, 29 U.S.C.A. § 157, with the result that the Company had engaged in unfair labor practices within the meaning of § 8(1) of the Act. It ordered the Company to cease and desist from giving effect to the contracts, from extending them or entering into new ones, from refusing to bargain and from interfering with the employees; and it required the Company to give notice accordingly and to bargain upon request. * * *

Contract in labor law is a term the implications of which must be determined from the connection in which it appears. Collective bargaining between employer and the representatives of a unit, usually a union, results in an accord as to terms which will govern hiring and work and pay in that unit. The result is not, however, a contract of employment except in rare cases; no one has a job by reason of it and no obligation to any individual ordinarily comes into existence from it alone. The negotiations between union and management result in what often has been called a trade agreement, rather than in a contract of employment. Without pushing the analogy too far, the agreement may be likened to the tariffs established by a carrier, to standard provisions prescribed by supervising authorities for insurance policies, or to utility schedules of rates and rules for service, which do not of themselves establish any relationships but which do govern the terms of the shipper or insurer or customer relationship whenever and with whomever it may be established. Indeed, in some European countries, contrary to American practice, the terms of a collectively negotiated trade agreement are submitted to a government department and if approved become a governmental regulation ruling employment in the unit.

After the collective trade agreement is made, the individuals who shall benefit by it are identified by individual hirings. The employer, except as restricted by the collective agreement itself and except that he must engage in no unfair labor practice or discrimination, is free to select those he will employ or discharge. But the terms of the employment already have been traded out. There is little left to individual agreement except the act of hiring. This hiring may be by writing or by word of mouth or may be implied from conduct. In the sense of contracts of hiring, individual contracts between the employer and employee are not forbidden, but indeed are necessitated by the collective bargaining procedure.

But, however engaged, an employee becomes entitled by virtue of the Labor Relations Act somewhat as a third party beneficiary to all benefits of the collective trade agreement, even if on his own he would yield to less favorable terms. The individual hiring contract is subsidiary to the terms of the trade agreement and may not waive any of its benefits, any more than a shipper can contract away the benefit of filed tariffs, the insurer the benefit of standard provisions, or the utility customer the benefit of legally established rates.

Concurrent existence of these two types of agreement raises problems as to which the National Labor Relations Act makes no express provision.   *   *   *

Individual contracts, no matter what the circumstances that justify their execution or what their terms, may not be availed of to defeat or delay the procedures prescribed by the National Labor Relations Act looking to collective bargaining, nor to exclude the contracting employee from a duly ascertained bargaining unit; nor may they be used to forestall bargaining or to limit or condition the terms of the collective agreement. "The Board asserts a public right vested in it as a public body, charged in the public interest with the duty of preventing unfair labor practices." National Licorice Co. v. National Labor Relations Board, 309 U.S. 350, 364, 60 S.Ct. 569, 577, 84 L.Ed. 799. Wherever private contracts conflict with its functions, they obviously must yield or the Act would be reduced to a futility.

It is equally clear since the collective trade agreement is to serve the purpose contemplated by the Act, the individual contract cannot be effective as a waiver of any benefit to which the employee otherwise would be entitled under the trade agreement. The very purpose of providing by statute for the collective agreement is to supersede the terms of separate agreements of employees with terms which reflect the strength and bargaining power and serve the welfare of the group. Its benefits and advantages are open to every employee of the represented unit, whatever the type or terms of his pre-existing contract of employment.

But it is urged that some employees may lose by the collective agreement, that an individual workman may sometimes have, or be capable of getting, better terms than those obtainable by the group and that his freedom of contract must be respected on that account.

We are not called upon to say that under no circumstances can an individual enforce an agreement more advantageous than a collective agreement, but we find the mere possibility that such agreements might be made no ground for holding generally that individual contracts may survive or surmount collective ones. The practice and philosophy of collective bargaining looks with suspicion on such individual advantages. Of course, where there is great variation in circumstances of employment or capacity of employees, it is possible for the collective bargain to prescribe only minimum rates or maximum hours or expressly to leave certain areas open to individual bargaining. But except as so provided, advantages to individuals may prove as disruptive of industrial peace as disadvantages. They are a fruitful way of interfering with organization and choice of representatives; increased compensation, if individually deserved, is often earned at the cost of breaking down some other standard thought to be for the welfare of the group, and always creates the suspicion of being paid at the long-range expense of the group as a whole. Such discriminations not infrequently amount to unfair labor practices. The workman is free, if he values his own bargaining position more than that of the group, to vote against representation; but the majority rules, and if it collectivizes the employment bargain, individual advantages or favors will generally in practice go in as a contribution to the collective result. We cannot except individual contracts generally from the operation of collective ones because some may be more individually advantageous. Individual contracts cannot subtract from collective ones, and whether under some circumstances they may add to them in matters covered by the collective bargain, we leave to be determined by appropriate forums under the laws of contracts applicable, and to the Labor Board if they constitute unfair labor practices. * * *

As so modified [in details not here material] the decree is
Affirmed.

MR. JUSTICE ROBERTS is of opinion that the judgment should be reversed.

Problems for Discussion

1.   Under Public Resolution 44 (H.J.Res. 375, 48 Stat. 1183, 73d Cong., 2d Sess.), Congress in 1934—acting pursuant to the short-lived National Industrial Recovery Act—created the "old" National Labor Relations Board with modest authority to enforce the statutory "right of employees to organize and to select their representatives for the purpose of collective bargaining." Neither the Act nor the Resolution, however, specifically provided for or defined the duty to bargain collectively. If the NLRA had been similarly designed, so that there was in substance a Section 7 but no Section 9(a), would the objectives of the former Section

be fostered—or frustrated—by *implying* a principle of exclusive representation by the majority representative? Does not free collective bargaining under Section 7 invite a pluralistic scheme of representation, with each labor organization bargaining only on behalf of its own supporters (and non-union workers continuing to bargain individually)? See Houde Engineering Corp., 1 N.L.R.B. (old series) 35 (1934).

2. Jones runs a small machine shop in a locality in which there is strong demand for skilled machinists. International Association of Machinists has been certified by the NLRB as the bargaining representative of Jones' employees. Jones has three skilled machinists, older men not connected with the union, who he fears may leave his employ. Jones wishes to offer them a wage increase, a special bonus, or perhaps a secret promise of a pension upon retirement, without discussing the matter with IAM. Jones has consulted your senior partner as his lawyer about the advisability of this step. Your senior seeks your recommendation. What advice would you give?

3. The Amalgamated Clothing and Textile Workers Union was elected the bargaining representative of the 1200 production and maintenance workers at the Southern Textile Company in Rocky Mount, North Carolina. Collective bargaining agreements were negotiated in 1977 and in 1979. After several bargaining sessions looking toward a new agreement to take effect in June 1981, deadlock was reached on a number of major issues, including the assignment of overtime (the company demanding that overtime be assigned among all employees by rotation and the union demanding that it be assigned by seniority). When the workers went on strike, Southern closed the plant, and it has been closed for about three weeks, during which time there has been informal contact between representatives of Southern and Amalgamated, but no formal bargaining sessions. There is some reason to believe that many employees may be willing to return to work if the situation is handled right by the company and its attorneys (including you). Southern would like your advice as to what it can and should do to get its mill in operation, and particularly as to whether it can take two proposed steps.

First, it wishes to send each employee a letter enclosing a ballot on which to indicate whether he or she wishes to return to work. The letter would state, in part: "Although we have requested on several occasions that you employees be given an opportunity to vote by secret ballot on the question of returning to work on the basis proposed by the company, the union has consistently refused to conduct such an election. We believe it is unfair and contrary to American principle for a minority of employees to keep a majority from gainful employment, and we propose to find out just how many employees want to return to work. The hours and working conditions which will prevail will be the same as those in effect under the expired union agreement. Employees who return to work on or before August 15 will find jobs available for them, but after that date full measures will be taken to fill all remaining vacancies from every available source. Negotiations with the union will continue and hopefully a new agreement can be reached without further economic strain for you and your family." The company also proposes to have its supervisors distribute handbills with the same message to strikers walking the picket lines. See Texas Co., 93 N.L.R.B. 1358 (1951), enforcement denied 198 F.2d 540 (9th Cir. 1952); NLRB v. Penokee Veneer Co., 168 F.2d 868 (7th Cir. 1948).

Second, the company wishes to invite all employees to a meeting, from which the union will be excluded. At the meeting, company representatives will set forth the union's and the company's respective positions on the overtime issue, will answer questions from the assembled employees regarding the company's proposal, and will (if legal) poll the employees as to their feelings about that proposal. Compare Obie Pacific, Inc., 196 N.L.R.B. 458 (1952), with Continental Oil Co., 194 N.L.R.B. 126 (1971).

Would you advise the company to take these contemplated actions? (You might also want to address the inquiry specifically put to you by the company president: "Isn't there anything in the United States Constitution or the labor laws which gives me the right to speak freely to my own workers?!)

EMPORIUM CAPWELL CO. v. WESTERN ADDITION COMMUNITY ORGANIZATION [2]

Supreme Court of the United States, 1975.
420 U.S. 50, 95 S.Ct. 977, 43 L.Ed.2d 12.

Opinion of the Court by Mr. Justice Marshall * * *.

This case presents the question whether, in light of the national policy against racial discrimination in employment, the National Labor Relations Act protects concerted activity by a group of minority employees to bargain with their employer over issues of employment discrimination. The National Labor Relations Board held that the employees could not circumvent their elected representative to engage in such bargaining. The Court of Appeals for the District of Columbia Circuit reversed and remanded, holding that in certain circumstances the activity would be protected. 485 F.2d 917. Because of the importance of the issue to the administration of the Act, we granted certiorari. 415 U.S. 913, 94 S.Ct. 1407, 39 L.Ed.2d 466. We now reverse.

I.

[The Emporium Capwell Company and the Department Store Employees Union were parties to a collective bargaining agreement

2. See Atleson, Work Group Behavior and Wildcat Strikes: The Causes and Functions of Industrial Disobedience, 34 Ohio St.L.Rev. 751 (1973); Cantor, Dissident Worker Action, After *The* *Emporium*, 29 Rutgers L.Rev. 35 (1975); Gould, The Status of Unauthorized and "Wildcat" Strikes Under the National Labor Relations Act, 52 Cornell L.Q. 672 (1967).

which contained a no-strike no-lockout clause, grievance and arbitration machinery, and a prohibition of employment discrimination by reason of race, color, creed, national origin, age, sex, or union activity.   In response to employee complaints that the company was discriminating on the basis of race in making assignments and promotions, the Union's secretary-treasurer, Walter Johnson, prepared a report which he submitted to the Company; the report referred to "the possibility of racial discrimination" as a matter of central concern and one which if not corrected might be potentially explosive.   At a meeting of Company employees convened by the Union (to which representatives of the California Fair Employment Practices Committee were invited), testimony about Company practices was taken down by a court reporter and Johnson stated that he had concluded the Company was discriminating and that the Union would process every discrimination grievance to arbitration if necessary.   Although some of the Company's employees at the meeting stated that contract procedures were inadequate to handle such a systemic grievance and that the Union should instead picket the Company, Johnson explained that the labor contract forbade that and stated that successful individual grievants would be helping all other employees who were victims of discrimination.

The Union then demanded that the Company convene the joint union-management Adjustment Board provided for in the contract, but when the Adjustment Board met, four of the vocal employees—James Hollins, Tom Hawkins and two others—refused to participate; Hollins read a statement objecting to reliance on individual grievances and demanding that the president of the Company meet with the four protestants to work out a broader agreement for dealing with the discrimination issue.   Hollins later unsuccessfully attempted to have discussions with the Company president, and soon after, he and Hawkins and several other dissident employees held a press conference at which they denounced the Company's policy as racist, reiterated their desire to deal directly with "the top management," and announced their intention to picket and institute a boycott of the store.

Some ten days later, Hollins, Hawkins and at least two other employees picketed the store throughout the day and distributed at the entrance handbills urging consumers not to patronize the store.[3]

3. The full text of the handbill read:
"* * BEWARE * * * * * BEWARE * *
* * BEWARE * *
"EMPORIUM SHOPPERS
" 'Boycott Is On' 'Boycott Is On'
'Boycott Is On'
"For years at The Emporium black, brown, yellow and red people have worked at the lowest jobs, at the lowest levels.   Time and time again we have seen intelligent, hard working brothers and sisters denied promotions and respect.

"The Emporium is a 20th Century colonial plantation.   The brothers and sisters are being treated the same way as our brothers are being treated in the slave mines of Africa.

First Johnson and then the Company warned these employees that they might be discharged if their activities continued, and when Hollins and Hawkins repeated their conduct they were terminated. After the filing of a Section 8(a)(1) charge by the Western Addition Community Organization, a local civil rights association to which Hollins and Hawkins belonged, an NLRB trial examiner found that they had resorted to concerted activity in the good-faith belief that the Company was discriminating against minority employees; he concluded, however, that their activity was not protected by Section 7 and that their discharges thus did not violate Section 8(a)(1).]

The Board, after oral argument, adopted the findings and conclusions of its Trial Examiner and dismissed the complaint. 192 NLRB 173. Among the findings adopted by the Board was that the discharged employees' course of conduct

> "was no mere presentation of a grievance, but nothing short of a demand that the [Company] bargain with the picketing employees for the entire group of minority employees." [4]

The Board concluded that protection of such an attempt to bargain would undermine the statutory system of bargaining through an exclusive, elected representative, impede elected unions' efforts at bettering the working conditions of minority employees "and place on the Employer an unreasonable burden of attempting to placate self-designated representatives of minority groups while abiding by the terms of a valid bargaining agreement and attempting in good faith to meet whatever demands the bargaining representative put forth under that agreement." [5]

"Whenever the racist pig at The Emporium injures or harms a black sister or brother, they injure and insult all black people. THE EMPORIUM MUST PAY FOR THESE INSULTS. Therefore, we encourage all of our people to take their money out of this racist store, until black people have full employment and are promoted justly through out The Emporium.

"We welcome the support of our brothers and sisters from the churches, unions, sororities, fraternities, social clubs, Afro-American Institute, Black Panther Party, WACO and the Poor Peoples Institute."

4. 192 NLRB, at 185. The evidence marshaled in support of this finding consisted of Hollins' meeting with the Company president in which he said that he wanted to discuss the problem perceived by minority employees; his statement that the picketers would not desist until the president treated with them; Hawkins' testimony that their purpose in picketing was to "talk to the top management to get better conditions"; and his statement that they wanted to achieve their purpose through "group talk and through the president if we could talk to him," as opposed to use of the grievance-arbitration machinery.

5. The Board considered but stopped short of resolving the question of whether the employees' invective and call for a boycott of the Company bespoke so malicious an attempt to harm their employer as to deprive

[handwritten margin notes: "ct of app", "NLRA should inc civil Rights Act", "burden on Bd to be sure er does not discriminate on basis of race"]

On respondent's petition for review the Court of Appeals reversed and remanded. The court was of the view that concerted activity directed against racial discrimination enjoys a "unique status" by virtue of the national labor policy against discrimination, as expressed in both the NLRA, see United Packinghouse Workers Union v. NLRB, 416 F.2d 1126, cert. den. 396 U.S. 903, 90 S.Ct. 216, 24 L.Ed.2d 179 (1969), and in Title VII of the Civil Rights Act of 1964, 42 U.S.C. §§ 2000e et seq. [42 U.S.C.A. §§ 2000e et seq.], and that the Board had not adequately taken account of the necessity to accommodate the exclusive bargaining principle of the NLRA to the national policy of protecting action taken in opposition to discrimination from employer retaliation.[6] The court recognized that protection of the minority group concerted activity involved in this case would interfere to some extent with the orderly collective-bargaining process, but it considered the disruptive effect on that process to be outweighed where protection of minority activity is necessary to full and immediate realization of the policy against discrimination. In formulating a standard for distinguishing between protected and unprotected activity, the majority held that the "Board should inquire, in cases such as this, whether the union was actually remedying the discrimination to the *fullest extent possible by the most expedient and efficacious means.* Where the union's efforts fall short of this high standard, the minority group's concerted activity cannot lose its section 7 protection." Accordingly, the court remanded the case for the Board to make this determination and, if it found in favor of the employees, to consider whether

---

[handwritten: ✱] them of the protection of the Act. The Board decision is therefore grounded squarely on the view that a minority group member may not by-pass the Union and bargain directly over matters affecting minority employees, and not at all on the tactics used in this particular attempt to obtain such bargaining.

Member Jenkins dissented on the ground that the employees' activity was protected by § 7 because it concerned the terms and conditions of their employment. Member Brown agreed but expressly relied upon his view that the facts revealed no attempt to bargain "but simply to urge [the Company] to take action to correct conditions of racial discrimination which the employees reasonably believed existed at The Emporium." 192 NLRB, at 179.

6. ✱   ✱   ✱

Section 704(a) of Title VII, 42 U.S.C. § 2000e–3(a) [42 U.S.C.A. § 2000e–3(a)] provides:

"It shall be an unlawful employment practice for an employer to discriminate against any of his employees or applicants for employment, for an employment agency, or joint labor-management committee controlling apprenticeship or other training or retraining, including on-the-job training programs, to discriminate against any individual, or for a labor organization to discriminate against any member thereof or applicant for membership, because he has opposed any practice made an unlawful employment practice by this subchapter, or because he has made a charge, testified, assisted, or participated in any manner in an investigation, proceeding, or hearing under this subchapter."

their particular tactics were so disloyal to their employer as to deprive them of § 7 protection under our decision in NLRB v. Local Union No. 1229, 346 U.S. 464, 74 S.Ct. 172, 98 L.Ed. 195 (1953).

II

Before turning to the central questions of labor policy raised by this case, it is important to have firmly in mind the character of the underlying conduct to which we apply them. As stated, the Trial Examiner and the Board found that the employees were discharged for attempting to bargain with the Company over the terms and conditions of employment as they affected racial minorities. Although the Court of Appeals expressly declined to set aside this finding, respondent has devoted considerable effort to attacking it in this Court, on the theory that the employees were attempting only to present a grievance to their employer within the meaning of the first proviso to § 9(a).[7] We see no occasion to disturb the finding of the Board. Universal Camera Corp. v. NLRB, 340 U.S. 474, 491, 71 S.Ct. 456, 95 L.Ed. 456 (1951). The issue, then, is whether such attempts to engage in separate bargaining are protected by § 7 of the Act or proscribed by § 9(a).

A

* * * Central to the policy of fostering collective bargaining, where the employees elect that course, is the principle of majority rule. See NLRB v. Jones & Laughlin Steel Corp., 301 U.S. 1, 57 S.Ct. 615, 81 L.Ed. 893, 108 A.L.R. 1352 (1937). If the majority

---

7. That proviso states:
"That any individual employee or a group of employees shall have the right at any time to present grievances to their employer and to have such grievances adjusted, without the intervention of the bargaining representative, as long as the adjustment is not inconsistent with the terms of a collective-bargaining contract or agreement then in effect * * *."

Respondent clearly misapprehends the nature of the "right" conferred by this section. The intendment of the proviso is to permit employees to present grievances and to authorize the employer to entertain them without opening itself to liability for dealing directly with employees in derogation of the duty to bargain only with the exclusive bargaining representative, a violation of § 8(a)(5). H.R.Rep.No. 245, 80th Cong., 1st Sess., p. 7 (1947);

H.R.Rep.No.510, 80th Cong., 1st Sess., p. 46 (1947) (Conference Comm). The Act nowhere protects this "right" by making it an unfair labor practice for an employer to refuse to entertain such a presentation, nor can it be read to authorize resort to economic coercion. This matter is fully explicated in Black-Clawson Co. v. Machinists, 313 F.2d 179 (C.A.2 1962). See also Republic Steel v. Maddox, 379 U.S. 650, 85 S.Ct. 614, 13 L.Ed.2d 580 (1965). If the employees' activity in the present case is to be deemed protected, therefore, it must be so by reason of the reading given to the main part of § 9(a), in light of Title VII and the national policy against employment discrimination, and not by burdening the proviso to that section with a load it was not meant to carry.

of a unit chooses union representation, the NLRA permits them to bargain with their employer to make union membership a condition of employment, thereby imposing their choice upon the minority. 29 U.S.C. §§ 157, 158(a)(3) [29 U.S.C.A. §§ 157, 158(a)(3)]. In establishing a regime of majority rule, Congress sought to secure to all members of the unit the benefits of their collective strength and bargaining power, in full awareness that the superior strength of some individuals or groups might be subordinated to the interest of the majority. Vaca v. Sipes, 386 U.S. 171, 182, 87 S.Ct. 903, 17 L.Ed.2d 842 (1967); J. I. Case Co. v. NLRB, 321 U.S. 332, 338–339, 88 L.Ed. 762, 64 S.Ct. 576 (1944); H.R.Rep. No. 972, 74th Cong., 1st Sess., 18, II Leg. Hist. of the NLRA 2974 (1935). As a result, "[t]he complete satisfaction of all who are represented is hardly to be expected." Ford Motor Co. v. Huffman, 345 U.S. 330, 338, 73 S.Ct. 681, 97 L.Ed. 1048 (1953).

* * *

In vesting the representatives of the majority with this broad power Congress did not, of course, authorize a tyranny of the majority over minority interests. First, it confined the exercise of these powers to the context of a "unit appropriate for the purposes of collective bargaining," i. e., a group of employees with a sufficient commonality of circumstances to ensure against the submergence of a minority with distinctively different interests in the terms and conditions of their employment. See Allied Chemical Workers v. Pittsburgh Plate Glass Co., 404 U.S. 157, 171, 92 S.Ct. 383, 30 L.Ed. 2d 341 (1971). Second, it undertook in the 1959 Landrum-Griffin amendments, 73 Stat. 519, to assure that minority voices are heard as they are in the functioning of a democratic institution. Third, we have held, by the very nature of the exclusive bargaining representative's status as representative of all unit employees, Congress implicitly imposed upon it a duty fairly and in good faith to represent the interests of minorities within the unit. Vaca v. Sipes, supra; Wallace Corp. v. NLRB, 323 U.S. 248, 89 L.Ed. 216, 65 S.Ct. 238 (1944); cf. Steele v. Louisville & N. R. Co., 323 U.S. 192, 65 S.Ct. 226, 89 L. Ed. 173 (1944). And the Board has taken the position that a union's refusal to process grievances against racial discrimination, in violation of that duty, is an unfair labor practice. Hughes Tool Co., 147 NLRB 1573 (1964); see Miranda Fuel Co., 140 NLRB 181 (1962), enforcement denied 326 F.2d 172 (C.A.2 1963). Indeed, the Board has ordered a union implicated by a collective-bargaining agreement in discrimination with an employer to propose specific contractual provisions to prohibit racial discrimination. See Local Union No. 12, United Rubber Workers of America v. NLRB, 368 F.2d 12 (C.A.5 1966) (enforcement granted).

B

Against this background of long and consistent adherence to the principle of exclusive representation tempered by safeguards for the protection of minority interests, respondent urges this Court to fashion a limited exception to that principle: employees who seek to bargain separately with their employer as to the elimination of racially discriminatory employment practices peculiarly affecting them, should be free from the constraints of the exclusivity principle of § 9(a). Essentially because established procedures under Title VII or, as in this case, a grievance machinery, are too time-consuming, the national labor policy against discrimination requires this exception, respondent argues, and its adoption would not unduly compromise the legitimate interests of either unions or employers.

Plainly, national labor policy embodies the principles of non-discrimination as a matter of highest priority, Alexander v. Gardner-Denver Co., 415 U.S. 36, 47, 94 S.Ct. 1011, 39 L.Ed.2d 147 (1974), and it is a commonplace that we must construe the NLRA in light of the broad national labor policy of which it is a part. See Textile Workers v. Lincoln Mills, 353 U.S. 448, 456–458, 77 S.Ct. 912, 1 L.Ed. 2d 972 (1957). These general principles do not aid respondent, however, as it is far from clear that separate bargaining is necessary to help eliminate discrimination. Indeed, as the facts of this case demonstrate, the proposed remedy might have just the opposite effect. The collective-bargaining agreement in this case prohibited without qualification all manner of invidious discrimination and made any claimed violation a grievable issue. The grievance procedure is directed precisely at determining whether discrimination has occurred. That orderly determination, if affirmative, could lead to an arbitral award enforceable in court. Nor is there any reason to believe that the processing of grievances is inherently limited to the correction of individual cases of discrimination. Quite apart from the essentially contractual question of whether the Union could grieve against a "pattern or practice" it deems inconsistent with the nondiscrimination clause of the contract, one would hardly expect an employer to continue in effect an employment practice that routinely results in adverse arbitral decisions.

The decision by a handful of employees to bypass the grievance procedure in favor of attempting to bargain with their employer, by contrast, may or may not be predicated upon the actual existence of discrimination. An employer confronted with bargaining demands from each of several minority groups would not necessarily, or even probably, be able to agree to remedial steps satisfactory to all at once. Competing claims on the employer's ability to accommodate each group's demands, e. g., for reassignments and promotions to a limited number of positions, could only set one group against the other even if it is not the employer's intention to divide and overcome them. Having divided themselves, the minority employees will not be in position to advance their cause unless it be by recourse *seriatim* to economic coercion, which can only have the effect of further dividing them along racial or other lines. Nor is the situation materially different where, as apparently happened here, self-designated representatives purport to speak for all groups that might consider themselves to be victims of discrimination. Even if in actual bargaining the various groups did not perceive their interests as divergent and further subdivide themselves, the employer would be bound to bargain with them in a field largely preempted by the current collective-bargaining agreement with the elected bargaining representative.

* * *

What has been said here in evaluating respondent's claim that the policy against discrimination requires § 7 protection for concerted efforts at minority bargaining has obvious implications for the related claim that legitimate employer and union interests would not be unduly compromised thereby. The court below minimized the impact on the Union in this case by noting that it was not working at cross-purposes with the dissidents, and that indeed it could not do so consistent with its duty of fair representation and perhaps its obligations under Title VII. As to the Company, its obligations under Title VII are cited for the proposition that it could have no legitimate objection to bargaining with the dissidents in order to achieve full compliance with that law.

This argument confuses the employees' substantive right to be free of racial discrimination with the procedures available under the NLRA for securing these rights. Whether they are thought to depend upon Title VII or have an independent source in the NLRA, they cannot be pursued at the expense of the orderly collective-bargaining process contemplated by the NLRA. The elimination of discrimination and its vestiges is an appropriate subject of bargaining, and an employer may have no objection to incorporating into a collective agreement the substance of his obligation not to discriminate in personnel decisions; the Company here has done as much, making any claimed dereliction a matter subject to the grievance-arbitration machinery as well as to the processes of Title VII. But that does not mean that he may not have strong and legitimate objections to bargaining on several fronts over the implementation of the right to be free of discrimination for some of the reasons set forth above. Similarly, while a union cannot lawfully bargain for the establishment or continuation of discriminatory practices, see Steele v. Louisville & N. R. Co., supra, 42 U.S.C. § 2000–2(c)(3) [42 U.S.C.A. § 2000–2(c)(3)], it has a legitimate interest in presenting a united front on this as on other issues and in not seeing its strength dissipated and its stature denigrated by subgroups within the unit separately pursuing what they see as separate interests. When union and employer are not responsive to their legal obligations, the bargain they have struck must yield pro tanto to the law, whether by means of conciliation through the offices of the EEOC, or by means of federal court enforcement at the instance of either that agency or the party claiming to be aggrieved.

Accordingly, we think neither aspect of respondent's contention in support of a right to short-circuit orderly, established processes for eliminating discrimination in employment is well-founded. The policy of industrial self-determination as expressed in § 7 does not require fragmentation of the bargaining unit along racial or other lines in order to consist with the national labor policy against discrimination. And in the face of such fragmentation, whatever its effect on discriminatory practices, the bargaining process that the principle of exclusive representation is meant to lubricate could not endure unhampered.

[In Part III of its opinion, the Court considered whether the exclusive-representation policies of the NLRA were to be subordinated to the very specific protection accorded by Title VII against employer reprisals for employee efforts to oppose unlawful discrimination. See note 7 supra. The Court, assuming arguendo that Section 704(a) protects employee picketing and the institution of a consumer boycott of an employer, held nonetheless that violations of that section were to be challenged under the procedures set forth in Title VII. To the employees' claim that NLRB unfair labor practice proceedings are more expeditious and effective than remedies involving the EEOC, the Court responded that this argument "is properly addressed to the Congress and not to this Court or the NLRB."]

MR. JUSTICE DOUGLAS, dissenting.

The Court's opinion makes these union members—and others similarly situated—prisoners of the union. The law, I think, was designed to prevent that tragic consequence. Hence, I dissent.

Petitioners, who are black and were members of a union through which they obtained employment by the Emporium, would seem to have suffered rank discrimination because of their race. They theoretically had a cause of action against their union for breach of its duty of fair representation spelled out in Steele v. Louisville R. Co., 323 U.S. 192, 65 S.Ct. 226, 89 L.Ed. 173. But as the law on that phase of the problem has evolved it would seem that the burden on the employee is heavy. See Vaca v. Sipes, 386 U.S. 171, 190, 87 S.Ct.

903, 17 L.Ed.2d 842, where it was held that the union action must be "arbitrary, discriminatory, and in bad faith."

The employees might also have sought relief under Title VII of the Civil Rights Act of 1964, which forbids discrimination in employment on the basis of "race, color, religion, sex or national origin."
* * *

In this case, the employees took neither of the foregoing courses, each fraught with obstacles, but picketed to protest Emporium's practices. I believe these were "concerted activities" protected under § 7 of the National Labor Relations Act. The employees were engaged in a traditional form of labor protest, directed at matters which are unquestionably a proper subject of employee concern. * * *

The Board has held that the employees were unprotected because they sought to confront the employer outside the grievance process, which was under union control. The Court upholds the Board, on the view that this result is commanded by the principle of "exclusive representation" embodied in § 9 of the NLRA. But in the area of racial discrimination the union is hardly in a position to demand exclusive control, for the employee's right to nondiscriminatory treatment does not depend upon union demand but is based on the law.
* * *

The law should facilitate the involvement of unions in the quest for racial equality in employment, but it should not make the individual a prisoner of the union. While employees may reasonably be required to approach the union first, as a kind of "exhaustion" requirement before resorting to economic protest, cf N.L.R.B. v. Tanner Motor Livery, 419 F.2d 216 (C.A.9 1969), they should not be under continued inhibition when it becomes apparent that the union response is inadequate. The Court of Appeals held that the employees should be protected from discharge unless the Board found on remand that the union had been prosecuting their complaints "to the fullest extent possible, by the most expeditious means." I would not disturb this standard. Union conduct can be oppressive even if not made in bad faith. The inertia of weak-kneed, docile union leadership can be as devastating to the cause of racial equality as aggressive subversion. Continued submission by employees to such a regime should not be demanded.

I would affirm the judgment below.

Problems for Discussion

1. Had there been no union and no collective bargaining agreement at the Emporium store, would not Hollins and Hawkins have been clearly engaging in "concerted activity for mutual aid or protection" protected by

Section 7? (Put aside the question whether their abusive terminology might warrant forfeiting this protection.) Does the fact that there *is* a designated union—which Hollins and Hawkins earnestly believe to be inadequately representing the interests of a substantial number of employees—make their peaceful concerted activity any less within the language, and the spirit, of Section 7? (As with the *J. I. Case* decision, is not Section 9(a) taking back important individual and group rights which Section 7 appears clearly to grant?)

2. Although the Board and the Supreme Court make much of the finding that Hollins and Hawkins had demanded to "bargain" with the company president, would the case have been decided any differently had it been found that this was not their purpose? What exactly was it about their activity which led to the conclusion that they sought to "bargain"?

3. Assume that Smith, a black employee of the Emporium Capwell Co., was passed over for a promotion which he claims was due him under the terms of the collective bargaining agreement. Believing that he can present his grievance more aggressively and effectively than can the union, Smith has written to the Company president to demand an interview and to demand that the promotion be given to him; his letter also asserts that if the labor contract as presently written does provide for the promotion of another in preference to him, the contract ought to be promptly changed. Smith states that he is willing to meet alone with the Company president, but that he would much prefer to have along with him employees Jones and Williams (who are also officers in the Western Addition Community Organization). You are counsel for the Company, and the president has consulted you as to the response he should give to Smith's letter. What issues do you see and what advice would you give your client?

NOTE ON THE LIMITS OF MAJORITY RULE

As *J. I. Case* and *Emporium Capwell* make clear, the interests and wishes of individuals and minority groups within the bargaining unit must be subordinated to the exclusive-bargaining status of the majority labor organization. It is inevitable that, on occasion, certain groups or individuals will believe that the bargaining representative is ignoring their interests. Does the law provide any recourse?

(1) In defining the *appropriate bargaining unit,* the Board will attempt to exclude groups of workers who have a conflict of interests, or who lack a community of interests, with the unit in which the election will be held. The excluded group will then be able to select their own majority representative, or no representative at all.

(2) The Board and the Supreme Court have deduced from the power given by the NLRA to the exclusive representative *a duty of fair representation.* The union is thus forbidden by law to bargain

for a contract or to process grievances in a manner which is hostile, or in bad faith, or arbitrary with regard to individuals or groups within the bargaining unit. The duty was first created in cases of racially segregated unions, where the majority union with exclusively white membership discriminated against black workers in the unit in negotiating terms of employment; this form of hostile and unreasonable discrimination was held to violate an implied duty of fair representation, for which the injured workers could sue in a federal district court. Thereafter, the NLRB held that a union violation of the duty of fair representation is also an unfair labor practice. It has been held unlawful for a union to draw distinctions in bargaining or grievance processing on the basis of race or sex, union membership (very clearly a violation of Section 8(b) (2)), dissidence within the union, or personal hostility to the individuals involved.

(3) Employees have the periodic right to vote out the union in a *decertification election*, whether the union was initially recognized informally or was the victor in an NLRB representation election. The frequency of such elections is, of course, limited by the election-bar and certification-bar rules and particularly by the contract-bar rule, by which the incumbent union can insulate itself against a decertification election for up to three years.

(4) The Landrum-Griffin Act of 1959 provides for what is known as a *bill of rights for union members*. Its purpose is to guarantee a substantial measure of democratic rights and procedures within the internal affairs of the union, so that minority groups within the union have the opportunity to modify union policies. Members are given the right to speak on all matters at union meetings, to vote for candidates for union office, and to be eligible to stand for election to union office (subject to "reasonable" union rules).

(5) A worker who is in the bargaining unit for which the majority union speaks *does not automatically have to become a member* of that union. A unit member must become a union "member" only if the employer and the union negotiate a collective bargaining provision making membership a condition of continued employment; this is known as a union-shop provision, and Congress has chosen to permit this one exception to the mandates of Section 8(a)(3) through the provisos to that section. The "membership" that the employer and the union may agree to require is no more than the obligation to pay to the union an amount equivalent to union dues; the theory is that all employees in the unit receive the benefits of the union's activities as bargaining representative and grievance processor, so that it is reasonable to require all employees to pay a "fee" for such services. Section 14(b) of the NLRA empowers

states to enact "right to work" laws which make such union-shop provisions unlawful and unenforceable (an unusual deference to state policy in the midst of a comprehensive scheme of federal regulation).

(6) On matters other than "wages, hours, and other terms or conditions of employment"—that is, on so-called *nonmandatory subjects*—there is no duty to bargain exclusively with the majority representative, and on these matters individual or minority-group bargaining can lawfully be carried on.

(7) As already noted in connection with *Emporium Capwell,* the proviso to Section 9(a) explicitly preserves to individual employees the right to *present and to process grievances.*

All of these limitations on majority rule are explored in greater detail elsewhere in this book.

B. THE DUTY TO BARGAIN IN GOOD FAITH [8]

In 1947, Congress defined what it meant for an employer or labor organization to be obligated to "bargain collectively," as required by Sections 8(a)(5) and 8(b)(3), respectively. Section 8(d) provides that

> "to bargain collectively is the performance of the mutual obligation of the employer and the representative of the employees to meet at reasonable times and confer in good faith with respect to wages, hours, and other terms and conditions of employment, or the negotiation of an agreement, or any question arising thereunder, and the execution of a written contract incorporating any agreement reached if requested by either party, but such obligation does not compel either party to agree to a proposal or require the making of a concession."

Clearly, the statute requires that certain conduct be objectively manifested. The parties must "meet at reasonable times and confer" and must if requested execute a writing that incorporates any agreement reached. As starkly clear as these directives seem, they are not free of ambiguity. How long an interval between meetings is "unreasonable"? Are there any circumstances under which the employer (or union) may be excused from meeting at all? It is, for example, generally understood that the parties are not obliged

8. See Cox, The Duty to Bargain in Good Faith, 71 Harv.L.Rev. 1401 (1958); Duvin, The Duty to Bargain: Law in Search of Policy, 64 Col.L.Rev. 248 (1964); Fleming, The Obligation to Bargain in Good Faith, 47 Va.L.Rev. 988 (1961); Gross, Cullen & Hanslowe, Good Faith in Labor Negotiations: Tests and Remedies, 53 Cornell L.Rev. 1009 (1968); Smith, Evolution of the "Duty to Bargain" Concept in American Law, 39 Mich.L.Rev. 1065 (1941).

to continue meeting once they have in good faith bargained to a deadlock or "impasse" and it appears that further discussions would be fruitless; until circumstances change sufficiently to break the impasse (most obviously, if one party modifies its demands and requests a meeting), the duty to bargain is satisfied without "meeting." The court in dictum in General Electric Co. v. NLRB, p. 304 supra, stated that in some rare instances a party could refuse to meet for negotiations if the composition of the bargaining team across the table was purposely selected in order to be disruptive and offensive. Even less clear than the duty to "meet" is the duty to "confer." Most of the Problems for Discussion which follow this Note invite analysis of that statutory requirement.

The duty to bargain prescribed by Section 8(d) encompasses not only the obligation to meet and confer with respect to wages, hours and terms and conditions of employment. It includes the obligation to bargain "in good faith." The reasons for this requirement have been described as follows:

> "It was not enough for the law to compel the parties to meet and treat without passing judgment upon the quality of the negotiations. The bargaining status of a union can be destroyed by going through the motions of negotiating almost as easily as by bluntly withholding recognition. The NLRB reports are filled with cases in which a union won an election but lacked the economic power to use the strike as a weapon for compelling the employer to grant it real participation in industrial government. As long as there are unions weak enough to be talked to death, there will be employers who are tempted to engage in the forms of bargaining without the substance. The concept of 'good faith' was brought into the law of collective bargaining as a solution to this problem." [9]

The duty to bargain "in good faith" has been defined in general terms on many occasions. A typical formulation is that of the Court of Appeals for the Ninth Circuit in N.L.R.B. v. Montgomery Ward & Co., 133 F.2d 676 (9th Cir. 1943), where the court described the duty as "an obligation * * * to participate actively in the deliberations so as to indicate a present intention to find a basis for agreement." Not only must the employer have "an open mind and a sincere desire to reach an agreement" but "a sincere effort must be made to reach a common ground." Is this a useful formulation? How literally can its application be made the basis

9. Cox, The Duty to Bargain in Good Faith, 71 Harv.L.Rev. 1401, 1412–13 (1958).

of decision? In reading the following cases, see if you can develop any preferable formulation.

Although bad faith may occasionally be demonstrated by the declarations of the party in question, proof must ordinarily be derived by drawing inferences from external conduct. In some cases, an argument may be made that bad faith can be inferred from the nature of the substantive proposals which the respondent has made during the negotiations. The *White* decision, infra, is illustrative. More often, an effort is made to determine bad faith from the tactics or procedures employed by the respondent in bargaining with the other party. In certain cases, the Board has sought to single out particular tactics used by the respondent as *per se* violations of the duty to bargain in good faith. See the *Insurance Agents, Katz* and *Truitt Mfg.* cases, infra. In other proceedings, a finding of bad faith has been based upon the totality of the bargaining tactics employed. See the *General Electric* case, infra.

Problems for Discussion

1. Because of past disputes, during the term of several contracts, about the intended meaning of contract provisions and about oral assurances given at past negotiation sessions, the company wishes to know whether it may condition bargaining in the future upon the presence in the bargaining room of a certified court stenographer who is to prepare a verbatim transcript of the proceedings. The union has already stated that it regards the presence of a stenographer in negotiations as an insult, that it objects to the practice, and that it is prepared to challenge it by filing a charge under Section 8(a)(5). Advise the company concerning the legality (and the wisdom) of its position. See Latrobe Steel Co. v. NLRB, 630 F.2d 171 (3d Cir. 1980). (Can the company lawfully "get the upper hand" simply by bringing in the stenographer as part of the company's bargaining team, or simply by turning on a tape recorder when negotiations begin?)

2. Immediately after its certification as collective bargaining representative of employees of the Ames Cotton Company, TWUA presented a proposed contract and asked for a conference with Ames's executives. At the conference TWUA explained its proposals and gave supporting reasons. Ames asked a good many questions about their meaning and effect and at the end of the conference its president said, "I am sure we understand your position, although we would be glad to meet again if you think there is anything which requires further clarification. However, we cannot agree to any of your demands. If there is no further business, we may as well adjourn." Has Ames committed an unfair labor practice?

3. Carolina Cotton Company engaged in collective bargaining with TWUA Local 53, the certified representative of its employees, and a tentative agreement was reached on nearly all the terms of a collective agree-

ment including wages. Several times during the negotiations Local 53 broached the subject of union security and asked the company to agree to put a union shop clause into the contract. On the first occasion Andrews, the vice president in charge of industrial relations, replied, "We will not sign a union shop contract. Our minds are made up. Let's not waste time arguing about it. I know all the arguments, and you know that I know them. I made them all and suggested every conceivable compromise during the ten years I was a federal conciliator. Now let's get back to business." Whenever the union came back to this subject, Andrews left the room saying, "You're just wasting time." Has the company violated Section 8(a) (5)?

4. The Union represents employees at a number of supermarkets in the metropolitan area, and recently won a representation election at the Ace Supermarket. At the first scheduled bargaining session, the Union representative handed over to the Ace negotiating team a copy of a collective bargaining agreement, which was said to be "the same contract that is signed by every market we represent; we can't make any changes with you, or else every other market in the area will expect to get the same changes, and we are not prepared to renegotiate with everybody else. We'll be glad to explain what the reasons are for each of these provisions, but you'll have to sign it as is." Has the Union violated Section 8(b)(3)?

WHITE v. NLRB

United States Court of Appeals, Fifth Circuit, 1958.
255 F.2d 564.

TUTTLE, CIRCUIT JUDGE. This is a petition by the individual petitioners, doing business as White's Uvalde Mines, to review and set aside an order of the National Labor Relations Board, and a cross-request by the Board that the order be enforced. * * *

[W]e find that we are at last required to determine whether, in an otherwise unassailable attitude of collective bargaining, the employer may nevertheless be found guilty of a failure to bargain in good faith solely upon a consideration of the content of the proposals and counter proposals of the parties. In other words may the charge of refusal to bargain in good faith be sustained solely by reference to the terms of the employment contract which management finally says it is willing to sign if such proposed contract could fairly be found to be one which would leave the employees in no better state than they were without it. For the purpose of considering this question we may assume that the Board could find that the terms of the contract insisted on by the company requiring the surrender by the employees of their right to strike and their agreeing to leave to management the right to hire and fire and fix wages in return for agreements by the company respecting grievances and security that gave the union little, if any, real voice in these important aspects of employment relations would in fact have left the union in no better position than if it had no contract. It is perfectly apparent that the company representatives approached the bargaining table with a full understanding of their obligations to meet with, and discuss with, representatives of the employees any terms and conditions of employment that either party put forward; that they must at least expose themselves to such argument and persuasion as could be put forward, and that they must try to seek an area of agreement at least as to some of the terms of employment; that if they were able to arrive at such agreement they must be willing to reduce it to writing and sign it. It is, of some significance that at the fourth of the six bargaining sessions, when challenged by the employees' bargaining agent the company's managing partner signed the company's proposed complete contract and tendered it to the union, which declined to accept it. The question is: Can the company's insistence on terms overall favorable to it in net result be taken as proof that it did not approach the bargaining table in good faith, but that it approached the bargaining table only to give the outward sign of compliance when it had already excluded the possibility of agreement? * * *

issue

We start with the statute which states specifically that the "obligation [to bargain collectively] does not compel either party to agree to a proposal or require the making of a concession." The Board, in its brief, recognizes this but fails to give effect to it in stating its contention. Cf. NLRB v. San Angelo Standard, 5 Cir., 228 F.2d 504. Immediately after outlining nine different points of difference between the parties,[10] the brief says:

obligation does not compel concession

10. It would extend this opinion too greatly to outline in detail the proposals and counter proposals and the responses of the parties to them at the seven different bargaining sessions. However, it would seem that the statement of the criticized actions of the company, as enumerated by counsel for the Board in its brief, is as strong a presentation of the Board's views as is available. With some comments added by the Court, the brief says:

"A fair summary of the Company's bargaining in this case reveals the following:

"1. The Company, while insisting on a 'no strike' clause with provisions for union liability in the case of breach, at first resisted a corresponding 'no lockout' clause, and after agreeing to such a clause refused at all times to

agree to a provision calling for corresponding liability in the event of its breach.

"2. As the courts have recognized, a union's contractual waiver of its statutory right to strike is normally accompanied by a provision that disputes between the parties will be settled by grievance procedures and arbitration rather than by such 'self-help' measures as strikes. But the Company in this case coupled its insistence on a no-strike clause with an insistence that matters going to arbitration must be decided in the Company's favor if there was any evidence that the Company's position was not arbitrary or capricious. Such limited arbitration would leave the Union 'hamstrung' in a dispute with the Company, unable

"We do not contend that any one of the foregoing specifications * * * [11] would standing alone constitute a refusal to bargain. We do urge, however, that on the record as a whole,[12] and in accord with such authorities as Majure v. NLRB, 5 Cir., 198 F.2d 735; NLRB v. Denton, 5 Cir.,

to strike or to secure a review on the merits by the arbitrators.

"3. The Company at no time acceded to any proposal for the selection of a neutral arbitrator, in the event the arbitrators chosen by the Union and the Company could not agree. [The company proposal was that the two arbitrators select the third.]

"4. In the absence of any contract, the Company could not lawfully change its wage rates or grant merit increases or alter shop rules relating to working conditions without first bargaining with the Union over those changes. But the Company insisted, as a condition of the contract, that the Union surrender its right to bargain about those matters, and leave the Company free to act in a manner which, but for the contract, would be violative of the law.

"5. Although the Company professed to find the matters of house rentals and physical examinations 'of no importance', it insisted that the contract contain no provision as to the Union's right to bargain over the rental rates of Company houses, and further insisted that the contract require the employees to submit to a physical examination by the Company doctor, whose word as to employment would be final. The Company's intransigent attitude over matters which it regarded as unimportant is itself suggestive of a want of good faith. [The company insisted that these matters were important to it, but not to the employees, because in neither respect had there been any complaint as to the company's attitude.]

"6. The Company rejected the Union's request that the contract provide for bargaining over the annual bonus, although in the absence of a contract such bonuses are matters over which bargaining is required. NLRB v. Niles-Bement-Pond Co., 2 Cir., 199 F. 2d 713.

"7. Admitting that its minimum wage rate was substantially lower than comparable rates in the area, the Company at first 'stood pat' on wages, and eventually offered an increase to less than that embodied in the amendment to the federal wage and hour law, then being debated in Congress. [The statement that the Company admitted its minimum rate was substantially lower than comparable rates is strongly contested by the Company. The proposed increase was a minimum of 90 cents per hour, which was the minimum actually enacted months later].

"8. Notwithstanding substantial concessions by the Union in the course of the negotiations, the Company characterized the Union's second proposal as 'about the same' as its first one, and the Union's third proposal as 'not substantially different'. Such a denial of the realities of the Union's efforts to compromise differences hardly comports with a good faith desire to bargain.

"9. Granting little beyond such bare requirements as a provision against discrimination, the Company took the attitude, expressed by its chief negotiator, that 'we are giving the contract, and that is something.' This attitude, we submit falls far short of what this Court has described as 'a duty * * * to enter into discussion with an open and fair mind, and a sincere purpose to find a basis of agreement touching wages and hours and conditions of employment, and if found to embody it in a contract as specific as possible * * *'. Globe Cotton Mills v. NLRB [5 Cir.], 103 F.2d 91, 94."

11. The omitted part is a parenthetical reference to a tenth item that occurred after the strike had collapsed and is not germane to this discussion.

12. We assume by this is meant "all nine of them together with the unilateral increase of wages" heretofore eliminated by us.

217 F.2d 567, 570, certiorari denied 348 U.S. 981 [75 S.Ct. 572, 99 L.Ed. 764]; NLRB v. Reed & Prince Mfg. Co., 1 Cir., 205 F.2d 131, certiorari denied 346 U.S. 887 [74 S.Ct. 139, 98 L.Ed. 391], and NLRB v. Century Cement Mfg. Co., 2 Cir., 208 F.2d 84, the Board could reasonably find that the Company had not approached the bargaining in the good faith spirit required by the Act."

Thus the Board is saying that although the statute says no concession need be made and no item need be agreed upon, if a company fails to concede *anything* substantial,[13] then this is too much, and such failure amounts to bad faith.

The language of the Courts is not, as it cannot be, in construing this difficult statute, entirely clear, but we find no case which precisely supports the proposition here asserted by the Board. The principal basis of the Board's attack here is the broad management function clause and the failure to agree to a real arbitration clause in which the arbitrators have final powers. The remaining provisions criticized by the Board could not conceivably be considered as proof of bad faith by the petitioners. As to the inclusion of a broad management functions clause and thus a refusal to permit matters relating to hiring, discharging, hours and working conditions to be subject to grievance procedures and arbitration, the Supreme Court has said:

> "Congress provided expressly that the Board should not pass upon the desirability of the substanti[ve] terms of labor agreements. Whether a contract should contain a clause fixing standards for such matters as work scheduling or should provide for more flexible treatment of such matters is an issue for determination across the bargaining table, not by the Board. If the latter approach is agreed upon, the extent of union and management participation in the administration of such matters is itself a condition of employment to be settled by bargaining.

> "Accordingly, we reject the Board's holding that bargaining for the management functions clause proposed by respondent was, per se, an unfair labor practice." National Labor Relations Board v. American National Insurance Co., 343 U.S. 395.[14]

---

13. Although it is here assumed that no net substantial concessions were made, the company vigorously asserts it made some of substance during the negotiations.

14. The terms of the management functions clause there before the Court was:
"The right to select and hire, to promote to a better position, to discharge, demote or discipline for cause, and to maintain discipline and efficiency of employees and to determine the schedules of work is recognized by both union and company as the proper responsibility and prerogative of management to be held and exercised by the company, and while it is agreed that an employee feeling himself to have been aggrieved by any decision of the company in respect to such mat-

If such a clause is not per se proof of failure to bargain in good faith then *a fortiori* insistence on physical examination by the company's own doctor, refusal to include terms of a Christmas bonus, a refusal to grant specified wage increases, refusal to "freeze" rent and utility charges on company-owned houses and like issues could not either separately or collectively constitute such proof.   *   *   *

[The court then distinguished two of its earlier decisions. In Majure v. NLRB, 198 F.2d 735 (5th Cir. 1952), the company not only insisted on an agreement wholly favorable to itself but also stated when bargaining that its workers had "no right to be in the union" and that "there was no place for a contract" at the company; although the company persistently refused to consider union requests for increased compensation and paid vacations, it later unilaterally granted a raise in its commission rates and granted paid vacations. In NLRB v. Denton, 217 F.2d 567 (5th Cir. 1954), the company made repeated statements that it "would never sign a contract with any union."]

We do not hold that under no possible circumstances can the mere content of the various proposals and counter proposals of management and union be sufficient evidence of a want of good faith to justify a holding to that effect. We can conceive of one party to such bargaining procedure suggesting proposals of such a nature or type or couched in such objectionable language that they would be calculated to disrupt any serious negotiations. A careful study of the record before us, and viewed with all the adverse emphasis the Board has placed upon the challenged actions of the company in its brief, footnote [10] supra, leaves us with the clear impression that the Board erred in finding adequate proof of a failure to bargain in good faith.

RIVES, CIRCUIT JUDGE, dissenting.   *   *   *   Collective bargaining is at the very heart and core of the Labor Management Relations Act. If, in any particular case, effective collective bargaining is not had and cannot be required, then in that case the Act is nothing. It follows that there must be some protection against "merely going through the motions of negotiating," "a predetermined resolve not to budge from an initial position," "surface bargaining" accompanied by "a purpose to defeat it and wilful obstruction of it," "shadow boxing to a draw," "giving the Union a runaround while purporting to be meeting with the Union for the purpose of collective bargaining."   *   *   *

ters, or the union in his behalf, shall have the right to have such decision reviewed by top management officials of the company under the grievance machinery hereinafter set forth, it is further agreed that the final decision of the company made by such top management officials shall not be further reviewable by arbitration."

Chief Judge Magruder, speaking for the First Circuit in NLRB v. Reed & Prince Mfg. Co., 1953, 205 F.2d 131, 134, 135, made an admirable expression of the same principle:

> "It is true, as stated in N.L.R.B. v. American National Ins. Co., 1952, 343 U.S. 395, 404, 72 S.Ct. 824, 829, 96 L.Ed. 1027, that the Board may not 'sit in judgment upon the substantive terms of collective bargaining agreements.' But at the same time it seems clear that if the Board is not to be blinded by empty talk and by the mere surface motions of collective bargaining, it must take some cognizance of the reasonableness of the positions taken by an employer in the course of bargaining negotiations. See Wilson & Co., Inc., v. N.L.R.B., 8 Cir., 1940, 115 F.2d 759, 763. See also Smith, The Evolution of the 'Duty to Bargain' Concept in American Law, 39 Mich.L.Rev. 1065, 1108 (1941). Thus if an employer can find nothing whatever to agree to in an ordinary current-day contract submitted to him, or in some of the union's related minor requests, and if the employer makes not a single serious proposal meeting the union at least part way, then certainly the Board must be able to conclude that this is at least some evidence of bad faith, that is, of a desire not to reach an agreement with the union. In other words, while the Board cannot force an employer to make a 'concession' on any specific issue or to adopt any particular position, the employer is obliged to make *some* reasonable effort in *some* direction to compose his differences with the union, if § 8(a) (5) is to be read as imposing any substantial obligation at all." * * *

Under all of the authorities, in determining whether *either* an employer or a labor organization has failed to bargain in good faith, the Board must necessarily consider its conduct at the bargaining table, and whether it has acted reasonably or arbitrarily.

In the present case, the Company insisted on a no-strike clause with provisions for Union liability in the case of breach. It further insisted that matters going to arbitration must be decided in the Company's favor if there is any evidence that the Company's position was not arbitrary or capricious. It declined to accede to any proposal for the selection of a neutral arbitrator in the event the arbitrators chosen by the Union and the Company could not agree. While thus insisting that the Union waive its statutory right to strike, the Company declined to give any substitute, such as effective arbitration. In the recent case of Textile Workers Union of America v. Lincoln Mills, 1957, 353 U.S. 448, 455, 77 S.Ct. 912, 917, 1 L.Ed.2d 972, the Supreme Court said: "Plainly the agreement to arbitrate grievance disputes is the *quid pro quo* for an agreement not to strike."

Even without a contract, the Company could not lawfully change its wage rates, grant merit increases, or alter shop rules relating to working conditions without first bargaining with the Union. Nevertheless, the Company insisted that the Union surrender its right to bargain about those matters and leave the Company free to act as it saw fit. There are many other instances of arbitrary and unreasonable action set forth in the fair and careful intermediate report of the Trial Examiner and the decision of the Board, which leave me convinced that the Board had a rational basis for its conclusion that the Company failed to bargain in good faith. The other violations on the part of the Company make that conclusion all the more reasonable. In my opinion, that is a conclusion peculiarly within the province of the Board and which the Board is more competent to arrive at than is this Court. I, therefore, respectfully dissent.

NLRB v. CUMMER-GRAHAM CO., 279 F.2d 757 (5th Cir. 1960). The employer insisted upon a no-strike clause but would not grant the union's request for an arbitration clause. The court of appeals reversed the Board's finding of a refusal to bargain in good faith. It conceded that in practice no-strike clauses were commonly accompanied by arbitration clauses; and that "if we were entitled to an opinion, which we are not," arbitration would be a desirable adjunct. But the court concluded that a party could lawfully insist on one without the other, and that "These are matters for management and labor to resolve, if they can, at the bargaining table. If they cannot there be decided, then neither Board nor Court can compel an agreement or require a concession."

CHEVRON OIL CO. v. NLRB, 442 F.2d 1067 (5th Cir. 1971). The court reversed the Board's finding of bad faith which had been based principally on the employer's position regarding management rights as well as a no-strike no-arbitration clause. The court held that the employer, which consistently refused to adopt a number of union counterproposals on these matters, was simply utilizing its economic strength to engage in hard bargaining with a weaker union. "In our opinion the matter at hand resolves itself into purely a question of hard bargaining between two parties who were possessed of disparate economic power: A relatively weak Union encountered a relatively strong Company. The Company naturally desired to use its advantage to retain as many rights as possible. We do not believe, however, that that desire is inconsistent with good faith bargaining."

CONTINENTAL INS. CO. v. NLRB, 495 F.2d 44 (2d Cir. 1974). The employer refused to include a conventional recognition clause, and insisted on one which would force the union not to organize or represent other company employees outside the unit; it retreated from its practice of granting severance pay, first stating its flat opposition and then making a proposal "so inadequate as to be patently disingenuous"; it imposed new and stringent requirements for vacations, and took what the court characterized as the "extraordinary" position that vacations were not an earned right but were designed to enable employees to do a better job for the employer; it proposed a grievance clause which defined a grievance as limited to an alleged violation of clear and unambiguous express contract provisions, and permitted the employer to determine whether cases would go to arbitration and who the arbitrator would be; its proposals on wages would give it the right at any time to grant increases in any amounts to any employees it wished. The effect of all of these employer demands, along with a sharply restricted right to strike also proposed, would clearly have been "to place the employees in a worse position than if they had no contract at all and to require the Union in effect to waive its right to represent employees with respect to disputes over employment conditions. The Board was fully justified in concluding that the proposal was not made in good faith."

VANDERBILT PRODUCTS, INC. v. NLRB, 297 F.2d 833 (2d Cir., 1961). In bargaining with the union, the company conditioned further negotiations on acceptance by the union of a completely open shop, with no obligation of any sort to become a union member; no checkoff provision; an absolute right on the part of the employer to discharge or lay off without restriction or seniority limitation; and a five-year term for the contract. On appeal, *held, per curiam,* the employer violated its duty to bargain in good faith. In its opinion, the court quoted the following passage from NLRB v. Reed & Prince Mfg. Co., 205 F.2d 131, 139 (1st Cir.), *cert. denied,* 346 U.S. 887 (1953): "It is difficult to believe that the Company with a straight face and in good faith could have supposed that this proposal had the slightest chance of acceptance by a self-respecting union, or even that it might advance the negotiations by affording a basis of discussion; rather, it looks more like a stalling tactic by a party bent upon maintaining the pretense of bargaining."

— again, 3rd cir

Problems for Discussion

1. On September 25, 1980, after negotiations had almost been concluded for an initial contract, the employer insisted that the contract provide for a termination date of January 12, 1981, the anniversary date of the union's certification by the NLRB. Is insistence upon such a short term an unfair labor practice or merely "hard bargaining"? If objectionable, is that because it evinces an unlawful state of mind, or because

it is contrary to a legislative policy of industrial stability, or for some other reason? See *Solo Cup Co.* v. *NLRB*, 332 F.2d 447 (4th Cir. 1964); *Star Expansion Indus. Corp.*, 164 N.L.R.B. 563 (1967). How should a similar case be analyzed when the employer insists upon a contract term of five years, as in the *Vanderbilt* case, supra?

2. Since 1942 Smith Cotton Company has recognized TWUA and entered into a series of collective bargaining agreements. None of the agreements provided for a union shop or the arbitration of unsettled grievances. However, all of the contracts contained a no-strike clause, and in other respects corresponded closely to the manufacturing company agreement in the Supplement. The last agreement expired December 31, 1980. TWUA proposed a ten percent wage increase, a union shop clause and an arbitration clause. In support of these demands, the union argued that 97% of all collective bargaining agreements contain arbitration provisions and that a majority of the textile companies bargaining with TWUA had already agreed to a ten percent increase. Smith rejected all three proposals, giving extensive arguments in support of its position. The union then modified its requests to the extent of asking a six percent wage increase, a maintenance of membership clause in lieu of the union shop provision, and arbitration of grievances. At the fourth conference the union intimated that it would consider a smaller wage increase, some limitation on the arbitration clause and a willingness to be "reasonable" about union security if the company would be "reasonable" about the other issues. The company stood pat. TWUA then said, "Make us some kind of a counter-proposal to take back to the members." The company adamantly refused to make any counter-proposal, other than to point to the expired contract as one it would be willing to sign. Has the company committed an unfair labor practice?

[If it has, the union may of course file charges and ultimately expect the Board to issue a cease-and-desist order. But the ramifications for the employees may be far greater. If, for example, the employees were to strike in response to the employer's position at the bargaining table, and the employer were to hire permanent replacements, the right of the strikers to be reinstated upon request in lieu of their replacements will depend upon whether the strike was precipitated by an employer unfair labor practice or simply by a niggardly but lawful bargaining position. See pp. 864–66, infra.]

3. In response to union requests for a "checkoff" provision, pursuant to which the employer would deduct from the paycheck of all employees so authorizing periodic union dues and remit them directly to the union, the employer has consistently replied that such a provision will under no circumstances be incorporated in the agreement. At various times, the employer has given one or more of these reasons: The checkoff involves costly bookkeeping procedures; it is not the company's policy to aid the union in dues collection, which is the union's job; there is an undesirable "psychological" factor when the employees receive their pay already reduced by the amount of union dues. (In fact, the checkoff would add no measurable amount to the employer's bookkeeping expenses, and it is

already making payroll deductions for federal and state income taxes, health insurance premiums and charitable contributions.) Is the employer's persistent refusal to grant the checkoff a refusal to bargain in good faith? Need the employer, provided that it is bargaining in good faith on all other matters under discussion, give *any* reason for its refusal to grant the checkoff provision? See *Alba-Waldensian, Inc.*, 167 N.L.R.B. 695 (1967); *Farmers Co-operative Gin Ass'n*, 161 N.L.R.B. 887 (1966).

If the employer is held to have bargained in bad faith, what remedy should the board issue? See *H. K. Porter Co. v. NLRB*, 397 U.S. 99, 90 S.Ct. 821, 25 L.Ed.2d 146 (1970).

4.   On July 20, 1980, the Steelworkers were certified as the exclusive bargaining representative of the employees of Jones Company. On August 1 the union requested a meeting on the earliest possible date for the purposes of collective bargaining. The company postponed any answer and then sent word to the union that it would be impossible to arrange a meeting before Labor Day. Finally a date was made for September 15. In the interim the union requested information concerning the wage rates, age, length of service, etc., of employees in the bargaining unit in order to bargain intelligently. The information was not furnished until October. During August the union also requested permission to post certain non-controversial notices on the bulletin boards and was told that no permission could be granted until the first conference. At the conference and thereafter the company avoided taking any definite position on the matter. At the September 15th meeting the union sought to begin the discussion by exploring the subjects normally covered by a collective agreement but the company insisted that the union immediately submit its contract proposals in writing. Beginning in October there were five conferences devoted to the contract submitted by the union. They were followed by seven more conferences running through February 1981. One union request was for a substantial wage increase. The company immediately offered fifty cents an hour on condition that there be no further negotiation about the subject. The union rejected the condition stating that it would regard all economic benefits as a single package and might be able to agree to the fifty cents once such matters as pensions, insurance and holidays were settled.

With respect to the grievance procedure the company objected to the union's proposal that an employee be accompanied by the shop steward at the first step and also resisted a clause calling for ultimate arbitration. The company insisted, however, upon a no-strike clause. The union gave some ground on these points but the company rejected its modified suggestion as too complex even though it was a very typical clause and even though the company did not point out where it was too complex and how it could be simplified. The company also insisted that any grievance procedure should include the Section 9(a) proviso recognizing the right of individual employees to present grievances directly to the employer but rejected the union's counter-offer that, if this proviso be included, the contract should also contain the following proviso giving the union the right to be present.

A request for six paid holidays was rejected on the ground that the company gave year-end bonuses, but when the union offered to take a contract clause calling for the bonuses, the company rejected the suggestion.

The discussion about the seniority, pensions and insurance was more fruitful, but there was no agreement and the company never communicated its final position to the union on the last issue.

After the first five meetings the company submitted its idea of a contract. It covered two pages. One granted recognition to the Steelworkers but qualified it by paraphrasing the first proviso in Section 9(a) of the Act without mention of the second. It also had a provision dealing with hours of work but said nothing about wages, pensions, insurance, holidays, a grievance procedure or other subjects covered by the bargaining.

Just after New Year's the union called a strike. Various conciliation services endeavored to get the parties together. The company rejected their proposals for compromise and insisted that more progress could be made by direct negotiations than through mediation.

Has the company violated Section 8(a) (5)? See *NLRB v. Reed & Prince Co.*, 205 F.2d 131 (1st Cir.), cert. denied 346 U.S. 887 (1953).

Note on the Duty to Disclose Information in Bargaining [15]

In NLRB v. TRUITT MFG. CO., 351 U.S. 149, 76 S.Ct. 753, 100 L.Ed. 1027 (1956), the Supreme Court was presented for the first time with the question whether the duty to bargain in good faith under Section 8(a)(5) requires an employer to turn over to the union upon demand information in the possession of the company which the union claims is important to informed bargaining. In that case, the employer had offered a 2½-cent-an-hour wage increase in the course of bargaining for a new labor contract, and contended that it "would break the company" to pay the 10-cent-an-hour increase sought by the union. When the union requested permission to have a certified public accountant examine the company's financial records to ascertain the merit of the claim of financial inability, the company refused, asserting both that the average wage at the company was higher than that of competing companies and that "confidential financial information concerning the affairs of this Company is not a matter of bargaining or discussing with the Union." The NLRB found a violation of Section 8(a) (5), stating that "it is settled law, that when an employer seeks to justify the refusal of a wage increase upon an economic basis, * * * good-faith bargaining under the Act requires that upon request the employer attempt to substantiate its economic position

15. See Huston, Furnishing Information as an Element of Employer's Good Faith Bargaining, 35 U.Det.L.J. 471 (1958); Miller, Employer's Duty to Furnish Economic Data to Unions— Revisited, 17 Lab.L.J. 272 (1966).

by reasonable proof." The Board ordered the employer to turn over the requested information.

The Court of Appeals for the Sixth Circuit refused enforcement. It concluded: "The statute requires good faith bargaining with respect to wages and other matters affecting the terms and conditions of employment, not with respect to matters which lie within the province of management, such as the financial condition of the company, its manufacturing costs or the payment of dividends. * * * To bargain in good faith does not mean that the bargainor must substantiate by proof statements made by him in the course of the bargaining. It means merely that he bargain with a sincere desire to reach an agreement. There can be no question but that the company here was bargaining in that spirit." The court distinguished an earlier decision in which the employer was ordered to furnish information about employee wages, a subject which was within the scope of mandatory bargaining and about which the Truitt Company had in fact offered information. The court also concluded that the Board's decision would require any company which resists a wage increase on economic grounds to open its books, a "concession" which Section 8(d) expressly provides shall not be necessary in bargaining.

The Supreme Court reversed and directed that the Board's order be enforced. Observing that both parties treated the company's ability to pay increased wages as highly relevant, the Court majority concluded that the Board "has a right to consider an employer's refusal to give information about its financial status. * * * Good-faith bargaining necessarily requires that claims made by either bargainer should be honest claims. This is true about an asserted inability to pay an increase in wages. If such an argument is important enough to present in the give and take of bargaining, it is important enough to require some sort of proof of its accuracy. And it would certainly not be farfetched for a trier of fact to reach the conclusion that bargaining lacks good faith when an employer mechanically repeats a claim of inability to pay without making the slightest effort to substantiate the claim. * * * We do not hold, however, that in every case in which economic inability is raised as an argument against increased wages it automatically follows that the employees are entitled to substantiating evidence. Each case must turn upon its particular facts. The inquiry must always be whether or not under the circumstances of the particular case the statutory obligation to bargain in good faith has been met."

In a separate opinion, Justice Frankfurter stated that Sections 8(a)(5) and 8(d) require "an honest effort to come to terms"; good faith means more than "merely going through the motions of negotiating; it is inconsistent with a predetermined resolve not to budge from an initial position. But it is not necessarily incompatible with stubbornness or even with what to an outsider may seem unreasonableness." Contending that a want of good faith must be found by examining the history of dealings and the full negotiations between the parties, Justice Frankfurter criticized the Board for creating a *per se* rule and making only one fact dispositive—the company's failure to substantiate by proof its claim of financial inability to pay a wage increase.

The Court later held that the duty to disclose "unquestionably extends beyond the period of contract negotiations and applies to labor-management relations during the term of an agreement." NLRB v. ACME INDUSTRIAL CO., 385 U.S. 432, 87 S.Ct. 565, 17 L.Ed.2d 495 (1967). In the *Acme* case, the union during the term of its labor contract inferred from the employer's removal of certain machinery from the plant that the employer was committing a breach of the contract, which had provisions dealing with subcontracting and with the removal of plant equipment. The union filed grievances and requested that the company supply it with information concerning the removal of plant equipment. The company's denial was found by the Board and ultimately by the Supreme Court to violate the duty to bargain, which the Court held to continue during the process of grievance settlement under an existing labor contract. The Court also held that the union need not wait to press its claim for information in an arbitration proceeding and that the Board was properly "acting upon the probability that the desired information was relevant, and that it would be of use to the union in carrying out its statutory duties and responsibilities" of administering the collective bargaining agreement.

Problems for Discussion

1. Was the Supreme Court in *Truitt* endorsing a test for "good faith bargaining" which turns upon the subjective state of mind of the parties, or upon their objective conduct at the bargaining table? (Or both?) What particular circumstances were present in that case to show a bad faith refusal to open the company's books which would not be present in every case in which the employer refuses to meet a union's wage demands partly for financial reasons?

2. The company president has privately acknowledged to company officials that she would be willing to grant the union a wage increase of ten percent. At the bargaining table, however, she has consistently stated that a wage increase of any more than eight percent is out of the question and would make it impossible for the company to remain competitive. She has

at a number of meetings turned down the union's requests for reconsideration. In the event that the union can prove all of the above facts, should the Board conclude that the company has violated Section 8(a)(5)? See Cincinnati Cordage & Paper Co., 141 N.L.R.B. 72 (1963). Would you as attorney for the company advise the president to make such statements at the bargaining table?

3. The Insurance Agents Union has been bargaining representative for all of the district agents of the Prudential Insurance Company for some twenty years. There are some 17,000 agents working for the Company in thirty-four states, in 478 administrative districts. The turnover rate of unit members is roughly 25 percent per year. During the most recent negotiations, the Union has asked Prudential to supply it with a list of names and addresses of all employees in the unit, urging that such information was "necessary and relevant to the Union's performance and fulfillment of its statutory functions and duties as collective bargaining representative of all these employees." Prudential has refused to furnish the list, asserting that its policy is not to disclose this information to any organization for any purpose and that the true motive of the Union is to use this list not for purposes of collective bargaining but rather to increase its membership and facilitate its dues collection. Must Prudential disclose the list to the Union? See *Prudential Ins. Co.* v. *NLRB*, 412 F.2d 77, cert. denied 396 U.S. 928 (2d Cir. 1969); *Utica Observer-Dispatch* v. *NLRB*, 229 F.2d 575 (2d Cir. 1956).

DETROIT EDISON CO. v. NLRB

Supreme Court of the United States, 1979.
440 U.S. 301, 99 S.Ct. 1123, 59 L.Ed.2d 333.

Mr. Justice Stewart delivered the opinion of the Court.

The duty to bargain collectively, imposed upon an employer by § 8(a)(5) of the National Labor Relations Act, includes a duty to provide relevant information needed by a labor union for the proper performance of its duties as the employees' bargaining representative. NLRB v. Truitt Mfg. Co., 351 U.S. 149; NLRB v. Acme Industrial Co., 385 U.S. 432. In this case an employer was brought before the Board to answer a complaint that it had violated this statutory duty when it refused to disclose certain information about employee aptitude tests requested by a union in order to prepare for arbitration of a grievance. The employer supplied the union with much of the information requested, but refused to disclose three items: the actual test questions, the actual employee answer sheets, and the scores linked with the names of the employees who received them. The Board, concluding that all the items requested were relevant to the grievance and would be useful to the union in processing it, ordered the employer to turn over all of the materials directly to the union, subject to certain restrictions on the union's use of the information. 218 NLRB 1024

(1975). A divided Court of Appeals for the Sixth Circuit ordered enforcement of the Board's order without modification. NLRB v. Detroit Edison Co., 560 F.2d 722 (1977).

We granted certiorari to consider an important question of federal labor law. * * *

[Detroit Edison Co. (the Company) is a public utility generating and distributing electric power in Michigan. The operating and maintenance employees in its Monroe, Michigan plant have been represented by Local 223 of the Utility Workers Union since 1971. The collective bargaining agreement provides for promotions within the bargaining unit to be based upon seniority "whenever the reasonable qualifications and abilities of the employee (sic) being considered are not significantly different." The Company had used aptitude tests to predict job performance since the late 1920s or early 1930s, and in the late 1950s it began to use such standardized and validated tests to predict performance at the job of Instrument Man B. In the late 1960s, the Company's industrial psychologists revalidated these latter tests, and modified their structure and their passing score. The Company administered these tests under assurances to the job applicants that their scores would be kept confidential; the Company's industrial psychologists deemed themselves ethically bound not to reveal the test questions or the actual scores to representatives of management or of the employees.

In 1971, ten Monroe unit employees bid on six Instrument Man B openings, but none received a passing score (denoted "acceptable") on the test, and the Company filled the jobs with applicants from outside the bargaining unit. The Union filed a grievance, claiming that the new testing procedure was unfair and that the Company had bypassed senior unit employees in breach of the labor agreement. Prior to arbitration, the Union requested various materials relating to the Instrument Man B testing program. The Company turned over copies of the test-validation study, but it declined to furnish the actual tests or the applicants' test papers or scores, relying on the need to protect the integrity of future tests and the privacy interests of the examinees.

The Union then filed the unfair labor practice charges involved in this case, claiming that the requested information was relevant and necessary to the arbitration, especially with regard to such issues as promotion criteria, testing procedures, examination scoring, and the job relatedness of the tests. The arbitration proceeded (on the understanding that the Union could reopen the case if it prevailed before the NLRB), and the Company disclosed the raw scores of examinees (without their names), sample questions, and a detailed explanation of the scoring system; the Company also offered to turn over the score of any employee signing a written waiver, but the Union declined to seek such waivers. The arbitrator upheld the Instrument Man B tests as reliable and fair, and as a valid predictor of performance, and he also expressed the view that the Union's position had not been impaired by lack of access to the actual test questions.

In the later unfair labor practice hearing before the Administrative Law Judge, the Company offered to turn over the test questions and answer sheets to a union-selected industrial psychologist (who would be obligated to preserve secrecy), but the Union rejected this compromise. The Administrative Law Judge found that the tests and scores would probably be relevant to the Union as collective bargaining agent and that employer fears of loss of employee privacy by disclosure to the Union were insubstantial. He therefore concluded that the Company had violated Section 8(a)(5), and he ordered that the test scores be given to the Union and that the test questions and answer sheets be disclosed to an expert intermediary.]

The Board, and the Court of Appeals for the Sixth Circuit in its decision enforcing the Board's order, ordered the Company to turn over all the material directly to the Union. They concluded that the Union should be able to determine for itself whether it needed a psychologist to interpret the test battery and answer sheets. Both recognized the Company's interest in maintaining the security of the tests, but both reasoned that appropriate restrictions on the Union's use of the materials would protect this interest.[16] Neither was receptive to the Company's claim that employee privacy and the professional obligations of the Company's industrial psychologists should outweigh the Union request for the employee-linked scores.

II

Because of the procedural posture of this case, the questions that have been preserved for our review are relatively narrow. * * * The first concerns the Board's choice of a remedy for the Company's

---

16. The Board, although it ordered the Company to supply the tests and answer sheets directly to the Union, incorporated by reference the Administrative Law Judge's restrictions on the Union's use of the materials. Under those restrictions, the Union was given the right "to use the tests and the information contained therein to the extent necessary to process and arbitrate the grievances, but not to copy the tests, or otherwise use them, for the purpose of disclosing the tests or the questions to employees who have in the past, or who may in the future take these tests, or to anyone (other than the arbitrator) who may advise the employees of the contents of the tests." After the conclusion of the arbitration, the Union was required to return "all copies of the battery of tests" to the Company. The Court of Appeals, in enforcing the Board's order, stated that the "restrictions on use of the materials and obligation to return them to Detroit Edison are part of the decision and order which we enforce." 560 F.2d 722, 726.

failure to disclose copies of the test battery and answer sheets. The second, and related, question concerns the propriety of the Board's conclusion that the Company committed an unfair labor practice when it refused to disclose, without a written consent from the individual employees, the test scores linked with the employee names.

A

We turn first to the question whether the Board abused its remedial discretion when it ordered the Company to deliver directly to the Union the copies of the test battery and answer sheets. The Company's position, stripped of the argument that it had no duty at all to disclose these materials, is as follows: It urges that disclosure directly to the Union would carry with it a substantial risk that the test questions would be disseminated. Since it spent considerable time and money validating the Instrument Man B tests and since its tests depend for reliability upon the examinee's lack of advance preparation, it contends that the harm of dissemination would not be trivial. The future validity of the tests is tied to secrecy, and disclosure to employees would not only threaten the Company's investment but would also leave the Company with no valid means of measuring employee aptitude. The Company also maintains that its interest in preserving the security of its tests is consistent with the federal policy favoring the use of validated, standardized and non-discriminatory employee selection procedures reflected in the Civil Rights Act of 1964.   *   *   *

A union's bare assertion that it needs information to process a grievance does not automatically oblige the employer to supply all the information in the manner requested. The duty to supply information under § 8(a)(5) turns upon "the circumstances of the particular case," NLRB v. Truitt Mfg. Co., 351 U.S. 149, 153, and much the same may be said for the type of disclosure that will satisfy that duty. See, e. g., American Cyanamid Co., 129 NLRB 683, 684 (1960). Throughout this proceeding, the reasonableness of the Company's concern for test secrecy has been essentially conceded. The finding by the Board that this concern did not outweigh the Union's interest in exploring the fairness of the Company's criteria for promotion did not carry with it any suggestion that the concern itself was not legitimate and substantial. Indeed, on this record—which has established the Company's freedom under the collective contract to use aptitude tests as a criterion for promotion, the empirical validity of the tests, and the relationship between secrecy and test validity—the strength of the company's concern has been abundantly demonstrated. The Board has cited no principle of national labor policy to warrant a remedy that would unnecessarily disserve this interest, and we are unable to identify one.

It is obvious that the remedy selected by the Board does not adequately protect the security of the tests. The restrictions barring the Union from taking any action that might cause the tests to fall into the hands of employees who have taken or are likely to take them are only as effective as the sanctions available to enforce them. In this instance, there is substantial doubt whether the Union would be subject to a contempt citation were it to ignore the restrictions. It was not a party to the enforcement proceeding in the Court of Appeals, and the scope of an enforcement order under § 10(e) is limited by Rule 65(d) of the Federal Rules of Civil Procedure making an injunction binding only "upon the parties to the action * * * and those persons in active concert or participation with them * * *." See Regal Knitwear Co. v. NLRB, 324 U.S. 9, 14. The Union, of course, did participate actively in the Board proceedings, but it is debatable whether that would be enough to satisfy the requirement of the Rule. * * * Moreover, the Union clearly would not be accountable in either contempt or unfair labor practice proceedings for the most realistic vice inherent in the Board's remedy—the danger of inadvertent leaks.

We are mindful that the Board is granted broad discretion in devising remedies to undo the effects of violations of the Act. NLRB v. Seven-Up Bottling Co., 344 U.S. 344, 346; Fibreboard Corp. v. NLRB, 379 U.S. 203, 216, and of the principle that in the area of federal labor law "the relationship of remedy to policy is peculiarly a matter for administrative competence." Phelps Dodge Corp. v. NLRB, 313 U.S. 177, 194. Nonetheless, the rule of deference to the Board's choice of remedy does not constitute a blank check for arbitrary action. The rule that Congress in § 10(e) has entrusted to the courts in reviewing the Board's petitions for enforcement of its orders is not that of passive conduit. See Fibreboard Corp. v. NLRB, supra, 379 U.S., at 216. The Board in this case having identified no justification for a remedy granting such scant protection to the Company's undisputed and important interests in test secrecy, we hold that the Board abused its discretion in ordering the Company to turn over the test battery and answer sheets directly to the Union.

B

The dispute over Union access to the actual scores received by named employees is in a somewhat different procedural posture, since the Company did on this issue preserve its objections to the basic finding that it had violated its duty under § 8(a)(5) when it refused disclosure. The Company argues that even if the scores were relevant to the Union's grievance (which it vigorously disputes), the Union's need for the information was not sufficiently weighty to require breach of the promise of confidentiality to the examinees, breach of its industrial psychologists' code of professional ethics, and potential embarrassment and harassment of at least some of the examinees. The Board responds that this information does satisfy the appropriate standard of "relevance," see NLRB v. Acme Industrial Inc., 385 U.S. 432, and that the Company, having "unilaterally" chosen to make a promise of confidentiality to the examinees, cannot rely on that promise to defend against a request for relevant information. The professional obligations of the Company's psychologists, it argues, must give way to paramount federal law. Finally, it dismisses as speculative the contention that employees with low scores might be embarrassed or harassed.

We may accept for the sake of this discussion the finding that the employee scores were of potential relevance to the Union's grievance, as well as the position of the Board that the federal statutory duty to disclose relevant information cannot be defeated by the ethical standards of a private group. Cf. Nash v. Florida Industrial Comm'n, 389 U.S. 235, 239. Nevertheless we agree with the Company that its willingness to disclose these scores only upon receipt of consents from the examinees satisfied its statutory obligations under § 8(a)(5).

The Board's position appears to rest on the proposition that union interests in arguably relevant information must always predominate over all other interests, however legitimate. But such an absolute rule has never been established,[17] and we decline to adopt such a rule here. There are situations in which an employer's conditional offer to disclose may be warranted. That we believe is one.

The sensitivity of any human being to disclosure of information that may be taken to bear on his or her basic competence is sufficiently well known to be an appropriate subject of judicial notice. There is nothing in this record to suggest that the Company promised the examinees that their scores would remain confidential in order to further parochial concerns or to frustrate subsequent union attempts to

[17] See Emeryville Research Center, Shell Development Co. v. NLRB, 441 F.2d 880 (CA9 1971) (refusal to supply relevant salary information in precise form demanded did not constitute violation of § 8(a)(5) when company's proposed alternatives were responsive to union's need); Shell Oil Co. v. NLRB, 457 F.2d 615 (CA9 1975) (refusal to supply employee names without employee consent not unlawful when company had well-founded fear that nonstriking employees would be harassed); cf. Kroger Co. v. NLRB, 399 F.2d 455 (CA6 1958) (no disclosure of operating ratio data when, under circumstances, interests of employer predominated); United Aircraft Corp., 192 NLRB 382, 390 (employer acted reasonably in refusing to honor generalized request for employee medical records without employee's permission), modified on other grounds, Lodges 743 and 1746 v. United Aircraft Corp., 534 F.2d 422 (CA2 1975).

process employee grievances. And it has not been suggested at any point in this proceeding that the Company's unilateral promise of confidentiality was in itself violative of the terms of the collective-bargaining agreement. Indeed, the Company presented evidence that disclosure of individual scores had in the past resulted in the harassment of some lower scoring examinees who had, as a result, left the Company.

Under these circumstances, any possible impairment of the function of the Union in processing the grievances of employees is more than justified by the interests served in conditioning the disclosure of the test scores upon the consent of the very employees whose grievance is being processed. The burden on the Union in this instance is minimal. The Company's interest in preserving employee confidence in the testing program is well founded.

 * * * Accordingly, we hold that the order requiring the Company unconditionally to disclose the employee scores to the Union was erroneous.

The judgment is vacated and the case remanded to the Court of Appeals for the Sixth Circuit for further proceedings consistent with this opinion.

It is so ordered.

Mr. Justice Stevens, concurring in part and dissenting in part.

This is a close case on both issues. With respect to the test battery and answer sheets, I agree with Mr. Justice White that we should respect the Board's exercise of its broad remedial discretion. On the other hand, I agree with the Court that the Union should not be permitted to invade the individual employees' interest in the confidentiality of their test scores without their consent. Accordingly, I join all but Part II–A of the Court's opinion and Part I of Mr. Justice White's dissent.

Mr. Justice White, with whom Mr. Justice Brennan and Mr. Justice Marshall join, dissenting.
    * * *

I.

 * * * The only issue here regarding the test questions and answer sheets is "whether the Board abused its *remedial* discretion when it ordered the Company to deliver directly to the Union the copies of the test battery and answer sheets." If, however, the basic impropriety of the Company's failure to divulge the materials to the Union is settled, the Board's *remedial* authority to compel conditional disclosure is abundantly clear. The Court is quite wrong in holding that the Board's order exceeded the agency's "broad discretionary

[remedial power]."   Fibreboard Corp. v. NLRB, 379 U.S. 203, 216 (1964).   For it is too well established that a decree fashioned by the Board to remedy violations of the Act "will not be disturbed 'unless it can be shown that the order is a patent attempt to achieve ends other than those which can fairly be said to effectuate the policies of the Act.'"   Ibid., quoting Virginia Elec. & Power Co. v. NLRB, 319 U.S. 533, 540 (1943).

       *   *   *

A

The Board ordered release of the test questions and answer sheets only on condition that the Union preserve their secrecy. Specifically, the Union was admonished not to copy the materials or to make them available to potential test takers or to others who might advise the employees of their content. The Court scoffs at the order, however, on the ground that "there is substantial doubt whether the Union would be subject to a contempt citation were it to ignore the restrictions." But the Board placed no reliance on contempt sanctions when it directed release, and there is scant reason for rejecting the Board's judgment that sanctions of that sort are unnecessary. The Board, in my view, had forceful and independent grounds for concluding that the Union would respect the confidentiality of the materials and take due precautions against inadvertent exposure.

The Union has enjoyed a long and extensive relationship with the employer that it would be loath to jeopardize by intentionally breaching the conditions of release. Cf. Fawcett Printing Corp., 201 NLRB 964, 974 (1973). Even if the Union had any incentive to publicize the examination questions, its ardor would be dampened by the likely long term consequences of that course; the Board exercises continuing authority over the Union's affairs, and it may well approve the Company's future insistence on rigorous secrecy, thus delimiting the Union's subsequent latitude in grievance processing.[18]   Moreover, dissemination of test materials to potential test takers might impair the interests of those employees who qualify fairly for a desired position, thus inviting their disapprobation.

The Company acknowledges, in any event, see Tr. of Oral Arg. 12, and the Court agrees, that the real concern is with inadvertent disclosure. Yet there is no basis for assuming that the Union would handle the materials so cavalierly as to chance accidental disclosure, given the gravity with which the issue has been treated by all con-

---

18. The Union's disregard of the conditions of release may also violate the Union's duty to bargain in good faith under § 8(b)(3) of the Act, 29 U.S.C. § 158(b)(3), Comment, Psychological Aptitude Tests and the Duty to Supply Information, 91 Harv.L.Rev. 869, 876 n. 49 (1978), subjecting the Union to appropriate sanctions.

cerned. Thus, in the circumstances of this case, the Board had ample grounds to expect Union cooperation. And this Court is ill equipped to fault the Board on a matter so plainly summoning the Board's keen familiarity with industrial behavior.

B

Besides overrating the hazards of direct release to the Union of the test questions, the Court undervalues the interests vindicated by that procedure. The Court asserts simply that the "Board has cited no principle of national labor policy to warrant a remedy that would unnecessarily disserve [the Company's interest in maintaining secrecy], and we are unable to identify one." The Board observed in its decision, however, that "[a]s the bargaining agent of the employees involved, it is the Union which is entitled to information which is necessary to its role as bargaining agent in the administration of the collective bargaining agreement." Detroit Edison Co., 218 NLRB 1024, 1024 (1975). The employer's "accommodation"—releasing the test questions solely to a psychologist—which the Court tacitly endorses, is fundamentally at odds with the basic structure of the bargaining process. Congress has conferred paramount representational responsibilities and obligations on the employees' freely chosen bargaining agent. Yet the Company's alternative would install a third-party psychologist as a partner, if not primary actor, in promotion-related grievance proceedings. * * *

II

The Court further concludes that the Company properly declined to disclose the examinees' test scores, associated with the employees' names, absent consent by the examinees themselves. * * * The Administrative Law Judge concluded that the Company had "produced no probative evidence that the employees' sensitivities are likely to be abused by disclosure of the scores." 218 NLRB, at 1035. When an employer resists the divulgence of materials relevant to employee grievances, I would think that the employer has the burden of establishing any justification for nondisclosure. The Court, however, presumes what yet remains to be shown.

Moreover, there is no basis in the governing statute or regulations for attributing ascendant importance to the employees' confidentiality interests. Whether confidentiality considerations should prevail in the circumstances of this case is, as the Company and majority agree, principally a matter of policy. But it cannot be gainsaid that the Board is the body charged in the first instance with the task of discerning and effectuating congressional policies in the labor-management area. Its judgments in that regard should not be lightly overturned. Yet the Court strikes its own balance according decisional weight to concerns having no asserted or apparent foundation in the statute it purports to construe or in other applicable legislation.

The Court lightly dismisses the Union's interest in receipt of the examinees' identified scores, with or without consent, by declaring the burdens involved as "minimal." The Administrative Law Judge noted, however, that the "Union's obligation is to represent the unit of employees as a whole[;] [the Company] may not frustrate this by requiring the Union to secure the consent of individuals in the unit in order to secure information relevant and reasonably necessary to the enforcement of the collective-bargaining agreement which exists for the benefit of all." 218 NLRB, at 1036. Were individual examinees to withhold consent, and thus prevent the Union from scrutinizing their scores in light of their demographic and occupational characteristics, the Union might be inhibited in its efforts to discern patterns or anomalies indicating bias in the operation of the tests. Thus, the Board directed divulgence of the scores to the employees' statutory bargaining representative to enable it effectively to fulfill its vital statutory functions. Such a limited intrusion, cf. Whalen v. Roe, 429 U.S. 589, 602 (1977), for the purpose of vindicating grave statutory policies, hardly signals an occasion for judicial intervention.[19]

III

In sum, I think the Board's resolution is sound and that the Sixth Circuit's judgment enforcing it should be sustained. I do not mean to suggest that the considerations advanced by the Company are without substance or that this case does not present a "difficult and delicate"

---

19. In other contexts, the courts have generally rejected claims of confidentiality as a basis for withholding relevant information. See General Electric Co. v. NLRB, 466 F.2d 1177 (CA6 1972) (wage data); NLRB v. Frontier Homes Corp., 371 F.2d 974 (CA8 1967) (selling price lists); Curtiss-Wright Corp. v. NLRB, 347 F.2d 61 (CA3 1965) (job evaluation and wage data); NLRB v. Item Co., 220 F.2d 956 (CA5) (wage data), cert. denied, 350 U.S. 836 (1955), 352 U.S. 917 (1956); cf. United Aircraft Corp., 192 NLRB 382, 390 (1971) (company physician's records not disclosable without employee's permission unless needed for a particular grievance), modified on other issues sub nom. Lodges 743 and 1746 v. United Aircraft Corp., 534 F.2d 422 (CA2 1975), cert. denied, 429 U.S. 825 (1976); Shell Oil Co. v. NLRB, 457 F.2d 615, 619 (CA9 1975) (refusal to furnish employees' names without consent was proper when it was "establish[ed] beyond cavil that there was a clear and present danger of harassment and violence"). See also Cowles Communications, Inc., 172 NLRB 1909 (1968) (employees' salaries and other particularized data about employees); Electric Auto-Lite Co., 89 NLRB 1192 (1950) (wage data); R. Gorman, Labor Law 417–418 (1976); Comment, 91 Harv.L. Rev., supra n. 3, at 873–874, and n. 35. In NLRB v. Wyman-Gordon Co., 394 U.S. 759 (1969), in another setting, a plurality of this Court observed:

"The disclosure requirement [imposed by the Board and concerning employees' names and addresses] furthers [statutory objectives] by encouraging an informed employee electorate and by allowing unions the right of access to employees that management already possesses. It is for the Board and not for this Court to weigh against this interest the asserted interest of employees in avoiding the problems that union solicitation may present."

Id., at 767. * * *

task of balancing competing claims. Cf. Beth Israel Hospital v. NLRB, 437 U.S., at 501. But, by virtue of that, this is precisely the kind of case in which "considerable deference" is owed the Board.

*   *   *

Problems for Discussion

1. Did the Court in *Detroit Edison* conclude that the Board had erred in formulating the applicable rule of law? in stating the factors to be considered in applying that rule? in weighing those factors and reaching a conclusion? On each of these matters, was the Board given the deference to which it was entitled?

2. Assume that in a plant in which employees are paid pursuant to the labor agreement on a straight-time basis, the employer has expressed an interest in the possibility of moving to an incentive system and has prepared a time study which shows what activities each employee must do on the job and how many units of production each employee can complete within a given period of time. The union has asked the employer to turn over the time study in order that the union can determine the desirability of an incentive method and can negotiate concerning the "standard" (i. e., the number of units expected from an average employee) and the rate of incentive pay for each unit beyond the standard. In negotiations for a new contract, the company contends that it need not turn over the time study, asserting that it is not relevant to the straight-time pay system which presently obtains, and that the study was prepared by an industrial consultant retained at considerable expense by the company and is therefore company property. Is the company's refusal to produce the time study a violation of Section 8(a)(5)?

If the company can demonstrate that the disclosure of the time study will also disclose a most valuable trade secret concerning the company's productive processes, will that be relevant in a proceeding under Section 8(a)(5) to require the disclosure of the study? See *Kroger Co.* v. *NLRB*, 399 F.2d 455 (6th Cir. 1968); *Curtiss-Wright Corp., Wright Aero. Div.* v. *NLRB*, 347 F.2d 61 (3d Cir. 1965).

3. Assume that the company and union in Problem 2 negotiate a new labor contract, in which incentive pay is substituted for straight-time pay. The contract gives the employer the power to initiate changes in "standards" (or minimum pay) as the content of a job is modified, but the union is permitted to file a grievance and submit the case to arbitration in the event it believes the new standard to be arbitrary or unfair. The company has announced a new standard for a particular job and the union has filed a grievance; it has also requested that the company turn over the time study, for it believes that data in the time study will bear out its claim that the standard is too onerous. Must the employer turn over the time study to the union?

Assume that the company turns over the time study to the union but the union, claiming that there is no demonstrably accurate method for determining standards (which is true), has asked the company to permit qualified persons elected by the union to conduct an independent time study so as better to evaluate the company's study and to decide whether to demand arbitration. If the company refuses and the union initiates proceedings under Section 8(a)(5), what should be the outcome of the case (including any order that the Board should issue)? See *Fafnir Bearing Co.* v. *NLRB*, 362 F.2d 716 (2d Cir. 1966).

NLRB v. INSURANCE AGENTS' INTERNATIONAL UNION

Supreme Court of the United States, 1960.
361 U.S. 477, 80 S.Ct. 419, 4 L.Ed.2d 454.

MR. JUSTICE BRENNAN delivered the opinion of the Court.

This case presents an important issue of the scope of the National Labor Relations Board's authority under § 8(b) (3) of the National Labor Relations Act, which provides that "It shall be an unfair labor practice for a labor organization or its agents * * * to refuse to bargain collectively with an employer, provided it is the representative of his employees * * *." The precise question is whether the Board may find that a union, which confers with an employer with the desire of reaching agreement on contract terms, has nevertheless refused to bargain collectively, thus violating that provision, solely and simply because during the negotiations it seeks to put economic pressure on the employer to yield to its bargaining demands by sponsoring on-the-job conduct designed to interfere with the carrying on of the employer's business.

Since 1949 the respondent Insurance Agents' International Union and the Prudential Insurance Company of America have negotiated collective bargaining agreements covering district agents employed by Prudential in 35 States and the District of Columbia. * * *

In January 1956 Prudential and the union began the negotiation of a new contract to replace an agreement expiring in the following March. Bargaining was carried on continuously for six months before the terms of the new contract were agreed upon on July 17, 1956. It is not questioned that, if it stood alone, the record of negotiations would establish that the union conferred in good faith for the purpose and with the desire of reaching agreement with Prudential on a contract.

However, in April 1956, Prudential filed a § 8(b) (3) charge of refusal to bargain collectively against the union. The charge was based upon actions of the union and its members outside the conference room, occurring after the old contract expired in March. The union had announced in February that if agreement on the terms of the new contract was not reached when the old contract expired, the union members would then participate in a "Work Without a Contract" program—which meant that they would engage in certain planned, concerted on-the-job activities designed to harass the company.

A complaint of violation of § 8(b) (3) issued on the charge and hearings began before the bargaining was concluded. It was developed in the evidence that the union's harassing tactics involved activities by the member agents such as these: refusal for a time to solicit new business, and refusal (after the writing of new business was resumed) to comply with the company's reporting procedures; refusal to participate in the company's "May Policyholders' Month Campaign"; reporting late at district offices the days the agents were scheduled to attend them, and refusing to perform customary duties at the offices, instead engaging there in "sit-in-mornings," "doing what comes naturally" and leaving at noon as a group; absenting themselves from special business conferences arranged by the company; picketing and distributing leaflets outside the various offices of the company on specified days and hours as directed by the union; distributing leaflets each day to policyholders and others and soliciting policyholders' signatures on petitions directed to the company; and presenting the signed policyholders' petitions to the company at its home office while simultaneously engaging in mass demonstrations there.

The hearing examiner found that there was nothing in the record, apart from the mentioned activities of the union during the negotiations, that could be relied upon to support an inference that the union had not fulfilled its statutory duty; in fact nothing else was relied upon by the Board's General Counsel in prosecuting the complaint. The hearing examiner's analysis of the congressional design in enacting the statutory duty to bargain led him to conclude that the Board was not authorized to find that such economically harassing activities constituted a § 8(b) (3) violation. The Board's opinion answers flatly "We do not agree" and proceeds to say " * * * the Respondent's reliance upon harassing tactics during the course of negotiations for the avowed purpose of compelling the Company to capitulate to its terms is the antithesis of reasoned discussion it was duty-bound to follow. Indeed, it clearly revealed an unwillingness to submit its demands to the consideration of the bargaining table where argument, persuasion, and the free interchange of views could take place. In such circumstances, the fact that the Respondent continued to confer with the Company and was desirous of concluding an agreement does not *alone* establish that it fulfilled its obligation to bargain in good faith * * *." 119 N.L.R.B., at 769, 770–771. Thus the Board's view is that irrespective of the union's good faith in conferring with the employer at the bargaining table for the purpose and with the desire of reaching agreement on contract terms, its tactics during the course of the negotiations constituted *per se* a violation of § 8(b) (3). Accordingly, as is said in the Board's brief, "The issue here * * * comes down to whether the Board is authorized under the Act to hold that such tactics, which the Act does not specifically forbid but Section does not protect, support a finding of a failure to bargain in good faith as required by Section 8(b) (3)."

First. * * * [T]he nature of the duty to bargain in good faith * * * imposed upon employers by § 8(5) of the original Act was not sweepingly conceived. The Chairman of the Senate Committee declared: "When the employees have chosen their organization, when they have selected their representatives, all the bill proposes to do is to escort them to the door of their employer and say, 'Here they are, the legal representatives of your employees.' What happens behind those doors is not inquired into, and the bill does not seek to inquire into it."

The limitation implied by the last sentence has not been in practice maintained—practically, it could hardly have been—but the underlying purpose of the remark has remained the most basic purpose of the statutory provision. That purpose is the making effective of the duty of management to extend recognition to the union; the duty of management to bargain in good faith is essentially a corollary of its duty to recognize the union. * * * Collective bargaining, then, is not simply an occasion for purely formal meetings between management and labor, while each maintains an attitude of "take it or leave it"; it presupposes a desire to reach ultimate agreement, to enter into a collective bargaining contract. See Heinz Co. v. National Labor Relations Board, 311 U.S. 514, 61 S.Ct. 320, 85 L.Ed. 309. This was the sort of recognition that Congress, in the Wagner Act, wanted extended to labor unions; recognition as the bargaining agent of the employees in a process that looked to the ordering of the parties' industrial relationship through the formation of a contract. See Local 24, International Brotherhood of Teamsters Union v. Oliver, 358 U.S. 283, 295, 79 S.Ct. 297, 304, 3 L.Ed.2d 312.

But at the same time, Congress was generally not concerned with the substantive terms on which the parties contracted. Cf. Terminal Railroad Ass'n v. Brotherhood of Railroad Trainmen, 318 U.S. 1, 6, 63 S.Ct. 420, 423, 87 L.Ed. 571. Obviously there is tension between the principle that the parties need not contract on any specific terms and a practical enforcement of the principle that they are bound to deal with each other in a serious attempt to resolve differences and reach a common ground. And in fact criticism of the Board's application of the "good-faith" test arose from the belief that it was forcing employers to yield to union demands if they were to avoid a successful charge of unfair labor practice. Thus, in 1947 in Congress the fear was expressed that the Board had "gone very far, in the guise of determining whether or not employers had bargained in good faith, in setting itself up as the judge of what concessions an employer must make and of the proposals and counterproposals that he may or may not make." H.R.Rep. No. 245, 80th Cong., 1st Sess., p. 19. Since the Board was not viewed by Congress as an agency which should exercise its powers to arbitrate the parties' substantive solutions of the issues in their bargaining, a check on this apprehended trend was provided by writing the good-faith test of bargaining into § 8(d) of the Act. * * *

Second. At the same time as it was statutorily defining the duty to bargain collectively, Congress, by adding § 8(b) (3) of the Act through the Taft-Hartley amendments, imposed that duty on labor organizations. Unions obviously are formed for the very purpose of bargaining collectively; but the legislative history makes it plain that Congress was wary of the position of some unions, and wanted to ensure that they would approach the bargaining table with the same attitude of willingness to reach an agreement as had been enjoined on management earlier. It intended to prevent employee representatives from putting forth the same "take it or leave it" attitude that had been condemned in management. 93 Cong.Rec. 4135, 4363, 5005.

Third. It is apparent from the legislative history of the whole Act that the policy of Congress is to impose a mutual duty upon the parties to confer in good faith with a desire to reach agreement, in the belief that such an approach from both sides of the table promotes the over-all design of achieving industrial peace. See National Labor Relations Board v. Jones & Laughlin Steel Corp., 301 U.S. 1, 45, 57 S.Ct. 615, 628, 81 L.Ed. 893. Discussion conducted under that standard of good faith may narrow the issues, making the real demands of the parties clearer to each other, and perhaps to themselves, and may encourage an attitude of settlement through give and take. The mainstream of cases before the Board and in the courts reviewing its orders, under the provisions fixing the duty to bargain collectively, is concerned with insuring that the parties approach the bargaining table with this attitude. But apart from this essential standard of conduct, Congress intended that the parties should have wide latitude in their negotiations, unrestricted by any governmental power to regulate the substantive solution of their differences. See Local 24, International Brotherhood of Teamsters Union v. Oliver, supra, 358 U.S. at page 295, 79 S.Ct. at page 304.

We believe that the Board's approach in this case—unless it can be defended, in terms of § 8(b) (3), as resting on some unique character of the union tactics involved here—must be taken as proceeding from an erroneous view of collective bargaining. It must be realized that collective bargaining, under a system where the Government does not attempt to control the results of negotiations, cannot be equated with an academic collective search for truth—or even with what might be thought to be the ideal of one. The parties—even granting the modification of views that may come from a realization of economic interdependence—still proceed from contrary and to an extent antagonistic viewpoints and concepts of self-interest. The system has not reached the ideal of the philosophic notion that perfect understanding among people would lead to perfect agreement among them on values. The presence of economic weapons in reserve, and their actual exercise on occasion by the parties, is part and parcel of the system that the Wagner and Taft-Hartley Acts have recognized. Abstract logical analysis might find inconsistency between the command of the statute to negotiate toward an agreement in good faith and the legitimacy of the use of economic weapons, frequently having the most serious effect upon individual workers and productive enterprises, to induce one party to come to the terms desired by the other. But the truth of the matter is that at the present statutory stage of our national labor relations policy, the two factors—necessity for good-faith bargaining between parties, and the availability of economic pressure devices to each to make the other party incline to agree on one's terms—exist side by side. One writer recognizes this by describing economic force as "a prime motive power for agreements in free collective bargaining." Doubtless one factor influences the other; there may be less need to apply economic pressure if the areas of controversy have been defined through discussion; and at the same time, negotiation positions are apt to be weak or strong in accordance with the degree of economic power the parties possess. A close student of our national labor relations laws writes: "Collective bargaining is curiously ambivalent even today. In one aspect collective bargaining is a brute contest of economic power somewhat masked by polite manners and voluminous statistics. As the relation matures, Lilliputian bonds control the opposing concentrations of economic power; they lack legal sanctions but are nonetheless effective to contain the use of power. Initially it may be only fear of the economic consequences of disagreement that turns the parties to facts, reason, a sense of responsibility, a responsiveness to government and public opinion, and moral principle; but in time these forces generate their own compulsions, and negotiating a contract approaches the ideal of informed persuasion." Cox, The Duty to Bargain in Good Faith, 71 Harv.L.Rev. 1401, 1409.

For similar reasons, we think the Board's approach involves an intrusion into the substantive aspects of the bargaining process—again, unless there is some specific warrant for its condemnation of the precise tactics involved here. The scope of § 8(b) (3) and the limitations on Board power which were the design of § 8(d) are exceeded, we hold, by inferring a lack of good faith not from any deficiencies of the union's performance at the bargaining table by reason of its attempted use of economic pressure, but solely and simply because tactics designed to exert economic pressure were employed during the course of the good-faith negotiations. Thus the Board in the guise of determining good or bad faith in negotiations could regulate

[margin note, top left: Bd could regulate]

[margin note, top right: Bd could regulate, but would have too much influence]

what economic weapons a party might summon to its aid. And if the
Board could regulate the choice of economic weapons that may be used
as part of collective bargaining, it would be in a position to exercise
considerable influence upon the substantive terms on which the parties contract. As the parties' own devices became more limited, the
Government might have to enter even more directly into the negotiation of collective agreements. Our labor policy is not presently erected on a foundation of government control of the results of negotiations. See S.Rep.No. 105, 80th Cong., 1st Sess., p. 2. Nor does it contain a charter for the National Labor Relations Board to act at large
in equalizing disparities of bargaining power between employer and
union.

Fourth. The use of economic pressure, as we have indicated,
is of itself not at all inconsistent with the duty of bargaining in good
faith. * * * The Board freely (and we think correctly) conceded
here that a "total" strike called by the union would not have subjected it to sanctions under § 8(b)(3), at least if it were called after
the old contract, with its no-strike clause, had expired. Cf. United
Mine Workers, supra. The Board's opinion in the instant case is not
so unequivocal as this concession (and therefore perhaps more logical). But in the light of it and the principles we have enunciated,
we must evaluate the claim of the Board to power, under § 8(b)(3),
to distinguish among various economic pressure tactics and brand
the ones at bar inconsistent with good-faith collective bargaining.
We conclude its claim is without foundation.

(a) The Board contends that the distinction between a total
strike and the conduct at bar is that a total strike is a concerted activity protected against employer interference by §§ 7 and 8(a)(1)
of the Act, while the activity at bar is not a protected concerted activity. We may agree *arguendo* with the Board that this Court's decision in the Briggs-Stratton case, International Union, U. A. W., A.
F. of L., Local 232 v. Wisconsin Employers Relations Board, 336 U.S.
245, 69 S.Ct. 516, 93 L.Ed. 651, establishes that the employee conduct
here was not a protected concerted activity. On this assumption the
employer could have discharged or taken other appropriate disciplinary action against the employees participating in these "slow-down,"
"sit-in," and arguably unprotected disloyal tactics. See National Labor Relations Board v. Fansteel Metallurgical Corp., 306 U.S. 240, 59
S.Ct. 490, 83 L.Ed. 627; National Labor Relations Board v. Local
No. 1229, Intern. B. of Electrical Workers, 346 U.S. 464, 74 S.Ct. 172,
98 L.Ed. 195. But surely that a union activity is not protected against
disciplinary action does not mean that it constitutes a refusal to bargain in good faith. The reason why the ordinary economic strike
is not evidence of a failure to bargain in good faith is not that it constitutes a protected activity but that, as we have developed, there is
simply no inconsistency between the application of economic pressure

[margin note, right: this is not a protected activity]

and good-faith collective bargaining. The Board suggests that since (on the assumption we make) the union members' activities here were unprotected, and they could have been discharged, the activities should also be deemed unfair labor practices, since thus the remedy of a cease-and-desist order, milder than mass discharges of personnel and less disruptive of commerce, would be available. The argument is not persuasive. There is little logic in assuming that because Congress was willing to allow employers to use self-help against union tactics, if they were willing to face the economic consequences of its use, it also impliedly declared these tactics unlawful as a matter of federal law. Our problem remains that of construing § 8(b) (3)'s terms, and we do not see how the availability of self-help to the employer has anything to do with the matter.

(b) The Board contends that because an orthodox "total" strike is "traditional" its use must be taken as being consistent with § 8(b) (3); but since the tactics here are not "traditional" or "normal," they need not be so viewed. Further, the Board cites what it conceives to be the public's moral condemnation of the sort of employee tactics involved here. But again we cannot see how these distinctions can be made under a statute which simply enjoins a duty to bargain in good faith. Again, these are relevant arguments when the question is the scope of the concerted activities given affirmative protection by the Act. But as we have developed, the use of economic pressure by the parties to a labor dispute is not a grudging exception to some policy of completely academic discussion enjoined by the Act; it is part and parcel of the process of collective bargaining. On this basis, we fail to see the relevance of whether the practice in question is time-honored or whether its exercise is generally supported by public opinion. It may be that the tactics used here deserve condemnation, but this would not justify attempting to pour that condemnation into a vessel not designed to hold it. The same may be said for the Board's contention that these activities, as opposed to a "normal" strike, are inconsistent with § 8(b) (3) because they offer maximum pressure on the employer at minimum economic cost to the union. One may doubt whether this was so here, but the matter does not turn on that. Surely it cannot be said that the only economic weapons consistent with good-faith bargaining are those which minimize the pressure on the other party or maximize the disadvantage to the party using them. The catalog of union and employer weapons that might thus fall under ban would be most extensive.

Fifth. These distinctions essayed by the Board here, and the lack of relationship to the statutory standard inherent in them, confirm us in our conclusion that the judgment of the Court of Appeals, setting aside the order of the Board, must be affirmed. For they make clear to us that when the Board moves in this area, with only § 8(b) (3) for support, it is functioning as an arbiter of the sort of economic weapons the parties can use in seeking to gain acceptance of their bargaining demands. It has sought to introduce some standard of properly "balanced" bargaining power, or some new distinction of justifiable and unjustifiable, proper and "abusive" economic weapons into the collective bargaining duty imposed by the Act. The Board's assertion of power under § 8(b) (3) allows it to sit in judgment upon every economic weapon the parties to a labor contract negotiation employ, judging it on the very general standard of that section, not drafted with reference to specific forms of economic pressure. We have expressed our belief that this amounts to the Board's entrance into the substantive aspects of the bargaining process to an extent Congress has not countenanced.

* * * Congress has been rather specific when it has come to outlaw particular economic weapons on the part of unions. [The Court here cited Sections 8(b)(4) and 8(b)(7).] * * * [I]t is clear to us that the Board needs a more specific charter than § 8(b)(3) before it can add to the Act's prohibitions here. * * * Congress might be of opinion that greater stress should be put on the role of "pure" negotiation in settling labor disputes, to the extent of eliminating more and more economic weapons from the parties' grasp, and perhaps it might start with the ones involved here; or in consideration of the alternatives, it might shrink from such an undertaking. But Congress' policy has not yet moved to this point, and with only § 8(b) (3) to lean on, we do not see how the Board can do so on its own.

Affirmed.

[MR. JUSTICE FRANKFURTER, joined by MR. JUSTICE HARLAN and MR. JUSTICE WHITTAKER, filed a separate opinion.]

Problems for Discussion

1. Are the *Truitt* and *Insurance Agents* cases logically consistent in their premises and reasoning? Do you agree with the latter?

2. The Business Agent of International Brotherhood of Teamsters called at the office of the President of Quincy Lumber Co., and told him, "Your employees have designated Teamsters as their bargaining agent. Here is the contract we sign with lumber yards. Sign on page 9." Quincy agreed to recognize Teamsters and bargain collectively, knowing that majority of the employees had joined the union. However, Quincy expressed a desire to discuss the terms of the contract. The Business Agent replied, "This is the same contract we sign with all lumber yards. We'll discuss it if you wish, but there's a car full of pickets across the street who'll shut the yard down if you don't sign now." If Quincy refused to sign could it obtain legal relief against the picketing?

NLRB v. KATZ [20]

Supreme Court of the United States, 1962.
369 U.S. 736, 82 S.Ct. 1107, 8 L.Ed.2d 230.

Mr. Justice Brennan delivered the opinion of the Court.

Is it a violation of the duty "to bargain collectively" imposed by § 8(a) (5) of the National Labor Relations Act for an employer, without first consulting a union with which it is carrying on bona fide contract negotiations, to institute changes regarding matters which are subjects of mandatory bargaining under § 8(d) and which are in fact under discussion? The National Labor Relations Board answered the question affirmatively in this case, in a decision which expressly disclaimed any finding that the totality of the respondents' conduct manifested bad faith in the pending negotiations. 126 N.L. R.B. 288. A divided panel of the Court of Appeals for the Second Circuit denied enforcement of the Board's cease-and-desist order, finding in our decision in Labor Board v. Insurance Agents' Union, 361 U.S. 477, 80 S.Ct. 419, a broad rule that the statutory duty to bargain cannot be held to be violated, when bargaining is in fact being carried on, without a finding of the respondent's subjective bad faith in negotiating. 289 F.2d 700. * * *

We find nothing in the Board's decision inconsistent with *Insurance Agents* and hold that the Court of Appeals erred in refusing to enforce the Board's order.

The respondents are partners engaged in steel fabricating under the firm name of Williamsburg Steel Products Company. * * * The first meeting between the company and the union took place on August 30, 1956. * * * It is undisputed that the subject of merit increases was raised at the August 30, 1956, meeting although there is an unresolved conflict as to whether an agreement was reached on joint participation by the company and the union in merit reviews, or whether the subject was simply mentioned and put off for discussion at a later date. It is also clear that proposals concerning sick leave were made. Several meetings were held during October and one in November, at which merit raises and sick leave were each discussed on at least two occasions. It appears, however, that little progress was made. * * *

Meanwhile, on April 16, 1957, the union had filed the charge upon which the General Counsel's complaint later issued. As amended and amplified at the hearing and construed by the Board, the complaint's

20. See Comment, Impasse in Collective Bargaining, 44 Texas L.Rev. 769 (1966); Schatzki, The Employer's Uni- lateral Act—A Per Se Violation— Sometimes, 44 Texas L.Rev. 470 (1966).

charge of unfair labor practices particularly referred to three acts by the company: unilaterally granting numerous merit increases in October 1956 and January 1957; unilaterally announcing a change in sick-leave policy in March 1957; and unilaterally instituting a new system of automatic wage increases during April 1957.   *   *   *

The second line of defense was that the Board could not hinge a conclusion that § 8(a) (5) had been violated on unilateral actions alone, without making a finding of the employer's subjective bad faith at the bargaining table; and that the unilateral actions were merely evidence relevant to the issue of subjective good faith. This argument prevailed in the Court of Appeals.   *   *   *

The duty "to bargain collectively" enjoined by § 8(a) (5) is defined by § 8(d) as the duty to "meet   *   *   *   and confer in good faith with respect to wages, hours, and other terms and conditions of employment." Clearly, the duty thus defined may be violated without a general failure of subjective good faith; for there is no occasion to consider the issue of good faith if a party has refused even to negotiate *in fact*—"to meet   *   *   *   and confer"—about any of the mandatory subjects. A refusal to negotiate *in fact* as to any subject which is within § 8(d), and about which the union seeks to negotiate, violates § 8(a) (5) though the employer has every desire to reach agreement with the union upon an over-all collective agreement and earnestly and in all good faith bargains to that end. We hold that an employer's unilateral change in conditions of employment under negotiation is similarly a violation of § 8(a) (5), for it is a circumvention of the duty to negotiate which frustrates the objectives of § 8(a) (5) much as does a flat refusal.

The unilateral actions of the respondent illustrate the policy and practical considerations which support our conclusion.

We consider first the matter of sick leave. A sick-leave plan had been in effect since May 1956, under which employees were allowed ten paid sick-leave days annually and could accumulate half the unused days, or up to five days each year. Changes in the plan were sought and proposals and counter-proposals had come up at three bargaining conferences. In March 1957, the company, without first notifying or consulting the union, announced changes in the plan, which reduced from ten to five the number of paid sick-leave days per year, but allowed accumulation of twice the unused days, thus increasing to ten the number of days which might be carried over. This action plainly frustrated the statutory objective of establishing working conditions through bargaining. Some employees might view the change to be a diminution of benefits. Others, more interested in accumulating sick-leave days, might regard the change as an improvement. If one view or the other clearly prevailed among the employees, the unilateral action might well mean that the employer had either uselessly dissipated trading material or aggravated the sick-leave issue. On the other hand, if the employees were more evenly divided on the merits of the company's changes, the union negotiators, beset by conflicting factions, might be led to adopt a protective vagueness on the issue of sick leave, which also would inhibit the useful discussion contemplated by Congress in imposing the specific obligation to bargain collectively.

Other considerations appear from consideration of the respondents' unilateral action in increasing wages. At the April 4, 1957 meeting, the employers offered, and the union rejected, a three-year contract with an immediate across-the-board increase of $7.50 per week, to be followed at the end of the first year and again at the end of the second by further increases of $5 for employees earning less than $90 at those times. Shortly thereafter, without having advised or consulted with the union, the company announced a new system of automatic wage increases whereby there would be an increase of $5 every three months up to $74.99 per week; an increase of $5 every six months between $75 and $90 per week; and a merit review every six months for employees earning over $90 per week. It is clear at a glance that the automatic wage increase system which was instituted unilaterally was considerably more generous than that which had shortly theretofore been offered to and rejected by the union. Such action conclusively manifested bad faith in the negotiations, Labor Board v. Crompton-Highland Mills, 337 U.S. 217, 69 S.Ct. 960, and so would have violated § 8(a) (5) even on the Court of Appeals' interpretation, though no additional evidence of bad faith appeared. An employer is not required to lead with his best offer; he is free to bargain. But even after an impasse is reached he has no license to grant wage increases greater than any he has ever offered the union at the bargaining table, for such action is necessarily inconsistent with a sincere desire to conclude an agreement with the union.[21]

The respondents' third unilateral action related to merit increases, which are also a subject of mandatory bargaining. Labor Board v. Allison & Co., 165 F.2d 766. The matter of merit increases had been raised at three of the conferences during 1956 but no final understanding had been reached. In January 1957, the company, without notice to the union, granted merit increases to 20 employees out of the approximately 50 in the unit, the increases ranging between $2 and $10. This action too must be viewed as tantamount to an outright refusal to negotiate on that subject, and therefore as a violation of § 8(a) (5), unless the fact that the January raises were in line with

21. Of course, there is no resemblance between this situation and one wherein an employer, after notice and consultation, "unilaterally" institutes a wage increase identical with one which the union has rejected as too low. See Labor Board v. Bradley Washfountain Co., 192 F.2d 144, 150–152; Labor Board v. Landis Tool Co., 193 F.2d 279.

the company's long-standing practice of granting quarterly or semi-annual merit reviews—in effect, were a mere continuation of the status quo—differentiates them from the wage increases and the changes in the sick-leave plan. We do not think it does. Whatever might be the case as to so-called "merit raises" which are in fact simply automatic increases to which the employer has already committed himself, the raises here in question were in no sense automatic, but were informed by a large measure of discretion. There simply is no way in such case for a union to know whether or not there has been a substantial departure from past practice, and therefore the union may properly insist that the company negotiate as to the procedures and criteria for determining such increases.

It is apparent from what we have said why we see nothing in Insurance Agents contrary to the Board's decision. The union in that case had not in any way whatever foreclosed discussion of any issue, by unilateral actions or otherwise. The conduct complained of consisted of partial-strike tactics designed to put pressure on the employer to come to terms with the union negotiators. We held that Congress had not, in § 8(b) (3), the counterpart of § 8(a) (5), empowered the Board to pass judgment on the legitimacy of any particular economic weapon used in support of genuine negotiations. But the Board *is* authorized to order the cessation of behavior which is in effect a refusal to negotiate, or which directly obstructs or inhibits the actual process of discussion, or which reflects a cast of mind against reaching agreement. Unilateral action by an employer without prior discussion with the union does amount to a refusal to negotiate about the affected conditions of employment under negotiation, and must of necessity obstruct bargaining, contrary to the congressional policy. It will often disclose an unwillingness to agree with the union. It will rarely be justified by any reason of substance. It follows that the Board may hold such unilateral action to be an unfair labor practice in violation of § 8(a) (5), without also finding the employer guilty of overall subjective bad faith. While we do not foreclose the possibility that there might be circumstances which the Board could or should accept as excusing or justifying unilateral action, no such case is presented here.

The judgment of the Court of Appeals is reversed and the case is remanded with direction to the court to enforce the Board's order.

It is so ordered.

MR. JUSTICE FRANKFURTER took no part in the decision of this case.

MR. JUSTICE WHITE took no part in the consideration or decision of this case.

NLRB v. INTERCOASTAL TERMINAL, INC., 286 F.2d 954 (5th Cir. 1961). During 1957, the union and employer engaged in contract negotiations. Among the clauses sought by the employer was a management prerogatives clause which would have had the effect, *inter alia,* of allowing it broad authority to change work-schedules. Negotiations failed to result in a contract, and on January 10, 1958, the employer wrote to the union suggesting that an impasse had perhaps been reached but that the company was willing to continue the negotiations and/or sign a contract embodying those clauses on which tentative agreement had already been reached. The union did not respond to this letter nor did it communicate further with the employer until July 1958. Thereafter, the employer unilaterally changed various work schedules and also rescinded the two-week vacations which it had announced in 1957 would be given to black employees. The Board found that both of these unilateral changes constituted unlawful refusals to bargain. On petition to enforce the Board's order, *held*, the changes in work schedules were not unlawful, since management merely acted in accordance with its proposal previously discussed with the union and since a genuine impasse existed in view of the union's failure to reply to the employer's letter of January 10. On the other hand, the revocation of vacations was unlawful since changes in the company's vacation policies were never discussed in the prior negotiations with the union.

Problems for Discussion

1. The rationale in *Katz* appears to be that the unilateral changes made by the employer, before impasse and without notice to the union, are comparable to a flat refusal to bargain on those subjects. Do you agree? Since negotiations on sick leave, wages and merit-pay increases were actually taking place, is there not some better justification for the Court's holding?

2. The Board's decision in *Katz*—as well as its decisions in *Insurance Agents* and *Truitt*—exhibit an inclination toward the fashioning of *per se* tests, in which a single objective act is thought so seriously to conflict with the duty to bargain (and so rarely to be justifiable) that it alone warrants a finding of a violation, regardless of the bargainer's subjective state of mind. Such rules not only facilitate planning by the parties in the plant and at the bargaining table, but they also facilitate adjudication and conformity to NLRB remedial orders. Can you reconcile the Supreme Court's rejection of such a *per se* approach in *Insurance Agents* and its endorsement of such an approach in *Katz*?

3. Assume that the employer is obligated under the collective bargaining agreement to provide full pay for certain holidays and to contribute 60% of the cost of the employees' group insurance. Suppose further that the contract has expired, that negotiations over a new agreement have not yet reached an impasse, and that the employer has suddenly announced,

without prior notification to the union, that it has discontinued holiday pay and the insurance contributions. What arguments would you make on behalf of the employer, and what disposition should the Board make in the event of a complaint charging the employer with violating Section 8(a) (5)? See *Local 155, Molders* v. *N.L.R.B.*, 442 F.2d 742 (D.C.Cir. 1971); *Crestline Co.*, 133 N.L.R.B. 256 (1961).

4. The employer, a painting contractor, and the Painters' Union have a collective bargaining agreement which provides that employees within the unit are to work seven hours a day, five days a week. Although the contract makes no mention of any production quota, it has been the tradition, known to all parties, that journeymen painters complete an average of 11.5 rooms per week. On May 7, at a special meeting of the Union, a resolution was adopted to the effect that no journeyman was to paint more than ten rooms per week, given the desire of the membership to safeguard the health and safety of the painters and to improve the quality of their work. (Violations of this work rule were to be punishable by fine.) The resolution was implemented, and the employer has asked whether the Union's action constitutes an unlawful refusal to bargain in good faith. Does it? *New York Dist. Council 9, Painters* v. *NLRB*, 453 F.2d 783, cert. denied 408 U.S. 930 (2d Cir. 1972).

NLRB v. GENERAL ELECTRIC CO.[22]

United States Court of Appeals, Second Circuit 1970.
418 F.2d 736.

IRVING R. KAUFMAN, CIRCUIT JUDGE.

Almost ten years after the events that gave rise to this controversy, we are called upon to determine whether an employer may be guilty of bad faith bargaining, though he reaches an agreement with the union, albeit on the company's terms. We must also decide if the company committed three specific violations of the duty to bargain by failing to furnish information requested by the union, by attempting to deal separately with IUE locals, and by presenting a personal accident insurance program on a take-it-or-leave-it basis.

* * *

[After a strike in 1946 which resulted in a settlement which the General Electric Company regarded as extremely costly, it developed a new bargaining policy referred to as Boulwarism (named after a vice president for personnel relations). The new plan was threefold. As negotiations approached, the Company would use its local management personnel to help determine the desires of the workforce on

22. See Cooper, Boulwarism and the Duty to Bargain in Good Faith, 20 Rutgers L.Rev. 653 (1966); Gross, Cullen & Hanslowe, Good Faith in Labor Negotiations: Tests and Remedies, 53 Cornell L.Rev. 1009 (1968); H. Northrup, Boulwarism (1964); Note, Boulwareism: Legality and Effect, 76 Harv.L.Rev. 807 (1963).

the type and level of economic benefits; these were translated by the Company into specific proposals, whose cost and effectiveness were researched in order to determine an attractive bargaining offer within the Company's means; the Company then attempted to "sell" its proposals to its employees and the general public through a publicity campaign in plant newspapers, bulletins, letters, television and radio announcements and personal contacts. The Company announced in negotiations that it rejected the usual "horse-trading" approach to bargaining, with each side eventually compromising initial unreasonable positions; it advertised its initial proposals as "fair" and "firm." Though willing to accept Union suggestions based on facts it might have overlooked, General Electric refused to change its position simply because the Union disagreed with it. The Company also pursued a policy of guaranteeing uniform terms among its several unions and between union and nonunion workers.

In late 1959, the Company began to solicit employee views in anticipation of the 1960 contract negotiations. It also, over the objections of the IUE, announced (in June 1960) that it was instituting an accident and life insurance plan for the Company's nonunion employees, and later granted these employees a modest pay increase. Once negotiations began, General Electric widely publicized its claim that the Union's demands were "astronomical" and that the Company rather than the Union was the best guardian of the employees' interests. When the Company presented its "firm, fair offer" to the Union, in August 1960, it declined to honor the Union's request to delay publicizing the offer to the employees in order to give the Union an opportunity to consider it and to propose changes. The Company also rebuffed several Union requests for information in the Company's possession, particularly cost studies (the Company arguing that it negotiated only about the level of benefits to the employees and not about their cost to the Company). When the Union asked to have certain proposed wage increases granted in the form of supplemental unemployment benefits, the Company representatives responded that they would look foolish were they to retreat from the proposal already widely publicized to the employees. When the Union went out on strike in early October 1960, the Company made certain proposals to particular local unions several days before those terms were offered to the coordinating committee which was bargaining on behalf of all of the Union's members in all locals. On October 22, the Union capitulated and signed a memorandum agreement with the Company, and on October 24 the strike ended.

Proceedings were then initiated against General Electric for violations of Section 8(a)(5). The trial examiner concluded that: (1) The company failed to bargain in good faith by its "take it or leave it" proposal in June 1960 concerning accident insurance; (2) the company also violated Section 8(a)(5) by its refusals to divulge information (particularly regarding the cost to the company of furnishing certain fringe benefits) promptly to the union; (3) the company also violated Section 8(a)(5) by dealing directly with various local unions while obligated to bargain with the IUE–GE Conference Board as representative of all locals; and (4) the "totality" of the company's behavior revealed an attitude inconsistent with the "good faith" required by Section 8(a)(5); the last finding was based on the trial examiner's earlier findings (which did not turn upon the company's lack of subjective good faith) along with such other factors as the calculated strategy of the company to place itself in a position where it was all but impossible to modify its offer to the union. The Board endorsed all of the above findings of the trial examiner, the last of them by a vote of 3-to-2. The Board's decision was rendered on December 16, 1964, and it was not until June 3, 1969 that the case was argued on appeal to the Court of Appeals for the Second Circuit. The intervening period was devoted to litigation regarding certain procedural matters and to unsuccessful settlement discussions: during that time, the company and union negotiated two labor contracts, in 1963 and 1966. The court of appeals enforced the Board's order with regard to the accident insurance proposal, the refusal to disclose information, and the direct dealings with the local unions. Judge Kaufman then turned in Part V of his opinion to the Board finding of an overall failure to bargain in good faith which, in the court's words, was "compounded like a mosaic of many pieces, but depending not on any one alone. They are together to be understood to comprise the 'totality of the circumstances.' "]

The Board * * * chose to find an overall failure of good faith bargaining in GE's conduct. Specifically, the Board found that GE's bargaining stance and conduct, considered as a whole, were designed to derogate the Union in the eyes of its members and the public at large. This plan had two major facets: first, a take-it-or-leave-it approach ("firm, fair offer") to negotiations in general which emphasized both the powerlessness and uselessness of the Union to its members, and second, a communications program that pictured the Company as the true defender of the employees' interests, further denigrating the Union, and sharply curbing the Company's ability to change its own position. * * *

GE argues forcefully that it made so many concessions in the course of negotiations—concessions which, under section 8(d), it was not obliged to make—that its good faith and the absence of a take-it-or-leave-it attitude were conclusively proven, despite any contrary indicia on which the Trial Examiner and the Board rely. The dissent proceeds under the misapprehension that we consider lack of major concessions as evidence of bad faith. Rather, we discuss them only because while the absence of concessions would not prove bad faith, their presence would, as GE claims, raise a strong inference of good faith. On close examination, however, few of the alleged concessions turn out to have a great deal of substance. Its offer of a wage re-opener accompanied its original proposal; the option to choose a vacation instead of a wage increase was included over the Union's objections (at least during the negotiating meetings), and changes in the Pension Plan were more in the nature of clarifications than actual shifts in position, or in any case involved issues of quite minor significance.

The Company's stand, however, would be utterly inexplicable without the background of its publicity program. Only when viewed in that context does it become meaningful. We have already indicated that one of the central tenets of "the Boulware approach" is that the "product" or "firm, fair offer" must be marketed vigorously to the "consumers" or employees, to convince them that the Company, and not the Union, is their true representative. GE, the Trial Examiner found, chose to rely "entirely" on its communications program to the virtual exclusion of genuine negotiations, which it sought to evade by any means possible. Bypassing the national negotiators in favor of direct settlement dealings with employees and local officials forms another consistent thread in this pattern. The aim, in a word, was to deal with the Union through the employees, rather than with the employees through the Union.

The Company's refusal to withhold publicizing its offer until the Union had had an opportunity to propose suggested modifications is indicative of this attitude. Here two interests diverged. The command of the Boulware approach was clear: employees and the general public must be barraged with communications that emphasized the generosity of the offer, and restated the firmness of GE's position. A genuine desire to reach a mutual accommodation might, on the other hand, have called for GE to await Union comments before taking a stand from which it would be difficult to retreat. GE hardly hesitated. It released the offer the next day, without waiting for Union comments on specific portions.

The most telling effect of GE's marketing campaign was not on the Union, but on GE itself. Having told its employees that it had made a "firm, fair offer," that there was "nothing more to come," and that it would not change its position in the face of "threats" or a strike, GE had in effect rested all on the expectation that it could institute its offer without significant modification. Properly viewed, then, its communications approach determined its take-it-or-leave-it bargaining strategy. Each was the natural complement of the other; if either were substantially changed, the other would in all probability have to be modified as well. It is only in this context that

GE's incomprehensible insistence on a January 1 starting date for the pension benefits, and the "explanations" that followed it, can be understood.

All this was brought into the open during the September 28 meeting. Virtually on the eve of the strike, Union negotiators were searching for a way to save face by reconstituting their SUB proposal within the outlines of the Company's costs. Far from being frivolous as the dissent seems to suggest, such last minute attempts at compromise are the stuff of which lasting accommodations and productive labor-management relations are made. The substance of the Company's response to this effort was well put by their chief negotiator, Philip Moore:

> "After all our months of bargaining and after telling the employees before they went to vote that this is it, we would look ridiculous to change it at this late date; and secondly the answer is no."

The Company, having created a view of the bargaining process that admitted of no compromise, was trapped by its own creation. It could no longer seek peace without total victory, for it had by its own words and actions branded any compromise a defeat.

GE urges that section 8(c), 29 U.S.C. § 158(c) (1964), prohibits the Board from considering its publicity efforts in passing on the legality of its bargaining conduct. The section reads:

> "(c) The expressing of any views, argument, or opinion, or the dissemination thereof, whether in written, printed, graphic, or visual form, shall not constitute or be evidence of an unfair labor practice under any of the provisions of this subchapter, if such expression contains no threat of reprisal or force or promise of benefit."

GE would have us read that section as a bar to the Board's use of any communications, in any manner, unless the communication itself contained a threat or a promise of benefit. The legislative history, past decisions, and the logic of the statutory framework, however, indicate a contrary conclusion.

The bald prohibition of section 8(c) invited comment when it was enacted, as well as later. Senator Taft replied to some of the criticism of the bill that bears his name:

> "It should be noted that this subsection is limited to 'views, arguments, or opinions' and does not cover instructions, directions, or other statements that would ordinarily be deemed relevant and admissible in courts of law." I Legislative History of the LMRA 1947, at 1541.

The key word is "relevant." The evil at which the section was aimed was the alleged practice of the Board in inferring the existence of an unfair labor practice from a totally unrelated speech or opinion delivered by an employer. Senator Taft later indicated, for example, in the context of a section 8(a)(3) discriminatory firing, that prior statements of the employer would have to be shown to "tie in" with the specific unfair labor practice. I Legislative History of the LMRA 1947, at 1545. Later references to the section described the barred statements as those which were "severable or unrelated," and "irrelevant or immaterial." II Legislative History of the LMRA 1947, at 429 (Senate Report), 549 (House Conference Report). The objective of 8(c) then, was to impose a rule of relevancy on the Board in evaluating the legality of statements by parties to a labor dispute. Its purpose was hardly to eliminate all communications from the Board's purview, for to do so would be to emasculate a statute whose structure depends heavily on evaluation of motive and intent. See e. g., §§ 8(a)(1), 8(a)(3), 8(a)(5). * * *

While it is clear that the Board is not to control the substantive terms of a collective bargaining contract, nonetheless the parties must do more than meet. Our Brother FRIENDLY makes much of the point that General Electric did bargain and reach an "agreement" with the Union. He says that prior 8(a)(5) cases demanded nothing less than a showing of no such desire to reach an agreement, and opines that without such a "definite standard" an 8(a)(5) violation may not be made out. Some cases have indeed spoken of the evil of a "desire not to reach an agreement with the Union" as crucial. While the dissenting opinion cites NLRB v. Reed & Prince Mfg. Co., 205 F.2d 131, 134 (1st Cir.), cert. denied 346 U.S. 887, 74 S.Ct. 139, 98 L.Ed. 391 (1953), * * * [i]n the case before Judge Magruder, Reed & Prince submitted a woefully inadequate and demeaning "offer" of a contract. Presumably, the Union could have seen no alternative but to accept it, and had it done so, our Brother FRIENDLY would have held that the Company bargained with a "desire to reach an agreement," and thus had not violated the proscriptions of § 8(a)(5). Judge Magruder, on the other hand, said that the "employer is obliged to make *some* reasonable effort in *some* direction to compose his differences with the union, if § 8(a) (5) is to be read as imposing any substantial obligation at all." 205 F.2d at 135. His point, of course, was that "desire to reach agreement" may mean different things to different people, but in the context of a meaningful and purposeful reading of section 8(a)(5) it must mean more than a willingness to sign a piece of paper. The statute does not say that any "agreement" reached will validate whatever tactics have been employed to exact it. * * * A pattern of conduct by which one party makes it virtually impossible for him to respond to the other—knowing that he is doing so deliberately—should be condemned by the same rationale that prohibits "going through the motions" with a "predetermined resolve not to budge from an initial position." See NLRB v. Truitt Mfg. Co. supra (concurring opinion). * * *

In order to avoid any misunderstanding of our holding, some additional discussion is in order. We do not today hold that an employer may not communicate with his employees during negotiations. Nor are we deciding that the "best offer first" bargaining technique is forbidden. Moreover, we do not require an employer to engage in "auction bargaining," or, as the dissent seems to suggest, compel him to make concessions, "minor" or otherwise. * * *

We hold that an employer may not so combine "take-it-or-leave-it" bargaining methods with a widely publicized stance of unbending firmness that he is himself unable to alter a position once taken. It is this specific conduct that GE must avoid in order to comply with the Board's order, and not a carbon copy of every underlying event relied upon by the Board to support its findings. Such conduct, we find, constitutes a refusal to bargain "in fact." NLRB v. Katz, 369 U.S. 736, 743, 82 S.Ct. 1107 (1962). It also constitutes, as the facts of this action demonstrate, an absence of subjective good faith, for it implies that the Company can deliberately bargain and communicate as though the Union did not exist, in clear derogation of the Union's status as exclusive representative of its members under section 9(a). See NLRB v. Herman Sausage Co., 275 F.2d 229, 234 (5th Cir. 1960).

* * * The petition for review is denied, and the petition for enforcement of the Board's order is granted.

WATERMAN, Circuit Judge (concurring). * * *

We recognize that a company is entitled to insist on the terms of its original offer if it believes that the union can be made to accept that offer. That GE refused to yield to union demands without giving reasons based upon cost, maintained a "stiff and unbending" posture, used a unilateral letter of intent when final agreement was reached, failed to make significant concessions, and publicized its offer without waiting for union suggestions do not indicate anything except that GE made and stood by what it conceived to be a fair, firm offer.

What makes these practices unfair is GE's "widely publicized stance of unbending firmness," that is, GE's communications to its employees that firmness was one of the company's independent policies. Two distinct evils derive from such publicity. First, publicity regarding firmness tends to make the company seal itself into its original position in such a way that, even if it wished to change that position at a later date, its pride and reputation for truthfulness are so at stake that it cannot do so. Second, publicity regarding firmness fixes in the minds of employees the idea that the company has set itself up as their representative and therefore that the union is superfluous. Doubtless these evils exist to some extent whenever a company makes, and stands by, a firm fair offer even when there is no company publicity of the kind here involved. However, it seems clear that publicity tends to amplify these undesirable tendencies to the point that, in a case such as this one, the amplification can well be construed to have been activated by a company motive not to bargain in good faith.

On the other side of the ledger there is very little positive good which can derive from company publicity which indicates that a company believes in firmness for firmness' sake. The free speech benefits of publicity in labor negotiations lie in the fact that informed employees will better know whether to vote for or against a strike and how to evaluate the union's performance on their behalf. These benefits can all be reaped by a company which advertises the terms of an offer and its belief that these terms are fair, without also stating that as a matter of policy it can never be persuaded to change the advertised terms. Such advertisement could only tend to convince employees that because firmness is a company policy it is also a company policy to ignore the union. A company, of course, can advertise its belief that its offer is fair, and that, at the particular time, it sees no reason to change its offer even to forestall a strike. This kind of statement is different from advertising that it is company policy never to change any offer in response to union pressure. * * *

FRIENDLY, CIRCUIT JUDGE (concurring and dissenting).

* * * [T]he majority of the Board was at pains to emphasize that its finding of overall bad faith was not based upon identifiable acts or failures to act that GE could avoid in the future but rather

> upon our review of (1) the Respondent's entire course of conduct, (2) its failure to furnish relevant information, (3) its attempts to deal separately with locals and to bypass the national bargaining representative, (4) the manner of its presentation of the accident insurance proposal, (5) the disparagement of the Union as bargaining representative by the communication program, (6) its conduct of the negotiations themselves, and (7) its attitude or approach as revealed by all these factors.

Such attempts to restrict communications (item 5) and lay down standards with respect to bargaining techniques, attitudes and approaches (items (6) and (7)), bring the Board into collision with § 8(c) and (d) and the important policies they embody. It is easy to understand that anyone reviewing this enormous record would emerge with a good deal of sympathy for the situation of the Union and distaste for the tactics of the employer; no one likes to see a person who regards himself as in a strong position pushing it unduly, even though the fairness of GE's offer is not challenged. But the Act does not empower the Board to translate such feelings into a finding of an unfair labor practice, and judicial sanction of such efforts to intrude into areas which Congress left to the parties may in the long run be quite as detrimental to unions as to employers. See NLRB v. Insurance Agents' Int'l Union, 361 U.S. 477, 80 S.Ct. 419, 4 L.Ed.2d 454 (1960). * * *

The danger of collision with § 8(c) or (d) arises only when the Board makes a finding of violation although the parties have sat down with each other and have not engaged in any proscribed tactic. Still I have no difficulty with the Board's making a finding of bad faith based on an entire course of conduct so long as the standard of bad faith is, in Judge Magruder's well-known phrase, a "desire not to reach an agreement with the Union." NLRB v. Reed & Prince Mfg. Co., 205 F.2d 131, 134 (1 Cir.), cert. denied 346 U.S. 887, 74 S.Ct. 139, 98 L.Ed. 391 (1953). In such instances, the difficulties inevitable in an examination of the "totality of the circumstances" and an order based upon them are outweighed by the definiteness of the standard, the consequent feasibility of compliance, and the necessity for such an order if the employer's duty to recognize the union is to be carried out in substance as well as in form. See, e. g., NLRB v. Montgomery Ward & Co., 133 F.2d 676, 146 A.L.R. 1045 (9th Cir. 1943). However, as Professor Cox remarked in a notable article which has been cited with approval by the Supreme Court, NLRB v. Insurance Agents' Union, supra, 361 U.S. at 489–490, 80 S.Ct. 419, and has not suffered from the lapse of a decade, it is "doubtful whether much is gained by retrospective review of the negotiations when the parties have actually bargained together." The Duty to Bargain in Good Faith, 71 Harv.L.Rev. 1401, 1439 (1958). Here the General Counsel conceded that GE entertained no such prohibited desire and, despite the majority's innuendoes concerning antiunion animus, the Trial Examiner rightly observed that no claim was "made in this case that the respondent was seeking to rid itself of the Union," with which it had been dealing for many years and expected to deal for many more. * * *

While the lead opinion makes much use of the "take-it-or-leave-it" phrase, it never defines this. I should suppose it meant a resolve to adhere to a position without even listening to and considering the views of the other side. To go further and say that a party, whether employer or union, who, after listening to and considering such proposals, violates § 8(a)(5) if he rejects them because of confidence in his own bargaining power, would ignore the explicit command of § 8(d) * * * *

It surely cannot be, for example, that a union intent on imposing area standards violates § 8(b)(3) if it refuses to heed the well-documented presentation of an employer who insists that acceptance of them will drive him out of business. Neither can it be that a union violates § 8(b)(3) if it insists on its demands because it knows the employer simply cannot stand a strike. It must be equally true that an employer is not to be condemned for "take-it-or-leave-it" bargaining when, after discussing the union's proposals and supporting arguments, he formulates what he considers a sufficiently attractive offer and refuses to alter it unless convinced an alteration is "right." Hence the Board correctly declined to affix the "take-it-or-leave-it" label which my Brother KAUFMAN uses.

Once we rid ourselves of the prejudice inevitably engendered by this catch-phrase, we reach the argument that a party violates § 8(a) (5) if he gets himself into a situation where he is "unable to alter a position once taken," even though he would otherwise be willing to do so. * * * I find no substantial evidence that GE got itself into the predicament the majority depicts. The best evidence to the contrary consists of the changes the Company in fact made. * * *

The Union's appraisals of the value of these concessions at the time is more impressive than the depreciation of them nine years after the event. Moreover, in appraising such concessions it is important to remember Judge Burger's caution that, although it may sometimes be necessary to consider "the reasonableness of parties' positions on particular issues to determine whether, under all the circumstances of the negotiation, a particular bargaining position was adopted for the purpose of frustrating negotiation generally and thus preventing an agreement," "the courts have been vigilant lest the examination of parties' positions to test good faith become a process of judging, directly or indirectly, the substantive terms of their proposals." United States Steelworkers of America v. NLRB, supra, 390 F.2d at 853 (dissenting opinion). By characterizing some of the changes as "of quite minor significance," the lead opinion does precisely that.

I find nothing on the other side substantial enough to outweigh this evidence that GE remained able to adopt changes it thought to be "right." * * *

An essential element to the Board's conclusion of GE's offending was the Company's publicity campaign. "The disparagement of the Union as bargaining representative" is item (5) in the Board's bill of particulars. The Board elaborated this by saying it is unlawful "for an employer to mount a campaign, as Respondent did, both before and during negotiations, for the purpose of disparaging and discrediting the statutory representative in the eyes of its employees, to exert pressure on the representative to submit to the will of the employer, and to create the impression that the employer rather than the union is the true protector of the employees' interests."

I find no warrant for such a holding in the language of the statute, its legislative history or decisions construing it. GE's communications fit snugly under the phrase "views, argument, or opinion" in § 8(c). The very archetypes of what Congress had in mind were communications by an employer to his workers designed to influence their decisions contrary to union views, and communications by unions to workers designed to influence their decisions contrary to employer views. The statute draws no distinctions between communications by an employer in an effort to head off organization and communications after organization intended to show that he is doing right by his employees and will do no more under the threat of a strike. Congress had enough faith in the common sense of the American working man to believe he did not need—or want—to be shielded by a government agency from hearing whatever arguments employers or unions desired to make to him. Freedom of choice by employees after hearing all relevant arguments is the cornerstone of the National Labor Relations Act. * * *

It is plain that GE's communications came under the protection of the statute, and not the exception which Senator Taft described. The word "relevant" in Senator Taft's speech cannot be blown up to such a degree as to render the amendment largely nugatory. * * *

The Examiner coined a phrase, echoed both by the Board and in the lead opinion, * * * namely, that GE's communications program was an attempt "to deal with the Union through the employees rather than with the employees through the Union." Somewhat parallel to this is the opinion's statement that the Company "deliberately bargain[ed] and communicate[d] as though the Union did not exist, in clear derogation of the Union's status as exclusive representative of its members under section 9(a)," * * *. Picturesque characterizations of this sort, at such sharp variance with the record, scarcely aid the quest for a right result. Members of Congress would probably be surprised to learn that being "exclusive representatives" means that interested parties may not go to constituents in an endeavor to influence the representatives to depart from positions they have taken. There can be nothing wrong in an employer's urging employees to communicate with their representatives simply because the communication is one the representatives do not want to hear. I thus find it impossible to accept the proposition that, by exercising its § 8(c) right to persuade the employees and by encouraging them to exercise their right to persuade their representatives, GE was somehow "ignoring the legitimacy and relevance of the Union's position as statutory representative of its members" * * *.

* * * No one denies that § 8(c) protects employer communications attempting to persuade employees that they should not strike because the offer fully meets their needs, because union leaders are seeking a strike for personal reasons, or because a strike will cost too much in lost pay. To prohibit an employer from adding that the mere fact of a strike would gain nothing in the way of further concessions would remove his most important and most relevant argument. * * *

It is doubtless true in labor as in other negotiations that the louder people shout, the harder it becomes for them to change their positions without unacceptable loss of face. In that sense any positive public declaration, whether by an employer or by a union, may run counter to the objective of securing industrial peace by promoting agreement. But the Board has been expressly prohibited from promoting peace by restricting speech. Conformably with the dictates of the First Amendment, Congress, when it enacted § 8(c), determined the dangers that free expression might entail for successful bargaining were a lesser risk than to have the Board police employer or union speech. * * *

The only standard of conduct set for GE by the Board's opinion is that a mix of the "fair, firm offer" technique pursued to an unknown point X, plus a communications program pursued to an equally unknown point Y, plus a number of additional items, Z_1, Z_2, and Z_3, is proscribed. This already sufficient confusion is now compounded by the difference in my brothers' efforts at elucidation.

In view of the general obscurity of what GE is and is not permitted to do, the Company could take little comfort from the majority's assurance that it will be given a full opportunity to show it has made a good faith effort at compliance before it is held in contempt. In fact, however, no contempt proceeding could be successfully maintained. For the Supreme Court has very recently declared, in the closely related context of an equitable decree with respect to work stoppages, that "The most fundamental postulates of our legal order forbid the imposition of a penalty for disobeying a command that defies comprehension." International Longshoremen's Ass'n Local

1291 v. Philadelphia Marine Trade Ass'n, 389 U.S. 64, 76, 88 S.Ct. 201, 208, 19 L.Ed.2d 236 (1967).

The venerable age this case has attained is a further reason for declining to churn up waters that already are troubled enough. * * * [A] court must have some discretion to decline to enforce a Labor Board order relating to practices nearly a decade in the past when, as here, the parties have engaged in bargaining, any harmful effect of the alleged unfair labor practice has been dissipated, the case was one of first impression, and there has thus been no "stubborn refusal to abide by the law." * * *

NLRB v. HERMAN SAUSAGE CO., 275 F.2d 229 (5th Cir. 1960): "If the insistence is genuinely and sincerely held, if it is not mere window dressing, it may be maintained forever though it produce a stalemate. Deep conviction, firmly held and from which no withdrawal will be made, may be more than the traditional opening gambit of a labor controversy. It may be both the right of the citizen and essential to our economic legal system * * * of free collective bargaining. The Government, through the Board, may not subject the parties to direction either by compulsory arbitration or the more subtle means of determining that the position is inherently unreasonable, or unfair, or impracticable, or unsound."

Problems for Discussion

1. The *General Electric* decision, in spite of the court's caveats, appears to contemplate labor negotiations in which each side as its initial position states proposals which are predictably unacceptable to the other, and through a process of "horsetrading" retreats gradually into a zone of possible acceptability. Expressed or implied are such sentiments on the part of the union as "Our people will settle for no less" and on the part of the company, "The company can offer no more"; but after trade-offs and sometimes threats, the union takes less and the company gives more. To the extent such a dynamic is required by law, is it reconcilable with the model of labor negotiations sketched out in the *Truitt* case, pp. 394–96, supra? Which is the more realistic model? The more desirable?

2. Consider again Problem 4 on page 384 and Problem 2 on page 415. How does the *General Electric* decision affect your analysis of those problems?

3. Suppose that an employer and a union bargained at length, with concessions being made on both sides, until the fifteenth negotiating session after three months, when the employer announced that it had made all the concessions it could and that its position thereafter would be firm. The employer then commenced an intensive campaign of publicity to convince employees that management's latest offer was fair, that the union's

remaining demands were irresponsible, and that a strike would represent a needless expenditure of the employees' and the company's money. Would this conduct constitute, or be evidence of, a refusal to bargain in good faith?

4. Most Board orders give the respondent some specific guidance regarding the conduct which must henceforth be avoided. Does the general bargaining order in *General Electric* satisfy that objective? What kind of conduct will violate it? How ought alleged violations of the general bargaining order be challenged?

C. Subjects of Collective Bargaining [23]

The desire of employees and unions to participate in entrepreneurial decisions often goes very far into the management of an enterprise because many decisions not directly related to wages, hours, or working conditions nonetheless have major implications for the employees as individuals or for the union as an organization or for both.

The substitution of business machines for clerks in the offices of an electric utility or insurance company would eliminate hundreds, if not thousands, of jobs; so would moving a plastics or textile manufacturing concern from Rhode Island to a new plant in Mississippi. Dropping a line of products as commercially unprofitable may cause temporary or even permanent unemployment for workers whose skills are limited. At least in theory cutting an advertising appropriation can have similar consequences.

In the case of a narrowly-based craft union, managerial decisions concerning the introduction of new equipment and changes in staffing patterns may sometimes have more effect on the organization than on the workers. When flight engineers are displaced from the cockpit of commercial aircraft, or when typesetters are displaced from the composing room of a newspaper, job security for the workers may be protected by transferring them to other jobs or eliminating jobs only by omitting to fill vacancies. But the unions involved can foresee their own demise if the crafts they represent are thus eliminated.

The range of putative subjects for collective bargaining is much wider than suggested by these illustrations, and covers such diverse matters as awarding individual merit increases in rate of pay,

---

23. See Christensen, New Subjects and New Concepts in Collective Bargaining, ABA Section of Labor Relations Law Proceedings 245 (1970); Cox and Dunlop, Regulation of Collective Bargaining by the National Labor Relations Board, 63 Harv.L.Rev. 389, 427 (1950); Fillion & Trebilcock, The Duty to Bargain Under ERISA, 17 Wm. & Mary L.Rev. 251 (1975); Modjeska, Guess Who's Coming to the Bargaining Table?, 39 Ohio St.L.J. 415 (1978); Note, Proper Subjects for Collective Bargaining: Ad Hoc v. Predictive Definition, 58 Yale L.J. 803 (1949); Oldham, Organized Labor, the Environment and the Taft-Hartley Act, 71 Mich.L.Rev. 936 (1973).

the location of a new plant, and the calculation of profits. Recent experiments have even involved the workers in structuring the very processes by which they manufacture their company's products and participating in the company's managing board.

The question who shall participate in a decision in the management of an enterprise is inextricably bound up with the question of the considerations to be given weight in reaching the decision. If the decision is treated as a management function, economic efficiency will usually have predominant weight. If the union participates, what it sees as the impact upon the men and women who compose the workforce may become a major factor. Labor and management are constantly allocating responsibility between themselves on such matters as individual merit increases, shift schedules, subcontracting, and plant removal. The question for the law student to consider is: What role if any does the law play—or can it most usefully play—in allocating the decisionmaking function?

The language of Sections 8(d) and 9(a) can easily be read as a command to bargain upon each and every subject embraced within the critical phrase, rates of pay, wages, hours, and other conditions of employment, but the words are scarcely compelling. Probably, neither Congress nor the public had any notion when the Wagner Act was adopted in 1935 that the law was undertaking to define the scope of collective bargaining. Senator Walsh, the Chairman of the Senate Labor Committee, had explained (79 Cong.Rec. 7660 (1935)):

> When the employees have chosen their organization, when they have selected their representatives, all the bill proposed to do is to escort them to the door of their employer and say 'Here they are, the legal representatives of your employees.' What happens behind those doors is not inquired into and the bill does not seek to inquire into it.

As an original question, therefore, it seems quite possible that the law might have come to be that a union and an employer who genuinely accepts the union as the employees' representative will be left to work out and, if necessary, to fight out between themselves whether any particular subject (such as pensions, merit increases or subcontracting) will be included in their negotiations and covered by their contract.

But the law has taken a different course. Two rules seem quite settled. *First,* the duty to bargain extends to each and every subject embraced within the statutory phrase, so that it is an unfair labor practice for either the employer or union to refuse to bargain about such a subject upon the request of the other. See NLRB v. Katz, 369 U.S. 736, 82 S.Ct. 1107, 8 L.Ed.2d 230 (1962), at p. 416 supra. *Second,* there are other subjects which fall outside the phrase, wages, hours and other terms and conditions of employment, and which, therefore, are not statutory. There is no duty to bargain about these topics. Under some circumstances, insisting upon bargaining to agreement on a non-statutory subject *may* be a *per se* violation of either Section 8(a)(5) or 8(b)(3). NLRB v. Wooster Div. of Borg-Warner Corp., see p. 448 infra.

The list of statutory subjects includes: (1) wages very broadly defined to include pensions, fringe benefits such as hospital and medical insurance, profit-sharing, stock purchases at less than market price, and all other forms of compensation; (2) work rules dealing with such subjects as seniority, work-loads and discipline; (3) matters of union status, such as the recognition clause, union shop, and check-off; and (4) perhaps some more or less peripheral items embraced under the heading "conditions of employment," such as subcontracting, technological change, volume of production, decentralization and plant location.

The list of non-statutory subjects includes proposals which are illegal under the National Labor Relations Act, such as the closed shop, Penello v. UMW, 88 F.Supp. 935 (D.D.C.1950); or inconsistent with NLRA duties, such as bargaining for an inappropriate unit, Douds v. ILA, 241 F.2d 278 (2d Cir. 1957), introducing a party other than the certified union, or derogating from the union's authority, NLRB v. Wooster Div. of Borg-Warner, p. 448 infra. Probably the non-statutory subjects include clauses which are illegal under other valid statutes or contrary to public policy. Finally, the non-mandatory or non-statutory subjects of bargaining include those of the more or less peripheral items mentioned above which are held not to be covered by the phrase "wages, hours, and other terms and conditions of employment."

The materials that follow focus upon two questions: (1) What are the statutory subjects and what are the principles according to which they are to be identified; and (2) What are the consequences of inclusion or exclusion of a particular subject. The two questions are interrelated because one cannot intelligently consider whether a particular topic—subcontracting of maintenance work, for example—should be a mandatory subject of collective bargaining without understanding what are the legal as well as the practical consequences of that decision. The task of classifying bargaining subjects as mandatory has arisen in at least three settings: (a) The union requests that the employer bargain about the subject, but the employer refuses; if the subject is within the statutory categories, the employer's refusal obviously constitutes a violation of Section 8(a)(5), but if the subject is non-statutory, there is no duty to bargain and the employer's refusal is privileged. (b) The employer without consulting with the union on the subject, implements a change in its operations; such a "unilateral" change will violate the Act if it relates to a mandatory subject but not otherwise. (c) The employer during negotiations takes a position on a subject, and demands that the union concede on that subject as a condition of reaching an agreement. Conversely, the union might take an adamant stand on an issue, and back its insistence with a strike.

All of the major cases that follow deal with the problem of characterizing a subject (sometimes during formal contract negotiations and sometimes not) as "mandatory" or "permissive." In the *Fibreboard* and *Pittsburgh Plate Glass* decisions—which were cases which combined the elements just described in fact-settings (a) and (b) —once the disputed subject was characterized, the legal consequences flowed readily. In the *American National Insurance* and *Borg-Warner* cases, which involved the employer's insistence on its position at the bargaining table, the Supreme Court had to decide not only how the subject matter should be characterized but also whether insistence was consistent with the statutory obligation to bargain in good faith. The answer to that latter question determines the relative spheres of collective-bargaining responsibility between government and private parties; or, to put it another way, it determines the extent to which private economic force can be used in support of bargaining demands and thus ultimately the substantive content of the labor contract. (The duty to bargain about a particular subject is often affected by any collective bargaining agreement which is in existence at the time. Although the issue of the duty to bargain during the contract term is considered in some degree in the *Pittsburgh Plate Glass* case, a more detailed discussion is reserved for a later point in this case book; see pp. 658–69, infra.)

COX AND DUNLOP, REGULATION OF COLLECTIVE
BARGAINING BY THE NATIONAL LABOR
RELATIONS BOARD

63 Harv.L.Rev. 389, 401–405, 407–411 (1950).

The [decided cases] * * * appear to commit the NLRB to defining the scope of collective bargaining. But it is uncertain whether the rulings represent an administrative determination that such matters fall within the area of joint responsibility, or merely mark out the range of topics about which management and union are to negotiate, leaving their classification among the three categories [for management to decide, for the union to decide, or for both to decide jointly] to the bargaining process.

To make the problem concrete we may refer again to the *Inland Steel* litigation. Inland announced the categorical position that there was no statutory duty to bargain with the Steelworkers about retirements and pensions and then refused to engage in further discussions. The NLRB held that the refusal violated section 8(a) (5). Let us suppose, however, that Inland had given the Steelworkers this answer:

"We recognize your authority to speak for the employees about pensions or any other subject and we are glad to discuss the matter with you. Our position is that the union should agree to give the company exclusive responsibility over pensions and retirements. The subjects are linked with corporate tax and financial policies and involve complex statistical inquiries. Moreover, our employees are represented in different units by 23 unions of which you are only one. It would be intolerable to bargain about a company pension plan each year with each of 23 unions. We will be glad to hear your views and to explain our thinking on the subject and if you convince us that we are wrong, we will of course go on to consider whether a new pension fund should be established and what its terms should be."

Would this position violate section 8(a) (5)?

The same question arises with respect to other subjects on which the NLRB has held employers must bargain. Does the NLRB's declaration that an employer must negotiate with the bargaining representative about the subcontracting of work mean that the union must be allowed to share in each decision as to what work may be let out and what work will be kept in the shop? Or may the employer bargain for a provision in the collective agreement either recognizing that this aspect of planning the work will be the exclusive function of management or calling for him to talk the matter over with the union but reserving the right to make the decision? The NLRB has also said that an employer is required to bargain about the scheduling of shifts. When the scheduling of shifts requires the careful synchronization of complicated processes, must management agree to fix the starting time of each shift by the give-and-take of bargaining or may it assert that the resolution of technological problems should be made the exclusive function of management by the terms of the collective bargaining agreement?

A priori the bare words of section 8(a) (5) are open to two conflicting interpretations, which may be stated somewhat argumentatively as follows: *First*. Section 8(a) (5) makes it an unfair labor practice "to refuse to bargain collectively" with the representative designated by a majority of the employees. Section 9(a) plainly declares that the representative's authority extends to "rates of pay, wages, hours of employment, or other conditions of employment." Therefore, the employer must bargain with respect to each such subject and, as in the *Inland Steel* case, a refusal to discuss a subject covered by the quoted phrase is an unfair labor practice. Nor can this duty be satisfied by going through the forms of bargaining; the employer must have an open mind and sincere desire to reach an agreement. But although an employer must discuss every subject embraced within section 9(a), he complies with the duty to bargain if he negotiates in good faith any question as to whether a specific term or condition of employment (1) should be established by the collective agreement; or (2) should be fixed periodically by joint management-union determination within the framework of the contract; or (3) should be left to management's discretion or individual bargaining without the intervention of the bargaining agent.

Second. Under sections 8(a) (5) and 9(a) an employer must bargain collectively with respect to each subject embraced within the quoted phrase. The essential policy of the statute is that industrial peace can be achieved by taking from management exclusive control over wages, hours, and the other aspects of the employment relationship defined by section 9(a). For that reason the Supreme Court and court of appeals have repeatedly held that section 8(a) (5) makes unilateral action by an employer an unfair labor practice. The employer who insists upon unilateral control of any "condition of employment" is therefore guilty of an unfair labor practice even though he backs his position by argument and negotiates in good faith.

The choice between these interpretations will determine how the line is to be drawn between the area of exclusive management functions on the one side and the sphere of joint management-union responsibility on the other. Similar questions will have to be decided in drawing a line between the sphere of joint responsibility and the union's internal affairs. Under the first interpretation the lines would be drawn by managements and unions in the course of their annual contract negotiations and, if they could not agree, by recourse to economic weapons. Under the second interpretation the line would be drawn by the NLRB and the courts. Since pensions and merit increases are held to be covered by section 9(a), management could not bargain for exclusive responsibility without running afoul of section 8(a) (5); decisions with respect to them would have to be joint decisions. Similarly the Board and courts would decide as issues of statutory construction whether letting subcontracts and scheduling shifts are management's functions or problems requiring joint determination.

*   *   *

Merit Increases. From its inception, collective bargaining has established a wage rate for each job classification or each craft. The terms "standard rate," "price list," or "scale" have been used to refer to these wage rates. Collective bargaining over wages has centered largely, although not exclusively, on proposed changes by one side or the other in these contract wage rates.

The issue inevitably arises in the practical operation of a business whether the contract rate may be exceeded by the employer for particular individual workmen. Some workers may possess superior skill. Such workers are scarce and employers are willing to pay more to attract them. Quality factors or personality may be decisive in some types of work. A single job classification or craft with a single rate may in fact include a variety of types of work, some of which require additional experience and training. A piecework or incentive system permits variations in individual earnings where performance is readily measurable. But under an hourly-rate method of wage payment the question must be answered whether the contract rate is a maximum as well as a minimum. The Webbs' answer, "The standard rate * * * is only a minimum, never a maximum." is generally accepted.

Collective bargaining has developed a variety of procedures to deal with these merit increases. At one end of the spectrum are those methods by which the parties have entirely or largely removed questions of increases above the scale from the area of joint determination by agreements vesting in management exclusive authority over such increases. At the other end are contracts giving the union sole responsibility for their distribution. Between the extremes lie the contracts placing such matters in the area of joint determination. The following contract provisions are illustrative of agreed assignment to management control:

"Where voluntary increases are given to employees on account of special skill, superior workmanship, or for other reasons, the Union shall be notified; such action on the part of the Employer shall be final and no other employee shall have the right to demand similar treatment." * * *

"Employees shall receive not less than the job rates for the work performed. * * *" (Agreement between Standard Oil Co. of Cal. and Oil Workers Int'l Union, Local 547, CIO, effective November 3, 1948).

There are many contracts which treat merit increases as falling within the area of joint control. For example:

"No increase shall be granted to any employee unless consented to by the union." * * *

The above reference to specific agreements indicates that collective bargaining has elected in numerous instances to exclude merit increases from the area of joint determination. These decisions have been made by aggressive unions, mature in collective bargaining, generally in situations where individual workers may have considerable individual bargaining power, or where qualitative factors of skill or personality are not readily standardized. It would indeed be a strange result of a law designed to "encourage collective bargaining" to preclude an employer in bargaining from taking a position on merit increases which had been accepted and incorporated in agreements between union and many other employers, including his competitors.

* * *

Subcontracting. Subcontracting here refers to the process by which a company purchases goods or services from another enterprise which it might otherwise have produced or performed at its own plants and facilities. In industries, such as clothing, garments, millinery, and shoes, where operations may readily be transferred among shops, collective bargaining has frequently developed detailed regulations covering subcontracting. In these highly competitive industries, with few obstacles to the entry of new firms, unlimited subcontracting could quickly affect union employment opportunities, the success of a strike, and the contract wage scale. In some other industries, such as basic steel and chemicals, the subcontracting issue has rarely, if ever, arisen in collective bargaining, and few contract provisions exist on the topic. The companies and most unions agree that the sole right to determine the extent of subcontracting is fully reserved in management rights clauses.

An examination of collective bargaining agreements again reveals a full spectrum of provisions extending from the detailed regulation of subcontracting by joint determination to contract terms which, in addition to general management rights clauses, specify exclusive management responsibility for subcontracting.   *   *   *

NLRB v. AMERICAN NATIONAL INSURANCE CO.

Supreme Court of the United States, 1952.
343 U.S. 395, 72 S.Ct. 824, 96 L.Ed. 1027.

MR. CHIEF JUSTICE VINSON delivered the opinion of the Court.

This case arises out of a complaint that respondent refused to bargain collectively with the representatives of its employees as required under the National Labor Relations Act, as amended.

The Office Employees' International Union A. F. of L., Local No. 27, certified by the National Labor Relations Board as the exclusive bargaining representative of respondent's office employees, requested a meeting with respondent for the purpose of negotiating an agreement governing employment relations. At the first meetings, beginning on November 30, 1948, the Union submitted a proposed contract covering wages, hours, promotions, vacations and other provisions commonly found in collective bargaining agreements, including a clause establishing a procedure for settling grievances arising under the contract by successive appeals to management with ultimate resort to an arbitrator.

On January 10, 1949 following a recess for study of the Union's contract proposals, respondent objected to the provisions calling for unlimited arbitration. To meet this objection, respondent proposed a so-called management functions clause listing matters such as promotions, discipline and work scheduling as the responsibility of management and excluding such matters from arbitration. The Union's representative took the position "as soon as [he] heard [the proposed clause]" that the Union would not agree to such a clause so long as it covered matters subject to the duty to bargain collectively under the Labor Act.

Several further bargaining sessions were held without reaching agreement on the Union's proposal or respondent's counterproposal to unlimited arbitration. As a result, the management functions clause was "by-passed" for bargaining on other terms of the Union's contract proposal. On January 17, 1949, respondent stated in writing its agreement with some of the terms proposed by the Union and, where there was disagreement, respondent offered counterproposals, including a clause entitled "Functions and Prerogatives of Management" along the lines suggested at the meeting of January 10th. The Union objected to the portion of the clause providing:

> "The right to select and hire, to promote to a better position, to discharge, demote or discipline for cause, and to maintain discipline and efficiency of employees and to determine the schedules of work is recognized by both union and company as the proper responsibility and prerogative of management to be held and exercised by the company, and while it is agreed that an employee feeling himself to have been aggrieved by any decision of the company in respect to such matters, or the union in his behalf, shall have the right to have such decision reviewed by top management officials of the company under the grievance machinery hereinafter set forth, it is further agreed that the final decision of the company made by such top management officials shall not be further reviewable by arbitration."

At this stage of the negotiations, the National Labor Relations Board filed a complaint against respondent based on the Union's charge that respondent had refused to bargain as required by the Labor Act and was thereby guilty of interfering with the rights of its employees guaranteed by Section 7 of the Act and of unfair labor practices under Sections 8(a)(1) and 8(a)(5) of the Act. While the proceeding was pending, negotiations between the Union and respondent continued with the management functions clause remaining an obstacle to agreement. * * * Finally, on January 13, 1950, after the Trial Examiner had issued his report but before decision by the Board, an agreement between the Union and respondent was signed. The agreement contained a management functions clause that rendered nonarbitrable matters of discipline, work schedules and other matters covered by the clause. The subject of promotions and demotions was deleted from the clause and made the subject of a special clause establishing a union-management committee to pass upon promotion matters.   *   *   *

The Board agreed with the Trial Examiner that respondent had not bargained in a good faith effort to reach an agreement with the Union [based on all of the circumstances, including a unilateral change in working conditions during bargaining]. But the Board rejected the Examiner's views on an employer's right to bargain for a management functions clause and held that respondent's action in bargaining for inclusion of any such clause "constituted, quite [apart from] Respondent's demonstrated bad faith, per se violations of Section 8(a)(5) and (1)." Accordingly, the Board not only ordered respondent in general terms to bargain collectively with the Union (par. 2(a)), but also included in its order a paragraph designed to prohibit bargaining for any management functions clause covering a condition of employment. (Par. 1(a)). 89 N.L.R.B. 185.   *   *   *

First. The National Labor Relations Act is designed to promote industrial peace by encouraging the making of voluntary agreements governing relations between unions and employers. The Act does not compel any agreement whatsoever between employees and employers. Nor does the Act regulate the substantive terms governing wages, hours and working conditions which are incorporated in an agreement.[24] The theory of the Act is that the making of voluntary labor agreements is encouraged by protecting employees' rights to organize for collective bargaining and by imposing on labor and management the mutual obligation to bargain collectively.   *   *   *

In 1947, the fear was expressed in Congress that the Board "has gone very far, in the guise of determining whether or not employers had bargained in good faith, in setting itself up as the judge of what concessions an employer must make and of the proposals and counterproposals that he may or may not make." Accordingly, the Hartley Bill, passed by the House, eliminated the good faith test and expressly provided that the duty to bargain collectively did not re-

---

24. Terminal Railroad Ass'n v. Trainmen, 318 U.S. 1, 6, 63 S.Ct. 420, 423, 87 L.Ed. 571 (1943):
"The Railway Labor Act, like the National Labor Relations Act, does not undertake governmental regulation of wages, hours, or working conditions. Instead it seeks to provide a means by which agreement may be reached with respect to them. The national interest expressed by those Acts is not primarily in the working conditions as such. So far as the Act itself is concerned these conditions may be as bad as the employees will tolerate or be made as good as they can bargain for. The Act does not fix and does not authorize anyone to fix generally applicable standards for working conditions.   *   *   *"

quire submission of counterproposals. As amended in the Senate and passed as the Taft-Hartley Act, the good faith test of bargaining was retained and written into Section 8(d) of the National Labor Relations Act. That Section contains the express provision that the obligation to bargain collectively does not compel either party to agree to a proposal or require the making of a concession.

Thus it is now apparent from the statute itself that the Act does not encourage a party to engage in fruitless marathon discussions at the expense of frank statement and support of his position. And it is equally clear that the Board may not, either directly or indirectly, compel concessions or otherwise sit in judgment upon the substantive terms of collective bargaining agreements.

Second. The Board offers in support of the portion of its order before this Court a theory quite apart from the test of good faith bargaining prescribed in Section 8(d) of the Act, a theory that respondent's bargaining for a management functions clause as a counterproposal to the Union's demand for unlimited arbitration was, "*per se*," a violation of the Act.

Counsel for the Board do not contend that a management functions clause covering some condition of employment is an illegal contract term. As a matter of fact, a review of typical contract clauses collected for convenience in drafting labor agreements shows that management functions clauses similar in essential detail to the clause proposed by respondent have been included in contracts negotiated by national unions with many employers.[25] The National War Labor Board, empowered during the last war "[t]o decide the dispute, and provide by order the wages and hours and all other terms and conditions (customarily included in collective-bargaining agreements)," ordered management functions clauses included in a number of agreements. Several such clauses ordered by the War Labor Board provided for arbitration in case of union dissatisfaction with the exercise of management functions, while others, as in the clause proposed by respondent in this case, provided that management decisions would be final. Without intimating any opinion as to the form of management functions clause proposed by respondent in this case or the desirability of including any such clause in a labor agreement, it is manifest that bargaining for management functions clauses is common collective bargaining practice.

25. * * *

Writers advocating inclusion of detailed management functions clauses in collective bargaining agreements urge the desirability of defining the respective functions of management and labor in matters such as work scheduling consistent with the needs of the particular industry. See Cox and Dunlop, Regulation of Collective Bargaining by the National Labor Relations Board, 63 Harv.L.Rev. 389 (1950) * * *

If the Board is correct, an employer violates the Act by bargaining for a management functions clause touching any condition of employment without regard to the traditions of bargaining in the particular industry or such other evidence of good faith as the fact in this case that respondent's clause was offered as a counterproposal to the Union's demand for unlimited arbitration. The Board's argument is a technical one for it is conceded that respondent would not be guilty of an unfair labor practice if, instead of proposing a clause that removed some matters from arbitration, it simply refused in good faith to agree to the Union proposal for unlimited arbitration. The argument starts with a finding, not challenged by the court below or by respondent, that at least some of the matters covered by the management functions clause proposed by respondent are "conditions of employment" which are appropriate subjects of collective bargaining under Sections 8(a) (5), 8(d) and 9(a) of the Act. The Board considers that employer bargaining for a clause under which management retains initial responsibility for work scheduling, a "condition of employment," for the duration of the contract is an unfair labor practice because it is "in derogation of" employees' statutory rights to bargain collectively as to conditions of employment.[26]

Conceding that there is nothing unlawful in including a management functions clause in a labor agreement, the Board would permit an employer to "propose" such a clause. But the Board would forbid bargaining for any such clause when the Union declines to accept the proposal, even where the clause is offered as a counterproposal to a Union demand for unlimited arbitration. Ignoring the nature of the Union's demand in this case, the Board takes the position that employers subject to the Act must agree to include in any labor agreement provisions establishing fixed standards for work schedules or any other condition of employment. An employer would be permitted to bargain as to the content of the standard so long as he agrees to freeze a standard into a contract. Bargaining for more flexible treatment of such matters would be denied employers even though the result may be contrary to common collective bargaining practice in the industry. The Board was not empowered so to disrupt collective bargaining practices. On the contrary, the term "bargain collectively" as used in the Act "has been considered to absorb and give statutory approval to the philosophy of bargaining as worked out in the labor movement in the United States." Order of Railroad Telegraphers v. Railway Express Agency, 321 U.S. 342, 346, 64 S.Ct. 582, 585, 88 L.Ed. 788 (1944).

26. The Board's argument would seem to prevent an employer from bargaining for a "no-strike" clause, commonly found in labor agreements, requiring a union to forego for the duration of the contract the right to strike expressly granted by Section 7 of the Act. However, the Board has permitted an employer to bargain in good faith for such a clause. Shell Oil Co., 77 N.L.R.B. 1306 (1948). This result is explained by referring to the "salutary objective" of such a clause. Bethlehem Steel Co., 89 N.L.R.B. 341, 345 (1950).

Congress provided expressly that the Board should not pass upon the desirability of the substantive terms of labor agreements. Whether a contract should contain a clause fixing standards for such matters as work scheduling or should provide for more flexible treatment of such matters is an issue for determination across the bargaining table, not by the Board. If the latter approach is agreed upon, the extent of union and management participation in the administration of such matters is itself a condition of employment to be settled by bargaining.

Accordingly, we reject the Board's holding that bargaining for the management functions clause proposed by respondent was, *per se*, an unfair labor practice. Any fears the Board may entertain that use of management functions clauses will lead to evasion of an employer's duty to bargain collectively as to "rates of pay, wages, hours and conditions of employment" do not justify condemning all bargaining for management functions clauses covering any "condition of employment" as *per se* violations of the Act. The duty to bargain collectively is to be enforced by application of the good faith bargaining standards of Section 8(d) to the facts of each case rather than by prohibiting all employers in every industry from bargaining for management functions clauses altogether.

Third. * * * Accepting as we do the finding of the court below that respondent bargained in good faith for the management functions clause proposed by it, we hold that respondent was not in that respect guilty of refusing to bargain collectively as required by the National Labor Relations Act. Accordingly, enforcement of paragraph 1(a) of the Board's order was properly denied.

MR. JUSTICE MINTON, with whom MR. JUSTICE BLACK and MR. JUSTICE DOUGLAS join, dissenting:

* * * This case is one where the employer came into the bargaining room with a demand that certain topics upon which it had a duty to bargain were to be removed from the agenda—that was the price the Union had to pay to gain a contract. There is all the difference between the hypothetical "management functions" clauses envisioned by the majority and this "management functions" clause as there is between waiver and coercion. No one suggests that an employer is guilty of an unfair labor practice when it proposes that it be given unilateral control over certain working conditions and the union accepts the proposal in return for various other benefits. But where, as here, the employer tells the union that the only way to obtain a contract as to wages is to agree not to bargain about certain other working conditions, the employer has refused to bargain about those other working conditions. * * *

An employer may not stake out an area which is a proper subject for bargaining and say, "As to this we will not bargain." To do so is a plain refusal to bargain in violation of § 8(a) (5) of the Act. If employees' bargaining rights can be cut away so easily, they are indeed illusory. I would reverse.

Problems for Discussion

1. The Court in *American National Insurance* appears to hold that it is unlawful for an employer to come to the bargaining table and state "Decisions about promotions and demotions are none of the union's business and I will not discuss the matter"; but that it is lawful for the employer to state "I will discuss with you today the matter of control over promotions and demotions, but it is my firm position that they are none of the union's business and that I will not discuss them with the union during the term of the contract." Is this a sensible distinction? Is it an administrable one?

2. What does the Court mean in *American National Insurance* when it states that the adoption of the Board's position would give the Board too great a measure of control over the substantive terms of the labor contract? Had the Board's position been adopted, would it be illegal for the employer to insist upon a merit-pay provision reposing in the employer exclusive power to award merit increases for high-quality work? To insist upon employer power to award such increases after "meeting and conferring" (but not bargaining to impasse) with the union? To insist upon employer power to award such increases after bargaining with the union to impasse? To insist upon employer power to award such increases subject to review by a neutral arbitrator for discrimination or arbitrariness? Compare the power of the Board to disapprove employer insistence on such clauses under the principles ultimately adopted by the Supreme Court.

3. Tender Meat Packing Company has long maintained a system of wage payment under which a wage bracket is established for every occupation. Each employee is paid at least the minimum for his occupation and then advanced within the bracket upon the basis of supervision's judgment of his individual ability and performance. Meat Cutters' Local 1678 has recently become the collective bargaining agent of Tender Meat's production and maintenance employees.

(a) May Tender Meat, if it negotiates in good faith concerning the wage brackets, lawfully refuse to discuss either the practice of granting individual merit increases or the increases to be granted particular individuals? *no*

(b) May Tender Meat lawfully continue, during negotiations, to grant individual merit increases within existing brackets? *?*

(c) Would it violate Sections 8(a)(5) and 8(d) for Tender Meat to insist that the contract contain a clause making the granting of individual merit increases a management function? *no*

NLRB v. WOOSTER DIVISION OF BORG–WARNER CORP.

Supreme Court of the United States, 1958.
356 U.S. 342, 78 S.Ct. 718, 2 L.Ed.2d 823.

MR. JUSTICE BURTON delivered the opinion of the Court.

In these cases an employer insisted that its collective-bargaining contract with certain of its employees include: (1) a "ballot" clause calling for a pre-strike secret vote of those employees (union and non-union) as to the employer's last offer, and (2) a "recognition" clause which excluded, as a party to the contract, the International Union which had been certified by the National Labor Relations Board as the employees' exclusive bargaining agent, and substituted for it the agent's uncertified local affiliate. The Board held that the employer's insistence upon either of such clauses amounted to a refusal to bargain, in violation of § 8(a) (5) of the National Labor Relations Act, as amended. The issue turns on whether either of these clauses comes within the scope of mandatory collective bargaining as defined in § 8(d) of the Act. For the reasons hereafter stated, we agree with the Board that neither clause comes within that definition. Therefore, we sustain the Board's order directing the employer to cease insisting upon either clause as a condition precedent to accepting any collective-bargaining contract.

Late in 1952, the International Union, United Automobile, Aircraft and Agricultural Implement Workers of America, CIO (here called International) was certified by the Board to the Wooster (Ohio) Division of the Borg-Warner Corporation (here called the company) as the elected representative of an appropriate unit of the company's employees. Shortly thereafter, International chartered Local No. 1239, UAW–CIO (here called the Local). Together the unions presented the company with a comprehensive collective-bargaining agreement. In the "recognition" clause, the unions described themselves as both the "International Union, United Automobile, Aircraft and Agricultural Implement Workers of America and its Local Union No. 1239, U. A. W.–C. I. O. * * *."

The company submitted a counter-proposal which recognized as the sole representative of the employees "Local Union 1239, affiliated with the International Union, United Automobile, Aircraft and Agricultural Implement Workers of America (UAW–CIO)." The unions' negotiators objected because such a clause disregarded the Board's certification of International as the employees' representative. The negotiators declared that the employees would accept no agreement which excluded International as a party.

The company's counterproposal also contained the "ballot" clause, * * * In summary, this clause provided that, as to all nonarbitrable issues (which eventually included modification, amendment or termination of the contract), there would be a 30-day negotiation period after which, before the union could strike, there would have to be a secret ballot taken among all employees in the unit (union and non-union) on the company's last offer. In the event a majority of the employees rejected the company's last offer, the company would have an opportunity, within 72 hours, of making a new proposal and having a vote on it prior to any strike. The unions' negotiators announced they would not accept this clause "under any conditions."

From the time that the company first proposed these clauses, the employees' representatives thus made it clear that each was wholly unacceptable. The company's representatives made it equally clear that no agreement would be entered into by it unless the agreement contained both clauses. In view of this impasse, there was little further discussion of the clauses, although the parties continued to bargain as to other matters. The company submitted a "package" proposal covering economic issues but made the offer contingent upon the satisfactory settlement of "all other issues * * *." The "package" included both of the controversial clauses. On March 15, 1953, the unions rejected that proposal and the membership voted to strike on March 20 unless a settlement were reached by then. None was reached and the unions struck. Negotiations, nevertheless, continued. On April 21, the unions asked the company whether the latter would withdraw its demand for the "ballot" and "recognition" clauses if the unions accepted all other pending requirements of the company. The company declined and again insisted upon acceptance of its "package," including both clauses. Finally, on May 5, the Local, upon the recommendation of International, gave in and entered into an agreement containing both controversial clauses.

In the meantime, International had filed charges with the Board claiming that the company, by the above conduct, was guilty of an unfair labor practice within the meaning of § 8(a) (5) of the Act.

* * * [The Board found a violation, and the Court of Appeals enforced the Board's order as to the "recognition" clause but refused enforcement as to the "ballot" clause.]

Read together, [Section 8(a) (5) and Section 8(d)] establish the obligation of the employer and the representative of its employees to bargain with each other in good faith with respect to "wages, hours, and other terms and conditions of employment * * *." The duty is limited to those subjects, and within that area neither party is legally obligated to yield. National Labor Relations Board v. American Insurance Co., 343 U.S. 395, 72 S.Ct. 824, 96 L.Ed. 1027. As to other matters, however, each party is free to bargain or not to bargain, and to agree or not to agree.

The company's good faith has met the requirements of the statute as to the subjects of mandatory bargaining. But that good faith does not license the employer to refuse to enter into agreements on the ground that they do not include some proposal which is not a mandatory subject of bargaining. We agree with the Board that such conduct is, in substance, a refusal to bargain about the subjects that are within the scope of mandatory bargaining. This does not mean that bargaining is to be confined to the statutory subjects. Each of the two controversial clauses is lawful in itself. Each would be enforceable if agreed to by the unions. But it does not follow that, because the company may propose these clauses, it can lawfully insist upon them as a condition to any agreement.

Since it is lawful to insist upon matters within the scope of mandatory bargaining and unlawful to insist upon matters without, the issue here is whether either the "ballot" or the "recognition" clause is a subject within the phrase "wages, hours, and other terms and conditions of employment" which defines mandatory bargaining. The "ballot" clause is not within that definition. It relates only to the procedure to be followed by the employees among themselves before their representative may call a strike or refuse a final offer. It settles no term or condition of employment—it merely calls for an advisory vote of the employees. It is not a partial "no-strike" clause. A "no-strike" clause prohibits the employees from striking during the life of the contract. It regulates the relations between the employer and the employees. See National Labor Relations Board v. American Insurance Co., supra, 343 U.S. at page 408, n. 22, 72 S.Ct. at page 831, 96 L.Ed. 1027. The "ballot" clause, on the other hand, deals only with relations between the employees and their unions. It substantially modifies the collective-bargaining system provided for in the statute by weakening the independence of the "representative" chosen by the employees. It enables the employer, in effect, to deal with its employees rather than with their statutory representative. Cf. Medo Photo Corp. v. National Labor Relations Board, 321 U.S. 678, 64 S.Ct. 830, 88 L.Ed. 1007.

The "recognition" clause likewise does not come within the definition of mandatory bargaining. The statute requires the company to bargain with the certified representative of its employees. It is an evasion of that duty to insist that the certified agent not be a party to the collective-bargaining contract. The Act does not prohibit the voluntary addition of a party, but that does not authorize the employer to exclude the certified representative from the contract. * * *

MR. JUSTICE FRANKFURTER joins this opinion insofar as it holds that insistence by the company on the "recognition" clause, in conflict with the provisions of the Act requiring an employer to bargain with the representative of his employees, constituted an unfair labor practice. He agrees with the views of MR. JUSTICE HARLAN regarding the "ballot" clause. The subject matter of that clause is not so clearly outside the reasonable range of industrial bargaining as to establish a refusal to bargain in good faith, and is not prohibited simply because not deemed to be within the rather vague scope of the obligatory provisions of § 8(d).

MR. JUSTICE HARLAN, whom MR. JUSTICE CLARK and MR. JUSTICE WHITTAKER join, concurring in part and dissenting in part.

I agree that the company's insistence on the "recognition" clause constituted an unfair labor practice, but reach that conclusion by a different route from that taken by the Court. However, in light of the finding below that the company bargained in "good faith," I dissent from the view that its insistence on the "ballot" clause can support the charge of an unfair labor practice. * * *

Preliminarily, I must state that I am unable to grasp a concept of "bargaining" which enables one to "propose" a particular point, but not to "insist" on it as a condition to agreement. The right to bargain becomes illusory if one is not free to press a proposal in good faith to the point of insistence. Surely adoption of so inherently vague and fluid a standard is apt to inhibit the entire bargaining process because of a party's fear that strenuous argument might shade into forbidden insistence and thereby produce a charge of an unfair labor practice. This watered-down notion of "bargaining" which the Court imports into the Act with reference to matters not within the scope of § 8(d) appears as foreign to the labor field as it would be to the commercial world. To me all of this adds up to saying that the Act limits *effective* "bargaining" to subjects within the three fields referred to in § 8(d), that is "wages, hours, and other terms and conditions of employment," even though the Court expressly disclaims so holding.

I shall discuss my difficulties with the Court's opinion in terms of the "ballot" clause. The "recognition" clause is subject in my view to different considerations.

I.

At the start, I question the Court's conclusion that the "ballot" clause does not come within the "other terms and conditions of employment" provision of § 8(d). The phrase is inherently vague and prior to this decision has been accorded by the Board and courts an expansive rather than a grudging interpretation. Many matters which might have been thought to be the sole concern of management are now dealt with as compulsory bargaining topics. E. g. National Labor Relations Board v. J. H. Allison & Co., 6 Cir., 165 F.2d 766, 3 A.L.R.2d 990 (merit increases). And since a "no-strike" clause is something about which an employer can concededly bargain to the point of insistence, see Shell Oil Co., 77 N.L.R.B. 1306, I find it difficult to understand even under the Court's analysis of this problem why the "ballot" clause should not be considered within the area of bargaining described in § 8(d). It affects the employer-employee relationship in much the same way, in that it may determine the timing of strikes or even whether a strike will occur by requiring a vote to ascertain the employees' sentiment prior to the union's decision.

Nonetheless I shall accept the Court's holding that this clause is not a condition of employment, for even though the union would accordingly not be *obliged* under § 8(d) to bargain over it, in my view it does not follow that the company was *prohibited* from insisting on its inclusion in the collective bargaining agreement. In other words, I think the clause was a permissible, even if not an obligatory, subject of good faith bargaining.

The legislative history behind the Wagner and Taft-Hartley Acts persuasively indicates that the Board was never intended to have power to prevent good faith bargaining as to any subject not violative of the provisions or policies of those Acts. * * *

The decision of this Court in 1952 in National Labor Relations Board v. American National Insurance Co., supra, was fully in accord with this legislative background in holding that the Board lacked power to order an employer to cease bargaining over a particular clause because such bargaining under the Board's view, entirely apart from a showing of bad faith, constituted *per se* an unfair labor practice. * * *

The most cursory view of decisions of the Board and the circuit courts under the National Labor Relations Act reveals the unsettled and evolving character of collective bargaining agreements. Provisions which two decades ago might have been thought to be the exclusive concern of labor or management are today commonplace in such agreements. The bargaining process should be left fluid, free from intervention of the Board leading to premature crystallization of labor agreements into any one pattern of contract provisions, so that these agreements can be adapted through collective bargaining to the changing needs of our society and to the changing concepts of the responsibilities of labor and management. What the Court does today may impede this evolutionary process. * * * I do not deny that there may be instances where unyielding insistence on a particular item may be a relevant consideration in the over-all picture in determining "good faith," for the demands of a party might in the context of a particular industry be so extreme as to constitute some evidence of an unwillingness to bargain. But no such situation is presented in this instance by the "ballot" clause. "No-strike" clauses, and other provisions analogous to the "ballot" clause limiting the right to strike, are hardly novel to labor agreements. And in any event the uncontested finding of "good faith" by the Trial Examiner forecloses that issue here.

Of course an employer or union cannot insist upon a clause which would be illegal under the Act's provisions, National Labor Relations

Board v. National Maritime Union, 2 Cir., 175 F.2d 686, or conduct itself so as to contravene specific requirements of the Act. Medo Photo Supply Corp. v. Labor Board, 321 U.S. 678, 64 S.Ct. 830, 88 L.Ed. 1007. But here the Court recognizes, as it must, that the clause is lawful under the Act, and I think it clear that the company's insistence upon it violated no statutory duty to which it was subject.

*   *   *

II.

The company's insistence on the "recognition" clause, which had the effect of excluding the International Union as a party signatory to agreement and making Local 1239 the sole contracting party on the union side, presents a different problem. In my opinion the company's action in this regard did constitute an unfair labor practice since it contravened specific requirements of the Act.

*   *   * The employer's duty to bargain with the representatives includes not merely the obligation to confer in good faith, but also " *   *   * the execution of a written contract incorporating any agreement reached if requested *   *   * " by the employees' representatives. § 8(d). I think it hardly debatable that this language must be read to require the company, if so requested, to sign any agreement reached with the same representative with which it is required to bargain. By conditioning agreement upon a change in signatory from the certified exclusive bargaining representative, the company here in effect violated this duty.

I would affirm the judgment of the Court of Appeals in both cases and require the Board to modify its cease and desist order so as to allow the company to bargain over the ballot clause.[27]

Problems for Discussion

1. A principal reason given for the Court's decision is that insistence upon a nonmandatory subject "is, in substance, a refusal to bargain about the subjects that are within the scope of mandatory bargaining." Do you agree? (Is this not also true of insistence upon one mandatory subject as a condition to agreeing upon other mandatory subjects?) Could the Court have articulated a more tenable rationale for barring insistence upon nonmandatory subjects in general, or for barring insistence upon the "ballot" and "recognition" clauses in Borg-Warner?

2. If you are attorney for a party which is very intent, in its labor negotiations, upon securing a concession from the other party on a matter which is not clearly a mandatory subject, what advice must you give, based on Borg-Warner? Consider explaining: (a) how the Board and courts

27. The Borg-Warner decision is discussed in Cox, Labor Decisions of the Supreme Court at the October Term, 1957, 44 Va.L.Rev. 1057, 1075 (1958); Note, 43 Minn.L.Rev. 1225 (1959).

will likely go about deciding whether the issue is mandatory or permissive; (b) how assertive your client may be at the bargaining table; (c) the wisdom and legality (and morality) of feigning insistence on an actually inconsequential mandatory subject, while "signaling" that the insistence will be dropped if the other party concedes on the matter that is strongly desired; and (d) the consequences if, for example, the employer insists on such a subject, and the employees respond with a strike during which they are "permanently" replaced, and they later seek reinstatement?

3.   On the question of the "ballot clause," do you agree more with the opinion of Mr. Justice Burton or that of Mr. Justice Harlan? Why is a no-strike clause a "mandatory" subject, and how materially different is the ballot clause? Is the ballot clause contrary to federal labor policy? Compare Sections 203(c) and 209(b) of the Labor Act.

4.   Can management lawfully insist to the point of impasse on a contract clause prohibiting either party from taking action to "interfere with, restrain or coerce by discipline, discharge, fine or otherwise" any employee who chooses to engage in or refrain from a strike? See *U.O.P. Norplex v. NLRB*, 445 F.2d 155 (7th Cir. 1971). Can the union lawfully insist upon such a provision?

5.   If the contract already has a union-shop provision, requiring all employees to join the union and pay dues, may the employer insist upon a provision that the union may not increase membership dues without the employer's consent?

PENELLO v. UNITED MINE WORKERS, 88 F.Supp. 935 (D.D.C., 1950).   A complaint filed under NLRA Section 10(j) alleged that during the 1950 negotiations concerning the national bituminous coal wage agreement the union insisted that any collective bargaining agreement with the employers provide for a closed shop and for a welfare and retirement fund to be administered so as to provide benefits only for members of the union. *Held*, that such insistence would violate NLRA Section 8(b) (3). Since the record showed it was probable that a violation would occur, a temporary injunction should issue.

DOUDS v. INTERNATIONAL LONGSHOREMEN'S ASS'N, 241 F.2d 278 (2d Cir. 1957).   In August, 1956, ILA and the New York Shipping Ass'n began to negotiate a contract to replace an expiring agreement covering longshoremen in the port of Greater New York. ILA demanded that the contract be expanded to cover the East and Gulf Coasts. During the bargaining NLRB conducted a representation proceeding in the course of which it confined the scope of the bargaining unit to the port of Greater New York and conducted an election in that unit which was won by ILA. After certification as the representative for employees in the port of Greater New York, ILA continued to demand an agreement covering the East and Gulf Coasts and when the Association refused, a strike was called to enforce the demand. Upon a charge filed by the Association, NLRB issued a complaint and sought a temporary injunction under Section 10(j) enjoining ILA from insisting upon a change in the bargaining unit. Upon appeal from an order granting the injunction, *held* that ILA was violating Section 8(b)(3). "This distinction between private bargaining over conditions of employment and the administrative determination of the unit appropriate for bargaining is clear. The parties cannot bargain meaningfully about wages or hours or conditions of employment unless they know the unit of bargaining. That question is for the Board to decide on a petition under Section 9(c) of the Act, and its decision is conclusive on the parties * * * although the decision may subsequently be changed.

"The machinery for initial decision and subsequent change is provided in the statute * * * The process of change not permitted by the Act is one that denies the Board this ultimate control of the bargaining unit and disrupts the bargaining process itself. This is precisely what occurs when, after the Board has decided what the appropriate bargaining unit is, one party over the objection of the other demands a change in that unit. Such a demand interferes with the required bargaining 'with respect to rates of pay, wages, hours and conditions of employment' in a manner excluded by the Act. It is thus a refusal to bargain in good faith within the meaning of Section 8(b)(3)."

NLRB v. DETROIT RESILIENT FLOOR DECORATORS LOCAL 2265, 317 F.2d 269 (6th Cir. 1963). After obtaining recognition from the employer, the union proposed that a contract be signed incorporating a provision which obligated the employer to contribute to a fund, already supported by a number of employers, which was devoted exclusively to "promoting, publicizing, and advancing the interests of the floor covering industry." Although the employer was a member of this industry, he resisted making such contributions. After prolonged discussion, however, the employer signed the agreement, subject to a reservation allowing him to contest the right of the union to insist upon the provision. The Board ruled that the provision was not a mandatory subject of bargaining. "An industry promotion fund seems to us to be outside of the employment relationship. It concerns itself rather with the relationship of employers to one another or, like advertising, with the relationship of an employer to the consuming public. The ability of an employer or an industry to meet changing conditions may, as the respondent argues, affect employees' opportunities in the long run, and labor organizations are understandably concerned with the future of the industries from which their members derive their livelihood. Such long-range prospects may also be affected by conditions and events of even more general applicability

such as developments on the economic or political scene, legislation, taxation, and foreign competition. Nothing prevents an employer and a union from joining voluntarily in a mutual effort to attempt to influence their industry's course of development, provided, of course, that other legislative enactments do not prohibit such activities. To hold, however, under this Act, that one party must bargain at the behest of another on any matter which might conceivably enhance the prospects of the industry would transform bargaining over the compensation, hours, and employment conditions of employees into a debate over policy objectives." On petition to enforce the Board's order, *held*, enforcement granted.

FORD MOTOR CO. (CHICAGO STAMPING PLANT) v. NLRB, 441 U.S. 488, 99 S.Ct. 1842, 60 L.Ed.2d 420 (1979). The UAW and its Local 588 represent the 3600 production employees at the Ford parts-stamping plant in Chicago Heights, Illinois. For many years, Ford provided in-plant food services, particularly cafeterias and vending machines, to its employees; these were operated by ARA Services, Inc. (with Ford having the right to review and approve the quality, quantity, and price of the food served). Labor contracts since 1967 expressly dealt with such matters as cafeteria supervision, the restocking of vending machines, and menu variety; but Ford always refused to bargain about in-plant food and beverage prices. In February 1976, Ford informed the Union that cafeteria and vending-machine prices would be increased, and rejected the Union's request to bargain over both price and services and to supply information relevant to Ford's involvement in food services.

The Board found this conduct to violate Section 8(a)(5) and ordered the Company to bargain and to provide the requested information. The court of appeals—although sharing the prevailing view in the courts that in-plant food prices were not a subject of mandatory bargaining—enforced the Board's order on the facts of the case, giving considerable weight to the fact that the length of the lunch period and the distance of restaurants made it impracticable for the employees to eat away from the plant (so that the in-plant food "can be viewed as a physical dimension of one's working environment").

The Supreme Court affirmed (making no special mention of the lack of reasonable eating alternatives). It observed that the Board has special expertise in classifying bargaining subjects as "terms or conditions of employment" and that "if its construction of the statute is reasonably defensible, it should not be rejected merely because the courts might prefer another view of the statute." The

Court held that "the Board's consistent view that in-plant food prices and services are mandatory bargaining subjects is not an unreasonable or unprincipled construction of the statute and that it should be accepted and enforced."

Since employees must eat at some point during the workday "the availability of food during working hours and the conditions under which it is to be consumed are matters of deep concern to workers." When management in its own interest provides in-plant feeding facilities, food prices and service "may reasonably be considered" a bargainable subject, for they are germane to the working environment. To require the employer to bargain will not "permit the Union to usurp managerial decisionmaking" and will serve the ends of the NLRA by funneling into collective bargaining (rather than strikes and other forms of economic warfare) substantial disputes which can arise over the pricing of in-plant food and beverages. The Court also observed that many contract provisions concerning in-plant food services have been negotiated, and that nonprice aspects of such services had been in the Ford agreement at this plant for many years. (It then set forth statistics on the percentage of companies providing in-plant food services, but no statistics on how many of those companies treated such matters in their labor contracts.)

To Ford's argument that food prices and service are too trivial to be made mandatory subjects of bargaining, the Court stated that the employees in this case were sufficiently upset about the matter, and that even minor increases in the cost of meals can amount over time to a substantial sum of money. To Ford's argument that it would be disruptive to secure approval in advance of every minor change in price or service, the Court responded: "[I]t is sufficient compliance with the statutory mandate if management honors a specific union request for bargaining about changes that have been made or are to be made." Moreover, problems arising from frequent changes can be anticipated in the collective bargaining agreement.

Problems for Discussion

1. How many unconvincing propositions can you detect in this abbreviated version of the *Ford Motor* decision? For example, should NLRB determinations about the scope of mandatory bargaining (a "question of law," is it not?) be judicially reversed only if "unprincipled" or not "reasonably defensible"? Should all matters of "deep concern" to employees be, by virtue of that fact, classified as mandatory subjects? Is it pertinent that many employers furnish cafeteria facilities (as distinguished from their bargaining about it)? Will classifying in-plant food prices

as mandatory subjects limit resort to strikes and other forms of economic warfare? Will a unilateral change in food prices at the Ford plant be lawful, absent subsequent demand for bargaining about it and refusal by the Company? (Whatever happened to the *Katz* case?)

2. Since 1965, the Ryder Technical Institute had paid its employees an annual Christmas bonus. The bonus for each employee was calculated according to a complex formula based on the employee's position and length of service, and recommendations from supervisors. In 1980, the Teamsters Union was certified as bargaining agent for all of Ryder's employees. A collective bargaining agreement was executed in October which made no mention of the Christmas bonuses. That December, the employer, without consulting with the Union, failed to give any Christmas bonuses. The Union filed a Section 8(a)(5) charge, claiming that Ryder had unilaterally changed wages without bargaining. The employer argued that the bonus was not a part of wages but rather a gift given at its discretion. How should the Administrative Law Judge rule? See *Radio Television Tech. School, Inc.* v. *NLRB*, 488 F.2d 457 (3d Cir. 1974).

3. Employees of the Silver Bell Mine are represented by the United Mine Workers. Seventy percent of the employees live in the town of Silver Bell, which is owned by the mining company, and nearly all of the residents of Silver Bell are employees of the mining company. The nearest concentration of housing not owned by the company is twenty-five miles from the mine. Rent for the company-owned housing was unchanged from 1964 until 1981, when the company, without bargaining with Union, raised all rents twenty-five percent. Has the mining company violated Section 8(a)(5)? See *American Smelting and Refining Co.* v. *NLRB*, 406 F.2d 552 (9th Cir.), cert. denied 395 U.S. 935 (1969).

4. Assume that the Oilworkers Union has been certified as the bargaining representative for the production workers at Ace Petroleum Corp., and that a first collective bargaining agreement is almost fully negotiated. The main sticking point has been the provision proposed by the Union for a three-step grievance procedure, with recourse from the third-step determination of the Vice-President for Personnel Relations to an impartial arbitrator, selected by both contracting parties. The Vice-President, who is also the Company's chief negotiator, refuses even to discuss such a provision, contending that the Company has made enough concessions, that it is enough that it intends to honor the contract, and that grievances will be resolved informally as they arise. The Union comes to you for advice about the wisdom and legality of striking over their proffered provision, which is given very high priority by the workers. Give your advice.

Assume, instead, that Ace has agreed to include some form of grievance and arbitration provision in the labor contract, but that a dispute has developed regarding the company's insistence that in the first step of the grievance procedure—an oral presentation of the grievance to the foreman —the aggrieved employee is not to be accompanied by a representative of the union. Would Ace's continued insistence violate the law? Consider NLRB v. J. Weingarten, Inc., at page 813 infra. See NLRB v. Tomco Communications, Inc., 567 F.2d 871 (9th Cir. 1978).

FIBREBOARD PAPER PRODUCTS CORP. v. NLRB [28]

Supreme Court of the United States, 1964.
379 U.S. 203, 85 S.Ct. 398, 13 L.Ed.2d 233.

MR. CHIEF JUSTICE WARREN delivered the opinion of the Court.

This case involves the obligation of an employer and the representative of his employees under §§ 8(a) (5), 8(d) and 9(a) of the National Labor Relations Act to "confer in good faith with respect to wages, hours, and other terms and conditions of employment." The primary issue is whether the "contracting out" of work being performed by employees in the bargaining unit is a statutory subject of collective bargaining under those sections.

Petitioner, Fibreboard Paper Products Corporation (the Company), has a manufacturing plant in Emeryville, California. Since 1937 the East Bay Union Machinists, Local 1304, United Steelworkers of America, AFL–CIO (the Union) has been the exclusive bargaining representative for a unit of the Company's maintenance employees. In September 1958, the Union and the Company entered the latest of a series of collective bargaining agreements which was to expire on July 31, 1959. The agreement provided for automatic renewal for another year unless one of the contracting parties gave 60 days' notice of a desire to modify or terminate the contract. On May 26, 1959, the Union gave timely notice of its desire to modify the contract and sought to arrange a bargaining session with Company representatives. On June 2, the Company acknowledged receipt of the Union's notice and stated: "We will contact you at a later date regarding a meeting for this purpose." As required by the contract, the Union sent a list of proposed modifications on June 15. Efforts by the Union to schedule a bargaining session met with no success until July 27, four days before the expiration of the contract, when the Company notified the Union of its desire to meet.

The Company, concerned with the high cost of its maintenance operation, had undertaken a study of the possibility of effecting cost savings by engaging an independent contractor to do the maintenance work. At the July 27 meeting, the Company informed the Union that it had determined that substantial savings could be effected by contracting out the work upon expiration of its collective bargaining agreements with the various labor organizations representing its maintenance employees. * * * After some discussion of the Company's right to enter a contract with a third party to do the work

---

28. See Platt, The Duty to Bargain as Applied to Management Decisions, 19 Lab.L.J. 143 (1968); Rabin, *Fibreboard* and the Termination of Bargaining Unit Work: The Search for Standards in Defining the Scope of the Duty to Bargain, 71 Colum.L.Rev. 803 (1971); Rabin, The Decline and Fall of *Fibre-* *board*, N.Y.U. 24th Annual Conf. on Labor 237 (1972); Schwarz, Plant Relocation or Partial Termination—The Duty to Decision-Bargain, 39 Fordham L.Rev. 81 (1970).

After reading the *Fibreboard* decision, the student should read *First Na-*

then being performed by employees in the bargaining unit, the meeting concluded with the understanding that the parties would meet again on July 30.

By July 30, the Company had selected Fluor Maintenance, Inc., to do the maintenance work. Fluor had assured the Company that maintenance costs could be curtailed by reducing the work force, decreasing fringe benefits and overtime payments, and by preplanning and scheduling the services to be performed. The contract provided * * * that the Company would pay Fluor the costs of the operation plus a fixed fee of $2,250 per month.

At the July 30 meeting, the Company's representative, in explaining the decision to contract out the maintenance work, remarked that during bargaining negotiations in previous years the Company had endeavored to point out through the use of charts and statistical information "just how expensive and costly our maintenance work was and how it was creating quite a terrific burden upon the Emeryville plant." He further stated that unions representing other Company employees "had joined hands with management in an effort to bring about an economical and efficient operation," but "we had not been able to attain that in our discussions with this particular Local." The Company also distributed a letter stating that "since we will have no employees in the bargaining unit covered by our present Agreement, negotiation of a new or renewed Agreement would appear to us to be pointless." On July 31, the employment of the maintenance employees represented by the Union was terminated and Fluor employees took over. That evening the Union established a picket line at the Company's plant.

The Union filed unfair labor practice charges against the Company, alleging violations of §§ 8(a) (1), 8(a) (3) and 8(a) (5). [T]he Board adhered to the Trial Examiner's finding that the Company's motive in contracting out its maintenance work was economic rather than anti-union but found nonetheless that the Company's "failure to negotiate with * * * [the Union] concerning its decision to subcontract its maintenance work constituted a violation of Section 8(a)(5) of the Act." [29] * * *

The Board ordered the Company to reinstitute the maintenance operation previously performed by the employees represented by the Union, to reinstate the employees to their former or substantially equivalent positions with back pay computed from the date of the Board's supplemental decision, and to fulfill its statutory obligation to bargain.

tional Maintenance Corp. v. NLRB, decided by the Supreme Court in June 1981, set forth in the Appendix to this casebook.

29. The Board did not disturb [the] holding that the Company had not

violated §§ 8(a)(1) or 8(a)(3), or [the] holding that the Company had satisfied its obligation to bargain about termination pay.

On appeal, the Court of Appeals for the District of Columbia Circuit granted the Board's petition for enforcement. * * * Because of the limited grant of certiorari, we are concerned here only with whether the subject upon which the employer allegedly refused to bargain—contracting out of plant maintenance work previously performed by employees in the bargaining unit, which the employees were capable of continuing to perform—is covered by the phrase "terms and conditions of employment" within the meaning of § 8(d).

The subject matter of the present dispute is well within the literal meaning of the phrase "terms and conditions of employment." See *Order of Railroad Telegraphers* v. *Chicago & N. W. R. Co.*, 362 U.S. 330, 80 S.Ct. 761. A stipulation with respect to the contracting out of work performed by members of the bargaining unit might appropriately be called a "condition of employment." The words even more plainly cover termination of employment which, as the facts of this case indicate, necessarily results from the contracting out of work performed by members of the established bargaining unit.

The inclusion of "contracting out" within the statutory scope of collective bargaining also seems well designed to effectuate the purposes of the National Labor Relations Act. One of the primary purposes of the Act is to promote the peaceful settlement of industrial disputes by subjecting labor-management controversies to the mediatory influence of negotiation. The Act was framed with an awareness that refusals to confer and negotiate had been one of the most prolific causes of industrial strife. *Labor Board* v. *Jones & Laughlin Steel Corp.*, 301 U.S. 1, 42–43, 57 S.Ct. 615, 626–627. To hold, as the Board has done, that contracting out is a mandatory subject of collective bargaining would promote the fundamental purpose of the Act by bringing a problem of vital concern to labor and management within the framework established by Congress as most conducive to industrial peace.

The conclusion that "contracting out" is a statutory subject of collective bargaining is further reinforced by industrial practices in this country. While not determinative, it is appropriate to look to industrial bargaining practices in appraising the propriety of including a particular subject within the scope of mandatory bargaining. *Labor Board* v. *American Nat'l Ins. Co.*, 343 U.S. 395, 408, 72 S.Ct. 824, 831. Industrial experience is not only reflective of the interests of labor and management in the subject matter but is also indicative of the amenability of such subjects to the collective bargaining process. Experience illustrates that contracting out in one form or another has been brought, widely and successfully, within the collective bargaining framework. Provisions relating to contracting out exist in numerous collective bargaining agreements, and "contracting out work is the basis of many grievances; and that type of claim is grist in the mills of the arbitrators." *United Steelworkers* v. *Warrior & Gulf Nav. Co.,* 363 U.S. 574, 584, 80 S.Ct. 1347, 1354. * * *

The facts of the present case illustrate the propriety of submitting the dispute to collective negotiation. The Company's decision to contract out the maintenance work did not alter the Company's basic operation. The maintenance work still had to be performed in the plant. No capital investment was contemplated; the Company merely replaced existing employees with those of an independent contractor to do the same work under similar conditions of employment. Therefore, to require the employer to bargain about the matter would not significantly abridge his freedom to manage the business.

The Company was concerned with the high cost of its maintenance operation. It was induced to contract out the work by assurances from independent contractors that economies could be derived by reducing the work force, decreasing fringe benefits, and eliminating overtime payments. These have long been regarded as matters peculiarly suitable for resolution within the collective bargaining framework, and industrial experience demonstrates that collective negotiation has been highly successful in achieving peaceful accommodation of the conflicting interests. Yet, it is contended that when an employer can effect cost savings in these respects by contracting the work out, there is no need to attempt to achieve similar economies through negotiation with existing employees or to provide them with an opportunity to negotiate a mutually acceptable alternative. The short answer is that, although it is not possible to say whether a satisfactory solution could be reached, national labor policy is founded upon the congressional determination that the chances are good enough to warrant subjecting such issues to the process of collective negotiation.

The appropriateness of the collective bargaining process for resolving such issues was apparently recognized by the Company. In explaining its decision to contract out the maintenance work, the Company pointed out that in the same plant other unions "had joined hands with management in an effort to bring about an economical and efficient operation," but "we had not been able to attain that in our discussions with this particular Local." Accordingly, based on past bargaining experience with this union, the Company unilaterally contracted out the work. While "the Act does not encourage a party to engage in fruitless marathon discussions at the expense of frank statement and support of his position," *Labor Board* v. *American Nat'l Ins. Co.,* 343 U.S. 395, 404, 72 S.Ct. 824, 829, it at least demands that the issue be submitted to the mediatory influence of collective negotiations. As the Court of Appeals pointed out, "it is not necessary that it be likely or probable that the union will yield or supply a feasible solution but rather that the union be afforded an opportunity to meet management's legitimate complaints that its maintenance was unduly costly."

We are thus not expanding the scope of mandatory bargaining to hold, as we do now, that the type of "contracting out" involved in this case—the replacement of employees in the existing bargaining unit with those of an independent contractor to do the same work under similar conditions of employment—is a statutory subject of collective bargaining under § 8(d). Our decision need not and does not encompass other forms of "contracting out" or "subcontracting" which arise daily in our complex economy.

The only question remaining is whether, upon a finding that the Company had refused to bargain about a matter which is a statutory subject of collective bargaining, the Board was empowered to order the resumption of maintenance operations and reinstatement with back pay. We believe that it was so empowered. * * * The Board's order will not be disturbed "unless it can be shown that the order is a patent attempt to achieve ends other than those which can fairly be said to effectuate the policies of the Act." *Virginia Elec. & Power Co.* v. *Labor Board*, 319 U.S. 533, 540, 63 S.Ct. 1214, 1218. Such a showing has not been made in this case.

There has been no showing that the Board's order restoring the *status quo ante* to insure meaningful bargaining is not well designed to promote the policies of the Act. Nor is there evidence which would justify disturbing the Board's conclusion that the order would not impose an undue or unfair burden on the Company.[30]

It is argued, nonetheless, that the award exceeds the Board's powers under § 10(c) in that it infringes the provision that "no order of the Board shall require the reinstatement of any individual as an employee who has been suspended or discharged, or the payment to him of any back pay, if such individual was suspended or discharged for cause * * *." The legislative history of the provision indicates that it was designed to preclude the Board from reinstating an individual who had been discharged because of misconduct.[31] There is no in-

---

30. The Board stated: "We do not believe that requirement [restoring the *status quo ante*] imposes an undue or unfair burden on Respondent. The record shows that the maintenance operation is still being performed in much the same manner as it was prior to the subcontracting arrangement. Respondent has a continuing need for the services of maintenance employees; and Respondent's subcontract is terminable at any time upon 60 days' notice." 138 NLRB, at 555, n. 19.

31. The House Report states that the provision was "intended to put an end to the belief, now widely held and certainly justified by the Board's decisions, that engaging in union activities carries with it a license to loaf, wander about the plants, refuse to work, waste time, break rules, and engage in incivilities and other disorders and misconduct." H.R.Rep. No. 245, 80th Cong., 1st Sess., 42 (1947). The Conference Report notes that under § 10(c) "employees who are discharged or suspended for interfering with other employees at work, whether or not in order to transact union business, or for engaging in activities, whether or not union activities, contrary to shop rules, or for Communist activities, or for other cause [interfering with war production] * * * will not be entitled to reinstatement." H.R.Conf.Rep. No. 510, 80th Cong., 1st Sess., 55 (1947).

dication, however, that it was designed to curtail the Board's power in fashioning remedies when the loss of employment stems directly from an unfair labor practice as in the case at hand.

The judgment of the Court of Appeals is affirmed.

MR. JUSTICE GOLDBERG took no part in the consideration or decision of this case.

MR. JUSTICE STEWART, with whom MR. JUSTICE DOUGLAS and MR. JUSTICE HARLAN join, concurring.

Viewed broadly, the question before us stirs large issues. The Court purports to limit its decision to "the facts of this case." But the Court's opinion radiates implications of such disturbing breadth that I am persuaded to file this separate statement of my own views.

* * * The Court most assuredly does not decide that every managerial decision which necessarily terminates an individual's employment is subject to the duty to bargain. Nor does the Court decide that subcontracting decisions are as a general matter subject to that duty. The Court holds no more than that this employer's decision to subcontract this work, involving "the replacement of employees in the existing bargaining unit with those of an independent contractor to do the same work under similar conditions of employment" is subject to the duty to bargain collectively. Within the narrow limitations implicit in the specific facts of this case, I agree with the Court's decision. * * *

The basic question is whether the employer failed to "confer in good faith with respect to * * * terms and conditions of employment" in unilaterally deciding to subcontract this work. This question goes to the scope of the employer's duty in the absence of a collective bargaining agreement.[32] It is true, as the Court's opinion points out, that industrial experience may be useful in determining the proper scope of the duty to bargain. See *Labor Board* v. *American Nat'l Ins. Co.*, 343 U.S. 395, 408, 72 S.Ct. 824, 831. But data showing that many labor contracts refer to subcontracting or that subcontracting grievances are frequently referred to arbitrators under collective bargaining agreements, while not wholly irrelevant, do not have much real bearing, for such data may indicate no more than that the parties have often considered it mutually advantageous

---

32. There was a time when one might have taken the view that the National Labor Relations Act gave the Board and the courts no power to determine the subjects about which the parties must bargain—a view expressed by Senator Walsh when he said that public concern ends at the bargaining room door. 79 Cong.Rec. 7659 (1939). See Cox and Dunlop, Regulation of Collective Bargaining by the NLRB, 63 Harv.L.Rev. 389. But too much law has been built upon a contrary assumption for this view any longer to prevail, and I question neither the power of the Court to decide this issue nor the propriety of its doing so.

to bargain over these issues on a permissive basis. In any event, the ultimate question is the scope of the duty to bargain defined by the statutory language.

It is important to note that the words of the statute are words of limitation. The National Labor Relations Act does not say that the employer and employees are bound to confer upon any subject which interests either of them; the specification of wages, hours, and other terms and conditions of employment defines a limited category of issues subject to compulsory bargaining. The limiting purpose of the statute's language is made clear by the legislative history of the present Act. As originally passed, the Wagner Act contained no definition of the duty to bargain collectively.[33] In the 1947 revision of the Act, the House bill contained a detailed but limited list of subjects of the duty to bargain, excluding all others. In conference the present language was substituted for the House's detailed specification. While the language thus incorporated in the 1947 legislation as enacted is not so stringent as that contained in the House bill, it nonetheless adopts the same basic approach in seeking to define a limited class of bargainable issues.

* * * [T]he Court's opinion seems to imply that any issue which may reasonably divide an employer and his employees must be the subject of compulsory collective bargaining.[34]

Only a narrower concept of "conditions of employment" will serve the statutory purpose of delineating a limited category of issues which are subject to the duty to bargain collectively. Seeking to effect this purpose, at least seven circuits have interpreted the statutory language to exclude various kinds of management decisions from the scope of the duty to bargain. In common parlance, the conditions of a person's employment are most obviously the various physical dimensions of his working environment. What one's hours are to be, what amount of work is expected during those hours, what periods of relief are available, what safety practices are observed, would all seem conditions of one's employment. There are other less tangible but no less important characteristics of a person's employment which might also be deemed "conditions"—most prominently the characteristic involved in this case, the security of one's employment. On one

33. However, it did recognize that the party designated by a majority of employees in a bargaining unit shall be their exclusive representative "for the purpose of collective bargaining in respect of rates of pay, wages, hours of employment, or other conditions of employment." (§ 9(a).)

34. The opinion of the Court seems to assume that the only alternative to compulsory collective bargaining is un-remitting economic warfare. But to exclude subjects from the ambit of compulsory collective bargaining does not preclude the parties from seeking negotiations about them on a permissive basis. And there are limitations upon the use of economic force to compel concession upon subjects which are only permissively bargainable. Labor Board v. Wooster Div. of Borg Warner Corp., 356 U.S. 343.

view of the matter, it can be argued that the question whether there is to be a job is not a condition of employment; the question is not one of imposing conditions on employment, but the more fundamental question whether there is to be employment at all. However, it is clear that the Board and the courts have on numerous occasions recognized that union demands for provisions limiting an employer's power to discharge employees are mandatorily bargainable. Thus, freedom from discriminatory discharge, seniority rights, the imposition of a compulsory retirement age, have been recognized as subjects upon which an employer must bargain, although all of these concern the very existence of the employment itself.

While employment security has thus properly been recognized in various circumstances as a condition of employment, it surely does not follow that every decision which may affect job security is a subject of compulsory, collective bargaining. Many decisions made by management affect the job security of employees. Decisions concerning the volume and kind of advertising expenditures, product design, the manner of financing, and of sales, all may bear upon the security of the workers' jobs. Yet it is hardly conceivable that such decisions so involve "conditions of employment" that they must be negotiated with the employees' bargaining representative.

In many of these areas the impact of a particular management decision upon job security may be extremely indirect and uncertain, and this alone may be sufficient reason to conclude that such decisions are not "with respect to * * * conditions of employment." Yet there are other areas where decisions by management may quite clearly imperil job security, or indeed terminate employment entirely. An enterprise may decide to invest in labor-saving machinery. Another may resolve to liquidate its assets and go out of business. Nothing the Court holds today should be understood as imposing a duty to bargain collectively regarding such managerial decisions, which lie at the core of entrepreneurial control. Decisions concerning the commitment of investment capital and the basic scope of the enterprise are not in themselves primarily about conditions of employment, though the effect of the decision may be necessarily to terminate employment. If, as I think clear, the purpose of § 8(d) is to describe a limited area subject to the duty of collective bargaining, those management decisions which are fundamental to the basic direction of a corporate enterprise or which impinge only indirectly upon employment security should be excluded from that area.

Applying these concepts to the case at hand, I do not believe that an employer's subcontracting practices are, as a general matter, in themselves conditions of employment. Upon any definition of the statutory terms short of the most expansive, such practices are not conditions—tangible or intangible—of any person's employment.

The question remains whether this particular kind of subcontracting decision comes within the employer's duty to bargain. On the facts of this case, I join the Court's judgment, because all that is involved is the substitution of one group of workers for another to perform the same task in the same plant under the ultimate control of the same employer. The question whether the employer may discharge one group of workers and substitute another for them is closely analogous to many other situations within the traditional framework of collective bargaining. Compulsory retirement, layoffs according to seniority, assignment of work among potentially eligible groups within the plant—all involve similar questions of discharge and work assignment, and all have been recognized as subjects of compulsory collective bargaining.

Analytically, this case is not far from that which would be presented if the employer had merely discharged all his employees and replaced them with other workers willing to work on the same job in the same plant without the various fringe benefits so costly to the company. While such a situation might well be considered a § 8(a) (3) violation upon a finding that the employer discriminated against the discharged employees because of their union affiliation, it would be equally possible to regard the employer's action as a unilateral act frustrating negotiation on the underlying questions of work scheduling and remuneration, and so an evasion of his duty to bargain on these questions, which are concededly subject to compulsory collective bargaining. Similarly, had the employer in this case chosen to bargain with the union about the proposed subcontract, negotiations would have inevitably turned to the underlying questions of cost, which prompted the subcontracting. Insofar as the employer frustrated collective bargaining with respect to these concededly bargaining issues by its unilateral act of subcontracting this work, it can properly be found to have violated its statutory duty under § 8(a) (5).

This kind of subcontracting falls short of such larger entrepreneurial questions as what shall be produced, how capital shall be invested in fixed assets, or what the basic scope of the enterprise shall be. In my view, the Court's decision in this case has nothing to do with whether any aspects of those larger issues could under any circumstances be considered subjects of compulsory collective bargaining under the present law.

I am fully aware that in this era of automation and onrushing technological change, no problems in the domestic economy are of greater concern than those involving job security and employment stability. Because of the potentially cruel impact upon the lives and fortunes of the working men and women of the Nation, these problems have understandably engaged the solicitous attention of government, of responsible private business, and particularly of organized labor. It is possible that in meeting these problems Congress may eventually decide to give organized labor or government a far heavier hand in controlling what until now have been considered the prerogatives of private business management. That path would mark a sharp departure from the traditional principles of a free enterprise economy. Whether we should follow it is, within constitutional limitations, for Congress to choose. But it is a path which Congress certainly did not choose when it enacted the Taft-Hartley Act.

ORDER OF R.R. TELEGRAPHERS v. CHICAGO & N.W. RY. CO., 362 U.S. 330 (1960). Plaintiff sought permission from public utility commissions in four states to discontinue various small stations where the traffic was not sufficient to warrant the expense of maintaining personnel. The union thereafter invoked section 6 of the Railway Labor Act and asked plaintiff to agree that no existing jobs would be eliminated by management without the agreement of the union. Plaintiff replied that this demand was not a proper subject for bargaining under the Railway Labor Act, and following unsuccessful negotiation on related matters the union struck. Plaintiff then sought to have the strike enjoined in the district court. On certiorari from a decision by the Court of Appeals sustaining the granting of an injunction by the district court, *held* (5–4), the district court had no jurisdiction to enjoin the strike under the Norris-LaGuardia Act. In reaching its decision, the Court found, *inter alia*, that the strike grew out of a "controversy concerning terms or conditions of employment" as defined in section 13(c) of the Norris-LaGuardia Act. "Plainly the controversy here relates to an effort on the part of the union to change the 'terms' of an existing collective bargaining agreement. * * * The employment of many of these station agents hangs on the number of railroad stations that will either be completely abandoned or consolidated with other stations * * * We cannot agree with the Court of Appeals that the union's effort to negotiate about the job security of its members 'represents an attempt to usurp legitimate managerial prerogative in the exercise of business judgment with respect to the most economical and efficient conduct of its operations.' [264 F.2d 254, 259 (1959)] It is too late now to argue that employees can have no collective voice to influence railroads to act in a way that will preserve the interests of the employees as well as the interests of the railroad and the public at large."

Problems for Discussion

1. The decision of the Board which was reviewed in the *Fibreboard* case by the Supreme Court resulted from a Board rehearing and reversal of an earlier decision on the same record. In its 1961 decision, the Board had dismissed the 8(a)(5) complaint because, under the law as then ob-

tained, the employer was held to violate that section in connection with a subcontracting decision only if its decision was motivated by anti-union animus (and thus a violation of section 8(a)(3) independently) or if it failed to bargain about the *effects* of its decision upon the employees (such as severance and accrued vacation or retirement pay) as opposed to the decision itself.   The Board found that the decision to subcontract was economically rather than discriminatorily motivated and that the employer in fact did bargain about the effects of the decision (i. e., severance pay). In 1962, with a change in membership stemming from new appointments by President Kennedy, the original decision was reconsidered and reversed, and the employer held in violation of Section 8(a)(5) for failing to bargain about the decision to subcontract itself.   Much the same reversal of Board policy occurred in the area of recognition picketing, witness the *Hod Carriers (Blinne)* case, at p. 704 infra.   Cases like *Dal-Tex, Hollywood Ceramics* and *Sewell*—at pp. 144, 159 and 178, supra, dealing with pre-election communications—were also a product of this shift in membership and in attitude.   What drawbacks and/or advantages do you see in having Board decisions reflect a changing composition of the Board, which in turn may reflect a changing political persuasion in the White House?   Are such shifts in decisionmaking more or less a source of concern than if found in a judicial tribunal?

2.   What exactly is required of the employer if it is held that a particular decision—subcontracting, partial shutdown, automation—is a "mandatory" subject, and must be negotiated with the union in good faith? Will this obligation likely interfere in any substantial manner with the employer's conduct of the business?   Should the ease—or difficulty—of complying with the duty to bargain on these decisions affect the judgment of the Board or courts in determining *whether* these decisions are mandatorily bargainable?   Is it relevant, for example, that the planning and implementation of these kinds of decisions are frequently best carried out in secrecy?

3.   Does the inclusion of a subject in the "mandatory" category increase or diminish resort to economic force on that subject?   Should the Board or courts, in determining whether an employer decision should be made the subject of mandatory bargaining, consider the implications such a determination would have for utilization by the parties of economic force in securing agreement?

4.   The opinion for the Court notes that the bargaining requirement relates only to this particular and limited kind of subcontracting and not necessarily to other kinds involving greater deployment of capital or personnel.   Can it also be fairly said that this decision should not necessarily govern even this limited kind of subcontracting when employed in a different kind of industry, in a different part of the country, with a different kind of employment pattern, and a different history of union activity? In other words, to what extent is the Board or Court conception of mandatory subjects a uniform and generalized one, to be applied regardless of industry, geography, employment market, union development and strength, and bargaining traditions?   Does the mode of operation of the Board— or the inherent limitations of workload—make it impossible for the Board

so to fashion its judgments as to account for these divergent patterns of industrial relations? Would it be desirable for the Board to do so if it could? (You might consider the same questions in connection with Board regulation of pre-election speech and literature, where the impact of statements about the social or economic consequences of unionization will no doubt drastically differ in different industrial settings.) Very much the same kind of problem is considered in the *American National Insurance* case, p. 441 supra.

———

It should be emphasized that a holding by the Board or a court that subcontracting is a "term or condition of employment" does not necessarily mean that the employer must first bargain with the union to impasse before implementing a decision to subcontract. The decision of the Fibreboard Company, for example, was effected at a time when no contract was in existence between it and the union. Had there been a contract, there may have been some provision which gave to the Company—perhaps in a "management rights" clause— the power to subcontract work. Such a clear provision might be deemed a "waiver" by the union of its statutory right to require the employer to bargain, and disputes over the meaning of such a provision would ordinarily be tested before an arbitrator. The duty to bargain during the contract term, and the relationship between that duty and contract arbitration, are considered in greater detail at pp. 658–69, infra.

Not only was there no contract provision on which the Fibreboard Company could rely, but its decision to subcontract worked a change in the status quo; it had apparently never subcontracted this kind of work before. When, however, an employer's decision to subcontract is consistent with past practice, it is that practice which will be treated as the status quo, and the employer is free to continue "unilaterally" to subcontract consistent with that status quo and need bargain only regarding a departure therefrom. The Board will also not likely find a duty to bargain when the subcontracting has a minimal or no impact on job security of workers in the bargaining unit. These principles were articulated by the Board in WESTINGHOUSE ELEC. CORP., 150 N.L.R.B. 1574 (1965). The employer in that case had for almost twenty-five years entered into thousands of subcontracts covering its maintenance operations as well as the manufacture of various components, tools and dies, and parts. Most of the maintenance jobs could have been done by the company's employees and many of the parts and components and the like could have been manufactured by the company itself. (In addition, the union had bargained unsuccessfully in three separate contract negotiations to obtain some limitation on management's power to subcontract.) The union filed a charge with the NLRB under Section 8(a)(5), claiming that these subcontracts constituted refusals to bargain in good faith. The Board concluded that, while the employer was obligated to bargain about its subcontracting practices should the union raise the issue at general contract negotiations, the employer was free to continue to make such subcontracting decisions as before without notice to or consultation with the union:

> "In sum—bearing in mind particularly that the recurrent contracting out of work here in question was motivated solely by economic considerations; that it comported with the traditional methods by which the Respondent conducted its business operations; that it did not during the period here in question vary significantly in kind or degree from what had been customary under past established practice; that it had no demonstrable adverse impact on employees in the unit; and that the Union had the opportunity to bargain about changes in existing subcontracting practices at general negotiating meetings—for all these reasons cumulatively, we conclude that Respondent did not violate its statutory bargaining obligation by failing to invite union participation in individual subcontracting decisions."

INTERNATIONAL UNION, UNITED AUTOMOBILE WORKERS v. NLRB (GENERAL MOTORS CORP.), 470 F.2d 422 (D.C.Cir. 1972). In addition to manufacturing trucks, GM owns and operates various facilities for the retail sale and servicing of GM trucks and truck parts. UAW represented the employees at one such facility, the Houston Truck Center. When UAW heard rumors that GM was engaged in negotiations to sell the Houston Truck Center to Trucks of Texas, Inc., an independent dealer, it asked that it be kept informed and given an opportunity to bargain, but the Center manager said he would not do so until any sale was consummated. UAW filed unfair labor practice charges. GM then proceeded to sign an agreement leasing the premises and selling all personal property at the Houston Center to Trucks of Texas, Inc. (Trucks), which agreed to operate a dealership pursuant to a GM franchise (which GM was free to terminate at any time). After Trucks announced that no jobs would be available to the present GM employees, GM discussed with the employees and the Union the benefits to which the terminated employees would be entitled.

The Board found no violation of Section 8(a)(5), holding that the transfer to Trucks was a "sale of the business" which was "at the core of entrepreneurial control." A divided court of appeals denied the UAW's petition for review.

UAW contended that *Fibreboard* should be read to embrace any management decision resulting in termination of employment, and that in any event this was in substance a "classical contracting out situation." The court disagreed, and approved the Board's characterization of the transfer as a sale, pursuant to a national GM policy, which was "fundamental to the basic direction of a corporate enterprise." Acknowledging that its task was to assure that the interests of employees were carefully balanced against the right of an employer to run its business, the court stated that "What UAW would have us do would turn over the management to it." [Do you agree?]

The court reviewed the appellate decisions in similar cases:

"In applying the case-by-case approach, the Courts of Appeals have looked to several factors to determine if a decision is one 'primarily about the conditions of employment' or is instead 'fundamental to the basic direction of a corporate enterprise.' If the decision appears to be primarily designed to avoid the bargaining agreement with the union or if it produces no substantial change in the operations of the employer, the courts have required bargaining. International Union, UAW v. NLRB, 127 U.S.App.D.C. 97, 381 F.2d 265 (1967), cert. denied 389 U.S. 857, 88 S.Ct. 82, 19 L.Ed.2d 122 ['contracting out' of one step in a two-step car-parking operation previously done by union employees]; Weltronic Co. v. NLRB, 419 F.2d 1120 (6 Cir. 1969), cert. denied 398 U.S. 938, 90 S.Ct. 1841, 26 L.Ed.2d 270 [transfer of work from a union plant to a non-union plant three miles away]. If the decision resulted in the termination of a substantial portion or a distinct line of the employer's business or involved a major change in the nature of its operations, no bargaining has been required. NLRB v. Drapery Mfg. Co., 425 F.2d 1026, 1028 (8 Cir. 1970) [shut down of a drapery manufacturing division of a company involving 'a major shift in capital investment' that was purely economically motivated]; NLRB v. Transmarine Navigation Corp., 380 F.2d 933 (9 Cir. 1967) [the operation of a terminal moved to another location with the company accepting minority interest in joint venture]; NLRB v. Royal Plating & Polishing Co., supra [one of two plants closed down]; see also NLRB v. Dixie Ohio Express Co., 409 F.2d 10 (6 Cir. 1969) [procedures for loading and unloading substantially altered]; NLRB v. Adams Dairy, Inc., 322 F.2d 553 (8 Cir. 1963), remanded in light of *Fibreboard,* 379 U.S. 644, 85 S.Ct. 613, 13 L.Ed.2d 550 (1965), reaffirmed, 350 F.2d 108 (8 Cir. 1965), cert. denied 382 U.S. 1011, 86 S.Ct. 619, 15 L.Ed.2d 526 [change in distribution method]; Machinists v. Northeast Airlines, 80 LRRM 2197 [airline merger]. The difficult cases have been those involving a small but not insubstantial proportion of the employer's business; in these cases, the results have often hinged on hints of anti-union animus. See, e. g., N. L. R. B. v. Johnson, 368 F.2d 549 (9 Cir. 1966) [floor covering company decided to subcontract installation services immediately after the negotiation of a collective bargaining agreement]; N. L. R. B. v. American Manufacturing Co., 351 F.2d 74 (5 Cir. 1965) [subcontracting of truck delivery portion of business where a clear showing of animosity toward union is present]."

The dissenting judge contended that the Board had not discharged its obligation under *Fibreboard* to balance the interests of employer and employees, but had simply characterized this transaction as a "sale" (which although perhaps sound as a matter of property law "may have little or nothing to do with the relative importance of the interests of management and employees in bargaining about the decision") and had through abstract speculation looked only to management's interest in avoiding bargaining. The Board had said: "Such managerial decisions at times require secrecy as well as the freedom to act quickly and decisively. They also involve subject areas as to which determinative financial and operational considerations are likely to be unfamiliar to the employees and their representatives." But, said the dissenting judge, the employer may confront problems of time and confidentiality regardless whether it is negotiating a subcontract or a sale or a franchise. The Board thus neglected to consider the specific interests of GM and the UAW in this particular case, in which "the most significant difference [with *Fibreboard*] is probably the choice of forms made by the draftsmen who prepared the documents."

Problems for Discussion

1. Western Steel Company has a large fabricating plant at Stockton, California. United Steelworkers, CIO, is the collective bargaining representative not only of the production and maintenance workers but also of all office and clerical workers. The office and clerical workers are in a separate bargaining unit but as a practical matter, Western and Steelworkers have made a practice of negotiating one contract covering both units. The present contract will expire in 40 days. Steelworkers has already presented its proposals for modifications which include inserting into the contract the following clause:

> The company agrees that it will not subcontract any work which might be done by employees in the bargaining units nor transfer to any new plant operations now being carried on at the Stockton plant. The company will not install new machinery or equipment displacing employees in the bargaining units without the prior consent of the union. In the event of disagreement, the issue shall be submitted to the permanent umpire for a final and binding decision.

Western's Stockton plant has been operating at capacity, but the company expects the normal growth of the economy on the West Coast to result in an increase in business. Western's directors are rumored to be considering proposals to build additions to the Stockton plant or, alternatively, to build a new plant at some location nearer the Southern California market. The rumors are accurate, but these plans look to the long range future and no final decisions are imminent. Western might act during the next year or it might not.

It is also known that Western has had experts from Remington Rand surveying its clerical work with a view to substituting business machines for a large part of the office work presently done by hand. Rumors are rife that 80 per cent of the jobs would be abolished in two office departments if Remington Rand can adapt its machines to Western's needs and rent them at a saving in cost.

(a) What position should Western's negotiators take with respect to the Steelworkers' demand at the next bargaining conference? May Western refuse even to discuss the matter? If not, what should be its position and how fully should it go into questions concerning subcontracting, plant location and the installation of business machines?

(b) Would Steelworkers be guilty of an unfair labor practice if it refused to sign any contract that did not contain a clause restricting the installation of office machines? Would it be advisable for Steelworkers to take the position that it does not insist upon any particular form of agreement but that its willingness to scale down its demand for wage increases will depend upon the job protection clauses?

2. Ozark Trailers, Inc. manufactures truck bodies at three plants in three states. Employees at Ozark's Missouri plant have been represented by the Allied Industrial Workers. Because of production inefficiencies at that plant, the number of units produced has fallen below that of the other two plants, and the quality of workmanship is substantially poorer. The Board of Directors of Ozark decided to shut down the Missouri plant permanently and has offered to bargain with the union about the treatment of employees at that plant (such as severance pay or transfer to other Ozark plants). However, Ozark refuses to discuss with the union the actual decision to shut down the Missouri plant or to reconsider that decision. Has Ozark violated Section 8(a)(5)? See *First National Maintenance Corp. v. NLRB*, —— U.S. ——, —— S.Ct. ——, —— L.Ed.2d —— (June 22, 1981) (set forth in the Appendix to this casebook).

3. Evaluate the following proposition: "There is no substantial justification for an employer's refusal to bargain about *any* decision to reshape the scope of the enterprise, including going out of business altogether. First, these decisions have a direct and dramatic impact upon the job security of the employees. Second, negotiations may convince the employer that there is no need to take the drastic measures contemplated. Third, there is no significant impairment of employer prerogatives, since there need simply be notice to the union and an opportunity for informed discussion; the employer is free to implement its decision after a bargaining impasse is reached. Fourth, employer discussion of these decisions

will, incidentally but usefully, provide assurance that its actions are not discriminatorily motivated. Fifth, on the matter of a complete shutdown, the *Darlington* case, page 242 supra, was decided under a statutory provision requiring anti-union animus to establish a violation, while the duty to bargain obtains even when the employer's decision is economically motivated." Did the Supreme Court give adequate attention to these arguments in *First National Maintenance Corp. v. NLRB*, set forth in the Appendix?

ALLIED CHEMICAL WORKERS v. PITTSBURGH PLATE GLASS CO.

Supreme Court of the United States, 1971.
404 U.S. 157, 92 S.Ct. 383, 30 L.Ed.2d 341.

MR. JUSTICE BRENNAN delivered the opinion of the Court.

Under the National Labor Relations Act, as amended, mandatory subjects of collective bargaining include pension and insurance benefits for active employees, and an employer's mid-term unilateral modification of such benefits constitutes an unfair labor practice. This cause presents the question whether a mid-term unilateral modification that concerns, not the benefits of active employees, but the benefits of already retired employees also constitutes an unfair labor practice. The National Labor Relations Board, one member dissenting, held that changes in retired employees' retirement benefits are embraced by the bargaining obligation and that an employer's unilateral modification of them constitutes an unfair labor practice in violation of §§ 8(a)(5) and (1) of the Act. 177 N.L.R.B. 911 (1969). The Court of Appeals for the Sixth Circuit disagreed and refused to enforce the Board's cease-and-desist order, 427 F.2d 936 (1970). We granted certiorari, 401 U.S. 907 (1971). We affirm the judgment of the Court of Appeals.

I

Since 1949, Local 1, Allied Chemical and Alkali Workers of America, has been the exclusive bargaining representative for the employees "working" on hourly rates of pay at the Barberton, Ohio, facilities of respondent Pittsburgh Plate Glass Co. In 1950, the Union and the Company negotiated an employee group health insurance plan, in which, it was orally agreed, retired employees could participate by contributing the required premiums, to be deducted from their pension benefits. * * *

[In negotiations for the 1962 and 1964 contracts, the Company agreed to make monthly contributions of two dollars and four dollars respectively toward the cost of medical insurance premiums for persons retiring after 1962. Medicare, a national health program, was enacted in November 1965 and shortly after, the Company announced its intention to cancel the negotiated health plan for retirees and to substitute supplemental Medicare coverage toward which it would pay three dollars per month. After the Union protested, the Company stated that it had reconsidered and had decided instead to write each retired employee, offering to pay the supplemental Medicare premium if the employee would withdraw from the negotiated plan. Over the Union's objections, the Company wrote to its 190 retirees, fifteen of whom elected to withdraw from the negotiated plan. The Union filed charges under Section 8(a)(5).]

[T]he Company was ordered to cease and desist from refusing to bargain collectively about retirement benefits and from making unilateral adjustments in health insurance plans for retired employees without first negotiating in good faith with the Union. The Company was also required to rescind, at the Union's request, any adjustment it had unilaterally instituted and to mail and post appropriate notices.

II

* * *

Together, [Sections 1, 8(a)(5), 8(d) and 9(a)] establish the obligation of the employer to bargain collectively, "with respect to wages, hours, and other terms and conditions of employment," with "the representatives of his employees" designated or selected by the majority "in a unit appropriate for such purposes." <u>This obligation extends only to the "terms and conditions of employment" of the employer's "employees" in the "unit appropriate for such purposes" that the union represents.</u> * * *

First. * * * We have repeatedly affirmed that the task of determining the contours of the term "employee" [in Section 2(3) of the NLRA] "has been assigned primarily to the agency created by Congress to administer the Act." NLRB v. Hearst Publications, 322 U.S. 111, 130 (1944). See also Iron Workers v. Perko, 373 U.S. 701, 706 (1963); NLRB v. Atkins & Co., 331 U.S. 398 (1947). But we have never immunized Board judgments from judicial review in this respect. "[T]he Board's determination that specified persons are 'employees' under this Act is to be accepted if it has 'warrant in the record' and a reasonable basis in law." NLRB v. Hearst Publications, supra, at 131.

In this cause we hold that the Board's decision is not supported by the law. The Act, after all, as § 1 makes clear, is concerned with the disruption to commerce that arises from interference with the organization and collective-bargaining rights of "workers"—not those who have retired from the work force. The inequality of bargaining power that Congress sought to remedy was that of the "working" man, and the labor disputes that it ordered to be subjected to collective bargaining were those of employers and their active employees. Nowhere in the history of the National Labor Relations Act is there any evidence that retired workers are to be considered as within the ambit of the collective-bargaining obligations of the statute.

To the contrary, the legislative history of § 2(3) itself indicates that the term "employee" is not to be stretched beyond its plain meaning embracing only those who work for another for hire. * * * The ordinary meaning of "employee" does not include retired workers; retired employees have ceased to work for another for hire.

The decisions on which the Board relied in construing § 2(3) to the contrary are wide of the mark. The Board enumerated "unfair labor practice situations where the statute has been applied to persons who have not been initially hired by an employer or whose employment has terminated. Illustrative are cases in which the Board has held that applicants for employment and registrants at hiring halls—who have never been hired in the first place—as well as persons who have quit or whose employers have gone out of business are 'employees' embraced by the policies of the Act." 177 N.L.R.B., at 913 (citations omitted). Yet all of these cases involved people who, unlike the pensioners here, were members of the active work force available for hire and at least in that sense could be identified as "employees." No decision under the Act is cited, and none to our knowledge exists, in which an individual who has ceased work without expectation of further employment has been held to be an "employee." * * *

Second. Section 9(a) of the Labor Relations Act accords representative status only to the labor organization selected or designated by the majority of employees in a "unit appropriate" "for the purposes of collective bargaining." * * *

In this cause, in addition to holding that pensioners are not "employees" within the meaning of the collective-bargaining obligations of the Act, we hold that they were not and could not be "employees" included in the bargaining unit. The unit determined by the Board to be appropriate was composed of "employees of the Employer's plant * * * working on hourly rates, including group leaders who work on hourly rates of pay * * *." Apart from whether retirees could be considered "employees" within this language, they obviously were not employees "working" or "who work" on hourly rates of pay. Although those terms may include persons on temporary or limited absence from work, such as employees on military duty, it would utterly destroy the function of language to read them as embracing those whose work has ceased with no expectation of return. * * *

Here, even if, as the Board found, active and retired employees have a common concern in assuring that the latter's benefits remain adequate, they plainly do not share a community of interests broad enough to justify inclusion of the retirees in the bargaining unit. Pensioners' interests extend only to retirement benefits, to the exclusion of wage rates, hours, working conditions, and all other terms of active employment. Incorporation of such a limited-purpose constituency in the bargaining unit would create the potential for severe internal conflicts that would impair the unit's ability to function and would disrupt the processes of collective bargaining. Moreover, the risk cannot be overlooked that union representatives on occasion might see fit to bargain for improved wages or other conditions favoring active employees at the expense of retirees' benefits.
* * *

Third. The Board found that bargaining over pensioners' rights has become an established industrial practice. But industrial practice cannot alter the conclusions that retirees are neither "employees" nor bargaining unit members. The parties dispute whether a practice of bargaining over pensioners' benefits exists and, if so, whether it reflects the views of labor and management that the subject is not merely a convenient but a mandatory topic of negotiation. But even if industry commonly regards retirees' benefits as a statutory subject of bargaining, that would at most, as we suggested in Fibreboard Corp. v. NLRB, 379 U.S. 203, 211 (1964), reflect the interests of employers and employees in the subject matter as well as its amenability to the collective-bargaining process; it would not be determinative. Common practice cannot change the law and make into bargaining unit "employees" those who are not.

III

Even if pensioners are not bargaining unit "employees," are their benefits, nonetheless, a mandatory subject of collective bargaining as "terms and conditions of employment" of the active employees who remain in the unit? The Board held, alternatively, that they are, on the ground that they "vitally" affect the "terms and conditions of employment" of active employees principally by influencing the value of both their current and future benefits. 177 N.L.R.B., at 915.[35] * * *

35. * * * The Board also noted "that changes in retirement benefits for retired employees affect the availability of employer funds for active employees." 177 N.L.R.B., at 915. That, again, is quite true. But countless other employer expenditures that concededly are not subjects of mandatory bargaining, such as supervisors' salaries and dividends, have a similar impact. The principle that underlies the Board's argument sweeps with far too broad a brush. The Board does suggest in its brief that pensioners' benefits are different from other employer expenses because they are nor-

Section 8(d) of the Act, of course, does not immutably fix a list of subjects for mandatory bargaining. See, e. g., Fibreboard Corp. v. N.L.R.B., supra, at 220–221 (STEWART, J., concurring) ; Richfield Oil Corp. v. NLRB, 97 U.S.App.D.C. 383, 389–390, 231 F.2d 717, 723–724 (1956). But it does establish a limitation against which proposed topics must be measured. In general terms, the limitation includes only issues that settle an aspect of the relationship between the employer and employees. See, e. g., NLRB v. Borg-Warner Corp., 356 U.S. 342 (1958). Although normally matters involving individuals outside the employment relationship do not fall within that category, they are not wholly excluded. In Teamsters Union v. Oliver, 358 U.S. 283 (1959), for example, an agreement had been negotiated in the trucking industry, establishing a minimum rental that carriers would pay to truck owners who drove their own vehicles in the carriers' service in place of the latter's employees. Without determining whether the owner-drivers were themselves "employees," we held that the minimum rental was a mandatory subject of bargaining, and hence immune from state antitrust laws, because the term "was integral to the establishment of a stable wage structure for clearly covered employee-drivers." United States v. Drum, 368 U.S. 370, 382–383, n. 26 (1962). Similarly, in Fibreboard Corp. v. NLRB, supra, at 215, we held that "the type of 'contracting out' involved in this case —the replacement of employees in the existing bargaining unit with those of an independent contractor to do the same work under similar conditions of employment—is a statutory subject of collective bargaining * * *." * * * We agree with the Board that the principle of *Oliver* and *Fibreboard* is relevant here; in each case the question is not whether the third-party concern is antagonistic to or compatible with the interests of bargaining-unit employees, but whether it vitally affects the "terms and conditions" of their employment. But we disagree with the Board's assessment of the significance of a change in retirees' benefits to the "terms and conditions of employment" of active employees.

The benefits that active workers may reap by including retired employees under the same health insurance contract are speculative and insubstantial at best. As the Board itself acknowledges in its brief, the relationship between the inclusion of retirees and the overall insurance rate is uncertain. Adding individuals increases the group experience and thereby generally tends to lower the rate, but including pensioners, who are likely to have higher medical expenses,

mally regarded as part of labor costs. The employer's method of accounting, however, hardly provides a suitable basis for distinction. In any case, the impact on active employees' compensation from changes in pensioners' benefits is, like the effect discussed in the text of including retirees under the same health insurance plan as active employees, too insubstantial to bring those changes within the collective-bargaining obligation.

may more than offset that effect. In any event, the impact one way or the other on the "terms and conditions of employment" of active employees is hardly comparable to the loss of jobs threatened in *Oliver* and *Fibreboard*. * * *

The mitigation of future uncertainty and the facilitation of agreement on active employees' retirement plans, that the Board said would follow from the union's representation of pensioners, are equally problematical. * * * By advancing pensioners' interests now, active employees * * * have no assurance that they will be the beneficiaries of similar representation when they retire. * * *

We recognize that "classification of bargaining subjects as 'terms [and] conditions of employment' is a matter concerning which the Board has special expertise." Meat Cutters v. Jewel Tea, 381 U.S. 676, 685–686 (1965). The Board's holding in this cause, however, depends on the application of law to facts, and the legal standard to be applied is ultimately for the courts to decide and enforce. We think that in holding the "terms and conditions of employment" of active employees to be *vitally* affected by pensioners' benefits, the Board here simply neglected to give the adverb its ordinary meaning. Cf. NLRB v. Brown, 380 U.S. 278, 292 (1965).

IV

The question remains whether the Company committed an unfair labor practice by offering retirees an exchange for their withdrawal from the already negotiated health insurance plan. * * * We need not resolve, however, whether there was a "modification" within the meaning of § 8(d), because we hold that even if there was, a "modification" is a prohibited unfair labor practice only when it changes a term that is a mandatory rather than a permissive subject of bargaining.

Paragraph (4) of § 8(d), of course, requires that a party proposing a modification continue "in full force and effect * * * all the terms and conditions of the existing contract" until its expiration. * * * The provision begins by defining "to bargain collectively" as meeting and conferring "with respect to wages, hours, and other terms and conditions of employment." It then goes on to state that "the duty to bargain collectively shall also mean" that mid-term unilateral modifications and terminations are prohibited. Although this part of the section is introduced by a "proviso" clause, * * * it quite plainly is to be construed *in pari materia* with the preceding definition. Accordingly, just as § 8(d) defines the obligation to bargain to be with respect to mandatory terms alone, so it prescribes the duty to maintain only mandatory terms without unilateral modification for the duration of the collective-bargaining agreement. * * *

The structure and language of § 8(d) point to a more specialized purpose than merely promoting general contract compliance. The conditions for a modification or termination set out in paragraphs (1) through (4) plainly are designed to regulate modifications and terminations so as to facilitate agreement in place of economic warfare. * * * When a proposed modification is to a permissive term, therefore, the purpose of facilitating accord on the proposal is not at all in point, since the parties are not required under the statute to bargain with respect to it. The irrelevance of the purpose is demonstrated by the irrelevance of the procedures themselves of § 8(d). Paragraph (2), for example, requires an offer "to meet and confer with the other party for the purpose of negotiating a new contract or a contract containing the proposed modifications." But such an offer is meaningless if a party is statutorily free to refuse to negotiate on the proposed change to the permissive term. The notification to mediation and conciliation services referred to in paragraph (3) would be equally meaningless, if required at all.[36] We think it would be no less beside the point to read paragraph (4) of § 8(d) as requiring continued adherence to permissive as well as mandatory terms. The remedy for a unilateral mid-term modification to a permissive term lies in an action for breach of contract, * * * not in an unfair-labor-practice proceeding.

As a unilateral mid-term modification of a permissive term such as retirees' benefits does not, therefore, violate § 8(d), the judgment of the Court of Appeals is

Affirmed.

MR. JUSTICE DOUGLAS dissents.

Problems for Discussion

1. Assume that the Company has for many years required that job applicants take a number of aptitude and psychological tests, and that the Union has regularly complained that these tests have not been validated and that they are culturally biased (resulting in the unfair exclusion of

36. The notification required by paragraph (3) is "of the existence of a dispute." Section 2(9) of the Act defines "labor dispute" to include "any controversy concerning terms, tenure or conditions of employment, or concerning the association or representation of persons in negotiating, fixing, maintaining, changing, or seeking to arrange terms or conditions of employment * * *." 49 Stat. 450, as amended, 29 U.S.C. § 152(9). Since controversies over permissive terms are excluded from the definition, a paragraph (3) notice might not be required in the case of a proposed modification to such a term even if § 8(d) applied.

minority-group applicants). At the current negotiations for a new labor agreement, the Union has proposed that the tests be eliminated or that the Union be a participant in designing them (or at least be given an opportunity to secure an impartial appraisal concerning their validity). If the Union were to insist to impasse on its position, or to strike over it, would it commit a violation of Section 8(b)(3)? Cf. Houston Chapter, Associated Gen. Contractors of America, Inc. v. NLRB, 143 N.L.R.B. 409 (1963), enf'd 349 F.2d 449 (5th Cir. 1965), cert denied 382 U.S. 1026, 86 S.Ct. 648, 15 L.Ed. 540 (1966).

Would the result be any different if the Union were to insist on a provision requiring that all job openings be filled by persons referred by the Union's hiring hall?

2. The Rubber Workers Union represents the production and maintenance employees of the Triple-R Company (Run-Right-Retreads), a mid-sized manufacturer of retread tires in Smalltown, Pennsylvania. Triple-R is the only significant company in town, employing almost two-thirds of the eligible workforce. Emissions from the plant have been polluting the air and water of the community; the plant itself, however, is fully ventilated. The Union seeks to add the following provision to the collective bargaining agreement: "Pollution Control—The Company shall not operate at any time without an emission-control system installed and operating. If the plant is closed because of an alleged violation of this provision, all employees covered by this agreement shall receive full compensation at their regular rate of pay for all time lost." The Union wishes to know whether it may only propose this provision, or may be adamant about it. What is your advice? See Oldham, Organized Labor, the Environment and the Taft-Hartley Act, 71 Mich.L.Rev. 936 (1973).

3. The company and the union have settled all terms of their forthcoming labor agreement, except for the union's demand that the agreement include a provision for "interest arbitration" in the event they cannot reach an agreement over new contract terms in subsequent agreements. Although the union has resorted to strikes in impasse situations in prior negotiations, it has concluded that this is costly for its members, both in terms of time lost on account of the strike and layoffs resulting from the company's routine stockpiling of inventory in anticipation of the strikes. To the union, the proffered interest arbitration clause would not only afford an added measure of job security but would also provide for a neutral arbiter to set contract terms fairly. The union is prepared to strike to compel the company to include the interest-arbitration provision in the otherwise settled labor contract. Would this be a violation of Section 8(b)(3)? Is *Pittsburgh Plate Glass* of any pertinence on this matter? See NLRB v. Columbus Printing Pressmen and Assistants' Union No. 252, 543 F.2d 1161 (5th Cir. 1976).

D. THE ROLE OF THE STRIKE AND THIRD–PARTY IMPASSE RESOLUTION

At the center of most discussions concerning collective bargaining is a debate about the necessity and utility of the strike. This debate has become particularly heated in recent years, with the prevalence of work stoppages among public employees, but it has been with us for decades in the private sector, particularly in industries (such as transportation, communications, steel, defense) which are generally regarded as vital to the national welfare. Although the peaceful work stoppage is one of the activities protected under the Labor Act by Section 7, a protection which is underlined in Section 13, it has also been the expressed desire of Congress to have disagreements at the bargaining table resolved without recourse to economic weapons. Several examples of these congressional expressions are Section 8(d), which provides that in all industries within the coverage of the Labor Act, contract renegotiations must be accompanied by notification of federal and state mediation agencies and by a "cooling off" period prior to resort to a strike or lockout; by Section 8(g), enacted in 1974, which requires mediation and a strike notice in contract disputes in private health care institutions, where a board of inquiry may be appointed to recommend a contract settlement; and by Sections 206 through 210 of the Taft-Hartley Act, which provide for the appointment of a presidential board of inquiry and for a strike-injunction and an eighty-day cooling off period when a strike (or lockout) threatens the national "health or safety."

This section of the casebook will consider: First, the premises underlying the American system of collective bargaining in the private sector, and the role of the strike in that system; second, the machinery that is available to resolve negotiating disputes by means short of a work stoppage, most particularly by mediation and other third-party procedures; and third, the impact of the strike upon the duty of the parties under Section 8 of the Labor Act to bargain in good faith.

1. The Premises of Collective Bargaining and the Role of the Strike.

Virtually all of the major strikes in the United States today grow out of conflicts concerning the terms and conditions of employment to be written into collective bargaining agreements. Disputes over unionization, or between two unions seeking to represent the same employees, are pretty well taken care of under the National Labor Relations Act. We have also found in grievance procedures ending in arbitration thoroughly satisfactory methods of handling disputes arising during the term of a collective bargaining contract. The unsolved problems generally involve wages or some related item such as insurance benefits and pensions. Thus they relate essentially to the price of labor.

At the present time our national labor policy is predicated on the belief that the price of labor should be fixed by collective bargaining save in those periods when wage stabilization measures are required to combat inflationary pressures.

Collective bargaining is a part of an economy founded on private enterprise. Wages and other terms and conditions of employment are determined not by the government but by the people concerned. Of course, the aggregation of large amounts in capital in corporations and somewhat later the combination of large numbers of workers into unions has made private negotiation of wages something quite different from what it was a hundred years ago. Also, government policies have undoubted effects on wage levels. But even when allowances are made for those forces, it remains essentially true that collective bargaining is a system for fixing the price of labor without government regulation of the whole structure of wages and prices. Moreover, most of the organized labor movement would not have it otherwise. Since the eighteen-eighties one of the strongest characteristics of the American labor movement has been its dedication to practical objectives which it has sought to obtain by private economic action within our existing society rather than by political reforms aimed at remaking our social and economic institutions. In this respect the American labor movement has been almost unique. European socialists like Harold Laski have railed at it for that reason, and one must recognize that there are signs of a shift toward reliance on political action. Whatever the portents, however, it is fair to say today that collective bargaining operates as a wage fixing mechanism within the framework of a private enterprise system.

You will ask then, how does collective bargaining work, why do management and union ever get together? The answers appear to be two. In the first place the long negotiations over the terms of a collective bargaining contract themselves tend to bring about agreement, or at least to narrow the area of disagreement. But the second factor that makes collective bargaining work is the strike. Everyone who has been in a tough wage negotiation where the stakes were high knows that the bargain is never struck until one minute before midnight when there is no place else to go, nothing left to do, no possible escape from choosing between a strike and a compromise. In the final analysis collective bargaining works as a method of fixing terms and conditions of employment only because there comes a time when both sides conclude that the risks of losses through a strike are so great that compromise is cheaper than economic battle. And when one side or both miscalculate and conclude that the risks are worth running and a strike occurs, it is settled only when each side is convinced that continuing the struggle will cost more than acceptance of the terms the other offers. To put it in a phrase, the strike or the fear of a strike is the motive power that makes collective bargaining operate.

In most industries we are ready enough to accept this way of fixing employees' wages. It works pretty well on the whole and such economic waste as results from strikes is more than offset by the advantages of leaving industry and labor free to work out their own agreements. The trouble comes in those industries where a strike becomes intolerable to the public long before the strike can serve its function of making the parties—management and labor—agree on a voluntary settlement of their differences. In such instances, we are confronted with a dilemma. So long as our labor policy is predicated on collective bargaining, we cannot wholly eliminate the risk of strikes. Nor can we discard collective bargaining without substituting for the private negotiation of wages a high degree of government regulation. We must pay for our freedom.

2. *Facilitation of Voluntary Agreements.*

Although this dilemma is most stark in vital industries, it exists in all. Congress has attempted to preserve the right to strike as a last resort but to encourage the parties first to exhaust all attempts at direct negotiation as well as third-party intervention in order to reach a settlement which will reflect the private interests of the parties.

Pre-Strike Notification. Section 8(d) provides elaborate procedural requirements designed to help settle labor disputes and, in particular, to avert hasty and ill-considered strikes. Section 8(d)(1) requires that any party desiring to terminate or modify an existing collective bargaining agreement must serve written notice on the other party at least sixty days prior to the expiration date of the contract or, if the contract provides no such date, sixty days prior to the time when the termination or modification is to be made. Section 8(d)(3) stipulates that within thirty days of submitting the written notice required by 8(d)(1), the moving party must inform the Federal Mediation and Conciliation Service together with any State or Territorial agency which is designed and empowered to mediate or conciliate the dispute. Finally, Section 8(d)(4) demands that the party continue

> in full force and effect without resorting to strike or lock-out, all the terms and conditions of the existing contract for a period of sixty days after such notice is given or until the expiration date of such contract, whichever occurs later * * *

A failure to comply with these provisions constitutes an unlawful refusal to bargain within the meaning of Section 8(a) (5) or Section 8(b) (3). In addition, Section 8(d) (4) provides that any employee who strikes within any notice period prescribed in Section 8(d) will lose his status as an employee of the employer concerned for the purposes of Sections 8, 9 and 10 of the Act unless and until he is reemployed by that employer.

These provisions have given rise to considerable legal controversy. For a long period, there was a question as to whether Section 8(d) might be applied to prohibit strikes to enforce demands which the union erroneously believed to be consistent with the existing collective bargaining agreement. In recent years, however, the Board has taken the view that a strike to terminate or modify the agreement occurs only when the union deliberately seeks an objective which it knows is contrary to the terms of the contract. Another problem under 8(d) arose in the *Mastro Plastics* case where the NLRB contended that employees who struck within sixty days of giving notice to their employer fell within the ban of 8(d) (4) even though their strike was in response to unfair labor practices by the employer rather than in furtherance of the union's bargaining demands. On certiorari to the Supreme Court, however, the Board was reversed and Section 8(d) was held to apply only to strikes designed to terminate or modify an existing contract. *Mastro Plastics Corp. v. NLRB*, 350 U.S. 270, 76 S.Ct. 349, 100 L.Ed. 309 (1956).

Another series of problems has arisen having to do with the relationship between Section 8(d) (3) and Sections 8(d) (1) and 8(d) (4). If the union does not notify federal and state mediation and conciliation agencies for more than thirty days after notifying the employer, must the union wait another thirty days before striking or merely wait sixty days after the original notice was served upon the employer? Even if an additional thirty days has elapsed prior to the strike, can the union still be held to have violated 8(d)(4) for failing to notify the government agencies within the prescribed thirty days? A number of different constructions of the Act have been suggested. The most strict would bar a union from striking after any late notice to the mediation agencies even if the union delays the strike for more than thirty days, and would require in order to validate any strike that a new sixty-day notice first be served on the employer and the cycle begun afresh. The most lenient construction would permit the union to wait for thirty days from notifying the mediation agencies before striking, that wait not only validating the strike but also cleansing the violation of Section 8(d)(3) resulting from the late notice. The construction which appears best to comport with the language of Section 8(d), and with its purpose of giving the mediation agencies thirty days within which to attempt to effect a settlement, is to hold the union responsible for the late notice under Section 8(d)(3) but to permit the union to strike if it waits at least thirty days after giving such notice. That position has been endorsed by the court of appeals in Local 219, Retail Clerks v. NLRB, 265 F.2d 814 (D.C.Cir. 1959).

In 1974, Congress eliminated from the Labor Act an exclusion for private nonprofit hospitals which had been a part of the Act since 1947. (Public Law 93–360 (July 26, 1974).) It also expressed a concern for the peculiar need in health care institutions for the uninterrupted rendition of services to the public and took a number of steps to facilitate the settlement of contract negotiation disputes beyond those already set forth in Section 8(d). First, a party wishing to terminate or modify a labor contract in a health care institution is to give the other party ninety days notice prior to contract expiration and sixty days notice to Federal and State mediation agencies (rather than sixty and thirty days, respectively). Moreover, even in the case of an initial contract (where there is no "termination or modification"), a thirty-day notice must be given the mediation agencies. Second, although the intervention of the mediation agencies in all other industries is at the discretion of those agencies, in health care institutions the Federal Mediation and Conciliation Service is directed to use its best efforts to effect a settlement, and the parties are directed to "participate fully and promptly in such meetings." Third, although the notice requirements of Section 8(d) speak in all other industries to notice of contract termination or modification and not explicitly to notice of a work stoppage, a new Section 8(g) now requires that in addition to the Section 8(d) notices a union must "before engaging in any strike, picketing or other concerted refusal to work at any health care institution" give a ten-day notice to the employer and to the Federal Mediation Service. Any individual participating in a strike within any of the periods established for health care institutions in Sections 8(d) and 8(g) is subject to the loss-of-status provision of the former section. (A new Section 213, relating to the role of the Federal Mediation Service in health care disputes, was also added to the Act in 1974, and provides that the Director of the Service may appoint an impartial Board of Inquiry to investigate the dispute and to make recommendations for its settlement; the Board is to report within fifteen days of its appointment, and for that period as well as for an additional fifteen-day period after it has issued its report, the parties must maintain the status quo and must refrain from strike or lockout. The Director may appoint such a Board only if he is of the opinion that "a threatened or actual strike or lockout affecting a health care institution will, if permitted to occur or to continue, substantially interrupt the delivery of health care in the locality concerned.")

Conciliation and Mediation. The Taft-Hartley Act established a new independent agency, known as the Federal Mediation and Conciliation Service. As we have already pointed out, sixty days prior to making any change in the terms and conditions of employment fixed by a collective agreement covering employees in an industry affecting interstate commerce, the party desiring a change must give notice to the other party, and thirty days thereafter must notify both the Federal Mediation and Conciliation Service and any State mediation agency. During the sixty day period it is an unfair labor practice to make any change in terms and conditions of employment (except by mutual agreement) or to call a strike. The Service may proffer its services in any labor dispute in an industry affecting interstate commerce but it is directed to avoid attempting to mediate disputes having only a minor effect on interstate commerce. In addition, the Service may intervene in grievance cases only in exceptional circumstances. Behind these restrictions lies the belief that State agencies should assume a larger role in settling labor controversies, and most of the industrial States have also established effective conciliation or mediation agencies.

Occasionally a distinction is drawn between conciliation and mediation: a conciliator is said to be merely an errand boy carrying messages between the parties whereas a mediator drives affirmatively toward a settlement by making his own proposals. But the difference is largely theoretical. By whatever name they may be called both have one end in view—that of bringing the parties to agree on the terms of a contract or, failing complete agreement, a voluntary submission to arbitration. Like every trade, mediation has its peculiar tricks, but basically the mediator depends on persuasion and on a thorough understanding of industrial relations to enable him to discover some basis for agreement.

At a joint conference, the mediator learns from both parties how they perceive the issues that separate them. Through a series of separate conferences, the mediator then explores intimately and confidentially all of the factors discussed in the joint meeting, and he induces the parties to analyze the obstacles to settlement and their own true priorities and feasible concessions. Essential to the successful pursuit of this task is the parties' firm understanding that what they say to the mediator in confidence will not be disclosed. Not infrequently, the mediator or conciliator learns that a deadlock has resulted from a misunderstanding concerning basic facts or of the position of the other party, of practices elsewhere or of the pertinent laws or administrative rulings. By dispelling these misunderstandings, either in individual or joint conferences, the mediator can restore the momentum toward settlement. He can also do this by suggesting compromises or alternative approaches to either side in reaching its own objectives; the hope is that rigid ways of thinking, which have caused the deadlock, will be dispelled and that new and imaginative approaches will be stimulated. Another way in which the mediator can facilitate bargaining is by conveying to one party that the other party, who is believed to be relying merely on rhetoric—the union threatening a strike or the company pleading incapacity—in fact really "means business." Also of importance is the fact that the mediator is able to impress upon both parties the requirements of the public interest, particularly in major disputes in either the private or public sector.

Fact-Finding Boards. Reliance has sometimes been placed on fact finding to supplement normal conciliation and mediation services. In the railway labor field this has become an integral part of the collective bargaining process, and that experience—along with more recent experiences under state public-sector bargaining legislation—was incorporated in the NLRA in the 1974 amendments dealing with private health care institutions. Under the Railway Labor Act, the National Mediation Board may enter into a negotiation after either party gives notice of an intended change in rates of pay, rules or working conditions, and if mediation fails, the President may—if the dispute threatens to deprive any section of the country of essential transportation service—appoint under Section 10 of the Act an Emergency Board to investigate the pertinent facts and report them to the President. Throughout the period of mediation and investigation, neither party may make any change in the conditions out of which the dispute arose, but thereafter there may be lawful resort to economic weapons.

A similar, but more condensed, time-table is set forth in a new Section 213 of the National Labor Relations Act, relating to the role of the Federal Mediation Service in health care disputes. The Director of the Service—if he or she is of the opinion that "a threatened or actual strike or lockout affecting a health care institution will, if permitted to occur or to continue, substantially interrupt the delivery of health care in the locality concerned"—may appoint an impartial board of inquiry to investigate the dispute and actually to make recommendations for its settlement. Throughout the pertinent period, the parties must maintain the status quo and must refrain from striking, locking out, or changing working conditions.

Although it is frequently suggested that such fact-finding boards, particularly those with powers to make recommendations for substantive contract terms, induce the parties to withhold their offers of compromise from the bargaining table and reserve them for the fact-finder, it is uncertain how often that is in fact the case. In any event, it seems fairly plain that on balance the fact-finding board is a sound procedure to have available for occasional use in achieving the settlement of labor controversies having significant public ramifications.

National Emergencies. Sections 206 through 210 of the Labor-Management Relations Act of 1947 set forth detailed procedures to govern strikes which are deemed to constitute a national emergency. The statute provides that if the President believes that an actual or threatened strike will imperil the national health or safety, he may impanel a board of inquiry. This board is expressly forbidden to make recommendations for the settlement of the dispute but is directed to investigate the causes and circumstances of the controversy. Having received the report of the board, the President may conclude that the strike is a threat to national health or safety whereupon he can direct the Attorney General to petition any appropriate district court for an injunction. If the district court finds that a strike affects all or a substantial part of an industry engaged in interstate commerce or in the production of goods for commerce and that the continuation of the strike will imperil the national health or safety, the Court shall have jurisdiction to enjoin the strike. Thereafter, bargaining between the parties continues with the aid of the Federal Mediation and Conciliation Service. Sixty days after the issuing of the injunction, the board of inquiry must submit a further report setting forth the current status of the dispute and the employer's last offer of settlement. Within the next fifteen days, a vote must be taken among the employees to determine whether they will agree to accept the last offer of the employer. Whether or not the foregoing measures have resulted in a settlement between the parties, the injunction must be dissolved after it has been in force for eighty days.

In 1959, these procedures were tested in the courts as a result of a strike by more than half a million steelworkers against some 97 steel companies. When stockpiles had dwindled and an estimated 250,000 men had been laid off in dependent industries, the President, having received a report from a board of inquiry, ordered the Attorney General to seek an injunction. After an injunction had been granted by the district court and affirmed by the Court of Appeals, the case was taken on certiorari to the Supreme Court. The union argued to the Court that the statute permitted injunctions only where the physical well-being of the citizenry was in jeopardy and where the judge in his discretion had determined that other techniques for averting the crisis were unavailing. These arguments were rejected by the Court in a per curiam decision which limited the role of the courts under the national emergency provisions to a determination of whether the national health or safety is imperiled by the strike. On the basis of the affidavits by experts and government officials, the Court concluded that critical defense needs were involved which constituted a threat to the national safety. UNITED STEELWORKERS v. UNITED STATES, 361 U.S. 391 (1959). The national emergency provisions have been invoked in a number of other industries, including coal, atomic energy, maritime, and telecommunications.

There is great diversity of opinion about the effectiveness of the national emergency dispute provision of the Taft-Hartley Act. There is general recognition of the futility of the clause calling for a vote on the employer's last offer of settlement. There is also wide support for giving emergency boards power to make recommendations as well as to report facts. There is less unanimity on the issues raised by the injunction provisions and on the desirability of seizure as an alternative remedy.

---

3. The Effect of a Strike Upon the Duty to Bargain

The use of the strike is "part and parcel" of the process of collective bargaining in the United States. The underlying theory, developed at pages 482–85 supra, is reflected in such decisions as NLRB v. Insurance Agents Int'l Union, at p. 408 supra. That case holds that, barring specific congressional outlawry, a union's resort during negotiations to a peaceful work stoppage—even if regarded as unconventional, peculiarly disruptive and indeed obnoxious by common standards—does not in itself violate the duty to bargain in good faith. (It may be, however, that such stoppages render the employees susceptible to discharge.) The question remains whether such union activity in some way modifies the duty of the employer so to bargain. Although it has been argued that a conventional peaceful strike is so disruptive of amicable relations between union and employer that it ought to relieve the employer of the duty to continue dealing at the bargaining table, that argument has been clearly and consistently rejected. As the court held in NLRB v. Rutter-Rex Mfg. Co., 245 F.2d 594 (5th Cir. 1957):

"The duty to bargain did not terminate with the calling or execution of the strike. The strike, or threat of it, so carefully recognized as a right in the Act, Section 13, 29 U.S. C.A. § 163, is a means of self-help allowed to a union as pressure in the bargaining process. How or why the strike is called, or how conducted, may well have significant effect upon the right of strikers for reinstatement or reemployment or in other respects not necessary to indicate. But the mere fact that a Union has without justification precipitated a strike does not make the union or the employees for whom it is the bargaining representative outlaws so that they forfeit all of the benefits of the Act. The calling of such a strike does not infect all that thereafter occurs with the virus of that action. A strike does not in and of itself suspend the bargaining obligation."

The strike in the *Rutter-Rex* case was a protected economic strike. Is the duty to bargain suspended when the union or employees engage in activities which are unprotected or unlawful? In

Phelps Dodge Copper Prods. Corp., 101 N.L.R.B. 360 (1952), the employer was held not to have violated the Act when it refused to continue contract negotiations while the union engaged in an unprotected slowdown. The Board held that the slowdown "negates the existence of honest and sincere dealing in the Union's contemporaneous request to negotiate in these circumstances. The Respondent was not required to indulge in the futile gesture of honoring the Union's request." Are there sound reasons for thus suspending the employer's duty to bargain? Can this holding survive the Supreme Court decision in *Insurance Agents*? See NLRB v. Katz, 369 U.S. 736, 82 S.Ct. 1107, 8 L.Ed.2d 230, 741 n. 7 (1962).

As will be developed in materials below, at pp. 833–36, the employer during the strike is entitled by law to hire temporary or even permanent replacements for the strikers in order to keep its business going. Appeals directly to employees to break ranks with the union, and appeals to strike replacements, raise questions of individual bargaining and the bypassing of the majority representative. (This has been considered at pp. 364–69, supra.) Such appeals might also hold out inducements which exceed those currently being offered to the union at the bargaining table, and may thus indicate that the employer is not using its best efforts to reach a settlement with the union. NLRB v. Katz, p. 416 supra. But it is sometimes difficult to tell whether the employer has offered such unlawfully extravagant terms to strikebreakers. Thus, in Pacific Gamble Robinson Co. v. NLRB, 186 F.2d 106 (6th Cir. 1951), the most recent wage offer to the union during a strike was a ten-cent increase to 87 cents an hour for starting employees and 98 cents an hour for workers employed for a year or more. The employer hired four nonunion replacements (who presumably did not satisfy the one-year requirement) at the rate of 98 cents an hour. The court of appeals reversed the finding of the Board that this action violated Section 8(a)(5):

> "The finding that the offer of 98 cents made to replacements after the strike was higher than that made to the union on August 15, and repeated on September 8, ignores the fact that the flat 98 cent rate which was all that was offered the replacements included no right of seniority or vacation with pay, no provision as to the length of the work week, as to overtime, arbitration, and none of the other valuable features of the contract. On the conceded facts the offer made to the union was much more advantageous than that made to the replacements."

At one time, the Board also held that an employer decision to subcontract work (rather than hire strikebreakers to do the work within the plant) in order to meet its orders during a strike was a mandatory subject about which the employer first had to bargain with the union to impasse. That holding was considered by the court of appeals in the following case.

HAWAII MEAT CO. v. NLRB

United States Court of Appeals, Ninth Circuit, 1963.
321 F.2d 397.

DUNIWAY, CIRCUIT JUDGE.

[Local 594 of the Meatcutters Union was certified as representative of all of the employees of the Company, which was engaged in the meat processing business. Included in the unit were several drivers and driver helpers. After some ten negotiating sessions in May and June 1960, it became apparent to the Company that a strike was imminent, and it entered into an agreement with one Fukumoto to assume the Company's delivery services in the event of a strike; Fukumoto was to rent the Company's trucks and provide its own personnel. The agreement was finally executed on July 1, when the strike began; it provided that the arrangement would continue until terminated by either party on thirty days' notice. The same day, the Company sent a letter to all employees, informing them of its intention to seek permanent replacements and of the fact that as of the next working day, July 5, "all of our delivery will be done by a trucking company we have made a contract with. There are no longer any delivery truck driver or driver helper jobs." Although the decision to subcontract was initially a means to keep Company operations going during the strike, either then or thereafter the Company also decided to make the arrangement permanent.]

The Board sustained most of the trial examiner's findings and squarely held that the company was obliged to bargain with the union about its decision to subcontract out its delivery work, even though the employer's decision may have been motivated by economic considerations, rather than by any opposition to the principles of collective bargaining. It therefore found it unnecessary to decide whether the subcontracting was motivated by retaliatory considerations, thus constituting a violation of section 8(a)(3). * * *

For the purpose of this decision, we assume, but do not decide, that the Board is correct in the position that it takes that an employer who proposes to subcontract work being done by members of the bargaining unit, thereby eliminating their jobs, must, in the absence of a strike, offer the union an opportunity to bargain about the proposed decision, and that if it does not do so, it violates section 8(a)(5). We also assume that if the employer decides to subcontract as a means of keeping its plant operating during an economic strike, and if thereafter a request is made to bargain upon such decision, the employer's duty to bargain, which is not terminated by the existence of a strike, embraces a duty to bargain about the question of whether, when the strike is over, he will continue the subcontract arrangement. The Board did not base its decision upon this ground.

Our answer is "no" to the narrow question which is presented to us, namely, whether a decision to subcontract, taken at the time an economic strike occurs, and made for the purpose of keeping the plant operating, constitutes a failure to bargain as required by the Act when after the strike begins, the employer does not, on its own motion, offer the union an opportunity to bargain about the decision to subcontract. * * *

We think that when an employer is confronted with a strike, his legal position is, in some respects, different from that which exists when no strike is expected or occurs. No case holds that a struck employer may not try to keep his business operating; on the contrary, it is quite clear that he has the right to do so. He may not use the strike as an excuse for committing unfair labor practices. (See, e. g., NLRB v. United States Cold Storage Corp., 5 Cir., 1953, 203 F.2d 924). But it does not follow that what this employer did to meet the strike was an unfair labor practice, even though it might have been one in the absence of a strike.

We think that a requirement that, upon the occurrence of a strike, and before putting into effect a subcontracting arrangement designed to keep the struck business operating, the employer must offer to bargain about the decision to subcontract, would effectively deprive the employer of this method of meeting the strike. A mere naked offer to bargain would not end the matter. The union could, by accepting the offer, deprive the employer of an effective means of meeting the strike for a period of time that might render it valueless to the struck employer. An employer is under no duty to offer to bargain, after a strike starts, about a decision to hire replacements for strikers, even on a permanent basis. (See NLRB v. Mackay Radio & Tel. Co., 1938, 304 U.S. 333, 58 S.Ct. 904, 82 L.Ed. 1381). In that case, the Supreme Court said:

> "Nor was it an unfair labor practice to replace the striking employees with others in an effort to carry on the business. Although § 13 provides, 'Nothing in this Act shall be construed so as to interfere with or impede or diminish in any way the right to strike,' it does not follow that an employer, guilty of no act denounced by the statute, has lost the right to protect and continue his business by supplying places left vacant by strikers. And he is not bound to discharge those

hired to fill the places of strikers, upon the election of the latter to resume their employment, in order to create places for them. The assurance by respondent to those who accepted employment during the strike that if they so desired their places might be permanent was not an unfair labor practice nor was it such to reinstate only so many of the strikers as there were vacant places to be filled." (Id. at 345–346, 58 S.Ct. at 910–911)

We think it no more proper for the Board to intrude upon the decision of the employer, in a strike situation, to keep going by subcontracting, than to intrude upon a decision to replace, permanently, individual strikers. This, we think, is consistent with the philosophy expressed by the Supreme Court in NLRB v. Insurance Agents' Union * * *

The Board's order is set aside; the petition to enforce the order is denied.

Problems for Discussion

1. Would there in fact have been a duty to bargain about the subcontracting of the employer's trucking operations absent a strike?

2. If there would have been such a duty, and this would thus be a "mandatory" subject, does the Labor Act permit a finding that it is *not* a mandatory subject in the midst of a strike—a strike which, somewhat ironically in light of the court's reliance on the *Insurance Agents* decision, is treated by that decision as "part and parcel" of the collective bargaining process?

3. Does the court's rationale justify a failure to bargain about subcontracting which ultimately proves to extend in time beyond the termination of the strike? About subcontracting which is intended so to extend? Does the cited passage from the Supreme Court decision in *Mackay Radio* support the court's conclusion?

4. Is the court not really holding—as shown by its reference to the *Insurance Agents* case (and by its quotation of passages from that case, omitted here, dealing with the allowable use of economic force during bargaining)—that requiring the employer to bargain about subcontracting or permanent replacements would simply encumber too greatly an important employer counterweapon to the strike? If that is indeed the essence of the court's decision, did it usurp a function which the Labor Act gives primarily to the National Labor Relations Board? Consider this question again after studying the materials at pp. 833–62, infra.

E.   BARGAINING REMEDIES [37]

H. K. PORTER CO. v. NLRB

Supreme Court of the United States, 1970.
397 U.S. 99, 90 S.Ct. 821, 25 L.Ed.2d 146.

MR. JUSTICE BLACK delivered the opinion of the Court.

After an election respondent United Steelworkers Union was, on October 5, 1961, certified by the National Labor Relations Board as the bargaining agent for certain employees at the Danville, Virginia, plant of the petitioner, H. K. Porter Co.   Thereafter negotiations commenced for a collective-bargaining agreement.   Since that time the controversy has seesawed between the Board, the Court of Appeals for the District of Columbia Circuit, and this Court.   This delay of over eight years is not because the case is exceedingly complex, but appears to have occurred chiefly because of the skill of the company's negotiators in taking advantage of every opportunity for delay in an act more noticeable for its generality than for its precise prescriptions.   The entire lengthy dispute mainly revolves around the union's desire to have the company agree to "check off" the dues owed to the union by its members, that is, to deduct those dues periodically from the company's wage payments to the employees. The record shows, as the Board found, that the company's objection to a checkoff was not due to any general principle or policy against making deductions from employees' wages.   The company does deduct charges for things like insurance, taxes, and contributions to charities, and at some other plants it has a checkoff arrangement for union dues.   The evidence shows, and the court below found, that the company's objection was not because of inconvenience, but solely on the ground that the company was "not going to aid and comfort the union."   Efforts by the union to obtain some kind of compromise on the checkoff request were all met with the same staccato response to the effect that the collection of union dues was the "union's business" and the company was not going to provide any assistance.

37.   See Gross, Cullen & Hanslowe, Good Faith in Labor Negotiations: Tests and Remedies, 53 Cornell L.Rev. 1009 (1968); McCulloch, Past, Present and Future Remedies Under Section 8(a)(5) of the NLRA, 19 Lab.L.J. 131 (1968); D. McDowell & K. Huhn, NLRB Remedies for Unfair Labor Practices (1976); McGuiness, Is the Award of Damages for Refusals to Bargain Consistent with National Labor Policy?, 14 Wayne L.Rev. 1086 (1968); Note, The Use of Section 10(j) of the Labor-Management Relations Act in Employer Refusal-to-Bargain Cases, 1976 U.Ill.L.F. 845 (1976); Morris, The Role of the NLRB and the Courts in the Collective Bargaining Process: A Fresh Look at the Conventional Wisdom and Unconventional Remedies, 30 Vand.L.Rev. 661 (1977); St. Antoine, A Touchstone for Labor Board Remedies, 14 Wayne L. Rev. 1039 (1968); Schlossberg & Silard, The Need for a Compensatory Remedy in Refusal-to-Bargain Cases, 14 Wayne L.Rev. 1059 (1968).

Based on this and other evidence the Board found, and the Court of Appeals approved the finding, that the refusal of the company to bargain about the checkoff was not made in good faith, but was done solely to frustrate the making of any collective-bargaining agreement.   * * *

[After further negotiations, and proceedings before the Board and the Court of Appeals, the Board ultimately] issued a supplemental order requiring the petitioner to "[g]rant to the Union a contract clause providing for the checkoff of union dues." 172 N.L.R.B. No. 72, 68 L.R.R.M. 1337. The Court of Appeals affirmed this order, H. K. Porter Co. v. NLRB, 134 U.S.App.D.C. 227, 414 F.2d 1123 (1969). We granted certiorari to consider whether the Board in these circumstances has the power to remedy the unfair labor practice by requiring the company to agree to check off the dues of the workers. 396 U.S. 817. For reasons to be stated we hold that while the Board does have power under the National Labor Relations Act, 61 Stat. 136, as amended, to require employers and employees to negotiate, it is without power to compel a company or a union to agree to any substantive contractual provision of a collective-bargaining agreement.

      * * *

The object of this Act was not to allow governmental regulation of the terms and conditions of employment, but rather to ensure that employers and their employees could work together to establish mutually satisfactory conditions. The basic theme of the Act was that through collective bargaining the passions, arguments, and struggles of prior years would be channeled into constructive, open discussions leading, it was hoped, to mutual agreement. But it was recognized from the beginning that agreement might in some cases be impossible, and it was never intended that the Government would in such cases step in, become a party to the negotiations and impose its own views of a desirable settlement.   * * *

In discussing the effect of [the addition of Section 8(d) in 1947], this Court said it is "clear that the Board may not, either directly or indirectly, compel concessions or otherwise sit in judgment upon the substantive terms of collective bargaining agreements." NLRB v. American Ins. Co., 343 U.S. 395, 404 (1952). Later this Court affirmed that view stating that "it remains clear that § 8(d) was an attempt by Congress to prevent the Board from controlling the settling of the terms of collective bargaining agreements." NLRB v. Insurance Agents, 361 U.S. 477, 487 (1960). The parties to the instant case are agreed that this is the first time in the 35-year history of the Act that the Board has ordered either an employer or a union to agree to a substantive term of a collective-bargaining agreement.

Recognizing the fundamental principle "that the National Labor Relations Act is grounded on the premise of freedom of contract," 128 U.S.App.D.C., at 349, 389 F.2d, at 300, the Court of Appeals in this case concluded that nevertheless in the circumstances presented here the Board could properly compel the employer to agree to a proposed checkoff clause. The Board had found that the refusal was based on a desire to frustrate agreement and not on any legitimate business reason. On the basis of that finding the Court of Appeals approved the further finding that the employer had not bargained in good faith, and the validity of that finding is not now before us. Where the record thus revealed repeated refusals by the employer to bargain in good faith on this issue, the Court of Appeals concluded that ordering agreement to the checkoff clause "may be the only means of assuring the Board, and the court, that [the employer] no longer harbors an illegal intent." 128 U.S.App.D.C., at 348, 389 F.2d at 299.

In reaching this conclusion the Court of Appeals held that § 8(d) did not forbid the Board from compelling agreement. That court felt that "[s]ection 8(d) defines collective bargaining and relates to a determination of whether a * * * violation has occurred and not to the scope of the remedy which may be necessary to cure violations which have already occurred." 128 U.S.App. D.C., at 348, 389 F.2d, at 299. We may agree with the Court of Appeals that as a matter of strict, literal interpretation that section refers only to deciding when a violation has occurred, but we do not agree that that observation justifies the conclusion that the remedial powers of the Board are not also limited by the same considerations that led Congress to enact § 8(d). It is implicit in the entire structure of the Act that the Board acts to oversee and referee the process of collective bargaining, leaving the results of the contest to the bargaining strengths of the parties. It would be anomalous indeed to hold that while § 8(d) prohibits the Board from relying on a refusal to agree as the sole evidence of bad-faith bargaining, the Act permits the Board to compel agreement in that same dispute. The Board's remedial powers under § 10 of the Act are broad, but they are limited to carrying out the policies of the Act itself. One of these fundamental policies is freedom of contract. While the parties' freedom of contract is not absolute under the Act, allowing the Board to compel agreement when the parties themselves are unable to agree would violate the fundamental premise on which the Act is based—private bargaining under governmental supervision of the procedure alone, without any official compulsion over the actual terms of the contract.

  * * * It may well be true, as the Court of Appeals felt, that the present remedial powers of the Board are insufficiently broad

to cope with important labor problems. But it is the job of Congress, not the Board or the courts, to decide when and if it is necessary to allow governmental review of proposals for collective-bargaining agreements and compulsory submission to one side's demands. The present Act does not envision such a process.

The judgment is reversed and the case is remanded to the Court of Appeals for further action consistent with this opinion.

Reversed and remanded.

MR. JUSTICE WHITE took no part in the decision of this case.

MR. JUSTICE MARSHALL took no part in the consideration or decision of this case.

MR. JUSTICE HARLAN, concurring.   *   *   *

MR. JUSTICE DOUGLAS, with whom MR. JUSTICE STEWART concurs, dissenting: *   *   *

[T]he Board has the power, where one party does not bargain in good faith, "to take such affirmative action *   *   * as will effectuate the policies" of the Act.   * * *

Here the employer did not refuse the checkoff for any business reason, whether cost, inconvenience, or what not. Nor did the employer refuse the checkoff as a factor in its bargaining strategy, hoping that delay and denial might bring it in exchange favorable terms and conditions. Its reason was a resolve to avoid reaching any agreement with the union.

In those narrow and specialized circumstances, I see no answer to the power of the Board in its discretion to impose the checkoff as "affirmative action" necessary to remedy the flagrant refusal of the employer to bargain in good faith.

The case is rare, if not unique, and will seldom arise.   *   *   *

Problems for Discussion

1. Was the employer well advised not to challenge the Board's finding that it had bargained in bad faith? Was that finding consistent with the federal policy most strongly emphasized by the Supreme Court, that is, the policy of non-interference by the federal government in setting the substantive terms of the labor contract? Is it an unfair labor practice for either party to insist on a position for which it has no "need"? Need *any* reason be adduced for a bargaining position if the proponent is simply strong enough to back that position with economic strength?

2. With the refusal-to-bargain finding now sustained in the *Porter* case, and the checkoff order overturned, what order *is* to issue against the Porter Company? Whatever the order is to be, would not a refusal by the Company to incorporate a checkoff provision be a violation of the order, so that the same issue of Board power would arise once more?

3. Strong Roofing Company had for several years been a member of the Roofing Contractors Association, which negotiates on behalf of its member companies with the Roofers Union. On August 15, the Association

and the Union reached an understanding on the terms of a collective bargaining agreement. On August 20, Strong withdrew from the Association and subsequently refused to sign the agreement negotiated by the Association. The Board found that Strong had violated Section 8(a)(5) of the Act, issued a cease-and-desist order, and ordered Strong to sign the contract and to pay "to the appropriate source any fringe benefits provided for in the above-described contract." The Board petitions the court of appeals for enforcement.

(a) Should the finding of a Section 8(a)(5) violation be sustained? (b) Strong contends that the Board exceeded its authority in ordering the payment of the fringe benefits. What are the employer's strongest arguments? Should that part of the Board's order be enforced? (c) If it is enforced, and there later arises a dispute about the meaning of the fringe-benefit provisions and therefore about the amounts due, how should that dispute be resolved? See *NLRB v. Strong Roofing & Insulating Co.*, 393 U.S. 357, 89 S.Ct. 541, 21 L.Ed.2d 546 (1969).

4. After an election among the over-the-road drivers employed by the American Manufacturing Company of Texas, the Teamsters were certified as the bargaining representative. Within the week, the company posted a notice that it had negotiated an agreement of sale of its trucks, that henceforth the company's products would be transported by an independent trucking firm, and that all of its drivers were immediately laid off. The Board sustained the union's charge of a Section 8(a)(5) violation, and ordered not only that the employer cease and desist from refusing to bargain and that it bargain with the union, but also that it resume trucking operations and offer reinstatement and backpay to all of the drivers laid off. American Manufacturing is a small firm, and the evidence indicates that it would cost the Company $150,000 to purchase a new fleet of trucks. It also appears that the Company has found it more economical to hire the outside firm than to transport its own products. Should the court enforce the order of reinstitution, reinstatement and backpay? See *NLRB v. American Mfg. Co.*, 351 F.2d 74 (5th Cir. 1965). Would your analysis differ if American had not sold the trucks but had instead leased them to an independent hauler and laid off its own drivers? See *Kronenberg d/b/a American Needle & Novelty Co.*, 206 N.L.R.B. 534 (1973).

5. Cooper Thermometer Company had for many years recognized the United Electrical Workers as bargaining representative for the production employees at its plant in Urbantown, Connecticut. As its current labor contract was nearing its termination date, Cooper announced that because the present facilities were inadequate and the cost of improving them exorbitant, he intended to move the Company's operations to Ruraltown, some 27 miles away (45 minutes by car, public transportation being unavailable). Cooper announced too his willingness to bargain with the Union regarding severance pay and other benefits upon the termination of the Urbantown employees. The Union requested that the Company (which the Union conceded was economically motivated) should bargain with the Union before making any agreement to purchase the Ruraltown facility, should extend full seniority rights to any employees transferring to Ruraltown, and should recognize the Union as bargaining representative there. The Company re-

fused to discuss any of those matters with the Union, and soon closed the Urbantown plant. Of the eighty Urbantown employees, only a handful applied for and took employment at Ruraltown, in view of the lower wages there and the costs of commuting.

Has the Company acted unlawfully? If so, what should the remedy be? See Cooper Thermometer Co. v. NLRB, 376 F.2d 684 (2d Cir. 1967).

EX–CELL–O CORPORATION

National Labor Relations Board, 1970.
185 N.L.R.B. 107.

[The United Automobile Workers requested recognition on August 3, 1964, but the Ex-Cell-O Corporation refused the request and the union petitioned for an election, which was held on October 22. The union won the election, but the company filed objections (regarding alleged union misrepresentations) which were overruled by the Acting Regional Director. The Board granted the company's request for review of that decision, which was ultimately affirmed by the Board on October 28, 1965, and the union was certified. The company informed the union that it would not bargain, as a means of securing court review of the Board's action, and a hearing on the union's charge under Sections 8(a)(1) and (5) was commenced on June 1, 1966. After an unsuccessful company attempt to secure an injunction against the Regional Director and the Trial Examiner, the latter closed the hearing on December 21, 1966 and issued his decision on March 2, 1967. The Trial Examiner found a refusal to bargain and recommended that a cease-and-desist order issue and that the company be directed to make its employees whole for any monetary losses suffered on account of the company's unlawful refusal. The Board granted the company's request for review as well as for oral argument, consolidated the *Ex-Cell-O* case with three cases raising similar issues, and invited briefs *amicus curiae* and participation in oral argument (in July 1967) by such organizations as the Chamber of Commerce of the United States, the National Association of Manufacturers, the AFL-CIO, the Teamsters and the NAACP Legal Defense Fund. The Board rendered its decision on August 25, 1970, in which it adopted the findings, conclusions and recommendations of the Trial Examiner as significantly modified in the opinion below.]

It is not disputed that Respondent refused to bargain with the Union, and we hereby affirm the Trial Examiner's conclusion that Respondent thereby violated Section 8(a)(1) and (5) of the Act. The compensatory remedy which he recommends, however, raises important issues concerning the Board's powers and duties to fashion appropriate remedies in its efforts to effectuate the policies of the National Labor Relations Act.

It is argued that such a remedy exceeds the Board's general statutory powers. In addition, it is contended that it cannot be granted because the amount of employee loss, if any, is so speculative that an order to make employees whole would amount to the imposition of a penalty. And the position is advanced that the adoption of this remedy would amount to the writing of a contract for the parties, which is prohibited by Section 8(d).

We have given most serious consideration to the Trial Examiner's recommended financial reparations Order, and are in complete agreement with his finding that current remedies of the Board designed to cure violations of Section 8(a)(5) are inadequate. A mere affirmative order that an employer bargain upon request does not eradicate the effects of an unlawful delay of 2 or more years in the fulfillment of a statutory bargaining obligation. It does not put the employees in the position of bargaining strength they would have enjoyed if their employer had immediately recognized and bargained with their chosen representative. It does not dissolve the inevitable employee frustration or protect the Union from the loss of employee support attributable to such delay. The inadequacy of the remedy is all the more egregious where, as in the recent N.L.R.B. v. Tiidee Products, Inc., case, the court found that the employer had raised "frivolous" issues in order to postpone or avoid its lawful obligation to bargain. We have weighed these considerations most carefully. For the reasons stated below, however, we have reluctantly concluded that we cannot approve the Trial Examiner's Recommended Order that Respondent compensate its employees for monetary losses incurred as a consequence of Respondent's determination to refuse to bargain until it had tested in court the validity of the Board's certification.

Section 10(c) of the Act directs the Board to order a person found to have committed an unfair labor practice to cease and desist and "to take such affirmative action including reinstatement of employees with or without back pay, as will effectuate the policies of this Act." This authority, as our colleagues note with full documentation, is extremely broad and was so intended by Congress. It is not so broad, however, as to permit the punishment of a particular respondent or a class of respondents. Nor is the statutory direction to the Board so compelling that the Board is without discretion in exercising the full sweep of its power, for it would defeat the purposes of the Act if the Board imposed an otherwise proper remedy that resulted in irreparable harm to a particular respondent and hampered rather than promoted meaningful collective bargaining. Moreover, as the Supreme Court recently emphasized, the Board's grant of power does not extend to compelling agreement. (H. K. Porter Co., Inc. v. N.L.R.B., 397 U.S. 99.) It is with respect to these three limitations upon the Board's power to remedy a violation of Section 8(a)(5) that we examine the UAW's requested remedy in this case.

The Trial Examiner concluded that the proposed remedy was not punitive, that it merely made the employees partially whole for losses occasioned by the Respondent's refusal to bargain, and was much less harsh than a backpay order for discharged employees, which might require the Respondent to pay wages to these employees as well as their replacements. Viewed solely in the context of an assumption of employee monetary losses resulting directly from the Respondent's violation of Section 8(a)(5), as finally determined in court, the Trial Examiner's conclusion appears reasonable. There are, however, other factors in this case which provide counterweights to that rationale. In the first place, there is no contention that this Respondent acted in a manner flagrantly in defiance of the statutory policy. On the contrary, the record indicates that this Respondent responsibly fulfills its legally established collective-bargaining obligations. It is clear that Respondent merely sought judicial affirmance of the Board's decision that the election of October 22, 1964, should not be set aside on the Respondent's objections. In the past, whenever an employer has sought court intervention in a representation proceeding the Board has argued forcefully that court intervention would be premature, that the employer had an unquestioned right under the statute to seek court review of any Board order before its bargaining obligation became final. Should this procedural right in 8(a)(5) cases be tempered by a large monetary liability in the event the employer's position in the representation case is ultimately found to be without merit? Of course, an employer or a union which engages in conduct later found in violation of the Act, does so at the peril of ultimate conviction and responsibility for a make-whole remedy. But the validity of a particular Board election tried in an unfair labor practice case is not, in our opinion, an issue on the same plane as the discharge of employees for union activity or other conduct in flagrant disregard of employee rights. There are wrongdoers and wrongdoers. Where the wrong in refusing to bargain is, at most, a debatable question, though ultimately found a wrong, the imposition of a large financial obligation on such a respondent may come close to a form of punishment for having elected to pursue a representation question beyond the Board and to the courts. * * *

In *Tiidee Products* the court suggested that the Board need not follow a uniform policy in the application of a compensatory remedy in 8(a)(5) cases. Indeed, the court noted that such uniformity in this area of the law would be unfair when applied "to unlike cases." The court was of the opinion that the remedy was proper where the employer had engaged in a "manifestly unjustifiable refusal to bargain" and where its position was "palpably without merit." [38]   *   *   *   [T]he court in *Tiidee Products* distinguished those cases in which the employer's failure to bargain rested on a "debatable question." With due respect for the opinion of the Court of Appeals for the District of Columbia, we cannot agree that the application of a compensatory remedy in 8(a)(5) cases can be fashioned on the subjective determination that the position of one respondent is "debatable" while that of another is "frivolous." What is debatable to the Board may appear frivolous to a court, and vice versa. Thus, the debatability of the employer's position in an 8(a) (5) case would itself become a matter of intense litigation.   *   *   *

It is argued that the instant case is distinguishable from *H. K. Porter* in that here the requested remedy merely would require an employer to compensate employees for losses they incurred as a consequence of their employer's *failure to agree* to a contract he *would* have agreed to *if* he had bargained in good faith. In our view, the distinction is more illusory than real. The remedy in *H. K. Porter* operates prospectively to bind an employer to a specific contractual term. The remedy in the instant case operates retroactively to impose financial liability upon an employer flowing from a *presumed* contractual agreement. The Board infers that the latter contract, though it never existed and does not and need not exist, was *denied* existence by the employer because of his refusal to bargain. In either case the employer has not agreed to the contractual provision for which he must accept full responsibility *as though he had agreed to it*. Our colleagues contend that a compensatory remedy is not the "writing of a contract" because it does not "specify new or continuing terms of employment and does not prohibit changes in existing terms and conditions." But there is no basis for such a remedy unless the Board finds, as a matter of fact, that a contract would have resulted from bargaining. The fact that the contract, so to speak, is "written in the air" does not diminish its financial impact upon the recalcitrant employer who, willy-nilly, is forced to accede to terms never mutually established by the parties. Despite the admonition of the Supreme Court that Section 8(d) was intended to mean what it says, i. e., that the obligation to bargain "does not compel either party to agree to a proposal or require the making of a

---

38. In these cases, at least, it would seem incumbent on the Board to utilize to the fullest extent its authority under Sec. 10(j) and (e) of the Act, thereby minimizing the pernicious delay in collective bargaining and consequent loss of benefits to the employees affected. See also Justice Harlan's concurrence in *H. K. Porter*, supra.

concession," one of the parties under this remedy is forced by the Government to submit to the other side's demands. It does not help to argue that the remedy could not be applied unless there was substantial evidence that the employer would have yielded to these demands during bargaining negotiations. Who is to say in a specific case how much an employer is prepared to give and how much a union is willing to take? Who is to say that a favorable contract would, in any event, result from the negotiations? And it is only the employer of such good will as to whom the Board might conclude that he, at least, would have given his employees a fair increase, who can be made subject to a financial reparations order; should such an employer be singled out for the imposition of such an order? To answer these questions the Board would be required to engage in the most general, if not entirely speculative, inferences, to reach the conclusion that employees were deprived of specific benefits as a consequence of their employer's refusal to bargain.

Much as we appreciate the need for more adequate remedies in 8(a)(5) cases, we believe that, as the law now stands, the proposed remedy is a matter for Congress, not the Board. In our opinion, however, substantial relief may be obtained immediately through procedural reform, giving the highest possible priority to 8(a)(5) cases combined with full resort to the injunctive relief provisions of Section 10(j) and (e) of the Act.

* * *

MEMBERS McCULLOCH AND BROWN, dissenting in part:

Although concurring in all other respects in the Decision and Order of the Board, we part company with our colleagues on the majority in that we would grant the compensatory remedy recommended by the Trial Examiner. Unlike our colleagues, we believe that the Board has the statutory authority to direct such relief and that it would effectuate the policies of the Act to do so in this case. * * *

The declared policy of the Act is to promote the peaceful settlement of disputes by encouraging collective bargaining and by protecting employee rights. To accomplish this purpose, Board remedies for violations of the Act should, on one hand, have the effect of preventing the party in violation from so acting in the future, and from enjoying any advantage he may have gained by his unlawful practices. But they must also presently dissipate the effects of violations on employee rights in order that the employees so injured receive what they should not have been denied. A Board order so devised is to be enforced by the courts "unless it can be shown that the order is a patent attempt to achieve ends other that those which can fairly be said to effectuate the policies of the Act."

Deprivation of an employee's statutory rights is often accompanied by serious financial injury to him. Where this is so, an order which only guarantees the exercise of his rights in the future often falls far short of expunging the effects of the unlawful conduct involved. Therefore, one of the Board's most effective and well-established affirmative remedies for unlawful conduct is an order to make employees financially whole for losses resulting from violations of the Act. Various types of compensatory orders have been upheld by the Supreme Court in the belief that "Making the workers whole for losses suffered on account of an unfair practice is part of the vindication of the public policy which the Board enforces." The most familiar of these is the backpay order used to remedy the effect of employee discharges found to be in violation of Section 8(a)(3) of the Act. While the cease-and-desist and reinstatement orders remedy the denial of the aggrieved employee's rights and protect the prospective exercise thereof, the backpay order repairs the financial losses which have been suffered, and, in thus making the employee whole, serves to recreate, as fully as possible, the conditions and relationships that would have been had there been no unfair labor practice. * * *

The Board has already recognized in certain refusal-to-bargain situations that the usual bargaining order is not sufficient to expunge the effects of an employer's unlawful and protracted denial of its employees' right to bargain. Though the bargaining order serves to remedy the loss of legal right and protect its exercise in the future, it does not remedy the financial injury which may also have been suffered. In a number of situations the Board has ordered the employer who unlawfully refused to bargain to compensate its employees for their resultant financial losses. Thus, some employers unlawfully refuse to sign after an agreement. The Board has in these cases ordered the employer to execute the agreement previously reached and, according to its terms, to make whole the employees for the monetary losses suffered because of the unlawful delay in its effectuation.

Similarly, in *American Fire Apparatus Co.*, the employer violated Section 8(a)(5) by unilaterally discontinuing payment of Christmas bonuses, and the Board concluded that only by requiring the bonuses to be paid could the violation be fully remedied.

* * * And in *Fibreboard Paper Products Corp.*, the employer unilaterally contracted out its maintenance operations in violation of Section 8(a)(5). The Board concluded that an order to bargain about this decision could not, by itself, adequately remedy the effects of the violation. It further ordered the employer to reinstate the employees and to make them whole for any loss of earnings suffered on account of the unlawful conduct. The Supreme

Court upheld the compensatory remedy, and stated that "There has been no showing that the Board's order restoring the *status quo ante* to insure meaningful bargaining is not well designed to promote the policies of the Act." * * *

The present case is but another example of a situation where a bargaining order by itself is not really adequate to remedy the effects of an unlawful refusal to bargain. The Union herein requested recognition on August 3, 1964, and proved that it represented a majority of employees 2½ months later in a Board-conducted election. Nonetheless, since October 1965 the employer, by unlawfully refusing to bargain with the Union, has deprived its employees of their legal right to collective bargaining through their certified bargaining representative.[39] While a bargaining order at this time, operating prospectively, may insure the exercise of that right in the future, it clearly does not repair the injury to the employees here, caused by the Respondent's denial of their rights during the past 5 years.

39. We find no merit in the Respondent's contention in the present case that, at least in a "technical" refusal-to-bargain situation, a compensatory remedy would penalize it for obtaining judicial review of the Board's representation proceedings. In Consolo v. Federal Maritime Commission, supra at 624–625, the Court rejected the same contention. Relying on a case involving the Board (NLRB v. Electric Vacuum Cleaner Company, Inc., 315 U.S. 685), the Court concluded that "At any rate it has never been the law that a litigant is absolved from liability for that time during which his litigation is pending" (Id. at 624–625) and noted (at 625) that the time of appeal allowed the respondent to continue its unlawful conduct thus in turn continue to injure the petitioner. That such a remedy would include the entire amount lost by the wronged party, instead of being reduced by the amount accruing while the violator was contesting the issue, no more makes the remedy penal in character under this Act than it does elsewhere. "The litigant must pay for his experience, like others who have tried and lost." Life & Casualty Ins. Co. v. McCray, 291 U.S. 566, 575.

There is no question of the right of an employer to test the legal propriety of a Board certification or to test its legal position respecting any issue of law or fact upon which a Board bargaining order is predicated: but it should not thereby realize benefits not usually flowing from such a proceeding. In other words, should an employer choose to await court action, and if its legal position be sustained, it would not only be absolved of the duty to bargain, but also of any monetary remedy arising out of the order contemplated herein; if, on the other hand, an employer be found to have rested its refusal to bargain on an erroneous view of law or fact, any loss to employees incurred by its continued adherence to that error should be borne by that employer and not by its employees. That is the risk taken by all litigants.

The employer's argument for tolling the compensatory period during the time he contests the violation is contrary to the policy of the Act in fostering the prompt commencement of collective bargaining, a policy shown explicitly in the denial of judicial review of the Board's representation proceedings. To allow the employer to avoid making his employees whole for the period bargaining was delayed by his litigating a mistaken view of the law would encourage such delay in the areas in which Congress particularly deemed speed to be essential.

In these refusal-to-bargain cases there is at least a legal injury. Potential employee losses incurred by an employer's refusal to bargain in violation of the Act are not limited to financial matters such as wages. Thus, it is often the case that the most important employee gains arrived at through collective bargaining involve such benefits as seniority, improved physical facilities, a better grievance procedure, or a right to arbitration. Therefore, even the remedy we would direct herein is not complete, limited as it is to only some of the monetary losses which may be measured or estimated. The employees would not be made whole for all the losses incurred through the employer's unfair labor practice. But, where the legal injury is accompanied by financial loss, the employees should be compensated for it.   *   *   *

This type of compensatory remedy is in no way forbidden by Section 8(d).[40] It would be designed to compensate employees for injuries incurred by them by virtue of the unfair labor practices and would not require the employer to accept the measure of compensation as a term of any contract which might result from subsequent collective bargaining. The remedy contemplated in no way "writes a contract" between the employer and the union, for it would not specify new or continuing terms of employment and would not prohibit changes in existing terms and conditions. All of these would be left to the outcome of bargaining, the commencement of which would terminate Respondent's liability.

Furthermore, this compensatory remedy is not a punitive measure. It would be designed to do no more than reimburse the employees for the loss occasioned by the deprivation of their right to be represented by their collective-bargaining agent during the period of the violation. The amount to be awarded would be only that which would reasonably reflect and be measured by the loss caused by the unlawful denial of the opportunity for collective bargaining. *   *   * Accordingly, as the reimbursement order sought herein is meant to enforce public policy, the Board's exercise of its discretion in ordering such a remedy would not be strictly confined to the same considerations which govern comparable awards in either equity courts or damage awards in legal actions. In the first place, it is well established that, where the defendant's wrongful act prevents exact determination of the amount of damage, he cannot plead such uncertainty in order to deny relief to the injured person, but rather

---

40. The provision in Sec. 8(d) that neither party is required to agree to a proposal or make a concession appears to have been designed not for the situation before us, but to preclude the Board from evaluating "the merits of the provisions of the parties" as a factor in determining whether bargaining was in good faith. House Conference Report, Legislative History, p. 538.

must bear the risk of the uncertainty which was created by his own wrong. The Board is often faced with the task of determining the precise amount of a make-whole order where the criteria are less than ideal, and has successfully resolved the questions presented.[41]

But even if a reimbursement order were judged by legal or equitable principles regarding damages, the remedy would not be speculative. It is well established that the rule which precludes recovery of "uncertain damages" refers to uncertainty as to the fact of injury, rather than to the amount. Where, as here, the employer has deprived its employees of a statutory right, there is by definition a legal injury suffered by them, and any uncertainty concerns only the amount of the accompanying reimbursable financial loss. * * *

Accordingly, uncertainty as to the amount of loss does not preclude a make-whole order proposed here, and some reasonable method or basis of computation can be worked out as part of the compliance procedure. These cannot be defined in advance, but there are many methods for determining the measurable financial gain which the employees might reasonably have expected to achieve, had the Respondent fulfilled its statutory obligation to bargain collectively. The criteria which prove valid in each case must be determined by what is pertinent to the facts. Nevertheless, the following methods for measuring such loss do appear to be available, although these are neither exhaustive nor exclusive. Thus, if the particular employer and union involved have contracts covering other plants of the employer, possibly in the same or a relevant area, the terms of such agreements may serve to show what the employees could probably have obtained by bargaining. The parties could also make comparisons with compensation patterns achieved through collective bargaining by other employees in the same geographic area and indus-

---

41. The problem most frequently arises when we must determine the amount of backpay due to unlawfully discharged employees. As we recently stated in connection with this issue (The Buncher Company, 164 NLRB 340, enfd. 405 F.2d 787 (C.A.3)):

In solving many of the problems which arise in backpay cases, the Board occasionally is required to adopt formulas which result in backpay determinations that are close approximations because no better basis exists for determining the exact amount due. However, the fact that the exact amount due is incalculable is no justification for permitting the Respondent to escape completely his legal obligation to compensate the victims of his discriminatory actions for the loss of earnings which they suffered. In general, courts have acknowledged that in solving such backpay problems, the Board is vested with wide discretion in devising procedures and methods which will effectuate the purposes of the Act and has generally limited its review to whether a method selected was "arbitrary or unreasonable in the circumstances involved," or whether in determining the amount, a "rational basis" was utilized.

try. Or the parties might employ the national average percentage changes in straight time hourly wages computed by the Bureau of Labor Statistics. * * *

In the instant case, as noted above, a *prima facie* showing of loss can readily be made out by measuring the wage and benefit increments that were negotiated for employees at Respondent's other organized plants against those given employees in this bargaining unit during the period of Respondent's unlawful refusal to bargain. Granted that the task of determining loss may be more difficult in other cases where no similar basis for comparison exists, this is not reason enough for the Board to shirk its statutory responsibilities, and no reason at all for it to do so in a case such as this where that difficulty is not present. * * *

Following the Board's *Ex-Cell-O* decision, the UAW petitioned the Court of Appeals for the District of Columbia Circuit for review of the Board's decision not to award monetary compensation. In UAW v. NLRB, 449 F.2d 1046 (D.C. Cir. 1971), the court reproved the Board for rejecting that court's decision in *Tiidee Products*. The court remanded the case to the Board for "express determinations whether Ex-Cell-O's objections to the certification were frivolous or fairly debatable, and whether 'make-whole' compensation or some other special remedy is appropriate." The court rejected the Board's argument that the Board and the courts would be unable to agree on what was "frivolous" litigation, and stated that "courts should accord the usual latitude to the Board" in determining whether litigation was as a matter of fact frivolous. However, before the Board had an opportunity to decide *Ex-Cell-O* on remand, the court of appeals issued a separate decision on the employer's petition for review of the Board's bargaining order. Ex-Cell-O Corp. v. NLRB, 449 F.2d 1058 (D.C. Cir. 1971). Enforcing the Board's order, the court conducted an independent evaluation of the record and concluded that the employer's objections were, in fact, "fairly debatable" and that therefore a compensatory award was inappropriate. Thus, six and one-half years after the election, the court enforced the Board's order that the employer bargain with the union that won that election.

Meanwhile, the Board wrestled with the *Tiidee* case on remand. It acknowledged that the decision of the court of appeals was the law of the case but concluded that it could not construct from the evidence the contract to which the parties would have agreed had the employer promptly bargained. Thus, it was impossible to calculate a compensatory award. Instead, the Board, noting the flagrant employer violations of the Act, ordered the employer to pay to the Board and the union the costs of litigation, to mail a copy of the Board-ordered notice to each employee, to give the union access to company bulletin boards, and to supply the union with an up-to-date list of employee names and addresses. TIIDEE PRODS., INC., 194 N.L. R.B. 1234 (1972). The Court of Appeals granted enforcement (except for reimbursement of the Board's litigation expenses), finding that the Board's inability to calculate a make-whole remedy was an adequate reason for not doing so. The court also found that the Board had used its expert and informed discretion to balance the difficulties of computation against the "relative ease and certainty" of calculating the costs of litigation. NLRB v. Tiidee Prods., Inc., 502 F.2d 349 (D.C. Cir. 1974), cert. denied 421 U.S. 991 (1975).

Problems for Discussion

1. Do you agree with the views of the majority of the Board or the dissenting members in the *Ex-Cell-O* case? In appraising those views, consider how you would reconstruct the agreement that the parties would have reached had the Company promptly bargained after the certification. The chart on the following page compares the terms and conditions obtaining at the Ex-Cell-O plant in Elwood, Indiana, at which the refusal-to-bargain occurred, and those obtaining under labor contracts at other Ex-Cell-O plants.

2. The Court of Appeals for the District of Columbia was willing to limit the "make-whole" order to the case of the "flagrant" refusal to bargain (as opposed to the case of the employer seeking to secure judicial review of "debatable" challenges to the union's status). Is this distinction a sound one?

3. On occasion, it has been suggested that a special Labor Court should be established (much like the Tax Court) to hear all appeals from decisions of the NLRB, the purpose being principally to eliminate the lack of expertise and the conflicts among the federal courts of appeals. Because Section 10(f) of the present Act permits any aggrieved party to seek review of Board orders in the District of Columbia, that court hears a significant number of labor cases, and is perhaps an institution which closely approximates a Labor Court (of appeals) in our present federal system. It was that Court which in the *Struksnes* case, p. 184, supra, remanded to the Board for more stringent rules on employer interrogation; which in *H. K. Porter*, p. 496, supra, suggested to the Board that it should consider ordering the employer to incorporate a checkoff provision in the labor contract; and which in *Ex-Cell-O* took issue with

	ELWOOD, INDIANA Employee Handbook (Revised 5–63)	BLUFFTON, OHIO 4–3–65 Agreement	LIMA, OHIO 4–1–65 Agreement	FOSTORIA, OHIO 4–1–65 Agreement	TRAVERSE CITY, MICH. 5–8–65 Agreement	DETROIT, MICH. 4–1–55 Agreement
Shift Premium	Afternoon $.12 Midnight $.16	Same*	Same	Same	Afternoon $.15 Midnight $.20	Afternoon $.16 Midnight $.20
Overtime	Daily, time and one half up to 10 hrs. and up to 8 hrs. on Saturdays. Double time for the excess and for Sundays and Holidays.	Same	Same	Same	Same	Same
Holidays	7 (8 in 1965 or 1966 (Tr. 181))	9	9	9	8 (9 in 1966)	8 (9 in 1966)
Vacations	Year's Hrs. Days Serv. Pay off 1　40　5 3　60　7 5　80　10 10　100　12	Year's Pay Days Serv. off 1　2%**　5 3　2.8%　7 5　4%　10 10　5%　12	Same as Bluffton	Year's Hrs. Days Serv. Pay off 1　40　5 3　60　7 5　80　10 10　100　12 15　120　15	Year's Pay Days Serv. off 1　2.5%　5 3　3.5%　5 5　5.5%　10 10　6%　12 15　7%　15	Same as Fostoria
Deferred Pay Plan	Additional $.05 per hour, payable on layoff, leave of absence, termination or retirement	None	None	None	None	None
Hospital & Surgical Insurance	Co. pays 75%***	Co. pays all, incl. after retirement	Same	Same	Same	Same
Group Life Insurance	$4500	$6000	Same	Same	$6500	$7000
Accidental Death	2250	3000	Same	Same	3250	3500
Sickness & Accident benefit	$40.25–45.50 per week	$60.00 per week	$50–65 per week	$50–65 per week	$65 per week	$70 per week
Bereavement Pay	No mention	Yes	Same	Same	Same	Same
Automatic Cost-of-living Adjustment	No mention	Yes	Same	Same	Same	Same
Supplemental Unemployment Benefits	No (TR. 182)	Yes	Same	Same	Same	Same

* Same as in column to the left.
** Percent of past year's earnings.
*** Co. subsequently absorbed a cost increase.

[B3745]

the Board's remedial modesty. In these, and other cases, something of a "dialogue" has developed between the Board and that court of appeals, with the court in many instances urging a more aggressive exercise of jurisdiction than appears to suit the Board.

What kinds of models of a Labor Court do you believe would be valuable and feasible? What would be their advantages and disadvantages? Should such a court hear labor cases arising from other agencies as well, such as arbitrators under collective bargaining agreements, or wage and hour cases from the Labor Department, or race and sex discrimination cases from the Equal Employment Opportunity Commission? See Morris, Labor Court: A New Perspective, N.Y.U. 24th Ann. Conf. on Labor 27 (1972).

II. ADMINISTRATION OF THE COLLECTIVE AGREEMENT

A. THE COLLECTIVE AGREEMENT AND THE GRIEVANCE PROCEDURE [1]

1. *The Collective Bargaining Agreement*

The anticipated, and usual, product of collective bargaining is a written agreement between the employer and the union. In part, this agreement sets down the relationship between those two parties, for example in provisions dealing with the recognition of the union as exclusive representative for employees in the bargaining unit or dealing with the resolution of contract disputes through a grievance procedure. In greatest measure, the labor contract sets down the relationship between the employer and its employees, and among the employees themselves. Thus, the contract will normally have provisions governing wages, hours, discipline, promotions and transfers, medical and health insurance, pensions, vacations and holidays, work assignments, seniority and the like. The labor agreement is not a contract of employment; employees are hired separately and individually, but the tenure and terms of their employment once in the unit are regulated by the provisions of the collective bargaining agreement.

The collective bargaining agreement shares with the ordinary commercial contract a number of common features of form and function. But the differences between the labor contract and the commercial contract are of far more profound significance. While the typical commercial contract is the creation of parties who have been joined in a voluntary arrangement sparked by mutual self-interest, the labor contract is the product of a bilateral relationship which is in large measure compelled by law, frequently against the wishes of one of the two parties. Most commercial contracts regulate the rights and duties of the parties for a single and transient transaction, or for a defined period of time. The labor contract, while fixed in

---

1. Excellent discussions of the importance of grievances and the role of a soundly conceived grievance procedure in their adjustment are to be found in Katz, Minimizing Disputes Through the Adjustment of Grievances, 12 Law and Contemporary Prob. 249 (1947); Selekman, Administering the Union Agreement, 23 Harv.Bus.Rev. 299 (1945); Selekman, Handling Shop Grievances, 23 Harv.Bus.Rev. 469 (1945).

For broader discussions concerning the nature of rights under a collective bargaining agreement, see Cox, Rights Under a Labor Agreement, 69 Harv.L. Rev. 601 (1956); Cox, The Legal Nature of Collective Bargaining Agreements, 57 Mich.L.Rev. 1 (1958); Feller, A General Theory of the Collective Bargaining Agreement, 61 Calif.L.Rev. 663 (1973); Summers, Collective Agreements and the Law of Contracts, 78 Yale L.J. 525 (1969).

duration, will usually govern the parties' relationship for a number of years and looks toward an indefinite period of continued dealing in the future. While the labor contract resembles the commercial contract in its form, in that it is technically an agreement between two signatory parties, it most pointedly shapes the rights and duties for a mass of third persons, the employees in the plant. Those employees spend a great part of their life doing the work which is the subject of the labor contract. By articulating or absorbing a host of rules and regulations for carrying on the day-to-day continuing activities of those employees, the labor contract functions more like a statute or a code of regulations than it does a bilateral agreement. Moreover, the union, although a legal entity with capacity to contract, does not speak for a single monolithic constituency but rather for an amalgam of workers who are skilled and unskilled, young and old, male and female, black and white, educated and uneducated, whose ambitions, needs and interests frequently come into conflict.

Because of many of these characteristics, the labor contract—burdened with the task of regulating a complex work community on a continuing basis—cannot reduce to writing each and every norm or rule that has been developed over time to govern the parties' activities. It is common to treat the collective bargaining agreement as comprised not only of the written and executed document but also of plant customs and industrial practices as well as of informal agreements and concessions made at the bargaining table but not reduced to writing. Moreover, many contract provisions contain purposeful ambiguities or silences, in the expectation that no dispute will arise over their meaning or that future disputes will be resolved in due course to the mutual satisfaction of the parties. The parties normally realize that resolution of contract disputes will require formal procedures, typically culminating in recourse to a neutral third party; by this process of grievance settlement and arbitration, the contract itself evolves and the process of collective bargaining continues. Both the labor contract and the commercial contract are negotiated subject to applicable rules of contract law and of public policy, but the labor contract is far more peculiarly enmeshed in a framework of regulatory laws—in part state law but always against the background of federal labor legislation, and in part conventional contract law but always against the background of the special history of labor-management relations in America. Because of this, there are a number of different decisionmaking agencies which are potentially implicated in the construction and application of the terms of the labor contract: state courts and federal courts, privately selected arbitrators, state administrative agencies, the National Labor Relations Board, and other federal agencies (such as the Equal Employment Opportunity Commission or the Department of Labor).

2. *The Grievance Procedure*

Most collective bargaining agreements make express provision for resolution of contract disputes not by a lawsuit in a civil court but rather through machinery which is internal to the plant or company. Some contracts define the term "grievance" very broadly to refer, for example, to "any dispute, disagreement or difference arising between any employee or the union and the company." More often, however, grievances are more narrowly defined as disputes relating in some manner to the proper interpretation or application of the collective agreement. Such a definition does not necessarily imply that a grievance must involve a matter that is explicitly covered by some term of the contract for, as just noted, the "agreement" of the parties is commonly understood to encompass unwritten past practices and informal understandings; the parties' relationship is constantly evolving and adapting to new and changing circumstances.

The typical agreement will provide for the presentation of a grievance, often orally but sometimes in writing, by the aggrieved employee or the union to the appropriate supervisor or foreman. If unresolved, the grievance will move to a higher level of supervision, and it is common to have a three or four step grievance procedure, in which the last in-company step involves dealings between high union officials (sometimes at the international level) and company officials (commonly at companywide levels outside the plant). The great majority of grievances are generally settled at the first stage; were it otherwise, higher management and union officials could easily become overburdened with the task of reviewing complaints.

An increasing number of agreements specify time limits within which grievances must be initiated, considered, and, if necessary, appealed to higher levels. Originally, the demand for time limits emanated from union officials who sought to prevent stalling tactics by management and to avoid impatience and dissatisfaction among the employees involved. But management has also become interested in preventing delay, particularly in cases involving discharges and layoffs where retroactive pay may be required in the event that the grievance is settled favorably to the union.

Agreements commonly provide that union representatives processing grievances will be given access to the plant premises and to plant personnel in order to obtain the information needed to prosecute the grievance. In addition, special provisions may be included with respect to union representatives, such as elected shop stewards or grievance committeemen, who are also employees of the company.

Thus, contracts commonly provide that such employees will be compensated for working time spent in processing grievances.

Further provisions are often included to safeguard the jobs of shop stewards or grievance committeemen and insure their continuity of service. For example, these employees may be given preferred seniority to protect them from layoffs, and management may be further restricted in transferring them to other plants or departments. (Are these forms of "job favoritism" unlawful, as discrimination which encourages union membership? See pp. 1091–96, infra.)

Although a wide variety of techniques may be employed, any grievance procedure can be expected to serve a number of distinct purposes affecting the union, the employer and the employees. The most straightforward function of the process, of course, is to provide a method for peacefully settling the complaints of employees, after mutual deliberation, and in so doing, to provide guidance for future cases by clarifying the terms of the contract. In the course of fulfilling this primary function, however, the grievance procedure may also serve other purposes. For example, the accumulation of grievances may pin-point ambiguities and trouble-spots in the agreement which can be taken up for discussion at the next contract negotiations. Moreover, the pattern of grievances may provide valuable information to higher management by identifying problems of supervision and personnel policy which may then be corrected before more serious trouble can arise. In some instances, the grievance procedure may also be used, for better or worse, as a strategic device. For example, certain unions may look upon the process as a technique with which to gradually extend the bargaining agreement by gaining concessions from management that stretch the literal provisions of the contract. In other cases, unions may press grievances with particular vigor in order to gain leverage in forthcoming contract negotiations or to satisfy constituents who are being appealed to by rival factions within the union.

In the light of experience in countless plants, it is clear beyond dispute that an effective, well-administered grievance procedure can play an indispensable role in improving the climate of labor relations and providing a measure of "industrial due process" to the individual worker. The advantages to be derived from these procedures have been summed up in the following terms by a distinguished panel of labor relations experts:[2]

> "The gains from this system are especially noteworthy
> because of their effect on the recognition and dignity of the
> individual worker. This system helps prevent arbitrary action on questions of discipline, layoff, promotion, and trans-

---

2. Independent Study Group for the Committee for Economic Development,   The Public Interest in National Labor Policy, p. 32 (1961).

fer, and sets up orderly procedures for the handling of grievances. Wildcat strikes and other disorderly means of protest have been curtailed and an effective work discipline generally established. In many situations, cooperative relationships marked by mutual respect between management and labor stand as an example of what can be done."

In order that the grievance procedure may achieve these objectives, there has developed a principle which can be capsulized in the phrase "Obey, and then grieve." The employer, it may be assumed, has issued a work rule or through its supervisors has given an employee an order which violates the employer's obligations under the collective bargaining agreement. Both industrial justice and plant efficiency can be secured if the wronged employees do not take it upon themselves to ignore the improper rule or order but rather obey it and file a grievance. The reasons behind this cardinal principle were set forth by the late Harry Shulman, professor and Dean of the Yale Law School, permanent umpire under the labor contract between the Ford Motor Company and the United Auto Workers, and commonly regarded as one of the great scholar/practitioners of the art of labor arbitration. In Ford Motor Co., 3 Lab.Arb. 779 (1944), Dean Shulman stated:

"The remedy under the contract for violation of right lies in the grievance procedure and only in the grievance procedure. To refuse obedience because of a claimed contract violation would be to substitute individual action for collective bargaining and to replace the grievance procedure with extra-contractual methods. And such must be the advice of the committeeman if he gives advice to employees. His advice must be that the safe and proper method is to obey supervision's instructions and to seek correction and redress through the grievance procedure. * * *

" *   *   *   [M]ore important, the grievance procedure is prescribed in the contract precisely because the parties anticipated that there would be claims of violations which would require adjustment. That procedure is prescribed for all grievances and not merely for doubtful ones. Nothing in the contract even suggests the idea that only doubtful violations need be processed through the grievance procedure and that clear violations can be resisted through individual self-help. The only difference between a 'clear' violation and a 'doubtful' one is that the former makes a clear grievance and the latter a doubtful one. But both must be handled in the regular prescribed manner. *   *   * "

B. GRIEVANCE ARBITRATION [3]

1. *The Nature and Functions of Labor Arbitration*

It has often been observed that the solving of disputes through arbitration probably antedates recorded history. Although in the field of labor relations, the practice is of relatively recent origin, at least in this country, arbitration provisions can today be found in an estimated 96% of all agreements. The reasons for the prevalence of grievance arbitration are clear enough. In part, its use has resulted from the emergence of powerful unions able to insist upon this procedure at the bargaining table. Many unions favor arbitration both because they believe that they will receive a more sympathetic hearing from an arbitrator and because they retain a lingering distrust of courts and "legalistic" procedures originating from judicial decisions prior to the passage of the Norris-LaGuardia Act. Perhaps a stronger reason for the spread of arbitration lies in the growing recognition by management as well as labor that arbitration represents the best available alternative for settling disputes under collective agreements. Since disagreements over the interpretation or application of these agreements arise frequently, it would be intolerable to management and impossibly burdensome to unions to resort to a strike in order to resolve their differences. A possible alternative would be to bring suit in a state or federal court (and this procedure may actually be followed under agreements which make no provision for arbitration). Nevertheless, crowded dockets make the process too cumbersome to be widely accepted.

Most commonly, the arbitration is conducted before an individual, although occasionally it will be a three-person panel (with each party appointing one member of the panel more as an advocate than as a neutral). Typically, the arbitrator is selected by the parties on an ad hoc basis to decide only a single case. In some of the larger industrial bargaining units, however, in light of the volume of grievances, a permanent umpire or referee will be selected, to be paid an annual retainer and to handle all of the cases going to arbitration under a given contract or group of contracts. Arbitrators come most frequently from the ranks of the legal profession or the teaching profession (most commonly, professors of law or business adminis-

3. Cox, Reflections Upon Labor Arbitration, 72 Harv.L.Rev. 1482 (1959); F. & E. Elkouri, How Arbitration Works (3d ed. 1973); O. Fairweather, Practice & Procedure in Labor Arbitration (1973); R. Fleming, The Labor Arbitration Process (1965); P. Hays, Labor Arbitration: A Dissenting View (1966); Shulman, Reason, Contract, and Law in Labor Relations, 68 Harv. L.Rev. 999 (1955); Symposium on Labor Arbitration, 10 Vand.L.Rev. 649 (1957); C. Updegraff, Arbitration and Labor Relations (3d ed. 1970).

tration or industrial relations), although there will sometimes be resort to a local clergyman or other respected person in the community. There are also a relatively small number of full-time professional labor arbitrators. Government or private organizations, primarily the Federal Mediation and Conciliation Service or the American Arbitration Association, facilitate the selection of an arbitrator by supplying the parties with lists of names of qualified persons from which the parties are to chose; not surprisingly, the parties will frequently research earlier arbitration decisions rendered by the persons on the list, in an effort to determine their "leanings."

There are some important differences between the ad hoc arbitrator and the permanent umpire. The latter over the course of time develops a familiarity with the parties, with the contract, with past negotiations, with the physical set-up of the plant and with plant practices. By virtue of this familiarity, he is sometimes expected by the parties (or assumes that he is expected) to consider the long-range implications of particular decisions and the overall working relationship between the parties, rather than to render a "literal" decision within the four corners of the written document. The ad hoc arbitrator, appointed to decide a single dispute, may not have this kind of familiarity and feels constrained to take a more particularistic or legalistic attitude toward the dispute, the parties and the agreement. Whether these differing attitudes are appropriate is, however, a source of considerable disagreement within the arbitral fraternity. Some observers have pointed out another difference between the permanent and the ad hoc arbitrator, noting the greater likelihood that the ad hoc arbitrator—whose future reemployment by the parties may depend on it—will render a decision which is excessively cautious about offending one party or the other and which tends to "split the difference." Support for this claim is said to be commonly found in discharge grievances, where the arbitrator will find the discharge to have been without just cause and will order the grievant reinstated, but without imposing on the company any liability for backpay.

In any event, whether the arbitrator is designated on a permanent or an ad hoc basis, he will sometimes be required to determine whether he is properly simply a creature of the parties whose function is to determine no more than what their private-contractual intentions are, or is more like a civil judge who can (or must) consider such "external" matters as law and public policy. This issue can arise when one party relies upon an explicit provision in the agreement and the other party claims that the arbitrator must find the provision to violate the National Labor Relations Act or Title VII of the 1964 Civil Rights Act and must refuse to give it effect. Here too, the arbitration fraternity is sharply split. The matter is further complicated by the fact that, as noted above, many arbitrators are not trained in the law but are selected rather for their expertise in industrial relations or because they are a respected "lay" figure in the community. An added source of difficulty are the statements in a number of judicial opinions to the effect that an arbitrator's award will be subject to court reversal if the arbitrator strays from the agreement and bases his opinion solely upon the assumed requirements of statutory or case law.

On the whole arbitration proceedings are more informal, more expeditious and less costly than civil litigation. The hearing itself may take place almost anywhere—in a conference room at the plant, in an office or even a hotel room. Frequently, the parties are not represented by lawyers (but by a full-time union representative and an industrial-relations or personnel executive for the company). Formal rules of evidence do not apply, and arbitrators tend to admit "for what it is worth" a substantial amount of evidence which would normally be objectionable as immaterial or hearsay. Although evidence is elicited by questioning witnesses and submitting documents, and witnesses will generally be examined and cross-examined in a more or less orderly fashion, the presentation of written or oral evidence is commonly quite informal and unstructured. In many cases, the purpose of the proceeding is as much to "ventilate" the grievance as it is to secure a favorable decision from the arbitrator. The arbitrator's decision, usually in writing, tends to be brief, undetailed, and untechnical; it will commonly be filed with the parties less than a month after the hearing. Written briefs are not common, and in almost all cases in which they are filed, are submitted after the hearing rather than before. Many of these informal qualities—which have always made arbitration a most attractive alternative to civil litigation—have been giving way in recent years to a greater "legalization" of the arbitration process, as lawyers have been called in to serve as arbitrators and as parties have increasingly called in legal counsel to represent them at hearings.

———

Cox, "Reflections Upon Labor Arbitration," 72 Harv.L.Rev. 1482, 1493, 1498–99 (1959): "The generalities, the deliberate ambiguities, the gaps, the unforeseen contingencies, and the need for a rule even though the agreement is silent all require a creativeness in contract administration which is quite unlike the attitude of one construing a deed, a promissory note, or a 300-page corporate trust indenture. The process of interpretation cannot be the same because the conditions which determine the character of the instruments are different. * * *

"At this point we may draw two conclusions:

"First, it is not unqualifiedly true that a collective-bargaining agreement is simply a document by which the union and employees have imposed upon management limited, express restrictions of its otherwise absolute right to manage the enterprise, so that an employee's claim must fail unless he can point to a specific contract provision upon which the claim is founded. There are too many people, too many problems, too many unforeseeable contingencies to make the words of the contract the exclusive source of rights and duties. One cannot reduce all the rules governing a community like an industrial plant to fifteen or even fifty pages. Within the sphere of collective bargaining, the institutional characteristics and the governmental nature of the collective-bargaining process demand a common law of the shop which implements and furnishes the context of the agreement. We must assume that intelligent negotiators acknowledged so plain a need unless they stated a contrary rule in plain words.

"Second, the 'interpretation and application' of a collective-bargaining agreement through grievance arbitration is not limited to documentary construction of language. The failure to recognize this truth probably explains much of the conflict between arbitral and judicial thinking. * * * Collective agreements, because of the institutional characteristics already mentioned, are less complete and more loosely drawn than many other contracts; therefore, there is much more to be supplied from the context in which they were negotiated. The governing criteria are not judge-made principles of the common law but the practices, assumptions, understandings, and aspirations of the going industrial concern. The arbitrator is not bound by conventional law although he may follow it. If we are to develop a rationale of grievance arbitration, more work should be directed towards identifying the standards which shape arbitral opinions; if the process is rational, as I assert, a partial systematization should be achievable even though scope must be left for art and intuition. I can pause only to note some of the familiar sources: legal doctrines, a sense of fairness, the national labor policy, past practice at the plant, and perhaps good industrial practice generally. Of these perhaps past practice is the most significant; witness the cases in which it is argued that a firmly established practice takes precedence even over the plain meaning of the words."

Problem for Discussion

In a collective bargaining agreement between Inland Container Corporation and the Paper Mill Workers, it was provided that job vacancies would be filled by management selection but that "if the qualifications are comparatively equal between two Regular Employees, Seniority shall prevail." An opening appeared for a job and though a regular employee, Torres, was the only applicant, the Company considered his experience insufficient and promoted an apprentice with less seniority. Torres submitted a grievance claiming he should have at least been given a fair trial in the new job. At the outset of the arbitration hearing, however, Torres stated unequivocally that he no longer desired promotion to the new job and would not accept it even if it were offered to him. Management then moved to dismiss the proceeding, but the union asked to continue and demanded that a decision be reached. What disposition would you make as arbitrator?

---

2. *Discharge and Discipline* [4]

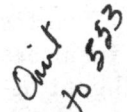

PHILADELPHIA TRANSPORTATION CO.

49 Lab.Arb. 606 (undated).

GERSHENFELD, ARBITRATOR:—This grievance has been processed to arbitration under the terms of the current Agreement between the Philadelphia Transportation Co. and Local 234, TWU, AFL–CIO. Mr. H. Aikens served as Company Arbitrator. Mr. E. Monaghan served as Union Arbitrator and the undersigned was designated Impartial Chairman.

Both prior to and at a hearing held on March 7, 1967, the Union requested a delay in the proceedings. The Union indicated that it was seeking a postponement inasmuch as the aggrieved, X——, was under criminal indictment for the same alleged offense for which he had been discharged by the Company on October 28, 1966. The Company discharged X—— on the charge of committing an indecent act with regard to Mrs. Y——. The act was alleged to have occurred in a darkened bus near the end of Bus Route A on September 30, 1966.

The Union felt that the arbitration hearing might serve to jeopardize X—— in court. The Company objected, arguing that the arbitration hearing was an independent forum provided for by contract between the parties. After some discussion and a meeting with Company- and Union-appointed Arbitrators, the undersigned Impartial Chairman ruled that it was appropriate to postpone the Union's portion of the case until after the court hearing in Montgomery County, Pennsylvania. The Company proceeded to present its case at the March 7, 1967 arbitration meeting. It should be noted that during the course of the session, the Union stipulated that, in the event of the reinstatement of X——, the Union was not seeking a back-pay liability beyond the date of March 7, 1967.

---

4. See Edwards, Due Process Considerations in Labor Arbitration, 25 Arb.J. 141 (1970); Note, Industrial Due Process and Just Cause for Discipline: A Comparative Analysis of the Arbitral and Judicial Decisional Processes, 6 U.C.L.A.L.Rev. 603 (1959); Summers, Individual Protection Against Unjust Dismissal: Time for a Statute, 62 Va.L.Rev. 481 (1976).

X＿＿ was tried in Montgomery County Court on June 23, 1967. The judge directed a verdict of not guilty on the charge of assault and battery with intent to ravish, and the jury found the defendant not guilty on the charge of indecent assault. An arbitration hearing was next held on July 5, 1967 at which the Union argued its case and both parties summarized their positions. The parties agreed to provide the Impartial Chairman with the notes of testimony in the trial of X＿＿. These notes of testimony were received on September 13, 1967. A meeting was held on September 25, 1967 involving the Impartial Chairman and the Company- and Union-appointed Arbitrators. The undersigned, after considering all pertinent evidence and argument, has prepared the Award and Opinion in this case.

The parties have stipulated that their Agreement contains a just [cause] clause" with respect to discharge. The issue, then, is:

Was X＿＿ properly discharged for just cause by the Company on October 28, 1966?

Company Position

1.   Any employee attempting or even suggesting an indecent act should be discharged. The business of the Company is public transportation, and it is imperative that the general public feel it can travel in Company vehicles free from advances by Company employees. The Company has previously discharged a man for making indecent remarks to two women, and that discharge (in 1965) still stands.

2.   The arbitration forum is an independent one. Whatever happens in the courts is not directly pertinent to this case. The Company believes that it has demonstrated via testimony of Mrs. Y＿＿ that an indecent act occurred and therefore the discharge of X＿＿ should be sustained. Further, in addition to the incidents precipitating the discharge, twice before X＿＿ showed a lack of propriety in requesting a kiss from Mrs. Y＿＿.

3.   The Company feels it significant that the Union has failed to place X＿＿ on the stand. If X＿＿ is innocent, why should he hesitate to give testimony?   *   *   *

Union Position

1.   It is the task of the Company to demonstrate the validity of the discharge. This has in no way been accomplished by the Company. Further, X＿＿ has been tried and found not guilty by a Montgomery County court. It is improper to overrule that decision, and X＿＿ should be restored to work with a back-pay award to March 7, 1967. The precedent in the Hill case applies.

2.   Mrs. Y's____ testimony is not creditable. For example, she testified in arbitration that X____ placed his hand in her pocket searching for a token, yet there is nothing in the record of the Justice of the Peace hearing to indicate that she said it. The fact that she waited three days after the alleged incident occurred to charge X____ also throws doubt on her credibility.

3.   The Union has a perfect right not to place X____ on the stand. However, the Union did make available the full notes of testimony from the court case which included X's____ testimony in court.
* * *

4.   X____ has an excellent work record. He has been with the Company for twenty-three years. The Union is precluded from introducing any evidence beyond a three-year period from the man's record but in those three years his record shows no lateness, no chargeable accidents and seven commendations from passengers and others who have examined and praised his work. This excellent record coupled with the not guilty verdict of the Montgomery County jury requires that X____ be restored to duty.

5.   Since there has been no clear proof of X's____ guilt, it is important that he be restored to duty with full back pay to March 7, 1967. Otherwise, bus drivers will believe that they are subject to discipline based on charges filed by passengers even when the charges have no merit.

Opinion

The Impartial Chairman is persuaded that the Company's position with regard to the independence of the arbitration forum *vis a vis* the Courts is basically sound. Under these terms, it is proper for the arbitration hearing to be used, *de novo*, to determine the propriety of the discharge imposed on X____ by the Company. However, it also is appropriate to note that the court decision finding X____ not guilty on two counts while not binding here may appropriately be introduced into the arbitration hearings in support of the Union position.

After studying all pertinent data, the Impartial Chairman accepts the court decisions as fairly representing the fact that X____ did not commit a crime in the legal sense of the word. However, after a careful review of all exhibits and testimony, the Impartial Chairman also believes that X____ did engage in some form of illicit behavior. There were instances where both the Company and the Union were able to pick holes in the testimony of the other party. Mrs. Y____, however, did tell a basically consistent story and the Impartial Chairman finds reason to believe that some improper act by X____ with regard to Mrs. Y____ did occur. In this connection, while the Union was not obligated to place X____ on the stand, it is somewhat surprising to find a man accused of as serious an act as the one before us, not defending himself.

If the Impartial Chairman believes that X___ acted improperly but did less than would qualify legally as a crime, the remaining question becomes the appropriateness of the penalty. X___ has been with the Company for some twenty-three years, and it was stipulated by the Company that his record was satisfactory. The Union added that X___ had frequently been commended for his work. This totality of background cannot be taken lightly. By the same token, neither can X's___ unfortunate behavior on September 30, 1966 be disregarded. On balance, the Impartial Chairman believes that X___ deserves another opportunity to re-establish himself in the industrial community at the company but that the imposition of severe discipline is appropriate in this case. Accordingly, X___ is ordered returned to work with no back pay and the Company is afforded the opportunity to re-assign X— to minimize his public contact or to eliminate the possibility for acts of this type to re-occur. While it is to be hoped that no repetition of this type of incident will ever again involve X—, it is important that the riding public be protected.

The Impartial Chairman believes that re-assignment within the Bus Division is within his purview as an Arbitrator and has ruled accordingly. The Impartial Chairman recognizes that re-assignment outside of the division requires the active cooperation of the parties inasmuch as they must jointly agree to modify the Agreement to protect his seniority. In the event that an appropriate assignment is not available for X___ in the Bus Division, the Impartial Chairman strongly urges the parties to work together in seeking an appropriate assignment for X___ and making the necessary contractual changes.

* * *

AWARD

X___ is hereby re-instated to a position with the Company without back compensation. The Company is afforded an opportunity for re-assignment of X___ within the Bus Division.

Problems for Discussion

1. What purposes are served by having the case heard and decided not by a single arbitrator but by three, with the company and union each appointing one member of the panel? Should these two latter panel members be expected to act as neutrals or as partisans? Should the "neutral" arbitrator feel free to attempt a mediated settlement of the grievance between his or her colleagues on the panel?

2. Was it sound procedure to hear the Company's evidence in March and the Union's evidence in July? What do you think was the Union's

case, in view of the fact that the grievant did not testify at the arbitration hearing? (Why not, in light of the intervening acquittal?) Who should bear the "burden of proof" in a discharge case—the Union, which is charging a contract breach, or the Company, which knowingly took the challenged action? Must the arbitrator be convinced of the grievant's culpability "beyond a reasonable doubt" in order to sustain the discharge?

3. Once the arbitrator determined that the grievant had indeed committed an offensive act upon a customer, was he not obliged to sustain the position of the Company that this was "just cause" for discharge? Apparently the only reason for not sustaining the discharge was the grievant's 23-year satisfactory work record; is that a proper basis for decision?

4. Since the grievant had been acquitted of two criminal charges arising from the same incident, what reasons can you give for not making these acquittals controlling on the issues before the arbitrator in the discharge case?

5. Was it proper for the arbitrator to award a remedy that neither party had asked for? Was it proper for the arbitrator to "suggest" that the Company might reassign the grievant?

OTIS ELEVATOR COMPANY

(Unpublished, 1961)

MIDONICK, ARBITRATOR:

There is submitted to me Grievance No. 3566, dated December 7, 1960, by which the Union challenges the discharge of Joseph Calise, an assembler at the Yonkers, New York, plant of the Company.

The Company admits the discharge on or about December 5, 1960, but sets up as a defense that the discharge took place as a result of flagrant violation of the Company's rule against gambling on its premises during working hours, and the resulting indictment, prosecution and conviction of Joseph Calise in the County Court of Westchester County. The certified copy of the conviction recites that on December 1, 1960, the said Joseph Calise was convicted of the crimes of "knowingly possessing policy slips (12/29/59) and knowingly possessing policy slips (12/28/59)", and upon the basis of such indictments and convictions said Joseph Calise was fined the sum of $125 on each indictment, and it was further ordered that if the fine were not paid that Joseph Calise be imprisoned in the Westchester County Penitentiary and Work House at hard labor, for the terms of 30 days on each Indictment, the sentences to run concurrently. The certified copy of the minutes further indicates that the fine of $250 was paid in Court at the time of sentencing on December 1, 1960. The conviction was for misdemeanors.

The arbitration clause under which I am proceeding is contained in the labor agreement between the Company and the Union, effective June 1, 1959, until May 30, 1961.

The arbitration clause of that agreement provides in Article VI, Section 2, as follows:

"Section 2. The decision of such arbitrator shall be final and binding upon the parties but the arbitrator shall not have the power to add to, subtract from, or modify the terms of this Agreement, or any Agreement supplemental thereto   *   *   *."

The substantive section of the agreement on discharges is to be found in Article IX, Section 11 as follows:

"Section 11. The Employer shall have the right to discharge any employee for just cause. The Union shall have the right to challenge the propriety of the discharge of any employee, except a probationary employee, and any such discharge shall be considered a grievance to be dealt with in accordance with the grievance procedure heretofore set forth in Article V. Employees discharged without just cause shall receive pay for all lost time unless an arbitrator rules otherwise."

The parties stipulated at the hearing that the following dispute is submitted to me: "Has Joseph Calise been discharged for just cause, and if not what shall the remedy be?"

There is little dispute about the facts.

A detective investigating from the office of the District Attorney of Westchester County spent approximately five weeks in the plant posing as an employee in an effort to discover the gambling activities about which the District Attorney had received complaints. The testimony of the detective was that he observed five men in the plant handling policy slips, and that one of them was Joseph Calise. Joseph Calise was the sole user of his own work bench, and at that bench the policy slips were discovered on the days which the indictment specified. Calise did not testify at the arbitration, and it was clear from testimony of admissions made by him that he did not deny his guilt. He does complain, however, as does the Union, that different and much harsher treatment is being meted out to Calise than to the other four employees evidently involved.

On cross-examination of the detective investigator, his testimony was that the sole distinction between Calise and the remaining four observed in possession of policy slips in the plant, was that his investigation "disclosed that these four other people were actually working for Mr. Calise."

The Union does not condone the practice of organized gambling; it deplores the practice and seeks to root it out as does the Company. The Union's argument here concerns the difference of treatment faced by Calise and the others, and more particularly the Union complains that the discipline awarded to Calise was too harsh.

The Union proved and argues that Calise had been a satisfactory employee in this plant for 24 long years prior to his discharge, that he had unbroken seniority for this period of time, that he has a wife dependent upon him as well as four small children ranging in age from one to eight, that he is 47 years of age, that the Company's pension plan gives him no fixed or vested rights until 20 years of service and his attaining age 50 while in the employ of the Company, the second of which conditions he has not met and as a result will lose all of his rights in the pension plan unless this arbitrator were to restore some or all of the rights, and that Calise has also been denied unemployment compensation on the ground that his own misconduct led to his discharge, that Calise is unable to find, because of the nature of the problem, other suitable employment if this discharge were allowed to stand. Taking all of these difficulties together, the Union argues that Calise, having paid his debt to society formally, is being overly punished by the severity and finality of the Company's action.

The Union argues further that they have made a thorough investigation of the potentiality for further harm to discipline in the plant if Calise were to be restored to his position. They are convinced that gambling will not resume in the plant and certainly not through any efforts of Calise. The Union introduced in evidence, without objection to its competency by the Company who merely objected to its relevancy and materiality, the following letter from Calise's parish priest:

"CHURCH OF CHRIST THE KING
Rectory
740 North Broadway
Yonkers, N. Y.

April 20, 1961

"TO WHOM IT MAY CONCERN:

"Joseph Calise of 50 Douglas Ave., Yonkers, N. Y. is a member of the Church of Christ the King, Yonkers, N. Y.

"Mr. Calise has appeared before me and does promise, swear, and hold to the position that if he is re-employed by Otis Co. of Yonkers, N. Y., he will not engage or aid in the crime for which he has been convicted, as long as he remains in the employ of Otis.

"I feel that this testimony of Mr. Calise is honest and that he can be counted on to be true to his word.

"With kindest best wishes and a prayer for a just decision, I remain,

"Respectfully
"Fr. JOHN J. FOLEY"

The Company answers these contentions by standing firmly by its decision to discharge Calise. The Company points out that it exercised restraint and moderation in connection with Calise's case in that they waited an entire year after the indictment before disciplining Calise at all, and that only after the official conviction did the Company undertake to rid itself of Calise. The Company argues quite strongly that if Calise were to be restored to his position in the plant without adequate punishment, that no Company rule would be enforceable because employees would expect too much leniency from arbitrators. * * *

It is my view that some leniency should be afforded to Calise in this situation so long as the Company's right to enforce its approriate rules is sanctioned with disciplinary action strong enough, although short of discharge, to serve as a sufficient deterrent.

In reinstating Calise to his former position with the Company as of July 3, 1961, I am mindful of the absence of proof of serious harm to the operations of the Company. It was evidently required for the detective assigned by the District Attorney's office of Westchester County, to pose as an employee for five weeks before the full extent of the activities with respect to policy numbers in this plant was evident to him. It must be, therefore, that these activities were conducted with considerable decorum and secretiveness indeed, and were successfully designed to avoid any disturbance of the even tenor of the plant operations. Nothing was visible except to the expert in policy slip detection. No planned Company operations were proved to have been in any way disturbed; no testimony of any foreman or other supervisor was offered to show any disruption, diminution, or curtailment of production that could be observed. I am also mindful that Calise's offense was a first offense.

This is not to say that the arbitrator in any way condones such illegal activities as policy numbers gambling. The Union also takes a strong position on the side of the Company in this respect. It is merely that the harm to the Company as such was limited compared with the kind of harm which would flow from violations of other types of rules and regulations.

In view of the Company's strong protestations that a strict measure of discipline must be meted out to Calise in order to maintain general discipline with respect to this and other rules, I have considered the entire arsenal of disciplines and sanctions. I feel that a seven-month disciplinary layoff from December 5, 1960, to July 3, 1961, without pay, without unemployment compensation and without counting those seven months as part of the seniority of Calise, would be sufficient punishment from all points of view—in view of the nature of his defense, in view of his punishment by public authority, limited to a conviction for misdemeanors and a fine of $250, in view of his heavy family obligations involving four young innocent children and a wife, in view of his fine record except for the activity here involved, and in view of the fact that his pension rights built up after decades of service would be otherwise lost. I am inclined to believe that a seven-month layoff without pay is adequate to maintain strict discipline without crossing over the line to harshness.

I also place a reasonable amount of weight on the balance of the scales favoring Calise, that the Company has not seen fit to discipline four others in the plant who had also been engaged in policy slip operations. Whether or not these four others, as was testified by the policy detective were "working for" Calise and despite the lack of prosecution by public authority, these four men were guilty also of violating the same rule against gambling in the plant. The failure of the Company to take any measures of discipline against them, instead fastening the entire burden upon the shoulders of Calise as an example to all men, becomes an additional basis to warrant some amelioration in the sanctions applied to Calise. It is partially on the basis of such condonation by the Company of gambling violations only mildly different in their nature and extent, that I must reduce the onus to be borne by Calise alone. I have therefore reinstated Calise as indicated in the award, after a seven-month no-pay layoff.

Despite the Company's fears of recurrence of violation of the rule against gambling, I am confident that no such difficulty will materialize. Having thus placed my own reputation as a seer in the balance, I am relieved that I will be sharing the risk, as it were, with the Company and the Union. All will be well, as it was during the year between the accusation of Calise and his conviction, during which year he remained on the job and without any evidence of further transgression. * * *

Award:

* * * Joseph Calise has not been discharged for just cause. There was just cause for substantial disciplinary action against Joseph Calise, but under all the circumstances, outright and final discharge is a disciplinary action with effects too harsh upon the grieving employee.

The remedy hereby awarded requires the Company to reinstate Joseph Calise to his former position on July 3, 1961, without back pay or other remuneration during the period of disciplinary layoff from December 5, 1960, through July 2, 1961, and without crediting Joseph Calise for any seniority or other benefits flowing from the labor agreement for such period of disciplinary layoff, but preserving nevertheless all of his seniority, pension rights and other benefits so that upon his reinstatement pursuant to this award he will be deemed to have taken an approved leave of absence for the period from December 5, 1960, through July 2, 1961, subject to the terms of this award.

Problems for Discussion

1. After reading only the facts of the case but not the opinion of the arbitrator on the merits, would you have believed the grievant to stand a substantial chance of securing reinstatement? If you actually believed the grievance to have been almost frivolous, what might have impelled you—for example, as counsel or international representative for the union—to press this case to arbitration? Do you think an arbitrator might have been more sympathetic to the grievant's case than would a trial-court judge? Even assuming a judge to have sustained the claim of the grievant on the merits, would reinstatement likely have been ordered?

2. What exactly is the asserted breach of contract which is being challenged through the contract grievance procedure? In passing on that question, should it be relevant to the arbitrator that: (a) the grievant possessed 24 years of seniority? (b) the grievant was three years away from retirement? (c) the grievant had four children? (d) the grievant's priest attested to his character in a letter? Would these factors be technically objectionable if introduced in a civil lawsuit against the company? In a criminal proceeding against the grievant? If there is a difference in the relevant issues of proof, how do you account for this difference?

3. Do you believe that the fact that the grievant had already been convicted in a criminal proceeding helped him or hurt him in the arbitration proceeding? Is it arguable that conviction for the commission of a crime on company premises is automatic and conclusive justification for discharge? Is it arguable that the arbitrator's task is only to determine whether the grievant *in fact* engaged in the criminal conduct but that once finding that he had the arbitrator is forbidden to "second-guess" the employer on the sanction imposed?

4. The arbitrator was swayed in some measure by the company's failure to discipline four other employees implicated in the gambling scheme. Should he have been? If examined in isolation the discipline of a single employee would be deemed for just cause, precisely why should it be relevant that the employer has treated other employees comparably situated less severely? Is the arbitrator's analysis of this issue likely to have a beneficent effect upon the employer's personnel policy?

5. Given the arbitrator's analysis of the merits, and the employer's treatment of the other implicated employees, is it arguable that the arbitrator's award was too *harsh* on the grievant? The "half-way" sanction adopted by the arbitrator is not uncommon in discharge cases. Is it rationally justifiable, or is it merely an expedient adopted by arbitrators to avoid alienating either party completely?

6. If the gambling activities that had led to Calise's conviction had been engaged in away from the Company's premises altogether, would that have justified some disciplinary action? Would your answer be different if, instead of working as a production employee for a company manufacturing elevators, Calise had worked as a security guard there, or had worked for a company operating a state-licensed casino?

———

COCA-COLA BOTTLING CO. OF BOSTON (Wallen, Arbitrator 1949). Although the contract contained no express provision limiting the Company's right of discipline and discharge, the Union claimed that the discharge of Edward Pierce was a breach of the agreement, but the Company claimed that the grievance was not arbitrable (since the contractual grievance procedure covered "any dispute as to the meaning of this agreement or respecting compliance with its terms"). The contract contained a management rights clause ("Except as there is contained in this agreement an express provision limiting the discretion of the Company, nothing herein contained shall be deemed to limit the Company in the exercise of the rights, functions and privileges of management"), an integration or "zipper" clause ("This contract contains the entire agreement between the parties * * * and no change in or amendment or addition to this contract shall be valid unless in writing signed by the parties hereto"), and a provision that "No arbitrator shall have the power to add to or subtract from the terms of this agreement." The neutral arbitrator (and the Union appointee) in a tripartite panel held that it was proper to imply a "just cause" limitation on management's power to discipline, and that the grievance was therefore arbitrable.

There was testimony before the panel that the subject of the Company's right to discharge without being accountable through the grievance and arbitration procedure was never raised in contract negotiations, and that the Company negotiator was content to be silent on the matter in view of the liberal powers apparently accorded by the contract. Although the contract in its terms neither gave the Company the unfettered right to discharge nor gave the Union the right to challenge a discharge, the neutral arbitrator concluded that a limitation on the right of discharge was implied in the labor agreement. Otherwise, several important provisions—such as those requiring that layoffs and recalls were to be determined by the seniority of the employees, and the grievance procedure itself—would be reduced to a nullity. Moreover, "the entire logic" of the collective bargaining agreement points toward protection of job security. "The meaning of the contract, when viewed as a whole, is that a limitation on the employer's right to discharge was created with the birth of the instrument." Such a conclusion did not improperly "add" to the terms of the contract, because the limit on the right of discharge was in fact an implied provision. Nor was the detailed management rights clause a defense, since "These expressions of the particular rights reserved to management imply the exclusion of others. If the Company, in agreeing to the [provision] had intended that it would cover the right to discharge at will, it almost certainly would have listed this right so rarely found in collective bargaining agreements, among the others which it specifically reserved."

The Company-designated arbitrator dissented, pointing out that, under the management rights clause, there could be no limit on the right of discharge absent an "express provision," and that there was "no provision in the written contract the meaning of which was in dispute and no provision in the written contract which the Union claimed had been violated by the Company," so that the grievance was nonarbitrable. The integration clause disspelled any claim that a limit on the right of discharge was "created with the birth of the instrument," and the view of the neutral arbitrator would require management to list every conceivable right it had previously enjoyed or might wish to enjoy in the future in order to secure such rights, an obviously untenable burden. The neutral had disregarded contract provisions to which the parties had agreed and wrote into the contract a provision on which they had never agreed.

Problems for Discussion

1.   Whose reasoning is the more convincing?

2.   Given how common "just cause" provisions are, would *you* as Company negotiator have perceived the obligation or the wisdom of clarifying the Company's position on the right of discharge?

3.   *Subcontracting* [5]

ALLIS-CHALMERS MFG. CO.

Arbitration Award, 1962.
39 Lab.Arb.Rep. 1213.

SMITH, ARBITRATOR.   [The union alleged that the Company had violated the contract by contracting out certain janitorial work on

---

5.   See Dash, The Arbitration of Subcontracting Disputes, 16 Ind. & Lab. Rel.Rev. 208 (1963); Greenbaum, The Arbitration of Subcontracting Disputes: An Addendum, 16 Ind. & Lab. Rel.Rev. 221 (1963); Fairweather, Implied Restrictions on Work Movements, 38 Notre Dame Law 518 (1963); Note, 39 Ind.L.J. 561 (1964): Wallen, How Issues of Subcontracting and Plant Removal Are Handled by Arbitrators, 19 Ind. & Lab.Rel.Rev. 265 (1965).

October 29 and 30, 1960 and certain work on components in early 1962.]

The initial question for decision is whether, as the Company contends, the claims made by the instant grievances fall outside the jurisdictional authority of the Referee. The Company relies upon Reference Paragraph 167 of the Agreement, which provided as follows:

The jurisdictional authority of the Impartial Referee is defined as and limited to the determination of any grievance which is a controversy between the parties or between the Company and employes covered by this agreement concerning compliance with any provision of this agreement and is submitted to him consistent with the provisions of this agreement.

The Company notes that the first step of the grievance procedure contemplates that an employee may present "any grievance concerning his employment," but asserts that this provision is much broader than the "arbitration clause" above quoted in that the latter limits arbitrable grievances to those which allege a violation of some express provision or provisions of the Agreement. The Company reasons that, inasmuch as the claim of the Union does not rest on any specific provision of the Agreement relating to the matter of subcontracting (or, more accurately, contracting out) of work encompassed by the defined bargaining unit, but, instead, rests on alleged implications derived from a composite of provisions (the definition of the bargaining unit, specified wage rates, seniority, etc.), the Referee has no jurisdiction.

This contention, in the Referee's judgment, is without merit and must be rejected. Without elaborating the point, it seems to the Referee that the Company is reading into Reference Paragraph 167 a limitation which is not there. The Paragraph does not state that a grievance must concern and involve a "provision" which explicitly touches the subject matter of the grievance. It simply says, in effect, that the grievance must involve a controversy concerning compliance with "any provision" of the Agreement. This language does not foreclose the consideration of a claim based on the theory that one or more cited provisions of the Agreement give rise to an implied limitation or restriction on managerial action. There can be no doubt that in the area of contractual obligations generally it is frequently necessary, in order to give effect to the intent of the parties, to determine whether the specific provisions of the agreement, fairly and properly construed, import obligations not specifically stated. This is true at least as much in the case of labor agreements as in the case of other kinds of contracts.

The Referee therefore concludes that the instant grievances present claims which are within his jurisdiction to decide. The basic issue is whether, from the provisions defining the bargaining unit, specifying the wage structure, providing seniority rights, and otherwise providing rights and benefits to employees, there arises an implied prohibition upon the contracting out of work of kinds normally and customarily done by employees in the bargaining unit. This is a contention which involves a controversy concerning compliance with a provision of the Agreement alleged to be implicit in the specified provisions.

Insofar as the Union's case is predicated, as it appears at least in part to be, on the broad proposition that the labor agreement, taken as a whole or in the light of the specific provisions cited, gives rise to an implied absolute and unqualified prohibition upon the contracting out of work normally and customarily performed by employees in the bargaining unit, the contention must be dismissed as untenable. The Referee considered this matter in Referee Case No. 8, 1959–1961 Agreement, Springfield Works, and there stated:

> The Referee has considered this general problem more than once. He is unable to accept as sound the broad proposition asserted by the Union that an absolute prohibition upon the contracting out of work done by bargaining unit employees can properly be implied from the "recognition," "wage" and "seniority" provisions of the contract. None of these provisions literally, historically, or in context is a guarantee to employees in the defined bargaining unit that the work which was there when the unit was first recognized will continue to be there. Rather, they assure that, insofar as persons are employed by the Company to perform work of the kinds which are included within the defined unit, there will be recognition by the Company of the Union as the bargaining representative of such persons, and that such persons will be entitled to the benefits of the wage, seniority, and other provisions of the labor agreement.   *   *   *

Little would be gained by attempting, here, to analyze the reported decisions, either as to the particular facts involved, or as to the statements of "principle" to be found in the opinions. As Bethlehem Steel Company Umpire Ralph T. Seward stated in 30 LA 678, after he had undertaken such an examination:

> Beyond revealing that other companies and unions have faced this same question of implied obligations—have presented similar arguments and voiced similar fears—the cases show little uniformity of either theoretical argument or ultimate decision. Within each group of decisions, moreover, there are conflicts of principle and approach. The Umpire has returned from his exploration of the cases a sadder—if not a wiser—man.   *   *   *

The present Referee, while rejecting the Union's view that there exists an absolute (implied) prohibition on the contracting out of work of kinds regularly and normally performed by bargaining unit employees, likewise rejects the Company's view that it has complete freedom in this respect. In the Springfield case he indicated that "a standard of 'good faith' may be applicable, difficult of definition as this may be." Upon further reflection, he is prepared now to say that he thinks this standard is implicit in the union-management relationship represented by the parties' Agreement, in view of the quite legitimate interests and expectations which the employees and the Union have in protecting the fruits of their negotiations with the Company.

"Past practice" in subcontracting for services and for the manufacturing of components may properly be taken into account as a factor negating the existence of any broad, implied limitation on subcontracting, but not as eliminating the restriction altogether. Moreover, an unsuccessful Union attempt to negotiate into the contract specific restrictions on subcontracting, as was the case in the parties' negotiations of their 1959–1961 Agreement, is likewise a fact which may help to support the claim that the parties have recognized that the Company has substantial latitude in the matter of subcontracting. Yet it would be unrealistic to interpret futile bargaining efforts as meaning the parties were in agreement that the Agreement implies no restriction at all. Parties frequently try to solidify through bargaining a position which they could otherwise take, or to broaden rights which otherwise might arguably exist. Thus, the Referee does not find either in the evidence of past practice, here adduced or in the history of the negotiations of the 1959–1961 Agreement, a satisfactory basis for concluding that the Company has complete, untrammeled freedom in the matter of subcontracting. Nor, incidentally, does he attach any special significance to the decisions of the National Labor Relations Board holding that the matter of subcontracting is a "bargainable" issue under the National Labor Relations Act. The parties did bargain on this subject without reaching agreement on any specific provision for inclusion in their Agreement. The question here is whether the Agreement they reached may properly be said to imply some kind of limitation on the Company's freedom to subcontract. In the Referee's judgment, some limitation may properly be implied, narrow though it may be.

Real difficulty arises, however, in attempting to lay down a set of specific criteria to be used in determining whether, in a subcontracting situation, an employer has acted in bad faith. Many arbitrators have sought to do this, and the wide variation in the results of their deliberations of itself casts some doubt on the wisdom of such efforts and suggests that detailed specification may best be left to the collective bargaining process. In general, it seems to the Referee that "good faith" is present when the managerial decision to contract out work is made on the basis of a rational consideration of factors related to the conduct of an efficient, economical operation, and with some regard for the interests, and expectations of the employees affected by the decision, and that "bad faith" is present when the decision is arbitrary (i. e., lacks any rational basis) or fails to take into account at all the interests and expectations of employees affected. Without attempting anything like a complete "catalog," the following would appear, at least prima facie, to be instances of bad faith: (1) To negotiate a collective agreement with the Union representative covering classifications of work while withholding from the Union the fact that the employer contemplates, in the immediate future, a major change in operations which will eliminate such work; (2) entering into a "subcontracting" arrangement which is a subterfuge, in the sense that the "employees" of the ostensible "subcontractor" become in substance the employees of the employer; (3) the commingling of employees of a subcontractor, working under a different set of wages or other working conditions, regularly and continuously with employees of the employer performing the same kinds of work; (4) contracting out work for the specific purpose of undermining or weakening the Union or depriving employees of employment opportunities. On the other hand, the Referee does not consider that it is *per se* arbitrary, unreasonable, or an act of bad faith to contract out work primarily to reduce production costs. After all, a prime managerial obligation is to conduct an efficient and profitable enterprise, and in doing so serve,.in the long run, the best interests of employees as well as stockholders.

The observations made above do not resolve cases. The facts of the particular case must be examined, especially in relation to the considerations underlying the managerial decision to contract out the work in question. Of necessity, the Referee, having taken the position that the managerial discretion is subject to the implied limitation that it must be exercised in good faith, cannot escape the necessity and responsibility for making a judgment on this matter. As a matter of procedure, it seems evident that management should explain *why* it made the decision, and that it is then appropriate for the Union to attempt either to show that the considerations motivating the decision, as disclosed by management, indicate bad faith, or else that other considerations of a kind indicating bad faith in fact motivated the decision.

The only part of the work undertaken by Don's Window Cleaning Company on October 29 and 30, 1960, which is here protested is floor cleaning. Company testimony is to the effect that this work (in addition to other work) was "let" to the outside contractor, rather than assigned at least in part to bargaining unit employees, on an overtime basis, because of these considerations: (1) The necessity of insuring that the work would be completed over the week-end; (2) lack of certainty as to when the floor washing would take place; (3) lack of certainty as to how many people would be required to do such work; (4) the difficulty of getting unit personnel to come in "on emergencies" or on overtime; (5) the inability of some of the unit personnel to handle "scrubbing machines"; (6) the necessity of coordinating the floor cleaning with the moving and other operations involved; (7) the limitations, under State law, of the number of hours which women could be required to work consecutively; and (8) safety factors. Economic considerations, such as the overtime premium payments which would have been required, were not, apparently, involved in the determination.

The Union does not claim that these considerations were not the factors motivating the decision. Its claim is that the Company judgment concerning some of them (e. g., the difficulty of coordinating the work of Company employees with the work of employees of the outside contractor) was unsound. It seems to the Referee, however, that the factors which management took into account were within the range of considerations which could rationally be taken into account, and that there is no evidence that the total judgment reached was either arbitrary or unreasonable, or failed to take into account the natural desires of unit personnel to avail themselves of an overtime opportunity. On the whole, the conclusion must be that there is no evidence of bad faith.

[The arbitrator then concluded that as to both the "operating mechanisms" and the "stationary contracts," the Company did the work through a subcontractor only because it would be less costly and more quickly completed than if the Company performed the work itself.]

As in the case of the janitorial work, the Referee concludes that the considerations which management took into account, although in these instances primarily or partially economic, indicate that its decisions were not arbitrary or unreasonable, and were not taken in bad faith. No ulterior purpose is indicated in terms either of the status of the Union or of employees in the bargaining unit, nor is there any showing, if this has relevance, that the effect of such subcontracting was to curtail bargaining unit jobs in any substantial way. The Referee repeats that, in his view, cost considerations as a basis for subcontracting, do not of themselves, necessarily indicate bad faith. Manufacturing operations commonly involve some contracting out or purchasing of components, or work thereon, and considerable flexibility in this regard is to be expected in the interest of an efficient and economically sound enterprise. It may fairly be presumed, indeed, that the Company on occasion takes contracts to supply components, or to perform work on components, for other manufacturing concerns. The existence of a substantial degree of managerial discretion, therefore, does not necessarily harm the employees of the Company.

They may actually gain thereby, rather than lose, in their over-all employment opportunities.

———

CARBIDE AND CARBON CHEMICALS CO., 24 Lab.Arb.Rep. 158 (1955). The union protested the subcontracting of certain painting work in 1954, although the company had contracted out over fifty maintenance jobs of various kinds without protest from the union during the preceding eight years. A majority of the tripartite panel denied the grievance. "The Parties were fully aware that this type of work was being contracted out over a period of many years and yet took no action to in any way modify the contractual language. The Board cannot do so now upon the request of one of the Parties."

PURE OIL CO., 38 Lab.Arb.Rep. 1042 (1962). The company in 1962 subcontracted various types of work, including occasional snowplowing together with certain maintenance, roustabout and well-pulling work. Some of these jobs could have been performed by the company's employees; others were non-recurring and would have required management to obtain equipment not then owned by the company. There was no record of subcontracting by the company prior to this time. The arbitrator ruled in favor of the company. "There is a well recognized and accepted statement of management's prerogatives which is that, in the absence of statutory restrictions, the Company has all rights which have not been specifically bargained away in a collective bargaining agreement. Management is restrained only to the extent that federal or state statutes, or a collective bargaining agreement with a union has specifically limited the free exercise of its powers. * * * Since we find no restrictive language in the parties' Agreement, and particularly no evidence that the Company has been seeking to cripple or destroy the Union, we find no basis for sustaining this grievance."

———

Problems for Discussion

1. The *Allis-Chalmers* case involved not only a dispute about whether the subcontracting violated a substantive contractual limitation upon management's power but also a dispute about whether *that* contract issue was intended by the company and the union to be resolved by an arbitrator. The latter issue, known as "substantive arbitrability," was argued to and decided by Arbitrator Smith himself. Is it at all strange for the arbitrator himself to determine whether he has the power to decide the underlying substantive contract dispute? Does the arbitrator's determination that he has jurisdiction predetermine in any way the outcome of the case on the merits? What is the recourse of the union in the event the employer refuses to submit even the issue of substantive arbitrability to the arbitrator? (See pp. 565–85, infra.)

2. As in the *Coca-Cola* case, p. 532 supra, the arbitrator in *Allis-Chalmers* acknowledges that the employer's discretion in operating its business may be subject to limitations which are not spelled out in the labor contract in express terms. Is the implying of such limitations equally appropriate in discipline cases and subcontracting cases? As to subcontracting cases, do you agree with the following observations of the arbitrator in *American Sugar Refining Co.*, 37 Lab.Arb. 334 (1961)?

"Arbitrators are not soothsayers and 'wise men' employed to dispense equity and good will according to their own notions of what is best for the parties, nor are they kings like Solomon with unlimited wisdom or courts of unlimited jurisdiction. Arbitrators are employed to interpret the working agreement as the parties themselves wrote it. * * * When an arbitrator finds that the parties have not dealt with the subject of contracting-out in their working agreement, but that the employer is nevertheless prohibited from contracting-out (a) unless he acts in good faith; (b) unless he acts in conformance with past practice; (c) unless he acts reasonably; (d) unless his act does not deprive a substantial number of employees of employment; (e) unless his acts were dictated by the requirements of the business; (f) if his act is barred by the recognition clause; (g) if his act is barred by the seniority provisions of the working agreement; or (h) if his act violates the spirit of the agreement, the arbitrator may be in outer space and reading the stars instead of the contract." (The arbitrator then denied the union's grievance on the ground that there was no language in the contract which mentioned subcontracting or otherwise limited management's right to operate the business efficiently.)

3. On the other hand, did not the arbitrator in *Allis-Chalmers* give the employer *too much* freedom to subcontract when he suggested that the employer there was free to subcontract when motivated in good faith by a desire to reduce labor costs? Why do not the typical provisions for wages, hours and workweek compel the conclusion that the employer may not lay off a worker and then use a subcontractor to get the same work performed for less (often by the very same worker who is hired by the subcontractor)? See *Continental Tenn. Lines, Inc.*, 72 Lab.Arb. 619 (1979).

4. Could the union have challenged the subcontracting by going to the National Labor Relations Board? What form could such challenge take? If the union were indeed to have a choice of forum for the prosecution of its case—arbitration or Board—what factors should go into making that choice? Should the Board proceed to rule on the case if an arbitrator has not yet done so? (See pp. 645–58, infra.) Should the arbitrator proceed to rule if the Board has not yet done so? See pp. 626–32, infra.)

---

4. *The Effect of Past Practice and Public Law* [6]

It has already been noted, see pp. 513–14, supra, that the "collective bargaining agreement" is not confined to the written terms

6. See Edwards, Labor Arbitration at the Crossroads: The Common Law of the Shop v. External Law, 32 Arb. J. 65 (1977); Feller, The Coming End of Arbitration's Golden Age, in Na-

tional Academy of Arbitrators, 29th Annual Proceedings 97 (1976); McLaughlin, Custom and Past Practice in Labor Arbitration, 18 Arb.J. 205 (1963); Meltzer, Ruminations About

of a document executed by the company and the union. As is demonstrated by the *Coca-Cola* case relating to discipline for cause, see p. 532, supra and the *Allis-Chalmers* case relating to subcontracting, see p. 533 supra, the agreement contains as well a set of unspoken rights and obligations. These rights and obligations go even beyond those which are implied from the express terms. Perhaps the most significant source of these unwritten rules are the customs and usages —or past practices—which represent the accepted way that employees are treated and the production processes are ordered. Since the press of negotiations and the complexity of the rules governing the workplace make it impossible to reduce all of these rules to writing, many of the parties' understandings are expressed only in the habits of the past: a rest break in mid-morning, early close-down of machines at the end of the workweek to allow time for cleaning and servicing, two workers on a task rather than three or one, paid time off to vote on Election Day, distributing overtime opportunities on a rotational basis rather than by seniority, the distribution of turkeys at Thanksgiving. What is the legal effect of these practices? Are they as binding as are the written terms? Are they, to the contrary, modifiable at will? How does one determine which practices are binding and which are not? How and when can otherwise binding past practices be terminated? These issues will be considered in the materials immediately following.

Another source of arbitral principles lying outside the written terms of the contract—and also considered below—are the rules of law laid down by legislatures and courts to regulate the conduct of private persons; some of these rules apply to society generally, such as the broad rules of torts, contracts and criminal law, while others apply to employers and employees, such as the rules regulating industrial safety and health, the freedom of employees to organize and bargain collectively, and the abolition of employment discrimination based upon race, sex, or national origin. What should be the position of the arbitrator when it is argued that these rules of statutory or court-made law modify or actually negate the terms of the written labor agreement?

The following materials can serve only as an introduction to the role of past practices and public law in the construction and application of the collective bargaining agreement.

PHILLIPS PETROLEUM CO.

24 Lab.Arb. 191 (1955).

MERRILL, ARBITRATOR:—For many years, perhaps for more than twenty, Phillips Petroleum Company has furnished electrical

Ideology, Law, and Labor Arbitration, 34 U.Chi.L.Rev. 545 (1967); Mittenthal, Past Practice and the Administration of Collective Bargaining Agreements, 59 Mich.L.Rev. 1017 (1961).

energy, generated at its DeNoya Power Plant, to employees living in and around the DeNoya Plant Camp. Some of these employees lived in company owned houses, which were rented at $4.00 per room per month, including utilities. Others lived in housing owned either by themselves or by others than the Company. To these houses, a flat rate of $1.00 per month is charged for electric service. These arrangements long antedated the achievement of bargaining representation by the local union which is the grievant in this case.

* * *

The contract does not specifically provide for the furnishing of electrical or other service by the Company. However, one provision states, in substance, that present rents for company housing or utility charges shall not be increased, except in connection with a general increase by the Company in such rents and charges. This provision did not appear in the first contract negotiated after the Union achieved its status as representative. It was introduced at some later time, which was not specifically identified at the hearing. Neither were the parties able to enlighten me concerning the nature of the bargaining which led to its inclusion. It appears that its presence in the contract has not made a difference in the wage rates prevailing in the bargaining unit. However, the Union asserted, and the Company did not seem to me seriously to deny, that, in bargaining negotiations, reference has been made to the availability of this service as one of the advantages resulting from employment with the Company in this area. * * *

For some time, conditions surrounding the rendition of this service have been growing unsatisfactory, certainly to the Company, perhaps to some of the "patrons". The Company's selection as Operator of the North Burbank Water Flood Unit has imposed an additional load upon its DeNoya plant. A survey of the situation led to the conclusion that the Company, for economic reasons, should terminate the service from that plant to all employees except those living at the DeNoya Camp, itself. A notice of intention so to do, dated June 18, 1954, was mailed to all such employees, and a definitive notice, specifying November 1 as time of termination, was sent under date of October 21, 1954. * * *

Positions of Parties

The Union, filing this grievance, declines to recognize the propriety of the discontinuance as a unilateral act by the Company. It insists that continued service is called for by the contract; that discontinuance, if desired, should have been bargained for through the procedure prescribed for amending that document; that, in any event, partial discontinuance, since the "discontinued" employees must pay a higher rate to private utilities, amounts to an increased rate for utilities which is not part of a general increase. The Company, on the other hand, contends that the electrical service, not being specifically mentioned in the contract as an emolument of employment, is a mere gratuity, which may be discontinued at any time; and that the contractual reference to charges for rents and utilities is merely a promise that, so long as the Company *does* elect to furnish these advantages, it will do so at a uniform rate to all who *are* served, but without any agreement that they shall be made available to all employees, or to all those who have received service in the past. * * *

Arbitrators' Rulings—* * * In a number of cases, arbitrators have regarded plant practices, even of long standing, as imposing no obligation of continuance on the employer if not embodied specifically in the collective bargaining contract. Le Roi Mfg. Co., 8 L.A. 350 (1947) (milk concession to union); Drug Products Co., 10 L.A. 804 (1948) (travel allowance to two particular employees); Globe-Union, Inc., 18 L.A. 320 (1951) (preparation of time-records by time-keepers rather than employees); American Zinc Co. of Ill., 18 L.A. 827 (1952) (helpers for skilled craftsmen); New York Trap Rock Corp., 19 L.A. 421 (1952) (extra pay for certain type of work). Of these five decisions, it is noteworthy that three are rendered by the same arbitrator, which detracts somewhat from the extent to which they should be regarded as establishing a general body of opinion. In addition, there may be added to this group a decision which ruled it a violation of a contract to change a "long existing practice or custom" without notice, though recognizing that a change on proper notice would be valid. Diamond Alkali Co., 3 L.A. 560 (1946).

On the other hand, a much stronger current of decision regards long standing plant practices, customs and usages as incorporated into the collective bargaining contract, unless expressly negatived by its terms. The theory upon which this view proceeds is expressed best by a few quotations:

> "A union-management contract is far more than words on paper. It is also all the oral understandings, interpretations and mutually acceptable habits of action which have grown up around it over the course of time. * * *

> "If any of these mutually acceptable methods of effectuating the contract become undesirable to either party, it should obtain the consent of the other party to revise the contract, in this larger sense, accordingly. The terms of a contract cannot be unilaterally changed during the time period it covers. * * *" Coca Cola Bottling Co., 9 L.A. 197 (1947) (custom to notify union and allow time for investigation before discharging employee for dishonesty).

"In the absence of a change in the contract, established practices under the old contract are given approval by the execution of the new and become, by construction, a part of the new contract." Republic Steel Corp., 3 L.A. 760 (1946) (computation of seniority). * * *

In addition to the decisions quoted from, many others apply the same doctrine. Goodyear Tire & Rubber Co., 1 L.A. 556 (1946) (wash-up time); International Shoe Co., 2 L.A. 201 (1946) (excuse of employee from Saturday work on account of religious scruples); West Pittston Iron Works, 3 L.A. 137 (1944) (paid lunch period— "plant practices and customs which existed at the time the contract was executed and which the parties did not contemplate changing, are by implication a part of the contract"); Libby, McNeill & Libby, 5 L.A. 564 (1946) (special piecework basis and standby allowances); Franklin Assn. of Chicago, 7 L.A. 614 (1947) (vacation pay, though not specified); Standard Oil Co. (Ind.), 14 L.A. 641 (1950) (job description, fixed by practice and custom); Ryan Aeronautical Co., 17 L.A. 395 (1951) (free milk); John Deere Waterloo Tractor Works, 18 L.A. 276 (1952) (clean-up time allowance to "incentive workers"); General Aniline & Film Corp., 19 L.A. 628 (1952) (job evaluation); International Minerals & Chem. Corp., 20 L.A. 248 (1953) (using production employees on construction work, when available). The principle has been applied against labor as well as against management. Cory Glass Coffee Brewer Co., 4 L.A. 426 (1946).

A third group of cases, recognizing that existing practices are accepted by contracts which do not restrict them, does not incorporate them fully into the contracts. By this view, the employer cannot, at his own volition, discontinue the prior practice. He must negotiate with the bargaining agent concerning his desire for modification or elimination. Western Air Lines, 9 L.A. 419 (1948) (downgrading); General Cable Corp., 17 L.A. 780 (1952) (paid supper time). If negotiations, conducted in good faith, bring no accord, the employer then may act without waiting for the close of the contractual term. Ryan Aeronautical Co., 17 L.A. 395 (1951) (free milk).

While the cases do not indicate that every last detail of existent plant practice is frozen into a collective bargaining agreement, they do not as yet seem clearly to indicate where the line is to be drawn. One arbitrator attempted to distinguish between matters affecting working conditions and gratuities. According to him, matters affecting working conditions are integrally related to time worked, or not worked, while gratuities are not so related. Gratuities may be withdrawn at will; practices as to working conditions become integral parts of the contract. As examples of matters affecting working conditions, he cites paid meal times, washing up periods, rest periods and coffee breaks. As gratuities, he cites parking spaces, music-while-you-work, Thanksgiving turkeys and free coffee. Fawick Airflex Co., 11 L.A. 666 (1948). But a comparison of the illustrations given with the items which various arbitrators have held not to be alterable unilaterally by the employer indicates that his distinction cannot be supported. Certainly, the employer's view that a practice is a gratuity is not decisive. Libby, McNeill & Libby, 5 L.A. 564 (1946); Franklin Assn. of Chicago, 7 L.A. 614 (1947). The test suggested is impracticable, because working time is not the only important consideration in working conditions. Perhaps the best test, though admittedly inexact, is that the usage, to achieve contractual status, must concern a "major condition of employment." General Aniline & Film Corp. 19 L.A. 628 (1952). And see Cox and Dunlop, "The Duty to Bargain Collectively During the Term of an Existing Agreement," 63 Harv.L.Rev. 1097, 1116–1125 (1950).

Conclusion—In the light of the decisions, as recited above, it seems to me that the current of opinion has set strongly in favor of the position that existing practices, in respect to major conditions of employment, are to be regarded as included within a collective bargaining contract, negotiated after the practice has become established and not repudiated or limited by it. This also seems to me the reasonable view, since the negotiators work within the frame of existent practice and must be taken to be conscious of it. Likely, they do not always think it necessary to spell it out. That principle would lead to a sustention of the grievance here involved. However, a still stronger case is presented where the contract, though not expressly embodying the practice, refers to it and contemplates its continuance. Cf. International Harvester Co., 20 L.A. 276 (1953). That, it seems to me, is the situation here. The stipulation respecting rents and utility charges recognizes an existing practice, and, by stipulating against any increase in charges except one of general application, clearly assumes that the practice will continue. I think this is borne out by the references to the practice in collective bargaining discussions and by the part it played in inducing the location of houses. Had this provision been deleted, it would have been an indication that the scope of the contract was being narrowed so as to exclude the practice. Corn Products Ref. Co., 7 L.A. 125 (1947). Cf. Connecticut Power Co., 14 L.A. 951 (1950). But here the stipulation has little significance, unless the service is to be continued, and I think that the principle applied by the arbitrators in the decisions which have been recited before supports the view that such continuance is part of the contractual obligation. * * *

Whatever may be the merits of the "negotiation rule" as applied to practices where the contract is absolutely silent, I am convinced that the "contractual incorporation" rule is the proper one when applied to a contract which contains stipulations based on and assuming the continuance of the existing practice. Any other rule, it seems to me, would defeat the justifiable expectations of the party in whose favor the practice runs. * * *

Remedy—* * * [T]he award will be, and is, that the grievance be sustained, and that the furnishing of electric service to employees outside the DeNoya Camp who have heretofore received such service in accordance with the established practice, at the rate of $1.00 per month, is declared to be a continuing obligation under the contract; that the Company shall make good its obligations to such employees to whom it has discontinued service by paying to them the difference between $1.00 per month and the rates actually charged by the utilities from whom service has been secured; that, for the future, the Company shall have the option either of restoring the service or of reimbursing the employees concerned in the same manner as provided for past service, it being understood that nothing in this award shall preclude the Company from exercising the privilege, secured to it by the contract, of instituting a general increase in its charge for this service, which, of course, must be applicable to all recipients.

Problems for Discussion

1. For twenty years, the Torrington Company had permitted its employees to take one hour off from work, with pay, to vote on Election Day. The policy was instituted unilaterally, and the Company continued it after the Metal Products Union was selected as the bargaining representative, even though the labor contract made no mention of it. In December 1980, when Mr. Torrington announced that this benefit would be discontinued, the Union sent a written protest. As the contract drew toward its expiration date of September 30, 1981, the parties began to negotiate a new agreement and at the first meeting, Mr. Torrington informed the Union that he did not intend to reestablish the Election Day benefit. The Union responded by including a contrary provision in its written demands at a meeting in early September. Later that month, both parties exchanged written proposals that the old contract be continued with specific amendments, but neither set of proposals mentioned the Election Day policy. When a new contract was signed in October 1981, it made no mention of the Election Day benefit. The first week in November, Mr. Torrington announced once again that there would be no paid time off to vote. The Union filed a grievance, which it has taken to arbitration. The labor contract provides for arbitration of disputes regarding "the interpretation or application of any provisions in this contract," and also provides that the arbitrator "shall have no power to add to, delete from or modify, in any way, any of the provisions of this agreement."

The Company has argued to the arbitrator that the grievance is not arbitrable and that if it is arbitrable it should be dismissed on the merits. How should the arbitrator rule? See Torrington Co. v. Metal Products Workers Local 1645, 362 F.2d 677 (2d Cir. 1966), at p. 597 infra.

2. Examine carefully each of the theories set forth in *Phillips Petroleum* for determining when past practices are binding on the employer and when they may be unilaterally terminated. On each of these theories, how should the arbitrator rule if an employer unilaterally discontinues the following practices of long standing? (a) Three workers have worked together to assemble a component which now, because of new technology, can be assembled by only one. (b) Workers have been given five minutes (paid) at the end of the workday to wash up, but now the use of computerized technology has eliminated the "dirty" feature of their work. (c) A Christmas bonus has been given for many years, measured by one-half of one week's wages for each employee. (d) Employees working in a plant utilizing precious metals, who were formerly permitted to leave the plant without a search, are new being subjected to electronic detection devices, in light of a substantial increase in pilferage of company materials.

MITTENTHAL, THE ROLE OF LAW IN ARBITRATION *

National Academy of Arbitrators, Proceedings of the
Twenty-First Annual Meeting 42 (1968).

* * * My concern here is with what arbitrators should do when asked to consider the law in resolving a grievance dispute.

* * * Howlett's view is based in part on the belief that "all applicable law" is, *by implication,* incorporated in "every agreement." Some courts and some arbitrators have drawn this implication. * * *

I find no merit in such an argument. * * * A judge has two functions to perform. He must interpret the contract; he must also determine the legal operation of the contract, that is, the legal remedies (if any) for its enforcement. He is, in other words, "concerned not only with the [contract] but also with the law that limits and governs it." It is only in connection with the legal operation of the contract that it is necessary for the judge to refer to any applicable constitution or statute. Realistically, what happens is that he interprets the contract and then imposes upon his interpretation the relevant rules of law. Given this view of judicial decision-making, there is no need to imply that the law is incorporated in the contract.

* * * [J]udges concern themselves with applicable law because they exercise the coercive power of the state and must deter-

---

mine the legal operation of the contract. Arbitrators, unlike judges, are not an arm of the state and do not determine the legal operation of the collective bargaining contract. We determine contract rights and questions of interpretation and application, nothing more. We are the servants of the parties, not the public. We derive our powers from the contract, not from the superior authority of the law. Hence, even if courts had a rational basis for implying that law is part of the contract, arbitrators would have no justification for doing the same. * * *

The typical contract does mention the law. It is not unusual for the parties to refer to statutory law regarding union security,[7] checkoff,[8] reemployment of veterans,[9] and supplemental unemployment benefits.[10] Those who draft such provisions are certainly aware of the impact of law upon employee rights. Their limited reference to the law suggests that they intend a limited role for the law. Their failure to state, in these circumstances, that all applicable law is part of the contract must have some significance. Thus, Howlett's implication seems inconsistent with the language found in most contracts.

Finally, even if the implication could somehow hurdle all of these objections, it would be confronted by the arbitration clause. Ordinarily, the arbitrator is confined to the interpretation and application of the agreement and forbidden to add to or modify the terms of the agreement. If he rules that the law is part of the contract, he must read into the parties' contract a new and indeterminate set of rights and duties. By doing so, however, he would be adding to the terms of the contract and thus ignoring the limitations on his authority. The purpose of a narrow arbitration clause is to limit us to questions of private rights which arise out of the contract. That purpose would certainly be defeated if we were to draw an implication which would transform arbitration into a forum for the vindication of not just private rights but public rights as well. In the absence of any evidence that the parties intend such a drastic departure from the normal arbitration system, the implication should be rejected.

7. E. g., "the foregoing provisions [union membership] shall be effective in accordance with and consistent with applicable provisions of federal and state law."

8. E. g., "the provisions of this [checkoff clause] shall be effective in accordance with and consistent with applicable provisions of federal law."

9. E. g., "the Company shall accord to each employee who applies for reem- ployment after conclusion of his military service with the United States such reemployment rights as he shall then be entitled to under then existing statutes."

10. E. g., "the [SUB] Plan and all rights and duties thereunder, shall be governed, construed and administered in accordance with the laws of the State of Ohio."

For these reasons, I find nothing in the collective bargaining contract to support the implication that the law is incorporated in the contract.

C. Where Contract and Law Conflict

Let me turn now to more specific problems. What should an arbitrator do where the contract and the law conflict, where an award affirming a clear contract obligation would require either party to violate a statutory command?

Professor Cox gave us an excellent example of this problem at an earlier meeting. He noted that after World War II a conflict developed between the Selective Service Act and contract seniority. This statute was interpreted by the Supreme Court to require employers to give veterans preference over nonveterans in the event of layoffs during the first year after their discharge from the armed forces. The typical contract gave veterans only the seniority they would have had if they had not been drafted. A dispute arose when an employer, in reducing the work force, retained a veteran and laid off a nonveteran even though he had more contract seniority. The nonveteran grieved, relying upon the contract. The employer defended his action, relying upon the law. Who should prevail?

There are two possible points of view. Cox tells us to deny this grievance—that is, to respect the law and ignore the contract.[11] He argues that:

> * * *   The parties to collective bargaining cannot avoid negotiating and carrying out their agreement within the existing legal framework. It is either futile or grossly unjust to make an award directing an employer to take action which the law forbids—futile because if the employer challenges the award the union cannot enforce it; unjust because if the employer complies he subjects himself to punishment by civil authority.

Furthermore, such an award demeans the arbitration process by inviting noncompliance, appeals to the courts, and reversal of the award.

Professor Meltzer, on the other hand, tells us to grant the grievance—that is, to respect the contract and ignore the law. His

11. Most arbitrators followed this course and held the statute to be controlling. See, e. g., International Harvester Co., 22 L.A. 583 (1954); Dow Chemical Co., 1 L.A. 70 (1945). Another example of this problem would be a situation where the contract requires the employer or the union to discriminate against employees in a manner prohibited by the NLRA.

argument includes three main points, each of which deserves some comment.

First, Meltzer says:

> There is * * * no reason to credit arbitrators with any competence, let alone any special expertise, with respect to the law, as distinguished from the agreement. A good many arbitrators lack any legal training at all, and even lawyer-arbitrators do not necessarily hold themselves out as knowledgeable about the broad range of statutory and administrative materials that may be relevant in labor arbitrations.

No one can quarrel with this description. Arbitrators are not omniscient. Most of us do not have the time, the energy, or the occasion to become truly knowledgeable about the law. But some of our members—Smith, Aaron, Cox, Meltzer himself, to name but a few—surely possess the necessary expertise. Such men are well equipped to decide grievance disputes which raise both contractual and legal questions. It is not unusual for the parties to fit the arbitrator to the dispute, to choose a man qualified by experience or learning for the particular task involved. An example of this is the use of industrial engineers to arbitrate time-study or incentive issues. There is no reason why the parties, when confronted by a difficult legal question, cannot exercise this same selectivity in finding a man with experience in both the contract and the law.

Second, Meltzer says:

> * * * an analogy to administrative tribunals is instructive. Such agencies consider themselves bound by the statutes entrusted to their administration and leave to the courts challenges to the constitutional validity of such statutes. Arbitrators should in general accord a similar respect to the agreement that is the source of their authority and should leave to the courts or other official tribunals the determination of whether the agreement contravenes a higher law.

This analogy is appealing. But another analogy can be constructed to support a different conclusion. For example, an administrative agency would refuse to enforce the terms of its enabling statute in a given case if enforcement would require conduct that is unlawful under some other statute. An arbitrator should likewise refuse to enforce a particular contract provision if enforcement would require action forbidden by the law. My point is not that Meltzer's analogy is wrong but rather that his analogy, by itself, is not sufficient reason to adopt his point of view.

Third, Meltzer says that "the parties typically call on an arbitrator to construe and not to destroy their agreement." His position is that an arbitrator is not construing the contract if he defers to the law and ignores the terms of the contract. He would adhere strictly to the contract even where it means requiring one of the parties to act unlawfully.

This is really the crux of the problem. No one would disagree with Meltzer's view that the arbitrator is supposed to construe, rather than destroy, the contract. The question is what exactly is the arbitrator doing when he takes notice of the conflict between the law and the contract and refuses to order the commission of an act required by contract but forbidden by law? Is he destroying the contract by refusing to issue such an order? I do not think so. A strong case can be made for the proposition that the arbitrator, when exercising this kind of restraint, is ordinarily construing the contract.

Consider some of the language in the typical contract. First, it is not unusual to find a "separability" or "saving" clause. Such a clause says that if any contract provision "shall be or become invalid or unenforceable" by reason of the law, "such invalidity or unenforceability shall not affect" the rest of the contract. The parties thus intend to isolate any invalidity so as to preserve the overall integrity of the contract. But they also recognize the fact that a contract provision can be held "invalid" or "unenforceable" because of a state or federal statute. They do not wish to be bound by an invalid provision. The implication seems clear that the arbitrator should not enforce a provision which is clearly unenforceable under the law.

Second, it is not unusual to find an arbitration clause which says the arbitrator's awards will be "final and binding" upon the employer, the union, and the employees concerned. If the arbitrator ignores the law and orders the employer to commit an unlawful act, he invites noncompliance and judicial intervention.[12] He knows that his award, under such circumstances, is not going to be "final and binding." Either the employer asks a court to reverse the award, or the employer refuses to comply and the union asks a court to affirm the award. In either event, the dispute continues beyond the grievance procedure. That could hardly be what the parties intended when they adopted arbitration as the final step in the grievance procedure as the means of terminating the dispute. The implication seems clear that the arbitrator must

---

12. A court would certainly set aside such an award. See Smith and Jones, "The Supreme Court and Labor Dispute Arbitration: The Emerging Federal Law," 63 Mich.L.Rev. 751, 804 (1965).

consider the law in this kind of situation if his award is to have the finality which the contract contemplates.[13]

Thus, it may well be that contracts can be construed to justify resort to the law to avoid an award which would require unlawful conduct.

On balance, the relevant considerations support Cox's view. The arbitrator should "look to see whether sustaining the grievance would require conduct the law forbids or would enforce an illegal contract; if so, the arbitrator should not sustain the grievance." This principle, however, should be carefully limited. It does not suggest that "an arbitrator should pass upon all the parties' legal rights and obligations" or that "an arbitrator should refuse to give effect to a contract provision merely because the courts would not enforce it." Thus, although the arbitrator's award may *permit* conduct forbidden by law but sanctioned by contract, it should not *require* conduct forbidden by law even though sanctioned by contract.

*   *   *

Problems for Discussion

1. The collective bargaining agreement provides: "In the interest of efficiency, order and cleanliness, no employee shall be permitted at any time anywhere on company property to distribute literature of any kind. Violators of this rule shall be subject to discipline." Three weeks prior to the election of union officers, Ralph Rebel stationed himself in the company parking lot prior to the beginning of his shift, and there distributed leaflets attacking the record of the incumbent union officials and urging the election of an insurgent slate of candidates. He was seen by a representative of the union, who informed him of the no-distribution rule in the labor contract. At the end of his shift, Rebel stationed himself in the parking lot once again, and distributed the leaflets. The union representative insisted that Rebel be disciplined, but the company has refused. The union filed a grievance, and the case is now before an arbitrator. The company has argued that the contract provision is unlawful on its face and that it cannot serve as the basis for a grievance. It therefore asks either that the grievance be declared nonarbitrable, or else that if the arbitrator reaches the merits she should rule against the union. What decision should the arbitrator render?

2. The collective bargaining agreement provides that job openings will be posted for bids and that the job will be awarded to the bidding

---

13. Note, however, that even if the arbitrator respects the law and refuses to order the employer to commit an unlawful act, the union might ask a court to set aside the award on the ground that the arbitrator exceeded his authority under the contract. No award is "final and binding" in the sense that it precludes parties from going to court and attempting to reverse the award on certain limited grounds.

employee with the most seniority with the company and who is able to perform the job. The company and the union have also for many years informally classified jobs in the plant as A jobs (for men only), B jobs (for women only) and C jobs (open to either men or women employees). When an A job recently opened up, a bid was submitted by Linda Rosario, who possessed more company seniority than the most senior male employee bidding on the job; nonetheless, the company invoked the tradition of sex-classified jobs and awarded the job to the most senior qualified male. The company asserted (and the union conceded) that the job has been classified as an A job because it requires a substantial amount of lifting of heavy cartons. Ms. Rosario filed a grievance protesting the failure to assign her the job—or the failure to permit her to demonstrate that she is capable of performing the job—and the union has processed her grievance to arbitration. The company claims that the past practice has been uniformly and notoriously applied so that it is binding on both parties, and also claims that the practice is consistent with, indeed dictated by, a state law enacted in 1932 barring the assignment of women to this kind of work. The union claims that the practice and the state law have been superseded by Title VII of the Civil Rights Act of 1964 which bars discrimination in working conditions on the basis of sex, and argues therefore that the only applicable rule concerning entitlement to promotions is the seniority provision of the labor contract, which requires the promotion of Ms. Rosario. Outline the opinion that the arbitrator should write in such a case.

C. JUDICIAL ENFORCEMENT OF COLLECTIVE AGREEMENTS [14]

Prior to the enactment of Section 301 of the Labor Management Relations Act in 1947 the State courts alone had jurisdiction over suits for breach of a collective bargaining agreement (except where there was diversity of citizenship), and any substantive rights and remedies were determined by State law. Legal rights and remedies were uncertain or ineffective or both, for a variety of reasons.

A union was not treated as a legal entity. In most jurisdictions a class action was necessary for the members to sue or be sued. Execution of a money judgment would have to be levied upon the individual property of the members.

14. See Bickel & Wellington, Legislative Purpose and the Judicial Process: The Lincoln Mills Case, 71 Harv.L.Rev. 1 (1957); Lesnick, Arbitration as a Limit on the Discretion of Management, Union, and NLRB: The Year's Major Developments, N.Y.U. 18th Annual Conf. on Labor 7 (1966); Smith & Jones, The Impact of the Emerging Federal Law of Grievance Arbitration on Judges, Arbitrators, and Parties, 52 Va.L.Rev. 831 (1966).

A significant and highly controversial appraisal of labor arbitration and the role of the courts in contract enforcement can be found in P. Hays, Labor Arbitration: A Dissenting View (1966); the author was an arbitrator himself, as well as a professor of labor law and later a federal circuit judge. The book is critically reviewed in Aaron, 42 Wash.L.Rev. 969 (1967); Dunau, 35 Amer.Scholar 774 (1966); Wallen, 81 Harv.L.Rev. 507 (1967).

There was grave doubt whether a collective agreement was enforceable at all and, if so, by and against whom it was enforceable.[15] One view was that a collective bargaining contract was only a "gentlemen's agreement" without legal effect. *E. g.*, Young v. Canadian No. Ry., [1931] A.C. 83. A second analysis allowed individual employees to sue the employer as third party beneficiaries of promises made by the employer to the union. *E. g.*, Yazoo & M.V.R. Co. v. Sideboard, 161 Miss. 4, 133 So. 669 (1931).

A third view was that the union negotiated as agent for its' members (or perhaps all the employees) as principals, so that the legal obligations ran directly between employees and employer. *E. g.*, A. R. Barnes & Co. v. Berry, 169 F. 225 (6th Cir. 1909). Under this view, presumably only the employees and employer could sue or be sued and the employer and any individual employee could negotiate different terms and conditions of employment. But see J. I. Case Co. v. NLRB, p. 364 supra. A fourth view argued that the agreement between employer and labor union had the effect of a custom which was to be presumed to be incorporated into each individual employment contract unless the presumption was negated. Piercy v. Louisville & N. Ry. Co., 198 Ky. 477, 248 S.W. 1042 (1923). The consequences of this view would seem to be much the same as the results of an agency analysis.

In the national debate upon labor policy leading to enactment of the Taft Hartley Act many employers and trade associations pressed for a law that would make collective bargaining agreements binding on unions. But disinterested observers were divided over the wisdom of giving the law a role to play in the enforcement of collective bargaining agreements. Dean Harry Shulman, a wise and experienced arbitrator and public member of many labor panels, urged keeping law out of the administration of collective bargaining agreements: [16]

> "[A]rbitration is an integral part of the system of self-government. And the system is designed to aid management in its quest for efficiency, to assist union leadership in its participation in the enterprise, and to secure justice

15. The early literature discussing the theoretical nature of collective bargaining contracts and individual hires is voluminous. *E. g.*, Burstein, *Enforcement of Collective Agreements by the Courts*, in 6 N.Y.U.Conf. on Labor 31 (1953); Gregory, *The Collective Bargaining Agreement: Its Nature and Scope*, 1949 Wash. U.L.Q. 3; Lenhoff, *The Present Status of Collective Contracts in the American Legal System*, 39 Mich.L.Rev. 1109 (1941); Rice, *Collective Labor Agreements in American Law*, 44 Harv.L.Rev. 572 (1931); Warns, *The Nature of the Collective Bargaining Agreement*, 3 Miami L.Q. 235 (1949); Witmer, *Collective Labor Agreements in the Courts*, 48 Yale L.J. 195 (1938); Note, 3 Buffalo L.Rev. 270 (1954).

16. Shulman, Reason, Contract, and Law in Labor Relations, 68 Harv.L. Rev. 999 (1955).

for the employees. It is a means of making collective bargaining work and thus preserving private enterprise in a free government. When it works fairly well, it does not need the sanction of the law of contracts or the law of arbitration. It is only when the system breaks down completely that the courts' aid in these respects is invoked. But the courts cannot, by occasional sporadic decision, restore the parties' continuing relationship; and their intervention in such cases may seriously affect the going systems of self-government. When their autonomous system breaks down, might not the parties better be left to the usual methods for adjustment of labor disputes rather than to court actions on the contract or on the arbitration award? I suggest that the law stay out—but, mind you, not the lawyers."

Professor Cox, writing shortly after LMRA Section 301 became law, expressed a somewhat different view:

"Litigation will not establish sound industrial relations. One unfortunate consequence of the enactment of Section 301 may be that it will temporarily encourage some employers to rush to court. It is comparatively rare, however, for persons to exercise their right to sue when, as a practical matter, they are bound in a continuing personal or commercial relationship, and there seems no reason to suppose that the practice would be different in the industrial world. But even though judicial processes are rarely invoked to enforce collective bargaining agreements, the voluntary acceptance of the mutual responsibilities to which collective bargaining gives rise should be encouraged by the law's recognition of the binding character of such agreements.[17]

"It is difficult to make an accurate appraisal, but casual observation leads me to the conclusion that in the overwhelming proportion of cases employers and labor unions accept arbitration in good faith and scrupulously comply with arbitration agreements and awards. Yet for a few years longer we will be unable to rely on honesty and good will as the sanction for all undertakings, and the absence of a statutory remedy allows any party with preponderant economic power to disregard the grievance procedures if he chooses. If a decline in business activity should reduce the economic power of unions, more companies might succumb to the temptation to refuse to arbi-

17. Cox, Some Aspects of the Labor Management Relations Act, 1947, 61 Harv.L.Rev. 274, 313 (1948).

trate doubtful cases. Conversely, it is not outside the realm of possibility for a union with a stranglehold on a business to assert its economic power in disregard of the agreement.[18] "

TEXTILE WORKERS UNION v. LINCOLN MILLS OF ALABAMA

Supreme Court of the United States, 1957.
353·U.S. 448, 77 S.Ct. 923, 1 L.Ed.2d 972.

MR. JUSTICE DOUGLAS delivered the opinion of the Court.

Petitioner-union entered into a collective bargaining agreement in 1953 with respondent-employer, the agreement to run one year and from year to year thereafter, unless terminated on specified notices. The agreement provided that there would be no strikes or work stoppages and that grievances would be handled pursuant to a specified procedure. The last step in the grievance procedure—a step that could be taken by either party—was arbitration.

This controversy involves several grievances that concern work loads and work assignments. The grievances were processed through the various steps in the grievance procedure and were finally denied by the employer. The union requested arbitration, and the employer refused. Thereupon the union brought this suit in the District Court to compel arbitration.

The District Court concluded that it had jurisdiction and ordered the employer to comply with the grievance arbitration provisions of the collective bargaining agreement. The Court of Appeals reversed by a divided vote. 230 F.2d 81. * * *

There has been considerable litigation involving § 301 [of the Labor Management Relations Act of 1947] and courts have construed it differently. There is one view that § 301(a) merely gives federal district courts jurisdiction in controversies that involve labor organizations in industries affecting commerce, without regard to diversity of citizenship or the amount in controversy. Under that view § 301(a) would not be the source of substantive law; it would neither supply federal law to resolve these controversies nor turn the federal judges to state law for answers to the questions. Other courts—the overwhelming number of them—hold that § 301 (a) is more than jurisdictional—that it authorizes federal courts to fashion a body of federal law for the enforcement of these collective bargaining agreements and includes within that federal law specific

---

18. Cox, Grievance Arbitration in the Federal Courts, 67 Harv.L.Rev. 591, 605–606 (1954).

performance of promises to arbitrate grievances under collective bargaining agreements. Perhaps the leading decision representing that point of view is the one rendered by Judge Wyzanski in Textile Workers Union of America (C.I.O.) v. American Thread Co., D.C., 113 F. Supp. 137. That is our construction of § 301(a), which means that the agreement to arbitrate grievance disputes, contained in this collective bargaining agreement, should be specifically enforced.

From the face of the Act it is apparent that § 301(a) and § 301 (b) supplement one another. Section 301(b) makes it possible for a labor organization, representing employees in an industry affecting commerce, to sue and be sued as an entity in the federal courts. Section 301(b) in other words provides the procedural remedy lacking at common law. Section 301(a) certainly does something more than that. Plainly, it supplies the basis upon which the federal district courts may take jurisdiction and apply the procedural rule of § 301- (b). The question is whether § 301(a) is more than jurisdictional.

The legislative history of § 301 is somewhat cloudy and confusing. But there are a few shafts of light that illuminate our problem.

The bills, as they passed the House and the Senate, contained provisions which would have made the failure to abide by an agreement to arbitrate an unfair labor practice. S.Rep. No. 105, 80th Cong., 1st Sess., pp. 20–21, 23; H.R.Rep. No. 245, 80th Cong., 1st Sess., p. 21. This feature of the law was dropped in Conference. As the Conference's Report stated, "Once parties have made a collective bargaining contract, the enforcement of that contract should be left to the usual processes of the law and not to the National Labor Relations Board." H.Conf.Rep. No. 510, 80th Cong., 1st Sess., p. 42.

Both the Senate and the House took pains to provide for "the usual processes of the law" by provisions which were the substantial equivalent of § 301(a) in its present form. Both the Senate Report and the House Report indicate a primary concern that unions as well as employees should be bound to collective bargaining contracts. But there was also a broader concern—a concern with a procedure for making such agreements enforceable in the courts by either party. * * *

Congress was also interested in promoting collective bargaining that ended with agreements not to strike. The Senate Report, supra, p. 16 states:

"If unions can break agreements with relative impunity, then such agreements do not tend to stabilize industrial relations. The execution of an agreement does not by itself promote industrial peace. The chief advantage which an employer can reasonably expect from a collective labor agreement is assurance of uninterrupted operation during the term of the agreement. Without some effective method of assuring freedom from economic warfare for the term of the agreement, there is little reason why an employer would desire to sign such a contract.

"Consequently, to encourage the making of agreements and to promote industrial peace through faithful performance by the parties, collective agreements affecting interstate commerce should be enforceable in the Federal courts. Our amendment would provide for suits by unions as legal entities and against unions as legal entities in the Federal courts in disputes affecting commerce."

Thus collective bargaining contracts were made "equally binding and enforceable on both parties." Id., p. 15. As stated in the House Report, supra, p. 6, the new provision "makes labor organizations equally responsible with employers for contract violation and provides for suit by either against the other in the United States district courts." To repeat, the Senate Report, supra, p. 17, summed up the philosophy of § 301 as follows: "Statutory recognition of the collective agreement as a valid, binding, and enforceable contract is a logical and necessary step. It will promote a higher degree of responsibility upon the parties to such agreements, and will thereby promote industrial peace."

Plainly the agreement to arbitrate grievance disputes is the *quid pro quo* for an agreement not to strike. Viewed in this light, the legislation does more than confer jurisdiction in the federal courts over labor organizations. It expresses a federal policy that federal courts should enforce these agreements on behalf of or against labor organizations and that industrial peace can be best obtained only in that way. * * *

It seems, therefore, clear to us that Congress adopted a policy which placed sanctions behind agreements to arbitrate grievance disputes, by implication rejecting the common-law rule, discussed in Red Cross Line v. Atlantic Fruit Co., 264 U.S. 109, 44 S.Ct. 274, 68 L.Ed. 582, against enforcement of executory agreements to arbitrate. We would undercut the Act and defeat its policy if we read § 301 narrowly as only conferring jurisdiction over labor organizations.

The question then is, what is the substantive law to be applied in suits under § 301(a)? We conclude that the substantive law to apply in suits under § 301(a) is federal law which the courts must fashion from the policy of our national labor laws. See Mendelsohn, Enforceability of Arbitration Agreements Under Taft-Hartley Section 301, 66 Yale L.J. 167. The Labor Management Relations Act expressly furnishes some substantive law. It points out what the parties may or may not do in certain situations. Other problems will lie in the penumbra of express statutory mandates. Some will lack express statutory sanction but will be solved by looking at the policy of the legislation and fashioning a remedy that will effectuate that policy. The range of judicial inventiveness will be determined by the nature of the problem. See Board of Commissioners of Jackson County v. United States, 308 U.S. 343, 351, 60 S.Ct. 285, 288, 84 L.Ed. 313. Federal interpretation of the federal law will govern, not state law. Cf. Jerome v. United States, 318 U.S. 101, 104, 63 S.Ct. 483, 485, 87 L.Ed. 640. But state law, if compatible with the purpose of § 301, may be resorted to in order to find the rule that will best effectuate the federal policy. See Board of Commissioners of Jackson County v. United States, supra, 308 U.S. at pages 351–352, 60 S.Ct. at pages 288–289. Any state law applied, however, will be absorbed as federal law and will not be an independent source of private rights.

It is not uncommon for federal courts to fashion federal law where federal rights are concerned. See Clearfield Trust Co. v. United States, 318 U.S. 363, 366–367, 63 S.Ct. 573, 574–575, 87 L.Ed. 838; National Metropolitan Bank v. United States, 323 U.S. 454, 65 S.Ct. 354, 89 L.Ed. 383. Congress has indicated by § 301(a) the purpose to follow that course here. There is no constitutional difficulty. Article III, § 2 extends the judicial power to cases "arising under * * * the Laws of the United States * * *." The power of Congress to regulate these labor-management controversies under the Commerce Clause is plain. Houston East & West Texas R. Co. v. United States, 234 U.S. 342, 34 S.Ct. 833, 58 L.Ed. 1341; National Labor Relations Board v. Jones & Laughlin Corp., 301 U.S. 1, 57 S.Ct. 615, 81 L.Ed. 893. A case or controversy arising under § 301(a) is, therefore, one within the purview of judicial power as defined in Article III.

The question remains whether jurisdiction to compel arbitration of grievance disputes is withdrawn by the Norris-LaGuardia Act, 47 Stat. 70, 29 U.S.C. § 101 et seq., 29 U.S.C.A. § 101 et seq. Section 7 of that Act prescribes stiff procedural requirements for issuing an injunction in a labor dispute. The kinds of acts which had given rise to abuse of the power to enjoin are listed in § 4. The failure to arbitrate was not a part and parcel of the abuses against which the Act was aimed. Section 8 of the Norris-LaGuardia Act does, indeed, indicate a congressional policy toward settlement of labor disputes by arbitration, for it denies injunctive relief to any person who has failed to make "every reasonable effort" to settle the dispute by negotiation, mediation, or "voluntary arbitration." Though a literal reading might bring the dispute within the terms of the Act (see Cox, Grievance Arbitration in the Federal Courts, 67 Harv.L.Rev. 591, 602–604), we see no justification in policy for restricting § 301(a) to damage suits, leaving specific performance of a contract to arbitrate grievance disputes to the inapposite procedural requirements of that Act. * * * The congressional policy in favor of the enforcement of agreements to arbitrate grievance disputes being clear, there is no reason to submit them to the requirements of § 7 of the Norris-LaGuardia Act. * * *

MR. JUSTICE BLACK took no part in the consideration or decision of this case.

MR. JUSTICE BURTON, whom MR. JUSTICE HARLAN joins, concurring in the result.

This suit was brought in a United States District Court under § 301 of the Labor Management Relations Act of 1947, 61 Stat. 156, 29 U.S.C. § 185, 29 U.S.C.A. § 185, seeking specific enforcement of the arbitration provisions of a collective-bargaining contract. * * * Having jurisdiction over the suit, the court was not powerless to fashion an appropriate federal remedy. The power to decree specific performance of a collectively bargained agreement to arbitrate finds its source in § 301 itself, and in a Federal District Court's inherent equitable powers, nurtured by a congressional policy to encourage and enforce labor arbitration in industries affecting commerce.

I do not subscribe to the conclusion of the Court that the substantive law to be applied in a suit under § 301 is federal law. At the same time, I agree with Judge Magruder in International Brotherhood v. W. L. Mead, Inc., 1 Cir., 230 F.2d 576, that some federal rights may necessarily be involved in a § 301 case, and hence that the constitutionality of § 301 can be upheld as a congressional grant to Federal District Courts of what has been called "protective jurisdiction."

[MR. JUSTICE FRANKFURTER dissented.]

LOCAL 174, TEAMSTERS v. LUCAS FLOUR CO.

Supreme Court of the United States, 1962.
369 U.S. 95, 82 S.Ct. 571, 7 L.Ed.2d 593.

MR. JUSTICE STEWART delivered the opinion of the Court.

The petitioner and the respondent (which we shall call the union and the employer) were parties to a collective bargaining contract within the purview of the National Labor Relations Act, 29 U.S.C.A. § 151 et seq. The contract contained the following provisions, among others:

"ARTICLE II

"The Employer reserves the right to discharge any man in his employ if his work is not satisfactory.

*   *   *   *   *   *   *   *   *   *

"ARTICLE XIV

"Should any difference as to the true interpretation of this agreement arise, same shall be submitted to a Board of Arbitration of two members, one representing the firm, and one representing the Union. If said members cannot agree, a third member, who must be a disinterested party shall be selected, and the decision of the said Board of Arbitration shall be binding. It is further agreed by both parties hereto that during such arbitration, there shall be no suspension of work.

"Should any difference arise between the employer and the employee, same shall be submitted to arbitration by both parties. Failing to agree, they shall mutually appoint a third person whose decision shall be final and binding."

In May of 1958 an employee named Welsch was discharged by the employer after he had damaged a new fork lift truck by running it off a loading platform and onto some railroad tracks. When a business agent of the union protested, he was told by a representative of the employer that Welsch had been discharged because of unsatisfactory work. The union thereupon called a strike to force the employer to rehire Welsch. The strike lasted eight days. After the strike was over, the issue of Welsch's discharge was submitted to arbitration. Some five months later the Board of Arbitration rendered a decision, ruling that Welsch's work had been unsatisfactory, that his unsatisfactory work had been the reason for his discharge, and that he was not entitled to reinstatement as an employee.

In the meantime, the employer had brought this suit against the union in the Superior Court of King County, Washington, asking damages for business losses caused by the strike. After a trial that court entered a judgment in favor of the employer in the amount of $6,501.60. On appeal the judgment was affirmed by Department One of the Supreme Court of Washington. * * * Expressly applying principles of state law, the court reasoned that the strike was a violation of the collective bargaining contract, because it was an attempt to coerce the employer to forego his contractual right to discharge an employee for unsatisfactory work. We granted certiorari to consider questions of federal labor law which this case presents. 365 U.S. 868, 81 S.Ct. 902, 5 L.Ed.2d 859. * * *

[For the reasons stated in Charles Dowd Box Co. v. Courtney, 368 U.S. 502, 82 S.Ct. 519, 7 L.Ed.2d 489 (1962)] we hold that the Washington Supreme Court was correct in ruling that it had jurisdiction over this controversy. There remain for consideration two other issues, one of them implicated but not specifically decided in Dowd Box. Was the Washington court free, as it thought, to decide this controversy within the limited horizon of its local law? If not, does applicable federal law require a result in this case different from that reached by the state court? * * *

It was apparently the theory of the Washington court, that, although Textile Workers Union v. Lincoln Mills, 353 U.S. 448, 77 S.Ct. 912, 1 L.Ed.2d 972, requires the federal courts to fashion, from the policy of our national labor laws, a body of federal law for the enforcement of collective bargaining agreements, nonetheless, the courts of the States remain free to apply individualized local rules when called upon to enforce such agreements. This view cannot be accepted. The dimensions of § 301 require the conclusion that substantive principles of federal labor law must be paramount in the area covered by the statute. Comprehensiveness is inherent in the process by which the law is to be formulated under the mandate of Lincoln Mills, requiring issues raised in suits of a kind covered by § 301 to be decided according to the precepts of federal labor policy.

More important, the subject matter of § 301(a) "is peculiarly one that calls for uniform law." Pennsylvania R. Co. v. Public Service Comm., 250 U.S. 566, 569, 40 S.Ct. 36, 37, 64 L.Ed. 1142; see Cloverleaf Butter Co. v. Patterson, 315 U.S. 148, 167–169, 62 S.Ct. 491, 501–503, 86 L.Ed. 754. The possibility that individual contract terms might have different meanings under state and federal law would inevitably exert a disruptive influence upon both the negotiation and administration of collective agreements. Because neither party could be certain of the rights which it had obtained or conceded, the process of negotiating an agreement would be made immeasurably more difficult by the necessity of trying to formulate contract provisions in such a way as to contain the same meaning under two or more systems of law which might someday be invoked in enforcing the contract. Once the collective bargain was made, the possibility of conflicting substantive interpretation under competing legal systems would tend to stimulate and prolong disputes as to its interpretation. Indeed, the existence of possibly conflicting legal concepts might substantially impede the parties' willingness to agree to contract terms providing for final arbitral or judicial resolution of disputes.

The importance of the area which would be affected by separate systems of substantive law makes the need for a single body of federal law particularly compelling. The ordering and adjusting of competing interests through a process of free and voluntary collective bargaining is the keystone of the federal scheme to promote industrial peace. State law which frustrates the effort of Congress to stimulate the smooth functioning of that process thus strikes at the very core of federal labor policy. With due regard to the many factors which bear upon competing state and federal interests in this area, California v. Zook, 336 U.S. 725, 730–731, 69 S.Ct. 841, 843–844, 93 L.Ed. 1005; Rice v. Santa Fe Elevator Corp., 331 U.S. 218, 230–231, 67 S.Ct. 1146, 1152, 91 L.Ed. 1447, we cannot but conclude that in enacting § 301 Congress intended doctrines of federal labor law uniformly to prevail over inconsistent local rules.

Whether, as a matter of federal law, the strike which the union called was a violation of the collective bargaining contract is thus the ultimate issue which this case presents. It is argued that there could be no violation in the absence of a no-strike clause in the contract explicitly covering the subject of the dispute over which the strike was called. We disagree.

The collective bargaining contract expressly imposed upon both parties the duty of submitting the dispute in question to final and binding arbitration. In a consistent course of decisions the Courts of Appeals of at least five Federal Circuits have held that a strike to settle a dispute which a collective bargaining agreement provides shall be settled exclusively and finally by compulsory arbitration constitutes a violation of the agreement. The National Labor Relations Board has reached the same conclusion. W. L. Mead, Inc., 113 N.L.R.B. 1040. We approve that doctrine. To hold otherwise would obviously do violence to accepted principles of traditional contract law. Even more in point, a contrary view would be completely at odds with the basic policy of national labor legislation to promote the arbitral process as a substitute for economic warfare. See United Steelworkers v. Warrior & Gulf Nav. Co., 363 U.S. 574, 80 S.Ct. 1347, 4 L.Ed.2d 1409.

What has been said is not to suggest that a no-strike agreement is to be implied beyond the area which it has been agreed will be exclusively covered by compulsory terminal arbitration. Nor is it to suggest that there may not arise problems in specific cases as to whether compulsory and binding arbitration has been agreed upon, and, if so, as to what disputes have been made arbitrable. But no such problems are present in this case. * * *

[MR. JUSTICE BLACK dissented.]

Problems for Discussion

1. In his dissent, Justice Black delivered the following comments on the construction of the contract by the majority.

"Both parties to collective bargaining discussions have much at stake as to whether there will be a no-strike clause in any resulting agreement. It is difficult to believe that the desire of employers to get such a promise and the desire of the union to avoid giving it are matters which are not constantly in the minds of those who negotiate these contracts. In such a setting, to hold—on the basis of no evidence whatever—that a union, without knowing it, impliedly surrendered the right to strike by virtue of "traditional contract law" or anything else is to me just fiction. * * *

"I have been unable to find any accepted principle of contract law—traditional or otherwise—that permits courts to change completely the nature of a contract by adding new promises that the parties themselves refused to make in order that the new court-made contract might better fit into whatever social, economic, or legal policies the courts believe to be so important that they should have been taken out of the realm of voluntary contract by the legislative body and furthered by compulsory legislation." 369 U.S. 95, 108, 109, 82 S.Ct. 571, 7 L.Ed.2d 593 (1962).

Would you disagree with the majority's conclusion on the basis of the points made by Justice Black? See Wellington, *Freedom of Contract and the Collective Bargaining Agreement*, 112 U.Pa.L.Rev. 467 (1964).

2.   During the term of a contract similar to the Lucas Flour agreement in all pertinent respects, an employer discharged Plum, a prominent union member, upon grounds which the employer deemed to constitute "just cause" within the meaning of a clause stipulating that there should be "no discharge without just cause" but which the union deemed insufficient. In response, the union called an immediate strike. Two hundred of 600 employees stopped work. After seeking unsuccessfully for three days to persuade the strikers to return to work the company declared the contract terminated, discharged the strikers, and hired replacements. The union filed grievances on behalf of Plum and the strikers. When the company refused to process the grievances, the union brought an action under Section 301 to compel arbitration. What judgment would you enter? See *Local 721 Packinghouse Workers* v. *Needham Packing Co.*, 376 U.S. 247 (1964). Would your answer be different if the company had merely refused to arbitrate Plum's grievance while the strike continued?

3.   In 1969, the employer terminated the employment of several employees who were covered by a collective bargaining agreement which provided, *inter alia,* that "Employees who qualified for a vacation in the previous year and whose employment is terminated for any reason before the vacation is taken will be paid that vacation at time of termination." However, the employer failed to pay the terminated employees their accumulated vacation pay, and in 1975, an action was brought against the employer in state court but was dismissed in 1977 because of unremedied pleading defects. In 1981, four years after the dismissal of that lawsuit and almost seven years after the employees had been terminated, the union filed suit in federal district court under Section 301. That section contains no statute of limitations. The employer contends that since the action was based partly upon the oral employment contract which each employee had made, the union is barred from coming into court now by the state six-year statute of limitations governing contracts not in writing. The union contends that the court should apply the state twenty-year statute of limitations governing written contracts since the dispute arose over a provision in the collective bargaining agreement, or alternatively that a suit in federal court cannot be barred by a statute of limitations enacted by a state and thus the court should fashion judicially a uniform statute of limitations for Section 301 suits that would permit the instant one to be adjudicated on the merits and not dismissed because of a procedural flaw. How should the federal court dispose of the employer's motion to dismiss? See *UAW* v. *Hoosier Cardinal Corp.*, 383 U.S. 696, 86 S.Ct. 1107 (1966).

UNITED STEELWORKERS OF AMERICA v.
AMERICAN MFG. CO.

Supreme Court of the United States, 1960.
363 U.S. 564, 80 S.Ct. 1343, 4 L.Ed.2d 1403.

MR. JUSTICE DOUGLAS delivered the opinion of the Court.

This suit was brought by petitioner union in the District Court to compel arbitration of a "grievance" that petitioner, acting for one Sparks, a union member, had filed with the respondent, Sparks' employer. * * * The agreement provided that during its term there would be "no strike," unless the employer refused to abide by a decision of the arbitrator. The agreement sets out a detailed grievance procedure with a provision for arbitration (regarded as the standard form) of all disputes between the parties "as to the meaning, interpretation and application of the provisions of this agreement." [19]

The agreement also reserves to the management power to suspend or discharge any employee "for cause." [20] It also contains a provision that the employer will employ and promote employees on the principle of seniority "where ability and efficiency are equal." [21] Sparks left his work due to an injury and while off work brought an action for compensation benefits. The case was settled, Sparks' physician expressing the opinion that the injury had made him 25% permanently partially disabled. That was on September 9. Two

---

19. The relevant arbitration provisions read as follows:
"Any disputes, misunderstandings, differences or grievances arising between the parties as to the meaning, interpretation and application of the provisions of this agreement, which are not adjusted as herein provided, may be submitted to the Board of Arbitration for decision. * * *
"The arbitrator may interpret this agreement and apply it to the particular case under consideration but shall, however, have no authority to add to, subtract from, or modify the terms of the agreement. Disputes relating to discharges or such matters as might involve a loss of pay for employees may carry an award of back pay in whole or in part as may be determined by the Board of Arbitration.
"The decision of the Board of Arbitration shall be final and conclusively binding upon both parties, and the parties agree to observe and abide by same. * * * "

20. "The Management of the works, the direction of the working force, plant layout and routine of work, including the right to hire, suspend, transfer, discharge or otherwise discipline any employee for cause, such cause being: infraction of company rules, inefficiency, insubordination, contagious disease harmful to others, and any other ground or reason that would tend to reduce or impair the efficiency of plant operation; and to lay off employees because of lack of work, is reserved to the Company, provided it does not conflict with this agreement. * * * "

21. This provision provides in relevant part:
"The Company and the Union fully recognize the principle of seniority as a factor on the selection of employees for promotion, transfer, lay-off, re-employment, and filling of vacancies, where ability and efficiency are equal. It is the policy of the Company to promote employees on that basis."

weeks later the union filed a grievance which charged that Sparks
was entitled to return to his job by virtue of the seniority provision
of the collective bargaining agreement. Respondent refused to arbitrate and this action was brought. The District Court held that
Sparks, having accepted the settlement on the basis of permanent partial disability, was estopped to claim any seniority or employment
rights and granted the motion for summary judgment. The Court
of Appeals affirmed, 264 F.2d 624, for different reasons. After
reviewing the evidence it held that the grievance is "a frivolous,
patently baseless one, not subject to arbitration under the collective
bargaining agreement." Id., at page 628. The case is here on a
writ of certiorari, 361 U.S. 881, 80 S.Ct. 152, 4 L.Ed.2d 118.

Section 203 (d) of the Labor Management Relations Act, 1947, 61
Stat. 154, 29 U.S.C. § 173(d), 29 U.S.C.A. § 173(d) states, "Final
adjustment by a method agreed upon by the parties is hereby declared
to be the desirable method for settlement of grievance disputes arising over the application or interpretation of an existing collective-
bargaining agreement. * * *" That policy can be effectuated
only if the means chosen by the parties for settlement of their differences under a collective bargaining agreement is given full play.

A state decision that held to the contrary announced a principle
that could only have a crippling effect on grievance arbitration. The
case was International Ass'n of Machinists v. Cutler-Hammer, Inc.,
271 App.Div. 917, 67 N.Y.S.2d 317, affirmed 297 N.Y. 519, 74 N.E.2d
464. It held that "If the meaning of the provision of the contract
sought to be arbitrated is beyond dispute, there cannot be anything
to arbitrate and the contract cannot be said to provide for arbitration." 271 App.Div. at page 918, 67 N.Y.S.2d at page 318. The
lower courts in the instant case had a like preoccupation with ordinary contract law. The collective agreement requires arbitration of
claims that courts might be unwilling to entertain. Yet in the
context of the plant or industry the grievance may assume propor-
tions of which judges are ignorant. Moreover, the agreement is to
submit all grievances to arbitration, not merely those that a court
may deem to be meritorious. There is no exception in the "no strike"
clause and none therefore should be read into the grievance clause,
since one is the *quid pro quo* for the other. The question is not
whether in the mind of a court there is equity in the claim. Arbitration is a stabilizing influence only as it serves as a vehicle for handling every and all disputes that arise under the agreement.

The collective agreement calls for the submission of grievances
in the categories which it describes irrespective of whether a court
may deem them to be meritorious. In our role of developing a meaningful body of law to govern the interpretation and enforcement of
collective bargaining agreements, we think special heed should be

given to the context in which collective bargaining agreements are negotiated and the purpose which they are intended to serve. See Lewis v. Benedict Coal Corp., 361 U.S. 459, 468, 80 S.Ct. 489, 495, 4 L.Ed.2d 442. The function of the court is very limited when the parties have agreed to submit all questions of contract interpretation to the arbitrator. It is then confined to ascertaining whether the party seeking arbitration is making a claim which on its face is governed by the contract. Whether the moving party is right or wrong is a question of contract interpretation for the arbitrator. In these circumstances the moving party should not be deprived of the arbitrator's judgment, when it was his judgment and all that it connotes that was bargained for.

The courts therefore have no business weighing the merits of the grievance considering whether there is equity in a particular claim, or determining whether there is particular language in the written instrument which will support the claim. The agreement is to submit all grievances to arbitration, not merely those the court will deem meritorious. The processing of even frivolous claims may have therapeutic values of which those who are not a part of the plant environment may be quite unaware.[22]

The union claimed in this case that the company had violated a specific provision of the contract. The company took the position that it had not violated that clause. There was, therefore, a dispute between the parties as to "the meaning, interpretation and application" of the collective bargaining agreement. Arbitration should have been ordered. When the judiciary undertakes to determine the merits of a grievance under the guise of interpreting the grievance procedure of collective bargaining agreements, it usurps a function which under that regime is entrusted to the arbitration tribunal.

Reversed.

MR. JUSTICE BRENNAN, MR. JUSTICE HARLAN, and MR. JUSTICE FRANKFURTER concurred (see page 574 *infra*).

---

22. Cox, Current Problems in the Law of Grievance Arbitration, 30 Rocky Mt.L.Rev. 247, 261 (1958) writes:
"The typical arbitration clause is written in words which cover, without limitation, all disputes concerning the interpretation or application of a collective bargaining agreement. Its words do not restrict its scope to meritorious disputes or two-sided disputes, still less are they limited to disputes which a judge will consider two-sided. Frivolous cases are often taken, and are expected to be taken, to arbitration. What one man considers frivolous another may find meritorious, and it is common knowledge in industrial relations circles that grievance arbitration often serves as a safety valve for troublesome complaints. Under these circumstances it seems proper to read the typical arbitration clause as a promise to arbitrate every claim, meritorious or frivolous, which the complainant bases upon the contract. The objection that equity will not order a party to do a useless act is outweighed by the cathartic value of arbitrating even a frivolous grievance and by the dangers of excessive judicial intervention."

[MR. JUSTICE WHITTAKER concurred, in a separate opinion, and MR. JUSTICE BLACK took no part in the consideration of the case.]

UNITED STEELWORKERS OF AMERICA v. WARRIOR & GULF NAVIGATION CO.

Supreme Court of the United States, 1960.
363 U.S. 574, 80 S.Ct. 1347, 4 L.Ed.2d 1409.

MR. JUSTICE DOUGLAS delivered the opinion of the Court.

Respondent transports steel and steel products by barge and maintains a terminal at Chicasaw, Alabama, where it performs maintenance and repair work on its barges. The employees at that terminal constitute a bargaining unit covered by a collective bargaining agreement negotiated by petitioner union. Respondent between 1956 and 1958 laid off some employees, reducing the bargaining unit from 42 to 23 men. This reduction was due in part to respondent contracting maintenance work, previously done by its employees, to other companies. The latter used respondent's supervisors to lay out the work and hired some of the laid-off employees of respondent (at reduced wages). Some were in fact assigned to work on respondent's barges. A number of employees signed a grievance which petitioner presented to respondent, the grievance reading:

"We are hereby protesting the Company's actions, of arbitrarily and unreasonably contracting out work to other concerns, that could and previously has been performed by Company employees.

"This practice becomes unreasonable, unjust and discriminatory in view of the fact that at present there are a number of employees that have been laid off for about 1 and ½ years or more for allegedly lack of work.

"Confronted with these facts we charge that the Company is in violation of the contract by inducing a partial lockout, of a number of the employees who would otherwise be working were it not for this unfair practice."

The collective agreement had both a "no strike" and a "no lockout" provision. It also had a grievance procedure which provided in relevant part as follows:

"Issues which conflict with any Federal statute in its application as established by Court procedure or matters which are strictly a function of management shall not be subject to arbitration under this section.

"Should differences arise between the Company and the Union or its members employed by the Company as to the meaning and application of the provisions of this Agreement, or should any local trouble of any kind arise, there shall be no suspension of work on account of such differences, but an earnest effort shall be made to settle such differences immediately [through a five-step grievance procedure culminating in arbitration]   *   *   *

broader than Com mfg goes beyond
K

Settlement of this grievance was not had and respondent refused arbitration. This suit was then commenced by the union to compel it.

The District Court granted respondent's motion to dismiss the complaint.   *   *   *   The Court of Appeals affirmed by a divided vote, 269 F.2d 633, 635, the majority holding that the collective agreement had withdrawn from the grievance procedure "matters which are strictly a function of management" and that contracting-out fell in that exception. The case is here on a writ of certiorari. 361 U.S. 912, 80 S.Ct. 255, 4 L.Ed.2d 183.

We held in Textile Workers v. Lincoln Mills, 353 U.S. 448, 77 S.Ct. 912, 923, 1 L.Ed.2d 972, that a grievance arbitration provision in a collective agreement could be enforced by reason of § 301(a) of the Labor Management Relations Act and that the policy to be applied in enforcing this type of arbitration was that reflected in our national labor laws. Id., 353 U.S. at pages 456–457, 77 S.Ct. at pages 917–918. The present federal policy is to promote industrial stabilization through the collective bargaining agreement. Id., 353 U.S. at pages 453–454, 77 S.Ct. at page 916. A major factor in achieving industrial peace is the inclusion of a provision for arbitration of grievances in the collective bargaining agreement.[23]

Thus the run of arbitration cases, illustrated by Wilko v. Swan, 346 U.S. 427, 74 S.Ct. 182, 98 L.Ed. 168 become irrelevant to our problem. There the choice is between the adjudication of cases or controversies in courts with established procedures or even special statutory safeguards on the one hand and the settlement of them in the more informal arbitration tribunal on the other. In the commercial case, arbitration is the substitute for litigation. Here arbitration is the substitute for industrial strife. Since arbitration of labor disputes has quite different functions from arbitration under an ordinary commercial agreement, the hostility evinced by courts toward arbitration of commercial agreements has no place here. For arbi-

23. Complete effectuation of the federal policy is achieved when the agreement contains both an arbitration provision for all unresolved grievances and an absolute prohibition of strikes, the arbitration agreement being the "*quid pro quo*" for the agreement not to strike. Textile Workers v. Lincoln Mills, 353 U.S. 448, 455, 77 S.Ct. 912, 917.

tration of labor disputes under collective bargaining agreements is part and parcel of the collective bargaining process itself.

The collective bargaining agreement states the rights and duties of the parties. It is more than a contract; it is a generalized code to govern a myriad of cases which the draftsmen cannot wholly anticipate. See Shulman, Reason, Contract, and Law in Labor Relations, 68 Harv.L.Rev. 999, 1004–1005. The collective agreement covers the whole employment relationship. It calls into being a new common law—the common law of a particular industry or of a particular plant. As one observer has put it: [24]

> " * * * [I]t is not unqualifiedly true that a collective-bargaining agreement is simply a document by which the union and employees have imposed upon management limited, express restrictions of its otherwise absolute right to manage the enterprise, so that an employee's claim must fail unless he can point to a specific contract provision upon which the claim is founded. There are too many people, too many problems, too many unforeseeable contingencies to make the words of the contract the exclusive source of rights and duties. One cannot reduce all the rules governing a community like an industrial plant to fifteen or even fifty pages. Within the sphere of collective bargaining, the institutional characteristics and the governmental nature of the collective-bargaining process demand a common law of the shop which implements and furnishes the context of the agreement. We must assume that intelligent negotiators acknowledged so plain a need unless they stated a contrary rule in plain words."

A collective bargaining agreement is an effort to erect a system of industrial self-government. When most parties enter into contractual relationship they do so voluntarily, in the sense that there is no real compulsion to deal with one another, as opposed to dealing with other parties. This is not true of the labor agreement. The choice is generally not between entering or refusing to enter into a relationship, for that in all probability pre-exists the negotiations. Rather it is between having that relationship governed by an agreed upon rule of law or leaving each and every matter subject to a temporary resolution dependent solely upon the relative strength, at any given moment, of the contending forces. The mature labor agreement may attempt to regulate all aspects of the complicated relationship, from the most crucial to the most minute over an extended period of time. Because of the compulsion to reach agreement and the breadth

---

24. Cox, Reflections Upon Labor Arbitration, 72 Harv.L.Rev. 1482, 1498–1499 (1959).

of the matters covered, as well as the need for a fairly concise and readable instrument, the product of negotiations (the written document) is, in the words of the late Dean Shulman, "a compilation of diverse provisions: some provide objective criteria almost automatically applicable; some provide more or less specific standards which require reason and judgment in their application; and some do little more than leave problems to future consideration with an expression of hope and good faith." Shulman, supra, at 1005. <u>Gaps may be left to be filled in by reference to the practices of the particular industry and of the various shops covered by the agreement.</u> Many of the specific practices which underlie the agreement may be unknown, except in hazy form, even to the negotiators. Courts and arbitration in the context of most commercial contracts are resorted to because there has been a breakdown in the working relationship of the parties; such resort is the unwanted exception. But the grievance machinery under a collective bargaining agreement is at the very heart of the system of industrial self-government. Arbitration is the means of solving the unforeseeable by molding a system of private law for all the problems which may arise and to provide for their solution in a way which will generally accord with the variant needs and desires of the parties. The processing of disputes through the grievance machinery is actually a vehicle by which meaning and content is given to the collective bargaining agreement.

Apart from matters that the parties <u>specifically exclude,</u> all of the questions on which the parties disagree must therefore come within the scope of the grievance and arbitration provisions of the collective agreement. The grievance procedure is, in other words, a part of the continuous collective bargaining process. It, rather than a strike, is the terminal point of a disagreement.

> "A proper conception of the arbitrator's function is basic. He is not a public tribunal imposed upon the parties by superior authority which the parties are obliged to accept. He has no general charter to administer justice for a community which transcends the parties. He is rather part of a system of self-government created by and confined to the parties. * * *" Shulman, supra, at 1016.

The labor arbitrator performs functions which are not normal to the courts; <u>the considerations which help him fashion judgments may indeed be foreign to the competence of courts.</u> The labor arbitrator's source of law is not confined to the express provisions of the contract, as the industrial common law—the practices of the industry and the shop—is equally a part of the collective bargaining agreement although not expressed in it. The labor arbitrator is usually chosen because of the parties' confidence in his knowledge of the common law of the shop and their trust in his personal judgment to bring to bear considerations which are not expressed in the contract as criteria for judgment. The parties expect that his judgment of a particular grievance will reflect not only what the contract says but, insofar as the collective bargaining agreement permits, such factors as the effect upon productivity of a particular result, its consequence to the morale of the shop, his judgment whether tensions will be heightened or diminished. For the parties' objective in using the arbitration process is primarily to further their common goal of uninterrupted production under the agreement, to make the agreement serve their specialized needs. The ablest judge cannot be expected to bring the same experience and competence to bear upon the determination of a grievance, because he cannot be similarly informed.

The Congress, however, has by § 301 of the Labor Management Relations Act, assigned the courts the duty of determining whether the reluctant party has breached his promise to arbitrate. For arbitration is a matter of contract and a party cannot be required to submit to arbitration any dispute which he has not agreed so to submit. Yet, to be consistent with congressional policy in favor of settlement of disputes by the parties through the machinery of arbitration, the judicial inquiry under § 301 must be strictly confined to the question whether the reluctant party did agree to arbitrate the grievance or agreed to give the arbitrator power to make the award he made. An order to arbitrate the particular grievance should not be denied unless it may be said with positive assurance that the arbitration clause is not susceptible to an interpretation that covers the asserted dispute. Doubts should be resolved in favor of coverage.[25]

We do not agree with the lower courts that contracting-out grievances were necessarily excepted from the grievance procedure of this agreement. To be sure the agreement provides that "matters which are strictly a function of management shall not be subject to arbitration." But it goes on to say that if "differences" arise or if "any local trouble of any kind" arises, the grievance procedure shall be applicable.

Collective bargaining agreements regulate or restrict the exercise of management functions; they do not oust management from the performance of them. Management hires and fires, pays and promotes, supervises and plans. All these are part of its function, and absent a collective bargaining agreement, it may be exercised freely except as limited by public law and by the willingness of employees

---

25. It is clear that under both the agreement in this case and that involved in American Manufacturing Co., 362 U.S. 564, 80 S.Ct. 1343, the question of arbitrability is for the courts to decide. Cf. Cox, Reflections Upon Labor Arbitration, 72 Harv.L.Rev. 1482, 1508–1509. Where the assertion by the claimant is that the parties excluded from court determination not merely the decision of the merits of the grievance but also the question of its arbitrability, vesting power to make both decisions in the arbitrator, the claimant must bear the burden of a clear demonstration of that purpose.

to work under the particular, unilaterally imposed conditions. A collective bargaining agreement may treat only with certain specific practices, leaving the rest to management but subject to the possibility of work stoppages. When, however, an absolute no-strike clause is included in the agreement, then in a very real sense everything that management does is subject to the agreement, for either management is prohibited or limited in the action it takes, or if not, it is protected from interference by strikes. This comprehensive reach of the collective bargaining agreement does not mean, however, that the language, "strictly a function of management" has no meaning.

"Strictly a function of management" might be thought to refer to any practice of management in which, under particular circumstances prescribed by the agreement, it is permitted to indulge. But if courts, in order to determine arbitrability, were allowed to determine what is permitted and what is not, the arbitration clause would be swallowed up by the exception. Every grievance in a sense involves a claim that management has violated some provision of the agreement.

Accordingly, "strictly a function of management" must be interpreted as referring only to that over which the contract gives management complete control and unfettered discretion. Respondent claims that the contracting-out of work falls within this category. Contracting-out work is the basis of many grievances; and that type of claim is grist in the mills of the arbitrators. A specific collective bargaining agreement may exclude contracting-out from the grievance procedure. Or a written collateral agreement may make clear that contracting-out was not a matter for arbitration. In such a case a grievance based solely on contracting-out would not be arbitrable. Here, however, there is no such provision. Nor is there any showing that the parties designed the phrase "strictly a function of management" to encompass any and all forms of contracting-out. In the absence of any express provision excluding a particular grievance from arbitration, we think only the most forceful evidence of a purpose to exclude the claim from arbitration can prevail, particularly where, as here, the exclusion clause is vague and the arbitration clause quite broad. Since any attempt by a court to infer such a purpose necessarily comprehends the merits, the court should view with suspicion an attempt to persuade it to become entangled in the construction of the substantive provisions of a labor agreement, even through the back door of interpreting the arbitration clause, when the alternative is to utilize the services of an arbitrator.

The grievance alleged that the contracting-out was a violation of the collective bargaining agreement. There was, therefore, a dispute "as to the meaning and application of the provisions of this Agreement" which the parties had agreed would be determined by arbitration.

The judiciary sits in these cases to bring into operation an arbitral process which substitutes a regime of peaceful settlement for the older regime of industrial conflict. Whether contracting-out in the present case violated the agreement is the question. It is a question for the arbiter, not for the courts.

Reversed.

MR. JUSTICE BRENNAN, MR. JUSTICE HARLAN and MR. JUSTICE FRANKFURTER, concurring. The issue in the Warrior Case is essentially no different from that in American, that is, it is whether the company agreed to arbitrate a particular grievance. In contrast to American, however, the arbitration promise here excludes a particular area from arbitration—"matters which are strictly a function of management." Because the arbitration promise is different, the scope of the court's inquiry may be broader. Here, a court may be required to examine the substantive provisions of the contract to ascertain whether the parties have provided that contracting out shall be a "function of management." If a court may delve into the merits to the extent of inquiring whether the parties have expressly agreed whether or not contracting out was a "function of management," why was it error for the lower court here to evaluate the evidence of bargaining history for the same purpose? Neat logical distinctions do not provide the answer. The Court rightly concludes that appropriate regard for the national labor policy and the special factors relevant to the labor arbitral process, admonish that judicial inquiry into the merits of this grievance should be limited to the search for an explicit provision which brings the grievance under the cover of the exclusion clause since "the exclusion clause is vague and arbitration clause quite broad." The hazard of going further into the merits is amply demonstrated by what the courts below did. On the basis of inconclusive evidence, those courts found that Warrior was in no way limited by any implied covenants of good faith and fair dealing from contracting out as it pleased—which would necessarily mean that Warrior was free completely to destroy the collective bargaining agreement by contracting out all the work.

The very ambiguity of the Warrior exclusion clause suggests that the parties were generally more concerned with having an arbitrator render decisions as to the meaning of the contract than they were in restricting the arbitrator's jurisdiction. The case might of course be otherwise were the arbitration clause very narrow, or the exclusion clause quite specific, for the inference might then be permissible that the parties had manifested a greater interest in confining the arbitrator; the presumption of arbitrability would then not have the same force and the Court would be somewhat freer to examine into the merits.

The Court makes reference to an arbitration clause being the quid pro quo for a no-strike clause. I do not understand the Court to mean that the application of the principles announced today depends upon the presence of a no-strike clause in the agreement.

MR. JUSTICE BLACK took no part in the consideration or decision of this case.

MR. JUSTICE WHITTAKER, dissenting. *   *   *

With respect, I submit that there is nothing in the contract here to indicate that the employer "signified [its] willingness" (Marchant, supra, 169 N.E. at 391) to submit to arbitrators whether it must cease contracting out work. Certainly no such intention is "made manifest by plain language" [as required by prior arbitration cases not involving a collective bargaining relation]. To the contrary, the parties by their conduct over many years interpreted the contracting out of major repair work to be "strictly a function of management," and if, as the concurring opinion suggests, the words of the contract can "be understood only by reference to the background which gave rise to their inclusion," then the interpretation given by the parties over 19 years to the phrase "matters which are strictly a function of management" should logically have some significance here. By their contract, the parties agreed that "matters which are strictly a function of management shall not be subject to arbitration." The union over the course of many years repeatedly tried to induce the employer to agree to a covenant prohibiting the contracting out of work, but was never successful. The union again made such an effort in negotiating the very contract involved here, and, failing of success, signed the contract, knowing, of course, that it did not contain any such covenant, but that, to the contrary, it contained, just as had the former contracts, a covenant that "matters which are strictly a function of management shall not be subject to arbitration." Does not this show that, instead of signifying a willingness to submit to arbitration the matter of whether the employer might continue to contract out work, the parties fairly agreed to exclude at least that matter from arbitration? * * *

Problems for Discussion

1. After the decision of the Supreme Court in *Warrior & Gulf*, is the arbitrator free to determine that the contract was intended to make subcontracting "strictly a function of management" and that the dispute before him is thus nonarbitrable? Assume that the arbitrator concludes that the dispute is arbitrable; is he then free to determine that subcontracting is a management function and hence not a breach of the agreement? The opinion of the arbitrator is reported at 36 Lab.Arb. 695 (1961).

2. Company has, for fourteen years, paid its employees a Christmas bonus, based upon each employee's regular earnings during the calendar

year. Union has represented plant employees for eight years, and has negotiated contracts containing a "standard" arbitration clause, which authorizes either party to take to arbitration any unsettled "dispute regarding
the meaning, interpretation or application of the provisions of this agreement" and forbids the arbitrator "to add to, subtract from, or modify the
terms of the agreement." Last Christmas, the employer, claiming hard
economic times, failed to give any employees a Christmas bonus. Union
has unsuccessfully asserted a claim of contract breach through the grievance procedure, and has brought an action in the federal district court to
compel arbitration. The Company has moved to dismiss. Should this motion be granted, on the following alternative assumptions?

(a) The contract (as have all its predecessor contracts) contains a provision: "It shall be within the complete discretion of Company whether to
make gifts or pay bonuses to employees." *No -*

(b) There is no contract language at all which explicitly deals with the
issue of bonuses (although there are conventional wage and other fringe-
benefit provisions). See Boeing Co. v. UAW, 231 F.Supp. 930 (E.D.Pa.
1964), aff'd mem. 349 F.2d 412 (3d Cir. 1965). *No*

(c) There is no contract language at all which explicitly deals with the
issue of bonuses, and the Company attempts to offer evidence that during
negotiations for the current contract the Union negotiator persistently
sought a provision requiring Company to pay a Christmas bonus and the
Company just as persistently refused. (Should the court grant Union's
motion to exclude this evidence as irrelevant?) *yes*

(d) There is no contract language at all which explicitly deals with the
issue of bonuses, and the Company attempts to offer evidence that during
negotiations for the current contract the Union and Company negotiators
agreed that disputes concerning any Company gifts or bonuses would not be
sent to arbitration but would instead be finally resolved at the level of the
Vice-President for Personnel Relations. (Should the court grant Union's
motion to exclude this evidence as irrelevant?) See Pacific Northwest Bell
Tel. Co. v. Communications Workers of America, 310 F.2d 244 (9th Cir.
1963). *no*

3.   Assume that a labor contract contains a recognition clause in the
customary form; provisions dealing with such familiar subjects as seniority, vacations, holidays, hours, wages and grievances; a provision barring
"coercion, intimidation, discrimination by the employer or union against
any employee because of membership or nonmembership in the union";
and an arbitration clause covering "any dispute concerning the interpretation, application, or alleged violation of any provisions of this agreement."
Assume, however, that there is no explicit provision dealing with employer
decisions to subcontract work or dealing with discharge for just cause,
and that there is no union-security clause. Should a court require the
company to arbitrate on demand of the union in the following cases?

(a) The company has refused the union's demand that all employees
be required, within thirty days of initial employment, to become and remain members of the union to the extent of paying the usual initiation

fee and dues. See *Consolidated Vultee Aircraft Corp.* v. *UAW*, 160 P.2d 113 (Cal.Dist.Ct. of App.1945).

(b) The company has subcontracted work which bargaining-unit employees have performed in the past. See *Local 483, Boilermakers* v. *Shell Oil Co.*, 369 F.2d 526 (7th Cir. 1966); *Allis Chalmers Mfg. Co.*, p. 614 supra.

(c) The company has discharged employee Pierce, and the union asserts that the discharge was arbitrary and unjustifiable. See *Coca-Cola Bottling Co. of Boston*, p. 532 supra.

4. A collective bargaining agreement covering the period July 1, 1978 through June 30, 1981 provided, *inter alia*, that: "In connection with the third year of this contract, it has been agreed that the contract may be reopened only for the negotiation of a wage increase and paid holidays as a fringe issue. Any notices to reopen the contract for either or both of these two issues during the third year are to be given in the same manner as that required by law to negotiate for a new contract." In the third year of the agreement negotiations were held briefly but when the company refused to agree to any wage increase or increase in the number of paid holidays, the union commenced an action to compel arbitration of the amount of a wage increase to be paid and number of paid holidays to be added. The contract contains the standard arbitration clause which authorizes either party to take to arbitration any unsettled "grievance or dispute regarding the meaning, interpretation or application of the provisions of this agreement." The contract also provides that the arbitrator "may interpret this agreement, but shall have no authority to add to, subtract from, or modify the terms of the agreement." The company has moved to dismiss the union's complaint. How should the court rule?

Would the result be different if the contract expressly provided that unresolved disputes about specific terms in the negotiation of a subsequent agreement were to be submitted to an arbitrator, who would have the authority to make a binding determination of new contract terms? See Milwaukee Newspaper & Graphic Communications Union Local 23 v. Newspapers, Inc., 586 F.2d 19 (7th Cir. 1978), cert. denied, 440 U.S. 971, 99 S.Ct. 1534, 59 L.Ed.2d 787 (1979); Winston-Salem Printing Pressmen and Assistants' Union No. 318 v. Piedmont Pub. Co., 393 F.2d 221 (4th Cir. 1968).

JOHN WILEY & SONS v. LIVINGSTON

Supreme Court of the United States, 1964.
376 U.S. 543, 84 S.Ct. 909, 11 L.Ed.2d 898.

MR. JUSTICE HARLAN delivered the opinion of the Court.

This is an action by a union, pursuant to § 301 of the Labor Management Relations Act, 29 U.S.C.A. § 185, to compel arbitration under a collective bargaining agreement. The major questions presented are (1) whether a corporate employer must arbitrate with a union under a bargaining agreement between the union and another corporation which has merged with the employer, and, if so, (2) whether the courts or the arbitrator is the appropriate body to decide whether procedural prerequisites which, under the bargaining agreement, condition the duty to arbitrate have been met. Because of the importance of both questions to the realization of national labor policy, we granted certiorari (373 U.S. 908, 83 S.Ct. 1300, 10 L.Ed.2d 411) to review a judgment of the Court of Appeals directing arbitration (313 F.2d 52), in reversal of the District Court which had refused such relief (203 F.Supp. 171). We affirm the judgment below, but, with respect to the first question above, on grounds which may differ from those of the Court of Appeals, whose answer to that question is unclear.

District 65, Retail, Wholesale and Department Store Union, AFL–CIO, entered into a collective bargaining agreement with Interscience Publishers, Inc., a publishing firm, for a term expiring on January 31, 1962. The agreement did not contain an express provision making it binding on successors of Interscience. On October 2, 1961, Interscience merged with the petitioner John Wiley & Sons, Inc., another publishing firm, and ceased to do business as a separate entity. There is no suggestion that the merger was not for genuine business reasons.

At the time of the merger Interscience had about 80 employees, of whom 40 were represented by this Union. It had a single plant in New York City, and did an annual business of somewhat over $1,000,-000. Wiley was a much larger concern, having separate office and warehouse facilities and about 300 employees, and doing an annual business of more than $9,000,000. None of Wiley's employees was represented by a union.

In discussions before and after the merger, the Union and Interscience (later Wiley) were unable to agree on the effect of the merger on the collective bargaining agreement and on the rights under it of those covered employees hired by Wiley. The Union's position was that despite the merger it continued to represent the covered Interscience employees taken over by Wiley, and that Wiley was obligated to recognize certain rights of such employees which had "vested" under the Interscience bargaining agreement. Such rights, more fully described below, concerned matters typically covered by collective bargaining agreements, such as seniority status, severance pay, etc. The Union contended also that Wiley was required to make certain pension fund payments called for under the Interscience bargaining agreement.

Wiley, though recognizing for purposes of its own pension plan the Interscience service of the former Interscience employees, asserted that the merger terminated the bargaining agreement for all purposes. It refused to recognize the Union as bargaining agent or to accede to the Union's claims on behalf of Interscience employees. All such employees, except a few who ended their Wiley employment with severance pay and for whom no rights are asserted here, continued in Wiley's employ.

No satisfactory solution having been reached, the Union, one week before the expiration date of the Interscience bargaining agreement, commenced this action to compel arbitration.

The threshold question in this controversy is who shall decide whether the arbitration provisions of the collective bargaining agreement survived the Wiley-Interscience merger, so as to be operative against Wiley. Both parties urge that this question is for the courts. Past cases leave no doubt that this is correct. * * * The duty to arbitrate being of contractual origin, a compulsory submission to arbitration cannot precede judicial determination that the collective bargaining agreement does in fact create such a duty. Thus, just as an employer has no obligation to arbitrate issues which it has not agreed to arbitrate, so *a fortiori*, it cannot be compelled to arbitrate if an arbitration clause does not bind it at all.

The unanimity of views about who should decide the question of arbitrability does not, however, presage, the parties' accord about what is the correct decision. Wiley, objecting to arbitration, argues that it never was a party to the collective bargaining agreement, and that, in any event, the Union lost its status as representative of the former Interscience employees when they were mingled in a larger Wiley unit of employees. The Union argues that Wiley, as successor to Interscience, is bound by the latter's agreement, at least sufficiently to require it to arbitrate. The Union relies on § 90 of the N. Y. Stock Corporation Law, McKinney's Consol.Laws, c. 59, which provides, among other things, that no "claim or demand for any cause" against a constituent corporation shall be extinguished by a consolidation. Alternatively, the Union argues that apart from § 90, federal law requires that arbitration go forward, lest the policy favoring arbitration frequently be undermined by changes in corporate organization.

Federal law, fashioned "from the policy of our national labor laws," controls. Textile Workers Union of America v. Lincoln Mills, 353 U.S. 448, 456, 77 S.Ct. 912, 918, 1 L.Ed.2d 972. State law may be utilized so far as it is of aid in the development of correct principles or their application in a particular case, id., 353 U.S. at 457, 77 S.Ct. 912, 1 L.Ed.2d 972, but the law which ultimately results is federal. We hold that the disappearance by merger of a corporate employer which has entered into a collective bargaining agreement with a union does not automatically terminate all rights of the employees covered by the agreement, and that, in appropriate circumstances, present here, the successor employer may be required to arbitrate with the union under the agreement.

This Court has in the past recognized the central role of arbitration in effectuating national labor policy. Thus, in Warrior & Gulf Navigation Co., supra, 363 U.S. at 578, 80 S.Ct. 1347, 1351, 4 L.Ed.2d 1409, arbitration was described as "the substitute for industrial strife," and as "part and parcel of the collective bargaining process itself." It would derogate from "[t]he federal policy of settling labor disputes by arbitration," United Steelworkers of America v. Enterprise Wheel & Car Corp., 363 U.S. 593, 596, 80 S.Ct. 1358, 1360, 4 L.Ed.2d 1424, if a change in the corporate structure or ownership of a business enterprise had the automatic consequence of removing a duty to arbitrate previously established; this is so as much in cases like the present, where the contracting employer disappears into another by merger, as in those in which one owner replaces another but the business entity remains the same.

Employees, and the union which represents them, ordinarily do not take part in negotiations leading to a change in corporate ownership. The negotiations will ordinarily not concern the well-being of the employees, whose advantage or disadvantage, potentially great, will inevitably be incidental to the main considerations. The objectives of national labor policy, reflected in established principles of federal law, require that the rightful prerogative of owners independently to rearrange their businesses and even eliminate themselves as employers be balanced by some protection to the employees from a sudden change in the employment relationship. The transition from one corporate organization to another will in most cases be eased and industrial strife avoided if employees' claims continue to be resolved by arbitration rather than by "the relative strength * * * of the contending forces," Warrior & Gulf, supra, 363 U.S. at 580, 80 S.Ct. at 1352, 4 L.Ed.2d 1409.

The preference of national labor policy for arbitration as a substitute for tests of strength between contending forces could be overcome only if other considerations compellingly so demanded. We find none. While the principles of law governing ordinary contracts would not bind to a contract an unconsenting successor to a contracting party,[26] a collective bargaining agreement is not an ordinary contract. " * * * [I]t is a generalized code to govern a myriad of cases which the draftsmen cannot wholly anticipate * * *. The collective agreement covers the whole employment relationship. It calls into being a new common law—the common law of a particular industry or of a particular plant." Warrior & Gulf, supra, 363 U.S. at 578–579, 80 S.Ct. at 1351, 4 L.Ed.2d 1409 (footnotes omitted). Cen-

---

26. But cf. the general rule that in the case of a merger the corporation which survives is liable for the debts and contracts of the one which disappears. 15 Fletcher, Private Corporations (1961 rev. ed.), § 7121.

tral to the peculiar status and function of a collective bargaining agreement is the fact, dictated both by circumstance, see id., 363 U.S. at 580, 80 S.Ct. 1347, 4 L.Ed.2d 1409, and by the requirements of the National Labor Relations Act, that it is not in any real sense the simple product of a consensual relationship. Therefore, although the duty to arbitrate, as we have said, supra, must be founded on a contract, the impressive policy considerations favoring arbitration are not wholly overborne by the fact that Wiley did not sign the contract being construed.[27] This case cannot readily be assimilated to the category of those in which there is no contract whatever, or none which is reasonably related to the party sought to be obligated. There was a contract, and Interscience, Wiley's predecessor, was party to it. We thus find Wiley's obligation to arbitrate this dispute in the Interscience contract, construed in the context of a national labor policy.

We do not hold that in every case in which the ownership or corporate structure of an enterprise is changed the duty to arbitrate survives. As indicated above, there may be cases in which the lack of any substantial continuity of identity in the business enterprise before and after a change would make a duty to arbitrate something imposed from without, not reasonably to be found in the particular bargaining agreement and the acts of the parties involved. So too, we do not rule out the possibility that a union might abandon its right to arbitration by failing to make its claims known. Neither of these situations is before the Court. Although Wiley was substantially larger than Interscience, relevant similarity and continuity of operation across the change in ownership is adequately evidenced by the wholesale transfer of Interscience employees to the Wiley plant, apparently without difficulty. The Union made its position known well before the merger and never departed from it. In addition, we do not suggest any view on the questions surrounding a certified union's claim to continued representative status following a change in ownership. See, e. g., National Labor Relations Board v. Aluminum Tubular Corp., 2 Cir., 299 F.2d 595, 598–600; National Labor Relations Board v. McFarland, 10 Cir., 306 F.2d 219; Cruse Motors, Inc., 105 N.L.R.B. 242, 247. This Union does not assert that it has any bargaining rights independent of the Interscience agreement; it seeks to arbitrate claims based on that agreement, now expired, not to negotiate a new agreement.[28]

---

27. Compare the principle that when a contract is scrutinized for evidence of an intention to arbitrate a particular kind of dispute, *national labor policy* requires, within reason, that "an interpretation that covers the asserted dispute," Warrior & Gulf, supra, 363 U.S. pp. 582–583, 80 S.Ct. pp. 1352, 1353, 4 L.Ed.2d 1409, be favored.

28. The fact that the Union does not represent a majority of an appropriate bargaining unit in Wiley does not prevent it from representing those employees who are covered by the agreement which is in dispute and out of which Wiley's duty to arbitrate arises. Retail Clerks Int'l Ass'n., Local Unions Nos. 128 and 633, v. Lion Dry Goods, Inc., 369 U.

Beyond denying its obligation to arbitrate at all, Wiley urges that the Union's grievances are not within the scope of the arbitration clause.

[The Court then listed the union's grievances, including whether the job security and grievance provisions were to continue in force, and whether "now and after January 30, 1962" Wiley was obligated to honor the contractual seniority rights of Interscience employees, to contribute to their pension fund, and to pay severance and vacation pay under the contract. The Court noted the very broad terms of the arbitration provision in the Interscience contract, and concluded that the subject matter of the grievances was dealt with in that contract and would have been arbitrable against Interscience had disputes arisen prior to the merger.] Wiley argues, however, that the Union's claims are plainly outside the scope of the arbitration clause: first, because the agreement did not embrace post-merger claims, and, second because the claims relate to a period beyond the limited term of the agreement.

In all probability, the situation created by the merger was one not expressly contemplated by the Union or Interscience when the agreement was made in 1960. Fairly taken, however, the Union's demands collectively raise the question which underlies the whole litigation: What is the effect of the merger on the rights of covered employees? It would be inconsistent with our holding that the obligation to arbitrate survived the merger were we to hold that the fact of the merger, without more, removed claims otherwise plainly arbitrable from the scope of the arbitration clause.

It is true that the Union has framed its issues to claim rights not only "now"—after the merger but during the term of the agreement—but also after the agreement expired by its terms. Claimed rights during the term of the agreement, at least, are unquestionably within the arbitration clause; we do not understand Wiley to urge that the Union's claims to all such rights have become moot by reason of the expiration of the agreement. As to claimed rights "after January 30, 1962," it is reasonable to read the claims as based solely on the Union's construction of the Interscience agreement in such

S. 17, 82 S.Ct. 541, 7 L.Ed.2d 503. There is no problem of conflict with another union, cf. L. B. Spear & Co., 106 N.L.R.B. 687, since Wiley had no contract with any union covering the unit of employees which received the former Interscience employees.

Problems might be created by an arbitral award which required Wiley to give special treatment to the former Interscience employees because of rights found to have accrued to them

under the Interscience contract. But the mere possibility of such problems cannot cut off the Union's right to press the employees' claims in arbitration. While it would be premature at this stage to speculate on how to avoid such hypothetical problems, we have little doubt that within the flexible procedures of arbitration a solution can be reached which would avoid disturbing labor relations in the Wiley plant.

a way that, had there been no merger, Interscience would have been required to discharge certain obligations notwithstanding the expiration of the agreement.   We see no reason why parties could not if they so chose agree to the accrual of rights during the term of an agreement and their realization after the agreement had expired. Of course, the Union may not use arbitration to acquire new rights against Wiley any more than it could have used arbitration to negotiate a new contract with Interscience, had the existing contract expired and renewal negotiations broken down.

Whether or not the Union's demands have merit will be determined by the arbitrator in light of the fully developed facts. It is sufficient for present purposes that the demands are not so plainly unreasonable that the subject matter of the dispute must be regarded as nonarbitrable because it can be seen in advance that no award to the Union could receive judicial sanction. See Warrior & Gulf, supra, 363 U.S. at 582–583, 80 S.Ct. 1347, 4 L.Ed.2d 1409.

Wiley's final objection to arbitration raises the question of so-called "procedural arbitrability."   The Interscience agreement provides for arbitration as the third stage of the grievance procedure. "Step 1" provides for "a conference between the affected employee, a Union Steward and the Employer, officer or exempt supervisory person in charge of his department."   In "Step 2," the grievance is submitted to "a conference between an officer of the Employer, or the Employer's representative designated for that purpose, the Union Shop Committee and/or a representative of the Union."   Arbitration is reached under "Step 3" "in the event that the grievance shall not have been resolved or settled in 'Step 2.' "   Wiley argues that since Steps 1 and 2 have not been followed, and since the duty to arbitrate arises only in Step 3, it has no duty to arbitrate this dispute. Specifically, Wiley urges that the question whether "procedural" conditions to arbitration have been met must be decided by the court and not the arbitrator.

We think that labor disputes of the kind involved here cannot be broken down so easily into their "substantive" and "procedural" aspects. Questions concerning the procedural prerequisites to arbitration do not arise in a vacuum; they develop in the context of an actual dispute about the rights of the parties to the contract or those covered by it. In this case, for example, the Union argues that Wiley's consistent refusal to recognize the Union's representative status after the merger made it "utterly futile—and a little bit ridiculous to follow the grievance steps as set forth in the contract." Brief, p. 41. In addition, the Union argues that time limitations in the grievance procedure are not controlling because Wiley's violations of the bargaining agreement were "continuing."   These arguments in response to Wiley's "procedural" claim are meaningless unless set in the background of the merger and the negotiations surrounding it.

Doubt whether grievance procedures or some part of them apply to a particular dispute, whether such procedures have been followed or excused, or whether the unexcused failure to follow them avoids the duty to arbitrate cannot ordinarily be answered without consideration of the merits of the dispute which is presented for arbitration. In this case, one's view of the Union's responses to Wiley's "procedural" arguments depends to a large extent on how one answers questions bearing on the basic issue, the effect of the merger; e. g., whether or not the merger was a possibility considered by Wiley and the Union during the negotiation of the contract. It would be a curious rule which required that intertwined issues of "substance" and "procedure" growing out of a single dispute and raising the same questions on the same facts had to be carved up between two different forums, one deciding after the other. Neither logic nor considerations of policy compel such a result.

Once it is determined, as we have, that the parties are obligated to submit the subject matter of a dispute to arbitration, "procedural" questions which grow out of the dispute and bear on its final disposition should be left to the arbitrator. Even under a contrary rule, a court could deny arbitration only if it could confidently be said not only that a claim was strictly "procedural," and therefore within the purview of the court, but also that it should operate to bar arbitration altogether, and not merely limit or qualify an arbitral award. In view of the policies favoring arbitration and the parties' adoption of arbitration as the preferred means of settling disputes, such cases are likely to be rare indeed. In all other cases, those in which arbitration goes forward, the arbitrator would ordinarily remain free to reconsider the ground covered by the court insofar as it bore on the merits of the dispute, using the flexible approaches familiar to arbitration. Reservation of "procedural" issues for the courts would thus not only create the difficult task of separating related issues, but would also produce frequent duplication of effort.

In addition, the opportunities for deliberate delay and the possibility of well-intentioned but no less serious delay created by separation of the "procedural" and "substantive" elements of a dispute are clear. While the courts have the task of determining "substantive arbitrability," there will be cases in which arbitrability of the subject matter is unquestioned but a dispute arises over the procedures to be followed. In all of such cases, acceptance of Wiley's position would produce the delay attendant upon judicial proceedings preliminary to arbitration. As this case, commenced in January 1962 and not yet committed to arbitration, well illustrates, such delay may entirely eliminate the prospect of a speedy arbitrated settlement of the dispute, to the disadvantage of the parties (who, in addition, will have to bear increased costs) and contrary to the aims of national labor policy.

No justification for such a generally undesirable result is to be found in a presumed intention of the parties. Refusal to order arbitration of subjects which the parties have not agreed to arbitrate does not entail the fractionating of disputes about subjects which the parties do wish to have submitted. Although a party may resist arbitration once a grievance has arisen, as does Wiley here, we think it best accords with the usual purposes of an arbitration clause and with the policy behind federal labor law to regard procedural disagreements not as separate disputes but as aspects of the dispute which called the grievance procedures into play. * * *

Affirmed.

MR. JUSTICE GOLDBERG took no part in the consideration or decision of this case.

When the underlying controversy in *Wiley* went to arbitration in 1970, the arbitrator treated the collective bargaining agreement provisions as in force until the Interscience employees were moved, during the term of the agreement, into the Wiley headquarters at which time their separate identity from the (other) Wiley employees was held to cease. INTERSCIENCE ENCYCLOPEDIA, INC., 55 Lab.Arb. 211, 218 (1970). The arbitrator stated that:

> "[W]here the industrial community has remained substantially intact after a change in ownership, the collective bargaining agreement is just as applicable to the enterprise as it was before the event. This was the 'substantial continuity of identity in the business enterprise before and after a change' in the ownership that the Court made prerequisite to obligating the unconsenting successor to arbitrate. The same reasoning would compel the persistence of the contract upon which the employees' rights are dependent, either to its contract termination date or until there is a change of conditions that altered the separate identity within the new business enterprise, whichever occurred sooner.
>
> "In the present case, this conversion took place on January 12, 1962 when the former Interscience employees were moved to the Wiley quarters and comingled with the larger Wiley contingent. As expressed in the Wiley letter of October 2, 1961, the former Interscience clerical and shipping employees became a minority accretion to an identical unit of Wiley employees for which the Union was not the chosen bargaining representative. With the loss of the elements

necessary for its viability, the collective agreement between
the Company and the Union ceased to be enforceable."

———

NOLDE BROS., INC. v. LOCAL 358, BAKERY & CONFECTIONERY
WORKERS UNION, 430 U.S. 243, 97 S.Ct. 1067, 51 L.Ed.2d 300 (1977).
The Company's bakery employees in Norfolk, Virginia, were covered
by a labor agreement with Local 358 of the Bakery and Confectionery Workers Union. The contract provided for arbitration of "any
grievance," for severance pay for all employees having three or more
years of service, and for vacation pay based on length of service and
amount of earnings. Negotiations for a new contract continued beyond August 27, 1973, which was the formal contract termination
date pursuant to the Union's termination notice. On August 31,
after the Union had rejected Nolde's most recent proposal and a
strike was imminent, Nolde announced that it was that day closing
the Norfolk bakery. The Company paid the terminated workers
their accrued wages and vacation pay, but rejected the Union's demand for severance pay as well as the Union's demand to arbitrate
that claim; the Company asserted that its obligation to arbitrate
terminated when the labor contract terminated. In a Section 301 action, the Supreme Court held that the duty to arbitrate the severance-
pay claim survived the termination of the contract, and affirmed the
decision of the court of appeals requiring Nolde to arbitrate.

Although Nolde claimed that its obligation for severance pay
terminated when the contract did, the Union claimed that the employees' right to such pay "vested" as they worked during the contract term so that they were entitled to it even if their actual severance from employment took place thereafter. The Court stated:
"[I]t is clear that, whatever the outcome, the resolution of that claim
hinges on the interpretation ultimately given the contract clause
providing for severance pay. The dispute therefore, although arising *after* the expiration of the collective-bargaining contract, clearly
arises *under* that contract." The Court acknowledged its prior decisions to the effect that the duty to arbitrate is a creature of the
labor contract and cannot be forced upon a party absent its contractual agreement to arbitrate. But this principle "does not require us to hold that termination of a collective-bargaining agreement automatically extinguishes a party's duty to arbitrate grievances arising under the contract. Carried to its logical conclusion
that argument would preclude the entry of a post-contract arbitration order even when the dispute arose during the life of the contract
but arbitration proceedings had not begun before termination.
The same would be true if arbitration processes began but were not
completed, during the contract's term. Yet it could not seriously

be contended in either instance that the expiration of the contract would terminate the parties' contractual obligation to resolve such a dispute in an arbitral, rather than a judicial forum."

The Court found the *Wiley* case instructive, for even though the union there sought arbitration regarding post-contract severance pay *before* the labor contract had terminated, "that factor was not dispositive in our determination of arbitrability." The severance-pay claim would have been arbitrable under the Nolde contract had it arisen during the contract term, and there is nothing in the arbitration provision which suggests an exclusion for disputes arising under the contract but based on events occurring after its termination. The termination of the contract does not undermine the reasons the parties had chosen to resolve their disputes through arbitration: confidence in the arbitration process, the arbitrator's presumed special competence, prompt and inexpensive resolution.

The Court noted the strong federal policy favoring arbitration of labor-contract disputes and stated that "the parties must be deemed to have been conscious of this policy," so that their failure to exclude from arbitration disputes arising after contract termination "affords a basis for concluding that they intended to arbitrate all grievances" arising from the contract. "In short, where the dispute is over a provision of the expired agreement, the presumptions favoring arbitrability must be negated expressly or by clear implication."

Justice Stewart (for Justice Rehnquist as well) dissented, pointing out that the policy fostering arbitration as a means of assuring harmony in a continuing labor-management relationship is inapt when the Company is closing its facility and when the contract's termination releases the Union from its obligation not to strike. The fact that the NLRB holds that the duty to arbitrate terminates with contract termination, so that the employer may unilaterally decline to arbitrate post-contract claims without first bargaining to impasse, demonstrates that there is no federal labor policy requiring an order to arbitrate in the instant case.

Problems for Discussion

1. Why is there a presumption that a court rather than the arbitrator is to determine questions of *substantive* arbitrability? Is it consistent with that presumption to presume that questions of *procedural* arbitrability are for the arbitrator rather than a court? Are the reasons for the latter presumption which are given by the Court in *Wiley* convincing? Are they not even more convincing when the issue is substantive arbitrability?

2. Evaluate the following proposition: "The question whether the termination of the Nolde Bros. contract relieved the Company of the duty to

arbitrate the Union's severance-pay claims is nothing more than an issue of procedural arbitrability. The *Wiley* decision requires that this question is to be determined by the arbitrator, and the Court in *Nolde* usurped arbitral authority when it decided this question itself."

3.   Assume that the Union in the *Nolde* case had chosen to press its claim for severance pay not through arbitration but by resort to a strike and picketing. (Presumably, this would take place at Nolde's other facilities, the Norfolk facility having been closed down.) Would such a post-termination strike be a violation of the Norfolk collective bargaining agreement? See Goya Foods, Inc., 238 N.L.R.B. 1465 (1978).

4.   On Wednesday, September 8, 1981, the employer, Milton Typesetters, promoted one Robert Finn to head typesetter. Michael Kingman, an employee with more seniority than Finn, felt that he should have received the promotion instead. The collective bargaining agreement provides a grievance procedure which can be instituted by any employee who believes "he or she has been unjustly dealt with provided that a grievance is filed within ten days." A grievance was filed on Kingman's behalf on Monday, September 21, the ninth working day. The employer refused to arbitrate contending that "within ten days" means not ten working days but ten calendar days and that the grievance had to have been filed by the 18th. The union has initiated a suit under Section 301 on Kingman's behalf to compel arbitration, contending that any procedural questions are to be decided by the arbitrator. Counsel for the employer contends that under *Wiley* there is the negative inference that where the merits (here seniority and promotion) and the procedural questions are not intertwined, the procedural questions are to be decided by the courts and not the arbitrator and that therefore the court should not compel the employer to arbitrate even the procedural question. How should the court rule? See *Tobacco Workers Local 317* v. *Lorillard Corp.*, 448 F.2d 949 (4th Cir. 1971).

Assume, instead, that the Milton labor contract is silent as to the time within which a grievance must be formally initiated. Assume too that the union does not file a grievance on Kingman's behalf until five months after the promotion of Finn. Upon a demand for arbitration and the Company's refusal, the union seeks an order to arbitrate from a federal court under Section 301. Milton defends by asserting that the traditional equity doctrine of laches should apply and should bar the union's claim because of its long delay in asserting it. Should the court address this defense or should it send it to an arbitrator? See Operating Engineers Local 150 v. Flair Builders, Inc., 406 U.S. 487, 92 S.Ct. 1710, 32 L.Ed.2d 248 (1972).

5.   Columbia Broadcasting System (CBS) has separate bargaining agreements with Local A as the representative of broadcasting technicians and Local B as the representative of recording engineers. The agreements with both locals contain typical arbitration clauses and expansive work-assignment provisions. When CBS recently assigned certain work, newly generated by computer technology, to the employees represented by Local A, Local B complained that this work was akin to that traditionally done by the workers in its unit and should instead be assigned to them. When CBS

rejected Local B's claim and its demand for arbitration, Local B brought an action under Section 301 to compel arbitration. CBS has joined Local A as defendant and in its answer has asserted: (1) that the action by Local B should be dismissed, since it would be unfair to CBS and to Local A if the court were to order arbitration with Local B in an arbitral forum which could not consider as well the contract rights of Local A; and, in the alternative, (2) that for the same reasons the court should compel a tripartite arbitration among CBS, Local A and Local B.

What ruling should the court make? See Columbia Broadcasting System, Inc. v. American Recording & Broadcasting Ass'n, 414 F.2d 1326 (2d Cir. 1969).

NOTE ON THE SUCCESSOR'S DUTY TO ARBITRATE [29]

The continuing impact of the *Wiley* decision concerning the obligations of the successor employer has been called into question by the Supreme Court itself, in two more recent decisions. The facts of NLRB v. BURNS INTERNATIONAL SECURITY SERVICES, INC., have already been set forth at pages 353–60, supra, as have excerpts from the Court's opinion holding that the successor employer, Burns, was obligated to bargain under Section 8(a)(5) with the union that had formerly represented the employees of the predecessor Wackenhut; those employees comprised a majority of the Burns bargaining unit. The Court held, however, that the duty to bargain with the predecessor's union did not carry with it the duty to abide by the terms of the predecessor's collective bargaining agreement. The Court at great length distinguished its earlier decision in *Wiley*, which was urged by the union as the principal support for its argument that "contract continuity" was essential to foster the statutory objectives of preserving industrial peace and sheltering the predecessor's employees against the economic impact of a business transfer.

First, the Court placed great weight upon the policy of Section 8(d) to encourage the parties to set contract terms themselves, through free collective bargaining, and not by government compulsion of unwanted provisions. The Court noted that the Board itself gives effect to this policy by permitting a newly certified union—during the period of an existing labor contract, made with a predeces-

---

29. See Goldberg, The Labor Law Obligations of a Successor Employer, 63 Nw.L.Rev. 735 (1969); Morris & Gaus, Successorship and the Collective Bargaining Agreement: Accommodating *Wiley* and *Burns*, 59 Va.L.Rev. 1359 (1973); Note, Contract Rights and the Successor Employer: The Impact of *Burns Security*, 71 Mich.L.Rev. 571 (1973); Note, Contractual Successorship: The Impact of *Burns*, 40 U.Chi. L.Rev. 617 (1973); Platt, The NLRB and the Arbitrator in Sale and Merger Situations, N.Y.U. 19th Annual Conf. on Labor 375 (1967); Severson & Willcoxon, Successorship Under *Howard Johnson*: Short Order Justice for Employees, 64 Calif.L.Rev. 795 (1976); Slicker, A Reconsideration of the Doctrine of Employer Successorship—A Step Toward a Rational Approach, 57 Minn.L.Rev. 1051 (1973).

sor union, but which no longer constitutes a "contract bar" to an election—to demand negotiations for a new contract. Second, the Court held that the "contract continuity" policies of *Wiley* were announced in a Section 301 case involving the special federal policy of arbitration as a substitute for industrial strife, while the *Burns* case arose under Section 8(a)(5) which is expressly limited by the provisions of Section 8(d). (The Court left unspoken the implication that Section 8(d) is properly to be treated as part of the federal law which should also shape the duty to arbitrate under Section 301.) Third, and without much explication, the Court observed that *Wiley* involved "a merger occurring against a background of state law that embodied the general rule that in merger situations the surviving corporation is liable for the obligations of the disappearing corporation" (a fact that the *Wiley* Court had consigned to a footnote) ; *Burns* involved no contractual dealings or purchase of assets between predecessor and successor companies, but merely a transfer of employees, "a wholly insufficient basis for implying either in fact or in law that Burns had agreed or must be held to have agreed to honor Wackenhut's collective-bargaining contract."

After once again emphasizing the statutory policy favoring free collective bargaining—including the establishment of contract terms through strikes and lockouts—and forbidding governmental imposition of contract terms contrary to the will of the parties, the Court noted its reluctance to burden either a union or a successor employer with the uneconomic or the inequitable provisions of a labor contract made with a predecessor employer.

> "[H]olding either the union or the new employer bound to the substantive terms of an old collective-bargaining contract may result in serious inequities. A potential employer may be willing to take over a moribund business only if he can make changes in corporate structure, composition of the labor force, work location, task assignment, and nature of supervision. Saddling such an employer with the terms and conditions of employment contained in the old collective-bargaining contract may make these changes impossible and may discourage and inhibit the transfer of capital. On the other hand, a union may have made concessions to a small or failing employer that it would be unwilling to make to a large or economically successful firm. The congressional policy manifest in the Act is to enable the parties to negotiate for any protection either deems appropriate, but to allow the balance of bargaining advantage to be set by economic power realities. Strife is bound to occur if the concessions that must be honored do not correspond to the relative economic strength of the parties.

"The Board's position would also raise new problems, for the successor employer would be circumscribed in exactly the same way as the predecessor under the collective-bargaining contract. It would seemingly follow that employees of the predecessor would be deemed employees of the successor, dischargeable only in accordance with provisions of the contract and subject to the grievance and arbitration provisions thereof. Burns would not have been free to replace Wackenhut's guards with its own except as the contract permitted. * * *

"In many cases, of course, successor employers will find it advantageous not only to recognize and bargain with the union but also to observe the pre-existing contract rather than to face uncertainty and turmoil. Also, in a variety of circumstances involving a merger, stock acquisition, reorganization, or assets purchase, the Board might properly find as a matter of fact that the successor had assumed the obligations under the old contract. * * * Such a duty does not, however, ensue as a matter of law from the mere fact that an employer is doing the same work in the same place with the same employees as his predecessor, as the Board had recognized until its decision in the instant case. * * * We accordingly set aside the Board's finding of a § 8(a)(5) unfair labor practice insofar as it rested on a conclusion that Burns was required to but did not honor the collective-bargaining contract executed by Wackenhut."

The force of *Wiley v. Livingston* was diminished yet further, more recently, in a case involving the very issue there litigated, that is, the duty of a successor company under Section 301 to arbitrate under the predecessor's labor contract. In HOWARD JOHNSON CO. v. DETROIT LOCAL JOINT EXEC. BD., 417 U.S. 249, 94 S.Ct. 2236, 41 L.Ed.2d 46 (1974), the Grissom family, which had operated a motel and restaurant as franchisees of Howard Johnson, transferred the business to Howard Johnson Co. by selling it the personal property and leasing to it the real property. Although Grissom had a labor contract covering its 53 employees, and that contract stipulated that it would be binding on Grissom's successors and assigns, Howard Johnson disclaimed the contract and any liabilities thereunder, and so informed the union. The Grissom employees were informed shortly before the formal transfer of the operation that they were to be terminated, and after independent and nondiscriminatory recruitment, Howard Johnson began doing business in exactly the same manner as before, with 45 employees, only nine of whom had worked for Grissom, and with a completely new set of supervisors. The union claimed that the refusal to hire the former

Grissom employees was a "lockout" in violation of the Grissom contract, which the union claimed bound Howard Johnson. While Grissom announced its willingness to arbitrate, Howard Johnson would not, and the union brought an action under Section 301. The Supreme Court refused to order arbitration. The Court chose to justify its denial of arbitration in *Howard Johnson* on a distinction of *Wiley*, in the process very severely undermining the precedential strength of that decision and injecting considerable uncertainty into the law governing the successor's duty to arbitrate.

The Court emphasized two factors which distinguished *Howard Johnson*. (1) Howard Johnson acquired the business not by merger but by purchase and rental of property from a company which continues to exist after the transfer. The Court conceded that "ordinarily" the analysis of successorship problems does not turn on whether there is a merger, consolidation or purchase of assets, but —without explaining why the circumstances were out of the ordinary —then proceeded to note that the controlling state corporate law governing the Interscience-Wiley merger (which made the survivor responsible for the predecessor's obligations) made a continued duty to arbitrate "fairly within the reasonable expectations of the parties." Moreover, a merger results in the "disappearance" of the predecessor while the Grissom sale and lease left Grissom amenable to a union action for breach of its labor contract. (2) Even more important, the Court held that while "continuity of identity in the business enterprise" was demonstrated in *Wiley* by the hiring of *all* of the Interscience employees, such continuity was lacking when Howard Johnson exercised its privilege to recruit a new workforce, without discrimination on the basis of union membership, which included only a small minority of the persons working for Grissom at the time of the transfer. The gist of the union's arbitration claim was not any vested rights of employees already hired by Howard Johnson but the claim to employment by former Grissom employees *not* hired. The Court announced an important principle:

> "This continuity of identity in the business enterprise necessarily includes, we think, a substantial continuity in the identity of the work force across the change in ownership.
> * * * This view is reflected in the emphasis most of the lower courts have placed on whether the successor employer hires a majority of the predecessor's employees in determining the legal obligations of the successor in § 301 suits under *Wiley*."

Thus, the Court held that "continuity in the workforce" is necessary in order to carry over the duty to arbitrate and that central to such continuity is the hiring of at least a majority of the predecessor's employees.

The Court, in passing, announced three other principles of importance to successorship cases. First, the duty to arbitrate will, as the duty to bargain, be readily imposed when the successor takes not in a bona fide transaction at arm's length but instead as an alter ego, or "disguised continuance of the old employer"; the employer's object is merely to avoid the contract without any substantial change in ownership. Second, the successor violates Section 8(a)(3) when it refuses to hire the predecessor's employees because of their union membership, activity or representation. (It might follow from this that it is also illegal to avoid hiring the predecessor's employees—regardless of union proclivities—in order to avoid arbitration, but this surely would be difficult to square with the Court's desire to free business purchasers of cumbersome contracts made by the predecessor.) Third, a court errs when it decides in the abstract whether a company is a "successor" and only then decides whether it is required to arbitrate or to bargain.

> "The question whether Howard Johnson is a 'successor' is simply not meaningful in the abstract. Howard Johnson is of course a successor employer in the sense that it succeeded to operation of a restaurant and motor lodge formerly operated by the Grissoms. But the real question in each of these 'successorship' cases is, on the particular facts, what are the legal obligations of the new employer to the employees of the former owner or their representative. The answer to this inquiry requires analysis of the interests of the new employer and the employees and of the policies of the labor laws in light of the facts of each case and the particular legal obligation which is at issue, whether it be the duty to recognize and bargain with the union, the duty to remedy unfair labor practices, the duty to arbitrate, etc. There is, and can be, no single definition of 'successor' which is applicable in every legal context. A new employer, in other words, may be a successor for some purposes and not for others."

Problems for Discussion

1. By what criteria is an arbitrator to decide whether and how far the successor company is bound by the substantive clauses of the old agreement? Was it logically consistent with the Supreme Court's decision in *Wiley v. Livingston* for the arbitrator to rule that Wiley, after the closing of the old Interscience plant, was not bound by any of the substantive clauses? Was not bound by the grievance and arbitration provisions?

2. Weber operated a retail coal and fuel oil business in Brooklyn, New York with 24 drivers and servicemen represented by Teamsters under

a collective agreement running until December 15, 1982, which contained provisions relating to seniority, grievances, job security, pensions, and other matters. There was also a conventional arbitration clause. On August 7, 1981 Humble, a fully integrated oil company with retail fuel oil customers, purchased all the assets and good will of Weber, and hired about half of Weber's employees. The Weber operations and accounts were completely absorbed into Humble's business and lost any separate identity. Humble's 518 employees in the New York area, including those in its retail fuel oil business, were represented by another union under a different collective agreement. The Teamsters demanded that Humble comply with its contract with Weber and, when Humble declined, demanded arbitration. Humble refused arbitration and the Teamsters brought an action under Section 301. Pending the litigation the NLRB determined that the former Weber employees had become part of the Humble bargaining unit. The district court, following *Wiley*, ordered arbitration. Humble appealed. What judgment should be entered? See *McGuire* v. *Humble Oil & Refining Co.*, 355 F.2d 352 (2d Cir. 1966). Cf. General Warehousemen and Helpers Local 767 v. Standard Brands, Inc., 579 F.2d 1282 (5th Cir. 1978).

UNITED STEELWORKERS OF AMERICA v. ENTERPRISE WHEEL & CAR CORP.[30]

Supreme Court of the United States, 1960.
363 U.S. 593, 80 S.Ct. 1358, 4 L.Ed.2d 1424.

Mr. Justice Douglas delivered the opinion of the Court.

Petitioner union and respondent during the period relevant here had a collective bargaining agreement which provided that any differences "as to the meaning and application" of the agreement should be submitted to arbitration and that the arbitrator's decision "shall be final and binding on the parties." Special provisions were included concerning the suspension and discharge of employees. The agreement stated:

> "Should it be determined by the Company or by an arbitrator in accordance with the grievance procedure that the employee has been suspended unjustly or discharged in violation of the provisions of this Agreement, the Company shall reinstate the employee and pay full compensation at the employee's regular rate of pay for the time lost."

---

30. See Aaron, Judicial Intervention in Labor Arbitration, 20 Stan.L.Rev. 41 (1967); Dunau, Three Problems in Labor Arbitration, 55 Va.L.Rev. 427 (1969); Jones, The Name of the Game is Decision—Some Reflections on "Arbitrability" and "Authority" in Labor Arbitration, 46 Texas L.Rev. 865 (1968); St. Antoine, Judicial Review of Labor Arbitration Awards, 75 Mich. L.Rev. 1137 (1977).

The agreement also provided:

"* * * It is understood and agreed that neither party will institute *civil suits or legal proceedings* against the other for alleged violation of any of the provisions of this labor contract; instead all disputes will be settled in the manner outlined in this Article III—Adjustment of Grievances."

A group of employees left their jobs in protest against the discharge of one employee. A union official advised them at once to return to work. An official of respondent at their request gave them permission and then rescinded it. The next day they were told they did not have a job any more "until this thing was settled one way or the other."

A grievance was filed; and when respondent finally refused to arbitrate, this suit was brought for specific enforcement of the arbitration provisions of the agreement. The District Court ordered arbitration. The arbitrator found that the discharge of the men was not justified, though their conduct, he said, was improper. In his view the facts warranted at most a suspension of the men for 10 days each. After their discharge and before the arbitration award the collective bargaining agreement had expired. The union, however, continued to represent the workers at the plant. The arbitrator rejected the contention that expiration of the agreement barred reinstatement of the employees. He held that the provision of the agreement above quoted imposed an unconditional obligation on the employer. He awarded reinstatement with back pay, minus pay for a 10-day suspension and such sums as these employees received from other employment.

Respondent refused to comply with the award. Petitioner moved the District Court for enforcement. The District Court directed respondent to comply. 168 F.Supp. 308. The Court of Appeals, while agreeing that the District Court had jurisdiction to enforce an arbitration award under a collective bargaining agreement held that the failure of the award to specify the amounts to be deducted from the back pay rendered the award unenforceable. That defect, it agreed, could be remedied by requiring the parties to complete the arbitration. It went on to hold, however, that an award for back pay subsequent to the date of termination of the collective bargaining agreement could not be enforced. It also held that the requirement for reinstatement of the discharged employees was likewise unenforceable because the collective agreement had expired. 269 F.2d 327.

The refusal of courts to review the merits of an arbitration award is the proper approach to arbitration under collective bargaining agreements. The federal policy of settling labor disputes by arbitration would be undermined if courts had the final say on the merits of the awards. As we stated in United Steelworkers of America v. Warrior & Gulf Navigation Co., 363 U.S. 574, 80 S.Ct. 1347, the arbitrators under these collective agreements are indispensable agencies in a continuous collective bargaining process. They sit to settle disputes at the plant level—disputes that require for their solution knowledge of the custom and practices of a particular factory or of a particular industry as reflected in particular agreements.[31]

When an arbitrator is commissioned to interpret and apply the collective bargaining agreement, he is to bring his informed judgment to bear in order to reach a fair solution of a problem. This is especially true when it comes to formulating remedies. There the need is for flexibility in meeting a wide variety of situations. The draftsmen may never have thought of what specific remedy should be awarded to meet a particular contingency. Nevertheless, an arbitrator is confined to interpretation and application of the collective bargaining agreement; he does not sit to dispense his own brand of industrial justice. He may of course look for guidance from many sources, yet his award is legitimate only so long as it draws its essence from the collective bargaining agreement. When the arbitrator's words manifest an infidelity to this obligation, courts have no choice but to refuse enforcement of the award.

The opinion of the arbitrator in this case, as it bears upon the award of back pay beyond the date of the agreement's expiration and reinstatement, is ambiguous. It may be read as based solely upon the arbitrator's view of the requirements of enacted legislation, which would mean that he exceeded the scope of the submission. Or it may be read as embodying a construction of the agreement itself, perhaps with the arbitrator looking to "the law" for help in determining the sense of the agreement. A mere ambiguity in the opinion accompanying an award, which permits the inference that the arbitrator may have exceeded his authority, is not a reason for refusing to enforce the award. Arbitrators have no obligation to the court to give their reasons for an award. To require opinions free of ambiguity may lead arbitrators to play it safe by writing no supporting opinions. This would be undesirable for a well reasoned opinion tends to engender confidence in the integrity of the process and aids in clarifying the

---

31. "Persons unfamiliar with mills and factories—farmers or professors, for example—often remark upon visiting them that they seem like another world. This is particularly true if, as in the steel industry, both tradition and technology have strongly and uniquely molded the ways men think and act when at work. The newly hired employee, the 'green hand,' is gradually initiated into what amounts to a miniature society. There he finds himself in a strange environment that assaults his senses with unusual sounds and smells and often with different 'weather conditions' such as sudden drafts of heat, cold, or humidity. He discovers that the society of which he only gradually becomes a part has of course a formal government of its own—the rules which management and the union have laid down —but that it also differs from or parallels the world outside in social classes, folklore, ritual, and traditions. * * *" Walker, Life in the Automatic Factory, 36 Harv.Bus.L.Rev. 111, 117.

underlying agreement. Moreover, we see no reason to assume that this arbitrator has abused the trust the parties confided in him and has not stayed within the areas marked out for his consideration. It is not apparent that he went beyond the submission. The Court of Appeals opinion refusing to enforce the reinstatement and partial back pay portions of the award was not based upon any finding that the arbitrator did not premise his award on his construction of the contract. It merely disagreed with the arbitrator's construction of it.

The collective bargaining agreement could have provided that if any of the employees were wrongfully discharged, the remedy would be reinstatement and back pay up to the date they were returned to work. Respondent's major argument seems to be that by applying correct principles of law to the interpretation of the collective bargaining agreement it can be determined that the agreement did not so provide, and that therefore the arbitrator's decision was not based upon the contract. The acceptance of this view would require courts, even under the standard arbitration clause, to review the merits of every construction of the contract. This plenary review by a court of the merits would make meaningless the provisions that the arbitrator's decision is final, for in reality it would almost never be final. This underlines the fundamental error which we have alluded to in United States Steelworkers of America v. American Manufacturing Co., 362 U.S. 564, 80 S.Ct. 1343. As we there emphasized the question of interpretation of the collective bargaining agreement is a question for the arbitrator. It is the arbitrator's construction which was bargained for; and so far as the arbitrator's decision concerns construction of the contract, the courts have no business overruling him because their interpretation of the contract is different from his.

We agree with the Court of Appeals that the judgment of the District Court should be modified so that the amounts due the employees may be definitely determined by arbitration. In all other respects we think the judgment of the District Court should be affirmed.

[The dissenting opinion of MR. JUSTICE WHITTAKER is omitted.]

TORRINGTON CO. v. METAL PRODUCTS WORKERS LOCAL 1645

United States Court of Appeals, Second Circuit, 1966.
362 F.2d 677.

LUMBARD, CHIEF JUDGE: * * * In its company newsletter of December 1962, Torrington announced that it was discontinuing its twenty-year policy of permitting employees time off with pay to vote on election days. This policy had been unilaterally instituted by the company and was not a part of the then-existing collective bargaining agreement, which contained an extremely narrow arbitration provision. The Union did not attempt to arbitrate this issue. Rather, on April 9, 1963, it filed a many-faceted complaint with the National Labor Relations Board which included a charge that the unilateral change of election day policy constituted an unfair labor practice.

The Union later dropped this charge, and the Board dismissed the entire complaint on July 29, 1963. In August, the parties began negotiations for a new collective bargaining agreement, as the old contract was due to expire September 27, 1963. At the first meeting, Torrington informed the Union that it did not intend to reestablish its paid time off for voting policy. The Union responded by including a contrary provision in its written demands presented at a meeting in August or early September.

At this point, the record is somewhat unclear as to the circumstances surrounding the negotiations. We know that in the written proposals made by Torrington (September 26) and by the Union (October 25), *each* suggested that the old contract be continued with specific amendments, none of which involved the election day policy. We know that a long and costly strike began when the old contract expired on September 27, that some employees worked during the strike, and that those employees were not given paid time off for the November 1963 elections. And it is conceded by all that the current contract, signed on January 18, 1964, contained, like the old, no mention of paid time off for voting.

When the 1964 elections became imminent, Torrington's understanding of its rights under the new contract was revealed by a union flier to the employees dated November 2, 1964. The Union reported that, "The Torrington Company has again stated that you will *not* be allowed the one hour time off for voting this year." This time, however, the Union was armed with a new weapon, for the new contract contained a much less restrictive arbitration clause.[32] Thus,

---

32. Relevant portions of Article V of the agreement are as follows:

"*Section 1.*—If a grievance is not settled after it has been processed through the three (3) steps described in Article IV above, and if it is a grievance with respect to the interpretation or application of any provisions in this contract and is not controlled by Section 1 of Article XIV, (Management) it may be submitted to arbitration in the manner herein provided * * *

"*Section 3.*—The arbitrator shall be bound by and must comply with all of the terms of this agreement and he shall have no power to add to, delete from or modify, in any way, any of the provisions of this agreement. The arbitrator shall not have the authority to determine the right of employees to merit increases. The arbitrator shall have no authority to set or determine wages except as provided by Section 21 of Article VI, Wages.

"*Section 4.*—The decision of the arbitrator shall be binding on both parties during the life of this agreement unless the same is contrary, in any way, to law."

on December 17, 1964, the Union filed the grievance which underlies this case. When no solution was reached by the parties, application was made to the American Arbitration Association for determination under its Voluntary Labor Arbitration Rules, and the arbitrator was selected by the parties. A hearing was held on May 19, 1965.

In his written decision, the arbitrator first held that the dispute was arbitrable under the new contract's arbitration clause even though the contract contained no express provision for paid time off for voting, a decision which is not challenged. * * * He then ruled that the benefit of paid time off to vote was a firmly established practice at Torrington, that the company therefore had the burden of changing this policy by negotiating with the Union, and that in the negotiations which culminated in the current bargaining agreement the parties did not agree to terminate this practice. Finding further that this employee benefit was not within management's prerogative under the "management functions" clause of the contract, the arbitrator held that employees who took time off to vote on November 3, 1964, or who worked on that day and had received an election benefit in 1962 must be paid a comparable benefit for Election Day 1964.

The company petitioned to vacate the award. * * * Judge Clarie held that the arbitrator had gone outside the terms of the contract and thus had exceeded his authority by reading the election day benefit into the new contract after the parties had negotiated the issue but had made no such provision in that contract.

The essence of the Union's argument on appeal is that, in deciding that the arbitrator exceeded his authority in making this award, the District Court exceeded the scope of its authority and improperly examined the merits of the arbitrator's award. The Union relies on the language in United Steelworkers of America v. Enterprise Wheel & Car Corp., 363 U.S. 593, 596, 80 S.Ct. 1358, 1360, 4 L.Ed.2d 1424 (1960), the third of the famous Steelworkers trilogy in which the Supreme Court outlined the proper role of the judiciary in labor arbitration cases, to the effect that the courts are not "to review the merits of an arbitration award."

I.

It is now well settled that a grievance is arbitrable "unless it may be said with positive assurance that the arbitration clause is not susceptible of an interpretation that covers the asserted dispute." United Steelworkers of America v. Warrior & Gulf Nav. Co., 363 U.S. at 582–583, 80 S.Ct. at 1353. A less settled question is the appropriate scope of judicial review of a specific arbitration award. Although the arbitrator's decision on the merits is final as to questions of law and fact, his authority is contractual in nature and is limited to the powers conferred in the collective bargaining agreement. For this reason, a number of courts have interpreted *Enterprise Wheel* as authorizing review of whether an arbitrator's award exceeded the limits of his contractual authority.

Torrington contends that the arbitrator exceeded his authority in this case by "adding" the election day bonus to the terms of the January 1964 agreement. However, the arbitrator held that such a provision was implied by the prior practice of the parties. In some cases, it may be appropriate exercise of an arbitrator's authority to resolve ambiguities in the scope of a collective bargaining agreement on the basis of prior practice, since no agreement can reduce all aspects of the labor-management relationship to writing. However, while courts should be wary of rejecting the arbitrator's interpretation of the implications of the parties' prior practice, the mandate that the arbitrator stay within the confines of the collective bargaining agreement * * * requires a reviewing court to pass upon whether the agreement authorizes the arbitrator to expand its express terms on the basis of the parties' prior practice. Therefore, we hold that the question of an arbitrator's authority is subject to judicial review, and that the arbitrator's decision that he has authority should not be accepted where the reviewing court can clearly perceive that he has derived that authority from sources outside the collective bargaining agreement at issue. See Textile Workers Union of America v. American Thread Co., 291 F.2d 894 (4 Cir. 1961).

II.

Unfortunately, as the dissenting opinion illustrates, agreeing upon these general principles does not make this case any easier. Certain it is that Torrington's policy of paid time off to vote was well established by 1962. On this basis, the arbitrator ruled that the policy must continue during the 1964 agreement because Torrington did not negotiate a contrary policy into that agreement. To bolster his decision, the arbitrator noted that Torrington's written demands of September 26, 1963, constituted the first occasion on which either party did not expressly insist that its election day position be adopted. Therefore, he concluded, it was the company which removed this question "from the table" and the company cannot complain if its policy under the old contract is now continued.

We cannot accept this interpretation of the negotiations. In the first place, as Judge Clarie stated, labor contracts generally state affirmatively what conditions the parties agree to, more specifically, what restraints the parties will place on management's freedom of action. While it may be appropriate to resolve a question never raised during negotiations on the basis of prior practice in the plant or industry, it is quite another thing to assume that the contract confers a specific benefit when that benefit was discussed during negotiations but omitted from the contract.

"[I]n entering into a collective agreement, in the negotiations for which as much care and deliberateness were exercised in respect to the omission as to the inclusion of various restraints and obligations, neither party agreed to submit to an arbitrator the question of whether it should be subjected to the very restraint or obligation which in negotiations the parties, by omitting it from the contract, agreed the contract should *not* subject it to." Freidin [Discussion of a Paper by Sam Kagel, in Arbitration and Public Policy 10, 14 (BNA 1961)].

The arbitrator's primary justification for reading the election day benefit into the 1964 agreement was that such a benefit corresponded to the parties' prior practice. But in this the arbitrator completely ignored the fact that the company had revoked that policy almost ten months earlier, by newsletter to the employees in December 1962 and by formal notice to the Union in April 1963. It was within the employer's discretion to make such a change since the narrow arbitration clause in the previous collective bargaining agreement precluded resort to arbitration by the Union. And there was no showing that Torrington's announcement was merely a statement of bargaining position and was not a seriously intended change in policy.

In light of this uncontroverted fact, and bearing in mind that the arbitrator has no jurisdiction to "add to" the 1964 agreement, we do not think it was proper to place the "burden" of securing an express contract provision in the 1964 contract on the company. At the start of negotiations, Torrington announced its intent to *continue* its previous change of election day policy. This was an express invitation to the Union to bargain with respect to this matter. After the Union failed to press for and receive a change in the 1964 agreement, the company was surely justified in applying in November 1964 a policy it had rightfully established in 1962, and had applied in November 1963 (during the strike).

In our opinion, the Union by pressing this grievance has attempted to have "added" to the 1964 agreement a benefit which it did not think sufficiently vital to insist upon during negotiations for the contract which ended a long and costly strike. We find this sufficiently clear from the facts as found by the arbitrator to agree with the district court that the arbitrator exceeded his authority by ruling that such a benefit was implied in the terms of that agreement. * * *

FEINBERG, CIRCUIT JUDGE (dissenting): * * * The arbitrator in this case concluded that both parties agreed at the bargaining table to continue the prior practice of paid time off for voting. It is clear that the new contract did not by its terms deal with the time off for voting issue. But the arbitrator reasoned that it was the company, not the union, that was trying to change the twenty-year old practice. It was the company that introduced the issue into the bargaining at the first negotiation meeting in August 1963, and insisted on a change in the practice. Thereafter, according to the arbitrator, the company "removed * * * [this demand] from the table * * *. Thus * * * both parties agreed that the old contract was to be continued except for certain changes among which was *not* a change in the practice of giving time off with pay for voting."

The arbitrator assumed that a collective bargaining agreement can include terms or conditions not made explicit in the written contract. This proposition is correct. In a prior appeal * * * this court said that the arbitration clause of the agreement could be applicable to a recall grievance if there were "some special agreement making it applicable or * * * some custom or common understanding which has that effect." Torrington Co. v. Metal Prods. Workers, 347 F.2d 93, 95 (2d Cir.), cert. denied 382 U.S. 940, 86 S.Ct. 394, 15 L.Ed.2d 351 (1965). This is a clear statement of the view that it is proper to look beyond the terms of a labor contract in interpreting it. In United Steelworkers of America v. Warrior & Gulf Nav. Co., 363 U.S. 574, 580, 80 S.Ct. 1317, 1352, 4 L.Ed.2d 1409 (1960), the Supreme Court said: "Gaps [in the "written document"] may be left to be filled in by reference to the practices of the particular industry and of the various shops covered by the agreement." Moreover, the difference between the earlier (1961–1963) and the new contract in this case is most significant. The arbitration article in the earlier contract contained the following limitations on the arbitrator's power:

> The Company's decisions will stand and will not be overruled by any arbitrator unless the arbitrator can find that the Company misinterpreted or violated the express terms of the agreement.
>
> * * * * * * * * * *
>
> No point not covered by this contract shall be subject to arbitration * * *.

After a 16-week strike in which the scope of the arbitration clause was an important issue (which, in itself, is unusual), these limitations on the arbitrator's power were excluded in the new contract. This was a clear recognition by the parties that there can be "implied" as well as "express" terms in the agreement. In this case, the arbitrator held that pay for time off for voting was a benefit which was such "an implied part of the contract." If so, then, of course, the arbitator did not "add to, delete from, or modify, in any way, any of the provisions of this agreement" in violation of the arbitration clause.

Thus, the arbitrator looked to prior practice, the conduct of the negotiation for the new contract and the agreement reached at the bargaining table to reach his conclusion that paid time off for voting was "an implied part of the contract." From all of this, I conclude that the arbitrator's award "draws its essence from the collective bargaining agreement" and his words do not "manifest an infidelity to this obligation." Once that test is met, the inquiry ends. Whether the arbitator's conclusion was correct is irrelevant because the parties agreed to abide by it, right or wrong. Nevertheless, the majority has carried the inquiry further and concerned itself with a minute examination of the merits of the award, which we are enjoined not to do. Thus, the majority opinion states that the arbitrator "ignored the fact that the company had revoked [its] * * * policy almost ten months earlier." Of course, the arbitrator was aware of the company's actions in December 1962 and April 1963 and referred to them in his opinion. And I would suppose that what significance to attach to these acts—e. g., whether the company could revoke its policy unilaterally—and to the bargaining held thereafter is exactly the sort of question the parties left to the arbitrator to decide.

––––––––––

Problems for Discussion

1. A collective bargaining agreement calls for making all layoffs in reverse order of seniority, and also requires that transfers and promotions be offered in order of seniority. One clause provides: "Seniority is defined to mean length of service with the Company since the last date of hire at whatever location and in whatever capacity employed." Ayres, an employee who had resigned on December 31, 1978, was rehired on September 15, 1980. As a result of a mistake, however, the company records gave her the seniority date of May 1, 1970, which was the date of her original employment prior to the resignation. The erroneous date was carried forward for five years in published seniority listings, and it was the basis upon which two grievances were adjusted. Thereafter, the company attempted to correct the list and offered a promotion to Bolcom, an employee whose seniority dated from May 1, 1978. Ayres filed a grievance, which was sustained by an arbitrator. The arbitrator held that the seniority list had become frozen despite the mistake, and stated that "There must come a time when past errors which have not been challenged or corrected by either party, or by individual employees, must be accepted as the agreed understanding and no longer subject to change." The arbitration provisions in the labor contract are the same as those in

the *Torrington* case. The employer has filed a motion in a federal trial court to vacate the arbitrator's award. What should be the court's decision?

2. The employer discharged an employee for falsifying records relating to hours of work, and the case was submitted to arbitration. The agreement provided that "employees may be discharged for proper cause" and that "if any grievance, arising out of any action taken by the Company in discharging * * * any employee, is carried to arbitration, the arbitrator shall not substitute his judgment for that of the management and shall only reverse the action or decision of the management if he finds that the Company's complaint against the employee is not supported by the facts, and that the management has acted arbitrarily and in bad faith or in violation of the express terms of this Agreement." The arbitrator handed down an award which simply stated that the employee was guilty of conduct which justified discipline, that "discharge was an excessive penalty for said misconduct" and that the employee was "entitled to be reinstated in his employment without [back] pay." The employer refused to abide by the award, and the union brought suit for enforcement in a federal district court. How should the court rule? See *Truck Drivers Local 784* v. *Ulry-Talbert Co.*, 330 F.2d 562 (8th Cir. 1964).

3. The Otis Elevator Company discharged an employee for violation of a company rule prohibiting gambling. The company acted after the employee in question had been convicted in a county court for the knowing possession of "policy slips" on the owner's premises during working hours. Following a hearing, an arbitrator ruled that despite the knowing violation of the company's rule, the employee had not been discharged for "just cause." Though some disciplinary action was appropriate, discharge was considered too severe a penalty in view of the employee's seniority, his four children, his good record, his punishment by the authorities and because of the lack of disciplinary action taken against other employees whom the arbitrator, though not the authorities, felt were guilty of the same offense. The arbitrator therefore ruled that the employee be reinstated without back pay. On a motion for preliminary injunction to enforce the arbitrator's award, the motion was denied. The court conceded that ordinarily, a judge is not free to consider the soundness of the arbitrator's decision. (The court here cited *Enterprise Wheel*.) But the "misconduct involved here was not just an infraction of a company rule. It was a crime * * * A collective bargaining agreement may well give an arbitrator power to dispense his own brand of industrial justice, but the contract, and his power under it are limited by, and must yield to, overriding public policy. This award clashes with that policy. It indulges crime, cripples an employer's power to support the law and impairs his right to prevent exposure to criminal liability. The award is, therefore, void and unenforceable." What decision should the court of appeals make on reviewing the action of the district court? See *Local 453 International Union of Elec. Workers* v. *Otis Elevator Co.*, 314 F.2d 25, (2d Cir.), cert. denied 373 U.S. 949 (1963).

4. The collective bargaining agreement between Company and Union provides: "Employees who do not maintain their membership in good standing in the Union shall be subject to immediate discharge." Union bylaws define "membership in good standing" to include regular attendance at Union meetings. Employee Jones is consistently absent from

membership meetings, and Union insists that Company discharge him, but Company refuses. The contract has a standard arbitration clause.

(a) Union commences an action in a federal district court to compel arbitration of its grievance. Should the court order arbitration? *yes*

(b) Assume that the grievance is sent to arbitration. How should the arbitrator rule? *no discharge, unless it is found by laws are line into eba*

(c) Assume that the arbitrator rules that Jones had failed to maintain his membership in good standing, that the labor contract thus requires Company to discharge him immediately, and that Company should therefore be ordered to do so. If Company brings an action to set aside the award—or if Union brings an action to confirm it—how should the court *affirm* decide? Cf. General Warehousemen and Helpers Local 767 v. Standard Brands, Inc., 579 F.2d 1282 (5th Cir. 1978).

Judicial Enforcement of the No-Strike Clause

With the reintroduction in the Taft-Hartley Act of 1947 of the federal judiciary as an important agency in regulating labor-management relations, and the emphasis in the same legislation upon the peaceful resolution of disputes concerning collective bargaining agreements, it became all but inevitable that the continuing vitality of the Norris-LaGuardia Act of 1932 would have to be tested. The earlier statute had been based upon the belief that judges were ill-equipped to pass judgment upon the social and economic issues involved in labor disputes and that strikes, boycotts and picketing were part of the competitive struggle for life which society tolerates because the freedom is worth more than it costs. There was no clear congressional attempt in 1947 to reconcile these two conflicting social and juridical philosophies, and the task of compromise and adjustment fell to the courts. That task was presented most starkly when a union instituted a strike during the term of a contract which provided that grievances would be determined by arbitration and that there would be no resort to strike or lockout during the contract term. A request for an injunction against the strike in breach of contract required a determination whether Section 4 of the Norris-LaGuardia Act was to be treated as limited in any way by Section 301 of the Labor Management Relations Act.

This statutory conflict was not altogether unprecedented in the sphere of federal labor legislation. The Railway Labor Act of 1926 imposed various duties upon employers, but established no agency to enforce them and left the problem of compliance to the courts. Neither the Norris-LaGuardia Act nor the 1934 amendments to the Railway Labor Act spoke specifically to the question of the injunctive powers of the federal courts in enforcing the mandates of the Railway Labor Act. In Virginian Ry. v. System Federation No. 40, 300 U.S. 515, 57 S.Ct. 592, 81 L.Ed. 789 (1937), the

Supreme Court rejected the argument that a mandatory injunction compelling an employer to recognize and bargain with a union offended Section 9 of the Norris-LaGuardia Act, holding instead that that Act could not render nugatory the specific provisions of the Railway Labor Act protecting employees from the interference, restraint or coercion of employers. Some years later, in Graham v. Brotherhood of Locomotive Firemen, 338 U.S. 232, 70 S.Ct. 14, 94 L.Ed. 22 (1949), the Court sustained the issuance of an injunction requiring the bargaining representative to represent fairly all employees within the bargaining unit; to preclude such relief because of the Norris-LaGuardia Act would mean that Congress intended to hold before employees the illusory right to nondiscriminatory representation by their bargaining agent while denying them any remedy for its violation.

Neither of the cases mentioned above involved an injunction which prohibited a *strike* by a labor union—the classic situation with which the Norris-LaGuardia Act was primarily concerned. This very situation, however, eventually came before the Supreme Court in BROTHERHOOD OF R. R. TRAINMEN V. CHICAGO RIVER & IND. R. R., 353 U.S. 30, 77 S.Ct. 635, 1 L.Ed.2d 622 (1957). There, a railroad union had asserted twenty-one contract grievances (almost all involving claims to additional compensation) which were ultimately submitted to the National Railroad Adjustment Board, and called a strike while the cases were pending before the Board. A permanent injunction was issued against the strike by a federal district court, and the union argued to the Supreme Court that the injunction violated the Norris-LaGuardia Act. The Court, however, sustained the injunction. It considered the history of the Railway Labor Act of 1926 and its failure to eliminate strikes over contract grievances (or so-called "minor disputes" under the Act), followed by the creation in 1934 of the Adjustment Board, whose jurisdiction to render binding grievance decisions could be invoked either by the railroad or the union. The Court characterized the latter provisions as erecting a system of "compulsory arbitration" and framed the question before it as whether the federal courts may enjoin a union "from striking to defeat the jurisdiction of the Adjustment Board." The Court concluded:

> "We hold that the Norris-LaGuardia Act cannot be read alone in matters dealing with railway labor disputes. There must be an accommodation of that statute and the Railway Labor Act so that the obvious purpose in the enactment of each is preserved. We think that the purposes of these Acts are reconcilable.

" *   *   *   [In the Norris-LaGuardia Act,] Congress
acted to prevent the injunctions of the federal courts from
upsetting the natural interplay of the competing economic
forces of labor and capital.   Rep. LaGuardia, during the
floor debates on the 1932 Act, recognized that the machinery of the Railway Labor Act channeled these economic
forces, in matters dealing with railway labor, into special
processes intended to compromise them.   Such controversies, therefore, are not the same as those in which the injunction strips labor of its primary weapon without substituting any reasonable alternative.   *   *   * "

(Strikes arising from "major disputes", that is the negotiation of
new contract terms, are not, however, unlawful under the Railway
Labor Act, and no injunction may issue when, under Section 13(c)
of the Norris-LaGuardia Act, there is a "controversy concerning
terms or conditions of employment."   Order of R. R. Telegraphers
v. Chicago & N. W. Ry., 362 U.S. 330, 80 S.Ct. 761, 4 L.Ed.2d 774
(1960), at p. 468, supra.)

With the enactment of the Labor Management Relations Act of
1947, providing for union unfair labor practices and NLRB cease
and desist orders and Board-initiated injunction actions, Congress
once again narrowed the freedom from injunctive relief which had
been expressed in such sweeping terms in Section 4 of the Norris-
LaGuardia Act.   Further possible conflicts were created by Section
301 of the LMRA, which raised the question whether the Norris-La-
Guardia Act precluded the use of injunctions to enforce claims arising out of a collective bargaining agreement.   In Textile Workers
Union v. Lincoln Mills, at p. 556, supra, the Supreme Court held that
Section 7 of the Norris-LaGuardia Act did not apply to a suit for
specific enforcement of a promise to arbitrate.   When the Court
then considered the more pointed issue whether a federal court could
enjoin a strike in violation of a no-strike clause in a collective bargaining agreement, the Court first held that no such injunction could
issue.   In SINCLAIR REFINING CO. v. ATKINSON, 370 U.S. 195, 82 S.Ct.
195, 8 L.Ed.2d 440 (1962), a divided Court affirmed a dismissal of
an injunction action brought by an employer against continued work
stoppages concerning contract grievances during the term of a labor contract providing for arbitration and for "no strikes or work
stoppages for any cause which is or may be the subject of a grievance."   The Court concluded that the contract-enforcement policy
underlying Section 301 "was not intended to have any such partially
repealing effect upon such a long-standing, carefully thought out

and highly significant part of this country's labor legislation as the Norris-LaGuardia Act."

The Court majority, through Mr. Justice Black, refused to engage in the "accommodation" of the anti-injunction principles of the Norris-LaGuardia Act when Congress had not done so in the Labor-Management Relations Act of 1947. Justice Black pointed out that when Congress intended to supersede the Norris-LaGuardia Act it did so explicitly, witness Section 10(h) of the Labor Act, and that injunctions under the Taft-Hartley Act were uniformly to be sought by the NLRB and not by private parties. Reference was also made to congressional bills which would expressly have repealed the Norris-LaGuardia Act in actions to enforce labor contracts but which failed of passage. The Court also distinguished several cases on which the plaintiff company had relied. The *Chicago River* case under the Railway Labor Act was held inapt, principally because the strike in that case was "in defiance of an affirmative duty, imposed upon the union by the Railway Labor Act itself, compelling unions to settle disputes as to the interpretation of an existing collective bargaining agreement, not by collective union pressures on the railroad but by submitting them to the Railroad Adjustment Board as the exclusive means of final determination of such 'minor' disputes." *Lincoln Mills* was distinguished because there the injunction was sought against a refusal to arbitrate and its issuance thus "did not enjoin any one of the kinds of conduct which the specific prohibitions of the Norris-LaGuardia Act withdrew from the injunctive powers of United States courts." Finally, *Lincoln Mills* and the *Steelworkers Trilogy* were held simply to be applications of the clear statutory directives of Section 301 and not to invite the development of a judge-made policy contrary to the directives of the Norris-LaGuardia Act; "The argument to the contrary seems to rest upon the notion that injunctions against peaceful strikes are necessary to make the arbitration process effective. But whatever might be said about the merits of this argument, Congress has itself rejected it."

Three dissenting Justices, in an opinion by Mr. Justice Brennan, would have read the Norris-LaGuardia Act and Section 301 of the Labor Management Relations Act as to authorize the issuance of an injunction against the strike in breach of contract. In a dramatic reversal of position, a majority of the Court eight years after *Sinclair* adopted the views of the dissenting Justices, in the following case.

BOYS MARKETS, INC. v. RETAIL CLERKS' LOCAL 770 [33]

Supreme Court of the United States, 1970.
398 U.S. 235, 90 S.Ct. 1583, 26 L.Ed.2d 199.

MR. JUSTICE BRENNAN delivered the opinion of the Court.

In this case we re-examine the holding of Sinclair Refining Co. v. Atkinson, 370 U.S. 195, 82 S.Ct. 1328, 8 L.Ed.2d 440 (1962), that the anti-injunction provisions of the Norris-LaGuardia Act preclude a federal district court from enjoining a strike in breach of a no-strike obligation under a collective-bargaining agreement, even though that agreement contains provisions, enforceable under § 301 (a) of the Labor Management Relations Act, 1947, for binding arbitration of the grievance dispute concerning which the strike was called. The Court of Appeals for the Ninth Circuit, considering itself bound by Sinclair reversed the grant by the District Court for the Central District of California of petitioner's prayer for injunctive relief. 416 F.2d 368 (1969). We granted certiorari. 396 U.S. 1000, 90 S.Ct. 572, 24 L.Ed.2d 492 (1970). Having concluded that Sinclair was erroneously decided and that subsequent events have undermined its continuing validity, we overrule that decision and reverse the judgment of the Court of Appeals.

I

In February 1969, at the time of the incidents that produced this litigation, petitioner and respondent were parties to a collective-bargaining agreement which provided, inter alia, that all controversies concerning its interpretation or application should be resolved by adjustment and arbitration procedures set forth therein and that, during the life of the contract, there should be "no cessation or stoppage of work, lock-out, picketing or boycotts * * *." The dispute arose when petitioner's frozen foods supervisor and certain members of his crew who were not members of the bargaining unit began to rearrange merchandise in the frozen food cases of one of petitioner's supermarkets. A union representative insisted that the food cases be stripped of all merchandise and be restocked by union personnel. When petitioner did not accede to the union's demand, a strike was called and the union began to picket petitioner's establishment. Thereupon petitioner demanded that the union cease the work stoppage and picketing and sought to

---

33. See Axelrod, The Application of the Boys Markets Decision in the Federal Courts, 16 B.C.Ind. & Com.L.Rev. 893 (1975); Comment, Boys Markets Injunctions Against Employers, 91 Harv.L.Rev. 715 (1978); Gould, On Labor Injunctions, Unions, and the Judges: the Boys Markets Case, 1970 Sup.Ct.Rev. 215; Vladeck, Boys Markets and National Labor Policy, 24 Vand.L.Rev. 93 (1970). See also Wellington & Albert, Statutory Interpretation and the Political Process: A Comment on Sinclair v. Atkinson, 72 Yale L.J. 1547 (1963).

invoke the grievance and arbitration procedures specified in the contract.

The following day, since the strike had not been terminated, petitioner filed a complaint in California Superior Court seeking a temporary restraining order, a preliminary and permanent injunction, and specific performance of the contractual arbitration provision. The state court issued a temporary restraining order forbidding continuation of the strike and also an order to show cause why a preliminary injunction should not be granted. Shortly thereafter, the union removed the case to the Federal District Court and there made a motion to quash the state court's temporary restraining order. In opposition, petitioner moved for an order compelling arbitration and enjoining continuation of the strike. Concluding that the dispute was subject to arbitration under the collective-bargaining agreement and that the strike was in violation of the contract, the District Court ordered the parties to arbitrate the underlying dispute and simultaneously enjoined the strike, all picketing in the vicinity of petitioner's supermarket, and any attempts by the union to induce the employees to strike or to refuse to perform their services.

II

At the outset, we are met with respondent's contention that *Sinclair* ought not to be disturbed because the decision turned on a question of statutory construction which Congress can alter at any time. Since Congress has not modified our conclusions in *Sinclair*, even though it has been urged to do so,[34] respondent argues that principles of *stare decisis* should govern the present case.

We do not agree that the doctrine of *stare decisis* bars a re-examination of *Sinclair* in the circumstances of this case. We fully recognize that important policy considerations militate in favor of continuity and predictability in the law. Nevertheless, as Mr. Justice Frankfurter wrote for the Court, "[S]*tare decisis* is a principle of policy and not a mechanical formula of adherence to the latest decision, however recent and questionable, when such adherence involves collision with a prior doctrine more embracing in its scope, intrinsically sounder, and verified by experience." Helvering v. Hallock, 309 U.S. 106, 119, 60 S.Ct. 444, 451, 84 L.Ed. 604 (1940). See Swift & Co. v. Wickham, 382 U.S. 111, 116, 86 S.Ct. 258, 261, 15 L.Ed.2d 194 (1965). It is precisely because *Sinclair* stands as a significant departure from our otherwise consistent emphasis upon the congressional policy to promote the peaceful settlement of labor disputes through arbitration and our efforts to accommodate and

34. See, e. g., Report of Special Atkinson-Sinclair Committee, A.B.A. Labor Relations Law Section—Proceedings 226 (1963) [hereinafter cited as A.B. A. *Sinclair* Report].

harmonize this policy with those underlying the anti-injunction provisions of the Norris-LaGuardia Act that we believe *Sinclair* should be reconsidered. Furthermore, in light of developments subsequent to *Sinclair,* in particular our decision in Avco Corp. v. Aero Lodge 735, 390 U.S. 557, 88 S.Ct. 1235, 20 L.Ed.2d 126 (1968), it has become clear that the *Sinclair* decision does not further but rather frustrates realization of an important goal of our national labor policy.

Nor can we agree that conclusive weight should be accorded to the failure of Congress to respond to *Sinclair* on the theory that congressional silence should be interpreted as acceptance of the decision. The Court has cautioned that "[i]t is at best treacherous to find in congressional silence alone the adoption of a controlling rule of law." Girouard v. United States, 328 U.S. 61, 69, 66 S.Ct. 826, 830, 90 L.Ed. 1084 (1946). Therefore, in the absence of any persuasive circumstances evidencing a clear design that congressional inaction be taken as acceptance of *Sinclair,* the mere silence of Congress is not a sufficient reason for refusing to reconsider the decision. Helvering v. Hallock, supra, 309 U.S. at 119–120, 60 S.Ct. at 451–452.

III

[The Court here referred to the *Lincoln Mills* case, in which it decided that substantive federal law was to apply in suits under Section 301 and that a union could obtain specific performance of an employer's promise to arbitrate grievances, consistent with the Norris-LaGuardia Act. The *Steelworkers Trilogy* emphasized the importance of arbitration to resolve labor-management disputes. Charles Dowd Box Co. v. Courtney, 368 U.S. 502, 82 S.Ct. 519, 7 L.Ed.2d 483 (1962), held that Congress in enacting Section 301 did not intend to disturb preexisting state-court jurisdiction over suits for violation of labor contracts, but rather to supplement that jurisdiction. The Court also mentioned the holding in *Lucas Flour* that in Section 301 actions brought in state courts, substantive federal law is to displace inconsistent local rules.]

Subsequent to the decision in *Sinclair,* we held in Avco Corp. v. Aero Lodge 735, supra, that § 301(a) suits initially brought in state courts may be removed to the designated federal forum under the federal question removal jurisdiction delineated in 28 U.S.C. § 1441. In so holding, however, the Court expressly left open the questions whether state courts are bound by the anti-injunction proscriptions of the Norris-LaGuardia Act and whether federal courts, after removal of a § 301(a) action, are required to dissolve any injunctive relief previously granted by the state courts. See generally General Electric Co. v. Local Union 191, 413 F.2d 964 (C.A. 5th Cir. 1969) (dissolution of state injunction required). Three Justices who concurred expressed the view that *Sinclair* should be reconsidered "upon an appropriate future occasion." 390 U.S. at 562, 88 S.Ct., at 1238 (Stewart, J., concurring).

The decision in *Avco*, viewed in the context of *Lincoln Mills* and its progeny, has produced an anomalous situation which, in our view, makes urgent the reconsideration of *Sinclair*. The principal practical effect of *Avco* and *Sinclair* taken together is nothing less than to oust state courts of jurisdiction in § 301(a) suits where injunctive relief is sought for breach of a no-strike obligation. Union defendants can, as a matter of course, obtain removal to a federal court,[35] and there is obviously a compelling incentive for them to do so in order to gain the advantage of the strictures upon injunctive relief which *Sinclair* imposes on federal courts. The sanctioning of this practice, however, is wholly inconsistent with our conclusion in *Dowd Box* that the congressional purpose embodied in § 301 (a) was to *supplement,* and not to encroach upon, the pre-existing jurisdiction of the state courts. It is ironic indeed that the very provision that Congress clearly intended to provide additional remedies for breach of collective-bargaining agreements has been employed to displace previously existing state remedies. We are not at liberty thus to depart from the clearly expressed congressional policy to the contrary.

On the other hand, to the extent that widely disparate remedies theoretically remain available in state, as opposed to federal, courts, the federal policy of labor law uniformity elaborated in *Lucas Flour Co.*, is seriously offended. This policy, of course, could hardly require, as a practical matter, that labor law be administered identically in all courts, for undoubtedly a certain diversity exists among the state and federal systems in matters of procedural and remedial detail, a fact that Congress evidently took into account in deciding not to disturb the traditional jurisdiction of the States. The injunction, however, is so important a remedial device, particularly in the arbitration context, that its availability or non-availability in various courts will not only produce rampant forum shopping and maneuvering from one court to another but will also greatly frustrate any relative uniformity in the enforcement of arbitration agreements.

Furthermore, the existing scheme, with the injunction remedy technically available in the state courts but rendered inefficacious by the removal device, assigns to removal proceedings a totally unintended function. While the underlying purposes of Congress in pro-

---

35. Section 301(a) suits require neither the existence of diversity of citizenship nor a minimum jurisdictional amount in controversy. All § 301(a) suits may be removed pursuant to 28 U.S.C. § 1441.

viding for federal question removal jurisdiction remain somewhat obscure, there has never been a serious contention that Congress intended that the removal mechanism be utilized to foreclose completely remedies otherwise available in the state courts. Although federal question removal jurisdiction may well have been intended to provide a forum for the protection of federal rights where such protection was deemed necessary or to encourage the development of expertise by the federal courts in the interpretation of federal law, there is no indication that Congress intended by the removal mechanism to effect a wholesale dislocation in the allocation of judicial business between the state and federal courts. Cf. City of Greenwood, Miss. v. Peacock, 384 U.S. 808, 86 S.Ct. 1800, 16 L.Ed.2d 944 (1966).

It is undoubtedly true that each of the foregoing objections to *Sinclair-Avco* could be remedied either by overruling *Sinclair* or by extending that decision to the States. While some commentators have suggested that the solution to the present unsatisfactory situation does lie in the extension of the *Sinclair* prohibition to state court proceedings, we agree with Chief Justice Traynor of the California Supreme Court that "whether or not Congress could deprive state courts of the power to give such [injunctive] remedies when enforcing collective bargaining agreements, it has not attempted to do so either in the Norris-LaGuardia Act or section 301." McCarroll v. Los Angeles County Dist. Council of Carpenters, 49 Cal.2d 45, 63, 315 P.2d 322, 332 (1957), cert. denied 355 U.S. 932, 78 S.Ct. 413, 2 L.Ed.2d 415 (1958). * * *

An additional reason for not resolving the existing dilemma by extending *Sinclair* to the States is the devastating implications for the enforceability of arbitration agreements and their accompanying no-strike obligations if equitable remedies were not available.[36] As we have previously indicated, a no-strike obligation, express or implied, is the *quid pro quo* for an undertaking by the employer to submit grievance disputes to the process of arbitration. See Textile Workers Union of America v. Lincoln Mills, supra, 353 U.S., at 455, 77 S.Ct. at 917. Any incentive for employers to enter into such an arrangement is necessarily dissipated if the principal and most expeditious method by which the no-strike obligation can be enforced is eliminated. While it is of course true, as respondent contends, that other avenues of redress, such as an action for damages, would

---

[36]. It is true that about one-half of the States have enacted so-called "little Norris-LaGuardia Acts" that place various restrictions upon the granting of injunctions by state courts in labor disputes. However, because many States do not bar injunctive relief for violations of collective-bargaining agreements, in only about 14 jurisdictions is there a significant Norris-LaGuardia-type prohibition against equitable remedies for breach of no-strike obligations. * * *

remain open to an aggrieved employer, an award of damages after a dispute has been settled is no substitute for an immediate halt to an illegal strike. Furthermore, an action for damages prosecuted during or after a labor dispute would only tend to aggravate industrial strife and delay an early resolution of the difficulties between employer and union.[37]

Even if management is not encouraged by the unavailability of the injunction remedy to resist arbitration agreements, the fact remains that the effectiveness of such agreements would be greatly reduced if injunctive relief were withheld. Indeed, the very purpose of arbitration procedures is to provide a mechanism for the expeditious settlement of industrial disputes without resort to strikes, lockouts, or other self-help measures. This basic purpose is obviously largely undercut if there is no immediate, effective remedy for those very tactics that arbitration is designed to obviate. Thus, because *Sinclair*, in the aftermath of *Avco*, casts serious doubt upon the effective enforcement of a vital element of stable labor-management relations—arbitration agreements with their attendant no-strike obligations—we conclude that *Sinclair* does not make a viable contribution to federal labor policy.

IV

We have also determined that the dissenting opinion in *Sinclair* states the correct principles concerning the accommodation necessary between the seemingly absolute terms of the Norris-LaGuardia Act and the policy considerations underlying § 301(a). 370 U.S., at 215, 82 S.Ct., at 1339. Although we need not repeat all that was there said, a few points should be emphasized at this time.

The literal terms of § 4 of the Norris-LaGuardia Act must be accommodated to the subsequently enacted provisions of § 301(a) of the Labor Management Relations Act and the purposes of arbitration. * * *

37. As the neutral members of the A.B.A. committee on the problems raised by *Sinclair* noted in their report:

"Under existing laws, employers may maintain an action for damages resulting from a strike in breach of contract and may discipline the employees involved. In many cases, however, neither of these alternatives will be feasible. Discharge of the strikers is often inexpedient because of a lack of qualified replacements or because of the adverse effect on relationships within the plant. The damage remedy may also be unsatisfactory because the employer's losses are often hard to calculate and because the employer may hesitate to exacerbate relations with the union by bringing a damage action. Hence, injunctive relief will often be the only effective means by which to remedy the breach of the no-strike pledge and thus effectuate federal labor policy." A.B.A. *Sinclair* Report 242.

The Norris-LaGuardia Act was responsive to a situation totally different from that which exists today. In the early part of this century, the federal courts generally were regarded as allies of management in its attempt to prevent the organization and strengthening of labor unions; and in this industrial struggle the injunction became a potent weapon that was wielded against the activities of labor groups. The result was a large number of sweeping decrees, often issued *ex parte*, drawn on an *ad hoc* basis without regard to any systematic elaboration of national labor policy. See Milk Wagon Drivers' Union, etc. v. Lake Valley Co., 311 U.S. 91, 102, 61 S.Ct. 122, 127, 85 L.Ed. 63 (1940).

In 1932 Congress attempted to bring some order out of the industrial chaos that had developed and to correct the abuses that had resulted from the interjection of the federal judiciary into union-management disputes on the behalf of management. See declaration of public policy, Norris-LaGuardia Act, § 2, 47 Stat. 70. Congress, therefore, determined initially to limit severely the power of the federal courts to issue injunctions "in any case involving or growing out of any labor dispute * * *." § 4, 47 Stat. 70. Even as initially enacted, however, the prohibition against federal injunctions was by no means absolute. See Norris-LaGuardia Act, §§ 7, 8, 9, 47 Stat. 71, 72. Shortly thereafter Congress passed the Wagner Act, designed to curb various management activities that tended to discourage employee participation in collective action.

As labor organizations grew in strength and developed toward maturity, congressional emphasis shifted from protection of the nascent labor movement to the encouragement of collective bargaining and to administrative techniques for the peaceful resolution of industrial disputes. This shift in emphasis was accomplished, however, without extensive revision of many of the older enactments, including the anti-injunction section of the Norris-LaGuardia Act. Thus it became the task of the courts to accommodate, to reconcile the older statutes with the more recent ones.

A leading example of this accommodation process is Brotherhood of Railroad Trainmen v. Chicago River & Ind. R. Co., 353 U.S. 30, 77 S.Ct. 635, 1 L.Ed.2d 622 (1957). There we were confronted with a peaceful strike which violated the statutory duty to arbitrate imposed by the Railway Labor Act. The Court concluded that a strike in violation of a statutory arbitration duty was not the type of situation to which the Norris-LaGuardia Act was responsive, that an important federal policy was involved in the peaceful settlement of disputes through the statutorily mandated arbitration procedure, that this important policy was imperiled if equitable remedies were not available to implement it, and hence that Norris-LaGuardia's policy of nonintervention by the federal courts should yield to the overriding interest in the successful implementation of the arbitration process.

The principles elaborated in *Chicago River* are equally applicable to the present case. To be sure, *Chicago River* involved arbitration procedures established by statute. However, we have frequently noted, in such cases as *Lincoln Mills,* the *Steelworkers Trilogy,* and *Lucas Flour,* the importance that Congress has attached generally to the voluntary settlement of labor disputes without resort to self-help and more particularly to arbitration as a means to this end. Indeed, it has been stated that *Lincoln Mills,* in its exposition of § 301 (a), "went a long way towards making arbitration the central institution in the administration of collective bargaining contracts."

The *Sinclair* decision, however, seriously undermined the effectiveness of the arbitration technique as a method peacefully to resolve industrial disputes without resort to strikes, lockouts, and similar devices. Clearly employers will be wary of assuming obligations to arbitrate specifically enforceable against them when no similarly efficacious remedy is available to enforce the concomitant undertaking of the union to refrain from striking. On the other hand, the central purpose of the Norris-LaGuardia Act to foster the growth and viability of labor organizations is hardly retarded— if anything, this goal is advanced—by a remedial device that merely enforces the obligation that the union freely undertook under a specifically enforceable agreement to submit disputes to arbitration.[38] We conclude, therefore, that the unavailability of equitable relief in the arbitration context presents a serious impediment to the congressional policy favoring the voluntary establishment of a mechanism for the peaceful resolution of labor disputes, that the core purpose of the Norris-LaGuardia Act is not sacrificed by the limited use of equitable remedies to further this important policy, and consequently that the Norris-LaGuardia Act does not bar the granting of injunctive relief in the circumstances of the instant case.

---

38. As well stated by the neutral members of the A.B.A. *Sinclair* committee: " * * * [T]he reasons behind the Norris-LaGuardia Act seem scarcely applicable to the situation * * * [in which a strike in volation of a collective-bargaining agreement is enjoined]. The Act was passed primarily because of widespread dissatisfaction with the tendency of judges to enjoin concerted activities in accordance with 'doctrines of tort law which made the lawfulness of a strike depend upon judicial views of social and economic policy.' * * * Where an injunc- tion is used against a strike in breach of contract, the union is not subjected in this fashion to judicially created limitations on its freedom of action but is simply compelled to comply with limitations to which it has previously agreed. Moreover, where the underlying dispute is arbitrable, the union is not deprived of any practicable means of pressing its claim but is only required to submit the dispute to the impartial tribunal that it has agreed to establish for this purpose." A.B.A. *Sinclair* Report 242.

V

Our holding in the present case is a narrow one. We do not undermine the vitality of the Norris-LaGuardia Act. We deal only with the situation in which a collective-bargaining contract contains a mandatory grievance adjustment or arbitration procedure. Nor does it follow from what we have said that injunctive relief is appropriate as a matter of course in every case of a strike over an arbitrable grievance. The dissenting opinion in *Sinclair* suggested the following principles for the guidance of the district courts in determining whether to grant injunctive relief—principles that we now adopt:

> "A District Court entertaining an action under § 301 may not grant injunctive relief against concerted activity unless and until it decides that the case is one in which an injunction would be appropriate despite the Norris-La-Guardia Act. When a strike is sought to be enjoined because it is over a grievance which both parties are con-tractually bound to arbitrate, the District Court may issue no injunctive order until it first holds that the contract *does* have that effect; and the employer should be ordered to arbitrate, as a condition of his obtaining an injunction against the strike. Beyond this, the District Court must, of course, consider whether issuance of an injunction would be warranted under ordinary principles of equity—whether breaches are occurring and will continue, or have been threatened and will be committed; whether they have caused or will cause irreparable injury to the employer; and whether the employer will suffer more from the denial of an injunction than will the union from its issuance." 370 U.S., at 228, 82 S.Ct., at 1346. (Emphasis in original.)

In the present case there is no dispute that the grievance in question was subject to adjustment and arbitration under the collective-bargaining agreement and that the petitioner was ready to proceed with arbitration at the time an injunction against the strike was sought and obtained. The District Court also concluded that, by reason of respondent's violations of its no-strike obligation, petitioner "has suffered irreparable injury and will continue to suffer irreparable injury." Since we now overrule *Sinclair*, the holding of the Court of Appeals in reliance on *Sinclair* must be reversed. Accordingly, we reverse the judgment of the Court of Appeals and remand the case with directions to enter a judgment affirming the order of the District Court.

MR. JUSTICE MARSHALL took no part in the decision of this case.

MR. JUSTICE STEWART, concurring.

When Sinclair Refining Co. v. Atkinson, 370 U.S. 195, 82 S.Ct. 1328, 8 L.Ed.2d 440, was decided in 1962, I subscribed to the opinion of the Court. Before six years had passed I had reached the conclusion that the *Sinclair* holding should be reconsidered, and said so in Avco Corp. v. Aero Lodge 735, 390 U.S. 557, 562, 88 S.Ct. 1235, 1238, 20 L.Ed.2d 126 (concurring opinion). Today I join the Court in concluding "that *Sinclair* was erroneously decided and that subsequent events have undermined its continuing validity * * *."

In these circumstances the temptation is strong to embark upon a lengthy personal *apologia*. But since MR. JUSTICE BRENNAN has so clearly stated my present views in his opinion for the Court today, I simply join in that opinion and in the Court's judgment. An aphorism of Mr. Justice Frankfurter provides me refuge: "Wisdom too often never comes, and so one ought not to reject it merely because it comes late." Henslee v. Union Planters Bank, 335 U.S. 595, 600, 69 S.Ct. 290, 293, 93 L.Ed. 259 (dissenting opinion).

MR. JUSTICE BLACK, dissenting. * * *

Although Congress has been urged to overrule our holding in *Sinclair*, it has steadfastly refused to do so. Nothing in the language or history of the two Acts has changed. Nothing at all has changed, in fact, except the membership of the Court and the personal views of one Justice. I remain of the opinion that *Sinclair* was correctly decided, and, moreover, that the prohibition of the Norris-LaGuardia Act is close to the heart of the entire federal system of labor regulation. In my view *Sinclair* should control the disposition of this case.

Even if the majority were correct, however, in saying that *Sinclair* misinterpreted the Taft-Hartley and Norris-LaGuardia Acts, I should be compelled to dissent. I believe that both the making and the changing of laws which affect the substantial rights of the people are primarily for Congress, not this Court. Most especially is this so when the laws involved are the focus of strongly held views of powerful but antagonistic political and economic interests. The Court's function in the application and interpretation of such laws must be carefully limited to avoid encroaching on the power of Congress to determine policies and make laws to carry them out.

* * * When the law has been settled by an earlier case then any subsequent "reinterpretation" of the statute is gratuitous and neither more nor less than an amendment: it is no different in effect from a judicial alteration of language that Congress itself placed in the statute. * * * If the Congress is unhappy with these powers as this Court defined them, then the Congress may act; this Court should not. The members of the majority have simply

decided that they are more sensitive to the "realization of an important goal of our national labor policy" than the Congress or their predecessors on this Court.   *   *   *

I dissent.

MR. JUSTICE WHITE dissents for the reasons stated in the majority opinion in Sinclair Refining Co. v. Atkinson, 370 U.S. 195, 82 S.Ct. 1328, 8 L.Ed.2d 440 (1962).

BUFFALO FORGE CO. v. UNITED STEELWORKERS OF AMERICA, 428 U.S. 397, 96 S.Ct. 3141 (1976).[39]   The Company operates three plant and office facilities, and had labor contracts covering its production and maintenance employees who were represented by the United Steelworkers and two Steelworker locals (the Union).   The contracts contained no-strike clauses ("There shall be no strikes, work stoppages or interruption or impeding of work") and a grievance and arbitration procedure which provided for arbitration of disputes concerning "the meaning and application of the provisions of this Agreement."   During the term of these contracts, clerical and technical employees (represented by the United Steelworkers and two other locals) went out on strike in a dispute arising from the negotiation of their first contract with the Company.   The Union endorsed a refusal by the production and maintenance workers to cross the picket lines established by the clerical and technical employees. The Company, claiming that this constituted a breach of the no-strike clause and that the Union should arbitrate whatever dispute caused this work stoppage by the production and maintenance employees, brought an action in the federal district court seeking damages and a preliminary injunction of the work stoppage.   The Union asserted that its work stoppage did not violate the no-strike clause and that it was prepared promptly to submit that question to arbitration. The district court concluded that the Norris-LaGuardia Act forbade the issuance of an injunction, since the action of the production and maintenance employees was not over an arbitrable grievance but was rather a sympathetic action in aid of the clerical workers; accordingly it was not enjoinable under the *Boys Markets* case.   The court of appeals affirmed the denial of the injunction and it was in turn affirmed by the Supreme Court, in a 5–4 decision.

Unlike *Boys Markets*, this was not a strike concededly in violation of the contract, with the object of avoiding arbitration of some

39. See Cantor, Buffalo Forge and Injunctions Against Employer Breaches of Collective Bargaining Agreements, 1980 Wisc.L.Rev. 247 (1980); Gould, On Labor Injunctions Pending Arbitration: Recasting *Buffalo Forge*, 30 Stanford L.Rev. 533 (1978); Smith, The Supreme Court, *Boys Markets* Labor Injunctions, and Sympathy Work Stoppages, 44 U.Chi.L.Rev. 321 (1977).

underlying dispute with the Company. *Boys Markets* allowed of an exception to Section 4 of the Norris-LaGuardia Act only for a strike which frustrated the federal policy favoring arbitration procedures designated by the parties to resolve their contract disputes. "The District Court found, and it is not now disputed, that the strike was not *over* any dispute between the Union and the employer that was even remotely subject to the arbitration provisions of the contract. The strike at issue was a sympathy strike in support of sister unions negotiating with the employer; neither its causes nor the issue underlying it were subject to the settlement procedures provided by the contract between the employer and respondents. The strike had neither the purpose nor the effect of denying or evading an obligation to arbitrate or of depriving the employer of his bargain." (The Court also stated, in dictum, that in a labor contract silent on the right to strike, a mandatory arbitration clause would not justify implying a commitment by the Union to refrain from engaging in sympathy strikes.) Whether the Union's work stoppage violated its no-strike promise was itself a dispute to be decided by an arbitrator and not by the district court, which is deprived by Section 4 of the Norris-LaGuardia Act of the power to enjoin the strike even pending the decision of the arbitrator. It would "cut deeply into the policy of the Norris-LaGuardia Act" if the federal court could hold hearings, make findings of fact, interpret the applicable contract provisions and issue injunctions to restore the status quo ante as to any arbitrable contract breaches falling within the shelter of Section 4. Were the courts to have power to enjoin, this would improperly influence the decision of the arbitrator as to the facts and the interpretation of the contract; it would also in many instances discourage one of the parties from seeking arbitration or as a practical matter permanently settle the issue, quite in the face of the federal policy to resolve the issue through arbitration.

    In a lengthy and careful dissenting opinion for four Justices, Mr. Justice Stevens argued that the district court had jurisdiction to enjoin the work stoppage by the production and maintenance employees. He contended that the central concerns of the Norris-LaGuardia Act related to union organization, recognition and contract negotiation, rather than to the enforcement of commitments already made in such contracts; that all of the reasons underlying the decision of the Court in *Boys Markets* were also applicable in the case of sympathy strikes in breach of contractual no-strike provisions; and that court-issued injunctions against such sympathy strikes pending their arbitration would not unduly interfere with the arbitral procedures designated by the parties.

    As the Supreme Court observed in the *Boys Markets* case, an employer whose business has been interrupted by a work stoppage in breach of a labor agreement may seek to secure damages in lieu of or in addition to an injunction. The Court has passed upon the question of liability of unions and their officers and members, in cases involving authorized strikes and "wildcat" strikes. Legislative guidance is provided in Sections 301(b) and (e), which the student should consult.

In ATKINSON v. SINCLAIR REFINING CO., 370 U.S. 238, 82 S.Ct. 1318, 8 L.Ed.2d 462 (1962), some 1000 employees struck, during the term of a contract with a no-strike clause, to protest the employer's docking of a total of $2.19 from the pay of three employees. The Court held that the first count of the employer's complaint, which sought damages of $12,500 from the signatory local and international unions, stated a cause of action under Section 301; the Court read the labor contract to make unavailable to the employer the grievance and arbitration procedure in the event of a contract breach by the unions, so that judicial recourse was appropriate. The second count of the complaint relied upon diversity-of-citizenship jurisdiction and claimed damages from twenty-four union committeemen as individuals for "fomenting, assisting and participating in" the strike. The Court read the third sentence of Section 301(b) as a congressional reaction to cases such as the *Danbury Hatters* case, page 33 supra, in which treble damages were awarded against union officers and members as individuals for a nationwide union-directed boycott, and foreclosure made on the homes of many of the members. "The national labor policy requires and we hold that when a union is liable for damages for violation of the no-strike clause, its officers and members are not liable for these damages."

More recently, in COMPLETE AUTO TRANSIT, INC. v. REIS, —— U.S. ——, 101 S.Ct. 1836, 68 L.Ed.2d 248 (1981), the Court was confronted with the more difficult question whether the same immunity of individual strikers against damage actions applies when they participate in a "wildcat" strike which is unauthorized by the signatory union and for which that union can therefore not be held liable in damages. Although such individual immunity would leave the employer with no financial remedy for loss of business during the wildcat strike, a divided Court held that Section 301(b), particularly when read in light of its legislative history, "clearly reveals Congress' intent to shield individual employees from liability for damages arising from their breach of the no-strike clause of a collective-bargaining agreement, whether or not the union participated in or authorized the illegality."

The legislative history revealed that Congress had rejected the imposition of liability for damages upon individuals engaging in various kinds of unlawful work stoppages and had opted instead to render such individuals unprotected by Section 7 of the NLRA and thus susceptible to discharge and other discipline by the employer. The Court concluded that such discipline, along with other sanctions —including union discipline of the wildcat strikers, and employer recourse through damages or an injunction against a union which participated in or authorized the strike—gave the employer adequate assurance of adherence to collective bargaining agreements. Two dissenting Justices contended that these sanctions were wholly inadequate protection for the employer against wildcat strikers and that Congress did not intend, in Section 301(b), to shelter individuals from personal accountability for damages resulting from their own individual conduct as distinguished from union-authorized conduct.

The standards to be used in determining the circumstances in which a union can be held responsible for breaching a no-strike clause—either in its own right or vicariously for the breach of another union—were articulated by the Supreme Court in CARBON FUEL CO. v. UNITED MINE WORKERS, 444 U.S. 212, 100 S.Ct. 410, 62 L.Ed.2d 394 (1979). There, Carbon Fuel Company was party to a labor contract with the United Mine Workers (UMWA) and its District 17; certain locals within District 17 violated the agreement by calling a total of forty-eight unauthorized or "wildcat" strikes. The company brought an action for damages not only against the locals but also against District 17 and the UMWA on the theory that they had a duty to use all reasonable means to stop the locals' "wildcat" stoppages.

The Supreme Court held that, although the locals may be liable in damages, District 17 and the UMWA were not, absent a showing that they adopted, encouraged or prolonged the strikes or were otherwise responsible by virtue of common law principles of agency. Sections 301(b) and (e) were held to supplant both the narrower test for union liability under Section 6 of the Norris-LaGuardia Act and the broader test of responsibility for employers under Section 2(2) of the Wagner Act ("any person acting in the interest of an employer"). Since District 17 and the UMWA were not liable vicariously for the locals' stoppages, Congress must also have intended to free them of direct liability for their own failure to respond to the stoppages absent their own instigation, support, ratification or encouragement. There was thus no liability for failure to use reasonable means to control the locals' actions in breach of contract.

———

Problems for Discussion

1. Carr Corporation and the Teamsters Union signed a two-year collective agreement on September 1, 1980. In May 1981, the Company discharged two employees, and the Union promptly called a strike. The following week, the Union filed a grievance claiming that the Company had

violated the "just cause" provision of the contract. (The contract provided for a grievance and arbitration procedure available to either party for "all disputes between the parties hereto" and also contained a no-strike no-lock-out clause.) Carr refused to process the grievance or indeed to deal at all with the Union, and when the Union instituted an action to compel arbitration, Carr counterclaimed for damages in the amount of $250,000 flowing from the strike. Carr has argued that the Union's strike is a material breach of the labor contract which both frees Carr of the reciprocal duty to arbitrate (and indeed the duty to recognize the Union) and gives rise to a cause of action for damages. The Union argues that, even if its strike does violate the contract, it does not discharge Carr of the duty to arbitrate either the two unjust discharges or the Union's liability for the strike. How should the court rule on the Union's suit to compel arbitration of the discharges and the Company's counterclaim for damages for the strike? See Drake Bakeries, Inc. v. Local 50, American Bakery & Confectionery Workers, 370 U.S. 254, 82 S.Ct. 1346, 8 L.Ed.2d 474 (1962); Local 721, United Packinghouse Food & Allied Workers v. Needham Packing Co., 376 U.S. 247, 84 S.Ct. 773, 11 L.Ed.2d 680 (1964).

2. Able Manufacturing Company and the Machinists Union have a labor contract which contains a four-step grievance procedure, beginning with consultations between the foreman and the shop steward and culminating in review by Able's Vice-President for Industrial Relations. There is no provision for arbitration of grievances which remain unresolved after step four, and the contract expressly gives the Union the right to strike at that point. A serious dispute arose recently regarding the Company's calculation of pay for a certain class of employees and, after the filing of a grievance and the failure to resolve the case at step one, the parties were preparing to proceed to step two when the Union instituted a strike. The Company has brought an action in the federal district court for an injunction against the strike. Should an injunction issue?

3. The workers in the Fiume Coalmine are represented by the Mine Workers Union, which has an agreement with the company providing for the arbitration of "any disputes" arising during the contract term but lacking any no-strike clause. A recent explosion in a nearby mine, which resulted in a number of deaths, has generated considerable concern among the workers and the Union officials. Yesterday, several miners detected a heavier density of fumes than that normally perceived, and the figures reflecting the airflow in the mine were barely at the level of acceptability under federal safety regulations. A meeting of the Union was called last night, and the members overwhelmingly voted not to go into the mines until a full and impartial safety investigation was conducted and conditions in the mine approved. The company contends that the Union's action is in violation of the contract and that the appropriate manner for the Union to challenge conditions in the mine is not by a work stoppage but rather by use of the grievance and arbitration machinery. The company has instituted an action in the federal district court for an injunction, and has requested that a temporary restraining order issue. What arguments should the Union make in defense? Should the injunction issue? (Consider the

relevance of Section 502 of the Labor Act.) See *Gateway Coal Co.* v. *UMW*, 414 U.S. 368, 94 S.Ct. 629, 38 L.Ed.2d 583 (1974).

4. In the labor contract between Power Tractors Corporation and the Auto Workers Union, there is an unqualified no-strike clause and a grievance and arbitration provision; however, because of some dissatisfaction in the past with arbitration decisions on matters of job reclassification, that issue has been explicitly excluded from the reach of the arbitration clause. During the contract term, a dispute arose on a reclassification issue and, after having exhausted the procedures for intra-company review, the Union has instituted a strike. The company has commenced an action in a state court for an injunction against the strike.

(a) Over the union's claim that *Boys Markets* is controlling and that a court may, under these facts, perhaps grant money damages, but not an injunction, the state court has in fact issued an injunction against continuation of the strike. Should the injunction be reversed on appeal?

(b) Assume, instead, that the strike concerns a grievance which is subject to the arbitration clause of the labor contract, but that the state court has refused to issue an injunction, relying on the state's "little Norris-LaGuardia Act" which has been broadly read by the courts of the state to bar strike injunctions even over arbitrable grievances. Should the court's order of dismissal be reversed?

5. Lever Brothers has for many years operated a soap-production plant in Baltimore, Maryland, where the employees are represented by the Chemical Workers Union. The labor contract there has an arbitration clause, and a provision which permits the company "permanently to eliminate, change or consolidate jobs, departments or divisions" and another provision which permits the company to "assign work to outside contractors" only after giving notice to the Union furnishing "full information regarding the reasons for the action." In June 1981, Lever Brothers advised the Union that it was permanently closing its Baltimore plant and transferring the work there to its Hammond, Indiana facility which was represented by the Oil Workers Union. The Chemical Workers Union filed a grievance, alleging violation of the "contracting out" provision (since there had been no notice or consultation), and it ultimately brought an action in the federal court. In that action, the Union sought not only an order to compel arbitration but also an injunction against the closing of the Baltimore plant and the transfer of the operations to Hammond. Should the court issue the injunction? See Lever Bros. v. International Chem. Workers Union, Local 217, 554 F.2d 115 (4th Cir. 1976).

D. THE ROLE OF THE NATIONAL LABOR RELATIONS BOARD AND THE ARBITRATOR DURING THE TERM OF A COLLECTIVE AGREEMENT

The execution of a collective agreement has substantial effect upon the rights and duties of employers and labor unions under the NLRA. For example, although the use of a peaceful strike or picketing in support of a claim by employees is normally protected under Section 7 of the Act, the bargaining representative may contractually waive this statutory privilege for itself and for all employees in the bargaining unit. A strike in violation of a no-strike promise will thus be treated as unprotected activity and will render the participating employees subject to discharge. Disputes between unions concerning the representation of employees in the plant, or concerning the assignment of work to employees already represented by these different unions, will normally be subject to resolution through the procedures of the National Labor Relations Board. But these procedures may be lawfully displaced if the interested parties can effect an adjustment of their claims through the collective bargaining process. An agreement waiving the right to bargain about statutory subjects or authorizing management to take unilateral action will effectively modify the employer's duties under Section 8(a)(5). It has indeed been suggested that the employer's duty to bargain has little independent significance during the life of a labor agreement, and that that duty is effectively discharged by complying with the grievance and arbitration procedures of the agreement. (Of course, as has already been noted, it has been held that there are certain statutory rights of such central significance to the legislative scheme that they cannot be effectively waived by contract. An example is the right of employees in the bargaining unit to engage in solicitation for or against unions outside of their working time. See NLRB v. Magnavox Co., at p. 121, supra. But such unwaivable statutory rights are rare.)

The reciprocal impact of the NLRA and the collective bargaining agreement is a complex subject, involving a consideration of two different sets of regulations for the conduct of the parties and two different sets of interpreting and enforcing institutions, on the one hand the Board and the federal courts of appeals and on the other the arbitrator and (or) the federal district courts. Two kinds of illustrative problems have been selected for detailed study: (1) The relationship between the Board's role in enforcing the NLRA and the arbitrator's role in enforcing the labor contract, and (2) the duty to bargain during the term of the labor contract.

1. Conduct Which Allegedly Violates Both the Contract and the Labor Act [40]

During the term of a collective agreement the same conduct may give rise to both unfair labor practice charges (or representa-

---

40. See Atleson, Disciplinary Discharges, Arbitration and NLRB Deference, 20 Buffalo L.Rev. 355 (1971); Comment, Judicial Review and the Trend   Toward More Stringent NLRB Standards on Arbitral Deferrals, 129 U.Pa. L.Rev. 738 (1981); Sovern, Section 301 and the Primary Jurisdiction of the

tion issues) and an arbitrable grievance. This might be the case if an employer discharges a shop steward allegedly because of his zealous prosecution of grievances. Or, an employer may bargain with one union rather than another on behalf of certain employees, or assign work to one group of employees and thereby precipitate a work stoppage by some other group represented by a different union under a different labor agreement. Or, management without bargaining with the union may contract out electrical repairs theretofore done by the maintenance department, with resulting layoffs of maintenance electricians.

Such disputes concerning alleged discriminatory discharge, representation or work-assignment issues, and unilateral employer action can be processed by the aggrieved union either through the NLRB or the contractual grievance and arbitration procedure. May the union choose either remedy it wishes and, one failing, pursue the other? Is the arbitrator stripped of jurisdiction to decide cases which touch upon statutory matters, or conversely is the Board without power to decide cases which invite a construction of the collective bargaining agreement? If such deference is not required, should either institution defer to the other as a matter of comity? (If the agreement is the rare one which does not provide for arbitration, parallel questions arise concerning the relationship between administrative and judicial remedies.) These are the issues addressed in the cases and abstracts immediately following.

[handwritten marginalia: what are res judicata effects]

CAREY v. WESTINGHOUSE ELEC. CORP.

Supreme Court of the United States, 1964.
375 U.S. 261, 84 S.Ct. 401, 11 L.Ed.2d 320.

MR. JUSTICE DOUGLAS delivered the opinion of the Court.

The petitioner union (IUE) and respondent employer (Westinghouse) entered into a collective bargaining agreement covering workers at several plants including one where the present dispute occurred. The agreement states that Westinghouse recognizes IUE and its locals as exclusive bargaining representatives for each of those units for which IUE or its locals have been certified by the National Labor Relations Board as the exclusive bargaining representative; and the agreement lists among those units for which IUE has been certified a unit of "all production and maintenance employees" at the plant where the controversy arose, "but excluding all salaried, technical * * * employees." The agreement also contains a grievance procedure for the use of arbitration in case of unresolved disputes, including those

NLRB, 76 Harv.L.Rev. 529 (1963); Wollett, The Agreement and the National Labor Relations Act: Courts, Arbitrators, and the NLRB—Who Decides What? 14 Lab.L.J. 1041 (1963); Note, The NLRB and Deference to Arbitration, 77 Yale L.J. 1191 (1968).

involving the "interpretation, application or claimed violation" of the agreement.

IUE filed a grievance asserting that certain employees in the engineering laboratory at the plant in question, represented by another union, Federation, which had been certified as the exclusive bargaining representative for a unit of "all salaried, technical" employees, excluding "all production and maintenance" employees, were performing production and maintenance work. Westinghouse refused to arbitrate on the ground that the controversy presented a representation matter for the National Labor Relations Board. IUE petitioned the Supreme Court of New York for an order compelling arbitration. That court refused. The Appellate Division affirmed, one judge dissenting, 15 A.D.2d 7, 221 N.Y.S.2d 303. The Court of Appeals affirmed, one judge dissenting, holding that the matter was within the exclusive jurisdiction of the Board since it involved a definition of bargaining units. 11 N.Y.2d 452, 230 N.Y.S.2d 703, 184 N.E.2d 298. The case is here on certiorari. 372 U.S. 957, 83 S.Ct. 1012, 10 L.Ed.2d 10.

We have here a so-called "jurisdictional" dispute involving two unions and the employer. But the term "jurisdictional" is not a word of a single meaning. In the setting of the present case this "jurisdictional" dispute could be one of two different, though related, species: either—(1) a controversy as to whether certain work should be performed by workers in one bargaining unit or those in another; or (2) a controversy as to which union should represent the employees doing particular work. If this controversy is considered to be the former, the National Labor Relations Act (61 Stat. 136, 73 Stat. 519, 29 U.S.C. § 151 et seq.) does not purport to cover all phases and stages of it. While § 8(b) (4) (D) makes it an unfair labor practice for a union to strike to get an employer to assign work to a particular group of employees rather than to another, the Act does not deal with the controversy anterior to a strike nor provide any machinery for resolving such a dispute absent a strike. The Act and its remedies for "jurisdictional" controversies of that nature come into play only by a strike or a threat of a strike. Such conduct gives the Board authority under § 10(k) to resolve the dispute.

Are we to assume that the regulatory scheme contains an *hiatus*, allowing no recourse to arbitration over work assignments between two unions but forcing the controversy into the strike stage before a remedy before the Board is available? The Board, as admonished by § 10(k), has often given effect to private agreements to settle disputes of this character; and that is in accord with the purpose as stated even by the minority spokesman in Congress —"that full opportunity is given the parties to reach a voluntary accommodation without governmental intervention if they so desire." 93 Cong.Rec. 4035; 2 Leg.Hist. L.M.R.A. (1947) 1046. And see National Labor Relations Board v. Radio and Television Broadcast Engineers Union, Local 1212 etc., 364 U.S. 573, 577, 81 S.Ct. 330, 5 L.Ed.2d 302. * * *

Grievance arbitration is one method of settling disputes over work assignments; and it is commonly used, we are told. To be sure, only one of the two unions involved in the controversy has moved the state courts to compel arbitration. So unless the other union intervenes, an adjudication of the arbiter might not put an end to the dispute. Yet the arbitration may as a practical matter end the controversy or put into movement forces that will resolve it. * * *

What we have said so far treats the case as if the grievance involves only a work assignment dispute. If, however, the controversy be a representational one, involving the duty of an employer to bargain collectively with the representative of the employees as provided in § 8(a) (5), further considerations are necessary. Such a charge, made by a union against the employer, would, if proved, be an unfair labor practice, as § 8(a) (5) expressly states. Or the unions instead of filing such a charge might petition the Board under § 9(c) (1) to obtain a clarification of the certificates they already have from the Board; and the employer might do the same. * * *

If this is truly a representation case, either IUE or Westinghouse can move to have the certificate clarified. But the existence of a remedy before the Board for an unfair labor practice does not bar individual employees from seeking damages for breach of a collective bargaining agreement in a state court, as we held in Smith v. Evening News Assn., 371 U.S. 195, 83 S.Ct. 267, 9 L.Ed.2d 246. We think the same policy considerations are applicable here; and that a suit either in the federal courts, as provided by § 301(a) of the Labor Management Relations Act of 1947 (61 Stat. 156, 29 U.S.C. § 185(a); Textile Workers v. Lincoln Mills, 353 U.S. 448, 77 S.Ct. 912, 1 L.Ed.2d 972), or before such state tribunals as are authorized to act (Charles Dowd Box Co. v. Courtney, 368 U.S. 502, 82 S.Ct. 519, 7 L.Ed.2d 483; Local 174, Teamsters, Chauffeurs, Warehousemen & Helpers of America v. Lucas Flour Co., 369 U.S. 95, 82 S.Ct. 571, 7 L.Ed.2d 593) is proper, even though an alternative remedy before the Board is available, which, if invoked by the employer, will protect him.

The policy considerations behind Smith v. Evening News Assn., supra, are highlighted here by reason of the blurred line that often exists between work assignment disputes and controversies over which of two or more unions is the appropriate bargaining unit. It may be claimed that A and B, to whom work is assigned as "technical," employees, are in fact "production and maintenance" employees; and if that charge is made and sustained the Board, under the decisions already noted, clarifies the certificate. But IUE may claim that when the work was assigned to A and B, the collective agreement was violated because "production and maintenance" employees, not "technical" employees, were entitled to it. As noted, the Board clarifies certificates where a certified union seeks to represent additional employees; but it will not entertain a motion to clarify a certificate where the union merely seeks additional work for employees already within its unit. See General Aniline & Film Corp., 89 N.L.R.B. 467; American Broadcasting Co., 112 N.L.R.B. 605; Employing Plasterers Assn., 118 N.L.R.B. 17. The Board's description of the line between the two types of cases is as follows:

> "* * * a Board certification in a representation proceeding is not a jurisdictional award; it is merely a determination that a majority of the employees in an appropriate unit have selected a particular labor organization as their representative for purposes of collective bargaining. It is true that such certification presupposes a determination that the group of employees involved constitute an appropriate unit for collective bargaining purposes, and that in making such determination the Board considers the general nature of the duties and work tasks of such employees. However, unlike a jurisdictional award, this determination by the Board does not freeze the duties or work tasks of the employees in the unit found appropriate. Thus, the Board's unit finding does not *per se* preclude the employer from adding to, or subtracting from, the employees' work assignments. While that finding may be determined by, it does not determine, job content; nor does it signify approval, in any respect, of any work task claims which the certified union may have made before this Board or elsewhere." Plumbing Contractors Assn., 93 N.L.R.B. 1081, 1087.

As the Board's decisions indicate, disputes are often difficult to classify. In the present case the Solicitor General, who appears *amicus*, believes the controversy is essentially a representational one. So does Westinghouse. IUE on the other hand claims it is a work assignment dispute. Even if it is in form a representation problem, in substance it may involve problems of seniority when lay-offs occur (see Sovern, Section 301 and the Primary Jurisdiction of the NLRB, 76 Harv.L.Rev. 529, 574-575 (1963)) or other aspects of work assignment disputes. If that is true, there is work for the arbiter whatever the Board may decide.

If by the time the dispute reaches the Board, arbitration has already taken place, the Board shows deference to the arbitral award, provided the procedure was a fair one and the results not repugnant to the Act.   * * *

Should the Board disagree with the arbiter, by ruling, for example, that the employees involved in the controversy are members of one bargaining unit or another, the Board's ruling would, of course, take precedence; and if the employer's action had been in accord with that ruling, it would not be liable for damages under § 301. But that is not peculiar to the present type of controversy. Arbitral awards construing a seniority provision (Carey v. General Electric Co., 2 Cir., 315 F.2d 499, 509–510), or awards concerning unfair labor practices, may later end up in conflict with Board rulings. See International Association of Machinists, 116 N.L.R.B. 645; Monsanto Chemical Co., supra. Yet, as we held in Smith v. Evening News Assn., supra, the possibility of conflict is no barrier to resort to a tribunal other than the Board.

However the dispute be considered—whether one involving work assignment or one concerning representation—we see no barrier to use of the arbitration procedure. If it is a work assignment dispute, arbitration conveniently fills a gap and avoids the necessity of a strike to bring the matter to the Board. If it is a representation matter, resort to arbitration may have a pervasive, curative effect even though one union is not a party.

By allowing the dispute to go to arbitration its fragmentation is avoided to a substantial extent; and those conciliatory measures which Congress deemed vital to "industrial peace" (Textile Workers v. Lincoln Mills, supra, 353 U.S. at 455, 77 S.Ct. 917) and which may be dispositive of the entire dispute, are encouraged. The superior authority of the Board may be invoked at any time. Meanwhile the therapy of arbitration is brought to bear in a complicated and troubled area.

Reversed.

MR. JUSTICE GOLDBERG took no part in the consideration or decision of this case.

MR. JUSTICE HARLAN, concurring.

I join the Court's opinion with a brief comment. As is recognized by all, neither position in this case is without its difficulties. Lacking a clear-cut command in the statute itself, the choice in substance lies between a course which would altogether preclude any attempt at resolving disputes of this kind by arbitration, and one which at worst will expose those concerned to the hazard of duplicative proceedings. The undesirable consequences of the first alternative are inevitable, those of the second conjectural. As between the two, I think the Court at this early stage of experience in this area rightly chooses the latter.

MR. JUSTICE BLACK, with whom MR. JUSTICE CLARK joins, dissenting. * * *

I agree with the New York court and would affirm its judgment. Stripped of obscurantist arguments, this controversy is a plain, garden-variety jurisdictional dispute between two unions. The Court today holds, however, that the National Labor Relations Act not only permits but compels Westinghouse to arbitrate the dispute with only one of the two warring unions. Such an arbitration could not, of course, bring about the "final and binding arbitration of grievance and disputes" that the Court says contributes to the congressional objectives in passing the Labor Act. * * *

The result of all this is that the National Labor Relations Board, the agency created by Congress finally to settle labor disputes in the interest of industrial peace, is to be supplanted in part by so-called arbitration which in its very nature cannot achieve a final adjustment of those disputes. One of the main evils it had been hoped the Labor Act would abate was jurisdictional disputes between unions over which union members would do certain work. The Board can make final settlements of such disputes. Arbitration between some but not all the parties cannot. I fear that the Court's recently announced leanings to treat arbitration as an almost sure and certain solvent of all labor troubles has been carried so far in this case as unnecessarily to bring about great confusion and to delay final and binding settlements of jurisdictional disputes by the Labor Board, the agency which I think Congress intended to do that very job.

I would affirm.

Problems for Discussion

1. Can a district court in a case such as *Carey* take any action (upon appropriate motion) to bring both unions before the arbitrator in a single proceeding? Can an arbitrator do so? See Jones, On Nudging and Shoving, etc., 79 Harv.L.Rev. 327 (1965).

2. The union contends that employee Williams has been delinquent in the payment of dues and that the employer is thus obligated to discharge her in accordance with the union-security provision of the labor contract. The employer, however, has refused to discharge Williams, asserting (1) that it does not believe that Williams was delinquent within the meaning of the contract and that it indeed believes that union officials have purposely made themselves unavailable to receive such dues, and (2) that in any event the union-security provision in the labor contract violates the National Labor Relations Act.

(a) If the union brings suit to compel arbitration under Section 301 of its claim that Williams must be discharged, how should the court rule? *arb*

(b) If the employer, while the Section 301 action is pending, files a charge against the union under Section 8(b)(2) of the NLRA, should the court grant a motion by the employer to stay arbitration?

(c) Should the Regional Director decline to issue a complaint against the union under Section 8(b)(2) until the arbitrator has ruled on the union's claim of contract breach?

(d) If the unfair labor practice case is actually decided by an Administrative Law Judge, adverse to the union, should the court in a Section 301 action order the employer to arbitrate? See *Kentile, Inc. v. Local 457, Rubber Workers,* 228 F.Supp. 541 (E.D.N.Y.1964).

(e) If the union's claim of contract breach reaches an arbitrator, who concludes that Williams had been delinquent in her dues and that the company was required by the contract to discharge her, may the employer—in an action by the union to enforce the arbitration award—properly defend upon the ground that the award requires it to commit an unfair labor practice?

NLRB v. C & C PLYWOOD CORP.

Supreme Court of the United States, 1967.
385 U.S. 421, 87 S.Ct. 559, 17 L.Ed.2d 486.

MR. JUSTICE STEWART delivered the opinion of the Court.

* * * In August 1962, the Plywood, Lumber, and Saw Mill Workers Local No. 2405 was certified as the bargaining representative of the respondent's production and maintenance employees. The agreement which resulted from collective bargaining contained the following provision:

"Article XVII

"WAGES

"A. A classified wage scale has been agreed upon by the Employer and Union, and has been signed by the parties and thereby made a part of the written agreement. The Employer reserves the right to pay a premium rate over and above the contractual classified wage rate to reward any particular employee for some special fitness, skill, aptitude or the like. The payment of such a premium rate shall not be considered a permanent increase in the rate of that position and may, at the sole option of the Employer, be reduced to the contractual rate * * *."

The agreement also stipulated that wages should be "closed" during the period it was effective and that neither party should be obligated to bargain collectively with respect to any matter not specifically referred to in the contract.[41] Grievance machinery was estab-

---

41. "ARTICLE XIV

"WAIVER OF DUTY TO BARGAIN

"The parties acknowledge that during negotiations which resulted in this Agreement, each had the unlimited right and opportunity to make demands and proposals with respect to any subject or matter of collective bargaining, and that the understanding and agreements arrived at by the parties after the exercise of that right and opportunity are set forth in this Agreement. Therefore, the Employer and

lished, but no ultimate arbitration of grievances or other disputes was provided.

Less than three weeks after this agreement was signed, the respondent posted a notice that all members of the "glue spreader" crews would be paid $2.50 per hour if their crews met specified bi-weekly (and later weekly) production standards, although under the "classified wage scale" referred to in the above quoted Art. XVII of the agreement, the members of these crews were to be paid hourly wages ranging from $2.15 to $2.29, depending upon their function within the crew. When the union learned of this premium pay plan through one of its members, it immediately asked for a conference with the respondent. During the meetings between the parties which followed this request, the employer indicated a willingness to discuss the terms of the plan, but refused to rescind it pending those discussions.

It was this refusal which prompted the union to charge the respondent with an unfair labor practice in violation of Sections 8(a) (5) and (1). The trial examiner found that the respondent had instituted the premium-pay program in good-faith reliance upon the right reserved to it in the collective agreement. He, therefore, dismissed the complaint. The Board reversed. Giving consideration to the history of negotiations between the parties, as well as the express provisions of the collective agreement, the Board ruled the union had not ceded power to the employer unilaterally to change the wage system as it had. For while the agreement specified different hourly pay for different members of the glue spreader crews and allowed for merit increases for "particular employee[s]," the employer had placed all the members of these crews on the same wage scale and had made it a function of the production output of the crew as a whole.

In refusing to enforce the Board's order, the Court of Appeals did not decide that the premium-pay provision of the labor agreement had been misinterpreted by the Board. Instead, it held the Board did not have jurisdiction to find the respondent had violated Section 8(a) of the Labor Act, because the "existence * * * of an unfair labor practice [did] not turn entirely upon the provisions of the Act, but arguably upon a good-faith dispute as to the correct meaning of the provisions of the collective bargaining agreement * * *." 351 F.2d, at 228.

* * *

Union, for the life of this Agreement, each voluntarily and unqualifiedly waives the right and each agree that the other shall not be obligated to bargain collectively with respect to any subject matter not specifically referred to or covered in this Agreement, even though such subjects or matters may not have been within the knowledge or contemplation of either or both of the parties at the time they negotiated or signed this Agreement."

In evaluating this contention, it is important first to point out that the collective bargaining agreement contained no arbitration clause. * * * Thus, the Board's action in this case was in no way inconsistent with its previous recognition of arbitration as "an instrument of national labor policy for composing contractual differences." International Harvester Co., 138 N.L.R.B., 923, 926 (1962), aff'd sub nom. Ramsey v. NLRB, 327 F.2d 784 (C.A.7th Cir.), cert. denied 377 U.S. 1003, 84 S.Ct. 1938, 12 L.Ed.2d 1052.

The respondent's argument rests primarily upon the legislative history of the 1947 amendments to the National Labor Relations Act. It is said that the rejection by Congress of a bill which would have given the Board unfair labor practice jurisdiction over all breaches of collective bargaining agreements shows that the Board is without power to decide any case involving the interpretation of a labor contract. We do not draw that inference from this legislative history.

When Congress determined that the Board should not have general jurisdiction over all alleged violations of collective bargaining agreements and that such matters should be placed within the jurisdiction of the courts, it was acting upon a principle which this Court had already recognized:

> "The Railroad Labor Act, like the National Labor Relations Act, does not undertake governmental regulation of wages, hours, or working conditions. Instead it seeks to provide a means by which agreement may be reached with respect to them."

Terminal Railroad Ass'n v. Brotherhood of Railroad Trainmen, 318 U.S. 1, 6, 63 S.Ct. 420, 423, 87 L.Ed. 571. To have conferred upon the National Labor Relations Board generalized power to determine the rights of parties under all collective agreements would have been a step toward governmental regulation of the terms of those agreements. We view Congress' decision not to give the Board that broad power as a refusal to take this step.

But in this case the Board has not construed a labor agreement to determine the extent of the contractual rights which were given the union by the employer. It has not imposed its own view of what the terms and conditions of the labor agreement should be. It has done no more than merely enforce a statutory right which Congress considered necessary to allow labor and management to get on with the process of reaching fair terms and conditions of employment—"to provide a means by which agreement may be reached." The Board's interpretation went only so far as was necessary to determine that the union did not agree to give up these statutory safeguards. Thus, the Board, in necessarily construing a labor agreement to decide this unfair labor practice case, has not exceeded the jurisdiction laid out for it by Congress. * * *

If the Board in a case like this had no jurisdiction to consider a collective agreement prior to an authoritative construction by the courts, labor organizations would face inordinate delays in obtaining vindication of their statutory rights. Where, as here, the parties have not provided for arbitration, the union would have to institute a court action to determine the applicability of the premium pay provision of the collective bargaining agreement. If it succeeded in court, the union would then have to go back to the Labor Board to begin an unfair labor practice proceeding. It is not unlikely that this would add years to the already lengthy period required to gain relief from the Board. Congress cannot have intended to place such obstacles in the way of the Board's effective enforcement of statutory duties. For in the labor field, as in few others, time is crucially important in obtaining relief. Amalgamated Clothing Workers of America v. Richman Bros. Co., 348 U.S. 511, 526, 75 S.Ct. 452, 460, 99 L.Ed. 600 (dissenting opinion).

The legislative history of the Labor Act, the precedent interpreting it, and the interest of its efficient administration thus all lead to the conclusion that the Board had jurisdiction to deal with the unfair labor practice charge in this case. We hold that the Court of Appeals was in error in deciding to the contrary.

The remaining question, not reached by the Court of Appeals, is whether the Board was wrong in concluding that the contested provision in the collective agreement gave the respondent no unilateral right to institute its premium pay plan. In reaching this conclusion, the Board relied upon its experience with labor relations and the Act's clear emphasis upon the protection of free collective bargaining. We cannot disapprove of the Board's approach. For the law of labor agreements cannot be based upon abstract definitions unrelated to the context in which the parties bargained and the basic regulatory scheme underlying that context. See Cox, The Legal Nature of Collective Bargaining Agreements, 57 Mich.L.Rev. 1 (1958). Nor can we say that the Board was wrong in holding that the union had not foregone its statutory right to bargain about the pay plan inaugurated by the respondent. For the disputed contract provision referred to increases for "particular employee[s]," not groups of workers. And there was nothing in it to suggest that the carefully worked out wage differentials for various members of the glue spreader crew could be invalidated by the respondent's decision to pay all members of the crew the same wage. * * *

Problems for Discussion

1. What should have been the decision of the Court if the collective bargaining agreement had contained an arbitration clause?

2. The union has a collective bargaining agreement covering the employees of the Acme Industrial Company at its plant in St. Louis. The agreement bars subcontracting which will cause the layoff of unit employees, and provides that employees who are laid off in the event plant equipment is moved to other company locations may transfer (with full seniority) to that location. Union representatives have learned that the company is removing certain machinery from the St. Louis plant and moving it to a plant in another state. Fearing that such action will result in a loss of jobs in St. Louis, the union has asked the company to turn over information about the removals, but the company has refused, claiming that no employees have been laid off, that the labor contract has not been violated and that therefore the union has no interest in learning such information. The union has filed a grievance under the contract and has once again asked the employer to turn over the desired information. The company has once again asserted that there is no breach of contract, that the union has thus failed to show any need for the information and that in any event whether it must turn over the information is itself a question of contract construction which must be eventually determined by an arbitrator. The union has now sought such information regarding the equipment removals by filing a Section 8(a)(5) charge with the NLRB, and the company has attacked the Board's jurisdiction to proceed. Does the Board have the power to rule upon the merits of the union's unfair labor practice claim? If it does have that power, how should the Board rule? See *NLRB* v. *Acme Industrial Co.*, 385 U.S. 432, 87 S.Ct. 565, 17 L.Ed.2d 495 (1967).

INTERNATIONAL HARVESTER CO.

National Labor Relations Board, 1962.
138 N.L.R.B. 923, enf'd sub nom. Ramsey v. NLRB,
327 F.2d 784 (7th Cir.), cert. denied 377 U.S.
1003 (1964).

[The collective agreement between International Harvester and United Automobile Workers contained clauses requiring union membership 30 days after employment and providing for the voluntary checkoff of union dues. Ramsey joined UAW in order to keep his job and authorized the checkoff of his dues.

In April 1958 Ramsey revoked the authorization for the checkoff. He did not pay the May and June dues. On July 1, 1958 UAW notified International Harvester that Ramsey was 60 days in default and requested "appropriate action." In accordance with the contract Ramsey was given 10 days to rectify his default, but he did not pay up the dues. On July 21, UAW filed a grievance complaining of International Harvester's failure to discharge Ramsey under the union shop clause. On August 1, the collective agreement expired. The union shop clause could not be renewed because of a State right-to-work law applicable to contracts executed after its enactment. On August 6, International Harvester rejected the grievance on the ground that a State court order—of dubious validity— barred enforcement of the union shop clause of the old contract.

During 1958–1959 the grievance was processed and unsuccessful efforts were made to settle it. In May 1959 the permanent umpire made an award holding (1) that Ramsey should have been discharged under the contract in July 1958; (2) that he should be treated as discharged as of that date but newly hired August 1, 1958 when the union shop clause became ineffective.

In 1961 Ramsey was laid off for lack of work under circumstances in which his old seniority would have yielded continuing employment. Ramsey then filed unfair labor practice charges alleging violations of sections 8(a) (3) and 8(b) (2).

After the usual proceedings the Trial Examiner held that sections 8(a) (3) and 8(b) (2) had been violated because there was no union shop clause in effect after August 1, 1958, at the time UAW repeated its demand for discrimination against Ramsey and International Harvester actually took action against him. The Trial Examiner's recommendation was based upon a line of prior NLRB decisions holding that a union security clause is a defense to charges of unlawful discrimination only if it is "in effect at the moment the attempted or actual action is taken."

The Board's opinion, after stating these facts, continued:]

* * *

There is no question that the Board is not precluded from adjudicating unfair labor practice charges even though they might have been the subject of an arbitration proceeding and award. Section 10(a) of the Act expressly makes this plain, and the courts have uniformly so held. However, it is equally well established that the Board has considerable discretion to respect an arbitration award and decline to exercise its authority over alleged unfair labor practices if to do so will serve the fundamental aims of the Act.

The Act, as has repeatedly been stated, is primarily designed to promote industrial peace and stability by encouraging the practice and procedure of collective bargaining. Experience has demonstrated that collective-bargaining agreements that provide for final and binding arbitration of grievances and disputes arising thereunder, "as a substitute for industrial strife," contribute significantly to the attainment of this statutory objective. Approval of the arbitral technique, which has become an effective and expeditious means of resolving labor disputes, finds expression in Section 203(d) of the Labor Management Relations Act, 1947. That provision declares: "Final adjustment by a method agreed upon by the parties is hereby declared to be the desirable method for settlement of grievance disputes arising over the application or interpretation of an existing collective-bargaining agreement." The Board has often looked to this declaration as a guideline in administering its Act.

If complete effectuation of the Federal policy is to be achieved, we firmly believe that the Board, which is entrusted with the administration of one of the many facets of national labor policy, should give hospitable acceptance to the arbitral process as "part and parcel of the collective bargaining process itself," and voluntarily withhold its undoubted authority to adjudicate alleged unfair labor practice charges involving the same subject matter, unless it clearly appears that the arbitration proceedings were tainted by fraud, collusion, unfairness, or serious procedural irregularities or that the award was clearly repugnant to the purpose and policies of the Act. As the Court has reminded the Board in another context but in language equally applicable to the situation here presented:

> * * * that the Board has not been commissioned to effectuate the policies of the Labor Relations Act so single-mindedly that it may wholly ignore other and equally important Congressional objectives. Frequently the entire scope of Congressional purpose calls for careful accommodation of one statutory scheme to another, and it is not too much to demand of an administrative body that it undertake this accommodation without excessive emphasis upon its immediate task.

Consistent with this reminder, and aware of the underlying objectives of the Act, the Board in the appropriate case has not permitted parties to bypass their specially devised grievance—arbitration machinery for resolving their disputes and where an arbitration award had already been rendered has held them to it.

From what has been said previously, it is quite clear that, in pursuing its grievance to arbitration, the Union in the present case was simply exercising a contractual right to have that tribunal vindicate its claim that the Company breached its obligation by refusing to enforce their concededly valid union-shop agreement to discharge Ramsey for failing to pay his regular membership dues. The Company did not challenge the Union's right to resort to arbitration and properly so, for this was the very procedure which the parties had agreed in their contract was "adequate to provide a fair and final determination of all grievances arising under the terms of this Contract," and which justified the Union's no-strike commitment.[42] Further-more, it is apparent that the parties' submission of their controversy was not only required by their agreement, but also, under established law, was mandatory and survived the contract term.

The record is clear that the issue of the Company's contractual obligation to comply with the Union's demand for Ramsey's discharge was fully and fairly litigated before an impartial arbitrator. In a well-reasoned and informed decision, the arbitrator sustained the Union's grievance. There is certainly not the slightest suggestion—nor is such a contention even urged—of fraud, collusion, or other irregularity on the part of any party to "railroad" Ramsey out of his job. Admittedly, Ramsey was in default in his dues payments which, under the contract at least, made him vulnerable to discharge. Although Ramsey was not given notice of the arbitration hearing, his interests were vigorously defended there by the Company, which had at all times supported Ramsey's position that he was not legally required to maintain his union membership and stubbornly resisted the Union's efforts to secure his removal from his job. For these reasons, we find no serious procedural infirmities in the arbitration proceedings which warrant disregarding the arbitrator's award. After all is said and done, "procedural regularity [is] not * * * an end in itself, but [is] * * * a means of defending substantive interests."

Nor do we find, as the Trial Examiner did, that the resolution of the legal issue before him was at variance with settled law and therefore clearly repugnant to the purposes of the Act. In the light of recent Board decisions and the rapidly developing body of Federal labor law reflected in the *Lincoln Mills* line of cases, the decisions relied upon by the Trial Examiner to support his finding are not conclusive. For example, they do not answer basic questions respecting the Union's contractual right to pursue arbitration to enforce its demand, first made *during the contract term*, for the discharge of Ramsey for failing to make dues payments as required by a concededly valid union-security agreement. However, we need not decide these questions

---

42. Article X, section 2. In Textile Workers Union of America, AFL–CIO v. Lincoln Mills of Alabama, 353 U.S. 448, 455, the Court observed: "Plainly the agreement to arbitrate grievance disputes is the *quid pro quo* for an agreement not to strike."

The present case is plainly distinguished from Gateway Transportation Co., 137 NLRB 1763, where the Board refused to give effect to an arbitration award because the arbitration proceeding did not measure up to the standards of fairness. There, unlike here, the employee contested the employer's right to discharge him and, although neither the union nor anyone else sponsored his cause, he was denied the opportunity to do so himself. In the present case, on the other hand, the Company was aligned in interest with Ramsey and both before and at the arbitration proceeding strenuously resisted the Union's asserted right to demand Ramsey's discharge. Indeed, the arbitration proceeding was initiated by the Union because the Company refused to heed its demand.

in determining to accept the arbitrator's award since it plainly appears to us that the award is not palpably wrong. To require more of the Board would mean substituting the Board's judgment for that of the arbitrator, thereby defeating the purposes of the Act and the common goal of national labor policy of encouraging the final adjustment of disputes, "as part and parcel of the collective bargaining process."

In sum, while an arbitrator's award concededly cannot oust the Board of its jurisdiction to adjudicate unfair labor practice charges, we conclude that, under the facts and circumstances herein, it will effectuate the policies of the Act to respect the award and dismiss the complaint in its entirety.

MEMBER RODGERS and MEMBER FANNING dissented.   *   *   *

SPIELBERG MFG. CO., 112 NLRB 1080 (1955). Following a lawful economic strike the employer refused to reinstate four strikers accused of misconduct. The union, which gained recognition and a contract in the settlement, agreed with the company to submit the four cases to arbitration and notified the four employees. The arbitration board sustained the company. The union or the four employees then filed unfair labor practice charges. *Held,* the complaint should be dismissed because of the arbitration award. " * * [T]he arbitration award is not * * * at odds with the statute. This does not mean that the Board would necessarily decide the issue of the alleged strike misconduct as the arbitration panel did. We do not pass upon that issue. * * * [T]he proceedings appear to have been fair and regular, all parties had agreed to be bound, and the decision of the arbitration panel is not clearly repugnant to the purposes and policies of the Act. In these circumstances we believe that the desirable objective of encouraging the voluntary settlement of labor disputes will be best served by our recognition of the arbitrators' award."

HONOLULU STAR BULLETIN, LTD., 123 NLRB 395 (1959). Van Kralingen was employed by the respondent in 1956 to work as an ad compositor. Thereafter, he took an active interest in union affairs. In particular, he made speeches and circulated documents attacking the overtime provisions of the collective bargaining agreement recently signed between respondent and the incumbent union. Toward the end of 1956 Van Kralingen was fired. The General Counsel for the Board contended that Van Kralingen was discharged for his activities in opposition to the overtime provisions, while the respondent claimed that he was fired for disorderly conduct. The respondent also argued that the Board should respect a prior decision upholding the discharge rendered by a joint conciliation and arbitration committee established by agreement between the parties to determine disputes of this kind. At the hearing before this committee, composed of two union and two management representatives, Van Kralingen was denied the right to be represented by counsel and was not permitted to record the proceedings by machine. In addition, he was not permitted to be present when the Company's supervisors testified concerning the reasons for his discharge, though he was later allowed to question one of the supervisors on the basis of a partial report of that supervisor's testimony. *Held*, the discharge was in violation of the Act, and the Board need not honor the decision of the committee since "the Board is not satisfied as to the fairness and regularity of the arbitration proceeding."

Following the Supreme Court decision in Carey v. Westinghouse Elec. Corp., p. 626 supra, that the arbitrator had jurisdiction to decide the grievance arising from the assignment of work that was allegedly "production and maintenance" work, the company filed with the NLRB a motion to clarify the certifications of the competing unions (IUE and Federation). The Board, however, chose to defer action pending the outcome of the arbitration proceeding. The arbitrator, resting his decision principally upon the wage level of the affected group of employees, determined that some of them should be treated as production and maintenance employees, to be represented by IUE, and the others as technical employees to be represented by Federation. After the rendition of the arbitrator's award, the Board assumed jurisdiction to clarify the unions' certifications. WESTINGHOUSE ELEC. CORP., 162 N.L.R.B. 768 (1967). The initial question addressed by the Board was the weight properly to be accorded an arbitration award which purported to resolve competing claims under two different labor contracts with one of the competing unions not a party to the arbitration proceeding, and which applied criteria other than those generally applied by the Board in making unit determinations. The Board decided that it was not appropriate to defer to the award of the arbitrator, as "the ultimate issue of representation could not be decided by the Arbitrator on the basis of his interpreting the contract under which he was authorized to act, but could only be resolved by utilization of Board criteria for making unit determinations." It was necessary, to warrant deference, that the arbitrator's award reflect use of Board standards and be consistent with them. "In this case apparently not all the evidence concerning all these standards was available to the Arbitrator for his consideration and appraisal, and his award reflects this deficiency." The Board concluded that the arbitrator's award rested solely on one criterion, an estimate of the skills of the employees involved, and neglected other significant factors usually considered in unit-determination cases, such as bargaining history, integration of operations within the group, and the progression of employees within the group from lower to higher grades. The Board, concluding that "while we give some consideration to the award, we do not think it would effectuate statutory policy to defer to it entirely," held that the disputed group of employees ought not be split and that they should be absorbed within the existing unit represented by the Federation.

Title VII of the Civil Rights Act of 1964, 42 U.S.C.A. § 2000e et seq., bars discrimination in employment on the basis (among other things) of race, and provides for a lawsuit by the aggrieved employee after there has been an opportunity for conciliation by the Equal Employment Opportunity Commission. In ALEXANDER v. GARDNER-DENVER CO., 415 U.S. 36 (1974), the Supreme Court considered a case in which an employer covered by the Act had a collective bargaining agreement which also barred discrimination on the basis of race, barred discharge without "just cause," and provided for arbitration of grievances. An employee who was discharged, allegedly for poor work, challenged the discharge through the grievance procedure; although the issue of race discrimination was presented to the arbitrator, he made no mention of it in his decision sustaining the discharge as based on "just cause" on account of poor work. The Supreme Court held that when the employee thereafter pursued an action in a federal court for violation of Title VII, he was entitled to a trial de novo on the issue of race discrimination. The Court held that prior resort to arbitration did not constitute an election of remedies or a waiver of judicial relief, and also that trial courts in Title VII actions were not obligated to "defer" to arbitration decisions which ruled upon the same transaction. Noting the analogy to the National Labor Relations Act, the Court stated that the employee's rights under the Civil Rights Act and under the labor contract were of a "distinctly separate nature" entitled to separate vindication; it also noted that the arbitrator's task was merely to effectuate the intent of the parties to the contract and not to invoke public laws. The Court stated that the arbitrator's task was to construe the law of the shop and not the law of the land; that the arbitrator was generally chosen for his familiarity with industrial relations and not with public law; that arbitration procedures were informal and did not accord the evidentiary guarantees present in civil trials; and that a principle of judicial deference to arbitration might induce employees to circumvent arbitration in race discrimination cases. The Court concluded: "The federal court should consider the employee's claim de novo. The arbitral decision may be admitted as evidence and accorded such weight as the court deems appropriate." What do you believe should be the impact of *Alexander v. Gardner-Denver Co.*, upon NLRB deference to arbitration decisions of the kind already considered in these materials? See also Barrentine v. Arkansas-Best Freight System, Inc., —— U.S. ——, 101 S.Ct. 1437, 67 L.Ed.2d 641 (1981) (wage claim under Fair Labor Standards Act).

[handwritten margin note: Decision may be evid]

——————

Problems for Discussion

1. How should the *International Harvester* case have been decided if the Board went back of the award to rule upon the merits?

2. Exactly what factor(s) in the *Honolulu Star Bulletin* case were likely responsible for the Board's refusal to defer to the decision of the arbitration committee? If any of these factors had existed in isolation, do you believe the Board would have reached the same conclusion?

3. Jones, an employee of the Star Corporation, was a member of the Electrical Workers Union and was its shop steward; in that capacity, he had been a vigorous advocate against the company in many grievances and had been responsible for securing several backpay awards against the company in substantial amounts. After a dispute with several company officials, one of them threatened to "get" Jones, and several days later Jones was discharged, allegedly for encouraging a work slowdown and for practicing race discrimination against workers in the bargaining unit. The Union filed a grievance concerning the discharge; throughout the grievance procedure and before the arbitrator, the Union felt confident that it could set aside the discharge by demonstrating that there was no substance to the company's claim regarding the slowdown and the race discrimination. Since the Union made no issue of the company threat to "get" Jones or of his vigorous efforts as shop steward, the arbitrator did not raise any question whether the company's asserted reasons were really a pretext for a discharge motivated by antiunion animus. The arbitrator sustained the discharge, and Jones filed a charge under Section 8(a)(3) for discriminatory discharge. Should the Board defer to the arbitration award and dismiss Jones' claim? See *NLRB v. General Warehouse Corp.*, 90 CCH L.C. ¶ 12656 (3d Cir. 1981); *Suburban Motor Freight, Inc.*, 247 N.L.R.B. No. 2 (1980). *[handwritten: yes]*

(a) Assume, instead, that the arbitrator had ruled that Jones was indeed responsible for the slowdown and the discrimination, but that discharge was too harsh a discipline; accordingly, Jones was ordered reinstated without backpay. When Jones files a charge under Section 8(a)(3), seeking reinstatement with full backpay, should the Regional Director issue a complaint? See *Amoco Texas Ref. Co.*, 251 N.L.R.B. No. 202 (1980). *[handwritten: no]*

(b) Assume, instead, that the arbitrator had ruled that Jones was unjustly discharged in breach of contract, and that he should be reinstated with backpay. Assume also that the Company has for two months refused to comply with the award, and that the Union has filed a charge with the NLRB of discriminatory discharge. Should the Regional Director issue a complaint? See *Local 715, IBEW v. NLRB (Malrite of Wisconsin, Inc.)*, 494 F.2d 1136 (D.C.Cir. 1974).

4. The Teamsters Union and the Television Technical School have a collective bargaining agreement which provides for a grievance procedure ending in arbitration. Although the contract makes no mention of Christmas bonuses, the School has for twenty years regularly given such a bonus (either $50 or $100 depending upon the employees' job and wage rate). Last December, during the contract term, the School for the first time withheld the bonus, without discussing the matter with the Union. When the Union insisted that the bonus was part of the compensation package which the School could not change without securing the agreement of the Union, the School rejected this proposition and the dispute ultimately reached an arbitrator. The arbitrator ruled that bonuses of the kind in question are universally understood as gifts or gratuities, the payment of which is wholly within the discretion of the employer; there being no express contractual limitation upon that discretion, it was an inherent management right to withhold the bonuses at any time without bargaining and without securing the Union's consent. The Union has brought the case to the NLRB, claiming that the School has violated Section 8(a)(5), while the School has argued that the duty to bargain has been satisfied by submitting the case to arbitration and securing a ruling supporting the position of the School. Should the Board defer to the decision of the arbitrator? See *Radio Television Technical School* v. *NLRB*, 488 F.2d 457 (3d Cir. 1973). Compare *Valley Ford Sales, Inc.*, 211 N.L.R.B. 834 (1974). yes

5. The Cafeteria Employees Union was on the ballot and unsuccessful in four successive representation elections among the New York City restaurants of the Horn and Hardart Company. Subsequently, Horn and Hardart, convinced that the Union actually did have majority support, executed a three-year labor contract recognizing it as bargaining representative for all full-time and regular part-time employees "at all Company locations in the New York metropolitan area." Horn and Hardart subsequently opened a cafeteria in Suffolk County, Long Island, and another in northern New Jersey. When the Cafeteria Employees Union claimed that these locations were within the coverage of the labor contract, Horn and Hardart protested, and the issue was submitted to arbitration. While arbitration was pending, the Retail Clerks Union presented a claim of representation to the Company for both locations, but neither that Union nor any Suffolk County or New Jersey employees were parties to the arbitration proceeding.

Shortly after the arbitrator rendered her decision sustaining the claim of the Cafeteria Employees Union, the Retail Clerks filed a petition for separate representation elections at the Suffolk County and northern New Jersey locations. In both NLRB proceedings, the Company (and the Cafeteria Employees Union as intervenor) moved to dismiss, asserting that the contract as construed by the arbitrator constituted a bar to a representation election. Should the Board dismiss the petitions for this reason? See NLRB v. Horn & Hardart Co., 439 F.2d 674 (2d Cir. 1971).

COLLYER INSULATED WIRE [43]

National Labor Relations Board, 1971.
192 N.L.R.B. 837.

* * *

The complaint alleges and the General Counsel contends that Respondent violated Section 8(a)(5) and (1) of the National Labor Relations Act, as amended, by making assertedly unilateral changes in certain wages and working conditions. Respondent contends that its authority to make those changes was sanctioned by the collective-bargaining contract between the parties and their course of dealing under that contract. Respondent further contends that any of its actions in excess of contractual authorization should properly have been remedied by grievance and arbitration proceeding[s], as provided in the contract. We agree with Respondent's contention that this dispute is essentially a dispute over the terms and meaning of the contract between the Union and the Respondent. For that reason, we find merit in Respondent's exceptions that the dispute should have been resolved pursuant to the contract and we shall dismiss the complaint. * * *

[The respondent company, a manufacturer of insulated electrical wiring, and the union had bargained collectively since 1937 and were operating under a labor contract covering the period April 1969 through July 1971. The contract authorized the employer to make certain changes in wage rates, subject to the grievance procedure, when job evaluations showed that the content of a job had changed; this applied both to production workers, paid on an incentive basis, and to skilled maintenance workers who were paid on a straight-time basis. During the contract term, the employer made three kinds of changes—in wages and job content—without securing the consent of the union. In November 1969, it increased the pay of the maintenance workers by twenty cents per hour in order to meet the higher

---

43. See Christensen, Private Judges, Public Rights: The Role of Arbitration in the Enforcement of the National Labor Relations Act, in The Future of Labor Arbitration in America (Correge et al., ed. 1976); Getman, Collyer Insulated Wire: A Case of Misplaced Modesty, 49 Ind.L.J. 57 (1973); Nash, Wilder & Banov, The Development of the *Collyer* Deferral Doctrine, 27 Vand.L.Rev. 23 (1974); Schatzki, NLRB Resolution of Contract Disputes Under Section 8(a)(5), 50 Texas L.Rev. 225 (1972); Zimmer, Wired for Collyer: Rationalizing NLRB and Arbitration Jurisdiction, 48 Ind.L.J. 141 (1973).

wage rate paid by other employers in the area; the union during contract negotiations had rejected a company proposal for a greater wage increase for maintenance workers than for production workers, and it had been agreed that further negotiations on the issue would be undertaken during the term of the contract. Also in November 1969, the company directed that the removal and cleaning of a gear used in an extruder machine to pack insulation onto the electrical wiring, a process formerly performed by two maintenance machinists, was to be performed thereafter by only one such machinist (with the assistance of a machine operator and helper). Finally, in November 1969 and February 1970, the company—again without bargaining with the union—implemented certain wage increases for extruder-machine operators. The union claimed that the company's actions constituted refusals to bargain in good faith, in violation of Sections 8(a)(5) and (1), while the company argued that they were authorized under the labor contract and that any union grievances should be processed through the contractual grievance procedure.]

II. RELEVANT CONTRACT PROVISIONS

The contract now in effect between the parties makes provision for adjustment by Respondent in the wages of its employees during the contract term. Those provisions appear to contemplate changes in rates in both incentive and nonincentive jobs. Thus, article IX, section 2, provides:

> The Corporation agrees to establish rates and differentials of pay for all employees according to their skill, experience and hazards of employment, and to review rates and differentials from time to time. * * * However, no change in the general scale of pay now in existence shall be made during the term of this Agreement. This Article IX is applicable to the general wage scale, but shall not be deemed to prevent adjustments in individual rates from time to time to remove inequalities or for other proper reasons.

Further evidence of the contractual intent to permit Respondent to modify job rates subject to review through the grievance and arbitration procedures is found in article XIII, section 3, paragraph b, covering new or changed jobs. That paragraph provides that the Union shall have 7 days to consider any new rating established by the Company and to submit objections. Thereafter, even absent Union agreement, it vests in the Company authority to institute a new pay rate. The Union, if dissatisfied, may then challenge the propriety of the rate by invoking the grievance procedure which culminates in arbitration.

Finally, the breadth of the arbitration provision makes clear that the parties intended to make the grievance and arbitration machinery the exclusive forum for resolving contract disputes. * * *

III. THE TRIAL EXAMINER'S DECISION

[The Trial Examiner found that the skill-factor pay increase for maintenance workers and the reassignment of duties at the extruder gear were not sanctioned by the labor contract and, because unilateral, were in violation of Section 8(a)(5). He found that the pay increase for extruder operators was sanctioned by the contract and past practice, and was therefore lawful.]

IV. DISCUSSION

We find merit in Respondent's exceptions that because this dispute in its entirety arises from the contract between the parties, and from the parties' relationship under the contract, it ought to be resolved in the manner which that contract prescribes. We conclude that the Board is vested with authority to withhold its processes in this case, and that the contract here made available a quick and fair means for the resolution of this dispute including, if appropriate, a fully effective remedy for any breach of contract which occurred. We conclude, in sum, that our obligation to advance the purposes of the Act is best discharged by the dismissal of this complaint.

In our view, disputes such as these can better be resolved by arbitrators with special skill and experience in deciding matters arising under established bargaining relationships than by the application by this Board of a particular provision of our statute. The necessity for such special skill and expertise is apparent upon examination of the issues arising from Respondent's actions with respect to the operators' rates, the skill factor increase, and the reassignment of duties relating to the worm gear removal. Those issues include, specifically: (a) the extent to which these actions were intended to be reserved to the management, subject to later adjustment by grievance and arbitration; (b) the extent to which the skill factor increase should properly be construed, under article IX of the agreement, as a "change in the general scale of pay" or, conversely, as "adjustments in individual rates * * * to remove inequalities or for other proper reason"; (c) the extent, if any, to which the procedures of article XIII governing new or changed jobs and job rates should have been made applicable to the skill factor increase here; and (d) the extent to which any of these issues may be affected by the long course of dealing between the parties. The determination of these issues, we think, is best left to discussions in the grievance procedure by the parties who negotiated the applicable provisions or, if such discussions do not resolve them, then to an arbitrator chosen under the agreement and authorized by it to resolve such issues.

The Board's authority, in its discretion, to defer to the arbitration process has never been questioned by the courts of appeals, or by the Supreme Court. Although Section 10(a) of the Act clearly vests the Board with jurisdiction over conduct which constitutes a violation of the provisions of Section 8, notwithstanding the existence of methods of "adjustment or prevention that might be established by agreement," nothing in the Act intimates that the Board must exercise jurisdiction where such methods exist. On the contrary in *Carey* v. *Westinghouse Electric Corporation*, 375 U.S. 261, 271 (1964), the Court indicated that it favors our deference to such agreed methods * * *.

The policy favoring voluntary settlement of labor disputes through arbitral processes finds specific expression in Section 203 (d) of the LMRA, in which Congress declared:

> Final adjustment by a method agreed upon by the parties is hereby declared to be the desirable method for settlement of grievance disputes arising over the application or interpretation of an existing collective-bargaining agreement.

And, of course, disputes under Section 301 of the LMRA called forth from the Supreme Court the celebrated affirmation of that national policy in the *Steelworkers* trilogy. * * *

The question whether the Board should withhold its process arises, of course, only when a set of facts may present not only an alleged violation of the Act but also an alleged breach of the collective-bargaining agreement subject to arbitration. Thus, this case like each such case compels an accommodation between, on the one hand, the statutory policy favoring the fullest use of collective bargaining and the arbitral process and on the other, the statutory policy reflected by Congress' grant to the Board of exclusive jurisdiction to prevent unfair labor practices.

We address the accommodation required here with the benefit of the Board's full history of such accommodations in similar cases. * * * Those cases reveal that the Board has honored the distinction between two broad but distinct classes of cases, those in which there has been an arbitral award, and those in which there has not.

In the former class of cases the Board has long given hospitable acceptance to the arbitral process. * * * The Board's policy was refined in *Spielberg Manufacturing Company*, where the Board established the now settled rule that it would limit its inquiry, in the presence of an arbitrator's award, to whether the procedures were fair and the results not repugnant to the Act.

In those cases in which no award had issued, the Board's guidelines have been less clear. At times the Board has dealt with the unfair labor practice, and at other times it has left the parties to their contract remedies. In an early case, *Consolidated Aircraft Corporation*, the Board, after pointing out that the charging party had failed to utilize the grievance procedures, stated:

> [I]t will not effectuate the statutory policy of encouraging the practice and procedure of collective bargaining for the Board to assume the role of policing collective contracts between employers and labor organizations by attempting to decide whether disputes as to the meaning and administration of such contracts constitute unfair labor practices under the Act. On the contrary, we believe that parties to collective contracts would thereby be encouraged to abandon their efforts to dispose of disputes under the contracts through collective bargaining or through the settlement procedures mutually agreed upon by them, and to remit the interpretation and administration of their contracts to the Board. We therefore do not deem it wise to exercise our jurisdiction in such a case, where the parties have not exhausted their rights and remedies under the contract as to which this dispute has arisen.

The Board has continued to apply the doctrine enunciated in *Consolidated Aircraft*, although not consistently.

Jos. Schlitz Brewing Company, is the most significant recent case in which the Board has exercised its discretion to defer. The underlying dispute in *Schlitz* was strikingly similar to the one now before us. In *Schlitz* the respondent employer decided to halt its production line during employee breaks. That decision was a departure from an established practice of maintaining extra employees, relief men, to fill in for regular employees during breaktime. The change resulted in, among other things, elimination of the relief man job classification. The change elicited a union protest leading to an unfair labor practice proceeding in which the Board ruled that the case should be "left for resolution within the framework of the agreed upon settlement procedures." The majority there explained its decision in these words:

> Thus, we believe that where, as here, the contract clearly provides for grievance and arbitration machinery, where the unilateral action taken is not designed to undermine the Union and is not patently erroneous but rather is based on a substantial claim of contractual privilege, and it appears

that the arbitral interpretation of the contract will resolve both the unfair labor practice issue and the contract interpretation issue in a manner compatible with the purposes of the Act, then the Board should defer to the arbitration clause conceived by the parties.   *   *   *

The circumstances of this case, no less than those in *Schlitz*, weigh heavily in favor of deferral.   Here, as in *Schlitz*, this dispute arises within the confines of a long and productive collective-bargaining relationship.   The parties before us have, for 35 years, mutually and voluntarily resolved the conflicts which inhere in collective bargaining.   Here, as there, no claim is made of enmity by Respondent to employees' exercise of protected rights.   Respondent here has credibly asserted its willingness to resort to arbitration under a clause providing for arbitration in a very broad range of disputes and unquestionably broad enough to embrace this dispute.

Finally, here, as in *Schlitz*, the dispute is one eminently well suited to resolution by arbitration.   The contract and its meaning in present circumstances lie at the center of this dispute.   In contrast, the Act and its policies become involved only if it is determined that the agreement between the parties, examined in the light of its negotiating history and the practices of the parties thereunder, did not sanction Respondent's right to make the disputed changes, subject to review if sought by the Union, under the contractually prescribed procedure.   That threshold determination is clearly within the expertise of a mutually agreed-upon arbitrator.   In this regard we note especially that here, as in *Schlitz*, the dispute between these parties is the very stuff of labor contract arbitration.   The competence of a mutually selected arbitrator to decide the issue and fashion an appropriate remedy, if needed, can no longer be gainsaid.

We find no basis for the assertion of our dissenting colleagues that our decision here modifies the standards established in *Spielberg* for judging the acceptability of an arbitrator's award.   *   *   *   It is true, manifestly, that we cannot judge the regularity or statutory acceptability of the result in an arbitration proceeding which has not occurred.   However, we are unwilling to adopt the presumption that such a proceeding will be invalid under *Spielberg* and to exercise our decisional authority at this juncture on the basis of a mere possibility that such a proceeding might be unacceptable under *Spielberg* standards.   That risk is far better accommodated, we believe, by the result reached here of retaining jurisdiction against an event which years of experience with labor arbitration have now made clear is a remote hazard.

Member Fanning's dissenting opinion incorrectly characterizes this decision as instituting "compulsory arbitration" and as creating an opportunity for employers and unions to "strip parties of statutory rights."

We are not compelling any party to agree to arbitrate disputes arising during a contract term, but are merely giving full effect to their own voluntary agreements to submit all such disputes to arbitration, rather than permitting such agreements to be sidestepped and permitting the substitution of our processes, a forum not contemplated by their own agreement.

Nor are we "stripping" any party of "statutory rights." The courts have long recognized that an industrial relations dispute may involve conduct which, at least arguably, may contravene both the collective agreement and our statute. When the parties have contractually committed themselves to mutually agreeable procedures for resolving their disputes during the period of the contract, we are of the view that those procedures should be afforded full opportunity to function. The long and successful functioning of grievance and arbitration procedures suggests to us that in the overwhelming majority of cases, the utilization of such means will resolve the underlying dispute and make it unnecessary for either party to follow the more formal, and sometimes lengthy, combination of administrative and judicial litigation provided for under our statute. At the same time, by our reservation of jurisdiction, infra, we guarantee that there will be no sacrifice of statutory rights if the parties' own processes fail to function in a manner consistent with the dictates of our law. * * *

V. REMEDY

Without prejudice to any party and without deciding the merits of the controversy, we shall order that the complaint herein be dismissed, but we shall retain jurisdiction * * * over this dispute solely for the purpose of entertaining an appropriate and timely motion for further consideration upon a proper showing that either (a) the dispute has not, with reasonable promptness after the issuance of this decision, either been resolved by amicable settlement in the grievance procedure or submitted promptly to arbitration, or (b) the grievance or arbitration procedures have not been fair and regular or have reached a result which is repugnant to the Act. * * *

MEMBER BROWN, concurring:
* * *

The deferral policy should be applied to disputes covered by the collective-bargaining agreement and subject to arbitration whether the disputes involve alleged violations of Section 8(a)(5), (3), or (1) or whether brought by the employer, the union, or an employee.
* * *

In my opinion deferral would serve only a limited purpose in representation cases. I have serious reservations about applying the same standards to representation cases as I would apply to unfair labor practices cases. For this reason I did not sign the *Raley's* case, in which the Board applied *Spielberg* principles to representation cases. Representation proceedings generally involve the very questions of whether there will be a collective-bargaining arrangement and, if so, to what extent. The standards for Board determinations of units are to assure employees the fullest freedom in exercising the rights guaranteed by the Act. Public interest considerations in the determination of the boundaries of the bargaining unit precludes, in my view, surrender of this function to private parties. * * *

One other area in which I would not defer to arbitration is where there has been a repudiation of the collective-bargaining process. In such a situation the desirability of encouraging resort to arbitration must yield to the Board's duty to protect the bargaining process. Deferral, of course, would not encourage bargaining where the very process of bargaining, including grievance arbitration, has been repudiated and is, in effect, nonexistent. * * *

MEMBER FANNING, dissenting:

* * * To establish the principle, as a matter of labor law, that the parties to a collective-bargaining agreement must, in part, surrender their protection under this statute as a consequence of agreeing to a provision for binding arbitration of grievances will, in my view, discourage rather than encourage the arbitral process in this country. Many may decide they cannot afford the luxury of such "voluntary" arbitration.

* * * I believe the majority's policy is contrary to the intent of Congress and, indeed, beyond the power of the Board. Section 10(a) of the Act clearly states that the Board's power to prevent unfair labor practices "shall not be *affected* by other means of adjustment or prevention that has been or may be established by agreement, law, or otherwise." (Emphasis supplied.) Moreover, under Section 14(c)(1), Congress in the amended Act specifically limited the extent to which the Board may exercise its discretion to refuse jurisdiction over any "class or category of employers" by providing: "That the Board shall not decline to assert jurisdiction over any labor dispute over which it would assert juridiction under the standards prevailing upon August 1, 1959."

Assuming *arguendo* the power of the Board to refuse to entertain charges in cases of this type, the policy of embarking upon such a program is open to serious question. Arbitrators are employed to interpret and apply a specific collective-bargaining agreement. Generally, they are loath to intrude into the area of public rights or national labor policy. These questions historically have been the prime concern of the Board, which was established by Congress exclusively for this purpose. Understandably, an arbitrator, paid jointly by a union and an employer to adjudicate their private rights and obligations, may be unwilling to suggest that one of them is in violation of the National Labor Relations Act and to direct a remedy appropriate to such a finding. The function of good arbitration involves not only the resolution of a particular dispute, but the fostering of a harmonious relationship between the parties to collective bargaining. To endow the arbitrator's award in all cases involving contract interpretation with the prior *imprimatur* of Board approval is, in my opinion, a disservice to the arbitrator, the parties before him, and the effectuation of a sound national labor policy.

Congress has said that arbitration and the voluntary settlement of disputes are the preferred method of dealing with certain kinds of industrial unrest. Congress has also said that the power of this Board to dispose of unfair labor practices is not to be affected by any other method of adjustment. Whatever these two statements mean, they do not mean that this Board can abdicate its authority wholesale. Clearly there is an accommodation to be made. The majority is so anxious to accommodate arbitration that it forgets that the first duty of this Board is to provide a forum for the adjudication of unfair labor practices. We have not been told that arbitration is the only method; it is one method. * * *

MEMBER JENKINS, dissenting:
* * *

Even if I perceived any statutory grant of discretion to the Board to prevent access to it because the arbitration route is available, I can see no policy reason for doing so. To do so does not prevent dual litigation of the same issue, for *Spielberg* already accomplishes this. That to do so will result in any economy of time or money is hardly to be expected.

In 1970, arbitration required 164.2 days from filing of the grievance to issuance of the arbitrator's award, and Board cases required 199 days from the filing of a charge to issuance of the Trial Examiner's decision. Even this rather small time difference is narrowing, as comparison with earlier years discloses. The expense of arbitration is heavy, averaging over $500 per day in 1970, even excluding attorneys' fees, stenographers, witnesses, and hearing room rental. Because of this high cost, as a respected scholar pointed out to the National Academy of Arbitrators:

> Small unions or financially weak firms may be "arbitrated to death" and thus legitimate interests of individual workers or managers may be bargained away because of lack of

funds to process cases. That this is happening, frequently
by design of the financially stronger party, is evident from
the many sources in our profession.

Both the time and expense may be increased by the necessity of filing a charge with the Board within 6 months of the alleged violation
in order to prevent Section 10(b) from barring Board review of the
award under *Spielberg*. To this must be added the time and expense
of the Board proceeding if review of the award is sought. And a
further suit to enforce the arbitration award is always a possibility.
* * *

Nor does arbitration provide an adequate remedy for violations
of the Act. It disposes only of the individual case, rather than settling a principle. It cannot provide a "cease and desist" remedy, as
the Board can. It cannot provide other means of effectuating the
purposes of the Act, such as posting of notices, or other types of
remedy. Unlike the Board's processes, it can be invoked only by the
union, and not by an individual. Thus arbitration cannot speak to
or affect future conduct (which may account for its "bogging down"
under sheer volume, as noted earlier), it cannot effectively protect
the public interest by providing adequate remedies for violations,
and it may sacrifice individual rights guaranteed by the Act because
it is not available to aggrieved individuals.

The majority is reading out of our jurisdiction the statutory protection against all unfair labor practices which may involve in part,
and perhaps distantly, the interpretation of a contract provision,
where the contract contains an arbitration clause. Most unfair labor
practices can be connected somehow to contract terms or existing
practices, by broad construction of general clauses, by the necessary
inquiry into existing practices, by "waiver," or otherwise. This decision will, of course, encourage the creation of such clauses where
they do not now exist. It will also permit unions and employers to
contract themselves almost entirely out of the Act by writing into
their agreements a provision that neither will violate any provision
of the Act, and any alleged such violation will be arbitrated. * * *
The result is that the Board here abdicates a major portion of its
statutory responsibility. It is small wonder that one respected
scholar has expressed concern that "the major problem in this area
is the reluctance of the NLRB to prevent attenuation of its powers
by a blind and placid acceptance of arbitration as an alternative,
rather than subordinate, forum." * * *

GENERAL AMERICAN TRANSP. CORP., 228 N.L.R.B. 808 (1977).
The employer terminated one Soape, the union's area steward,

allegedly for lack of work. The labor contract listed as a function of management the layoff of employees for lack of work "provided, however, that the contractor will not use these rights for the purposes of discrimination against any employee." The contract had a grievance and arbitration procedure governing disputes involving the application or interpretation of the agreement. Soape alleged that he was discharged because of his concerted activities, specifically attending area contract negotiations and filing a complaint with OSHA. Soape filed charges under Sections 8(a)(3) and (1)—contrary to the directions of a union official, who asserted that his proper remedy was through the grievance procedure—the General Counsel issued a complaint, and the Administrative Law Judge, refusing to defer the case, found Soape's discharge to be an unfair labor practice. The NLRB held, 3 to 2, that the Judge was correct in declining to defer to the grievance-arbitration procedure of the contract.

Members Fanning and Jenkins, who had dissented in *Collyer*, reiterated their opposition to the deferral doctrine articulated in that case, concluding (as they had done throughout the intervening six years) that "we believe that the Board has a statutory duty to hear and to dispose of unfair labor practices and that the Board cannot abdicate or avoid its duty by seeking to cede its jurisdiction to private tribunals." These two members asserted that their position was particularly compelling in cases arising under Section 8(a)(3), since the statutory protection against discrimination "is clearly an individual, as contrasted with a union or group, right," and since so-called voluntary arbitration is "a sham in cases, like the instant case, where the charging party is an individual discriminatee seeking to enforce his individual rights." It is erroneous to presume, said Members Fanning and Jenkins, that because the contract barred discrimination by the employer, the arbitrator's decision would also resolve the claim of unfair labor practice; the mere fact that an arbitrator finds that there was "just cause" to discharge an employee does not negate the possibility that the employer was using such "cause" as a pretext for a discharge actually caused by support for the union. Statistics on NLRB deferrals since *Collyer* show that the Board still must review arbitration awards to determine whether to defer, and that "The reduction in our workload is insignificant and the sacrifice of statutory protection is substantial."

Chairman Murphy, although believing that the NLRB does indeed have the power under the Act to defer to grievance-arbitration machinery, concluded that such deferral was proper when "the dispute is essentially between the contracting parties" under Section 8(a)(5) or 8(b)(3), but not when there is a claim of deprivation of an individual's Section 7 rights. In these latter cases—under Sections 8(a)(1), (a)(3), (b)(1)(A), and (b)(2)—the key issue is not whether the conduct is permitted by the contract, but whether it is coercive or unlawfully motivated, and "in these situations, an arbitrator's resolution of the contract issue will not dispose of the unfair labor practice allegation." "Statutory rights, unlike rights created by contract, cannot lawfully be reduced or eliminated either by the employer, the union, or by both. By the same token, an allegation that an employee's statutory rights have been invaded by the employer, the union, or by both ought not to be adjudicated by the very party or parties charged with the wrongdoing." A union purporting to act on behalf of a discriminatee may not have the resources to investigate and prosecute fully; it has the discretion (within the bounds of the duty of fair representation) to abandon or trade off the grievance; even when the union proceeds to arbitration, the aggrieved employee is an outsider, with no standing to participate as a party or to have his own counsel or to examine witnesses or submit evidence; and the arbitrator is generally authorized to determine only whether the employee had engaged in certain conduct and whether the contract permitted discipline therefor. "If the employee claimed that the discipline was in reprisal for having engaged in protected concerted activities under Section 7, the arbitrator either would not or could not reach that issue without exceeding the power given him by the contract."

Members Penello and Walther dissented, adhering to their position in *Collyer*, which they asserted had been endorsed by courts of appeals and had already been extended by the Board to cases of discriminatory discharge (in a decision which Chairman Murphy stated should be overruled). Deferral in Section 8(a)(3) cases was appropriate, said the two dissenters, at least where, as in the instant case, there was a long-established and stable collective bargaining relationship and there was no pattern of employer subversion of Section 7 rights. To deny deferral here, as Chairman Murphy has done, is inconsistent with the *Spielberg* doctrine, under which there have been frequent deferrals to arbitration awards involving alleged anti-union discrimination, and ignores the expertise of arbitrators in handling "just cause" cases, in which there is often a need to determine the issue of pretext. The dissenters criticized several of the arguments made by Chairman Murphy, and pointed out that deferral policies under *Collyer* have already taken into account many of her concerns: the Board has refused to defer where the interests of the aggrieved employee and of the union are adverse or where the employer has in substance rejected the principals of collective bargaining, and it has also asserted jurisdiction to decide the merits when, after deferral, the respondent has refused to go to arbitration or an arbitrator's award has failed

to meet the *Spielberg* standards. Pointing to the same post-*Collyer*
statistics as had Members Fanning and Jenkins, the dissenting
Members concluded that *Collyer* has encouraged resort to grievance-
arbitration procedures, has expedited the disposition of some disputes, many of which have been resolved in the grievance procedure
short of arbitration, and has lightened the workload of the Board.

Problems for Discussion

1.   Are you convinced that the Board acts in violation of a statutory
mandate, and in excess of its authority, when it chooses to defer hearing
a case until there has been an opportunity to have it processed through
contractual grievance procedures?   On the other hand, are you convinced
that the reasons for deferring in Section 8(a)(3) cases are substantially
as compelling as the reasons for deferring in Section 8(a)(5) cases?
Which, if any, of Chairman Murphy's arguments (for a different treatment of these two kinds of cases) do you find persuasive?

2.   If the Board will defer to arbitration awards already rendered,
under *International Harvester* and *Spielberg*, in refusal-to-bargain cases
and discrimination cases, is it rational to refuse to defer in advance, either under the facts of *Collyer* or the facts of *General American Transp.*?

3.   O'Connell was an employee of the National Radio Company, and
was a member of and shop steward for the Electrical Workers Union. Two
months ago, the Company—relying on a contract provision giving management the right to control the scheduling, assignment and performance
of work—announced a rule requiring that union representatives authorized by the contract to handle grievances on company time must make
a record of their activities on such matters and must turn over this record
to the Company at the end of each week. O'Connell claimed that the
Company had no authority to promulgate such a rule and refused to
prepare and submit the required reports, for which he was given a disciplinary warning and then discharged. (The labor contract provides that
the Company may discipline or discharge only for "just cause" and that
it may not discriminate against employees on account of union membership or activities.)   The Union has filed charges against the Company for
violating Sections 8(a)(3) and 8(a)(5). It argues that O'Connell was
discharged for engaging in activity protected by Section 7; that there
was no warrant in the labor contract for the rule adopted by the Company;
and that, in any event, any such rule would be invalid under the decision
of the Supreme Court in the *Magnavox* case (at p. 121, supra). Should the
Regional Director decline to issue a complaint, in light of the assurances
of the Company that it is willing to process the matter through the grievance procedures of the labor contract?   See *National Radio Co.*, 198 N.L.
R.B. 527 (1972). Should be first arb.

4.   When the Supreme Court in the *Carey* case, p. 626 supra, ordered
that arbitration should proceed in the dispute between the IUE and
the Federation, and the Company thereafter asked the Board to clarify

the certifications of those competing unions, ought the Board have stayed its proceedings pending the outcome of the arbitration? Consider as well the Horn & Hardart problem (problem 5 at p. 644 supra); if the representation petition had been filed before the arbitrator had rendered her decision construing the recognition clause of the labor contract, ought the Board have deferred action on the petition pending arbitration?

---

2.   The Duty to Bargain During the Term of an Existing Agreement [44]

The major thrust of Section 8(a)(5) when it was originally enacted in 1935 was to compel the employer, after a union had been properly designated as majority employee representative, to acknowledge it as a partner in setting wages, hours and working conditions. The employer was not to be permitted to frustrate the employees' designation simply by refusing outright to recognize and bargain with the union. The question remains whether the duty to bargain is thus discharged upon the execution of the labor contract or whether it imposes upon the parties obligations independent of the contract during the contract term. During congressional consideration of the Taft-Hartley amendments of 1947, it was suggested that any contract breach should be treated as an unfair labor practice, remediable by the NLRB (in contrast to an arbitrator), but that proposal was rejected. Section 8(d), enacted in 1947, defines the duty to bargain collectively as including the duty to "confer in good faith" with respect to "any question arising" under a labor contract; it also forbids either party during the contract term to "terminate or modify such contract" unless notice is given to the other party sixty days prior to the contract termination date (with notice to federal and state mediation agencies to follow within thirty days) and all contract terms maintained in full force, without strike or lockout, until the expiration of a cooling-off period. Section 8(d) also provides that

> "the duties so imposed shall not be construed as requiring either party to discuss or agree to any modification of the terms and conditions contained in a contract for a fixed period, if such modification is to become effective before such terms and conditions can be reopened under the provisions of the contract."

While it is obvious that Congress intended that the labor contract is to serve as an instrument of stability and repose during its term, it has never been altogether clear how much the Board—in contrast to the arbitrator and the courts—was to play a role in im-

44.   Nelson & Howard, The Duty to Bargain During the Term of an Existing Agreement, 27 Lab.L.J. 573 (1976).

plementing that congressional intention. Thus, while an employer refusal to arbitrate a contract grievance might arguably be a refusal to "confer in good faith" on a "question arising" under the contract, remediable by the Board, the normal procedure is to treat this simply as the breach of a contract promise to arbitrate, remediable by a court action under Section 301. Similarly, while a strike during the term of a contract in support of demands which an arbitrator would not sustain might be viewed as a strike to "modify" the contract—called without complying with the notice and cooling-off provisions of Section 8(d)—most such strikes are treated as union efforts to support a good-faith claim as to the meaning of the contract terms (and not their "modification"), which are actionable, if at all, not through the NLRB but through the grievance and arbitration procedures of the contract.

The argument has indeed often been made that, during the contract term, all claims which might otherwise be characterized as refusals to bargain—such as, most typically, unilateral changes by the employer in wages and working conditions—should be treated instead as matters of contract administration to be resolved through grievance arbitration. In effect, it is argued that compliance with the grievance and arbitration procedures during the contract term is itself satisfaction of the duty to bargain, with the arbitrator serving as "agent" of both parties in resolving disputes concerning working conditions. The decision of the Board in the *Collyer* case, at p. 645 supra, might arguably be viewed as a step in the direction of channeling refusal-to-bargain claims during the contract term through the arbitration machinery as claimed breaches of contract.

The following materials consider the relationship between the statutory obligation to bargain and the rights and duties set forth in collective bargaining agreements.

Problem for Discussion

Hyde Supermarkets, Inc. signed a collective bargaining agreement (containing, among other things, recognition and arbitration clauses) after several months of negotiations with the union chosen by a majority of employees in a Board election. Two weeks later, a group of employees —claiming to represent the nearly unanimous views of the workers in the bargaining unit—went to Hyde and asserted that the union had done such a poor job in negotiations that the employees wished to disclaim the union and the contract and to rely in the future, as in the past, on Hyde's fairness in setting working conditions. Hyde promptly informed the union of this incident, and that it no longer intended to recognize the union as bargaining representative or the contract as binding. The union has filed a Section 8(a)(5) charge with the NLRB. Has the employer committed an unfair labor practice? If so, what remedial order should the Board issue?   See *NLRB* v. *Hyde*, 339 F.2d 568 (9th Cir. 1965).

JACOBS MANUFACTURING CO.

National Labor Relations Board, 1951.
94 N.L.R.B. 1214.

* * *   In July 1948, the Respondent and the Union executed a 2-year bargaining contract which, by its terms, could be reopened 1 year after its execution date for discussion of "wage rates."   In July 1949 the Union invoked the reopening clause of the 1948 contract, and thereafter gave the Respondent written notice of its "wage demands."   In addition to a request for a wage increase, these demands included a request that the Respondent undertake the entire cost of an existing group insurance program, and another request for the establishment of a pension plan for the Respondent's employees.   When the parties met thereafter to consider the Union's demands, the Respondent refused to discuss the Union's pension and insurance requests on the ground that they were not appropriate items of discussion under the reopening clause of the 1948 contract.

The group insurance program to which the Union alluded in its demands was established by the Respondent before 1948.   It was underwritten by an insurance company, and provided life, accident, health, surgical, and hospital protection.   All the Respondent's employees were eligible to participate in the program, and the employees shared its costs with the Respondent.   When the 1948 contract was being negotiated, the Respondent and the Union had discussed changes in this *insurance program*, and had agreed to increase certain of the benefits as well as the costs.   However, neither the changes thereby effected, nor the insurance program itself, was mentioned in the 1948 contract.

As indicated by the Union's request, there was no pension plan for the Respondent's employees in existence in 1949.   The subject of *pensions*, moreover, had not been discussed during the 1948 negotiations;   and, like insurance, that subject is not mentioned in the 1948 contract.

a.   For the reasons stated below, Chairman Herzog and Members Houston and Styles agree with the Trial Examiner's conclusion that the Respondent violated Section 8(a)(5) of the Act by refusing to discuss the matter of *pensions* with the Union.   * * *

We are satisfied   * * *   that the 1948 contract did not in itself impose on the Respondent any obligation to discuss pensions or insurance.   The reopening clause of that contract refers to *wage rates*, and thus its intention appears to have been narrowly limited to matters directly related to the amount and manner of compensation for work. For that reason, a requirement to discuss pensions or insurance cannot be predicated on the language of the contract.

On the other hand, a majority of the Board believes that, regardless of the character of the reopening clause, the Act itself imposed upon the Respondent the duty to discuss *pensions* with the Union during the period in question.

It is now established as a principle of law that the matter of pensions is a subject which falls within the area where the statute requires bargaining. And, as noted above, the 1948 contract between the Respondent and the Union was silent with respect to the subject of pensions; indeed, the matter had never been raised or discussed by the parties. The issue raised, therefore, is whether the Respondent was absolved of the obligation to discuss pensions because of the limitation contained in Section 8(d) of the amended Act dealing with the duty to discuss or agree to the modification of an existing bargaining contract. The pertinent portion of Section 8(d) of the Act provides:

> *   *   *   the duties so imposed shall not be construed as requiring either party to discuss or agree to any modification of the terms and conditions contained in a contract for a fixed period, if such modification is to become effective before such terms and conditions can be reopened under the provisions of the contract.

*   *   *   The crucial point at issue here   *   *   *   is the construction to be given the phrase "terms and conditions *contained in* a contract." (Emphasis supplied.) The Board, in the *Tide Water* case [Tide Water Assoc. Oil Co., 85 N.L.R.B. 1096], concluded that the pertinent portion of Section 8(d)

> *refers to terms and conditions which have been integrated and embodied into a writing.*   *   *   *   With respect to unwritten terms dealing with "wages, hours and other terms and conditions of employment," the obligation remains on both parties to bargain continuously.

Thus, as already construed by this Board in the *Tide Water* case, Section 8(d) does not itself license a party to a bargaining contract to refuse, during the life of the contract, to discuss a bargainable subject unless it has been made a part of the agreement itself. Applied here, therefore, the *Tide Water* construction of Section 8(d) means that the Respondent was obligated to discuss the Union's pension demand.

Members Houston and Styles have carefully reexamined the Board's construction of Section 8(d) in the *Tide Water* case, and are persuaded that the view the Board adopted in the *Tide Water* case best effectuates the declared policy of the Act. Chairman Herzog, while joining in the result with respect to the obligation to bargain here concerning pensions—never previously discussed by the parties—joins in the rationale herein *only* to the extent that it is consistent with his views separately recited below, concerning the insurance program.

By making mandatory the discussion of bargainable subjects not already covered by a contract, the parties to the contract are encouraged to arrive at joint decisions with respect to bargainable matters, that, at least to the party requesting discussion, appear at the time to be of some importance. The Act's policy of "encouraging the practice and procedure of collective bargaining" is consequently furthered. A different construction of Section 8(d) in the circumstances—one that would permit a party to a bargaining contract to avoid discussion when it was sought on subject matters not contained in the contract—would serve, at its best, only to dissipate whatever the good will that had been engendered by the previous bargaining negotiations that led to the execution of a bargaining contract; at its worst, it could bring about the industrial strife and the production interruptions that the policy of the Act also seeks to avert.

The significance of this point cannot be overemphasized. It goes to the heart of our disagreement with our dissenting colleague, Member Reynolds. His dissent stresses the need for "contract stability," and asserts that the furtherance of sound collective bargaining requires that the collective bargaining agreement be viewed as fixing, for the term of the contract, all aspects of the employer-employee relationship, and as absolving either party of the obligation to discuss, during that term, even those matters which had never been raised, or discussed in the past. We could hardly take issue with the virtue of "contract stability," at least in the abstract, and we would certainly agree that everyone is better off when, in negotiating an agreement, the parties have been able to foresee what all the future problems may be, to discuss those problems, and either to embody a resolution of them in the contract, or to provide that they may not be raised again during the contract. But we are here concerned with the kind of case in which, for one reason or another, this has *not* been done, and the question is what best effectuates the policies of the Act in *such* a case.   *   *   *

The construction of Section 8(d) adopted by the Board in the *Tide Water* case serves also to simplify, and thus to speed, the bargaining process. It eliminates the pressure upon the parties at the time when a contract is being negotiated to raise those subjects that may not then be of controlling importance, but which might in the future assume a more significant status. It also assures to both unions and employers that, if future conditions require some agreement as to matters about which the parties have not sought, or have not been able to obtain agreement, then some discussion of those matters will be forthcoming when necessary.

We cannot believe that Congress was unaware of the foregoing considerations when it amended the Act by inserting Section 8(d), or that it sought, by the provision in question, to freeze the bargaining relationship by eliminating any mandatory discussion that might lead to the addition of new subject matter to an existing contract. What Section 8(d) does do is to reject the pronouncements contained in some pre-1947 Board and court decisions—sometimes *dicta*, sometimes necessary to the holding—to the effect that the duty to bargain continues even as to those matters upon which the parties have reached agreement and which are set forth in the terms of a written contract. But we believe it does no more. Those bargainable issues which have never been discussed by the parties, and which are in no way treated in the contract, remain matters which both the union and the employer are obliged to discuss at any time.

In so holding, we emphasize that under this rule, no less than in any other circumstance, the duty to bargain implies only an obligation to *discuss* the matter in question in good faith with a sincere purpose of reaching some agreement. It does not require that either side agree, or make concessions. And if the parties originally desire to avoid later discussion with respect to matters not specifically covered in the terms of an executed contract, they need only so specify in the terms of the contract itself. Nothing in our construction of Section 8(d) precludes such an agreement, entered into in good faith, from foreclosing future discussion of matters not contained in the agreement.[45]

---

45. For an example of a contract in which such a provision was incorporated, see the contract between United Automobile Workers of America and General Motors Corporation, which states:

* * *

(154) The parties acknowledge that during the negotiations which resulted in this agreement, each had the unlimited right and opportunity to make demands and proposals with respect to any subject or matter not removed by law from the area of collective bargaining, and that the understandings and agreements arrived at by the parties after the exercise of that right and opportunity are set forth in this agreement. Therefore, the Corporation and the Union, for the life of this agreement, each voluntarily and unqualifiedly waives the right, and each agrees that the other shall not be obligated, to bargain collectively with respect to any subject or matter not specifically referred to or covered in this agreement, even though such subjects or matter may not have been within the knowledge or contemplation of either or both of the parties at the time that they negotiated or signed this agreement.

b.   Chairman Herzog, for reasons set forth in his separate opinion, believes that—unlike the pensions issue—the Respondent was under no obligation to bargain concerning the *group insurance program.*[46]

However, Members Houston and Styles—a minority of the Board on this issue—are of the further opinion that the considerations discussed above leading to the conclusion that the Respondent was obligated to discuss the matter of pensions, also impel the conclusion that the Respondent was obligated to discuss the Union's group insurance demand.   *   *   *

Members Houston and Styles believe, moreover, that the view adopted by Chairman Herzog on the insurance issue is subject to the same basic criticism as is the view of Member Reynolds—it exalts "contract stability" over industrial peace; it eliminates mandatory collective bargaining on subjects about which one of the parties *now* wants discussion, and concerning which it may well be willing to take economic action if discussion is denied, solely because the matter has once been discussed in a manner which may warrant an inference that the failure to mention that subject in the contract was part of the bargain.   Members Houston and Styles are constrained to reject the view of Chairman Herzog for the further reason that it would establish a rule which is administratively unworkable, and would inject dangerous uncertainty into the process of collective bargaining. Apart from the extremely difficult problems of proof—illustrated in this very case—which would constantly confront the Board in cases of this type, the parties to collective bargaining negotiations would always be faced with this question after a subject has been *discussed* —"Have we really *negotiated,* or are we under an obligation to discuss the subject further if asked to?"   To this query the rule of the *Tide Water* case gives a clear and concise answer: "You are obligated to discuss any bargainable subject upon request unless you have reduced your agreement on that subject to writing or unless you have agreed in writing not to bargain about it during the term of the contract."   Members Houston and Styles would apply that rule without deviation.   *   *   *

CHAIRMAN HERZOG, concurring in part:

I believe that this Respondent was *not* under a duty to discuss the Union's *group insurance* demand.   The individual views which

---

46. *Members Reynolds* and *Murdock* would also find that the Respondent was not obligated to discuss the group insurance program. Their views on the matter likewise are set forth in their separate opinions * * *. The complaint is therefore *dismissed* as to this aspect of the case.

lead me, by a different road, to the result reached on this issue by Members Reynolds and Murdock, are as follows:

Unlike the issue of pensions, concerning which the contract is silent and the parties did not negotiate at all in 1948, the subject of group insurance was fully discussed while the Respondent and the Union were negotiating the agreement.   True, that agreement is silent on the subject, so it cannot literally be said that there is a term "contained in" the 1948 contract relating to the group insurance program.   The fact remains that during the negotiations which preceded its execution, the issue was consciously explored.   The record reveals that the Union expressly requested that the preexisting program be changed so that the Respondent would assume its entire cost, the very proposal that was again made as part of the 1949 midterm demand which gave rise to this case.   The Respondent rejected the basic proposal on this first occasion, but agreement was then reached—although outside the written contract—to increase certain benefits under the group insurance program.

In my opinion, it is only reasonable to assume that rejection of the Union's basic proposal, coupled in this particular instance with enhancement of the substantive benefits, constituted a part of the contemporaneous "bargain" which the parties made when they negotiated the entire 1948 contract.   In the face of this record as to what the parties discussed and did, I believe that it would be an abuse of this Board's mandate to throw the weight of Government sanction behind the Union's attempt to disturb, in midterm, a bargain sealed when the original agreement was reached.

To hold otherwise would encourage a labor organization—or, in a Section 8(b)(3) case, an employer—to come back, time without number, during the term of a contract, to demand resumed discussion of issues which, although perhaps not always incorporated in the written agreement, the other party had every good reason to believe were put at rest for a definite period.   * * *   That would serve only to stimulate uncertainty and evasion of commitments at a time when stability should be the order of the day.

MEMBER REYNOLDS, concurring separately and dissenting in part:

* * *   [I]t is my opinion that Section 8(d) imposes no obligation on either party to a contract to bargain on any matter during the term of the contract except as the express provisions of the contract may demand.   This is a result reasonably compatible with the particular Section 8(d) language involved, as well as with Section 8(d) as a whole.   Moreover, not only does the result accord stability and dignity to collective bargaining agreements, but it also gives substance to the practice and procedure of collective bargaining.

It is well established that the function of collective bargaining agreements is to contribute stability, so essential to sound industrial relations.   Contractually stabilized industrial relations enable employers, because of fixed labor costs, to engage in sound long-range production planning, and employees, because of fixed wage, seniority, promotion, and grievance provisions, to anticipate secure employment tenure.   Hence, when an employer and a labor organization have through the processes of collective bargaining negotiated an agreement containing the terms and conditions of employment for a definite period of time, their total rights and obligations emanating from the employer-employee relationship should remain fixed for that time.   Stabilized therefore are the rights and obligations of the parties with respect to all bargainable subjects whether the subjects are or are not specifically set forth in the contract.   To hold otherwise and prescribe bargaining on unmentioned subjects would result in continued alteration of the total rights and obligations under the contract, thus rendering meaningless the concept of contract stability.

That a collective bargaining agreement stabilizes all rights and conditions of employment is consonant with the generally accepted concept of the nature of such an agreement.   The basic terms and conditions of employment existing at the time the collective bargaining agreement is executed, and which are not specifically altered by, or mentioned in, the agreement, are part of the *status quo* which the parties, by implication, consider as being adopted as an essential element of the agreement.   This view is termed "reasonable and logical," and its widespread endorsement as sound industrial relations practice makes it a general rule followed in the arbitration of disputes arising during the term of a contract.   The reasonableness of the approach is apparent upon an understanding of collective bargaining techniques.   Many items are not mentioned in a collective bargaining agreement either because of concessions at the bargaining table or because one of the parties may have considered it propitious to forego raising one subject in the hope of securing a more advantageous deal on another.   Subjects traded off or foregone should, under these circumstances, be as irrevocably settled as those specifically covered and settled by the agreement.   To require bargaining on such subjects during midterm debases initial contract negotiations.   *   *   *

Eliminating the duty to bargain in midterm concerning items not mentioned in the contract does not mean that the collective bargaining process ends with the negotiation of the contract.   Day-to-day grievances and other disputes arising out of the employer-employee relationship are ever present.   The settlement of these matters is part and parcel of the collective bargaining process, and it is in this regard that there remains upon the parties the continuing duty to bargain collectively.   *   *   *   Collective bargaining during the term of the contract therefore would be mandatory only with respect to administering or interpreting the terms of the contract in accordance with the procedure outlined in the contract.   *   *   *

MEMBER MURDOCK, dissenting in part:

I am unable to agree with my colleagues of the majority that by refusing to discuss pensions and insurance with the Union under the particular circumstances of this case, the Respondent violated Section 8(a)(5) of the Act.

Despite the fact that the reopening clause in the contract which the Union here invoked was limited to "wage rates," the Union included insurance and pensions in its demands thereunder in addition to a wage increase.   In my view the Respondent properly took the position that the parties were meeting pursuant to the reopening provision of the contract to discuss wage *rates* and that pensions and insurance were not negotiable thereunder and would not be discussed at that time.   *   *   *

[In NLRB v. Jacobs Mfg. Co., 196 F.2d 680 (2d Cir. 1952), the court of appeals agreed that the company was obligated to bargain about pensions because that issue was not mentioned in the written agreement and had not been discussed in negotiations.   The court did not, however, decide whether discussion of a subject during negotiations relieves the employer of the duty to bargain, upon union request, for the insertion of a new contract provision in midterm.   The Board has generally held that a union in the latter situation will not be deemed to have "waived" its right to have the employer discuss a subject in mid-term unless it has rather clearly manifested an intention to relinquish that right, for example through explicit statements at the bargaining table or by explicit contract provisions; but the Board's application of this principle, and even its adherence to it, has been far from consistent.   See Pepsi-Cola Distrib. Co., 241 N.L.R.B. No. 136 (1979).]

Problems for Discussion

1.   Assume that in the middle of the contract term, the Jacobs Manufacturing Company announces a change in the employee share of premiums for the health insurance plan and a change in the benefits.   It does not notify the union or bargain in advance of this announcement.   Has the Company violated Section 8(a)(5)?   In formulating an answer, consider: (a) whether the holding in *Jacobs* means that the Company may lawfully make this change?   (b) whether the "integration clause" at footnote 45

of the Board's opinion would make such a change lawful? (c) whether the *Katz* decision, at p. 416 supra, would make such a change unlawful? and (d) whether Section 8(d) (particularly the "termination or modification" provisions) would make such a change unlawful?

2.   Assume that in the middle of the contract term, Jacobs Manufacturing Company informs the union that it is imperative to make such changes in the health insurance plan and that it wishes to give the union an opportunity to discuss the matter before doing so. The union, however, has refused to discuss the matter at all, and after frequent futile overtures by the Company to meet about the issue, the Company implements the change in the insurance plan. The union files a charge of violation of Section 8(a)(5). Does the charge have merit? Consider the same questions as in Problem 1. See *Oak-Cliff-Golman Baking Co.*, 207 N.L.R.B. 1063 (1973).

3.   Assume that pursuant to the Board's decision, the Jacobs Co. bargains with the union upon request concerning a pension plan, and that an impasse is reached after two months. (The date is still in the midst of the contract term.) May the union strike? May the union strike after it gives the appropriate notices required under Section 8(d)? Compare *United Packinghouse Workers*, 89 N.L.R.B. 310 (1950), with *Local 3 Packinghouse Workers* v. *NLRB*, 210 F.2d 325 (8th Cir.) cert. denied 348 U.S. 822 (1954).

4.   Suppose that a labor contract sets forth the terms of a pension and retirement plan and that, during the contract term, the employer declares that it will thereafter terminate the payment of pension moneys to retirees and will instead devote them to the construction of a convalescent home for aged former employees. Would such action violate Section 8(a)(5)? If not, would there be any legal recourse for aggrieved parties, and who would have standing to pursue that legal recourse? See *Allied Chem. Workers* v. *Pittsburgh Plate Glass Co.*, p. 475, supra.

[COLLYER INSULATED WIRE, p. 645 supra]

Problems for Discussion

1.   Consider Problem 1, immediately above. When the union files a charge under Section 8(a)(5) challenging the Company's change in the premiums and benefits of the health insurance plan, should the Regional Director issue a complaint? (Assume the Jacobs contract contains a grievance and arbitration provision. Are there any other assumptions that must be made in order to answer this question?)

2.   Consider the facts of the *Westinghouse* case, at p. 470 supra. If the union were today to file charges under Section 8(a)(5) regarding the company's subcontracting of maintenance and production work, should the Regional Director issue a complaint? What argument might you make on behalf of the union that *Collyer* is not controlling?

3. Assume that an employer has subcontracted certain maintenance work for the first time, and that the labor contract has no specific provision dealing with subcontracting but does have a recognition clause, wage and seniority provisions, a conventional management rights clause (which among other things gives management the privilege to manage the business, to assign work and to discipline for just cause), and grievance and arbitration provisions. Assume also that the union asserts that the subcontracting violated the labor contract, and that an arbitrator renders an award for the company, endorsing a position similar to that of the arbitrator in *Allis-Chalmers* (p. 533 supra) or *Pure Oil* (p. 539 supra). If the union files timely charges under Section 8(a)(5) for unilateral subcontracting, should a complaint issue, and if so how should the Board rule? How would you argue for the union that the Board ought not defer to the decision of the arbitrator?

If the Board ought not defer to such an award after its rendition, should it also refuse to "Collyerize" the Section 8(a)(5) charges in advance of arbitration?

Part Four

STRIKES, BOYCOTTS AND PICKETING

As already noted in the historical materials, supra, peaceful strikes, picketing and boycotts were commonly outlawed in the state courts through judicially developed principles of tort law. Some courts found these concerted activities tantamount to threats of unlawful violence regardless of the employees' objectives, and other courts developed a catalogue of objectionable purposes which would warrant an injunction. Federal courts were at the same time utilizing the vague mandates of the Sherman Act to proscribe (criminally as well as through injunction and treble damages) peaceful union activities with interstate ramifications.

A gradual appreciation by common law courts of the interests of workers, reinforced in a number of states by anti-injunction statutes, led to a retreat from judicial intervention in the 1920s and 1930s. Parallel action at the federal level reached its high point with the enactment in 1932 of the Norris-LaGuardia Act, and with major Supreme Court decisions in 1940 narrowing the reach of the Sherman Act in labor-management disputes. That year, the Court also decided Thornhill v. Alabama, at page 675 infra, which appeared to give constitutionally protected status to peaceful picketing as a form of free speech.

By 1947, however, the American public—as reflected in congressional action—concluded that certain peaceful union pressure had been used abusively and should be outlawed. The most objectionable forms of pressure were declared to be unfair labor practices. The Supreme Court retreated from the broadest ramifications of *Thornhill,* so that much federal and state regulation of union activities was now immune from constitutional attack. Moreover, the labor injunction was revived under the Taft-Hartley Act as an acceptable remedial device (albeit subject to strict limitations regarding to whom and when it was available). At the same time, the National Labor Relations Board and the federal courts were grappling with the question of allowable employer self-help measures in response to peaceful concerted activity.

The materials that follow deal with three major issues: (1) the constitutional limitations, if any, on the power of the state and federal governments to regulate strikes, picketing, and boycotts;

(2) the legality of these concerted activities under the National Labor Relations Act; and (3) the limitations imposed by Sections 8 (a)(1) and 8(a)(3) of the NLRA upon the employer's right to discipline, discharge or otherwise interfere with employees who engage in concerted activities. (The relationship between federal statutory law and the lawmaking and adjudicating power of the states is reserved for more comprehensive treatment in Part Six of the casebook. Suffice it to say at this point that the power of the states to regulate strikes, picketing, and boycotts involving enterprises subject to the jurisdiction of the NLRB has been severely limited, or preempted, as a result of the labor legislation enacted by Congress. These preemption principles emerged at precisely the same time as the *Thornhill* case was losing its force as a curb upon state power through "freedom of speech" principles.)

I. CONSTITUTIONAL LIMITATIONS [1]

At least two constitutional doctrines affect the power of the federal or State governments to restrict the use of concerted action to enforce the demands of a labor union against an employer, or other employees, or a competing labor organization: (1) the concept of "due process" developed under the Fifth and Fourteenth Amendments, and (2) the freedom of communication protected against undue federal restriction by the First Amendment and, through the Fourteenth Amendment, against unwarranted curtailment by a State.

A. FIFTH AND FOURTEENTH AMENDMENTS

The Fifth and Fourteenth Amendments guarantee that no one shall be deprived of "life, liberty or property without due process of law." There has been little litigation concerning the application of these provisions to strike action as distinguished from picketing. Perhaps the leading Supreme Court decision on the question— rendered in a rather unusual factual context—is DORCHY v. KANSAS, 272 U.S. 306, 47 S.Ct. 86, 71 L.Ed. 248 (1926), in which Mr. Justice Brandeis delivered a unanimous opinion for the Court. There, a Kansas statute, while reserving to individual employees the right to quit at any time, made it a crime "to induce others to quit their employment for the purpose and with the intent to hinder, delay, limit or suspend the operation of" mining. Dorchy, as vice-president of a local of the United Mine Workers, was convicted, and sen-

---

1. See Cox, Strikes, Picketing and the Constitution, 4 Vanderbilt L.Rev. 574 (1951); Gregory, Constitutional Limitations on the Regulation of Union and Employer Conduct, 49 Mich.L.Rev. 191 (1950).

tenced to fine and imprisonment, for calling a strike designed to compel a mine company to pay a two-year-old disputed claim to an individual no longer employed by the company. Dorchy attacked the statute as in violation of the Fourteenth Amendment, claiming that the strike was a "liberty" protected by the Constitution. The Court upheld the statute as applied:

> "The right to carry on business—be it called liberty or property—has value. To interfere with this right without just cause is unlawful. The fact that the injury was inflicted by a strike is sometimes a justification. But a strike may be illegal because of its purpose, however orderly the manner in which it is conducted. To collect a stale claim due to a fellow member of the union who was formerly employed in the business is not a permissible purpose. In the absence of a valid agreement to the contrary, each party to a disputed claim may insist that it be determined only by a court. * * * To enforce payment by a strike is clearly coercion. The Legislature may make such action punishable criminally, as extortion or otherwise. * * * And it may subject to punishment him who uses the power or influence incident to his office in a union to order the strike. Neither the common law, nor the Fourteenth Amendment confers the absolute right to strike."

The Court has since cited *Dorchy* approvingly (see UAW v. Wisconsin Employment Rel. Bd., 336 U.S. 245, 69 S.Ct. 516, 93 L.Ed. 651 (1949)), and there is little question—especially in light of the Court's decisions on picketing, to be discussed shortly, where there is the further constitutional concern for freedom of speech—that there is no absolute right to strike. The State courts have sustained numerous restrictions.

None of the cases, however, clearly examines in detail the interest of the employees, in order to determine whether their interest in striking for the purpose of securing better terms and conditions of employment is entitled to some degree of constitutional protection. On principle it would seem that the interest of employees in freedom to strike is cognizable under the Fifth and Fourteenth Amendments. Recourse to a strike involves the withholding of personal service and the association of individuals into a group. Withholding personal service is surely an exercise of "liberty" in the constitutional sense; and so too, recent Supreme Court cases have held, is the freedom to associate in labor organizations. The fact that the strike is a weapon—a form of self-help—used to advance the workers' interest in wages, hours and other terms and conditions of employment does not militate against the claim to some degree of constitutional protection. A constitution which assures the owner of property an opportunity to obtain a reasonable return on his capital surely must recognize the worker's interest in the conditions under which he labors and the price he receives for his work.

It may clarify these generalizations to illustrate them in caricature. Let us suppose that in the State of Ames cotton is king. There would seem little room to doubt the power of the Ames legislature (leaving aside questions of federal preemption) to require employers and employees to submit to a State Board of Arbitration for final and binding decision, without strike or lockout, any labor dispute threatening to interrupt the ginning, compressing or storing of cotton during the harvesting season. This is not an unreasonable method of securing the uninterrupted operation of businesses which, in Ames, might well be deemed essential to the public welfare. But suppose that the Ames legislature, instead of providing for compulsory arbitration, were to enact a statute, the sole consequence of which was to make it a crime for the employees of any employer engaged in ginning, compressing or storing of cotton to strike as a result of a labor dispute. No Ames statute fixes minimum wages or provides for compulsory arbitration. Economic conditions would affect the impact of the legislation and might save it from invalidity if the labor market were sufficiently tight for the laws of supply and demand to protect the individual laborer. In communities where employment opportunities were more limited, however, the consequence would be to compel the workers to accept whatever wage the employer offered. Should not the supposed statute be held unconstitutional, therefore, on the ground that it arbitrarily and capriciously sacrifices the employees' interest in a fair wage by depriving them of their only effective weapon in the competition over the division of the joint product of capital and labor?

If it is correct to conclude that a restriction upon strikes is invalid under the Fifth or Fourteenth Amendment unless the requirements of substantive "due process" are satisfied, the constitutionality of each individual restriction can be determined only after analyzing in detail the needs which gave rise to the challenged legislation in order to determine whether they reasonably justify such a restriction. Although that issue has been with us for more than half a century, it has become particularly pressing in the last two decades which have witnessed an expansion in the rendition of governmental services to the public and in the proportion of the national workforce comprised of federal, state, county and municipal employees, and a more dramatic expansion in the unionization of these employees. Unionization and collective bargaining in the public sector cannot be treated in detail in this casebook, but it should be noted here that there have been a number of court tests of the constitutionality of the very common legislative ban upon strikes by public employees. Such absolute strike prohibitions have consistently been sustained against constitutional attack. Greatest emphasis is placed upon the unique (and monopolistic) position of government in the rendition of essential services and upon the serious societal disruption that would result were governmental services to be interrupted by work stoppages.

The decision that perhaps most seriously addresses the claim of constitutional protection for the right of public employees to strike is POSTAL CLERKS v. BLOUNT, 325 F.Supp. 879 (D.D.C.), aff'd mem. 404 U.S. 802 (1971), in which a three-judge panel upheld a blanket statutory ban upon strikes by federal employees. The majority, noting that the right to strike in the private sector was given not by the Constitution but by federal legislation, observed that the denial of the strike to public employees was rooted in public interest and in long historical tradition. This denial—even taken alongside the statutory protection for private employees—was held not to be arbitrary or irrationally discriminatory, given the interest in assuring "the continuing functioning of the Government without interruption, to protect public health and safety or for other reasons." The majority did, however, assume that public employees had a constitutional right to organize in labor organizations. The concurring judge found this fundamental right to be so intertwined with the right to strike as to raise a serious question whether the latter right was not also constitutionally sanctioned:

> "A union that never strikes, or which can make no credible threat to strike may wither away in ineffectiveness. * * * I do not suggest that the right to strike is co-equal with the right to form labor organizations. * * * But I do believe that the right to strike is, at least, within constitutional concern and should not be discriminatorily abridged without substantial or 'compelling' justification."

Although he believed that the right to strike under the Constitution should turn not on whether the employer was a private employer or a governmental agency but rather upon the essentiality of the services rendered, the concurring judge acknowledged that this was an extremely difficult line to draw (particularly for a court) and that both history and judicial precedent compelled at least as an expedient that the distinction between public and private employees be regarded as crucial.

B.   PICKETING AND FREEDOM OF COMMUNICATION [2]

THORNHILL v. ALABAMA

Supreme Court of the United States, 1940.
310 U.S. 88, 60 S.Ct. 736, 84 L.Ed. 1093.

MR. JUSTICE MURPHY delivered the opinion of the Court.

Petitioner, Byron Thornhill, was convicted in the Circuit Court of Tuscaloosa County, Alabama, of the violation of Section 3448 of the State Code of 1923. The Code Section reads as follows: "§ 3448. Loitering or picketing forbidden.—Any person or persons, who, without a just cause or legal excuse therefor, go near to or loiter about the premises or place of business of any other person, firm, corporation, or association of people, engaged in a lawful business, for the purpose or with intent of influencing, or inducing other persons not to trade with, buy from, sell to, have business dealings with, or be employed by such persons, firm, corporation, or association, or who picket the works or place of business of such other persons, firms, corporations, or associations of persons, for the purpose of hindering, delaying, or interfering with or injuring any lawful business or enterprise of another, shall be guilty of a misdemeanor; but nothing herein shall prevent any person from soliciting trade or business for a competitive business." * * *

Statute

The proofs consist of the testimony of two witnesses for the prosecution. It appears that petitioner on the morning of his arrest was seen "in company with six or eight other men" "on the picket line" at the plant of the Brown Wood Preserving Company. Some weeks previously a strike order had been issued by a Union, apparently affiliated with The American Federation of Labor, which had as members all but four of the approximately one hundred employees of the plant. Since that time a picket line with two picket posts of six to eight men each had been maintained around the plant twenty-four hours a day. * * * There is no testimony indicating the nature of the dispute between the Union and the Preserving Company, or the course of events which led to the issuance of the strike order, or the nature of the effort for conciliation.

2. In addition to the authorities cited in the footnote on p. 768 supra, see Gregory, Peaceful Picketing and Freedom of Speech, 26 A.B.A.J. 709 (1940); Teller, Picketing and Free Speech, 56 Harv.L.Rev. 180 (1942); Dodd, Picketing and Free Speech: A Dissent, 56 Harv.L.Rev. 513 (1943); Teller, Picketing and Free Speech: A Reply, 56 Harv.L.Rev. 532 (1943); Jaffe, In Defense of the Supreme Court's Picket-ing Doctrine, 41 Mich.L.Rev. 1037 (1943); Cox, The Influence of Mr. Justice Murphy on Labor Law, 48 Mich. L.Rev. 767 (1950); Jones, Free Speech: Pickets on the Grass, Alas! Amidst Confusion, a Consistent Principle, 29 S.Cal.L.Rev. 137 (1956); Samoff, Picketing and the First Amendment: "Full Circle" and "Formal Surrender," 9 Lab.L.J. 889 (1958).

The Company scheduled a day for the plant to resume operations. One of the witnesses, Clarence Simpson, who was not a member of the Union, on reporting to the plant on the day indicated, was approached by petitioner who told him that "they were on strike and did not want anybody to go up there to work." None of the other employees said anything to Simpson, who testified: "Neither Mr. Thornhill nor any other employee threatened me on the occasion testified to. Mr. Thornhill approached me in a peaceful manner, and did not put me in fear; he did not appear to be mad." "I then turned and went back to the house, and did not go to work." The other witness, J. M. Walden, testified: "At the time Mr. Thornhill and Clarence Simpson were talking to each other, there was no one else present, and I heard no harsh words and saw nothing threatening in the manner of either man." For engaging in some or all of these activities, petitioner was arrested, charged, and convicted as described. [By appropriate motions he raised and the courts below ruled on the constitutional questions considered herein.]

First.   The freedom of speech and of the press, which are secured by the First Amendment against abridgment by the United States, are among the fundamental personal rights and liberties which are secured to all persons by the Fourteenth Amendment against abridgment by a state.

The safeguarding of these rights to the ends that men may speak as they think on matters vital to them and that falsehoods may be exposed through the processes of education and discussion is essential to free government. Those who won our independence had confidence in the power of free and fearless reasoning and communication of ideas to discover and spread political and economic truth. Noxious doctrines in those fields may be refuted and their evil averted by the courageous exercise of the right of free discussion. Abridgment of freedom of speech and of the press, however, impairs those opportunities for public education that are essential to effective exercise of the power of correcting error through the processes of popular government. Compare United States v. Carolene Products, 304 U.S. 144, 152, 153n * * *. It is imperative that, when the effective exercise of these rights is claimed to be abridged, the courts should "weigh the circumstances" and "appraise the substantiality of the reasons advanced" in support of the challenged regulations. Schneider v. State, 308 U.S. 147, 161, 162, 60 S.Ct. 146, 150, 151, 84 L.Ed. 155.

Second.   The section in question must be judged upon its face. * * *

Third.   Section 3448 has been applied by the State courts so as to prohibit a single individual from walking slowly and peacefully back and forth on the public sidewalk in front of the premises of an employer, without speaking to anyone, carrying a sign or placard on a staff above his head stating only that the employer did not employ union men affiliated with the American Federation of Labor; the purpose of the described activity was concededly to advise customers and prospective customers of the relationship existing between the employer and its employees and thereby to induce such customers not to patronize the employer. O'Rourke v. City of Birmingham, 27 Ala.App. 133, 168 So. 206, certiorari denied 232 Ala. 355, 168 So. 209. The statute as thus authoritatively construed and applied leaves room for no exceptions based upon either the number of persons engaged in the proscribed activity, the peaceful character of their demeanor, the nature of their dispute with an employer, or the restrained character and the accurateness of the terminology used in notifying the public of the facts of the dispute.

* * * It is apparent that one or the other of the offenses [defined in Section 3448] comprehends every practicable method whereby the facts of a labor dispute may be publicized in the vicinity of the place of business of an employer. The phrase "without a just cause or legal excuse" does not in any effective manner restrict the breadth of the regulation; the words themselves have no ascertainable meaning either inherent or historical. * * * The vague contours of the term "picket" are nowhere delineated.[3] * * * In sum, whatever the means used to publicize the facts of a labor dispute, whether by printed sign, by pamphlet, by word of mouth or otherwise, all such activity without exception is within the inclusive prohibition of the statute so long as it occurs in the vicinity of the scene of the dispute.

Fourth. We think that Section 3448 is invalid on its face.

* * * Freedom of discussion, if it would fulfill its historic function in this nation, must embrace all issues about which infor-

---

3. See Hellerstein, Picketing Legislation and the Courts (1931), 10 No.Car. L.Rev. 158, 186n:

"A picketer may: (1) Merely observe workers or customers. (2) Communicate information, e. g., that a strike is in progress, making either true, untrue or libelous statements. (3) Persuade employees or customers not to engage in relations with the employer: (a) through the use of banners, without speaking, carrying true, untrue or libelous legends; (b) by speaking, (i) in a calm, dispassionate manner, (ii) in a heated, hostile manner, (iii) using abusing epithets and profanity, (iv) yelling loudly, (v) by persisting in making arguments when employees or customers refuse to listen; (c) by offering money or similar inducements to strike breakers. (4) Threaten employees or customers: (a) by the mere presence of the picketer; the presence may be a threat of, (i) physical violence, (ii) social ostracism, being branded in the community as a 'scab', (iii) a trade or employees' boycott, i. e., preventing workers from securing employment and refusing to trade with customers, (iv) threatening injury to property; (b) by verbal threats. (5) Assaults and use of violence. (6) Destruction of property. (7) Blocking of entrances and interference with traffic. The picketer may engage in a combination of any of the types of conduct enumerated above. The picketing may be carried on singly or in groups; it may be directed to employees alone or to customers alone or to both. It may involve persons who have contracts with the employer or those who have not or both."

mation is needed or appropriate to enable the members of society to cope with the exigencies of their period.

since dissemination of info, is protected

In the circumstances of our times the dissemination of information concerning the facts of a labor dispute must be regarded as within that area of free discussion that is guaranteed by the Constitution. Hague v. C. I. O., 307 U.S. 496, 59 S.Ct. 954, 83 L.Ed. 1423; Schneider v. State, 308 U.S. 147, 155, 162, 163, 60 S.Ct. 146, 151, 84 L.Ed. 155. See Senn v. Tile Layers Union, 301 U.S. 468, 478, 57 S.Ct. 857, 862, 81 L.Ed. 1229. It is recognized now that satisfactory hours and wages and working conditions in industry and a bargaining position which makes these possible have an importance which is not less than the interests of those in the business or industry directly concerned. The health of the present generation and of those as yet unborn may depend on these matters, and the practices in a single factory may have economic repercussions upon a whole region and affect widespread systems of marketing. The merest glance at State and Federal legislation on the subject demonstrates the force of the argument that labor relations are not matters of mere local or private concern. Free discussion concerning the conditions in industry and the causes of labor disputes appears to us indispensable to the effective and intelligent use of the processes of popular government to shape the destiny of modern industrial society. The issues raised by regulations, such as are challenged here, infringing upon the right of employees effectively to inform the public of the facts of a labor dispute are part of this larger problem.

* * * It may be that effective exercise of the means of advancing public knowledge may persuade some of those reached to refrain from entering into advantageous relations with the business establishment which is the scene of the dispute. Every expression of opinion on matters that are important has the potentiality of inducing action in the interests of one rather than another group in society. But the group in power at any moment may not impose penal sanctions on peaceful and truthful discussion of matters of public interest merely on a showing that others may thereby be persuaded to take action inconsistent with its interests. Abridgment of the liberty of such discussion can be justified only where the clear danger of substantive evils arises under circumstances affording no opportunity to test the merits of ideas by competition for acceptance in the market of public opinion. We hold that the danger of injury to an industrial concern is neither so serious nor so imminent as to justify the sweeping proscription of freedom of discussion embodied in Section 3448.

The State urges that the purpose of the challenged statute is the protection of the community from the violence and breaches of the peace, which, it asserts, are the concomitants of picketing. The power and the duty of the State to take adequate steps to preserve the peace and to protect the privacy, the lives, and the property of its residents cannot be doubted. But no clear and present danger of destruction of life or property, or invasion of the right of privacy, or breach of the peace can be thought to be inherent in the activities of every person who approaches the premises of an employer and publicizes the facts of a labor dispute involving the latter. We are not now concerned with picketing en masse or otherwise conducted which might occasion such imminent and aggravated danger to these interests as to justify a statute narrowly drawn to cover the precise situation giving rise to the danger. Compare American Steel Foundries v. Tri-City Council, 257 U.S. 184, 205, 42 S.Ct. 72, 77, 66 L.Ed. 189, 27 A.L.R. 360. Section 3448 in question here does not aim specifically at serious encroachments on these interests and does not evidence any such care in balancing these interests against the interest of the community and that of the individual in freedom of discussion on matters of public concern. * * * The danger of breach of the peace or serious invasion of rights of property or privacy at the scene of a labor dispute is not sufficiently imminent in all cases to warrant the legislature in determining that such place is not appropriate for the range of activities outlawed by Section 3448.

Reversed.

MR. JUSTICE MCREYNOLDS is of opinion that the judgment below should be affirmed.

TEAMSTERS, LOCAL 695 v. VOGT, INC.

Supreme Court of the United States, 1957.
354 U.S. 284, 77 S.Ct. 1166.

MR. JUSTICE FRANKFURTER delivered the opinion of the Court.

This is one more in the long series of cases in which this Court has been required to consider the limits imposed by the Fourteenth Amendment on the power of a State to enjoin picketing. The case was heard below on the pleadings and affidavits, the parties stipulating that the record contained "all of the facts and evidence that would be adduced upon a trial on the merits * * *." Respondent owns and operates a gravel pit in Oconomowoc, Wisconsin, where it employs 15 to 20 men. Petitioner unions sought unsuccessfully to induce some of respondent's employees to join the unions and commenced to picket the entrance to respondent's business with signs reading, "The men on this job are not 100% affiliated with the A. F. L." "In consequence," drivers of several trucking companies refused to deliver and haul goods to and from respondent's plant, causing substantial damage to respondent. Respondent thereupon sought an injunction to restrain the picketing. * * *

[The State Supreme Court, in affirming the grant of the injunction against the picketing,] held that "One would be credulous indeed to believe under the circumstances that the Union had no thought of coercing the employer to interfere with its employees in their right to join or refuse to join the defendant Union." Such picketing, the court held, was for "an unlawful purpose," since Wis.Stat. § 111.06(2)(b) made it an unfair labor practice for an employee individually or in concert with others to "coerce, intimidate or induce any employer to interfere with any of his employes in the enjoyment of their legal rights * * * or to engage in any practice with regard to his employes which would constitute an unfair labor practice if undertaken by him on his own initiative." * * *

unfair labor practice, so had unlawful purpose

* * * It is not too surprising that the response of States—legislative and judicial—to use of the injunction in labor controversies should have given rise to a series of adjudications in this Court relating to the limitations on state action contained in the provisions of the Due Process Clause of the Fourteenth Amendment. It is also not too surprising that examination of these adjudications should disclose an evolving, not a static, course of decision.

The series begins with Truax v. Corrigan, 257 U.S. 312, 42 S.Ct. 124, 66 L.Ed. 254, in which a closely divided Court found it to be violative of the Equal Protection Clause—not of the Due Process Clause —for a State to deny use of the injunction in the special class of cases arising out of labor conflicts. The considerations that underlay that case soon had to yield, through legislation and later through litigation, to the persuasiveness of undermining facts. Thus, to remedy the abusive use of the injunction in the federal courts, see Frankfurter and Greene, The Labor Injunction, the Norris-LaGuardia Act, 47 Stat. 70, 29 U.S.C. § 101, 29 U.S.C.A. § 101, withdrew, subject to qualifications, jurisdiction from the federal courts to issue injunctions in labor disputes to prohibit certain acts. Its example was widely followed by state enactments.

fed cts only have juris to issue injunction in certain circ

Apart from remedying the abuses of the injunction in this general type of litigation, legislatures and courts began to find in one of the aims of picketing an aspect of communication. This view came to the fore in Senn v. Tile Layers Union, 301 U.S. 468, 57 S.Ct. 857, 81 L.Ed. 1229, where the Court held that the Fourteenth Amendment did not prohibit Wisconsin from authorizing peaceful stranger picketing by a union that was attempting to unionize a shop and to induce an employer to refrain from working in his business as a laborer.

Although the Court had been closely divided in the Senn case, three years later, in passing on a restrictive instead of permissive state statute, the Court made sweeping pronouncements about the right to picket in holding unconstitutional a statute that had been applied to ban all picketing, with "no exceptions based upon either the number of persons engaged in the proscribed activity, the peaceful character of their demeanor, the nature of their dispute with an employer, or the restrained character and the accurateness of the terminology used in notifying the public of the facts of the dispute." Thornhill v. Alabama, 310 U.S. 88, 99, 60 S.Ct. 736, 743, 84 L.Ed. 1093. As the statute dealt at large with all picketing, so the Court broadly assimilated peaceful picketing in general to freedom of speech, and as such protected against abridgment by the Fourteenth Amendment.

These principles were applied by the Court in A. F. L. v. Swing, 312 U. S. 321, 61 S.Ct. 568, 85 L.Ed. 855, to hold unconstitutional an injunction against peaceful picketing, based on a State's common-law policy against picketing when there was no immediate dispute between employer and employee. On the same day, however, the Court upheld a generalized injunction against picketing where there had been violence because "it could justifiably be concluded that the momentum of fear generated by past violence would survive even though future picketing might be wholly peaceful." Milk Wagon Drivers Union v. Meadowmoor Dairies, 312 U.S. 287, 294, 61 S.Ct. 552, 555, 85 L.Ed. 836.

Soon, however, the Court came to realize that the broad pronouncements, but not the specific holding, of Thornhill had to yield "to the impact of facts unforeseen," or at least not sufficiently appreciated. Cf. People v. Charles Schweinler Press, 214 N.Y. 395, 108 N.E. 639, L.R.A. 1918A, 1124; 28 Harv.L.Rev. 790. Cases reached the Court in which a State had designed a remedy to meet a specific situation or to accomplish a particular social policy. These cases made manifest that picketing, even though "peaceful," involved more than just communication of ideas and could not be immune from all state regulation. "Picketing by an organized group is more than free speech, since it involves patrol of a particular locality and since the very presence of a picket line may induce action of one kind or another, quite irrespective of the nature of the ideas which are being disseminated," Bakery and Pastry Drivers Local v. Wohl, 315 U.S. 759, 776, 62 S.Ct. 816, 819, 86 L.Ed. 1178 (concurring opinion); see Carpenters and Joiners Union, etc. v. Ritter's Cafe, 315 U.S. 722, 725–728, 62 S.Ct. 807, 808–810, 86 L.Ed. 1143.

These latter two cases required the Court to review a choice made by two States between the competing interests of unions, employers, their employees, and the public at large. In the Ritter's Cafe case, Texas had enjoined as a violation of its antitrust law picketing of a restaurant by unions to bring pressure on its owner with respect to the use of nonunion labor by a contractor of the restaurant owner in the construction of a building having nothing to do with the restaurant. The Court held that Texas could, consistent with the Fourteenth Amendment, insulate from the dispute a neutral establishment that industrially had no connection with it. This type of picketing certainly involved little, if any, "communication." * * *

The implied reassessments of the broad language of the Thornhill case were finally generalized in a series of cases sustaining injunctions against peaceful picketing, even when arising in the course of a labor controversy, when such picketing was counter to valid state policy in a domain open to state regulation. The decisive reconsideration came in Giboney v. Empire Storage & Ice Co., 336 U.S. 490, 69 S.Ct. 684, 93 L.Ed. 834. A union, seeking to organize peddlers, picketed a wholesale dealer [Empire] to induce it to refrain from selling to nonunion peddlers. The state courts, finding that such an agreement would constitute a conspiracy in restraint of trade in violation of the state antitrust laws, enjoined the picketing. This Court affirmed unanimously. * * * [We] concluded that it was "clear that appellants were doing more than exercising a right of free speech or press. * * * They were exercising their economic power together with that of their allies to compel Empire to abide by union rather than by state regulation of trade." Id., 336 U.S. at page 503, 69 S.Ct. at page 691.

The following Term, the Court decided * * * Building Service Emp. Intern. Union v. Gazzam, 339 U.S. 532 * * *. Following an unsuccessful attempt at unionization of a small hotel and refusal by the owner to sign a contract with the union as bargaining agent, the union began to picket the hotel with signs stating that the owner was unfair to organized labor. The State, finding that the object of the picketing was in violation of its statutory policy against employer coercion of employees' choice of bargaining representative, enjoined picketing for such purpose. This Court affirmed, rejecting the argument that "the Swing case, supra, is controlling. * * * In that case this Court struck down the State's restraint of picketing based solely on the absence of an employer-employee relationship. An adequate basis for the instant decree is the unlawful objective of the picketing, namely, coercion by the employer of the employees' selection of a bargaining representative. Peaceful picketing for any lawful purpose is not prohibited by the decree under review." Id., 339 U.S. at page 539, 70 S.Ct. at page 788.

A similar problem was involved in Local Union No. 10, United Ass'n of Journeymen, Plumbers and Steamfitters, etc. v. Graham, 345 U.S. 192, 73 S.Ct. 585, 587, 97 L.Ed. 946, where a state court had enjoined, as a violation of its "Right to Work" law, picketing that advertised that nonunion men were being employed on a building job. This Court found that there was evidence in the record supporting a conclusion that a substantial purpose of the picketing was to put pressure on the general contractor to eliminate nonunion men from the job and, on the reasoning of the cases that we have just discussed, held that the injunction was not in conflict with the Fourteenth Amendment.

This series of cases, then, established a broad field in which a State, in enforcing some public policy, whether of its criminal or its civil law, and whether announced by its legislature or its courts, could constitutionally enjoin peaceful picketing aimed at preventing effectuation of that policy.

*   *   *

Of course, the mere fact that there is "picketing" does not automatically justify its restraint without an investigation into its conduct and purposes. State courts, no more than state legislatures, can enact blanket prohibitions against picketing. Thornhill v. Alabama and A. F. L. v. Swing, supra. The series of cases following Thornhill and Swing demonstrate that the policy of Wisconsin enforced by the prohibition of this picketing is a valid one. In this case, the circumstances set forth in the opinion of the Wisconsin Supreme Court afford a rational basis for the inference it drew concerning the purpose of the picketing. No question was raised here concerning the breadth of the injunction, but of course its terms must be read in the light of the opinion of the Wisconsin Supreme Court, which justified it on the ground that the picketing was for the purpose of coercing the employer to coerce his employees. "If astuteness may discover argumentative excess in the scope of the [injunction] beyond what we constitutionally justify by this opinion, it will be open to petitioners to raise the matter, which they have not raised here, when the [case] on remand [reaches] the [Wisconsin] court." International Brotherhood of Teamsters Union v. Hanke, 339 U.S., at pages 480–481, 70 S.Ct. at page 779.

Therefore, having deemed it appropriate to elaborate on the issues in the case, we affirm.

Affirmed.

MR. JUSTICE WHITTAKER took no part in the consideration or decision of this case.

MR. JUSTICE DOUGLAS, with whom THE CHIEF JUSTICE and MR. JUSTICE BLACK concur, dissenting.

The Court has now come full circle. In Thornhill v. Alabama, 310 U.S. 88, 102, 60 S.Ct. 736, 744, 84 L.Ed. 1093, we struck down a state ban on picketing on the ground that "the dissemination of information concerning the facts of a labor dispute must be regarded as within that area of free discussion that is guaranteed by the Constitution." Less than one year later, we held that the First Amendment protected organizational picketing on a factual record which cannot be distinguished from the one now before us. A. F. L. v. Swing, 312 U.S. 321, 61 S.Ct. 568, 85 L.Ed. 855. Of course, we have always recognized that picketing has aspects which make it more than speech. Bakery and Pastry Drivers Local v. Wohl, 315 U.S. 769, 776–777, 62 S.Ct. 816, 819, 820, 86 L.Ed. 1178 (concurring opinion). That difference underlies our decision in Giboney v. Empire Storage & Ice Co., 336 U.S. 490, 69 S.Ct. 684, 93 L.Ed. 834. There, <u>picketing was an essential part of "a single and integrated course of conduct, which was in violation of Missouri's valid law."</u> * * *

But where, as here, there is no rioting, no mass picketing, no violence, no disorder, no fisticuffs, no coercion—indeed nothing but speech —the principles announced in Thornhill and Swing should give the advocacy of one side of a dispute First Amendment protection.

The retreat began when, in International Brotherhood of Teamsters Union v. Hanke, 339 U.S. 470, 70 S.Ct. 773, 94 L.Ed. 995, four members of the Court announced that all picketing could be prohibited if a state court decided that that picketing violated the State's public policy. The retreat became a rout in Local Union No. 10, United Ass'n of Journeymen, Plumbers and Steamfitters, etc. v. Graham, 345 U.S. 192, 73 S.Ct. 585, 97 L.Ed. 946. It was only the "purpose" of the picketing which was relevant. The state court's characterization of the picketers' "purpose" had been made well-nigh conclusive. Considerations of the proximity of picketing to conduct which the State could control or prevent were abandoned, and no longer was it necessary for the state court's decree to be narrowly drawn to prescribe a specific evil. Id., 345 U.S. at pages 201–205, 73 S.Ct. at pages 589–591 (dissenting opinion).

Today, the Court signs the formal surrender. State courts and state legislatures cannot fashion blanket prohibitions on all picketing. But, for practical purposes, the situation now is as it was when Senn v. Tile Layers Union, 301 U.S. 468, 57 S.Ct. 857, 81 L.Ed. 1229, was decided. State courts and state legislatures are free to decide whether to permit or suppress any particular picket line for any reason other than a blanket policy against all picketing. I would adhere to the principle announced in Thornhill. I would adhere to the result reached in Swing. I would return to the test enunciated in Giboney—that this form of expression can be regulated only to the extent that it forms an essential part of a course of conduct which the State can regulate or prohibit. I would reverse the judgment below.

Problems for Discussion

1. In Mobile, Alabama, members of a maritime union picketed a dock adjacent to a Liberian cargo ship. The pickets carried signs and distributed handbills protesting substandard wages paid foreign seamen and urging readers to patronize only American vessels. The signs and handbills clearly stated that the dispute was limited to the Liberian ship. Stevedoring companies which service the ship and others at the port sought an injunction in state court against the picketing. At a hearing, the state court found that members of the Longshoremen's Union employed by the stevedoring companies refused to cross the picket lines. As ships in port were unable to unload, other ships became stranded in the harbor without

a place to dock. The picketing threatened to disrupt the eighty percent of the stevedores' business which depends on foreign shipping. A union picket captain testified to hopes that the port would become cluttered with foreign ships unable to load or unload, forcing the docks to shut down. Furthermore, there was a risk of massive loss of agricultural crops which required immediate shipping, since all grain storage facilities in the Mobile area were full. Thus, the picketing threatened to disrupt the economy not only of Mobile, but of the entire state. May the picketing and handbilling be constitutionally enjoined? (Do not consider questions of federal preemption under the NLRB.) See *American Radio Ass'n* v. *Mobile S.S. Ass'n*, 419 U.S. 215, 95 S.Ct. 409, 42 L.Ed.2d 399 (1974).

2. Assume that in the above problem the dockside picketing and handbilling took place adjacent to a Yugoslavian cargo ship that was preparing to take on a shipment of wheat to be transported to the Soviet Union. The unions engaging in such activity are longshore and maritime unions supporting the call of the AFL–CIO for interruption of the recent "grain deal" in which millions of tons of wheat have been sold to the Soviet Union. The AFL–CIO opposition is articulated as rooted in differences of social and governmental philosophy. Assume that all of the commercial interruption outlined in problem 1 occurs here. May a state court constitutionally enjoin the picketing and handbilling? Would the result be different if the AFL–CIO opposition was partly based upon the desire to have any such grain shipments carried on American vessels instead?

3. Assume that a union, attempting to organize a small restaurant (outside of the discretionary jurisdiction of the NLRB), refrains from picketing but instead places the restaurant on the local labor council's "Do Not Patronize List" which is widely disseminated through union newspapers and similar channels. Could a state court enjoin such publication? If so, how ought the injunction be worded? Would the case stand on any different footing in a state having a labor relations act which included provisions identical to Sections 7, 8(c) and 8(b)(1) of the NLRA? Cf. *NLRB* v. *International Ass'n of Machinists*, 263 F.2d 796 (9th Cir. 1959).

HUDGENS v. NLRB [4]

Supreme Court of the United States, 1976.
424 U.S. 507, 96 S.Ct. 1029, 47 L.Ed.2d 196.

MR. JUSTICE STEWART delivered the opinion of the Court.

A group of labor union members who engaged in peaceful primary picketing within the confines of a privately owned shopping center were threatened by an agent of the owner with arrest for criminal trespass if they did not depart. The question presented is whether this threat violated the National Labor Relations Act, as amended 61 Stat. 136, 29 U.S.C. § 151 et seq. The National Labor

---

4. See Note, Shopping Center Picketing: The Impact of *Hudgens v. NLRB*, 45 Geo.Wash.L.Rev. 812 (1977).

Relations Board concluded that it did, 205 N.L.R.B. 628, and the Court of Appeals for the Fifth Circuit agreed. 501 F.2d 161. We granted certiorari because of the seemingly important questions of federal law presented. 420 U.S. 971, 95 S.Ct. 1391, 43 L.Ed.2d 651.

I

The petitioner, Scott Hudgens, is the owner of the North DeKalb Shopping Center, located in suburban Atlanta, Ga. The center consists of a single large building with an enclosed mall. Surrounding the building is a parking area which can accommodate 2,640 automobiles. The shopping center houses 60 retail stores leased to various businesses. One of the lessees is the Butler Shoe Company. Most of the stores, including Butler's, can be entered only from the interior mall.

In January 1971, warehouse employees of the Butler Shoe Company went on strike to protest the company's failure to agree to demands made by their union in contract negotiations. The strikers decided to picket not only Butler's warehouse but its nine retail stores in the Atlanta area as well, including the store in the North DeKalb Shopping Center. On January 22, 1971, four of the striking warehouse employees entered the center's enclosed mall carrying placards which read, "Butler Shoe Warehouse on Strike, AFL–CIO, Local 315." The general manager of the shopping center informed the employees that they could not picket within the mall or on the parking lot and threatened them with arrest if they did not leave. The employees departed but returned a short time later and began picketing in an area of the mall immediately adjacent to the entrances of the Butler store. After the picketing had continued for approximately 30 minutes, the shopping center manager again informed the picketers that if they did not leave they would be arrested for trespassing. The picketers departed. * * *

[Upon charges filed by the union, the NLRB held that Hudgens had violated Section 8(a)(1), and the Board's order was enforced by the court of appeals. In the decisions of the administrative law judge, the Board and the court of appeals—as well as in the arguments of counsel at each stage—there was considerable ambiguity as to whether the rights of the picketers were to rest solely upon Section 7 of the Labor Act or more broadly upon a constitutional right, sustained in earlier Court decisions, to enter upon "private" property (including shopping center property) having certain attributes of "public" property.] * * * * 5

5. * * * Section 8(a)(1) makes it an unfair labor practice for "an employer" to "restrain, or coerce employees" in the exercise of their § 7 rights. While Hudgens was not the employer of the employees involved in this case, it seems to be undisputed that he was an employer engaged in commerce within the meaning of § 2(6) and (7) of the Act, 29 U.S.C. § 152(6) and

* * * In the present posture of the case the most basic question is whether the respective rights and liabilities of the parties are to be decided under the criteria of the National Labor Relations Act alone, under a First Amendment standard, or under some combination of the two. It is to that question, accordingly, that we now turn.

It is, of course, a commonplace that the constitutional guarantee of free speech is a guarantee only against abridgment by government, federal or state. * * * But even truisms are not always unexceptionably true, and an exception to this one was recognized almost 30 years ago in the case Marsh v. Alabama, 326 U.S. 501, 66 S.Ct. 276, 90 L.Ed. 265. In *Marsh,* a Jehovah's Witness who had distributed literature without a license on a sidewalk in Chickasaw, Ala., was convicted of criminal trespass. Chickasaw was a so-called company town, wholly owned by the Gulf Shipbuilding Corporation. It was described in the Court's opinion as follows: " * * * the town and its shopping district are accessible to and freely used by the public in general and there is nothing to distinguish them from any other town and shopping center except the fact that the title to the property belongs to a private corporation."

The Court pointed out that if the "title" to Chickasaw had "belonged not to a private but to a municipal corporation and had appellant been arrested for violating a municipal ordinance rather than a ruling by those appointed by the corporation to manage a company town it would have been clear that appellant's conviction must be reversed." 326 U.S., at 504, 66 S.Ct., at 277. Concluding that Gulf's "property interests" should not be allowed to lead to a different result in Chickasaw, which did "not function differently from any other town," 326 U.S., at 506–508, 66 S.Ct., at 279, the Court invoked the First and Fourteenth Amendments to reverse the appellant's conviction.

It was the *Marsh* case that in 1968 provided the foundation for the Court's decision in Amalgamated Food Employees Union Local 590 v. Logan Valley Plaza, Inc., 391 U.S. 308, 88 S.Ct. 1601, 20 L.Ed.2d 603. That case involved peaceful picketing within a large shopping center near Altoona, Pa. One of the tenants of the shopping center was a retail store that employed a wholly nonunion staff. Members of a local union picketed the store, carrying signs proclaiming that it was nonunion and that its employees were not receiving union wages or other union benefits. The picketing took place on the shopping center's property in the immediate vicinity of the store. A Pennsylvania court issued an injunction that re-

(7). The Board has held that a statutory "employer" may violate § 8(a) (1) with respect to employees other than his own. See Austin Co., 101 N.L.R.B. 1257, 1258–1259. See also § 2(13) of the Act, 29 U.S.C. § 152(13).

quired all picketing to be confined to public areas outside the shopping center, and the Supreme Court of Pennsylvania affirmed the issuance of this injunction. This Court held that the doctrine of the *Marsh* case required reversal of that judgment.

The Court's opinion pointed out that the First and Fourteenth Amendments would clearly have protected the picketing if it had taken place on a public sidewalk * * *. The Court's opinion then reviewed the *Marsh* case in detail, emphasized the similarities between the business block in Chickasaw, Ala., and the Logan Valley shopping center and unambiguously concluded:

> "The shopping center here is clearly the functional equivalent of the business district of Chickasaw involved in *Marsh*." 391 U.S., at 318, 88 S.Ct., at 1608.

Upon the basis of that conclusion, the Court held that the First and Fourteenth Amendments required reversal of the judgment of the Pennsylvania Supreme Court.

There were three dissenting opinions in the *Logan Valley* case, one of them by the author of the Court's opinion in *Marsh*, Mr. Justice Black. His disagreement with the Court's reasoning was total:
* * *

> "The question is, Under what circumstances can private property be treated as though it were public? The answer that *Marsh* gives is when that property has taken on *all* the attributes of a town, i. e., 'residential buildings, streets, a system of sewers, a sewage disposal plant and a "business block" on which business places are situated.' 326 U.S., at 502, 66 S.Ct., at 277. I can find nothing in *Marsh* which indicates that if one of these features is present, e. g., a business district, this is sufficient for the Court to confiscate a part of an owner's private property and give its use to people who want to picket on it." * * *

Four years later the Court had occasion to reconsider the *Logan Valley* doctrine in Lloyd Corp. v. Tanner, 407 U.S. 551, 92 S.Ct. 2219, 33 L.Ed.2d 131. That case involved a shopping center covering some 50 acres in downtown Portland, Ore. On a November day in 1968 five young people entered the mall of the shopping center and distributed handbills protesting the then ongoing American military operations in Vietnam. Security guards told them to leave, and they did so, "to avoid arrest." 407 U.S., at 556, 92 S.Ct., at 2223. They subsequently brought suit in a federal district court, seeking declaratory and injunctive relief. The trial court ruled in their favor, holding that the distribution of handbills on the shopping center's property was protected by the First and Fourteenth Amendments. The Court of Appeals for the Ninth Circuit affirmed the judgment, 446 F.2d 545, expressly relying on this Court's *Marsh* and *Logan Valley* decisions. This Court reversed the judgment of the Court of Appeals.

The Court in its *Lloyd* opinion did not say that it was overruling the *Logan Valley* decision. Indeed a substantial portion of the Court's opinion in *Lloyd* was devoted to pointing out the differences between the two cases, noting particularly that, in contrast to the handbilling in *Lloyd*, the picketing in *Logan Valley* had been specifically directed to a store in the shopping center and the picketers had had no other reasonable opportunity to reach their intended audience. 407 U.S., at 561–567, 92 S.Ct., at 2225–2228. But the fact is that the reasoning of the Court's opinion in *Lloyd* cannot be squared with the reasoning of the Court's opinion in *Logan Valley*.

It matters not that some members of the Court may continue to believe that the *Logan Valley* case was rightly decided. Our institutional duty is to follow until changed the law as it now is, not as some members of the Court might wish it to be. And in the performance of that duty we make clear now, if it was not clear before, that the rationale of *Logan Valley* did not survive the Court's decision in the *Lloyd* case. Not only did the *Lloyd* opinion incorporate lengthy excerpts from two of the dissenting opinions in *Logan Valley*, 407 U.S., at 562–563, 565, 92 S.Ct., at 2225–2226, 2227; the ultimate holding in *Lloyd* amounted to a total rejection of the holding in *Logan Valley*:

"* * * Respondents contend * * * that the property of a large shopping center is 'open to the public,' serves the same purposes as a 'business district' of a municipality, and therefore has been dedicated to certain types of public use. The argument is that such a center has sidewalks, streets, and parking areas which are functionally similar to facilities customarily provided by municipalities. It is then asserted that all members of the public, whether invited as customers or not, have the same right of free speech as they would have on the similar public facilities in the streets of a city or town.

"The argument reaches too far. The Constitution by no means requires such an attenuated doctrine of dedication of private property to public use. The closest decision in theory, Marsh v. Alabama, supra, involved the assumption by a private enterprise of all of the attributes of a state-created municipality and the exercise by that enterprise of semi-official municipal functions as a delegate of the State. In effect, the owner of the company town was performing the full spectrum of municipal powers and stood in the shoes of the State. In the instant case there is no comparable assumption or exercise of municipal functions or power." 407 U.S., at 568–569, 92 S.Ct., at 2229 (footnote omitted).

* * *

"We hold that there has been no such dedication of Lloyd's privately owned and operated shopping center to public use as to entitle respondents to exercise therein the asserted First Amendment rights. * * *" 407 U.S., at 570, 92 S.Ct., at 2229.

If a large self-contained shopping center *is* the functional equivalent of a municipality, as *Logan Valley* held, then the First and Fourteenth Amendments would not permit control of speech within such a center to depend upon the speech's content. * * * "[A]bove all else, the First Amendment means that government has no power to restrict expression because of its message, its ideas, its subject matter, or its content." Police Department of Chicago v. Mosley, 408 U.S. 92, 95, 92 S.Ct. 2286, 2290, 33 L.Ed.2d 212. It conversely follows, therefore, that if the respondents in the *Lloyd* case did not have a First Amendment right to enter that shopping center to distribute handbills concerning Vietnam, then the respondents in the present case did not have a First Amendment right to enter this shopping center for the purpose of advertising their strike against the Butler Shoe Company.

We conclude, in short, that under the present state of the law the constitutional guarantee of free expression has no part to play in a case such as this.

III

From what has been said it follows that the rights and liabilities of the parties in this case are dependent exclusively upon the National Labor Relations Act. Under the Act the task of the Board, subject to review by the courts, is to resolve conflicts between § 7 rights and private property rights, "and to seek a proper accommodation between the two." Central Hardware Co. v. NLRB, 407 U.S. 539, 543, 92 S.Ct. 2238, 2241, 33 L.Ed.2d 122. What is "a proper accommodation" in any situation may largely depend upon the content and the context of the § 7 rights being asserted. The task of the Board and the reviewing courts under the Act, therefore, stands in conspicuous contrast to the duty of a court in applying the standards of the First Amendment, which requires "above all else" that expression must not be restricted by government "because of its message, its ideas, its subject matter, or its content."

In the *Central Hardware* case, and earlier in the case of NLRB v. Babcock & Wilcox Co., 351 U.S. 105, 76 S.Ct. 679, 100 L.Ed. 975, the Court considered the nature of the Board's task in this area under the Act. Accommodation between employees' § 7 rights and employers' property rights, the Court said in *Babcock & Wilcox,* "must be obtained with as little destruction of one as is consistent with the maintenance of·the other." 351 U.S., at 112, 76 S.Ct., at 684.

Both *Central Hardware* and *Babcock & Wilcox* involved organizational activity carried on by nonemployees on the employers' property.[6] The context of the § 7 activity in the present case was different in several respects which may or may not be relevant in striking the proper balance. First, it involved lawful economic strike activity rather than organizational activity. * * * Second, the § 7 activity here was carried on by Butler's employees (albeit not employees of its shopping center store), not by outsiders. See NLRB v. Babcock & Wilcox Co., 351 U.S., at 111–113, 76 S.Ct., at 683–685. Third, the property interests impinged upon in this case were not those of the employer against whom the § 7 activity was directed, but of another.

The *Babcock & Wilcox* opinion established the basic objective under the Act: accommodation of § 7 rights and private property rights "with as little destruction of one as is consistent with the maintenance of the other." The locus of that accommodation, however, may fall at differing points along the spectrum depending on the nature and strength of the respective § 7 rights and private property rights asserted in any given context. In each generic situation, the primary responsibility for making this accommodation must rest with the Board in the first instance. See NLRB v. Babcock & Wilcox, 351 U.S., at 112, 76 S.Ct., at 684; cf. NLRB v. Erie Resistor Corp., 373 U.S. 221, 235–236, 83 S.Ct. 1139, 1149–1150, 10 L.Ed.2d 308; NLRB v. Truckdrivers Union, 353 U.S. 87, 97, 77 S.Ct. 643, 648, 1 L.Ed.2d 676. "The responsibility to adapt the Act to changing patterns of industrial life is entrusted to the Board." NLRB v. Weingarten, Inc., 420 U.S. 251, 266, 95 S.Ct. 959, 968, 43 L.Ed.2d 171.

For the reasons stated in this opinion, the judgment is vacated and the case is remanded to the Court of Appeals with directions to remand to the National Labor Relations Board, so that the case may ·be there considered under the statutory criteria of the National La-`bor Relations Act alone.

It is so ordered.

Vacated and remanded.

6. A wholly different balance was struck when the organizational activity was carried on by employees already rightfully on the employer's property, since the employer's management interests rather than his property interests were there involved. Republic Aviation Corp. v. NLRB, 324 U.S. 793, 65 S.Ct. 982, 89 L.Ed. 1372. This difference is "one of substance." NLRB v. Babcock & Wilcox Co., 351 U.S., at 113, 76 S.Ct., at 685.

[MR. JUSTICE POWELL wrote a separate concurring opinion in which he joined the Court's opinion but noted that *Logan Valley* had not technically been overruled by the *Lloyd* case; he observed, however, that *Logan Valley* was in substance irreconcilable with Marsh v. Alabama and thus was a very weak case initially. MR. JUSTICE WHITE wrote a separate opinion concurring in the judgment but not the opinion of the Court; he too found *Logan Valley* not to have been overruled by the *Lloyd* case, but he would in any event find the *Hudgens* case distinguishable from *Logan Valley*, since he did not believe that the pickets in *Hudgens* were conveying information regarding the very store they were picketing. MR. JUSTICE STEVENS took no part in the consideration of this case.]

MR. JUSTICE MARSHALL, with whom MR. JUSTICE BRENNAN joins, dissenting.

* * * [The dissenting opinion first criticized the opinion of the Court for reaching out to decide a constitutional question and to overrule *Logan Valley* when the decisions of the Board and the court of appeals had clearly rested on a construction of Section 7 of the Labor Act so that the Supreme Court could have disposed of the case on purely statutory grounds. The two dissenting Justices, in construing the statute, employed the test of *Babcock & Wilcox* and would have affirmed the conclusion of the court of appeals that the picketers could not effectively communicate with the patrons of the Butler Shoe Store in Hudgens' mall through advertising in newspapers, radio, television, mail, handbills or billboards or by picketing on public rights-of-way adjoining the shopping center. They then turned to the constitutional issue which had been addressed by the Court.]

The Court adopts the view that *Marsh* has no bearing on this case because the privately owned property in *Marsh* involved all the characteristics of a typical town. But there is nothing in *Marsh* to suggest that its general approach was limited to the particular facts of that case. The underlying concern in *Marsh* was that traditional public channels of communication remain free, regardless of the incidence of ownership. Given that concern, the crucial fact in *Marsh* was that the company owned the traditional forums essential for effective communication; it was immaterial that the company also owned a sewer system and that its property in other respects resembled a town.

In *Logan Valley* we recognized what the Court today refuses to recognize—that the owner of the modern shopping center complex, by dedicating his property to public use as a business district, to some extent displaces the "State" from control of historical First Amendment forums, and may acquire a virtual monopoly of places suitable for effective communication. The roadways, parking lots and walkways of the modern shopping center may be as essential for effective speech as the streets and sidewalks in the municipal or company-owned town. I simply cannot reconcile the Court's denial of any role for the First Amendment in the shopping center with *Marsh's* recognition of a full role for the First Amendment on the streets and sidewalks of the company-owned town.

My reading of *Marsh* admittedly carried me farther than the Court in *Lloyd*, but the *Lloyd* Court remained responsive in its own way to the concerns underlying *Marsh*. *Lloyd* retained the availability of First Amendment protection when the picketing is related to the function of the shopping center, and when there is no other reasonable opportunity to convey the message to the intended audience. Preserving *Logan Valley* subject to *Lloyd's* two related criteria guaranteed that the First Amendment would have application in those situations in which the shopping center owner had most clearly monopolized the forums essential for effective communication. This result, although not the optimal one in my view, Lloyd Corp. v. Tanner, 407 U.S. 551, 570, 579–583, 92 S.Ct. 2219, 2229, 2234–2236, 33 L.Ed. 2d 131 (Marshall, J., dissenting), is nonetheless defensible.

In *Marsh*, the private entity had displaced the "state" from control of all the places to which the public had historically enjoyed access for First Amendment purposes, and the First Amendment was accordingly held fully applicable to the private entity's conduct. The shopping center owner, on the other hand, controls only a portion of such places, leaving other traditional public forums available to the citizen. But the shopping center owner may nevertheless control all places essential for the effective undertaking of some speech-related activities—namely, those related to the activities of the shopping center. As for those activities, then, the First Amendment ought to have application under the reasoning of *Marsh*, and that was precisely the state of the law after *Lloyd*. * * *

On remand, 230 N.L.R.B. 414 (1977), the NLRB held that Hudgens—by threatening through its agent to cause the arrest of Butler's warehouse employees engaged in picketing Butler's retail outlet in Hudgens' Mall—violated Section 8(a)(1). The Board considered the three differences between the instant fact situation and the situations in *Babcock & Wilcox* and *Central Hardware*: the nature of the activity, the persons engaging therein, and the title to the property. This case involves economic strike activity rather than organizational activity, but both are protected by Section 7, so that "economic activity deserves at least equal deference." Similarly, because the picketers here were employees of the company whose store they were picketing, they are entitled to at least as much protection as the nonemployee union organizers in *Babcock,* where the organizers were accorded rights only to the extent necessary to promote the rights of the employees who were their intended audience.

" * * * A further distinction between organizational and economic strike activity becomes apparent when the focus shifts to the characteristics of the audience at which the Section 7 activity in question is directed. In an organizational campaign, the group of employees whose support the union seeks is specific and often is accessible by means of communication other than direct entry of the union organizers onto the employer's property, such as meeting employees on the street, home visits, letters, and telephone calls.

Here, the pickets' intended audience comprised two distinct groups: (1) those members of the buying public who might, when seeing Butler's window display inside the Mall, think of doing business with that one employer, and (2) the employees at the Butler store. Although the non-striking employees at the Butler store were obviously a clearly defined group, the potential customers (the more important component of the intended audience) became established as such only when individual shoppers decide to enter the store.

Hudgens contends that *Babcock & Wilcox* should be read to require, that, if television, radio, and newspaper advertising is available, the picketers' Section 7 rights must yield to property rights regardless of the expense involved and regardless of the fact that such forms of communication, in order to reach the intended audience, necessarily must also reach the general populace. As to these contentions, the Administrative Law Judge found, and we agree, that the mass media, appropriately used by the North DeKalb Center and its merchants to attract customers from the Metropolitan Atlanta area, are not "reasonable" means of communication for employee pickets seeking to publicize their labor dispute with a single store in the Mall. * * *

* * * As to Hudgens' suggestion that the pickets could have used public streets and sidewalks, the Administrative Law Judge pointed out that Butler is only 1 of 60 stores fronting on the same common inside walkways, that the closest public area—i. e., not privately owned—is 500 feet away from the store, and that a message announced orally or by picket sign at such a distance from the focal

point would be too greatly diluted to be meaningful. Further, we find merit in the General Counsel's contentions that safety considerations, the likelihood of enmeshing neutral employers, and the fact that many people become members of the pickets' intended audience on impulse all weigh against requiring the pickets to remove to public property, or even to the sidewalks surrounding the Mall."

[handwritten: outside message would be diluted]

As for the third consideration mentioned by the Supreme Court in *Hudgens*—that the property rights impinged upon were not those of the employer (Butler) but of another—the Board concluded: "[W]e find that, under the circumstances here, Hudgens' property right to exclude certain types of activity on his Mall must yield to the Section 7 right of lawful primary economic picketing directed against an employer doing business on that Mall." The walkways in the Mall, although privately owned, are essentially open to the public; had the picketers not been carrying signs they too would have been within the scope of Hudgens' invitation to the public. Nor is Hudgens a neutral bystander. He is financially interested in the success of each lessee in the Mall, inasmuch as part of his rent is based upon their gross sales; moreover, "in maintaining the comfort, cleanliness, and security of the Mall, Hudgens is, in a real sense, acting for the shopkeepers who lease their store locations from him. To this degree, he is their agent * * *"

[handwritten: 1. walkways are public]

[handwritten: 2. Hudgens financially interested]

[handwritten: pseudo agency relationship]

"[I]n finding that the *Babcock & Wilcox* criteria are satisfied and that, in these circumstances, Hudgens' property rights must yield to the pickets' Section 7 rights, we are simply subjecting the businesses on the Mall to the same risk of Section 7 activity as similar businesses fronting on public sidewalks now endure. In leasing the shops to the merchants, Hudgens necessarily submitted his own property rights to whatever activity, lawful and protected by the Act, might be conducted against the merchants had they owned, instead of leased, the premises. * * * A contrary holding would enable employers to insulate themselves from Section 7 activities by simply moving their operations to leased locations on private malls, and would thereby render Section 7 meaningless as to their employees."

[handwritten: voluntarily submitted]

Problems for Discussion

1. Diamond Sugar Company owns a 2,000-acre tract of land in Georgia, which it uses as a sugar plantation. During harvest season, it employs 380 migrant laborers to harvest the sugar cane. Those laborers live in

rows of shacks erected on the Company's land. There is a general store on the plantation, the rudiments of an athletic field, a mess hall and a social hall which serves as a canteen, a movie-exhibition house and a church. A doctor and nurse also live on the plantation and service the needs of the workers there. The employees work six days a week, ten hours a day. Because of the poor quality of the living conditions and the food, malnutrition and illness are well above normal. On Friday and Saturday nights, the Company supplies a bus (which is usually filled to a capacity of 60) to take the workers into the next town, 40 miles away, to enjoy what there is of local night life.

Several young attorneys working for Community Legal Services in the State of Georgia have adopted a program to educate rural workers in their legal rights and on matters of health, sanitary conditions and the like. On three occasions, they approached the plantation manager to gain access to the workers in their cabins at the end of the work day, but this was refused. Most recently, the attorneys assumed fictitious names and appearances and gained access to the plantation property, but were promptly discovered, and were ejected from the property with the aid of the local sheriff. They threatened to use every legal means to gain access to the property in order to organize and educate the workers, and the plantation manager has asserted that he will use every legal means to keep them out.

There is no applicable statute which would entitle the CLS attorneys to have access to the plantation property. Do they, however, have a constitutional right to do so for this purpose? See Petersen v. Talisman Sugar Corp., 478 F.2d 73 (5th Cir. 1973). Can you anticipate (and refute) any arguments that the Diamond Sugar Company might make in support of a constitutional right to *exclude* the CLS attorneys? See *PruneYard Shopping Center v. Robins*, 447 U.S. 74, 100 S.Ct. 2035, 64 L.Ed.2d 741 (1980).

2. Assume that the facts are essentially the same, but that the organization seeking access to the plantation property is the Farm Workers Union, and it desires both to distribute authorization cards and to picket in order to induce employees to join and the company to bargain. Would this change the constitutional rights of the parties? See *Association de Trabajadores Agricolas de Puerto Rico v. Green Giant Co.*, 518 F.2d 130 (3d Cir. 1975); *Agricultural Labor Relations Bd. v. Superior Court*, 16 Cal. 3d 392, 128 Cal.Rptr. 183, 546 P.2d 687 (1976).

3. Assume that the facts are essentially the same, but that the organization seeking access to the plantation property is the Teamsters Union, which is attempting to organize certain workers on the plantation whose work there brings them within the jurisdiction of the National Labor Relations Board. The Union desires both to distribute authorization cards and to picket in order to induce employees to join and the Company to bargain. Does their exclusion by Diamond Sugar Co. constitute a violation of Section 8(a)(1) of the NLRA?

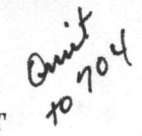

II. THE NATIONAL LABOR RELATIONS ACT

A. UNION UNFAIR PRACTICES AFFECTING ORGANIZATION [1]

C. S. SMITH METROPOLITAN MARKET CO. v. LYONS

Supreme Court of California, 1940.
16 Cal.2d 389, 106 P.2d 414.

EDMONDS, JUSTICE. Injunctive relief granted an employer in a controversy with union labor over picketing occasioned this appeal. The market company had no union men employed and the purpose of the picketing was to bring about the establishment of a closed shop in its meat departments.

[The market company owns and operates seven retail markets in southern California. It was picketed at its Long Beach stores by members of the Amalgamated Meat Cutters Union. When the picketing began, there was no dispute between the market company and its employees, apparently none of whom was a member of any labor union or sought to become one. The president had offered to pay the union initiation fee for any employee who desired to join the union, but none accepted the offer. At no time did the company engage in acts of intimidation or discrimination against union members. The purpose of the picketing was to compel the company's meat employees to join the union, to compel the discharge of those who refused, and to compel the company to enter into a closed-shop agreement. The union already had closed-shop agreements with a number of markets and butcher shops in Long Beach, which promised to pay union wages and to close on Sunday; some of the unionized employers did not, however, adhere to union standards. The Smith Market Company paid its butchers more than union scale, with hours of employment less than the union schedule elsewhere in Long Beach; there was a finding that the company would not change its working conditions to the detriment of its employees if the union's picketing were to be abandoned. The picketing resulted in a loss of business to the company and induced other companies and their employees to refrain from selling or delivering merchandise there. The state trial court issued an injunction.]

---

1. For a general discussion of organizational picketing see Lauritzen, Organizational Picket Line—Coercion, 3 Stanford L.Rev. 413 (1951); Tobriner, Organizational Picket Line—Lawful Economic Pressure, 3 id. 423 (1951). For discussions concerning the effects of Section 8(b) (7), see Comment, Picketing for Area Standards: An Exception to Section 8(b) (7), 1968 Duke L.J. 767; Dunau, Some Aspects of the Current Interpretation of Section 8(b) (7), 52 Geo.L.J. 220 (1964); Meltzer, Organizational Picketing and the NLRB: Five on a Seesaw, 30 U.Chi.L.Rev. 78 (1962); Rosen, Area Standards Picketing, 23 Lab.L.J. 67 (1972); Shawe, Federal Regulation of Recognition Picketing, 52 Geo.L.J. 248 (1964).

The gravamen of the charge against the appellants under the findings in the present case is a conspiracy to damage the market company by intentionally interfering with its business. However, * * * the interference with the employer's business must * * * be considered in its relation to the purposes of the appellants.

The law does not invariably give relief against acts causing loss and the field of business competition furnishes numerous examples of intentional infliction of damage without legal remedy. [The court here cited numerous authorities.]

* * * In the absence of legislation laying down rules for the contest * * * or outside the scope of such legislation, business men are apparently free to inflict damage in the struggle of competition so long as they abstain from violence, fraud or other unlawful conduct. "Every one who enters the field of competition desires and plans to draw custom from his competitors. Unless his acts are unlawful, his avarice is not actionable." American Auto Ass'n v. Amer. Auto Owners Ass'n, supra, 216 Cal. at page 142, 13 P.2d at page 715, 83 A.L.R. 699. "The fact that the methods used were ruthless, or unfair, in a moral sense, does not stamp them as illegal. It has never been regarded as the duty or province of the courts to regulate practices in the business world beyond the point of applying legal or equitable remedies in cases involving acts of oppression or deceit which are unlawful. Any extension of this jurisdiction must come through legislative action." Katz v. Kapper, supra, 7 Cal.App. 2d at page 6, 44 P.2d at page 1062. The justification for such conduct is said to be that free competition is generally considered worth more to society than it costs. Holmes, J., dissenting in Vegelahn v. Guntner, 1896, 167 Mass. 92, 106, 44 N.E. 1077, 35 L.R.A. 722, 57 Am.St.Rep. 443.

The foregoing principles are applicable and have been applied to competition in the field of labor. The use of any of the lawful methods of concerted action in this field—stopping work, persuading others not to work, interfering with advantageous trade relations— all necessarily cause economic loss not only to the parties directly affected but to customers and often to the public generally. Nevertheless, in the struggle for existence the fact of damage to others, intentionally inflicted, does not warrant injunctive relief against workmen any more than it does against business men, if it is inflicted in pursuit of a legally justifiable object. Parkinson v. Building Trades Council, [154 Cal. 581, 98 P. 1027].

The underlying reason beneath these rules is a widespread belief in competition, free enterprise, and equality of opportunity. Statutes such as the Cartwright Act and the Fair Trade Act, supra, represent interference with the free play of competition in specific situations where the legislature has concluded that the competitive struggle has become unequal or unfair. And the inequality of bargaining power between employer and employee has long been fully recognized by legislation curtailing the employer's freedom to bargain with his employees as he chooses. For example, California has statutes dealing with compensation (Labor Code, secs. 200–452), working hours (secs. 510–856, Id.), women and minors (secs. 1171–1398, Id.), immigrants (secs. 1460–1486, Id.), employment agencies (secs. 1550–1681, Id.), unemployment relief (secs. 2010–2183, Id.), health (secs. 2260–2606, Id.), employment relations (secs. 2700–3091, Id.), workmen's compensation and insurance (secs. 3201–6002, Id.), and safety in employment (secs. 6300–7601, Id.).

Even more significant is section 923 of the Labor Code which declares the legislative policy of this state in favor of collective action by workmen. That section likewise declares the legislative reasons for favoring such a policy. Individual workmen, it is said, are not free to exercise actual liberty of contract in bargaining for work with employers. This is so because the latter have been permitted "to organize in the corporate and other forms of capital control" of great economic strength. Hence, in order to equalize bargaining power it is said to be necessary that workmen be permitted to organize and to engage in "concerted activities for the purposes of collective bargaining or other mutual aid or protection". This is not an effort by the legislature to destroy free competition; it is rather an attempt to insure an equality of bargaining power upon which the benefits of competition and free enterprise rest, and thus to secure to the individual workman a larger measure of freedom in his dealings with employers of labor. In other words combination and organization are permissible on both sides, and the determination of terms and conditions of employment is to be left to bargaining and competition by these organizations in a free and unrestricted market.

* * * [T]he determinative issue is whether the workmen are demanding something which is reasonably related to employment and to the purposes of collective bargaining. More specifically, the propriety of lawful concerted action depends upon whether the workmen have such an interest in the employment relationship that the attainment of their object will benefit them directly or will enhance their bargaining power.

The members of a labor organization may have a substantial interest in the employment relations of an employer although none of them is or ever has been employed by him. The reason for this is that the employment relations of every employer affect the working conditions and bargaining power of employees throughout the industry in which he competes. Hence, where union and nonunion employees are engaged in a similar occupation and their respective employers are engaged in trade competition one with another, the efforts of the union to extend its membership to the employments in which it has no foothold is not an unreasonable aim.

Modern industry is not organized on a single shop basis, and it is a logical corollary of the collective bargaining principle that independent labor organizations should be permitted to grow and extend their bargaining power beyond the single shop. The market for a product may be so competitive that one producer cannot maintain higher labor standards resulting in higher costs than those maintained by his nonunion competitors.

Nor is the interest of the union in extending its organization any less substantial where the labor standards of the nonunion shop are on an equality with those of its union competitors. Under these circumstances it may reasonably be believed vital to union interests to organize such a shop, for there can be no doubt that the receipt by other workmen of equivalent benefits without suffering correlative union responsibility serves to create intraunion unrest and disaffections.

Tested by these principles, it is apparent in the present case that the members of the butchers' union have a substantial interest in the employment relations of the market company. The findings show that the union had contracts with a number of other markets and butcher shops in Long Beach under which they agreed to employ only members of the union and to comply with union standards of employment, including the union scale of wages and hours and night and Sunday closing of butcher shops. It was also found that not all of the markets with which the union had contracts adhere to union standards of employment. On this point the evidence shows that these shops refuse to comply with union standards until their competitors are unionized. It is immaterial that the respondent pays its butchers more than the union scale with hours of employment less than those fixed by the union. The market company's president admitted that he would not sign a union contract if it required night and Sunday closing, although a city ordinance provided that butcher shops be closed at such times. Under these circumstances, it is clear that the continued operation of the respondent's shops under nonunion conditions had an immediate effect upon both the working conditions and bargaining power of all the union butchers employed in Long Beach. The appellants were, therefore, privileged to direct against the market company any peaceful form of concerted action within their control.

[The Court then cited numerous precedents, some of which upheld the right of unions to picket nonunion shops and some of which held that such picketing should be enjoined.]

But in this state, ever since the decision in the Parkinson case [154 Cal. 581, 98 P. 1027] the courts have recognized the right of labor unions to engage in concerted action to obtain a union shop, or, in other words, to strengthen their bargaining power. The fear that they have grown so strong as to endanger vital civil liberties and disrupt the functioning of our economic system is an argument exclusively for the consideration of the legislature. * * *

The judgment is reversed and the trial court is directed to dismiss the action.

We concur: GIBSON, C. J.; CARTER, J.; MOORE, Justice pro tem.

CURTIS and SHENK, JJ., and MARKS, Justice pro tem. (dissenting).

We dissent for the reasons stated in the dissenting opinions in the case of McKay v. Retail Automobile Salesmen's Local Union No. 1067, Cal.Sup., 106 P.2d 373. [The following passages are excerpts from the dissent in the *McKay* case.]

* * * Throughout the discussion of respondents is the underlying thesis that its actions in this particular have been motivated by the desire to further the best interests of workingmen in general and to promote a higher social order, and in this regard it insists that its actions are justified in the instant case upon the ground that a closed shop is an important means of maintaining the combined bargaining power of the workers. Assuming that closed shops are for the best interests of workingmen in their negotiations with their employers, as their bargaining power is greater, nevertheless, it would appear that there are certain fundamental rights important to workingmen as individuals, which are so important as to outweigh any advantage of a closed shop procured by coercive activities. One of these rights is the right of an individual to ally himself with a group of his own seeking, and to select a representative for negotiations with his employer in whom he has faith and confidence. To have forced upon him membership in an association to which he is antagonistic, and to have imposed upon him as a representative, an agency which he does not desire, is so violative of his freedom of action and his liberty as an individual as to need no apology for the defense of these rights, and to justify the enactment by the legislature of a statute intended to preserve these rights to him. We cannot but believe that the rights of an individual as a citizen, are as highly important to him as his rights as a member of a social class, and should be as carefully preserved.

Nothing herein said can or should be construed as antagonistic to the principle of collective bargaining which has come to play an important part in our industrial life. However, we are convinced that the growth of the labor union has been based upon the principle of voluntary association of workers and not upon the combination of one group of workers over another group by coercion, and that insistence upon such voluntary association will in the long run work to the benefit rather than the detriment of organized labor.

* * * It appears from the allegations of the complaint, and cannot be disputed, that the plaintiff employees are under the jurisdiction of the National Labor Relations Board. The Howard Automobile Company as their employer is engaged in interstate commerce and is likewise subject to the operation of the federal act. Under that act such an employer is forbidden to interfere in any way with the union affiliations of his employees. The employer, in this case, the Howard Automobile Company, is proscribed by the federal act from even suggesting to its employees, the plaintiffs herein, that they join or do not join a union. Yet if the judgment in this case is to stand, that company must submit to activities on the part of the defendant unions, the result of which is to compel it to require its employees to join the picketing union or be discharged from their employment. If the company refuses to accede to the demand of the picketing union to violate the federal law it must suffer the loss of its business. If the company violates that law, as demanded by the picketing union, it is punishable thereunder. * * * Such an interpretation placed on the law makes of it a weapon of coercion and intimidation to be wielded at the whim and caprice of a group not possessed of legislative authority and not subject to any legal control or restraint.

Furthermore, * * * the right of the plaintiff employees to organize their own union and to select their own bargaining representatives is recognized by both state and federal law.

The picketing which the plaintiff employees are here seeking to enjoin is contrary to their rights under both laws, is therefore picketing for an unlawful purpose, and as such should be subject to the injunctive processes of the courts of this state.

Problems for Discussion

1. Compare this case with Plant v. Woods, at p. 25 supra. Would Justice Holmes be pleased with the outcome of the *Smith Metropolitan Markets* case? Would the intervening enactment of the National Labor Relations Act justify a reconsideration and reversal of the Holmes position? Does the NLRA as it was written at that time reinforce, or undermine, the claims of the Meat Cutters Union to continue picketing?

(Whatever the impact of the NLRA, hindsight makes it clear that since the picketing by the Meat Cutters Union was within the regulatory concerns of Congress, the state labor laws of California should have been preempted and the case dismissed. Preemption theory had not really begun to develop as early as 1940, however, so that the court's assertion of jurisdiction would not have been regarded as unusual.)

2. The California legislature had enacted a state version of the Norris-LaGuardia Act by the time this case was decided. Assuming the language to be comparable to that in the federal statute, how could the dissenting state Justices get around it?

3. Would the California court have likely reached the same conclusion if the Smith Market Company was already lawfully recognizing the Retail Clerks Union as bargaining representative for all of its store employees, including those in the meat department, and the Meat Cutters were picketing for the purpose of forcing the company to withdraw recognition, breach the labor contract, and recognize the Meat Cutters (arguably a minority union and arguably for an inappropriate bargaining unit)?

4. Articulate the respective interests of all of the parties concerned (including the public) in the *Smith* case and in the hypothetical variation in Problem 3. Can a state court weigh these interests for purposes of fashioning a tort rule, or can this properly be done only by a legislature? (Note once again the echoes of Justices Holmes and Brandeis.)

Federal policy pertaining to union efforts to organize employees has undergone several distinct changes. In passing the original Wagner Act Congress rejected the argument that mutuality required a grant of protection against interference, coercion and restraint by labor organizations as well as by employers; and although this decision was often defended on the ground that it would bring about federal intervention in matters better regulated by local police authorities, the true ground of objection was that such a measure would be inconsistent with the policy of encouraging union organization and collective bargaining.

> This erroneously conceived mutuality argument that since employers are to be prohibited with interfering with organization of workers, employees and labor organizations should be no more active than employers in the organization of employees is untenable; *this would defeat the very object of the bill.* [S.Rep. 573, 74th Cong., 1st Sess., p. 16.]

It soon became apparent, however, that the law could not in good conscience compel an employer to bargain with one union as the certified representative of his employees and at the same time protect the right of another union to picket in order to compel the employer to recognize it as the bargaining representative of the same employees. Hence, in passing the Taft-Hartley amendments of 1947, Congress included a provision, Section 8(b) (4) (C), which made it unlawful for a minority union to engage in a strike for recognition in defiance of the certification of another union as the bargaining representative of the employees in question.

In addition to Section 8(b) (4) (C), Congress amended Section 7 to guarantee to employees, not only the right to form, join or assist labor organizations, but "the right to refrain from any or all such activities." Moreover, Section 8(b) (1) was inserted making it an unfair labor practice for a labor organization or its agents to restrain or coerce employees in the exercise of rights guaranteed by Section 7.

For many years it seemed possible that Section 8(b) (1) might prohibit a minority union from picketing for recognition regardless of whether any other union had already been certified. After having rejected this view during the earlier years of the Taft-Hartley Act, the National Labor Relations Board reversed its position in 1957 and declared that picketing under these circumstances restrained and coerced employees in the exercise of their rights under Section 7. DRIVERS LOCAL 639 (CURTIS BROS.), 119 N.L.R.B. 232 (1957). When the issue reached the Supreme Court, however, the Board was reversed with the Court emphasizing the protection given to the right to strike in Section 13 of the NLRA and cautioning against an "expansive reading" of general provisions in such a way as to limit that right. NLRB v. Drivers Local 639, 362 U.S. 274, 80 S.Ct. 706, 4 L.Ed.2d 710 (1960).

In 1959, Congress addressed itself specifically to the question of organization and recognition picketing by adding Section 8(b) (7) to the National Labor Relations Act. Although the Supreme Court has not had occasion to rule upon any of the numerous problems that are raised by this Section, the position of the National Labor Relations Board is revealed in the opinions which follow.

HOD CARRIERS LOCAL 840 (BLINNE CONSTRUCTION CO.)

National Labor Relations Board, 1962.
135 NLRB 1153.

[In 1961, the Board held that the respondent union had violated Section 8(b)(7)(C), but—after the composition of the Board changed, as a result of new appointments by President Kennedy—the Board later granted the motion of the union to reconsider the case.]

Before proceeding to determine the application of Section 8 (b) (7) (C) to the facts of the instant case, it is essential to note the interplay of the several sections of Section 8(b) (7), of which subparagraph (C) is only a constituent part.

The Section as a whole, as is apparent from its opening phrases, prescribes limitations only on picketing for an object of "recognition" or "bargaining" (both of which terms will hereinafter be subsumed under the single term "recognition") or for an object of organization. Picketing for other objects is not proscribed by this

Section. Moreover, not all picketing for recognition or organization is proscribed. A "currently certified" union may picket for recognition or organization of employees for whom it is certified. And even a union which is not certified is barred from recognition or organizational picketing only in three general areas. The first area, defined in subparagraph (A) of Section 8(b) (7), relates to situations where another union has been lawfully recognized and a question concerning representation cannot appropriately be raised. The second area, defined in subparagraph (B), relates to situations where, within the preceding twelve months a "valid election" has been held.

The intent of subparagraphs (A) and (B) is fairly clear. Congress concluded that where a union has been lawfully recognized and a question concerning representation cannot appropriately be raised, or where the employees within the preceding twelve months have made known their views concerning representation, both the employer and the employees are entitled to immunity from recognition or organization picketing for prescribed periods.

Congress did not stop there, however. Deeply concerned with other abuses, most particularly "blackmail" picketing, Congress concluded that it would be salutary to impose even further limitations on picketing for recognition or organization. Accordingly, subparagraph (C) provides that even where such picketing is not barred by the provisions of (A) or (B) so that picketing for recognition or organization would otherwise be permissible, such picketing is limited to a reasonable period not to exceed thirty days unless a representation petition is filed prior to the expiration of that period. Absent the filing of such a timely petition, continuation of the picketing beyond the reasonable period becomes an unfair labor practice. On the other hand, the filing of a timely petition stays the limitation and picketing may continue pending the processing of the petition. Even here, however, Congress by the addition of the first proviso to subparagraph (C) made it possible to foreshorten the period of permissible picketing by directing the holding of an expedited election pursuant to the representation petition.

The expedited election procedure is applicable, of course, only in a Section 8(b) (7) (C) proceeding, i. e., where a Section 8(b) (7) (C) unfair labor practice charge has been filed. Congress rejected efforts to amend the provisions of Section 9(c) of the Act so as to dispense generally with pre-election hearings. Thus, in the absence of a Section 8(b) (7) (C) unfair labor practice charge, a union will not be enabled to obtain an expedited election by the mere device of engaging in recognition or organizational picketing and filing a representation petition.[2] And on the other hand, a

---

2. Congress plainly did not intend such a result. See Congressman Barden's statement (105 Daily Cong.Rec., A. 8062, September 2, 1959; 2 L.H. 1813).

picketing union which files a representation petition pursuant to the mandate of Section 8(b) (7) (C) and to avoid its sanctions will not be propelled into an expedited election, which it may not desire, merely because it has filed such a petition. In both the above situations, the normal representation procedures are applicable; the showing of a substantial interest will be required, and the pre-election hearing directed in Section 9(c) (1) will be held.

This, in our considered judgment, puts the expedited election procedure prescribed in the first proviso to subparagraph C in its proper and intended focus. That procedure was devised to shield aggrieved employers and employees from the adverse effects of prolonged recognition or organizational picketing. Absent such a grievance, it was not designed either to benefit or to handicap picketing activity. As District Judge Thornton aptly stated in *Reed v. Roumell,* 185 F.Supp. 4 (E.D.Mich.1961), "If [the first proviso] were intended to confer a primary or independent right to an expedited election entirely separated from the statutory scheme, it would seem that such intention would have manifested itself in a more forthright manner, rather than in the shy seclusion of Section 8(b) (7) (C)."

Subparagraphs (B) and (C) serve different purposes. But it is especially significant to note their interrelationship. Congress was particularly concerned, even where picketing for recognition or organization was otherwise permissible, that the question concerning representation which gave rise to the picketing be resolved as quickly as possible. It was for this reason that it provided for the filing of a petition pursuant to which the Board could direct an expedited election in which the employees could freely indicate their desires as to representation. If, in the free exercise of their choice, they designate the picketing union as their bargaining representative, that union will be certified and it will by the express terms of Section 8(b) (7) be exonerated from the strictures of that Section. If, conversely, the employees reject the picketing union, that union will be barred from picketing for twelve months thereafter under the provisions of subparagraph (B).

The scheme which Congress thus devised represents what that legislative body deemed a practical accommodation between the right of a union to engage in legitimate picketing for recognition or organization and abuse of that right. One caveat must be noted in that regard. The Congressional scheme is, perforce, based on the premise that the election to be conducted under the first proviso to subparagraph (C) represents the free and uncoerced choice of

And the Board has ruled further that a charge filed by a picketing union or a person "fronting" for it may not be utilized to invoke an expedited election. *Claussen Baking Company,* 11–RC–1329, May 5, 1960. See also *Reed v. Roumell,* cited infra.

the employee electorate. Absent such a free and uncoerced choice, the underlying question concerning representation is not resolved and, more particularly, subparagraph (B) which turns on the holding of a "valid election" does not become operative.

There remains to be considered only the second proviso to subparagraph (C). In sum, that proviso removes the time limitation imposed upon, and preserves the legality of, recognition or organizational picketing falling within the ambit of subparagraph (C), where that picketing merely advises the public that an employer does not employ members of, or have a contract with, a union unless an effect of such picketing is to halt pickups or deliveries, or the performance of services. Needless to add, picketing which meets the requirements of the proviso also renders the expedited election procedure inapplicable.

Except for the final clause in Section 8(b)(7) which provides that nothing in that Section shall be construed to permit any act otherwise proscribed under Section 8(b) of the Act, the foregoing sums up the limitations imposed upon recognition or organizational picketing by the Landrum-Griffin amendments. However, at the risk of laboring the obvious, it is important to note that structurally, as well as grammatically, subparagraphs (A), (B), and (C) are subordinate to and controlled by the opening phrases of Section 8(b)(7). In other words, the thrust of all the Section 8(b) (7) provisions is only upon picketing for an object of recognition or organization, and not upon picketing for other objects. Similarly, both structurally and grammatically, the two provisos in subparagraph (C) appertain only to the situation defined in the principal clause of that subparagraph.

Having outlined, in concededly broad strokes, the statutory framework of Section 8(b) (7) and particularly subparagraph (C) thereof, we may appropriately turn to a consideration of the instant case which presents issues going to the heart of that legislation.

The relevant facts may be briefly stated. On February 2, 1960, all three common laborers employed by Blinne at the Fort Leonard Wood job site signed cards designating the Union to represent them for purposes of collective bargaining. The next day the Union demanded that Blinne recognize the Union as the bargaining agent for the three laborers. Blinne not only refused recognition but told the Union it would transfer one of the laborers, Wann, in order to destroy the Union's majority.[3] Blinne carried out this threat and transferred Wann five days later, on February 8. Following this refusal to recognize the Union and the transfer of Wann the Union

---

3. Blinne's assumption that this transfer would destroy the Union's majority was in error. However, that error has no significance in this case.

started picketing at Fort Wood. The picketing, which began on February 8, immediately following the discharge of Wann, had three announced objectives: (1) recognition of the Union; (2) payment of the Davis-Bacon scale of wages; and (3) protest against Blinne's unfair labor practices in refusing to recognize the Union and in threatening to transfer and transferring Wann.

[margin note: objectives of picketing]

The picketing continued, with interruptions due to bad weather, until at least March 11, 1960, a period of more than thirty days from the date the picketing commenced. The picketing was peaceful, only one picket was on duty, and the picket sign he carried read "C. A. Blinne Construction Company, unfair." The three laborers on the job (one was the replacement for Wann) struck when the picketing started.

The Union, of course, was not the certified bargaining representative of the employees. Moreover, no representation petition was filed during the more than thirty days in which picketing was taking place. On March 1, however, about three weeks after the picketing commenced and well within the statutory thirty-day period, the Union filed unfair labor practice charges against Blinne, alleging violations of Section 8(a) (1), (2), (3) and (5). On March 22, the Regional Director dismissed the Section 8(a) (2) and (5) charges, whereupon the Union forthwith filed a representation petition under Section 9(c) of the Act. Subsequently, on April 20, the Regional Director approved a unilateral settlement agreement with Blinne with respect to the Section 8(a) (1) and (3) charges which had not been dismissed. In the settlement agreement, Blinne neither admitted nor denied that it had committed unfair labor practices.[4]

[margin note: not certified; no petition filed]

General Counsel argues that a violation of Section 8(b) (7) (C) has occurred within the literal terms of that provision because (1) the Union's picketing was concededly for an object of obtaining recognition; (2) the Union was not currently certified as the representative of the employees involved; and (3) no petition for representation was filed within 30 days of the commencement of the picketing. Inasmuch as the Union made no contention that its recognition picketing was "informational" within the meaning of the second proviso to subparagraph (C) or that it otherwise comported with the strictures of that proviso, General Counsel contends that a finding of unfair labor practice is required.

[margin note: 8(b)(7)(c) violated]

* * * Respondent advances two major contentions. The first is that Section 8(b) (7) (C) does not apply to picketing by a

4. Although the transcript in these proceedings for obvious reasons makes no reference to the disposition of the representation petition filed by the Union on March 22, it is a matter of public record and known to the parties that the petition was dismissed on April 26, 1960, for the reason that, "the unit sought appears to be inappropriate and is also expected to go out of existence within about four months."

majority union in an appropriate unit; the second is that employer *defenses to 8(b)(7)(c)* unfair labor practices are a defense to a charge of a Section 8(b) (7) violation. We deal with the contentions in that order.

Respondent, urging the self-evident proposition that a statute should be read as a whole, argues that Section 8(b) (7) (C) was not *majority status in app unit* designed to prohibit picketing for recognition by a union enjoying majority status in an appropriate unit. Such picketing is for a lawful purpose inasmuch as Sections 8(a) (5) and 9(a) of the Act specifically impose upon an employer the duty to recognize and bargain with a union which enjoys that status. Accordingly, Respondent contends, absent express language requiring such a result, Section 8(b) (7) (C) should not be read in derogation of the duty so imposed.

There is grave doubt that the argument here made is apposite in this case.[5] But, assuming its relevance, we find it to be without merit. To be sure, the legislative history is replete with references that Congress in framing the 1959 amendments was primarily concerned with "blackmail" picketing where the picketing union represented none or few of the employees whose allegiance it sought. Legislative references susceptible to an interpretation that Congress was concerned with the evils of majority picketing are sparse. Yet it cannot be gainsaid that Section 8(b) (7) by its explicit language exempts only "currently certified" unions from its proscriptions. Cautious as we should be to avoid a mechanical reading of statutory terms in involved legislative enactments, it is difficult to avoid giving the quoted words, essentially words of art, their natural construction. Moreover, such a construction is consonant with the underlying statutory scheme which is to resolve disputed issues of majority status, whenever possible, by the machinery of a Board election. Absent unfair labor practices or pre-election misconduct warranting the setting aside of the election, majority unions will presumably not be prejudiced by such resolution. On the other hand, the admitted difficulties of determining majority status without such an election are obviated by this construction.

Congress was presumably aware of these considerations. In *no Con intent to broaden exemption* any event, there would seem to be here no valid considerations, requiring that Congress be assumed to have intended a broader exemption than the one it actually afforded.

We turn now to the second issue, namely, whether employer unfair labor practices are a defense to a Section 8(b) (7) (C) vio-

---

5. The argument here is based, as it must be, on the premise that Respondent not only represented a majority of the employees but that this majority status was in an appropriate unit. The latter proposition is by no means established. The Trial Examiner "assumed" the existence of an appropriate unit for purposes of his analysis. The dismissal of the Section 8(a) (5) charge and, particularly, the subsequent dismissal of the representation petition and the reason given therefor tend to invalidate his assumption.

lation. As set forth in the original Decision and Order, the Union argues that Blinne was engaged in unfair labor practices within the meaning of Section 8(a) (1) and (3) of the Act; that it filed appropriate unfair labor practice charges against Blinne within a reasonable period of time after the commencement of the picketing; that it filed a representation petition as soon as the Section 8(a) (2) and 8(a) (5) allegations of the charges were dismissed; that the Section 8(a) (1) and (3) allegations were in effect sustained and a settlement agreement was subsequently entered into with the approval of the Board; and that, therefore, this sequence of events should satisfy the requirements of Section 8(b) (7) (C).

The majority of the Board in the original Decision and Order rejected this argument. Pointing out that the representation petition was concededly filed more than thirty days after the commencement of the picketing, the majority concluded that the clear terms of Section 8(b)(7)(C) had been violated.

* * * It seems fair to say that Congress was unwilling to write an exemption into Section 8(b) (7) (C) dispensing with the necessity for filing a representation petition wherever employer unfair labor practices were alleged. The fact that the bill as ultimately enacted by the Congress did not contain the amendment to Section 10(*l*) which the Senate had adopted in S. 1555 [which would have made any Section 8(a) unfair labor practice, and not just a violation of Section 8(a) (2), a defense under Section 8(b) (7)] cogently establishes that this reluctance was not due to oversight. On the other hand, it strains credulity to believe that Congress proposed to make the rights of unions and employees turn upon the results of an election which, because of the existence of unremedied unfair labor practices, is unlikely to reflect the true wishes of the employees.

We do not find ourselves impaled on the horns of this dilemma. Upon careful reappraisal of the statutory scheme we are satisfied that Congress meant to require, and did require, in a Section 8(b) (7) (C) situation, that a representation petition be filed within a reasonable period, not to exceed thirty days. By this device machinery can quickly be set in motion to resolve by a free and fair election the underlying question concerning representation out of which the picketing arises. This is the normal situation, and the situation which the statute is basically designed to serve.

There is legitimate concern, however, with the abnormal situation, that is, the situation where because of unremedied unfair labor practices a free and fair election cannot be held. We believe Congress anticipated this contingency also. Thus, we find no mandate in the legislative scheme to compel the holding of an election pursuant to a representation petition where, because of unremedied unfair labor practices or for other valid reason, a free and uncoerced election cannot be held. On the contrary, the interrelated provisions of sub-paragraphs (B) and (C), by their respective references to a "valid election" and to a "certif[ication of] results" presuppose that Congress contemplated only a fair and free election. Only after such an election could the Board certify the results and only after such an election could the salutary provisions of subparagraph (B) become operative.

In our view, therefore, Congress intended that, except to the limited extent set forth in the first proviso,[6] the Board in Section 8(b) (7) (C) cases follow the tried and familiar procedures it typically follows in representation cases where unfair labor practice charges are filed. That procedure, as already set forth, is to hold the representation case in abeyance and refrain from holding an election pending the resolution of the unfair labor practice charges. Thus, the fears that the statutory requirement for filing a timely petition will compel a union which has been the victim of unfair labor practices to undergo a coerced election are groundless. No action will be taken on that petition while unfair labor practice charges are pending, and until a valid election is held pursuant to that petition, the union's right to picket under the statutory scheme, is unimpaired.

On the other side of the coin, it may safely be assumed that groundless unfair labor practice charges in this area, because of the statutory priority accorded Section 8(b) (7) violations, will be quickly dismissed. Following such dismissal an election can be directed forthwith upon the subsisting petition, thereby effectuating the Congressional purpose. Moreover, the fact that a timely petition is on file will protect the innocent union, which through mistake of fact or law has filed a groundless unfair labor practice charge, from a finding of a Section 8(b) (7) (C) violation. Thus, the policy of the entire Act is effectuated and all rights guaranteed by its several provisions are appropriately safeguarded. See *Mastro Plastics Corp. v. N. L. R. B.*, 350 U.S. 270, 285, 76 S.Ct. 349, 359.

The facts of the instant case may be utilized to demonstrate the practical operation of the legislative scheme. Here the union had filed unfair labor practice charges alleging violations by the employer of Section 8(a) (1), (2), (3) and (5) of the Act. General Counsel found the allegations of Section 8(a) (2) and (5) violations groundless. Hence had these allegations stood alone and had a timely petition been on file, an election could have been directed forthwith and the underlying question concerning representation out of which

---

6. As already noted, that proviso en-ables the Board to dispense with the preelection hearing prescribed in Sec-tion 9(c) (1), and to dispense also with the requirement of a showing of sub-stantial interest.

the picketing arose could have been resolved pursuant to the statutory scheme. The failure to file a timely petition frustrated that scheme.[7]

On the other hand, the Section 8(a) (1) and (3) charges were found meritorious. Under these circumstances, and again consistent with uniform practice, no election would have been directed notwithstanding the currency of a timely petition; the petition would be held in abeyance pending a satisfactory resolution of the unfair labor practice charges.[8] The aggrieved union's right to picket would not be abated in the interim and the sole prejudice to the employer would be the delay engendered by its own unfair labor practices. The absence of a timely petition, however, precludes disposition of the underlying question concerning representation which thus remains unresolved even after the Section 8(a) (1) and (3) charges are satisfactorily disposed of. Accordingly, to condone the refusal to file a timely petition in such situations would be to condone the flouting of a legislative judgment. Moreover, and most important, to impose a lesser requirement would fly in the face of the public interest which prompted that judgment.

Because we read Section 8(b) (7) (C) as requiring in the instant case the filing of a timely petition and because such a petition was admittedly not filed until more than thirty days after the commencement of the picketing, we find that Respondent violated Section 8(b) (7) (C) of the Act. As previously noted, it is undisputed that "an object" of the picketing was for recognition.[9] It affords

7. We would, however, have had a much different case here if the Section 8(a)(5) charge had been found meritorious so as to warrant issuance of a complaint. A representation petition assumes an unresolved question concerning representation. A Section 8(a) (5) charge, on the other hand, presupposes that no such question exists and that the employer is wrongfully refusing to recognize or bargain with a statutory bargaining representative. Because of this basic inconsistency, the Board has over the years uniformly refused to entertain representation petitions where a meritorious charge of refusal to bargain has been filed and, indeed, has dismissed any representation petition which may already have been on file. The same considerations apply where a meritorious Section 8(a) (5) charge is filed in a Section 8(b) (7) (C) context. * * * So here, if a meritorious Section 8(a) (5) charge had been filed, a petition for representation would not have been required. * * *

8. The Board's practice of declining to entertain, or dismissing, representation petitions does not apply to situations involving unlawful interference or unlawful discrimination. The inconsistency latent in the refusal to bargain situation is not present in the latter situations and uniform practice has been merely to hold such petitions in abeyance.

9. The counterpart provision of Section 8(b) (7) as passed by the Senate in S. 1555 limited its impact to situations where recognition was "the object" of picketing. See 1 L.H. 583. The bill as enacted, however, follows the pattern of Section 8(b) (4) and broadens the proscription to conduct which has "an object" which is forbidden. See *Denver Building and Construction Trades Council* v. *NLRB*, 341 U.S. 675, 688, 689, 71 S.Ct. 943, 951 (1951).

Respondent no comfort that its picketing was also in protest against the discriminatory transfer of an employee and against payment of wages at a rate lower than that prescribed by law. Had Respondent confined its picketing to these objectives rather than, as it did, include a demand for recognition, we believe none of the provisions of Section 8(b) (7) would be applicable.[10] Under the circumstances here, however, Section 8(b) (7) (C) is applicable.

Accordingly, having concluded as in the original decision herein that a violation of Section 8(b) (7) (C) has occurred, albeit for differing reasons, we reaffirm the Order entered therein.

PHILIP RAY RODGERS and BOYD LEEDOM, MEMBERS, wrote separate opinions reaffirming the majority opinion originally rendered in this case. 130 NLRB 587 (1961).

MEMBER FANNING, concurred in part and dissented in part.

Problems for Discussion

1. Assume that a representative of the Hotel and Restaurant Employees Union nails a sign to a telephone pole next to the entrance to the

10. As noted at the outset, Section 8(b) (7) is directed only at recognition and organizational picketing and not at picketing for other objects including so-called protest picketing against unfair labor practices. There is ample legislative history to substantiate the proposition that Congress did not intend to outlaw picketing against unfair labor practices as such. See, for example, 105 Daily Cong.Rec. 5756, 5766, 15121, 15907, 16400, 16541; 2 L.H. 1361, 1384, 1429, 1714. Absent other evidence (such as is present in this case) of an organizational, recognition or bargaining objective it is clear that Congress did not consider picketing against unfair labor practices as such to be also for proscribed objectives and, hence, outlawed. Parenthetically it follows that a cease-and-desist order issued against picketing in violation of Section 8(b) (7) will enjoin only picketing for recognition, bargaining, or organization and will not be a bar to protest picketing against unfair labor practices.

We are aware that this analysis runs counter to what the majority of the Board had held in *Lewis Food Company*, 115 NLRB 890, namely, that a strike to compel reinstatement of a discharged employee was necessarily a strike to force or require the employer "to recognize and bargain" with the union as to such matter. Implicit in that holding was the broader proposition that any strike or picketing in support of a demand which could be made through the process of collective bargaining was a strike or picketing for recognition or bargaining. Included in this category, presumably, would be picketing against substandard wages or working conditions in a competing plant, or a strike in support of an economic demand at a bargaining table where neither recognition nor willingness to bargain are really in issue but only the reluctance of the employer to grant the particular economic demand. * * * We might well concede that in the long view all union activity, including strikes and picketing, has the ultimate economic objective of organization and bargaining. But we deal here not with abstract economic ideology. Congress itself has drawn a sharp distinction between recognition and organizational picketing and other forms of picketing, thereby recognizing, as we recognize, that a real distinction does exist. See *Cox, op. cit, supra,* 266. The *Lewis Food* issue and its ramifications are not crucial in this case. Moreover, the *Lewis Food* case itself has now been reversed in any event. *Fanelli Ford Sales,* 133 NLRB No. 163; see also *Miratti's Inc.,* 132 NLRB No. 48, and *Andes Candies, Inc.,* 133 NLRB No. 65.

Jones Cafeteria and sits nearby, speaking to customers only if spoken to and simply observing those who enter and leave the cafeteria. The sign states that the cafeteria is "Unfair" and "Refuses to Recognize" the union. Assuming that the union lost a valid election two weeks ago, does this conduct by the union representative constitute an unfair labor practice?

2. In September, after a period of picketing for recognition, the union lost a representation election by a substantial margin. The day after the election results were certified, the company discharged employees Arthur and Bemis, who had been active union supporters. The union promptly protested the discharges in a telephone call to the company, asserting that they were caused by hostility to the union and that they were otherwise arbitrary and without just cause. Just as promptly, the union filed a charge under Section 8(a)(3) and resumed picketing; its new picket signs read "Company Unfair. Discriminates Against Union Workers." After an investigation of the Section 8(a)(3) charge by the Regional Office, the Regional Director in November determined that Arthur and Bemis were discharged for reasons other than union activity and declined to issue a complaint. The union nonetheless continued to picket. May it do so without violating Section 8(b)(7)(B)? See Waiters Local 500 (Mission Valley Inn), 140 N.L.R.B. 433 (1963).

3. The Hotel and Restaurant Employees Union has placed a solitary representative outside the entrance to Jones Cafeteria, who passes out leaflets to prospective patrons urging them not to enter the cafeteria because Jones is "unfair" and "pays substandard wages." An election was conducted by the NLRB two weeks ago in which a majority of Jones' employees voted against having the Hotel and Restaurant Employees represent them. Can Jones succeed in preventing the union from posting such a representative outside his cafeteria?

4. Giant Markets opened a new store in April and immediately recognized the Retail Clerks Union as bargaining representative for all of its employees. A contract was negotiated and was signed in September. In October, members of the Meat Cutters Union began picketing the Giant store, carrying signs stating "Giant Store Unfair to Meat-Counter Employees. Does Not Meet Area Standards." Since the meat counter employees were included within the bargaining unit and were subject to the contract with the Retail Clerks Union, Giant filed a charge under Section 8(b)(7)(A) and the Regional Director issued a complaint. The following facts were stipulated at the hearing before the Administrative Law Judge. Counsel for Giant conferred with counsel for the Meat Cutters in order to inquire what the area standards were that Giant was expected to meet. He was told that the Meat Cutters expected Giant to pay its meat counter employees the prevailing wage rates under Meat Cutter labor contracts and to meet the prevailing benefits regarding health, welfare and pension plans. Counsel for the Meat Cutters also produced an illustrative area contract, from which recognition and union-shop clauses had been stricken; provisions dealing with grievance-processing and arbitration were left unstricken. Counsel for the Meat Cutters reiterated that Giant was not being required to agree to the contract but only to "meet its standards," at which point the picketing would cease. The Meat

Cutters frequently circulated letters in trade publications explaining that the picketing was aimed only at forcing the store to meet area standards.

Should the Judge find that the picketing violates the Labor Act? (Has Giant Markets violated the Labor Act?)   Cf. *NLRB* v. *Retail Clerks Local 889 (State-Mart, Inc.)*, 166 N.L.R.B. 818 (1967), enf'd 404 F.2d 855 (5th Cir. 1968).

5.   Martin's Shoe Factory has never bargained with a union, and no union election has ever been conducted among its employees.   The Leather Workers Union began to solicit among the Martin employees and soon supplemented a demand for recognition by picketing, which continued for a week.   When the picketing failed to turn away many of the factory workers, tempers flared on the picket line, and a pattern of serious threats and violence emerged;   several workers were physically assaulted by picketers, and damage was done to employee automobiles in the adjacent lot.   This violence continued throughout the second week of picketing, at which time the company filed a charge under Section 8(b)(7)(C). Should the Regional Director issue a complaint and seek a district court injunction pursuant to Section 10(*l*)?

Assume that upon the employer's statement of intention to file an unfair labor practice charge, the union withdraws its pickets.   One month later, however, picketing resumes (accompanied by a request for recognition) and continues peacefully for two more weeks.   Can the company secure relief against the picketing at this time?

The rather convoluted language of section 8(b)(7)(C) is capped by two provisos, one dealing with the expedited election (discussed in the *Blinne* case) and the other with informational picketing.   The placement of the second proviso—which relates only to picketing under subsection (C)—has given rise to questions concerning its relationship to the principal ban of section 8(b)(7).   One such question, considered by the Board soon after the 1959 amendments, is whether picketing, in order to be sheltered by the proviso, must be "purely" informational and free of any recognitional object or whether even recognition picketing may be validated if the requirements of the proviso are otherwise satisfied.   In the so-called *Crown Cafeteria* case, the Board in 1961 initially held that the proviso sheltered only "purely" informational picketing which lacked an object of recognition or organization, but it reversed itself in a supplemental decision in 1962, after a change in Board membership.   *Local Jt. Exec. Bd. of Hotel Employees*, 130 N.L.R.B. 570 (1961), supplemental decision 135 N.L.R.B. 1183 (1962).   In that case, the employer rebuffed the union's demands for recognition and for hiring through the union's hiring hall, and the union picketed the public entrance to the cafeteria;   the picket signs were addressed to "members of organized labor and their friends" and stated that the cafeteria was nonunion and that the cafeteria should not be patronized. The Trial Examiner concluded that the picketing, which went on for more than a reasonable period of time, was nonetheless lawful because it did not have the effect of inducing any stoppage of goods or services. A divided Board at first reversed the Trial Examiner. The Board majority held:

"We regard the Trial Examiner's and our dissenting colleagues' construction of the Act as undermining the carefully worked out program established by Congress in Section 8(b) (7). We cannot believe that Congress meant to permit recognition picketing merely because the picketing also takes the form of truthfully advising the public that the employer is non-union, or does not have a union contract. Rather, we believe that Congress was careful to state that picketing will be permitted only if it is for "the" purpose of so advising the public. Indeed the ban against picketing is particularly applicable in the present situation, where the Union did not represent the majority of the employees, and the only lawful course for Crown to follow was to refuse to recognize the Union, as it did. * * *

"We are satisfied that Congress added the proviso only to make clear that purely informational picketing, which publicizes the lack of a union contract or the lack of union organization, and which has no present object of recognition, should not be curtailed " * * * unless an effect of such picketing is to induce any individual employed by any other person in the course of his employment, not to pick up, deliver or transport any goods or not to perform any services." But that is not the situation in this case. As the Trial Examiner found, apart from the picketing, the Union was in fact demanding present recognition from Crown. * * *

"Consideration of the result of the Trial Examiner's, and our dissenting colleagues', contrary construction of the proviso convinces us of their error. They would permit present recognition picketing whenever the labor organization is careful to indicate by its picket signs only an ostensible purpose of advising the public. However, this would render meaningless, at the whim of a picketing union, the stated objective of Section 8(b) (7). The resulting nullification of the whole of Section 8(b) (7) (C) would most certainly result in an absurd situation. * * *."

The two dissenting Board members would have affirmed the decision of the Trial Examiner upholding the picketing, and a Board majority ultimately did so on reconsideration by adopting what had been the dissenting opinion. (The Board's supplemental decision and order were affirmed in Smitley v. NLRB, 327 F.2d 351 (9th Cir. 1964).) Excerpts from that opinion follow.

* * *

"Section 8(b)(7)(C), in its present form, was proposed in conference as a compromise to the House version of the bill in this area of legislation. That version was substantially as enacted, but *without* the proviso. From the structure of the section as it emerged from conference, it seems clear that Congress intended to permit a kind of picketing which, but for the proviso, would have come within the prohibition of the section. It logically follows that the intent was to exclude from the ban picketing which, while it embraced the proscribed object of recognition or organization, was nonetheless permitted because it met two specific conditions. The first condition was, as already stated, "of truthfully advising the public (including consumers) that an employer does not employ members of, or have a contract with, a labor organization." The second condition was added immediately after the first, i. e., "unless an effect of such picketing is to induce any individual employed by any other person in the course of his employment not to pick up, deliver or transport any goods or not to perform any services." In other words, Congress, by way of compromise, excluded from its prohibition recognition or organization picketing that met these two conditions. * * *

"To read the proviso the way our colleagues do would, it seems to us, have the patent effect of creating a new unfair labor practice not within the contemplation of Congress. For, if it is an unfair labor practice when a union does *not* engage in recognition or organization picketing if "an effect of such picketing is to induce any individual employed by any other person in the course of his employment not to pick up, deliver or transport any goods or not to perform any services," the prohibition obviously embraces an area wholly *outside* the statutory intendment. Even a casual reading of Section 8(b) (7) and its legislative history makes it abundantly clear that Congress was dealing solely with recognition and organization picketing. It could have dealt with other forms of picketing in that section, but did not. To hold that a work stoppage would convert non-recognition and non-organization picketing into an unfair labor practice under Section 8(b) (7) (C) is to write into the 1959 amendments an additional unfair labor practice. This, we feel is evident, Congress clearly did not do. * * *"

NLRB v. LOCAL 3, INTERNATIONAL BHD. OF ELECTRICAL WORKERS

United States Court of Appeals, Second Circuit, 1963.
317 F.2d 193.

ANDERSON, DISTRICT JUDGE.
* * *

[The General Services Administration awarded a contract to one Picoult to renovate the Federal Post Office Building in Brooklyn.

Local 3 protested the award of this work to Picoult, which chose to deal with a different union. Local 3 instituted picketing of the building, including side and rear delivery areas which were not traversed by the general public. On two occasions, deliveries to Picoult by employees of other companies were turned away by the picket line. The union claimed that its object was to have the subcontract let to a company which recognized it as bargaining representative and, failing that, simply to oust Picoult. The Board found the picketing to violate Section 8(b)(7)(C) and sought court enforcement of its order.]

One of the principal difficulties in construing and applying subparagraph (C) is that Section 8(b)(7) contains the partially synonymous words, "object" and "purpose", used in two distinct contexts but to which much of the same evidence is relevant. These are: "where an object thereof is forcing or requiring an employer to recognize or bargain * * *" and "for the purpose of truthfully advising the public * * *." It does not necessarily follow that, where an object of the picketing is forcing or requiring an employer to recognize or bargain, the purpose of the picketing, in the context of the second proviso, is not truthfully to advise the public, etc. The union may legitimately have a long range or strategic objective of getting the employer to bargain with or recognize the union and still the picketing may be permissive. This proviso gives the union freedom to appeal to the unorganized public for spontaneous popular pressure upon an employer; it is intended, however, to exclude the invocation of pressure by organized labor groups or members of unions, as such.

The permissible picketing is, therefore, that which through the dissemination of certain allowed representations, is designed to influence members of the unorganized public, as individuals, because the impact upon the employer by way of such individuals is weaker, more indirect and less coercive.

In this connection what is meant by "advising the public," as used in the second proviso, is highly pertinent. Congress expressly provided that the word "public" should not be so narrowly construed as to exclude consumers, but the whole context of the phrase in which it appears makes it clear that it was not intended to be so broadly defined as to include organized labor groups which, at a word or signal from the picketeers, would impose economic sanctions upon the employer; otherwise Section 8(b)(7) would be, in effect, almost entirely emasculated. By this latest amendment to the Taft-Hartley Act Congress sought to circumscribe a kind of picketing which, by its nature, could in most cases bring an employer to his knees by threatening the destruction of his business and which, because of the attendant loss of employment, had a material tendency to coerce employees in their freedom to accept or reject union membership or freely select the union they wanted to represent them.

Professor Cox of Harvard, now Solicitor General, who worked with the Senate Labor Committee Chairman on the Section 8(b)(7) amendment to the Taft-Hartley Act, has said,

> "Picketing before a union election is divided by section 8(b)(7) into two categories: (1) picketing which halts pick-ups or deliveries by independent trucking concerns or the rendition of services by the employees of other employers, and (2) picketing which appeals only to employees in the establishment and members of the public. * * * The theory is that the former class of picketing is essentially a signal to organized economic action backed by group discipline. Such economic pressure, if continued, causes heavy loss and increases the likelihood of the employer's coercing the employees to join the union. In the second type of picketing, the elements of communication predominate. If the employer loses patronage, it is chiefly because of the impact of the picket's message upon members of the public acting as individuals * * *." The Landrum-Griffin Amendments to the National Labor Relations Act, 44 Minnesota Law Review 257.

Although the two categories are described by him in terms of the *effect* of each, the express language of the second proviso uses the words "for the purpose of" and it is difficult to see how they can be ignored. Nevertheless, the description of the two categories is helpful in gaining insight to the second proviso. The concepts of "signal" picketing and "publicity" picketing should be used in characterizing the union's tactical purpose rather than in describing the picketing's effect. Yet purpose can be determined only through what is said and done under certain circumstances; and the effect of the picketing is one of the circumstances considered in determining in any case what the purpose was in so far as it is the natural and logical consequence of what the picketeers are saying and doing.

The effect might fall short of "inducing any individual employed by any other person in the course of his employment, not to pick up, deliver or transport any goods or not to perform any services" and still be evidence of non-permissive purpose, such as display of qualifying signs accompanied by hostile gestures; or speech directed to persons unconnected with organized labor and not employees of secondary employers, such as a casual passer-by; or, for example, by forming a shoulder to shoulder picket line across an entrance which affected only members of the unorganized public who were not employees of a secondary employer.

Under the second proviso it is the difference in purpose which determines which is permissible picketing and which is not. In its context the second proviso means in terms of "signal" and "publicity" picketing that while most picketing with a "signaling" purpose is proscribed, most picketing for publicity is protected; the exceptions are that signal picketing is permissible when an object thereof is not forcing or requiring an employer to recognize or bargain, and publicity picketing is proscribed when it communicates more than the limited information expressly permitted by the second proviso or when it is apparently the purpose to advise organized labor groups or their members as shown by signal effects, unless there is persuasive proof that those effects are inspired by the employer who is seeking thereby to prevent legitimate second-proviso picketing by the union.

The Board must, therefore, approach its conclusion as to whether or not the picketing was "for the purpose of truthfully advising the public" by way of a finding of whether or not the union's tactical purpose was to signal economic action, backed by organized group discipline.

Accordingly the case is remanded.

Problems for Discussion

The following problems arise from the recent dispute between Widgets, Inc. and the International Union of Widgeteers (IUW). The union has been seeking to organize and represent the employees of Widgets.

(1) IUW stations pickets at both consumer entrances and delivery entrances, the signs reading: "FRIENDS OF THE LABOR MOVEMENT —WIDGETS, INC. UNFAIR, REFUSES TO RECOGNIZE IUW. DO NOT PATRONIZE. DO NOT CROSS THIS PICKET LINE." Throughout the first two weeks of picketing the Teamsters refuse to make deliveries. Widgets, Inc. thereupon files a charge under § 8(b)(7)(C). Evaluate the likelihood of success.

(2) IUW pickets patrol only the consumer entrances, having been told by the Union leaders to stay away from delivery entrances. The picket signs read: "THIS IS TO INFORM PUBLIC THAT WIDGETS, INC. DOES NOT HAVE A CONTRACT WITH IUW. PLEASE DO NOT PATRONIZE." IUW leaders have informed the Teamsters to continue deliveries. They have also placed advertisements in local newspapers, stating that the purpose of the picketing is solely to inform the public that Widgets, Inc. does not employ Union labor. The picketing continues for two months. Can Widgets, Inc. secure relief under § 8(b)(7)?

(3) Same facts as in Problem 2, except that over the two-month period in which the picketing takes place, three truck drivers refuse to make deliveries, and one window washer refuses to enter the plant building to do his job. Is there a violation of § 8(b)(7)(C)?

(4) The IUW has just lost an election at Widgets. One week after certification of the results, the union begins picketing the customer entrance to the Widgets store. Two union organizers walk back and forth carrying signs stating: "WIDGETS, INC. DOES NOT HAVE A CONTRACT WITH THE IUW, AFL–CIO. DO NOT PATRONIZE." There is a separate entrance for employees and deliveries, which is not picketed. No deliveries are interrupted, and no one is threatened or physically prevented from entering the store. Nevertheless, business is sharply curtailed, and Mr. Widgets files a charge with the Regional Director alleging a violation of Section 8(b)(7). Should a complaint issue? Are there any constitutional obstacles to the Board's finding that the picketing violates the Labor Act and issuing a cease-and-desist order?

B. SECONDARY PRESSURE

1. *Under the Taft-Hartley Act* [11]

The provisions of the National Labor Relations Act prohibiting the secondary boycott were first inserted during the Taft-Hartley amendments of 1947. The core of the prohibition was contained in Section 8(b)(4)(A), which during the further amendment of the Labor Act in 1959 was carried forward with minor changes to become what is now Section 8(b)(4)(B). (In many of the cases that follow, the reference to Section 8(b)(4)(A) is to the 1947 text rather than to the section presently so labeled.) The outlawry of the secondary boycott was not, however, new to the law. Most states at common law treated the secondary boycott as an illegal exercise of coercion against a person who was "uninvolved" in the labor dispute of another company. E. g., Bricklayers' Union v. Seymour Ruff & Sons, 160 Md. 483, 154 A. 52 (1931). The secondary boycott which affected the delivery or receipt of goods in interstate commerce was also consistently held to contravene the Sherman Antitrust Act and not to be saved by the labor-exempting provisions of the Clayton Act. Duplex Printing Press Co. v. Deering, 254 U.S. 443, 41 S.Ct. 172, 65 L.Ed. 349 (1921). The United States Supreme Court, however, in 1941 read the Norris-LaGuardia Act to shelter the secondary boycott from antitrust liability, both civil and criminal. United States v. Hutcheson, 312 U.S. 219, 61 S.Ct. 463, 85 L.Ed. 788 (1941). After a short-lived exemption from the antitrust laws—and indeed arguable affirmative endorsement in Section 7 of the Wagner Act of 1935 —Congress came full circle in 1947 and declared the secondary boycott an unfair labor practice. Not only can the Board issue a cease-

---

11. See Goetz, Secondary Boycotts and the LMRA: A Path Through the Swamp, 19 U.Kan.L.Rev. 651 (1971); Koretz, Federal Regulation of Secondary Picketing, 59 Col.L.Rev. 125 (1959); Lesnick, The Gravamen of the Secondary Boycott, 62 Colum.L. Rev. 1363 (1962); St. Antoine, What Makes Secondary Boycotts Secondary?, Southwestern Legal Foundation, 11th Ann.Inst. on Labor Law 5 (1965).

and-desist order, but even in advance of a Board hearing on the merits the Regional Director is to secure an injunction against probable violations of Section 8(b)(4)(B), pursuant to Section 10(*l*) of the Labor Act; Congress went so far as to declare the secondary boycott a federal tort remediable by an action for compensatory damages under Section 303.

Although Congress did not use the term "secondary boycott" in Section 8(b)(4) but attempted rather to spell out in detail certain proscribed conduct, the legislative history leaves no doubt that it was seeking to outlaw what had become known at common law (and in industrial parlance) as the secondary boycott. At its core, the secondary boycott is the application of economic pressure upon a person with whom the union has no dispute regarding its own terms of employment in order to induce that person to cease doing business with another employer with whom the union does have such a dispute. Thus, a union may seek to organize the employees at Company P, or may seek to extract economic concessions during a collective bargaining negotiation with Company P. An inducement of P's employees to engage in a work stoppage would be treated as "primary" concerted activity, and a request to Company S which buys the product of Company P to refrain from doing so would be a "primary" product boycott. In either situation the object is to cut off P's business and thereby to force an earlier capitulation to the union's demands. But if the request to Company S is unsuccessful, and the union attempts to coerce in turn that company to cease buying from (or supplying) Company P—and that coercion takes the form of appealing to S's employees to engage in a work stoppage or to S's customers to boycott S's product—the union's pressure becomes "secondary." The attempted withdrawal of services or patronage from S (generically referred to as a "boycott") pressures a person with whom the union has no underlying quarrel and whose employment relations it does not seek to alter. The object, just as in the primary boycott, is to fracture the ongoing business relationship between Company P and its suppliers or purchasers in order to make it increasingly costly for that company to resist the union's demands.

The reader should consider, at this point, why it is that there has for so long been a deeply ingrained opposition in law to the secondary boycott. In our social and economic system, we place a high value upon the freedom of individuals and groups to use peaceful methods to exert pressure on others to take lawful action, such as the withdrawal of patronage. Especially sympathetic is the case where the peaceful method used has as a substantial component the communication of pertinent information. Of course, there is sympathy for the "uninvolved" or "neutral" secondary employer, in at least as great a degree as there is for the primary employer who is "responsible" for the workers' grievances. But what factors induce a court or a legislature to conclude that direct picketing pressure on the former is to be curbed through the sanctions of our legal system? Does the decision to outlaw the secondary boycott commend itself to our sense of justice or utility as readily as does the decision (under Sections 8(a)(1) and 8(b)(1)) to outlaw, for example, physical or economic coercion of individual employees for the purpose of affecting their allegiance to a union?

Although it is generally rather clear whether a picketed company is a primary or secondary employer, there are some situations which give rise to close questions of characterization. Assume, for example, that employees working for a carpentry subcontractor on a construction site wish to secure for themselves the work of preparing doors for installation by trimming door edges and by carving out areas to receive hardware. When their employer brings "prefitted doors" to the jobsite for installation, the carpenters refuse to handle or install them. This is surely a work stoppage designed to pressure the carpentry subcontractor to boycott the manufacturer of the pre-fitted doors. Is this an illegal secondary boycott? As a starting point for analysis, the student should ask which company is the one whose personnel policy is being challenged by the union. Should the labelling of one or the other company as Company P or Company S turn upon whether the carpenters have traditionally done this work at the jobsite, or are seeking to acquire this work for the first time? Should it turn upon whether the carpentry subcontractor is free to purchase doors that are not prefitted, or is rather obligated by the specifications in its agreement with the general contractor to purchase pre-fitted doors? These issues are explored in greater detail below, at pages 776–86.

Confidence in identifying the secondary boycott also breaks down when the union's inducement of a boycott takes place neither completely at the location of Company P (the primary situs) through an appeal to P's employees or customers nor completely at the location of Company S (the secondary situs) through an appeal to S's employees or customers. It is quite common, for example, that picketing conducted at the primary situs and directed to primary employees will also turn away deliveries or pickups to be made by employees of secondary companies. Although to that extent the picketing may induce a brief work stoppage of secondary employees and an interruption in the business of the secondary employer, these effects have commonly been accepted as an "incident" of lawful primary picketing. Cf. N.L.R.B. v. International Rice Milling Co., 341 U.S. 665, 71 S.Ct. 961, 95 L.Ed. 1277 (1951). But picketing appeals even in the vicinity of primary employees may have a proliferating impact upon secondary employees and employers when the primary employees are working alongside employees of other companies at property owned by those other companies or by third persons. For example, as in the *Denver Building* case, infra, picketing against one subcontractor at a construction site may induce a work stoppage among employees of other subcontractors and interrupt deliveries of materials to the entire jobsite. Even picketing at the primary plant may be thought to exert undue pressure upon employees of independent contractors rendering services there, as was the issue in the *General Electric* case, pp. 738–46 infra.

The statute contains little or nothing in its own terms to aid in the identification of the secondary boycott in such close cases. Even the central policy behind outlawing the secondary boycott—to shield "neutral" employers from pressures arising from labor disputes "not their own"—stops short of offering a clear answer. At base, the drawing of the line between primary and secondary activity in these borderline cases will be informed by the values and attitudes of the line-drawer, particularly that person's concern on the one hand for minimizing economic combat or on the other hand for maximizing the access of workers to peaceful measures for the furtherance of employee or union interests.

NLRB v. DENVER BLDG. & CONST. TRADES COUNCIL

Supreme Court of the United States, 1951.
341 U.S. 675, 71 S.Ct. 943, 95 L.Ed. 1284.

MR. JUSTICE BURTON delivered the opinion of the Court.

The principal question here is whether a labor organization committed an unfair labor practice, within the meaning of § 8(b) (4) (A) of the National Labor Relations Act, 49 Stat. 449, 29 U.S.C. § 151, 29 U.S.C.A. § 151, as amended by the Labor Management Relations Act, 1947, by engaging in a strike, an object of which was to force the general contractor on a construction project to terminate its contract with a certain subcontractor on that project. For the reasons hereafter stated, we hold that such an unfair labor practice was committed.

[Doose & Lintner, a general contractor on a construction site, awarded the electrical subcontract (in the amount of $2,300) to Gould & Preisner, which proved to be the only nonunion subcontractor at that site. Representatives of the craft unions whose members worked at the site, and of the Denver Building and Construction Council with which those unions were affiliated, informed Doose & Lintner that continued use of Gould & Preisner would result in picketing of the site and a refusal to work alongside such nonunion labor. After a single picket had patrolled for two weeks (carrying a placard stating "This Job Unfair to Denver Building and Construction Trades Council") and had turned away all of the workers except those of Gould & Preisner, Doose & Lintner finally ordered its electrical subcontractor off the job. Immediately thereafter, the picket was removed and all union employees resumed work. Gould & Preisner filed charges against the respondent Council and unions, alleging their inducement of a strike by the employees of the general contractor and other subcontractors, an object of which was to force Doose & Lintner to cease doing business with Gould & Preisner. The NLRB held the respondents' activity to be secondary, but the court of appeals found it to be primary and refused to enforce the Board's cease-and-desist order.]

While § 8(b) (4) does not expressly mention "primary" or "secondary" disputes, strikes or boycotts, that section often is referred to in the Act's legislative history as one of the Act's "secondary boycott sections." The other is § 303, 61 Stat. 158, 29 U.S.C. (Supp. III) § 187, 29 U.S.C.A. § 187, which uses the same language in defining the basis for private actions for damages caused by these proscribed activities.

Senator Taft, who was the sponsor of the bill in the Senate and was the Chairman of the Senate Committee on Labor and Public Welfare in charge of the bill, said, in discussing this section: " * * * under the provisions of the Norris-LaGuardia Act [29 U.S.C.A. § 101 et seq.], it became impossible to stop a secondary boycott or any other kind of a strike, no matter how unlawful it may have been at common law. All this provision of the bill does is to reverse the effect of the law as to secondary boycotts. It has been set forth that there are good secondary boycotts and bad secondary boycotts. Our committee heard evidence for weeks and never succeeded in having anyone tell us any difference between different kinds of secondary boycotts. So we have so broadened the provision dealing with secondary boycotts as to make them an unfair labor practice." 93 Cong.Rec. 4198. * * *

At the same time that §§ 7 and 13 safeguard collective bargaining, concerted activities and strikes between the primary parties to a labor dispute, § 8(b) (4) restricts a labor organization and its agents in the use of economic pressure where an object of it is to force an employer or other person to boycott someone else.

A. We must first determine whether the strike in this case had a proscribed object. The conduct which the Board here condemned is readily distinguishable from that which it declined to condemn in the Rice Milling case, 341 U.S. 665, 71 S.Ct. 961. There the accused union sought merely to obtain its own recognition by the operator of a mill, and the union's pickets near the mill sought to influence two employees of a customer of the mill not to cross the picket line. In that case we supported the Board in its conclusion that such conduct was no more than was traditional and permissible in a primary strike. The union did not engage in a strike against the customer. It did not encourage concerted action by the customer's employees to force the customer to boycott the mill. It did not commit any unfair labor practice proscribed by § 8(b) (4).

In the background of the instant case there was a long-standing labor dispute between the Council and Gould & Preisner due to the latter's practice of employing nonunion workmen on construction jobs in Denver. The respondent labor organizations contend that they engaged in a primary dispute with Doose & Lintner alone, and that they sought simply to force Doose & Lintner to make the project an all-union job. If there had been no contract between Doose & Lintner and Gould & Preisner there might be substance in their contention that the dispute involved no boycott. If, for example, Doose & Lintner had been doing all the electrical work on this project through its own nonunion employees, it could have replaced them with union men and thus disposed of the dispute. However, the existence of the Gould & Preisner subcontract presented a materially different situation. The nonunion employees were employees of Gould & Preisner. The only way that respondents could attain their purpose was to force Gould & Preisner itself off the job. This, in turn, could be done only through Doose & Lintner's termination of Gould & Preisner's subcontract. The result is that the Council's strike, in order to attain its ultimate purpose, must have included among its objects that of forcing Doose & Lintner to terminate that subcontract. On that point, the Board adopted the following finding: "That *an* object, if not the only object, of what transpired with respect to * * * Doose & Lintner was to force or require them to cease doing business with Gould & Preisner seems scarcely open to question, in view of all of the facts. And it is clear at least as to Doose & Lintner, that that purpose was achieved." (Emphasis supplied.) 82 N.L.R.B. at 1212.

We accept this crucial finding. It was an object of the strike to force the contractor to terminate Gould & Preisner's subcontract.

B. We hold also that a strike with such an object was an unfair labor practice within the meaning of § 8(b) (4) (A).

It is not necessary to find that the *sole* object of the strike was that of forcing the contractor to terminate the subcontractor's contract. This is emphasized in the legislative history of the section. See also, National Labor Relations Board v. Wine, Liquor & Distillery Workers Union, 2 Cir., 178 F.2d 584, 586, 16 A.L.R.2d 762.

We agree with the Board also in its conclusion that the fact that the contractor and subcontractor were engaged on the same construction project, and that the contractor had some supervision over the subcontractor's work, did not eliminate the status of each as an independent contractor or make the employees of one the employees *were separate ers* of the other. The business relationship between independent contrac- tors is too well established in the law to be overridden without clear language doing so. The Board found that the relationship between Doose & Lintner and Gould & Preisner was one of "doing business" and we find no adequate reason for upsetting that conclusion.

Finally, § 8(c) safeguarding freedom of speech has no significant application to the picket's placard in this case. Section 8(c) does *1st Amend does not applicable* not apply to a mere signal by a labor organization to its members, or to the members of its affiliates, to engage in an unfair labor practice such as a strike proscribed by § 8(b) (4) (A). That the placard was merely such a signal, tantamount to a direction to strike, was found by the Board. " * * * the issues in this case turn upon acts by labor organizations which are tantamount to directions and instruc- tions to their members to engage in strike action. The protection *protection of FC does not apply in §64/A* afforded by Section 8(c) of the Act to the expression of 'any views, argument or opinion' does not pertain where, as here, the issues raised under Section 8(b) (4) (A) turn on official directions or instructions to a union's own members." 82 N.L.R.B. at 1213.

* * * The judgment of the Court of Appeals accordingly is reversed and the case is remanded to it for procedure not inconsistent with this opinion.

MR. JUSTICE JACKSON would affirm the judgment of the Court of Appeals.

MR. JUSTICE DOUGLAS, with whom MR. JUSTICE REED joins, dis- senting. *Dissent*

The employment of union and nonunion men on the same job is a basic protest in trade union history. That was the protest here. The union was not out to destroy the contractor because of his antiunion attitude. The union was not pursuing the contractor to other jobs. All the union asked was that union men not be compelled to work alongside nonunion men on the same job. As Judge Rifkind stated in an analogous case, "the union was not extending its activity to a front remote from the immediate dispute but to one intimately and indeed inextricably united to it."

The picketing would undoubtedly have been legal if there had been no subcontractor involved—if the general contractor had put nonunion men on the job. The presence of a subcontractor does not alter one whit the realities of the situation; the protest of the union is precisely the same. In each the union was trying to protect the job on which union men were employed. If that is forbidden, the Taft- Hartley Act makes the right to strike, guaranteed by § 13, dependent on fortuitous business arrangements that have no significance so far as the evils of the secondary boycott are concerned. I would give scope to both § 8(b) (4) and § 13 by reading the restrictions of § 8(b)

(4) to reach the case where an industrial dispute spreads from the job to another front.

The Court's decision in *Denver Building* was the object of sustained attack by organized labor, particularly in the construction trades, and led to almost twenty-five years of effort to secure a legislative overruling. Any number of bills were introduced in both Houses of Congress to authorize so-called common situs picketing by unions seeking to organize (or engaged in a dispute with) construction subcontractors. It was not until 1975 that such legislation —encumbered with numerous exceptions and provisions—was able to pass both Houses (see H.R. 5900, 94th Cong., 1st Sess. (1975)) but the victory of the construction unions was short-lived, for President Ford vetoed the legislation, condemning it as highly controversial and likely to lead to continued inflation in the construction industry. The major thrust of the bill that passed Congress was to amend Section 8(b)(4) with a proviso to the effect that that Section was not to

> be construed to prohibit any strike or refusal to perform services or any inducement of any individual employed by any person to strike or refuse to perform services at the site of the construction, alteration, painting, or repair of a building * * * and directed at any of several employers who are in the construction industry and are jointly engaged as joint venturers or in the relationship of contractors and subcontractors in such construction, alteration, painting, or repair at such site * * *.

The accompanying legislative reports (see H.R.Rep.No.94-371, 94th Cong., 1st Sess. (1975)) declared that it was the object of Congress to overrule the *Denver Building* decision, "its spirit and its progeny"; to endorse the analysis of Mr. Justice Douglas in dissent; and "to grant construction workers the same rights under the NLRA as are enjoyed by other workers." The report declared that "The present law ignores the economic reality of the integral relationship between contractors and subcontractors in construction, and imposes greater restrictions on the union right of concerted action in the construction industry than in other areas of employment." The presidential veto, which Congress failed to override, leaves the *Denver Building* decision as the authoritative interpretation of Section 8(b)(4)(B) in the construction industry.

Problems for Discussion

1. Employees of Acme Supermarket are represented by the Retail Clerks Union and are on strike for increased contract benefits. The

union has established a picket line at the consumer entrances, employee entrances and at the pickup and loading platforms at the rear of the store. Deliverymen from Bond Bakers, approaching the rear platform to make deliveries of bread and cake, refuse to cross the picket line or to complete deliveries. Is the union violating Section 8(b)(4)(B)?

2.   Assume instead that the Acme employees picket not only the Acme site but also at the Bond Bakery, labelling Bond "Unfair" for continuing attempts to sell its merchandise at Acme Supermarket. Is the union violating Section 8(b)(4)(B)?

3.   Employees of Acme Supermarket are on strike, and have set up a picket line at the Acme store. The object of the strike is to force Acme to stop purchasing bread and cakes from Bond and instead to assign such baking work to a group of Acme employees now working in a modest back-of-the-store baking operation; and also to force Acme to stop purchasing from Bond while Bond remains non-union (the Clerks Union is trying to organize the Bond employees). Is the union violating Section 8(b)(4)(B)?

4.   The Retail Clerks Union represents all of the Acme employees in a single bargaining unit which excludes four employees working at a bakery counter, who bake, wrap, and otherwise prepare baked goods for sale at that counter and on the store's regular merchandise shelves. The Bakers Union has demanded that Acme recognize it as representative of the four employees, but Acme has refused. The bakery employees, and other representatives of the Bakers Union, are picketing Acme and turning away employees represented by the Retail Clerks, as well as customers. Is the Bakers Union violating Section 8(b)(4)(B)?

5.   The scenario is the same as in problem (4), except that the bakery counter is run not by Acme but by Bond Bread, as a separate concession, with the four workers employed by Bond. The Bakers Union pickets for recognition and turns away Acme employees and customers. Is the Bakers Union violating Section 8(b)(4)(B)?

SAILORS' UNION OF THE PACIFIC
(MOORE DRY DOCK CO.)

National Labor Relations Board, 1950.
92 N.L.R.B. 547.

[A certain contract to transport gypsum had been withdrawn from an American ship, which employed members of the Sailors' Union of the Pacific, and given to the *S.S. Phopho,* a Panamanian flagship owned by the corporation Samsoc. The *Phopho* was tied at the Moore Dry Dock to be converted to enable it to carry gypsum. By February 16, 1950, a substantial portion of the crew had been hired, none of the crew being members of the Sailors' Union. The wages they had contracted for were less than half of the union scale. This crew began work, training, cleaning the ship, and preparing the ship for departure. On February 16, the union demanded that Samsoc recognize it as bargaining agent for the crew of the *Phopho*, which Samsoc refused to do. The next day, pickets arrived at the entrance to Moore Dry Dock, carrying signs declaring the *Phopho* to be unfair. The union requested permission to picket on Moore property adjacent to the ship, but permission was denied.

The picketing had no effect on members of the crew of the *Phopho*, since they were quartered on the ship, and their shipping articles provided for resolution of all labor disputes by Panamanian officials. The effect on Moore employees, however, was marked. The Sailors' Union sent letters to the unions representing Moore employees, explaining the nature of the dispute and requesting that no work be done on the *Phopho*. Both the picket signs and the letters emphasized that the dispute was with Samsoc and limited to the *Phopho*. By February 21, all work on the *Phopho* by Moore employees had ceased. Moore employees did continue to work on other ships at the Moore dock. Moore then filed Section 8(b)(4) charges.]

Section 8(b)(4)(A) is aimed at secondary boycotts and secondary strike activities. It was not intended to proscribe primary action by a union having a legitimate labor dispute with an employer. Picketing at the premises of a primary employer is traditionally recognized as primary action even though it is "necessarily designed to induce and encourage third persons to cease doing business with the picketed employer." * * * Hence, if Samsoc, the owner of the *S.S. Phopho*, had had a dock of its own in California to which the *Phopho* had been tied up while undergoing conversion by Moore Dry Dock employees, picketing by the Respondent at the dock site would unquestionably have constituted *primary* action, even though the Respondent might have expected that the picketing would be more effective in persuading Moore employees not to work on the ship than to persuade the seamen aboard the *Phopho* to quit that vessel. The difficulty in the present case arises therefore, not because of any difference in picketing objectives, but from the fact that the *Phopho* was not tied up at its own dock, but at that of Moore, while the picketing was going on in front of the Moore premises.

In the usual case, the *situs* of a labor dispute is the premises of the primary employer. Picketing of the premises is also picketing of the *situs* * * * But in some cases the *situs* of the dispute may not be limited to a fixed location; it may be ambulatory. * * * [W]e hold in the present case that, as the *Phopho* was the place of employment of the seamen, it was the *situs* of the dispute between Samsoc and the Respondent over working conditions aboard that vessel.

When the *situs* is ambulatory, it may come to rest temporarily at the premises of another employer. The perplexing question is: Does the right to picket follow the *situs* while it is stationed at the premises of a secondary employer, when the only way to picket that *situs* is in front of the secondary employer's premises? Admittedly, no easy answer is possible. Essentially the problem is one of balancing the right of a union to picket at the site of its dispute as against the right of a secondary employer to be free from picketing in a controversy in which it is not directly involved.

When a secondary employer is harboring the *situs* of a dispute between a union and a primary employer, the right of neither the union to picket nor of the secondary employer to be free from picketing can be absolute. The enmeshing of premises and *situs* qualifies both rights. In the kind of situation that exists in this case, we believe that picketing of the premises of a secondary employer is primary if it meets the following conditions: (a) The picketing is strictly limited to times when the *situs* of dispute is located on the secondary employer's premises; (b) at the time of the picketing the primary employer is engaged in its normal business at the *situs*; (c) the picketing is limited to places reasonably close to the location of the *situs*; and (d) the picketing discloses clearly that the dispute is with the primary employer. All these conditions were met in the present case. * * *

[In explaining how the second of these four conditions was satisfied, the Board observed: "The multitudinous steps of preparation, including hiring and training a crew and putting stores aboard, are as much a part of the normal business of a ship as the voyage itself."]

We believe that our dissenting colleagues' expressions of alarm are based on a misunderstanding of our decision. We are not holding, as the dissenters seem to think, that a union which has a dispute with a shipowner over working conditions of seamen aboard a ship may lawfully picket the premises of an independent shipyard to which the shipowner has delivered his vessel for overhaul and repair. We are only holding that, if a shipyard permits the owner of a vessel to use its dock for the purpose of readying the ship for its regular voyage by hiring and training a crew and putting stores aboard ship, a union representing seamen may then, within the careful limitations laid down in this decision, lawfully picket in front of the shipyard premises to advertise its dispute with the shipowner. * * *

Under the circumstances of this case, we therefore find that the picketing practice followed by the Respondent was primary and not secondary and therefore did not violate Section 8(b)(4)(A) of the Act.

[The dissenting opinion of MEMBERS REYNOLDS and MURDOCH is omitted.]

Problem for Discussion

Acme Supermarket employees are on strike for increased contract benefits. Acme gets its bread and cakes from Bond Bakers by pickups from Bond made by an Acme employee driving an Acme truck. The Acme driver reports to work each morning at 6:00 A.M. to assist unloading shipments of frozen vegetables. At 8:00 A.M. as he begins his daily drive to the Bond Bakery, the driver has been accompanied by a car transporting two Acme strikers, who alight from their car and picket around the Acme truck while it is taking on baked goods at the Bond loading platform. The picketing ceases when the bread has been loaded, and the truck returns to Acme with the strikers following. After the bread is unloaded, the truck returns to Bond to make another pickup, with the strikers continuing to follow. At 1:00 P.M. the truckdriver returns to Acme, and spends the next two hours servicing the truck and cleaning the garage and loading platform. Is the union representing the strikers violating Section 8(b)(4) (B)?

DOUDS v. METROPOLITAN FEDERATION OF ARCHITECTS [12]

District Court, Southern District of New York, 1948.
75 F.Supp. 672.

RIFKIND, DISTRICT JUDGE. This is a petition brought by Charles T. Douds, Regional Director of the Second Region of the National Labor Relations Board to enjoin the respondent, Metropolitan Federation of Architects, Engineers, Chemists and Technicians, Local 231, United Office & Professional Workers of America, C. I. O., from engaging in certain activities alleged to be in violation of Section 8(b) (4) (A) of the National Labor Relations Act, as amended by § 101 of the Labor Management Relations Act of 1947, Public Law 101, 80th Congress, popularly known as the Taft-Hartley Act, 29 U.S.C.A. § 158(b) (4) (A). * * *

The testimony offered by the petitioner, the respondent, and the charging party at the hearings established the following facts:

Ebasco Services, Inc. is a corporation engaged, since 1905, in the business of supplying engineering services, such as planning and designing and drafting plans, for industrial and public utility installations. During the year ending September 1, 1947, the respondent union was the bargaining agent for Ebasco's employees. On that day the agreement between Ebasco and the union expired. A new agreement was not reached and a strike against Ebasco was commenced on September 5, 1947.

12. See Asher, Secondary Boycott—Allied, Neutral and Single Employers, 52 Geo.L.J. 406 (1964); Levin, "Wholly Unconcerned": The Scope and Meaning of the Ally Doctrine Under Section 8(b)(4) of the NLRA, 119 U.Pa.L. Rev. 283 (1970); Comment, Unions, Conglomerates, and Secondary Activity Under the NLRA, 129 U.Pa.L.Rev. 221 (1980).

James P. O'Donnell and Guy M. Barbolini in 1946 organized a partnership, styled Project Engineering Company, herein called "Project". Its business is identical with Ebasco's—planning and designing and drafting plans for industrial installations although they seem to have specialized in chemical and petroleum plants. The partnership had an inception completely independent of Ebasco or its influence. There is no common ownership of any kind. It was through Project's solicitations that Ebasco first employed the partnership. An open contract dated December 19, 1946 marked the beginning of their business relations.

Prior to August, 1946, Ebasco never subcontracted any of its work. Subsequent to that date it subcontracted some of its work. At the time the strike was called, part of Ebasco's work had been let out to Project. An appreciable percentage of Project's business for some months antedating the strike consisted of work secured from Ebasco. After the strike had begun, an even greater percentage—about 75%—of its work was Ebasco's. Some work, which had been begun by Ebasco's workers, was transferred, after the commencement of the strike, in an unfinished condition to Project for completion.

In a brochure printed and distributed by Ebasco before the strike to its prospective customers, Ebasco represented itself as having available the services of a number of draftsmen and designers, which included the personnel of Project and of other subcontractors. The contract price of all the work done by Project for Ebasco was computed by adding to the compensation of the men engaged on Ebasco work a factor for overhead and profits. In their business relationship it was the practice of Project to furnish Ebasco with time sheets, showing the number of hours each of the former's employees spent on Ebasco work. Ebasco's statements to its customers contained the time spent by technicians, with no distinction made between the work done by Ebasco employees and subcontractors' employees.

Ebasco supervisory personnel made regular visits to Project to oversee the work on the subcontracts. After the strike was called and the work subcontracted increased, these visits increased in frequency and numbers of personnel involved. Ebasco supervisory personnel, whose subordinates were on strike, continued to supervise their "jobs", at Project's plant, where such work had been transferred. The working hours of Project employees were increased after the commencement of the Ebasco strike.

Delegations representing the respondent union approached the charging party on more than one occasion and asked, among other things, that it refuse to accept work which had come "off the boards" of Ebasco.

On October 28, 1947, respondent union ordered Project picketed and such picketing has continued since that day. The pickets carry signs which denominate Project a scab shop for Ebasco. A number of resignations at Project are attributable to the picketing.

The number of pickets has usually been reasonable and the picketing was ordinarily unaccompanied by violence. * * * Project continues to do engineering work for Ebasco—the kind of work which Ebasco employees themselves would be doing if they were not striking. * * *

One of the prohibitions of Section 8(b) (4) (A) of the Act is: "It shall be an unfair labor practice for a labor organization * * * to * * * encourage the employees of any employer to engage in, a strike * * * where an object thereof is * * * requiring * * * any * * * person * * * to cease doing business with any other person."

Is Project "doing business" with Ebasco within the meaning of the Act? The term is not defined in the Act itself. Section 2, 29 U.S. C.A. § 152, contains thirteen definitions, but none of doing business. * * * To find the limitations to which "doing business" must be confined recourse may be had to the legislative history to discover the mischief which Congress intended to remedy. In describing the "necessity for legislation" the House Committee on Education and Labor reported, Report No. 245, pp. 4–5:

"The employers' plight has likewise not been happy. * * *

"His business on occasions has been virtually brought to a standstill by disputes to which he himself was not a party and in which he himself had no interest." * * *

During the Congressional debates on the Bill, Senator Pepper objected to the provisions relating to the secondary boycott and stated an illustration in which he thought it would be unjust to apply them. Senator Taft, in reply, said: "I do not quite understand the case which the Senator has put. This provision makes it unlawful to resort to a secondary boycott to injure the business of a third person who is wholly unconcerned in the disagreement between an employer and his employees." (April 29, 1947, p. 4323 of the Congressional Record, Vol. 93.)

Examination of these expositions of Congressional purpose indicates that the provision was understood to outlaw what was theretofore known as a secondary boycott. It is to the history of the secondary boycott, therefore, that attention should be directed and it is in the light of that history that the term "doing business" should be evaluated. See Hellerstein, Secondary Boycotts in Labor Disputes, 1938, 47 Yale Law J. 341; Gromfine, Labor's Use of Secondary Boycotts, 1947, 15 Geo. Washington Law Rev. 327.

When the term is read with the aid of the glossary provided by the law of secondary boycott it becomes quite clear that Project cannot claim to be a victim of that weapon in labor's arsenal. To suggest that Project had no interest in the dispute between Ebasco and its employees is to look at the form and remain blind to substance. In every meaningful sense it had made itself party to the contest. Manifestly it was not an innocent bystander, nor a neutral. It was firmly allied to Ebasco and it was its conduct as ally of Ebasco which directly provoked the union's action.

Significant is the unique character of the contract between Ebasco and Project. Ebasco did not buy any articles of commerce from Project. Ebasco did not retain the professional services of Project. Ebasco "bought" from Project, in the words of the basic contract, "services of your designers and draftsmen * * * to work under the direction and supervision of the Purchaser." The purchase price consisted of the actual wages paid by Project plus a factor for overhead and profit. In practice the terms and implications of the agreement were fully spelled out. Ebasco supplied both direction and supervision of a detailed and pervasive character. It established the maximum wage rates for which it would be charged. Invoices were in terms of manhours, employee by employee. Daily tally was taken of the number of men at work on Ebasco assignments and communicated to Ebasco. The final product, the plans and drawings, were placed upon forms supplied by Ebasco, bearing its name, and were thus delivered to Ebasco's clients as Ebasco's work. In advertising its services to the industries which it served Ebasco held itself out as "having available" a number of designers and draftsmen which included those employed by Project.

True enough, the contract prescribes that "all employees furnished by the seller shall at all times be and remain employees of the seller". I do not, however, draw therefrom the inference advocated by the petitioner and the charging party. The very need for such a provision emphasizes the realization of the parties that they were doing business on terms which cast a shadow of doubt upon the identity of the employer. Without question, Ebasco and Project were free to contract who, as between themselves, should be subject to the burden and possessed of the privileges that attach to the employer of those on Project's payroll. But the law is not foreclosed by such agreements to examine the reality relevant to the purposes of a particular statute. Cf. Rutherford Food Corp. v. McComb, 1947, 331 U.S. 722, 67 S.Ct. 1473; N. L. R. B. v. Hearst Publications, Inc., 1944, 322 U.S. 111, 64 S.Ct. 851, 88 L.Ed. 1170.

I am unable to hold that corporate ownership or insulation of legal interests between two businesses can be conclusive as to neutrality or disinterestedness in a labor dispute.

The evidence is abundant that Project's employees did work, which, but for the strike of Ebasco's employees, would have been done by Ebasco. The economic effect upon Ebasco's employees was precisely that which would flow from Ebasco's hiring strikebreakers to work on its own premises. The conduct of the union in inducing Project's employees to strike is not different in kind from its conduct in inducing Ebasco's employees to strike. If the latter is not amenable to judicial restraint, neither is the former. In encouraging a strike at Project the union was not extending its activity to a front remote from the immediate dispute but to one intimately and indeed inextricably united to it. See Bakery Drivers Local v. Wohl, 1942, 315 U. S. 769, 62 S.Ct. 816, 86 L.Ed. 1178; cf. Carpenters Union v. Ritter's Cafe, 1942, 315 U.S. 722, 62 S.Ct. 807, 86 L.Ed. 1143.

* * * It must be apparent that a construction of the Act which outlaws the kind of union activity here involved would almost certainly cast grave doubts upon its constitutionality. It is preferable to interpret the disputed section so as restrain only that kind of union activity which does not enjoy constitutional immunity.

The case at bar is not an instance of a secondary boycott.

For these reasons it is clear that there has been no violation of Section 8(b) (4) (A) and the court is therefore without power to grant the requested relief. * * *

Problems for Discussion

1. Repairmen for Royal Typewriter are on strike for higher wages. Royal Typewriters are sold with a one-year warranty. The duties of the repairmen are to repair typewriters under warranty and also to repair typewriters leased from Royal. During the strike, Royal instructs customers needing repairs to have the repairs performed by another company of the customer's choice. The customers are told to send the repair bills to Royal, which in turn agrees to pay the company performing the repairs. Accordingly, one of Royal's major customers, Vick Chemical Co., arranges to have extensive repairs performed by Tytell Typewriter Co., for which Royal agrees to pay in installments. While such repair work is being performed, Royal employees picket both Vick and Tytell, seeking to force Tytell to stop performing Royal repairs. Does the picketing of Tytell violate § 8(b)(4)(B)? Does the picketing of Vick? See NLRB v. Business Mach. Bd. (Royal Typewriter Co.), 228 F.2d 553 (2d Cir. 1956).

Suppose Royal agreed with Vick that Vick would pay Tytell for the repair work and that Royal would then reimburse Vick. Tytell has no dealings with Royal and is unaware of the strike. Could Tytell then be lawfully picketed by the Royal employees?

2. The Union of Marine Cooks and Stewards is involved in a labor dispute with the Irwin-Lyons Lumber Co. Irwin-Lyons cuts logs, the Ace Company transports the logs down a river to the Irwin-Lyons mills, where the logs are sawed into lumber, and then the lumber is carried from the mill in a ship by Irwin-Lyons. The dock for the ship is the

situs of the labor dispute. The union pickets operations of the Ace Company, causing the Ace Company to cease carrying Irwin-Lyons logs under threat of a work stoppage. The individuals who own the Ace Company also own 75% of the stock in Irwin-Lyons, many of them in about the same ratio. The same person is president of both companies and another is secretary-treasurer of both. Irwin-Lyons is an Oregon corporation, and the Ace Company is a public utility operating under franchise from the State of Oregon. Does the picketing of the Ace Company violate § 8(b)(4)(B)? See *National Union of Marine Cooks (Irwin-Lyons Co.)*, 87 N.L.R.B. 54 (1949).

3. Members of the American Federation of Television and Radio Artists (AFTRA) are on strike against WBAL–TV, Baltimore, which is owned by the Hearst Corporation. AFTRA pickets the Baltimore News American, a newspaper owned by Hearst. The publisher of the News American files a Section 8(b)(4)(B) charge and the Regional Director issues a complaint. The Administrative Law Judge determines the following facts regarding the structure of the Hearst Corporation.

Hearst has its headquarters in New York and comprises twenty divisions, which are not separately incorporated. The News American and WBAL are controlled by different divisions. No member of the management of either division sits on the board of directors of Hearst and there is no overlap between the management of the two divisions. The management of each division has substantially complete control of the day-to-day operation of the division. Hearst does not influence the editorial policies of either the newspaper or the television station, although it does make certain news services and columns available to both. Both the television station and the newspaper employ their own news-gathering staffs. When one division advertises on the other's medium, it pays the going commercial rate. Both divisions employ the same labor lawyer, but they pursue separate labor relations policies without interference from New York. Each division controls its own budget, but must obtain approval from Hearst for capital expenditures in excess of $10,000.

(a) Is AFTRA violating Section 8(b)(4)(B) by picketing the News American? See *AFTRA* v. *NLRB*, 462 F.2d 887 (D.C. Cir. 1972).

(b) Would your analysis differ materially if the Hearst Corporation operated the newspaper and television station not through divisions but rather through separately incorporated, wholly-owned subsidiaries?

(c) In the event you conclude that the picketing violates the Labor Act, what remedies are available to the injured parties? Under each of the remedies you can contemplate, who will determine whether the News American is an "ally" of the struck television station?

LOCAL 761, INTERNATIONAL UNION OF ELECTRICAL WORKERS v. NLRB [13]

Supreme Court of the United States, 1961.
366 U.S. 667, 81 S.Ct. 1285, 6 L.Ed.2d 592.

MR. JUSTICE FRANKFURTER delivered the opinion of the Court.

Local 761 of the International Union of Electrical, Radio and Machine Workers, AFL–CIO was charged with a violation of § 8(b) (4) (A) of the Taft-Hartley Act, 61 Stat. 136, 141, upon the following facts.

General Electric Corporation operates a plant outside of Louisville, Kentucky, where it manufactures washers, dryers, and other electrical household appliances. The square-shaped, thousand-acre, unfenced plant is known as Appliance Park. A large drainage ditch makes ingress and egress impossible except over five roadways across culverts, designated as gates.

Since 1954, General Electric sought to confine the employees of independent contractors, described hereafter, who work on the premises of the Park, to the use of Gate 3–A and confine its use to them. The undisputed reason for doing so was to insulate General Electric employees from the frequent labor disputes in which the contractors were involved. Gate 3–A is 550 feet away from the nearest entrance available for General Electric employees, suppliers, and deliverymen. Although anyone can pass the gate without challenge, the roadway leads to a guardhouse where identification must be presented. Vehicle stickers of various shapes and colors enable a guard to check on sight whether a vehicle is authorized to use Gate 3–A. Since January 1958, a prominent sign has been posted at the gate which states: "GATE 3–A FOR EMPLOYEES OF CONTRACTORS ONLY—G. E. EMPLOYEES USE OTHER GATES." On rare occasions, it appears, a General Electric employee was allowed to pass the guardhouse, but such occurrence was in violation of company instructions. There was no proof of any unauthorized attempts to pass the gate during the strike in question.

The independent contractors are utilized for a great variety of tasks on the Appliance Park premises. Some do construction work on new buildings; some install and repair ventilation and heating equipment; some engage in retooling and rearranging operations necessary to the manufacture of new models; others do "general maintenance work." These services are contracted to outside employers either because the company's employees lack the necessary skill or manpower, or because the work can be done more economically by independent contractors. The latter reason determined the

13. See Zimmerman, Secondary Picketing and the Reserved Gate: The *General Electric* Doctrine, 47 Va.L. Rev. 1164 (1961).

contracting of maintenance work for which the Central Maintenance department of the company bid competitively with the contractors. While some of the work done by these contractors had on occasion been previously performed by Central Maintenance, the findings do not disclose the number of employees of independent contractors who were performing these routine maintenance services, as compared with those who were doing specialized work of a capital-improvement nature.

The Union, petitioner here, is the certified bargaining representative for the production and maintenance workers who constitute approximately 7,600 of the 10,500 employees of General Electric at Appliance Park. On July 27, 1958, the Union called a strike because of 24 unsettled grievances with the company. Picketing occurred at all the gates, including Gate 3–A, and continued until August 9 when an injunction was issued by a Federal District Court. The signs carried by the pickets at all gates read: "LOCAL 761 ON STRIKE G. E. UNFAIR." Because of the picketing, almost all of the employees of independent contractors refused to enter the company premises.

Neither the legality of the strike or of the picketing at any of the gates except 3–A is in dispute, nor that the picketing was other than peaceful in nature. The sole claim was that the picketing before the gate exclusively used by employees of independent contractors was conduct proscribed by § 8(b) (4) (A).

The Trial Examiner recommended that the Board dismiss the complaint. He concluded that the limitations on picketing which the Board had prescribed in so-called "common situs" cases were not applicable to the situation before him, in that the picketing at Gate 3–A represented traditional primary action which necessarily had a secondary effect of inconveniencing those who did business with the struck employer. He reasoned that if a primary employer could limit the area of picketing around his own premises by constructing a separate gate for employees of independent contractors, such a device could also be used to isolate employees of his suppliers and customers, and that such action could not relevantly be distinguished from oral appeals made to secondary employees not to cross a picket line where only a single gate existed.

The Board rejected the Trial Examiner's conclusion, 123 N.L. R.B. 1547. It held that since only the employees of the independent contractors were allowed to use Gate 3–A, the Union's object in picketing there was "to enmesh these employees of the neutral employers in its dispute with the Company" thereby constituting a violation of § 8(b) (4) (A) because the independent employees were encouraged to engage in a concerted refusal to work "with an object of forcing the independent contractors to cease doing business with the Company."

The Court of Appeals for the District of Columbia granted enforcement of the Board's order * * *.

I.

Section 8(b) (4) (A) of the National Labor Relations Act provides that it shall be an unfair labor practice for a labor organization

> " * * * to engage in, or to induce or encourage the employees of any employer to engage in a strike or a concerted refusal in the course of their employment to use, manufacture, process, transport, or otherwise handle or work on any goods, articles, materials, or commodities or to perform any services, where an object thereof is: (A) forcing or requiring * * * any employer or other person * * * to cease doing business with any other person * * *."

can't be literally construed

This provision could not be literally construed; otherwise it would ban most strikes historically considered to be lawful, so-called primary activity. "While § 8(b) (4) does not expressly mention 'primary' or 'secondary' disputes, strikes or boycotts, that section often is referred to in the Act's legislative history as one of the Act's 'secondary boycott sections.' " Labor Board v. Denver Building Council, 341 U.S. 675, 686, 71 S.Ct. 943, 950. "Congress did not seek, by § 8(b) (4), to interfere with the ordinary strike * * *." Labor Board v. International Rice Milling Co., 341 U.S. 665, 672, 71 S.Ct. 961, 965. The impact of the section was directed toward what is known as the secondary boycott whose "sanctions bear, not upon the employer who alone is a party to the dispute, but upon some third party who has no concern in it." International Brotherhood of Electrical Workers v. Labor Board, 181 F.2d 34, 37. Thus the section "left a striking labor organization free to use persuasion, including picketing, not only on the primary employer and his employees but on numerous others. Among these were secondary employers who were customers or suppliers of the primary employer and persons dealing with them * * * and even employees of secondary employers so long as the labor organization did not * * * 'induce or encourage the employees of any employer to engage in a strike or a concerted refusal in the course of their employment' * * *." Labor Board v. Local 294, International Brotherhood of Teamsters, 284 F.2d 887, 889. * * *

Important as is the distinction between legitimate "primary activity" and banned "secondary activity," it does not present a glaringly bright line. The objectives of any picketing include a desire to influence others from withholding from the employer their services or trade. See Sailors' Union of the Pacific (Moore Dry Dock), 92 N.L.R.B. 547. "[I]ntended or not, sought for or not, aimed for or not, employees of neutral employers do take action sympathetic with strikers and do put pressure on their own employers." Seafarers International Union v. Labor Board, 105 U.S.App.D.C. 211, 265 F.2d 585, 590. "It is clear that, when a union pickets an employer with whom it has a dispute, it hopes, even if it does not intend, that all persons will honor the picket line, and that hope encompasses the employees of neutral employers who may in the course of their employment (deliverymen and the like) have to enter the premises." Id., at 591. "Almost all picketing, even at the situs of the primary employer and surely at that of the secondary, hopes to achieve the forbidden objective, whatever other motives there may be and however small the chances of success." Local 294, supra, at 890. But picketing which induces secondary employees to respect a picket line is not the equivalent of picketing which has an object of inducing those employees to engage in concerted conduct against their employer in order to force him to refuse to deal with the struck employer. Labor Board v. International Rice Milling, supra.

However difficult the drawing of lines more nice than obvious, the statute compels the task. * * * The nature of the problem, as revealed by unfolding variant situations, inevitably involves an evolutionary process for its rational response, not a quick, definitive formula as a comprehensive answer. And so, it is not surprising that the Board has more or less felt its way during the fourteen years in which it has had to apply § 8(b) (4) (A), and has modified and reformed its standards on the basis of accumulating experience. "One of the purposes which lead to the creation of such boards is to have decisions based upon evidential facts under the particular statute made by experienced officials with an adequate appreciation of the complexities of the subject which is entrusted to their administration." Republic Aviation Corp. v. Labor Board, 324 U.S. 793, 800, 65 S.Ct. 982, 986.

II.

The early decisions of the Board following the Taft-Hartley amendments involved activity which took place around the secondary employer's premises. For example in Wadsworth Building Co., supra, the union set up a picket line around the situs of a builder who had contracted to purchase prefabricated houses from the primary employer. The Board found this to be illegal secondary activity. See also Printing Specialties Union (Sealbright Pacific), 82 N.L.R.B. 271. In contrast, when picketing took place around the premises of the primary employer the Board regarded this as valid primary activity. In Oil Workers International Union (Pure Oil Co.), 84 N.L. R.B. 315, Pure had used Standard's dock and employees for loading its oil onto ships. The companies had contracted that, in case of a strike against Standard, Pure employees would take over the loading of Pure oil. The union struck against Standard and picketed the dock, and Pure employees refused to cross the picket line. The Board held this to be a primary activity, although the union's action induced the Pure employees to engage in a concerted refusal to handle Pure products at the dock. The fact that the picketing was confined to the vicinity of the Standard premises influenced the Board not to find that an object of the activity was to force Pure to cease doing business with Standard, even if such was a secondary effect.

> "A strike, by its very nature, inconveniences those who customarily do business with the struck employer. Moreover, any accompanying picketing of the employer's premises is necessarily designed to induce and encourage third persons to cease doing business with the picketed employer. It does not follow, however, that such picketing is therefore proscribed by Section 8(b) (4) (A) of the Act." 84 N.L.R.B., at 318. * * *

In United Electrical Workers (Ryan Construction Corp.), 85 N.L.R.B. 417, Ryan had contracted to perform construction work on a building adjacent to the Bucyrus plant and inside its fence. A separate gate was cut through the fence for Ryan's employees which no employee of Bucyrus ever used. The Board concluded that the union—on strike against Bucyrus—could picket the Ryan gate, even though an object of the picketing was to enlist the aid of Ryan employees, since Congress did not intend to outlaw primary picketing.

> "When picketing is wholly at the premises of the employer with whom the union is engaged in a labor dispute, it cannot be called 'secondary' even though, as is virtually always the case, an object of the picketing is to dissuade all persons from entering such premises for business reasons. It makes no difference whether 1 or 100 other employees wish to enter the premises. It follows in this case that the picketing of Bucyrus premises, which was primary because in support of a labor dispute *with Bucyrus*, did not lose its character and become 'secondary' at the so-called Ryan gate because Ryan employees were the only persons regularly entering Bucyrus premises at that gate." 85 N.L.R.B., at 418. See also General Teamsters (Crump, Inc.), 112 N.L.R.B. 311.

Thus, the Board eliminated picketing which took place around the situs of the primary employer—regardless of the special circumstances involved—from being held invalid secondary activity under § 8(b) (4) (A).

However, the impact of the new situations made the Board conscious of the complexity of the problem by reason of the protean forms in which it appeared. This became clear in the "common situs" cases—situations where two employers were performing separate tasks on common premises. The Moore Dry Dock case, supra, laid out the Board's new standards in this area. There, the union picketed outside an entrance to a dock where a ship, owned by the struck employer, was being trained and outfitted. Although the premises picketed were those of the secondary employer, they constituted the only place where picketing could take place; furthermore, the objectives of the picketing were no more aimed at the employees of the secondary employer—the dock owner—than they had been in the Pure Oil and Ryan cases. The Board concluded, however, that when the situs of the primary employer was "ambulatory" there must be a balance between the union's right to picket and the interest of the secondary employer in being free from picketing. It set out four standards for picketing in such situations which would be presumptive of valid primary activity: (1) that the picketing be limited to times when the situs of dispute was located on the secondary premises, (2) that the primary employer be engaged in his normal business at the situs, (3) that the picketing take place reasonably close to the situs, and (4) that the picketing clearly disclose that the dispute was only with the primary employer. These tests were widely accepted by reviewing federal courts. * * *

In Local 55 (PBM), 108 N.L.R.B. 363, the Board for the first time applied the Dry Dock test although the picketing occurred at premises owned by the primary employer. There, an insurance company owned a tract of land that it was developing, and also served as the general contractor. A neutral subcontractor was also doing work at the site. The union, engaged in a strike against the insurance company, picketed the entire premises, characterizing the entire job as unfair, and the employees of the subcontractor walked off. The Court of Appeals for the Tenth Circuit enforced the Board's order which found the picketing to be illegal on the ground that the picket signs did not measure up to the Dry Dock standard that they clearly disclose that the picketing was directed against the struck employer only. 218 F.2d 226.

The Board's application of the Dry Dock standards to picketing at the premises of the struck employer was made more explicit in Retail Fruit & Vegetable Clerks (Crystal Palace Market), 116 N.L.R.B. 856. The owner of a large common market operated some of the shops within, and leased out others to independent sellers. The union, although given permission to picket the owner's individual stands, chose to picket outside the entire market. The Board held that this action was violative of § 8(b) (4) (A) in that the union did not attempt to minimize the effect of its picketing, as required in a common-situs case, on the operations of the neutral employers utilizing the market. "We believe * * * that the foregoing principles should apply to all common situs picketing, including cases where, as here, the picketed premises are owned by the primary employer." 116 N.L.R.B., at 859. The Ryan case, supra, was overruled to the extent it implied the contrary. The Court of Appeals for the Ninth Circuit, in enforcing the Board's order, specifically approved its disavowance of an ownership test. 249 F.2d 591. The Board made clear that its decision did not affect situations where picketing which had effects on neutral third parties who dealt with the employer occurred at premises occupied solely by him. "In such cases, we adhere to the rule established by the Board * * * that more latitude be given to picketing at such separate primary premises than at premises occupied in part (or entirely) by secondary employers." 116 N.L.R.B., at 860, n. 10.

In rejecting the ownership test in situations where two employers were performing work upon a common site, the Board was naturally guided by this Court's opinion in Rice Milling, in which we indicated that the location of the picketing at the primary employer's premises was "not necessarily conclusive" of its legality. 341 U.S., at 671. Where the work done by the secondary employees is unrelated to the normal operations of the primary employer, it is difficult to perceive how the pressure of picketing the entire situs is any less on the neutral employer merely because the picketing takes place at property owned by the struck employer. The application of the Dry Dock tests to limit the picketing effects to the employees of the employer against whom the dispute is directed carries out the "dual congressional objectives of preserving the right of labor organizations to bring pressure to bear on offending employers in primary labor disputes and of shielding unoffending employers and others from pressures in controversies not their own." Labor Board v. Denver Building Council, supra, at 692.

III.

From this necessary survey of the course of the Board's treatment of our problem, the precise nature of the issue before us emerges. With due regard to the relation between the Board's function and the scope of judicial review of its rulings, the question is whether the Board may apply the Dry Dock criteria so as to make unlawful picketing at a gate utilized exclusively by employees of independent contractors who work on the struck employers' premises. The effect of such a holding would not bar the union from picketing at all gates used by the employees, suppliers, and customers of the struck employer. Of course an employer may not, by removing all his employees from the situs of the strike, bar the union from publicizing its cause, see Local 618 v. Labor Board, 249 F.2d 332. The basis of the Board's decision in this case would not remotely have that effect, nor any such tendency for the future.

The Union claims that if the Board's ruling is upheld, employers will be free to erect separate gates for deliveries, customers, and re-

placement workers which will be immunized from picketing. This
fear is baseless. The key to the problem is found in the type of work
that is being performed by those who use the separate gate. It is
significant that the Board has since applied its rationale, first stated
in the present case, only to situations where the independent workers
were performing tasks unconnected to the normal operations of the
struck employer—usually construction work on his buildings. In
such situations, the indicated limitations on picketing activity respect
the balance of competing interests that Congress has required the
Board to enforce. On the other hand, if a separate gate were devised
for regular plant deliveries, the barring of picketing at that location
would make a clear invasion on traditional primary activity of appealing to neutral employees whose tasks aid the employer's everyday
operations. The 1959 Amendments to the National Labor Relations
Act, which removed the word "concerted" from the boycott provisions,
included a proviso that "nothing contained in this clause (B) shall be
construed to make unlawful, where not otherwise unlawful, any
primary strike or primary picketing." 29 U.S.C.A. (Sup. I, 1959)
§ 158(b)(4)(B). The proviso was directed against the fear that the
removal of "concerted" from the statute might be interpreted so that
"the picketing at the factory violates section 8(b) (4) (A) because
the pickets induce the truck drivers employed by the trucker not to
perform their usual services where an object is to compel the trucking
firm not to do business with the * * * manufacturer during the
strike." Analysis of the bill prepared by Senator Kennedy and Representative Thompson, 105 Cong.Rec. 16589.

    In a case similar to the one now before us, the Court of Appeals
for the Second Circuit sustained the Board in its application of § 8(b)
(4) (A) to a separate-gate situation. "There must be a separate gate,
marked and set apart from other gates; the work done by the men who
use the gate must be unrelated to the normal operations of the employer, and the work must be of a kind that would not, if done when the
plant were engaged in its regular operations, necessitate curtailing
those operations." United Steelworkers v. Labor Board, Doc.No.
26252, decided May 3, 1961. These seem to us controlling considerations.

                                IV.

    The foregoing course of reasoning would require that the judg-
ment below sustaining the Board's order be affirmed but for one consideration, even though this consideration may turn out not to affect
the result. The legal path by which the Board and the Court of Appeals reached their decisions did not take into account that if Gate
3–A was in fact used by employees of independent contractors who
performed conventional maintenance work necessary to the normal
operations of General Electric, the use of the gate would have been
a mingled one outside the bar of § 8(b) (4) (A). In short, such mixed

use of this portion of the struck employer's premises would not bar picketing rights of the striking employees. While the record shows some such mingled use, it sheds no light on its extent. It may well turn out to be that the instances of these maintenance tasks were so insubstantial as to be treated by the Board as *de minimis*. We cannot here guess at the quantitative aspect of this problem. It calls for Board determination. For determination of the questions thus raised, the case must be remanded by the Court of Appeals to the Board.

Reversed.

THE CHIEF JUSTICE and MR. JUSTICE BLACK concur in the result. MR. JUSTICE DOUGLAS, dissented. * * *

Problems for Discussion

1. The Retail Clerks Union at the Acme Supermarket has called a strike for increased contract benefits, but the market is continuing in operation through the use of supervisory personnel. In an effort to separate deliverymen from the picketing Acme employees, Acme constructs a delivery platform at the edge of its parking lot and erects signs directing deliverymen to the platform through an unused driveway which is at all points considerably distant from the store and from customer and employee entrances. Nonetheless, a group of picketers station themselves at the driveway entrance, where no Acme employees are located, and turn away Bond Bakery delivery trucks. Is the Union violating Section 8(b)(4)(B)?

2. The scenario is the same as in problem 1, except that the driveway is reserved exclusively for employees of Concreet Construction Company, which is building for Acme (at the rear of its parking lot) a quick-food-service stand which will dispense sandwiches and hot snacks at lunch and dinner hours. The Concreet employees are turned away by the Acme picket line. Is the Union violating Section 8(b)(4)(B)?

3. The scenario is the same, except that Acme closes its market because of the serious curtailment of business caused by the picketing. A week later, the employees of Fashion Interiors appear at the driveway; they intend to occupy the supermarket building for a week, replacing linoleum with carpeting, installing new lighting fixtures, and repainting. The picketing by the Retail Clerks continues, both at the supermarket building and at the driveway, at a time when no other employees or customers are there, and the employees of Fashion Interiors are turned away and refuse to return to work. Is the Union violating Section 8(b)(4)(B)?

The very complex relationship among the decisions in Denver Building, pp. 724–28 supra, Moore Dry Dock, pp. 729–31, and General Electric, pp. 738–46 was explored by both the Board and a court of appeals in MARKWELL & HARTZ, INC. v. NLRB, 387 F.2d 79

(5th Cir. 1967), *enforcing* 155 N.L.R.B. 319 (1965). There, Markwell & Hartz (M&H) was the general contractor for a construction project in Louisiana. Employees of M&H were represented by the UMW and were assigned about eighty percent of the work on the project. The remainder of the work was assigned to two subcontractors, Binnings (pile-driving) and Barnes (electrical work). Employees of Binnings and Barnes were represented by the Trades Council.

A dispute arose between M&H and the Trades Council, the latter demanding recognition as bargaining agent for M&H employees. The Council began picketing the project on October 17, 1963. By November 16, M&H, desiring to insulate the subcontractors from the labor dispute, had built four separate gates, three for the exclusive use of the subcontractors, their employees and suppliers, and the fourth for M&H employees and suppliers. Despite the fact that the gates were clearly marked, the Trades Council continued to picket all four gates. Employees of Binnings and of Barnes refused to cross the picket lines, and M&H assigned its own workers to complete the pile-driving.

M&H filed a charge under Section 8(b)(4)(B), resulting in the issuance of a cease and desist order against picketing of the three subcontractors' gates. The Trades Council argued that its picketing was within the protection of the *General Electric* separate-gate doctrine, and that *General Electric* had sub silentio overruled the *Denver Building* decision. The Board rejected that argument, concluding that *General Electric* was inapplicable because it was limited to situations in which the struck employer was the owner of the premises. Since M&H did not own the construction site and since the subcontractors were to be regarded as neutrals, the common-situs rules of *Moore Dry Dock* were held applicable and the picketing was found not to comply with those rules. *Moore Dry Dock* was deemed to require that the "timing and location of the picketing * * * be tailored to reach the employees of the primary employer, rather than those of the neutral employer * * *," while the picketing of the subcontractors' gates was clearly addressed to the employees of Binnings and Barnes and was designed to force those subcontractors to cease doing business with M&H.

The court of appeals enforced the Board's order against the Trades Council, with each of the three judges writing a separate opinion announcing a separate basis for decision.

Judge Connally concluded that, applying the tests of *General Electric*, the work performed by a subcontractor is not "related" to the work of the general contractor, so that separate-gate picketing is not allowable. He also rejected an argument by the Trades Council that *Denver* should apply only to the situation where the labor dispute is with the subcontractor and the general contractor is the neutral (which was the situation in *Denver,* the converse of the situation in *Markwell & Hartz*). Thus, the Trades Council was obligated to limit its picketing to the single M&H gate in accordance with *Moore Dry Dock* and *General Electric.*

Judge Rives reached the same result by a different line of reasoning. He concluded that the work performed by the subcontractors must have been related to the work of M&H since M&H employees were able to take over the pile-driving when Binnings employees walked off the job. Judge Rives believed, however, that *Denver Building* applied to common-situs picketing on the premises of a third party, while *General Electric* applied only to picketing on the premises of the struck company. The picketing involved in *Markwell & Hartz* thus came within the *Denver* rule and had to be limited to the single gate.

In a lengthy dissent, Judge Wisdom rejected Judge Rives' conclusion that *General Electric* applied only when the struck company owned the premises where the picketing occurred. He could see no logical distinction in the two situations and could find no language in *General Electric* to support such a distinction. He concluded that *General Electric* modified *Denver Building* to the extent that the decision in *Denver* was reached without considering the "relatedness" of the work performed by the subcontractor. *Denver* could not be cited for a holding on "relatedness" since that issue was not dealt with. The court of appeals and the Board were, he argued, applying more rigid standards to the construction industry than to other industries. "Any prime contractor would be able to frustrate the purposes of picketing by opening gates reserved for his subcontractors." The touchstone should be the "relatedness" of the work in the building industry as in others. Since the Board had made no finding on the issue of relatedness, the case should be remanded for such a finding.

[For an application of *Markwell & Hartz* and the other principal cases discussed therein, see Carpenters Local 470 (Mueller-Anderson, Inc.), 224 N.L.R.B. 315 (1976), enf'd, 564 F.2d 1360 (9th Cir. 1977).]

2.   The 1959 Amendments [14]

The 1959 amendments to Section 8(b)(4) were designed to close certain loopholes in the Taft-Hartley secondary boycott provisions. As enacted in 1947, those provisions made it an unfair labor practice for a labor organization to "encourage the employees of any employer" to engage in a strike or a "concerted refusal" to process, transport or otherwise handle goods where an object was to force one person to cease doing business with another. It had been held that the use of the terms "employees" and "employer" as defined in Section 2 of the Labor Act permitted a union to induce a secondary work stoppage by minor supervisors, farm workers, governmental and railway employees, and workers at nonprofit private hospitals. Congress closed this loophole in 1959 by banning a union inducement of a secondary work stoppage by "any individual employed by any person engaged in commerce or in an industry affecting commerce." Congress also in 1959 struck the word "concerted" from what had been Section 8(b)(4)(A) of the Taft-Hartley Act, and thus brought within the secondary boycott ban a union inducement of a single individual (e. g., one truck driver) to refrain from transporting or handling goods produced by or destined for the primary employer. By a more significant amendment, Congress added a second proscribed method for effecting a secondary boycott; in addition to the inducement of a work stoppage, Congress now forbade a union "to threaten, coerce, or restrain any person engaged in commerce or in an industry affecting commerce" where the union's objective was secondary. This was incorporated in the newly numbered Section 8(b)(4)(B) as subsection (ii), while the work-stoppage ban was carried forward as subsection (i).

The prohibitions of the 1959 amendments were narrowly construed by the Supreme Court in NLRB v. SERVETTE, INC., 377 U.S. 46, 84 S.Ct. 1098, 12 L.Ed.2d 121 ((1964). This case involved a strike against Servette, a wholesale distributor to retail supermarket chains. Representatives of the striking union sought to support the strike by requesting supermarket managers to stop stocking Servette products. These requests were backed by a warning that handbills, urging customers not to purchase Servette products, would be distributed in front of stores selling Servette products. In some

14. See Engel, Secondary Consumer Picketing—Following the Struck Product, 52 Va.L.Rev. 189 (1966); Lewis, Consumer Picketing and the Court—The Questionable Yield of *Tree Fruits*, 49 Minn.L.Rev. 479 (1965); Minch, Consumer Picketing: Reassessing the Concept of Employer Neutrality, 65 Calif.L.Rev. 172 (1977); Note, Picketing and Publicity Under Section 8(b)(4) of the LMRA, 73 Yale L.J. 1265 (1964); Shalov, The Landrum-Griffin Amendments: Labor's Use of the Secondary Boycott, 45 Corn.L.Q. 724 (1960).

instances, such handbills were distributed.   Servette filed a Section 8(b)(4) charge, but the Board dismissed the complaint.   It held that subsection (i) was not violated because supermarket managers were not "individuals" within the meaning of that subsection and thus that inducements aimed at managers were not proscribed.   The "threat" of handbilling and the actual handbilling were held not prohibited by subsection (ii) because handbilling was protected by the publicity proviso added to the Act in the 1959 amendments.   The court of appeals reversed, finding violations in both the requests to the managers and the handbilling.   The Supreme Court reinstated the Board's order dismissing the complaint, but for different reasons from those relied on by the Board.

The Supreme Court agreed with the court of appeals that the word "individual" included supermarket managers.   But the Court found no illegal inducement.   Section 8(b)(4)(i) was held to prohibit only encouraging someone to refuse to perform his duties.   The managers were not being encouraged to withhold their services but rather to make a managerial decision within their authority.   Encouraging or inducing someone to make such a decision was held not to violate subsection (i).   The Court found support for this interpretation in the legislative history of the 1959 statute, which evidenced no congressional intention to expand the type of conduct outlawed under subsection (i), and also in the structure of the statute; if subsection (i) had been intended to prohibit appeals to managers making managerial decisions, then subsection (ii) prohibiting threats to managers making decisions would have been superfluous.

The Court also agreed with the Board that the proviso protected the union's distribution of handbills.   The court of appeals had concluded that the proviso did not protect the handbilling because the proviso in terms protects only publicity concerning "products * * produced by an employer with whom the labor organization has a primary dispute * * *."   Servette was a distributor and had not "produced" any goods.   The Supreme Court, however, referring to the legislative purpose, gave a broad reading to the word "produced" in the proviso so as to encompass distribution:

"The proviso was the outgrowth of a profound Senate concern that the unions' freedom to appeal to the public for support of their case be adequately safeguarded. * * * It would fall far short of achieving this basic purpose if the proviso applied only in situations where the union's labor dispute is with the manufacturer or processor.   Moreover, a primary target of the 1959 amendments was the secondary boycotts conducted by the Teamsters Union, which ordinarily represents employees not of manufacturers, but of motor carriers. There is nothing in the legislative history which suggests that the protection of the proviso was intended to be any narrower in coverage than the prohibition to which it is an exception, and we see no basis for attributing such an incongruous purpose to Congress."

The "threat" of handbilling was thus not prohibited by subsection (ii) because the "statutory protection for the distribution of handbills would be undermined if a threat to engage in protected conduct were not itself protected."

— See supp

NLRB v. FRUIT AND VEGETABLE PACKERS, LOCAL 760

Supreme Court of the United States, 1964.
377 U.S. 58, 84 S.Ct. 1063, 12 L.Ed.2d 129.

MR. JUSTICE BRENNAN delivered the opinion of the Court.

* * * The question in this case is whether the respondent unions violated [Section 8(b)(4)(ii)(B) of the NLRB as amended] when they limited their secondary picketing of retail stores to an appeal to the customers of the stores not to buy the products of certain firms against which one of the respondents was on strike.

Issue

Respondent Local 760 called a strike against fruit packers and warehousemen doing business in Yakima, Washington.[15] The struck firms sold Washington State apples to the Safeway chain of retail stores in and about Seattle, Washington. Local 760, aided by respondent Joint Council, instituted a consumer boycott against the apples in support of the strike. They placed pickets who walked back and forth before the customers' entrances of 46 Safeway stores in Seattle. The pickets—two at each of 45 stores and three at the 46th store—wore placards and distributed handbills which appealed to Safeway customers, and to the public generally, to refrain from buying Washington State apples, which were only one of numerous food products sold in the stores. Before the pickets appeared at any store, a letter was delivered to the store manager informing him that the picketing was only an appeal to his customers not to buy Washington State apples, and that the pickets were being expressly instructed "to patrol peacefully in front of the consumer entrances of the store, to stay away from the delivery entrances and not to interfere with the work of your employees, or with deliveries to or pickups from your store." A copy of written instructions to the pickets—which included the explicit

---

15. The firms, 24 in number, are members of the Tree Fruits Labor Relations Committee, Inc., which acts as the members' agent in labor disputes and in collective bargaining with unions which represent employees of the members. The strike was called in a dispute over terms of the renewal of a collective bargaining agreement.

statement that "you are also forbidden to request that the customers not patronize the store"—was enclosed with the letter. Since it was desired to assure Safeway employees that they were not to cease work, and to avoid any interference with pickups or deliveries, the pickets appeared after the stores opened for business and departed before the stores closed. At all times during the picketing, the store employees continued to work, and no deliveries or pickups were obstructed. Washington State apples were handled in normal course by both Safeway employees and the employees of other employers involved. Ingress and egress by customers and others was not interfered with in any manner.

[The NLRB found the union's conduct to violate § 8(b)(4), which the Board read to bar all consumer picketing in front of a secondary establishment. The Court of Appeals set aside the Board's order, holding that Safeway could not be "coerced" unless the picketing had a substantial economic impact on its business.]

The Board's reading of the statute—that the legislative history and the phrase "other than picketing" in the proviso reveal a congressional purpose to outlaw all picketing directed at customers at a secondary site—necessarily rested on the finding that Congress determined that such picketing always threatens, coerces or restrains the secondary employer. We therefore have a special responsibility to examine the legislative history for confirmation that Congress made that determination. Throughout the history of federal regulation of labor relations, Congress has consistently refused to prohibit peaceful picketing except where it is used as a means to achieve specific ends which experience has shown are undesirable. "In the sensitive area of peaceful picketing Congress has dealt explicitly with isolated evils which experience has established flow from such picketing." National Labor Relations Board v. Drivers etc. Local Union, 362 U.S. 274, 284, 80 S.Ct. 706, 712, 4 L.Ed.2d 710. We have recognized this congressional practice and have not ascribed to Congress a purpose to outlaw peaceful picketing unless "there is the clearest indication in the legislative history," ibid., that Congress intended to do so as regards the particular ends of the picketing under review. Both the congressional policy and our adherence to this principle of interpretation reflect concern that a broad ban against peaceful picketing might collide with the guarantees of the First Amendment.

We have examined the legislative history of the amendments to § 8(b)(4), and conclude that it does not reflect with the requisite clarity a congressional plan to proscribe all peaceful consumer picketing at secondary sites, and, particularly, any concern with peaceful picketing when it is limited, as here, to persuading Safeway customers not to buy Washington State apples when they traded in the Safeway stores. All that the legislative history shows in the way of an "iso-

proscribed conduct

lated evil" believed to require proscription of peaceful consumer picketing at secondary sites was its use to persuade the customers of the secondary employer to cease trading with him in order to force him to cease dealing with, or to put pressure upon, the primary employer. This narrow focus reflects the difference between such conduct, and peaceful picketing at the secondary site directed only at the struck product. In the latter case, the union's appeal to the public is confined to its dispute with the primary employer, since the public is not asked to withhold its patronage from the secondary employer, but only to boycott the primary employer's goods. On the other hand, a union appeal to the public at the secondary site not to trade at all with the secondary employer goes beyond the goods of the primary employer, and seeks the public's assistance in forcing the secondary employer to cooperate with the union in its primary dispute.[16] This is not to say that this distinction was expressly alluded to in the debates. It is to say, however, that the consumer picketing carried on in this case is not attended by the abuses at which the statute was directed.

The story of the 1959 amendments, which we have detailed at greater length in our opinion filed today in National Labor Relations Board v. Servette, Inc., 375 U.S. 46, 84 S.Ct. 1098, begins with the original § 8(b) (4) of the Taft-Hartley Act. Its prohibition, in pertinent part, was confined to the inducing or encouraging of "the employees of any employer to engage in, a strike or a concerted refusal * * * [to] handle * * * any goods * * *" of a primary employer. This proved to be inept language. Three major loopholes were revealed. Since only inducement of "employees" was proscribed, direct inducement of a supervisor or the secondary employer by threats of labor trouble was not prohibited. Since only a "strike or concerted refusal" was prohibited, pressure upon a single employee was not forbidden. Finally, railroads, airlines and municipalities were not "employers" under the Act and therefore inducement or encouragement of their employees was not unlawful. * * *

[Justice Brennan examined the history of the 1959 legislation in the Senate. He observed that the bills which did pass the Senate

---

16. The distinction between picketing a secondary employer merely to "follow the struck goods," and picketing designed to result in a generalized loss of patronage, was well established in the state cases by 1940. The distinction was sometimes justified on the ground that the secondary employer, who was presumed to receive a competitive benefit from the primary employer's nonunion, and hence lower, wage scales, was in "unity of interest" with the primary employer, Goldfinger v. Feintuch, 276 N.Y. 281, 286, 11 N.E. 2d 910, 116 A.L.R. 477; Newark Lad-der & Bracket Sales Co. v. Furniture Workers Union Local 66, 125 N.J.Eq. 99, 4 A.2d 49; Johnson v. Milk Drivers & Dairy Employees Union, Local 854, 195 So. 791 (Ct.App.La.), and sometimes on the ground that picketing restricted to the primary employer's product is "a primary boycott against the merchandise." Chiate v. United Cannery Agricultural Packing and Allied Workers of America, 2 CCH Lab.Cas. 125, 126 (Cal.Super.Ct.). See I Teller, Labor Disputes and Collective Bargaining § 123 (1940).

in prior years contained no amendments to Section 8(b)(4), and that the proposals of certain individual Senators were not designed to curb consumer picketing.]

The House history * * * confirms our conclusion. From the outset the House legislation included provisions concerning secondary boycotts. The Landrum-Griffin bill, which was ultimately passed by the House, embodied the Eisenhower Administration's proposals as to secondary boycotts. The initial statement of Congressman Griffin in introducing the bill which bears his name, contains no reference to consumer picketing in the list of abuses which he thought required the secondary boycott amendments. Later in the House debates he did discuss consumer picketing, but only in the context of its abuse when directed against shutting off the patronage of a secondary employer.

In the debates before passage of the House bill he stated that the amendments applied to consumer picketing of customer entrances to retail stores selling goods manufactured by a concern under strike, if the picketing were designed to "coerce or to restrain the employer of [the] second establishment, to get him not to do business with the manufacturer * * *," and further that, "of course, this bill and any other bill is limited by the constitutional right of free speech. If the purpose of the picketing is to *coerce the retailer not to do business* with the manufacturer—then such a boycott could be stopped." (Italics supplied.)

* * * There is thus nothing in the legislative history prior to the convening of the Conference Committee which shows any congressional concern with consumer picketing beyond that with the "isolated evil" of its use to cut off the business of a secondary employer as a means of forcing him to stop doing business with the primary employer. When Congress meant to bar picketing *per se,* it made its meaning clear; for example, § 8(b)(7) makes it an unfair labor practice, "to picket or cause to be picketed * * * any employer * * *." In contrast, the prohibition of § 8(b)(4) is keyed to the coercive nature of the conduct, whether it be picketing or otherwise.

Senator Kennedy presided over the Conference Committee. He and Congressman Thompson prepared a joint analysis of the Senate and House bills. This analysis pointed up the First Amendment implications of the broad language in the House revisions of § 8(b)(4) stating,

"The prohibition [of the House bill] reaches not only picketing but leaflets, radio broadcasts and newspaper advertisements, thereby interfering with freedom of speech.

" * * * one of the apparent purposes of the amendment is to prevent unions from appealing to the general public as consumers for assistance in a labor dispute. This is a basic infringement upon freedom of expression."

This analysis was the first step in the development of the publicity proviso, but nothing in the legislative history of the proviso alters our conclusion that Congress did not clearly express an intention that amended § 8(b) (4) should prohibit all consumer picketing. Because of the sweeping language of the House bill, and its implications for freedom of speech, the Senate conferees refused to accede to the House proposal without safeguards for the right of unions to appeal to the public, even by some conduct which might be "coercive." The result was the addition of the proviso. But it does not follow from the fact that some coercive conduct was protected by the proviso, that the exception "other than picketing" indicates that Congress had determined that all consumer picketing was coercive.

No Conference Report was before the Senate when it passed the compromise bill, and it had the benefit only of Senator Kennedy's statement of the purpose of the proviso. He said that the proviso preserved "the right to appeal to consumers by methods other than picketing asking them to refrain from buying goods made by nonunion labor *and* to refrain from trading with a retailer who sells such goods. * * * We were not able to persuade the House conferees to permit picketing in front of that secondary shop, but were able to persuade them to agree that the unions shall be free to conduct informational activity short of picketing. In other words, the union can hand out handbills at the shop * * * and can carry on all publicity short of having ambulatory picketing * * *." (Italics supplied.) This explanation does not compel the conclusion that the Conference Agreement contemplated prohibiting any consumer picketing at a secondary site beyond that which urges the public, in Senator Kennedy's words, to "refrain from trading with a retailer who sells such goods." To read into the Conference Agreement, on the basis of a single statement, an intention to prohibit all consumer picketing at a secondary site would depart from our practice of respecting the congressional policy not to prohibit peaceful picketing except to curb "isolated evils" spelled out by the Congress itself.

Peaceful consumer picketing to shut off all trade with the secondary employer unless he aids the union in its dispute with the primary employer, is poles apart from such picketing which only persuades his customers not to buy the struck product. The proviso indicates no more than that the Senate conferees' constitutional doubts led Congress to authorize publicity other than picketing which persuades the customers of a secondary employer to stop all trading with him, but not such publicity which has the effect of cutting off his deliveries or inducing his employees to cease work. On the other hand, picketing which persuades the customers of a secondary employer to stop all trading with him was also to be barred.

legislative

In sum, the legislative history does not support the Board's finding that Congress meant to prohibit all consumer picketing at a secondary site, having determined that such picketing necessarily threatened, coerced or restrained the secondary employer. Rather, the history shows that Congress was following its usual practice of legislating against peaceful picketing only to curb "isolated evils."

opposition

This distinction is opposed as "unrealistic" because, it is urged, all picketing automatically provokes the public to stay away from the picketed establishment. The public will, it is said, neither read the signs and handbills, nor note the explicit injunction that "This is not a strike against any store or market." Be that as it may, our holding today simply takes note of the fact that a broad condemnation of peaceful picketing, such as that urged upon us by petitioners, has never been adopted by Congress, and an intention to do so is not revealed with that "clearest indication in the legislative history," which we require. National Labor Relations Board v. Drivers, etc. Local Union, supra.

within letter of statute, but not within spirit

We come then to the question whether the picketing in this case, confined as it was to persuading customers to cease buying the product of the primary employer, falls within the area of secondary consumer picketing which Congress did clearly indicate its intention to prohibit under § 8(b) (4) (ii). We hold that it did not fall within that area, and therefore did not "threaten, coerce, or restrain" Safeway. While any diminution in Safeway's purchases of apples due to a drop in consumer demand might be said to be a result which causes respondents' picketing to fall literally within the statutory prohibition, "it is a familiar rule that a thing may be within the letter of the statute and yet not within the statute, because not within its spirit nor within the intention of the makers." Holy Trinity Church v. United States, 143 U.S. 457, 459, 12 S.Ct. 511, 512, 36 L.Ed. 226. See United States v. American Trucking Ass'ns, 310 U.S. 534, 543–544, 60 S.Ct. 1059, 1063–1064, 84 L.Ed. 1345. When consumer picketing is employed only to persuade customers not to buy the struck product, the union's appeal is closely confined to the primary dispute. The site of the appeal is expanded to include the premises of the secondary employer, but if the appeal succeeds, the secondary employers' purchases from the struck firms are decreased only because the public has diminished its purchases of the struck product. On the other hand, when consumer picketing is employed to persuade customers not to trade at all with the secondary employer, the latter stops buying the struck product, not because of a falling demand, but in response to pressure designed to inflict injury on his business generally. In such case, the union does more than merely follow the struck product; it creates a separate dispute with the secondary employer.

result of picketing

We disagree therefore with the Court of Appeals that the test of "to threaten, coerce, or restrain" for the purposes of this case is whether Safeway suffered or was likely to suffer economic loss. A violation of § 8(b) (4) (ii) (B) would not be established, merely because respondents' picketing was effective to reduce Safeway's sales of Washington State apples, even if this led or might lead Safeway to drop the item as a poor seller.

The judgment of the Court of Appeals is vacated and the case is remanded with direction to enter judgment setting aside the Board's order. It is so ordered.

MR. JUSTICE DOUGLAS took no part in the consideration or decision of this case.

MR. JUSTICE BLACK, concurring.

Because of the language of § 8(b) (4) (ii) (B) of the National Labor Relations Act and the legislative history set out in the opinions of the Court and of my BROTHER HARLAN, I feel impelled to hold that Congress, in passing this section of the Act, intended to forbid the striking employees of one business to picket the premises of a neutral business where the purpose of the picketing is to persuade customers of the neutral business not to buy goods supplied by the struck employer. Construed in this way, as I agree with BROTHER HARLAN that it must be, I believe, contrary to his view, that the section abridges freedom of speech and press in violation of the First Amendment. * * *

In short, we have neither a case in which picketing is banned because the picketers are asking others to do something unlawful nor a case in which *all* picketing is, for reasons of public order, banned. Instead, we have a case in which picketing, otherwise lawful, is banned only when the picketers express particular views. The result is an abridgment of the freedom of these picketers to tell a part of the public their side of a labor controversy, a subject the free discussion of which is protected by the First Amendment.

I cannot accept my BROTHER HARLAN'S view that the abridgment of speech and press here does not violate the First Amendment because other methods of communication are left open. This reason for abridgment strikes me as being on a par with holding that governmental suppression of a newspaper in a city would not violate the First Amendment because there continue to be radio and television stations. First Amendment freedoms can no more validly be taken away by degrees than by one fell swoop.

MR. JUSTICE HARLAN, whom MR. JUSTICE STEWART joins, dissenting. * * *

Nothing in the statute lends support to the fine distinction which the Court draws between general and limited product picketing. The enactment speaks pervasively of "threatening, coercing, or restraining any person"; the proviso differentiates only between modes of expression, not between types of secondary consumer picketing. For me, the Court's argument to the contrary is very unconvincing.

The difference to which the Court points between a secondary employer merely lowering his purchases of the struck product to the degree of decreased consumer demand and such an employer ceasing to purchase one product because of consumer refusal to buy any products, is surely too refined in the context of reality. It can hardly be supposed that in all, or even most, instances the result of the type of picketing involved here will be simply that suggested by the Court. Because of the very nature of picketing there may be numbers of persons who will refuse to buy at all from a picketed store, either out of economic or social conviction or because they prefer to shop where they need not brave a picket line. Moreover, the public can hardly be expected always to know or ascertain the precise scope of a particular picketing operation. Thus in cases like this, the effect on the secondary employer may not always be limited to a decrease in his sales of the struck product. And even when that is the effect, the employer may, rather than simply reducing purchases from the primary employer, deem it more expedient to turn to another producer whose product is approved by the union.

The distinction drawn by the majority becomes even more tenuous if a picketed retailer depends largely or entirely on sales of the struck product. If, for example, an independent gas station owner sells gasoline purchased from a struck gasoline company, one would not suppose he would feel less threatened, coerced, or restrained by picket signs which said "Do not buy X gasoline" than by signs which said "Do not patronize this gas station." To be sure Safeway is a multiple article seller, but it cannot well be gainsaid that the rule laid down by the Court would be unworkable if its applicability turned on a calculation of the relation between total income of the secondary employer and income from the struck product.

The Court informs us that "Peaceful consumer picketing to shut off all trade with the secondary employer unless he aids the union in its dispute with the primary employer, is poles apart from such picketing which only persuades his customers not to buy the struck product." The difference was, it is stated, "well established in the state cases by 1940," that is before the present federal enactment. In light of these assertions, it is indeed remarkable that the Court not only substantially acknowledges that the statutory language does not itself support this distinction but cites no report of Congress, no statement of a legislator, not even the view of any of the many commentators in the area, in any way casting doubt on the applicability of § 8(b) (4) (ii) (B) to picketing of the kind involved here.

The Court's distinction fares no better when the legislative history of § 8(b) (4) (ii) (B) is examined. Even though there is no Senate, House, or Conference Report which sheds light on the matter, that hardly excuses the Court blinding itself to what the legislative and other background materials do show. Fairly assessed they, in my opinion, belie Congress' having made the distinction upon which the Court's thesis rests. Nor can the Court find comfort in the generalization that " 'In the sensitive area of peaceful picketing Congress has dealt explicitly with isolated evils which experience has established flow from such picketing';" in enacting the provisions in question Congress *was* addressing itself to a particular facet of secondary boycotting not dealt with in prior legislation, namely, peaceful secondary consumer picketing. I now turn to the materials which illuminate what Congress had in mind.

It is clear that consumer picketing in connection with secondary boycotting was at the forefront of the problems which led to the amending of the Taft-Hartley Act by the Labor-Management Reporting and Disclosure Act of 1959.   *   *   *

Reporting on the compromise reached by the Conference Committee on the Kennedy-Ervin and Landrum-Griffin bills, Senator Kennedy, who chaired the Conference Committee, stated:

> "[T]he House bill prohibited the union from carrying on any kind of activity to disseminate informational material to secondary sites. They could not say that there was a strike in a primary plant.   *   *   *   "Under the language of the conference [ultimately resulting in present § 8(b) (4) (ii) (B)] we agreed there would not be picketing at a secondary site. What was permitted was the giving out of handbills or information through the radio, and so forth." 105 Cong. Rec. 17720, II Leg.Hist. 1389.   *   *   *

Senator Kennedy spoke further on the Conference bill and particularized the union rights protected by the Senate conferees:

> "(c) The right to appeal to consumers by methods other than picketing asking them to refrain from buying goods made by nonunion labor and to refrain from trading with a retailer who sells such goods.
>
> "Under the Landrum-Griffin bill it would have been impossible for a union to inform the customers of a secondary employer that that employer or store was selling goods which were made under racket conditions or sweatshop conditions, or in a plant where an economic strike was in progress. We were not able to persuade the House conferees to permit picketing in front of that secondary shop, but we were able to persuade them to agree that the union shall be free to conduct informational activity short of picketing. In other words, the union can hand out handbills at the shop, can place advertisements in newspapers, can make announcements over the radio, and can carry on all publicity

short of having ambulatory picketing in front of a secondary site." 105 Cong.Rec. 17898–17899, II Leg.Hist. 1432.

The Court does not consider itself compelled by these remarks to conclude that the Conference Committee meant to prohibit *all* secondary consumer picketing. A fair reading of these comments, however, can hardly leave one seriously in doubt that Senator Kennedy believed this to be precisely what the Committee had done; the Court's added emphasis on the word "and" is, I submit, simply grasping at straws, if indeed the phrase relied on does not equally well lend itself to a disjunctive reading. Cf. DeSylva v. Ballentine, 351 U.S. 570, 573, 76 S.Ct. 974, 976, 100 L.Ed. 1415. The complicated role the Court assigns to the publicity proviso makes even less understandable its failure to accord to the remarks of Senator Kennedy their proper due. The proviso, according to the Court's interpretation, is unnecessary in regard to picketing designed to effect a boycott of the primary product and comes into play only if a complete boycott of the secondary employer is sought. Had this ingenious interpretation been intended, would not Senator Kennedy, who was at pains to emphasize the scope of activities still left to unions, have used it to refute the criticisms of Senator Morse made only shortly before?
* * *

The majority relies on remarks made by Congressman Griffin, the bill's cosponsor. When read in context what seems significant about them is that the Congressman nowhere suggests that there can be some kind of consumer picketing which does not coerce or restrain the secondary employer. Nor does he intimate any constitutional problem in prohibiting picketing that follows the struck product.   * * *

In the light of the foregoing, I see no escape from the conclusion that § 8(b) (4) (ii) (B) does prohibit *all* consumer picketing. There are, of course, numerous times in the debates of both houses in which consumer picketing is referred to generally or the reference is made with an example of an appeal to consumers not to purchase at all from the secondary employer. But it is remarkable that every time the possibility of picketing of the sort involved in this case was considered, it was assumed to be prohibited by the House bill. Admittedly, in the House, appeals to refrain from purchase of the struck product were discussed only by opponents of the House bill; however, only one of two inferences can be drawn from the silence of the bill's supporters. Either the distinction drawn by this Court was not considered of sufficient significance to require comment, or the proponents recognized a difference between the two types of consumer picketing but assumed that the bill encompassed both. Under either supposition, the conclusion reached by the Court in regard to the picketing involved here is untenable.

Under my view of the statute the constitutional issue is therefore reached. Since the Court does not discuss it, I am content simply to state in summary form my reasons for believing that the prohibitions of § 8(b) (4) (ii) (B), as applied here, do not run afoul of constitutional limitations. This Court has long recognized that picketing is "inseparably something more [than] and different" from simple communication. Hughes v. Superior Court, 339 U.S. 460, 464, 70 S.Ct. 718, 721, 94 L.Ed. 985; see, e. g., Building Service Employees v. Gazzam, 339 U.S. 532, 537, 70 S.Ct. 784, 787, 94 L.Ed. 1045; Bakery Drivers v. Wohl, 315 U.S. 769, 776, 62 S.Ct. 816, 819, 86 L.Ed. 1178 (concurring opinion of DOUGLAS, J.). Congress has given careful and continued consideration to the problems of labor-management relations, and its attempts to effect an accommodation between the right of unions to publicize their position and the social desirability of limiting a form of communication likely to have effects caused by something apart from the message communicated, are entitled to great deference. The decision of Congress to prohibit secondary consumer picketing during labor disputes is, I believe, not inconsistent with the protections of the First Amendment, particularly when, as here, other methods of communication are left open.

Contrary to my BROTHER BLACK, I think the fact that Congress in prohibiting secondary consumer picketing has acted with a discriminating eye is the very thing that renders this provision invulnerable to constitutional attack. That Congress has permitted other picketing which is likely to have effects beyond those resulting from the "communicative" aspect of picketing does not, of course, in any way lend itself to the conclusion that Congress here has aimed to "prevent dissemination of information about the facts of a labor dispute." Even on the highly dubious assumption that the "non-speech" aspect of picketing is always the same whatever the particular context, the social consequences of the "non-communicative" aspect of picketing may certainly be thought desirable in the case of "primary" picketing and undesirable in the case of "secondary" picketing, a judgment Congress has indeed made in prohibiting secondary but not primary picketing.

I would enforce the Board's order.

Problem for Discussion

Employees of Bond Bakery, represented by the Bakers Union, are on strike for higher wages. A representative of the Union approaches the manager of Acme Supermarket and requests that he cease stocking Bond Bread. The representative informs the manager that if he does not comply, the Union will distribute handbills in front of Acme to Acme customers. He shows the manager a sample handbill which reads: "Acme sells Bond Bread. Bond employees on strike. Do not patronize Acme Supermarket." The manager refuses to comply. The Union responds by distributing handbills only at customer entrances and by taking out a full-page advertisement in the local newspaper. This activity turns away customers and induces two deliverymen not to complete deliveries to Acme. Do any of the Union's activities violate Section 8(b)(4)(B)?

In NLRB v. Retail Store Employees Union, Local 1001 (Safeco Title Ins. Co.), 447 U.S. 607, 100 S.Ct. 2372, 65 L.Ed.2d 377 (1980), the Supreme Court retreated somewhat from the broad permission given in *Tree Fruits* to product picketing at the secondary site. Safeco Title Insurance Company did business with five small title companies, which searched land titles, performed escrow services and sold title insurance; over 90 percent of their gross incomes derived from the sale of Safeco insurance. When contract negotiations between Safeco and the Union reached an impasse, the employees went on strike and picketed not only at Safeco's office in Seattle but also at each of the five local title companies. Handbills (the legality of which was not contested) were distributed asking consumers to cancel their Safeco policies; the picket signs, which were challenged through charges under Section 8(b)(4)(ii) (B), declared that Safeco had no contract with the Union. The Board held that since the Safeco insurance policies accounted for substantially all of the title companies' business, the picketing was calculated to induce customers not to patronize the neutral title companies at all. The court of appeals, en banc, refused to enforce the Board's order, holding that picketing appeals limited to the primary product were lawful, regardless of the severity of the consequences to the neutral. A divided Supreme Court reversed and remanded for enforcement of the Board's order.

The Court noted the distinction in *Tree Fruits* between picketing which shuts off all trade with the secondary employer unless that employer aids the union in its dispute with the primary employer, and picketing which merely persuades the customers of the secondary employer not to buy the struck product; the former is unlawful, but the latter is not. The Court observed, however, that in many instances the effects of product picketing and of a total secondary boycott may be the same; it gave the illustration of picketing appeals at a housing subdivision (the neutral) urging prospective purchasers not to buy the houses built by the primary employer, a general contractor. The Court concluded that in the clash of interests between the neutral employer and a union seeking to picket at a "one-product secondary site," Congress decided that the former should prevail. Unlike *Tree Fruits*, where the picketing was directed against one item of many being sold by the neutral retailer, and where the union's success would result in declining sales of only the boycotted product, "secondary picketing against consumption of the

primary product [purveyed by the title companies, i. e., the Safeco insurance] leaves responsive consumers no realistic option other
than to boycott the title companies altogether"; the title companies
stop using Safeco insurance "not because of a falling demand, but in
response to pressure designed to inflict injury on [their] business
generally."

The Court majority therefore concluded: "Product picketing
that reasonably can be expected to threaten neutral parties with
ruin or substantial loss simply does not square with the language or
the purpose of § 8(b)(4)(ii)(B). Since successful secondary picketing would put the title companies to a choice between their survival
and the severance of their ties with Safeco, the picketing plainly
violates the statutory ban on the coercion of neutrals" with the object of forcing them to cease doing business with the primary employer. The Court also concluded that such a statutory ban upon
the total boycott of a neutral "imposes no impermissible restrictions upon constitutionally protected speech."

In a particularly significant footnote, the Court majority speculated on how its newly announced rule would be applied: "If secondary picketing were directed against a product representing a
major portion of a neutral's business, but significantly less than
that represented by a single dominant product, neither *Tree Fruits*
nor today's decision necessarily would control. The critical question
would be whether, by encouraging customers to reject the struck
product, the secondary appeal is reasonably likely to threaten the
neutral party with ruin or substantial loss. Resolution of the question in each case will be entrusted to the Board's expertise."

In separate concurring opinions, Justices Blackmun and Stevens, criticizing the perfunctory manner in which the Court majority had rejected the constitutional challenge, set forth more detailed
reasons for so holding. Justice Blackmun believed that Congress
had given effect to substantial governmental interests by striking a
"delicate balance between union freedom of expression and the
ability of neutral employers, employees, and consumers to remain
free from coerced participation in industrial strife." Justice Stevens
emphasized the greater governmental freedom in regulating picketing than, for example, handbilling; the former depends more on
the persuasiveness of the picket's physical presence and "calls for
an automatic response to a signal, rather than a reasoned response
to an idea." The Congressional ban sustained in this case is, moreover, limited in geographical scope and is "sufficiently justified by
the purpose to avoid embroiling neutrals in a third party's labor
dispute."

Justice Brennan dissented, for himself and Justices White and
Marshall. He believed the product picketing at the title companies

to have been lawful under *Tree Fruits,* since the appeal did not attempt to induce a boycott of any product originating from nonprimary sources. "The *Tree Fruits* test reflects the distinction between economic damage sustained by the secondary firm solely by virtue of its dependence upon the primary employer's goods, and injuries inflicted upon interests of the secondary firm that are unrelated to the primary dispute—injuries that are calculated to influence the secondary retailer's conduct with respect to the primary dispute." The latter pressure places the economic interests of the secondary employer in jeopardy beyond the extent of the risk it has assumed by handling the primary employer's product, and spreads the disruptive impact of the primary dispute even to other businesses which sell nonprimary products to the secondary retailer. Justice Brennan attempted to point out other failings in the Court's analysis: the extent of harm to the neutral's business, and hence the coercion to cease dealing with the primary, is not necessarily congruent with the percentage of the secondary firm's business made up by the primary product; a single-product retailer will be badly harmed economically by a successful primary boycott, even when there is no appeal at the neutral site at all; whatever the percentage of its business constituted by the primary product, the neutral "necessarily assumes the risks of interrupted supply or declining sales" flowing from the manufacturer's labor problems; and the vague standard announced by the Court leaves a union uncertain, at least without access to the neutral's balance sheets, whether its product boycott will be lawful.

Problems for Discussion

1. Is the Court's reasoning in *Safeco* intelligible? Why should it be unlawful to employ product picketing to inflict economic injury on the neutral retailer precisely comparable to that which would flow from a successful strike at the primary company?

2. Is the Court's standard in *Safeco* for lawful product picketing (absence of "ruin or substantial loss" for the neutral retailer) intelligible? What facts must be available to the union's counsel in order that he or she may provide sound advice on whether product picketing may be carried out at the secondary site? (Will those facts likely be available?) Considering that peaceful product picketing which is found unlawful under *Safeco* may be enjoined, and may lead to substantial compensatory damage awards under Section 303, is the vagueness of the Court's standard subject to serious challenge under the First Amendment to the Federal Constitution (an issue not directly addressed by the Court)?

3. The United Steelworkers are on strike against the Bay Refining Division of Dow Chemical Co., which produces Bay Gasoline. The Steelworkers picket three gasoline stations which sell Bay Gas, carrying signs

which read: "BOYCOTT BAY GAS" and "BAY GAS MADE BY SCABS." The three stations are owned by Central Michigan Petroleum, Inc., Rupp Oil Co., and Alexander, Inc., respectively. Dow does not own any interest in or exert any control over any of the three stations. The Central Michigan station earns 98% of its revenues from the sale of Bay Gas and other Dow products. The Rupp station is also a General Tire dealership and earns 85% of its revenues from the sale of Dow products. The Alexander station is also a General Tire dealership and in addition sells another brand of fuel; 60% of its revenues are earned from the sale of gas, and 75% of gas sales are sales of Bay Gas. Does the picketing of any or all of these stations violate Section 8(b)(4)(B)? See *Local 14055, Steelworkers v. NLRB (Dow Chemical Co.)*, 524 F.2d 853 (D.C.Cir. 1975), vacated and remanded, 429 U.S. 807, 97 S.Ct. 42, 50 L.Ed.2d 68 (1976), complaint dismissed, 229 N.L.R.B. 302 (1977).

4. Could a union engaged in a dispute with a refrigeration company lawfully pass out handbills to customers of a supermarket (or picket there), if the supermarket utilizes the services of the company to install and repair refrigeration facilities? See *Local 142, Plumbers Union*, 133 N.L.R.B. 307 (1961).

Would it be legal for that supermarket to be picketed by striking employees of the company which supplies the supermarket with paper bags? How should the picket signs be worded to maximize the union's chances for success? See *Kroger Co. v. NLRB*, 647 F.2d 634 (6th Cir. 1980).

5. Would it be lawful for striking employees of a meat packing company to picket in front of a retail supermarket, or in front of a fast-food hamburger store, pointing out that the "scab meat" is part of the hamburger meat being sold in the supermarket or being consumed in the store? Compare *Amalgamated Packinghouse Workers (Packerland Packing Co.)*, 218 N.L.R.B. 853 (1975), with *Local 248, Meat Cutters (Milwaukee Meat Packers Ass'n)*, 230 N.L.R.B. 189 (1977).

3.   Hot Cargo Clauses [17]

Suppose that the Teamsters Union succeeded in persuading all the trucking concerns in a given area to agree that they would not require their employees to handle the goods of any employer who became involved in a labor dispute. If a labor dispute arose involving the ABC

17. See Comment, Hot Cargo Clauses: The Scope of Section 8(e), 71 Yale L.J. 158 (1961); Comment, Subcontracting Clauses and Section 8(e) of the National Relations Act, 62 Mich. L.Rev. 1176 (1964); Feldacker, Subcontracting Restrictions and the Scope of Sections 8(b)(4)(A) and (B) and of 8(e) of the National Labor Relations Act, 17 Lab.L.J. 170 (1966); Hickey, Subcontracting Clauses Under Section 8(e) of the NLRA, 40 Notre Dame Lawyer 377 (1965); Lesnick, Job Security and Secondary Boycotts: The Reach of NLRA §§ 8(b)(4) and 8(e), 113 U.Pa.L.Rev. 1000 (1965); Note, A Rational Approach to Secondary Boycotts and Work Preservation, 57 Va.L.Rev. 1280 (1971); St. Antoine, Secondary Boycotts and Hot Cargo: A Study in Balance of Power, 40 U. Det.L.J. 189 (1962); Shalov, The Landrum-Griffin Amendments: Labor's Use of the Secondary Boycott, 45 Corn.L.Q. 724 (1960).

Furniture Store, would it be an unfair labor practice for the Teamsters to induce the trucking employees to refuse to handle ABC furniture in view of the agreements signed with their employers? For six or seven years, these "hot cargo" agreements were held to legitimize the secondary boycott, but in 1957 the Supreme Court held that such clauses could not serve as a valid defense in a case such as the one just described. LOCAL 1976, CARPENTERS v. NLRB (SAND DOOR & PLYWOOD CO.), 357 U.S. 93, 78 S.Ct. 1011, 2 L.Ed.2d 1186 (1958). On the other hand, said the Court, if the truckers were to abide by their agreements voluntarily, without the Teamsters having to induce their employees not to work, there would be only a primary boycott rather than a violation of the Taft-Hartley Act.

Many observers felt that this was an impractical distinction. The effect upon the furniture company was the same whether or not the union induced the employees of the truckers not to handle the goods. Furthermore, one might wonder how voluntary was the truckers' participation in the primary boycott. Would a "hot cargo" agreement have been signed in the first place except under pressure from the Teamsters, and if a trucker should abide by the agreement when the occasion arose, was this not so because he feared that if he did not comply the Teamsters would be more demanding in the next negotiations or might remind the trucker of his failure to perform his part of the contract whenever he asked the union to help put a stop to a wildcat strike? The only way to deal with such pressures was to nip them in the bud by prohibiting the agreements themselves. This was the theory upon which the Senate voted to outlaw "hot cargo" contracts in the trucking industry during the deliberations preceding the 1959 amendments to the NLRA. In the House the prohibition was extended to all agreements by which an employer agrees with a labor organization not to handle or use the goods of another person. Eventually, a decision was reached to enact what is now Section 8(e) of the National Labor Relations Act.

NATIONAL WOODWORK MFR'S ASS'N v. NLRB

Supreme Court of the United States, 1967.
386 U.S. 612, 87 S.Ct. 1250, 18 L.Ed.2d 357.

MR. JUSTICE BRENNAN delivered the opinion of the Court.
* * *

Frouge Corporation, a Bridgeport, Connecticut concern, was the general contractor on a housing project in Philadelphia. Frouge had a collective bargaining agreement with the Carpenters' International Union under which Frouge agreed to be bound by the rules and regulations agreed upon by local unions with contractors in areas in which Frouge had jobs. Frouge was therefore subject to the provision of a collective bargaining agreement between the Union and an organization of Philadelphia contractors, the General Building Contractors Association, Inc. A sentence in a provision of that agreement entitled Rule 17 provides that " * * * no member of the District Council will handle * * * any doors * * * which have been fitted prior to being furnished on the job. * * * " Frouge's Philadelphia project called for 3,600 doors. Customarily, before the doors could be hung on such projects, "blank" or "blind" doors would be mortised for the knob, routed for the hinges, and beveled to make them fit between jambs. These are tasks traditionally performed in the Philadelphia area by the carpenters employed on the jobsite. However, precut and prefitted doors ready to hang may be purchased from door manufacturers. Although Frouge's contract and job specifications did not call for premachined doors, and "blank" or "blind" doors could have been ordered, Frouge contracted for the purchase of premachined doors from a Pennsylvania door manufacturer which is a member of the National Woodwork Manufacturers Association, petitioner in No. 110 and respondent in No. 111. The Union ordered its carpenter members not to hang the doors when they arrived at the jobsite. Frouge thereupon withdrew the prefabricated doors and substituted "blank" doors which were fitted and cut by his carpenters on the job-site.

The National Woodwork Manufacturers Association and another filed charges with the National Labor Relations Board against the Union alleging that by including the "will not handle" sentence of Rule 17 in the collective bargaining agreement the Union committed the unfair labor practice under § 8(e) of entering into an "agreement * * * whereby * * * [the] * * * employer * * * agrees to cease or refrain from handling * * * any of the products of any other employer * * *," and alleging further that in enforcing the sentence against Frouge, the Union committed the unfair labor practice under § 8(b) (4) (B) of "forcing or requiring any person to cease using * * * the products of any other * * * manufacturer * * *." The National Labor Relations Board dismissed the charges, 149 N.L.R.B. 646. The Board adopted the findings of the Trial Examiner that the "will not handle" sentence in Rule 17 was language used by the parties to protect and preserve cutting out and fitting as unit work to be performed by the jobsite carpenters. * * * The Court of Appeals for the Seventh Circuit reversed the Board. * * * We granted certiorari. * * *

I.

Even on the doubtful premise that the words of § 8(e) unambiguously embrace the sentence of Rule 17, this does not end inquiry into Congress' purpose in enacting the section. It is a "familiar rule, <u>that a thing may be within the letter of the statute and yet</u> <u>not within the statute, because not within its spirit nor within the in-</u> <u>tention of its makers.</u>"   Holy Trinity Church v. United States, 143 U.S. 457, 459.   * * *

Strongly held opposing views have invariably marked controversy over labor's use of the boycott to further its aims by involving an employer in disputes not his own.   But congressional action to deal with such conduct has stopped short of proscribing identical activity having the object of pressuring the employer for agreements regulating relations between him and his own employees.   That Congress meant §§ 8(e) and 8(b) (4) (B) to prohibit only "secondary" objectives clearly appears from an examination of the history of congressional action on the subject; we may, by such an examination, "reconstitute the gamut of values current at the time when the words were uttered."

[The Court then traced the outlawry of the secondary boycott under the Sherman Act, its protection under the Norris-LaGuardia Act, and its outlawry once again under what is now Section 8(b) (4) (B); it emphasized that the latter section was directed at the secondary boycott as conventionally defined, that is, union pressure on a "neutral" employer to induce it to cease doing business with a "primary" employer with whom the union has its dispute.]

Despite this virtually overwhelming support for the limited reading of § 8(b) (4) (A), the Woodwork Manufacturers Association relies on Allen Bradley Co. v. Local Union No. 3, etc., Electrical Workers, 325 U.S. 797, 65 S.Ct. 1533, as requiring that the successor section, § 8(b) (4) (B), be read as proscribing the District Council's conduct in enforcing the "will not handle" sentence of Rule 17 against Frouge.   The Association points to the references to *Allen Bradley* in the legislative debates leading to the enactment of the predecessor § 8(b) (4) (A).   We think that this is an erroneous reading of the legislative history.   *Allen Bradley* held violative of the antitrust laws a combination between Local 3 of the International Brotherhood of Electrical Workers and both electrical contractors and manufacturers of electrical fixtures in New York City to restrain the bringing in of such equipment from outside the city.   The contractors obligated themselves to confine their purchases to local manufacturers, who in turn obligated themselves to confine their New York City sales to contractors employing members of the local, this scheme supported by threat of boycott by the contractors' employees.   While recognizing that the union might have had an immunity for its contribution to the trade boycott had it acted alone, citing *Hutcheson,* supra, <u>the Court held immunity was not intended</u> <u>by the Clayton or Norris-LaGuardia Acts in cases in which the</u>

union's activity was part of a larger conspiracy to abet contractors and manufacturers to create a monopoly.

The argument that the references to *Allen Bradley* in the debates over § 8(b) (4) (A) have broader significance in the determination of the reach of that section is that there was no intent on Local 3's part to influence the internal labor policies of the boycotted out-of-state manufacturers of electrical equipment. There are three answers to this argument: *First*, the boycott of out-of-state electrical equipment by the electrical contractors' employees was not in pursuance of any objective relating to pressuring their employers in the matter of *their* wages, hours, and working conditions; there was no work preservation or other primary objective related to the union employees' relations with their contractor employers. On the contrary, the object of the boycott was to secure benefits for the New York City electrical manufacturers and their employees. "This is a secondary object because the cessation of business was being used tactically, with an eye to its effect on conditions elsewhere." *Second*, and of even greater significance on the question of the inferences to be drawn from the references to *Allen Bradley*, Senator Taft regarded the Local 3 boycott as in effect saying, "We will not permit any material made by any other union or by any non-union workers to come into New York City and be put into any building in New York City." 93 Cong.Rec. 4199, II 1947 Leg.Hist. 1107. This clearly shows that the Senator viewed the pressures applied by Local 3 on the employers of its members as having solely a secondary objective. The Senate Committee Report echoes the same view:

> "[It is] an unfair labor practice for a union to engage in the type of secondary boycott that has been conducted in New York City by local No. 3 of the IBEW, whereby electricians have refused to install electrical products of manufacturers employing electricians who are members of *some other labor organization other than local No. 3.*" S. Rep. No. 105, 80th Cong., 1st Sess., 22, I 1947 Leg.Hist. 428. (Emphasis supplied.)

Other statements on the floor of Congress repeat the same refrain. *Third*, even on the premise that Congress meant to prohibit boycotts such as that in *Allen Bradley* without regard to whether they were carried on to affect labor conditions elsewhere, the fact is that the boycott in *Allen Bradley* was carried on not as a shield to preserve the jobs of Local 3 members, traditionally a primary labor activity, but as a sword, to reach out and monopolize all the manufacturing job tasks for Local 3 members. It is arguable that Congress may have viewed the use of the boycott as a sword as different from labor's traditional concerns with wages, hours, and working conditions. But the boycott in the present case was not used as a sword; it was a shield carried solely to preserve the members' jobs. We therefore have no occasion today to decide the questions which might arise where the workers carry on a boycott to reach out to monopolize jobs or acquire new job tasks when their own jobs are not threatened by the boycotted product. * * *

In effect Congress, in enacting § 8(b) (4) (A) of the Taft-Hartley Act, returned to the regime of *Duplex Printing Press Co.* and *Bedford Stone Cutters,* supra, and barred as a secondary boycott union activity directed against a neutral employer, including the immediate employer when in fact the activity directed against him was carried on for its effect elsewhere.

Indeed, Congress in rewriting § 8(b) (4) (A) as § 8(b) (4) (B) took pains to confirm the limited application of the section to such "secondary" conduct. The word "concerted" in former § 8(b) (4) (A) was deleted to reach secondary conduct directed to only one individual. This was in response to the Court's holding in National Labor Relations Board v. International Rice Milling Co., 341 U.S. 665, 71 S.Ct. 961, that "concerted" required proof of inducement of two or more employees. But to make clear that the deletion was not to be read as supporting a construction of the statute as prohibiting the incidental effects of traditional primary activity, Congress added the proviso that nothing in the amended section "shall be construed to make unlawful, where not otherwise unlawful, any primary strike or primary picketing." Many statements and examples proffered in the 1959 debates confirm this congressional acceptance of the distinction between primary and secondary activity.

II.

The Landrum-Griffin Act amendments in 1959 were adopted only to close various loopholes in the application of § 8(b) (4) (A) which had been exposed in Board and court decisions. * * *

Section 8(e) simply closed still another loophole. In Local 1976, United Brotherhood of Carpenters, etc. v. National Labor Relations Board (Sand Door), 357 U.S. 93, 78 S.Ct. 1011, the Court held that it was no defense to an unfair labor practice charge under § 8(b) (4) (A) that the struck employer had agreed, in a contract with the union, not to handle nonunion material. However, the Court emphasized that the mere execution of such a contract provision (known as a "hot cargo" clause because of its prevalence in Teamsters Union contracts), or its voluntary observance by the employer, was not unlawful under § 8(b) (4) (A). Section 8(e) was designed to plug this gap in the legislation by making the "hot cargo" clause itself unlawful. The *Sand Door* decision was believed by Congress not only to create the possibility of damage actions against employers for breaches of "hot cargo" clauses, but also to create a situation in which such clauses might be employed to exert subtle pressures upon employers to engage in "voluntary" boycotts. Hearings in late 1958 before the Senate Select Committee explored seven cases of "hot cargo" clauses in Teamster union contracts, the use of which the Committee found conscripted neutral employers in Teamster organizational campaigns.

This loophole closing measure likewise did not expand the type of conduct which § 8(b) (4) (A) condemned. Although the language of § 8(e) is sweeping, it closely tracks that of § 8(b) (4) (A), and just as the latter and its successor § 8(b) (4) (B) did not reach employees' activity to pressure their employer to preserve for themselves work traditionally done by them, § 8(e) does not prohibit agreements made and maintained for that purpose.

The legislative history of § 8(e) confirms this conclusion. The Kennedy-Ervin bill as originally reported proposed no remedy for abuses of the "hot cargo" clauses revealed at the hearings of the Select Committee. Senators Goldwater and Dirksen filed a minority report urging that a prohibition against "hot cargo" clauses should be enacted to close that loophole. Their statement expressly acknowledged their acceptance of the reading of § 8(b) (4) (A) as applicable only "to protect genuinely neutral employers and their employees, not themselves involved in a labor dispute, against economic coercion designed to give a labor union victory in a dispute with some other employer." They argued that a prohibition against "hot cargo" clauses was necessary to further that objective. They were joined by Senator McClellan, Chairman of the Select Committee, in their proposal to add such a provision. Their statements in support consistently defined the evil to be prevented in terms of agreements which obligated neutral employers not to do business with other employers involved in labor disputes with the union. Senator Gore initially proposed, and the Senate first passed, a "hot cargo" amendment to the Kennedy-Ervin bill which outlawed such agreements only for "common carriers subject to Part II of the Interstate Commerce Act." This reflected the testimony at the Select Committee hearings which attributed abuses of such clauses primarily to the Teamsters Union. Significantly, such alleged abuses by the Teamsters invariably involved uses of the clause to pressure neutral trucking employers not to handle goods of other employers involved in disputes with the Teamsters Union.

The House Labor Committee first reported out a bill containing a provision substantially identical to the Gore amendment. The House Report expressly noted that since that proposal tracked the language of § 8(b) (4) (A) "it preserved the established distinction between primary activities and secondary boycotts." The substitute Landrum-Griffin bill, however, expanded the proposal to cover all industry and not common carriers alone. * * * An analysis of the substitute bill submitted by Representative Griffin referred to the need to plug the various loopholes in the "secondary boycott" provisions, one of which is the "hot cargo" agreement. In Conference Committee, the Landrum-Griffin application to all industry, and not just to common carriers, was adopted. * * *

In addition to all else, "the silence of the sponsors of [the] Amendments is pregnant with significance * * *." National Labor Relations Board v. Fruit & Vegetable Packers, etc., supra, 377 U.S. at 66, 84 S.Ct. at 1068. Before we may say that Congress meant to strike from workers' hands the economic weapons traditionally used against their employers' efforts to abolish their jobs, that meaning should plainly appear. "[I]n this era of automation and onrushing technological change, no problems in the domestic economy are of greater concern than those involving job security and employment stability. Because of the potentially cruel impact upon the lives and fortunes of the working men and women of the Nation, these problems have understandably engaged the solicitous attention of government, of responsible private business, and particularly of organized labor." Fibreboard Paper Prods. Corp. v. National Labor Relations Board, 379 U.S. 203, 225, 85 S.Ct. 398, 411, 13 L.Ed.2d 233 (concurring opinion of Stewart, J.). We would expect that legislation curtailing the ability of management and labor voluntarily to negotiate for solutions to these significant and difficult problems would be preceded by extensive congressional study and debate, and consideration of voluminous economic, scientific, and statistical data. The silence regarding such matters in the Eighty-sixth Congress is itself evidence that Congress, in enacting § 8(e), had no thought of prohibiting agreements directed to work preservation * * *.

Moreover, our decision in *Fibreboard Paper Prods. Corp.,* supra implicitly recognizes the legitimacy of work preservation clauses like that involved here. Indeed, in the circumstances presented in *Fibreboard,* we held that bargaining on the subject was made mandatory by § 8(a) (5) of the Act, concerning as it does "terms and conditions of employment." *Fibreboard* involved an alleged refusal to bargain with respect to the contracting-out of plant maintenance work previously performed by employees in the bargaining unit. * * * It would therefore be incongruous to interpret § 8(e) to invalidate clauses over which the parties may be mandated to bargain and which have been successfully incorporated through collective bargaining in many of this Nation's major labor agreements.

Finally, important parts of the historic accommodation by Congress of the powers of labor and management are §§ 7 and 13 of the

National Labor Relations Act. * * * Section 13 preserves the right to strike, of which the boycott is a form, except as specifically provided in the Act. In the absence of clear indicia of congressional intent to the contrary, these provisions caution against reading statutory prohibitions as embracing employee activities to pressure their own employers into improving the employees' wages, hours, and working conditions. * * *

The Woodwork Manufacturers Association and *amici* who support its position advance several reasons, grounded in economic and technological factors, why "will not handle" clauses should be invalid in all circumstances. Those arguments are addressed to the wrong branch of government. * * *

III.

The determination whether the "will not handle" sentence of Rule 17 and its enforcement violated § 8(e) and § 8(b) (4) (B) cannot be made without an inquiry into whether, under all the surrounding circumstances, the Union's objective was preservation of work for Frouge's employees, or whether the agreements and boycott were tactically calculated to satisfy union objectives elsewhere. Were the latter the case, Frouge, the boycotting employer, would be a neutral bystander, and the agreement or boycott would, within the intent of Congress, become secondary. There need not be an actual dispute with the boycotted employer, here the door manufacturer, for the activity to fall within this category, so long as the tactical object of the agreement and its maintenance is that employer, or benefits to other than the boycotting employees or other employees of the primary employer thus making the agreement or boycott secondary in its aim. The touchstone is whether the agreement or its maintenance is addressed to the labor relations of the contracting employer *vis-à-vis* his own employees. This will not always be a simple test to apply. But "[h]owever difficult the drawing lines more nice than obvious, the statute compels the task." Local 761, Inter. Union of Electrical, etc., Workers v. National Labor Relations Board, 366 U.S. 667, 674, 81 S.Ct. 1285, 1290.

That the "will not handle" provision was not an unfair labor practice in this case is clear. The finding of the Trial Examiner, adopted by the Board, was that the objective of the sentence was preservation of work traditionally performed by the job-site carpenters. This finding is supported by substantial evidence, and therefore the Union's making of the "will not handle" agreement was not a violation of § 8(e).

Similarly, the Union's maintenance of the provision was not a violation of § 8(b) (4) (B). The Union refused to hang prefabricated doors whether or not they bore a union label, and even refused to install prefabricated doors manufactured off the jobsite by members of the Union. This and other substantial evidence supported the finding that the conduct of the Union on the Frouge jobsite related solely to preservation of the traditional tasks of the jobsite carpenters. * * *

[The concurring opinion of MR. JUSTICE HARLAN has been omitted.]

MR. JUSTICE STEWART, whom MR. JUSTICE BLACK, MR. JUSTICE DOUGLAS, and MR. JUSTICE CLARK join, dissenting. * * *

The Court concludes that the Union's conduct in this case falls outside the ambit of § 8(b) (4) because it had an ultimate purpose that it characterizes as "primary" in nature—the preservation of work for union members. But § 8(b) (4) is not limited to boycotts that have as their only purpose the forcing of any person to cease using the products of another; it is sufficient if that result is "an object" of the boycott. Legitimate union objectives may not be accomplished through means proscribed by the statute. See National Labor Relations Board v. Denver Bldg. & Const. Trades Council, 341 U.S. 675, 688–689, 71 S.Ct. 943, 951, 95 L.Ed. 1284. Without question, preventing Frouge from using Mohawk's prefitted doors was "an object" of the Union's conduct here.

It is, of course, true that courts have distinguished "primary" and "secondary" activities, and have found the former permitted despite the literal applicability of the statutory language. See Local 761, Intern. Union of Electrical, etc., Workers v. National Labor Relations Board, 366 U.S. 667, 81 S.Ct. 1285. But the Court errs in concluding that the product boycott conducted by the Union in this case was protected primary activity. As the Court points out, a typical form of secondary boycott is the visitation of sanctions on Employer A, with whom the union has no dispute, in order to force him to cease doing business with Employer B, with whom the union does have a dispute. But this is not the only form of secondary boycott that § 8(b) (4) was intended to reach. The Court overlooks the fact that a product boycott for work preservation purposes has consistently been regarded by the courts, and by the Congress that passed the Taft-Hartley Act, as a proscribed "secondary boycott."

* * *

A proper understanding of the purpose of Congress in enacting § 8(b) (4) in that year requires an appreciation of the impact of this Court's 1945 decision in Allen Bradley Co. v. Local Union No. 3, IBEW, 325 U.S. 797, 65 S.Ct. 1533. * * * Just as in the case before us, the union enforced the product boycott to protect the work opportunities of its members. The Court found the antitrust laws applicable to the union's role in the scheme, but solely on the ground that the union had conspired with the manufacturers and contractors. Significantly for present purposes, the Court stated that "had there been no union-contractor-manufacturer combination the union's actions here * * * would not have been violations of the Sherman Act." 325 U.S., at 807, 65 S.Ct., at 1539. The Court further indicated that, by itself, a bargaining agreement authorizing the product boycott in question would not transgress the antitrust laws. 325 U.S., at 809, 65 S.Ct., at 1539. In conclusion, the Court recognized that allowing unions to effect product boycotts might offend sound public policy, but indicated that the remedy lay in the hands of the legislature * * *

Congress responded when it enacted the Taft-Hartley Act. * * * Two years after the *Allen Bradley* decision, the 80th Congress prohibited such product boycotts, but did so through the Taft-Hartley Act rather than by changing the antitrust laws. * * * It is entirely understandable that Congress should have sought to prohibit product boycotts having a work preservation purpose. Unlike most strikes and boycotts, which are temporary tactical maneuvers in a particular labor dispute, work preservation product boycotts are likely to be permanent, and the restraint on the free flow of goods in commerce is direct and pervasive, not limited to goods manufactured by a particular employer with whom the union may have a given dispute. * * *

The Court seeks to avoid the thrust of this legislative history stemming from *Allen Bradley* by suggesting that in the present case, the product boycott was used to preserve work opportunities traditionally performed by the Union, whereas in *Allen Bradley* the boycott was originally designed to create new job opportunities. But it is misleading to state that the union in *Allen Bradley* used the product boycott as a "sword." The record in that case establishes that the boycott was undertaken for the defensive purpose of restoring job opportunities lost in the depression. Moreover, the Court is unable to cite anything in *Allen Bradley,* or in the Taft-Hartley Act and its legislative history, to support a distinction in the applicability of § 8(b) (4) based on the origin of the job opportunities sought to be preserved by a product boycott. The Court creates its sword and shield distinction out of thin air; nothing could more clearly indicate that the Court is simply substituting its own concepts of desirable labor policy for the scheme enacted by Congress. * * *

In 1959 Congress enacted § 8(e) to ensure that § 8(b) (4)'s ban on boycotts would not be circumvented by unions that obtained management's agreement to practices which would give rise to a § 8(b) (4) violation if the union attempted unilaterally to enforce their observance. * * * Since, as has been shown, the product boycott enforced by the union in the case before us violates § 8(b) (4) (B), it follows that Rule 17, the provision in the collective bargaining agreement applied to authorize this same boycott by agreement, equally violates § 8(e). * * *

Finally, the Court's reliance on Fibreboard Paper Products Corp. v. National Labor Relations Board, 379 U.S. 203, 85 S.Ct. 398, 13 L.Ed.2d 233, is wholly misplaced. * * * [Unlike *Fibreboard*, which was limited to an employer's decision to contract out maintenance work within the plant,] an employer's decision as to the products he wishes to buy presents entirely different issues. That decision has traditionally been regarded as one within management's discretion, and *Fibreboard* does not indicate that it is a mandatory subject of collective bargaining, much less a permissible basis for a product boycott made illegal by federal labor law.

The relevant legislative history confirms and reinforces the plain meaning of the statute and establishes that the Union's product boycott in this case and the agreement authorizing it were both unfair labor practices. In deciding to the contrary, the Court has substituted its own notions of sound labor policy for the word of Congress. There may be social and economic arguments for changing the law of product boycotts established in § 8, but those changes are not for this Court to make.

I respectfully dissent.

NLRB v. ENTERPRISE ASS'N OF STEAM AND GENERAL PIPEFITTERS (AUSTIN CO.), 429 U.S. 507, 97 S.Ct. 891, 51 L.Ed.2d 1 (1977).[18] The Pipefitters Union signed a collective bargaining agreement with a heating and air-conditioning contractor (Hudik), providing that the threading and cutting of internal piping in climate-control units installed by Hudik would be performed at the jobsite by Hudik's employees covered by the contract; this was work traditionally performed by those employees. Hudik was then awarded a subcontract by Austin, the general contractor on a construction project known as the Norwegian Home for the Aged. Austin's job specifications, incorporated in the subcontract, provided for the installation of prefabricated climate-control units with internal piping already cut and threaded at the factory

18. See Leslie, Right to Control: A Study in Secondary Boycotts and La- bor Antitrust, 89 Harv.L.Rev. 904 (1976).

by the employees of the manufacturer, Slant/Fin. When these units arrived at the jobsite, Hudik's employees refused to install them; the union representative claimed that the use of those units was in violation of the labor contract. Austin, the general contractor, filed charges with the NLRB for violation of Section 8(b) (4)(B).

Although the Board found the labor-contract provision lawful under Section 8(e), it concluded that the refusal to handle was an unlawful secondary boycott not sheltered by the contract: the object of the work stoppage by the Hudik employees was either to force Austin not to use the units with prethreaded piping or to force Hudik to terminate the subcontract with Austin, which the Board regarded as the primary employer since it (and not Hudik) controlled the assignment of internal piping work. The court of appeals reversed, holding that the union's purpose was to force Hudik to abide by a lawful, primary work-preservation provision in the labor contract. A divided Supreme Court agreed (6-to-3) with the Board and reversed the court of appeals.

The Court (through Mr. Justice White) concluded that the jobsite work-preservation clause was lawful, but that the contract could not render lawful a work stoppage which was itself secondary and unlawful. "Regardless of whether an agreement is valid under § 8(e), it may not be enforced by means that would violate § 8(b) (4)." (The dissenting Justices agreed with this proposition, but disagreed with the majority's conclusion that the stoppage was a secondary boycott.) The key issue was whether the product boycott was addressed to Hudik's labor relations among its own employees, or whether the union's conduct was "tactically calculated to satisfy [its] objectives elsewhere" (quoting from *National Woodwork*). The Board properly followed *National Woodwork* by looking to "the totality of the circumstances" to determine whether the union's objective was exclusively that of work preservation, giving weight (albeit not conclusive weight) to the fact that Hudik lacked the "right of control" over the use of prethreaded piping at the time the union applied its pressure. "There is ample support in the record for the Board's resolution of this question. * * * It is uncontrovertible that the work at this site could not be secured by pressure on Hudik alone and that the union's work objectives could not be obtained without exerting pressure on Austin as well. That the union may also have been seeking to enforce its contract and to convince Hudik that it should bid on no more jobs where prepiped units were specified does not alter the fact that the union refused to install the Slant/Fin units and asserted that the piping work on the Norwegian Home job belonged to its members. It was not error for the Board to conclude that the union's objectives were not confined to the employment relationship with Hudik but included the object of influencing Austin in a manner prohibited by § 8(b) (4)(B)."

The dissenting Justices read *National Woodwork* to establish the principles that "If the purpose of a contract provision, or of economic pressure on an employer, is to secure benefits for that employer's own employees, it is primary; if the object is to affect the policies of some other employer toward his employees, the contract or its enforcement is secondary." But the majority disagreed: "The distinction between primary and secondary activity does not always turn on which group of employees the union seeks to benefit. There are circumstances under which the union's conduct is secondary when one of its purposes is to influence directly the conduct of an employer other than the struck employer. In these situations, a union's efforts to influence the conduct of the nonstruck employer are not rendered primary simply because it seeks to benefit the employees of the struck employer. *National Woodwork* itself embraced the view that the union's conduct would be secondary if its tactical object was to influence another employer."

The dissenters relied upon the Board's own finding that the object of the Pipefitters Union was to preserve the work traditionally done by the Hudik employees, and contended that under *National Woodwork* such work preservation is a legitimate primary objective; the work stoppage in the instant case was therefore lawful. It is inconsistent with that case to hold that, because Austin and not Hudik had the "right to control" the assignment of the work of cutting and threading the internal piping, the Union's pressure must have been directed at Austin. Hudik was by no means a "neutral." After making an agreement with its employees to satisfy their concern about work preservation, it defied those obligations by voluntarily accepting a subcontract which it knew disabled it from keeping its bargain with the union. Even after entering into the subcontract, Hudik was not a "neutral" because it was in a position to negotiate with the union about such substitutes for compliance as premium pay to replace the lost work. "In short, the agreement in this case, as the Board found, was for a primary purpose; pressure brought to compel Hudik to agree to it would have been primary; and pressure brought to enforce it when Hudik breached it, whether by ordering prefabricated units himself, as in *National Woodwork*, or by entering a contract that required him to breach it, was no less primary."

Problem for Discussion

Which, if any, of the following courses of action would be available to the Pipefitters Union to achieve their objectives in the labor contract with Hudik?

(a) File a grievance and take the case to arbitration under the appropriate provisions of the labor contract?

(b) Demand that Hudik discuss the payment of premium rates for the installation of each climate-control unit with prethreaded piping?

(c) Refuse to handle such units until Hudik agrees to incorporate such a premium-pay provision in the contract? See *Carpenters Local 742 (J. L. Simmons Co.)*, 237 N.L.R.B. 564 (1978).

(d) Picket the general contractor Austin, or the entire construction site, until the general contractor altered the specifications for the climate-control units? (i. e., Should Austin exult in its victory, and in the apparent holding of the Supreme Court that it rather than Hudik is the primary employer?)

MEAT & HIGHWAY DRIVERS, LOCAL 710 v. NLRB

United States Court of Appeals, District of Columbia Circuit, 1964.
335 F.2d 709.

WRIGHT, CIRCUIT JUDGE. The National Labor Relations Board has found that certain subcontracting clauses of petitioner's bargaining agreements and proposals are void under § 8(e) of the Labor Act, and that economic action to obtain their provisions violated § 8 (b) (4) (i) (ii) (A) and (B). The subcontracting clauses involved will be referred to as the work allocation clause,[19] the union standards clause,[20] and the union signatory clauses.[21] By votes of 3–2, 4–1, and 5–0, respectively, the Board found these clauses to be secondary, and thus unlawful. The union petitions to review and set aside the Board's decision and the Board cross-petitions for enforcement.

The union here represents truck drivers employed by Wilson, Armour, Swift, and other Chicago packing companies who deliver

19. This clause provides, in pertinent part, that truck shipments by each meat packer to its customers within Chicago be made from a Chicago distribution facility of the employer "by employees covered by this agreement."

* * *

20. This clause provides, in pertinent part, that in the event the packer does not have sufficient equipment to make all local deliveries itself, "it may contract with any cartage company whose truckdrivers enjoy the same or greater wages and other benefits as provided in this agreement for the making of such deliveries."

21. One such union signatory clause required that both shipments into Chicago, and local overflow work, be made only by carriers "party to the Central States or other Over-The-Road Teamster Motor Freight Agreement." The union acquiesces in the Board's finding that this clause violates § 8(e).

* * *

meat and meat products in the Chicago area. The factual background of the dispute, as to which there is general agreement, is well stated in the separate opinion of Chairman McCulloch of the Board:

"For at least 20 years, meat packers in Chicago have agreed with [the union] that deliveries of meat products by truck within the Chicago area would be made directly by the packers, using their own equipment driven by employees represented by [the union]. During most of this period, deliveries to customers in the Chicago area originated from the packers' plant in Chicago. Toward the end of the last decade, extensive changes in the distribution of meat products were effected as the major packers moved much of their slaughtering and processing operations outside of Chicago. The relocation of Swift, Armour, and Wilson, the three major packers, caused a sharp reduction in employment both of inside plant workers and of local drivers. Of about 330 truckdrivers employed by Swift, Armour, and Wilson at the beginning of the prior contract term in May 1958, only 80 were still employed 3 years later when negotiations began for a new agreement. Drivers employed by the packers continued to make deliveries from the remaining plant facilities in Chicago to customers within a 50 mile radius, but deliveries to customers within the same area were increasingly being made by over-the-road drivers whose runs originated from the packers' facilities outside the Chicago area. It was to the problem of recovering the jobs lost by the local drivers in the Chicago area and retaining those still performed there that the Union addressed itself in the 1961 negotiations."

The Union proposals for the bargaining agreement, which were found by the Board to violate § 8(e), include the work allocation clause which requires that all deliveries in Chicago, whether from within the city or from out of state, be made by local employees covered by the agreement. Under this provision the packing companies would be required to divide into two stages their shipments from out of state to Chicago consignees, terminating the interstate segment at the Chicago terminal.

The Board found that the delivery of out-of-state shipments to Chicago consignees was work historically performed, not by local drivers who were members of the bargaining unit, but by over-the-road drivers employed by interstate carrier. Thus, according to the Board, since such deliveries were not bargaining unit work, they could not be the subject of a clause which would allocate that work to the bargaining unit; to do so would require the packers to cease doing business, at least in part, with the interstate carriers, violating § 8 (e). In short, the Board says that the work allocation clause here provides for "work acquisition," not "work preservation," and consequently it is secondary in nature, falling outside the ambit of the cases declaring certain subcontracting clauses primary.

Resolution of the difficult issue of primary *versus* secondary activity, as it relates to this case, involves consideration of two factors: (1) jobs fairly claimable by the bargaining unit, and (2) preservation of those jobs for the bargaining unit. If the jobs are fairly claimable by the unit, they may, without violating either § 8(e) or § 8(b) (4) (A) or (B), be protected by provision for, and implementation of, no-subcontracting or union standards clauses in the bargaining agreements. Activity and agreements which directly protect fairly claimable jobs are primary under the Act. Incidental secondary effects of such activity and agreement do not render them illegal. Thus the "cease doing business" language in § 8(e) cannot be read literally because inherent in all subcontracting clauses, even those admittedly primary, is refusal to deal with at least some contractors.

Applying these principles to the work allocation clause here, we find that delivery in the Chicago area, irrespective of origin of the shipment, is work fairly claimable by the union. It has been said "that a union has always been free to bargain for the expansion of the employment opportunities within the bargaining unit." Comment, 62 Mich.L.Rev. 1176, 1190 (1964). The work here claimed is of a type which the men in the bargaining unit have the skills and experience to do. It would be difficult to deny that "[a] clause covering non-traditional work may be just as consecrated to the primary objective of bettering the lot of the bargaining unit employees and just as foreign to the congressional purpose for section 8(e) as those clauses involving only the work traditionally done within the bargaining unit." Id. at 1189.

Moreover, in the case before us, we have not work acquisition but work recapture. * * * Most of the packing houses have been moved out of Chicago, so that now most of the shipments for the area are out-of-state shipments. It is understandable, therefore, that the union, in bargaining for a new agreement, turned its attention to these out-of-state shipments in an effort to require that the last leg thereof be made by local drivers. Thus the union, under its new proposal, is attempting not only to retain jobs for local drivers, but to recapture some of the work lost by the movement of packing houses out of Chicago. Unquestionably, this work is fairly claimable by the local drivers, and their union's efforts in their behalf in that direction fall easily within the legitimate area of collective bargaining. We agree with Chairman McCulloch, joined by Member Brown, in dissenting from the opinion of the Board on this point:

"Deliveries to consignees in the Chicago area, regardless of origin, can justifiably be considered to be work of the employees within [the union's] unit. Even if it had never been customarily performed by unit members when it was part of an interstate haul, it is nevertheless so closely allied—and is in part identical—to the local deliveries previously recognized for almost 20 years to be unit work as to make bargaining about it mandatory. To hold otherwise is to say that a union may not seek to bargain with an employer either about the quantum of work, or the qualifications of its members to perform closely related work, whenever technological changes or mere changes in methods of distribution are to be effected."

Since we view this attempt on the part of the union to maintain and regain the local delivery jobs for members of the bargaining unit as a typical primary activity, we hold the work allocation clause valid under § 8(e), and economic activity to obtain it lawful under § 8 (b) (4).

The union proposal also contained a union standards subcontracting clause which read:

"In the event that the Employer does not have sufficient equipment at any given time to deliver his then current sales or consignments within the Chicago city limits, it may contract with any cartage company whose truckdrivers enjoy the same or greater wages and other benefits as provided in this agreement for the making of such deliveries." [22]

The Board's basic reason for finding the subcontracting clause illegal is its view that a work standards clause accords "the Union a veto over the decision as to who may receive the signatory employer's subcontracts" by defining "the persons with whom the signatory employer may and may not do business." This view, given primary place in the Board's decision and utilized as the major argument in its brief on this point, follows the distinction that clauses which regulate "who" may receive subcontracting work are secondary, while only clauses which regulate "when" subcontracting occurs are primary. This court has rejected that distinction in a line of cases cited in the margin.[23] We have considered the matter once more and re-adopt the principles of these cases.   *   *   *

---

22. * * * We take it that the phrase "same or greater wages and other benefits" requires only that total cost to the employer be the same or greater. Thus the temptation of cheap labor is removed without requiring details identical with the union contract.

23. * * *

Member Brown of the Board, who relied on Retail Clerks Union Local 770 v. N. L. R. B., dissented from the Board's decision that the provision here involved violated § 8(e). He said:

"In thus limiting the class of persons to whom the assigned work of the con-

tract unit may be subcontracted, the Union's purpose, so far as this record reveals, is not to limit the employer in the persons with whom he does business in order to further a dispute at another employer's establishment, or to protest objectionable conditions at another employer's establishment, or to improve the conditions of the employees of another employer. Rather, the Union's objective was to accommodate the business needs of the employer while at the same time protecting the welfare of employees in the packer bargaining unit it represents.

" * * * [This clause] recognizes realistically that situations sometimes do

To protect unit work by partially deterring such employer conduct, this clause would at least remove from the employer the temptation of cheap labor through substandard contractors. This is a usual function of a standards clause, as discussed in our prior opinions. We need not assume that an employer would use such a tactic as here discussed; it is enough that the union could fear it, and seek such a clause to prevent it.

An additional reason for the Board's decision, not argued to us in the Board's brief, but given as supporting grounds ("moreover") in the Board's opinion, is that the union's object in bargaining for this clause was to aid union members generally, rather than members of the unit. We agree that such an object is secondary. See Orange Belt District Council of Painters No. 48 v. NLRB, supra.

But a finding as to the object of one party to the contract is insufficient (standing alone) to support the conclusion that the contract itself violates § 8(e). Under § 8(e), what the Congress has prohibited are certain contract terms, and—as contrasted with § 8(b) (4) — the union's object is not an element of the unfair labor practice. To conclude that a contract term falling within the letter of § 8(e) properly falls within its prohibition, there must be either a finding that *[to violate § (e)]* both parties understood and acquiesced in a secondary object for the term, or a finding that secondary consequences within § 8(e)'s intendment would probably flow from the clause, in view of the economic history and circumstances of the industry, the locality, and the parties. * * *

Certain contracts long in force between the union and some of the Chicago packers contain the following union signatory clause: *[union signatory clause]*

"Livestock, meat and meat products for delivery by truck to a distance not exceeding 50 miles from the Chicago Stock Yards, whether to final destination or point of transfer, shall be delivered by the Company in their own equipment except when there is a lack of equipment at individual plants or branches, *and then all effort will be*

arise when the packer may have drivers of his own available but insufficient equipment to carry out his operations. In such situations, the [clause] would permit the packer to contract with a cartage company; but only when the cartage company maintains the same or better labor standards. The [clause] thus discourages the packer's use of a cartage company as a device for undermining the work and standards which the packer had agreed to maintain for his employees. Accordingly, the [clause] serves both the packer's interest in flexibility and the Union's interest in preventing that flexibility from undercutting the job security of the packer's own employees through subcontracting their work for performance under substandard conditions.

" * * * [A]s noted previously, my colleagues would agree that a no-subcontracting agreement to preserve the work of the bargaining unit employees is lawful even though it absolutely precludes subcontracting of the work to other employers. Reason would dictate a similar result here in view of the similar object of the clause under consideration and where incidental effects are even less restrictive. * * * "

made to contract a cartage company who employs members of Local No. 710. * * *" (Emphasis supplied.)

While the work allocation features of this paragraph are valid, the provision requiring or encouraging a boycott of cartage companies who do not have union contracts is a violation of § 8(e). To make the selection of subcontractors turn upon union approval bears only a tenuous relation to the legitimate economic concerns of the employees in the unit, and enables the union to use secondary pressure in its dispute with the subcontractors. We therefore hold this provision void under § 8(e).

With reference to this union signatory clause, the union raises the issue of the scope of the ban. The Board found objectionable only the provision "and then all effort will be made to contract a cartage company who employs members of Local No. 710." Nevertheless, its order ran against the entire clause. The union argues that the objectionable portion should be excised, leaving the remainder of the clause intact as a viable promise capable of enforcement in keeping with the sense of the contract. Excision of the objectionable language would give the employers greater latitude under the contract. Thus excision should be acceptable to them. And the union, certainly, would rather see the language deleted than lose the benefit of the remainder of the clause. Deletion, then would leave the total collective bargaining agreement in a state close to the actual agreement of the parties. And deletion would satisfy totally the requirements of § 8(e). Accordingly, we hold that the Board should not invalidate more of the contract than is unlawful, "where the excess may be severed and separately condemned as it can here." Labor Board v. Rockaway News Co., 345 U.S. 71, 79, 73 S.Ct. 519, 31 LRRM 2432 (1953).
* * *

Problems for Discussion

1. Consider the legality of each of the following labor-contract provisions, and whether it is necessary to have further information in particular cases. (You may assume that none of the provisions is sheltered by the clothing-industry and construction-industry provisos to Section 8 (e).)

(a) Employer shall refrain from using piping which is trimmed by any other company prior to shipment to the jobsite.

(b) Employer shall refrain from using piping which is trimmed by any other company so long as there are unit employees who are on layoff and who are competent to perform such trimming work at the jobsite.

(c) Employer shall refrain from using piping which is trimmed by any company whose employees do not enjoy the same or greater wages and other benefits as provided in this agreement for the performance of such trimming work.

(d) It shall not be a violation of this agreement nor a cause for discipline if employees refuse to work on, install or handle piping which has been manufactured by any company which does not employ members of this Union.

(e) No employee shall be required to perform any service on goods received at the jobsite which service would, but for the existence of a labor dispute involving any other company, be performed by the employees of such other company.

(f) No employee shall be required to perform any service or work on goods which have been shipped to the jobsite from or by any other company currently involved in a labor dispute.

(g) Employer shall not require any employee to cross or work behind any lawful picket line, whether at this Employer or any other employer and whether the picket line is of this Union or of any other union.

2. In *Enterprise Association,* page 776 supra, the Court majority criticized the manner in which the dissenters distinguished between primary and secondary pressure by stating: "[U]nder the theory of the dissent, * * * striking workers may legally demand that their employer cease doing business with another company even if the union's object is to obtain new work so long as that work is for the benefit of the striking employees. If, for example, Hudik had in the past used prepiped units without opposition from the union, and the union had demanded that Hudik not fulfill its contract with Austin on the Norwegian Home job—all for the benefit of Hudik employees—it would appear that the dissenters' approach would exonerate the union. * * * We disagree, for the union's object would necessarily be to force Hudik to cease doing business with Austin, not to preserve, but to aggrandize, its own position and that of its members. Such activity is squarely within the statute. Here, of course, the union sought to acquire work that it never had and that its employer had no power to give it, namely, the piping work on units specified by any contractor or developer who prefers and uses prepiped units."

Does this render no longer tenable the suggestion of the District of Columbia Circuit in the *Meat & Highway Drivers* case that work-acquisition provisions are primary and lawful if the work in question is "fairly claimable" by the members of the signatory union? Is the Supreme Court view, and the "sword-shield" distinction in *National Woodwork,* in any degree understandable, given the purposes of the secondary boycott provisions of the NLRA?

3. The Retail Clerks Union has a contract with Hughes Market which contains a clause that provides that Hughes "agrees that any employees performing bargaining unit work set forth in this Agreement, within its establishments, including employees of lessees, shall be members of [the bargaining unit of Hughes employees represented by the Retail Clerks]."

During the term of the contract, Hughes leases a portion of its premises to Saba Drugs, a prescription-writing pharmacy. Saba is completely walled off and is an entirely separate operation from Hughes, selling different products. Saba is a nonunion store. The Retail Clerks Union demands that Hughes terminate the lease with Saba unless the Saba employees join the bargaining unit represented by the Union. Hughes responds that the contract provision does not cover this situation, and that if it does it is illegal under Section 8(e).

The Union also demands that Hughes cease permitting employees of Canada Dry Corp. to stock soda in the market. During the twenty years that Hughes has been open, Canada Dry employees have always stocked their own soda when making deliveries, while Hughes employees have stocked Coca-Cola and other brand sodas. The employer concedes that this work is covered by the contract clause, but maintains that the clause violates Section 8(e).

Assume that the case comes before the NLRB on charges filed by Hughes. Should the Board sustain the validity of the contract provision as it relates to the work done by the Saba employees? (Would it be important to know whether the labor contract contains an arbitration provision?) Should the Board sustain the validity of the provision as it relates to the work done by the Canada Dry employees? Must the provision be "rewritten" in order to be valid, and ought the Board do so? See *Canada Dry Corp.* v. *NLRB*, 421 F.2d 907 (6th Cir. 1970); *Retail Clerks Local 770 (Hughes Market, Inc.)*, 218 N.L.R.B. 680 (1975).

The Clothing-Industry and Construction-Industry Provisos.

Section 8(e) excludes from its ban hot cargo clauses of two kinds: agreements by jobbers or manufacturers in the clothing industry not to subcontract work to nonunion contractors, and agreements by construction employers not to subcontract jobsite work to nonunion contractors. These two provisos in Section 8(e) have somewhat different origins and reach. In the clothing industry in the first decades of this century, manufacturers would frequently, in order to avoid unionization and higher wages, subcontract the work of cutting and sewing the fabric to "outside" contractors, whose operations were mobile, short-lived and difficult to unionize; "jobbers" also emerged, having no employees of their own but being primarily in the business of assigning work to contractors. The only practicable way for the clothing unions to improve the working conditions of the great preponderance of workers in the industry (some eighty percent worked for the contractors) was to secure agreements from the manufacturers and jobbers not to contract out work to nonunion shops. See Greenstein v. National Skirt & Sportswear Ass'n, 178 F.Supp. 681 (S.D.N.Y.1960). In realization of this economic reality, and of the integrated business relationship of the subcontractor and the manufacturer or jobber, Congress authorized hot cargo clauses in the clothing industry. Indeed, it went further and in Section 8(e) eliminated the clothing industry from the reach even of Section 8(b)(4)(B) and the totality of secondary boycott prohibitions. Thus, not only is it lawful in that industry to enter into an agreement not to contract work to nonunion shops, but it is also lawful for a union to induce a work stoppage to secure such an agreement (which would, if the agreement were illegal, otherwise violate Section 8(b)(4)(A)) and to induce a work stoppage the object of which is actually to force the manufacturer or jobber to cease doing business that it is presently doing with a nonunion contractor (which would, were it not for the expansive proviso, otherwise violate Section 8(b)(4)(B)).

Because of the frictions traditionally created by the presence in the construction industry of union and nonunion employees working side-by-side at the jobsite, Section 8(e) expressly exempts from its ban hot cargo provisions "relating to the contracting or subcontracting of work to be done at the site of the construction." If, however, the construction employer agrees to refrain from accepting at the jobsite materials made elsewhere by a nonunion company, such an agreement is not sheltered by the proviso and will be held to violate Section 8(e). Since a work stoppage to obtain an unlawful hot cargo agreement violates Section 8(b)(4)(A), a strike to obtain a hot cargo clause relating to jobsite work is lawful, while a strike to obtain a hot cargo clause relating to work done elsewhere will violate Section 8(b)(4)(A) and may be the subject of an action for damages under Section 303 of the Labor Act. In contrast to the clothing industry, there is no explicit proviso in Section 8(e) which removes altogether the construction industry from the reach of Section 8(b)(4). The significance is that a strike which is designed not to secure a hot cargo clause but to enforce it—and thus to sever immediately the business relationship between the employer and a nonunion contractor—will be banned by Section 8(b)(4)(B). This will be true even if the nonunion employer is performing work at the jobsite; the strike to compel a cessation is unlawful, but an employer agreement is lawful, as is a lawsuit or a demand for arbitration, or any other measure short of a work stoppage or threats or coercion generated by the union. NORTHEASTERN INDIANA BLDG. & CONSTR. TRADES COUNCIL, 148 N.L.R.B. 854 (1964), enf't denied on other grounds 352 F.2d 696 (D.C.Cir. 1966).

The most recent major pronouncement on the reach of the construction-industry proviso to Section 8(e) was made by the Supreme Court in CONNELL CONSTR. CO. v. PLUMBERS, LOCAL 100, 421 U.S. 616, 95 S.Ct. 1830, 44 L.Ed.2d 418 (1975). There, Plumbers Local 100, seeking to organize plumbing and mechanical subcontractors in the Dallas, Texas area, picketed at a major construction project under the supervision of general contractor Connell, until it secured an agreement that Connell would use only mechanical subcontractors whose employees were represented by Local 100. The union had no interest in organizing any of Connell's own employees and had no conventional collective bargaining agreement with Connell. Connell brought an action, under federal and state antitrust laws, to enjoin the enforcement of the hot cargo agreement and any future union picketing aimed at enforcement. The Supreme Court, although it held that state antitrust regulation was ousted by federal labor law, held that the agreement was not exempt from the federal antitrust laws since it may have eliminated competition among mechanical subcontractors on bases other than wages and conditions of employment.

The Court rejected the union's argument that the hot cargo agreement, which was expressly limited to subcontracted mechanical work to be performed at the jobsite, was within the construction-industry proviso to Section 8(e) and therefore "permitted" under the federal labor law. Turning to the legislative history of Section 8(e) and the objective of Congress to authorize hot cargo agreements designed to eliminate the need of union members to work alongside nonunion employees at the jobsite, the Court concluded that the agreement between Local 100 and the "stranger" general contractor did not fall within the shelter of the proviso. The union represented no employees of Connell who would be discomfited by working alongside nonunion mechanical employees; the agreement, while designed to assure that mechanical work would be performed only by members of Local 100, would not assure that these members would avoid working alongside other nonunion crafts at the jobsite; and the object of the agreement was not even to organize subcontractor employees at a particular jobsite but was more generally to unionize mechanical subcontractors in the Dallas area. The Court doubted that Congress intended to shelter hot cargo agreements with contractors who were "strangers" to the union, thereby giving construction unions "an almost unlimited organizational weapon" in achieving "top-down" organizing against the wishes of employees. It concluded that the authorization given by the proviso to Section 8(e) "extends only to agreements in the context of collective-bargaining relationships and * * * possibly to common-situs relationships on particular jobsites as well."

Problem for Discussion

Acme Construction Company is a general contractor engaged in the business of building homes and commercial office buildings. It has on its payroll some fifty carpenters who are represented by the United Brotherhood of Carpenters and Joiners of America. Although it uses these carpenters on most of its construction work, Acme often fully subcontracts distant projects to nonunion firms. In addition, it completely subcontracts some small local residential jobs to Smith Construction Co., whose carpenters are represented by a small independent carpenters' union.

In its latest round of contract negotiations with the United Brotherhood, Acme has received a proposal for the following provision: "Acme agrees that neither it nor any of its subcontractors at a jobsite will subcontract any work to be done at the site of construction, alteration, painting or repair of a building, structure or other work except to a person, firm or corporation which is party to a current labor agreement with the union signatory to this agreement."

Acme has consulted you and wishes to know whether it is lawful to include such a provision in its labor agreement. What is your response? See Pacific Northwest Chapter of Associated Builders & Contractors, Inc. v. NLRB (Woelke & Romero Framing, Inc.), 107 L.R.R.M. 2065, 91 CCH Lab.Cas. ¶ 12,712 (9th Cir. 1981) (en banc); Donald Schriver, Inc. v. NLRB, 635 F.2d 859 (D.C.Cir. 1980), cert. denied, ── U.S. ──, 101 S.Ct. 2058, 68 L.Ed.2d 357 (1981).

How would your analysis be affected, if at all, were the proposed clause to be presented to Acme by representatives of the independent carpenters' union after Acme subcontracts a local project jointly to Smith Construction Co. and a nonunion firm?

C. WORK ASSIGNMENT DISPUTES [24]   *Omit to 799*

NLRB v. RADIO AND TELEVISION BROADCAST ENGINEERS LOCAL 1212

Supreme Court of the United States, 1961.
364 U.S. 573, 81 S.Ct. 330, 5 L.Ed.2d 302.

MR. JUSTICE BLACK delivered the opinion of the Court.

This case, in which the Court of Appeals refused to enforce a cease-and-desist order of the National Labor Relations Board, grew out of a "jurisdictional dispute" over work assignments between the respondent union composed of television "technicians," and another union [Local 1, International Alliance of Theatrical Stage Employees], composed of "stage employees." Both of these unions were certified bargaining agents for their respective Columbia Broadcasting System employee members and had collective bargaining agreements in force with that company, but neither the certifications nor the agreements clearly apportioned between the employees

----

24. See Atleson, The NLRB and Jurisdictional Disputes: The Aftermath of CBS, 53 Geo.L.J. 93 (1964); Cohen, The NLRB and Section 10(k): A Study of the Reluctant Dragon, 14 Lab.L.J. 905 (1963); Farmer & Powers, The Role of the National Labor Relations Board in Resolving Jurisdictional Disputes, 46 Va.L.Rev. 660 (1960); Leslie, The Role of the NLRB and the Courts in Resolving Union Jurisdictional Disputes, 75 Colum.L.Rev. 1470 (1975); O'Donoghue, Jurisdictional Disputes in the Construction Industry Since *CBS*, 52 Geo.L.J. 314 (1964); Player, Work Assignment Disputes Under Section 10(k): Putting the Substantive Cart Before the Procedural Horse, 52 Texas L.Rev. 417 (1974); Sussman, Section 10(k): Mandate for Change?, 47 B.U.L.Rev. 201 (1967).

represented by the two unions the work of providing electric lighting for television shows. This led to constant disputes, extending
over a number of years, as to the proper assignment of this work,
disputes that were particularly acrimonious with reference to "remote lighting," that is, lighting for telecasts away from the home
studio. Each union repeatedly urged Columbia to amend its bargaining agreement so as specifically to allocate remote lighting to
its members rather than to members of the other union. But, as the
Board found, Columbia refused to make such an agreement with
either union because "the rival locals had failed to agree on the resolution of this jurisdictional dispute over remote lighting." Thus
feeling itself caught "between the devil and the deep blue," Columbia
chose to divide the disputed work between the two unions according
to criteria improvised apparently for the sole purpose of maintaining peace between the two. But, in trying to satisfy both of the
unions, Columbia has apparently not succeeded in satisfying either.
During recent years, it has been forced to contend with work stoppages by each of the two unions when a particular assignment was
made in favor of the other.

The precise occasion for the present controversy was the decision
of Columbia to assign the lighting work for a major telecast from the
Waldorf-Astoria Hotel in New York City to the stage employees.
When the technicians' protest of this assignment proved unavailing,
they refused to operate the cameras for the program and thus forced
its cancellation. This caused Columbia to file the unfair labor practice charge which started these proceedings, claiming a violation of
§ 8(b)(4)(D) of the Taft-Hartley Act. That section clearly makes
it an unfair labor practice for a labor union to induce a strike or a
concerted refusal to work in order to compel an employer to assign
particular work to employees represented by it rather than to employees represented by another union, unless the employer's assignment is in violation of "an order or certification of the Board determining the bargaining representative for employees performing such
work * * *." Obviously, if § 8(b) (4) (D) stood alone, what this
union did in the absence of a Board order or certification entitling its
members to be assigned to these particular jobs would be enough to
support a finding of an unfair labor practice in a normal proceeding
under § 10(c) of the Act. But when Congress created this new type
of unfair labor practice by enacting § 8(b) (4) (D) as part of the
Taft-Hartley Act in 1947, it also added § 10(k) to the Act. Section
10(k), set out below, quite plainly emphasizes the belief of Congress
that it is more important to industrial peace that jurisdictional disputes be settled permanently than it is that unfair labor practice sanctions for jurisdictional strikes be imposed upon unions. Accordingly, § 10(k) offers strong inducements to quarrelling unions to settle
their differences by directing dismissal of unfair labor practice

charges upon voluntary adjustment of jurisdictional disputes. And even where no voluntary adjustment is made, "the Board is empowered and directed," by § 10(k), "to hear and determine the dispute out of which such unfair labor practice shall have arisen," and upon compliance by the disputants with the Board's decision the unfair labor practice charges must be dismissed.

In this case respondent failed to reach a voluntary agreement with the stage employees union so the Board held the § 10(k) hearing as required to "determine the dispute." The result of this hearing was a decision that the respondent union was not entitled to have the work assigned to its members because it had no right to it under either an outstanding Board order or certification, as provided in § 8 (b) (4) (D), or a collective bargaining agreement.[25] The Board refused to consider other criteria, such as the employer's prior practices and the custom of the industry, and also refused to make an affirmative award of the work between the employees represented by the two competing unions. The respondent union refused to comply with this decision, contending that the Board's conception of its duty "to determine the dispute" was too narrow in that this duty is not at all limited, as the Board would have it, to strictly legal considerations growing out of prior Board orders, certifications or collective bargaining agreements. It urged, instead, that the Board's duty was to make a final determination, binding on both unions, as to which of the two union's employees was entitled to do the remote lighting work, basing its determination on factors deemed important in arbitration proceedings, such as the nature of the work, the practices and customs of this and other companies and of these and other unions, and upon other factors deemed relevant by the Board in the light of its experience in the field of labor relations. On the basis of its decision in the § 10(k) proceeding and the union's challenge to the validity of that decision, the Board issued an order under § 10(c) directing the union to cease and desist from striking to compel Columbia to assign remote lighting work to its members. The Court of Appeals for the Second Circuit refused to enforce the cease-and-desist order, accepting the respondent's contention that the Board had failed to make the kind of determination that § 10(k) requires. The Third and Seventh Circuits have construed § 10(k) the same way, while the Fifth Circuit has

25. This latter consideration was made necessary because the Board has adopted the position that jurisdictional strikes in support of contract rights do not constitute violations of § 8(b) (4) (D) despite the fact that the language of that section contains no provision for special treatment of such strikes. See Local 26, International Fur Workers, 90 N.L.R.B. 1379. The Board has explained this position as resting upon the principle that "to fail to hold as controlling * * * the contractual preemption of the work in dispute would be to encourage disregard for observance of binding obligations under collective-bargaining agreements and invite the very jurisdictional disputes Section 8(b) (4) (D) is intended to prevent." National Association of Broadcast Engineers, supra, n. 46, at page 364.

agreed with the Board's narrower conception of its duties. Because of this conflict and the importance of this problem, we granted certiorari.

We agree with the Second, Third and Seventh Circuits that § 10 (k) requires the Board to decide jurisdictional disputes on their merits and conclude that in this case that requirement means that the Board should affirmatively have decided whether the technicians or the stage employees were entitled to the disputed work. The language of § 10 (k), supplementing § 8(b) (4) (D) as it does, sets up a method adopted by Congress to try to get jurisdictional disputes settled. The words "hear and determine the dispute" convey not only the idea of hearing but also the idea of deciding a controversy. And the clause "the dispute out of which such unfair labor practice shall have arisen" can have no other meaning except a jurisdictional dispute under § 8(b) (4) (D) which is a dispute between two or more groups of employees over which is entitled to do certain work for an employer. To determine or settle the dispute as between them would normally require a decision that one or the other is entitled to do the work in dispute. Any decision short of that would obviously not be conducive to quieting a quarrel between two groups which, here as in most instances, is of so little interest to the employer that he seems perfectly willing to assign work to either if the other will just let him alone. This language also indicates a congressional purpose to have the Board do something more than merely look at prior Board orders and certifications or a collective bargaining contract to determine whether one or the other union has a clearly defined statutory or contractual right to have the employees it represents perform certain work tasks. For, in the vast majority of cases, such a narrow determination would leave the broader problem of work assignments in the hands of the employer, exactly where it was before the enactment of § 10(k)—with the same old basic jurisdictional dispute likely continuing to vex him, and the rival unions, short of striking, would still be free to adopt other forms of pressure upon the employer. The § 10(k) hearing would therefore accomplish little but a restoration of the preexisting situation, a situation already found intolerable by Congress and by all parties concerned. If this newly granted Board power to hear and determine jurisdictional disputes had meant no more than that, Congress certainly would have achieved very little to solve the knotty problem of wasteful work stoppages due to such disputes. * * *

The Taft-Hartley Act as originally offered contained only a section making jurisdictional strikes an unfair labor practice. Section 10(k) came into the measure as the result of an amendment offered by Senator Morse which, in its original form, proposed to supplement this blanket proscription by empowering and directing the Board either "to hear and determine the dispute out of which such unfair labor practice shall have arisen or to appoint an arbitrator to hear and determine such dispute * * *." That the purpose of this amendment was to set up machinery by which the underlying jurisdictional dispute would be settled is clear and, indeed, even the Board concedes this much. The authority to appoint an arbitrator passed the Senate but was eliminated in conference, leaving it to the Board alone "to hear and determine" the underlying jurisdictional dispute. * * *

The Board contends, however, that this interpretation of § 10(k) should be rejected, despite the language and history of that section. In support of this contention, it first points out that § 10(k) sets forth no standards to guide it in determining jurisdictional disputes on their merits. * * * But administrative agencies are frequently given rather loosely defined powers to cope with problems as difficult as those posed by jurisdictional disputes and strikes. It might have been better, as some persuasively argued in Congress, to intrust this matter to arbitrators. But Congress, after discussion and consideration, decided to intrust this decision to the Board. It has had long experience in hearing and disposing of similar labor problems. With this experience and a knowledge of the standards generally used by arbitrators, unions, employers, joint boards and others in wrestling with this problem, we are confident that the Board need not disclaim the power given it for lack of standards. Experience and common sense will supply the grounds for the performance of this job which Congress has assigned the Board. * * *

We conclude therefore that the Board's interpretation of its duty under § 10(k) is wrong and that under that section it is the Board's responsibility and duty to decide which of two or more employee groups claiming the right to perform certain work tasks is right and then specifically to award such tasks in accordance with its decision. Having failed to meet that responsibility in this case, the Board could not properly proceed under § 10(c) to adjudicate the unfair labor practice charge. The Court of Appeals was therefore correct in refusing to enforce the order which resulted from that proceeding.

Affirmed.

Problem for Discussion

Consider the following situations and determine whether any of them would involve jurisdictional strikes within the meaning of 8(b) (4) (D):

    a. A union pickets to secure the reemployment of strikers whom the employer has replaced.

    b. A union strikes to induce the employer to sign a new collective bargaining contract which includes a clause carried over from the old agreement recognizing the union's right to perform certain types of jobs.

    c. A union strikes to compel the employer to allow his own drivers to load his trucks instead of continuing to have this work done by employees of the independent warehouses from which he obtains his supplies.

In its first major decision on work-assignment disputes after the *CBS* case, MACHINISTS LOCAL 1743 (J. A. JONES CONSTR. CO.), 135 N.L.R.B. 1402 (1962), the Board enumerated some of the criteria it would utilize in resolving such disputes and indicated how it conceived of the decisional process:

> "At this beginning stage in making jurisdictional awards as required by the Court, the Board cannot and will not formulate general rules for making them. Each case will have to be decided on its own facts. The Board will consider all relevant factors in determining who is entitled to the work in dispute, e. g., the skills and work involved, certifications by the Board, company and industry practice, agreements between unions and between employers and unions, awards of arbitrators, joint boards, and the AFL-CIO in the same or related cases, the assignment made by the employer, and the efficient operation of the employer's business. This list of factors is not meant to be exclusive, but is by way of illustration. The Board cannot at this time establish the weight to be given the various factors. Every decision will have to be an act of judgment based on common sense and experience rather than on precedent. It may be that later, with more experience in concrete cases, a measure of weight can be accorded the earlier decisions."

In that case, a contractor had assigned the operation of electrically driven cranes to electricians represented by the IBEW, over the claim of the Machinists' Union that the cranes should be operated by employees in the machine shop whom that union represented. Testing the respective union claims against its newly announced criteria, the Board found that the electricians rather than the machinists were entitled to operate the cranes. The Board was cautious in the wording of its award, presumably because an award formulated in terms of union membership might have raised problems of union discrimination under Section 8(a)(3); the Board concluded, "In making this determination, we are assigning the disputed work to electricians, who are represented by the IBEW, but not to the IBEW or its members."

Problem for Discussion

Suppose that a newspaper has traditionally employed a keyboard-operated linotype machine to create type but that the paper has recently introduced a photo-composition method to perform this function. The new method involves certain skills, such as photography and darkroom work, which are familiar to employees belonging to the Newspaper Guild and the Photo Engravers. But the function of creating type has traditionally been performed by members of the Typographical Union, although these members have not previously done work requiring the skills employed in the new process. Since some of these members may well lose their jobs if they cannot perform the photo-composition work, the union has undertaken to train them for this function. Moreover, the employer is willing to assign the work to the Typographical Union. Should the Board uphold this assignment, relying principally on the threat to the jobs of the members of this union? *See Philadelphia Typographical Union, Local 2*, 142 N.L.R.B. 36 (1963).

The Enforcement of Work-Assignment Awards

Assume that in the problem just above, the NLRB awards the photo-composition work to members of the Newspaper Guild, but the employer continues to insist on assigning the work to members of the Typographical Union (who remain willing to perform the work in spite of the Board's award). What action may the Guild take in order to induce the employer to comply with the Board's award? One course of action might be to file a grievance under the Guild labor contract with the newspaper company; but even if the Guild prevails (must the arbitrator acquiesce in the Board's earlier work-assignment award?), the arbitrator's award is not self-executing, and it may take time to secure a judicial confirmation, enforceable in contempt proceedings. Alternatively does the Guild have any recourse against either the company or the Typographical Union before the NLRB itself? Has either committed an unfair labor practice by refusing to abide by the Board's award? Would either be in contempt? The Guild might decide that the most expeditious way to wrest the disputed work from the typographers is to strike and picket at the newspaper company. Is it lawful to do so?

The Supreme Court has recently spoken to these matters, in NLRB v. PLASTERERS LOCAL UNION 79, 404 U.S. 116, 92 S.Ct. 360, 30 L.Ed.2d 312 (1971): "[T]he § 10(k) decision standing alone, binds no one. No cease-and-desist order against either union or employer results from such a proceeding; the impact of the § 10(k) decision is felt in the § 8(b)(4)(D) hearing because for all practical purposes the Board's award determines who will prevail in the unfair labor practice proceeding. If the picketing union persists in its conduct despite a § 10(k) decision against it, a § 8(b)(4)(D) complaint issues and the union will likely be found guilty of an unfair labor practice and be ordered to cease and desist. On the other hand, if that union wins the § 10(k) decision and the employer does not comply, the employer's § 8(b)(4)(D) case evaporates and the charges he filed against the picketing union will be dismissed. Neither the employer nor the employees to whom he has assigned the work are legally bound to observe the § 10(k) decision, but both will lose their § 8(b)(4)(D) protection against the picketing which may, as it did here, shut down the job. The employer will be under intense pressure, practically, to conform to the Board's decision. This is the design of the Act; Congress provided no other way to implement the Board's § 10(k) decision." [Read Section 8(b)(4)(D) carefully to see why it is that the case under that section "evaporates" against continued picketing by the union which prevails in the Section 10(k) proceeding.]

Assume instead—referring again to the problem immediately above—that the Board in its Section 10(k) hearing awards the disputed work to the typographers (in accordance with the company's initial assignment), that the Guild strikes and pickets with the object of securing a reassignment, that the company's earlier-filed charges against the Guild are the subject of a Board unfair labor practice hearing, and that the Board decides that the Guild has violated Section 8(b)(4)(D). If the Guild believes that the Board has grievously erred in making its work-assignment award, can it secure judicial review of that award, and if so when? It has clearly been held that Section 10(k) awards are not directly reviewable by the federal courts, since they are not final orders; the Guild must precipitate a Section 8(b)(4)(D) proceeding by continued striking or picketing, and then must seek judicial review of the Board's cease-and-desist order in that proceeding. NLRB v. INTERNATIONAL LONGSHOREMEN'S & WAREHOUSEMEN'S UNION, LOCAL No. 50, 504 F.2d 1209 (9th Cir. 1974), cert. denied 420 U.S. 973, 95 S.Ct. 1393, 43 L.Ed.2d 652 (1975). [Examine Section 10(l) of the Act to see whether the Regional Director could seek a district court injunction against the Guild for its continued picketing. This would provide another avenue for judicial review of the Board's 10(k) award, would it not?]

In the case just cited, there was a dispute between the Longshoremen's Union and the Operating Engineers over the operation of a barge-mounted floating crane used to load logs onto ships. The Longshoremen struck when the employer assigned the work initially to the Operating Engineers, and when the employer reassigned the work to the members of the striking union, a Section 10(k) proceeding ensued and the Board awarded the work to the Operating Engineers. When the employer refused to abide by that award, the Board proceeded with its Section 8(b)(4)(D) case against the Longshoremen (because of its earlier strike), found a violation, and issued an order which it sought to have enforced in the federal court of appeals. The court said that it was constrained to adopt the Board's fact findings if they were supported by substantial evidence on the whole record, and to adopt the Board's conclusion as to work assignment unless it was arbitrary and capricious. The court acknowledged that courts of appeals "have been reluctant to deny enforcement to Board orders stemming from § 10(k) proceedings. We have been able to find only fourteen reported cases decided since *CBS* and *Jones* in which circuit courts have reviewed the merits of a § 10(k) decision. In each of these cases, the Board's work award was sustained, as the Courts of Appeals have granted the Board broad leeway in carrying out its *CBS* mandate."

Nonetheless, the court refused to enforce the Board's order against the Longshoremen. It noted how consistently the Board "always disclaims reliance upon any particular factor by asserting that the decision was made '[u]pon the entire record, and after full consideration of all relevant factors,'" and how in the instant case "the Board moved almost aimlessly from factor to factor without making explicit how much weight a particular factor was given or in some instances even which union the factor favored." The court noted that even the Board had conceded that the factors of Board certifications, industry practice, labor contracts, employer preference and Board precedent had favored the Longshoremen. It rebuked the Board for not giving weight to an arbitration award under the Longshoremen's contract holding that the disputed work was covered by that contract. [The Board does not consider itself precluded by an arbitration proceeding that does not include the adversary union in a jurisdictional dispute. Is that not a reasonable position?] The court also observed that, in spite of the great weight consistently placed by the Board on the employer's preference, it had failed to do so here. [The Board justified this by the fact that the employer's "preference" appears to have been dictated by the Longshoremen's work stoppage.]

The court concluded: "Many commentators have examined the Board's 10(k) decisions and have been dismayed by the Board's failure to articulate any decisionmaking standards. * * * While the practice may be easy and comfortable for the Board, it makes judicial review virtually impossible, because the decision is totally unprincipled. * * * The time has come, however, for the Board to accord a measure of weight to its past decisions and to establish some rational principles governing the weight that it gives

to the various factors it considers in § 10(k) hearings.   *   *   *
We do not quarrel with the Board's consistent reliance upon employer preference, collective bargaining contracts and to a lesser degree other factors.   *   *   *   What we do object to is the Board's
refusal to acknowledge the extraordinary importance of these two
factors in its § 10(k) decisionmaking process.   *   *   *   The Board
must be given the first opportunity to use its accumulated expertise
and make a principled rather than an arbitrary award of the work
in light of the correct construction of the contract.   In exercising
this discretion, it will not suffice for the Board again to merely list
the relevant factors and then come to a conclusion without explaining why it comes to that conclusion.   *   *   *   [W]hen the Board
decides that certain factors take precedence over others, it must explain why and reconcile its decisions with its past judgments.   Otherwise, § 10(k) will not bring the desired stability to the process by
which jurisdictional disputes are resolved, and the courts will be
unable to determine whether or not the Board's decisions are arbitrary and capricious."

On remand, 223 N.L.R.B. 1034 (1976), the NLRB reaffirmed
its decision to award the disputed work to employees represented by
the Operating Engineers and its conclusion that the Longshoremen
had violated Section 8(b)(4)(D).   The Board disclaimed giving undue emphasis in its work-assignment decisions to the employer's
preference, and it explained why it gave little weight to the decision
of the arbitrator under the Longshoremen's contract and little weight
to the company's preference on the facts of this case.   It made no
effort to generalize about, or to give weighted priority to, the various factors it considered in making its work assignment.   Was the
Board delinquent in failing to respond specifically to the directive
of the court of appeals to articulate a more principled decision?
Was the court unreasonable in expecting the Board to do so?

Congressional Preference for Private Resolution

Congress in Section 10(k) contemplated governmental resolution of the work-assignment dispute only as a last resort in the event
private resolution failed.   Thus, that section provides that the hearing will not proceed at all if, within ten days of receiving notice of
the filing of the Section 8(b)(4)(D) charge, "the parties to such
dispute submit to the Board satisfactory evidence that they have
adjusted, or agreed upon methods for the voluntary adjustment of,
the dispute."

This statutory language was interpreted by the United States
Supreme Court in NLRB v. PLASTERERS LOCAL UNION NO. 79,
404 U.S. 116, 92 S.Ct. 360, 30 L.Ed.2d 312 (1971).   There, Texas
State Tile & Terrazzo Company (Texas State), a construction con-

tractor engaged in the business of installing tile, had a labor contract with the Tile Setters Union and used members of that union to lay tile and also to apply mortar on floors, walls and ceilings to receive tile. The Plasterers Union, which had no contract with Texas State (which employed no members of that union), sent a letter to Texas State, claiming that the work of applying the mortar on a particular construction project then under way was the work of the Plasterers Union and not the Tile Setters. When Texas State refused to re-assign the mortaring work, the Plasterers submitted their claim to the National Joint Board for the Settlement of Jurisdictional Disputes, an arbitration panel established in 1948 by agreement between groups of building contractors and the Building and Construction Trades Department of the AFL–CIO. Both the Plasterers Union and the Tile Setters were, as members of the Building Trades Department, bound by the award of the Joint Board, which after a hearing awarded the work to the Plasterers, pursuant to a 1917 agreement and 1924 arbitration award between the two international unions. Texas State which had never stipulated to being bound by the decisions of the Joint Board did not participate in the Joint Board proceedings. It refused to respect the award to the Plasterers Union and to take the assigned work away from the Tile Setters.

When the Plasterers began to picket at the job site at which Texas State was working, charges were filed under Section 8(b)(4)(D), and the regional director promptly gave notice of a hearing under Section 10(k), in which both unions participated. Although acknowledging the Joint Board award to the Plasterers, the NLRB "after taking into account and balancing all relevant factors" awarded the work to the Tile Setters. When the Plasterers refused to abide by the 10(k) award, Section 8(b)(4)(D) proceedings resulted in a finding against them of an unfair labor practice. Cross-petitions to enforce and to review the NLRB order brought the case to the Supreme Court.

The principal contention of the Plasterers Union, in both the Section 10(k) hearing and the Section 8(b)(4)(D) proceeding, was that the NLRB could not properly hear the dispute because, under the former section, the "parties" to the dispute (i. e., the Plasterers and the Tile Setters) had, by taking the case before the Joint Board, "adjusted, or agreed upon methods for the voluntary adjustment of, the dispute." The Supreme Court disagreed, and held that the employer in a work-assignment dispute is also a "party" whose participation in "voluntary adjustment" is necessary before the NLRB is required to stay its hand. The Court pointed out that Texas State was not disinterested in the outcome of the work-assignment dispute: it had a labor contract with the Tile Setters specifically covering the disputed work (and neither employed members of the Plasterers Union nor had a contract with that Union); it thought it more efficient and less costly, and more consistent with industry practice, to use the same craft to apply the adhesive before applying the tile; and it believed that it would lose a substantial amount of its plastering work to plastering contractors if that work were awarded to the Plasterers Union. The Court concluded:

"It may be that in some cases employers have no stake in how a jurisdictional dispute is settled and are interested only in prompt settlement. Other employers, as shown by this cause, are not neutral and have substantial economic interests in the outcome of the § 10(k) proceeding. A change in work assignment may result in different terms or conditions of employment, a new union to bargain with, higher wages or costs, and lower efficiency or quality of work. In the construction industry, in particular, where employers frequently calculate bids on very narrow margins, small cost differences are likely to be extremely important. * * * The usual focus of the legislative debates [relating to Sections 8(b)(4)(D) and 10(k)] was on ways of protecting the employer from the economic havoc of jurisdictional strikes. But it does not follow from statements condemning the economically deleterious effects of inter-union strife that Congress intended an employer to have no say in a decision that may, practically, affect his business in a radical way. * * * It is clear that Congress intended to protect employers and the public from the detrimental economic impact of 'indefensible' jurisdictional strikes. It would therefore be myopic to transform a procedure that was meant to protect employer interests into a device that could injury them."

———

D.   FEATHERBEDDING AND MAKE–WORK ARRANGEMENTS [26]

"Featherbedding" is the name given to employee practices which create or spread employment by "unnecessarily" maintaining or increasing the number of employees used, or the amount of time consumed, to work on a particular job. It may take the form of minimum-crew regulations on the railroad, make-work rules such as the setting and prompt destruction of unneeded "bogus" type in the newspaper industry, stand-by pay for musicians when a radio station broadcasts music from phonograph records, or production ceilings for work on the assembly line or at the construction site. Most of these practices stem from a desire on the part of employees for job security in the face of technological improvements

---

26. See Aaron, Governmental Restraints on Featherbedding, 5 Stan. L.Rev. 680 (1953); Note, Drafting Problems and the Regulation of Featherbedding—an Imagined Dilemma, 73 Yale L.J. 812 (1964).

or, as in the case of painters going over with a dry brush pipe already painted prior to delivery to the worksite, in the face of employer subcontracting. In addition to job security, employees often justify such practices as required by minimum standards of health and safety (e. g., minimum-crew and production-ceiling limitations). These practices are "enforced" against uncooperative employees by union fines or, when there is no union on the scene, by social ostracism; and against uncooperative employers by contract remedies if the practices have been incorporated in a collective bargaining agreement and also by the use of concerted activities, such as the strike, picketing and boycott.

In spite of employee assertions that these so-called featherbedding practices are directly related to job security, health and safety, most courts at common law found these practices to be economically wasteful and without any legitimate employee justification. E. g., Austin v. Painters Dist. Council 22, 339 Mich. 462, 64 N.W.2d 550 (1954), cert. denied 348 U.S. 979 (1955) (injunction granted against refusal to work with paint rollers, found not dangerous to employee health or safety); Opera on Tour, Inc. v. Weber, 285 N.Y. 348, 34 N.E.2d 349, cert. denied 314 U.S. 615 (1941) (injunction granted against strike induced by musicians in protest against use by traveling opera company of phonograph records rather than live orchestra). It was, indeed, not until 1942 that it was definitely held that such practices and supportive concerted activities were immune against federal antitrust proceedings under the Sherman Act; the union was held to be engaged in peaceful concerted activities in a dispute relating to conditions of employment and thus protected by the Norris-LaGuardia Act and by Section 20 of the Clayton Act. United States v. American Fed'n of Musicians, 47 F.Supp. 304 (N.D.Ill.1942), aff'd per curiam 318 U.S. 741 (1943).

At about the same time, however, Congress—in protest against certain particularly serious abuses committed by the musicians' union in the broadcasting industry—amended the Communications Act of 1934 by the Lea Act of 1946 (or anti-Petrillo Act, named in dubious honor of the then-president of the union), 47 U.S.C. § 506. The Act provides for fine and imprisonment for imposing restrictions on the recording of phonograph records for broadcast and, more relevantly, for inducing radio broadcasters to employ "any persons in excess of the number of employees needed * * * to perform actual services" or to pay more than once for services performed or to pay "for services * * * which are not to be performed." (The full text is provided at pp. 806–07, infra.) Another federal statute (the Hobbs Act) makes criminal the use or attempted use of extortion of money—by "actual or threatened force, violence, or fear"—which "obstructs, delays, or affects commerce" (18 U.S.C.

§ 1951, an amendment to the Federal Anti-Racketeering Act of 1934); it has been held by the Supreme Court to outlaw threats of union force or violence designed to induce an employer to pay for unwanted services of a particular class of laborers on a construction site. United States v. Green, 350 U.S. 415, 76 S.Ct. 522, 100 L.Ed. 494 (1956). Both the Lea Act and the Hobbs Act have lain dormant for more than twenty years, unused as weapons against feather-bedding. This might be said to demonstrate both the difficulty of drafting legislation which bars the use of all featherbedding prac-tices thought generally to be objectionable, and the unwisdom of criminalizing union activities which may be separated only slightly from peaceful pressure designed to promote the job security or safe-ty of employees.

With at least some of these concerns in mind, Congress enacted Section 8(b)(6) as part of the Taft-Hartley amendments. That Sec-tion requires that a distinction be drawn between the employment of an unnecessary number of workers, all of whom perform actual services, and the payment of compensation to stand-bys. The House bill proscribed both practices: Section 12(a)(3) declared it to be un-lawful to call or engage in a strike an object of which was to compel an employer to engage in a "featherbedding practice"; the latter term was defined to include requiring an employer either (a) to employ any person "in excess of the number of employees reasonably required by such employer to perform actual services," or (b) to pay "any money or other thing of value for services * * * which are not to be performed." (H.R.Rep.No.245, 80th Cong., 1st Sess. 25, 50, 61 (1947).) The Senate conferees objected to the first of these two clauses on the ground that "it was almost impossible for the courts to determine the exact number of men required in hun-dreds of industries and all kinds of functions." (93 Cong.Rec. 6601, 6603 (June 5, 1947).) Apparently the objection prevailed, for only the second clause was carried forward into the conference agreement. Thus, the legislative history makes it clear that labor unions remain free to press for make-work devices and to oppose the introduction of labor-saving machinery, but it would be an unfair labor practice to take action to establish stand-by arrangements or otherwise se-cure payments for which no work is required.

NLRB v. GAMBLE ENTERPRISES, INC.

Supreme Court of the United States, 1953.
345 U.S. 117, 73 S.Ct. 560, 97 L.Ed. 864.

MR. JUSTICE BURTON delivered the opinion of the Court.
* * * For generations professional musicians have faced a shortage in the local employment needed to yield them a livelihood.

They have been confronted with the competition of military bands, traveling bands, foreign musicians on tour, local amateur organizations and, more recently, technological developments in reproduction and broadcasting. To help them conserve local sources of employment, they developed local protective societies. Since 1896, they also have organized and maintained on a national scale the American Federation of Musicians, affiliated with the American Federation of Labor. By 1943, practically all professional instrumental performers and conductors in the United States had joined the Federation, establishing a membership of over 200,000, with 10,000 more in Canada.

The Federation uses its nationwide control of professional talent to help individual members and local unions. It insists that traveling band contracts be subject to its rules, laws and regulations. Article 18, § 4, of its By-Laws provides: "Traveling members cannot, without the consent of a Local, play any presentation performances in its jurisdiction unless a local house orchestra is also employed."   ·

From this background we turn to the instant case. For more than 12 years the Palace Theater in Akron, Ohio, has been one of an interstate chain of theaters managed by respondent, Gamble Enterprises, Inc., which is a Washington corporation with its principal office in New York. Before the decline of vaudeville and until about 1940, respondent employed a local orchestra of nine union musicians to play for stage acts at that theater. When a traveling band occupied the stage, the local orchestra played from the pit for the vaudeville acts and, at times augmented the performance of the traveling band.

Since 1940, respondent has used the Palace for showing motion pictures with occasional appearances of traveling bands. Between 1940 and 1947, the local musicians, no longer employed on a regular basis, held periodic rehearsals at the theater and were available when required. When a traveling band appeared there, respondent paid the members of the local orchestra a sum equal to the minimum union wages for a similar engagement but they played no music.

The Taft-Hartley Act, containing § 8(b) (6), was passed, over the President's veto, June 23, 1947, and took effect August 22. Between July 2 and November 12, seven performances of traveling bands were presented on the Palace stage. Local musicians were neither used nor paid on those occasions. They raised no objections and made no demands for "stand-by" payments. However, in October, 1947, the American Federation of Musicians, Local No. 24 of Akron, Ohio, here called the union, opened negotiations with respondent for the latter's employment of a pit orchestra of local musicians whenever a traveling band performed on the stage. The pit orchestra was to play overtures, "intermissions" and "chasers" (the latter while patrons were leaving the theater). The union required acceptance of this proposal as a condition of its consent to local appearances of traveling bands. Respondent declined the offer and a traveling band scheduled to appear November 20 cancelled its engagement on learning that the union had withheld its consent. * * * [The union continued to block the appearance of traveling bands throughout the latter half of 1949, when no agreement could be reached on the union's demand that Gamble Enterprises employ a local orchestra for some number of engagements correlated to the number of traveling band appearances.]

In 1949, respondent filed charges with the National Labor Relations Board asserting that the union was engaging in the unfair labor practice defined in § 8(b) (6). [After the usual proceedings the Board dismissed the complaint, but the court of appeals reversed, holding that the union had violated Section 8(b) (6).]

We accept the finding of the Board, made upon the entire record, that the union was seeking actual employment for its members and not mere "stand-by" pay. The Board recognized that, formerly, before § 8(b) (6) had taken effect, the union had received "stand-by" payments in connection with traveling band appearances. Since then, the union has requested no such payments and has received none. It has, however, requested and consistently negotiated for actual employment in connection with traveling band and vaudeville appearances. It has suggested various ways in which a local orchestra could earn pay for performing competent work and, upon those terms, it has offered to consent to the appearance of traveling bands which are Federation-controlled. Respondent, with equal consistency, has declined these offers as it had a right to do.

Since we and the Board treat the union's proposals as in good faith contemplating the performance of actual services, we agree that the union has not, on this record, engaged in a practice proscribed by § 8(b) (6). It has remained for respondent to accept or reject the union's offers on their merits in the light of all material circumstances. We do not find it necessary to determine also whether such offers were "in the nature of an exaction." We are not dealing here with offers of mere "token" or nominal services. The proposals before us were appropriately treated by the Board as offers in good faith of substantial performances by competent musicians. There is no reason to think that sham can be substituted for substance under § 8 (b) (6) any more than under any other statute. Payments for "standing-by," or for the substantial equivalent of "standing-by," are not payments for services performed, but when an employer receives a bona fide offer of competent performance of relevant services, it remains for the employer, through free and fair negotiation, to determine whether such offer shall be accepted and what compensation shall be paid for the work done.

The judgment of the Court of Appeals, accordingly, is reversed and the cause is remanded to it.

JACKSON, J., dissenting:

* * *   [T]he Court holds that so long as some exertion is performed or offered by the employees, no matter how useless or unwanted, it can never be said that there is an exaction "for services which are not performed or not to be performed." This language undoubtedly presents difficulties of interpretation, but I am not persuaded that it is so meaningless and empty in practice as the Court would make it. Congress surely did not enact a prohibition whose practical application would be restricted to those without sufficient imagination to invent some "work."

Before this Act, the union was compelling the theatre to pay for no work. When this was forbidden, it sought to accomplish the same result by compelling it to pay for useless and unwanted work. * * * Such subterfuge should not be condoned.

MR. JUSTICE CLARK, with whom THE CHIEF JUSTICE joins, dissenting. * * *

AMERICAN NEWSPAPER PUBLISHERS ASSOCIATION v. NLRB, 345 U.S. 100, 73 S.Ct. 552, 97 L.Ed. 852 (1953). This case involved a claim by newspaper publishers that the International Typographical Union was violating Section 8(b)(6). The union insisted on the inclusion in all collective bargaining agreements of a provision for the setting of "bogus" type—that is, the setting of type and then the prompt destruction of that type in the melting box—for standard advertisements supplied to the newspapers in a form ready for direct use.

As in the *Gamble* case, the Court read the proscriptions of Section 8(b)(6) narrowly in concluding that the Union was not in violation of the Act. The Court noted that the setting of bogus type was a longstanding practice, dating back to the nineteenth century, instituted to provide job security for union members. This work was to be performed only in slack periods so that it did not interfere with other work performed by union members. The Court traced the history of the statute and concluded that the statute was aimed only at prohibiting the "exaction" of payment when no services at all were performed. Noting that Congress intended to relieve the Board and the courts of the task of determining whether workers were "reasonably required," the Court held that "Section 8(b)(6) leaves to collective bargaining the determination of what, if any, work, including bona fide 'made work,' shall be included as compensable services and what rate of compensation shall be paid for it."

Problems for Discussion

1. During contract negotiations, Bond Bakers and the Bakers' Union have reached agreement on all contract provisions except those covering severance pay, vacation pay, and call-in pay. (Production at Bond fluctuates from day-to-day depending on the number of orders Bond receives from its customers, so that some members of the bargaining unit work only when orders are high.) The union then goes on strike over those three issues. Bond files a Section 8(b)(6) charge, claiming that vacation pay, severance pay, and especially call-in pay are, by definition, payments for which no services are performed. Assuming the Regional Director issues a complaint, how should the Administrative Law Judge rule in this case?

As to severance pay, do you agree with the following statement? [27]

"It is submitted that Section 8(b)(6) should not be held to forbid a union from seeking contracts for severance pay. When an employee devotes his labor to a particular enterprise, he assumes for the benefit of his employer the risk of temporary unemployment between displacement from one job and finding another. Acceptance of this risk is an inseparable part of the services rendered. Under an agreement calling for severance pay the employer undertakes, in effect, to insure its employees against the risk, in consideration of their contribution to the enterprise. Moreover, since insecurity hampers the growth of sound plant relationships and reduces productivity, arrangements for severance pay probably increase the value of the services rendered. Thus, under Section 64 of the Bankruptcy Act any sum received by an employee as dismissal compensation 'is a part of his wage.' To place a contrary interpretation on Section 8(b)(6) would outlaw one of the most promising voluntary solutions for the problem of transitional unemployment."

2. A Teamsters local has a contract with the J.R. Stevenson Corp., a construction company, under which Stevenson promises to supply a heated trailer with a telephone to a shop steward of the union and to pay that steward $20,000 per year. Arnold Korwin is assigned by the Teamsters as the steward to work in the trailer. His only duty is to check drivers making deliveries to the construction site to make sure that they are carrying union cards. He also runs up a telephone bill of about $100 per month which Stevenson is required to pay. When the contract expires, Mr. Stevenson discharges Korwin and refuses to bargain with the Teamsters, but the Teamsters picket the construction site, halting all deliveries, until Stevenson signs a new contract and rehires Korwin. Have the Teamsters violated Section 8(b)(6)? If so, what should the remedy be? See *Local 456, Teamsters (J.R. Stevenson Corp.)*, 212 N.L. R.B. 968 (1974).

3. A 1946 amendment to the Communications Act of 1934, 48 Stat. 1064, 1102 (60 Stat. 89, 47 U.S.C.A. § 506), provided as follows:

"(a) It shall be unlawful, by the use or express or implied threat of the use of force, violence, intimidation, or duress, or by the use or express or

---

27. Cox, Some Aspects of the Labor-
Management Relations Act, 1947, 61
Harv.L.Rev. 288–89 (1947).

implied threat of the use of other means, to coerce, compel or constrain
or attempt to coerce, compel, or constrain a licensee—

"(1) to employ or agree to employ, in connection with the conduct of
the broadcasting business of such licensee, any person or persons in excess
of the number of employees needed by such licensee to perform actual services; or

"(2) to pay or give or agree to pay or give any money or other thing
of value in lieu of giving, or on account of failure to give employment to
any person or persons * * * in excess of the number of employees needed by such licensee to perform actual services * * * "

Section (b) made it unlawful to use any of the means proscribed in Section
(a) to coerce a licensee or any other person to pay any exaction for the
privilege of manufacturing, selling or using recordings or electrical repro-
ductions "or any other articles, equipment, machines or materials used or
intended to be used in broadcasting" or in preparing or presenting a program for broadcasting; or to accede to or impose any comparable restrictions for the purpose of preventing or limiting the use of such articles, etc.
in broadcasting or programs.[28]

Suppose that Section (a) were broadened to apply to all businesses
covered by the NLRA. Would the statute be constitutional as applied to a
peaceful strike or peaceful picketing? Would you favor such an amendment?

E.   VIOLENCE AND UNION RESPONSIBILITY

At one time, picketing was regarded as in itself so intimidating
as to constitute "moral coercion" akin to physical coercion and
threats of violence. Vegelahn v. Guntner, 167 Mass. 92, 44 N.E.
1077 (1896). That view has been discarded, at first by common law
judges such as Justice Holmes, then by legislatures including the
federal Congress, and later by the Supreme Court which in 1940 declared in Thornhill v. Alabama, 310 U.S. 88, 60 S.Ct. 736, 84 L.Ed.
1093 that picketing represented a form of communication of information protected by the First Amendment to the Constitution. But
serious violence to person and property will on occasion be committed
in the course of a strike or picketing, and such violence is not constitutionally immune from governmental regulation in the public interest. Milk Wagon Drivers Local 753 v. Meadowmoor Dairies, Inc.,
312 U.S. 287, 61 S.Ct. 552, 85 L.Ed. 836 (1941).

---

28. For a discussion of the activities
of the A. F. of M. against which this
statute was directed, see Countryman,
The Organized Musicians, 16 U. of Chi.
L.Rev. 56, 239 (1948–49). For a discussion of the interplay between statutory protection and collective bargaining protection for musicians displaced by recordings, see Gorman,
The Recording Musician and Union
Power: A Case Study of the American Federation of Musicians, at Committee Print No. 15, Subcommittee on
Courts of the Comm. on the Judiciary.
H.Rep., 95th Cong., 2d Sess. 1071
(1978). On strikes against labor saving devices, see Teller, Focal Problems in American Labor Law—Opera
on Tour, Inc., v. Weber, 28 Va.L.Rev.
727 (1942).

Violence during a strike or picketing may subject the union and employees to several sanctions.

First, if the employees engaging in violence are employed by the company which is their object, they may be discharged or otherwise disciplined for their misconduct which, although concerted, is not within the shelter of Section 7 or 8(a)(1) of the Labor Act. See pp. 823–25, infra.

Second, state courts may enjoin or issue a judgment of damages—compensatory and punitive—against a union or individuals found to have engaged in such violence. Criminal prosecution may also be in order.

Third, if the misconduct can be charged to a union, it may be found to violate Section 8(b)(1)(A) of the Labor Act. Thus, just as with employer violence unlawful under Section 8(a)(1), a union violates Section 8(b)(1) when its agents use physical violence— or threats of physical violence—to force an employee to engage in concerted activity which he would otherwise resist. Perry Norvell Co., 80 N.L.R.B. 225 (1948). Although, as will be considered more fully at pp. 929–33, infra, NLRB jurisdiction to regulate union activity ordinarily ousts state-court jurisdiction over the same matter, the deeply felt need for local authorities to stem violence, regardless of its coexistence with a labor dispute, has been held to warrant congruent exercise of state law with Board power under Section 8(b)(1). Ordinary principles of agency law will be invoked by the NLRB to determine union responsibility for the conduct of its agents in cases of violence. Thus, if threats to strikebreakers, or physical injury to them, are effected by officers or employees of the union within the general scope of their activities on behalf of the union—even though contrary to specific instructions—the union may be held responsible under Section 8(b)(1). LONGSHOREMEN'S LOCAL 6 (SUNSET LINE & TWINE CO.), 79 N.L.R.B. 1487 (1948) (since union business agent was acting in furtherance of the strike, and he had authority to direct the strike and picketing, union is responsible for his assault and threats against nonstrikers). Reference should also be made to Section 2(13) of the Labor Act: "In determining whether any person is acting as an 'agent' of another person so as to make such other person responsible for his acts, the question of whether the specific acts performed were actually authorized or subsequently ratified shall not be controlling."

In cases in which the union is held to violate Section 8(b)(1)(A) by causing or threatening physical violence, the Board will issue a cease-and-desist order but will not require the union to reimburse the employee victims either for loss of pay (caused by the union's blocking access to the plant) or for physical or mental injury. Although this refusal to grant monetary damages against the union is controversial and has divided the Board—particularly in cases of flagrant and aggravated violence—the Board has adhered to this policy for some twenty-five years. The reasons were recently reiterated in UNION DE TRONQUISTAS LOCAL 901 (LOCK JOINT PIPE & CO.), 202 N.L.R.B. 399 (1973). The Board noted that, while it deplores violence in the course of a strike or picketing, the award of substantial monetary damages against the union will unduly interfere with the policy of the Labor Act to protect concerted activities. Emotions run high in times of industrial combat; the violent conduct of isolated individuals might all too readily be attributed to the union; the large number of employees refraining from work will both create serious problems of proof as to the reasons therefor and generate the risk of enormous backpay liability for the union. The Board also asserted that remedies against the union for violation of Section 8(b)(1)(A) for strike violence were sufficient deterrent: the Board may ultimately issue a cease-and-desist order, court-enforceable through the contempt sanction; while the case is pending before the Board, an injunction may be sought under Section 10(j) in aggravated cases; and the union seeking to enforce its bargaining rights through violent action may be denied a bargaining order and forced to demonstrate its majority support in a secret-ballot election. Moreover, the employee suffering physical or mental injury may secure redress against the union in a state-court tort action.

Do you share the Board's reticence to award damages, in cases of union violence contrary to Section 8(b) (1), for loss of pay and for physical or mental injury to employees? Ought the Board make *some* exceptions to its absolute bar?

F. REMEDIES FOR UNION UNFAIR LABOR PRACTICES

Along with the ban upon certain union-induced concerted activities, which Congress enacted in 1947 and expanded in 1959, came the revival in modified form of the labor injunction. In view of Congress' special objection to the secondary boycott (including the hot cargo agreement), strikes in support of work-assignment demands, and unlawfully protracted recognition picketing, Congress provided in Section 10(*l*) of the Labor Act that the Regional Director is obligated to request a temporary injunction in the event a charge is filed against a union for such violations and the charge is believed by the Regional Director to have merit. (Section 10(*l*) should be studied, with attention given to the kind of union activity it reaches, the timing of the injunction request, the function of the federal district court, the limitations upon the issuance of an injunction and the procedures to be employed.)   Many cases arising from union-induced strikes and picketing are promptly handled through the injunction procedures of Section 10(l) and in many instances the injunction effectively terminates the dispute, without completion of the unfair labor practice proceeding before the Administrative Law Judge and the Board.

Union unfair labor practices not covered within Section 10(l) are subject to the injunction procedures of Section 10(j)—as are all employer unfair labor practices.   Examples of union conduct which have been enjoined under Section 10(j) are strikes initiated without complying with the notification and cooling-off requirements of Section 8(d), inducement of employer discrimination against non-members, and violence or mass picketing in violation of Section 8(b)(1).   The Section 10(j) injunction differs from that under Section 10(l) in two major respects: it may not be sought by the Regional Director until after a complaint has been issued at the Regional Office and only after authorization by the five-member Board, and—more important—the decision to petition for the 10(j) injunction lies within the discretion of the Regional Director and is not mandated by the Labor Act.   Although the federal district court will generally issue an injunction under Section 10(l) whenever it is determined that there is reasonable cause to believe Section 8(b)(4) or 8(b)(7) has been violated, the court will generally require additional proof of need for the injunction when it is sought under Section 10(j).   The requirements for issuance of the 10(j) injunction—and the fact that it is sought and issued very infrequently—have already been discussed, at pages 258–59, supra.

Not only did Congress in the Taft-Hartley amendments provide for the intervention of the federal district courts by way of injunction against union unfair labor practices, but it also took the unusual step of singling out union unfair labor practices under Section 8(b)(4) and declaring them in Section 303 to be federal torts which may be remedied by actions in federal and state trial courts for damages for past economic harm caused to the employer.   Such an action may be brought, in the case of a secondary boycott for example, either by the "neutral" employer or by the "primary" employer.   United Brick Workers v. Deena Artware, Inc., 198 F.2d 637 (6th Cir.), cert. denied 344 U.S. 897 (1952).   More generally, a cause of action has been accorded third persons who have suffered rather direct and foreseeable economic injury as a result of the union's illegal activity.   Thus, recovery was permitted for business losses suffered by an exclusive area sales agent of the primary employer in a secondary-boycott situation, even though that sales agent was not the object of the unlawful picketing.   W. J. Milner & Co. v. IBEW Local 349, 476 F.2d 8 (5th Cir. 1973).   But see UMW v.

Osborne Mining Co., 279 F.2d 716 (6th Cir.), cert. denied 364 U.S. 881 (1960). Assuming a proper party plaintiff, common law principles developed under the law of torts dictate liability in a Section 303 action for all injuries proximately flowing from the illegal conduct. Thus, the aggrieved party may recover for loss of a lease suffered because of the illegal union activity and for loss of business profits which can be ascertained with reasonable certainty, Riverside Coal Co. v. UMW, 410 F.2d 267 (6th Cir.), cert. denied 396 U.S. 846 (1969); for time and money spent in attempting to have the picketing stopped, Abbott v. Local 142 Journeymen of Pipe Fitting Industry, 429 F.2d 786 (5th Cir. 1970); and for such losses as the rental value of idled equipment and amounts paid as salaries of supervisory personnel for the period of the work stoppage, and daily liquidated damages under a contract with a third party to the extent that late performance resulted from the boycott, Wells v. Union of Operating Engineers, 206 F.Supp. 414 (W.D.Ky.), aff'd 303 F.2d 73 (6th Cir. 1962).

Both the language and the legislative history of Section 303 demonstrate that the damages under that section are to be limited, as a matter of federal law, to compensatory damages. Punitive damages may not be awarded for violation of that section. Teamsters Local 20 v. Morton, 377 U.S. 252 (1964). Nor may an injunction issue, for that form of relief may be sought or issued only by the NLRB. Amalgamated Ass'n of Street Employees v. Dixie Motor Coach Corp., 170 F.2d 902 (8th Cir. 1949). If, however, the court considers along with the Section 303 claim a proper claim for violation of state law—most commonly, for violence in the course of a strike or picketing—the court does have the power to award punitive damages or an injunction, if that would be proper under state law, but only with regard to the violent conduct under consideration as distinguished from the peaceful (although illegal) conduct of the union in violation of Section 8(b)(4).

Court remedies under Section 303 and Board remedies under Section 8(b)(4) are independent. Choosing one remedy does not constitute a waiver of the other; both remedies may be pursued simultaneously in the two different forums; and recovery under Section 303 need not await a Board determination of illegality under Section 8(b)(4). International Longshoremen's Union v. Juneau Spruce Corp., 342 U.S. 237, 72 S.Ct. 235, 96 L.Ed. 275 (1952). Indeed, it is possible that the Board will find a union not to have committed an unfair labor practice while a judge and jury will conclude that the union—in the same transaction—has violated Section 303, with both determinations being affirmed by the court of appeals. NLRB v. Deena Artware, Inc., 198 F.2d 645 (6th Cir. 1952), cert. denied 345 U.S. 906 (1953); United Brick Workers v. Deena Artware, Inc., 198 F.2d 637 (6th Cir.), cert. denied 344 U.S. 897 (1952). There has, however, been some tendency in the recent cases to conclude that a union which has been held by the Board after a full and fair hearing to have violated Section 8(b)(4) will be collaterally estopped in a later proceeding under Section 303 to challenge the Board's findings. E. g., Paramount Transp. System v. Chauffeurs Local 150, 436 F.2d 1064 (9th Cir. 1971).

III. RIGHTS OF STRIKERS UNDER THE NATIONAL LABOR RELATIONS ACT [1]

A. PROTECTED AND UNPROTECTED CONCERTED ACTIVITY

When employees engage in concerted activity, one legal issue presented is whether the union which has endorsed such activity is responsible for committing an unfair labor practice and, if so, what remedy may be imposed by the NLRB. That issue has just been considered in these materials. But not all concerted activity is union-inspired and not much of it is outlawed by Section 8(b) of the Labor Act; in many instances, the employees are less concerned with Board remedies than they are with the employer's own remedies of self-help, the most serious being discharge from employment. Although the Wagner Act was primarily aimed at guaranteeing employees the rights to form, join and assist labor organizations and to bargain collectively through representatives of their own choosing, Section 7 also guarantees "the right to engage in other concerted activities for the purpose of collective bargaining or other mutual aid or protection * * *." Section 8(a)(1) prohibits employer action which coerces, restrains or interferes with the exercise of this right. Section 8(a)(3) also outlaws employer discouragement of union membership—which has been broadly construed to encompass concerted activity protected by Section 7 in support of a labor organization—which is accomplished by "discrimination."

When employees engage in concerted activity and the employer takes some responsive action, two sorts of questions arise: First, what kinds of activities in which employees engage are protected by Section 7? Second, given employee action which is protected concerted activity, does Section 8(a)(1) or (3) make any employer act which discourages it unfair and unlawful, or only those acts

---

1. See Cantor, Dissident Worker Action, After *The Emporium*, 29 Rutgers L.Rev. 35 (1975); Cox, The Right to Engage in Concerted Activities, 26 Ind.L.J. 319 (1951); Getman, The Protection of Economic Pressure by Section 7 of the National Labor Relations Act, 115 U.Pa.L.Rev. 1195 (1967); Schatzki, Some Observations and Suggestions Concerning a Misnomer—"Protected" Concerted Activities, 47 Texas L.Rev. 378 (1969).

which interfere "unduly" or "unreasonably" or "without justification"? If the latter, is it for the Board or the courts to strike the balance? These two questions will be considered in order in this and the following section of the casebook.

As the language of Section 7 makes rather clear on its face, it is not necessary to have a union sponsoring concerted activity, or anywhere on the scene, in order that such activity be protected as "concerted activities for * * * mutual aid or protection." In NLRB v. WASHINGTON ALUMINUM CO., 370 U.S. 9, 82 S.Ct. 1099, 8 L.Ed.2d 298 (1962), the Supreme Court held that employees who had staged a spontaneous walkout because they believed it was too cold to continue to work had engaged in protected activity, even though they were not unionized or seeking to unionize and they had not presented any specific demand to their employer. The Court therefore found their discharge to violate Section 8(a)(1). Nonetheless, activity to be protected against discharge must be "concerted" and must be designed to advance the employees' "mutual aid or protection." What do these terms mean? Are they meant to confine the protections afforded by the statute, as well as to expand them?

The phrase "concerted activities * * * for mutual aid or protection" was given a generous interpretation by the Supreme Court in NLRB v. J. WEINGARTEN, INC., 420 U.S. 251, 95 S.Ct. 959, 43 L.Ed.2d 171 (1975). There, an employee was suspected of being responsible for cash shortages and was called to an interview with the store manager; the manager interrogated her in the presence of a security specialist and refused her requests to call in the union steward or some other union representative. The Board held that the employer's exertion of pressure on the employee to submit to the interview, which she had reasonable fear would result in her discipline, constituted coercion of the employee in the exercise of "concerted activities * * * for mutual aid or protection." The Court began its analysis by noting that the employee's request for assistance by the union representative was within the literal coverage of the statutory phrase. It then continued: "This is true even though the employee alone may have an immediate stake in the outcome; he seeks 'aid or protection' against a perceived threat to his employment security. The union representative whose participation he seeks is however safeguarding not only the particular employee's interest, but also the interests of the entire bargaining unit by exercising vigilance to make certain that the employer does not initiate or continue a practice of imposing punishment unjustly. The representative's presence is an assurance to other employees in the bargaining unit that they too can obtain his aid and protection if called upon to attend a like interview. Concerted activity for mutual aid or protection is therefore as present here as it was held to be in NLRB v. Peter Cailler Kohler Swiss Chocolates Co., 130 F.2d 503, 505–506 (1942), cited with approval by this Court in Houston Insulation Contractors Assn. v. NLRB, 386 U.S. 664, 668–669, 87 S.Ct. 1278, 18 L.Ed.2d 389 (1967):

> *Concerted activity for mutual aid* [handwritten margin note]
>
> 'When all the other workmen in a shop make common cause with a fellow workman over his separate grievance, and go out on strike in his support, they engage in a 'concerted activity' for 'mutual aid or protection,' although the aggrieved workman is the only one of them who has any immediate stake in the outcome. The rest know that by their action each of them assures himself, in case his turn ever comes, of the support of the one whom they are all then helping; and the solidarity so established is 'mutual aid' in the most literal sense, as nobody doubts.'

"The Board's construction plainly effectuates the most fundamental purposes of the Act. In § 1, 29 U.S.C. § 151 [29 U.S.C.A. § 151], the Act declares that it is a goal of national labor policy to protect 'the exercise by workers of full freedom of association, self-organization, and designation of representatives of their own choosing, for the purpose of * * * mutual aid or protection.' To that end the Act is designed to eliminate the 'inequality of bargaining power between employees * * * and employers.' Ibid. Requiring a lone employee to attend an investigatory interview which he reasonably believes may result in the imposition of discipline perpetuates the inequality the Act was designed to eliminate and bars recourse to the safeguards the Act provided 'to redress the perceived imbalance of economic power between labor and management.' American Ship Building Co. v. NLRB, 380 U.S. 300, 316, 85 S.Ct. 955, 13 L.Ed.2d 855 (1965)."

For similar reasons, the Court held that a union representative who seeks upon request to accompany the employee to a so-called investigatory interview may not be disciplined for such conduct. International Ladies' Garment Workers' Union v. Quality Mfg. Co., 420 U.S. 276, 95 S.Ct. 972, 43 L.Ed.2d 189 (1975).

Problems for Discussion

1. An employee of a non-union company, acting on his own initiative, went to his employer and said, "The boys are wondering when you are going to give us a raise." The employer replied that the employee was lucky simply to have a job, and soon after discharged him. Has the employer violated Section 8(a)(1) or (3)? See Maietta Trucking Co., 194 N.L.R.B. 794 (1971).

Would your analysis and answer differ if the employee were instead working for a unionized company and, on his own initiative, he pointed out certain provisions of the collective bargaining agreement which he contended entitled him to a pay increase? Compare NLRB v. Interboro Contractors, Inc., 388 F.2d 495 (2d Cir. 1968), with Ontario Knife Co. v. NLRB, 637 F.2d 840 (2d Cir. 1980).

If two employees had complained to the employer in each of the problem-cases above, would they have been protected by the NLRA against discharge? Should the outcome be different if only one employee so complains? Should the term "concerted activities" in Section 7 be read as a term of limitation on individual rights, given the legislative roots and the purposes of the Act?

2. Acting on rumors that the employer had inadequate funds in its checking account to cover the paychecks just issued to them, three employees during their lunch hour drove to the employer's bank and one of them, Amy Able, went inside to inquire of the bank manager regarding the employer's account balance. At a cocktail party that night, the bank manager informed the company president of Ms. Able's inquiry, and the next morning, Ms. Able was told by the president (who was unaware of the involvement of the other two employees) to "punch the time clock for the last time, and never show your face around here again!" Advise Ms. Able on her rights under the Labor Act to get back her job. See Air Surrey Corp. v. NLRB, 601 F.2d 256 (6th Cir. 1979).

3. Does Section 7 protect the right of an employee in a non-union company, confronted with an employer demand to appear for an interview concerning the distribution of narcotics on company property, to insist upon the presence and assistance of a co-worker (a first-year law student) at the interview? See Anchortank, Inc., 239 N.L.R.B. 430 (1978).

Does Section 7 protect the right of an employee in a unionized company to insist upon the presence of the shop steward at a meeting in which the plant manager is to inform the employee of a final decision to terminate him because of his use of drugs on company property? See NLRB v. Certified Grocers of California, Ltd., 587 F.2d 449 (9th Cir. 1978).

4. During a hotly contested mayoral campaign in the city of North Industry, a group of employees of Acme Manufacturing Co. formed an association known as "Mayer for Mayor." Mayer was a candidate running on a fairly well elaborated campaign platform, one of the planks of which was municipal tax incentives to bring new industry to the city and to revitalize older industrial establishments. Although the president of Acme was sympathetic to candidate Mayer, he ordered employees associated with "Mayer for Mayor" to refrain from circulating petitions and campaign literature on the company parking lot before and after working hours. These employees have consulted you about their right to distribute such material nonetheless. What is your advice? See Local 174, UAW v. NLRB (Firestone Steel Prods. Co.), 106 L.R.R.M. 2561, 90 CCH Lab.Cas. ¶ 12602 (D.C.Cir. 1981).

Would your advice be the same if these employees sought instead to distribute literature of the Communist Party. including its newspaper, The Daily Worker? See Ford Motor Co. (Rouge Complex), 233 N.L.R.B. 698 (1977).

EASTEX, INC. v. NLRB

Supreme Court of the United States, 1978.
437 U.S. 556, 98 S.Ct. 2505, 57 L.Ed.2d 428.

MR. JUSTICE POWELL delivered the opinion of the Court.

issue — Employees of petitioner sought to distribute a union newsletter in nonworking areas of petitioner's property during nonworking time urging employees to support the union and discussing a proposal to incorporate the state "right-to-work" statute into the state constitution and a presidential veto of an increase in the federal minimum wage. The newsletter also called on employees to take action to protect their interests as employees with respect to these two issues. The question presented is whether petitioner's refusal to allow the distribution violated § 8(a)(1) of the National Labor Relations Act

* * *

contents of newsletter — [In March and April 1974, certain employees of the Company and officers of Local 801 of the United Paperworkers International Union (the collective bargaining representative of the Company's production employees) sought to distribute a union newsletter in nonworking areas of the plant./ The first and fourth sections of the newsletter urged employees to support the Union and extolled the benefits of union solidarity. The second section encouraged employees to write their state legislators to oppose incorporating the state "right to work" law (which bans union shop agreements) into a revised state constitution; the newsletter warned that such incorporation could weaken unions. The third section of the newsletter, after noting the President's veto of a bill increasing the federal minimum wage and comparing the increase in prices and profits in the oil industry, urged the employees to register to vote in federal elections and to support candidates sympathetic to labor/ Company officials refused all requests to circulate the newsletter in nonworking areas of the plant, and the Union filed an unfair labor practice charge.

The Board and the court of appeals concluded that the employer violated Section 8(a)(1). They rejected the Company's claim that, because the newsletter was not directed at conditions in the workplace over which the employer had control, its distribution was not for the "mutual aid and protection" of the employees. They also concluded that the Company had shown no "special circumstances" which would justify a ban upon employees solicitation in nonworking areas of the plant on nonworking time.]

II

Two distinct questions are presented. The first is whether, apart from the location of the activity, distribution of the newsletter is the kind of concerted activity that is protected from employer interference by §§ 7 and 8(a)(1) of the National Labor Relations Act. If it is, then the second question is whether the fact that the activity takes place on petitioner's property gives rise to a countervailing interest that outweighs the exercise of § 7 rights in that location. * * *

A

Section 7 provides that "[e]mployees shall have the right * * * to engage in * * * concerted activities for the purpose of collective bargaining or other mutual aid or protection * * *." Petitioner contends that the activity here is not within the "mutual aid or protection" language because it does not relate to a "specific dispute" between employees and their own employer "over an issue which the employer has the right or power to affect." Brief for Petitioner 13. In support of its position, petitioner asserts that the term "employees" in § 7 refers only to employees of a particular employer, so that only activity by employees on behalf of themselves or other employees of the same employer is protected. Id., at 18, 24. Petitioner also argues that the term "collective bargaining" in § 7 "indicates a direct bargaining relationship whereas 'other mutual aid or protection' must refer to activities of a similar nature * * *." Id., at 24. Thus, in petitioner's view, under § 7 "the employee is only protected for activity within the scope of the employment relationship." Id., at 13. Petitioner rejects the idea that § 7 might protect any activity that could be characterized as "political," and suggests that the discharge of an employee who engages in any such activity would not violate the Act.

We believe that petitioner misconceives the reach of the "mutual aid or protection" clause. The "employees" who may engage in concerted activities for "mutual aid or protection" are defined by § 2(3) of the Act, 29 U.S.C.A. § 152(3), to "include any employee, and shall not be limited to the employees of a particular employer, unless the Act explicitly states otherwise * * *." This definition was intended to protect employees when they engage in otherwise proper concerted activities in support of employees of employers other than their own. In recognition of its intent, the Board and the courts long have held that the "mutual aid or protection" clause encompasses such activity.[2] Petitioner's argument on this point ignores the language of the Act and its settled construction.

2. E. g., Fort Wayne Corrugated Paper Co. v. NLRB, 111 F.2d 869, 874 (CA7 1940), enforcing 11 N.L.R.B. 1, 5–6 (1939) (right to assist in organizing another employer's employees); NLRB v. J. G. Boswell Co., 136 F.2d 585, 595 (CA9 1943), enforcing 35 N.L. R.B. 968 (1941) (right to express sympathy for striking employees of another employer); Redwing Carriers, Inc., 137 N.L.R.B. 1545, 1546–1547 (1962), enforced sub nom. Teamster

We also find no warrant for petitioner's view that employees lose their protection under the "mutual aid or protection" clause when they seek to improve terms and conditions of employment or otherwise improve their lot as employees through channels outside the immediate employee-employer relationship. The 74th Congress knew well enough that labor's cause often is advanced on fronts other than collective bargaining and grievance settlement within the immediate employment context. It recognized this fact by choosing, as the language of § 7 makes clear, to protect concerted activities for the somewhat broader purpose of "mutual aid or protection" as well as for the narrower purposes of "self-organization" and "collective bargaining." Thus, it has been held that the "mutual aid or protection" clause protects employees from retaliation by their employers when they seek to improve working conditions through resort to administrative and judicial forums, and that employees' appeals to legislators to protect their interests as employees are within the scope of this clause. To hold that activity of this nature is entirely unprotected—irrespective of location or the means employed—would leave employees open to retaliation for much legitimate activity that could improve their lot as employees. As this could "frustrate the policy of the Act to protect the right of workers to act together to better their working conditions," NLRB v. Washington Aluminum Co., 370 U.S. 9, 14, 82 S.Ct. 1099, 1102, 8 L.Ed.2d 298 (1962), we do not think that Congress could have intended the protection of § 7 to be as narrow as petitioner insists.[3]

Local 79 v. NLRB, 117 U.S.App.D.C. 84, 325 F.2d 1011 (1963), cert. denied, 377 U.S. 905, 84 S.Ct. 1165, 12 L.Ed.2d 176 (1964) (right to honor picket line of another employer's employees); NLRB v. Alamo Express Co., 430 F.2d 1032, 1036 (CA5 1970), cert. denied, 400 U.S. 1021, 91 S.Ct. 584, 27 L.Ed.2d 633 (1971), enforcing 170 N.L.R.B. 315 (1968) (accord); Washington State Service Employees State Council No. 18, 188 N.L.R.B. 957, 959 (1971) (right to demonstrate in support of another employer's employees); Yellow Cab, Inc., 210 N.L.R.B. 568, 569 (1974) (right to distribute literature in support of another employer's employees). We express no opinion, however, as to the correctness of the particular balance struck between employees' exercise of § 7 rights and employers' legitimate interests in any of the above-cited cases.

3. Petitioner relies upon several cases said to construe § 7 more narrowly

than do we. NLRB v. Leslie Metal Arts Co., 509 F.2d 811 (CA6 1975), and Shelly & Anderson Furniture Mfg. Co. v. NLRB, 497 F.2d 1200 (CA9 1974), both quote the same treatise for the proposition that to be protected under § 7, concerted activity must seek "a specific remedy" for a "work-related complaint or grievance." 509 F.2d, at 813, and 497 F.2d, at 1202–1203, quoting 18B Business Organizations, T. Kheel, Labor Law § 10.02[3], at 10–21 (1973). It was unnecessary in those cases to decide whether the protection of § 7 went beyond the treatise's formulation, for the activity in both cases was held to be protected. Moreover, in stating its "rule," the treatise relied upon takes no note of the cases cited in nn. 13, 15, and 16, supra. Compare R. Gorman, Labor Law 296–302 (1976). The Courts of Appeals for the Sixth and Ninth Circuits themselves have taken a broader view of the "mutual aid or protection" clause than the reference to the treatise in

It is true, of course, that some concerted activity bears a less immediate relationship to employees' interests as employees than other such activity. We may assume that at some point the relationship becomes so attenuated that an activity cannot fairly be deemed to come within the "mutual aid or protection" clause. It is neither necessary nor appropriate, however, for us to attempt to delineate precisely the boundaries of the "mutual aid or protection" clause. That task is for the Board to perform in the first instance as it considers the wide variety of cases that come before it.[4]   Republic Aviation Corp. v. NLRB, 324 U.S. 793, 798, 65 S.Ct. 982, 985, 89 L.Ed. 1372 (1945); Phelps Dodge Corp. v. NLRB, 313 U.S. 177, 194, 61 S.Ct. 845, 852, 85 L.Ed. 1271 (1941). To decide this case, it is enough to determine whether the Board erred in holding that distribution of the second and third sections of the newsletter is for the purpose of "mutual aid or protection."

The Board determined that distribution of the second section, urging employees to write their legislators to oppose incorporation of the state "right-to-work" statute into a revised state constitution, was protected because union security is "central to the union concept of strength through solidarity" and "a mandatory subject of bargaining in other than right-to-work states." 215 N.L.R.B., at 274. The newsletter warned that incorporation could affect employees adversely "by weakening Unions and improving the edge business has at the bargaining table." The fact that Texas already has a "right-to-work" statute does not render employees' interest in this matter any less strong, for, as the Court of Appeals noted, it is "one thing to face a

---

the above-cited cases would seem to suggest. See, e. g., Kellogg Co. v. NLRB, 457 F.2d 519, 522–523 (CA6 1972), and cases there cited; Kaiser Engineers v. NLRB, 538 F.2d 1379, 1384–1385 (CA9 1976). * * *

This leaves only G&W Electric Specialty Co. v. NLRB, 360 F.2d 873 (CA7 1966), which refused to enforce a Board order because the concerted activity there—circulation of a petition concerning management of an employee-run credit union—"involved no request for any action upon the part of the Company and did not concern a matter over which the Company had any control." Id., at 876. G&W Electric cites no authority for its narrowing of § 7, and it ignores a substantial weight of authority to the contrary, including the Seventh Circuit's own prior holding in Fort Wayne Corrugated Paper Co. v. NLRB, 111 F.2d

869, 874 (1940). See n. [2], *supra*. We therefore do not view any of these cases as persuasive authority for petitioner's position.

4. * * * In addition, even when concerted activity comes within the scope of the "mutual aid or protection" clause, the forms such activity permissibly may take may well depend on the object of the activity. "The argument that the employer's lack of interest or control affords a legitimate basis for holding that a subject does not come within 'mutual aid or protection' is unconvincing. The argument that economic pressure should be unprotected in such cases is more convincing." Getman, The Protection of Economic Pressure By Section 7 of the National Labor Relations Act, 115 U.Pa.L.Rev. 1195, 1221 (1967).

legislative scheme which is open to legislative modification or repeal" and "quite another thing to face the prospect that such a scheme will be frozen in a concrete constitutional mandate." 550 F.2d, at 205. We cannot say that the Board erred in holding that this section of the newsletter bears such a relation to employees' interests as to come within the guarantee of the "mutual aid or protection" clause. * * *

The Board held that distribution of the third section, criticizing a presidential veto of an increase in the federal minimum wage and urging employees to register to vote to "defeat our enemies and elect our friends," was protected despite the fact that petitioner's employees were paid more than the vetoed minimum wage. It reasoned that the "minimum wage inevitably influences wage levels derived from collective bargaining, even those far above the minimum," and that "concern by [petitioner's] employees for the plight of other employees might gain support for them at some future time when they might have a dispute with their employer." 215 N.L.R.B., at 274 (internal quotation marks omitted). We think that the Board acted within the range of its discretion in so holding. Few topics are of such immediate concern to employees as the level of their wages. The Board was entitled to note the widely recognized impact that a rise in the minimum wage may have on the level of negotiated wages generally, a phenomenon that would not have been lost on petitioner's employees. The union's call, in the circumstances of this case, for these employees to back persons who support an increase in the minimum wage, and to oppose those who oppose it, fairly is characterized as concerted activity for the "mutual aid or protection" of petitioner's employees and of employees generally.

In sum, we hold that distribution of both the second and the third sections of the newsletter is protected under the "mutual aid or protection" clause of § 7.

B

The question that remains is whether the Board erred in holding that petitioner's employees may distribute the newsletter in nonworking areas of petitioner's property during nonworking time. Consideration of this issue must begin with the Court's decisions in Republic Aviation Corp. v. NLRB, 324 U.S. 793, 65 S.Ct. 982, 89 L.Ed. 1372 (1945), and NLRB v. Babcock & Wilcox Co., 351 U.S. 105, 76 S.Ct. 679, 100 L.Ed. 975 (1956). * * *

It is apparent that the instant case resembles Republic Aviation rather closely. * * * The only possible ground of distinction is that part of the newsletter in this case does not address purely organizational matters, but rather concerns other activity protected by § 7. The question, then, is whether this difference required the Board to apply a different rule here than it applied in Republic Aviation.

* * * In the first place, petitioner's reliance on its property right is largely misplaced. Here, as in *Republic Aviation*, petitioner's employees are "already rightfully on the employer's property," so that in the context of this case it is the "employer's management interests rather than [its] property interests" that primarily are implicated. [Hudgens v. NLRB, 424 U.S. 507, at 521–22 n. 10, 96 S.Ct. 1029, at 1037 n. 10.] As already noted, petitioner made no attempt to show that its management interests would be prejudiced in any way by the exercise of § 7 rights proposed by its employees here. Even if the mere distribution by employees of material protected by § 7 can be said to intrude on petitioner's property rights in any meaningful sense, the degree of intrusion does not vary with the content of the material. Petitioner's only cognizable property right in this respect is in preventing employees from bringing literature onto its property and distributing it there —not in choosing which distributions protected by § 7 it wishes to suppress. * * * It is apparent that the complexity of the Board's rules and the difficulty of the Board's task might be compounded greatly if it were required to distinguish not only between literature that is within and without the protection of § 7, but also among subcategories of literature within that protection. * * *

We need not go so far in this case, however, as to hold that the *Republic Aviation* rule properly is applied to every in-plant distribution of literature that falls within the protective ambit of § 7. This is a new area for the Board and the courts which has not yet received mature consideration. * * * For this reason, we confine our holding to the facts of this case.

Petitioner concedes that its employees were entitled to distribute a substantial portion of his newsletter on its property. In addition, as we have held above, the sections to which petitioner objected concern activity which petitioner, in the absence of a countervailing interest of its own, is not entitled to suppress. Yet petitioner made no attempt to show that its management interests would be prejudiced in any manner by distribution of these sections, and in our view any incremental intrusion on petitioner's property rights from their distribution together with the other sections would be minimal. Moreover, it is undisputed that the Union undertook the distribution in order to boost its support and improve its bargaining position in upcoming contract negotiations with petitioner. Thus, viewed in context, the distribution was closely tied to vital concerns of the Act. In these circumstances, we hold that the Board did not err in applying the *Republic Aviation* rule to the facts of this case. The judgment of the Court of Appeals therefore is

Affirmed.

[In a dissenting opinion joined by the Chief Justice, Justice Rehnquist formulated the question before the Court as "whether Congress has authorized the Board to displace an employer's right to prevent the distribution on his property of political material concerning matters over which he has no control." He criticized the Court for deferring to the NLRB's imposition of a substantial burden on the property rights of the employer, absent any Court precedent and absent an "unmistakable expression" of congressional approval.]

Even assuming that employees are engaged in "concerted" activity for "mutual aid or protection" it does not necessarily follow that such activity is immune from discipline. The broad language of Section 7 has never been read without qualification, for it could not seriously be argued that industrial sabotage (e. g., destroying company equipment or products) even in the cause of unionization or improvement in working conditions ought to be sheltered by the Labor Act against immediate dismissal. With no legislative guidelines thus to distinguish between "protected" and "unprotected" concerted activity, the Board and courts have assumed the task of drawing that distinction. Although the decisions have been informed by the knowledge that classification one way or the other will render the employees either immune from or susceptible to discharge, they offer very little by way of analysis or even by way of a realization that the Board is engaging in a lawmaking enterprise of major dimensions. The cases rather assume that employees ought not be protected from employer self-help when their conduct is either in violation of law or is so fundamentally contrary to the dictates of the employment relationship as to warrant characterization as "indefensible," or "reprehensible" or "disloyal."

Thus, concerted activity—even for mutual aid and protection—will be held to fall without the protection of Section 7 if its objective is contrary to the terms or spirit of the National Labor Relations Act or allied federal legislation. For example, if the object of the striking employees is to induce the employer to discharge a worker because he is a dissident voice within the union, the union commits an unfair labor practice by seeking to compel the employer to violate Section 8(a)(3), and the participating employees are deemed to be unprotected against summary discharge. It has also been held lawful for an employer to discharge workers who have engaged in a work stoppage the object of which is to force the employer to grant an immediate wage increase at a time when federal regulations barred such an increase without the prior authorization of a wage-stabilization agency. American News Co., 55 N.L.R.B. 1302 (1944).

As earlier materials in this book have demonstrated, a union's use of economic pressure in support of demands falling outside the scope of mandatory bargaining (i. e., "wages, hours and other terms or conditions of employment") will constitute a refusal to bargain in good faith. Employees participating in such concerted activity are thus engaging in unprotected activity and are liable to immediate discharge. A number of cases have dealt with the issue whether the termination or replacement of a particular supervisor constitutes a mandatory subject or a permissive subject (within the prerogative of the employer), the characterization ultimately determining not so much the outlawry of the union's activity but rather the legality of the employer's resort to discipline against striking employees. E. g., Dobbs Houses, Inc. v. NLRB, 325 F.2d 531 (5th Cir. 1964). Also unprotected is strike activity, at or near the end of the term of a labor contract, which is directed at the modification of contract terms but which has not been preceded by the formal notification of the other party and of state and federal mediation agencies, and the cooling-off periods, mandated by Section 8(d) of the Labor Act. (That Section is considered in greater detail at pp. 485–87, supra.) Section 8(d) is (along with a companion Section 8(g) governing concerted activities in health care institutions) unique in that it shows Congress explicitly declaring that employees who engage in such a premature strike are amenable to immediate discharge; Congress relieved the Board of drawing such an implication from the Act, by clearly divesting such strikers of their status as "employees" within the unfair labor practice and representation sections of the Act.

More common than the cases in which activity is deemed unprotected because of the employees' objective are cases in which activity is held to fall without Section 7 because of the method of protest utilized by the employees. If that method is in direct violation of federal law—for example, it is a secondary boycott in violation of Section 8(b)(4) or is a shipboard work stoppage contrary to the mutiny provisions of the federal Criminal Code—the employees may be discharged. See Southern S. S. Co. v. NLRB, 316 U.S. 31, 62 S.Ct. 886, 86 L.Ed. 1246 (1942). (*Held*, NLRB abuses its discretion under Section 10(c) by reinstating mutineers. "It is sufficient for this case to observe that the Board has not been commissioned to effectuate the policies of the Labor Relations Act so single-mindedly that it may wholly ignore other and equally important Congressional objectives."). The use of methods deemed contrary to the "spirit" although not the terms of the federal Labor Act will be regarded as unprotected. Perhaps the major decision on this point is that of the Supreme Court in EMPORIUM CAPWELL CO. v. WESTERN ADDITION COMMUNITY ORGANIZATION, 420 U.S. 50, 95 S.Ct. 977, 43 L.Ed.2d 12 (1975), at p. 369, supra. In that case—which could be usefully restudied at this point—the Court held that the employer was not forbidden by the Labor Act to discharge two employees who (without the endorsement of the incumbent union) engaged in peaceful picketing and leafletting designed to induce the employer to bargain with them with a view toward altering its policies on the hiring and promotion of minority-group workers. Even the laudable objective of eliminating race discrimination in employment was held not to supersede the exclusive-representation principles of the Labor Act, and the peaceful concerted activity was held unprotected against discharge. And, although a strike during the term of a labor contract, in violation of a no-strike clause, is not prohibited by the Labor Act, it is unprotected and may be met with employer discipline. NLRB v. Sands Mfg. Co., 306 U.S. 332, 59 S.Ct. 508, 83 L.Ed. 682 (1939). (Through an even more extended exercise in lawmaking, however, the Supreme Court has held that a no-strike clause in a collective bargaining agreement should be narrowly construed so as not to bar a strike in protest of a serious employer unfair labor practice; such unfair labor practice strikes during the contract term are thus generally treated as protected activities. Mastro Plastics Corp. v. NLRB, 350 U.S. 270, 76 S.Ct. 349, 100 L.Ed. 309 (1956).)

If strikers engage in concerted activities which violate the criminal and tort laws of the state, that too will render their conduct unprotected. Perhaps the most famous illustration is NLRB v. Fansteel Metallurgical Corp., 306 U.S. 240, 59 S.Ct. 490, 83 L.Ed. 627 (1939), in which employees, in violation of a state-court injunction, engaged in a prolonged sitdown strike, forcible seizure of the plant, and destruction of the employer's property. The Supreme Court upheld the discharge of the strikers. The same will be true when the strikers engage in actual and threatened violence on the picket line or at the homes of fellow workers. E. g., NLRB v. Thayer Co., 213 F.2d 748 (1st Cir. 1954), see p. 866, infra. There will be some point, however, at which conduct on the picket line will be sufficiently "tolerable" when tested by the norms of industrial confrontation such that the policies inherent in Section 7 must supersede even those of state criminal and tort law. As the NLRB has observed: "[T]he emotional tension of a strike almost inevitably gives rise to a certain amount of disorder and * * * conduct on a picket line cannot be expected to approach the etiquette of the drawing room or breakfast table." Republic Creosoting Co., 19 N.L.R.B. 267 (1940). Analogous issues will be raised when employees make accusations or comments concerning the employer which in other contexts might be regarded as defamatory, or when they engage in their activity on company property in a manner which in other contexts would be deemed trespassory. It is initially the task of the Board to draw the line between conduct sheltered by Section 7 and conduct which should be deemed unprotected because of its closeness to assault, slander or trespass. The Board or a court will sometimes explain its result in such instances simply by labeling the conduct as "indefensible" or "reprehensible" or "irresponsible."

This label has also been appended to employee protests which are timed to create an uncommon risk of injury to the employer's plant or equipment, or of spoilage to the company's goods or to goods of others which the company is processing. For example, the court in NLRB v. Marshall Car Wheel Co., 218 F.2d 409 (5th Cir. 1955), called the employees' conduct "irresponsible" and hence unprotected when they walked out of the plant at a time when molten iron was being held in a cupola which would be subjected to costly damage were the iron retained there for a long period of time. The Supreme Court has also treated as unprotected sporadic and unannounced work stoppages which maximize the pressure on the employer, because of its inability to plan its business affairs in anticipation of such stoppages, while minimizing the sacrifice for the employees, who remain on the payroll. See NLRB v. Insurance Agents Int'l Union, 361 U.S. 477, 80 S.Ct. 419, 4 L.Ed.2d 454 (1960), at p. 408, supra.

The Supreme Court decision in the *Jefferson Standard* case, which follows, finds the Court dealing with concerted activities which raise a number of the issues outlined in this Note. Does the Court illuminate the standards by which such activity is to be judged as protected or unprotected against discharge?

NLRB v. LOCAL 1229, IBEW

(JEFFERSON STANDARD BROADCASTING CO.)

Supreme Court of the United States, 1953.
346 U.S. 464, 74 S.Ct. 172, 98 L.Ed. 195.

MR. JUSTICE BURTON delivered the opinion of the Court.

The issue before us is whether the discharge of certain employees by their employer constituted an unfair labor practice, within the meaning of §§ 8(a) (1) and 7 of the Taft-Hartley Act, justifying their reinstatement by the National Labor Relations Board. For the reason that their discharge was "for cause" within the meaning of § 10 (c) of that Act, we sustain the Board in not requiring their reinstatement.

In 1949, the Jefferson Standard Broadcasting Company (here called the company) was a North Carolina corporation engaged in interstate commerce. Under a license from the Federal Communications Commission, it operated, at Charlotte, North Carolina, a 50,000-watt radio station, with call letters WBT. It broadcasts 10 to 12 hours daily by radio and television. The television service, which it started July 14, 1949, representing an investment of about $500,000, was the only such service in the area. Less than 50% of the station's programs originated in Charlotte. The others were piped in over leased wires, generally from New York, California or Illinois from several different networks. Its annual gross revenue from broadcasting operations exceeded $100,000 but its television enterprise caused it a monthly loss of about $10,000 during the first four months of that operation, including the period here involved. Its rates for television advertising were geared to the number of receiving sets in the area. Local dealers had large inventories of such sets ready to meet anticipated demands.

The company employed 22 technicians. In December 1948, negotiations to settle the terms of their employment after January 31, 1949, were begun between representatives of the company and of the respondent Local Union No. 1229, International Brotherhood of Electrical Workers, American Federation of Labor (here called the union). The negotiations reached an impasse in January 1949, and the existing contract of employment expired January 31. The technicians, nevertheless, continued to work for the company and their collective-bargaining negotiations were resumed in July, only to break down again July 8. The main point of disagreement arose from the union's demand for the renewal of a provision that all discharges from employment be subject to arbitration and the company's counterproposal that such arbitration be limited to the facts material to each discharge, leaving it to the company to determine whether those facts gave adequate cause for discharge.

July 9, 1949, the union began daily peaceful picketing of the company's station. Placards and handbills on the picket line charged the company with unfairness to its technicians and emphasized the company's refusal to renew the provision for arbitration of discharges. The placards and handbills named the union as the representative of the WBT technicians. The employees did not strike. They confined their respective tours of picketing to their off-duty hours and continued to draw full pay. There was no violence or threat of violence and no one has taken exception to any of the above conduct.

But on August 24, 1949, a new procedure made its appearance. Without warning, several of its technicians launched a vitriolic attack on the quality of the company's television broadcasts. Five thousand handbills were printed over the designation "WBT Technicians." These were distributed on the picket line, on the public square two or three blocks from the company's premises, in barber shops, restaurants and busses. Some were mailed to local businessmen. The handbills made no reference to the union, to a labor controversy or to collective bargaining. They read:

"Is Charlotte A Second-Class City?"

"You might think so from the kind of Television programs being presented by the Jefferson Standard Broadcasting Co. over WBTV. Have you seen one of their television programs lately? Did you know that all the programs presented over WBTV are on film and may be from one day to five years old. There are no local programs presented by WBTV. You cannot receive the local baseball games, football games or other local events because WBTV does not have the proper equipment to make these pickups. Cities like New York, Boston, Philadelphia, Washington receive such programs nightly. Why doesn't the Jefferson Standard Broadcasting Company purchase the needed equipment to bring you the same type of programs enjoyed by other leading American cities? Could it be that they consider Charlotte a second-class community and only entitled to the pictures now being presented to them?

"WBT Technicians"

This attack continued until September 3, 1949, when the company discharged ten of its technicians, whom it charged with sponsoring or distributing these handbills. The company's letter discharging them tells its side of the story.[5]

5. "Dear Mr. * * *,
"When you and some of our other technicians commenced early in July to picket against this Company, we felt that your action was very ill-considered. We were paying you a salary of * * * per week, to say nothing of other benefits which you receive as an employee of our Company, such as time-and-a-half pay for all work beyond eight hours in any one day, three weeks vacation each year with full pay, unlimited sick leave with full pay, liberal life insurance and hospitalization, for you and your family, and retirement and pension benefits unexcelled anywhere. Yet when we were unable to agree upon the terms of a contract with your Union, you began to denounce us publicly as 'unfair.'

"And ever since early July while you have been walking up and down the street with placards and literature attacking us, you have continued to hold your job and receive your pay and all the other benefits referred to above.

"Even when you began to put out propaganda which contained many untruths about our Company and great deal of personal abuse and slander, we still continued to treat you exactly as before. For it has been our understanding that under our labor laws, you have a very great latitude in trying to make the public believe that your employer is unfair to you.

"Now, however, you have turned from trying to persuade the public that we are unfair *to you* and are trying to persuade the public that we give inferior service *to them.* While we are struggling to expand into and develop a new field, and incidentally losing large sums of money in the process, you are busy trying to turn customers and the public against us in every possible way, even handing out leaflets on the public street advertising that our operations are 'second-class,' and endeavoring in various ways to hamper and totally destroy our business. Certainly we are not required by law or common sense to keep you in our employment and pay you a substantial salary while you thus do your best to tear down and bankrupt our business.

"You are hereby discharged from our employment. Although there is nothing requiring us to do so, and the circumstances certainly do not call for our doing so, we are enclosing a check payable to your order for two weeks' advance or severance pay.

"Very truly yours,
"Jefferson Standard Broadcasting
Company
"By: Charles H. Crutchfield
"*Vice President*
"Enclosure"

September 4, the union's picketing resumed its original tenor and, September 13, the union filed with the Board a charge that the company, by discharging the above-mentioned ten technicians, had engaged in an unfair labor practice. The General Counsel for the Board filed a complaint based on those charges and, after hearing, a trial examiner made detailed findings and a recommendation that all of those discharged be reinstated with back pay. 94 N.L.R.B. 1507, 1527. The Board found that one of the discharged men had neither sponsored nor distributed the "Second-Class City" handbill and ordered his reinstatement with back pay. It then found that the other nine had sponsored or distributed the handbill and held that the company, by discharging them for such conduct, had not engaged in an unfair labor practice. The Board, accordingly, did not order their reinstatement. One member dissented. Id., at 1507 et seq. Under § 10(f) of the Taft-Hartley Act, the union petitioned the Court of Appeals for the District of Columbia Circuit for a review of the Board's order and for such a modification of it as would reinstate all ten of the discharged technicians with back pay. That court remanded the cause to the Board for further consideration and for a finding as to the "unlawfulness" of the conduct of the employees which had led to their discharge. 91 U.S.App.D.C. 333, 202 F.2d 186.[6] We granted certiorari because of the importance of the case in the administration of the Taft-Hartley Act. 345 U.S. 947, 73 S.Ct. 865.

In its essence, the issue is simple. It is whether these employees, whose contracts of employment had expired, were discharged "for cause." * * *

The company's letter shows that it interpreted the handbill as a demonstration of such detrimental disloyalty as to provide "cause" for its refusal to continue in its employ the perpetrators of the attack. We agree.

Section 10(c) of the Taft-Hartley Act expressly provides that "No order of the Board shall require the reinstatement of any individual as an employee who has been suspended or discharged, or the payment to him of any back pay, if such individual was suspended or discharged for cause." There is no more elemental cause for discharge of an employee than disloyalty to his employer. It is equally

---

6. The Court of Appeals said: "Protection under § 7 of the Act * * * is withdrawn only from those concerted activities which contravene either (a) specific provisions or basic policies of the Act or of related federal statutes, or (b) specific rules of other federal or local law that is not incompatible with the Board's governing statute. * * *
* * * * * *

"We think the Board failed to make the finding essential to its conclusion that the concerted activity was unprotected. Sound practice in judicial review of administrative orders precludes this court from determining 'unlawfulness' without a prior consideration and finding by the Board." 91 U.S. App.D.C., at pages 335, 336, 202 F.2d at pages 188, 189.

elemental that the Taft-Hartley Act seeks to strengthen, rather than to weaken, that cooperation, continuity of service and cordial contractual relation between employer and employee that is born of loyalty to their common enterprise.

Congress, while safeguarding, in § 7, the right of employees to engage in "concerted activities for the purpose of collective bargaining or other mutual aid or protection," did not weaken the underlying contractual bonds and loyalties of employer and employee. The conference report that led to the enactment of the law said:

"[T]he courts have firmly established the rule that under the existing provisions of section 7 of the National Labor Relations Act, employees are not given any right to engage in unlawful or other improper conduct.

" * * * Furthermore, in section 10(c) of the amended act, as proposed in the conference agreement, it is specifically provided that no order of the Board shall require the reinstatement of any individual or the payment to him of any back pay if such individual was suspended or discharged for cause, and this, of course, applies with equal force whether or not the acts constituting the cause for discharge were committed in connection with a concerted activity." H. R.Rep.No. 510, 80th Cong., 1st Sess. 38–39.

This has been clear since the early days of the Wagner Act. [Citations omitted.] The above cases illustrate the responsibility that falls upon the Board to find the facts material to such decisions. The legal principle that insubordination, disobedience or disloyalty is adequate cause for discharge is plain enough. The difficulty arises in determining whether, in fact, the discharges are made because of such a separable cause or because of some other concerted activities engaged in for the purpose of collective bargaining or other mutual aid or protection which may not be adequate cause for discharge. Cf. National Labor Relations Board v. Peter Cailler Kohler Swiss Chocolates Co., 2 Cir., 130 F.2d 503.

In the instant case the Board found that the company's discharge of the nine offenders resulted from their sponsoring and distributing the "Second-Class City" handbills of August 24—September 3, issued in their name as the "WBT Technicians." Assuming that there had been no pending labor controversy, the conduct of the "WBT Technicians" from August 24 through September 3 unquestionably would have provided adequate cause for their disciplinary discharge within the meaning of § 10(c). Their attack related itself to no labor practice of the company. It made no reference to wages, hours or working conditions. The policies attacked were those of finance and public relations for which management, not technicians, must be responsible. The attack asked for no public sympathy or support. It was a continuing attack, initiated while off duty, upon the very interests which the attackers were being paid to conserve and develop. Nothing could be further from the purpose of the Act than to require an employer to finance such activities. Nothing would contribute less to the Act's declared purpose of promoting industrial peace and stability.

The fortuity of the coexistence of a labor dispute affords these technicians no substantial defense. While they were also union men and leaders in the labor controversy, they took pains to separate those categories. In contrast to their claims on the picket line as to the labor controversy, their handbill of August 24 omitted all reference to it. The handbill diverted attention from the labor controversy. It attacked public policies of the company which had no discernible relation to that controversy. The only connection between the handbill and the labor controversy was an ultimate and undisclosed purpose or motive on the part of some of the sponsors that, by the hoped-for financial pressure, the attack might extract from the company some future concession. A disclosure of that motive might have lost more public support for the employees than it would have gained, for it would have given the handbill more the character of coercion than of collective bargaining. Referring to the attack, the Board said "In our judgment, these tactics, in the circumstances of this case, were hardly less 'indefensible' than acts of physical sabotage." 94 N.L.R. B., at 1511. In any event, the findings of the Board effectively separate the attack from the labor controversy and treat it solely as one made by the company's technical experts upon the quality of the company's product. As such, it was as adequate a cause for the discharge of its sponsors as if the labor controversy had not been pending. The technicians, themselves, so handled their attack as thus to bring their discharge under § 10(c).

The Board stated "We * * * do not decide whether the disparagement of product involved here would have justified the employer in discharging the employees responsible for it, had it been uttered in the context of a conventional appeal for support of the union in the labor dispute." Id., at 1512, n. 18. This underscored the Board's factual conclusion that the attack of August 24 was not part of an appeal for support in the pending dispute. It was a concerted separable attack purporting to be made in the interest of the public rather than in that of the employees.

We find no occasion to remand this cause to the Board for further specificity of findings. Even if the attack were to be treated, as the Board has not treated it, as a concerted activity wholly or partly within the scope of those mentioned in § 7, the means used by the technicians in conducting the attack have deprived the attackers of the protection of that section, when read in the light and context of the purpose of the Act.

Accordingly, the order of the Court of Appeals remanding the cause to the National Labor Relations Board is set aside, and the cause is remanded to the Court of Appeals with instructions to dismiss respondent's petition to modify the order of the Board. It is so ordered.

Order set aside and cause remanded with instructions.

MR. JUSTICE FRANKFURTER, whom MR. JUSTICE BLACK and MR. JUSTICE DOUGLAS join, dissenting. * * * On this central issue—whether the Court of Appeals rightly or wrongly found that the Board applied an improper criterion—this Court is silent. It does not support the Board in using "indefensible" as the legal litmus nor does it reject the Court of Appeals' rejection of that test. This Court presumably does not disagree with the assumption of the Court of Appeals that conduct may be "indefensible" in the colloquial meaning of that loose adjective, and yet be within the protection of § 7.

Instead, the Court, relying on § 10(c) which permits discharges "for cause," points to the "disloyalty" of the employees and finds sufficient "cause" regardless of whether the handbill was a "concerted activity" within § 7. Section 10(c) does not speak of discharge "for disloyalty." If Congress had so written that section, it would have overturned much of the law that had been developed by the Board and the courts in the twelve years preceding the Taft-Hartley Act. The legislative history makes clear that Congress had no such purpose but was rather expressing approval of the construction of "concerted activities" adopted by the Board and the courts. Many of the legally recognized tactics and weapons of labor would readily be condemned for "disloyalty" were they employed between man and man in friendly personal relations. In this connection it is significant that the ground now taken by the Court, insofar as it is derived from the provision of § 10(c) relating to discharge "for cause," was not invoked by the Board in justification of its order.

To suggest that all actions which in the absence of a labor controversy might be "cause"—or, to use the words commonly found in labor agreements, "just cause"—for discharge should be unprotected, even when such actions were undertaken as "concerted activities for the purpose of collective bargaining", is to misconstrue legislation designed to put labor on a fair footing with management. Furthermore, it would disregard the rough and tumble of strikes, in the course of which loose and even reckless language is properly discounted.

"Concerted activities" by employees and dismissal "for cause" by employers are not disassociated legal criteria under the Act. They are like the two halves of a pair of shears. Of course, as the Conference Report on the Taft-Hartley Act said, men on strike may be guilty of conduct "in connection with a concerted activity" which properly constitutes "cause" for dismissal and bars reinstatement. But § 10(c) does not obviate the necessity for a determination whether the distribution of the handbill here was a legitimate tool in the labor dispute or was so "improper," as the Conference Report put it, as to be denied the protection of § 7 and to constitute a discharge "for cause." It is for the Board, in the first instance, to make these evaluations, and a court of appeals does not travel beyond its proper bounds in asking the Board for greater explicitness in light of the correct legal standards for judgment.

The Board and the courts of appeals will hardly find guidance for future cases from this Court's reversal of the Court of Appeals, beyond that which the specific facts of this case may afford. More than that, to float such imprecise notions as "discipline" and "loyalty" in the context of labor controversies, as the basis of the right to discharge, is to open the door wide to individual judgment by Board members and judges. One may anticipate that the Court's opinion will needlessly stimulate litigation. * * *

Problems for Discussion

1. After negotiations for a new contract had failed, the employees of the Patterson-Sargent Company struck. The Company, a paint manufacturer, continued to operate by using its supervisors on production jobs, whereupon various employees distributed circulars which were entitled "Beware Paint Substitute." The circulars warned customers that Patterson-Sargent paints were not being made by "the well-trained experienced employees who have made the paint you have always bought" and that the paint might peel, crack, blister or scale. The final sentence pointed out to customers that they would be informed when they could again buy Patterson-Sargent paint made by the regular employees. The Company discharged those employees who had distributed the circulars and refused to reinstate them when the strike was over. Has the Company violated Section 8(a) (3)? See *Patterson-Sargent Company*, 115 NLRB 1627 (1956).

2. Maxine Lomax was a low-level supervisor directly in charge of the work of a number of employees in the men's and women's clothing department of the Thriftee Department Store. Ms. Lomax was discharged by Thriftee after a dispute about her working hours. She was well-liked by many of the employees, who frequently turned to her for assistance in her capacity as supervisor; she would often relieve employees at their counter and floor positions, and would help them out when they were unusually busy or when they were temporarily called away from the store on urgent business. Her presence was clearly a boost to employee morale. On the day that Ms. Lomax was discharged, some twenty employees appealed to the management of Thriftee to reconsider the discharge and to rehire Ms. Lomax, but when management refused, the employees walked out. Thriftee promptly announced that the employees were discharged and refused to process their applications for reinstatement, submitted several days later. Has Thriftee violated Section 8(a)(1)? See *Plastilite Corp.*, 153 N.L.R.B. 180 (1965), mdf'd on other grounds 375 F.2d 343 (8th Cir. 1967).

3.　Assume that in Problem 2, after being informed by Thriftee that Ms. Lomax would not be rehired, the employees secretly decided to stage their walkout several days later, the date of the storewide Labor Day sale, in order to have the maximum effect on Thriftee's business. The employees reported for work as usual, including the morning of the Labor Day sale, but walked out in a group at 11 a. m. that day, announcing their intention not to return until Ms. Lomax was rehired. Thriftee was not able to service the customers, and the doors were closed at noon. Thriftee immediately informed the striking employees of their discharge, citing the irreparable harm to customer relations by the work stoppage at such a busy time. Does that affect the determination of the legality of the discharges? See *Dobbs Houses, Inc.* v. *NLRB*, 325 F.2d 531 (5th Cir. 1963).

4.　Employee Thompson was active in organizing a union and in gathering authorization cards. He was also active in campaigning for better working conditions, to a degree that the company believed to be extreme. For example, Thompson was often heard to state that it was he who had helped to build up the company and that he could also tear it down if management did not improve conditions. Thompson also charged the company president, Cummings, with having made a small payoff to the president of a competing union in order to defeat unionization. Cummings, citing Thompson's "threats against the company and false and malicious rumors about me," discharged him. Is the discharge lawful? What further information, if any, is it necessary to know? See *NLRB* v. *Cement Transp., Inc.*, 490 F.2d 1024 (6th Cir. 1974).

B.　EMPLOYER RESPONSES TO CONCERTED ACTIVITIES [7]

NLRB v. MACKAY RADIO & TELEGRAPH CO.

Supreme Court of the United States, 1938.
304 U.S. 333, 58 S.Ct. 904, 82 L.Ed. 1381.

MR. JUSTICE ROBERTS delivered the opinion of the Court.

[Respondent, a California corporation engaged in the transmission of foreign and interstate communications, maintains an office at San Francisco where it employs upwards of sixty supervisors, operators and clerks, many of whom are members of Local 3 of the Ameri-

---

7.　See Christensen & Svanoe, Motive and Intent in the Commission of Unfair Labor Practices: The Supreme Court and the Fictive Formality, 77 Yale L.J. 1269 (1968); Getman, Section 8(a)(3) of the NLRA and the Effort to Insulate Free Employee Choice, 32 U.Chi.L.Rev. 735 (1965); Janofsky, New Concepts in Interference and Discrimination Under the NLRA—The Legacy of *American Ship Building* & *Great Dane Trailers*, 70 Colum.L.Rev. 81 (1970); Martin, The Rights of Economic Strikers to Reinstatement: A Search for Certainty, 1970 Wis.L.Rev. 1062; Note, Intent, Effect, Purpose, and Motive as Applicable Elements to § 8(a)(1) and § 8(a)(3) Violations of the NLRA, 7 Wake Forest L.Rev. 616 (1971); Oberer, The Scienter Factor in Sections 8(a)(1) and (3) of the Labor Act: of Balancing, Hostile Motive, Dogs and Tails, 52 Corn.L.Q. 491 (1967).

can Radio Telegraphists, a national labor organization; respondent's parent company, whose headquarters were in New York, deals with representatives of the national organization. In September, 1935, in view of the unsatisfactory state of negotiations for a new collective bargaining agreement, the national officers called a strike which took effect at midnight on October 4 (and which ultimately lasted only three days). Respondent, in order to maintain service, brought employees from other offices to fill the places of the San Francisco strikers. When the strike proved unsuccessful in other parts of the country, a number of San Francisco employees became convinced that they should return to work before their places were filled by new men. Respondent informed them that they might return to work in a body but that since it had promised eleven men brought to San Francisco an opportunity to remain there if they desired, the return of the strikers would have to be handled in such a way as not to displace the eleven. Later one of respondent's officials gave the striking employees a list on which the names of eleven strikers were checked off as ineligible for reinstatement until their applications were approved by the New York office. When it turned out that only five of the new men wished to stay in San Francisco, six of the eleven checked off resumed their work without challenge. The remaining five, who were prominent in the activities of the union and in connection with the strike, were not reinstated in the course of the next three weeks. Local 3 thereupon filed charges with the Board.

The Board concluded that respondent by refusing to reinstate the five men in question, "thereby discharging said employees," discriminated in regard to tenure of employment in violation of section 8(1) and (3). Accordingly the Board ordered their reinstatement with back pay. The Circuit Court of Appeals set aside the order of the Board.]

We hold that we have jurisdiction; that the Board's order is within its competence and does not contravene any provision of the Constitution. * * *

Second. Under the findings the strike was a consequence of, or in connection with, a current labor dispute as defined in section 2(9) of the act, 29 U.S.C.A. § 152(9). That there were pending negotiations for the execution of a contract touching wages and terms and conditions of employment of point-to-point operators cannot be denied. * * *

Third. The strikers remained employees under section 2(3) of the act, 29 U.S.C.A. § 152(3), which provides: "The term 'employee' shall include * * * any individual whose work has ceased as a consequence of, or in connection with, any current labor dispute or because of any unfair labor practice, and who has not obtained any other regular and substantially equivalent employment * * *."

Within this definition the strikers remained employees for the purpose of the act and were protected against the unfair labor practices denounced by it.

Fourth. It is contended that the Board lacked jurisdiction because respondent was at no time guilty of any unfair labor practice. * * * There is no evidence and no finding that the respondent was guilty of any unfair labor practice in connection with the negotiations in New York. On the contrary, it affirmatively appears that the respondent was negotiating with the authorized representatives of the union. Nor was it an unfair labor practice to replace the striking employees with others in an effort to carry on the business. Although section 13 of the act, 29 U.S.C.A. § 163, provides, "Nothing in this Act [chapter] shall be construed so as to interfere with or impede or diminish in any way the right to strike," it does not follow that an employer, guilty of no act denounced by the statute, has lost the right to protect and continue his business by supplying places left vacant by strikers. And he is not bound to discharge those hired to fill the places of strikers, upon the election of the latter to resume their employment, in order to create places for them. The assurance by respondent to those who accepted employment during the strike that if they so desired their places might be permanent was not an unfair labor practice, nor was it such to reinstate only so many of the strikers as there were vacant places to be filled. But the claim put forward [by the Board] is that the unfair labor practice indulged by the respondent was discrimination in reinstating striking employees by keeping out certain of them for the sole reason that they had been active in the union. As we have said, the strikers retained, under the act, the status of employees. Any such discrimination in putting them back to work is, therefore, prohibited by section 8.

Fifth. The Board's findings as to discrimination are supported by evidence. * * * The Board found, and we cannot say that its finding is unsupported, that, in taking back six of the eleven men and excluding five who were active union men, the respondent's officials discriminated against the latter on account of their union activities and that the excuse given that they did not apply until after the quota was full was an afterthought and not the true reason for the discrimination against them.

As we have said, the respondent was not bound to displace men hired to take the strikers' places in order to provide positions for them. It might have refused reinstatement on the grounds of skill or ability, but the Board found that it did not do so. It might have resorted to any one of a number of methods of determining which of its striking employees would have to wait because five men had taken permanent positions during the strike, but it is found that the preparation and use of the list, and the action taken by respondent, was with the purpose to discriminate against those most active in the union. There is evidence to support these findings. * * *

Seventh. The affirmative relief ordered by the Board was within its powers and its order was not arbitrary or capricious. * * *

MR. JUSTICE CARDOZO and MR. JUSTICE REED took no part in the consideration or decision of this case.

Problems for Discussion

1. Does not the permanent replacement of strikers (and the retention of non-strikers) constitute the clearest conceivable "discrimination in regard to hire or tenure of employment" which discourages union membership and activities? How, then, can the Court conclude that such replacement does not violate the Act? Is there any support for an exception in the text of the Act? In its purposes?

Could the General Counsel have prevailed on this issue if he had demonstrated that the employer could have kept the business going with merely temporary replacements? (How protracted was the strike?) That the employer was really motivated by a desire to break the union?

2. Notice that this case involves the replacement of "economic" strikers—that is, strikers who are using the stoppage as a means of extracting some bargaining concession from the employer. Can this case be used as a precedent when an economic striker, rather than being permanently replaced, is discharged outright?

Can this case be used as a precedent when the employee being permanently replaced is not an economic striker but is rather an "unfair labor practice striker," i. e., where the stoppage is a protest against an unfair labor practice committed by the employer? What arguments can be made to permit the unfair labor practice striker to be reinstated after an attempted permanent replacement (and thus to "bump" the replacement)? On the other hand, what arguments can be made for treating the economic striker *more* favorably than the unfair labor practice striker?

NLRB v. ERIE RESISTOR CO.

Supreme Court of the United States, 1963.
373 U.S. 221, 83 S.Ct. 1139, 10 L.Ed.2d 308.

MR. JUSTICE WHITE delivered the opinion of the Court.

[During a strike over the terms of a new collective bargaining agreement the company, which was under intense competitive pressure, continued production with the aid of non-strikers. Later, the company hired replacements to whom it promised some form of super-seniority at the end of the strike. Later but still during the strike, the company announced that the super-seniority would take the form of adding twenty years to the length of a worker's actual service for purposes of future layoffs and recalls (but not for other employee benefits based on seniority). The offer was extended to strikers who would return to work. In a short time, a substantial number of the strikers went back to work, and the union capitulated and signed a new contract and a settlement agreement (which left the company's super-seniority plan in effect pending the final disposition of unfair labor practice charges). The company then reinstated those strikers whose jobs had not been filled, and at about the same time the union received some 173 resignations from membership (out of an initial unit of 478 employees). Although within a few weeks the company's workforce had returned to nearly its pre-strike size, some nine months later it had slipped back to nearly half that size; many employees laid off during this cutback were reinstated strikers who had not been credited with super-seniority.

The union filed charges challenging both the super-seniority plan and the later layoffs. The NLRB held that specific evidence of the Respondent's discriminatory motivation is not required to establish the alleged violations of the Act, and that the employer's argument (accepted by the Trial Examiner) that its overriding purpose in granting super-seniority was to keep its plant open and that business necessity justified its conduct was unacceptable since "to excuse such conduct would greatly diminish, if not destroy, the right to strike guaranteed by the Act, and would run directly counter to the guarantees of Sections 8(a) (1) and (3) that employees shall not be discriminated against for engaging in protected concerted activities." Accordingly, the Board declined to make findings as to the specific motivation of the plan or its business necessity in the circumstances here. The Court of Appeals rejected as unsupportable the rationale of the Board that a preferential seniority policy is illegal however motivated.

> "We are of the opinion that inherent in the right of an employer to replace strikers during a strike is the concomitant right to adopt a preferential seniority policy which will assure the replacements some form of tenure, provided the policy is adopted *solely* to protect and continue the business of the employer. We find nothing in the Act which proscribes such a policy. Whether the policy adopted by the Company in the instant case was illegally motivated we do not decide. The question is one of fact for decision by the Board." 303 F.2d, at 364.

It consequently denied the Board's petition for enforcement and remanded the case for further findings.]

We think the Court of Appeals erred in holding that, in the absence of a finding of specific illegal intent, a legitimate business purpose is always a defense to an unfair labor practice charge. Cases in this Court dealing with unfair labor practices have recognized the relevance and importance of showing the employer's intent or motive to discriminate or to interfere with union rights. But specific evidence of such subjective intent is "not an indispensable element of proof of violation." Radio Officers Union of Commercial Telegraphers Union, A. F. L. v. National Labor Relations Board, 347 U.S. 17, 44, 74 S.Ct. 323, 98 L.Ed. 455. "Some conduct may by its very nature contain the implications of the required intent; the natural foreseeable consequences of certain action may warrant the inference. * * * The existence of discrimination may at times be inferred by the Board, for 'it is permissible to draw on experience in factual inquiries.'" Local 357, International Brotherhood of Teamsters, Chauffeurs, Warehousemen and Helpers of America v. National Labor Relations Board, 365 U.S. 667, 675, 81 S.Ct. 835, 839, 6 L.Ed.2d 11.

Though the intent necessary for an unfair labor practice may be shown in different ways, proving it in one manner may have far different weight and far different consequences than proving it in another. When specific evidence of a subjective intent to discriminate or to encourage or discourage union membership is shown, and found, many otherwise innocent or ambiguous actions which are normally incident to the conduct of a business may, without more, be converted into unfair labor practices. [The Court cited cases involving hiring, discharge, subcontracting, and plant removal.] Such proof itself is normally sufficient to destroy the employer's claim of a legitimate business purpose, if one is made, and provides strong support to a finding that there is interference with union rights or that union membership will be discouraged. Conduct which on its face appears to serve legitimate business ends in these cases is wholly impeached by the showing of an intent to encroach upon protected rights. The employer's claim of legitimacy is totally dispelled.

The outcome may well be the same when intent is founded upon the inherently discriminatory or destructive nature of the conduct itself. The employer in such cases must be held to intend the very consequences which foreseeably and inescapably flow from his actions and if he fails to explain away, to justify or to characterize his actions as something different than they appear on their face, an unfair labor practice charge is made out. Radio Officers Union of Commercial Telegraphers Union, A. F. L. v. National Labor Relations Board, supra. But as often happens, the employer may counter by claiming that his actions were taken in the pursuit of legitimate business ends and that his dominant purpose was not to discriminate or to invade union rights but to accomplish business objectives acceptable under the Act. Nevertheless his conduct *does* speak for itself—it *is* discriminatory and it *does* discourage union membership and whatever the claimed overriding justification may be, it carries with it unavoidable consequences which the employer not only foresaw but which he must have intended. As is not uncommon in human experience, such situations present a complex of motives and preferring one motive to another is in reality the far more delicate task, reflected in part in decisions of this Court of weighing the interests of employees in concerted activity against the interest of the employer in operating his business in a particular manner and of balancing in the light of the Act and its policy the intended consequences upon employee rights against the business ends to be served by the employer's conduct. This essentially is the teaching of the Court's prior cases dealing with this problem and, in our view, the Board did not depart from it.

The Board made a detailed assessment of super-seniority and, to its experienced eye, such a plan had the following characteristics:

(1) Super-seniority affects the tenure of all strikers whereas permanent replacement, proper under Mackay, affects only those who are, in actuality, replaced. It is one thing to say that a striker is subject to loss of his job at the strike's end but quite another to hold that in addition to the threat of replacement, all strikers will at best return to their jobs with seniority inferior to that of the replacements and of those who left the strike.

(2) A super-seniority award necessarily operates to the detriment of those who participated in the strike as compared to nonstrikers.

(3) Super-seniority made available to striking bargaining unit employees as well as to new employees is in effect offering individual benefits to the strikers to induce them to abandon the strike.

(4) Extending the benefits of super-seniority to striking bargaining unit employees as well as to new replacements deals a crippling blow to the strike effort. At one stroke, those with low seniority have the opportunity to obtain the job security which ordinarily only long years of service can bring, while conversely, the accumulated seniority of older employees is seriously diluted. This combination of threat and promise could be expected to undermine the strikers' mutual interest and place the entire strike effort in jeopardy. The history of this strike and its virtual collapse following the

announcement of the plan emphasize the grave repercussions of super-seniority.

(5) Super-seniority renders future bargaining difficult, if
not impossible, for the collective bargaining representative.   Unlike the replacement granted in Mackay
which ceases to be an issue once the strike is over, the
plan here creates a cleavage in the plant continuing
long after the strike is ended.   Employees are henceforth divided into two camps: those who stayed with
the union and those who returned before the end of the
strike and thereby gained extra seniority.   This breach
is reemphasized with each subsequent layoff and stands
as an ever-present reminder of the dangers connected
with striking and with union activities in general.

In the light of this analysis, super-seniority by its very terms
operates to discriminate between strikers and non-strikers, both during and after a strike, and its destructive impact upon the strike
and union activity cannot be doubted.   The origin of the plan, as respondent insists, may have been to keep production going and it may
have been necessary to offer super-seniority to attract replacements
and induce union members to leave the strike.   But if this is true,
accomplishment of respondent's business purpose inexorably was
contingent upon attracting sufficient replacements and strikers by
offering preferential inducements to those who worked as opposed
to those who struck.   We think the Board was entitled to treat this
case as involving conduct which carried its own indicia of intent and
which is barred by the Act unless saved from illegality by an overriding business purpose justifying the invasion of union rights.
*   *   *

*   *   *   In view of the deference paid the strike weapon by
the federal labor laws and the devastating consequences upon it
which the Board found was and would be precipitated by respondent's inherently discriminatory super-seniority plan, we cannot say
the Board erred in the balance which it struck here.   Although the
Board's decisions are by no means immune from attack in the courts
as cases in the Court amply illustrate, e. g., National Labor Relations Board v. Babcock & Wilcox Co., 351 U.S. 105, 76 S.Ct. 679, 100
L.Ed. 975; National Labor Relations Board v. United Steelworkers,
357 U.S. 357, 78 S.Ct. 1268, 2 L.Ed.2d 1383; National Labor Relations Board v. Insurance Agents, 361 U.S. 477, 80 S.Ct. 419, 4 L.Ed.
2d 454, its findings here are supported by substantial evidence, Universal Camera Corp. v. National Labor Relations Board, 340 U.S.
474, 71 S.Ct. 456, 95 L.Ed. 456, its explication is not inadequate,
irrational or arbitrary, compare Phelps Dodge Corp. v. National

Labor Relations Board, 313 U.S. 177, 196–197, 61 S.Ct. 845, 853–854, 85 L.Ed. 1271; National Labor Relations Board v. United Steelworkers, supra, and it did not exceed its powers or venture into an area barred by the statute. Compare National Labor Relations Board v. Insurance Agents, supra. * * *

Problems for Discussion

1. Are you convinced by the conclusion that super-seniority for returning strikers is so much more devastating than permanent replacement of strikers?

2. Is it fair to capsulize the Court's decision in *Erie Resistor* as follows: (a) Intention to discriminate against union members, or to deprive employees of statutory rights, is not necessary to a violation of Sections 8(a)(1) and (3); (b) the NLRA permits the Board to weigh the severity of different employer responses to union activity and to outlaw those which have too devastating an impact on that activity, regardless of the absence of an employer's discriminatory motive; and (c) the federal courts are to give great deference to the Board's exercise of judgment in this weighing process? Do any of these propositions survive the decision of the Court in *American Shipbuilding*, page 842 infra?

In NLRB v. TRUCK DRIVERS LOCAL 449 (BUFFALO LINEN), 353 U.S. 87, 77 S.Ct. 643, 1 L.Ed.2d 676 (1957), the Court had, before *Erie Resistor*, deferred to the expertise of the Board in adjusting the interests of employers and their workers in the use of economic weapons. There, a number of laundry concerns were joined in a multi-employer association, which bargained with a single union for a comprehensive labor agreement for the employees at all of the companies. During negotiations, the union called a strike at only one of the companies, hoping to secure a favorable settlement with that company while all other competing companies remained in business and then to utilize this "whipsaw" technique on each company in turn. Upon the strike at the one company, however, the other members of the employer association locked out their employees, and the union claimed that the lockout was in violation of Sections 8(a)(1) and (3) of the Labor Act. The Board had in prior cases authorized a lockout only when reasonably believed necessary by the employer to anticipate a strike which would otherwise have been timed to cause undue harm to the employer's equipment or business. To these so-called defensive lockouts, the Board in this case added the multi-employer lockout as a legitimate employer response to union concerted activity, and the Supreme Court upheld the decision of the Board. It stated:

> "Although the Act protects the right of the employees to strike in support of their demands, this protection is not

so absolute as to deny self-help by employers when legitimate interests of employees and employers collide. Conflict may arise, for example, between the right to strike and the interest of small employers in preserving multi-employer bargaining as a means of bargaining on an equal basis with a large union and avoiding the competitive disadvantages resulting from nonuniform contractual terms. The ultimate problem is the balancing of the conflicting legitimate interests. The function of striking that balance to effectuate national labor policy is often a difficult and delicate responsibility, which the Congress committed primarily to the National Labor Relations Board, subject to limited judicial review.

"The Court of Appeals recognized that the National Labor Relations Board has legitimately balanced conflicting interests by permitting lockouts where economic hardship was shown. The court erred, however, in too narrowly confining the exercise of Board discretion to the cases of economic hardship. We hold that in the circumstances of this case the Board correctly balanced the conflicting interests in deciding that a temporary lockout to preserve the multi-employer bargaining basis from the disintegration threatened by the Union's strike action was lawful."

AMERICAN SHIPBUILDING CO. v. NLRB [8]

Supreme Court of the United States, 1965.
380 U.S. 300, 85 S.Ct. 955, 13 L.Ed.2d 855.

MR. JUSTICE STEWART delivered the opinion of the Court.

The American Shipbuilding company operates four shipyards on the Great Lakes—at Chicago, at Buffalo, and at Toledo and Lorain, Ohio. The company is primarily engaged in the repairing of ships, a highly seasonal business concentrated in the winter months when the freezing of the Great Lakes renders shipping impossible. What limited business is obtained during the shipping season is frequently such that speed of execution is of the utmost importance to minimize immobilization of the ships.

---

8. See Baird, Lockout Law: The Supreme Court and the NLRB, 38 Geo. Wash.L.Rev. 396 (1970); Bernhardt, Lockouts: An Analysis of Board and Court Decisions Since Brown and American Ship, 57 Corn.L.Rev. 211 (1972); Feldesman & Koretz, Lockouts, 46 B.U.L.Rev. 329 (1966); Meltzer, Lockouts Under the LMRA: New Shadows on an Old Terrain, 28 U. Chi.L.Rev. 614 (1961); Oberer, Lockouts and the Law: The Importance of America Shipbuilding and Brown Food, 51 Cornell L.Q. 193 (1966).

Since 1952 the employer has engaged in collective bargaining with a group of eight unions. Prior to the negotiations here in question, the employer had contracted with the unions on five occasions, each agreement having been preceded by a strike. The particular chapter of the collective bargaining history with which we are concerned opened shortly before May 1, 1961, when the unions notified the company of their intention to seek modification of the current contract, due to expire on August 1. * * *

[O]n August 9, after extended negotiations, the parties separated without having resolved substantial differences on the central issues dividing them and without having specific plans for further attempts to resolve them—a situation which the trial examiner found was an impasse. Throughout the negotiations, the employer displayed anxiety as to the unions' strike plans, fearing that the unions would call a strike as soon as a ship entered the Chicago yard or delay negotiations into the winter to increase strike leverage. The union negotiator consistently insisted that it was his intention to reach an agreement without calling a strike; however, he did concede incomplete control over the workers—a fact borne out by the occurrence of a wildcat strike in February 1961. Because of the danger of an unauthorized strike and the consistent and deliberate use of strikes in prior negotiations, the employer remained apprehensive of the possibility of a work stoppage.

In light of the failure to reach an agreement and the lack of available work, the employer decided to lay off certain of his workers. On August 11 the employees received a notice which read: "Because of the labor dispute which has been unresolved since August 1, 1961, you are laid off until further notice." The Chicago yard was completely shut down and all but two employees laid off at the Toledo yard. A large force was retained at Lorain to complete a major piece of work there and the employees in the Buffalo yard were gradually laid off as miscellaneous tasks were completed. Negotiations were resumed shortly after these layoffs and continued for the following two months until a two-year contract was agreed upon on October 27. The employees were recalled the following day.

[After the usual unfair labor practice proceedings the Board concluded, 3–2 that the employer "by curtailing its operations at the South Chicago yard with the consequent layoff of the employees coerced employees in the exercise of their bargaining rights in violation of Section 8(a) (1) of the Act, and discriminated against its employees within the meaning of Section 8(a) (3) of the Act." [9] The

---

9. Although the complaint stated a violation of § 8(a)(5) as well, the Board made no findings as to this claim, believing that there would have been no point in entering a bargaining order because the parties had long since executed an agreement. The passage quoted in the text of this

decision followed established Board precedent.] "The Board has held that, absent special circumstances, an employer may not during bargaining negotiations either threaten to lock out or lock out his employees in aid of his bargaining position. Such conduct the Board has held presumptively infringes upon collective bargaining rights of employees in violation of Section 8(a) (1), and the lockout, with its consequent layoff, amounts to a discrimination within the meaning of Section 8(a) (3). In addition, the Board has held that such conduct subjects the Union and employees it represents to unwarranted and illegal pressure and creates an atmosphere in which the free opportunity for negotiation contemplated by Section 8(a) (5) does not exist." Quaker State Oil Refining Co., 121 N.L.R.B. 334, 337.

In analyzing the status of the bargaining lockout under §§ 8(a) (1) and 8(a) (3) of the National Labor Relations Act, it is important that the practice with which we are here concerned be distinguished from other forms of temporary separation from employment. No one would deny that an employer is free to shut down his enterprise temporarily for reasons of renovation or lack of profitable work unrelated to his collective bargaining situation. Similarly, we put to one side cases where the Board has concluded on the basis of substantial evidence that the employer has used a lockout as a means to injure a labor organization or to evade his duty to bargain collectively. Hopwood Retinning Co., 4 N.L.R.B. 922; Scott Paper Box Co., 81 N.L.R.B. 535. What we are here concerned with is the use of a temporary layoff of employees solely as a means to bring economic pressure to bear in support of the employer's bargaining position, after an impasse has been reached. This is the only issue before us, and all that we decide.

To establish that this practice is a violation of § 8(a) (1), it must be shown that the employer has interfered with, restrained, or coerced employees in the exercise of some right protected by § 7 of the Act. The Board's position is premised on the view that the lockout interferes with two of the rights guaranteed by § 7: the right to bargain collectively and the right to strike. In the Board's view, the use of the lockout "punishes" employees for the presentation of and adherence to demands made by their bargaining representatives and so coerces them in the exercise of their right to bargain collectively. It is important to note that there is here no allegation that the employer used the lockout in the service of designs inimical to the process of collective bargaining. There was no evidence and no finding that the employer was hostile to his employees banding together for collective bargaining or that the lockout was designed to discipline them

opinion below from NLRB v. Insurance Agents' Int'l Union, 361 U.S. 477, 80 S.Ct. 419, 4 L.Ed.2d 454 (1960), *infra*, has even more direct application to the § 8(a)(5) question. * * *

for doing so. It is therefore inaccurate to say that the employer's intention was to destroy or frustrate the process of collective bargaining. What can be said is that he intended to resist the demands made of him in the negotiations and to secure modification of these demands. We cannot see that this intention is in any way inconsistent with the employees' rights to bargain collectively.

Moreover, there is no indication, either as a general matter or in this specific case, that the lockout will necessarily destroy the unions' capacity for effective and responsible representation. The unions here involved have vigorously represented the employees since 1952, and there is nothing to show that their ability to do so has been impaired by the lockout. Nor is the lockout one of those acts which is demonstrably so destructive of collective bargaining that the Board need not inquire into employer motivation, as might be the case, for example, if an employer permanently discharged his unionized staff and replaced them with employees known to be possessed of a violent antiunion animus. Cf. Labor Board v. Erie Resistor Corp., 373 U.S. 221, 83 S.Ct. 1139. The lockout may well dissuade employees from adhering to the position which they initially adopted in the bargaining, but the right to bargain collectively does not entail any "right" to insist on one's position free from economic disadvantage. Proper analysis of the problem demands that the simple intention to support the employer's bargaining position as to compensation and the like be distinguished from a hostility to the process of collective bargaining which could suffice to render a lockout unlawful. See Labor Board v. Brown, 380 U.S. 278, 85 S.Ct. 980.

The Board has taken the complementary view that the lockout interferes with the right to strike protected under §§ 7 and 13 of the Act in that it allows the employer to pre-empt the possibility of a strike and thus leave the union with "nothing to strike against." Insofar as this means that once employees are locked out, they are deprived of their right to call a strike against the employer because he is already shut down, the argument is wholly specious, for the work stoppage which would have been the object of the strike has in fact occurred. It is true that recognition of the lockout deprives the union of exclusive control of the timing and duration of work stoppages calculated to influence the result of collective bargaining negotiations, but there is nothing in the statute which would imply that the right to strike "carries with it" the right exclusively to determine the timing and duration of all work stoppages. The right to strike as commonly understood is the right to cease work—nothing more. No doubt a union's bargaining power would be enhanced if it possessed not only the simple right to strike but also the power exclusively to determine when work stoppages shall occur, but the Act's provisions are not indefinitely elastic, content-free forms to be shaped in whatever manner the Board might think best conforms to the proper balance of bargaining power.

Thus, we cannot see that the employer's use of a lockout solely in support of a legitimate bargaining position is in any way inconsistent with the right to bargain collectively or with the right to strike. Accordingly, we conclude that on the basis of the findings made by the Board in this case, there has been no violation of § 8(a) (1).

Section 8(a) (3) prohibits discrimination in regard to tenure or other conditions of employment to discourage union membership. Under the words of the statute there must be both discrimination and a resulting discouragement of union membership. It has long been established that a finding of violation under this section will normally turn on the employer's motivation. See Labor Board v. Brown, 380 U.S. 278, 85 S.Ct. 980; Radio Officers' Union v. Labor Board, 347 U.S. 17, 43, 74 S.Ct. 323, 337; Labor Board v. Jones & Laughlin Steel Corp., 301 U.S. 1, 46, 57 S.Ct. 615, 628. Thus when the employer discharges a union leader who has broken shop rules, the problem posed is to determine whether the employer has acted purely in disinterested defense of shop discipline or has sought to damage employee organization. It is likely that the discharge will naturally tend to discourage union membership in both cases, because of the loss of union leadership and the employees' suspicion of the employer's true intention. But we have consistently construed the section to leave unscathed a wide range of employer actions taken to serve legitimate business interests in some significant fashion, even though the act committed may tend to discourage union membership. See, e. g., Labor Board v. Mackay Radio & Telegraph Co., 304 U.S. 333, 347, 58 S.Ct. 904, 911. Such a construction of § 8(a) (3) is essential if due protection is to be accorded the employer's right to manage his enterprise. See Textile Workers v. Darlington Mfg. Co., 380 U.S. 263, 85 S.Ct. 994.

This is not to deny that there are some practices which are inherently so prejudicial to union interests and so devoid of significant economic justification that no specific evidence of intent to discourage union membership or other antiunion animus is required. In some cases, it may be that the employer's conduct carries with it an inference of unlawful intention so compelling that it is justifiable to disbelieve the employer's protestations of innocent purpose. Radio Officers' Union v. Labor Board, supra, 347 U.S., at 44–45, 74 S.Ct. at 337–338; Labor Board v. Erie Resistor Corp., supra. Thus where many have broken a shop rule, but only union leaders have been discharged, the Board need not listen too long to the plea that shop discipline was simply being enforced. In other situations, we have described the process as the "far more delicate task * * * of weighing the interests of employees in concerted activity against the interest of the employer in operating his business in a particular manner * * *." Labor Board v. Erie Resistor Corp., supra, 373 U.S. at 229, 83 S.Ct. at 1145.

But this lockout does not fall into that category of cases arising under § 8(a) (3) in which the Board may truncate its inquiry into employer motivation. As this case well shows, use of the lockout does not carry with it any necessary implication that the employer acted to discourage union membership or otherwise discriminate against union members as such. The purpose and effect of the lockout was only to bring pressure upon the union to modify its demands. Similarly, it does not appear that the natural tendency of the lockout is severely to discourage union membership while serving no significant employer interest. In fact, it is difficult to understand what tendency to discourage union membership or otherwise discriminate against union members was perceived by the Board. There is no claim that the employer locked out only union members, or locked out any employee simply because he was a union member; nor is it alleged that the employer conditioned rehiring upon resignation from the union. * * *

To find a violation of § 8(a) (3) then, the Board must find that the employer acted for a proscribed purpose. Indeed, the Board itself has always recognized that certain "operative" or "economic" purposes would justify a lockout. But the Board has erred in ruling that only these purposes will remove a lockout from the ambit of § 8 (a) (3), for that section requires an intention to discourage union membership or otherwise discriminate against the union. There was not the slightest evidence and there was no finding, that the employer was actuated by a desire to discourage membership in the union as distinguished from a desire to affect the outcome of the particular negotiations in which he was involved. We recognize that the "union membership" which is not to be discouraged refers to more than the payment of dues and that measures taken to discourage participation in protected union activities may be found to come within the proscription. Radio Officers' Union v. Labor Board, supra, 347 U.S., at 39–40, 74 S.Ct., at 335. However, there is nothing in the Act which gives employees the right to insist on their contract demands, free from the sort of economic disadvantage which frequently attends bargaining disputes. Therefore, we conclude that where the intention proven is merely to bring about a settlement of a labor dispute on favorable terms, no violation of § 8(a) (3) is shown.

The conclusions which we draw from analysis of §§ 8(a) (1) and 8(a) (3) are consonant with what little of relevance can be drawn from the balance of the statute and its legislative history. In the original version of the Act, the predecessor of § 8(a) (1) declared it an unfair labor practice "[t]o attempt, by interference, influence, restraint, favor, coercion, or lockout, or by any other means, to impair the right of employees guaranteed in section 4." * * * [It is clear that the Senate] Committee was concerned with the status of the lockout and that the bill, as reported and as finally enacted, contained no prohibition on the use of the lockout as such.

Although neither § 8(a) (1) nor § 8(a) (3) refers specifically to the lockout, various other provisions of the Labor Management Relations Act do refer to the lockout, and these references can be interpreted as a recognition of the legitimacy of the device as a means of applying economic pressure in support of bargaining positions. Thus 29 U.S.C.A. § 158(d) (4) prohibits the use of strike or lockout unless requisite notice procedures have been complied with; 29 U.S.C.A. § 173(c) directs the Federal Mediation and Conciliation Service to seek voluntary resolution of labor disputes without resort to strikes or lockouts; and 29 U.S.C.A. §§ 176, 178, authorize procedures whereby the President can institute a board of inquiry to forestall certain strikes or lockouts. The correlative use of the terms "strike" and "lockout" in these sections contemplates that lockouts will be used in the bargaining process in some fashion. This is not to say that these provisions serve to define the permissible scope of a lockout by an employer. That, in the context of the present case, is a question ultimately to be resolved by analysis of §§ 8(a) (1) and 8 (a) (3).

The Board has justified its ruling in this case and its general approach to the legality of lockouts on the basis of its special competence to weigh the competing interests of employers and employees and to accommodate these interests according to its expert judgment. "The Board has reasonably concluded that the availability of such a weapon would so substantially tip the scales in the employer's favor as to defeat the Congressional purpose of placing employees on a par with their adversaries at the bargaining table." To buttress its decision as to the balance struck in this particular case, the Board points out that the employer has been given other weapons to counterbalance the employees' power of strike. The employer may permanently replace workers who have gone out on strike, or by stockpiling and subcontracting, maintain his commercial operations while the strikers bear the economic brunt of the work stoppage. Similarly, the employer can institute unilaterally the working conditions which he desires once his contract with the union has expired. Given these economic weapons, it is argued, the employer has been adequately equipped with tools of economic self-help.

There is of course no question that the Board is entitled to the greatest deference in recognition of its special competence in dealing with labor problems. In many areas its evaluation of the competing interests of employer and employee should unquestionably be given conclusive effect in determining the application of §§ 8(a) (1), (a) (3), and (a) (5). However, we think that the Board construes its functions too expansively when it claims general authority to define national labor policy by balancing the competing interests of labor and management.

While a primary purpose of the National Labor Relations Act was to redress the perceived imbalance of economic power between labor and management, it sought to accomplish that result by conferring certain affirmative rights on employees and by placing certain enumerated restrictions on the activities of employers. The Act prohibited acts which interfered with, restrained, or coerced employees in the exercise of their rights to organize a union, to bargain collectively, and to strike; it proscribed discrimination in regard to tenure and other conditions of employment to discourage membership in any labor organization. The central purpose of these provisions was to protect employee self-organization and the process of collective bargaining from disruptive interferences by employers. Having protected employee organization in countervailance to the employers' bargaining power, and having established a system of collective bargaining whereby the newly coequal adversaries might resolve their disputes, the Act also contemplated resort to economic weapons should more peaceful measures not avail. Sections 8(a) (1) and 8(a) (3) do not give the Board a general authority to assess the relative economic power of the adversaries in the bargaining process and to deny weapons to one party or the other because of its assessment of that party's bargaining power. Labor Board v. Brown, 380 U.S. 278, 85 S.Ct. 980. In this case the Board has, in essence, denied the use of the bargaining lockout to the employer because of its conviction that use of this device would give the employer "too much power." In so doing, the Board has stretched §§ 8(a) (1) and 8(a) (3) far beyond their functions of protecting the rights of employee organization and collective bargaining. What we have recently said in a closely related context is equally applicable here:

> "[W]hen the Board moves in this area * * * it is functioning as an arbiter of the sort of economic weapons the parties can use in seeking to gain acceptance of their bargaining demands. It has sought to introduce some standard of properly 'balanced' bargaining power, or some new distinction of justifiable and unjustifiable proper and 'abusive' economic weapons into * * * the Act. * * * We have expressed our belief that this amounts to the Board's entrance into the substantive aspect of the bargaining process to an extent Congress has not countenanced." Labor Board v. Insurance Agents' International Union, 361 U.S. 477, 497–498, 80 S.Ct. 419, 431.

We are unable to find that any fair construction of the provisions relied on by the Board in this case can support its finding of an unfair labor practice. Indeed, the role assumed by the Board in this area is fundamentally inconsistent with the structure of the Act and the function of the sections relied upon. The deference owed to an expert tribunal cannot be allowed to slip into a judicial inertia which results in the unauthorized assumption by an agency of major policy decisions properly made by Congress. Accordingly, we hold that an employer violates neither § 8(a) (1) nor § 8(a) (3) when, after a bargaining impasse has been reached, he temporarily shuts down his plant and lays off his employees for the sole purpose of bringing economic pressure to bear in support of his legitimate bargaining position.

Reversed.

[Mr. Justice White concurred in the reversal, but only because the record required the conclusion that the employer's purpose was not to exert economic pressure against the union but rather to avoid a strike which it reasonably feared would occur at a particularly disadvantageous time. He criticized the Court for unnecessarily passing upon the legality of the bargaining lockout and for overturning the Board's conclusion that the value of the bargaining lockout to the employer was here outweighed by its damaging consequences for the employees' right to bargain and to strike. Justice White rejected the conclusion of the majority that discriminatory motive was necessary to make out a violation, and said that even though the employer's conduct may have been in the pursuit of legitimate business ends, it unavoidably and foreseeably discouraged protected activity. "The balance and accommodation of 'conflicting legitimate interests' in labor relations does not admit of a simple solution and a myopic focus on the true intent or motive of the employer has not been the determinative standard of the Board or this Court. * * * The test is clearly one of choosing among several motivations or purposes and weighing the respective interests of employers and employees. And I think that is the standard the Court applies to the bargaining lockout in this case, but without heeding the fact the balance is for the Board to strike in the first instance."

Mr. Justice Goldberg, joined by the Chief Justice, also concurred in the result and also on the theory that this was a defensive lockout, designed to anticipate a threatened strike so as to avoid "economic injury over and beyond the loss of business normally incident to a strike upon the termination of the collective bargaining agreement." The Justice pointed out that bargaining lockouts can arise under many different circumstances and that it was unwise to suggest that they were always per se lawful; earlier NLRB decisions "properly take into account, in determining the legality of lockouts under the labor statutes, such factors as the length, character and history of the collective bargaining relation between the union and the employer, as well as whether a bargaining impasse has been reached." Here, the employer had a long history of collective bargaining, was confronted with a history of past strikes, had locked out only after bargaining in good faith to impasse, and reasonably feared a strike at an unusually harmful time. The test to apply in these cases was not that announced by the majority—whether employer conduct not actually motivated by antiunion bias is "demonstrably so destructive of collective bargaining" or "so prejudicial to union interests and so devoid of significant economic justification"—but rather "whether the legitimate economic interests of the employer justify his interference with the rights of his employees—a test involving 'the balancing of the conflicting legitimate interests,'" and one which is "committed primarily to the National Labor Relations Board, subject to limited judicial review."]

Problems for Discussion

1. Would the result in *American Shipbuilding* be the same if the employer locked out the employees prior to an impasse? See Darling & Co., 171 N.L.R.B. 801 (1968), enf'd sub nom. Lane v. NLRB, 418 F.2d 1208 (D.C.Cir. 1969).

2. The labor contract between the Ottawa Silica Company and the union was due to expire on May 31, 1975. Prior to that time, the union and the company met several times to try to reach a settlement on a contract, and sent various written proposals and counterproposals to each other. These efforts, however, were to no avail and it was clear that either a strike or lockout would occur. On May 31, the company gave the union its final proposals. Before a vote could be taken, the company announced a lockout to commence on June 1. The lockout remained in effect for five days, during which time the company continued normal operations by temporarily replacing the employees with sales, supervisory, and management personnel. On June 5, 1975, the union agreed to the contract terms offered by the employer, and promptly filed unfair labor practice charges. Did Ottawa Silica violate Sections 8(a)(1) and/or 8(a) (3) by staging the lockout and using temporary replacements during the period of the lockout? Compare *Ottawa Silica Co.* v. *NLRB*, 197 N.L.R.B. 449 (1972), enf'd mem. 482 F.2d 945 (6th Cir. 1973), with *Inland Trucking Co.* v. *N.L.R.B.*, 179 N.L.R.B. 350 (1969), enf'd 440 F.2d 562 (7th Cir. 1971).

NLRB v. GREAT DANE TRAILERS, INC.

Supreme Court of the United States, 1967.
388 U.S. 26, 87 S.Ct. 1792, 18 L.Ed.2d 1027.

MR. CHIEF JUSTICE WARREN delivered the opinion of the Court.
* * * The respondent company and the union entered into a collective bargaining agreement which was effective by its terms until March 31, 1963. The agreement contained a commitment by the company to pay vacation benefits to employees who met certain enumerated qualifications. In essence, the company agreed to pay specified vacation benefits to employees who, during the preceding year, had worked at least 1,525 hours. It was also provided that, in the case of a "lay-off, termination or quitting," employees who had

served more than 60 days during the year would be entitled to pro-rata shares of their vacation benefits. Benefits were to be paid on the Friday nearest July 1 of each year.

The agreement was temporarily extended beyond its termination date, but on April 30, 1963, the union gave the required 15 days' notice of intention to strike over issues which remained unsettled at the bargaining table. Accordingly, on May 16, 1963, approximately 350 of the company's 400 employees commenced a strike which lasted until December 26, 1963. The company continued to operate during the strike, using nonstrikers, persons hired as replacements for strikers, and some original strikers who had later abandoned the strike and returned to work. On July 12, 1963, a number of the strikers demanded their accrued vacation pay from the company. The company rejected this demand, basing its response on the assertion that all contractual obligations had been terminated by the strike and, therefore, none of the company's employees had a right to vacation pay. Shortly thereafter, however, the company announced that it would grant vacation pay—in the amounts and subject to the conditions set out in the expired agreement—to all employees who had reported for work on July 1, 1963. The company denied that these payments were founded on the agreement and stated that they merely reflected a new "policy" which had been unilaterally adopted. * * * Violations of § 8(a) (3) and (1) were charged. A hearing was held before a trial examiner who found that the company's action in regard to vacation pay constituted a discrimination in terms and conditions of employment which would discourage union membership, as well as an unlawful interference with protected activity. He held that the company had violated § 8(a) (3) and (1) and recommended that it be ordered to cease and desist from its unfair labor practice and to pay the accrued vacation benefits to strikers. The Board, after reviewing the record, adopted the Trial Examiner's conclusions and remedy. * * *

The Court of Appeals held that, although discrimination between striking and nonstriking employees had been proved, the Board's conclusion that the company had committed an unfair labor practice was not well-founded inasmuch as there had been no affirmative showing of an unlawful motivation to discourage union membership or to interfere with the exercise of protected rights. Despite the fact that the company itself had not introduced evidence of a legitimate business purpose underlying its discriminatory action, the Court of Appeals speculated that it might have been motivated by a desire "(1) to reduce expenses; (2) to encourage longer tenure among present employees; or (3) to discourage early leaves immediately before vacation periods."

* * *

The unfair labor practice charged here is grounded primarily in § 8(a) (3) which requires specifically that the Board find a discrimination and a resulting discouragement of union membership. American Ship Building Co. v. National Labor Relations Board, 380 U.S. 300, 311, 85 S.Ct. 955, 963, 13 L.Ed.2d 855 (1965). There is little question but that the result of the company's refusal to pay vacation benefits to strikers was discrimination in its simplest form. Compare Republic Aviation Corp. v. National Labor Relations Board, 324 U.S. 793, 65 S.Ct. 982, 89 L.Ed. 1372 (1945), with Local 357, Intern. Broth. of Teamsters, Chauffeurs, Warehousemen and Helpers of America v. National Labor Relations Board, 365 U.S. 667, 81 S.Ct. 835, 6 L.Ed.2d 11 (1961). Some employees who met the conditions specified in the expired collective bargaining agreement were paid accrued vacation benefits in the amounts set forth in that agreement, while other employees who also met the conditions but who had engaged in protected concerted activity were denied such benefits. Similarly, there can be no doubt but that the discrimination was capable of discouraging membership in a labor organization within the meaning of the statute. Discouraging membership in a labor organization "includes discouraging participation in concerted activities * * * such as a legitimate strike." National Labor Relations Board v. Erie Resistor Corp., 373 U.S. 221, 233, 83 S.Ct. 1139, 1148, 10 L.Ed.2d 308 (1963). The act of paying accrued benefits to one group of employees while announcing the extinction of the same benefits for another group of employees who are distinguishable only by their participation in protected concerted activity surely may have a discouraging effect on either present or future concerted activity.

But inquiry under § 8(a) (3) does not usually stop at this point. The statutory language "discrimination * * * to * * * discourage" means that the finding of a violation normally turns on whether the discriminatory conduct was motivated by an anti-union purpose. American Ship Building Co. v. National Labor Relations Board, 380 U.S. 300, 85 S.Ct. 955 (1965). It was upon the motivation element that the Court of Appeals based its decision not to grant enforcement, and it is to that element which we now turn. In three recent opinions we considered employer motivation in the context of asserted § 8(a) (3) violations. American Ship Building Co. v. National Labor Relations Board, supra; National Labor Relations Board v. Brown, 380 U.S. 278, 85 S.Ct. 980, 13 L.Ed.2d 839 (1965); and National Labor Relations Board v. Erie Resistor Corp., supra.
* * *

From this review of our recent decisions, several principles of controlling importance here can be distilled. First, if it can reasonably be concluded that the employer's discriminatory conduct was "inherently destructive" of important employee rights, no proof of antiunion motivation is needed and the Board can find an unfair labor practice even if the employer introduces evidence that the conduct was motivated by business considerations. Second, if the adverse effect of the discriminatory conduct on employee rights is "comparatively slight," an antiunion motivation must be proved to sustain the charge *if* the employer has come forward with evidence of legitimate and substantial business justifications for the conduct. Thus, in either situation, once it has been proved that the employer engaged in discriminatory conduct which could have adversely affected employee rights to *some* extent, the burden is upon the employer to establish that it was motivated by legitimate objectives since proof of motivation is most accessible to him.

Applying the principles to this case then, it is not necessary for us to decide the degree to which the challenged conduct might have affected employee rights. As the Court of Appeals correctly noted, the company came forward with no evidence of legitimate motives for its discriminatory conduct. 363 F.2d at 134. The company simply did not meet the burden of proof, and the Court of Appeals misconstrued the function of judicial review when it proceeded nonetheless to speculate upon what *might have* motivated the company. Since discriminatory conduct carrying a potential for adverse effect upon employee rights was proved and no evidence of a proper motivation appeared in the record, the Board's conclusions were supported by substantial evidence. Universal Camera Corp. v. National Labor Relations Board, 340 U.S. 474, 71 S.Ct. 456, 95 L.Ed. 456 (1951), and should have been sustained.

* * *

MR. JUSTICE HARLAN, whom MR. JUSTICE STEWART joins, dissenting. * * *

The "legitimate and substantial business justification" test may be interpreted as requiring only that the employer come forward with a nonfrivolous business purpose in order to make operative the usual requirement of proof of antiunion motive. If this is the result of today's decision, then the Court has merely penalized Great Dane for not anticipating this requirement when arguing before the Board. * * *

On the other hand, the use of the word "substantial" in the burden of proof formulation may give the Board a power which it formerly had only in § 8(a) (3) cases like *Erie Resistor*, supra. The Board may seize upon that term to evaluate the merits of the employer's business purposes and weigh them against the harm that befalls the union's interests as a result of the employer's action. If this is the Court's meaning, it may well impinge upon the accepted principle that "the right to bargain collectively does not entail any 'right' to insist on one's position free from economic disadvantage." American Ship Building Co. v. National Labor Relations Board, supra, at 309, 85 S.Ct. at 962. Employers have always been free to take reasonable measures which discourage a strike by pressuring the economic interests of employees, including the extreme measure of hiring permanent replacements, without having the Board inquire into the "substantiality" of their business justifications. National Labor Relations Board v. McKay Radio & Telegraph Co., 304 U.S. 333, 58 S.Ct. 904, 82 L.Ed. 1381. If the Court means to change this rule, though I assume it does not, it surely should not do so without argument of the point by the parties and without careful discussion. * * *

Problems for Discussion

1. Would the result be different if the employer had testified that it did not give vacation pay to strikers in order to reduce its costs of production?

2. General Electronics, presently a non-union company, has for many years given its employees paid holidays on Thanksgiving Day and the Friday after. It has also had a rule of long standing, which it has set forth in the company's employee handbook: "No employee shall be eligible for holiday pay if he fails to work all of his scheduled hours on the workdays immediately preceding and following such holiday, unless the absence is excused by personal illness, injury in the course of employment, death in the immediate family, or a reason determined to be equivalent by the Director of Labor Relations."

On November 15, IUE Local 333—which had made considerable progress in gathering authorization cards among plant employees—called a lawful strike to support its demands for recognition and for a general pay increase. General Electronics continued to operate, despite picketing, and urged all employees to continue to work. At first nearly all employees respected the picket line, but on the Wednesday preceding Thanksgiving Day, 103 of the 390 employees reported for work. Over the weekend, General promised pay for the two-day holiday to any employee who worked on Monday, the first scheduled workday following the holiday. That day 305 employees worked. General paid them all holiday pay but refused to pay the remaining 85 employees.

Can the Union secure holiday pay for those 85 employees? *yes*

3. A two-year collective bargaining agreement between the United States Pipe and Foundry Company and the union was due to expire on November 30, 1980. The employer and the union met at various times throughout October and November without reaching an agreement. However, the employees continued to work after the contract had expired on the basis of the last contract proposals by the Company. Since an impasse had been reached, the Company announced that certain changes would be

made, effective December 19. These changes included a cancellation of a wage increase put into effect at the expiration of the prior contract and the cancellation of some employee benefits such as paid holidays and vacation pay. The employees nevertheless continued to work until the employer instituted a total lockout on January 31, 1981. On May 13, 1981, a new agreement was signed and the lockout was ended. Did the Company violate the Labor Act by its withdrawal of benefits on December 19, 1980? If it did, will the ensuing total lockout of January 31 also be a violation of the Act? Compare *United States Pipe and Foundry Co.*, 180 N.L.R.B. 325 (1969), enf'd sub nom. *Local 155, Molders v. NLRB*, 143 U.S.App.D.C. 20, 442 F.2d 742 (D.C.Cir. 1971), with *NLRB v. Great Falls Employers' Council, Inc.*, 277 F.2d 772 (9th Cir. 1960).

4. The Pittsburgh-Des Moines Steel Company had a practice of giving annual Christmas bonuses to its employees. These bonuses were based on a five-factor formula: (1) overall results, (2) overall productivity, (3) results at each individual plant (the company had five plants), (4) productivity at each individual plant, and (5) continuity of work effort at each individual plant. In 1981, the maintenance unit at one of the company's plants engaged in an economic strike for 57 days. Consequently, the productivity at their plant was lower than normal. All employees in the company's five plants received Christmas bonuses except for the one unit which went out on strike. Has the company violated the Labor Act? See *Pittsburgh-Des Moines Steel Co.* v. *NLRB*, 284 F.2d 74 (9th Cir. 1960).

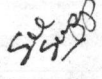

LAIDLAW CORP.[10]

National Labor Relations Board, 1968.
171 N.L.R.B. 1366.

[The Union on January 10, 1966 voted to reject the Company's wage offer and notified the Company of its intention to strike on January 12. On January 11, the plant manager announced that any striking employees who were replaced would "lose forever your right to employment by this company." The strike began on January 12, and on January 14 one Massey, a striker, applied for reinstatement but was told that his job had been filled and that even if he were reemployed he would be paid not at the wage rate obtaining at the time of the strike but rather at the rate paid a new hire. On January 18, Massey was informed of an opening in his job classification and was asked to return, but with treatment as a new employee; Massey refused to return on that basis and continued to strike. At a union meeting on February 10, many of the strikers voted to return to work, and they made unconditional application to do so on February 11; other strikers submitted such applications

---

10. See Finkin, The Truncation of *Laidlaw* Rights by Collective Agreements, 3 Ind.Rel.L.J. 591 (1979).

soon after. The Company announced that it had hired replacements for most of the strikers and that those strikers were not entitled to reinstatement. Although the Company did hire a number of the striker-applicants for vacancies existing at the time of their application, reinstatement applications were considered only on the date of application, and if there were excess vacancies on any later date they were filled by new hires, no check being made of the earlier reinstatement applications of February 11. Beginning on February 16, the Company notified the strikers (except those reinstated or declining reinstatement) of their termination as of the date of their written applications. It continued, however, to advertise for permanent help and a number of new employees were hired due to turnover, created in part by the departure of some permanent replacements. At a union meeting of February 20, a group of strikers protested the termination notices and the failure to reinstate most of the strikers, and decided to renew their strike effort on February 21 in protest against the Company's alleged unfair labor practice.

The Trial Examiner found that Massey was not entitled to reinstatement on January 14 when his job was filled by a permanent replacement, but that he remained an employee within Section 2(3) of the Labor Act and was thus entitled to full reinstatement when he reapplied at a time when the position was vacant. The Trial Examiner also concluded that the termination of the other strikers also violated Sections 8(a)(1) and (3), since they remained employees under the Act, their applications for reinstatement were continuous, they were entitled to full reinstatement when vacancies in their jobs later arose, and they were discriminated against when the Company hired new employees rather than offer positions to the strikers. It was also held that the failure to reinstate strikers as of February 11 converted the strike as of that date from an economic strike to an unfair labor practice strike.]

We concur in the conclusions of the Trial Examiner and in the relief granted Respondent's employees. In so doing we rely particularly on the principles set forth in N.L.R.B. v. Fleetwood Trailer Co., [389 U.S. 375 (1967)] in which the Supreme Court discussed the rights of economic strikers to reinstatement and the responsibility of employers to fully reinstate economic strikers, absent "legitimate and substantial business justifications," in a situation where production increased and more jobs were reestablished.

In *Fleetwood*, the employer was held to have violated the Act by failing to reinstate strikers and by hiring new employees for jobs which were reestablished when the employer resumed full production some 2 months after the strikers applied for reinstatement. In so finding, the Court pointed out that by virtue of Section 2(3) of the Act, an individual whose work ceases due to a labor dispute remains an employee if he has not obtained other regular or substantially equivalent employment, and that an employer refusing to reinstate strikers must show that the action was due to legitimate and substantial business justification. The Court further held that the burden of proving such justification was on the employer and also pointed out that the primary responsibility for striking a proper balance between the asserted business justifications and the invasion of employee rights rests with the Board rather than the courts. The Court also noted that an act so destructive of employee rights, without legitimate business justification, is an unfair labor practice without reference to intent or improper motivation. Furthermore, the Court explicitly rejected the argument, asserted by the employer in *Fleetwood* (389 U.S. at 380–381) and relied upon by the Respondent in the instant case, that reinstatement rights are determined at the time of initial application.

> It was clearly error to hold that the right of the strikers to reinstatement expired on August 20, when they first applied. *This basic right to jobs cannot depend on job availability as of the moment when applications are filed.* The right to reinstatement does not depend upon technicalities relating to application. On the contrary, *the status of the striker as an employee continues until he has obtained "other regular and substantially equivalent employment."* [Emphasis supplied.]

Application of these principles to the case before us makes it evident that the results reached by the Trial Examiner were correct, even though he did not have the benefit of the Supreme Court's *Fleetwood* decision, which issued subsequently.

Thus, in the case of Massey, he remained an employee when he rejoined the strike after his first effort to be reinstated was rejected even though at that particular moment he had been replaced. The right to reinstatement did not expire when the original application was made. When the position again became vacant, Massey, an economic striker who was still an employee, was available and entitled to full reinstatement unless there were legitimate and substantial business justifications for the failure to offer complete reinstatement. However, it is evident that no such justifications existed, for in fact Respondent needed and desired Massey's services, and it was Respondent who sought out Massey when the vacancy occurred. But its offer of employment as a new employee or as an employee with less than rights accorded by full reinstatement (such as denial of seniority) was wholly unrelated to any of its economic needs, could only penalize Massey for engaging in concerted activity, was inherently destructive of employee interests, and thus was unresponsive to the requirements of the statute, N.L.R.B. v. Erie Resistor Corp. In these circumstances there was no valid reason why Massey should not have been offered complete reinstatement, and Respondent's failure to do so was in violation of Section 8(a)(3) and (1) of the Act.

[The Board also held that Massey's fellow strikers were also treated unlawfully when they were not reinstated after February 11, pursuant to their request, as job openings arose. This was true if the strike after that date was converted into an unfair labor practice strike or even if it remained an economic strike (in which case their right to reinstatement would be precisely the same as Massey's).]

* * * As Respondent brought forward no evidence of business justification for refusing to reinstate these experienced employees while continuing to advertise for and hire new unskilled employees, we find such conduct was inherently destructive of employee rights. This right of reinstatement continued to exist so long as the strikers had not abandoned the employ of Respondent for other substantial and equivalent employment. Moreover, having signified their intent to return by their unconditional application for reinstatement and by their continuing presence, it was incumbent on Respondent to seek them out as positions were vacated. Having failed to fulfill its obligation to reinstate the employees to their jobs as vacancies arose, the Respondent thereby violated Section 8(a)(3) and (1) of the Act.

In arriving at our decision we are cognizant of a number of earlier cases in which the Board * * * in essence * * * held that an economic striker's right to full reinstatement is determined at the time application for reinstatement is made, and that if a replacement occupies the position at that particular moment, the striker is henceforth entitled only to nondiscriminatory consideration as an applicant for new employment. But, as we have noted previously, the Supreme Court in *Fleetwood* and *Great Dane* has now held that the right to the job does not depend on its availability at the precise moment of application, and that strikers retain their status as employees who are *entitled to reinstatement* absent substantial business justification, and regardless of union animus.

The underlying principle in both *Fleetwood* and *Great Dane, supra,* is that certain employer conduct, standing alone, is so inherently destructive of employee rights that evidence of specific anti-union motivation is not needed.[11] Specifically in *Fleetwood,* the

---

11. See also NLRB v. Erie Resistor Corp., supra.

Even if a finding of antiunion motivation is necessary, the employer's preference for strangers over tested and competent employees is sufficient basis for inferring such motive, and we, in agreement with the Trial Examiner, would do so if we considered motive material.

Court found that hiring new employees in the face of outstanding applications for reinstatement from striking employees is presumptively a violation of the Act, irrespective of intent unless the employer sustains his burden by showing legitimate and substantial reasons for his failure to hire the strikers. A similar parallel exists here which requires application of the same principle. When job vacancies arose as the result of the departure of permanent replacements, Respondent could not lawfully ignore outstanding applications for reinstatement from strikers and hire new applicants absent legitimate and substantial business reasons,[12] irrespective of intent. Moreover, we find, in accord with the Trial Examiner, that Respondent was in fact discriminatorily motivated when it implemented its avowed policy of not considering or hiring strikers once they had been replaced or if no vacancy existed on the date of application.[13]

We hold, therefore, that economic strikers who unconditionally apply for reinstatement at a time when their positions are filled by permanent replacements: (1) remain employees; and (2) are entitled to full reinstatement upon the departure of replacements unless they have in the meantime acquired regular and substantially equivalent employment, or the employer can sustain his burden of proof that the failure to offer full reinstatement was for legitimate and substantial business reasons. * * *

The decision of the Board was upheld in Laidlaw Corp. v. NLRB, 414 F.2d 99 (7th Cir. 1969) cert. denied 397 U.S. 920 (1970), and has since been endorsed by other courts of appeals. On review, the Laidlaw Corporation argued that even if the Board was correct in finding that its refusal to grant reinstatement was unlawful it was an abuse of the Board's discretion to apply that newly declared principle of law to Laidlaw and to impose a substantial backpay award against the company in spite of the fact that its conduct was lawful at the time it was performed. The company relied on a number of cases which held that in certain situations the Board's adoption of a new rule or policy may not be applied retroactively where its practical effect is to create a hardship on the employer disproportionate to the public ends to be accomplished. The court, however, disagreed: "In the case before us, we believe that the importance

---

12. E. g., as may be justified by a change in an employer's operations or where striker applicants lack requisite skills.

13. A refusal to consider or reinstate strikers once they have been replaced when vacancies thereafter occur is in effect a "delayed" discrimination which does not assume a mantle of lawfulness merely because certain lawful conduct, the hiring of a permanent replacement, intervened.

of protecting the statutory rights of Laidlaw's employees outweighs the fact that the company may have relied on a prior Board rule or policy. We are in agreement with the statement made by the General Counsel in his brief: 'Unless the disadvantaged strikers are compensated, they will have been penalized for exercising statutorily protected rights and the effect of discouraging future such exercises will not be completely dissipated. In these circumstances, it was not arbitrary or capricious for the Board to conclude that complete vindication of employee rights should take precedence over the employer's reliance on prior Board law.' "

Problems for Discussion

1. What is now the reach of the *MacKay Radio* doctrine, given the decision of the Board in *Laidlaw* which has been widely endorsed in the federal courts of appeals? Were the *MacKay* issue—the employer's right to hire permanent replacements for economic strikers—to arise afresh today, what would be the likely decision, given the decision of the Supreme Court in *Great Dane Trailers* and that of the Board in *Laidlaw*?

2. Is it lawful for an employer on the eve of a strike to state to its employees, as did the Laidlaw Corporation, that strikers will be permanently replaced and forever lose their employment status with the company?

3. A majority of the employees at Magnar Research Co. went out on strike on February 1, 1980 over new contract terms. The company hired permanent replacements for most of the strikers, and on July 1, 1980, most of the strikers applied unconditionally for reinstatement. The company informed them that no jobs were available because of the replacements but that they would be placed on a preferential hiring list. On July 1, 1981, however, the company informed the many former strikers who had not yet been returned to work that their preferential hiring status was terminated and that henceforth they would be considered for job openings in competition with new applicants; the company stated that one year had passed since their application for reinstatement, and that it was too burdensome to keep records for any longer period or to attempt to contact former employees thereafter, given the usual changes in addresses and telephone numbers. Does this announced termination of preferential hiring rights violate Sections 8(a)(1) and (3)?

Assume that, in terminating the preferential hiring rights of former strikers, the company relied upon a clause in the then expired (and since renewed) labor contract which provided that an employee who was laid off would lose his seniority rights for purposes of recall one year after the date of layoff. Would this modify the analysis under Sections 8(a) (1) and (3)? See *Brooks Research & Mfg., Inc.*, 202 N.L.R.B. 634 (1973).

4. Assume that in the preceding problem, when the strikers applied for reinstatement on July 1, 1980, Magnar entered into an agreement

with the union providing for the reinstatement of all of the strikers and the "bumping" of their replacements (who had been given oral assurances of permanent employment). If the latter workers file charges under Sections 8(a)(3) and 8(b)(2), should unfair labor practice complaints against Magnar and the union be issued by the Regional Director?

Employee Refusals to Cross Picket Lines

A particularly vexing problem in determining the reach of protection under Sections 8(a)(1) and (3) has been the treatment of employees who refuse to cross a picket line. If the picket line is at his own company, the employee who honors it and refuses to report to work will be deemed—if the picket line is the product of a lawful strike or picketing—to be a participant in that same activity and to be protected against discipline under Section 8(a)(1). If, however, the picket line is illegal—for example, it is incident to a secondary boycott in violation of Section 8(b)(4)—the employee making common cause with the picketers will himself be engaging in unprotected activity and will be amenable to discharge. The more difficult problem arises when the employee respects a lawful picket line (whether or not sponsored by his own union) at another company. While it is generally agreed that his decision to honor that picket line, even though made "as an individual," is "concerted" activity for "mutual aid or protection," there is disagreement as to whether it is protected or unprotected activity. The NLRB tends to treat such conduct as protected, while the federal courts of appeals have divided on the issue. One must dig rather deeply in the reported cases to find fully articulated reasons on either side of the issue.

Reasons for protecting the refusal to cross a lawful picket line established elsewhere are that this represents a showing of support for others in the labor movement who may some day be called upon to give comparable support when the now "lone" employee is himself a participant in lawful concerted activity; this conduct has also been made the special object of congressional concern in a proviso to Section 8(b)(4), declaring that it shall not be illegal (somewhat different from declaring that it shall be protected) to honor a picket line established at another company by the bargaining representative there; and, finally, to respect a picket line at another company is not designed to exert continuing and hurtful economic pressure on one's employer to make concessions in bargaining. Those who argue that respecting the picket line elsewhere should be treated as unprotected activity can point out that it smacks of the secondary boycott, with the employer of the refusing employee suffering pro tanto a work stoppage as a result of a labor dispute to which it is not a party and over which it has no control. Moreover, the refusal to cross the picket line can be treated as a breach of the employment contract, with the employee violating his employer's directions to work, instead picking and choosing the work that he wishes to do while remaining on the company payroll. NLRB v. L. G. Everist, Inc., 334 F.2d 312 (8th Cir. 1964).

If the refusal to cross a picket line elsewhere is unprotected activity, the employer may of course discharge the recalcitrant employee. If, however, the refusal is protected activity—somewhat akin to participation in an economic strike at one's own plant—then the employer's response to that refusal is confined by law. Thus, it has been held that (assuming the honoring of the picket line to be protected activity) the employee may not be discharged; although it has been held lawful for the employer to terminate that person's employment "where it is clear from the record that the employer acted only to preserve efficient operation of his business, and terminated the services of the employees only so it could immediately or within a short period thereafter replace them with others willing to perform the scheduled work." Redwing Carriers, Inc., 137 N.L.R.B. 1545 (1962), enf'd 325 F.2d 1011 (D.C.Cir. 1963), cert. denied 377 U.S. 905 (1964). Similarly, it has been held that the employer may not discharge an employee for refusal to cross a picket line to make a delivery when, at the time of the discharge, the delivery—which was a "one shot" delivery and required no work on a continuing basis at the picketed company—had already been completed by a supervisory employee. Thurston Motor Lines, 166 N.L. R.B. 862 (1967).

Problems for Discussion

1. Overnite Transportation Company is engaged in interstate freight transportation from its central terminal. Its employees are assigned no particular route but rather deliver freight according to assignments at the terminal and respond to radio calls in their trucks to make additional pickups at various locations. Last week, employee Styles received a radio call to pick up freight at the Warren Company, but when Styles arrived at the Warren plant and saw a picket line there, he drove past and made other pickups and deliveries at other locations. In the afternoon, Styles returned to the Warren plant to see whether conditions there had changed, but when he saw that they had not, he radioed in to the terminal and told the dispatcher that he could not in good conscience make the assigned pickup through the picket line. When the dispatcher promptly relayed this message to the terminal manager, the manager just as promptly informed Styles over his truck radio that he could not tolerate employees deciding which pickups and deliveries to make and which routes to drive, and that he should return to the terminal immediately and collect a final paycheck. Is it legal for the company thus to terminate Styles' employ-

ment? Are there any other facts necessary to make an informed conclusion? See *N.L.R.B.* v. *Overnite Transp. Co.*, 154 N.L.R.B. 127 (1965), enf'd in part 124 U.S.App.D.C. 289, 364 F.2d 682 (D.C.Cir. 1966).

2. During a strike at Montgomery Ward's Chicago mail order house, orders were rerouted from Chicago to the Kansas City house, where the employees are represented by the same union as at Chicago. Three employees at the Kansas City location refused to process mail orders which they believed were being routed from Chicago, and they were discharged for doing so. Are the discharges illegal? *NLRB* v. *Montgomery Ward & Co.*, 157 F.2d 486 (8th Cir. 1946).

NOTE ON UNFAIR LABOR PRACTICE STRIKES [14]

In many cases coming before the Board, such as *Laidlaw Corp.*, p. 856, supra, it has been plain that the employer's unfair labor practices caused the employees to initiate or prolong a strike, and in such cases the Board has quite uniformly ordered the employer to reinstate the striking employees to their former positions, discharging if necessary replacements hired during the strike. In MATTER OF BROWN SHOE CO., 1 N.L.R.B. 803 (1936), for example, the Board found that the respondent's arbitrary termination of a seniority agreement with the union in violation of section 8(1) was responsible for the strike at its plant on October 14, 1935. In order to restore the status quo in existence before the strike, the Board directed that the Brown Shoe Co. offer reinstatement to its striking employees and, upon request, enter into negotiations for the purpose of collective bargaining in respect to seniority arrangements. The reason for such order was set forth in the decision as follows:

> "The strike at the Salem plant on October 14 was caused by the respondent's conduct in arbitrarily terminating the seniority agreement with the union and by other antiunion conduct for which we have found it to be responsible. Moreover, we have found that the violent breaking of the picket line on the day of the strike was caused by the respondent, this conduct amounting to interference, restraint, and coercion of its employees in the exercise of their right to concerted activities for mutual aid and protection. An order requiring the respondent to cease and desist from such conduct will not wholly restore the union to at least the position it occupied in the Salem plant on the day of the strike. We, shall, therefore, in order to restore the status quo, order the respondent to offer reinstatement to those employees at the Salem plant who went out on strike on October 14, and to

14. See Note, Strike Misconduct: An Illusory Bar to Reinstatement, 72 Yale L.J. 182 (1962); Note, The Unfair Labor Practice Strike: A Critique and a Proposal for Change, 46 N.Y.U.L. Rev. 988 (1971).

that end, if necessary, to displace employees hired since October 14 to take the places of strikers."

In effect, the Board treats more favorably employees striking to protest conduct for which the NLRA provides a peaceful administrative remedy than employees who have no comparable means to better their terms of employment. Do you think that this is wise or unwise administrative policy?

Unfair labor practice strikers have also been treated somewhat more favorably than economic strikers concerning their rights to vote in representation elections held during the strike. Both economic and unfair labor practice strikers may vote, but the privilege of the economic striker expires if the election is held more than twelve months from the commencement of the strike. W. Wilton Wood, Inc., 127 N.L.R.B. 1675 (1959). And, since economic strikers are not entitled to "bump" their permanent replacements, such replacements may vote (in addition to the strikers), Rudolph Wurlitzer Co., 32 N.L.R.B. 163 (1941); but replacements for unfair labor practice strikers may not, Tampa Sand & Material Co., 137 N.L.R.B. 1549 (1962). The latter principle prevents the employer from committing an unfair labor practice and precipitating a strike, hiring replacements unsympathetic to the union and having them vote out the union in a representation election.

These distinctions in voting and reinstatement rights of economic and unfair labor practice strikers make it important on occasion to determine the "cause" of a strike. This issue is often complicated when a strike is initiated over bargaining demands or demands for recognition but, during the course of the strike, the employer commits unfair labor practices, e. g., refusing to bargain with a certified union or discriminatorily discharging a union supporter. Such an employer unfair labor practice will be held to "convert" the strike if it can be determined that the employer's action prolonged the strike beyond the date it would have terminated in due course as an economic strike. The *Laidlaw Corp.* case, at p. 856, supra, shows the Board applying the "conversion" doctrine, and finding that what had begun as a strike over bargaining demands became an unfair labor practice strike when it was prolonged by the union's vote to protest the employer's outright termination of strikers seeking reinstatement. The Board applied the usual rule that strikers who are permanently replaced during the economic phase of the strike are not entitled to immediate reinstatement, while strikers replaced after the date of conversion are.

The characterization of a strike as an unfair labor practice strike may also be important in determining whether there must be compliance with the notification and cooling-off requirements of

Section 8(d) of the Labor Act or whether a strike violates a no-strike promise in a collective bargaining agreement. These issues were addressed by the Supreme Court in MASTRO PLASTICS CORP. v. NLRB, 350 U.S. 270, 76 S.Ct. 349, 100 L.Ed. 309 (1956). In that case, an incumbent union had notified the employer of its intention to modify their labor contract; this notice was given in compliance with Section 8(d) which provides for a sixty-day waiting period for striking subsequent to a notice requesting "termination or modification" of a contract. One month after the notice was given, the employer discharged an employee for union activity, and the union called a strike to protest the discharge. The employer then discharged the strikers, arguing that their strike during the sixty-day cooling off period caused them to forfeit their status as "employees" under the Act (as stipulated by Section 8(d)) so that they were liable to immediate discharge; and that the strike was in breach of the contract's no-strike clause, and was thus also unprotected activity for which they could be discharged. The Court rejected both these arguments, resting on the Board's finding that the strike was precipitated by the unlawful discharge. Its object was thus not "termination or modification" of the contract within Section 8(d), so that compliance with the sixty-day waiting period was not necessary and participation in the strike did not expose the strikers to the loss-of-status provision of that Section. The Court also held that the conventional no-strike clause in a labor contract should be read to bar only economic strikes and not unfair labor practice strikes. The strikers were ordered reinstated with backpay.

The distinctions noted above between economic strikers and unfair labor practice strikers assume that the strikers have engaged in no conduct which falls beyond the protection of Section 7. When strikers do engage in such unprotected conduct, there is yet another distinction made in the law, once again in favor of the unfair labor practice striker and his right to reinstatement. The following case deals with that issue.

N L R B v. THAYER CO.

United States Court of Appeals, First Circuit, 1954.
213 F.2d 748.

[The company, in its two plants, sponsored in the early 1940s the formation of "workers' councils" in opposition to the United Furniture Workers. When, in the fall of 1948, the Furniture Workers attempted to organize once again and in fact demanded recognition as bargaining representative, the company threatened to discharge the union organizers and to close down its plants. These tactics were successful in one plant, where the company signed a new labor contract with the employer-dominated workers' council; in the other plant, the company first had to withhold the usual Christmas bonus and in January 1949 discharge seventeen employees before it sought employee approval of the contract with the workers' council. These discharges resulted in a strike at both plants, accompanied by intensive picketing. Large concentrations of pickets circled both plants (as many as 60 at one plant and 160 at the other) at the beginning and end of the workday, but usually the number of pickets was far less. The picket lines were fairly well-behaved, and nonstriking workers were able to enter and leave the plants without serious incident. The company took the position that the strike was illegal and that all strikers could lawfully be discharged; in addition, it secured an injunction against the picketing from a state court, which concluded that there was violence and destruction of property. Soon after, the pickets reapplied for their jobs, but 86 were refused reinstatement in addition to the 17 workers whose discharge in January 1949 had precipitated the strike. The NLRB concluded that the strike and picketing were protected by Section 7, and ordered that all 103 workers be reinstated.]

MAGRUDER, CHIEF JUDGE.

* * * It must be remembered that the employees were engaged in a strike provoked by unfair labor practices. This means, of course, that under ordinary circumstances if such strikers apply for their jobs at the termination of the strike, they must be returned to their old positions irrespective of the effect that such reinstatement may have upon the tenure of new employees hired as replacements. See, *e. g.*, NLRB v. Remington Rand, Inc., 130 F.2d 919, 927, 928 (C.A.2d, 1942). Where a strike is not caused by an unfair labor practice but is economic in nature, the employer need not discharge replacements in order to rehire strikers. NLRB v. Mackay Radio & Telegraph Co., 304 U.S. 333, 345, 58 S.Ct. 904, 82 L.Ed. 1381 (1938); NLRB v. Jackson Press, Inc., 201 F.2d 541, 546 (C.A. 7th, 1953). However, even in the situation of an economic strike, to avoid committing an 8(a)(1) unfair labor practice, the employer generally must rehire those strikers whose positions have not been filled and must refrain from disciplining them for the concerted activity. Home Beneficial Life Ins. Co. v. NLRB, 159 F.2d 280 (C.A. 4th, 1947); General Electric Co., 80 NLRB 174 (1948).

There is an exception to the latter generalization. If an economic strike as conducted is not concerted activity within the protection of § 7, then the employer is free to discharge the participating employees for the strike activity and the Board is powerless to order their reinstatement, see, *e. g.*, NLRB v. Indiana Desk Co., 149 F.2d 987 (C.A.7th, 1945). This is so because, if the particular collective action is not a protected § 7 activity, the employer commits no unfair labor practice by thus terminating the employment relation. He has not interfered with, restrained or coerced employees in the exercise of their rights guaranteed in § 7.   See Cox, The Right to Engage in Concerted Activities, 26 Ind.L.J. 319, 320 (1951).   Therefore, since the power of the Board to order reinstatement under § 10(c) is dependent upon its finding that an unfair labor practice has been committed, and since by hypothesis the economic strike was not caused by an unfair labor practice, it becomes crucial to the question of reinstatement of an economic striker to inquire whether the strike as conducted constituted concerted activity within the protection of § 7.

On the other hand where, as in the instant case, the strike was caused by an unfair labor practice, the power of the Board to order reinstatement is not necessarily dependent upon a determination that the strike activity was a "concerted activity" within the protection of § 7.   Even if it was not, the National Labor Relations Board has power under § 10(c) to order reinstatement if the discharges were not "for cause" [15] and if such an order would effectuate the policies of the Act.   Of course the discharge of strikers engaged in non-Section 7 activities often may be for cause, or their reinstatement may not effectuate the policies of the Act, but in certain circumstances it may.   The point is that where collective action is precipitated by an unfair labor practice, a finding that that action is not protected under § 7 does not, *ipso facto*, preclude an order reinstating employees who have been discharged because of their participation in the unprotected activity.

The respondents apparently have not recognized this subtlety, and failure to do so seems to have influenced their reasoning with respect to the effect of the state court decision.

[The court then considered, and rejected, the argument of the respondents that the state court finding that the strike was conducted in an illegal manner was equivalent to a finding that the strikers were not entitled to reinstatement and was res judicata in the proceeding before the Board.   Even if the state court finding could be deemed equivalent to one that the strike and picketing fell outside the protection of Section 7, that would not be dispositive of the issues in the instant case, that is, whether there was "cause" for discharge and if not, whether reinstatement would effectuate the policies of the Act.   These latter issues were not (and could not have been)

---

15. The "for cause" proviso added to § 10(c) in 1947 is applicable where the employee is engaged in collective action as well as where he acts alone, H.R.Rep.No.510, 80th Cong., 1st Sess., 38–39; and it would seem that where an employee is discharged because he engaged in collective action and the discharge is found to be "for cause", the action is not the type protected under § 7.   NLRB v. Local Union No. 1229, Int. Brotherhood of Electrical Workers, 346 U.S. 464, 74 S.Ct. 172, 98 L.Ed. 195 (1953).   However, a determination that an employee is not engaged in a § 7 activity does not necessarily mean that, if he is discharged for his participation in the unprotected action, the discharge is "for cause".   That depends on the surrounding circumstances.   What is *cause* in one situation may not be in another.

litigated in the state court, and there were thus no pertinent findings which could apply as res judicata or collateral estoppel.]

Thus we think that the state court decision did not necessarily preclude a reinstatement order, and we pass to a consideration of whether reinstatement was a proper remedy in view of the Board's own findings of fact. * * *

* * * It ordinarily may be assumed that the Board, as a part of the process of determining whether reinstatement would effectuate the policies of the Act, will balance the severity of the employer's unfair labor practice which provoked the industrial disturbance against whatever employee misconduct may have occurred in the course of the strike. Thus in reaching its decision the Board weighs two groups of facts. Such a decision has little value as a precedent in a subsequent Labor Board case because of the nuances of fact inevitable in the later situation. Therefore, if this court should conclude that the strike activity was not protected conduct under § 7, our disposition should be to remand the case to the Board in order to allow that body to make the primary administrative determination—which it has not yet made—whether under the circumstances the non-Section 7 activity was cause for discharge, and if not whether reinstatement is an appropriate remedy under the circumstances.

In our view, we need not remand the case for this purpose with respect to most of the employees ordered reinstated, for we agree with the Board that generally the conduct of the strikers on the picket line was protected collective action within the meaning of § 7.

If the pickets "restrained" or "coerced" other employees in the exercise of their rights under § 7 of the Act, and if union responsibility therefor could be demonstrated, the picketing would constitute a union unfair labor practice and therefore would not be a protected concerted activity under § 7. Nor would the same conduct by the picketing employees, even though not attributable to the union, be protected.[16]

* * * [E]xcept for isolated incidents discussed below, the non-strikers were not restrained or coerced in the exercise of their rights under § 7, and therefore the pickets were engaged in concerted activity protected by § 7.

16. "Although section 8(b) regulates only the conduct of labor organizations and section 7 deals with the rights of employees, it seems plain that the group activities which section 8(b) forbids a labor organization to lead must fall outside the protection of section 7 when employees engage in them either with or without the direction of a union. To hold otherwise would disregard legislative history [H.R.Rep. No. 510, 80th Cong., 1st Sess., 37–40 (1947)] and create an unwarranted anomaly." Cox, [The Right to Engage in Concerted Activities, 26 Ind. L.J. 319] at 325.

Certain strikers, however, participated in activities which we find were coercive, and therefore not within the scope of § 7. The trial examiner, in recommending the reinstatement of such strikers, took into consideration the fact that "the strike resulted from the flagrant unfair labor practices of Respondent Companies". This seems perfectly proper—not in justifying the employees' conduct or in concluding that their action was protected under § 7—but in deciding whether or not their discharge was "for cause" and whether their reinstatement would effectuate the policies of the Act.

The Board, as we have noted, made reinstatement turn exclusively on whether the employees' conduct was within § 7. It therefore apparently disregarded, and properly, under its approach, the fact that the strike was touched off by an unfair labor practice.

Since we disagree with the Board on some of these individual incidents, we shall remand where we disagree, with instructions that the Board decide whether under the circumstances there was cause for the respondents' refusal to rehire the particular strikers involved in the non-Section 7 activity, and if not whether reinstatement of these employees would effectuate the policies of the Act.

We hold that the following incidents were coercive in nature and calculated to instill fear of physical harm in the non-striker victims, and are therefore not activities protected under § 7: (1) The visit to the home of George Andrews, a non-striker, by 20 or 30 men in five automobiles for the purpose of persuading Andrews to respect the picket line; (2) a similar visit to the home of James Thompson; (3) two visits by three carloads of pickets to the home of Joe Tatro for the purpose of persuading Tatro to join the strike; (4) two visits to the home of Zigmand Maliska by five cars full of strikers, for the purpose of persuading Maliska to respect the picket line; (5) a visit by five strikers at 6:30 A.M. to Theodore Raffa's home to persuade Raffa to join the strike; and (6) an attack upon Cornelius Magner, a non-striker, by 17 or 18 pickets in front of the H. N. Thayer Company. * * *

On remand of the *Thayer* case, 115 N.L.R.B. 1591 (1956), the Board indicated that it would not follow the rationale of the court in future cases. When it adhered to its position in a case arising from a long, bitter and violent dispute between the Auto Workers and the Kohler Company, the Board was once again reversed on appeal. Local 833, UAW v. NLRB, 300 F.2d 699 (D.C.Cir.), cert. denied 370 U.S. 911 (1962). The following year, in Blades Mfg. Corp., 144 N.L.R.B. 561 (1963), the Board acceded and announced that it would thereafter follow the decision of the First Circuit in *Thayer*.

Part Five
LABOR AND THE ANTI-TRUST LAWS [1]

It will be recalled that the Supreme Court held, in Loewe v. Lawlor, 208 U.S. 274 (1908), that the Sherman Act applied to combinations of workers, and affirmed a judgment for damages. See page 33, supra. In 1914 the Clayton Act granted private persons the right to injunctive relief against violations of the Sherman Act. Congress had in mind suits against trusts and similar corporate combinations, but the new remedy was soon seized upon by employers seeking to put a speedy end to strikes and picketing. Although Sections 6 and 20 of the Clayton Act were widely believed to curtail the labor injunction, Duplex Printing Press Co. v. Deering, p. 44, supra, limited them to disputes between an employer and its own employees.

The usefulness of the Sherman Act as a strike-breaking weapon was curtailed, until 1937, by decisions holding that certain strikes at manufacturing establishments did not have the necessary relationship to interstate commerce to come under federal authority. Apparently coverage depended upon the strikers' purpose. If a union made up of employees at a manufacturing establishment called a strike for the purpose of raising their wages or improving their working conditions, the combination did not violate the Sherman Act even though shipments in interstate commerce were halted or reduced. E.g., United Leather Workers v. Herkert & Meisel Trunk Co., 265 U.S. 457 (1924). However, if a union which had organized some establishments in an industry were to call an organizational strike or institute a boycott in order to organize non-union factories and protect its members against the competition of cheap, non-union goods, then the strike would be unlawful. Coronado Coal Co. v. United Mine Workers of America, 268 U.S. 295 (1925); Alco-

1. See Cox, Labor and the Antitrust Laws—A Preliminary Analysis, 104 U. Pa.L.Rev. 252 (1955); Cox, Labor and the Antitrust Laws: Pennington and Jewel Tea, 46 B.U.L.Rev. 317 (1966); Leslie, Right to Control: A Study in Secondary Boycotts and Labor Antitrust, 89 Harv.L.Rev. 904 (1976); Meltzer, Labor Unions, Collective Bargaining, and the Antitrust Laws, 32 U.Chi.L.Rev. 659 (1965); Note, Union-Subcontractor Work Preservation Agreements: The Risk of Antitrust Liability, 45 Geo.Wash.L.Rev. 757 (1977); St. Antoine, Collective Bargaining and the Antitrust Laws, Industrial Relations Research Ass'n, 19th Annual Winter Meeting Proceedings 66 (1966); Sovern, Some Ruminations on Labor, the Antitrust Laws and *Allen Bradley*, 13 Lab.L.J. 957 (1962); Winter, Collective Bargaining and Competition: The Application of Antitrust Standards to Union Activities, 73 Yale L.J. 14 (1963).

Zander Co. v. Amalgamated Clothing Workers of America, 35 F.2d
203 (E.D.Pa.1929).

It is unlikely that this distinction could have survived the expanded concept of interstate commerce which developed after NLRB
v. Jones & Laughlin Steel Corp., p. 77, supra. Moreover, it was not
at all clear why—in light of the objectives of the federal anti-trust
laws—a work stoppage designed to raise wages was unobjectionable
while a work stoppage designed to organize a nonunion company
was commonly considered unlawful. In any event, the union which
engaged in such organizational strikes was often moved not only by
a desire to improve wages and working conditions and gain membership in the struck plant but also by a desire to consolidate organizational victories elsewhere. Nor was it clear why—tested by antitrust policy—a union could lawfully stop the flow of goods into
commerce by inducing a work stoppage at the manufacturer's plant
but could not lawfully do so by inducing a work stoppage among the
employees of the consumer. The effect of the decisions noted above
was to render subject to injunction in the federal courts two basic
tactics used by unions attempting to organize: "stranger" picketing
at the nonunion company in an industry in which some companies
were already organized, and the secondary boycott.

The enactment by Congress of the Wagner Act in 1935 generated a conflict of federal policies. The anti-trust laws were designed
to encourage manufacturers to compete for public favor at least
in part through lower prices; this generated pressures on manufacturers to minimize the costs incurred for the factors of production, among which was labor. A strict application of anti-trust policy would induce employers, through individualized bargaining,
constantly to bid down the cost of labor (i. e., wages paid) and to secure a competent workforce at the lowest wage that the market
would allow. The national labor laws, on the other hand, were based
on the congressional judgment that just such individual bargaining and subsistence working conditions caused industrial strife and
interruptions in the flow of interstate commerce. Congress's remedy
was to foster collective bargaining, which was "anti-competitive" in
at least two respects. First, wage demands were thus stabilized
within a single plant, geographic area or industry; competition was
removed from the labor market. Second, and as a result, competition in pricing was restricted in the product market, to the extent
that product prices among competitors were determined by the
costs incurred by the manufacturers in purchasing labor. In short,
unionization, collective bargaining and standardization of wages and
working conditions are inherently inconsistent with many of the
assumptions at the heart of anti-trust policy.

This conflict has been explored by the Supreme Court in several cases. The *Apex Hosiery* case, immediately below, represented an attempt by the Court to bring order and direction to this field of law, while the *Hutcheson* case shows the Court taking a dramatically different approach. The subsequent cases reveal the sharply divided views of the modern Court.

APEX HOSIERY CO. v. LEADER

Supreme Court of the United States, 1940.
310 U.S. 469, 60 S.Ct. 982, 84 L.Ed. 1311, 128 A.L.R. 1044.

MR. JUSTICE STONE delivered the opinion of the Court.

Petitioner, a Pennsylvania corporation, is engaged in the manufacture, at its factory in Philadelphia, of hosiery, a substantial part of which is shipped in interstate commerce. It brought the present suit in the federal district court for Eastern Pennsylvania against respondent Federation, a labor organization, and its officers, to recover treble the amount of damage inflicted on it by respondents in conducting a strike at petitioner's factory alleged to be a conspiracy in violation of the Sherman Anti-Trust Act, 26 Stat. 209, 15 U. S.C. sec. 1, 15 U.S.C.A. sec. 1.   *   *   *

[The Federation, with only eight members among the Apex Company's 2500 workers, instigated a violent strike (aided by employees from other Philadelphia companies) in support of its demands for a closed shop. The plant was forcibly seized and occupied for some seven weeks, during which time the strikers wrecked machinery and did other substantial damage to company property and equipment. For nearly three months, none of Apex's hosiery could be shipped in interstate commerce; the strike prevented the shipment of some $800,000 worth of finished hosiery, 80 percent of which was to be shipped outside the state. A jury trial resulted in a verdict of $237,310, which the district court trebled in entering judgment for the petitioner in excess of $711,000. The court of appeals reversed, concluding that the effect of the strike upon interstate commerce (less than three percent of the total output of the American hosiery industry) was insubstantial and also that the evidence failed to show an intent on the part of the respondents to restrain interstate commerce.]

A point strongly urged in behalf of respondents in brief and argument before us is that Congress intended to exclude labor organizations and their activities wholly from the operation of the Sherman Act. To this the short answer must be made that for the thirty-two years which have elapsed since the decision of Loewe v. Lawlor, 208 U.S. 274, 28 S.Ct. 301, 52 L.Ed. 488, 13 Ann.Cas.

815, this Court, in its efforts to determine the true meaning and application of the Sherman Act has repeatedly held that the words of the act, "Every contract, combination * * * or conspiracy, in restraint of trade or commerce" do embrace to some extent and in some circumstances labor unions and their activities; and that during that period Congress, although often asked to do so, has passed no act purporting to exclude labor unions wholly from the operation of the Act. On the contrary Congress has repeatedly enacted laws restricting or purporting to curtail the application of the Act to labor organizations and their activities, thus recognizing that to some extent not defined they remain subject to it. * * *

While we must regard the question whether labor unions are to some extent and in some circumstances subject to the Act as settled in the affirmative, it is equally plain that this Court has never thought the Act to apply to all labor union activities affecting interstate commerce. The prohibitions of the Sherman Act were not stated in terms of precision or of crystal clarity and the Act itself did not define them. In consequence of the vagueness of its language, perhaps not uncalculated, the courts have been left to give content to the statute, and in the performance of that function it is appropriate that courts should interpret its words in the light of its legislative history and of the particular evils at which the legislation was aimed. * * *

The critical words which circumscribe the judicial performance of this function so far as the present case is concerned are "Every * * * combination * * * or conspiracy, in restraint of trade or commerce." Since in the present case, as we have seen, the natural and predictable consequence of the strike was the restraint of interstate transportation the precise question which we are called upon to decide is whether that restraint resulting from the strike maintained to enforce union demands by compelling a shutdown of petitioner's factory is the kind of "restraint of trade or commerce" which the Act condemns.

In considering whether union activities like the present may fairly be deemed to be embraced within this phrase, three circumstances relating to the history and application of the Act which are of striking significance must first be taken into account. The legislative history of the Sherman Act as well as the decisions of this Court interpreting it, show that it was not aimed at policing interstate transportation or movement of goods and property. * * * It was another and quite a different evil at which the Sherman Act was aimed. It was enacted in the era of "trusts" and of "combinations" of businesses and of capital organized and directed to control of the market by suppression of competition in the marketing of goods and services, the monopolistic tendency of which had be-

come a matter of public concern.   The end sought was the prevention
of restraints to free competition in business and commercial transactions which tended to restrict production, raise prices or otherwise
control the market to the detriment of purchasers or consumers of
goods and services, all of which had come to be regarded as a special form of public injury.   *   *   *

A second significant circumstance is that this Court has never
applied the Sherman Act in any case, whether or not involving labor
organizations or activities unless the Court was of opinion that there
was some form of restraint upon commercial competition in the marketing of goods or services and finally this Court has refused to
apply the Sherman Act in cases like the present in which local strikes
conducted by illegal means in a production industry prevented interstate shipment of substantial amounts of the product but in which
it was not shown that the restrictions on shipments had operated to
restrain commercial competition in some substantial way.   *   *   *

The common law doctrines relating to contracts and combinations in restraint of trade were well understood long before the enactment of the Sherman law.   They were contracts for the restriction
or suppression of competition in the market, agreements to fix prices,
divide marketing territories, apportion customers, restrict production and the like practices, which tend to raise prices or otherwise
take from buyers or consumers the advantages which accrue to them
from free competition in the market.   Such contracts were deemed
illegal and were unenforcible at common law.   *   *   *   In enacting
the Sherman law [Congress] took over that concept by condemning
such restraints wherever they occur in or affect commerce between
the states.   They extended the condemnation of the statute to restraints effected by any combination in the form of trust or otherwise, or conspiracy, as well as by contract or agreement, having those
effects on the competitive system and on purchasers and consumers
of goods or services which were characteristic of restraints deemed
illegal at common law, and they gave both private and public remedies
for the injuries flowing from such restraints.   *   *   *

The question remains whether the effect of the combination or
conspiracy among respondents was a restraint of trade within the
meaning of the Sherman Act.   This is not a case of a labor organization being used by combinations of those engaged in an industry as
the means or instrument for suppressing competition or fixing
prices.   See United States v. Brims, 272 U.S. 549, 47 S.Ct. 169, 71
L.Ed. 403; Local 167 v. United States, 291 U.S. 293, 54 S.Ct. 396,
78 L.Ed. 804.   Here it is plain that the combination or conspiracy did
not have as its purpose restraint upon competition in the market for
petitioner's product.   Its object was to compel petitioner to accede

to the union demands and an effect of it, in consequence of the strikers' tortious acts, was the prevention of the removal of petitioner's product for interstate shipment. So far as appears the delay of these shipments was not intended to have and had no effect on prices of hosiery in the market * * *

A combination of employees necessarily restrains competition among themselves in the sale of their services to the employer; yet such a combination was not considered an illegal restraint of trade at common law when the Sherman Act was adopted, either because it was not thought to be unreasonable or because it was not deemed a "restraint of trade." Since the enactment of the declaration in § 6 of the Clayton Act that "the labor of a human being is not a commodity or article of commerce * * * nor shall such [labor] organizations or the members thereof, be held or construed to be illegal combinations or conspiracies in restraint of trade, under the anti-trust laws", it would seem plain that restraints on the sale of the employee's services to the employer, however much they curtail the competition among employees, are not in themselves combinations or conspiracies in restraint of trade or commerce under the Sherman Act.

* * * Furthermore, successful union activity, as for example consummation of a wage agreement with employers, may have some influence on price competition by eliminating that part of such competition which is based on differences in labor standards. Since, in order to render a labor combination effective it must eliminate the competition from non-union made goods, see American Steel Foundries v. Tri-City Central Trades Council, 257 U.S. 184, 209, 42 S.Ct. 72, 78, 66 L.Ed. 189, 27 A.L.R. 360, an elimination of price competition based on differences in labor standards is the objective of any national labor organization. But this effect on competition has not been considered to be the kind of curtailment of price competition prohibited by the Sherman Act. * * *

[The Court then traced its decisions holding secondary boycotts unlawful under the Sherman Act, including Duplex Printing Press Co. v. Deering, 254 U.S. 443, 41 S.Ct. 172 (1921), page 44, supra, and Bedford Cut Stone Co. v. Journeyman Stone Cutters' Ass'n, 274 U.S. 37, 47 S.Ct. 522 (1927). The Court noted that in Loewe v. Lawlor, page 33, supra, the Court drew an analogy to an unlawful conspiracy to circulate a "blacklist" designed to induce retailers not to deal with specified wholesalers. It then observed that in all such cases of secondary boycotts, "the effort of the union was to compel unionization of an employer's factory, not by a strike in his factory but by restraining by the boycott or refusal to work on the manufactured product purchases of his product in interstate commerce in competition with the like product of union shops."]

It will be observed that in each of these cases where the Act was held applicable to labor unions, the activities affecting interstate commerce were directed at control of the market and were so widespread as substantially to affect it.   There was thus a suppression of competition in the market by methods which were deemed analogous to those found to be violations in the non-labor cases.   * * * That the objective of the restraint in the boycott cases was the strengthening of the bargaining position of the union and not the elimination of business competition—which was the end in the non-labor cases—was thought to be immaterial because the Court viewed the restraint itself, in contrast to the interference with shipments caused by a local factory strike, to be of a kind regarded as offensive at common law because of its effect in curtailing a free market and it was held to offend against the Sherman Act because it effected and was aimed at suppression of competition with union made goods in the interstate market.

Both the Duplex Printing Co. and Bedford Stone cases followed the enactment of the Clayton Act and the recognition of the "rule of reason" in the Standard Oil case supra.   The applicability of that rule to restraints upon commerce effected by a labor union in order to promote and consolidate the interests of its union was not considered.[2]   But an important point considered and decided by the Court in both cases was that nothing in the Clayton Act precluded the relief granted.   We are not now concerned with the merits of either point.   The only significance of the two cases for present purposes is that in each the Court considered it necessary, in order to support its decision, to find that the restraint operated to suppress competition in the market.

If, without such effects on the market, we were to hold that a local factory strike, stopping production and shipment of its product interstate, violates the Sherman law, practically every strike in modern industry would be brought within the jurisdiction of the federal courts, under the Sherman Act, to remedy local law violations. The Act was plainly not intended to reach such a result, its language does not require it, and the course of our decisions precludes it.   The maintenance in our federal system of a proper distribution between

2. Whether the interest of the labor unions in these cases in maintaining and extending their respective organizations, rendered the restraint reasonable as a means of attaining that end within the common law rule, or brought the restraints within the rule of reason developed and announced in the Standard Oil case, was not discussed and we need not consider it here.   Restraints upon the competitive marketing of a manufacturer's product brought about by an agreement between the employer and his employees in order to secure continuous employment of the employees was held to be within the rule of reason and therefore not an unreasonable restraint of trade in National Ass'n of Window Glass Manufacturers v. United States, 263 U.S. 403, 44 S.Ct. 148, 68 L.Ed. 358.

state and national governments of police authority and of remedies private and public for public wrongs is of far-reaching importance. An intention to disturb the balance is not lightly to be imputed to Congress. The Sherman Act is concerned with the character of the prohibited restraints and with their effect on interstate commerce. It draws no distinction between the restraints effected by violence and those achieved by peaceful but oftentimes quite as effective means. Restraints not within the Act, when achieved by peaceful means, are not brought within its sweep merely because, without other differences, they are attended by violence.

[The dissenting opinion is omitted.]

Problems for Discussion

1. After *Apex Hosiery*, is it safe to say that any concerted activities by nonemployees with an organizational or recognitional objective will be immune from anti-trust liability? What advice could you give, for example, regarding the use of a secondary boycott with such an objective?

2. After *Apex Hosiery*, would a labor union be subject to anti-trust liability for inducing a refusal among its members to work on goods which had been assembled by another company, in support of demands that its members should do the assembling themselves? Or for inducing a refusal to use paint sprayers rather than paint brushes? Or for inducing a refusal to exhibit motion pictures that have been produced in foreign countries (or that are pornographic)?

3. If strikes or picketing may be used to achieve the objectives set forth in Problem 2, with immunity from the anti-trust laws, does it follow that an agreement between the employer and the union—in which the employer acquiesces in the union's demands because of the union's pressures—will also be immune from anti-trust liability? What would be the basis for such an immunity?

4. In reaching his conclusion that the Sherman Act ought not be read to outlaw concerted activities in support of unionization and wage demands, might Justice Stone in *Apex Hosiery* have made use of the then recent enactment of the National Labor Relations Act (and of the 1926 Railway Labor Act)? Would it be proper for the Court to rely upon the action of Congress in 1935 to assess the scope of congressional action taken in 1890?

UNITED STATES v. HUTCHESON

Supreme Court of the United States, 1941.
312 U.S. 219, 61 S.Ct. 463, 85 L.Ed. 788.

[The opinions are printed at pages 63–68, supra.]

ALLEN BRADLEY CO. v. LOCAL 3, IBEW, 325 U.S. 797, 65 S.Ct. 1533, 89 L.Ed. 1939 (1945). Local 3 of the International Brotherhood of Electrical Workers had jurisdiction over the metropolitan district of New York only. Some of its members were employed by New York manufacturers of electrical equipment and others by contractors engaged in installing such equipment in the New York area. In order to enlarge employment opportunities for union members working in local manufacturing establishments, the union obtained closed-shop contracts with those manufacturers. In addition, by means of strikes and boycotts, it put pressure on the contractors to agree not to purchase equipment except from local manufacturers having such contracts. These agreements with individual employers were subsequently expanded into a local industry-wide understanding which resulted in the setting up of agencies composed of representatives of the unions, the manufacturers and the contractors for the purpose of boycotting recalcitrant local manufacturers and contractors and excluding from the metropolitan area all equipment manufactured elsewhere, including that manufactured in factories which had collective bargaining agreements with other locals of the IBEW. Plaintiffs, manufacturers of electrical equipment in other cities, brought suit in a federal court against the New York local union, its officials and members, and obtained both a declaratory judgment to the effect that the combination of the union and the employers was a violation of the Sherman Act and a broadly phrased injunction, which included a provision forbidding all persons, including union officials, to induce union members not to install plaintiff's products. This decision was reversed by the Circuit Court of Appeals for the Second Circuit, which held "the activities which cannot be forbidden to Local 3 acting by itself are not to be interdicted because other groups join with them to the same end." 145 F.2d 215.

The Supreme Court held that the Sherman Act had been violated, but that the injunction should be limited to activities in which the union engaged in combination "with any person, firm or corporation which is a non-labor group." Mr. Justice Black, writing for himself and six other members of the Court, stated—

"Aside from the fact that the labor union here acted in combination with the contractors and manufacturers, the means it adopted to contribute to the combination's purpose fall squarely within the 'specified acts' declared by § 20 not to be violations of federal law. For the union's contribution to the trade boycott was accomplished through threats that unless their employers bought their goods from local manufacturers the union laborers would terminate the 'relation of employment' with them and cease to perform 'work or labor' for them; and through their 'recommending, advising, or persuading others by peaceful and lawful means' not to 'patronize' sellers of the boycotted electrical equipment. Consequently, under our holdings in the *Hutcheson* case and other cases which followed it, had there been no union-contractor-manufacturer combination the union's actions here, coming as they did within the exemptions of the Clayton and Norris-LaGuardia Acts, would not have been violations of the Sherman Act.   *   *   *

"We have been pointed to no language in any act of Congress or in its reports or debates, nor have we found any, which indicates that it was ever suggested, considered, or legislatively determined that labor unions should be granted an immunity such as is sought in the present case.   It has been argued that this immunity can be inferred from the union's right to make bargaining agreements with its employer.   Since union members can without violating the Sherman Act strike to enforce a union boycott of goods, it is said they may settle the strike by getting their employers to agree to refuse to buy the goods.   Employers and the union did here make bargaining agreements in which the employers agreed not to buy goods manufactured by companies which did not employ the members of Local No. 3.   We may assume that such an agreement standing alone would not have violated the Sherman Act.   But it did not stand alone. It was but one element in a far larger program in which contractors and manufacturers united with one another to monopolize all the business in New York City, to bar all other business men from that area, and to charge the public prices above a competitive level.   It is true that victory of the union in its disputes, even had the union acted alone, might have added to the cost of goods, or might have resulted in individual refusals of all of their employers to buy electrical equipment not made by Local No. 3.   So far as the union might have achieved this result acting alone, it would have been the natural consequence of labor union activities exempted by the Clayton Act from the coverage of the Sherman Act.   But when the unions participated with a combination of business men who had complete power to eliminate all competition among themselves and to prevent all competition from others, a situation was created not included within the exemptions of the Clayton and Norris-LaGuardia Acts."

UNITED MINE WORKERS OF AMERICA v. PENNINGTON

Supreme Court of the United States, 1965.
381 U.S. 657, 85 S.Ct. 1585, 14 L.Ed.2d 626.

MR. JUSTICE WHITE delivered the opinion of the Court.   *   *   *

[In an action against the Phillips Brothers Coal Company, brought by trustees of the United Mine Workers Welfare and Retirement Fund for royalty payments allegedly due under a 1950 wage agreement (as amended), the Company filed an answer and a cross claim in which it asserted that the UMW, the trustees and certain large coal operators had conspired to restrain and monopolize inter-

state commerce in violation of Sections 1 and 2 of the Sherman Act; the Company claimed actual damages in the amount of $100,000.] The allegations of the cross claim were essentially as follows: Prior to the 1950 Wage Agreement between the operators and the union, severe controversy had existed in the industry, particularly over wages, the welfare fund and the union's efforts to control the working time of its members. Since 1950, however, relative peace has existed in the industry, all as the result of the 1950 Wage Agreement and its amendments and the additional understandings entered into between UMW and the large operators. Allegedly the parties considered overproduction to be the critical problem of the coal industry. The agreed solution was to be the elimination of the smaller companies, the larger companies thereby controlling the market. More specifically, the union abandoned its efforts to control the working time of the miners, agreed not to oppose the rapid mechanization of the mines which would substantially reduce mine employment, agreed to help finance such mechanization and agreed to impose the terms of the 1950 agreement on all operators without regard to their ability to pay. The benefit to the union was to be increased wages as productivity increased with mechanization, these increases to be demanded of the smaller companies whether mechanized or not.
* * *

The complaint survived motions to dismiss and after a five-week trial before a jury, a verdict was returned in favor of Phillips and against the trustees and the union, the damages against the union being fixed in the amount of $90,000, to be trebled under 15 U.S.C.A. § 15 (1958 ed.). The trial court set aside the verdict against the trustees but overruled the union's motion for judgment notwithstanding the verdict or in the alternative for a new trial. The Court of Appeals affirmed. * * *

I.

We first consider UMW's contention that the trial court erred in denying its motion for a directed verdict and for judgment notwithstanding the verdict, since a determination in UMW's favor on this issue would finally resolve the controversy. The question presented by this phase of the case is whether in the circumstances of this case the union is exempt from liability under the antitrust laws. We think the answer is clearly in the negative and that the union's motions were correctly denied.

The antitrust laws do not bar the existence and operation of labor unions as such. Moreover, § 20 of the Clayton Act, 38 Stat. 738, and § 4 of the Norris-LaGuardia Act, 47 Stat. 70, permit a union, acting alone, to engage in the conduct therein specified without violating the Sherman Act. United States v. Hutcheson   * * *

But neither § 20 nor § 4 expressly deals with arrangements or agreements between unions and employers. Neither section tells us whether any or all such arrangements or agreements are barred or permitted by the antitrust laws. Thus Hutcheson itself stated:

> "So long as a union acts in its self-interest *and does not combine with non-labor groups,* the licit and the illicit under § 20 are not to be distinguished by any judgment regarding the wisdom or unwisdom, the rightness or wrongness, the selfishness or unselfishness of the end of which the particular union activities are the means." 312 U.S., at 232, 61 S.Ct. at 466. (Emphasis added.)

And in Allen Bradley Co. v. Local Union No. 3, IBEW, 325 U.S. 797, 65 S.Ct. 1533, 89 L.Ed. 1939, this Court made explicit what had been merely a qualifying expression in Hutcheson and held that "when the unions participated with a combination of business men who had complete power to eliminate all competition among themselves and to prevent all competition from others, a situation was created not included with the exemptions of the Clayton and Norris-LaGuardia Acts." Id., 325 U.S. at 809, 65 S.Ct. at 1540. * * *

If the UMW in this case, in order to protect its wage scale by maintaining employer income, had presented a set of prices at which the mine operators would be required to sell their coal, the union and the employers who happened to agree could not successfully defend this contract provision if it were challenged under the antitrust laws by the United States or by some party injured by the arrangement. Cf. Allen Bradley Co. v. Local Union No. 3, IBEW, 325 U.S. 797, 65 S.Ct. 1533, 89 L.Ed. 1939; * * * In such a case, the restraint on the product market is direct and immediate, is of the type characteristically deemed unreasonable under the Sherman Act and the union gets from the promise nothing more concrete than a hope for better wages to come.

Likewise, if as is alleged in this case, the union became a party to a collusive bidding arrangement designed to drive Phillips and others from the TVA spot market, we think any claim to exemption from antitrust liability would be frivolous at best. For this reason alone the motions of the unions were properly denied.

A major part of Phillips' case, however, was that the union entered into a conspiracy with the large operators to impose the agreed-upon wage and royalty scales upon the smaller, nonunion operators, regardless of their ability to pay and regardless of whether or not the union represented the employees of these companies, all for the purpose of eliminating them from the industry, limiting production and pre-empting the market for the large, unionized operators. The

UMW urges that since such an agreement concerned wage standards, it is exempt from the antitrust laws.

It is true that wages lie at the very heart of those subjects about which employers and unions must bargain and the law contemplates agreements on wages not only between individual employers and a union but agreements between the union and employers in a multi-employer bargaining unit. National Labor Relations Board v. Truck Drivers Union, 353 U.S. 87, 94–96, 77 S.Ct. 643, 646–647, 1 L.Ed.2d 676. The union benefit from the wage scale agreed upon is direct and concrete and the effect on the product market, though clearly present, results from the elimination of competition based on wages among the employers in the bargaining unit, which is not the kind of restraint Congress intended the Sherman Act to proscribe. Apex Hosiery Co. v. Leader, 310 U.S. 469, 503–504,|60 S.Ct. 982, 997, 84 L. Ed. 1311; see Adams Dairy Co. v. St. Louis Dairy Co., 260 F.2d 46 (C.A.8th Cir. 1958). We think it beyond question that a union may conclude a wage agreement with the multi-employer bargaining unit without violating the antitrust laws and that it may as a matter of its own policy, and not by agreement with all or part of the employers of that unit, seek the same wages from other employers.

This is not to say that an agreement resulting from union-employer negotiations is automatically exempt from Sherman Act scrutiny simply because the negotiations involve a compulsory subject of bargaining, regardless of the subject or the form and content of the agreement. Unquestionably the Board's demarcation of the bounds of the duty to bargain has great relevance to any consideration of the sweep of labor's antitrust immunity, for we are concerned here with harmonizing the Sherman Act with the national policy expressed in the National Labor Relations Act of promoting "the peaceful settlement of industrial disputes by subjecting labor-management controversies to the mediatory influence of negotiation," Fibreboard Paper Prods. Corp. v. National Labor Relations Board, 379 U.S. 203, 211, 85 S.Ct. 398, 403, 13 L.Ed.2d 233. But there are limits to what a union or an employer may offer or extract in the name of wages, and because they must bargain does not mean that the agreement reached may disregard other laws. Local 24 of Intern. Broth. of Teamsters, etc. v. Oliver, 358 U.S. 283, 296, 79 S.Ct. 297, 304, 3 L.Ed.2d 312; United Brotherhood of Carpenters v. United States, 330 U.S. 395, 399–400, 67 S.Ct. 775, 778, 91 L.Ed. 973.

We have said that a union may make wage agreements with a multi-employer bargaining unit and may in pursuance of its own union interests seek to obtain the same terms from other employers. No case under the antitrust laws could be made out on evidence limited to such union behavior.[3] But we think a union forfeits its exemption from the antitrust laws when it is clearly shown that it has agreed with one set of employers to impose a certain wage scale on other bargaining units. One group of employers may not conspire to eliminate competitors from the industry and the union is liable with the employers if it becomes a party to the conspiracy. This is true even though the union's part in the scheme is an undertaking to secure the same wages, hours or other conditions of employment from the remaining employers in the industry.

We do not find anything in the national labor policy that conflicts with this conclusion. This Court has recognized that a legitimate aim of any national labor organization is to obtain uniformity of labor standards and that a consequence of such union activity may be to eliminate competition based on differences in such standards. Apex Hosiery Co. v. Leader, 310 U.S. 469, 503, 60 S.Ct. 982, 997, 84 L.Ed. 1311. But there is nothing in the labor policy indicating that the union and the employers in one bargaining unit are free to bargain about the wages, hours and working conditions of other bargaining units or to attempt to settle these matters for the entire industry. On the contrary, the duty to bargain unit by unit leads to a quite different conclusion. The union's obligation to its members would seem best served if the union retained the ability to respond to each bargaining situation as the individual circumstances might warrant, without being strait-jacketed by some prior agreement with the favored employers. * * *

On the other hand, the policy of the antitrust laws is clearly set against employer-union agreements seeking to prescribe labor standards outside the bargaining unit. One could hardly contend, for example, that one group of employers could lawfully demand that the union impose on other employers wages that were significantly higher than those paid by the requesting employers, or a system of computing wages that, because of differences in methods of production, would be more costly to one set of employers than to another. The anticompetitive potential of such a combination is obvious, but is little more severe than what is alleged to have been the purpose and effect of the conspiracy in this case to establish wages at a level

3. Unilaterally, and without agreement with any employer group to do so, a union may adopt a uniform wage policy and seek vigorously to implement it even though it may suspect that some employers cannot effectively compete if they are required to pay the wage scale demanded by the union. The union need not gear its wage demands to wages which the weakest units in the industry can afford to pay. Such union conduct is not alone sufficient evidence to maintain a union-employer conspiracy charge under the Sherman Act. There must be additional direct or indirect evidence of the conspiracy. There was, of course, other evidence in this case, but we indicate no opinion as to its sufficiency.

that marginal producers could not pay so that they would be driven from the industry. And if the conspiracy presently under attack were declared exempt it would hardly be possible to deny exemption to such avowedly discriminatory schemes.

From the viewpoint of antitrust policy, moreover, all such agreements between a group of employers and a union that the union will seek specified labor standards outside the bargaining unit suffer from a more basic defect, without regard to predatory intention or effect in the particular case. For the salient characteristic of such agreements is that the union surrenders its freedom of action with respect to its bargaining policy. Prior to the agreement the union might seek uniform standards in its own self-interest but would be required to assess in each case the probable costs and gains of a strike or other collective action to that end and thus might conclude that the objective of uniform standards should temporarily give way. After the agreement the union's interest would be bound in each case to that of the favored employer group. It is just such restraints upon the freedom of economic units to act according to their own choice and discretion that run counter to antitrust policy. See, e. g., Associated Press v. United States, 326 U.S. 1, 19, 65 S.Ct. 1416, 1424, 89 L.Ed. 2013; Fashion Originators' Guild v. Federal Trade Comm'n, 312 U.S. 457, 465, 61 S.Ct. 703, 706, 85 L.Ed. 949; Anderson v. Shipowners Assn., 272 U.S. 359, 364–365, 47 S.Ct. 125, 71 L.Ed. 298.

Thus the relevant labor and antitrust policies compel us to conclude that the alleged agreement between UMW and the large operators to secure uniform labor standards throughout the industry, if proved, was not exempt from the antitrust laws.   *   *   *

[The decision below was nonetheless reversed and the case was remanded for further proceedings, because the trial court had erred in admitting evidence that the defendants had, as part of their conspiracy, attempted to influence the Secretary of Labor. Eastern R.R. Presidents Conference v. Noerr Motor Freight, Inc., 365 U.S. 127, 81 S.Ct. 523, 5 L.Ed.2d 464 (1961), had held that "joint efforts to influence public officials do not violate the antitrust laws even though intended to eliminate competition."]

MR. JUSTICE DOUGLAS, with whom MR. JUSTICE BLACK, and MR. JUSTICE CLARK agree, concurring.

As we read the opinion of the Court, it reaffirms the principles of Allen Bradley Co. v. Local Union, No. 3, IBEW, 325 U.S. 797, 65 S.Ct. 1533, 89 L.Ed. 1939, and tells the trial judge:

First. On the new trial the jury should be instructed that if there were an industry-wide collective bargaining agreement whereby employers and the union agreed on a wage scale that exceeded the financial ability of some operators to pay and that if it was made for the purpose of forcing some employers out of business, the union as well as the employers who participated in the arrangement with the union should be found to have violated the antitrust laws.

Second. An industry-wide agreement containing those features is prima facie evidence of a violation.

Congress can design an oligopoly for our society, if it chooses. But business alone cannot do so as long as the antitrust laws are enforced. Nor should business and labor working hand-in-hand be allowed to make that basic change in the design of our so-called free enterprise system. * * *

MR. JUSTICE GOLDBERG, with whom MR. JUSTICE HARLAN and MR. JUSTICE STEWART join, dissenting from the opinion but concurring in the reversal in [UMW v. Pennington] and concurring in the judgment of the Court in [Local 189, Meat Cutters v. Jewel Tea Co.] [Excerpts from the opinion of Mr. Justice Goldberg relevant to the *Pennington* case are set forth here; excerpts relevant to the *Jewel Tea* case are set forth with the other opinions in that case, below.]

* * * [B]oth Pennington and Jewel Tea, as the Court in Pennington, and my Brother WHITE's opinion in Jewel Tea acknowledge, involve conventional collective bargaining on wages, hours, and working conditions—mandatory subjects of bargaining under the National Labor Relations Act, 49 Stat. 452, as amended, 29 U.S.C. § 158(d) (1958 ed.). Yet the Mine Workers' activity in Pennington was held subject to an antitrust action by two lower courts. This decision was based upon a jury determination that the Union's economic philosophy is undesirable, and it resulted in an award against the Union of treble damages of $270,000 and $55,000 extra for respondent's attorneys' fees. In Jewel Tea, the Union has also been subjected to an antitrust suit in which a court of appeals, with its own notions as to what butchers are legitimately interested in, would subject the Union to a treble damage judgment in an as yet undetermined amount.

Regretfully these cases, both in the lower courts and in expressions in the various opinions filed today in this Court, as I shall demonstrate, constitute a throwback to past days when courts allowed antitrust actions against unions and employers engaged in conventional collective bargaining, because "a judge considered" the union or employer conduct in question to be "socially or economically" objectionable. Duplex Printing Press Co. v. Deering, supra, 254 U.S. at 485, 41 S.Ct. at 183 (dissenting opinion of Mr. Justice Brandeis). It is necessary to recall that history to place the cases before us in proper perspective.

[Mr. Justice Goldberg then traced the history of the application of the Sherman Act to labor unions, adverting to the major Supreme Court decisions construing that Act and the Clayton and Norris-LaGuardia Acts. He observed that the Wagner Act sought affirmatively to protect and encourage unionization and collective bargaining and that it also sought to narrow the role of the judiciary in formulating labor policy. He also noted that the Taft-Hartley Act outlawed certain specific union activities and did not test legality by subjective judgments of the union's purpose or effect.]

In my view, this history shows a consistent congressional purpose to limit severely judicial intervention in collective bargaining under cover of the wide umbrella of the antitrust laws, and, rather, to deal with what Congress deemed to be specific abuses on the part of labor unions by specific proscriptions in the labor statutes. * * * Following the sound analysis of Hutcheson, the Court should hold that, in order to effectuate congressional intent, collective bargaining activity concerning mandatory subjects of bargaining under the Labor Act is not subject to the antitrust laws. This rule flows directly from the Hutcheson holding that a union acting as a union, in the interests of its members, and not acting to fix prices or allocate markets in aid of an employer conspiracy to accomplish these objects, with only indirect union benefits, is not subject to challenge under the antitrust laws. To hold that mandatory collective bargaining is completely protected would effectuate the congressional policies of encouraging free collective bargaining, subject only to specific restrictions contained in the labor laws, and of limiting judicial intervention in labor matters via the antitrust route—an intervention which necessarily under the Sherman Act places on judges and juries the determination of "what public policy in regard to the industrial struggle demands." Duplex Printing Press Co. v. Deering, supra, 254 U.S., at 485, 41 S.Ct., at 183 (dissenting opinion of Mr. Justice Brandeis). See Winter, Collective Bargaining and Competition: The Application of Antitrust Standards to Union Activities, 73 Yale L.J. 14 (1963). * * * This national scheme would be virtually destroyed by the imposition of Sherman Act criminal and civil penalties upon employers and unions engaged in such collective bargaining. To tell the parties that they must bargain about a point but may be subject to antitrust penalties if they reach an agreement is to stultify the congressional scheme.

Moreover, mandatory subjects of bargaining are issues as to which union strikes may not be enjoined by either federal or state courts. To say that the union can strike over such issues but that both it and the employer are subject to possible antitrust penalties for making collective bargaining agreements concerning them is to assert that Congress intended to permit the parties to collective bargaining to wage industrial warfare but to prohibit them from peacefully settling their disputes. This would not only be irrational but would fly in the face of the clear congressional intent of promoting "the peaceful settlement of industrial disputes by subjecting labor-management controversies to the mediatory influence of negotiation." Fibreboard Paper Prods. Corp. v. National Labor Relations Board, 379 U.S. 203, 211, 85 S.Ct. 398, 403, 13 L.Ed.2d 233. * * *

* * * Since collective bargaining inevitably involves and requires discussion of the impact of the wage agreement reached with a particular employer or group of employers upon competing employers, the effect of the Court's decision will be to bar a basic element of collective bargaining from the conference room. If a union and employer are prevented from discussing and agreeing upon issues which are, in the great majority of cases, at the central core of bargaining, unilateral force will inevitably be substituted for rational discussion and agreement. Plainly and simply, the Court would subject both unions and employers to antitrust sanctions, criminal as well as civil, if in collective bargaining they concluded a wage agreement and, as part of the agreement, the union has undertaken to use its best efforts to have this wage accepted by other employers in the industry. Indeed, the decision today even goes beyond this. Under settled antitrust principles which are accepted by the Court as appropriate and applicable, which were the basis for jury instructions in Pennington, and which will govern it upon remand, there need not be direct evidence of an express agreement. Rather the existence of such an agreement, express or implied, may be inferred from the conduct of the parties.

* * * The rational thing for an employer to do, when faced with union demands he thinks he cannot meet, is to explain why, in economic terms, he believes that he cannot agree to the union requests. Indeed, the Labor Act's compulsion to bargain in good faith requires that he meaningfully address himself to the union's requests. See National Labor Relations Board v. Truitt Mfg. Co., 351 U.S. 149, 76 S.Ct. 753, 100 L.Ed. 1027. A recurring and most understandable reason given by employers for their resistance to union demands is that competitive factors prevent them from accepting the union's proposed terms. Under the Court's holding today, however, such a statement by an employer may start both the employer and union on the road to antitrust sanctions, criminal and civil. For a jury may well interpret such discussion and subsequent union action as showing an implicit or secret agreement to impose uniform standards on other employers. * * *

Furthermore, in order to determine whether, under the Court's standard, a union is acting unilaterally or pursuant to an agreement with employers, judges and juries will inevitably be drawn to try to determine the purpose and motive of union and employer collective bargaining activities. The history I have set out, however, makes clear that Congress intended to foreclose judges and juries from roaming at large in the area of collective bargaining, under cover of the antitrust laws, by inquiry into the purpose and motive of the employer and union bargaining on mandatory subjects. Such roaming at large, experience shows, leads to a substitution of judicial for congressional judgment as to how collective bargaining should operate. * * *

In Pennington, central to the alleged conspiracy is the claim that hourly wage rates and fringe benefits were set at a level designed to eliminate the competition of the smaller nonunion companies by making the labor cost too high for them to pay. Indeed, the trial judge charged that there was no violation of the Sherman Act in the establishing of wages and welfare payments through the national contract, "provided" the mine workers and the major coal producers had not agreed to fix "high" rates "in order to drive the small coal operators out of business." Under such an instruction, if the jury found the wage scale too "high" it could impute to the union the unlawful purpose of putting the nonunion operators out of business. It is clear that the effect of the instruction therefore, was to invite 12 jurymen to become arbiters of the economic desirability of the wage scale in the Nation's coal industry. The Court would sustain the judgment based on this charge and thereby put its stamp of approval on this role for courts and juries. * * * It is clear, as experience shows, that judges and juries neither have the aptitude nor possess the criteria for making this kind of judgment.
* * *

* * * [L]abor contracts establishing more or less standardized wages, hours, and other terms and conditions of employment in a given industry or market area are often secured either through bargaining with multi-employer associations or through bargaining with market leaders that sets a "pattern" for agreements on labor standards with other employers. These are two similar systems used to achieve the identical result of fostering labor peace through the negotiation of uniform labor standards in an industry. Yet the Court makes antitrust liability for both unions and employers turn on which of these two systems is used. It states that uniform wage agreements may be made with multi-employer units but an agreement cannot be made to affect employers outside the formal bargaining unit. I do not believe that the Court understands the effect of its ruling in terms of the practical realities of the automobile, steel, rubber, shipbuilding, and numerous other industries which follow the policy of pattern collective bargaining. See Chamber-

lain, Collective Bargaining 259–263 (1951)   *   *   *. I also do not understand why antitrust liability should turn on the form of unit determination rather than the substance of the collective bargaining impact on the industry.   *   *   *

     *   *   * Where there is an "agreement" to seek uniform wages in an industry, in what item is competition restrained? The answer to this question can only be that competition is restrained in employee wage standards.   *   *   *

     As I have already discussed, however, if one thing is clear, it is that Congress has repudiated the view that labor is a commodity and thus there should be competition to see who can supply it at the cheapest price.   *   *   * The kind of competition which is suppressed by employer-union agreement on uniform wages can only be competition between unions to see which union will agree to supply labor at a lower rate, or competition between employers in the sale of their products based on differences in labor costs. Neither type of "suppression," I submit, can be supported as a restraint of trade condemned by the antitrust laws. No one, I think, believes that Congress intended that there be an economic system under which unions would compete with each other to supply labor at the lowest possible cost.   *   *   *

Problems for Discussion

     1. Embry Aeronautical University, having submitted the low bid, is announced to be the successor of its competitor Ross Aviation, Inc. to a contract with the Army for the rendering of flight-training services. Prior to Embry's succession, Ross abandons its longstanding resistance to the unionization of its employees and negotiates a high-wage contract with Local 2003, International Association of Machinists. It is expected by Embry, the Army, Ross and Ross's employees that Embry will employ all or most of the Ross employees, as did Ross with respect to the workforce of its predecessor. However, given the low bid which won it the Army contract, Embry cannot afford the costly wage agreement. Both Ross and the union are aware of this fact; Ross hopes to regain the Army contract for itself by inducing a default by Embry. Embry does indeed default and brings suit against Ross and the union alleging that the wage agreement is a violation of the anti-trust laws. The union raises the labor exemption as its defense and distinguishes the *Pennington* case on two grounds: (1) here the wage contract was only with Ross, a single employer, and thus was not part of a multiemployer conspiracy; (2) the contract was simply to be extended to Embry, a successor employer in the same bargaining unit, and thus had no "extra-unit" impact. What result? See *Embry-Riddle Aeronautical Univ.* v. *Ross Aviation, Inc.*, 504 F.2d 896 (5th Cir. 1974).

     2. The Milk Drivers Union represents delivery employees of dairies and milk dealers in the Chicago area. Associated Milk Dealers, Inc.

(AMDI) is a nonprofit association which represents independently owned milk dealers in negotiating collective bargaining agreements. When the Union and AMDI agree upon an area contract, individual milk dealers (not AMDI) sign the agreement. The current three-year contract, which covers wages, hours, contributions to benefit funds, arbitration of disputes, etc., was concluded after negotiations attended by the Union, AMDI, Chicago Area Dairymen's Association (another employer association) and a number of individual employers. The contract also contains a "most favored nation" clause which permits a signatory milk dealer automatically to adopt the terms of an agreement between the Union and any other milk dealer if such terms are more advantageous to the other milk dealer than are the terms of the standard contract. The reason for the clause is apparent in a market of one union and numerous employers: it allows those employers who sign the contract to do so without fear of prejudice which might result to them if the union then turns to remaining employers and agrees to a different contract more favorable to the latter. Diamond Food Stores has just entered the Chicago milk processing market and its subdivision Hillfarm Dairy has signed a contract with the Union on terms allegedly more favorable than those of the standard contract. AMDI wishes to invoke the "most favored nation" clause and adopt the terms of the Hillfarm agreement. The Union contends that the anti-trust laws prohibit the enforcement of the "most favored nation" clause. Is the Union's contention correct? *Associated Milk Dealers, Inc.* v. *Milk Drivers Local 753*, 422 F.2d 546 (7th Cir. 1970).

LOCAL 189, MEAT CUTTERS v. JEWEL TEA CO.

Supreme Court of the United States, 1965.
381 U.S. 676, 85 S.Ct. 1596, 14 L.Ed.2d 640.

MR. JUSTICE WHITE announced the judgment of the Court and delivered an opinion in which THE CHIEF JUSTICE and MR. JUSTICE BRENNAN join.

Like United Mine Workers v. Pennington, this case presents questions regarding the application of §§ 1 and 2 of the Sherman Antitrust Act, 26 Stat. 209, as amended, 15 U.S.C.A. §§ 1–2 (1958 ed.), to activities of labor unions. In particular, it concerns the lawfulness of the following restriction on the operating hours of food store meat departments contained in a collective agreement executed after joint multi-employer, multi-union negotiations:

> "Market operating hours shall be 9:00 a. m. to 6:00
> p. m. Monday through Saturday, inclusive. No cus-
> tomer shall be served who comes into the market
> before or after the hours set forth above."

[Since shortly after the turn of the century, the working hours of Chicago butchers have been a source of great contention. A strike in 1919 eliminated the 81-hour, 7-day week, and subsequent labor contracts reduced working hours by 1947 to the 9 a. m. to 6 p. m. period contained in current agreements. Since 1920, the labor agreements similarly provided for a limitation upon the hours during which customers could be served. In the 1957 contract negotiations between locals of the Amalgamated Meat Cutters and representatives of Chicago retailers of fresh meat (both "self-service" markets, where meat was available for sale on a prepackaged self-service basis, and "service" markets, where meat could be custom-cut), an agreement was reached on the marketing-hour restrictions between the unions and the Associated Food Retailers of Greater Chicago, representing *inter alia* 300 meat dealers. Jewel Tea Co., however, sought a modification of the marketing-hour provision so as to allow for Friday night operations, but it relented and signed the standard agreement when the unions threatened to strike. In 1958, Jewel brought suit against the unions, certain union officers, Associated and one of its officers, seeking invalidation of the contract provision as a violation of Sections 1 and 2 of the Sherman Act. The gist of the complaint was an alleged conspiracy between the unions and Associated to prevent the retail sale of fresh meat after 6 p. m.]

The complaint stated that in recent years the prepackaged, self-service system of marketing meat had come into vogue, that 174 of Jewel's 196 stores were equipped to vend meat in this manner, and that a butcher need not be on duty in a self-service market at the time meat purchases were actually made. The prohibition of night meat marketing, it was alleged, unlawfully impeded Jewel in the use of its property and adversely affected the general public in that many persons find it inconvenient to shop during the day. An injunction, treble damages and attorney's fees were demanded.

The trial judge held the allegations of the complaint sufficient to withstand a motion to dismiss made on the grounds, *inter alia*, that (a) the "alleged restraint [was] within the exclusive regulatory scope of the National Labor Relations Act and [was] therefore outside the jurisdiction of the Court" and (b) the controversy was within the labor exemption to the antitrust laws. That ruling was sustained on appeal. Jewel Tea Co. v. Local Unions Nos. 189, etc., Amalgamated Meat Cutters, AFL–CIO, 274 F.2d 271 (C.A.7th Cir. 1960), cert. denied, 362 U.S. 936, 80 S.Ct. 757. After trial, however, the District Judge ruled the "record was devoid of any evidence to support a finding of a conspiracy" between Associated and the unions to force the restrictive provision on Jewel. Testing the unions' action standing alone, the trial court found that even in self-service markets removal of the limitation on marketing hours either would inaugurate longer hours and night work for the butchers or would result in butchers' work being done by others unskilled in the trade. Thus, the court concluded, the unions had imposed the marketing hours limitation to serve their own interests respecting conditions of employment, and such action was clearly within the labor exemption of the Sherman Act established by Hunt v. Crumboch, 325 U.S. 821, 65 S.Ct. 1545; United States v. Hutcheson, 312 U.S. 219, 61 S.Ct. 463; United States v. American Federation of Musicians, 318 U.S. 741, 63 S.Ct. 665. Alternatively, the District Court ruled that even if this was not the case, the arrangement did not amount to an unreasonable restraint of trade in violation of the Sherman Act.

The Court of Appeals reversed the dismissal of the complaint as to both the unions and Associated. * * * We granted certiorari on the unions' petition, 379 U.S. 812, 85 S.Ct. 66, and now reverse the Court of Appeals.

[The Court opened its opinion by rejecting the union's argument that the case was within the exclusive primary jurisdiction of the NLRB.]

II.

Here, as in United Mine Workers v. Pennington, the claim is made that the agreement under attack is exempt from the antitrust laws. We agree, but not on the broad grounds urged by the union.

It is well at the outset to emphasize that this case comes to us stripped of any claim of a union-employer conspiracy against Jewel. The trial court found no evidence to sustain Jewel's conspiracy claim and this finding was not disturbed by the Court of Appeals. We therefore have a situation where the unions, having obtained a marketing-hours agreement from one group of employers, has successfully sought the same terms from a single employer, Jewel, not as a result of a bargain between the unions and some employers directed against other employers, but pursuant to what the unions deemed to be in their own labor union interests. * * *

We pointed out in Pennington that exemption for union-employer agreements is very much a matter of accommodating the coverage of the Sherman Act to the policy of the labor laws. Employers and unions are required to bargain about wages, hours and working conditions, and this fact weighs heavily in favor of antitrust exemption for agreements on these subjects. But neither party need bargain about other matters and either party commits an unfair labor practice if it conditions its bargaining upon discussions of a nonmandatory subject. Labor Board v. Borg-Warner Corp., 356 U.S. 342, 78 S.Ct. 718. Jewel, for example, need not have bargained about or agreed to a schedule of prices at which its meat would be sold and the union could not legally have insisted that it do so. But if the union had made such a demand, Jewel had agreed and the United States or an injured party had challenged the agreement under the antitrust laws, we seriously doubt that either the union or Jewel could claim immunity by reason of the labor exemption, whatever substantive questions of violation there might be.

Thus the issue in this case is whether the marketing-hours restriction, like wages, and unlike prices, is so intimately related to wages, hours and working conditions that the unions' successful attempt to obtain that provision through bona fide, arms-length bargaining in pursuit of its own labor union policies, and not at the behest of or in combination with nonlabor groups, falls within the protection of the national labor policy and is therefore exempt from the Sherman Act.[5] We think that it is.

The Court of Appeals would classify the marketing hours restriction with the product-pricing provision and place both within the reach of the Sherman Act. In its view, labor has a legitimate interest in the number of hours it must work but no interest in whether the hours fall in the daytime, in the nighttime or on Sundays. "[T]he furnishing of a place and advantageous hours of employment for the butchers to supply meat to customers are the prerogatives of the employer." 331 F.2d 547, 549. That reasoning would invalidate with respect to both service and self-service markets the 1957 provision that "eight hours shall constitute the basic work day, Monday through Saturday; *work to begin at 9:00 a. m. and stop at 6:00 p. m.* * * *" as well as the marketing hours restriction.

Contrary to the Court of Appeals, we think that the particular hours of the day and the particular days of the week during which employees shall be required to work are subjects well within the realm of "wages, hours, and other terms and conditions of employment" about which employers and unions must bargain. National Labor Relations Act § 8(d); see Timken Roller Bearing Co., 70 N.L.R.B. 500, 504, 515–516, 521 (1946), rev'd on other grounds, 161 F.2d 949 (C.A.6th Cir. 1947) (employer's unilateral imposition of Sunday work was refusal to bargain); Massey Gin & Machine Works, Inc., 78 N.L. R.B. 189, 195, 199 (same; change in starting and quitting time); Camp & McInnes, Inc., 100 N.L.R.B. 524, 532 (same; reduction of lunch hour and advancement of quitting time). And, although the effect on competition is apparent and real, perhaps more so than in

5. The crucial determinant is not the form of the agreement—e. g., prices or wages—but its relative impact on the product market and the interests of union members. Thus in Teamsters Union v. Oliver, 358 U.S. 283, 79 S.Ct. 297, we held that federal labor policy precluded application of state anti-trust laws to an employer-union agreement that when leased trucks were driven by their owners, such owner-drivers should receive, in addition to the union wage, not less than a pre-scribed minimum rental. Though in form a scheme fixing prices for the supply of leased vehicles, the agreement was designed "to protect the negotiated wage scale against the possible undermining through diminution of the owner's wages for driving which might result from a rental which did not cover his operating costs." Id., at 293–294. As the agreement did not embody a " 'remote and indirect approach to the subject of wages' * * * but a direct frontal attack upon a problem thought to threaten the maintenance of the basic wage structure established by the collective bargaining contract," id., at 294, the paramount federal policy of encouraging collective bargaining proscribed application of the state law.

the case of the wage agreement, the concern of union members is immediate and direct. Weighing the respective interests involved, we think the national labor policy expressed in the National Labor Relations Act places beyond the reach of the Sherman Act union-employer agreements on when, as well as how long, employees must work. An agreement on these subjects between the union and the employers in a bargaining unit is not illegal under the Sherman Act, nor is the union's unilateral demand for the same contract of other employers in the industry.

Disposing of the case, as it did, on the broad grounds we have indicated, the Court of Appeals did not deal separately with the marketing hours provision, as distinguished from hours of work, in connection with either service or self-service markets. The dispute here pertains principally to self-service markets. * * *

If it were true that self-service markets could actually operate without butchers, at least for a few hours after 6 p. m., that no encroachment on butchers' work would result and that the workload of butchers during normal working hours would not be substantially increased, Jewel's position would have considerable merit. For then the obvious restraint on the product market—the exclusion of self-service stores from the evening market for meat—would stand alone, unmitigated and unjustified by the vital interests of the union butchers which are relied upon in this case. In such event the limitation imposed by the union might well be reduced to nothing but an effort by the union to protect one group of employers from competition by another, which is conduct that is not exempt from the Sherman Act. Whether there would be a violation of §§ 1 and 2 would then depend on whether the elements of a conspiracy in restraint of trade or an attempt to monopolize had been proved.[6]

Thus the dispute between Jewel and the unions essentially concerns a narrow factual question: Are night operations without butchers, and without infringement of butchers' interests, feasible? The District Court resolved this factual dispute in favor of the unions. It found that "in stores where meat is sold at night it is impractical to operate without either butchers or other employees. Someone must arrange, replenish and clean the counters and supply customer services." Operating without butchers would mean that "their work would be done by others unskilled in the trade," and "would involve

6. One issue, for example, would be whether the restraint was unreasonable. Judicial pronouncements regarding the reasonableness of restraints on hours of business are relatively few. Some cases appear to have viewed such restraints as tantamount to limits on hours of work and thus reasonable, even though contained in agreements among competitors. * * *

The decided cases * * * do not appear to offer any easy answer to the question whether in a particular case an operating hours restraint is unreasonable.

an increase in workload in preparing for the night work and cleaning the next morning." 215 F.Supp., at 846. Those findings were not disturbed by the Court of Appeals, which, as previously noted, proceeded on a broader ground. Our function is limited to reviewing the record to satisfy ourselves that the trial judge's findings are not clearly erroneous. Fed.Rules Civ.Proc., 52(a).

The trial court had before it evidence concerning the history of the unions' opposition to night work, the development of the provisions respecting night work and night operations, the course of collective negotiations in 1957, 1959, and 1961 with regard to those provisions, and the characteristics of meat marketing insofar as they bore on the feasibility of night operations without butchers. * * *

The unions' evidence with regard to the practicability of night operations without butchers was accurately summarized by the trial judge as follows:

> "[I]n most of plaintiff's stores outside Chicago, where night operations exist, meat cutters are on duty whenever a meat department is open after 6 P.M. * * * Even in self-service departments, ostensibly operated without employees on duty after 6 P.M., there was evidence that requisite customer services in connection with meat sales were performed by grocery clerks. In the same vein, defendants adduced evidence that in the sale of delicatessen items, which could be made after 6 P.M. from self-service cases under the contract, 'practically' always during the time the market was open the manager, or other employees, would be rearranging and restocking the cases. There was also evidence that even if it were practical to operate a self-service meat market after 6 P.M. without employees, the night operations would add to the workload in getting the meats prepared for night sales and in putting the counters in order the next day." 215 F.Supp., at 844.

[The Justices concluded that the findings of the district judge were not clearly erroneous.]

Reversed.

MR. JUSTICE DOUGLAS, with whom MR. JUSTICE BLACK and MR. JUSTICE CLARK concur, dissenting.

If we followed Allen Bradley Co. v. Local Union No. 3, 325 U.S. 797, 65 S.Ct. 1533, 89 L.Ed. 1939 we would hold with the Court of Appeals that this multi-employer agreement with the union not to sell meat between 6 p. m. and 9 a. m. was not immunized from the antitrust laws and that respondent's evidence made out a prima facie case that it was in fact a violation of the Sherman Act.

   If, in the present case, the employers alone agreed not to sell meat from 6 p. m. to 9 a. m., they would be guilty of an anticompetitive practice, barred by the antitrust laws. * * * In the circumstances of this case the collective bargaining agreement itself, of which the District Court said there was clear proof, was evidence of a conspiracy among the employers with the unions to impose the marketing-hours restriction on Jewel via a strike threat by the unions. This tended to take from the merchants who agreed among themselves their freedom to work their own hours and to subject all who, like Jewel, wanted to sell meat after 6 p. m. to the coercion of threatened strikes, all of which if done in concert only by businessmen would violate the antitrust laws. * * * Some merchants relied chiefly on price competition to draw trade; others employed courtesy, quick service, and keeping their doors open long hours to meet the convenience of customers. The unions here induced a large group of merchants to use their collective strength to hurt others who wanted the competitive advantage of selling meat after 6 p. m. Unless Allen Bradley is either overruled or greatly impaired, the unions can no more aid a group of businessmen to force their competitors to follow uniform store marketing hours than to force them to sell at fixed prices. Both practices take away the freedom of traders to carry on their business in their own competitive fashion. * * *

   JUSTICE GOLDBERG, JUSTICE STEWART and JUSTICE HARLAN, concurring.

                              * * *

   The judicial expressions in Jewel Tea represent another example of the reluctance of judges to give full effect to congressional purpose in this area and the substitution by judges of their views for those of Congress as to how free collective bargaining should operate. In this case the Court of Appeals would have held the Union liable for the Sherman Act's criminal and civil penalties because in the court's social and economic judgment, the determination of the hours at which meat is to be sold is a "proprietory" matter within the exclusive control of management and thus the Union had no legitimate interest in bargaining over it. My Brother DOUGLAS, joined by MR. JUSTICE BLACK and MR. JUSTICE CLARK, would affirm this judgment apparently because the agreement was reached through a multi-employer bargaining unit. But, as I have demonstrated above, there is nothing even remotely illegal about such bargaining. Even if an independent conspiracy test were applicable to the Jewel Tea situation, the simple fact is that multi-employer bargaining conducted at arm's length does not constitute union abetment of a business combination. It is often a self-defensive form of employer bargaining designed to match union strength.

My Brother WHITE, joined by THE CHIEF JUSTICE and MR. JUSTICE BRENNAN, while not agreeing with my Brother DOUGLAS, would reverse the Court of Appeals. He also, however, refuses to give full effect to the congressional intent that judges should not, under cover of the Sherman Act umbrella, substitute their economic and social policies for free collective bargaining. My Brother WHITE recognizes that the issue of the hours of sale of meat concerns a mandatory subject of bargaining based on the trial court's findings that it directly affected the hours of work of the butchers in the self-service markets, and therefore, since there was a finding that the Union was not abetting an independent employer conspiracy, he joins in reversing the Court of Appeals. In doing so, however, he apparently draws lines among mandatory subjects of bargaining, presumably based on a judicial determination of their importance to the worker, and states that not all agreements resulting from collective bargaining based on mandatory subjects of bargaining are immune from the antitrust laws, even absent evidence of union abetment of an independent conspiracy of employers. Following this reasoning, my Brother WHITE indicates that he would sustain a judgment here, even absent evidence of union abetment of an independent conspiracy of employers, if the trial court had found "that self-service markets could actually operate without butchers, at least for a few hours after 6 p. m., that no encroachment on butchers' work would result and that the workload of butchers during normal working hours would not be substantially increased * * *." Such a view seems to me to be unsupportable. It represents a narrow, confining view of what labor unions have a legitimate interest in preserving and thus bargaining about. Even if the self-service markets could operate after 6 p. m., without their butchers and without increasing the work of their butchers at other times, the result of such operation can reasonably be expected to be either that the small, independent, service markets would have to remain open in order to compete, thus requiring their union butchers to work at night, or that the small, independent, service markets would not be able to operate at night and thus would be put at a competitive disadvantage. Since it is clear that the large, automated self-service markets employ less butchers per volume of sales than service markets do, the Union certainly has a legitimate interest in keeping service markets competitive so as to preserve jobs. Job security of this kind has been recognized to be a legitimate subject of union interest. * * * Putting the opinion of the Court in Pennington together with the opinions of my Brothers DOUGLAS and WHITE in Jewel Tea, it would seem that unions are damned if their collective bargaining philosophy involves acceptance of automation (Pennington) and are equally damned if their collective bargaining philosophy involves resistance to automation (Jewel Tea). Again, the wisdom of a union adopting either philosophy is not for judicial determination.   *   *   *

My view that Congress intended that collective bargaining activity on mandatory subjects of bargaining under the Labor Act not be subject to the antitrust laws does not mean that I believe that Congress intended that activity involving all nonmandatory subjects of bargaining be similarly exempt. That direct and overriding interest of unions in such subjects as wages, hours, and other working conditions, which Congress has recognized in making them subjects of mandatory bargaining is clearly lacking where the subject of the agreement is price-fixing and market allocation. Moreover, such activities are at the core of the type of anticompetitive commercial restraint at which the antitrust laws are directed. * * *

Problems for Discussion

1. In the *National Woodwork* case, at page 766 supra, the full text of Rule 17 in the labor contract between the Union and the general contractor Frouge provided: "No employee shall work on any job on which cabinet work, fixtures, millwork, sash, doors, trim or other detailed millwork is used unless the same is Union-made and bears the Union Label of the United Brotherhood of Carpenters and Joiners of America. No member of this District Council will handle material coming from a mill where cutting out and fitting has been done for butts, locks, letter plates, or hardware of any description, nor any doors or transoms which have been fitted prior to being furnished on the job, including base, chair, rail, picture moulding, which has been previously fitted." [The NLRB held that the first sentence was a union-signatory provision which violated Section 8(e), and the Union did not challenge that conclusion on judicial review. The second sentence was, of course, upheld by the Supreme Court.]

Consider the following questions under the antitrust laws:

(a) Had the association of general contractors, with which the Union was negotiating, refused to include Rule 17 in their labor contract, and had the Union struck and picketed the contractors, could the Union's conduct have been enjoined as a violation of the Sherman Act? Would the Union be liable for treble damages?

(b) Could the general contractors (or Frouge as an individual contractor), once having agreed to include Rule 17 in the labor contract, successfully invalidate it by an action under the Sherman Act? Might your answer to this question depend upon whether this provision had been included in the contract with the general contractors at the urging of manufacturers of cabinets, fixtures and the like, whose sales had been increasingly undercut by cheaper cabinets, etc. supplied by nonunion manufacturers (and who had informed the Union that they could not continue to pay union wages while losing these sales)—as opposed to having been incorporated at the insistence of the Union? See United States v. Brims, 272 U.S. 549, 47 S.Ct. 169, 71 L.Ed. 403 (1926).

(Is the sentence in Rule 17 which is more obviously unlawful under Section 8(e) for that reason more obviously lawful under the Sherman Act? At the least, is it sound to argue that the more moderate remedies provided for unlawful hot cargo provisions under Section 8(e) should be deemed to "preempt" the more severe sanctions available under the Sherman Act?)

(c) If these refusal-to-handle provisions had not been incorporated in the labor contract, but had instead been for many years a part of the constitution of the Carpenters' Union and thus binding on its members, could they be invalidated under the Sherman Act? Would a refusal to handle, actually carried out at the job site pursuant to the Union's constitution, violate the Sherman Act? See Bedford Cut Stone Co. v. Journeymen Stone Cutters' Ass'n, 274 U.S. 37, 47 S.Ct. 522, 71 L.Ed. 916 (1927).

Reconsider all of these questions after studying the *Connell* case, immediately below.

2. Some years ago a new firm, Adams Dairy Company, began business in the St. Louis metropolitan area. While most dairy companies were then principally engaged in door-to-door sales, Adams devoted its energies to high-volume sales, in half-gallon and gallon paper cartons, to food markets. By spending less on containers and utilizing many fewer drivers than its competitors, Adams was able to charge prices substantially below prevailing levels for home-delivered milk. After Adams was organized by the Milk Drivers Union, the union began contract negotiations on behalf of the milk wagon drivers employed by the St. Louis dairies including Adams (which were members of a multiemployer association). The union has insisted upon dramatic wage increases at various increasing levels of quantity of milk delivered, such that the wages and commissions of the Adams deliverymen would be doubled as a result of the new agreement. The union has argued that higher pay is needed to compensate for the strain imposed by virtue of the heavy loading and unloading required by Adams, even though none of the drivers has complained and even though the drivers are already earning almost $20,000 a year; moreover, the union claims that its wage demands are also a valid means of work-spreading and generating more jobs. Adams believes that the union is simply trying to make it economically impossible to continue to charge low prices. It also believes that the other dairies are prepared to sign the agreement, since (because of their low-bulk deliveries) they will not be seriously injured by the sharply graduated pay scale sought by the union.

Adams wishes to know: (a) Whether there is any way that the union can be prevented from striking to enforce its demands, and (b) whether, if the other dairies sign the proposed contract, a court action is available to challenge the wage provision. See *Adams Dairy Co. v. St. Louis Dairy Co.*, 260 F.2d 46 (8th Cir. 1958).

CONNELL CONSTR. CO. v. PLUMBERS LOCAL 100 [7]

Supreme Court of the United States, 1975.
421 U.S. 616, 95 S.Ct. 1830, 44 L.Ed.2d 418.

MR. JUSTICE POWELL delivered the opinion of the Court.

The building trades union in this case supported its efforts to organize mechanical subcontractors by picketing certain general contractors, including Petitioner. The union's sole objective was to compel the general contractors to agree that in letting subcontracts for mechanical work they would deal only with firms that were parties to the union's current collective-bargaining agreement. The union disclaimed any interest in representing the general contractors' employees. In this case the picketing succeeded, and Petitioner seeks to annul the resulting agreement as an illegal restraint on competition under federal and state law. The union claims immunity from federal antitrust statutes and argues that federal labor regulation pre-empts state law.

I

Local 100 is the bargaining representative for workers in the plumbing and mechanical trades in Dallas. When this litigation began, it was party to a multiemployer bargaining agreement with the Mechanical Contractors Association of Dallas, a group of about 75 mechanical contractors. That contract contained a "most favored nation" clause, by which the union agreed that if it granted a more favorable contract to any other employer it would extend the same terms to all members of the Association.

Connell Construction Company is a general building contractor in Dallas. It obtains jobs by competitive bidding and subcontracts all plumbing and mechanical work. Connell has followed a policy of awarding these subcontracts on the basis of competitive bids, and it has done business with both union and nonunion subcontractors. Connell's employees are represented by various building trade unions. Local 100 has never sought to represent them or to bargain with Connell on their behalf.

In November 1970, Local 100 asked Connell to agree that it would subcontract mechanical work [to be performed at the construction site] only to firms that had a current contract with the union. * * * When Connell refused to sign this agreement, Local 100 stationed a single picket at one of Connell's major construction sites.

---

7. Comment, Broadening Labor's Antitrust Liability While Narrowing its Construction Industry Proviso Protection, 27 Cath.U.L.Rev. 305 (1978); King & Smith, Labor Relations and Antitrust: Developments After *Connell*, 3 Ind.Rel.L.J. 605 (1979); St. Antoine, *Connell*: Antitrust Law at the Expense of Labor Law, 62 Va.L.Rev. 603 (1976).

About 150 workers walked off the job, and construction halted. Connell filed suit in state court to enjoin the picketing as a violation of Texas antitrust laws. Local 100 removed the case to federal court. Connell then signed the subcontracting agreement under protest. It amended its complaint to claim that the agreement violated §§ 1 and 2 of the Sherman Act, 15 U.S.C. §§ 1, 2, and was therefore invalid. Connell sought a declaration to this effect and an injunction against any further efforts to force it to sign such an agreement.

By the time the case went to trial, Local 100 had submitted identical agreements to a number of other general contractors in Dallas. Five others had signed, and the union was waging a selective picketing campaign against those who resisted.

The District Court held that the subcontracting agreement was exempt from federal antitrust laws because it was authorized by the construction industry proviso to § 8(e) of the National Labor Relations Act, 29 U.S.C. § 158(e). The court also held that federal labor legislation pre-empted the State's antitrust laws. 78 L.R.R.M. 3012 (ND Tex.1971). The Court of Appeals for the Fifth Circuit affirmed, 483 F.2d 1154 (CA 5 1973), with one judge dissenting. It held that Local 100's goal of organizing nonunion subcontractors was a legitimate union interest and that its efforts toward that goal were therefore exempt from federal antitrust laws. On the second issue, it held that state law was pre-empted under San Diego Building Trades Council v. Garmon, 359 U.S. 236, 79 S.Ct. 773, 3 L.Ed.2d 775 (1959). We granted certiorari on Connell's petition. 416 U.S. 981, 94 S.Ct. 2381, 40 L.Ed.2d 757. We reverse on the question of federal antitrust immunity and affirm the ruling on state law pre-emption.

II

The basic sources of organized labor's exemption from federal antitrust laws are §§ 6 and 20 of the Clayton Act, 15 U.S.C. § 17 and 29 U.S.C. § 52, and the Norris-LaGuardia Act, 29 U.S.C. §§ 104, 105, and 113. These statutes declare that labor unions are not combinations or conspiracies in restraint of trade, and exempt specific union activities, including secondary picketing and boycotts, from the operation of the antitrust laws. See United States v. Hutcheson, 312 U.S. 219, 61 S.Ct. 463, 85 L.Ed. 788 (1941). They do not exempt concerted action or agreements between unions and nonlabor parties. UMW v. Pennington, 381 U.S. 657, 662, 85 S.Ct. 1585, 1589, 14 L. Ed.2d 626 (1965). The Court has recognized, however, that a proper accommodation between the congressional policy favoring collective bargaining under the NLRA and the congressional policy favoring free competition in business markets requires that some union-employer agreements be accorded a limited nonstatutory exemption from antitrust sanctions. Meat Cutters Local 189 v. Jewel Tea Co., 381 U.S. 676, 85 S.Ct. 1596, 14 L.Ed.2d 640 (1965).

The nonstatutory exemption has its source in the strong labor policy favoring the association of employees to eliminate competition over wages and working conditions. Union success in organizing workers and standardizing wages ultimately will affect price competition among employers, but the goals of federal labor law never could be achieved if this effect on business competition were held a violation of the antitrust laws. The Court therefore has acknowledged that labor policy requires tolerance for the lessening of business competition based on differences in wages and working conditions. See UMW v. Pennington, supra, 381 U.S. at 666, 85 S.Ct. at 1591; *Jewel Tea,* supra, 381 U.S. at 692–693, 85 S.Ct. at 1603–1604 (opinion of Mr. Justice White). Labor policy clearly does not require, however, that a union have freedom to impose direct restraints on competition among those who employ its members. Thus, while the statutory exemption allows unions to accomplish some restraints by acting unilaterally, e. g., American Federation of Musicians v. Carroll, 391 U.S. 99, 88 S.Ct. 1562, 20 L.Ed.2d 460 (1968), the nonstatutory exemption offers no similar protection when a union and a nonlabor party agree to restrain competition in a business market. See Allen Bradley Co. v. IBEW Local 3, 325 U.S. 797, 806–811, 65 S.Ct. 1533, 1538–1541, 89 L.Ed. 1939 (1945); Cox, Labor and the Antitrust Laws—A Preliminary Analysis, 104 U.Pa.L.Rev. 252 (1955); Meltzer, Labor Unions, Collective Bargaining, and the Antitrust Laws, 32 U.Chi.L.Rev. 659 (1965).

In this case Local 100 used direct restraints on the business market to support its organizing campaign. The agreements with Connell and other general contractors indiscriminately excluded nonunion subcontractors from a portion of the market, even if their competitive advantages were not derived from substandard wages and working conditions but rather from more efficient operating methods. Curtailment of competition based on efficiency is neither a goal of federal labor policy nor a necessary effect of the elimination of competition among workers. Moreover, competition based on efficiency is a positive value that the antitrust laws strive to protect.

The multiemployer bargaining agreement between Local 100 and the Association, though not challenged in this suit, is relevant in determining the effect that the agreement between Local 100 and Connell would have on the business market. The "most favored nation" clause in the multiemployer agreement promised to eliminate competition between members of the Association and any other subcontractors that Local 100 might organize. By giving members of the Association a contractual right to insist on terms as favorable as those given any competitor, it guaranteed that the union would make no agreement that would give an unaffiliated contractor a competitive advantage over members of the Association. Subcontractors in the Association thus stood to benefit from any extension of Local 100's organization, but the method Local 100 chose also had the effect of sheltering them from outside competition in that portion of the market covered by subcontracting agreements between general contractors and Local 100. In that portion of the market, the restriction on subcontracting would eliminate competition on all subjects covered by the multiemployer agreement, even on subjects unrelated to wages, hours and working conditions.

Success in exacting agreements from general contractors would also give Local 100 power to control access to the market for mechanical subcontracting work. The agreements with general contractors did not simply prohibit subcontracting to any nonunion firm; they prohibited subcontracting to any firm that did not have a contract with Local 100. The union thus had complete control over subcontract work offered by general contractors that had signed these agreements. Such control could result in significant adverse effects on the market and on consumers, effects unrelated to the union's legitimate goals of organizing workers and standardizing working conditions. For example, if the union thought the interests of its members would be served by having fewer subcontractors competing for the available work, it could refuse to sign collective-bargaining agreements with marginal firms. Cf. UMW v. Pennington, supra. Or, since Local 100 has a well-defined geographical jurisdiction, it could exclude "travelling" subcontractors by refusing to deal with them. Local 100 thus might be able to create a geographical enclave for local contractors, similar to the closed market in *Allen Bradley*, supra.

This record contains no evidence that the union's goal was anything other than organizing as many subcontractors as possible.[8] This goal was legal, even though a successful organizing campaign ultimately would reduce the competition that unionized employers face from nonunion firms. But the methods the union chose are not immune from antitrust sanctions simply because the goal is legal. Here Local 100, by agreement with several contractors, made nonunion subcontractors ineligible to compete for a portion of the available work. This kind of direct restraint on the business market

8. There was no evidence that Local 100's organizing campaign was connected with any agreement with members of the multiemployer bargaining unit, and the only evidence of agreement among those subcontractors was the "most favored nation" clause in the collective-bargaining agreement. In fact, Connell has not argued the case on a theory of conspiracy between the union and unionized subcontractors. It has simply relied on the multiemployer agreement as a factor enhancing the restraint of trade implicit in the subcontracting agreement it signed.

has substantial anticompetitive effects, both actual and potential, that would not follow naturally from the elimination of competition over wages and working conditions. It contravenes antitrust policies to a degree not justified by congressional labor policy, and therefore cannot claim a nonstatutory exemption from the antitrust laws.

There can be no argument in this case, whatever its force in other contexts, that a restraint of this magnitude might be entitled to an antitrust exemption if it were included in a lawful collective-bargaining agreement. Cf. UMW v. Pennington, supra, 381 U.S. at 664–665, 85 S.Ct. at 1590, 1591; *Jewel Tea,* supra, 381 U.S. at 689–690, 85 S.Ct. at 1601–1602 (opinion of Mr. Justice White); id., at 709–713, 732–733, 85 S.Ct. 1614, 1616, 1626–1627 (opinion of Mr. Justice Goldberg). In this case, Local 100 had no interest in representing Connell's employees. The federal policy favoring collective bargaining therefore can offer no shelter for the union's coercive action against Connell or its campaign to exclude nonunion firms from the subcontracting market.

[In Part III of the Court's opinion, Justice Powell considered the union's claim that its contract was explicitly allowed by the construction-industry proviso to Section 8(e), which removes from the ban of that Section "hot cargo" clauses relating to the subcontracting of work to be performed at a construction site. Observing that the scope of Section 8(e) was not exclusively to be determined by the NLRB and that a court could do so in the context of a federal antitrust action, the Court held that Section 8(e) "does not allow this type of agreement." The Court studied the legislative history of that Section and found that the permission to use "hot cargo" agreements for jobsite work was not for the purpose of entitling unions "to use subcontracting agreements as a broad organizational weapon" but rather "to alleviate the frictions that may arise when union men work continuously alongside nonunion men on the same construction site."]

Local 100 does not suggest that its subcontracting agreement is related to any of these policies. * * * The union admits that it sought the agreement solely as a way of pressuring mechanical subcontractors in the Dallas area to recognize it as the representative of their employees.

If we agreed with Local 100 that the construction industry proviso authorizes subcontracting agreements with "stranger" contractors, not limited to any particular jobsite, our ruling would give construction unions an almost unlimited organizational weapon. The unions would be free to enlist any general contractor to bring economic pressure on nonunion subcontractors, as long as the agreement recited that it only covered work to be performed on some jobsite somewhere. The proviso's jobsite restriction then would serve only to prohibit agreements relating to subcontractors that deliver their work complete to the jobsite.

It is highly improbable that Congress intended such a result. One of the major aims of the 1959 Act was to limit "top-down" organizing campaigns, in which unions used economic weapons to force recognition from an employer regardless of the wishes of his employees. * * *

These careful limits on the economic pressure unions may use in aid of their organizational campaigns would be undermined seriously if the proviso to § 8(e) were construed to allow unions to seek subcontracting agreements, at large, from any general contractor vulnerable to picketing. Absent a clear indication that Congress intended to leave such a glaring loophole in its restrictions on "top-down" organizing, we are unwilling to read the construction industry proviso as broadly as Local 100 suggests. Instead, we think its authorization extends only to agreements in the context of collective-bargaining relationships and in light of congressional references to the *Denver Building Trades* problem, possibly to common-situs relationships on particular jobsites as well.

Finally, Local 100 contends that even if the subcontracting agreement is not sanctioned by the construction industry proviso and therefore is illegal under § 8(e), it cannot be the basis for anti-trust liability because the remedies in the NLRA are exclusive. This argument is grounded in the legislative history of the 1947 Taft-Hartley amendments. Congress rejected attempts to regulate secondary activities by repealing the antitrust exemptions in the Clayton and Norris-LaGuardia Acts, and created special remedies under the labor law instead. It made secondary activities unfair labor practices under § 8(b)(4), and drafted special provisions for preliminary injunctions at the suit of the NLRB and for recovery of actual damages in the district courts. Sections 10(*l*), 303; 29 U.S.C. §§ 160(*l*), 187. But whatever significance this legislative choice has for antitrust suits based on those secondary activities prohibited by § 8(b)(4), it has no relevance to the question whether Congress meant to preclude antitrust suits based on the "hot-cargo" agreements that it outlawed in 1959. There is no legislative history in the 1959 Congress suggesting that labor-law remedies for § 8(e) violations were intended to be exclusive, or that Congress thought allowing antitrust remedies in cases like the present one would be inconsistent with the remedial scheme of the NLRA.

We therefore hold that this agreement, which is outside the context of a collective-bargaining relationship and not restricted to a particular jobsite, but which nonetheless obligates Connell to subcontract work only to firms that have a contract with Local 100, may be the basis of a federal antitrust suit because it has a potential for restraining competition in the business market in ways that would not follow naturally from elimination of competition over wages and working conditions.

[In Part IV of its opinion, the Court held that although the agreement between the union and Connell was subject to federal antitrust law, state antitrust law was to be preempted. "Because employee organization is central to federal labor policy and regulation of organizational procedures is comprehensive, federal law does not admit the use of state antitrust law to regulate union activity that is closely related to organizational goals. * * * Of course, other agreements between unions and nonlabor parties may yet be subject to state antitrust laws. See Teamsters Local 24 v. Oliver, supra, 358 U.S. at 295–297, 79 S.Ct. at 304–305. The governing factor is the risk of conflict with the NLRA or with federal labor policy."]

V

Neither the District Court nor the Court of Appeals decided whether the agreement between Local 100 and Connell, if subject to the antitrust laws, would constitute an agreement that restrains trade within the meaning of the Sherman Act. The issue was not briefed and argued fully in this Court. Accordingly, we remand for consideration whether the agreement violated the Sherman Act.[9]

Reversed in part and remanded.

[The dissenting opinions of JUSTICES DOUGLAS and STEWART, on behalf of a total of four justices, have been omitted.]

Problems for Discussion

1. If Connell had sought injunctive relief not against the enforcement of the disputed contract clause but rather against the union's picket-

9. In addition to seeking a declaratory judgment that the agreement with Local 100 violated the antitrust laws, Connell sought a permanent injunction against further picketing to coerce execution of the contract in litigation. Connell obtained a temporary restraining order against the picketing on January 21, 1971, and thereafter executed the contract —under protest—with Local 100 on March 28, 1971. So far as the record in this case reveals, there has been no further picketing at Connell's construction sites. Accordingly, there is no occasion for us to consider whether the Norris-LaGuardia Act forbids such an injunction where the specific agreement sought by the union is illegal, or to determine whether, within the meaning of the Norris-LaGuardia Act, there was a "labor dispute" between these parties. If the Norris-LaGuardia Act were applicable to this picketing, injunctive relief would not be available under the antitrust laws. See United States v. Hutcheson, 312 U.S. 219, 61 S.Ct. 463, 85 L.Ed. 788 (1941). If the agreement in question is held on remand to be invalid under federal antitrust laws, we cannot anticipate that Local 100 will resume picketing to obtain or enforce an illegal agreement.

ing to secure that clause, would the Norris-LaGuardia Act forbid the issuance of such an injunction?

2.   Is the Court's objection to the union's tactics rooted principally in anti-trust policy or principally in a disdain for coercive "top-down" organizing campaigns?   If it is the latter, ought not the appropriate remedies be those provided in the Labor Act rather than those provided in the Sherman Act?   (What exactly would the remedies be under either statute?)   Can the result in *Connell* be squared with the Court's earlier decision in *Apex Hosiery*?

3.   Unions in the clothing industry have, over time, been unsuccessful in organizing employees of contractors, who receive fabric from the jobbers or manufacturers and cut and sew it to make a finished garment which is then returned to the jobbers or manufacturers.   Organization is difficult because the contractors work in out-of-the-way lofts, are extremely mobile (since their primary capital equipment is sewing machines) and do not work on any one project for too long a time.   This has permitted the non-union contractors to pay very little, to require long hours and generally to operate under "sweatshop" conditions.   To organize the contractors effectively, the unions in the "needle trade" have entered into agreements with the jobbers or manufacturers (who *can* be organized) containing provisions barring the use of nonunion contractors.   One such agreement is that between the National Skirt and Sportswear Association (the Association) and the International Ladies' Garment Workers' Union (the Union).   It provides that the employer members of the Association are to maintain a union shop for employees doing manufacturing work on the employer's premises; that if manufacturing work is contracted out, it will be sent only to contractors operating union shops organized by the ILGWU; and that payments to contractors are to be sufficient to pay their workers in accordance with the agreement between the Association and the Union and in addition a reasonable amount to cover overhead.   Certain manufacturers who are party to the agreement have brought an action in a federal court seeking a declaration that these contract provisions are illegal and unenforceable, and an injunction against their enforcement by the Union.   What should be the court's disposition of the case?   See Greenstein v. National Skirt & Sportswear Ass'n, 178 F.Supp. 681 (S.D.N.Y.1959).

4.   Long John Silver's (Silver's) is a fast-food seafood restaurant chain, which has had two restaurants in the Pittsburgh area built by Muko Builders, Inc., a non-union company.   During construction of the two buildings, and subsequently during their operation, they were picketed by representatives of the Southwestern Pennsylvania Building and Construction Trades Council (Trades Council), an association of construction unions.   The president of Silver's requested a meeting with representatives of the Trades Council, in an effort to terminate the picketing.   The result of the meeting was an agreement that Silver's would invite bids for the construction of future restaurant buildings only from unionized contractors certified by the Trades Council; the Trades Council in turn terminated the picketing.   Silver's asked Muko if it would build as a union contractor, but Muko refused, and it subsequently was not asked to bid on any further

jobs for Silver's.   Silver's subsequently built twelve additional restaurants, all by union contractors.   Muko can show that the prices for those new restaurants aggregated over $250,000 more than Muko would have charged (while projecting a significant profit) ; that Muko's employees (who function primarily as supervisors, with the actual construction being done through subcontractors) are paid at prevailing wage rates; and that the Trades Council has never made any effort to organize Muko's employees.

Muko has brought an action against Silver's and the Trades Council under the federal antitrust laws, seeking an injunction and treble damages. The defendants have moved for summary judgment.   Should the motion be granted?   See Larry V. Muko, Inc., v. Southwestern Pennsylvania Bldg. & Constr. Trades Council, 609 F.2d 1368 (3d Cir. 1979).

AMERICAN FEDERATION OF MUSICIANS V. CARROLL, 391 U.S. 99, 88 S.Ct. 1561, 20 L.Ed.2d 460 (1968).   The AFM has bylaws and regulations governing so-called "club date" engagements (one-time engagements such as weddings and commencements) of its members, some of whom function as band leaders (usually playing an instrument as well) and some of whom function as instrumentalists or "sidemen."   Among other things, the union bylaws and regulations required leaders to engage a minimum number of sidemen; required leaders to charge purchasers of music (e. g., the father of the bride) a minimum price, composed of union-scale wages for sidemen, twice that for the leader, and an additional eight percent to cover taxes, insurance, and other expenses of the leader; required leaders to use a specific contract form in dealing with purchasers of music; required a leader to charge an additional ten percent when his band played outside its territory.   In effect, these regulations substituted for collective bargaining agreements with one-time music purchasers, since such agreements would be impracticable.   The AFM provisions were challenged by certain union members who functioned principally as band leaders, and who brought an action for injunctive relief and treble damages under the Sherman Act.

The Supreme Court agreed with the lower courts that the union's bylaws and regulations did not constitute a combination with a "non-labor group" but rather were exempt as affecting only a "labor" group within the Norris-LaGuardia Act, and that the complaint was properly dismissed.   Although the band leaders were functioning technically as independent contractors in arranging performing dates, and as employers of the sidemen, they were properly treated as a labor group, given their competition with "employee" members of the union regarding jobs, wages and the like.

The Court stated: "The District Court found that the orchestra leaders performed work and functions which actually or potentially affected the hours, wages, job security, and working conditions of

[AFM] members. These findings have substantial support in the evidence and in the light of the job and wage competition thus established, both courts correctly held that it was lawful for petitioners to pressure the orchestra leaders to become union members, * * * to insist upon a closed shop, * * * to impose the minimum employment quotas complained of, * * * to require the orchestra leaders to use the Form B contract, * * * and to favor local musicians by requiring that higher wages be paid to musicians from outside a local's jurisdiction * * *."

The court of appeals had disagreed with the trial court as to the legality of the "price list," holding it beyond the labor exemption because of its concern with "prices" rather than "wages." The Supreme Court, however, stated that it was "not dispositive of the question that petitioners' regulation in form establishes price floors. The critical inquiry is whether the price floors in actuality operate to protect the wages of the * * * sidemen." If the leaders were themselves to undercut the wage scale or other union regulations, this would put pressure on the union members they compete with to correspondingly lower their own demands. Even when the band leader was simply leading a group in a club-date engagement and not performing on an instrument and displacing an employee-musician, the price list was within the exemption from the antitrust laws. By fixing a reasonable amount over the sum of the minimum wages paid the sidemen, to cover the leader's costs in setting up the engagement, the union's price list insured that no part of the labor costs of the leader or the sidemen would be diverted for overhead or other non-labor costs. "In other words, the price of the product—here the price for an orchestra for a club-date—represents almost entirely the scale wages of the sidemen and the leader. Unlike most industries, except for the 8% charge, there are no other costs contributing to the price. Therefore, if leaders cut prices, inevitably wages must be cut." The Court viewed its analysis as supported by the opinions of Justices White and Goldberg in the *Jewel Tea* case (as well as by the opinion of the Court in Teamsters Union v. Oliver, see page 920, infra).

Problems for Discussion

1. A large number of fishermen in the Northwest, and persons working under them, have formed the Pacific Coast Fishermen's Union, which bargains collectively with fish processors and canners concerning the sale of fish to them. Union regulations require member fishermen to sell their catch only to processors and canners who agree to a standard purchase contract; this contract requires the buyer not to purchase fish from nonmembers of the Union, and also stipulates price, payment and

quantity terms governing the sale of fish from Union members. Apart from making these sales, the fishermen have no dealings with the signatory canners and processors. Columbia River Packers, Inc., a processor-canner, refuses to acquiesce in the provision requiring exclusive dealing with union fishermen, and brings suit under the antitrust laws, charging that the Union is really an association of fish dealers seeking to monopolize the northwest fish industry. Can the Union raise the labor exemption as a defense? See Columbia River Packers Ass'n v. Hinton, 315 U.S. 143, 62 S.Ct. 520, 86 L.Ed. 750 (1942).

2.   Paper companies with mills in the area of Mobile, Alabama, secure their supplies of pulpwood from various parties known as "dealers" who in turn obtain their supply from pulpwood "producers." The "producers" —working ordinarily with a crew of up to three other persons whom they employ—cut, load and haul cord wood designated by the "dealer," who generally acquires rights from the landowner to cut standing timber. The dealer leases trucks, saws and other necessary equipment to the producer (who ordinarily cannot afford to buy them), and gives the producer credit (against future moneys owed to the producers for wood supplied) for gas, tires, and the like. The dealers also deduct from the price they pay the producers for wood amounts required by law for workmen's compensation, liability insurance and the like. Producers do not sell directly to the paper mills but must do business through a dealer.

The producers have organized themselves as the Gulf Coast Pulpwood Association, and have engaged in a work stoppage and picketing of the dealers, in support of demands concerning the price and conditions of sale of pulpwood. The paper companies bring an action under the Sherman Act to enjoin the activities of the Association. May an injunction issue? See Scott Paper Co. v. Gulf Coast Pulpwood Ass'n, 85 L.R.R.M. 2978, 72 CCH Lab.Cas. ¶ 14031 (S.D.Ala.1973), aff'd 491 F.2d 119 (5th Cir. 1974).

(After thirty days, could a meritorious charge be filed with the NLRB against the Association for violation of Section 8(b)(7)? Could the paper companies proceed both in court and before the NLRB?)

*

Part Six

FEDERALISM AND LABOR RELATIONS[1]

Since the late 1940s, Supreme Court decisions have expanded the reach of congressional authority under the power to regulate interstate commerce, and Congress has increasingly regulated labor-management relations and conditions in the workplace. It has therefore become increasingly necessary for the courts—faced for the most part with congressional silence on the issue—to fit these rapidly growing labor laws into a federal system in which the sum of governmental power is shared between the states and the nation. Few issues have given rise to as much litigation in the appellate courts or to as much contrariety of judicial opinion.

In order to begin to understand the question of accommodating federal labor policy and state policies, it is well to recall a few elementary premises concerning the federal system. Article I, Section 8 of the United States Constitution gives to Congress the power "To regulate Commerce * * * among the several States" and "To make all Laws which shall be necessary and proper for carrying into Execution the foregoing Powers." The entire residue of regulatory power, so far as it may affect labor relations, was left to the States. Under the philosophy of constitutional interpretation prevailing prior to 1937, this meant for all practical purposes that industrial relations were governable only by the States. In 1908 the Supreme Court held, in Adair v. United States, 208 U.S. 161, 28 S.Ct. 277, 52 L.Ed. 436 (1908), that the federal government could not constitutionally protect organizational activities on interstate railroads because there was no "possible legal or logical connection * * * between an employé's membership in a labor organization and the carrying on of interstate commerce." In 1936 the Court declared

1. See Come, Federal Preemption of Labor-Management Relations: Current Problems in the Application of *Garmon*, 56 Va.L.Rev. 1435 (1970); Cox, Federalism in the Law of Labor Relations, 67 Harv.L.Rev. 1297 (1954); Cox, Labor Law Preemption Revisited, 85 Harv.L.Rev. 1337 (1972); Cox, Recent Developments in Federal Labor Law Preemption, 41 Ohio St.L.J. 277 (1980); Lesnick, Preemption Reconsidered: The Apparent Reaffirmation of *Garmon*, 72 Colum.L.Rev. 469 (1972); McCoid, Notes on a "G-String": A Study of the "No Man's Land" of Labor Law, 44 Minn.L.Rev 205 (1959); Meltzer, The Supreme Court, Congress and State Jurisdiction Over Labor Relations, 59 Columbia L.Rev. 6, 269 (1959); Michelman, State Power to Govern Concerted Employee Activities, 74 Harv.L.Rev. 641 (1961).

that the Congress lacked power to regulate the labor standards under which bituminous coal was produced. Carter v. Carter Coal Co., 298 U.S. 238, 56 S.Ct. 855, 80 L.Ed. 1160 (1936). The necessary implication of these decisions was that under our system of federalism, relations between employer and employee were governed exclusively by State statutes and judicial decisions. By 1937 the body of State law in this general field was not inconsiderable, although there was little protection of union organization and a mass of restrictions upon strikes, picketing, and other concerted activities.

In 1937 constitutional interpretation broke through the conceptualism of the preceding decades and embraced Mr. Justice Holmes' pragmatic philosophy: "[C]ommerce among the States is not a technical legal conception, but a practical one, drawn from the course of business." Swift & Co. v. United States, 196 U.S. 375, 398, 25 S.Ct. 276, 280, 49 L.Ed. 518 (1905). In NLRB v. Jones & Laughlin Steel Corp., 301 U.S. 1, 57 S.Ct. 615, 81 L.Ed. 893 (1937), the Court confirmed the newly asserted power of the national government to regulate labor relations in production industries. Thereafter a series of decisions expanded federal power over labor relations so far[2] that it is sometimes said, with only minimum exaggeration, that there is no business in which employment relations are not potentially subject to federal control. During the 1950s for example, the Court upheld the application of the NLRA to small local retailers of automobiles. Howell Chevrolet Co. v. NLRB, 346 U.S. 482, 74 S.Ct. 214 (1954).

The constitutional decisions allocating to Congress power to enact labor legislation mean (1) that the national government may regulate labor relations, including strikes, boycotts, and picketing, and (2) that it may forbid the application of State laws, whether statutory or judge-made. Both propositions are true beyond dispute, but they are only permissive. The national government may choose not to exercise its power over labor relations or to use only part. The choice may be made by Congress or left to an administrative agency. Neither the allocation of constitutional power to Congress nor even the actual enactment of federal legislation necessarily excludes the jurisdiction of State tribunals or the application of State law. Thus, the enormous expansion of national power over industrial relations which began in 1937 raised three groups of questions.

First, how far out along the range of infinitely small gradations from interstate railroads and basic steel producers to corner drugstores and delicatessens should actual federal regulation of labor relations extend? Although in the early years of the adminis-

2. The cases are reviewed in Stern, The Commerce Clause and the National Economy, 1933–1946, 59 Harv.L. Rev. 645, 883 (1946).

tration of the NLRA, it was assumed that the Board's jurisdiction was congruent with Congress's power under the Constitution to regulate interstate commerce, the burden on the Board that would accompany the exercise of such a vast jurisdiction (as well as the budgetary implications) convinced the Board to decline to exercise its jurisdiction over smaller businesses having only local significance. In 1959, Congress as part of the Landrum-Griffin Act declared in Section 14(c) of the NLRA that the Board was not to contract its jurisdiction beneath the levels announced in 1958. The jurisdictional standards now utilized by the Board are set forth in detail at pages 89–90, supra.

A second major question bearing on federalism in labor law is what tribunals have jurisdiction and what law applies to the labor relations of those businesses over which the NLRB can, but declines to, exercise jurisdiction? When the Board in the 1950s set its own jurisdiction at a level beneath that which it could statutorily assert over interstate commerce, it assumed that state tribunals and state law would regulate the business which it declined to regulate. But in Guss v. Utah Labor Relations Bd., 353 U.S. 1, 77 S.Ct. 598, 1 L.Ed.2d 601 (1957), the Supreme Court held this assumption to be incorrect, thus creating a "no man's land" in which the federal agency declined to act (partly from choice but partly for lack of funds and personnel) but from which the states were excluded by federal legislation. The Board's response was to announce expanded jurisdictional guidelines in 1958, in order that "more individuals, labor organizations and employers may invoke the rights and protections afforded by the statute." Siemons Mailing Service, 122 N.L.R.B. 81 (1958). As to the "no man's land" that still remained, Congress in 1959 declared in Section 14(c) that state courts and agencies may assert jurisdiction over labor disputes which the Board declines to regulate as outside its discretionary jurisdiction. Although Congress did not explicitly declare whether state tribunals are in these proceedings to apply federal or local law, it is generally understood that state law may be applied. E. g., Kempf v. Carpenters and Joiners Local Union No. 1273, 229 Or. 337, 367 P.2d 436 (1961).

On occasion, the question will be raised before the state court or agency whether a given employer actually fails to meet the NLRB's jurisdictional standards. The Board has thus far left state tribunals free to determine this question, and thus their own jurisdiction, under Section 14(c), but has arranged to render advisory opinions in particular cases at the request of either of the parties to the proceeding or the state court or agency involved. NLRB Rules & Regulations, 29 C.F.R. § 102.98 (1975).

The third and final issue of federalism in labor law is the most complex. How far does actual federal regulation of the labor relations of a business exclude the application of inconsistent, parallel, or supplementary state law? To the extent that federal law is exclusive, where does one draw the line between the "labor relations' subject only to federal law and the permissible subjects of state regulation? May a state punish violence or trespass on the picket line? May a state give a union organizer or a company official a remedy in tort for libelous statements made by the other, or a union member a remedy against the union for wrongful expulsion or for willfully securing his or her discharge or non-hiring? It is to this third issue that these materials now turn.

PREEMPTION OF STATE LABOR LAW: AN OVERVIEW

Labor law grew up initially as a body of judge-made rules regulating the concerted activities of employees by limiting the means to which they might resort and the objectives for which they might strike, picket or boycott. The rules were state law—private law in the sense that they were invoked in actions for damages or suits for injunctions in which no government agency was involved, but public regulation in the sense that they embodied the judges' notions of public policy in dealing with concerted activities. Little attention was given to the potential conflict between these state laws and policies and the provisions of the Wagner Act of 1935, since the principal concerns of the federal act were questions of representation and employer unfair labor practices, and not limitations upon unions. (It is now apparent that Section 7 created a federal right to engage in concerted activities immune from state interference but this implication of the NLRA passed virtually unnoticed until 1949.) By 1947—when Congress did outlaw certain union activity, and by which time the Supreme Court had vastly expanded the effective reach of the federal labor laws and of the NLRB—duplication and collision between state and federal law were becoming common. According to conventional "preemption" theory, the courts in determining whether state regulation is allowable in the face of federal legislation attempt to divine "the intent of Congress." Although Supreme Court decisions left Congress free to determine the reach of state authority over labor-management relations, Congress—with such limited exceptions as Section 14(b) of the Taft-Hartley Act, permitting individual states to outlaw union-shop provisions which would otherwise be valid under the NLRA—remained silent, thus transferring the issue back to the Court.

Federal-state preemption issues are difficult to resolve in most substantive areas of the law, but they are particularly complicated in the area of labor-management relations. Superimposed upon the general clash between centralized and local authorities are two added factors: the existence of a presumably expert and experienced federal administrative agency, charged since the enactment of the NLRA in 1935 with the tasks of regulating representation elections and conducting unfair labor practice proceedings; and the historically rooted suspicion of judges (all judges, but particularly state-court judges) for their alleged insensitivity, if not hostility, to the goals of the labor movement.

Two principal theories have developed, over the past twenty-five years, to justify sharp restrictions upon state jurisdiction and state lawmaking in the field of labor law. These theories (and others) have been articulated by the Supreme Court in different cases, and by different Justices in the same case. The relationship between the two theories, and the weight the Court will give them, are unstable. But they are the starting point for analysis of preemption issues and of the cases that follow.

One theory—which might be referred to as the "substantive rights" theory—holds that state courts and state law may not curtail conduct of employers or unions which Congress seeks affirmatively to protect or at least to permit. A state court could not, for example, enjoin a peaceful strike by a lawfully recognized union asserting wage demands in a contract renegotiation. Nor could a state outlaw, for example, a no-subcontracting provision which is the product of lawful mandatory bargaining under the National Labor Relations Act. This "substantive rights" theory does not rely for its applicability upon the existence or nonexistence of an expert administrative agency enforcing the NLRA; the inferred curtailment of state authority would follow even had the enforcement of the NLRA been left with the federal courts. Notice too that this theory appears not to impair the authority of the states to provide sanctions for employer or union conduct which is prohibited under the unfair labor practice provisions of the NLRA; additional state remedies would not impair any protection or permission afforded by federal law.

Although the general outlines of this rationale for preemption are plain enough, questions and qualifications leap quickly to mind. These are dealt with in the cases that follow. For example, what if there is a dispute in the state court as to whether the defendant's conduct is protected, the NLRB and federal court precedents not being all that clear? Should the state court decide whether the conduct is *actually* protected, or should it simply dismiss when there is an *arguable* claim of protection? An answer to that will depend upon such factors as one's confidence in the sensitivity of state-court judges (or members of state administrative agencies) to federal law and policies, the availability of Supreme Court review for erroneous state decisions, and one's assessment of the expertise of the NLRB on the issue (and thus the urgency of having that agency determine close issues of protection vel non). Another question that leaps to mind is how a decisionmaker is to determine whether conduct which is not affirmatively protected under Section 7 (e. g., "quickie" strikes or slowdowns) is nonetheless "intended" by Congress to be "permitted," in the sense that an employer is not to be able to resort to state courts but only to its own lawful self-help economic weapons. A final question worth raising at this point about the "substantive rights" theory is whether it is in fact indifferent to state regulation of conduct which Congress has declared to be an unfair labor practice. If, for example, Congress "intends" that the typical unfair labor practice is to be remedied through rather modest measures (e. g., a cease-and-desist order but no compensatory damages), does this not reflect a "substantive" policy of protection which would be impaired if the state were to make available compensatory relief or, worse yet, criminal sanctions?

A second theory which has been articulated in the Supreme Court decisions might be called the "primary jurisdiction" theory. It assumes that Congress in the NLRA not only protected certain conduct and prohibited other conduct, but also created an administrative agency—expert, experienced, peculiarly sensitive to federal values in the area of labor-management relations, and possessed of delicately balanced remedial authority. Under this theory, states could not regulate conduct which is clearly protected, or even conduct which is clearly prohibited. Indeed, conduct which is arguably but not clearly protected would also have to go unregulated, since it is the NLRB which is the designated agency for making this determination; the same is true for conduct which is arguably but not clearly prohibited by the unfair labor practice provisions of the Act.

Under this theory too, questions and qualifications quickly come to mind. Are there not some circumstances—most clearly where the accused party is engaging in violence—in which the states have a legitimate and weighty interest in outlawing certain conduct and affording remedies, in spite of the fact that the federal government and the NLRB do so as well? Are there not cases where a holding that the state courts must stay their hand, because the matter should be determined by the NLRB, will effectively deprive the aggrieved party of any forum at at all? For example, an employee's claim that the employer or union has acted tortiously might be dismissed by the state court, on the ground that the alleged conduct is or might be an unfair labor practice, while the Regional Director might choose (perhaps for reasons having little to do with the merits) not to proceed with the issuance of a complaint under Section 8. Or, conversely, the state court might be convinced the defendant's conduct is arguably protected, and dismiss the action for that reason, while the NLRB may for all practical purposes be unable to rule on the issue of protection (since this issue is brought to the Board only when an employer or union takes the initiative to coerce or discriminate against another person for protected activity). Is it rational to refuse giving effect to a strongly felt state policy whenever the defendant claims that its conduct *may* be protected by federal law, while affording no realistic opportunity to have the question of protection vel non actually litigated before the expert administrative agency?

It is obvious that the issues of federal-state conflict which are raised in the labor area are varied and complex. The cases that follow show the Court not only attempting to apply various theories to resolve specific substantive problems, but also grappling for a principle which can be readily applied in general categories of cases. The Court has tried to resist a technique of analysis which would simply take the form of weighing the significance of the state policy against the incursion it would make upon federal policy; were this vague test to be utilized on a case-by-case basis, there would be a great sacrifice of predictability. On the other hand, the Court has also tried to resist a technique of analysis which gives such uniform priority to federal concerns as to interfere unduly with legitimate state interests.

———

Certain preemption principles have been well established. For example, a state may not decide questions of representation in any business affecting commerce over which the NLRB can exercise jurisdiction. Bethlehem Steel Co. v. New York State Labor Relations Bd., 330 U.S. 767, 67 S.Ct. 1026, 91 L.Ed. 1234 (1947); La Crosse Tel. Corp. v. Wisconsin Employment Relations Bd., 336 U.S. 18, 69 S.Ct. 379, 93 L.Ed. 463 (1949). Representation cases turn on administrative policy concerning the time for and fairness of elections, the composition of the bargaining unit, and the eligibility of voters. Were a state agency to decide these matters, there might be established a pattern of representation inconsistent with federal policy, even though the NLRB has not acted in the particular case. Nor may a state purport to adjudicate and remedy employer unfair labor practices in a business over which the NLRB can exercise jurisdiction. In Plankinton Packing Co. v. Wisconsin Employment Relations Bd., 338 U.S. 953, 70 S.Ct. 491, 94 L.Ed. 588 (1950), Wisconsin had found a packinghouse guilty of discriminatory discharges and ordered reinstatement and backpay; the Supreme Court set the order aside without opinion. There is no reason for distinguishing between this unfair labor practice and others, whether committed by an employer or by a union.

Most of the cases involving state authority to regulate labor relations have involved either collective bargaining or concerted employee activities. A state may, for example, attempt to regulate the collective bargaining process, or the labor contract ultimately executed, when these touch upon matters of local concern, such as safety, discrimination in hiring and retention, wages and hours, and restraint of trade. The last-mentioned state policy was tested in the following case.

LOCAL 24, TEAMSTERS v. OLIVER

Supreme Court of the United States, 1959.
358 U.S. 283, 79 S.Ct. 297, 3 L.Ed.2d 312.

[This action was commenced in an Ohio state court by one Revel Oliver, a member of Teamsters Local 24, who worked as a truck-driver of a truck owned by him. He secured employment by leasing his truck to certain interstate carriers, which paid him both for his driving services and for the truck rental. Collective bargaining in the trucking industry in the midwest, including Ohio, was carried out between an association of motor carriers and a council of Teamster locals. The labor contract, effective February 1, 1955, contained an Article XXXII which regulated the minimum rental (and certain other terms) when a motor vehicle was leased to a carrier by an owner-driver working in the carrier's service. Since 1938, the union had sought some control over the terms of such truck rentals, since the union claimed that the carriers were undermining the wage scale of the drivers employed by them, and for whom the union negotiated, by leasing vehicles from an owner-driver at a rental which returned to the owner-driver less than his actual costs of operation; as a result, the net wage received by the owner-driver (although nominally he received the negotiated wage) was actually a wage reduced by the excess of his operating expenses over the rental he received. The negotiated minimum rental had been a compromise between the union's desire to abolish all owner-operators (who were allegedly using part of their wages for the upkeep of their vehicles) and the carriers' desire to have no limitations at all.

Oliver, seeking to have the Ohio court strike down the minimum-rental provision in the labor contract, brought an action against both the Teamsters council and the carrier association. The court held Article XXXII to violate the Ohio antitrust law, since it constituted a price-fixing agreement between a union and a nonlabor group which imposed restrictions upon articles of commerce (i. e., the leased vehicles) and barred an owner of those articles from reasonable freedom of action in dealing with them. (At trial, the carriers joined with Oliver in attacking Article XXXII.) To the union's claim that Ohio could not overturn an agreement made pursuant to the duty to bargain under the National Labor Relations Act, the state court held that the Labor Act could not "be reasonably construed to permit this remote and indirect approach to the subject of wages." The state court issued a permanent injunction barring the use of Article XXXII or of any future contract to alter Oliver's present rental agreement with the carriers or to determine the rate to be charged for the use of Oliver's equipment. The Supreme Court granted certiorari.]

MR. JUSTICE BRENNAN delivered the opinion of the Court.

* * * [T]he point of the Article is obviously not price fixing but wages. The regulations embody not the "remote and indirect approach to the subject of wages" perceived by the Court of Common Pleas but a direct frontal attack upon a problem thought to threaten the maintenance of the basic wage structure established by the collective bargaining contract. The inadequacy of a rental which means that the owner makes up his excess costs from his driver's wages not only clearly bears a close relation to labor's efforts to improve working conditions but is in fact of vital concern to the carrier's employed drivers; an inadequate rental might mean the progressive curtailment of jobs through withdrawal of more and more carrier-owned vehicles from service. Cf. Bakery and Pastry Drivers and Helpers Local 802 of International Brotherhood of Teamsters v. Wohl, 315 U.S. 769, 771, 62 S.Ct. 816, 817, 86 L.Ed. 1178. It is not necessary to attempt to set precise outside limits to the subject matter properly included within the scope of mandatory collective bargaining, cf. National Labor Relations Board v. Wooster Division of Borg-Warner Corp., 356 U.S. 342, 78 S.Ct. 718, 2 L.Ed.2d 823, to hold, as we do, that the obligation under § 8(d) on the carriers and their employees to bargain collectively "with respect to wages, hours, and other terms and conditions of employment" and to embody their understanding in "a written contract incorporating any agreement reached," found an expression in the subject matter of Article XXXII. See Timken Roller Bearing Co., 70 N.L.R.B. 500, 518, reversed on other grounds, 6 Cir., 161 F.2d 949. And certainly bargaining on this subject through their representatives was a right of the employees protected by § 7 of the Act.

Second. We must decide whether Ohio's antitrust law may be applied to prevent the contracting parties from carrying out their agreement upon a subject matter as to which federal law directs them to bargain. Little extended discussion is necessary to show that Ohio law cannot be so applied. We need not concern ourselves today with a contractual provision dealing with a subject matter that the parties were under no obligation to discuss; the carriers as employers were under a duty to bargain collectively with the union as to the subject matter of the Article, as we have shown. The goal of federal labor policy, as expressed in the Wagner and Taft-Hartley Acts, is the promotion of collective bargaining; to encourage the employer and the representative of the employees to establish, through collective negotiation, their own charter for the ordering of industrial relations, and thereby to minimize industrial strife. See National Labor Relations Board v. Jones & Laughlin Steel Corp., 301 U.S. 1, 45, 57 S.Ct. 615, 628, 81 L.Ed. 893; National Labor Relations Board v. American National Ins. Co., 343 U.S. 395, 401–402, 72 S.Ct. 824, 828, 96 L.Ed. 1027. Within the area in which collective bargaining was required, Congress was not concerned with the substantive terms upon which the parties agreed. Cf. Terminal Railroad Ass'n of St. Louis v. Brotherhood of Railroad Trainmen, 318 U.S. 1, 6, 63 S.Ct. 420, 423, 87 L.Ed. 571. The purposes of the Acts are served by bringing the parties together and establishing conditions under which they are to work out their agreement themselves. To allow the application of the Ohio antitrust law here would wholly defeat the full realization of the congressional purpose. The application would frustrate the parties' solution of a problem which Congress has required them to negotiate in good faith toward solving, and in the solution of which it imposed no limitations relevant here. * * * We believe that there is no room in this scheme for the application here of this state policy limiting the solutions that the parties' agreement can provide to the problems of wages and working conditions. Cf. State of California v. Taylor, 353 U.S. 553, 566, 567, 77 S.Ct. 1037, 1044, 1045, 1 L.Ed. 2d 1034. Since the federal law operates here, in an area where its authority is paramount to leave the parties free, the inconsistent application of state law is necessarily outside the power of the State. * * * Of course, the paramount force of the federal law remains even though it is expressed in the details of a contract federal law empowers the parties to make, rather than in terms in an enactment of Congress. See Railway Employes' Dept. v. Hanson, 351 U.S. 225, 232, 76 S.Ct. 714, 718, 100 L.Ed. 1112. Clearly it is immaterial that the conflict is between federal labor law and the application of what the State characterizes as an antitrust law. " * * * Congress has sufficiently expressed its purpose to * * * exclude state prohibition, even though that with which the federal law is concerned as a matter of labor relations be related by the State to the more inclusive area of restraint of trade." Weber v. Anheuser-Busch, Inc., 348 U.S. 468, 481, 75 S.Ct. 480, 488, 99 L.Ed. 546. We have not here a case of a collective bargaining agreement in conflict with a local health or safety regulation; the conflict here is between the federally sanctioned agreement and state policy which seeks specifically to adjust relationships in the world of commerce. If there is to be this sort of limitation on the arrangements that unions and employers may make with regard to these subjects, pursuant to the collective bargaining provisions of the Wagner and Taft-Hartley Acts, it is for Congress, not the States, to provide it.

Reversed.

[The dissenting opinion of MR. JUSTICE WHITTAKER is omitted.]

The CHIEF JUSTICE, MR. JUSTICE FRANKFURTER and MR. JUSTICE STEWART took no part in the consideration or decision of this case.

STATE REGULATION OF PENSION PLANS

In MALONE v. WHITE MOTOR CORP., 435 U.S. 497, 98 S.Ct. 1185, 55 L.Ed.2d 443 (1978), the Supreme Court considered a challenge to the Private Pension Benefit Protection Act of Minnesota (the State Pension Act), on the ground that it conflicted with the federal policy of free collective bargaining expressed in the National Labor Relations Act. A pension plan, bargained between the Company and the United Auto Workers, provided that pension benefits were to be payable only from a specific pension fund, and that the Company reserved the power to terminate the plan at any time; the Company did, however, give assurances to the Union at bargaining sessions in 1968 and 1971 that, should the Company terminate the pension plan, eligible employees would receive certain designated payments (below those set forth in the written plan). In early 1974, Minnesota enacted its State Pension Act, which in effect "vested" the rights of employees covered by existing pension plans, and imposed a "pension funding charge" on employers to guarantee that full pension payments would be made when covered employees reached normal retirement age. A few weeks later, the Company terminated its pension plan. Appellant Malone, Commissioner of Labor and Industry of the State of Minnesota, investigated the pension plan termination, and certified a pension funding charge in the amount of more than $19 million against the Company, to comply with the State Pension Act; this charge would operate as a lien on the assets of the Company. The Company filed suit in the federal district court, asserting on a number of constitutional grounds that the Minnesota pension funding charge should be overturned.

The district court denied the Company's motion for partial summary judgment (or in the alternative a preliminary injunction) on its claim that the Minnesota law was preempted by virtue of the Supremacy Clause. The Court of Appeals for the Eighth Circuit reversed, and the Supreme Court heard the case pursuant to its mandatory appellate jurisdiction.

The Company argued (and the court of appeals had agreed) that the State Pension Act purported to override the terms of the collectively bargained pension plan in at least three ways: it granted employees vested rights not available under the plan; although the pension plan provided that benefits were to be paid only out of the pension fund, the Act required payment from the general assets of the employer to the extent of any deficiency in the fund; the Act imposed liability for employer payments after termination of the plan in amounts beyond those specifically guaranteed pursuant to collective bargaining. The Supreme Court concluded, however, 6 to 3, that the State Pension Act was not preempted by federal law. (The Court acknowledged that since the enactment by Congress of the Federal Employee Retirement Income Security Act (ERISA), effective January 1, 1975, state law regarding pension plans covered by that federal act is expressly preempted; the operative events in this case, however, took place in 1974.)

The Court rested its conclusion upon the provisions and the legislative history of the federal Welfare and Pension Plans Disclosure Act of 1958, which convinced the Court that "Congress at that time recognized and preserved state authority to regulate pension plans, including those plans which were the product of collective bargaining." The 1958 federal Disclosure Act was designed to eliminate corruption in the administration of welfare and pension funds and to provide covered employees with information about the assets and income of those funds; this was to be effected, however, only through reporting and disclosure requirements. The substantive regulation of such funds was, the Court concluded, left by Congress to the states. Section 10 of the federal Disclosure Act expressly stated that state laws regulating welfare and pension plans were not to be preempted, and many comments in committee reports and on the floor of Congress adverted to the salutary state regulation of these plans through laws already in existence and likely to be enacted in the near future. "Congress was concerned with many of the same issues as are involved in this case—unexpected termination; inadequate funding; unfair vesting requirements. In preserving generally state laws 'affecting the operation or administration of employee welfare or pension benefit plans,' 72 Stat. 1003, Congress indicated that the States had and were to have authority to deal with these problems. * * * Although Congress came to a quite different conclusion in 1974 when ERISA was adopted, the 1958 Disclosure Act clearly anticipated a broad regulatory role for the States. In light of this history, we cannot hold that the Pension Act is nevertheless implicitly pre-empted by the collective-bargaining provisions of the NLRA. Congress could not have intended that bargained-for plans, which were among those that had given rise to the very problems that had so concerned Congress, were to be free from either state or federal regulation insofar as their substantive provisions were concerned. The [state] Pension Act seeks to protect the accrued benefits of workers in the event of plan termination and to insure that the assets and prospective income of the plan are sufficient to guarantee the benefits promised—exactly the kind of problems which the 85th Congress hoped that the States would solve."

The Court also distinguished the *Oliver* case, in which it had earlier held that states were not to limit "the solutions that the parties' agreement can provide to the problems of wages and working conditions." The *Oliver* decision had acknowleged that a different conclusion would be warranted when Congress had evidently permitted states to regulate the issue in question. "Congress clearly envisioned the exercise of state regulation power over pension funds, and we do not depart from *Oliver* in sustaining the Minnesota statute."

In separate dissenting opinions (joined by the Chief Justice), Justices Stewart and Powell argued that it was improper for the Court to conclude that because Congress had in 1958 failed substantively to regulate pension plans this constituted an indication that the States were free to do so. Both opinions relied on the *Oliver* decision, and Justice Powell specifically noted that the State Pension Act had mandated substantive pension-plan principles which would interfere with the process and the terms of collective bargaining on a mandatory subject; he was particularly concerned about the retroactive application of the state law in the midterm of a pension plan and collective bargaining agreement, "significantly changing the economic balance reached by the parties at the bargaining table."

[In Allied Structural Steel Co. v. Spannaus, 438 U.S. 234, 98 S.Ct. 2716, 57 L.Ed.2d 727 (1978), the Supreme Court declared the Minnesota Private Pension Benefits Protection Act unconstitutional when applied retroactively to pension plans already in existence. The statute was held to violate Article I, Section 10 of the federal Constitution, the so-called Contracts Clause: "No State shall * * * pass any * * * Law impairing the Obligation of Contracts."]

Problems for Discussion

1. Assume that there had been no 1958 federal Disclosure Act to suggest congressional tolerance of state pension laws similar to that considered in the *Malone* case, so that the Court would have had to apply traditional preemption analysis and the principles of the *Oliver* case. How should the *Malone* case have been decided?

2. A statute in the state of Franklin prohibits discrimination by an employer against an employee on grounds of age, with no "ceiling" on the

protected age-range. (The federal age-discrimination act bars such discrimination only against employees up to 70 years of age; it does not explicitly address the issue of preemption of state age-discrimination laws affording greater protection.) Suppose that a labor union requested an employer to sign a collective agreement providing for compulsory retirement at age 70. Has the employer a duty to bargain upon the subject? Could a court of the state of Franklin properly enjoin a strike called to compel the employer to execute such an agreement? Cf. Massachusetts Elec. Co. v. Massachusetts Comm'n Against Discrimination, 375 Mass. 160, 375 N.E. 2d 1192 (1978).

3. The Steelworkers Union has negotiated a labor contract with the Apex Steel Company. Among its terms are certain standards for work dress in the interest of safety; stipulations deal with the wearing of gloves, goggles and uniforms. Although the Company pointed out that the state safety code imposed yet more stringent dress requirements, the Union (while agreeing that this was apparently true) persuaded the Company that compliance with the state standards would unduly encumber the workers. The Industrial Safety Board of the state has issued a charge against the Company and the Union, and is about to commence hearings which may ultimately result in the imposition of fines and other penalties for noncompliance with the state safety standards. The Company and Union seek your advice as to whether the jurisdiction of the state Board may be attacked at the outset.

––––––––––

Until 1949, it was generally supposed that the large body of state law regulating the *concerted activities* of employees was applicable to all businesses whether they were engaged in interstate or intrastate activities. This supposed clarity was disturbed by two developments. Section 7 of the National Labor Relations Act was interpreted to guarantee the right to engage in "concerted activities for mutual aid or protection" not only against employer interference but by inference also against curtailment by the states. See International Union, UAW Local 232 v. Wisconsin Employment Relations Bd., 336 U.S. 245, 258, 69 S.Ct. 516, 523, 93 L.Ed. 651 (1949); Hill v. Florida ex rel. Watson, 325 U.S. 538, 65 S.Ct. 1373, 89 L.Ed. 1782 (1945). The Taft-Hartley amendments created union unfair labor practices which superimposed federal regulation upon the existing state law of strikes and picketing. To understand the consequences of these developments it is necessary to distinguish among three categories of employee activities under federal law.

One group is made up of the strikes, picketing, and similar activities protected by Section 7 of the NLRA. Peaceful strikes for higher wages are obvious examples, but the category includes nearly all normal peaceful labor activities not forbidden by, or contrary to, the policy of the NLRA or other federal law. A second group is made up of the strikes, picketing, and similar conduct forbidden by

Section 8(b). Between these two categories lies a group of concerted activities neither protected nor prohibited by federal statute; the slowdown, "quickie" stoppages, and strikes in breach of contract are clearcut illustrations. The Supreme Court's initial treatment of these "unprotected" concerted activities was to permit states to outlaw and to enjoin them: "There is no existing or possible conflict or overlapping between the authority of the Federal and State Boards, because the Federal Board has no authority either to investigate, approve or forbid the union conduct in question. This conduct is governable by the State or it is entirely ungoverned." INTERNATIONAL UNION, UAW LOCAL 232 v. WISCONSIN EMPLOYMENT RELATIONS BD. (BRIGGS-STRATTON CO.), 336 U.S. 245, 69 S.Ct. 516, 93 L.Ed. 651 (1949).

The *Oliver* case, supra, and the Problems below provide a framework for analyzing the proper role of the states in regulating protected concerted activities. The *Garmon* and *Lockridge* cases, infra, devote their principal attention to the role of the states in regulating conduct prohibited under the NLRA. The *Lodge 76, Machinists* case, infra, considers whether the *Briggs-Stratton* decision concerning state outlawry of "unprotected" concerted activities warrants continued endorsement in a more sophisticated age of preemption analysis.

Problems for Discussion

1. When workers employed at a Chrysler Corporation plant in Michigan went on strike in support of demands for a new collective bargaining agreement, the company sought an injunction in a Michigan state court, claiming that the union had not complied with the state's labor mediation law. The law, enacted to "preserve industrial peace" within the state, required that before employees could engage in a work stoppage they had to seek the services of a state mediation agency and had to subject the question of the strike to a majority vote. In the injunction action, the defendant union and employees have argued that the Michigan law is unconstitutional and have moved to dismiss the action. Should the motion be granted? See *UAW* v. *O'Brien*, 339 U.S. 454, 70 S.Ct. 781, 94 L.Ed. 978 (1950).

2. The Milwaukee Gas & Light Company has for many years negotiated labor agreements with the Electrical Workers Union. The Company is privately owned, and the Union initially secured bargaining rights through an election supervised by the NLRB. When the most recent contract negotiations reached an impasse, the Union announced its intention to strike, and the Company promptly initiated a proceeding with the Wisconsin Employment Relations Board; the Board in turn secured a state-court restraining order requiring the union to "desist and refrain" from going on strike. This order was entered pursuant to the state's Public Utility Anti-Strike Law which states, in part: "It shall be unlawful for any group of employees

of a public utility employer acting in concert to call a strike or go out on strike, or to cause any work stoppage or slowdown which would cause an interruption of an essential service." The union has appealed the issuance of the injunction. Should the injunction be vacated? See *Street Employees Div. 998* v. *Wisconsin Employment Rel. Bd.*, 340 U.S. 383, 71 S.Ct. 359, 95 L.Ed. 364 (1951).

Assume, in the above Problem, that the state Governor, acting pursuant to a state statute, proclaims that the strike would jeopardize the public health and welfare and orders that the state "take possession" of the Company's operations "for use and operation by the state in the public interest." No property is actually transferred to the state, and the internal management and organization of the Company are unchanged. The Governor then seeks an injunction against the strike under a state statute outlawing any work stoppage to enforce demands against the state or any work stoppage at a company seized in accordance with state law. Should the court issue a permanent injunction against the strike? *Street Employees Div. 1287* v. *Missouri*, 374 U.S. 74, 83 S.Ct. 1657, 10 L.Ed.2d 763 (1963).

3. Shortly after the Meat Cutters began an organizing campaign among the employees of the meat department of the Jack and Jill Supermarket, the company began to interrogate the employees coercively, to engage in surveillance of union meetings and to threaten the most active union supporters with discharge. The union filed charges against the company under Section 8(a)(1), which were sustained by the Administrative Law Judge; it also set up a picket line at the store advising the public that it was protesting the company's unfair labor practices. The company thereupon sought an injunction from a state court, claiming that there was mass picketing and intimidation of customers, in violation of state law. Although the state court found no violence or breach of the peace, it issued an injunction which limited the number of pickets at the store and which enjoined the picketers from handing out certain handbills and conversing with customers. Meanwhile, the Board adopted the findings of the Administrative Law Judge, found that the company had violated Section 8(a)(1) and issued a cease and desist order. It also filed suit in a federal district court seeking to restrain the enforcement of the state injunction and claiming that the NLRB had exclusive jurisdiction. Should the district court issue such an order? See *NLRB* v. *Nash-Finch Co.*, 404 U.S. 138, 92 S.Ct. 373, 30 L.Ed.2d 328 (1972).

Assume, in the above case, that as soon as the company commenced its state-court action for an injunction against the union, the union filed a complaint in the federal district court seeking an order to the employer to withdraw its injunction action. Should the federal court so order? See *Amalgamated Clothing Workers* v. *Richman Bros.*, 348 U.S. 511, 75 S.Ct. 452, 99 L.Ed. 600 (1955).

SAN DIEGO BUILDING TRADES COUNCIL v. GARMON

Supreme Court of the United States, 1959.
359 U.S. 236, 79 S.Ct. 773, 3 L.Ed.2d 775.

MR. JUSTICE FRANKFURTER delivered the opinion of the Court.

This case is before us for the second time. The present litigation began with a dispute between the petitioning unions and respondents, co-partners in the business of selling lumber and other materials in California. Respondents began an action in the Superior Court for the County of San Diego, asking for an injunction and damages. Upon hearing, the trial court found the following facts. In March of 1953 the unions sought from respondents an agreement to retain in their employ only those workers who were already members of the unions, or who applied for membership within thirty days. Respondents refused, claiming that none of their employees had shown a desire to join a union, and that, in any event, they could not accept such an arrangement until one of the unions had been designated by the employees as a collective bargaining agent. The unions began at once peacefully to picket the respondents' place of business, and to exert pressure on customers and suppliers in order to persuade them to stop dealing with respondents. The sole purpose of these pressures was to compel execution of the proposed contract. The unions contested this finding, claiming that the only purpose of their activities was to educate the workers and persuade them to become members. On the basis of its findings, the court enjoined the unions from picketing and from the use of other pressures to force an agreement, until one of them had been properly designated as a collective bargaining agent. The court also awarded $1,000 damages for losses found to have been sustained.

[The California state court concluded that the unions were violating Section 8(b)(2) of the NLRA, so that their conduct was not privileged; it issued an injunction and awarded damages. In a certiorari proceeding, the United States Supreme Court reversed, holding that the state injunction would conflict with the authority of the NLRB to issue cease-and-desist orders. On remand, the California court sustained the award of damages for violation of state law, and the Supreme Court once again granted certiorari "to determine whether the California court had jurisdiction to award damages arising out of peaceful union activity which it could not enjoin."]

In determining the extent to which state regulation must yield to subordinating federal authority, * * * [w]e have necessarily been concerned with the potential conflict of two law-enforcing authorities, with the disharmonies inherent in two systems, one federal, the other state, of inconsistent standards of substantive law

and differing remedial schemes. But the unifying consideration of
our decisions has been regard to the fact that Congress has entrusted administration of the labor policy for the Nation to a centralized administrative agency, armed with its own procedures, and
equipped with its specialized knowledge and cumulative experience
* * *.

Administration is more than a means of regulation; administration is regulation. We have been concerned with conflict in its broadest sense; conflict with a complex and interrelated federal scheme of
law, remedy, and administration. Thus, judicial concern has necessarily focused on the nature of the activities which the States have
sought to regulate, rather than on the method of regulation adopted.
When the exercise of state power over a particular area of activity
threatened interference with the clearly indicated policy of industrial
relations, it has been judicially necessary to preclude the States from
acting. However, due regard for the presuppositions of our embracing federal system, including the principle of diffusion of power
not as a matter of doctrinaire localism but as a promoter of democracy, has required us not to find withdrawal from the States of power
to regulate where the activity regulated was a merely peripheral concern of the Labor Management Relations Act. See International
Ass'n of Machinists v. Gonzales, 356 U.S. 617, 78 S.Ct. 923, 2 L.Ed.2d
1018. Or where the regulated conduct touched interests so deeply
rooted in local feeling and responsibility that, in the absence of compelling congressional direction, we could not infer that Congress had
deprived the States of the power to act.

When it is clear or may fairly be assumed that the activities
which a State purports to regulate are protected by § 7 of the National
Labor Relations Act, or constitute an unfair labor practice under
§ 8, due regard for the federal enactment requires that state jurisdiction must yield. To leave the States free to regulate conduct so
plainly within the central aim of federal regulation involves too great
a danger of conflict between power asserted by Congress and requirements imposed by state law. Nor has it mattered whether the States
have acted through laws of broad general application rather than laws
specifically directed towards the governance of industrial relations.
Regardless of the mode adopted, to allow the States to control conduct
which is the subject of national regulation would create potential
frustration of national purposes.

At times it has not been clear whether the particular activity
regulated by the States was governed by § 7 or § 8 or was, perhaps,
outside both these sections. But courts are not primary tribunals to
adjudicate such issues. It is essential to the administration of the
Act that these determinations be left in the first instance to the National Labor Relations Board. What is outside the scope of this
Court's authority cannot remain within a State's power and state

jurisdiction too must yield to the exclusive primary competence of the Board. See, e. g., Garner v. Teamsters, etc. Union, 346 U.S. 485, especially at pages 489–491, 74 S.Ct. 161, at pages 165–166, 98 L.Ed. 228; Weber v. Anheuser-Busch, Inc., 348 U.S. 468, 75 S.Ct. 480, 99 L.Ed. 546.

The case before us is such a case. The adjudication in California has throughout been based on the assumption that the behavior of the petitioning unions constituted an unfair labor practice. This conclusion was derived by the California courts from the facts as well as from their view of the Act. It is not for us to decide whether the National Labor Relations Board would have, or should have, decided these questions in the same manner. When an activity is arguably subject to § 7 or § 8 of the Act, the States as well as the federal courts must defer to the exclusive competence of the National Labor Relations Board if the danger of state interference with national policy is to be averted.

To require the States to yield to the primary jurisdiction of the National Board does not ensure Board adjudication of the status of a disputed activity. If the Board decides, subject to appropriate federal judicial review, that conduct is protected by § 7, or prohibited by § 8, then the matter is at an end, and the States are ousted of all jurisdiction. Or, the Board may decide that an activity is neither protected nor prohibited, and thereby raise the question whether such activity may be regulated by the States.[3] However, the Board may also fail to determine the status of the disputed conduct by declining to assert jurisdiction, or by refusal of the General Counsel to file a charge, or by adopting some other disposition which does not define the nature of the activity with unclouded legal significance. This was the basic problem underlying our decision in Guss v. Utah Labor Relations Board, 353 U.S. 1, 77 S.Ct. 598, 609, 1 L.Ed.2d 601. In that case we held that the failure of the National Labor Relations Board to assume jurisdiction did not leave the States free to regulate activities they would otherwise be precluded from regulating. It follows that the failure of the Board to define the legal significance under the Act of a particular activity does not give the States the power to act. In the absence of the Board's clear determination that an activity is neither protected nor prohibited or of compelling precedent applied to essentially undisputed facts, it is not for this Court to decide whether such activities are subject to state jurisdiction. The withdrawal of this narrow area from possible state activity follows from our decisions in Weber and Guss. The govern-

3. See International Union, United Auto Workers, etc. v. Wisconsin Employment Relations Board, 336 U.S. 245, 69 S.Ct. 516, 93 L.Ed. 651. The approach taken in that case, in which the Court undertook for itself to determine the status of the disputed activity, has not been followed in later decisions, and is no longer of general application.

ing consideration is that to allow the States to control activities that are potentially subject to federal regulation involves too great a danger of conflict with national labor policy.

In the light of these principles the case before us is clear. Since the National Labor Relations Board has not adjudicated the status of the conduct for which the State of California seeks to give a remedy in damages, and since such activity is arguably within the compass of § 7 or § 8 of the Act, the State's jurisdiction is displaced.

Nor is it significant that California asserted its power to give damages rather than to enjoin what the Board may restrain though it could not compensate. Our concern is with delimiting areas of conduct which must be free from state regulation if national policy is to be left unhampered. Such regulation can be as effectively exerted through an award of damages as through some form of preventive relief. The obligation to pay compensation can be, indeed is designed to be, a potent method of governing conduct and controlling policy. Even the States' salutary effort to redress private wrongs or grant compensation for past harm cannot be exerted to regulate activities that are potentially subject to the exclusive federal regulatory scheme. See Garner v. Teamsters, etc. Union, 346 U.S. 485, 492–497, 74 S.Ct. 161, 166–169, 98 L.Ed. 228. It may be that an award of damages in a particular situation will not, in fact, conflict with the active assertion of federal authority. The same may be true of the incidence of a particular state injunction. To sanction either involves a conflict with federal policy in that it involves allowing two law-making sources to govern. In fact, since remedies form an ingredient of any integrated scheme of regulation, to allow the State to grant a remedy here which has been withheld from the National Labor Relations Board only accentuates the danger of conflict.

It is true that we have allowed the States to grant compensation for the consequences, as defined by the traditional law of torts, of conduct marked by violence and imminent threats to the public order. International Union, United Automobile, Aircraft and Agricultural Implement Workers, etc. v. Russell, 356 U.S. 634, 78 S.Ct. 932, 2 L.Ed.2d 1030; United Construction Workers, etc. v. Laburnum Const. Corp., 347 U.S. 656, 74 S.Ct. 833, 98 L.Ed. 1025. We have also allowed the States to enjoin such conduct. Youngdahl v. Rainfair, Inc., 355 U.S. 131, 78 S.Ct. 206, 2 L.Ed.2d 151; United Automobile Aircraft and Agricultural Implement Workers, etc. v. Wisconsin Employment Relations Board, 351 U.S. 266, 76 S.Ct. 794, 100 L.Ed. 1162. State jurisdiction has prevailed in these situations because the compelling state interest, in the scheme of our federalism, in the maintenance of domestic peace is not overridden in the absence of clearly expressed congressional direction. We recognize that the opinion in United Construction Workers, etc. v. Laburnum Const. Corp., 347 U.S. 656, 74 S.Ct. 833, 835, 98 L.Ed. 1025, found support in the fact that the state remedy had no federal counterpart. But that decision was determined, as is demonstrated by the question to which review was restricted, by the "type of conduct" involved, i. e., "intimidation and threats of violence." In the present case there is no such compelling state interest.

The judgment below is reversed.

Reversed.

[Mr. Justice Harlan concurred, for himself and three other Justices, not because the union's activity was an unfair labor practice but rather because it was arguably protected by Section 7. He stated that "The threshold question in every labor pre-emption case is whether the conduct with respect to which a State has sought to act is, or may fairly be regarded as, federally protected activity," since such activity must be beyond the reach of state power. He claimed that the Court majority had read the *Russell* and *Laburnum* cases too narrowly in construing them to mean that state tort law was not preempted because it was violence that the state was regulating. Rather, the violence in those cases was relevant for a broader reason: it rendered the defendants' conduct beyond the protection of Section 7. Assuming this conduct to have been prohibited and thus within the regulatory power of the NLRB, a strict theory of primary jurisdiction would have dictated displacement of state power to grant relief; but the Court in those two earlier cases probed further in order to determine whether there was any conflict between state remedies and the NLRA, and concluded that there was none, since the NLRB affords no remedy for past injury caused by violent unfair labor practices. State remedies for conduct not protected by Section 7 should thus survive if there is no conflict between them and federal administrative remedies. "The Court's opinion in this case cuts deeply into the ability of States to furnish an effective remedy under their own laws for the redress of past nonviolent tortious conduct which is not federally protected, but which may be deemed to be, or is, federally prohibited. Henceforth the States must withhold access to their courts until the National Labor Relations Board has determined that such unprotected conduct is not an unfair labor practice, a course which, because of unavoidable Board delays, may render state redress ineffective. And in instances in which the Board declines to exercise its jurisdiction, the States are entirely deprived of power to afford any relief. * * * Solely because it is fairly debatable whether the conduct here involved is federally protected, I concur in the result of today's decision."]

AMALGAMATED ASS'N OF STREET EMPLOYEES v. LOCKRIDGE, 403 U.S. 274, 91 S.Ct. 1909, 29 L.Ed.2d 473 (1971). Lockridge had been employed by Western Greyhound Lines from May 1943 until November 1959, and was a member of the Street Employees Union. The labor contract required that all employees become and remain Union members as a condition of employment. Section 91 of the Union's constitution and bylaws provided that a member delinquent in paying monthly dues for fifteen days became a member "not in good standing," and that a two-month delinquency would lead to suspension from membership. Prior to September 1959, Lockridge's dues had been forwarded directly to the Union pursuant to a checkoff clause in the labor contract, but that month he effectively revoked his checkoff authorization, thus requiring him to mail dues to the Union's office. He failed to do so in October 1959, and on November 2, the Union's secretary-treasurer suspended Lockridge from membership and secured his discharge by Western Greyhound. The Union refused to accept the tender on November 10 of Lockridge's October and November dues. Lockridge filed suit in the Idaho courts alleging that the Union had acted willfully and maliciously in breach of the contract (reflected in the constitution and bylaws) between member and Union by stripping him of his union membership and his job on account of dues delinquency of only one month. The Idaho court, relying on a Supreme Court decision, IAM v. GONZALES, 356 U.S. 617, 78 S.Ct. 923, 2 L.Ed.2d 1018 (1958), upheld the claim of breach of contract, and among other things ordered that Lockridge be reinstated in the Union and paid more than $32,000 compensatory damages for loss of wages. The Supreme Court granted certiorari and reversed, relying principally on its decision in the *Garmon* case.

The Court majority, in an opinion by Mr. Justice Harlan, began by noting that the Idaho court had conceded that the Union's conduct violated Sections 8(b)(1)(A) and 8(b)(2) and probably caused the employer to violate Section 8(a)(3). The Court noted that preemption of state law stems not merely from Congress's enactment of a different set of substantive rules of labor law. "It sought as well to restructure fundamentally the processes for effectuating that policy, deliberately placing the responsibility for applying and developing this comprehensive legal system in the hands of an expert administrative body rather than the federalized judicial system. Thus, that a local court, while adjudicating a labor dispute also within the jurisdiction of the NLRB, may purport to apply legal rules identical to those prescribed in the federal Act or may eschew the authority to define or apply principles specifically developed to regulate labor relations does not mean that all relevant potential for debilitating conflict is absent." After observing that Congress had not explicitly dictated the extent of preemption of state law, and that it was important that any preemption standard be capable of relatively easy application on other than a case-by-case basis, the Court stated that "treating differently judicial power to deal with conduct protected by the Act from that prohibited by it would   *   *   *   be unsatisfactory.   Both areas equally involve conduct whose legality is governed by federal law, the application of which Congress committed to the Board, not courts."   The Court repudiated its earlier attempts to articulate preemption criteria which had been improperly tolerant of state jurisdiction; examples of unsound tests were those which turned upon whether the state remedy was not provided under the NLRA, or which would permit the application of general common law rules (as opposed to state rules specifically designed to regulate labor relations).

Justice Harlan rejected the theories of the Idaho court for justifying an exception to preemption.   That Lockridge's complaint charged a breach of contract rather than an unfair labor practice is beside the point, since "it is the conduct being regulated, not the formal description of governing legal standards, that is the proper focus of concern."   Moreover the state, in purporting to interpret contractual terms, was not dealing with an issue different from that which would be presented to the NLRB, i. e., the Union's discrimination against Lockridge.   Had the Board attempted to determine whether Lockridge's discharge was for reasons other than nonpayment of dues, it would routinely inquire into the proper construction of the Union constitution and bylaws in order to ascertain whether the Union properly found him to have been delinquent in his dues-paying responsibilities; had a violation of Section 8(b)(2) been made out, the Board would not treat the Union's good-faith misapplication of its rules as a defense.

The Court also distinguished the *Gonzales* case, on which the Idaho courts had relied.   There, a state court found that an expulsion from the union was in violation of the constitution and bylaws, and ordered reinstatement to union membership and damages for lost wages.   The Supreme Court had held that the principal remedy was the reinstatement and that the damages could be awarded to "fill out" this equity award.   Moreover, *Garmon* was decided the following year and "clearly did not fully embrace the technique of the prior case   *   *   *   It seems evident that the full-blown rationale of *Gonzales* could not survive the rule of *Garmon*."   Finally, two post-*Garmon* decisions of the Court—LOCAL 100, UNITED ASS'N OF JOURNEYMEN V. BORDEN, 373 U.S. 690, 83 S.Ct. 1423, 10 L.Ed.2d 638 (1963), and LOCAL 207, BRIDGE WORKERS V. PERKO, 373 U.S. 701, 83 S.Ct. 1429, 10 L.Ed.2d 646 (1963)—on facts similar to *Gonzales* resulted in preemption.   *Gonzales* was there treated as a case which focused on "purely internal union matters" (the constitution and bylaws, and the principal remedy of reinstatement to the union), matters normally left to state law and having only a "tangential and remote" relationship to the NLRA. *Borden* and *Perko*, however, like *Lockridge* itself, concerned alleged interference with the plaintiff's employment relations; Lockridge's case was "based solely upon the procurement of his discharge from employment" and "turned upon the construction of the applicable union security clause, a matter as to which   *   *   *   federal concern is pervasive and its regulation complex."

Mr. Justice Douglas dissented. He would limit *Garmon* to disputes between a union and an employer, where the possible hiatus between a preempted state court and a slow-moving NLRB can be filled by resort to economic power. An individual employee in a dispute with a union has no such recourse, and exclusive resort to the NLRB may be expensive, time-consuming or totally unavailing (should the General Counsel refuse to issue a complaint). When the quarrel of the employee with his union relates not to his job but to his suspension of union membership by virtue of the union's contract breach, this is a matter the regulation of which has not been undertaken by federal law, and a suit should lie in a state court.

Mr. Justice White wrote a dissenting opinion, in which the Chief Justice joined. He pointed out the significant number of instances in which the presumed congressional goal of a uniform national labor policy fashioned and applied by a single centralized agency has been deemed outweighed by the need to do justice in state tribunals or through state substantive law: court enforcement of collective bargaining agreements and arbitration promises, and court enforcement of the union's duty of fair representation, even though the defendant's conduct may constitute an unfair labor practice; judicial remedies for secondary boycotts under Section 303 of the NLRA; state jurisdiction under Section 14(c) in cases falling in (what was under the *Guss* decision) the "no man's land" over which the NLRB could have asserted but declined to assert jurisdiction; state authority under Section 14(b) to outlaw union-shop agreements otherwise authorized under the NLRA; and state prohibitions of union violence which may also violate Section 8(b)(1).

Mr. Justice White would add to this list actions under state law by union members to enforce, as contracts, union constitutions and bylaws. Congress specifically denied preemption in such cases in the Landrum-Griffin Act of 1959, and the *Gonzalez* case (which Justice White thought was spuriously distinguished by the Court majority) also so holds. "Here, Lockridge was discharged for alleged nonpayment of dues in accordance with the union constitution and brought suit alleging that he had in fact not been unduly tardy and that union's action was a breach of the contract. The face of the complaint did not implicate federal law. If the Idaho court were allowed to proceed, it would not have purported to adjudicate an unfair labor practice by reference to federal law, but, if it found the conduct unprotected by federal law, * * * would have enforced rights and obligations created by the union constitution." To hold that the NLRB must have exclusive power to adjudicate this case because the union's alleged conduct is, or may be, an unfair labor practice is "wooden logic."

Nor should Idaho's jurisdiction be preempted by the fact that the union's conduct might arguably have been protected under Section 7; the "arguably protected" branch of the *Garmon* doctrine should be rejected, urged Justice White for it "blindly preempts other tribunals" even though it is virtually impossible to secure an NLRB determination on this question in the first instance unless the employer deliberately commits an unfair labor practice through coercion or discrimination. Conduct arguably prohibited can be brought before the NLRB by the aggrieved party by filing a charge, but the Board will not determine whether employee or union conduct is actually *protected* unless the employer resorts to self-help in the hope that an unfair labor practice charge will be filed and the Board will find the union or employee conduct to be unprotected. "There seems little point in a doctrine that, in the name of national policy encourages the commission of unfair labor practices * * *. I would permit the state court to entertain the action and if the union defends on the ground that its conduct is protected by federal law, to pass on that claim at the outset of the proceeding. If the federal law immunizes the challenged union action, the case is terminated; but if not, the case is adjudicated under state law."

Problems for Discussion

1. *Garmon* and *Lockridge* suggest that a defendant in a state court case will maximize its chances for a dismissal if it concedes that its conduct is an unfair labor practice under Section 8(b). Is the defendant's attorney well advised to make such a concession? Can it be used adversely in a later-filed unfair labor practice case before the NLRB?

If the defendant's conduct is concededly prohibited under the NLRA, then the only reluctance to uphold state court jurisdiction will stem from a concern about differing remedies. Is that generally a strong enough concern to warrant preemption of state relief? Would *Garmon* and *Lockridge* therefore have been better articulated as "substantive right" cases rather than "primary jurisdiction" cases?

2. *Garmon* and *Lockridge* conclude that when the defendant's conduct is only *arguably* prohibited, state court jurisdiction should be preempted because it is for the expert NLRB to determine whether the conduct is actually prohibited (and to order proper remedies) rather than the inexpert

state courts. Might not a better rationale have been that state courts may err by holding actually prohibited some conduct which is in fact actually *protected*—so that once again the "substantive right" theory would better explain these decisions, rather than the "primary jurisdiction" theory?

(By the way, is the Court's fear consistent with the fact that Congress in Section 303 has given jurisdiction to state judges and juries to rule upon secondary boycott cases, perhaps the most complex category of unfair labor practice cases under the NLRA?)

3.   Assume that in the *Lockridge* case, a similarly situated fellow employee of the plaintiff was suspended from union membership and discharged by Greyhound in early November 1959, and that he promptly filed an unfair labor practice charge in the regional office, only to have the regional director refuse to issue a complaint because "it appears that there is insufficient evidence of violations." (This in fact occurred.) Should this have induced the Supreme Court in *Lockridge* to render a different decision? Is it humane to erect a system of jurisprudence in which an employee such as Lockridge, with nearly seventeen years of seniority with Greyhound, is afforded no forum at all in which the merits of his claim can be addressed? (Will there be a sympathetic forum in arbitration under the collective bargaining agreement, or in intra-union appeals, or anywhere else?)

LODGE 76, MACHINISTS v. WISCONSIN EMPLOYMENT RELATIONS COMM'N

Supreme Court of the United States, 1976.
427 U.S. 132, 96 S.Ct. 2548, 49 L.Ed.2d 396.

MR. JUSTICE BRENNAN delivered the opinion of the Court.

The question to be decided in this case is whether federal labor policy pre-empts the authority of a state labor relations board to grant an employer covered by the National Labor Relations Act an order enjoining a union and its members from continuing to refuse to work overtime pursuant to a union policy to put economic pressure on the employer in negotiations for renewal of an expired collective-bargaining agreement.

A collective-bargaining agreement between petitioner Local 76 (the Union) and respondent, Kearney and Trecker Corporation (the employer) was terminated by the employer pursuant to the terms of the agreement on June 19, 1971. Good-faith bargaining over the terms of a renewal agreement continued for over a year thereafter, finally resulting in the signing of a new agreement effective July 23, 1972. A particularly controverted issue during negotiations was the employer's demand that the provision of the expired agreement under which, as for the prior 17 years, the basic workday was seven and one-half hours, Monday through Friday, and the basic workweek was 37½ hours, be replaced with a new provision providing a basic workday of eight hours and a basic workweek of 40 hours, and that the terms on which overtime rates of pay were payable be changed accordingly.

A few days after the old agreement was terminated the employer unilaterally began to make changes in some conditions of employment provided in the expired contract, e. g., eliminating the checkoff of Union dues, eliminating the Union's office in the plant and eliminating Union lost time. No immediate change was made in the basic workweek or workday, but in March 1972, the employer announced that it would unilaterally implement, as of March 13, 1972, its proposal for a 40-hour week and eight-hour day. The Union response was a membership meeting on March 7 at which strike action was authorized and a resolution was adopted binding union members to refuse to work any overtime, defined as work in excess of seven and one-half hours in any day or 37½ hours in any week. Following the strike vote, the employer offered to "defer the implementation" of its workweek proposal if the Union would agree to call off the concerted refusal to work overtime. The Union, however, refused the offer and indicated its intent to continue the concerted ban on overtime. Thereafter, the employer did not make effective the proposed changes in the workday and workweek before the new agreement became effective on July 23, 1972. Although all but a very few employees complied with the Union's resolution against acceptance of overtime work during the negotiations, the employer did not discipline, or attempt to discipline, any employee for refusing to work overtime.

Instead, while negotiations continued, the employer filed a charge with the National Labor Relations Board that the Union's resolution violated § 8(b)(3) of the National Labor Relations Act, 29 U.S.C. § 158(b)(3). The Regional Director dismissed the charge on the ground that the "policy prohibiting overtime work by its member employees does not appear to be in violation of the Act" and therefore was not conduct cognizable by the Board under NLRB v. Insurance Agents Intern'l Union, 361 U.S. 477, 80 S.Ct. 419, 4 L.Ed.2d 454 (1960). However, the employer also filed a complaint before the Wisconsin Employment Relations Commission charging that the refusal to work overtime constituted an unfair labor practice under state law. The Union filed a motion before the Commission to dismiss the complaint for want of "jurisdiction over the subject matter" in that jurisdiction over "the activity of the [union] complained of [is] pre-empted by" the National Labor Relations Act. App. 11. The motion was denied and the Commission adopted the Conclusion of Law of its Examiner that "the concerted refusal to work overtime is not an activity which is arguably protected under Section 7 or arguably prohibited under Section 8 of the National Labor Relations Act, as amended and * * * therefore the * * * Commission is not preempted from asserting its jurisdiction to regulate said conduct." The Commission also adopted the further Conclusion of Law that the Union "by authorizing * * * the concerted refusal to work overtime * * * engaged in a concerted effort to interfere with production and * * * committed an unfair labor practice within the meaning of Section 111.06(2)(h) * * * " [4] The Commission thereupon entered an order that the Union, *inter alia*, "[i]mmediately cease and desist from authorizing, encouraging or condoning any concerted refusal to accept overtime assignments * * *." The Wisconsin Circuit Court affirmed and entered judgment enforcing the Commission's order. The Wisconsin Supreme Court affirmed the Circuit Court. 67 Wis.2d 13, 226 N.W.2d 203 (1975). We granted certiorari, 423 U.S. 890, 96 S.Ct. 186, 46 L.Ed.2d 121 (1975). We reverse.

I

 * * *

Cases that have held state authority to be pre-empted by federal law tend to fall into one of two categories: (1) those that reflect the concern that "one forum would enjoin, as illegal, conduct which the other forum would find legal" and (2) those that reflect the concern "that the [application of state law by] state courts would restrict the exercise of rights guaranteed by the Federal Acts." Automobile Workers v. Russell, 356 U.S. 634, 644, 78 S.Ct. 932, 938, 2 L.Ed.2d 1030 (1958). "[I]n referring to decisions holding state laws preempted by the NLRA, care must be taken to distinguish preemption based on federal protection of the conduct in question * * * from that based predominantly on the primary jurisdiction of the National Labor Relations Board * * *, although the two are often not easily separable." Brotherhood of Railroad Trainmen v. Jacksonville Terminal Co., 394 U.S. 369, 383 n. 19, 89 S.Ct. 1109, 1118, 22 L.Ed.2d 344 (1969). Each of these distinct aspects of labor law pre-emption has had its own history in our decisions to which we now turn.

We consider first pre-emption based predominantly on the primary jurisdiction of the Board. This line of pre-emption analysis

---

4. Wis.Stat. § 111.06(2) provides:
    "It shall be an unfair labor practice for an employee individually or in concert with others:
     *   *   *   *   *   *
    "(h) To take unauthorized possession of the property of the employer or to engage in any concerted effort to interfere with production except by leaving the premises in an orderly manner for the purpose of going on strike."

was developed in San Diego Unions v. Garmon, 359 U.S. 236, 79 S.Ct. 773, 3 L.Ed.2d 775, and its history was recently summarized in Amalgamated Association of Street, Electric Railway & Motor Coach Employees v. Lockridge, 403 U.S. 274, 290–291, 91 S.Ct. 1909, 1920, 29 L.Ed.2d 473 (1971)   *   *   *.

However, a second line of pre-emption analysis has been developed in cases focusing upon the crucial inquiry whether Congress intended that the conduct involved be unregulated because left "to be controlled by the free play of economic forces." NLRB v. Nash-Finch Co., 404 U.S. 138, 144, 92 S.Ct. 373, 377, 30 L.Ed.2d 328 (1971).[5] Concededly this inquiry was not made in 1949 in the so-called *Briggs-Stratton* case, Automobile Workers v. Wisconsin Board, 336 U.S. 245, 69 S.Ct. 516, 93 L.Ed. 651 (1949), the decision of this Court heavily relied upon by the court below in reaching its decision that state regulation of the conduct at issue is not pre-empted by national labor law. In *Briggs-Stratton*, the union, in order to bring pressure on the employer during negotiations, adopted a plan whereby union meetings were called at irregular times during working hours without advance notice to the employer or any notice as to whether or when the workers would return. In a proceeding under the Wisconsin Employment Peace Act, the Wisconsin Employment Relations Board issued an order forbidding the union and its members from engaging in concerted efforts to interfere with production by those methods. This Court did not inquire whether Congress meant that such methods should be reserved to the union "to be controlled by the free play of economic forces." Rather, because

5. See Cox, Labor Law Preemption Revisited, 85 Harv.L.Rev. 1337, 1352 (1972):
"An appreciation of the true character of the national labor policy expressed in the NLRA and the LMRA indicates that in providing a legal framework for union organization, collective bargaining, and the conduct of labor disputes, Congress struck a balance of protection, prohibition, and laissez-faire in respect to union organization, collective bargaining, and labor disputes that would be upset if a state could enforce statutes or rules of decision resting upon its views concerning accommodation of the same interests."
Cf. Lesnick, Preemption Reconsidered: The Apparent Reaffirmation of *Garmon*, 72 Col.L.Rev. 469, 478, 480 (1972):
"[T]he failure of Congress to prohibit a certain conduct * * * war-

rant[s a] * * * negative inference that it was deemed proper, indeed desirable—at least, desirable to be left for the free play of contending economic forces. Thus, the state is not merely filling a gap when it outlaws what federal law fails to outlaw; it is denying one party to an economic contest a weapon that Congress meant him to have available.

*   *   *   *   *

"The premise is * * * that Congress judged whether the conduct was illicit or legitimate, and that 'legitimate' connotes, not simply that federal law is neutral, but that the conduct is to be assimilated to the large residual area in which a regime of free collective bargaining—'economic warfare' if you prefer—is thought to be the course of regulatory wisdom."

these methods were "neither made a right under federal law nor a violation of it" the Court held that there "was no basis for denying to Wisconsin the power, in governing her internal affairs, to regulate" such conduct. Id., at 265, 69 S.Ct., at 527.

However, the *Briggs-Stratton* holding that state power is not pre-empted as to peaceful conduct neither protected by § 7 nor prohibited by § 8 of the federal Act, a holding premised on the statement that "[t]his conduct is either governable by the State or it is entirely ungoverned," id., at 254, 69 S.Ct., at 521, was undercut by subsequent decisions of this Court. For the Court soon recognized that a particular activity might be "protected" by federal law not only where it fell within § 7, but also when it was an activity that Congress intended to be "unrestricted by *any* governmental power to regulate" because it was among the permissible "economic weapons in reserve * * * actual exercise [of which] on occasion by the parties is part and parcel of the system that the Wagner and Taft-Hartley Acts have recognized." NLRB v. Insurance Agents, 361 U.S., at 488, 489, 80 S.Ct., at 426, 427 (emphasis added). "[T]he legislative purpose may * * * dictate that certain activity 'neither protected nor prohibited' be privileged against state regulation." Hanna Mining Co. v. Marine Engineers, 382 U.S., at 187, 86 S.Ct., at 331.

II

Insurance Agents, supra, involved a charge of a refusal by the union to bargain in good faith in violation of § 8(b)(3) of the Act. * * *

[The Court here discussed, and quoted at length from, its opinion in *Insurance Agents*; see pp. 408–15, supra.] We noted further that "Congress has been rather specific when it has come to outlaw particular economic weapons on the part of unions" and "the activities here involved have never been specifically outlawed by Congress." Id., at 498, 80 S.Ct., at 432. Accordingly, the Board's claim "to power * * * to distinguish among various economic pressure tactics and brand the ones at bar inconsistent with good-faith collective bargaining," id., at 492, 80 S.Ct., at 428, was simply inconsistent with the design of the federal scheme in which "the use of economic pressure by the parties to a labor dispute is * * * part and parcel of the process of collective bargaining." Id., at 495, 80 S. Ct., at 430.

The Court had earlier recognized in pre-emption cases that Congress meant to leave some activities unregulated and to be controlled by the free play of economic forces. Garner v. Teamsters, Chauffeurs and Helpers Local Union, 346 U.S. 485, 74 S.Ct. 161, 98 L.Ed.

228, in finding pre-empted state power to restrict peaceful recognitional picketing, said:

> "The detailed prescription of a procedure for restraint of specified types of picketing would seem to imply that other picketing is to be free of other methods and sources of restraint. For the policy of the Labor Management Relations Act is not to condemn all picketing but only that ascertained by its prescribed process to fall within its prohibition. Otherwise it is implicit in the Act that the public interest is served by freedom of labor to use the weapon of picketing. For a state to impinge on the area of labor combat designed to be free is quite as much an obstruction of federal policy as if the state were to declare picketing free for purposes or by methods which the federal Act prohibits." Id., at 499–500, 74 S.Ct., at 170–171.

* * * [T]he analysis of *Garner* and *Insurance Agents* came full bloom in the pre-emption area in Local 20, Teamsters, Chauffeurs & Helpers Union v. Morton, 377 U.S. 252, 84 S.Ct. 1253, 12 L.Ed.2d 280 (1964), which held pre-empted the application of state law to award damages for peaceful union secondary picketing. Although *Morton* involved conduct neither "protected nor prohibited" by § 7 or § 8 of the NLRA, we recognized the necessity of an inquiry whether " 'Congress occupied the field and closed it to state regulation.' " Id., at 258, 84 S.Ct., at 1257. Central to *Morton's* analysis was the observation that "[i]n selecting which forms of economic pressure should be prohibited * * *, Congress struck the 'balance * * * between the uncontrolled power of management and labor to further their respective interests,' " id., at 258–259, 84 S.Ct., at 1258, and that:

> "This weapon of self-help, permitted by federal law, formed an integral part of the petitioner's effort to achieve its bargaining goals during negotiations with the respondent. Allowing its use is a part of the balance struck by Congress between the conflicting interests of the union, the employees, the employer and the community. * * * If the Ohio law of secondary boycott can be applied to proscribe the same type of conduct which Congress focused upon but did not proscribe when it enacted § 303, the inevitable result would be to frustrate the congressional determination to leave this weapon of self-help available, and to upset the balance of power between labor and management expressed in óur national labor policy. 'For a state to impinge on the area of labor combat designed to be free is quite as much an obstruction of federal policy as if the state

were to declare picketing free for purposes or by methods which the federal Act prohibits.' Garner v. Teamsters Union, 346 U.S. 485, 500, 74 S.Ct. 161, 98 L.Ed. 228." *Morton,* supra, at 259–260, 84 S.Ct., at 1258.

Although many of our past decisions concerning conduct left by Congress to the free play of economic forces address the question in the context of union and employee activities, self-help is of course also the prerogative of the employer because he too may properly employ economic weapons Congress meant to be unregulable.   *   *   * "[R]esort to economic weapons should more peaceful measures not avail" is the right of the employer as well as the employee, American Ship Building Co. v. NLRB, 380 U.S., at 317, 85 S.Ct., at 966, and the State may not prohibit the use of such weapons or "add to an employer's federal legal obligations in collective bargaining" any more than in the case of employees. Cox, Labor Law Preemption Revisited, 85 Harv.L.Rev. 1337, 1365 (1972). See, e. g. Beasley v. Food Fair, Inc., 416 U.S. 653, 94 S.Ct. 2023, 40 L.Ed.2d 443 (1974). Whether self-help economic activities are employed by employer or union, the crucial inquiry regarding pre-emption is the same: whether "the exercise of plenary state authority to curtail or entirely prohibit self-help would frustrate effective implementation of the Act's processes." Railroad Trainmen v. Jacksonville Terminal Co., 394 U.S., at 380, 89 S.Ct., at 1116.

III

There is simply no question that the Act's processes would be frustrated in the instant case were the State's ruling permitted to stand. The employer in this case invoked the Wisconsin law because unable to overcome the union tactic with its own economic self-help means. Although it did employ economic weapons putting pressure on the union when it terminated the previous agreement,   *   *   * it apparently lacked sufficient economic strength to secure its bargaining demands under "the balance of power between labor and management expressed in our national labor policy," Teamsters Union v. Morton, 377 U.S., at 260, 84 S.Ct., at 1258.[6] But the economic weakness of the affected party cannot justify state aid contrary to federal law for, "as we have developed, the use of economic pressure

---

6.   Cf. *Cox,* supra, n. [5], at 1347: "[In *Briggs-Stratton,*] the Court was beguiled by the fallacy of supposing that a Congress which allowed an employer to discharge his employees for engaging in a series of 'quickie' strikes surely would not preclude the employer's pursuing what the Court regarded as the relatively mild sanction of legal redress through state courts. In fact, most employers facing a union with the strength and discipline to call a series of 'quickie' strikes would lack the economic power to discharge union members, leaving legal redress the more efficient sanction."

by the parties to a labor dispute is not a grudging exception [under] * * * the [federal] Act; it is part and parcel of the process of collective bargaining." *Insurance Agents*, 361 U.S., at 495, 80 S.Ct., at 430. The state action in this case is not filling "a regulatory void which Congress plainly assumed would not exist," Hanna Mining Co. v. Marine Engineers, 382 U.S., at 196, 86 S.Ct., at 335 (Brennan, J., concurring). Rather, it is clear beyond question that Wisconsin "[entered] into the substantive aspects of the bargaining process to an extent Congress has not countenanced." NLRB v. Insurance Agents, supra, at 498, 80 S.Ct., at 432.

Our decisions hold that Congress meant that these activities, whether of employer or employees, were not to be regulable by States any more than by the NLRB, for neither States nor the Board are "afforded flexibility in picking and choosing which economic devices of labor and management would be branded as unlawful." Ibid. Rather, both are without authority to attempt to "introduce some standard of properly 'balanced' bargaining power," id., at 497, 80 S.Ct., at 431, or to define "what economic sanctions might be permitted negotiating parties in an 'ideal' or 'balanced' state of collective bargaining." Id., at 500, 80 S.Ct., at 433. To sanction state regulation of such economic pressure deemed by the federal Act 'desirabl[y] * * * left for the free play of contending economic forces, * * * is not merely [to fill] a gap [by] outlaw[ing] what federal law fails to outlaw; it is denying to one party to an economic contest a weapon that Congress meant him to have available." Lesnick, Preemption Reconsidered: The Apparent Reaffirmation of *Garmon*, 72 Col.L.Rev. 469, 478 (1972). Accordingly, such regulation by the State is impermissible because it " 'stands as an obstacle to the accomplishment and execution of the full purposes and objectives of Congress.' " Hill v. Florida, 325 U.S. 538, 542, 65 S.Ct. 1373, 1375, 89 L.Ed. 1782 (1945).

IV

There remains the question of the continuing vitality of *Briggs-Stratton*. San Diego Unions v. Garmon, 359 U.S., at 245 n. 4, 79 S. Ct., at 780, made clear that the *Briggs-Stratton* approach to pre-emption is "no longer of general application." See also *Insurance Agents*, 361 U.S. at 493 n. 23, 80 S.Ct., at 429. We hold today that the ruling of *Briggs-Stratton*, permitting state regulation of partial strike activities such as are involved in this case is likewise "no longer of general application." * * *

Although we are not unmindful of the demands of *stare decisis* and the "important policy considerations militat[ing] in favor of continuity and predictability in the law", Boys Markets, Inc. v. Retail Clerks, 398 U.S. 235, 240, 90 S.Ct. 1583, 1587, 26 L.Ed.2d 199 (1970), *Briggs-Stratton* "stands as a significant departure from our * * * emphasis upon the congressional policy" central to the statutory scheme it has enacted, and since our later decisions make plain that *Briggs-Stratton* "does not further but rather frustrates realization of an important goal of our national labor policy," *Boys Market*, supra, at 241, 90 S.Ct., at 1587, *Briggs-Stratton* is expressly overruled. Its authority "has been 'so restricted by our later decisions' * * * that [it] must be regarded as having 'been worn away by the erosion of time' * * * and of contrary authority." United States v. Raines, 362 U.S. 17, 26, 80 S.Ct. 519, 524, 4 L.Ed.2d 524 (1960). * * *

Reversed.

MR. JUSTICE POWELL, with whom THE CHIEF JUSTICE joins, concurring.

* * * I write to make clear my understanding that the Court's opinion does not * * * preclude the States from enforcing, in the context of a labor dispute, "neutral" state statutes or rules of decision: state laws that are not directed toward altering the bargaining positions of employers or unions but which may have an incidental effect on relative bargaining strength. Except where Congress has specifically provided otherwise, the States generally should remain free to enforce, for example, their law of torts or of contracts, and other laws reflecting neutral public policy.[7] See Cox, Labor Law Preemption Revisited, 85 Harv.L.Rev. 1337, 1355–1356 (1972).

With this understanding, I join the opinion of the Court.

MR. JUSTICE STEVENS, with whom MR. JUSTICE STEWART and MR. JUSTICE REHNQUIST join, dissenting. * * *

If Congress had focused on the problems presented by partial strike activity, and enacted special legislation dealing with this subject matter, but left the form of the activity disclosed by this record unregulated, the Court's conclusion would be supported by Teamsters Union v. Morton, 377 U.S. 252, 84 S.Ct. 1253, 12 L.Ed.2d 280. But this is not such a case. Despite the numerous statements in the Court's opinion about Congress' intent to leave partial strike activity wholly unregulated, I have found no legislative expression of any such intent nor any evidence that Congress has scrutinized such activity. * * *

7. State laws should not be regarded as neutral if they reflect an accommodation of the special interests of employers, unions, or the public in areas such as employee self-organization, labor disputes, or collective bargaining.

If adherence to the rule of *Briggs-Stratton* would permit the States substantially to disrupt the balance Congress has struck between union and employer, I would readily join in overruling it. But I am not persuaded that partial strike activity is so essential to the bargaining process that the States should not be free to make it illegal. * * *

Problem for Discussion

The Railway Labor Act provides that in the event of a deadlock in the negotiation of new working conditions, the National Mediation Board is to be called in to attempt to settle the dispute without disruption of rail service; failing a settlement after mediation, the Act contemplates the possible use of peaceful economic weapons. There are no unfair labor practice provisions analogous to those in the National Labor Relations Act, and no administrative agency formally responsible for hearing charges of illegal conduct under the Act. After protracted but fruitless negotiations, with the intervention of the National Mediation Board, the Florida East Coast Railway Company (FEC) unilaterally changed its employees' rates of pay and working conditions. In response, the operating employees called a strike and picketed various locations at which FEC carried on its business, including the rail terminal owned by the Jacksonville Terminal Company. The Terminal Company, seeking to limit the physical scope of the picketing—which was being carried on at all of the entrances to the terminal—secured a state-court injunction barring picketing except at entrances reserved for FEC employees. The court concluded that, in spite of the tolerance of the Railway Labor Act for peaceful strikes and picketing in "major" disputes (i. e., over contract negotiations), Congress could not have intended to permit the kind of secondary boycott that would result from picketing elsewhere than at the FEC entrances. The case has reached the United States Supreme Court, where the union argues that the federal Constitution requires the dismissal of the complaint. What are the union's arguments? How should the Court rule? See *Brotherhood of R.R. Trainmen* v. *Jacksonville Terminal Co.*, 394 U.S. 369, 89 S.Ct. 1109, 22 L.Ed.2d 344 (1969).

The *Wisconsin Employment Relations Commission* case placed particular emphasis on the likely intention of Congress to shelter the union activity involved there against government regulation; but it also acknowledged that other Court decisions have rested on a theory of primary jurisdiction and it suggested that both theories have vitality and that a claim of preemption can be sustained if soundly based on either. The cases studied thus far, therefore, appear to carve out an almost boundless territory for preemption of state law and state jurisdiction. At the same time, however, either the Court or Congress has provided for a number of issues as to which the NLRB does not have exclusive jurisdiction: where the activity regulated is "a merely peripheral concern of the Labor Management Relations Act," violence and other conduct which "touches interests deeply rooted in local feeling and responsibility," and the actions itemized by Justice White dissenting in the *Lockridge* case. (In many of those actions, however, it should be noted that the applicable substantive rules of law which are to be applied in the state courts are federal rather than state rules, such as in actions for breach of a labor contract, actions for breach of the duty of fair representation, and claims against secondary boycotts under Section 303.)

More recently, there appears to have been a retreat from the broadest implications of the Supreme Court decisions already read, and the articulation by the Court of new considerations which justtify state intervention in labor disputes. For some, this conjures up images of a return to unwanted and unsympathetic judicial intrusion in peaceful industrial confrontations, generally to the disadvantage of the union movement. For others, this trend (if such there be) reflects a just desire to afford some fair forum and expeditious relief against clear violations of private rights. The three cases that follow—along with the *Malone* case, at page 923 supra —illustrate this recent development. Not surprisingly, the Court is sharply split on almost all of these issues. (These cases are discussed in Cox, Recent Developments in Federal Labor Law Preemption, 41 Ohio St.L.J. 277 (1980).)

FARMER v. UNITED BHD. OF CARPENTERS AND JOINERS OF AMERICA, LOCAL 25

Supreme Court of the United States, 1977.
430 U.S. 290, 97 S.Ct. 1056, 51 L.Ed.2d 338.

MR. JUSTICE POWELL delivered the opinion of the Court.

The issue in this case is whether the National Labor Relations Act, as amended, pre-empts a tort action brought in state court by a union member against the union and its officials to recover damages for the intentional infliction of emotional distress.

I

Petitioner Richard T. Hill [8] was a carpenter and a member of Local 25 of the United Brotherhood of Carpenters and Joiners of America. Local 25 (the Union) operates an exclusive hiring hall for em-

---

8. Hill died after the petition for a writ of certiorari was granted. On June 1, 1976, Joy A. Farmer, special adminis-　trator of Hill's estate, was substituted as petitioner. We will refer to Hill as the petitioner.

ployment referral of carpenters in the Los Angeles area. In 1965, Hill was elected to a three-year term as vice president of the Union. Shortly thereafter sharp disagreement developed between Hill and the Union Business Agent, Earl Daley, and other Union officials over various internal Union policies. According to Hill, the Union then began to discriminate against him in referrals to employers, prompting him to complain about the hiring hall operation within the Union and to the District Council and the International Union. Hill claims that as a result of these complaints he was subjected to a campaign of personal abuse and harassment in addition to continued discrimination in referrals from the hiring hall.[9]

In April of 1969 petitioner filed in Superior Court for the County of Los Angeles an action for damages against the Union, the District Council and the International with which the Union was affiliated, and certain officials of the Union, including Business Agent Daley. In count two of his amended complaint, Hill alleged that the defendants had intentionally engaged in outrageous conduct, threats, and intimidation, and had thereby caused him to suffer grievous emotional distress resulting in bodily injury. In three other counts, he alleged that the Union had discriminated against him in referrals for employment because of his dissident intra-Union political activities, that the Union had breached the hiring hall provisions of the collective-bargaining agreement between it and a contractors association by failing to refer him on a nondiscriminatory basis, and that the failure to comply with the collective-bargaining agreement also constituted a breach of his membership contract with the Union. He sought $500,-000 in actual, and $500,000 in punitive, damages.

The Superior Court sustained a demurrer to the allegations of discrimination and breach of contract on the ground that federal law pre-empted state jurisdiction over them, but allowed the case to go to trial on the allegations in count two. Hill attempted to prove that the Union's campaign against him included "frequent public ridicule," "incessant verbal abuse," and refusals to refer him to jobs in accordance with the rules of the hiring hall. The defendants countered with evidence that the hiring hall was operated in a nondiscriminatory manner. The trial court instructed the jury that in order to recover damages Hill had to prove by a preponderance of the evidence that the defendants intentionally and by outrageous conduct had caused him to suffer severe emotional distress. The court defined severe emotional distress as "any highly unpleasant mental reaction such as fright, grief, shame, humiliation, embarrassment, anger, chagrin,

9. According to Hill, the Union accomplished this discrimination by removing his name from the top of the out-of-work list and placing it at the bottom, by referring him to jobs of short duration when more desirable work was available, and by referring him to jobs for which he was not qualified.

disappointment, or worr[y]." The injury had to be "severe," which in this context meant

> "substantial or enduring, as distinguished from transitory or trivial. It must be of such a substantial quantity or enduring quality that no reasonable man in a civilized society should be expected to endure it. Liability does not extend to mere insults, indignities, annoyances, petty or other trivialities."

The court also instructed that the National Labor Relations Board (the Board) would not have jurisdiction to compensate petitioner for injuries such as emotional distress, pain and suffering, and medical expenses, nor would it have authority to award punitive damages. The court refused to give a requested instruction to the effect that the jury could not consider any evidence regarding discrimination with respect to employment opportunities or hiring procedures.

The jury returned a verdict of $7,500 actual damages and $175,-000 punitive damages against the Union, the District Council, and Business Agent Daley, and the trial court entered a judgment on the verdict.

The California Court of Appeal reversed. 49 Cal.App.3d 614, 122 Cal.Rptr. 722. Relying on this Court's decisions in Motor Coach Employees v. Lockridge, 403 U.S. 274, 91 S.Ct. 1909, 29 L.Ed.2d 473 (1971); Plumbers' Union v. Borden, 373 U.S. 690, 83 S.Ct. 1423, 10 L. Ed.2d 638 (1963); Iron Workers v. Perko, 373 U.S. 701, 83 S.Ct. 1429, 10 L.Ed.2d 646 (1963); and San Diego Building Trades Council v. Garmon, 359 U.S. 236, 79 S.Ct. 773, 3 L.Ed.2d 775 (1959), the Court of Appeal held that the state courts had no jurisdiction over the complaint since the "crux" of the action concerned employment relations and involved conduct arguably subject to the jurisdiction of the National Labor Relations Board. The Court remanded "with instructions to render judgment for the defendants and dismiss the action." 49 Cal.App.3d, at 631, 122 Cal.Rptr., at 732. The California Supreme Court denied review.

We granted certiorari to consider the applicability of the preemption doctrine to cases of this nature, 423 U.S. 1086, 96 S.Ct. 876, 47 L.Ed.2d 96 (1976). For the reasons set forth below we vacate the judgment of the Court of Appeal and remand for further proceedings.

II

* * * Judicial experience with numerous approaches to the pre-emption problem in the labor law area eventually led to the general rule set forth in *Garmon*, 359 U.S., at 244, 79 S.Ct., at 779, and recently reaffirmed in both *Lockridge*, 403 U.S., at 291, 91 S.Ct., at

1920, and Lodge 76, International Association of Machinists and Aerospace Workers v. Wisconsin Employment Relations Comm'n, 427 U.S. 132, 138–141, 96 S.Ct. 2548, 2552–2553, 49 L.Ed.2d 396 (1976):

> "When it is clear or may fairly be assumed that the activities which a State purports to regulate are protected by § 7 of the National Labor Relations Act, or constitute an unfair labor practice under § 8, due regard for the federal enactment requires that state jurisdiction must yield. To leave the States free to regulate conduct so plainly within the central aim of federal regulation involves too great a danger of conflict between power asserted by Congress and requirements imposed by state law." 359 U.S., at 244, 79 S.Ct., at 779.

But the same considerations that underlie the *Garmon* rule have led the Court to recognize exceptions in appropriate classes of cases. * * *

The nature of the inquiry is perhaps best illustrated by Linn v. Plant Guard Workers, 383 U.S. 53, 86 S.Ct. 657, 15 L.Ed.2d 582 (1966). Linn, an assistant manager of Pinkerton's National Detective Agency, filed a diversity action in federal court against a union, two of its officers, and a Pinkerton employee, alleging that the defendants had circulated a defamatory statement about him in violation of state law. If unfair labor practice charges had been filed, the Board might have found that the union violated § 8 by intentionally circulating false statements during an organizational campaign, or that the issuance of the malicious statements during the campaign had such a significant effect as to require that the election be set aside. Under a formalistic application of *Garmon*, the libel suit could have been pre-empted.

But a number of factors influenced the Court to depart from the *Garmon* rule. First, the Court noted that the underlying conduct— the intentional circulation of defamatory material known to be false —was not protected under the Act, 383 U.S., at 61, 86 S.Ct., at 662, and there was thus no risk that permitting the state cause of action to proceed would result in state regulation of conduct that Congress intended to protect. Second, the Court recognized that there was " 'an overriding state interest' " in protecting residents from malicious libels, and that this state interest was " 'deeply rooted in local feeling and responsibility.' " Id., at 61, 62, 86 S.Ct., at 663. Third, the Court reasoned that there was little risk that the state cause of action would interfere with the effective administration of national labor policy. The Board's § 8 unfair labor practice proceeding would focus only on whether the statements were misleading or coercive; whether the statements also were defamatory would be of no relevance to the Board's performance of its functions. Id., at 63, 86 S.Ct., at 663. Moreover, the Board would lack authority to provide the defamed individual with damages or other relief. Ibid. Conversely, the state law action would be unconcerned with whether the statements were coercive or misleading in the labor context, and in any event the court would have power to award Linn relief only if the statements were defamatory. Taken together, these factors justified an exception to the pre-emption rule.

The Court was careful, however, to limit the scope of that exception. To minimize the possibility that state libel suits would either dampen the free discussion characteristic of labor disputes or become a weapon of economic coercion, the Court adopted by analogy the standards enunciated in New York Times Co. v. Sullivan, 376 U.S. 254, 84 S.Ct. 710, 11 L.Ed.2d 686 (1964), and held that state damage actions in this context would escape pre-emption only if limited to defamatory statements published with knowledge or reckless disregard of their falsity. The Court also held that a complainant could recover damages only upon proof that the statements had caused him injury, including general injury to reputation, consequent mental suffering, alienation of associates, specific items of pecuniary loss, or any other form of harm recognized by state tort law. The Court stressed the responsibility of the trial judge to assure that damages were not excessive.

Similar reasoning underlies the exception to the pre-emption rule in cases involving violent tortious activity. Nothing in the federal labor statutes protects or immunizes from state action violence or the threat of violence in a labor dispute, Automobile Workers v. Russell, 356 U.S. 634, 640, 78 S.Ct. 932, 935, 2 L.Ed.2d 1030 (1958); id., at 649, 78 S.Ct., at 941 (Warren, C. J., dissenting); United Construction Workers v. Laburnum Construction Corp., 347 U.S. 656, 666, 74 S.Ct. 833, 838, 98 L.Ed. 1025 (1954), and thus there is no risk that state damage actions will fetter the exercise of rights protected by the NL RA. On the other hand, our cases consistently have recognized the historic state interest in "such traditionally local matters as public safety and order and the use of streets and highways." Allen-Bradley Local v. Wisconsin Employment Relations Board, 315 U.S. 740, 749, 62 S.Ct. 820, 825, 86 L.Ed. 1154 (1942). And, as with the defamation actions preserved by Linn, state court actions to redress injuries caused by violence or threats of violence are consistent with effective administration of the federal scheme: such actions can be adjudicated without regard to the merits of the underlying labor controversy. Automobile Workers v. Russell, supra, 356 U.S., at 649, 78 S. Ct., at 941 (Warren, C. J., dissenting).

Although cases like *Linn* and *Russell* involve state law principles with only incidental application to conduct occurring in the course of a labor dispute, it is well settled that the general applicability of a state cause of action is not sufficient to exempt it from pre-emption. "[I]t [has not] mattered whether the States have acted through laws of broad general application rather than laws specifically directed towards the governance of industrial relations." [10] *Garmon,* 359 U.S., at 246, 79 S.Ct., at 779. Instead, the cases reflect a balanced inquiry into such factors as the nature of the federal and state interests in regulation and the potential for interference with federal regulation. As was said in Vaca v. Sipes, 386 U.S., at 180, 87 S.Ct., at 911, our cases "demonstrate that the decision to pre-empt federal and state court jurisdiction over a given class of cases must depend upon the nature of the particular interests being asserted and the effect upon the administration of national labor policies of concurrent judicial and administrative remedies."

III

In count two of his amended complaint, Hill alleged that the defendants had intentionally engaged in "outrageous conduct, threats, intimidation, and words" which caused Hill to suffer "grievous mental and emotional distress as well as great physical damage." In the context of Hill's other allegations of discrimination in hiring hall referrals, these allegations of tortious conduct might form the basis for unfair labor practice charges before the Board. On this basis a rigid application of the *Garmon* doctrine might support the conclusion of the California courts that Hill's entire action was preempted by federal law. Our cases indicate, however, that inflexible application of the doctrine is to be avoided, especially where the state has a substantial interest in regulation of the conduct at issue and the State's in-

10. In Plumbers' Union v. Borden, 373 U.S. 690, 83 S.Ct. 1423, 10 L.Ed.2d 638 (1963), for example, an employee sued his union, which operated a hiring hall, claiming that the union had arbitrarily refused to refer him for employment on one particular occasion. He alleged that the union's conduct constituted both tortious interference with his right to contract for employment and breach of a promise, implicit in his membership arrangement with the union, not to discriminate unfairly against any member or deny him the right to work. Under these circumstances, concurrent state court jurisdiction would have impaired significantly the functioning of the federal system. If unfair labor practice charg-

es had been filed, the Board might have concluded that the refusal to refer Borden was due to a lawful hiring hall practice, see Teamsters Local 357 v. Labor Board, 365 U.S. 667, 81 S.Ct. 835, 6 L.Ed.2d 11 (1961). Board approval of various hiring hall practices would be meaningless if state courts could declare those procedures violative of the contractual rights implicit between a member and his union. Accordingly, the state cause of action was pre-empted under *Garmon.* Similar reasoning prompted the Court to apply the *Garmon* rule in the companion case of Iron Workers v. Perko, 373 U.S. 701, 83 S.Ct. 1429, 10 L.Ed.2d 646 (1963).

terest is one that does not threaten undue interference with the federal regulatory scheme. With respect to Hill's claims of intentional infliction of emotional distress, we cannot conclude that Congress intended exclusive jurisdiction to lie in the Board.

No provision of the National Labor Relations Act protects the "outrageous conduct" complained of by petitioner Hill in the second count of the complaint. Regardless of whether the operation of the hiring hall was lawful or unlawful under federal statutes, there is no federal protection for conduct on the part of union officers which is so outrageous that "no reasonable man in a civilized society should be expected to endure it." Thus, as in Linn v. Plant Guard Workers, 383 U.S. 53, 86 S.Ct. 657, 15 L.Ed.2d 582 (1966), and Automobile Workers v. Russell, 356 U.S. 634, 78 S.Ct. 932, 2 L.Ed.2d 1030 (1958), permitting the exercise of state jurisdiction over such complaints does not result in state regulation of federally protected conduct.

The State, on the other hand, has a substantial interest in protecting its citizens from the kind of abuse of which Hill complained. That interest is no less worthy of recognition because it concerns protection from emotional distress caused by outrageous conduct, rather than protection from physical injury, as in *Russell*, or damage to reputation, as in *Linn*. Although recognition of the tort of intentional infliction of emotional distress is a comparatively recent development in state law, see Prosser, Law of Torts, 49–50, 56 (4th ed.), our decisions permitting the exercise of state jurisdiction in tort actions based on violence or defamation have not rested on the history of the tort at issue, but rather on the nature of the State's interest in protecting the health and well-being of its citizens.

There is, to be sure, some risk that the state cause of action for infliction of emotional distress will touch on an area of primary federal concern. Hill's complaint itself highlights this risk. In those counts of the complaint that the trial court dismissed, Hill alleged discrimination against him in hiring hall referrals, which were also alleged to be violations of both the collective-bargaining agreement and the membership contract. These allegations, if sufficiently supported before the National Labor Relations Board, would make out an unfair labor practice and the Superior Court considered them preempted by the federal Act.[11] Even in count two of the complaint Hill

---

11. Whether a hiring hall practice is discriminatory and therefore violative of federal law is a determination Congress has entrusted to the Board. See Teamsters Local v. Labor Board, 365 U.S. 667, 81 S.Ct. 835, 6 L.Ed.2d 11 (1961). Whether there is federal preemption with respect to allegations of breach of a *contractual* obligation depends upon the nature of the obligation and the alleged breach. See Motor Coach Employees v. Lockridge, 403 U.S., at 292–297, 298–301, 91 S.Ct., at 1920–1923, 1925. Casting a complaint in terms of breach of a *membership agreement* does not necessarily insulate a state court action from application of the pre-emption doctrine.

made allegations of discrimination in "job-dispatching procedures" and "work assignments" which, standing alone, might well be preempted as the exclusive concern of the Board. The occurrence of the abusive conduct, with which the state tort action is concerned, in such a context of federally prohibited discrimination suggests a potential for interference with the federal scheme of regulation.

Viewed, however, in light of the discrete concerns of the federal scheme and the state tort law, that potential for interference is insufficient to counterbalance the legitimate and substantial interest of the State in protecting its citizens. If the charges in Hill's complaint were filed with the Board, the focus of any unfair labor practice proceeding would be on whether the statements or conduct on the part of union officials discriminated or threatened discrimination against him in employment referrals for reasons other than failure to pay union dues. Whether the statements or conduct of the respondents also caused Hill severe emotional distress and physical injury would play no role in the Board's disposition of the case, and the Board could not award Hill damages for pain, suffering, or medical expenses. Conversely, the state court tort action can be adjudicated without resolution of the "merits" of the underlying labor dispute. Recovery for the tort of emotional distress under California law requires proof that the defendant intentionally engaged in outrageous conduct causing the plaintiff to sustain mental distress. State Rubbish Collectors Assn. v. Siliznoff, 38 Cal.2d 330, 240 P.2d 282 (1952); Alcorn v. Anbro Engineering, Inc., 2 Cal.3d 493, 86 Cal.Rptr. 88, 468 P.2d 216 (1970). The state court need not consider, much less resolve, whether a union discriminated or threatened to discriminate against an employee in terms of employment opportunities. To the contrary, the tort action can be resolved without reference to any accommodation of the special interests of unions and members in the hiring hall context.

On balance, we cannot conclude that Congress intended to oust state court jurisdiction over actions for tortious activity such as that alleged in this case. At the same time, we reiterate that concurrent state court jurisdiction cannot be permitted where there is a realistic threat of interference with the federal regulatory scheme. Union discrimination in employment opportunities cannot itself form the underlying "outrageous" conduct on which the state court tort action is based; to hold otherwise would undermine the pre-emption principle. Nor can threats of such discrimination suffice to sustain state

See n. 10, supra. Allegations of breach of the contract between the union and the employer stand on different ground, since, as noted earlier § 301 of the Labor-Management Relations Act, 61 Stat. 156, 29 U.S.C.A. § 185, authorizes suits for breach of a *collective-bargaining agreement* even if the breach is an unfair labor practice within the Board's jurisdiction.

court jurisdiction. It may well be that the threat, or actuality, of employment discrimination will cause a union member considerable emotional distress and anxiety. But something more is required before concurrent state court jurisdiction can be permitted. Simply stated, it is essential that the state tort be either unrelated to employment discrimination or a function of the particularly abusive manner in which the discrimination is accomplished or threatened rather than a function of the actual or threatened discrimination itself.[12]

Two further limitations deserve emphasis. Our decision rests in part on our understanding that California law permits recovery only for emotional distress sustained as a result of "outrageous" conduct. The potential for undue interference with federal regulation would be intolerable if state tort recoveries could be based on the type of robust language and clash of strong personalities that may be commonplace in various labor contexts. We also repeat that state trial courts have the responsibility in cases of this kind to assure that the damages awarded are not excessive. See Linn v. Plant Guard Workers, 383 U. S., at 65–66, 86 S.Ct., at 664.

IV

Although the second count of petitioner's complaint alleged the intentional infliction of emotional distress, it is clear from the record that the trial of that claim was not in accord with the standards discussed above. The evidence supporting the verdict in Hill's favor focuses less on the alleged campaign of harassment, public ridicule, and verbal abuse, than on the discriminatory refusal to dispatch him to any but the briefest and least desirable jobs; and no appropriate instruction distinguishing the two categories of evidence was given to the jury. See n. 12, supra. The consequent risk that the jury verdict represented damages for employment discrimination rather than for instances of intentional infliction of emotional distress precludes reinstatement of the judgment of the Superior Court.

The Judgment of the Court of Appeal is vacated, and the case is remanded to that court for further proceedings not inconsistent with this opinion.

It is so ordered.

12. In view of the potential for interference with the federal scheme of regulation, the trial court should be sensitive to the need to minimize the jury's exposure to evidence of employment discrimination in cases of this sort. Where evidence of discrimination is necessary to establish the context in which the state claim arose, the trial court should instruct the jury that the fact of employment discrimination (as distinguished from attendant tortious conduct under state law) should not enter into the determination of liability or damages.

Problems for Discussion

1. In determining whether or not the Union is liable in tort, will most juries succeed in separating the Union's discriminatory referral practices, as such, from the abusive manner in which those practices were implemented? In determining compensatory damages, will most juries succeed in ignoring the wronged employee's loss of earnings, resulting from hiring hall non-referrals?

Does the Court's decision not invite resort to state courts and juries to determine substantially the same issues which the NLRB would address in a Section 8(b)(2) proceeding? If so, is this at all salutary? Is it constitutional?

2. Reexamine the synopses of the different opinions written by the Justices in the *Lockridge* case, page 934 supra, and compare them with the Court's unanimous decision in *Farmer*. Has *Lockridge* been effectively overruled? Consult particularly footnotes 10 and 11 of the *Farmer* opinion. Have *Borden* and *Perko* now been re-construed to stand for the proposition that preemption is appropriate in such cases not because of NLRB primary jurisdiction over unfair labor practices but rather because of likely federal protection for the union's conduct?

3. In the *Lockridge* case, the complaint was in two counts, one charging that the suspension from union membership was a contractual violation of the union constitution and bylaws, and the other charging that the union "acted wantonly, wilfully and wrongfully and without just cause, and * * * deprived plaintiff of his * * * employment with Greyhound Corporation * * * and plaintiff has been harassed and subject to mental anguish." Had the trial court sustained the jury's verdict under the latter theory (rather than under the theory of contract breach), should the Supreme Court have decided the case differently?

Had Lockridge been able to prove that his suspension from union membership and his discharge resulted not from a mere misinterpretation by the union of the constitution, bylaws and labor contract but rather from bad faith and hostility on the part of the union (did not the record in fact suggest precisely that?), would there not have been a justiciable claim in the state court for breach of the federal duty of fair representation?

4. After studying the materials on the Duty of Fair Representation, infra, the student should consider the following question: Could plaintiff Hill have sued, in a state court, for breach of the duty of fair representation, and claimed among other elements of relief money damages for emotional suffering? If this would permit the jury to address both the "discrimination" and "abusive manner" issues, and to award full damages, why did the Court in *Farmer* struggle so hard to justify state-court jurisdiction?

5. In the proceedings below in *Farmer*, the state trial court entered a judgment, based on a jury verdict, in the amount of $7,500 actual damages and $175,000 punitive damages. Had the issue been properly raised on appeal, should the judgment for punitive damages have been reversed? Com-

pare IBEW v. Foust, page 1000 infra, which holds that punitive damages may not be awarded against a union for violating its duty of fair representation.

6. A union, recently certified as bargaining representative for the company's production and maintenance workers, initiated a vigorous campaign to organize those within the bargaining unit who had not yet become members. Part of its campaign was the publication in its newsletter of a list of names of those in the unit who had not yet applied for membership, with the term "Scabs" predominantly displayed at the head of the list. After having twice seen his name on this list, Austin, a nonunion employee, informed union officials that he intended to sue the union if this coercive listing was continued. Thereafter, the list appeared again, this time with a definition, borrowed from the author Jack London: "After God had finished the rattlesnake, the toad and the vampire, He had some awful substance left with which He made a scab. A scab is a two-legged animal with a corkscrew soul, a water brain and a combination backbone of jelly and glue * * *." Austin promptly instituted an action against the union in the state court for defamation. The union moved to dismiss, arguing that state-court jurisdiction was preempted by the National Labor Relations Act. Should the union's motion be granted? See *Old Dominion Branch 496, Letter Carriers* v. *Austin*, 418 U.S. 264, 94 S.Ct. 2770, 41 L.Ed.2d 745 (1974).

SEARS, ROEBUCK & CO. v. SAN DIEGO COUNTY DIST. COUNCIL OF CARPENTERS

Supreme Court of the United States, 1978.
436 U.S. 180, 98 S.Ct. 1745, 56 L.Ed.2d 209.

MR. JUSTICE STEVENS delivered the opinion of the Court.

The question in this case is whether the National Labor Relations Act, as amended, deprives a state court of the power to entertain an action by an employer to enforce state trespass laws against picketing which is arguably—but not definitely—prohibited or protected by federal law.

I

On October 24, 1973, two business representatives of respondent Union visited the department store operated by petitioner (Sears) in Chula Vista, Cal., and determined that certain carpentry work was being performed by men who had not been dispatched from the Union hiring hall. Later that day, the Union agents met with the store manager and requested that Sears either arrange to have the work performed by a contractor who employed dispatched carpenters or agree in writing to abide by the terms of the Union's master labor agreement with respect to the dispatch and use of carpenters. The

Sears manager stated that he would consider the request, but he never accepted or rejected it.

Two days later the Union established picket lines on Sears' property. The store is located in the center of a large rectangular lot. The building is surrounded by walkways and a large parking area. A concrete wall at one end separates the lot from residential property; the other three sides adjoin public sidewalks which are adjacent to the public streets. The pickets patrolled either on the privately owned walkways next to the building or in the parking area a few feet away. They carried signs indicating that they were sanctioned by the "Carpenters Trade Union." The picketing was peaceful and orderly.

Sears' security manager demanded that the Union remove the pickets from Sears' property. The Union refused, stating that the pickets would not leave unless forced to do so by legal action. On October 29, Sears filed a verified complaint in the Superior Court of California seeking an injunction against the continuing trespass; the court entered a temporary restraining order enjoining the Union from picketing on Sears' property. The Union promptly removed the pickets to the public sidewalks. On November 21, 1973, after hearing argument on the question whether the Union's picketing on Sears' property was protected by state or federal law, the court entered a preliminary injunction. The California Court of Appeals affirmed. While acknowledging the pre-emption guidelines set forth in San Diego Union v. Garmon, 359 U.S. 236, 79 S.Ct. 773, 3 L.Ed.2d 775, the court held that the Union's continuing trespass fell within the longstanding exception for conduct which touched interests so deeply rooted in local feeling and responsibility that pre-emption could not be inferred in the absence of clear evidence of congressional intent.

The Supreme Court of California reversed. It concluded that the picketing was arguably protected by § 7 because it was intended to secure work for Union members and to publicize Sears' undercutting of the prevailing area standards for the employment of carpenters. The court reasoned that the trespassory character of the picketing did not disqualify it from arguable protection, but was merely a factor which the National Labor Relations Board would consider in determining whether or not it was in fact protected. The court also considered it "arguable" that the Union had engaged in recognitional picketing subject to § 8(b)(7)(C) of the Act which could not continue for more than 30 days without petitioning for a representation election. Because the picketing was both arguably protected by § 7 and arguably prohibited by § 8, the court held that state jurisdiction was pre-empted under the *Garmon* guidelines.

Since the Wagner Act was passed in 1935, this Court has not decided whether, or under what circumstances, a state court has power to enforce local trespass laws against a union's peaceful picketing. The obvious importance of this problem led us to grant certiorari in this case.   430 U.S. 905, 97 S.Ct. 1172, 51 L.Ed.2d 580.

II

We start from the premise that the Union's picketing on Sears' property after the request to leave was a continuing trespass in violation of state law. We note, however, that the scope of the controversy in the state court was limited. Sears asserted no claim that the picketing itself violated any state or federal law. It sought simply to remove the pickets from its property to the public walkways, and the injunction issued by the state court was strictly confined to the relief sought. Thus, as a matter of state law, the location of the picketing was illegal but the picketing itself was unobjectionable.

As a matter of federal law, the legality of the picketing was unclear. Two separate theories would support an argument by Sears that the picketing was prohibited by § 8 of the NLRA and a third theory would support an argument by the Union that the picketing was protected by § 7.   Under each of these theories the Union's purpose would be of critical importance.

If an object of the picketing was to force Sears into assigning the carpentry work away from its employees to Union members dispatched from the hiring hall, the picketing may have been prohibited by § 8(b)(4)(D). Alternatively, if an object of the picketing was to coerce Sears into signing a prehire or members-only type agreement with the Union, the picketing was at least arguably subject to the prohibition on recognitional picketing contained in § 8(b)(7)(C). Hence, if Sears had filed an unfair labor practice charge against the Union, the Board's concern would have been limited to the question whether the Union's picketing had an objective proscribed by the Act; the location of the picketing would have been irrelevant.

On the other hand, the Union contends that the sole objective of its action was to secure compliance by Sears with area standards, and therefore the picketing was protected by § 7. Longshoremen v. Ariadne Co., 397 U.S. 195, 90 S.Ct. 872, 25 L.Ed.2d 218. Thus, if the Union had filed an unfair labor practice charge under § 8(a)(1) when Sears made a demand that the pickets leave its property, it is at least arguable that the Board would have found Sears guilty of an unfair labor practice.

Our second premise, therefore is that the picketing was both arguably prohibited and arguably protected by federal law. The case is not, however, one in which "it is clear or may fairly be assumed" that the subject matter which the state court sought to regulate—that is, the location of the picketing—is either prohibited or protected by the Federal Act.

III

In San Diego Building Trades Council v. Garmon, 359 U.S. 236, 79 S.Ct. 773, 3 L.Ed.2d 775, the Court made two statements which have come to be accepted as the general guidelines for deciphering the unexpressed intent of Congress regarding the permissible scope of state regulation of activity touching upon labor-management relations. The first related to activity which is clearly protected or prohibited by the federal statute. The second articulated a more sweeping prophylactic rule:

> "When an activity is arguably subject to § 7 or § 8 of the Act, the States as well as the federal courts must defer to the exclusive competence of the National Labor Relations Board if the danger of state interference with national policy is to be averted." Id., at 245, 79 S.Ct., at 780.

 * * * [T]he Court has refused to apply the *Garmon* guidelines in a literal, mechanical fashion. This refusal demonstrates that "the decision to pre-empt * * * state court jurisdiction over a given class of cases must depend upon the nature of the particular interests being asserted and the effect upon the administration of national labor policies" of permitting the state court to proceed. Vaca v. Sipes, 386 U.S. 171, 180, 87 S.Ct. 903, 911, 17 L.Ed.2d 842.

With this limitation in mind, we turn to the question whether pre-emption is justified in a case of this kind under either the arguably protected or the arguably prohibited branch of the *Garmon* doctrine. While the considerations underlying the two categories overlap, they differ in significant respects and therefore it is useful to review them separately. We therefore first consider whether the arguable illegality of the picketing as a matter of federal law should oust the state court of jurisdiction to enjoin its trespassory aspects. Thereafter, we consider whether the arguably protected character of the picketing should have that effect.

IV

 * * *

The leading case holding that when an employer grievance against a union may be presented to the National Labor Relations Board it is not subject to litigation in a state tribunal is Garner v. Teamsters Union, 346 U.S. 485, 74 S.Ct. 161, 98 L.Ed. 228. *Garner* involved peaceful organizational picketing which arguably violated

§ 8(b)(2) of the Federal Act. A Pennsylvania equity court held that the picketing violated the Pennsylvania Labor Relations Act and therefore should be enjoined. The State Supreme Court reversed because the union conduct fell within the jurisdiction of the National Labor Relations Board to prevent unfair labor practices.

This Court affirmed because Congress had "taken in hand this particular type of controversy * * * [i]n language almost identical to parts of the Pennsylvania statute," 346 U.S., at 488, 74 S.Ct., at 165. * * * The reason for pre-emption was clearly articulated:

"Congress evidently considered that centralized administration of specially designed procedures was necessary to obtain uniform application of its substantive rules and to avoid these diversities and conflicts likely to result from a variety of local procedures and attitudes toward labor controversies. Indeed, Pennsylvania passed a statute the same year as its labor relations Act reciting abuses of the injunction in labor litigations attributable more to procedure and usage than to substantive rules. A multiplicity of tribunals and a diversity of procedures are quite as apt to produce incompatible or conflicting adjudications as are different rules of substantive law. * * * "The conflict lies in remedies * * *. [W]hen two separate remedies are brought to bear on the same activity, a conflict is imminent." Id., at 498–499, 74 S.Ct., at 170.

This reasoning has its greatest force when applied to state laws regulating the relations between employees, their union, and their employer. It may also apply to certain laws of general applicability which are occasionally invoked in connection with a labor dispute. Thus, a State's antitrust law may not be invoked to enjoin collective activity which is also arguably prohibited by the Federal Act. Capital Service, Inc. v. Labor Board, 347 U.S. 501, 74 S.Ct. 699, 98 L.Ed. 887; Weber v. Anheuser Busch, Inc., 348 U.S. 468, 75 S.Ct. 480, 99 L.Ed. 546. In each case, the pertinent inquiry is whether the two potentially conflicting statutes were "brought to bear on precisely the same conduct." Id., at 479, 75 S.Ct., at 487.[13]

13. "Respondent argues that Missouri is not prohibiting the IAM's conduct for any reason having to do with labor relations but rather because that conduct is in contravention of a state law which deals generally with restraint of trade. It distinguishes *Garner* on the ground that there the State and Congress were both attempting to regulate labor relations as such.

"We do not think this distinction is decisive. In *Garner* the emphasis was not on two conflicting labor statutes but rather on two similar remedies, one state and one federal, brought to bear on precisely the same conduct." 348 U.S., at 479, 75 S.Ct., at 487.

Motor Coach Employees v. Lockridge, 403 U.S. 274, 91 S.Ct. 1909, 29 L.Ed.2d 473, reaffirmed the notion that state regulation of activity arguably prohibited by the federal Act cannot avoid preemption simply because it is pursuant to a law of general application. * * *

On the other hand, the Court has allowed a State to enforce certain laws of general applicability even though aspects of the challenged conduct were arguably prohibited by § 8 of the Taft-Hartley Act. Thus, for example, the Court has upheld state-court jurisdiction over conduct that touches "interests so deeply rooted in local feeling and responsibility that, in the absence of compelling congressional direction, we could not infer that Congress had deprived the States of the power to act." San Diego Building Trades Council v. Garmon, 359 U.S. 236, 244, 79 S.Ct. 773, 779, 3 L.Ed.2d 775.
* * *

[In Farmer v. United Broth. of Carpenters and Joiners, 430 U.S. 290, 97 S.Ct. 1056, 51 L.Ed.2d 338 (1977),] the Court identified those factors which warranted a departure from the general preemption guidelines in the "local interest" cases. Two are relevant to the arguably *prohibited* branch of the *Garmon* doctrine. First, there existed a significant state interest in protecting the citizen from the challenged conduct. Second, although the challenged conduct occurred in the course of a labor dispute and an unfair labor practice charge could have been filed, the exercise of state jurisdiction over the tort claim entailed little risk of interference with the regulatory jurisdiction of the Labor Board. Although the arguable federal violation and the state tort arose in the same factual setting, the respective controversies presented to the state and federal forums would not have been the same.

The critical inquiry, therefore, is not whether the State is enforcing a law relating specifically to labor relations or one of general application but whether the controversy presented to the state court is identical to (as in *Garner*) or different from (as in *Farmer*) that which could have been, but was not, presented to the Labor Board. For it is only in the former situation that a state court's exercise of jurisdiction necessarily involves a risk of interference with the unfair labor practice jurisdiction of the Board which the arguably prohibited branch of the *Garmon* doctrine was designed to avoid.[14]

Pre-emption was required in the Court's view because the state court was exercising jurisdiction over a controversy which was virtually identical to that which could have been presented to the Board. Permitting the state court to exercise jurisdiction pursuant to a law of general application in these circumstances would have entailed a " 'real and immediate' potential for conflict with the federal scheme * * *." Farmer v. Carpenters, 430 U.S., at 301 n. 10, 97 S.Ct., at 1064.

An identical result would undoubtedly obtain were an employer subjected to recognitional or secondary picketing to seek injunctive relief in state court on the theory that the union was tortiously interfering with his freedom to contract. Cf. Retail Clerks International Ass'n v. J. J. Newberry Co., 352 U.S. 987, 77 S.Ct. 386, 1 L.Ed.2d 367, reversing, 78 Idaho 85, 298 P.2d 375 (1956).

14. While the distinction between a law of general applicability and a law expressly governing labor relations is, as we have noted, not dispositive for preemption purposes, it is of course apparent that the latter is more likely

In the present case, the controversy which Sears might have presented to the Labor Board is not the same as the controversy presented to the state court. If Sears had filed a charge, the federal issue would have been whether the picketing had a recognitional or work reassignment objective; decision of that issue would have entailed relatively complex factual and legal determinations completely unrelated to the simple question whether a trespass had occurred. Conversely, in the state action, Sears only challenged the location of the picketing; whether the picketing had an objective proscribed by federal law was irrelevant to the state claim. Accordingly, permitting the state court to adjudicate Sears' trespass claim would create no realistic risk of interference with the Labor Board's primary jurisdiction to enforce the statutory prohibition against unfair labor practices.

The reasons why pre-emption of state jurisdiction is normally appropriate when union activity is arguably prohibited by federal law plainly do not apply to this situation; they therefore are insufficient to preclude a State from exercising jurisdiction limited to the trespassory aspects of that activity.

V

The question whether the arguably protected character of the Union's trespassory picketing provides a sufficient justification for pre-emption of the state court's jurisdiction over Sears' trespass claim involves somewhat different considerations.

Apart from notions of "primary jurisdiction," there would be no objection to state courts and the NLRB exercising concurrent jurisdiction over conduct prohibited by the Federal Act. But there is a constitutional objection to state court interference with conduct actually protected by the Act. Considerations of federal supremacy, therefore, are implicated to a greater extent when labor-related activity is protected than when it is prohibited. Nevertheless, several considerations persuade us that the mere fact that the Union's trespass was *arguably* protected is insufficient to deprive the state court of jurisdiction in this case.

The first is the relative unimportance in this context of the "primary jurisdiction" rationale articulated in *Garmon*. In theory, of course, that rationale supports pre-emption regardless of which section of the NLRA is critical to resolving a controversy which may be subject to the regulatory jurisdiction of the NLRB. Indeed, at first

to involve the accommodation which Congress reserved to the Board. It is also evident that enforcement of a law of general applicability is less likely to generate rules or remedies which conflict with federal labor policy than the invocation of a special remedy under a state labor relations law.

blush, the primary jurisdiction rationale provides stronger support for pre-emption in this case when the analysis is focused upon the arguably protected, rather than the arguably prohibited, character of the Union's conduct. For to the extent that the Union's picketing was arguably protected, there existed a potential overlap beween the controversy presented to the state court and that which the Union might have brought before the NLRB. Prior to granting any relief from the Union's continuing trespass, the state court was obligated to decide that the trespass was not actually protected by federal law, a determination which might entail an accommodation of Sears' property rights and the Union's § 7 rights. In an unfair labor practice proceeding initiated by the Union, the Board might have been required to make the same accommodation.

Although it was theoretically possible for the accommodation issue to be decided either by the state court or by the Labor Board, there was in fact no risk of overlapping jurisdiction in this case. The primary jurisdiction rationale justifies pre-emption only in situations in which an aggrieved party has a reasonable opportunity either to invoke the Board's jurisdiction himself or else to induce his adversary to do so. In this case, Sears could not directly obtain a Board ruling on the question whether the Union's trespass was federally protected. Such a Board determination could have been obtained only if the Union had filed an unfair labor practice charge alleging that Sears had interfered with the Union's § 7 right to engage in peaceful picketing on Sears' property. By demanding that the Union remove its pickets from the store's property, Sears in fact pursued a course of action which gave the Union the opportunity to file such a charge. But the Union's response to Sears' demand foreclosed the possibility of having the accommodation of § 7 and property rights made by the Labor Board; instead of filing a charge with the Board, the Union advised Sears that the pickets would only depart under compulsion of legal process.

In the face of the Union's intransigence, Sears had only three options: permit the pickets to remain on its property; forcefully evict the pickets; or seek the protection of the State's trespass laws. Since the Union's conduct violated state law, Sears legitimately rejected the first option. Since the second option involved a risk of violence, Sears surely had the right—perhaps even the duty—to reject it. Only by proceeding in state court, therefore, could Sears obtain an orderly resolution of the question whether the Union had a federal right to remain on its property.

The primary jurisdiction rationale unquestionably requires that when the same controversy may be presented to the state court or the NLRB, it must be presented to the Board. But that rationale does not extend to cases in which an employer has no acceptable method of invoking, or inducing the Union to invoke, the jurisdiction of the Board. We are therefore persuaded that the primary jurisdiction rationale does not provide a *sufficient* justification for pre-empting state jurisdiction over arguably protected conduct when the party who could have presented the protection issue to the Board has not done so and the other party to the dispute has no acceptable means of doing so.[15]

This conclusion does not, however, necessarily foreclose the possibility that pre-emption may be appropriate. The danger of state interference with federally protected conduct is the principal concern of the second branch of the *Garmon* doctrine. To allow the exercise of state jurisdiction in certain contexts might create a significant risk of misinterpretation of federal law and the consequent prohibition of protected conduct. In those circumstances, it might be reasonable to infer that Congress preferred the costs inherent in a jurisdictional hiatus to the frustration of national labor policy which might accompany the exercise of state jurisdiction. Thus, the acceptability of "arguable protection" as a justification for pre-emption in a given class of cases is, at least in part, a function of the strength of the argument that § 7 does in fact protect the disputed conduct.

The Court has held that state jurisdiction to enforce its laws prohibiting violence, defamation, the intentional infliction of emotional distress, or obstruction of access to property, is not pre-empted by the NLRA. But none of those violations of state law involves protected conduct. In contrast, some violations of state trespass laws may be actually protected by § 7 of the Federal Act.

In NLRB v. Babcock & Wilcox, 351 U.S. 105, 76 S.Ct. 679, 100 L.Ed. 975, for example, the Court recognized that in certain circumstances nonemployee union organizers may have a limited right of access to an employer's premises for the purpose of engaging in organization solicitation. And the Court has indicated that *Babcock* extends to § 7 rights other than organizational activity, though the "locus" of the "accommodation of § 7 rights and private property rights * * * may fall at differing points along the spectrum depending on the nature and strength of the respective § 7 rights and private property rights asserted in any given context." Hudgens v. NLRB, 424 U.S. 507, 96 S.Ct. 1029, 47 L.Ed.2d 196.

---

15. * * * "So long as employers are effectively denied determinations by the NLRB as to whether 'arguably protected' picketing is actually protected except when an employer is willing to threaten or use force to deal with picketing, I would hold that only labor activity determined to be actually, rather than arguably, protected under federal law should be immune from state judicial control. To this extent San Diego Building Trades Council v. Garmon, 359 U.S. 236, 79 S.Ct. 773, 3 L.Ed.2d 775 (1959), should be reconsidered." Longshoremen v. Ariadne Co., 397 U.S., at 201–202, 90 S.Ct., at 875 (Mr. Justice White, concurring).

For purpose of analysis we must assume that the Union could have proved that its picketing was, at least in the absence of a trespass, protected by § 7. The remaining question is whether under *Babcock* the trespassory nature of the picketing caused it to forfeit its protected status. Since it cannot be said with certainty that, if the Union had filed an unfair labor practice charge against Sears, the Board would have fixed the locus of the accommodation at the unprotected end of the spectrum, it is indeed "arguable" that the Union's peaceful picketing, though trespassory, was protected. Nevertheless, permitting state courts to evaluate the merits of an argument that certain trespassory activity is protected does not create an unacceptable risk of interference with conduct which the Board, and a court reviewing the Board's decision, would find protected. For while there are unquestionably examples of trespassory union activity in which the question whether it is protected is fairly debatable, experience under the Act teaches that such situations are rare and that a trespass is far more likely to be unprotected than protected.

Experience with trespassory organizational solicitation by nonemployees is instructive in this regard. While *Babcock* indicates that an employer may not always bar nonemployee union organizers from his property, his right to do so remains the general rule. To gain access, the union has the burden of showing that no other reasonable means of communicating its organizational message to the employees exists or that the employer's access rules discriminate against union solicitation. That the burden imposed on the Union is a heavy one is evidenced by the fact that the balance struck by the Board and the courts under the *Babcock* accommodation principle has rarely been in favor of trespassory organizational activity.

Even on the assumption that picketing to enforce area standards is entitled to the same deference in the *Babcock* accommodation analysis as organizational solicitation,[16] it would be unprotected in most

16. This assumption, however, is subject to serious question. Indeed, several factors make the argument for protection of trespassory area standards picketing as a category of conduct less compelling than that for trespassory organizational solicitation. First, the right to organize is at the very core of the purpose for which the NLRB was enacted. Area standards picketing, in contrast, has only recently been recognized as a § 7 right. Hod Carriers Local 41 (Calumet Contractors Assn.), 133 N.L.R.B. 512. Second, *Babcock* makes clear that the interests being protected by according limited access rights to nonemployee, union organizers are not those of the organizers but of the employees located on the employer's property. The Court indicated that "no * * * obligation is owed nonemployee organizers"; any right they may have to solicit on an employer's property is a derivative of the right of that employer's employees to exercise their organization rights effectively. Area standards picketing, on the other hand, has no such vital link to the employees located on the employer's property. While such picketing may have a beneficial effect on the compensation of those employees, the rationale for protecting area standards picketing is that a union has a legitimate interest in protecting the wage standards of its members who are employed by competitors of the picketed employer.

instances. While there does exist some risk that state courts will on occasion enjoin a trespass that the Board would have protected, the significance of this risk is minimized by the fact that in the cases in which the argument in favor of protection is the strongest, the union is likely to invoke the Board's jurisdiction and thereby avoid the state forum. Whatever risk of an erroneous state court adjudication does exist is outweighed by the anomalous consequence of a rule which would deny the employer access to any forum in which to litigate either the trespass issue or the protection issue in those cases in which the disputed conduct is least likely to be protected by § 7.

If there is a strong argument that the trespass is protected in a particular case, a union can be expected to respond to an employer demand to depart by filing an unfair labor practice charge; the protection question would then be decided by the agency experienced in accommodating the § 7 rights of unions and the property rights of employers in the context of a labor dispute. But if the argument for protection is so weak that it has virtually no chance of prevailing, a trespassing union would be well advised to avoid the jurisdiction of the Board and to argue that the protected character of its conduct deprives the state court of jurisdiction.

As long as the union has a fair opportunity to present the protection issue to the Labor Board, it retains meaningful protection against the risk of error in a state tribunal. In this case the Union failed to invoke the jurisdiction of the Labor Board, and Sears had no right to invoke that jurisdiction and could not even precipitate its exercise without resort to self-help. Because the assertion of state jurisdiction in a case of this kind does not create a significant risk of prohibition of protected conduct, we are unwilling to presume that Congress intended the arguably protected character of the Union's conduct to deprive the California courts of jurisdiction to entertain Sears' trespass action.[17]

---

17. The fact that Sears demanded that the Union discontinue the trespass before it initiated the trespass action is critical to our holding. While it appears that such a demand was a precondition to commencing a trespass action under California law, see Pet. for Cert. A–4, in order to avoid a valid claim of pre-emption it would have been required as a matter of federal law in any event.

The Board has taken the position that "a resort to court action * * * does not violate § 8(a)(1)." NLRB v. Nash-Finch Co., 404 U.S., at 142, 92 S.Ct., at 376. If the employer were not required to demand discontinuation of the trespass before proceeding in state court and the Board did not alter its position in cases of this kind, the union would be deprived of an opportunity to present the protection issue to the agency created by Congress to decide such questions. While the union's failure to invoke the Board's jurisdiction should not be a sufficient basis for pre-empting state jurisdiction, the employer should not be permitted to deprive the union of an opportunity to do so.

The judgment of the Supreme Court of California is therefore reversed and the case is remanded to that court for further proceedings not inconsistent with this opinion.

[The separate concurring opinions of Justices Blackmun and Powell are omitted.]

MR. JUSTICE BRENNAN, with whom MR. JUSTICE STEWART and MR. JUSTICE MARSHALL join, dissenting.

The Court concedes that both the objective and the location of the Union's peaceful, nonobstructive picketing of Sears' store may have been protected under the National Labor Relations Act. Therefore, despite the Court's transparent effort to disguise it, faithful application of the principles of labor law pre-emption established in San Diego Trades Council v. Garmon, 359 U.S. 236, 79 S.Ct. 773, 3 L.Ed.2d 775 (1959), would compel the conclusion that the California Superior Court was powerless to enjoin the Union from picketing on Sears' property: that the trespass was arguably protected is determinative of the state court's lack of jurisdiction, whether or not pre-emption limits an employer's remedies. * * * [T]he *Garmon* test has proved to embody an entirely acceptable, and probably the best possible, accommodation of the competing state-federal interests. That an employer's remedies in consequence may be limited, while anomalous to the Court, produces no positive social harm; on the contrary, the limitation on employer remedies is fully justified both by the ease of application of the test by thousands of state and federal judges and by its effect of averting the danger that state courts may interfere with national labor policy. In sharp contrast, today's decision creates the certain prospect of state-court interference that may seriously erode § 7's protections of labor activities. Indeed, the most serious objection to the decision today is not that it is contrary to the teachings of *stare decisis* but rather that the Court's attempt to create a narrow exception to the principles of *Garmon* promises to be applied by the lower courts so as to disserve the interests protected by the national labor laws.

I

* * * As to arguably prohibited picketing, there is a risk that the state court might misinterpret or misapply the federal prohibition and restrain conduct that Congress may have intended to be free from governmental restraint. But, even when state courts can be depended upon accurately to determine whether conduct is in fact prohibited, local adjudication may disrupt the congressional scheme by resulting in different forms of relief than would adjudication by the NLRB. * * * This aspect of *Garmon* has never operated as a flat prohibition. There are circumstances in which

state courts can be depended upon accurately to determine whether the underlying conduct is prohibited and in which Congress cannot be assumed to have intended to oust state-court jurisdiction. Illustrative are decisions holding that States may regulate mass picketing, obstructive picketing, or picketing that threatens or results in violence, * * * in view of the historic state interest in "such traditionally local matters as public safety and order" * * *. Our decisions leave no doubt that exceptions to the *Garmon* principle are to be recognized only in comparable circumstances. See Farmer v. United Broth. of Carpenters and Joiners, 430 U.S. 290, 297–301, 97 S.Ct. 1056, 1061–1064, 51 L.Ed.2d 338 (1977); Vaca v. Sipes, 386 U.S. 171, 87 S.Ct. 903, 17 L.Ed.2d 842 (1967); Linn v. United Plant Guard Workers, Local 114, 383 U.S. 53, 86 S.Ct. 657, 15 L.Ed.2d 582 (1966).

When, on the other hand, the underlying conduct may be *protected* by the Act, the danger of permitting local adjudications is not that timing or form of relief might be different than the Board would administer, but rather that the local court might restrain conduct that is in fact protected by the Act. This might result not merely from attitudinal differences but even more from unfair procedures or lack of expertise in labor relations matters. The present case illustrates both the nature and magnitude of the danger. Because the location of employee picketing is often determinative of the meaningfulness of the employees' ability to engage in effective communication with their intended audience, employees often have the right to engage in picketing at particular locations, including the private property of another. See Hudgens v. NLRB, 424 U.S. 507, 96 S.Ct. 1029, 47 L.Ed.2d 196 (1975); Scott Hudgens, 230 N.L.R.B. No. 73 (1977); cf. NLRB v. Babcock & Wilcox Co., supra. The California Superior Court here entered an order, *ex parte*, broad enough to prohibit all effective picketing of Sears' store for a period of 35 days. * * * Since labor disputes are usually short lived, this possibly erroneous order may well have irreparably altered the balance of the competing economic forces by prohibiting the Union's use of a permissible economic weapon at a crucial time. Obviously it is not lightly to be inferred that a Congress that provided elaborate procedures for restraint of prohibited picketing and that failed to provide an employer with a remedy against otherwise unprotected picketing could have contemplated that local tribunals with histories of insensitivity to the organizational interests of employees be permitted effectively to enjoin protected picketing.

* * * In any instance in which it can seriously be maintained that the congressionally established scheme protects the employee activity, the assessment of the relative weight of the com-

peting state and federal interests has to be regarded as having been made by Congress. By drafting the statute so as to permit a Board determination that the underlying conduct is in fact within the ambit of § 7's protections, Congress necessarily indicated its view that the historic state interest in regulating the conduct, however defined, may have to yield to the attainment of other objectives and that the State interest thus must be regarded as less than compelling. * * *

II

The present case illustrates both the necessity of this flat rule and the danger of even the slightest deviation from it. The present case of course is a classic one for pre-emption. The question submitted to the state court was whether the Union had a protected right to locate peaceful nonobstructive pickets on the privately owned walkway adjacent to Sears' retail store or on the privately owned parking lot a few feet away.

A

That the trespass was arguably protected could scarcely be clearer. NLRB v. Babcock & Wilcox Co., supra, 351 U.S., at 112, 76 S.Ct., at 684, indicates that trespassory § 7 activity is protected when "reasonable efforts * * * through other available channels" will not enable the Union to reach its intended audience. This standard, which was developed in the context of a rather different factual situation, is but an application of more general principles. "[T]he basic objective of the Act [is] the accommodation of § 7 rights and private property rights 'with as little destruction of one as is consistent with the maintenance of the other.' The locus of that accommodation, however, may fall at differing points along the spectrum depending on the nature and strength of the respective § 7 rights and private property rights asserted in any given context." Hudgens v. NLRB, supra, 424 U.S., at 552, 96 S.Ct., at 1037–38, quoting NLRB v. Babcock & Wilcox Co., supra, 351 U.S., at 112, 76 S.Ct., at 684; see Scott Hudgens, supra, at 7–8.

Here, it can seriously be contended that the locus of the accommodation should be on the side of permitting the trespass. The § 7 interest is strong: the object of the picketing was arguably protected on one of two theories—as "area standards" or as "recognitional" picketing—and the record suggests that the relocation of the picketing to the nearest public area—a public sidewalk 150 to 200 feet away— may have so diluted the picketing's impact as to make it virtually meaningless. The private property interest, in contrast, was exceedingly weak. The picketing was confined to a portion of Sears' property which was open to the public and on which Sears had permitted solicitations by other groups. Thus, while Sears to be sure owned the property, it resembled public property in many respects. Indeed, while Sears' legal position would have been quite different if the lot and walkways had been owned by the city of Chula Vista, it is doubtful that Sears would have been any less angered or upset by the picketing if the property had in fact been public.

But the Court refuses to follow the simple analysis that has been sanctioned by the decisions of the last 20 years. Its reasons for discarding prior teachings, apparently, is a belief that faithful application of *Garmon* to the generic situation presented by this case causes positive social harm. I disagree.

* * * In this circumstance, I think the denial to the employer of a remedy is an entirely acceptable social cost for the benefits of a pre-emption rule that avoids the danger of state-court interference with national labor policy. The Court's arguments to the contrary are singularly unpersuasive. * * * [T]he * * * Court places no great reliance on the likelihood of violence. But the only other reason advanced for a conclusion that *Garmon* produces socially intolerable results is that it is "anomalous" to deny an employer a trespass remedy. Since the Act extensively regulates the conditions under which an employer's proprietary rights must yield to the exercise of § 7 rights, I am at a loss as to why the anomaly here is any greater than that which results from the pre-emption of state remedies against tortious conspiracies, compare § 7 of the Act, with F. Frankfurter and N. Greene, The Labor Injunction, supra, at 26–39, or from the pre-emption of state remedies against non-malicious libels. See Linn v. Plant Guard Workers, supra.

B

That this Court's departure from *Garmon* creates a great risk that protected picketing will be enjoined is amply illustrated by the facts of this case and by the task that was assigned to the California Superior Court. To decide whether the location of the Union's picketing rendered it unlawful, the state court here had to address a host of exceedingly complex labor law questions, which implicated nearly every aspect of the Union's labor dispute with Sears and which were uniquely within the province of the Board. Because it had to assess the "relative strength of the § 7 right," see NLRB v. Hudgens, supra, 424 U.S., at 522, 96 S.Ct., at 1038, its first task necessarily was to determine the nature of the Union's picketing. This picketing could have been characterized in one of three ways: as protected area standards picketing; as prohibited picketing to compel a reassignment of work; or as recognitional picketing that is protected at the outset but prohibited if no petition for a representative election is filed within a reasonable time, not to exceed 30 days. * * * Notably, if the state court concluded that the picketing was prohibited by § 8(b)(4)— or unprotected by § 7 on any other theory—that determination would have been conclusive against respondent: whether or not the state court agreed with the Union's contention that effective communication required that picketing be located on Sears' premises, the court would enjoin the trespassory picketing on the ground that no protected § 7 interest was involved. Obviously, since even the Court admits that the characterization of the picketing "entail[s] relatively complex factual and legal determinations," there is a substantial danger that the state court, lacking the Board's expertise and specialized sensitivity to labor relations matters, would err at the outset and effectively deny respondent the right to engage in any effective § 7 communication.

But even if the state court correctly assesses the § 7 interest, there are a host of other pitfalls. A myriad of factors are or could be relevant to determining whether § 7 protected the trespass: e. g., whether and to what extent relocating the picketing on the nearest public property 150 feet away would have diluted its impact; whether the picketing was characterized as recognitional or area standards; whether or the extent to which Sears had opened the property up to the public or permitted similar solicitation on it; whether it mattered that the picketers did not work for Sears, etc. And if relevant, each of these factors would suggest a number of subsidiary inquiries.

It simply cannot be seriously contended that the thousands of judges, state and federal, throughout the United States can be counted upon accurately to identify the relevant considerations and give each the proper weight in accommodating the respective rights. * * *

[The dissenting Justices also challenged the Court's assertion that trespassory activity by nonemployees will more likely than not be unprotected, and the Court's assertion that unions will be able, by recourse to the National Labor Relations Board, to avoid the adverse consequences of state court jurisdiction.]

IV

* * * [W]hat is far more disturbing than the specific holding in this case is its implications for different generic situations. Whatever the shortcomings of *Garmon*, none can deny the necessity for a rule in this complex area that is capable of uniform application by the lower courts. The Court's new exception to *Garmon* cannot be expected to be correctly applied by those courts and thus most inevitably will threaten erosion of the goal of uniform administration of the national labor laws. * * * It is no answer that errors remain correctible while this Court sits. The burden that will be

thrown upon this Court finally to decide, on an *ad hoc*, generic situation by generic situation basis, whether the employer had a "reasonable opportunity" to obtain a Board determination and, if not, whether the risk of interference outweighs the anomaly of denying the employer a remedy, should give us pause. Inconsistency and error in decisions below may compel review of an inordinate number of cases, lest lower court adjudications threaten irretrievable injury to interests protected by § 7. * * *

Problems for Discussion

1. Is it fair to conclude that, after *Sears*, if conduct is *arguably* protected (and what concerted activity, except for the most egregious, will not be?), state courts will have jurisdiction to construe Section 7 and all NLRB and judicial precedents thereunder; jurisdiction to construe them erroneously, subject only to the remote and long-delayed possibility of correction by the United States Supreme Court; and jurisdiction to issue an injunction mistakenly—unless and until the union "invokes the jurisdiction" of the National Labor Relations Board? Is this consistent with prior Supreme Court decisions?

Is it fair to conclude that, after *Farmer* and *Sears*, the only clearly preempted cases are those in which the plaintiff concedes that the defendant's conduct is clearly protected under Section 7 (and that these cases will be very rare indeed)? Is this consistent with prior Supreme Court decisions? (Consider particularly footnote 15 in the Court's opinion.)

2. How promptly must the state court hold a hearing on the question whether the defendant's conduct is actually protected under Section 7 of the NLRA? Is the state court free to issue an ex parte temporary restraining order without a full adversary hearing on this issue?

3. In state court cases in which the defendant's conduct is arguably protected under Section 7, when will the state court have to stay (or dismiss) the proceeding: When a charge is filed with the NLRB against the employer? When the regional director issues a complaint? When the NLRB requests (or secures) an injunction against the employer pursuant to Section 10(j)? When an Administrative Law Judge (or the NLRB) concludes that the employees' conduct is actually protected?

4. Is the vitality of the Board's decision on remand in Scott Hudgens, supra page 693, impaired by the Court's discussion regarding the lack of Section 7 protection for most trespassory concerted activity?

5. During contract negotiations between the Steelworkers and the Pepsi-Cola Company covering workers at the Miami plant, several employees participated in a work slowdown and were immediately discharged. This triggered a march by nearly 100 employees away from their work stations and to the office of the plant manager. After listening to the em-

ployee protests concerning the discharges, the plant manager announced
that the discharged employees would not be reinstated and he demanded
that the workers return to their work stations or leave the plant.   The
workers returned to their stations but remained there, without working, for
the few hours remaining in their shift.   They did not attempt to damage or
to seize the plant machinery or property, and left the plant at the end of
their shift when ordered to do so by police officers called by the employer.
The employer, alleging that the union and employees had engaged in an unlawful trespassory "sitdown" strike, brought an action for damages.   The
defendants have moved to dismiss the action as beyond the jurisdiction of
the state court.   Should the action be dismissed?   Cf. *NLRB* v. *Pepsi-Cola
Bottling Co.*, 449 F.2d 824 (5th Cir. 1971) cert. denied 407 U.S. 910 (1972).

Would your analysis be affected if the company could prove that certain
minor damage was done to some plant machinery when the employees resisted the attempts of certain foremen to drag them physically from their
work stations?

NEW YORK TEL. CO. v. NEW YORK DEPT. OF LABOR

Supreme Court of the United States, 1979.
440 U.S. 519, 99 S.Ct. 1328, 59 L.Ed.2d 553.

MR. JUSTICE STEVENS announced the judgment of the Court and
an opinion in which MR. JUSTICE WHITE and MR. JUSTICE REHNQUIST
joined.

The question presented is whether the National Labor Relations
Act, as amended, implicitly prohibits the State of New York from paying unemployment compensation to strikers.

Communication Workers of America, AFL–CIO (CWA) represents about 70% of the nonmanagement employees of companies affiliated with the Bell Telephone Company.   In June of 1971, when
contract negotiations had reached an impasse, CWA recommended a
nationwide strike.   The strike commenced on July 14, 1971, and, for
most workers, lasted only a week.   In New York, however, the 38,000
CWA members employed by petitioners remained on strike for seven
months.

New York's unemployment insurance law normally authorizes the
payment of benefits after approximately one week of unemployment.
If a claimant's loss of employment is caused by "a strike, lockout, or
other industrial controversy in the establishment in which he was employed," § 592.1 of the law suspends the payment of benefits for an
additional seven-week period.   In 1971, the maximum weekly benefit
of $75 was payable to an employee whose base salary was at least
$149 per week.

After the eight-week waiting period, petitioners' striking employees began to collect unemployment compensation. During the ensuing five months more than $49 million in benefits were paid to about 33,000 striking employees at an average rate of somewhat less than $75 per week. Because New York's unemployment insurance system is financed primarily by employer contributions based on the benefits paid to former employees of each employer in past years, a substantial part of the cost of these benefits was ultimately imposed on petitioners.

Petitioners brought suit in the United States District Court for the Southern District of New York against the state officials responsible for the administration of the unemployment compensation fund. They sought a declaration that the New York statute authorizing the payment of benefits to strikers conflicts with federal law and is therefore invalid, an injunction against the enforcement of § 592.1, and an award recouping the increased taxes paid in consequence of the disbursement of funds to their striking employees. After an eight-day trial, the District Court granted the requested relief. * * * The Court of Appeals for the Second Circuit reversed. * * *

The importance of the question led us to grant certiorari. 435 U.S. 941. We now affirm. Our decision is ultimately governed by our understanding of the intent of the Congress that enacted the National Labor Relations Act on July 5, 1935, and the Social Security Act on August 14 of the same year. * * *

I

* * * [T]here is no claim in this case that New York has sought to regulate or prohibit any conduct subject to the regulatory jurisdiction of the Labor Board under § 8. Nor are the petitioning employers pursuing any claim of interference with employee rights protected by § 7. The State simply authorized striking employees to receive unemployment benefits, and assessed a tax against the struck employers to pay for some of those benefits, once the economic warfare between the two groups reached its ninth week. Accordingly, beyond identifying the interest in national uniformity underlying the doctrine, the cases comprising the main body of labor pre-emption law are of little relevance in deciding this case.

There is, however, a pair of decisions in which the Court has held that Congress intended to forbid state regulation of economic warfare between labor and management, even though it was clear that none of the regulated conduct on either side was covered by the federal statute. In Teamsters Union v. Morton, 377 U.S. 252, the Court held that an Ohio court could not award damages against a union for peaceful secondary picketing even though the union's conduct was neither protected by § 7 nor prohibited by § 8. Because Congress had focused upon this type of conduct and elected not to proscribe it when § 303 of the Labor Management Relations Act was enacted, the Court inferred a deliberate legislative intent to preserve this means of economic warfare for use during the bargaining process.

More recently, in Lodge 76 v. Wisconsin Employment Relations Comm'n, 427 U.S. 132, the Court held that the state commission could not prohibit a union's concerted refusal to work overtime. Although this type of partial strike activity had not been the subject of special congressional consideration, as had the secondary picketing involved in Morton, the Court nevertheless concluded that it was a form of economic self-help that was "part and parcel of the process of collective bargaining," id., at 149 (quoting NLRB v. Insurance Agents, 361 U.S. 477, 495), that Congress implicitly intended to be governed only by the free play of economic forces. The Court identified the crucial inquiry in its pre-emption analysis in Lodge 76 as whether the exercise of state authority to curtail or entirely prohibit self-help would frustrate effective implementation of the policies of the National Labor Relations Act.

The economic weapons employed by labor and management in Morton, Lodge 76, and the present case are similar, and petitioners rely heavily on the statutory policy, emphasized in the former two cases, of allowing the free play of economic forces to operate during the bargaining process. Moreover, because of the two-fold impact of § 592.1, which not only provides financial support to striking employees but also adds to the burdens of the struck employers, we must accept the District Court's finding that New York's law, like the state action involved in Morton and Lodge 76, has altered the economic balance between labor and management.

But there is not a complete unity of state regulation in the three cases. Unlike Morton and Lodge 76, as well as the main body of labor pre-emption cases, the case before us today does not involve any attempt by the State to regulate or prohibit private conduct in the labor-management field. It involves a state program for the distribution of benefits to certain members of the public. Although the class benefited is primarily made up of employees in the State and the class providing the benefits is primarily made up of employers in the State, and although some of the members of each class are occasionally engaged in labor disputes, the general purport of the program is not to regulate the bargaining relationships between the two classes but instead to provide an efficient means of insuring employment security in the State. It is therefore clear that even though the statutory policy underlying Morton and Lodge 76 lends support to petitioners' claim, the holdings in those cases are not controlling. The Court is being asked to extend the doctrine of labor law pre-emption into a new area.

II

The differences between state laws regulating private conduct and the unemployment benefits program at issue here are important from a pre-emption perspective. For a variety of reasons, they suggest an affinity between this case and others in which the Court has shown a reluctance to infer a pre-emptive congressional intent.

Section 591.1 is not a "State law regulating the relations between employees, their union and their employer," as to which the reasons underlying the pre-emption doctrine have their "greatest force." Sears, [Roebuck & Co. v. Carpenters, 436 U.S. 180,] at 193. Instead, as discussed below, the statute is a law of general applicability. Although that is not a sufficient reason to exempt it from pre-emption, Farmer v. Carpenters, 430 U.S. 290, 300, our cases have consistently recognized that a congressional intent to deprive the States of their power to enforce such general laws is more difficult to infer than an intent to pre-empt laws directed specifically at concerted activity. See Farmer, supra, at 302; Sears, supra, at 194–195; Cox, [Labor Law Pre-emption Revisited, 85 Harv.L.Rev. 1337,], at 1356–1357.

Because New York's program, like those in other States, is financed in part by taxes assessed against employers, it is not strictly speaking a public welfare program. It nevertheless remains true that the payments to the strikers implement a broad state policy that does not primarily concern labor-management relations, but is implicated whenever members of the labor force become unemployed. Unlike most States, New York has concluded that the community interest in the security of persons directly affected by a strike outweighs the interest in avoiding any impact on a particular labor dispute.

As this Court has held in a related context, such unemployment benefits are not a form of direct compensation paid to strikers by their employer; they are disbursed from public funds to effectuate a public purpose. Labor Board v. Gullett Gin Co., 340 U.S. 361, 364–365. This conclusion is no less true because New York has found it most efficient to base employer contributions to the insurance program on "experience ratings." Id., at 365. Although this method makes the struck, rather than all, employers primarily responsible for financing striker benefits, the employer-provided monies are nonetheless funneled through a public agency, mingled with other—and clearly public—funds, and imbued with a public purpose. There are obvious reasons, in addition, why the pre-emption doctrine should not "hinge on the myriad provisions of state unemployment compensation laws." Ibid.

New York's program differs from State statutes expressly regulating labor-management relations for another reason. The program is structured to comply with a federal statute, and as a consequence is financed, in part, with federal funds. The federal subsidy mitigates the impact on the employer of any distribution of benefits. More importantly, as the Court has pointed out in the past, the federal statute authorizing the subsidy provides additional evidence of Congress' reluctance to limit the States' authority in this area. * * *

Title IX of the Social Security Act of 1935, supra, established the participatory federal unemployment compensation scheme. The statute authorizes the provision of federal funds to States having programs approved by the Secretary of Labor. In Ohio Bureau of Employment Services v. Hodory, 431 U.S. 471, 97 S.Ct. 1898, 52 L.Ed.2d 513 (1977), an employee who was involuntarily deprived of his job because of a strike claimed a federal right under Title IX to collect benefits from the Ohio Bureau. Specifically, he contended that Ohio's statutory disqualification of claims based on certain labor disputes was inconsistent with a federal requirement that all persons involuntarily unemployed must be eligible for benefits.

Our review of both the statute itself and also its legislative history convinced us that Congress had not intended to prescribe the nationwide rule that Hodory urged us to adopt. The voluminous history of the Social Security Act made it abundantly clear that Congress intended the several States to have broad freedom in setting up the types of unemployment compensation that they wish. We further noted that when Congress wished to impose or forbid a condition for compensation, it did so explicitly; the absence of such an explicit condition was therefore accepted as a strong indication that Congress did not intend to restrict the States' freedom to legislate in this area.

 * * * Congress has been sensitive to the importance of the States' interest in fashioning their own unemployment compensation programs and especially their own eligibility criteria.[18] It is therefore appropriate to treat New York's statute with the same deference that we have afforded analogous state laws of general applicability that protect interests "deeply rooted in local feeling and responsibili-

---

18. The force of the legislative history discussed in [earlier court decisions dealing with the Social Security Act] comes close to removing this case from the pre-emption setting altogether. In light of those decisions, the case may be viewed as presenting a potential conflict between two federal statutes —Title IX of the Social Security Act and the NLRA—rather than between federal and state regulatory statutes. But however the conflict is viewed, its ultimate resolution depends on an analysis of congressional intent.

ty." With respect to such laws, we have stated "that, in the absence of compelling congressional direction, we could not infer that Congress had deprived the States of the power to act." San Diego Building Trades Council v. Garmon, 359 U.S. 236, 244.

III

Pre-emption of state law is sometimes required by the terms of a federal statute. See, e. g., Ray v. Atlantic Richfield, 435 U.S. 151, 173–179. This, of course, is not such a case. Even when there is no express pre-emption, any proper application of the doctrine must give effect to the intent of Congress. Malone v. White Motor Co., 435 U.S. 497, 504. In this case there is no evidence that the Congress that enacted the National Labor Relations Act in 1935 intended to deny the States the power to provide unemployment benefits for strikers. Cf. Hodory, supra, at 482. Far from the compelling congressional direction on which pre-emption in this case would have to be predicated, the silence of Congress in 1935 actually supports the contrary inference that Congress intended to allow the States to make this policy determination for themselves.

New York was one of the five States that had an unemployment insurance law before Congress passed the Social Security and the Wagner Acts in the summer of 1935. Although the New York law did not then assess taxes against employers on the basis of their individual experience, it did authorize the payment of benefits to strikers out of a general fund financed by assessments against all employers in the State. The junior Senator from New York, Robert Wagner, was a principal sponsor of both the National Labor Relations Act and the Social Security Act; the two statutes were considered in Congress simultaneously and enacted into law within five weeks of one another; and the Senate Report on the Social Security Bill, in the midst of discussing the States' freedom of choice with regard to their unemployment compensation laws, expressly referred to the New York statute as a qualifying example. Even though that reference did not mention the subject of benefits for strikers, it is difficult to believe that Senator Wagner and his colleagues were unaware of such a controversial provision, particularly at a time when both unemployment and labor unrest were matters of vital national concern.   *   *   *

Subsequent events confirm our conclusion that the congressional silence in 1935 was not evidence of an intent to pre-empt the States' power to make this policy choice. On several occasions since the 1930's Congress has expressly addressed the question of paying benefits to strikers, and especially the effect of such payments on federal labor policy.[19] On none of these occasions has it suggested that such

---

19. Congress twice has considered and rejected amendments to existing laws that would have excluded strikers from receiving unemployment benefits.

payments were already prohibited by an implicit federal rule of law. Nor, on any of these occasions has it been willing to supply the prohibition. The fact that the problem has been discussed so often supports the inference that Congress was well aware of the issue when the Wagner Act was passed in 1935, and that it chose, as it has done since, to leave this aspect of unemployment compensation eligibility to the States.

In all events, a State's power to fashion its own policy concerning the payment of unemployment compensation is not to be denied on the basis of speculation about the unexpressed intent of Congress. New York has not sought to regulate private conduct that is subject to the regulatory jurisdiction of the National Labor Relations Board. Nor, indeed, has it sought to regulate any private conduct of the parties to a labor dispute. Instead, it has sought to administer its unemployment compensation program in a manner that it believes best effectuates the purposes of that scheme. In an area in which Congress has decided to tolerate a substantial measure of diversity, the fact that the implementation of this general state policy affects the relative strength of the antagonists in a bargaining dispute is not a sufficient reason for concluding that Congress intended to pre-empt that exercise of State power.

The House version of the Labor Management Relations Act of 1947 included a provision denying § 7 rights under the NLRA to any striking employee who accepted unemployment benefits from the State. H.R. 3020, § 2(3), 80th Cong., 1st Sess. This provision, which responded to public criticism of Pennsylvania's payment of benefits to striking miners in 1946, was rejected by the Senate and deleted by the Conference Committee. H.R. Cong.Rep.No.510, 80th Cong., 1st Sess., 32–33 (1947). Although the deletion was not explained, the House Minority Report suggests a reason: "Under the Social Security Act the determination [of eligibility] was advisedly left to the States." H.R.Rep.No.245, 80th Cong., 1st Sess., 68 (1947).

In 1969, the Nixon Administration proposed an amendment to the Social Security Act that would have excluded strikers from unemployment compensation eligibility. Speaking in opposition to the proposal, Congressman Mills made the following comment:
"We have tried to keep from prohibiting the States from doing the things the States believe are in the best interest of their people. There are a lot of decisions in this whole program which are left to the States.
"For example, there are two States, I recall, which will pay unemployment benefits when employees are on strike, but only two out of 50 make that decision. That is their privilege to do so * * *. I would not vote for it * * *, but if the State wants to do it we believe they ought to be given latitude to enable them to write the program they want." 115 Cong.Rec. 34106 (1969). Congress rejected the proposal.

On two other occasions, Congress has confronted the problem of providing purely federal unemployment and welfare benefits to persons involved in labor disputes. In both instances, it has drawn the eligibility criteria broadly enough to encompass strikers. 45 U.S.C.A. § 354(a–2)(iii) (Railway Unemployment Insurance Act); 7 U.S.C.A. § 2014(c) (Food Stamp Act). It thereby rejected the argument that such eligibility forces the Federal Government "to take sides in labor disputes." H.R. Rep.No.1402, 91st Cong., 2d Sess., 11 (1970).

The judgment of the Court of Appeals is

Affirmed.

[In a separate concurring opinion, Mr. Justice Brennan concluded that the legislative histories of the NLRA and the Social Security
Act provided sufficient evidence of congressional intent not to pre-
empt state unemployment compensation laws providing for payments
to strikers. He therefore disclaimed reliance upon the more general
preemption principles emanating from the *Morton* and *Machinists*
cases. He questioned Justice Stevens' distinguishing of those cases
on the ground that they dealt with statutes regulating private conduct
rather than conferring public benefits; Justice Brennan could not understand why the former kind of statute should be subjected to greater scrutiny. Nor could Justice Brennan agree with Justice Stevens
that the New York statute was clearly a "law of general applicability"
(even assuming that to be relevant to preemption analysis). Justice
Brennan joined more enthusiastically in the assertion of Justice Stevens that the New York law was of the kind which evinced a policy
"deeply rooted in local feeling and responsibility," and in his suggestion that this case was more one of conflicting federal statutes than
of federal-state preemption.]

MR. JUSTICE BLACKMUN, with whom MR. JUSTICE MARSHALL
joins, concurring in the judgment.

I concur in the result. I agree with that portion of Part III of
the Court's opinion where the conclusion is reached that Congress has
made its decision to permit a State to pay unemployment benefits to
strikers. (Whether Congress has made that decision wisely is not for
this Court to say.) Because I am not at all certain that the Court's
opinion is fully consistent with the principles recently enunciated in
Machinists v. Wisconsin Emp. Rel. Comm'n, 427 U.S. 132 (1976), I
refrain from joining the opinion's pre-emption analysis. * * *

[The] requirement that petitioner must demonstrate "compelling
congressional direction" in order to establish pre-emption is not, I believe, consistent with the pre-emption principles laid down in Machinists. * * * Where the exercise of state authority to curtail, prohibit, or enhance self-help " 'would frustrate effective implementation of the Act's processes,' " 427 U.S., at 148, quoting Railroad
Trainmen v. Jacksonville Terminal Co., 394 U.S. 369, 380 (1969), I
believe Machinists compels the conclusion that Congress intended
to pre-empt such state activity, unless there is evidence of congressional intent to tolerate it.

* * *

I believe this conclusion to be applicable to a case where a State
alters the balance struck by Congress by conferring a benefit on a

broadly defined class of citizens rather than by regulating more explicitly the conduct of parties to a labor-management dispute. The crucial inquiry is whether the exercise of state authority "frustrates the effective implementation of the Act's processes," not whether the State's purpose was to confer a benefit on a class of citizens.   *   *   *

In summary, in the adjudication of this case, I would not depart from the path marked out by the Court's decision in Machinists. Because, however, I believe the evidence justifies the conclusion that Congress has decided to permit New York's unemployment compensation law, notwithstanding its impact on the balance of bargaining power, I concur in the Court's judgment.

MR. JUSTICE POWELL, with whom THE CHIEF JUSTICE and MR. JUSTICE STEWART join, dissenting.

The Court's decision substantially alters, in the State of New York, the balance of advantage between management and labor prescribed by the National Labor Relations Act (the NLRA). It sustains a New York law that requires the employer, after a specified time, to pay striking employees as much as 50% of their normal wages. In so holding, the Court substantially rewrites the principles of pre-emption that have been developed to protect the free collective bargaining which is the essence of federal labor law.   *   *   *

II

  *   *   *   Nothing in the NLRA or its legislative history indicates that Congress intended unemployment compensation for strikers, let alone employer financing of such compensation, to be part of the legal structure of collective bargaining. The New York law therefore alters significantly the bargaining balance prescribed by Congress in that law. The decision upholding it cannot be squared with Morton and Lodge 76, where far less intrusive state statutes were invalidated because they "upset the balance of power between labor and management expressed in our national labor policy." Morton, supra, at 260.

The Court's opinion seeks to avoid this conclusion by ignoring the fact that the petitioners are not challenging the entire New York unemployment compensation law but only that portion of it that provides for benefits for striking employees. Although the Court characterizes the State's unemployment compensation law as "a law of general applicability" that "implement[s] a broad state policy that does not primarily concern labor-management relations," this description bears no relation to reality when applied to the challenged provisions of the law. Those provisions are "of general applicability" only if that term means—contrary to what the Court itself says—generally applicable only to labor-management relations. It would be difficult to think of a law more specifically focused on labor-management relations than one that compels an employer to finance a strike against itself.

Even if the challenged portion of the New York statute properly could be viewed as part of a law of "general applicability," this generality of the law would have little or nothing to do with whether it is pre-empted by the NLRA. * * * The "crucial inquiry regarding pre-emption" is whether the application of the state law in question " 'would frustrate the effective implementation of the NLRA's processes.' " Lodge 76, supra, at 147–148, quoting Railroad Trainmen v. Jacksonville Terminal Co., 394 U.S. 369, 380 (1969). * * * It is self-evident that the "potential [of the New York law] for interference" (Morton, supra, at 260) with the federally protected economic balance between management and labor is direct and substantial.

The Court has identified several categories of state laws whose application is unlikely to interfere with federal regulatory policy under the NLRA. Farmer v. Carpenters, supra, at 296–297. Mr. Justice Frankfurter described one of these categories in broad terms in Garmon, supra, at 243–244:

> "[States retain authority to regulate] where the regulated conduct touche[s] interests so deeply rooted in local feeling and responsibility that, in the absence of compelling congressional direction, we could not infer that Congress had deprived the States of the power to act."

The Court, attempting to draw support from the foregoing generalization, mistakenly treats New York's requirement that employers pay benefits to striking employees as state action "deeply rooted in local feeling and responsibility." But the broad language from Garmon has been applied only to a narrow class of cases. * * * The provisions of the New York law at issue here have nothing in common with the state laws protecting against personal torts or violence to property that have defined the "local feeling and responsibility" exception to pre-emption.

III

The challenged provisions of the New York law cannot, consistently with prior decisions of this Court, be brought within the "local feeling and responsibility" exception to the pre-emption doctrine. The principles of Morton and Lodge 76 therefore require pre-emption in this case unless in some other law Congress has modified the policy of the NLRA. The Court, acknowledging the need to look beyond the NLRA to support its conclusion, relies primarily on the Social Security Act. In that Act, adopted only five weeks after the passage of the

NLRA, it finds an indication that Congress did intend that the States be free to make unemployment compensation payments part of the collective-bargaining relationship structured by the NLRA. But it is extremely unlikely that little over a month after enacting a detailed and carefully designed statute to structure industrial relations, the Congress would alter so dramatically the balance struck in that law. It would be even more remarkable if such a change were made, as the Court suggests, without any explicit statutory expression, and indeed absent any congressional discussion whatever of the problem.   *   *   *

A much more cautious approach to implied amendments of the NLRA is required if the Court is to give proper effect to the legislative judgments of the Congress. Having once resolved the balance to be struck in the collective-bargaining relationship, and having embodied that balance in the NLRA, Congress should not be expected by the Court to reaffirm the balance explicitly each time it later enacts legislation that may touch in some way on the collective-bargaining relationship. Absent explicit modification of the NLRA, or clear inconsistency between the terms of the NLRA and a subsequent statute, the Court should assume that Congress intended to leave the NLRA unaltered. This assumption is especially appropriate in considering the intent of Congress when it enacted the Social Security Act just five weeks after completing its deliberations on the NLRA.

IV

*   *   *   I would hold, as it seems to me our prior decisions compel, that the New York statute contravenes federal law. It would then be open to the elected representatives of the people in Congress to address this issue in the way that our system contemplates.

Problems for Discussion

1. Had there been no specific legislative history evincing congressional toleration of variant state unemployment-compensation policies, how would this case have been decided in the Supreme Court, and by what vote? Is there not a contradiction between the retreat from preemption reflected in *Farmer* and *Sears* (relating to arguably protected and prohibited activities) and the rather broad preemption principles announced by most of the Justices in *New York Telephone* (relating to unprotected activities)?

2. Assume that New York (or some other state) were to amend its unemployment compensation law to provide for the payment of benefits equal to 100 percent of strikers' wages, to commence with the first day of the strike. Would the Court conclude that this state law was valid?

STATE REGULATION OF UNIONIZATION BY SUPERVISORS

Section 2(3) of the National Labor Relations Act excludes from the coverage of the Act "any individual employed as a supervisor," a term which is defined in Section 2(11). At the same time as supervisors were excluded, Congress in 1947 provided, in Section 14 (a), that "Nothing herein shall prohibit any individual employed as a supervisor from becoming or remaining a member of a labor organization, but no employer subject to this Act shall be compelled to deem individuals defined herein as supervisors as employees for the purpose of any law, either national or local, relating to collective bargaining." The implications of these sections for the continued vitality of state law governing unionization and collective bargaining by supervisors have been considered by the Supreme Court in several cases.

In MARINE ENGINEERS BENEFICIAL ASS'N v. INTERLAKE S.S. Co., 370 U.S. 173, 82 S.Ct. 1237, 8 L.Ed.2d 418 (1962), the union (MEBA) had picketed one of Interlake's ships, causing longshore employees of another company to refuse to unload the vessel. The picketing was enjoined by a state court, in spite of claims of NLRA preemption, on the ground that MEBA represented "supervisors" and hence was not a "labor organization" subject to the Act at all. On certiorari, the Supreme Court reversed. There was some question whether MEBA was clearly outside the latter statutory definition, since it to some extent represented employees as well; in fact, the NLRB had already ruled in other cases (one arising under Section 8(b) and the other a representation election proceeding) that MEBA was a "labor organization." The Court held that the task of deciding what is a "labor organization" requires the same expertise that the NLRB must bring to bear in deciding the applicability of Sections 7 and 8 of the Act. Hence, the courts must defer to the Board whenever a reasonably arguable case can be made that a union is a "labor organization" within the meaning of the Act.

Preemption problems continue, however, even after there has been a definitive determination that particular workers are "supervisors" outside of the coverage of the NLRA, as is the union in which they seek to organize.

In HANNA MINING CO. v. DISTRICT 2, MARINE ENGINEERS BENEFICIAL ASS'N, 382 U.S. 181, 86 S.Ct. 327, 15 L.Ed.2d 254 (1965), a union (MEBA) had represented licensed marine engineers employed by Hanna, which operated a fleet of vessels carrying cargo in the Great Lakes area. The labor contract terminated in July 1962, and during August negotiations, a majority of the marine engineers informed Hanna in writing that they no longer wished to be represented by MEBA. When Hanna thereupon declined to negotiate further absent evidence through a secret ballot of MEBA's majority status, the union began to picket a number of Hanna ships causing interference with loading and unloading activities by dock workers.

Hanna's petition for an NLRB election was dismissed on the stated ground that the engineers were "supervisors" excluded by Section 2(11) from the coverage of the NLRA election provisions. Hanna's charge of a secondary boycott in violation of Section 8(b)(4)(B), alluding to the inducement of work stoppages among dock workers, was also dismissed, since the Regional Director and General Counsel concluded the picketing was primary. In a third attempt in September 1962 to bring the matter before the NLRB, Hanna filed charges of illegal recognitional picketing under Section 8(b)(7), but the Regional Director and General Counsel also dismissed this charge because MEBA was seeking to organize and represent "supervisors" and not "employees." The picketing ended when winter brought an end to shipping, but resumed again in the spring of 1963, whereupon Hanna sought an injunction from a Wisconsin state court; Hanna claimed that the picketing had the improper objective of forcing MEBA's representation on unwilling engineers. The state court action was dismissed for lack of jurisdiction, but the Supreme Court reversed and remanded.

Because of the statutory exclusion of supervisors, the Court concluded that "activity designed to secure organization or recognition of supervisors cannot be protected by § 7 of the Act, arguably or otherwise," and that picketing to compel representation of supervisors is not prohibited by Section 8(b). Therefore, the *Garmon* decision would not require preemption of state regulation. But "the question arises whether Congress nonetheless desired that in their peaceful facets these efforts remain free from state regulation as well as Board authority." MEBA argued that the 1947 exclusion of supervisors from the NLRA, and the concurrent enactment of Section 14(a) disclaiming congressional intent to prohibit union membership by supervisors, signified "a federal policy of *laissez-faire* toward supervisors ousting state as well as Board authority, and more particularly, that to allow the Wisconsin injunction would obliterate the opportunity for supervisor unions that Congress expressly reserved." The Supreme Court rejected this argument, and held that Wisconsin courts had the jurisdiction to enjoin the MEBA picketing.

"This broad argument fails utterly in light of the legislative history, for the Committee reports reveal that Congress' propelling intention was to relieve employers from any compulsion under the Act and under state law to countenance or bargain with any union of supervisory employees. Whether the legislators fully realized that their method of achieving this result incidentally freed supervisors' unions from certain limitations under the newly enacted § 8 (b) is not wholly clear, but certainly Congress made no considered decision generally to exclude state limitations on supervisory organizing. As to the portion of § 14(a) quoted above, some legislative history suggests that it was not meant to immunize any conduct at all but only to make it 'clear that the amendments to the act do not prohibit supervisors from joining unions * * *.' S.Rep. No. 105, 80th Cong., 1st Sess., p. 28; H.R.Conf.Rep. No. 510, 80th Cong., 1st Sess., p. 60 ('[T]he first part of this provision [§ 14(a)] was included presumably out of an abundance of caution.'). However, even assuming that § 14(a) also itself intended to make it clear that state law could not prohibit supervisors from joining unions, the section would have no application to the present facts; for picketing by a minority union to extract recognition by force of such pressures is decidedly not a *sine qua non* of collective bargaining, as indeed its limitation by § 8(b)(7) in nonsupervisor situations attests."

In a converse situation—in which supervisors seeking to unionize commenced a state-court action against employer resort to self-help measures (there, discharge of the supervisors)— the Supreme Court held that state remedies *were* barred, by inference from federal law. Despite the surface inconsistency with *Hanna Mining*, the outcome and reasoning of the Court in BEASLEY v. FOOD FAIR OF NORTH CAROLINA, INC., 416 U.S. 653, 94 S.Ct. 2023, 40 L.Ed.2d 443 (1974), are in reality quite consistent with the earlier case.

In *Beasley*, the plaintiffs (petitioners for certiorari) were managers of meat departments in Food Fair supermarkets in the Winston-Salem, North Carolina area. Shortly after the Meat Cutters union won a representation election among the meat department employees, and the petitioners had joined the union, Food Fair discharged them, allegedly for their union membership. The union filed unfair labor practice charges with the NLRB, but the Regional Director and the General Counsel refused to issue a complaint, stating that the petitioners were "supervisors" excluded from the protection of the NLRA. Petitioners then brought an action against Food Fair for damages for violation of North Carolina's right-to-work law, which provides: "No person shall be required by an employer to abstain or refrain from membership in any labor union or labor organization as a condition of employment or continuation of employment." The North Carolina Supreme Court affirmed a summary judgment for Food Fair, concluding that Section 14(a) of the Labor Act ("no employer * * * shall be compelled to deem individuals defined herein as supervisors as employees for the purpose of any law, either national or local, relating to collective bargaining") prohibited the supervisors' enforcement of the North Carolina Law.   The Supreme Court affirmed.

The Court, finding that the Labor Act provided no protection for supervisors against discharge because of union membership, formulated the question before it as whether Congress "should be taken as having also precluded North Carolina from affording petitioners its state damages remedy for such discharges."   The Court found Section 14(a) to accord the employer freedom—under federal and state law—to decline to deal with unionized supervisors.   That Section, along with the exclusion of supervisors effected through the 1947 amendments of Sections 2(3) and 2(11), rested on Congress's belief that supervisors were "management obliged to be loyal to their employer's interests" whose loyalty might be impaired by unionization (especially when in the same unit or union with rank-and-file employees).   Congress intended to free the employer from the "perceived imbalance in labor-management relationships" that came when supervisors served "two masters with opposed interests."   The Court concluded that the North Carolina right-to-work law would improperly pressure Food Fair to treat the petitioner-managers as employees, and endorsed the position of the North Carolina Supreme Court: "To permit a state law to deprive an employer of his right to discharge his supervisor for membership in a union would completely frustrate the congressional determination to leave this weapon of self-help to the employer."

Problems for Discussion

1.   In light of the Court's analysis in the *Wisconsin Employment Relations Commission* case, page 938, supra, do you think that the Court would today justify its decision in *Hanna* in somewhat different terms? Does the *Wisconsin* case provide a principle regarding the allowable role of State law that would embrace both *Hanna* and *Beasley*?

2.   The Committee of Interns and Residents (CIR) is a union of housestaff personnel at various hospitals; its membership consists of doctors receiving post-graduate training.   From 1957 to 1974, CIR had bargaining rights for these doctors at institutions under the jurisdiction of the New York State Labor Relations Board (SLRB).   In 1974, Congress amended the NLRA so as to extend its coverage to private nonprofit health care institutions.   Congress's principal reasons for so amending the Act were the increasing degree of interstate activities of such institutions, and the increasing concern that health care services would be less subject to interruption if employees were accorded statutory protection for organizing and collective bargaining.

In 1975, CIR petitioned the National Labor Relations Board for an election at the Tranquil Medical Center.   The Board dismissed the petition, because of its conclusion that—although the Center was an "employer" covered by the NLRA—the housestaff personnel in the requested bargaining unit were not "employees" of the Center but were rather students there, engaged not so much in a working relationship as in an educational program. Within the week, CIR petitioned for an election with the State Labor Relations Board, which ordered that an election be held. An action was then brought in a federal court by the NLRB to enjoin both CIR and the New York SLRB from proceeding with the election. Should the injunction issue? See NLRB v. Committee of Interns & Residents, 566 F.2d 810 (2d Cir. 1977), cert. denied 435 U.S. 904, 98 S.Ct. 1449, 55 L.Ed.2d 495 (1978).

What if, instead, CIR induced a strike and picketing among the housestaff personnel, to compel the Medical Center to recognize CIR as bargaining representative, and the Center commenced an action in a state court for an injunction? Would the court have jurisdiction to issue the injunction?

Part Seven

THE INDIVIDUAL AND THE UNION

INTRODUCTION

After the passage of the Railway Labor Act and the National Labor Relations Act, our national labor policy was preoccupied for a number of years with the formation of unions and the operation of collective bargaining as a system of labor-management relations. The interests of the union were widely assumed to be synonymous with those of the employees it represented; any concern with individual rights and internal union affairs tended to be submerged by the overriding need to strengthen labor organizations so that they might better support the interests of the workers. Hence, the relationships between union officials and their organization and between the organization and its members were largely left to State courts, where trade unions were lumped in the general category of voluntary unincorporated associations along with churches, social clubs and fraternal organizations.

As unions increased in wealth and size in the friendly environment of the Wagner Act, a growing concern was expressed that the power of unions might be improperly used to further the private ends of union leaders. Warnings were also uttered to the effect that union power could sometimes be employed to run roughshod over the rights of the individual worker. Some recognition was given to these dangers by the Supreme Court in *Steele v. Louisville & Nashville R. Co.*, p. 994, infra, where the Court implied a duty on the part of the exclusive bargaining representative to represent fairly all members of the bargaining unit. On the other hand, Congress paid little heed to these problems. Legislative proposals were sometimes advanced to protect the individual union member, but they evoked scant interest. During the nineteen fifties, however, increasing attention was paid to the internal affairs of unions. At last, the entire subject erupted before the public through a series of revelations elicited by a Select Committee of the Senate (the McClellan Committee) during an investigation of union activities. In the course of these hearings, witnesses provided numerous examples of the misuse of union funds by labor leaders, the signing of "sweetheart" contracts by union officials in return for bribes from employers, the use of violence and fraud in union elections and similar abuses. Though only a small fraction of American unions were tainted, the impression on the public was vivid and there was increasing clamor for corrective legislation.

Following these events, Congress enacted legislation regulating the internal affairs of unions. This statute, entitled the Labor and Management Reporting and Disclosure Act (LMRDA), was built on certain basic premises:

First, union leaders had abused their power in the ways already described.

Second, since the government had been partially responsible for the growth of unions and for their power over those they represented, the government had an obligation to see that these abuses were eliminated.

Third, while these abuses ought not to be tolerated, responsibility for reform should rest predominantly with unions and their members in the interest of preserving the initiative and self determination of the labor movement. For this reason, primary emphasis was placed upon democratic processes within unions as an instrument of reform.

In furthering these premises, Congress took action along three lines. In the first place, provisions were enacted to insure democratic procedures. Periodic, fair elections were required, and individual members were guaranteed the right to run for office, to vote, to nominate candidates, to criticize union officials and policies, etc. Union members were allowed to initiate actions to enforce these obligations though they were obliged first to seek redress through the internal processes of the union. In the second place, unions were required to submit information relating to their financial and internal operations while union officials were compelled to disclose any money or other remuneration which they received from the employers with whom their union bargained. By requiring disclosure of such information and by insisting upon periodic, fair elections, Congress doubtless hoped to provide union members with the means to rid themselves of corrupt leadership. As a further step toward this end, however, Congress enacted a final group of provisions directly prohibiting certain actions on the part of union officials. Thus, Congress forbade expenditures of union funds for purposes not authorized in the union constitution, barred persons recently convicted of specified crimes from holding union office, prohibited unions from making loans over two thousand dollars to their officers and employees, and so forth.

The problems of regulating the relationship between the union and its members are manifold and complex. The materials in this part are designed to point out some of these difficulties and to reveal something of what the law has done and may come to do in coping with them. We have divided the materials into five chapters.

(1) The first chapter deals with the minimum obligation of a bargaining representative to represent fairly all of the employees in the bargaining unit. Collective bargaining inevitably involves conflicts of interests between different groups of workers. Even when the bargaining unit is defined by the NLRB in a way which gives all possible homogeneity to the employees in the unit, they cannot be exactly alike. The negotiation and administration of collective bargaining agreements involve repeated decisions as to whose interests should be preferred. Shall there be provision for more liberal pensions or for a larger wage increase? How large a wage premium should be given to skilled members of the unit? Should employees displaced by a plant closing be put at the bottom of the seniority list at the plant to which they transfer? Should the union press the grievance of a senior employee who claims that a junior employee given a promotion in fact lacks superior ability? To what extent should the law scrutinize such decisions by the union—decisions which are sometimes mindful of the race or sex, or the union membership, or the personal connections, or the political influence within the union, of the disadvantaged workers?

(2) The second chapter is devoted to the problem of "union security," and explores such matters as the extent to which employees can be compelled, upon pain of termination of employment, to join or contribute moneys to a union; and the uses to which the union is free to devote such moneys. Also considered are the benefits that the employer may lawfully accord to persons referred for jobs through union hiring halls or to persons serving as union officials.

(3) The third chapter takes up the question of the powers of unions to discipline their members. On what legal theory can a disciplined employee obtain redress from his union? What limitations will the courts impose upon the reasons for which discipline may be imposed? What procedural safeguards will the union have to provide in meting out discipline?

(4) The fourth chapter describes the requirements which have been laid down in the Labor Management Reporting and Disclosure Act (LMRDA) to insure periodic free elections for union officers.

(5) The final chapter seeks to draw together a number of miscellaneous safeguards which have been provided by the LMRDA in order to prevent corruption and related abuses by union officials.

I. THE RIGHT TO FAIR REPRESENTATION [1]

A. THE BASIC RIGHT AND REMEDIES

STEELE v. LOUISVILLE & NASHVILLE R. CO.

Supreme Court of the United States, 1944.
323 U.S. 192, 65 S.Ct. 226, 89 L.Ed. 173.

MR. CHIEF JUSTICE STONE delivered the opinion of the Court.

The question is whether the Railway Labor Act, 48 Stat. 1185, 45 U.S.C. § 151 et seq., 45 U.S.C.A. § 151 et seq., imposes on a labor organization, acting by authority of the statute as the exclusive bargaining representative of a craft or class of railway employees, the duty to represent all the employees in the craft without discrimination because of their race, and, if so, whether the courts have jurisdiction to protect the minority of the craft or class from the violation of such obligation.

* * * Petitioner, a Negro, is a locomotive fireman in the employ of respondent railroad, suing on his own behalf and that of his fellow employees who, like petitioner, are Negro firemen employed by the Railroad. Respondent Brotherhood, a labor organization, is, as provided under § 2, Fourth of the Railway Labor Act, the exclusive bargaining representative of the craft of firemen employed by the Railroad and is recognized as such by it and the members of the craft. The majority of the firemen employed by the Railroad are white and are members of the Brotherhood, but a substantial minority are Negroes who, by the constitution and ritual of the Brotherhood, are excluded from its membership. As the membership of the Brotherhood constitutes a majority of all firemen employed on respondent Railroad, and as under § 2, Fourth, the members because they are the majority have the right to choose and have chosen the Brotherhood to represent the craft, petitioner and other Negro firemen on the road have been required to accept the Brotherhood as their representative for the purposes of the Act.

On March 28, 1940, the Brotherhood, purporting to act as representative of the entire craft of firemen, without informing the Negro

1. See Axelrod & Kaufman, Mansion House—Bekins—Handy Andy: The National Labor Relations Board's Role in Racial Discrimination Cases, 45 Geo.Wash.L.Rev. 675 (1977); Clark, The Duty of Fair Representation: A Theoretical Structure, 51 Texas L.Rev. 1119 (1973); Cox, The Duty of Fair Representation, 2 Vill. L.Rev. 151 (1957); Finkin, The Limits of Majority Rule in Collective Bargaining, 64 Minn.L.Rev. 183 (1980); Leiken, The Current and Potential Equal Employment Role of the NLRB, 1971 Duke L.J. 833; Murphy, The Duty of Fair Representation Under Taft-Hartley, 30 Mo.L.Rev. 373 (1965); Sherman, Union's Duty of Fair Representation and the Civil Rights Act of 1964, 49 Minn.L.Rev. 771 (1965); Sovern, The National Labor Relations Act and Racial Discrimination, 62 Colum.L.Rev. 563 (1962); Wellington, Union Democracy and Fair Representation: Federal Responsibility in a Federal System, 67 Yale L.J. 1327 (1958).

firemen or giving them opportunity to be heard, served a notice on respondent Railroad and on twenty other railroads operating principally in the southeastern part of the United States. The notice announced the Brotherhood's desire to amend the existing collective bargaining agreement in such manner as ultimately to exclude all Negro firemen from the service. By established practice on the several railroads so notified only white firemen can be promoted to serve as engineers, and the notice proposed that only "promotable", i. e., white, men should be employed as firemen or assigned to new runs or jobs or permanent vacancies in established runs or jobs.

On February 18, 1941, the railroads and the Brotherhood, as representative of the craft, entered into a new agreement which provided that not more than 50% of the firemen in each class of service in each seniority district of a carrier should be Negroes; that until such percentage should be reached all new runs and all vacancies should be filled by white men; and that the agreement did not sanction the employment of Negroes in any seniority district in which they were not working. The agreement reserved the right of the Brotherhood to negotiate for further restrictions on the employment of Negro firemen on the individual railroads. On May 12, 1941, the Brotherhood entered into a supplemental agreement with respondent Railroad further controlling the seniority rights of Negro firemen and restricting their employment. The Negro firemen were not given notice or opportunity to be heard with respect to either of these agreements, which were put into effect before their existence was disclosed to the Negro firemen.

Until April 8, 1941, petitioner was in a "passenger pool", to which one white and five Negro firemen were assigned. These jobs were highly desirable in point of wages, hours and other considerations. Petitioner had performed and was performing his work satisfactorily. Following a reduction in the mileage covered by the pool, all jobs in the pool were, about April 1, 1941, declared vacant. The Brotherhood and the Railroad, acting under the agreement, disqualified all the Negro firemen and replaced them with four white men, members of the Brotherhood, all junior in seniority to petitioner and no more competent or worthy. As a consequence petitioner was deprived of employment for sixteen days and then was assigned to more arduous, longer, and less remunerative work in local freight service. In conformity to the agreement, he was later replaced by a Brotherhood member junior to him, and assigned work on a switch engine, which was still harder and less remunerative, until January 3, 1942. On that date, after the bill of complaint in the present suit had been filed, he was reassigned to passenger service. * * *

[The complaint sought, among other things, an injunction against enforcement of the labor agreements between the Railroad and the Brotherhood and damages against the Brotherhood. The Supreme Court of Alabama concluded that the complaint stated no cause of action. It held that the Railroad was obligated by statute to bargain with the Brotherhood as the majority representative of the craft, and that the Brotherhood had the statutory power both to create and to destroy the plaintiff's seniority rights. It construed the Railway Labor Act as imposing no duty on the Brotherhood to protect the rights of minorities from discrimination or unfair treatment, however gross.]

If, as the state court has held, the Act confers this power on the bargaining representative of a craft or class of employees without any commensurate statutory duty toward its members, constitutional questions arise. For the representative is clothed with power not unlike that of a legislature which is subject to constitutional limitations on its power to deny, restrict, destroy or discriminate against the rights of those for whom it legislates and which is also under an affirmative constitutional duty equally to protect those rights. If the Railway Labor Act purports to impose on petitioner and the other Negro members of the craft the legal duty to comply with the terms of a contract whereby the representative has discriminatorily restricted their employment for the benefit and advantage of the Brotherhood's own members, we must decide the constitutional questions which petitioner raises in his pleading.

But we think that Congress, in enacting the Railway Labor Act and authorizing a labor union, chosen by a majority of a craft, to represent the craft, did not intend to confer plenary power upon the union to sacrifice, for the benefit of its members, rights of the minority of the craft, without imposing on it any duty to protect the minority. Since petitioner and the other Negro members of the craft are not members of the Brotherhood or eligible for membership, the authority to act for them is derived not from their action or consent but wholly from the command of the Act. Section 2, Fourth, provides: "Employees shall have the right to organize and bargain collectively through representatives of their own choosing. The majority of any craft or class of employees shall have the right to determine who shall be the representative of the craft or class for the purposes of this Act * * *." * * *

Section 2, Second, requiring carriers to bargain with the representative so chosen, operates to exclude any other from representing a craft. Virginian R. Co. v. System Federation, supra, 300 U.S. 545, 57 S.Ct. 598, 81 L.Ed. 789. The minority members of a craft are thus deprived by the statute of the right, which they would otherwise possess, to choose a representative of their own, and its members cannot bargain individually on behalf of themselves as to matters which are properly the subject of collective bargaining. Order of Railroad Telegraphers v. Railway Express Agency, 321 U.S. 342, 64 S.Ct. 582, and see under the like provisions of the National Labor Relations Act, J. I. Case Co. v. National Labor Relations Board, 321 U.S. 332, 64 S.Ct. 576, 88 L.Ed. 762, and Medo Photo Supply Corp. v. National Labor Relations Board, 321 U.S. 678, 64 S.Ct. 830, 88 L.Ed. 1007. * * *

Unless the labor union representing a craft owes some duty to ᴶepresent non-union members of the craft, at least to the extent of not discriminating against them as such in the contracts which it makes as their representative, the minority would be left with no means of protecting their interests, or indeed, their right to earn a livelihood by pursuing the occupation in which they are employed. While the majority of the craft chooses the bargaining representative, when chosen it represents, as the Act by its term makes plain, the craft or class, and not the majority. The fair interpretation of the statutory language is that the organization chosen to represent a craft is to represent all its members, the majority as well as the minority, and it is to act for and not against those whom it represents. It is a principle of general application that the exercise of a granted power to act in behalf of others involves the assumption toward them of a duty to exercise the power in their interest and behalf, and that such a grant of power will not be deemed to dispense with all duty toward those for whom it is exercised unless so expressed.

We think that the Railway Labor Act imposes upon the statutory representative of a craft at least as exacting a duty to protect equally the interests of the members of the craft as the Constitution imposes upon a legislature to give equal protection to the interests of those for whom it legislates. Congress has seen fit to clothe the bargaining representative with powers comparable to those possessed by a legislative body both to create and restrict the rights of those whom it represents, cf. J. I. Case Co. v. National Labor Relations Board, supra, 321 U.S. 335, 64 S.Ct. 579, 88 L.Ed. 762, but it has also imposed on the representative a corresponding duty. We hold that the language of the Act to which we have referred, read in the light of the purposes of the Act, expresses the aim of Congress to impose on the bargaining representative of a craft or class of employees the duty to exercise fairly the power conferred upon it in behalf of all those for whom it acts, without hostile discrimination against them.

This does not mean that the statutory representative of a craft is barred from making contracts which may have unfavorable effects on some of the members of the craft represented. Variations in the terms of the contract based on differences relevant to the authorized purposes of the contract in conditions to which they are to be applied, such as differences in seniority, the type of work performed, the competence and skill with which it is performed, are within the scope of the bargaining representation of a craft, all of whose members are not identical in their interest or merit. [Citations omitted.] Without attempting to mark the allowable limits of differences in the terms of contracts based on differences of conditions to which they apply, it is enough for present purposes to say that the statutory power to represent a craft and to make contracts as to wages, hours and working conditions does not include the authority to make among members of the craft discriminations not based on such relevant differences. Here the discriminations based on race alone are obviously irrelevant and invidious. Congress plainly did not undertake to authorize the bargaining representative to make such discriminations. [Citations omitted.]

The representative which thus discriminates may be enjoined from so doing, and its members may be enjoined from taking the benefit of such discriminatory action. No more is the Railroad bound by or entitled to take the benefit of a contract which the bargaining representative is prohibited by the statute from making. In both cases the right asserted, which is derived from the duty imposed by the statute on the bargaining representative, is a federal right implied from the statute and the policy which it has adopted. It is the federal statute which condemns as unlawful the Brotherhood's conduct. "The extent and nature of the legal consequences of this condemnation, though left by the statute to judicial determination, are nevertheless to be derived from it and the federal policy which it has adopted." Deitrick v. Greaney, 309 U.S. 190, 200, 201, 60 S.Ct. 480, 485, 84 L.Ed. 694. [Other citations omitted.]

So long as a labor union assumes to act as the statutory representative of a craft, it cannot rightly refuse to perform the duty, which is inseparable from the power of representation conferred upon it, to represent the entire membership of the craft. While the statute does not deny to such a bargaining labor organization the right to determine eligibility to its membership, it does require the union, in collective bargaining and in making contracts with the carrier, to represent non-union or minority union members of the craft without hostile discrimination, fairly, impartially, and in good faith. Wherever necessary to that end, the union is required to consider requests of nonunion members of the craft and expressions of their views with respect to collective bargaining with the employer and to give to them notice of and opportunity for hearing upon its proposed action. * * *

In the absence of any available administrative remedy, the right here asserted, to a remedy for breach of the statutory duty of the bargaining representative to represent and act for the members of a craft, is of judicial cognizance. That right would be sacrificed or obliterated if it were without the remedy which courts can give for breach of such a duty or obligation and which it is their duty to give in cases in which they have jurisdiction. * * *

We conclude that the statute contemplates resort to the usual judicial remedies of injunction and award of damages when appropriate for breach of that duty.

The judgment is accordingly reversed and remanded for further proceedings not inconsistent with this opinion.

Reversed.

MR. JUSTICE BLACK concurs in the result.   [The concurring opinion of MR. JUSTICE MURPHY is omitted.]

Problem for Discussion

On the St. Louis Railway, two groups of employees performed virtually the same duties: (1) "brakemen," who were represented by the Brotherhood of Railway Trainmen (BRT), a labor organization which systematically excluded blacks, and (2) "train porters," all of whom were blacks represented by another union.   (The events took place prior to the enactment of the 1964 Civil Rights Act which announced for the first time a Congressional ban upon race discrimination in membership by a union.) The railroad and the BRT negotiated a contract forbidding the railroad to assign train porters to do work "generally recognized as brakemen's duties." Since ninety-five percent of a train porter's work met this description, the clause virtually required the railroad to discharge porters, thus eliminating blacks from this class of service.   Simon Howard, one of the porters, brought an action in a federal district court to enjoin the BRT from enforcing the contract.   There is no dispute about the facts, and both parties have moved for summary judgment.   How should the court decide?   See *Brotherhood of Railway Trainmen* v. *Howard*, 343 U.S. 768, 72 S.Ct. 1022, 96 L.Ed. 1283 (1952).

FORD MOTOR CO. v. HUFFMAN, 345 U.S. 330, 73 S.Ct. 681, 97 L.Ed. 1048 (1953).   Plaintiff sued to have certain provisions of a collective bargaining agreement declared invalid.   In their contract, the company and the United Automobile Workers agreed to give seniority credit for military service to employees who completed a probationary period of six months with Ford, even though they had not worked for Ford before the war.   This went beyond the requirement of a federal statute that seniority continue to accrue for persons whose service for Ford was interrupted by military duty.   The effect of this pre-employment seniority credit was to give greater seniority to certain employees who were first employed by Ford at a time subsequent to plaintiff's employment but who were credited with seniority based on their prior military service.   The plaintiff asserted that the union had violated its duty of fair representation by discriminating on the basis of a factor not ordinarily considered directly relevant to wages and working conditions. The Supreme Court *held* that the disputed provisions did not evidence a breach of the union's duty of fair representation. It stressed the discretion of the union to make reasonable distinctions among employees and concluded that the seniority credit was "within the reasonable bounds of relevancy." The Court observed:

> "Inevitably differences arise in the manner and degree to which the terms of any negotiated agreement affect individual employees and classes of employees. The mere existence of such differences does not make them invalid. The complete satisfaction of all who are represented is hardly to be expected. A wide range of reasonableness must be allowed a statutory bargaining representative in serving the unit it represents, subject always to complete good faith and honesty of purpose in the exercise of its discretion. * * * Seniority rules governing promotions, transfers, layoffs and similar matters may, in the first instance, revolve around length of competent service. Variations acceptable in the discretion of bargaining representatives, however, may well include differences based upon such matters as the unit within which seniority is to be computed, the privileges to which it shall relate, the nature of the work, the time at which it is done, the fitness, ability or age of the employees, their family responsibilities, injuries received in course of service, and time or labor devoted to related public service, whether civil or military, voluntary or involuntary."

———

In INTERNATIONAL BHD. OF ELEC. WORKERS v. FOUST, 442 U.S. 42, 99 S.Ct. 2121, 60 L.Ed.2d 698 (1979), the Supreme Court held (in a decision that was clearly intended to construe the NLRA as well) that the Railway Labor Act does not contemplate the award of punitive damages against a union which violates its duty of fair representation (in this case, by untimely filing a grievance for a discharged employee).

Respondent Foust was discharged for alleged medical reasons; the collective bargaining agreement required the presentation of grievances within sixty days from the occurrence giving rise thereto. Foust's attorney first contacted the union about the grievance fifty-two days after the discharge, and by the time intra-union communications were undertaken and the grievance filed, ten more days had elapsed. The railroad and the National Railroad Adjustment Board denied the grievance as untimely. Foust sued the union for breach of the duty of fair representation, and the district court entered a judgment, based on a jury verdict, for $40,000 actual damages and

$75,000 punitive damages. The court of appeals held that punitive damages could be awarded but only if the union acted wantonly or in reckless disregard of an employee's rights. The Supreme Court granted certiorari to resolve a conflict in the circuits regarding punitive damages in fair representation cases (and therefore, did not review either the finding of breach of that duty in this case or the award of compensatory damages).

In an opinion by Justice Marshall, for five Justices, the Court concluded that any positive value to be served by permitting punitive damage awards was offset by "the possibility that punitive awards could impair the financial stability of unions and unsettle the careful balance of individual and collective interest which this Court has previously articulated in the unfair representation area." The Court read earlier cases to adopt a principle of compensation of wronged individual employees in fair-representation cases "without compromising the collective interest of union members in protecting limited funds." The broad discretion of juries to award punitive damages would make the "impact of these windfall recoveries * * * unpredictable and potentially substantial." The depletion of union treasuries, with the resulting impairment of the union's effectiveness as collective bargaining representative, "is simply too great a price for whatever deterrent effect punitive damages may have."

The Court also feared that the threat of punitive damages would unduly interfere with the salutary exercise of union discretion in handling and settling grievances, and with the resulting strengthening of employer confidence in the union. Unions would be pressured to process frivolous grievances or resist fair settlements, threatening disruption of the "responsible decision-making essential to peaceful labor relations."

Treating the NLRA and the Railway Labor Act as articulating the same basic policies on this issue, the Court concluded: "[W]e hold that such [punitive] damages may not be assessed against a union that breaches its duty of fair representation by failing properly to pursue a grievance."

Four Justices, in a concurring opinion by Justice Blackmun, agreed that punitive damages ought not be awarded in the present case, where the union's delinquency was at worst negligent or grossly negligent. When, however, the union's breach of its duty of fair representation is rooted, for example, in intentional racial discrimination or deliberate personal animus, punitive damages would serve as a deterrent, an acceptable objective in duty of fair representation cases. The concurring Justices criticized the Court for announcing a per se rule barring punitive damages when the record did not necessitate such a broad (and unsound) disposition.

The Duty of Fair Representation and the NLRB

Nearly two decades passed after the Supreme Court had decided the *Steele* case, and had held that courts could enforce a union's duty of fair representation, before the National Labor Relations Board held the breach of that duty to be an unfair labor practice. Of course, if a union induced an employer to discipline an employee because he or she was not a member of the union, that would violate Sections 8(a)(3) and 8(b)(2). It was in NLRB v. MIRANDA FUEL Co., 140 N.L.R.B. 181 (1962), enf't denied, 326 F.2d 172 (2d Cir. 1963), that the Board held that such union-induced discipline is also an unfair labor practice when the individual employee is targeted for invidious or capricious reasons apart from nonmembership. The Board concluded that the freedom of employees from such union conduct was a right impliedly granted by Section 7 of the NLRA, and that such union conduct foreseeably encouraged union membership. The breach of the duty of fair representation thus violated Sections 8(b)(1)(A) and 8(b)(2). A divided court of appeals denied enforcement, but mustered no majority on the question whether the union's breach was indeed an unfair labor practice.

Even the Board itself continued to be divided on the issue, as demonstrated by the opinions in INDEPENDENT METAL WORKERS, LOCAL 1 (HUGHES TOOL CO.), 147 N.L.R.B. 1573 (1964). There, the Board issued a joint certification as bargaining representative to Local 1 of the Independent Metal Workers Union, which was an all-white local, and Local 2, which had only black members. An initial contract allocated certain jobs to white employees and other (inferior) jobs to black employees. A second contract, which amended and extended the first, was signed by the company and Local 1, over the objection of Local 2. That contract provided for the creation of new apprenticeships, to be awarded to white employees only. When the application of a black worker, Ivory Davis, for an apprenticeship position was rejected by the Company, Davis wrote the president of Local 1 asking that local to represent him in processing a grievance; Davis received no reply. He filed unfair labor practice charges against Local 1, and Local 2 moved to rescind the certification issued to Locals 1 and 2 on account of the discrimination by Local 1 against black workers as well as the existence of segregated locals. A majority of the Board decided to grant the requested relief, rescinding the certification and finding violations of Sections 8(b)(1), (2) and (3). Two Board members concurred in the rescission of the certification, and also in the finding of a violation of Section 8(b)(1)(A) on the theory that the refusal to represent Davis because he was not a member of the union was specifically condemned by the Labor Act; they expressly declined to rest a Section 8(b)(1)(A) violation on a violation of the duty of fair representation or on discrimination on account of race. These two members dissented, moreover, from the conclusion that Sections 8(b)(2) and (3) had been violated by Local 1. Excerpts from the separate opinion of these two members follow:

> "[N]either Section 7 nor Section 8(b)(1)(A) mentions a duty of fair representation. The majority in the *Miranda* case, reaffirmed here, found a right to fair representation implied in Section 7 on the basis of the bargaining representative's implied duty of fair representation derived from its status as bargaining representative under Section 9.
>
> There are a number of reasons why this conclusion based on verbal logic does not, in our opinion, represent the intent of Congress, which is after all the goal of statutory construction. Section 7 was part of the Wagner Act which in its unfair labor practice section was aimed only at employer conduct. The Wagner Act also contained the present Section 9(a). It hardly seems reasonable to infer, in these circumstances, that Section 7 contained a protected implied right to fair representation against the bargaining representative, when the entire Wagner Act did not make any conduct by a labor organization unlawful. Section 7 was continued substantially unchanged in the Taft-Hartley Act except for the addition of the "right to refrain" clause, which is not material to our problem. Although the Taft-Hartley Act ad ed union unfair labor practices to the list of prohibited conduct, neither the Act nor the legislative history contains any mention of the duty of fair representation, despite the fact that the *Steele* and *Wallace* decisions were well known, having issued 3 years previously. Again, although in the interval between the dates of the Taft-Hartley and Landrum-Griffin Acts, there were additional court decisions and articles by learned commentators in the law journals [2] dealing with the legal problems of fair

---

2. Cox's leading article, ["The Duty of Fair Representation," 2 Vill.L.Rev. 151 (1957)], appeared in 1957, 2 years before the passage of the Landrum-Griffin Act.

On May 5, 1953, Senator Ives for himself and Senators Smith, Aiken, Griswold, Purtell, Goldwater, Murray, Neely, Douglas, Lehman, and Kennedy introduced a bill to amend the National Labor Relations Act so as to make it an unfair labor practice for either an employer or a union to discriminate against an employee "on account of race, religion, color, national origin, or ancestry." The bill would also have made it an unfair labor practice for a labor organization to discriminate against or segregate any person otherwise eligible for membership "on account of race, religion, color, national origin, or ancestry." S. 1831, 83d Cong., 1st sess. The bill was referred to the Committee on Labor and Public Welfare, but was not reported out.

representation, Congress made no change in the wording of Section 7, and ignored the problem completely in adding a "Bill of Rights" section to the existing statute. * * *

"There is another and more important reason why the Board should not undertake to police a union's administration of its duties without a clear mandate from Congress. The purpose of the Act is primarily to protect the organizational rights of employees. But apart from the obligation to bargain in good faith, "Congress intended that the parties would have wide latitude in their negotiations, unrestricted by any governmental power to regulate the substantive solution of their differences." Before *Miranda,* it was assumed that contract or grievance decisions by employers and unions were immune from examination by the Board unless they were influenced by union considerations. But, under the underlying reasoning of the *Miranda* majority and that of the present decision, the Board is now constituted a tribunal to which every employee who feels aggrieved by a bargaining representative's action, whether in contract negotiations or in grievance handling, may appeal, regardless of whether the decision has been influenced in whole or in part by considerations of union membership, loyalty, or activity. The Board must determine on such appeal, without statutory standards, whether the representative's decision was motivated by "unfair or irrelevant or invidious" considerations and therefore to be set aside, or was within the "wide range of reasonableness * * * allowed a statutory representative in serving the unit it represents * * *" and to be sustained. Inevitably, the Board will have to sit in judgment on the substantive matters of collective bargaining, the very thing the Supreme Court has said the Board must not do, and in which it has no special experience or competence. This is not exaggeration. * * *

"In our dissent in *Miranda,* we expressed the view that 8(b)(2) outlaws only discrimination related to "union membership, loyalty, the acknowledgment of union authority or the performance of union obligations." This position was endorsed by a majority holding of the court of appeals in reversing the Board decision in *Miranda.* We adhere to that view.

"In the present case, the only unfair labor practice alleged is the failure of Respondent Union to process Ivory Davis' grievance. As both the Trial Examiner and the majority admit, the General Counsel did not affirmatively put in issue the legality of the collective-bargaining contract between Hughes Tool and Respondent Union. We cannot perceive how the mere refusal to process a grievance on behalf of an employee, unaccompanied by any request to or demand upon the employer and not based on a contract itself alleged to be violative of Section 8(b)(2) of the Act can be said to "cause or attempt to cause" an employer to do anything, much less to discriminate against an employee in violation of Section 8(a)(3). * * *

"The majority has adopted the Trial Examiner's finding that Respondent Union's refusal to process Ivory Davis' grievance also violated Section 8(b)(3). It seems to us that Section 8(b)(3) prescribes a duty owed by a union to employers and not to employees. * * *

"The legislative history of Section 8(b)(3) shows conclusively that this section was intended to be a counterpart of Section 8(a)(5), and under the latter the bargaining duty is owed entirely to the union * * *."

Direct endorsement of NLRB jurisdiction over the duty of fair representation was given by the Court of Appeals for the Fifth Circuit in LOCAL 12, UNITED RUBBER WORKERS v. NLRB, 368 F.2d 12 (1967), a case which like *Steele* involved race discrimination. The union represented workers at the East Gadsden, Alabama, plant of Goodyear Tire & Rubber Company. Although the labor contract provided for plantwide seniority, without regard to race or sex, on such matters as promotions, transfers, layoffs and recalls, a custom had developed of regulating those matters through three separate seniority ladders—white male, black male, and female. Also as a matter of unwritten custom, plant facilities such as lunchrooms, restrooms and showers were racially segregated.

In 1960 and 1961, eight black workers were laid off while white persons with less or no seniority were put to work on "white jobs." Although these black workers appealed to Local 12 to invoke the contractual grievance procedure against their layoffs and the segregated facilities, the local (including its executive board and full membership) refused to do so; but this decision was reversed in March 1962 by the President of the International Union. At the same time, Goodyear and Local 12 agreed that racially segregated seniority practices would end and that the complainants should be reinstated. When, however, Local 12 continued to refuse to process their grievances for backpay for the pre-March layoffs, as well as the grievances concerning the continued segregated plant facilities, the black workers filed unfair labor practice charges against the local.

The NLRB found that the local had violated Sections 8(b)(1)
(A), 8(b)(2), and 8(b)(3), and the court of appeals enforced the
Board's order requiring Local 12 to take the grievances to arbitration and to propose specific contractual provisions prohibiting racial
discrimination in the plant. The court concluded that the breach of
the duty of fair representation was in itself an unfair labor practice, and that that duty obtains just as much when the union processes grievances as when it negotiates an agreement initially.

> "Even in the administration stage of the bargaining
> contract, when the necessity of adjusting competing em-
> ployee claims may not be as pressing as during the negotia-
> tion stage where rigorous scrutiny of each compromise
> might frustrate the act's policy of encouraging industrial
> peace, the union must necessarily retain a broad degree of
> discretion in processing individual grievances. Thus, where
> the union, after a good faith investigation of the merits of
> a grievance, concludes that the claim is insubstantial and
> refuses to encumber further its grievance channels by con-
> tinuing to process the unmeritorious claim, its duty of fair
> representation may well be satisfied. Such good-faith ef-
> fort to represent fairly the interests of individual em-
> ployees, however, is not evidenced in this controversy. To
> the contrary, Local 12 in open disregard of the recom-
> mendations of its International President has continued to
> refuse to represent the vital interests of a segment of its
> membership. The claims with regard to back pay and seg-
> regation of plant facilities clearly concern meritorious is-
> sues involving wages and conditions of employment, issues
> with respect to which these employees have relinquished to
> the union as exclusive bargaining agent their individual
> rights to negotiate. See J. I. Case Co. v. NLRB, 1944, 321
> U.S. 332, 64 S.Ct. 576, 88 L.Ed. 762. Neither does the mere
> fact that the act provides that an individual employee may
> present his claim directly to the employer diminish the
> union's duty of fair representation, for admittedly the
> grievance of a single employee can have little force in the
> absence of support from his bargaining representative.
> Conley v. Gibson, 1957, 355 U.S. 41, 45, 78 S.Ct. 99, 102, 2
> L.Ed.2d 80, 84.

> " * * * We thus conclude that where the record dem-
> onstrates that a grievance would have been processed to
> arbitration but for arbitrary and discriminatory reasons,
> the refusal to so process it constitutes a violation of the
> union's duty to represent its members 'without hostile dis-

crimination, fairly, impartially, and in good faith.' Steele v. Louisville & N. R. R., supra, 323 U.S. at 204, 65 S.Ct. at 233, 89 L.Ed. at 184.

"Similarly, with respect to the grievances concerning the segregated nature of plant facilities, the union not only refused to process such claims but actively opposed desegregation of shower and toilet facilities. It is impossible for us to look upon such conduct as anything other than an effort to discriminate against Negro employees with respect to conditions of employment. As exclusive representative of all employees in the bargaining unit, Local 12's statutory obligation required it 'to make an honest effort to serve the interests of all of those members, without hostility to any.' Ford Motor Co. v. Huffman, supra, 345 U.S. at 337, 73 S.Ct. at 686, 97 L.Ed. at 1057. * * *

"[We are convinced] that Local 12, in refusing to represent the complainants in a fair and impartial manner, thereby violated section 8(b)(1)(A) by restraining them in the exercise of their section 7 right to bargain collectively through their chosen representatives. The mere fact that Local 12's conduct may not have directly resulted in encouraging or discouraging union membership does not persuade us to alter our determination, for the language of section 8(b)(1)(A), unlike certain other provisions of section 8, is not restricted to discrimination which encourages or discourages union membership. * * *

"Moreover, the Board's recent assertions that fair representation constitutes an essential element of section 7 employee rights are even more convincing in light of the similarity in language between section 7 and section 2 of the Railway Labor Act, from which the Supreme Court in *Steele* perceived congressional intent to impose such duty of fair representation upon the bargaining representative. In that case, the Court reasoned that since the jurisdiction of the Railway Adjustment Board did not encompass disputes between employees and unions, the remedy must necessarily be sought in the courts. Since the National Labor Relations Board has, however, been given jurisdiction over employee-union disputes, the Court's logic in *Steele*, reinforced by the Board's express desire to assume jurisdiction, further supports our conclusion that unfair representation cases are properly subject to Board jurisdiction. Significantly, the violation of every other duty imposed by the act, including the general duty to bargain collectively,

has been designated an unfair labor practice, and we find
no compelling reason to conclude that a breach of the duty
of fair representation was intended to represent a single,
narrow exception to Board jurisdiction. * * * "

In the years since the *Rubber Workers* decision, the federal
courts of appeals have come routinely to accept the proposition that
breach of the duty of fair representation is a union unfair labor
practice remediable through the procedures of the NLRB. Although
the Supreme Court has not squarely so ruled, it has in Vaca v. Sipes,
infra page 1020, assumed that NLRB jurisdiction exists and has made
that a cornerstone of its decision without raising any serious questions about the matter.

When a union has been found to violate the duty of fair representation by discriminating on the basis of race or sex in contract
negotiation or grievance processing, the Board may as a remedy revoke that union's certification. In the *Hughes Tool* case, supra, the
Board revoked the certification of the majority union because of its
racial discrimination in negotiating and grievance processing and,
independently, because of its classification or segregation in union
membership on racial grounds (which may not automatically violate the duty of fair representation). Moreover, although a collective bargaining agreement executed by a majority union will normally bar the holding of a representation election during its term
(up to three years), the Board will dispense with this contract-bar
rule when the agreement contains provisions which are racially discriminatory on their face. PIONEER BUS CO., 140 N.L.R.B. 54 (1962).
These principles, however, operate only to strip rights from an incumbent union, which by virtue of its incumbency might still have
an entrenched majority position—and thus continued bargaining
rights—in spite of the dropping of the contract bar or the revocation of certification.

For a time, the Board held that certain forms of union discrimination could be raised by an employer even prior to the union's certification. In Bekins Moving & Storage Co., 211 N.L.R.B. 138
(1974), a divided Board held that an elected union would be disqualified from certification if the employer could prove in the election proceeding that the union discriminated *in membership* along
lines of race or national origin; a Board majority believed that certification of such a union would be tantamount to unconstitutional
governmental discrimination. *Bekins* was soon overruled, in HANDY
ANDY, INC., 228 N.L.R.B. 447 (1977), in which the Board concluded
that it would be premature to permit an employer to challenge a
union's right to certification prior to that union's having an opportunity to demonstrate its freedom from discrimination based on race,

sex or national origin in contract negotiations and in grievance processing. By permitting challenges in the context of certification proceedings, *Bekins* had induced many employers to allege discrimination merely for the purpose of delaying collective bargaining and it had in any event no impact upon unions which had enough power to compel bargaining regardless of certification. In the election proceeding, certification is to be granted as a simple declaration of the union's majority status; if there is a subsequent violation of the union's duty of fair representation, however, this can be challenged in unfair labor practice proceedings, with one available remedy being revocation of the union's certification. "We conclude that our statutory function of eliminating invidious discrimination by labor organizations is best served by scrutinizing their activities when they are subject to our adversary procedures and remedial orders."

The Board's position in *Handy Andy* was endorsed by the Court of Appeals for the District of Columbia Circuit in a case involving alleged sex discrimination by a union seeking certification. In BELL & HOWELL CO. v. NLRB, 598 F.2d 136 (D.C.Cir. 1979), cert. denied 442 U.S. 942, 99 S.Ct. 2885, 61 L.Ed.2d 312, the court concluded that the purposes of the NLRA and of the duty of fair representation will best be achieved through unfair labor practice proceedings and remedies rather than through initial withholding of certification. As to the constitutional issue of governmental involvement when certifying a union which allegedly engages in unlawful sex discrimination, "[T]he effect of certification is to [impose] an affirmative obligation on the private association not to discriminate. Far from authorizing and encouraging discrimination, certification subjects the union to additional sanctions for any future discrimination."

Two courts of appeals have, however, concluded that the Constitution indeed requires not only that the NLRB withhold certification from a union which unlawfully discriminates on the basis of race in membership or in contract negotiation or administration elsewhere, but also that the NLRB must permit an employer to assert and prove such discrimination by way of a defense to the union's refusal-to-bargain charge under Section 8(a)(5). See NLRB v. MANSION HOUSE CENTER MANAGEMENT CORP., 473 F.2d 471 (8th Cir. 1973); NLRB v. HEAVY LIFT SERV., INC., 607 F.2d 1121 (5th Cir. 1979), cert. denied, —— U.S. ——, 101 S.Ct. 82, 66 L.Ed.2d 25 (1980). Even though the union which is the charging party has undisputed majority support, these courts conclude that an NLRB order to bargain would reinforce the union's discrimination with the imprimatur of the federal government.

Problems for Discussion

1.   Do you agree with the court in the *Rubber Workers* case that a violation of the duty of fair representation is properly treated as an unfair labor practice, or do you agree instead with the dissenting Board members in the *Hughes Tool* case? Which subsection of Section 8(b) furnishes the most sound basis for concluding that a violation of the duty of fair representation is an unfair labor practice?

2.   Assuming that a union's violation of the duty of fair representation violates Section 8(b) of the Labor Act, would the complaining individuals also have a judicial remedy in a state or federal court? See Vaca v. Sipes, p. 1020, infra. In the absence of diversity of citizenship, what would be the basis for federal jurisdiction? What factors should be taken into account by the aggrieved employees in determining whether to file an unfair labor practice charge or to initiate a lawsuit in a state or federal court?

3.   Two locals of the Glass Blowers Association serve as joint bargaining representatives for the employees at the plant of the Glimmer Glass Company. Membership in Local 106 is restricted to men, and Local 245 limits its membership to women. The current labor contract between the unions and Glimmer—negotiated and ratified by members of both locals—makes no distinctions because of sex or local union membership and provides that there will be no discrimination in the administration of the contract on the basis of race, sex or national origin. However, the unions' rules provide that the grievances of female employees may be processed only by Local 245 and those of men only by Local 106; the disposition of the grievances, however, affects both male and female employees. Are the unions violating the duty of fair representation? If so, what should be the remedy? See *NLRB* v. *Local 106, Glass Bottle Blowers*, 520 F.2d 693 (6th Cir. 1975).

4.   The union representing hotel employees at a number of hotels and motels in Southern California counts among its members a substantial number of Mexican-born workers who have come to this country only recently and who understand very little English; nor are they acquainted with the practices of American labor-management relations. These workers have complained to the union that the union meetings ought not be conducted exclusively in English, that a Spanish-language copy of the collective bargaining agreement should be prepared and made available to all employees, and that a Spanish-speaking individual should be designated by the union to assist the employees in their adjustment to the workplace and in the understanding of their rights under the labor contract. The union officials have refused to take such steps, and have noted that neither the union nor the company discriminates against any members of the union in the negotiation or administration of the labor contract. A Spanish-speaking member of the union has filed a complaint against the union in a federal court, alleging the above facts, and the union has moved to dismiss the action. How should the court rule? See *Retana* v. *Apartment & Elevator Operators Local 14*, 453 F.2d 1018 (9th Cir. 1972).

———

STRICK CORP.

National Labor Relations Board, 1979.
241 N.L.R.B. 210.

[The production and maintenance employees at the Berwick plant of Strick Corporation, a manufacturer of truck trailers, had for several years been represented jointly by the United Automobile Workers International Union and UAW Local 664. Under the terms of a three-year labor contract terminating September 19, 1975, employees were forbidden to strike, seniority was to be terminated upon "discharge for cause," and a grievance and arbitration procedure was available. In 1973 and 1974, there were four work stoppages in violation of the contract; the last of these, in July 1974, stemmed from the discharge of twelve employees who left work to attend a union meeting contrary to the instructions of their supervisor. These discharges resulted in a union meeting at which a wide range of demands were formulated, and ultimately more than 200 workers participated in the strike, in spite of the company's insistence that the grievances of the twelve dischargees could be processed through the contractual grievance procedure. On July 24, 1974, the company sent individual telegrams to all participants in the strike, discharging them.

The unions grieved the discharges of the strikers, with the company contending that their participation in a wildcat strike in breach of contract was cause for termination. After an arbitration hearing, at which the strikers were represented by union counsel, the arbitrator in November 1974 found that there was just cause for the strikers' discharge and permanent replacement but that to deny them "the right to return to employment [to fill vacancies as they occur] with this Company and to again enjoy the benefits of the seniority they acquired when previously employed by it" was unnecessarily punitive. He ordered that strikers applying for reinstatement were to be placed on a reemployment list and, upon reemployment, were to be given the seniority they had at the time of their discharge.

By January 1975, the employees at work for Strick were almost exclusively the workers who did not join the strike and the permanent replacements for the strikers. Pursuant to the union-security provisions of the existing labor contract, they became dues paying union members; they were sharply critical of the local and international union leaders, who had been rather indifferent to this newly constituted workforce but who finally decided, fueled by rumored decertification activity, to call a membership meeting to elect a new shop committee.

In the meantime, Strick's Director of Industrial Relations, Mr. Walsh, proclaimed the company's resistance to the arbitrator's award, asserting that the wildcat strikers did not deserve to be returned to work and that there would be friction in the plant if they were to work side by side with the replacements. When contract renewal negotiations began in July 1975, Walsh insisted upon the inclusion of a contract provision (Clause 21.01) which would supersede all prior arbitration awards. When he made it clear to the international representative at the negotiations, Mr. Clouser, that such a provision was indispensable and that the company was prepared to take a strike over it—and as Mr. Clouser appreciated that actively employed members of the unit and their shop committee could be expected to support the proffered provision (since it would enhance their relative seniority compared to the discharged strikers)—the unions ultimately relented; after securing advice of counsel, they on September 18, 1975 agreed to a clause stating that "The seniority provisions of this agreement supercede and cancel all prior agreements and/or arbitration awards granting or denying seniority or reemployment rights to individuals." Clouser felt that he could not conduct a strike over the contract without the support of the current workforce (nonstrikers and permanent replacements), that to resist Clause 21.01 would result in no contract, and that ultimately the unions might lose their status as bargaining representative.

Clouser and the unions' shop committee submitted the contract to a membership ratification meeting; the discharged strikers were neither notified nor otherwise offered an opportunity to participate in the vote. After the contract was approved and executed, the company hired no new employees (including the discharged strikers) until January 23, 1979. Had it honored the arbitration award, however, it would have by that time recalled many of the strikers. Several filed unfair labor practice charges, against the company for violating Sections 8(a)(3) and (1), and against the union for violating Sections 8(b)(1)(A) and 8(b)(2).]

INTERMEDIATE REPORT OF THE ADMINISTRATIVE LAW JUDGE

* * * [T]he element of majority rule embedded in the concept of free collective bargaining may frequently collide with the duty of fair representation where the latter is invoked on behalf of those adversely affected through the give and take of negotiations. Neither individual rights nor the interest in fostering a free system of collective bargaining should be preferred at the expense of the other. Accommodation of these competing interests may only be realized by imposing an evidentiary burden upon the party seeking to upset a duly negotiated agreement, that the labor organization did in fact act upon arbitrary, invidious, or discriminatory grounds.

With these general principles in mind, and taking full account of the realities, in the light of the credible testimony on this record, I am convinced that the Union harbored no animus against the strikers, and that it entered the 1975 negotiations with no interest to be served by curtailment of their rights. Faced with the Employer's adamant position in negotiations, it ultimately agreed under conditions in which the only employees who could effectively bring pressure upon the Employer would be asked to strike in support of a position which threatened their own job security and with which they disagreed. Furthermore, any failure to agree on the Unions' part would most certainly have deferred benefits for the actively employed replacements and nonstrikers. There could be little doubt, in September 1975, when negotiations drew to a close that forestalled negotiations over Article 21:01 would, to put it mildly, endanger the Unions' representative status at Berwick. While representatives of the Unions wavered in their testimony in this respect, I am convinced that to avoid the obvious consequences of provoking an impasse over this issue and in the interest of self-preservation the Unions ultimately accepted.

Both the General Counsel and the Charging Parties contend that the foregoing afforded no justification for offending the rights of the strikers, urging that " * * * a political threat to a union's security does not justify the sacrifice of the employment interests of a politically weaker group of employees." The substance of their claim is that labor organizations generally are enjoined by the duty of fair representation from sacrificing individual employment rights to enhance their own status. For support, the General Counsel and Charging Parties rely heavily upon Red Ball Motor Freight, 157 NLRB 1237, enforced 379 F.2d 137 (C.A.D.C., 1967); and Barton Brands, Limited, 213 NLRB 640.

In *Red Ball*, the issue arose in the context of a merger of two distinct working complements, represented by different labor organizations, into a single integrated operation. It was agreed that the election process of the NLRB would be utilized to resolve the competing claims for representation. During the preelection campaign, the union which formerly represented the larger group offered assurances to those employees that, if designated, it would, through the process of negotiation, provide them with a higher seniority ranking than would be afforded employees previously represented by the other union. In finding that this statement constituted coercion within the meaning of Section 8(b)(1)(A) of the Act, it was concluded that the duty of fair representation was violated by such preelection statements since no reasonable basis for the discrimination proposed against the smaller group was demonstrated and because the promised action did " * * * not reflect the kind of compromise between competing interests which collective bargaining daily requires, but would serve the interest of UTE and the majority of the employees in the unit it [UTE] sought to represent with hostility to those of the minority."

In *Barton Brands, Ltd., supra,* the Board found a breach of the duty of fair representation growing out of negotiations which took place after the merger of separate bargaining units. Initially seniority of employees in the newly integrated unit was dovetailed. However, during subsequent contract negotiations, the union proposed, and ultimately obtained the employer's assent to a provision endtailing for purposes of seniority, the employees whose prior employment was in the smaller unit. The administrative law judge initially dismissed the complaint in its entirety. The Board reversed, finding that the Union violated Section 8(b)(2) and 8(b)(1) (A) and that the Employer violated Section 8(a)(3) and 8(a)(1) of the Act concluding that the Union breached its duty of fair representation by effecting a reduction in seniority at the expense of a smaller group of employees. The Board described the basis for the union's action as follows: "[T]he motivation for the Union's stand was to assure the election of Ken Cecil by the numerically superior Barton employees at the expense of the small minority of former Glenco employees." 213 NLRB at page 641.[3]

Barton Brands, supra, and *Red Ball, supra,* afford no clear cut answer to the issue under consideration here. Detrimental action against segments of a bargaining unit to bolster the political stature of a union official or to enable a labor organization to obtain advantage over a rival union with respect to a pending question concerning representation has little resemblance to the motivation on which Respondent-Unions acted herein. Here, we have an incumbent representative, acting out of the institutional consideration of self-preservation under most extenuating circumstances. While there can be no question but that, in the process, the union repre-

---

3. The Circuit Court of the United States for the Seventh Circuit in Barton Brands, Ltd. v. N. L. R. B., 529 F. 2d 793, 797 (1976), disagreed with the Board, and concluded that the record did not support a basis for imputing the above-described motivation to the union. The Court reasoned that the union official was not acting within the scope of his authority, and therefore his motivation was not chargeable to the union as a whole. Nonetheless, the Court remanded the proceeding to the Board for consideration of whether its decision might be sustained on other grounds. Thereafter, the Board reaffirmed its original findings, after concluding, within the framework of the Court's remand, that the Union failed to make the required showing necessary to absolve it of liability; i. e., that the negotiated endtailing of the seniority of the smaller group was based upon objective justification. As for the Employer, the Board similarly concluded that the Employer failed to demonstrate that its entry in that agreement was based upon legitimate business considerations. See Barton Brands, Ltd., 228 NLRB 889 (1977).

sentatives knowingly disadvantaged one category of employees, the inquiry does not end there. Under the precedents, the action by the Union must be found to have been an "arbitrary sacrifice of a group of employees' rights in favor of another stronger more politically favored group * * *." See Gainey v. Brotherhood of Railway and Steamship Clerks, etc., 313 F.2d 318, 324 (C.A.3, 1963).

Basic statutory policies might well be offended by any notion that arbitrary conduct is inherent in a labor organization's effort to preserve its representative status at the expense of certain employees. To so hold would clash with the desirability of maintaining the stability of existing collective-bargaining relationships, long recognized as a central objective of the Act. Consistent with such objective, over the years, concepts have been devised by the Board to implement that policy, which apply often at the expense of even a majority of employees in a particular bargaining unit. Included are the Board's contract bar rule, the presumption of continuing majority, and the principle that an established relationship is invulnerable to challenge within 1-year after certification or a reasonable period of time if established pursuant to informal recognition. To serve these same ends, it would seem that, at the very least, a labor organization's action in the interest of preserving its representative status—an ever present concern upon those on the union side of the negotiating table—should only be condemned after careful thought as to the standard of responsibility which should rightfully emerge from all surrounding facts. Consistent therewith it is concluded that a negotiated change to the detriment of a segment of the bargaining unit in the interest of avoiding decertification lacks the inherent strain of arbitrariness.

With the foregoing in mind, I find that the discharged strikers should be relegated to whatever remedies might be available to them under Section 301 of the Act. The factors set forth below lead to the conclusion that the duty of fair representation was not violated herein.

Thus, the Unions' necessity to preserve their status as exclusive representative was occasioned by forces which were not of their own making. They neither inspired, abetted, nor condoned the conduct of the dischargees which robbed all substance from the contractual assurance provided the Employer that during 1972–1975, production would continue unabated by disruptive influences of work stoppages. Similarly the proposal to abrogate the arbitration award was contrived, injected into the negotiations and insisted upon as the price for a new contract, all solely by the Employer. The Unions were caught up in that drift of events when on September 18, 1975, they assented to the Employer's proposal 21.01.

True, at that time the discharged strikers, by virtue of the arbitration award, had a reasonable expectancy of future unemployment [sic] and as such were within the class benefiting from the duty of fair representation. Any definition of what that duty entailed, however, must take account of the conflicting interest of the other segment in the represented unit, who also fell within the protective scope of that doctrine. Thus, nonstrikers and replacements by virtue of the collective-bargaining agreement under which they were employed, and the union security provisions thereof, were required to become union members. It is not inconceivable that many of them crossed the picket lines and reported to work under the assumption that their future job security would not be threatened by individuals discharged because of their participation in the unlawful strike. For, the collective-bargaining agreement in effect at that time specifically provided that seniority shall be broken, "if an employee is discharged for good cause." Under such a clause there would be no reason for them to assume that an arbitrator would conclude that strikers, though discharged for cause, are entitled to seniority superior to theirs. Their support of the Employer's position on clause 21.01 was predicated upon more than an outright power grab.

More significant, however, to assessment of the degree of responsibility to be imposed upon the Unions are the hard practical considerations, which bore directly upon the Unions' position in the 1975 negotiations, and the relative standing of the represented groups with respect to those conditions. The dischargees had no interest whatever in timely culmination of the negotiations for their participation in ultimate benefits was inchoate and perhaps even conditional. On the other hand, any prolongation of the negotiations would be at the expense of the actively employed nonstrikers and replacements. To them, continued resistance by their representative to proposal 21.01 meant deferred enjoyment of other agreed-upon benefit gains. Yet, this was the sole group, in a position, to impose economic restraints upon the Employer in the event of impasse. The Unions were in no position to marshal support from the latter in furtherance of a bargaining position which, if successfully maintained, would weaken the job security of that group.

Such irreconcilable conflict within a represented unit and its radiating effects at the negotiating table, hardly provides an ideal format for application of technical legal conceptions. No term or condition of employment potentially is more divisive than seniority. Any negotiated change in an existing seniority structure doubtless operates to disadvantage certain unit numbers. In such circumstances, the exclusive representative is asked to serve two masters, and overzealous attentiveness to egality [sic] ought not be practiced by the authorities to the point whereby such considerations are superficially applied so as to confuse the duties of a fiduciary with the more stringent standards applicable to insurers.

Respondent-Unions in this case preferred agreement to inertia, and their having done so, albeit, at the expense of the dischargees, was not in disharmony with the pragmatics of collective bargaining.

Considering all the foregoing, I find that the record does not substantiate that the Union, in *yielding* to the Employer's demand and acting in a fashion consistent with the interest of all actively employed elements in the bargaining unit, breached any standard of responsibility owing to the discharged strikers. It is my further conclusion that there is no merit in the General Counsel's contention that the 8(b)(2) and 8(b)(1)(A) allegations are nonetheless substantiated by reason of the Unions' failure to notify the discharged strikers of the agreement reached and to allow their participation in the ratification process. Here, the Unions' contract settlement was based on hard practical considerations inoffensive to statutory interests. It was at that juncture that the "die was legitimately cast." Any reversal of that conclusion must rest upon imposition of a duty of notification, which if adhered to, would have required the Unions to invite a knowingly meaningless, yet potentially explosive confrontation between the conflicting groups. Allowing the dischargees to participate in the ratification process could inflame and obstruct, even though that group could not alleviate the conditions leading to the Unions' agreement. Having found that in the particular circumstances of this case, Respondent-Unions' deference to the actively employed work force did not entail a breach of any fiduciary obligation, the notice issue is controlled thereby. That view should not be altered, through indirection, by giving overarching weight to matters which, in the circumstances, would derogate from, rather than facilitate the process of collective bargaining. Accordingly, it is concluded that the 8(b)(1)(A) and 8(b)(2) allegations are not substantiated by the Unions' failure to afford the discharged strikers notice of and an opportunity to participate in the ratification process.

Based upon the foregoing, and as no independent evidence exists that Respondent-Employer pressed for abrogation of the arbitration award for reasons violative of Section 8(a)(3) and (1) of the Act, said allegations have not been substantiated by a preponderance of the evidence, and dismissal thereof shall be recommended.
* * *

DECISION OF THE BOARD

* * * While we agree with the Administrative Law Judge's ultimate finding that Respondent Unions did not violate their duty of fair representation, we regard as irrelevant the fact that the Unions may have lost the support of the then-working unit members if the Unions had failed to accede to the Employer's demand for a contract clause abrogating the arbitrator's award giving rise to this controversy. The only issue presented herein is whether the Unions acted arbitrarily or in bad faith in *acquiescing* in the Employer's demand for the clause. Given the particular circumstances herein, including the Employer's adamant demand for the clause, the Employer's avowed intention to "take a strike" if the Unions failed to agree to the clause, the desire of the working employees and their shop committee that the clause be included, and the probable ineffectiveness of a strike in opposition to the clause and the fact that resistance of the clause further would delay implementation of the new contract and its improved benefits thus resulting in detriment to working employees, we conclude that the Union was faced with a "Hobson's choice," and in making its decision did not act arbitrarily or in bad faith.

The record reveals that the Unions at all times actively pursued the rights of the discharged employees. Thus, the Unions promptly filed and processed the grievance giving rise to the arbitration award, and provided an attorney to argue before the arbitrator on behalf of the dischargees. The Unions also paid the dischargees' expenses related to the State of Pennsylvania's denial to them of unemployment compensation, and, on appeal of that denial, provided them with the services of its attorney. * * *

On the basis of the foregoing, we find that, by acquiescing in the Employer's demand, the Unions "acted upon wholly relevant considerations, not upon capricious or arbitrary factors," and accordingly have not breached their duty of fair representation.

Problems for Discussion

1. Assume, contrary to the facts of the *Strick* case, that it was the union rather than the company which initially proposed that seniority rights of the former strikers be extinguished in order that the strike replacements would have greater seniority for purposes of future layoffs and recalls. Assume that this demand was formulated by the union's bargaining team based upon a majority vote at a membership meeting. Would the union's demand (and the subsequent inclusion of such a provision in the labor contract by a willing employer) violate its duty of fair representation? To the extent that the *Red Ball* and *Barton Brands* so suggest, are those decisions soundly based? In short, why should a union not be free—absent invidious discrimination or personal hostility—to take any position supported by a democratic, majority vote of the union members?

2. In the *Strick* case, the Board in reviewing the Administrative Law Judge chose to place no weight on the fact that the union's leaders feared

decertification if they did not capitulate to the company's demand to over-turn the arbitrator's award. Why—absent invidious discrimination or personal hostility—is that not a fully appropriate criterion for a union to consider in negotiating a collective bargaining agreement?

3. Was the union's insistent attempt to use the grievance and arbitration procedure to secure reinstatement of the discharged strikers, with full seniority, a violation of the union's duty of fair representation owed to the strike replacements? When any union, after a strike is ended, negotiates a strike-settlement agreement which provides for the ouster of strike replacements, does it violate its duty of fair representation? (Does the employer commit an unfair labor practice by laying off the replacements and recalling the former strikers?)

4. With the advent of recorded music, a relatively small number of members of the American Federation of Musicians—based principally in New York City and Los Angeles—have made phonograph records and tapes along with soundtrack recording for films shown in theatres and on television; the result has been the displacement of "live" musicians from theatres, radio and television. The President and Executive Committee of the AF of M—seeking to soften the brunt of such "technological unemployment"—have negotiated agreements with large users of recorded music (such as record manufacturers and motion picture studios) which provide for very limited wage increases for the recording musicians and a substantial amount of money to be paid (per record and per film) into a fund to be disbursed to musicians across the country who participate in performances at schools, parks, fairs and the like. The New York and Los Angeles musicians have brought an action against the Union, claiming breach of the duty of fair representation. How should the court rule? Cf. *Atkinson v. Superior Ct. of Cal.*, 310 P.2d 145 (Cal.Dist. Ct.App.), vacated, 49 Cal.2d 338, 316 P.2d 960 (1957), app. dismissed, 357 U.S. 569 (1958).

5. Fair representation issues have often arisen (as in *Red Ball* and *Barton Brands*) when through acquisition, consolidation or merger, employees who have accrued seniority at two different work locations find themselves working at the same location. The question becomes whether all of the workers from the acquired location are to be "endtailed" on the composite seniority list, or whether (through one of a number of different equitable formulas) they are to be "dovetailed" so that the brunt of future layoffs will be shared among all of the employees in the new composite unit. The two cited cases stand for the proposition that a union breaches the duty of fair representation when it decides to endtail employees when the sole purpose is to win an election by appealing to the numerically larger number of voters.

(a) Would the result be different if the union reaches the decision to endtail after a thorough and protracted discussion of the positions of both conflicting groups of employees? See *Price v. International Bhd. of Teamsters*, 457 F.2d 605 (3d Cir. 1972).

(b) Is the case against the union in a dovetailing-endtailing decision affected by the fact that a preexisting labor agreement expressly provides for the dovetailing of seniority rights of absorbed employees, but that when there is a consolidation during the contract term, the union's bargaining and grievance committee agrees with the employer to amend the contract so as to provide for endtailing?

(c) Is the case against the union stronger or weaker in a situation in which a union is elected bargaining representative in a multiplant bargaining unit and negotiates an agreement providing for endtailing in the event of a merger, consolidation or shutdown, and the agreement is ratified by the membership; two years later, during the contract term, one of the plants is shut down and the employees there are transferred to other plants, where they are placed at the bottom of the seniority list?

B. THE INDIVIDUAL AND HIS GRIEVANCE [4]

VACA v. SIPES

Supreme Court of the United States, 1967.
386 U.S. 171, 87 S.Ct. 903, 17 L.Ed.2d 842.

MR. JUSTICE WHITE delivered the opinion of the Court.

On February 13, 1962, Benjamin Owens filed this class action against petitioners, as officers and representatives of the National Brotherhood of Packinghouse Workers and of its Kansas City Local No. 12 (the Union), in the Circuit Court of Jackson County, Missouri. Owens, a Union member, alleged that he had been discharged from his employment at Swift & Company's (Swift) Kansas City Meat Packing Plant in violation of the collective bargaining agreement then in force between Swift and the Union, and that the Union had "arbitrarily, capriciously and without just or reasonable reason or cause" refused to take his grievance with Swift to arbitration under the fifth step of the bargaining agreement's grievance procedures. * * *

I.

In mid-1959, Owens, a long-time high blood pressure patient, became sick and entered a hospital on sick leave from his employ-

4. See Report of A.B.A. Committee on Improvement of Administration of Union-Management Contracts, 50 Nw. L.Rev. 143 (1955); Blumrosen, Legal Protection for Critical Job Interests: Union-Management Authority Versus Employee Autonomy, 13 Rutgers L. Rev. 631 (1959); Cox, Rights Under a Labor Agreement, 69 Harv.L.Rev. 601 (1956); Dunau, Employee Participation in the Grievance Aspects of Collective Bargaining, 50 Colum.L. Rev. 731 (1950); Feller, A General Theory of the Collective Bargaining Agreement, 61 Calif.L.Rev. 663 (1973); Hanslowe, The Collective Agreement and the Duty of Fair Representation, 14 Lab.L.J. 1052 (1963); Lewis, Fair Representation in Grievance Administration: Vaca v. Sipes, 1967 Sup.Ct. Rev. 81; Summers, Individual Rights in Collective Agreements: A Preliminary Analysis, 9 Buffalo L.Rev. 239 (1960); Summers, The Individual Employee's Rights Under the Collective Agreement: What Constitutes Fair Representation, 126 U.Pa.L.Rev. 251 (1977).

ment with Swift. After a long rest during which his weight and blood pressure were reduced, Owens was certified by his family physician as fit to resume his heavy work in the packing plant. However, Swift's company doctor examined Owens upon his return and concluded that his blood pressure was too high to permit reinstatement. After securing a second authorization from another outside doctor, Owens returned to the plant, and a nurse permitted him to resume work on January 6, 1960. However, on January 8, when the doctor discovered Owens' return, he was permanently discharged on the ground of poor health. * * *

II.

Petitioners challenge the jurisdiction of the Missouri courts on the ground that the alleged conduct of the Union was arguably an unfair labor practice and within the exclusive jurisdiction of the NLRB. * * * For the reasons which follow, we reject this argument.

It is now well established that, as the exclusive bargaining representative of the employees in Owens' bargaining unit, the Union had a statutory duty fairly to represent all of those employees, both in its collective bargaining with Swift, see Ford Motor Co. v. Huffman, 345 U.S. 330, 73 S.Ct. 681, 97 L.Ed. 1048; Syres v. Oil Workers International Union, 350 U.S. 892, 76 S.Ct. 152, 100 L.Ed. 785, and in its enforcement of the resulting collective bargaining agreement, see Humphrey v. Moore, 375 U.S. 335, 84 S.Ct. 363, 11 L.Ed.2d 370. * * * Under this doctrine, the exclusive agent's statutory authority to represent all members of a designated unit includes a statutory obligation to serve the interests of all members without hostility or discrimination toward any, to exercise its discretion with complete good faith and honesty, and to avoid arbitrary conduct. Humphrey v. Moore, 375 U.S., at 342, 84 S.Ct., at 367. It is obvious that Owens' complaint alleged a breach by the Union of a duty grounded in federal statutes, and that federal law therefore governs his cause of action. e. g., Ford Motor Co. v. Huffman, supra.

Although N.L.R.A. § 8(b) was enacted in 1947, the NLRB did not until *Miranda Fuel* interpret a breach of a union's duty of fair representation as an unfair labor practice. * * * [P]etitioners argue that Owens' state court action was based upon Union conduct that is arguably proscribed by N.L.R.A. § 8(b), was potentially enforceable by the NLRB, and was therefore pre-empted under the *Garmon* line of decisions.

A. * * * [A]s a general rule, neither state nor federal courts have jurisdiction over suits directly involving "activity [which] is arguably subject to § 7 or § 8 of the Act." San Diego Building Trades Council v. Garmon, 359 U.S., at 245, 79 S.Ct., at 780.

This pre-emption doctrine, however, has never been rigidly applied to cases where it could not fairly be inferred that Congress intended exclusive jurisdiction to lie with the NLRB. Congress itself has carved out exceptions to the Board's exclusive jurisdiction: [Justice White here enumerated actions under Section 303 of the LMRA, claims of contract breach under Section 301, actions in which the NLRB declines to assert jurisdiction by virtue of Section 14 of the Act, and cases involving a "merely peripheral concern" of the Act or "deeply rooted" state interests.]

A primary justification for the pre-emption doctrine—the need to avoid conflicting rules of substantive law in the labor relations area and the desirability of leaving the development of such rules to the administrative agency created by Congress for that purpose— is not applicable to cases involving alleged breaches of the union duty of fair representation. The doctrine was judicially developed in *Steele* and its progeny, and suits alleging breach of the duty remained judicially cognizable long after the NLRB was given unfair labor practice jurisdiction over union activities by the L.M.R.A. Moreover when the Board declared in *Miranda Fuel* that a union's breach of its duty of fair representation would henceforth be treated as an unfair labor practice, the Board adopted and applied the doctrine as it had been developed by the federal courts. See 140 N.L. R.B., at 184–186. Finally, as the dissenting Board members in *Miranda Fuel* have pointed out, fair representation duty suits often require review of the substantive positions taken and policies pursued by a union in its negotiation of a collective bargaining agreement and in its handling of the grievance machinery; as these matters are not normally within the Board's unfair labor practice jurisdiction, it can be doubted whether the Board brings substantially greater expertise to bear on these problems than do the courts, which have been engaged in this type of review since the *Steele* decision.

In addition to the above considerations, the unique interests served by the duty of fair representation doctrine have a profound effect, in our opinion, on the applicability of the pre-emption rule to this class of cases. * * * Were we to hold, as petitioners and the government urge, that the courts are preempted by the NLRB's *Miranda Fuel* decision of this traditional supervisory jurisdiction, the individual employee injured by arbitrary or discriminatory union conduct could no longer be assured of impartial review of his complaint, since the Board's General Counsel has unreviewable discretion to refuse to institute an unfair labor practice complaint. See United Electrical Contractors Ass'n v. Ordman, 366 F.2d 776, C.A.2d Cir.,

Sept. 23, 1966, cert. denied, 385 U.S. 1026, 87 S.Ct. 753, 17 L.Ed.2d 674 (Jan. 17, 1967). The existence of even a small group of cases in which the Board would be unwilling or unable to remedy a union's breach of duty would frustrate the basic purposes underlying the duty of fair representation doctrine. For these reasons, we cannot assume from the NLRB's tardy assumption of jurisdiction in these cases that Congress, when it enacted N.L.R.A. § 8(b) in 1947, intended to oust the courts of their traditional jurisdiction to curb arbitrary conduct by the individual employee's statutory representative.

B. There are also some intensely practical considerations which foreclose pre-emption of judicial cognizance of fair representation duty suits, considerations which emerge from the intricate relationship between the duty of fair representation and the enforcement of collective bargaining contracts. For the fact is that the question of whether a union has breached its duty of fair representation will in many cases be a critical issue in a suit under L.M.R.A. § 301 charging an employer with a breach of contract. To illustrate, let us assume a collective bargaining agreement that limits discharges to those for good cause and that contains no grievance, arbitration or other provisions purporting to restrict access to the courts. If an employee is discharged without cause, either the union or the employee may sue the employer under L.M.R.A. § 301. * * *

* * * [I]f the wrongfully discharged employee himself resorts to the courts before the grievance procedures have been fully exhausted, the employer may well defend on the ground that the exclusive remedies provided by such a contract have not been exhausted. Since the employee's claim is based upon breach of the collective bargaining agreement, he is bound by terms of that agreement which govern the manner in which contractual rights may be enforced. For this reason, it is settled that the employee must at least attempt to exhaust exclusive grievance and arbitration procedures established by the bargaining agreement. Republic Steel Corp. v. Maddox, 379 U.S. 650, 85 S.Ct. 614, 13 L.Ed.2d 580. However, because these contractual remedies have been devised and are often controlled by the union and the employer, they may well prove unsatisfactory or unworkable for the individual grievant. The problem then is to determine under what circumstances the individual employee may obtain judicial review of his breach-of-contract claim despite his failure to secure relief through the contractual remedial procedures. * * *

We think that [one] situation when the employee may seek judicial enforcement of his contractual rights arises if, as is true here, the union has sole power under the contract to invoke the higher stages of the grievance procedure, *and* if, as is alleged here, the employee-plaintiff has been prevented from exhausting his contractual remedies by the union's *wrongful* refusal to process the grievance. It is true that the employer in such a situation may have done nothing to prevent exhaustion of the exclusive contractual remedies to which he agreed in the collective bargaining agreement. But the employer has committed a wrongful discharge in breach of that agreement, a breach which could be remedied through the grievance process to the employee-plaintiff's benefit were it not for the union's breach of its statutory duty of fair representation to the employee. To leave the employee remediless in such circumstances would, in our opinion, be a great injustice. We cannot believe that Congress, in conferring upon employers and unions the power to establish exclusive grievance procedures, intended to confer upon unions such unlimited discretion to deprive injured employees of all remedies for breach of contract. Nor do we think that Congress intended to shield employers from the natural consequences of their breaches of bargaining agreements by wrongful union conduct in the enforcement of such agreements. Cf. Richardson v. Texas & N. O. R. R., 242 F.2d 230, 235–236 (C.A.5th Cir.).

For these reasons, we think the wrongfully discharged employee may bring an action against his employer in the face of a defense based upon the failure to exhaust contractual remedies, provided the employee can prove that the union as bargaining agent breached its duty of fair representation in its handling of the employee's grievance. We may assume for present purposes that such a breach of duty by the union is an unfair labor practice, as the NLRB and the Fifth Circuit have held. The employee's suit against the employer, however, remains a § 301 suit, and the jurisdiction of the courts is no more destroyed by the fact that the employee, as part and parcel of his § 301 action, finds it necessary to prove an unfair labor practice by the union, than it is by the fact that the suit may involve an unfair labor practice by the employer himself. The court is free to determine whether the employee is barred by the actions of his union representative, and, if not, to proceed with the case. And if, to facilitate his case, the employee joins the union as a defendant, the situation is not substantially changed. The action is still a § 301 suit, and the jurisdiction of the courts is not pre-empted under the *Garmon* principle. This, at the very least, is the holding of Humphrey v. Moore with respect to pre-emption, as petitioners recognize in their brief. And, insofar as adjudication of the union's breach of duty is concerned, the result should be no different if the employee, as Owens did here, sues the employer and the union in separate actions. There would be very little to commend a rule which would permit the Missouri courts to adjudicate the Union's conduct in an action against Swift but not in an action against the Union itself.

For the above reasons, it is obvious that the courts will be compelled to pass upon whether there has been a breach of the duty of fair representation in the context of many § 301 breach-of-contract actions. If a breach of duty by the union and a breach of contract by the employer are proven, the court must fashion an appropriate remedy. Presumably, in at least some cases, the union's breach of duty will have enhanced or contributed to the employee's injury. What possible sense could there be in a rule which would permit a court that has litigated the fault of employer and union to fashion a remedy only with respect to the employer? Under such a rule, either the employer would be compelled by the court to pay for the union's wrong—slight deterrence, indeed, to future union misconduct —or the injured employee would be forced to go to two tribunals to repair a single injury. Moreover, the Board would be compelled in many cases either to remedy injuries arising out of a breach of contract, a task which Congress has not assigned to it, or to leave the individual employe without remedy for the union's wrong. Given the strong reasons for not pre-empting duty of fair representation suits in general, and the fact that the courts in many § 301 suits must adjudicate whether the union has breached its duty, we conclude that the courts may also fashion remedies for such a breach of duty.

It follows from the above that the Missouri courts had jurisdiction in this case. * * *

III.

Petitioners contend, as they did in their motion for judgment notwithstanding the jury's verdict, that Owens failed to prove that the Union breached its duty of fair representation in its handling of Owens' grievance. Petitioners also argue that the Supreme Court of Missouri, in rejecting this contention, applied a standard that is inconsistent with governing principles of federal law with respect to the Union's duty to an individual employee in its processing of grievances under the collective bargaining agreement with Swift. We agree with both contentions.

A.

* * * [T]he question which the Missouri Supreme Court thought dispositive of the issue of liability was whether the evidence supported Owens' assertion that he had been wrongfully discharged by Swift, regardless of the Union's good faith in reaching a contrary conclusion. This was also the major concern of the plaintiff at trial: the bulk of Owens' evidence was directed at whether he was medically fit at the time of discharge and whether he had performed heavy work after that discharge.

A breach of the statutory duty of fair representation occurs
only when a union's conduct toward a member of the collective bargaining unit is arbitrary, discriminatory, or in bad faith. * * *
Though we accept the proposition that a union may not arbitrarily
ignore a meritorious grievance or process it in perfunctory fashion,
we do not agree that the individual employee has an absolute right
to have his grievance taken to arbitration regardless of the provisions of the applicable collective bargaining agreement. In L.M.R.A.
§ 203(d), 29 U.S.C.A. § 173(d), Congress declared that "Final adjustment by a method agreed upon by the parties is * * * the
desirable method for settlement of grievance disputes arising over
the application or interpretation of an existing collective-bargaining
agreement." In providing for a grievance and arbitration procedure
which gives the union discretion to supervise the grievance machinery and to invoke arbitration, the employer and the union contemplate that each will endeavor in good faith to settle grievances
short of arbitration. Through this settlement process, frivolous
grievances are ended prior to the most costly and time-consuming
step in the grievance procedures. Moreover, both sides are assured
that similar complaints will be treated consistently, and major problem areas in the interpretation of the collective bargaining contract
can be isolated and perhaps resolved. And finally, the settlement
process furthers the interest of the union as statutory agent and as
coauthor of the bargaining agreement in representing the employees
in the enforcement of that agreement. See Cox, Rights Under a Labor Agreement, 69 Harv.L.Rev. 601 (1956).

If the individual employee could compel arbitration of his grievance regardless of its merit, the settlement machinery provided by
the contract would be substantially undermined, thus destroying the
employer's confidence in the union's authority and returning the individual grievant to the vagaries of independent and unsystematic
negotiation. Moreover, under such a rule, a significantly greater
number of grievances would proceed to arbitration. This would
greatly increase the cost of the grievance machinery and could so
overburden the arbitration process as to prevent it from functioning
successfully. See NLRB v. Acme Ind. Co., 385 U.S. 432, 438, 87
S.Ct. 565, 569, 17 L.Ed.2d 495; Ross, Distressed Grievance Procedures and Their Rehabilitation, in Labor Arbitration and Industrial
Change, Proceedings of the 16th Annual Meeting, National Academy
of Arbitrators 104 (1963). It can well be doubted whether the parties to collective bargaining agreements would long continue to provide for detailed grievance and arbitration procedures of the kind
encouraged by L.M.R.A. § 203(d), supra, if their power to settle the
majority of grievances short of the costlier and more time-consuming steps was limited by a rule permitting the grievant unilaterally

to invoke arbitration.   Nor do we see substantial danger to the interests of the individual employee if his statutory agent is given the contractual power honestly and in good faith to settle grievances short of arbitration.   For these reasons, we conclude that a union does not breach its duty of fair representation, and thereby open up a suit by the employee for breach of contract, merely because it settled the grievance short of arbitration.   *   *   *

For these same reasons, the standard applied here by the Missouri Supreme Court cannot be sustained.   For if a union's decision that a particular grievance lacks sufficient merit to justify arbitration would constitute a breach of the duty of fair representation because a judge or jury later found the grievance meritorious, the union's incentive to settle such grievances short of arbitration would be seriously reduced.   The dampening effect on the entire grievance procedure of this reduction of the union's freedom to settle claims in good faith would surely be substantial.   Since the union's statutory duty of fair representation protects the individual employee from arbitrary abuses of the settlement device by providing him with recourse against both employer (in a § 301 suit) and union, this severe limitation on the power to settle grievances is neither necessary nor desirable.   Therefore, we conclude that the Supreme Court of Missouri erred in upholding the verdict in this case solely on the ground that the evidence supported Owens' claim that he had been wrongfully discharged.

B.

Applying the proper standard of union liability to the facts of this case, we cannot uphold the jury's award, for we conclude that as a matter of federal law the evidence does not support a verdict that the Union breached its duty of fair representation.   *   *   *

In administering the grievance and arbitration machinery as statutory agent of the employees, a union must, in good faith and in a nonarbitrary manner make decisions as to the merits of particular grievances.   See Humphrey v. Moore, 375 U.S. 335, 349–350, 84 S.Ct. 363, 371–372, 11 L.Ed.2d 370; Ford Motor Co. v. Huffman, 345 U.S. 330, 337–339, 73 S.Ct. 681, 685–687, 97 L.Ed. 1048.   In a case such as this, when Owens supplied the Union with medical evidence supporting his position, the Union might well have breached its duty had it ignored Owens' complaint or had it processed the grievance in a perfunctory manner.   See Cox, Rights under a Labor Agreement, 69 Harv.L.Rev., at 632–634.   But here the Union processed the grievance into the fourth step, attempted to gather sufficient evidence to prove Owens' case, attempted to secure for Owens less vigorous work at the plant, and joined in the employer's efforts to have Owens rehabilitated. Only when these efforts all proved unsuccessful did the Union conclude both that arbitration would be fruitless and that the grievance should be dismissed. There was no evidence that any Union officer was personally hostile to Owens or that the Union acted at any time other than in good faith. Having concluded that the individual employee has no absolute right to have his grievance arbitrated under the collective bargaining agreement at issue, and that a breach of the duty of fair representation is not established merely by proof that the underlying grievance was meritorious, we must conclude that that duty was not breached here.

IV.

In our opinion, there is another important reason why the judgment of the Missouri Supreme Court cannot stand. Owens' suit against the Union was grounded on his claim that Swift had discharged him in violation of the applicable collective bargaining agreement. In his complaint, Owens alleged "that, as a direct result of said wrongful breach of said contract, by employer * * *. Plaintiff was damaged in the sum of Six Thousand, Five Hundred ($6,500.00) Dollars per year, continuing until the date of trial." For the Union's role in "preventing Plaintiff from completely exhausting administrative remedies," Owens requested, and the jury awarded, compensatory damages for the above-described breach of contract plus punitive damages of $3,000. R., at 6. We hold that such damages are not recoverable from the Union in the circumstances of this case.

The appropriate remedy for a breach of a union's duty of fair representation must vary with the circumstances of the particular breach. In this case, the employee's complaint was that the Union wrongfully failed to afford him the arbitration remedy against his employer established by the collective bargaining agreement. But the damages sought by Owens were primarily those suffered because of the employer's alleged breach of contract. Assuming for the moment that Owens had been wrongfully discharged, Swift's only defense to a direct action for breach of contract would have been the Union's failure to resort to arbitration, compare Republic Steel Corp. v. Maddox, 379 U.S. 650, 85 S.Ct. 614, 13 L.Ed.2d 58, with Smith v. Evening News Assn., 371 U.S. 195, 83 S.Ct. 267, 9 L.Ed.2d 246, and if that failure was itself a violation of the Union's statutory duty to the employee, there is no reason to exempt the employer from contractual damages which he would otherwise have had to pay. The difficulty lies in fashioning an appropriate scheme of remedies.

Petitioners urge that an employee be restricted in such circumstances to a decree compelling the employer and the union to arbitrate the underlying grievance. It is true that the employee's action is based on the employer's alleged breach of contract plus the union's alleged wrongful failure to afford him his contractual remedy of arbitration. For this reason, an order compelling arbitration should be viewed as one of the available remedies when a breach of the union's duty is proved. But we see no reason inflexibly to require arbitration in all cases. In some cases, for example, at least part of the employee's damages may be attributable to the union's breach of duty, and an arbitrator may have no power under the bargaining agreement to award such damages against the union. In other cases, the arbitrable issues may be substantially resolved in the course of trying the fair representation controversy. In such situations, the court should be free to decide the contractual claim and to award the employee appropriate damages or equitable relief.

A more difficult question is, what portion of the employee's damages may be charged to the union: in particular, may an award against a union include, as it did here, damages attributable solely to the employer's breach of contract? We think not. Though the union has violated a statutory duty in failing to press the grievance, it is the employer's unrelated breach of contract which triggered the controversy and which caused this portion of the employee's damages. The employee should have no difficulty recovering these damages from the employer, who cannot, as we have explained, hide behind the union's wrongful failure to act; in fact, the employer may be (and probably should be) joined as a defendant in the fair representation suit, as in Humphrey v. Moore, supra. It could be a real hardship on the union to pay these damages, even if the union were given a right of indemnification against the employer. With the employee assured of direct recovery from the employer, we see no merit in requiring the union to pay the employer's share of the damages.[5]

The governing principle, then, is to apportion liability between the employer and the union according to the damage caused by the fault of each. Thus, damages attributable solely to the employer's

---

5. We are not dealing here with situations where a union has affirmatively caused the employer to commit the alleged breach of contract. In cases of that sort where the union's conduct is found to be an unfair labor practice the NLRB has found an unfair labor practice by the employer, too, and has held the union and the employer jointly and severally liable for any back pay found owing to the particular employee who was the subject of their joint discrimination. E. g., Imparato Stevedoring Corp., 113 N.L.R.B. 883 (1955); Squirt Distrib. Co., 92 N.L.R.B. 1667 (1951); H. M. Newman, 85 N.L.R.B. 725 (1949). Even if this approach would be appropriate for analogous § 301 and breach-of-duty suits, it is not applicable here. Since the Union played no part in Swift's alleged breach of contract and since Swift took no part in the Union's alleged breach of duty, joint liability for either wrong would be unwarranted.

breach of contract should not be charged to the union, but increases if any in those damages caused by the union's refusal to process the grievance should not be charged to the employer. In this case, even if the Union had breached its duty, all or almost all of Owens' damages would still be attributable to his allegedly wrongful discharge by Swift. For these reasons, even if the Union here had properly been found liable for a breach of duty, it is clear that the damage award was improper.

Reversed.

MR. JUSTICE FORTAS, with whom THE CHIEF JUSTICE and MR. JUSTICE HARLAN join, concurring in the result.

* * * There is no basis for failure to apply the pre-emption principles in the present case * * *. The relationship between the union and the individual employee with respect to the processing of claims to employment rights under the collective bargaining agreement is fundamental to the design and operation of federal labor law. It is not "merely peripheral," as the Court's opinion states. * * * This is not an action by the employee against the employer, and the discussion of the requisites of such an action is, in my judgment, unnecessary. * * * The Court holds—and I think correctly if the issue is to be reached—that the union could not be required to pay damages measured by the breach of the employment contract, because it was not the union but the employer that breached the contract. I agree; but I suggest that this reveals the point for which I contend: that the employee's claim against the union is not a claim under the collective bargaining agreement, but a claim that the union has breached its statutory duty of fair representation. This claim, I submit, is a claim of unfair labor practice and it is within the exclusive jurisdiction of the NLRB. * * *

If we look beyond logic and precedent to the policy of the labor relations design which Congress has provided, court jurisdiction of this type of actions seems anomalous and ill-advised. We are not dealing here with the interpretation of a contract or with an alleged breach of an employment agreement. As the Court in effect acknowledges, we are concerned with the subtleties of a union's statutory duty faithfully to represent employees in the unit, including those who may not be members of the union. The Court—regrettably, in my opinion—ventures to state judgments as to the metes and bounds of the reciprocal duties involved in the relationship between the union and the employee. In my opinion, this is precisely and especially the kind of judgment that Congress intended to entrust to the Board and which is well within the pre-emption doctrine that this Court has prudently stated. * * *

Accordingly, I join the judgment of reversal, but on the basis stated.

MR. JUSTICE BLACK, dissenting.

The Court today opens slightly the courthouse door to an employee's incidental claim against his union for breach of its duty of fair representation, only to shut it in his face when he seeks direct judicial relief for his underlying and more valuable breach-of-contract claim against his employer. This result follows from the Court's announcement in this case, involving an employee's suit against his union, of a new rule to govern an employee's suit against his employer. The rule is that before an employee can sue his employer under § 301 of the L.M.R.A. for a simple breach of his employment contract, the employee must prove not only that he attempted to exhaust his contractual remedies, but that his attempt to exhaust them was frustrated by "arbitrary, discriminatory or * * * bad faith" conduct on the part of his union. With this new rule and its result, I cannot agree.

The Court recognizes as it must, that the jury in this case found at least that Benjamin Owens was fit for work, that his grievance against Swift was meritorious, and that Swift breached the collective bargaining agreement when it wrongfully discharged him. * * * Owens, who now has obtained a judicial determination that he was wrongfully discharged, is left remediless, and Swift, having breached its contract, is allowed to hide behind, and is shielded by, the union's conduct. I simply fail to see how it should make one iota of difference, as far as the "unrelated breach-of-contract" by Swift is concerned, whether the union's conduct is wrongful or rightful. Neither precedent nor logic support the Court's new announcement that it does.

Certainly, nothing in Republic Steel Corp. v. Maddox, 379 U.S. 650, 85 S.Ct. 614, supports this new rule. That was a case where the aggrieved employee attempted to "completely sidestep available grievance procedures in favor of a lawsuit." Id., at 653, 85 S.Ct. at 616. Noting that "it cannot be said * * * that contract grievance procedures are inadequate to protect the interests of an aggrieved employee until the employee has attempted to implement the procedures and found them so," ibid., the Court there held that the employee "must *attempt* use of the contract grievance procedure," id., at 652, 85 S.Ct. at 616, and "must afford the union the opportunity to act on his behalf," id., at 653, 85 S.Ct. at 616. * * * Here, of course, Benjamin Owens did not "completely sidestep available grievance procedures in favor of a lawsuit." With complete respect for the union's authority and deference to the contract grievance procedures, he not only gave the union a chance to act on his behalf, but in every way possible tried to convince it that his claim was meritorious and should be carried through the fifth step to arbitration. In short, he did everything the Court's opinion in *Maddox* said he should do, and yet now the Court says so much is not enough.

* * *

. * * * If the Court here were satisfied with merely holding that in this situation the employee cannot recover damages from the union unless the union breached its duty of fair representation, then it would be one thing to say that the union did not do so in making a good-faith decision not to take the employee's grievance to arbitration. But if, as the Court goes on to hold, the employee cannot sue his employer for breach of contract unless his failure to exhaust contractual remedies is due to the union's breach of its duty of fair representation, then I am quite unwilling to say that the union's refusal to exhaust such remedies—however non-arbitrary—does not amount to a breach of its duty. Either the employee should be able to sue his employer for breach of contract after having attempted to exhaust his contractual remedies, or the union should have an absolute duty to exhaust contractual remedies on his behalf. The merits of an employee's grievance would thus be determined by either a jury or an arbitrator. Under today's decision it will never be determined by either.

* * * The Court suggests three reasons for giving the union this almost unlimited discretion to deprive injured employees of all remedies for breach of contract. The first is that "frivolous grievances" will be ended prior to time-consuming and costly arbitration. But here no one, not even the union, suggests that Benjamin Owens' grivance was frivolous. The union decided not to take it to arbitration simply because the union doubted the chance of success. Even if this was a good-faith doubt, I think the union had the duty to present this contested, but serious claim to the arbitrator whose very function is to decide such claims on the basis of what he believes to be right. Second, the Court says that allowing the union to settle grievances prior to arbitration will assure consistent treatment of "major problem areas in interpretation of collective bargaining contracts." But can it be argued that whether Owens was "fit to work" presents a major problem in the interpretation of the collective bargaining agreement? The problem here was one of interpreting medical reports, not a collective bargaining agreement, and of evaluating other evidence of Owens' physical condition. I doubt whether consistency is either possible or desirable in determining whether a particular employee is able to perform a particular job. Finally, the Court suggests that its decision "furthers the interests of the union as statutory agent." I think this is the real reason for today's decision which entirely overlooks the interests of the injured employee, the only one who has anything to lose. Of course, anything which gives the union life and death power over those whom it is supposed to represent furthers its "interests." I simply fail to see how the union's legitimate role as statutory agent is undermined by requiring it to prosecute all serious grievances to a conclusion or by allowing the injured employee to sue his employer after he has given the union a chance to act on his behalf.

Henceforth, in almost every § 301 breach-of-contract suit by an employee against an employer, the employee will have the additional burden of proving that the union acted "arbitrarily or in bad faith." The Court never explains what is meant by this vague phrase or how trial judges are intelligently to translate it to a jury. Must the employee prove that the union in fact acted arbitrarily, or will it be sufficient to show that the employee's grievance was so meritorious that a reasonable union would not have refused to carry it to arbitration? Must the employee join the union in his § 301 suit against the employer, or must he join the employer in his unfair representation suit against the union? However these questions are answered, today's decision, requiring the individual employee to take on both the employer and the union in every suit against the employer and to prove not only that the employer breached its contract, but that the union acted arbitrarily, converts what would otherwise be a simple breach-of-contract action into a three-ring donnybrook. It puts an intolerable burden on employees with meritorious grievances and means they will frequently be left with no remedy. Today's decision, while giving the worker an ephemeral right to sue his union for breach of its duty of fair representation, creates insurmountable obstacles to block his far more valuable right to sue his employer for breach of the collective bargaining agreement.

UNION NEWS CO. v. HILDRETH, 295 F.2d 658 (6th Cir. 1962). Plaintiff Gladys Hildreth had been employed for ten years at the soda and lunch counter of the defendant Union News Company in a Detroit railroad station. The labor contract between the Company and the Hotel and Restaurant Employees Union provided that no employee was to be discharged except for just cause. Between early 1957 and early 1958, the Company noted cash shortages at the lunch counter; an examination by Union representatives of the Company's business records caused them to concur in the Company's judgment that one or more of the counter employees was being dishonest in handling money. Although the Company's manager suggested that the entire counter crew (of eleven or twelve employees) should be terminated, the Union prevailed upon the Company not to take such drastic action; instead, both Company and Union agreed to a temporary layoff and replacement of five of the counter employees for the purpose of seeing whether the cash picture would improve. Plaintiff Hildreth was among the five employees thus laid off in March 1958. When the cash picture improved in March and April, the Union agreed that the Company's experiment had proved its point, and that the replacement of the five employees could be made permanent. Although Ms. Hildreth met with Union officials—including the grievance committee and ultimately the executive board —in an effort to convince them that her discharge was unjust, the Union chose not to press a grievance on her behalf. The Company did not acquiesce in demands by Ms. Hildreth's attorney to permit her to process her grievance directly. Ms. Hildreth secured a jury verdict in the amount of $5,000 in her action for wrongful discharge in breach of the collective bargaining agreement. The judgment of the trial court was, however, reversed on appeal.

Although the court of appeals found no evidence that Ms. Hildreth had acted dishonestly, it also found no evidence that the Union and the Company had acted fraudulently, collusively or in bad faith. The court thus concluded that, by virtue of the Union's authority as exclusive bargaining representative, the Union and the Company could "mutually conclude, as a part of the bargaining process, that the circumstances shown by the evidence provided just cause for the layoff and discharge of plaintiff and other of defendant's employees. * * * Unless such bilateral decisions, made in good faith, and after unhurried consideration between a Union and an employer, be sustained in court, the bargaining process is a mirage, without the efficacy contemplated by the philosophy of the law which makes its use compulsory." The court noted that the parties were obligated by law to continue the process of collective bargaining even during the contract term, in the interpretation and administration of that contract. It held that the parties did not, "through retroactive compromise, settle or wipe out a vested and already existing grievance or cause of action of an employee," which would be beyond the Union's power; rather, the Union agreed with the employer that the "just cause" provision of the contract was properly construed to embrace the situation at the Company's lunch counter. The labor contract itself gave the Union the responsibility to construe its terms on behalf of the employees. "We consider that the Union was acting in the *collective* interest of those who by law and contract the Union was charged with protecting. * * * Under the philosophy of collective responsibility an employer who bargains in good faith should be entitled to rely upon the promises and agreements of the Union representatives with whom he must deal under the compulsion of law and contract. The collective bargaining process should be carried on between parties who can mutually respect and rely upon the authority of each other."

SIMMONS v. UNION NEWS CO., 382 U.S. 884, 86 S.Ct. 165, 15 L.Ed.2d 125 (1965). The Supreme Court denied certiorari to review a court of appeals decision for the Union News Company in a case, brought by one Simmons, arising from the same incident of "group discharge" that was litigated in the *Hildreth* case. Mr. Justice Black wrote an opinion, in which Chief Justice Warren concurred, dissenting from the denial of certiorari. Excerpts from his opinion follow. "The courts below refused to make their own determination of whether Miss Hildreth's and petitioner's discharges were made for 'just cause.' Instead, they allowed the employer's defense that 'just cause' was simply what the employer and the union jointly wanted it to be. * * *

"This case points up with great emphasis the kind of injustice that can occur to an individual employee when the employer and the union have such power over the employee's claim for breach of contract. Here no one has claimed from the beginning to the end of the Hildreth lawsuit or this lawsuit that either of these individuals was guilty of any kind of misconduct justifying her discharge. * * Moreover, petitioner alleges that she was prepared to show that subsequent to her discharge, the office girl who counted the money received at the lunch counter was found to be embezzling those funds and was discharged for it. Miss Hildreth had worked for respondent for nine and one-half years, and petitioner for fifteen years, prior to their discharges. There is no evidence that respondent had ever been dissatisfied with their work before the company became disappointed with its lunch counter about a year prior to the discharges. Yet both were discharged for 'just cause,' as determined not by a court but by an agreement of the company and the union.

"I would not construe the National Labor Relations Act as giving a union and an employer any such power over workers. In this case there has been no bargain made on behalf of all the workers represented by the union. Rather there has been a sacrifice of the rights of a group of employees based on the belief that some of them might possibly have been guilty of some kind of misconduct that would reduce the employer's profits. Fully recognizing the right of the collective bargaining representative to make a contract on the part of the workers for the future, I cannot believe that those who passed the Act intended to give the union the right to negotiate away alleged breaches of a contract claimed by individual employees.

"The plain fact is that petitioner has lost her job, not because of any guilt on her part, but because there is a suspicion that some one of the group which was discharged was guilty of misconduct. The sum total of what has been done here is to abandon the fine, old American ideal that guilt is personal. Our system of jurisprudence should not tolerate imposing on the innocent punishment that should be laid on the guilty. If the construction of the labor law given by the courts below is to stand, it should be clearly and unequivocally announced by this Court so that Congress can, if it sees fit, consider this question and protect the just claims of employees from the joint power of employers and unions."

At the heart of Mr. Justice Black's disagreement with the Court in Vaca v. Sipes and Simmons v. Union News Co. is a felt distinction between the negotiation of new contract terms and the settlement of grievances arising under an existing labor agreement. New contract terms are of a "legislative" quality, which speak broadly and prospectively to issues of general import for whole classes of employees, and which are formulated, declared and ratified typically in an open and visible manner; the orderly adjustment of interests within the bargaining unit requires that the union be the exclusive representative and that individual negotiations be outlawed. (Such was the philosophy articulated in J. I. Case Co. v. NLRB, 321 U.S. 332, 64 S.Ct. 576, 88 L.Ed. 762 (1944).) On the other hand, claims arising under an existing agreement have a more "vested" quality about them; they may arise under fairly clear contractual provisions, on which individuals have rested their expectations; grievance adjustment will often arise from such idiosyncratic fact situations that no broad contractual norms will be at stake and no other substantial employee interests undermined. Grievance settlements by the union may often be ad hoc and achieved through informal processes of low visibility. It is said that all of these elements make it appropriate—and not at all disruptive—to permit the aggrieved employee to pursue his or her contract claim directly against the employer, either by lawsuit or by the contractual grievance machinery culminating in arbitration. Indeed, there are references in a number of judicial decisions, including those of Justice Black, to the proviso to Section 9(a) of the Labor Act, which some have read to *entitle* aggrieved employees to press their contract claims directly whenever the union declines to do so (even in good faith).

For example, in Hughes Tool Co. v. NLRB, 56 N.L.R.B. 981 (1944), enf'd 147 F.2d 69 (5th Cir. 1945), the proviso was read to entitle the aggrieved employee to present grievances by appearing at every stage of the grievance procedure: "If, at any level of the established grievance procedure, there is an agreement between the employer, the exclusive representative, and the individual or group, disposition of the grievance is thereby achieved. Failing agreement of all three parties, any dissatisfied party may carry the grievance through subsequent machinery until the established grievance procedure is exhausted." See also Donnelly v. United Fruit Co., 40 N.J. 61, 190 A.2d 825 (1963). Is it not clear that this interpretation of the proviso has been squarely rejected by the Supreme Court in *Vaca v. Sipes,* and also more recently and explicitly in *Emporium Capwell Co. v. Western Addition Community Organization,* supra page 373, note 7?

Consider also the broader underlying distinction between contract negotiation and grievance adjustment, and the suggestion that the union's authority in the latter process is much more restricted. Justice Goldberg spoke to this issue in his concurring opinion in HUMPHREY v. MOORE, 375 U.S. 335, 352–53, 84 S.Ct. 363, 11 L.Ed.2d 370 (1964), a case in which a joint union-management panel resolved a contract grievance by agreeing to construe a provision in the labor contract to allow dovetailing of seniority rosters (when there was a serious issue as to the effect of the provision):

> "A mutually acceptable grievance settlement between an employer and a union, which is what the decision of the Joint Committee was, cannot be challenged by an individual dissenting employee under § 301(a) on the ground that the parties exceeded their contractual powers in making the settlement. * * * [T]he existing labor contract is the touchstone of an arbitrator's powers. But the power of the union and the employer jointly to settle a grievance dispute is not so limited. The parties are free by joint action to modify, amend and supplement their original collective bargaining agreement. They are equally free, since '[t]he grievance procedure is * * * a part of the continuous collective bargaining process,' to settle grievances not falling within the scope of the contract. [United Steelworkers v. Warrior & Gulf Navigation Co., 363 U.S. 574, 581 (1960).] In this case, for example, had the dispute gone to arbitration, the arbitrator would have been bound to apply the existing agreement and to determine whether the merger-absorption clause applied. However, even in the absence of such a clause, the contracting parties—the multiemployer unit and the union—were free to resolve the dispute by amending the contract to dovetail seniority lists or to achieve the same result by entering into a grievance settlement. The presence of the merger-absorption clause did not restrict the right of the parties to resolve their dispute by joint agreement applying, interpreting, or amending the contract. There are too many unforeseeable contingencies in a collective bargaining rela-

tionship to justify making the words of the contract the exclusive source of rights and duties.

" * * * If collective bargaining is to remain a flexible process, the power to amend by agreement and the power to interpret by agreement must be coequal.

"It is wholly inconsistent with this Court's recognition that '[t]he grievance procedure is * * * a part of the continuous collective bargaining process,' United Steelworkers of America v. Warrior & Gulf Navigation Co., 363 U.S., at 581, 80 S.Ct., at 1352, to limit the parties' power to settle grievances to the confines of the existing labor agreement, or to assert, as the Court now does, that an individual employee can claim that the collective bargaining contract is violated because the parties have made a grievance settlement going beyond the strict terms of the existing contract."

Problems for Discussion

1. Suppose that Johnson, a carpenter in a plant-wide unit covered by a collective bargaining agreement, was called out to do maintenance work on a high roof on Labor Day 1965 as a result of hurricane damage. He worked from 7:00 a. m. to 7:00 p. m. His usual rate of pay is $4.00 an hour. The collective bargaining agreement contains the following provisions:

"Eight hours' work between the hours of 8 o'clock a. m. and 5 o'clock p. m. shall constitute the regularly scheduled workday.

"All work in excess of eight hours a day and work performed outside of the regularly scheduled working hours shall be paid at time and a half the regular rate of pay.

"When maintenance men are required to perform work at heights above 50 feet, they shall be paid double time.

"Double time shall be paid for all work on the following holidays: New Year's Day, Memorial Day * * * Labor Day. * * *"

The company paid Johnson $8.00 an hour for this work. It might be contended that he should have been paid $16.00 for each of eight hours between 8 a. m. and 5 p. m., $24.00 for the ninth hour, and $36.00 for the work outside normal hours, a total of $224 for the day. Various other interpretations and calculations are possible that would reduce the pyramiding.

(a) May the company discuss the grievance with Johnson alone?

(b) If Johnson refuses to sign a grievance form, has the union any remedy under the grievance procedure?

(c) If Johnson accepts a compromise, does it bind the union?

(d) If the union accepts a compromise in grievance discussions (for example, an interpretation that gives Johnson only the premiums for high and holiday work), does it bind Johnson? If not, what recourse does Johnson have?

2. The chairman of the union's grievance committee has come to you for advice. A grievance initiated by employee Curth has been processed through the first three steps of the contractual grievance procedure; it remains unsettled, and arbitration is now available to the union on demand. Although the grievance committee believes there is some merit to Curth's grievance, it has concluded that it ought not proceed to arbitration. This judgment was based on the fact that the Curth grievance arose in a somewhat unique factual setting, that an arbitration victory will therefore not be of important precedential value, and, most important, that the union is in serious financial straits and an arbitration will consume a substantial proportion of its funds. The committee decided that it was more important to conserve those funds either for a grievance of more general significance or for the next collective bargaining negotiation. The chairman of the committee wishes to know whether, on these facts, the union is free to decline to take Curth's grievance to arbitration. What is your response? *Curth* v. *Faraday, Inc.*, 401 F.Supp. 678 (E.D.Mich.1975). (If a court were to find this action by the union to be a violation of the duty of fair representation, what remedy should be ordered?)

3. Assume that in Problem 2, Curth proceeds initially against the union for breach of the duty of fair representation, by filing a charge under Section 8(b)(1)(A) with the NLRB. Assume too that the NLRB concludes that the union committed no unfair labor practice. In the event Curth then sues the company for breach of the labor contract, can the company successfully assert the determination by the NLRB as a defense? (Would it matter whether the NLRB determination took the form of a refusal by the General Counsel to issue a complaint against the union, or instead took the form of a judgment on the merits by an Administrative Law Judge and the full NLRB?)

Conversely, if the NLRB found that the union had violated its duty of fair representation, will that finding be preclusive in Curth's court action under Section 301 against the company?

HINES v. ANCHOR MOTOR FREIGHT, INC., 424 U.S. 554, 96 S.Ct. 1048, 47 L.Ed.2d 231 (1976). Anchor discharged eight truckdrivers for dishonesty, claiming that in seeking reimbursement for overnight motel expenses, they had presented to the company receipts which overstated their actual room charges. At a later meeting attended by the drivers and their union, the company produced these receipts along with motel registration cards showing a lower room rate for the night in question, a notarized statement of the motel clerk asserting that the registration cards were accurate, and the motel owner's affidavit containing the same assertion as well as his statement that the drivers had been furnished with inflated receipts. The union claimed that the drivers were innocent and that their discharge was not for "just cause" as required by the collective bargaining agreement; and it asked that the case be submitted to the joint company-union arbitration committee. The union took no steps to investigate the motel, and at the hearing no evidence other than the drivers' assertion of their own innocence was presented by the union to challenge the company's documents.

The committee denied the grievance. The drivers then retained an attorney who secured a statement from the motel owner to the effect that the discrepancy between the receipts and the registration cards could in theory have been attributable to the motel clerk's intentional understatement on the cards and his pocketing of the difference.

The drivers brought an action against Anchor for unjust discharge in breach of contract, and against the union for breach of its duty of fair representation by virtue of its alleged failure, arbitrarily and in bad faith, to investigate their case properly. A deposition of the motel clerk revealed that he had in fact falsified the registration records and that it was he and not the drivers who had pocketed the difference between the sum on the registration cards and the sum on the receipts.

Although the District Judge granted summary judgment for both Anchor and the union (holding that at worst the union's conduct exhibited bad judgment), the court of appeals reversed the judgment as to the union, finding sufficient facts to sustain a possible inference of bad faith or arbitrary conduct. The higher court, however, affirmed the summary judgment for Anchor; it relied on the labor-contract provision making a grievance-committee decision "final and binding," and it concluded that the company had engaged in no misconduct in the grievance procedure.

The Supreme Court, assuming without deciding that the reversal of the summary judgment for the union was correct, held (6–2) that it necessarily followed that the summary judgment for Anchor had to be reversed, and that the finality provisions of the labor contract were no defense. Relying on *Vaca v. Sipes*, the Court concluded that just as the union's breach of the duty of fair representation in settling a grievance before arbitration relieves the employee in the Section 301 action against the employer of the duty to exhaust the grievance procedures, so too does the union's subversion of the arbitration process itself remove the bar of the arbitrator's decision.

The Court stated:

"Under the rule announced by the Court of Appeals, unless the employer is implicated in the Union's malfeasance or has otherwise caused the arbitral process to err, petitioners would have no remedy against Anchor even though they are successful in proving the Union's bad faith, the falsity of the charges against them and the breach of contract by Anchor by discharging without cause. This rule would apparently govern even in circumstances where it is shown that a union has manufactured the evidence and knows from the start that it is false; or even if, unbeknownst to the employer, the union has corrupted the arbitrator to the detriment of disfavored union members. As is the case where there has been a failure to exhaust, however, we cannot believe that Congress intended to foreclose the employee from his § 301 remedy otherwise available against the employer if the contractual processes have been seriously flawed by the union's breach of its duty to represent employees honestly and in good faith and without invidious discrimination or arbitrary conduct.

* * *

"Petitioners are not entitled to relitigate their discharge merely because they offer newly discovered evidence that the charges against them were false and that in fact they were fired without cause. The grievance processes cannot be expected to be error-free. The finality provision has sufficient force to surmount occasional instances of mistake. But it is quite another matter to suggest that erroneous arbitration decisions must stand even though the employee's representation by the Union has been dishonest, in bad faith or discriminatory; for in that event error and injustice of the grossest sort would multiply. The contractual system would then cease to qualify as an adequate mechanism to secure individual redress for damaging failure of the employer to abide by the contract. Congress has put its blessing on private dispute settlement arrangements provided in collective agreements, but it was anticipated, we are sure, that the contractual machinery would operate within some minimum levels of integrity. In our view, enforcement of the finality provision where the arbitrator has erred is conditioned upon the Union's having satisfied its statutory duty fairly to represent the employee in connection with the arbitration proceedings. Wrongfully discharged employees would be left without jobs and without a fair opportunity to secure an adequate remedy. * * *

"Petitioners, if they prove an erroneous discharge and the Union's breach of duty tainting the decision of the joint committee, are entitled to an appropriate remedy against the employer as well as the Union. * * *"

Problems for Discussion

1. The Court in *Hines* did not consider whether the union had in fact violated its duty of fair representation in its preparation and presen-

tation of the discharge grievance before the arbitrator. Given the manner in which the Court defines that duty in this case, did the Union in fact violate it?

2.   In the *Hines* case, the Supreme Court appears not to contemplate that the relief against the Anchor Company is to take the form of an order to re-submit the discharge grievances to arbitration; rather, those grievances are to be presented to the trial court. Is that a sound approach? If the trial court ultimately concludes that the dischargees were terminated wrongfully in breach of contract (contrary to the intervening arbitration award in the company's favor), should the court enter a judgment against the company for backpay for the full period from the date of discharge until the date of the judgment? What should be the liability of the union?

3.   Pete Velasquez has been a member of the International Longshoremen's Association and served as an official in an ILA local for two years. In June 1981, the employers' association which bargained with and signed a labor contract with the ILA instituted a grievance proceeding, charging that Velasquez had been responsible for instigating illegal work stoppages. In October, the claim was considered by an arbitrator, and was upheld; the award of the arbitrator "deregistered" Velasquez, which had the effect of depriving him of longshore work anywhere on the Pacific coast. On the same day, the same arbitrator rendered a decision in another grievance, this time in the union's favor, which limited the amount of lifting of heavy sacks to be done by all employees covered by the labor contract. Velasquez has secured information which leads him to believe that the two arbitration decisions were the product of an informal "swapping" agreement between the union and the employers, with the union sacrificing the Velasquez case in order to secure a decision that would benefit all workers in the unit. He has instituted an action against the union in a federal court, claiming breach of the duty of fair representation and alleging the above facts; the union has moved to dismiss the complaint. Should the motion be granted? See *Local 13, Longshoremen v. Pacific Maritime Ass'n*, 441 F.2d 1061 (9th Cir.), cert. denied, 404 U.S. 1061 (1971).

If the case were to go to trial, would Velasquez prevail if he could demonstrate that the "swapping" was done because he was disliked by union officials? Would it be *necessary* to prove this?

Would the union's conduct be any less subject to challenge had the "swapping" of grievances been effected informally between union and company representatives at the third step of the grievance procedure, prior to any arbitration proceedings?

Could the union win the case by demonstrating that the Velasquez grievance lacked merit?

4.   Employee Holodnak had published a letter in a local newspaper of a political group and was discharged for violating a company rule barring false or malicious statements concerning the company; the letter had attacked, among others, the company, the union, judges and arbitrators. The union assisted Holodnak in challenging his discharge through the grievance procedure, and provided an attorney to represent him in arbitration. At the

arbitration proceeding, the attorney conceded the validity of the company's rule; he did not urge the arbitrator to construe the rule strictly; he did not assert that the rule posed problems under the First Amendment, in view of the fact that almost all of the company's work was done pursuant to defense contracts with the United States Government; and he failed to intercede when the arbitrator on several occasions subjected Holodnak to questioning which Holodnak found offensive, inquisitorial and biased. The arbitrator ultimately sustained the discharge and denied the grievance. Holodnak now brings an action against the union for violation of its duty of fair representation, claiming that the attorney's performance was grossly inadequate. Should the court grant the union's motion for summary judgment? See *Holodnak v. Avco-Lycoming Div., Avco Corp.*, 381 F.Supp. 191 (D.Conn. 1974), mdf'd on other grounds 514 F.2d 285 (2d Cir. 1975). (If the court were to find the union's conduct to be a violation of the duty of fair representation, what remedy should be ordered?)

5. The labor contract between the Hussmann Refrigerator Company and Local 138 of the Steelworkers Union provides: "The Company recognizes the principle of seniority based upon the total length of continuous service with the Company. Seniority, skill and ability to perform the work required shall be considered by the Company in making promotions, transfers, layoffs and recalls. Where skill and ability to perform are substantially equal, seniority shall govern." The Company posted four job openings, and ultimately decided—after reviewing the personnel files of the eight employees bidding for the promotion—to award the positions to employees Morris, Newcomb, Oliver and Parker. These four had less seniority than four other bidders, Archer, Biddle, Carrington and DeVito, all of whom claimed that they had skill and ability equal to the successful bidders and all of whom convinced the Local to file grievances on their behalf. The union's grievance committee decided ultimately to proceed to arbitration. The union gave no notice of the hearing date to Morris, Newcomb, Oliver and Parker, and they did not appear before the arbitrator. The foreman, however, did testify on behalf of the Company, and gave the reasons why he believed that those four had skill and ability "head and shoulders" above the grievants, who testified on their own behalf. The arbitrator concluded that grievants Carrington and DeVito possessed skill and ability substantially equal to the four awardees, and directed the Company to promote them. The Company did so, by "bumping" and demoting Oliver and Parker.

Oliver and Parker have brought an action in a federal court against the Company for breach of contract and against the Local for breach of the duty of fair representation.

(a) Assume that the union decided to press the grievance of Archer, Biddle, Carrington and DeVito solely on the grounds that they were the four most senior bidders, that seniority is an objective principle for which unions have long fought, and that the claim that the awardees have greater skill and ability is not for the union to assess but rather for the employer to demonstrate before the arbitrator. Has the union violated its duty of fair representation? See *Smith v. Hussmann Refrigerator Co.*, 619 F.2d 1229 (8th Cir.) (en banc), cert. denied, —— U.S. ——, 101 S.Ct. 116, 66 L.Ed.2d 46 (1980).

(b) Assume, instead, that the union made a thorough investigation of the skill and ability of grievants Archer, Biddle, Carrington and De-Vito, and decided to press the grievance of these senior employees only after concluding that they were equal in skill and ability to the four awardees. In arguing that the union nonetheless violated its duty of fair representation, Oliver and Parker have asserted: "Where the interests of two groups of employees are diametrically opposed to each other and the union espouses the cause of one in the arbitration, it follows as a matter of law that there has been no fair representation of the other group. This is true even though, in choosing the cause of which group to espouse, the union acts completely objectively and with the best of motives. The old adage, that one cannot serve two masters, is particularly applicable to such a situation." Are Oliver and Parker correct? See *Clark v. Hein-Werner Corp.*, 8 Wis.2d 264, 99 N.W.2d 132 (1959).

(c) Did the union breach the duty of fair representation by failing to inform Oliver and Parker of the arbitration hearing and by failing to afford them an opportunity to testify there?

(d) Assume that the court concludes that there has been a breach of the union's duty of fair representation. Should the court then decide for itself (with a jury?) whether Oliver and Parker have substantially greater skill and ability than grievants Carrington and DeVito? What weight if any should be given the decision of the arbitrator?

(e) Assume that the court agrees with the arbitrator, finds that plaintiff-awardees Oliver and Parker were properly bumped and demoted, and that the employer did not breach the labor contract by doing so. Does this mean that, although the union may have violated its duty of fair representation, it is not liable for any remedy?

————

In a significant and thoughtful article, Professor Clyde W. Summers has, by examining the decided cases and reasoning from first principles, elicited the following "emerging principles of fair representation." See "The Individual Employee's Rights Under the Collective Agreement: What Constitutes Fair Representation?" in 126 Univ. of Pennsylvania L.Rev. 251, 279 (1977). Do you agree with Professor Summers that these principles "protect the individual's right to representation in grievance handling, and, at the same time, allow the union sufficient freedom to fulfill its function in administering the agreement"?

1. The individual employee has a right to have clear and unquestioned terms of the collective agreement that have been made for his benefit, followed and enforced until the agreement is properly amended. For the union to refuse to follow and enforce the rules and standards it has established on behalf of those it repre-

sents is arbitrary and constitutes a violation of its fiduciary obligation.

2.   The individual employee has no right to insist on any particular interpretation of an ambiguous provision in a collective agreement, for the union must be free to settle a grievance in accordance with any reasonable interpretation of the ambiguous provision.   However, the individual has a right that ambiguous provisions be applied consistently and that the provision mean the same when applied to him as when applied to other employees.   Settlement of similar grievances on different terms is discriminatory and violates the union's duty to represent all employees equally.

3.   The union has no duty to carry every grievance to arbitration; the union can sift out grievances that are trivial or lacking in merit.   However, the individual's right to equal treatment includes equal access to the grievance procedure and arbitration for similar grievances of equal merit.

4.   The individual employee has a right to have his grievance decided on its own merits.   The union violates its duty to represent fairly when it trades an individual's meritorious grievance for the benefit of another individual or of the group.   Majority vote does not necessarily validate grievance settlements, but may instead, make the settlement suspect as based on political power and not the merits of the grievance.

5.   Settlement of grievances for improper motives such as personal hostility, political opposition, or racial prejudice constitutes bad faith regardless of the merit of the grievance.   The union thereby violates its duty to represent fairly by refusing to process the grievance even though the employer may not have violated the agreement.

6.   The union can make good faith judgments in determining the merits of a grievance, but it owes the employees it represents the duty to use reasonable care and diligence both in investigating grievances in order to make that judgment, and in processing and presenting grievances on their behalf.

———

CLAYTON v. INTERNATIONAL UNION, UNITED AUTOMOBILE WORKERS

Supreme Court of the United States, 1981.
—— U.S. ——, —— S.Ct. ——, —— L.Ed.2d ——.

JUSTICE BRENNAN delivered the opinion of the Court.

An employee seeking a remedy for an alleged breach of the collective-bargaining agreement between his union and employer must attempt to exhaust any exclusive grievance and arbitration procedures established by that agreement before he may maintain a suit against his union or employer under § 301(a) of the Labor-Management Relations Act of 1947, 29 U.S.C. § 185(a). Republic Steel Corp. v. Maddox, 379 U.S. 650, 652–653 (1965); see Hines v. Anchor Motor Freight, Inc., 424 U.S. 554, 563 (1976); Vaca v. Sipes, 386 U.S. 171, 184 (1967). The question presented by this case is whether, and in what circumstances, an employee alleging that his union breached its duty of fair representation in processing his grievance, and that his employer breached the collective-bargaining agreement, must also attempt to exhaust the internal union appeals procedures established by his union's constitution before he may maintain his suit under § 301.

I

After eight years in the employ of ITT Gilfillan, Clifford E. Clayton, a member of the United Automobile, Aerospace and Agricultural Implement Workers of America (UAW) and a shop steward of its Local 509, was dismissed for violating a plant rule prohibiting defined misbehavior. Pursuant to the mandatory grievance and arbitration procedure established by the collective-bargaining agreement between ITT and Local 509, Clayton asked his union representative to file a grievance on his behalf on the ground that his dismissal was not for just cause. The union investigated Clayton's charges, pursued his grievance through the third step of the grievance procedure, and made a timely request for arbitration. It then withdrew the request, choosing not to proceed to arbitration. Clayton was notified of the union's decision after the time for requesting arbitration had expired.

The UAW requires every union member "who feels aggrieved by any action, decision, or penalty imposed upon him" by the union to exhaust internal union appeals procedures before seeking redress from a "civil court or governmental agency." UAW Constitution, Art. 33, § 12. These procedures, established by Arts. 32 and 33 of the UAW Constitution and incorporated into Art. IV of Local 509's bylaws, direct the employee first to seek relief from the membership of his local. Art. 33, § 3. If not satisfied with the result obtained there, the employee may further appeal to the International Executive Board of the UAW, and eventually to either the Constitutional Convention Appeals Committee or to a Public Review Board composed of "impartial persons of good public repute" who are not members or employees of the union. Arts. 32, 33, §§ 3–11.

Clayton did not file a timely internal appeal from his local's decision not to seek arbitration of his grievance.[6] Instead, six months after the union's withdrawal of its request for arbitration, Clayton filed this action under § 301(a) of the Labor-Management Relations Act of 1947, 29 U.S.C. § 185(a), in the District Court for the Central District of California. He alleged that the union had breached its duty of fair representation by arbitrarily refusing to pursue his grievance past the third step of the grievance procedure, and that the employer had breached the collective-bargaining agreement by discharging him without just cause.[7]

Both the union and the employer pleaded as an affirmative defense Clayton's failure to exhaust the internal union appeals procedure. * * *

The Courts of Appeals are divided over whether an employee should be required to exhaust internal union appeals procedures before bringing suit against a union or employer under § 301. Some hold that the employee's failure to exhaust internal union procedures may not be asserted as a defense by an employer. Others permit the defense to be asserted by an employer if the internal appeals procedures could result in reactivation of the grievance. With respect to a union, some courts hold that the employee's failure to exhaust is excused if union officials would be so hostile to an employee that he could not hope to obtain a fair hearing. Others would also excuse the employee's failure to exhaust if the substantive relief available through the internal procedures would be less than that available against the union in his § 301 action.

We granted certiorari to resolve the conflict. —— U.S. —— (1980). We reverse the dismissal of Clayton's suit against the union and affirm the reversal of the dismissal of his suit against the employer. We hold that where an internal union appeals procedure cannot result in reactivation of the employee's grievance or an award of the complete relief sought in his § 301 suit, exhaustion will not be required with respect to either the suit against the employer or the suit against the union.

6. Under Art. 33, § 3 of the UAW Constitution, Clayton had 30 days from the date the union withdrew its request for arbitration to initiate the internal union appeals procedures.

7. To prevail in an action under § 301 against either the employer or the union, an employee must ordinarily establish both that the union breached its duty of fair representation and that the employer breached the collective-bargaining agreement. Hines v. Anchor Motor Freight, Inc., 424 U. S. 554, 570–571 (1976).

II

Clayton's employer and union contend that exhaustion of the UAW procedures, like exhaustion of contractual grievance and arbitration procedures, will further national labor policy and should be required as a matter of federal common law. Their argument, in brief, is that an exhaustion requirement will enable unions to regulate their internal affairs without undue judicial interference and that it will also promote the broader goal of encouraging private resolution of disputes arising out of a collective-bargaining agreement.

We do not agree that the policy of forestalling judicial interference with internal union affairs is applicable to this case.[8] This policy has been strictly limited to disputes arising over *internal* union matters such as those involving the interpretation and application of a union constitution. As we stated in NLRB v. Marine Workers, 391 U.S. 418 (1968), the policy of deferring judicial consideration of internal union matters does not extend to issues "in the public domain and beyond the internal affairs of the union." *Id.*, at 426, n. 8. Here, Clayton's dispute against his union is based upon an alleged breach of the union's duty of fair representation. This allegation raises issues rooted in statutory policies extending far beyond internal union interests. See United Parcel Service, Inc. v. Mitchell, —— U.S. ——, ——, n. 2 (STEWART, J., concurring); Hines v. Anchor Motor Freight, Inc., *supra*, 424 U.S., at 562; Vaca v. Sipes, *supra*, 386 U.S., at 182; Humphrey v. Moore, 375 U.S. 335 (1964).

Our analysis, then, focuses on that aspect of national labor policy that encourages private rather than judicial resolution of disputes arising over collective-bargaining agreements. Concededly, a requirement that aggrieved employees exhaust internal remedies might lead to nonjudicial resolution of some contractual grievances. For example, an employee who exhausts internal union procedures might decide not to pursue his § 301 action in court, either because the union offered him a favorable settlement, or because it demonstrated that his underlying contractual claim was without merit. However, we decline to impose a universal exhaustion requirement lest employees with meritorious § 301 claims be forced to exhaust themselves and their resources by submitting their claims to potentially lengthy in-

8. This policy has its statutory roots in § 101(a)(4) of the Landrum-Griffin Act, 29 U.S.C. § 411(a)(4), which is part of the subchapter of the Act entitled "Bill of Rights of Members of Labor Organizations." Section 101 (a)(4) provides:
  "No labor organization shall limit the right of any member thereof to institute an action in any court, . . . *Provided*, That any such member may be required to exhaust reasonable hearing procedures (but not to exceed a four-month lapse of time) within such organization, before instituting legal . . . proceedings against such organizations or any officer thereof. . . ."

ternal union procedures that may not be adequate to redress their underlying grievances.

As we stated in NLRB v. Marine Workers, *supra*, 391 U.S., at 426, and n. 8, courts have discretion to decide whether to require exhaustion of internal union procedures. In exercising this discretion, at least three factors should be relevant: first, whether union officials are so hostile to the employee that he could not hope to obtain a fair hearing on his claim; second, whether the internal union appeals procedures would be inadequate either to reactivate the employee's grievance or to award him the full relief he seeks under § 301; and third, whether exhaustion of internal procedures would unreasonably delay the employee's opportunity to obtain a judicial hearing on the merits of his claim. If any of these factors are found to exist, the court may properly excuse the employee's failure to exhaust.

Clayton has not challenged the finding of the lower courts that the UAW internal appeals procedures are fair and reasonable. He concedes that he could have received an impartial hearing on his claim had he exhausted the internal union procedures. See Glover v. St. Louis-San Francisco R. Co., 393 U.S. 324, 330–331 (1969). Accordingly, our inquiry turns to the second factor, whether the relief available through the union's internal appeals procedures is adequate.

In his suit under § 301, Clayton seeks reinstatement from his employer and monetary relief from both his employer and his union. Although the UAW Constitution does not indicate on its face what relief is available through the internal union appeals procedures,[9] the parties have stipulated that the Public Review Board can award backpay in an appropriate case, and the two decisions of the Public Review Board reprinted in the Joint Appendix both resulted in awards of backpay. It is clear, then, that at least some monetary relief may be obtained through the internal appeals procedure.[10]

It is equally clear that the union can neither reinstate Clayton in his job, nor reactivate his grievance. Article IX of the collective-bargaining agreement between Local 509 and ITT Gilfillan provides that the union may obtain arbitration of a grievance only if it gives "notice . . . to the Company in writing within fifteen (15) working days after the date of the Company's decision at Step 3 of the Grievance Procedure." By the time Clayton learned of his union's

9. The UAW Constitution states only that the Constitutional Convention Appeals Committee has "the authority to consider and decide all appeals submitted to it," Art. 33, § 8, and that the Public Review Board has the "authority and duty to make final and binding decisions on all cases appealed to it," Art. 32, § 3(a), and to "dispose of all facets of the appeal." Art. 33, § 11.

10. The record does not indicate whether this monetary relief includes backpay only, or whether it also may include prospective monetary relief and incidental or punitive damages, relief that Clayton is apparently seeking in his § 301 action.

decision not to pursue the grievance to arbitration, this 15-day time limit had expired. Accordingly, the union could not have demanded arbitration even if the internal appeal had shown Clayton's claim to be meritorious. The union was bound by its earlier decision not to pursue Clayton's grievance past the third stage of the grievance and arbitration procedure.[11] For the reasons that follow, we conclude that these restrictions on the relief available through the internal UAW procedures render those procedures inadequate.[12]

Where internal union appeals procedures can result in either complete relief to an aggrieved employee or reactivation of his grievance, exhaustion would advance the national labor policy of encouraging private resolution of contractual labor disputes. In such cases, the internal union procedures are capable of fully resolving meritorious claims short of the judicial forum. Thus, if the employee received the full relief he requested through internal procedures, his § 301 action would become moot, and he would not be entitled to a judicial hearing. Similarly, if the employee obtained reactivation of his grievance through internal union procedures, the policies underlying *Republic Steel* would come into play, and the employee would be required to submit his claim to the collectively-bargained dispute-resolution procedures.[13] In either case, exhaustion of internal remedies could result in final resolution of the employee's contractual grievance through private rather than judicial avenues.

By contrast, where an aggrieved employee cannot obtain either the substantive relief he seeks or reactivation of his grievance, national labor policy would not be served by requiring exhaustion of internal remedies. In such cases, exhaustion would be a useless gesture: it would delay judicial consideration of the employee's § 301 action, but would not eliminate it. The employee would still be required to pursue judicial means to obtain the relief he seeks under § 301. Moreover, exhaustion would not lead to significant savings in judicial re-

11. * * *
Although most collective-bargaining agreements contain similarly strict time limits for seeking arbitration of grievances, there are some exceptions. The UAW informs us that "[s]ome employers and union have, through collective bargaining, agreed to allow the reinstatement of withdrawn grievances where a union tribunal reverses the union's initial decision. This is true, for example, in the current UAW contracts with the major automobile and agricultural implement manufacturers." UAW Brief 18, n. 40. In such cases, the relief available through the union's internal appeal procedures would presumably be adequate.

12. Accordingly, we need not discuss the third factor, whether exhaustion of the union's otherwise adequate internal appeals procedures would unreasonably delay the employee's opportunity to obtain a judicial hearing on the merits of his claim.

13. In addition, by reactivating the grievance, the union might be able to rectify the very wrong of which the employee complains—a breach of the duty of fair representation caused by the union's refusal to seek arbitration —and the employee would then be unable to satisfy the precondition to a § 301 suit against the employer.

sources, because regardless of the outcome of the internal appeal, the employee would be required to prove *de novo* in his § 301 suit that the union breached its duty of fair representation and that the employer breached the collective-bargaining agreement. As we recently stated, one of the important federal policies underlying § 301 is the "relatively rapid disposition of labor disputes." United Parcel Service, Inc. v. Mitchell, *supra*, —— U.S., at ——, quoting United Auto Workers v. Hoosier Cardinal Corp., 383 U.S. 696, 707 (1966). This policy is undermined by an exhaustion requirement unless the internal procedures are capable of either reactivating the employee's grievance or of redressing it.

In reliance upon the Court of Appeals' opinion in this case, the UAW contends that even if exhaustion is not required with respect to the employer, it should be required with respect to the union, because the relief Clayton seeks *against the union* in his § 301 suit is available through internal union procedures. We disagree. While this argument might have force where the employee has chosen to bring his § 301 suit only against the union, the defense should not be available where, as here, the employee has filed suit against both the union and the employer. A trial court requiring exhaustion with respect to the suit against the union, but not with respect to the suit against the employer, would be faced with two undesirable alternatives. If it stayed the action against the employer pending resolution of the internal appeals procedures, it would effectively be requiring exhaustion with respect to the suit against the employer, a result we have held would violate national labor policy. Yet if it permitted the action against the employer to proceed, and tolled the running of the statute of limitations in the suit against the union until the internal procedures had been exhausted, it could very well find itself with two separate § 301 suits, based on the same facts, proceeding at different paces in its courtroom. As we suggested in Vaca v. Sipes, *supra*, 386 U.S., at 197, this is a result that should be avoided if possible. The preferable approach is for the court to permit the employee's § 301 action to proceed against both defendants, despite the employee's failure to exhaust, unless the internal union procedures can reactivate the grievance or grant the relief that would be available in the employee's § 301 suit against both defendants.

III

* * *

In this case, the internal union appeals panels cannot reactivate Clayton's grievance and cannot grant Clayton the reinstatement relief he seeks under § 301. We therefore hold that Clayton should not have been required to exhaust internal union appeals procedures prior to bringing suit against his union and employer under § 301.

Affirmed in part, reversed in part.

JUSTICE POWELL, with whom THE CHIEF JUSTICE joins, dissenting.

I join JUSTICE REHNQUIST'S dissent, and write briefly to emphasize a rationale—suggested by an *amicus curiae*—that is consistent both with national labor policy and the relevant precedents.

In briefest summary, I would hold that in the circumstances of this case no issue concerning the breach of the union's statutory duty of fair representation properly can be said to arise *at all*. The union has not made a final determination whether to pursue arbitration on Clayton's behalf. Clayton should not be able to claim a breach of duty by the union until the union has had a full opportunity to make this determination. No such opportunity exists until Clayton exhausts the procedures available for resolving that question. Thus, as Clayton cannot claim a breach of duty by the union, he cannot bring a breach of contract suit under § 301 against his employer.

In my view, the asserted distinction in a tripartite case such as this one between contractual and internal union remedies, is immaterial. The situation presented in this case is well within the doctrine, underlying Republic Steel Corp. v. Maddox, 379 U.S. 650 (1965), that employees must pursue all procedures established for determining whether a union will go forward with a grievance. * * *

JUSTICE REHNQUIST, with whom THE CHIEF JUSTICE, JUSTICE STEWART, and JUSTICE POWELL join, dissenting.

* * * The Court's opinion today rights what I view as the principal error in the decision below by requiring the actions against the employer and union to proceed simultaneously. The Court reaches this conclusion by holding that in this particular case the exhaustion defense should not be available to either the union or employer. I, however, view differently than does the Court the benefits to be obtained from requiring exhaustion in this case, and would require Clayton to exhaust his intraunion remedies before proceeding against either his union or employer. * * *

The Court creates a three prong test for determining when a district court should exercise its discretion and require exhaustion of intraunion remedies. * * * [N]o prior case of this Court has held that exhaustion should not be required unless the internal union remedies can provide all the substantive relief requested or reactivation of the grievance. The principal difficulty with the Court's opinion lies in its framing of this second criterion which reflects much too narrow a view of the purposes of the exhaustion defense and the benefits which will likely result from requiring exhaustion in a case where a union has established a means for reviewing the manner in which it has represented an employee during a grievance.

The exhaustion of intraunion remedies, even where those remedies cannot provide reinstatement or reactivation of a grievance, does promote private resolution of labor disputes. Resort to the intraunion appeals procedures provides the union with its first opportunity to focus on the issue of fair representation—as opposed to the alleged breach of the collective-bargaining agreement. Resort to the union appeals procedures gives the union an opportunity to satisfy the employee that its decision not to pursue a grievance was correct. If successful on this score, litigation is averted. Where a union determines through its appeals procedure that it mishandled an employee's grievance, litigation may also be averted because at that point both the union and the employer have a strong incentive to pursue private resolution of the grievance. Even where a collective-bargaining agreement does not provide for reactivation of a grievance, it is reasonable to assume that many employers, when confronted with both a determination by a union that it had breached its duty of fair representation and the immediate prospect of an employee commencing litigation, would seriously consider voluntarily reactivating the grievance procedure to avoid the additional burden and costs of litigation. Should litigation nonetheless occur, exhaustion may well have narrowed the factual and legal issues to be decided and thus result in a savings of judicial resources. A fact that should also not be discounted is that the conscientious handling by a union of an employee's intraunion appeal cannot help but enhance the union's prestige with its employees. Cf. Republic Steel Corp. v. Maddox, 379 U.S. 650, 653 (1965). Exhaustion promotes union democracy and self-government as well as the broader policy of non-interference with internal union affairs. A union's incentive to maintain internal procedures which provide substantial procedural protection and which can afford significant substantive relief will be greatly undermined if an employee can simply bypass the procedures at will.

The error in the Court's analysis results in part from its apparent belief that intraunion remedies must provide a complete substitute for either the courts or the contract grievance procedure in order to be deemed "adequate." The purpose of intraunion remedies, however, is quite different. These remedies are provided to facilitate or encourage the private resolution of disputes, not to be a complete substitute for the courts. Intraunion remedies can serve this purpose so long as they have the capacity to address whether the union wrongfully handled the grievance. Obviously, if a union appeals procedure cannot address this question, exhaustion should not be required.

An additional question which is also of great importance is whether a union should ever be found to have breached its duty of fair representation when a union member shuns an appeals procedure which is both mandated by the union constitution and established for the purpose of allowing the union to satisfy its duty of fair representation. It seems to me not at all unreasonable to say that a union should have the right to require its members to give it the first opportunity to correct its own mistakes. * * *

Section 101(a)(4) [see note 8 supra] reflects what I believe to be the reasonable compromise Congress reached when trying to balance two somewhat competing interests—furtherance of the national labor policy in favor of private resolution of disputes on the one hand and the desire not to unduly burden or "exhaust" an individual employee with time-consuming procedures on the other. It is fair to say that § 101(a)(4) represents Congress' judgment that limiting access to the courts for at least 4 months is not an unreasonable price to pay in exchange for the previously mentioned benefits exhaustion may provide.

The language of § 101(a)(4) also goes a long way to satisfy the third prong of the test set forth by the Court today. Exhaustion of internal union precedures should not be required where such would unreasonably delay an employee's opportunity to obtain a judicial hearing on the merits of his claim. *Ante*, at 9. Intraunion procedures which take years to complete serve no worthwhile purpose in the overall scheme of promoting the prompt and private resolution of claims. But a requirement that an employee not be permitted to go to court without first having pursued an intraunion appeal for at least 4 months does substantially further this national labor policy without placing any unfair burden on an employee. As such, I think all interested parties would be well served by a requirement that employees exhaust their intraunion procedures for this limited period of time prescribed by Congress.

Problem for Discussion

Assume that in the *Hines* case, page 1039 supra, the discharged truckdrivers waited two and one-half years after the adverse decision of the arbitration committee before bringing an action against the employer for breach of the labor contract and against the union for breach of the duty of fair representation. You have been asked whether their action is barred by the statute of limitations. Is it?

You know that there is no explicit congressional statute of limitations for court actions of this kind, but you know that: (a) the state limitations period for actions to vacate arbitration awards is ninety days; (b) the statute of limitations for unfair labor practice proceedings before the NLRB is six months; (c) the state limitations period in tort actions is one year; (d) the state limitations period for actions on oral contracts (such as oral contracts of employment) is two years; (e) the state limitations period for "actions based on a statute" is three years; and (f) the state limitations period for actions on written contracts is six years. See *United Parcel Service, Inc. v. Mitchell,* —— U.S. ——, 101 S.Ct. 1559, 67 L.Ed.2d 732 (1981).

II. UNION SECURITY AND THE ENCOURAGEMENT OF UNION ACTIVITY

Unions in this country have traditionally faced a major problem in maintaining and increasing their membership. They have been met with greater and more persistent opposition from employers than their counterparts have faced in most other industrialized, democratic countries. And even apart from employer resistance, it is probably correct to state that employees in this country have generally been less easy to organize than has been true abroad. Finally, the labor movement in the United States has been marked throughout most of its history by rivalries between individual unions, and these rivalries have often taken the form of spirited contests to obtain new members at the expense of other labor organizations. For all these reasons, unions in this country have long striven to achieve 100% membership and to obtain this goal through contractual arrangements with employers which would make union membership a condition of employment for each employee in the unit. The notion of compulsory membership has inevitably created troublesome questions of principle—questions which have been raised not only by employers wishing to weaken the power of unions but by others not immediately involved in the field of labor relations in this country. With this background, the law has responded in a variety of ways to regulate the use of union security arrangements.

The materials below deal with the following issues:

(1) Under what circumstances may an employer and union lawfully agree that all employees shall, as a condition of employment, become members of the union or contribute financial support to the union? Are any limits imposed by the federal Constitution or by the Labor Act upon the use that may be made by a union of moneys contributed pursuant to a union security agreement?

(2) What power may be exercised by the states to limit the use of union security agreements?

(3) To what extent may unions lawfully exert control over the hiring process through the negotiation with the employer of hiring-hall agreements?

(4) To what extent, if any, may union officials be accorded preferred job status under the collective bargaining agreement?

A.   UNION SECURITY AND THE USE OF UNION DUES [1]

NLRB v. GENERAL MOTORS CORP.

Supreme Court of the United States, 1963.
373 U.S. 734, 83 S.Ct. 1453, 10 L.Ed.2d 670.

MR. JUSTICE WHITE delivered the opinion of the Court.

The issue here is whether an employer commits an unfair labor practice (National Labor Relations Act, § 8(a) (5)), when he refuses to bargain with a certified union over the union's proposal for the adoption of the "agency shop." More narrowly, since the employer is not obliged to bargain over a proposal that he commit an unfair labor practice, the question is whether the agency shop is an unfair labor practice under § 8(a) (3) of the Act or else is exempted from the prohibitions of that section by the proviso thereto. We have concluded that this type of arrangement does not constitute an unfair labor practice and that it is not prohibited by § 8.

Respondent's employees are represented by the United Automobile, Aerospace and Agricultural Implement Workers of America, UAW, in a single, multi-plant, company-wide unit. The 1958 agreement between union and company provides for maintenance of membership and the union shop. These provisions were not operative, however, in such states as Indiana where state law prohibited making union membership a condition of employment.

In June 1959, the Indiana intermediate appellate court held that an agency shop arrangement would not violate the state right-to-work law. Meade Elec. Co. v. Hagberg, 129 Ind.App. 631, 159 N.E.2d 408 (1959). As defined in that opinion, the term "agency shop" applies to an arrangement under which all employees are required as a condition of employment to pay dues to the union and pay the union's initiation fee, but they need not actually become union members. The union thereafter sent respondent a letter proposing the negotiation of a contractual provision covering Indiana plants "generally similar to that set forth" in the *Meade* case. Continued employment in the Indiana plants would be conditioned upon the payment of sums equal to the initiation fee and regular monthly dues paid by the union members. The intent of the proposal, the NLRB concluded, was not to require membership but to make membership available at the employees' option and on nondiscriminatory terms. Employees choosing not to join would make the required payments and, in accordance with union custom, would share in union expenditures for strike benefits,

---

1. See Hopfl, The Agency Shop Question, 49 Cornell L.Q. 478 (1964); Mayer, Union Security and the Taft-Hartley Act, 1961 Duke L.J. 505; Rosen- thal, The National Labor Relations Act and Compulsory Unionism, 1954 Wis.L.Rev. 53.

educational and retired member benefits, and union publications and promotional activities, but they would not be entitled to attend union meetings, vote upon ratification of agreements negotiated by the union, or have a voice in the internal affairs of the union. The respondent made no counterproposal, but replied to the union's letter that the proposed agreement would violate the National Labor Relations Act and that respondent must therefore "respectfully decline to comply with your request for a meeting" to bargain over the proposal.

[The NLRB held the agency shop provision lawful under Section 8(a)(3) and a subject of mandatory bargaining; the employer was held to violate Section 8(a)(5) and was ordered to bargain about the provision. The court of appeals, however, set aside the Board's order. It held that a provision requiring the payment of an agency fee equivalent to union dues as a condition of employment was not within the proviso to Section 8(a)(3) permitting a requirement of "membership" as a condition of employment. It found the agency shop provision to be unlawful and concluded that the employer was not required to bargain concerning its inclusion in the labor contract.]

Section 8(3) under the Wagner Act was the predecessor to § 8 (a) (3) of the present law. Like § 8(a) (3), § 8(3) forbade employers to discriminate against employees to compel them to join a union. Because it was feared that § 8(3) and § 7, if nothing were added to qualify them, might be held to outlaw union-security arrangements such as the closed shop, see 79 Cong. Rec. 7570 (statement of Senator Wagner), 7674 (statement of Senator Walsh); H.R. Rep. No. 972, p. 17; H.R.Rep. No. 1147, p. 19, the proviso to § 8(3) was added expressly declaring:

> "*Provided*, That nothing in this act * * * or in any other statute of the United States, shall preclude an employer from making an agreement with a labor organization * * * to require as a condition of employment membership therein, if such labor organization is the representative of the employees as provided in section 9(a) * * *."

The prevailing administrative and judicial view under the Wagner Act was or came to be that the proviso to § 8(3) covered both the closed and union shop, as well as less onerous union security arrangements, if they were otherwise legal. The NLRB construed the proviso as shielding from an unfair labor practice charge less severe forms of union-security arrangements than the closed or the union shop, including an arrangement in *Public Service Co. of Colorado*, 89 NLRB 418, requiring nonunion members to pay to the union $2 a month "for the support of the bargaining unit." And in Algoma Plywood & Veneer Co. v. Wisconsin Employment Relations Board, 336 U.S. 301, 307, 93 L.Ed. 691, 69 S.Ct. 584 (1949), which involved a maintenance of membership agreement, the Court, in commenting on petitioner's contention that the proviso of § 8(3) affirmatively protected arrangements within its scope, *cf*. Garner v. Teamsters, C. & H. Union, 346 U.S. 485, 98 L.Ed. 228, 74 S.Ct. 161 (1953), said of its purpose: "The short answer is that § 8(3) merely disclaims a national policy hostile to the closed shop *or other forms of union-security agreement*." (Emphasis added.)

When Congress enacted the Taft-Hartley Act, it added * * * to the language of the original proviso to § 8(3) * * *. These additions were intended to accomplish twin purposes. On the one hand, the most serious abuses of compulsory unionism were eliminated by abolishing the closed shop. On the other hand, Congress recognized that in the absence of a union-security provision "many employees sharing the benefits of what unions are able to accomplish, like collective bargaining, will refuse to pay their share of the cost." S.Rep.No.105, 80th Cong., 1st Sess., p. 6, 1 Leg.Hist.L.M.R.A. 412. Consequently, under the new law "employers would still be permitted to enter into agreements requiring all employees in a given bargaining unit to become members thirty days after being hired" but "expulsion from a union cannot be a ground of compulsory discharge if the worker is not delinquent in paying his initiation fees or dues". S.Rep.No.105, p. 7, 1 Leg.Hist.L.M.R.A. 413. The amendments were intended only to "remedy the most serious abuses of compulsory union membership and yet give employers and unions who feel that such agreements promoted stability by eliminating 'free riders' the right to continue such arrangements." Ibid. As far as the federal law was concerned, all employees could be required to pay their way. The bill "abolishes the closed shop but permits voluntary agreements for requiring such forms of compulsory membership as the union shop or maintenance of membership * * *." S.Rep.No.105, p. 3, 1 Leg. Hist.L.M.R.A. 409.

We find nothing in the legislative history of the Act indicating that Congress intended the amended proviso to § 8(a) (3) to validate only the union shop and simultaneously to abolish, in addition to the closed shop, all other union-security arrangements permissible under state law. There is much to be said for the Board's view that, if Congress desired in the Wagner Act to permit a closed or union shop and in the Taft-Hartley Act the union shop, then it also intended to preserve the status of less vigorous, less compulsory contracts, which demanded less adherence to the union.

Respondent, however, relies upon the express words of the proviso which allow employment to be conditioned upon "membership": since the union's proposal here does not require actual membership but demands only initiation fees and monthly dues it is not saved by the proviso. This position, of course, would reject administrative decisions concerning the scope of § 8(3) of the Wagner Act, *e. g., Public* Service Co. of Colorado, supra, reaffirmed by the Board under the Taft-Hartley amendments, American Seating Co., 98 NLRB 800. Moreover the 1947 amendments not only abolished the closed shop but also made significant alterations in the meaning of "membership" for the purposes of union security contracts. Under the second proviso to § 8(a) (3), the burdens of membership upon which employment may be conditioned are expressly limited to the payment of initiation fees and monthly dues. It is permissible to condition employment upon membership, but membership insofar as it has significance to employment rights, may in turn be conditioned only upon payment of fees and dues. "Membership" as a condition of employment is whittled down to its financial core. This Court has said as much before in Radio Officers' Union v. NLRB, 347 U.S. 17, 41, 98 L.Ed. 455, 74 S.Ct. 323 (1954):

> " * * * This legislative history clearly indicates that Congress intended to prevent utilization of union security agreements for any purpose other than to compel payment of union dues and fees. Thus, Congress recognized the validity of unions' concern about 'free riders,' i. e., employees who receive the benefits of union representation but are unwilling to contribute their fair share of financial support to such union, and gave the unions the power to contract to meet that problem while withholding from unions the power to cause the discharge of employees for any other reason * * *."

We are therefore confident that the proposal made by the union here conditioned employment upon the practical equivalent of union "membership," as Congress used that term in the proviso to § 8(a) (3). The proposal for requiring the payment of dues and fees imposes no burdens not imposed by a permissible union shop contract and compels the performance of only those duties of membership which are enforceable by discharge under a union shop arrangement. If an employee in a union shop unit refuses to respect any union-imposed obligations other than the duty to pay dues and fees, and membership in the union is therefore denied or terminated, the condition of "membership" for § 8(a) (3) purposes is nevertheless satisfied and the employee may not be discharged for nonmembership even though he is not a formal member. * * *

In short, the employer categorically refused to bargain with the union over a proposal for an agreement within the proviso to § 8(a) (3) and as such, lawful, for the purposes of this case. By the same token, § 7, and derivatively § 8(a) (1), cannot be deemed to forbid the employer to enter such agreements, since it too is expressly limited by the § 8(a) (3) proviso. We hold that the employer was not excused from his duty to bargain over the proposal on the theory that his acceding to it would necessarily involve him in an unfair labor practice. * * *

Reversed and remanded.

MR. JUSTICE GOLDBERG took no part in the consideration or decision of this case.

Problems for Discussion

1. The Teamsters and the Ace Trucking Company have executed a collective bargaining agreement which provides that thirty days after being hired, each employee is to become a "member in good standing" of the Teamsters Union and pay the Union initiation fee and monthly dues. Employee Jones was a member of the Union at the time the labor contract was executed, but he became discontented with Union leadership and policies, and he has tendered his resignation from membership; he announces that he does not intend to be bound by the obligations of membership—such as attendance at Union meetings and subjection to the Union constitution and bylaws—but he does continue to tender his monthly dues payments. The Union, however, declares that in view of his resignation, it will not accept his tender of dues, and the Company complies with the Union's demand that Jones be discharged. Has the Act been violated? *NLRB v. Hershey Foods Corp.,* 513 F.2d 1083 (9th Cir. 1975).

2. Martin was employed by the Eclipse Lumber Company and was a member of the Woodworkers Union; the labor contract contained no union security provision. During the term of that contract, Martin refused to pay to the Union an amount which the Union had assessed against all members in order to create a fund for contributions to certain political candidates for state office; for this he was fined, and rather than pay the fine he resigned from membership. Some years later, the Company and the Union negotiated a labor contract which contained a provision requiring all employees to become and remain members of the Union. Although Martin applied for membership, he was told that membership would be extended only if he paid the fine. He refused to pay the fine, and the company discharged him upon the Union's request. Has the Labor Act been violated? See *NLRB v. Eclipse Lumber Co.,* 199 F.2d 684 (9th Cir. 1953). Would the result be different if the Union had demanded that Martin pay, as a condition of membership, not the fine but rather a contribution to the Union's strike fund (to be used to pay benefits to members in the event of a future strike)? See *NLRB v. Die & Tool Makers,* 231 F.2d 298, cert. denied 352 U.S. 833 (7th Cir. 1956).

3. The contract between the Smith Mfg. Co. and the Electrical Workers Union contains a union shop provision, and employee Gray joined the Union thirty days after being placed on the payroll. Union dues are $10 per month, but members who attend monthly Union meetings are granted a $2 refund at the meeting. Gray has thus insisted on tendering no more than $8 to the Union each month in satisfaction of his dues obligation, asserting

that the other $2 is actually a fine for nonattendance at Union meetings. The Union has refused the tender of $8 and has asked the Company to discharge Gray. The Company wishes to know whether it may do so without violating the Labor Act. May it? Is Section 8(b)(5) of the Act pertinent? Compare *NLRB* v. *Leece-Neville Co.*, 140 N.L.R.B. 56 (1963), enf'd 330 F. 2d 242 (6th Cir.), cert. denied 379 U.S. 819 (1964), with *Local 171, Ass'n of Western Pulp Workers (Boise Cascade Corp.)*, 165 N.L.R.B. 971 (1967).

Would it be lawful for the Union to provide that "full members" who are temporarily off the payroll because of illness or other disability may satisfy their monthly dues obligation by paying only fifty cents—but not to extend this privilege to "agency-fee payers"? See *Machinists Dist. Lodge 720* v. *NLRB (McDonnell Douglas Corp.)*, 626 F.2d 119 (9th Cir. 1980).

4. For years, the contract between Triangle Publications and the Television Broadcasters Union has contained a union shop provision; the Union initiation fee for all new employees (who generally receive roughly $200 per week) has been $100. The Union has become concerned about the loss of work for its members resulting from the Company's greater use of part-time employees. In order to curtail this practice, the Union recently raised its initiation fee to $500, payable $300 immediately and $200 in two monthly payments. This has made it extremely difficult for part-time employees to become Union members as required by the collective bargaining agreement. The Company has filed a charge against the Union for violation of Sections 8(b)(2) and (5) of the Labor Act. Has the Union violated either Section? See *NLRB* v. *Television Broadcasting Studio Employees Local 804*, 315 F.2d 398 (3d Cir. 1963).

In one industry—building and construction—the statute takes account of special circumstances and reduces the grace period for acquiring union "membership" under a union shop provision or for beginning to pay union dues under an agency shop provision. In the building and construction industry, a given employer works on different jobs in different localities, performs work of brief duration and hires a transient workforce (often through a union-controlled hiring hall) typically highly organized along craft lines. A construction employer also must be in a position to know what wage rates to anticipate in different places in order that it may intelligently compute its contract bids. These factors render unsuitable the full-dressed representation election conducted by the NLRB and the usual month-long statutory grace period for union security provisions and invite dealing with a particular union even before the employee complement has been hired. Congress therefore, in the Landrum-Griffin amendments of 1959, enacted Section 8(f) of the Labor Act in order to broaden the powers of construction employers and unions to make union security agreements (like all others, subject to outlawry by state right-to-work laws) in two pertinent respects: The agreement will be lawful even if:

> (1) the majority status of such labor organization has not been established under the provisions of section 9 of this Act prior to the making of such agreement, or (2) such agreement requires as a condition of employment, membership in such labor organization after the seventh day following the beginning of such employment or the effective date of the agreement, whichever is later * * *.

Since these union shop arrangements may be negotiated before the union demonstrates majority support within the employer's bargaining unit, and indeed before employees are hired at all, they are known as "pre-hire agreements."

Problems for Discussion

The Baker Construction Company has negotiated and signed a labor contract with the Operating Engineers Union, at a time when the workforce has not yet been hired and the Union lacks certified status. One month later, a second union petitions for a representation election, which the Operating Engineers contend is untimely because of the contract-bar rule. Should the petition be dismissed?

If the second union had instead produced authorization cards from a majority of the employees, and the Company withdrew recognition from the Operating Engineers and extended recognition to the second union, would the Operating Engineers have a meritorious claim that the Company had violated Section 8(a)(5)?

Would your answers be different if, at the time of the petition (or recognition demand) by the second union, a majority of Company employees had joined the Operating Engineers pursuant to a union shop provision in the prehire agreement?

See *NLRB v. Local 103, Bridge Workers (Higdon Constr. Co.)*, 434 U.S. 335, 98 S.Ct. 651, 54 L.Ed.2d 586 (1978); *NLRB v. Irvin*, 475 F.2d 1265 (3d Cir. 1973).

INTERNATIONAL ASSOCIATION OF MACHINISTS v. STREET

Supreme Court of the United States, 1961.
367 U.S. 740, 81 S.Ct. 1784, 6 L.Ed.2d 1141.

MR. JUSTICE BRENNAN delivered the opinion of the Court.

A group of labor organizations, appellants here, and the carriers comprising the Southern Railway System, entered into a union-shop agreement pursuant to the authority of § 2, Eleventh of the

Railway Labor Act.² The agreement requires each of the appellees, employees of the carriers, as a condition of continued employment, to pay the appellant union representing his particular class or craft the dues, initiation fees and assessments uniformly required as a condition of acquiring or retaining union membership. The appellees, in behalf of themselves and of employees similarly situated, brought this action in the Superior Court of Bibb County, Georgia, alleging that the money each was thus compelled to pay to hold his job was in substantial part used to finance the campaigns of candidates for federal and state offices whom he opposed, and to promote the propagation of political and economic doctrines, concepts and ideologies with which he disagreed. The Superior Court found that the allegations were fully proved and entered a judgment and decree enjoining the enforcement of the union-shop agreement on the ground that § 2, Eleventh violates the Federal Constitution to the extent that it permits such use by the appellants of the funds exacted from employees. The Supreme Court of Georgia affirmed, 215 Ga. 27, 108 S.E.2d 796. On appeal to this Court under 28 U.S.C. § 1257(1), 28 U.S.C.A. § 1257(1), we noted probable jurisdiction, 361 U.S. 807, 80 S.Ct. 84, 4 L.Ed.2d 54.

I.

The Hanson Decision.

We held in Railway Employes' Dept. v. Hanson, 351 U.S. 225, 76 S.Ct. 714, 100 L.Ed. 1112, that enactment of the provision of § 2, Eleventh authorizing union-shop agreements between interstate railroads and unions of their employees was a valid exercise by Congress of its powers under the Commerce Clause and did not violate the First Amendment or the Due Process Clause of the Fifth Amendment. It is argued that our disposition of the First Amendment

2. 64 Stat. 1238, 45 U.S.C. § 152, Eleventh, 45 U.S.C.A. § 152, Eleventh. The section provides:
"Eleventh. Notwithstanding any other provisions of this chapter, or of any other statute or law of the United States, or Territory thereof, or of any State, any carrier or carriers as defined in this chapter and a labor organization or labor organizations duly designated and authorized to represent employees in accordance with the requirements of this chapter shall be permitted—
"(a) to make agreements, requiring, as a condition of continued employment, that within sixty days following the beginning of such employment, or the effective date of such agreements, whichever is the later, all employees shall become members of the labor organization representing their craft or class: *Provided*, That no such agreement shall require such condition of employment with respect to employees to whom membership is not available upon the same terms and conditions as are generally applicable to any other member or with respect to employees to whom membership was denied or terminated for any reason other than the failure of the employee to tender the periodic dues, initiation fees, and assessments (not including fines and penalties) uniformly required as a condition of acquiring or retaining membership. * * *"

claims in Hanson disposes of appellees' constitutional claims in this case adversely to their contentions. We disagree. As appears from its history, that case decided only that § 2, Eleventh, in authorizing collective agreements conditioning employees' continued employment on payment of union dues, initiation fees and assessments, did not on its face impinge upon protected rights of association. * * * We said: "It is argued that compulsory membership will be used to impair freedom of expression. But that problem is not presented by this record. * * * [I]f the exaction of dues, initiation fees, or assessments is used as a cover for forcing ideological conformity or other action in contravention of the First Amendment, this judgment will not prejudice the decision in that case. For we pass narrowly on § 2, Eleventh of the Railway Labor Act. We only hold that the requirement for financial support of the collective-bargaining agency by all who receive the benefits of its work is within the power of Congress under the Commerce Clause and does not violate either the First or the Fifth Amendments." * * *

The record in this case is adequate squarely to present the constitutional questions reserved in Hanson. These are questions of the utmost gravity. However, the restraints against unnecessary constitutional decisions counsel against their determination unless we must conclude that Congress, in authorizing a union shop under § 2, Eleventh, also meant that the labor organization receiving an employee's money should be free, despite that employee's objection, to spend his money for political causes which he opposes. Federal statutes are to be so construed as to avoid serious doubt of their constitutionality. "When the validity of an act of the Congress is drawn in question, and even if a serious doubt of constitutionality is raised, it is a cardinal principle that this Court will first ascertain whether a construction of the statute is fairly possible by which the question may be avoided." Crowell v. Benson, 285 U.S. 22, 62, 52 S.Ct. 285, 296, 76 L.Ed. 598. Each named appellee in this action has made known to the union representing his craft or class his dissent from the use of his money for political causes which he opposes. We have therefore examined the legislative history of § 2, Eleventh in the context of the development of unionism in the railroad industry under the regulatory scheme created by the Railway Labor Act to determine whether a construction is "fairly possible" which denies the authority to a union, over the employee's objection, to spend his money for political causes which he opposes. We conclude that such a construction is not only "fairly possible" but entirely reasonable, and we therefore find it unnecessary to decide the correctness of the constitutional determinations made by the Georgia courts.

II.

The Rail Unions and Union Security.

The history of union security in the railway industry is marked *first,* by a strong and long-standing tradition of voluntary unionism on the part of the standard rail unions; *second,* by the declaration in 1934 of a congressional policy of complete freedom of choice of employees to join or not to join a union; *third,* by the modification of the firm legislative policy against compulsion, but only as a specific response to the recognition of the expenses and burdens incurred by the unions in the administration of the complex scheme of the Railway Labor Act.   *   *   *

[Mr. Justice Brennan recounted the history leading to the amendment of the Railway Labor Act in 1934. The "regular" train unions urged that they be allowed to enter into labor contracts requiring membership in them as a condition of employment but that this privilege be denied to "company" unions. This proposal was, however, rejected by Congress, which approved the principle of freedom of choice for all railroad workers regarding union membership; the amended Act forbade all carriers to "require any person seeking employment to sign any contract or agreement promising to join or not to join a labor organization." During World War II, when major contract negotiations reached an impasse, in part over the issue of union security, a Presidential Emergency Board recommended against a membership requirement, concluding that it was both illegal under the Railway Labor Act and also unnecessary, in light of the unions' membership strength and their recognition by the carriers. When the issue of union security was revived in Congress in 1950, it was viewed in light of Congress's rejection of the principle of compulsory arbitration of new contract terms in the railroad industry and its emphasis upon the amicable adjustment of disputes between carriers and unions through free collective bargaining leading to a labor contract. Although this policy had been embodied in the Railway Labor Act since 1926, with its provisions requiring bargaining and resort to the National Mediation Board to assist in the resolution of impasses, new responsibilities had been imposed on rail unions in 1934, when Congress provided for representation elections, for exclusive representation on behalf of all employees in the craft or class, and for arbitration of contract grievances before the National Railroad Adjustment Board to which the unions were to appoint representatives.]

Performance of these functions entails the expenditure of considerable funds. Moreover, this Court has held that under the statutory scheme, a union's status as exclusive bargaining representative carries with it the duty fairly and equitably to represent all employees of the craft or class, union and nonunion. Steele v. Louisville & N. R. Co., 323 U.S. 192, 65 S.Ct. 226; Tunstall v. Brotherhood of Locomotive Firemen & Enginemen, 323 U.S. 210, 65 S.Ct. 235, 89 L.Ed. 187. The principal argument made by the unions in 1950 was based on their role in this regulatory framework. They maintained that because of the expense of performing their duties in the congressional scheme, fairness justified the spreading of the costs to all employees who benefited. They thus advanced as their purpose the elimination of the "free riders"—those employees who obtained the benefits of the unions' participation in the machinery of the Act without financially supporting the unions. * * *

This argument was decisive with Congress. * * *

These considerations overbore the arguments in favor of the earlier policy of complete individual freedom of choice. As we said in Railway Employes' Dept. v. Hanson, supra, 351 U.S. at page 235, 76 S.Ct. at page 720, "[t]o require, rather than to induce, the beneficiaries of trade unionism to contribute to its costs may not be the wisest course. But Congress might well believe that it would help insure the right to work in and along the arteries of interstate commerce. No more has been attempted here. * * * The financial support required relates * * * to the work of the union in the realm of collective bargaining." The conclusion to which this history clearly points is that § 2, Eleventh contemplated compulsory unionism to force employees to share the costs of negotiating and administering collective agreements, and the costs of the adjustment and settlement of disputes. One looks in vain for any suggestion that Congress also meant in § 2, Eleventh to provide the unions with a means for forcing employees, over their objection, to support political causes which they oppose.

III.

The Safeguarding of Rights of Dissent.

To the contrary, Congress incorporated safeguards in the statute to protect dissenters' interests. Congress became concerned during the hearings and debates that the union shop might be used to abridge freedom of speech and beliefs. The original proposal for authorization of the union shop was qualified in only one respect. It provided "That no such agreement shall require such condition of employment with respect to employees to whom membership is not available upon the same terms and conditions as are generally applicable to any other member * * *." This was primarily designed to prevent discharge of employees for nonmembership where the union did not admit the employee to membership on racial grounds. See House Hearings, p. 68; Senate Hearings, pp. 22–25. But it was strenuously protested that the proposal provided no protection for an employee who disagreed with union policies or leadership. It was argued, for example, that "the right of free speech is at stake. * * A man could feel that he was no longer able freely to express himself because he could be dismissed on account of criticism of the union * * *." House Hearings, p. 115; see also Senate Hearings, pp. 167–169, 320. Objections of this kind led the rail unions to propose an addition to the proviso to § 2, Eleventh to prevent loss of job for lack of union membership "with respect to employees to whom membership was denied or terminated for any reason other than the failure of the employee to tender the periodic dues, fees, and assessments uniformly required as a condition of acquiring or retaining membership." House Hearings, p. 247. * * *

A congressional concern over possible impingements on the interests of individual dissenters from union policies is therefore discernible. It is true that opponents of the union shop urged that Congress should not allow it without explicitly regulating the amount of dues which might be exacted or prescribing the uses for which the dues might be expended. We may assume that Congress was also fully conversant with the long history of intensive involvement of the railroad unions in political activities. But it does not follow that § 2, Eleventh places no restriction on the use of an employee's money, over his objection, to support political causes he opposes merely because Congress did not enact a comprehensive regulatory scheme governing expenditures. For it is abundantly clear that Congress did not completely abandon the policy of full freedom of choice embodied in the 1934 Act, but rather made inroads on it for the limited purpose of eliminating the problems created by the "free rider." That policy survives in § 2, Eleventh in the safeguards intended to protect freedom of dissent. Congress was aware of the conflicting interests involved in the question of the union shop and sought to achieve their accommodation. * * * We respect this congressional purpose when we construe § 2, Eleventh as not vesting the unions with unlimited power to spend exacted money. We are not called upon to delineate the precise limits of that power in this case. We have before us only the question whether the power is restricted to the extent of denying the unions the right, over the employee's objection, to use his money to support political causes which he opposes. Its use to support candidates for public office, and advance political programs, is not a use which helps defray the expenses of the negotiation or administration of collective agreements, or the expenses entailed in the adjustment of grievances and disputes. In other words, it is a use which falls clearly outside the reasons advanced by the unions and accepted by Congress why authority to make union-shop agreements was justified. On the other hand, it is equally clear that it is a use to support activities within the area of dissenters' interests which Congress enacted the proviso to protect. We give § 2, Eleventh the construction which achieves both congressional purposes when we hold, as we do, that § 2, Eleventh is to be construed to deny the unions, over an employee's objection, the power to use his exacted funds to support political causes which he opposes. * * *

IV.

The Appropriate Remedy.

Under our view of the statute, however, the decision of the court below was erroneous and cannot stand. The appellees who have participated in this action have in the course of it made known to their respective unions their objection to the use of their money for the support of political causes. In that circumstance, the respective unions were without power to use payments thereafter tendered by them for such political causes. However, the union-shop agreement itself is not unlawful. Railway Employes' Dept. v. Hanson, supra. * * * If their money were used for purposes contemplated by § 2, Eleventh, the appellees would have no grievance at all. We think that an injunction restraining enforcement of the union-shop agreement is therefore plainly not a remedy appropriate to the violation of the Act's restriction on expenditures. Restraining the collection of all funds from the appellees sweeps too broadly, since their objection is only to the uses to which some of their money is put. Moreover, restraining collection of the funds as the Georgia courts have done might well interfere with the appellant unions' performance of those functions and duties which the Railway Labor Act places upon them to attain its goal of stability in the industry. * * *

Since the case must therefore be remanded to the court below for consideration of a proper remedy, we think that it is appropriate to suggest the limits within which remedial discretion may be exercised consistently with the Railway Labor Act and other relevant public policies. As indicated, an injunction against enforcement of the union shop itself through the collection of funds is unwarranted. We also think that a blanket injunction against all expenditures of funds for the disputed purposes, even one conditioned on cessation of improper expenditures, would not be a proper exercise of equitable discretion. * * * Moreover, the fact that these expenditures are made for political activities is an additional reason for reluctance to impose such an injunctive remedy. Whatever may be the powers of Congress or the States to forbid unions altogether to make various types of political expenditures, as to which we express no opinion here, many of the expenditures involved in the present case are made for the purpose of disseminating information as to candidates and programs and publicizing the positions of the unions on them. As to such expenditures an injunction would work a restraint on the expression of political ideas which might be offensive to the First Amendment. For the majority also has an interest in stating its views without being silenced by the dissenters. To attain the appropriate reconciliation between majority and dissenting interests in the area of political expression, we think the courts in administering the Act should select remedies which protect both interests to the maximum extent possible without undue impingement of one on the other.

Among possible remedies which would appear appropriate to the injury complained of, two may be enforced with a minimum of administrative difficulty and with little danger of encroachment on the legitimate activities or necessary functions of the unions. Any remedies, however, would properly be granted only to employees who have made known to the union officials that they do not desire their funds to be used for political causes to which they object. The safeguards of § 2, Eleventh were added for the protection of dissenters' interest, but dissent is not to be presumed—it must affirmatively be made known to the union by the dissenting employee. The union receiving money exacted from an employee under a union-shop agreement should not in fairness be subjected to sanctions in favor of an employee who makes no complaint of the use of his money for such activities. * * *

One remedy would be an injunction against expenditure for political causes opposed by each complaining employee of a sum, from those moneys to be spent by the union for political purposes, which is so much of the moneys exacted from him as is the proportion of the union's total expenditures made for such political activities to the union's total budget. The union should not be in a position to make up such sum from money paid by a nondissenter, for this would shift a disproportionate share of the costs of collective bargaining to the dissenter and have the same effect of applying his money to support such political activities. A second remedy would be restitution to each individual employee of that portion of his money which the union expended, despite his notification, for the political causes to which he had advised the union he was opposed. There should be no necessity, however, for the employee to trace his money up to and including its expenditure; if the money goes into general funds and no separate accounts of receipts and expenditures of the funds of individual employees are maintained, the portion of his money the employee would be entitled to recover would be in the same proportion that the expenditures for political purposes which he had advised the union he disapproved bore to the total union budget.

The judgment is reversed and the case is remanded to the court below for proceedings not inconsistent with this opinion.

Reversed and remanded.

MR. JUSTICE DOUGLAS, concurring.

* * * If an association is compelled, the individual should not be forced to surrender any matters of conscience, belief, or expression. He should be allowed to enter the group with his own flag flying, whether it be religious, political, or philosophical; nothing that the group does should deprive him of the privilege of preserving and expressing his agreement, disagreement, or dissent, whether it coincides with the view of the group, or conflicts with it in minor or major ways; and he should not be required to finance the promotion of causes with which he disagrees. * * *

The collection of dues for paying the costs of collective bargaining of which each member is a beneficiary is one thing. If, however, dues are used, or assessments are made, to promote or oppose birth control, to repeal or increase the taxes on cosmetics, to promote or oppose the admission of Red China into the United Nations, and the like, then the group compels an individual to support with his money causes beyond what gave rise to the need for group action.

I think the same must be said when union dues or assessments are used to elect a Governor, a Congressman, a Senator, or a President. It may be said that the election of a Franklin D. Roosevelt rather than a Calvin Coolidge might be the best possible way to serve the cause of collective bargaining. But even such a selective use of union funds for political purposes subordinates the individual's First Amendment rights to the views of the majority. I do not see how that can be done, even though the objector retains his rights to campaign, to speak, to vote as he chooses. For when union funds are used for that purpose, the individual is required to finance political projects against which he may be in rebellion. The furtherance of the common cause leaves some leeway for the leadership of the group. As long as they act to promote the cause which justified bringing the group together, the individual cannot withdraw his financial support merely because he disagrees with the group's strategy. If that were allowed, we would be reversing the Hanson case *sub silentio*. * * *

MR. JUSTICE BLACK, dissenting.
* * *

* * * I think the Court is once more "carrying the doctrine of avoiding constitutional questions to a wholly unjustifiable extreme." In fact, I think the Court is actually rewriting § 2, Eleventh to make it mean exactly what Congress refused to make it mean. The very legislative history relied on by the Court appears to me to prove that

its interpretation of § 2, Eleventh is without justification. For that history shows that Congress with its eyes wide open passed that section, knowing that its broad language would permit the use of union dues to advocate causes, doctrines, laws, candidates and parties, whether individual members objected or not. Under such circumstances I think Congress has a right to a determination of the constitutionality of the statute it passed, rather than to have the Court rewrite the statute in the name of avoiding decision of constitutional questions. * * *

There is, of course, no constitutional reason why a union or other private group may not spend its funds for political or ideological causes if its members voluntarily join it and can voluntarily get out of it. Labor unions made up of voluntary members free to get in or out of the unions when they please have played important and useful roles in politics and economic affairs. How to spend its money is a question for each voluntary group to decide for itself in the absence of some valid law forbidding activities for which the money is spent. But a different situation arises when a federal law steps in and authorizes such a group to carry on activities at the expense of persons who do not choose to be members of the group as well as those who do. Such a law, even though validly passed by Congress, cannot be used in a way that abridges the specifically defined freedoms of the First Amendment. And whether there is such abridgment depends not only on how the law is written but also on how it works.

There can be no doubt that the federally sanctioned union-shop contract here, as it actually works, takes a part of the earnings of some men and turns it over to others, who spend a substantial part of the funds so received in efforts to thwart the political, economic and ideological hopes of those whose money has been forced from them under authority of law. This injects federal compulsion into the political and ideological processes, a result which I have supposed everyone would agree the First Amendment was particularly intended to prevent. And it makes no difference if, as is urged, political and legislative activities are helpful adjuncts of collective bargaining. * * *

I would therefore hold that § 2, Eleventh of the Railway Labor Act, in authorizing application of the union-shop contract to the named protesting employees who are appellees here, violates the freedom of speech guarantee of the First Amendment. * * *

MR. JUSTICE FRANKFURTER, whom MR. JUSTICE HARLAN joins, dissenting.

* * *

I completely defer to the guiding principle that this Court will abstain from entertaining a serious constitutional question when a statute may fairly be construed so as to avoid the issue, but am unable to accept the restrictive interpretation that the Court gives to § 2, Eleventh of the Railway Labor Act. * * *

The statutory provision cannot be meaningfully construed except against the background and presupposition of what is loosely called political activity of American trade unions in general and railroad unions in particular—activity indissolubly relating to the immediate economic and social concerns that are the *raison d'être* of unions. It would be pedantic heavily to document this familiar truth of industrial history and commonplace of trade-union life. To write the history of the Brotherhoods, the United Mine Workers, the Steel Workers, the Amalgamated Clothing Workers, the International Ladies Garment Workers, the United Auto Workers, and leave out their so-called political activities and expenditures for them, would be sheer mutilation. Suffice it to recall a few illustrative manifestations. The AFL, surely the conservative labor group, sponsored as early as 1893 an extensive program of political demands calling for compulsory education, an eight-hour day, employer tort liability, and other social reforms. The fiercely contested Adamson Act of 1916, 39 Stat. 721, see Wilson v. New, 243 U.S. 332, 37 S.Ct. 298, 61 L.Ed. 755, was a direct result of railway union pressures exerted upon both the Congress and the President. More specifically, the weekly publication "Labor"—an expenditure under attack in this case—has since 1919 been the organ of the railroad brotherhoods which finance it. Its files through the years show its preoccupation with legislative measures that touch the vitals of labor's interests and with the men and parties who effectuate them. This aspect—call it the political side— is as organic, as inured a part of the philosophy and practice of railway unions as their immediate bread-and-butter concerns.

Viewed in this light, there is a total absence in the text, the context, the history and the purpose of the legislation under review of any indication that Congress, in authorizing union-shop agreements, attributed to unions and restricted them to an artificial, non-prevalent scope of activities in the expenditure of their funds. An inference that Congress legislated regarding expenditure control in contradiction to prevailing practices ought to be better founded than on complete silence. The aim of the 1951 legislation, clearly stated in the congressional reports, was to eliminate "free riders" in the industry—to make possible "the sharing of the burden of maintenance by all of the beneficiaries of union activity." To suggest that this language covertly meant to encompass any less than the maintenance of those activities normally engaged in by unions is to withdraw life from law and to say that Congress dealt with artificialities and not with railway unions as they were and as they functioned. * * *

I cannot attribute to Congress that *sub silentio* it meant to bar railway unions under a union-shop agreement from expending their funds in their traditional manner. How easy it would have been to give at least a hint that such was its purpose. The claim that these expenditures infringe the appellees' constitutional rights under the First Amendment must therefore be faced. *   *   *

[W]e unanimously held that the plaintiffs in Hanson had not been denied any right protected by the First Amendment. Despite our holding, the gist of the complaint here is that the expenditure of a portion of mandatory funds for political objectives denies free speech—the right to speak or to remain silent—to members who oppose, against the constituted authority of union desires, this use of their union dues. No one's desire or power to speak his mind is checked or curbed. The individual member may express his views in any public or private forum as freely as he could before the union collected his dues. Federal taxes also may diminish the vigor with which a citizen can give partisan support to a political belief, but as yet no one would place such an impediment to making one's views effective within the reach of constitutionally protected "free speech." *   *   *

But were we to assume, *arguendo,* that the plaintiffs have alleged a valid constitutional objection if Congress had specifically ordered the result, we must consider the difference between such compulsion and the absence of compulsion when Congress acts as platonically as it did, in a wholly non-coercive way. Congress has not commanded that the railroads shall employ only those workers who are members of authorized unions. Congress has only given leave to a bargaining representative, democratically elected by a majority of workers, to enter into a particular contractual provision arrived at under the give-and-take of duly safeguarded bargaining procedures. *   *   * When we speak of the Government "acting" in permitting the union shop, the scope and force of what Congress has done must be heeded. There is not a trace of compulsion involved—no exercise of restriction by Congress on the freedom of the carriers and the unions. On the contrary, Congress expanded their freedom of action. Congress lifted limitations upon free action by parties bargaining at arm's length.

The plaintiffs have not been deprived of the right to participate in determining union policies or to assert their respective weight in defining the purposes for which union dues may be expended. *   *   *

In conclusion, then, we are asked by union members who oppose these expenditures to protect their right to free speech—although they are as free to speak as ever—against governmental action which has permitted a union elected by democratic process to bargain for a union shop and to expend the funds thereby collected for purposes which are controlled by internal union choice. To do so would be to mutilate a scheme designed by Congress for the purpose of equitably sharing the cost of securing the benefits of union exertions; it would greatly embarrass if not frustrate conventional labor activities which have become institutionalized through time. To do so is to give constitutional sanction to doctrinaire views and to grant a miniscule claim constitutional recognition.

* * *

[The separate opinion of MR. JUSTICE WHITTAKER is omitted.]

———

Two years after its decision in the *Street* case, the Supreme Court clarified its position on the appropriate remedies, in BROTHERHOOD of RY. CLERKS v. ALLEN, 373 U.S. 113, 83 S.Ct. 1158, 10 L.Ed. 2d 235 (1963). The Court held that while no claim is made out against the union unless the employee makes known to the union his objection to the expenditure of his dues money for political causes, "It would be impracticable to require a dissenting employee to allege and prove each distinct union political expenditure to which he objects; it is enough that he manifests his opposition to *any* political expenditures by the union." To implement the Court's earlier suggested remedies, a determination must be made of what expenditures in the record are political expenditures and the proportion which such expenditures bear to total union expenditures; "basic considerations of fairness" compel the union, with access to the pertinent facts and records, to prove the portion of political to total expenditures, and not the individual employees. A comparable amount of the individual's total dues and fees could be ordered refunded if already paid; and future exactions could be reduced accordingly. The Court invited the defendant unions to consider the adoption of some internal union plan providing for the designation of political expenditures, the manifestation of objections by members unwilling to contribute to such expenditures and an appropriate reduction in the moneys exacted from such objecting members. A few International unions have in fact adopted such plans, thereby providing an internal remedy for members (or non-members subject to valid agency shop agreements) to challenge the use of their dues money for political causes they oppose.

In SEAY v. McDONNELL DOUGLAS CO., 371 F.Supp. 754 (C.D. Cal.1973), the court made an attempt, in extended dictum, to deal with the elusive problem left unresolved by the Supreme Court of defining the kinds of "political" expenses which cannot lawfully be taxed against an unconsenting employee. The court stated:

"Dissenting employees in an agency fee situation should not be required to support financially union expenditures as follows:

"One, for payments to or on behalf of any candidate for public office in connection with his campaign for election to such public office, or

"Two, for payments to or on behalf of any political party or organization, or

"Three, for the holding of any meeting or the printing or distribution of any literature or documents in support of any such candidate or political party or organization. * * *

"[E]xpenditures for other purposes * * * are sufficiently germane to collective bargaining to require dissenting employees who are subject to union shop or agency fee agreements to bear their share of that burden."

Problems for Discussion

1.   William Buckley is a noted newspaper and television journalist, author, and sometime political candidate. He is a member of the bargaining unit at his television station which is represented by AFTRA (American Federation of Television and Radio Artists); AFTRA and the company have negotiated a collective bargaining agreement which requires all employees in the bargaining unit to become members of the union. Buckley claims that thus conditioning his right to continued employment in the media upon his joining AFTRA is an infringement of the rights accorded him by the First Amendment to the Federal Constitution. He brings an action against AFTRA and his employer to enjoin their enforcement of the union shop provision. What defenses do you believe should be raised by the defendants? How should the case be decided? See *Buckley* v. *AFTRA*, 496 F.2d 305 (2d Cir.), cert. denied 419 U.S. 1093 (1974).

2.   Linscott is employed by the Miller Falls Company, which recently negotiated an agreement with the United Electrical Workers containing a union shop provision. Linscott is a Seventh Day Adventist. She argues that it is contrary to the fundamental tenets of her religion to join any union. Those tenets hold that individuals must not join with a class of persons (whether capital or labor), but must rather remain free at all times to choose as an individual the best way to discharge his or her responsibilities to God; joining the union would deprive her of her power of personal decision and would bind her with persons of different convictions to adhere to the same policy, contrary to her individual conscience. Because of these religious beliefs, Linscott refused to join the union but offered to pay an amount equivalent to union dues to a nonreligious charity. The union, however, refused this proposal, and demanded and secured her discharge. Does she have legal means whereby to secure reinstatement or damages?

Consider first a challenge to the constitutionality under the First Amendment of imposing a union shop provision upon a person with Ms. Linscott's beliefs. See *Linscott* v. *Miller Falls Co.*, 440 F.2d 14 (1st Cir.), cert. denied 404 U.S. 872, 92 S.Ct. 77, 30 L.Ed.2d 116 (1971); *Gray* v. *Gulf, M. & O. R. R.*, 429 F.2d 1064 (5th Cir. 1970), cert. denied 400 U.S. 1001, 91 S.Ct. 461, 27 L.Ed.2d 451 (1971).

Consider also a challenge under the Civil Rights Act of 1964. Section 703(a) makes it unlawful for an employer to "discharge any individual * * * because of such individual's * * * religion," and Section 703 (c) makes it unlawful for a union to exclude or expel from membership or "otherwise to discriminate against, any individual because of his * * * religion," or to cause an employer to discriminate in a manner unlawful under the section. Section 701(j) of the Act provides: "The term 'religion' includes all aspects of religious observance and practice, as well as belief, unless an employer demonstrates that he is unable to reasonably accommodate to an employee's or prospective employee's religious observance or practice without undue hardship on the conduct of the employer's business." Compare Cooper v. General Dynamics, Convair Aerospace Div., 533 F.2d 163 (5th Cir. 1976), cert. denied 433 U.S. 908, 97 S.Ct. 2972, 53 L.Ed.2d 1091 (1977), with Anderson v. General Dynamics, Convair Aerospace Div., 589 F.2d (9th Cir. 1978), cert. denied 442 U.S. 921, 99 S.Ct. 2848, 61 L.Ed.2d 290 (1979), and Burns v. Southern Pac. Transp. Co., 589 F.2d 403 (9th Cir. 1978), cert. denied 439 U.S. 1072, 99 S.Ct. 843, 59 L.Ed.2d 38 (1979).

3. In 1974, Congress brought within the coverage of the Labor Act nonprofit health care institutions (which had formerly been explicitly excluded from the definition of "employer" in Section 2(2)). At the same time, Congress enacted a new Section 19, which announced an exception to the principles normally governing union security agreements. Section 19 exempts members of a bona fide religious organization, which has historically held conscientious objections to joining or financially supporting labor organizations, from the obligation to join or pay moneys to the bargaining representative—provided such persons pay an equal sum to a nonreligious charity. The apparent reason was to avoid disrupting charitable hospitals controlled by Seventh Day Adventists, for so long outside the union security provisions of the NLRA, by subjecting employees there to discharge. Can you formulate any constitutional challenges to Section 19? Could it be put to good use (by which party) in the action by Mr. Buckley in Problem 1? Could it be put to good use (by which party) in the action by Ms. Linscott in Problem 2?

B. STATE RIGHT-TO-WORK LAWS [3]

Between 1944 and 1947—when the proviso to Section 8(3) of the Wagner Act sheltered union security agreements as potent as the closed shop—twelve states enacted so-called right-to-work laws (either by statute or by constitutional amendment) which provided in substance that employees were not to be required to join a un-

3. See Grodin & Beeson, State Right-to-Work Laws and Federal Labor Policy, 52 Calif.L.Rev. 95 (1964); Henderson, The Confrontation of Federal Preemption and State Right to Work Laws, 1967 Duke L.J. 1079; Kuhn, Right-to-Work Laws—Symbols or Substance?, 14 Ind. & Lab.Rel.Rev. 587 (1961); F. Meyers, Right to Work in Practice (1959); P. Sultan, Right-to-Work Laws (1958).

ion as a condition of receiving or retaining a job. Today, such laws obtain in nineteen states, most of them in the more agricultural states of the south and midwest. (These states are Alabama, Arizona, Arkansas, Florida, Georgia, Iowa, Kansas, Mississippi, Nebraska, Nevada, North Carolina, North Dakota, South Carolina, South Dakota, Tennessee, Texas, Utah, Virginia, and Wyoming; Louisiana's law applies only to agricultural workers, who fall outside the reach of the federal Labor Act.) The wording of these state provisions varies a good deal. Some states bar (1) discrimination in employment so as to encourage union membership; (2) an employment "monopoly" by a labor union; (3) "combinations" or "conspiracies" to deprive persons of employment because of nonmembership; (4) strikes or picketing to obtain an unlawful agreement; or (5) conspiracies to cause the discharge or denial of employment to an individual by inducing other persons to refuse to work with him because of his nonmembership. Most right-to-work states simply declare unlawful any agreement which conflicts with the policy that the right of persons to work shall not be denied or abridged on account of membership or nonmembership in any labor organization, or any agreement requiring union membership (or paying dues to a union) as a condition of employment. The remedy provided under most such state laws is damages for persons injured by the violation; many provide for injunctive relief; and some make violations a misdemeanor subject to criminal penalties.

The purpose of these laws appears in part to be the protection of employee freedom and in part to be the attraction of new business to a union-free and thus presumably lower-wage environment. The question whether these state laws could flourish under a federal law that authorized the union shop as a force for industrial stability was definitively addressed by Congress in the Taft-Hartley amendments of 1947. In spite of the strong preemptive implications of the Wagner Act (not articulated to any substantial degree by the Supreme Court until the mid-1950's), Congress established a preserve for state right-to-work laws by enacting Section 14(b) of the Labor Act:

> Nothing in this Act shall be construed as authorizing the execution or application of agreements requiring membership in a labor organization as a condition of employment in any State or Territory in which such execution or application is prohibited by State or Territorial law.

Shortly after the Taft-Hartley Act, a union's constitutional attack on a state right-to-work law was rebuffed by the Supreme Court in Lincoln Fed. Union 19129 v. Northwestern Iron & Metal Co., 335 U.S. 525, 69 S.Ct. 251, 93 L.Ed. 212 (1949). Just as, some years before, the Court had endorsed the union argument that a state constitutionally could, in the reasonable pursuit of industrial peace, outlaw contracts which *forbade* joining a union (the so-called yellow dog contract), the Court now marshalled the same considerations to reject the union argument that states could not constitutionally outlaw contracts which *compelled* the joining of a union. It only remained to determine how these state laws were to be interwoven with the federal statutory fabric, and on this issue the Supreme Court was to speak in two 1963 decisions, once again giving rather broad scope to the right-to-work laws.

In Retail Clerks, Local 1625 v. Schermerhorn, 373 U.S. 746, 83 S.Ct. 1461, 10 L.Ed.2d 678 (1963), the state court had interpreted its right-to-work law to outlaw not only the union shop (requiring employees to become members) but also the agency shop (requiring employees to give the union only financial support). The union argued that Section 14(b) did not cede to the states the power to invalidate the agency shop since this was not an agreement "requiring membership in a labor organization." The Court quickly rejected this argument, holding that the only kind of "membership" which may lawfully be demanded of an employee is his payment of a service fee to the union measured by periodic dues and initiation fees, and that thus the agency shop is the "practical equivalent" of an agreement requiring "membership," both under the proviso to Section 8(a)(3), NLRB v. General Motors, 373 U.S. 734, 83 S.Ct. 1453, 10 L.Ed.2d 670 (1963), which made the agency shop lawful under federal law, and under Section 14(b), which authorized states to prohibit it. The Court proceeded to address the union's second argument which was that, even if its agency shop provision was invalid —because banned by the state right-to-work law—its execution and enforcement would violate Sections 8(a)(3) and 8(b)(2) and could thus be addressed only by the National Labor Relations Board. By 1963, the law of federal preemption had indeed been sufficiently developed and rather clearly compelled the ouster of state-court jurisdiction over conduct which arguably or actually was a federal unfair labor practice. San Diego Bldg. Trades Council v. Garmon, 359 U.S. 236, 79 S.Ct. 773, 3 L.Ed.2d 775 (1959). On this issue, the Court sought the benefit of reargument and the views of the NLRB.

After reargument, the Court, in Retail Clerks, Local 1625 v. Schermerhorn, 375 U.S. 96, 84 S.Ct. 219, 11 L.Ed.2d 179 (1963), concluded that the state-court injunction against the enforcement of the agency shop agreement was a valid remedy. Congress, by acknowledging that states could prohibit union security agreements which the federal law would protect, "chose to abandon any search for uniformity in dealing with the problems of state laws barring the execution and application of agreements authorized by Section

14(b) and decided to suffer a medley of attitudes and philosophies on the subject." Congress gave the states such overriding power that it would be anomalous to conclude that only the NLRB had the power to implement state policy. But the Court was cautious to note that the state-court injunction may run only against the "execution or application" (in the words of Section 14(b)) of a union security agreement; the state is not free to enjoin a strike or picketing the object of which is to *secure* a union shop or agency shop agreement. While it may seem strange to direct the states to permit concerted activity for a contract clause while authorizing the states to enjoin the enforcement of the clause after the concerted activity has been successful, the Court took no note of the anomaly and merely reiterated that state power "begins *only with actual negotiation and execution of the type of agreement described by Section 14(b)*. Absent such an agreement, conduct arguably an unfair labor practice would be a matter for the National Labor Relations Board under *Garmon*." Perhaps the Court was concerned that certain concerted activity which Congress clearly sought to protect—such as peaceful picketing designed to induce employees to become members, at least when not outlawed by Section 8(b)(7), and peaceful informational picketing designed to communicate to the public that a company is nonunion—would be too readily outlawed by state courts, particularly when a number of state right-to-work laws are extremely broadly drawn and provide in some instances for severe sanctions (including criminal penalties).

A continuing campaign has been waged both for and against the enactment of state "right to work" laws authorized by Section 14(b). Unions have stressed several points in resisting such legislation. Primary emphasis, of course, has been placed upon the argument that unions—unlike other voluntary associations—must represent members and non-members alike so that those who do not join are "free riders," accepting valuable benefits without cost. Unions also stress the fact that the National Labor Relations Act prohibits various abuses of union security and reduces the union shop to little more than an obligation to pay dues. Reference is frequently made to the experience under the union shop authorization elections that were required for a time under the NLRA; in the 46,117 authorization elections, the union shop prevailed in 97.1% of the contests with 91% of the employees voting in favor. Finally, unions argue that the union shop contributes to harmonious labor-management relations by minimizing the insecurity of labor representatives and reducing the temptation of the employer to undermine the union and thus exacerbate the relationship.

Employers respond to these arguments by stressing "the basic rights of an individual to get and keep a job without having to pay tribute to any organization in order to make a living." In answer to the unions' "free-loader" argument, it is urged that many employees may wish to refrain from joining a union or paying dues for genuine reasons of conscience. Regardless of the size of the majority favoring compulsory union membership, the rights of these individuals should be respected. In addition to this question of principle, employers argue that unions are already too powerful and will become more so if "right to work" laws are repealed. Finally, the argument is often made that the right of employees to shift allegiance to a different union will be impaired, as a practical matter, if all must become members of the incumbent union. As a result, corrupt and ineffective unions will be perpetuated to the detriment of the employees involved.

Problem for Discussion

In the collective bargaining agreement between the General Contractors Association in Houston, Texas and the Laborers Union, there is a provision for hiring exclusively through referrals by the union-operated hiring hall. The hiring-hall provision expressly bars discrimination in referrals because of union membership or nonmembership, giving priority to workers with greatest seniority in service for the contractors and general work experience in the trade. Smith works as a laborer, but has for years strongly resisted becoming a member of the Union. He believes as a matter of principle that hiring should be done by the employers and not controlled by the Union, and that Union control over the hiring process exerts subtle and unlawful pressures on workers to become union members. He points to the Texas right-to-work law, barring hiring on the basis of union membership or nonmembership. He wishes to know whether he can successfully attack the contractual hiring-hall provision in the Texas courts as in violation of state law. What advice would you give him? See *NLRB v. Houston Chapter, Assoc. Gen. Contractors*, 349 F.2d 449 (5th Cir. 1965) cert. denied 382 U.S. 1026 (1966).

C.   THE UNION HIRING HALL [4]

In certain industries—most notably, maritime, longshoring and construction—unions provide what is in effect a job-referral service and act as a clearinghouse between employees seeking work and employers seeking workers. These industries are characterized by irregular and short-lived employment opportunities. For example, an electrical subcontractor in the construction business may have no regular employee force but rather seek qualified electricians to go to the jobsite on one date to install wires across the studded substructure of the house and will later send electricians (not always the same ones) back after the walls have been completed in order

---

4. See Fenton, Union Hiring Halls Under the Taft-Hartley Act, 9 Lab.L.J. 505 (1958); Rains, Construction Trades Hiring Halls, 10 Lab.L.J. 363 (1959).

to install switchplates and fixtures. A shipowner may seek to employ a crew for a transoceanic run and return, or for a shorter run to some port along the same coast; after a long time at sea, the crewmen may not wish to ship out again but may rather prefer some days on shore to be spent with family or friends. It would be time-consuming and uneconomical for the many employers in these industries to hire on their own and for the many employees individually to search for employment. The solution that has been worked out over time is the union-operated hiring hall, which receives from the employers requests for workers and provides workers who are qualified and available. The service can be rendered at no cost to the employer, and the union recoups its cost from membership dues and hiring-hall fees of nonmembers. The union and employer may agree that the hiring hall is "nonexclusive," that is, that the employer is free to reject persons referred by the union and may hire from other sources; or may agree to make the hiring hall the exclusive method of recruitment. The union is expected to distribute work opportunities in accordance with some equitable principle; work on board ship will commonly be assigned in accordance with the seniority of the workers in their service within the hall's jurisdiction, and work on shore in loading and unloading ships will commonly be on a rotary basis, with work assigned to the employees who earliest completed their last preceding job and are thus at the top of a first-come first-served list. In industries where seniority with a given employer cannot be utilized to achieve job security, the union hiring hall can afford comparable benefits.

Union control over the referral process has frequently, however, tempted union officials to engage in invidious discrimination—to give preference in referrals to union members rather than to nonmembers, or to give preference to those union members who are most zealous in their attendance at meetings or in their support of the incumbent officials, or simply to friends, relatives or persons of the same color. The union-operated hiring hall thus frequently went hand-in-hand with the closed shop, where union membership in good standing was a condition of referral and thus of employment; the union could control the volume and qualifications of the work force at the source. To the extent that the parties make union membership a condition of referral and employment, such an agreement would clearly constitute a violation by the employer of Section 8(a)(3)—since it would lack the thirty-day grace period for joining the union, which makes the union shop lawful under the proviso to that section—and a violation of Section 8(b)(2) by the union. But exclusive referral or preference of union members is not a necessary adjunct of the union-operated hiring hall, and it has been the task of the Board and the courts to test the hiring hall against the directive in those two sections barring "discrimination." The key issue is thus whether the hiring hall arrangement, as written or as implemented in practice, works a union-induced discrimination which encourages union membership.

LOCAL 357, TEAMSTERS v. NLRB

Supreme Court of the United States, 1961.
365 U.S. 667, 81 S.Ct. 835, 6 L.Ed.2d 11.

MR. JUSTICE DOUGLAS delivered the opinion of the Court.

Petitioner union (along with the International Brotherhood of Teamsters and a number of other affiliated local unions) executed a three-year collective bargaining agreement with California Trucking Associations which represented a group of motor truck operators in California. The provisions of the contract relating to hiring of casual or temporary employees were as follows:

> "Casual employees shall, wherever the Union maintains a dispatching service, be employed only on a seniority basis in the Industry whenever such senior employees are available. An available list with seniority status will be kept by the Unions, and employees requested will be dispatched upon call to any employer who is a party to this Agreement. Seniority rating of such employees shall begin with a minimum of three months service in the Industry, *irrespective of whether such employee is or is not a member of the Union.*

> "Discharge of any employee by any employer shall be grounds for removal of any employee from seniority status. No casual employee shall be employed by any employer who is a party to this Agreement in violation of seniority status if such employees are available and if the dispatching service for such employees is available. The employer shall first call the Union or the dispatching hall designated by the Union for such help. In the event the employer is notified that such help is not available, or in the event the employees called for do not appear for work at the time designated by the employer, the employer may hire from any other available source." (Emphasis added.)

Accordingly the union maintained a hiring hall for casual employees. One Slater was a member of the union and had customarily used the hiring hall. But in August 1955 he obtained casual employment with an employer who was party to the hiring-hall agreement without being dispatched by the union. He worked until sometime in November of that year, when he was discharged by the employer on complaint of the union that he had not been referred through the hiring-hall arrangement.

Slater made charges against the union and the employer. Though, as plain from the terms of the contract, there was an express provision that employees would not be discriminated against because they were or were not union members, the Board found that the hiring-hall provision was unlawful *per se* and that the discharge of Slater on the union's request constituted a violation by the employer of § 8(a) (1) and § 8(a) (3) and a violation by the union of § 8(b) (2) and § 8(b) (1) (A) of the National Labor Relations Act, as amended by the Taft-Hartley Act, 61 Stat. 140–141, as amended, 29 U.S.C. § 158, 29 U.S.C.A. § 158. The Board ordered, *inter alia,* that the company and the union cease giving any effect to the hiring-hall agreement; that they jointly and severally reimburse Slater for any loss sustained by him as a result of his discharge; and that they jointly and severally reimburse all casual employees for fees and dues paid by them to the union beginning six months prior to the date of the filing of the charge. 121 N.L.R.B. 1629.

The union petitioned the Court of Appeals for review of the Board's action, and the Board made a cross-application for enforcement. That court set aside the portion of the order requiring a general reimbursement of dues and fees. By a divided vote it upheld the Board in ruling that the hiring-hall agreement was illegal *per se.* 275 F.2d 646. Those rulings are here on certiorari, 363 U.S. 837, 80 S.Ct. 1610, 4 L.Ed.2d 1723, one on the petition of the union, the other on petition of the Board.

Our decision in Local 60, United Broth. of Carpenters, etc., v. National Labor Relations Board, 365 U.S. 651, 81 S.Ct. 875, is dispositive of the petition of the Board that asks us to direct enforcement of the order of reimbursement. [The Supreme Court in that case found that the reimbursement remedy was "punitive" and hence beyond the Board's remedial power under Section 10(c) since there was no basis for concluding that all the casual employees involved, many of whom were union members of long standing, would have refused to pay dues to the union had it refrained from committing unlawful acts under Section 8(b) (2).]

The other aspect of the case goes back to the Board's ruling in Mountain Pacific Chapter, 119 N.L.R.B. 883. That decision, rendered in 1958, departed from earlier rulings and held, Abe Murdock dissenting, that the hiring-hall agreement, despite the inclusion of a nondiscrimination clause, was illegal *per se:*

> "Here the very grant of work at all depends solely upon union sponsorship, and it is reasonable to infer that the arrangement displays and enhances the Union's power and control over the employment status. Here all that appears is unilateral union determination and subservient employer action with no aboveboard explanation as to the reason for it, and it is reasonable to infer that the Union will be guided in its

concession by an eye towards winning compliance with a membership obligation or union fealty in some other respect. The Employers here have surrendered all hiring authority to the Union and have given advance notice via the established hiring hall to the world at large that the Union is arbitrary master and is contractually guaranteed to remain so. From the final authority over hiring vested in the Respondent Union by the three AGC chapters, the inference of the encouragement of union membership is inescapable." Id., 896.

The Board went on to say that a hiring-hall arrangement to be lawful must contain protective provisions. Its views were stated as follows:

"We believe, however, that the inherent and unlawful encouragement of union membership that stems from unfettered union control over the hiring process would be negated, and we would find an agreement to be non-discriminatory on its face, only if the agreement explicitly provided that:

"(1) Selection of applicants for referral to jobs shall be on a nondiscriminatory basis and shall not be based on, or in any way affected by, union membership, bylaws, rules, regulations, constitutional provisions, or any other aspect or obligation of union membership, policies, or requirements.

"(2) The employer retains the right to reject any job applicant referred by the union.

"(3) The parties to the agreement post in places where notices to employees and applicants for employment are customarily posted, all provisions relating to the functioning of the hiring arrangement, including the safeguards that we deem essential to the legality of an exclusive hiring agreement." Id., 897.

The Board recognizes that the hiring hall came into being "to eliminate wasteful, time-consuming, and repetitive scouting for jobs by individual workmen and haphazard uneconomical searches by employers." Id., 896, n. 8. The hiring hall at times has been a useful adjunct to the closed shop. But Congress may have thought that it need not serve that cause, that in fact it has served well both labor and management—particularly in the maritime field and in the building and construction industry. In the latter the contractor who frequently is a stranger to the area where the work is done requires a "central source" for his employment needs; and a man looking for a job finds in the hiring hall "at least a minimum guarantee of continued employment."

Congress has not outlawed the hiring hall, though it has outlawed the closed shop except within the limits prescribed in the *provisos* to

§ 8(a) (3).   Senator Taft made clear his views that hiring halls are useful, that they are not illegal *per se,* that unions should be able to operate them so long as they are not used to create a closed shop:

> "In order to make clear the real intention of Congress, it should be clearly stated that the hiring hall is not necessarily illegal. The employer should be able to make a contract with the union as an employment agency. The union frequently is the best employment agency. The employer should be able to give notice of vacancies, and in the normal course of events to accept men sent to him by the hiring hall. He should not be able to bind himself, however, to reject nonunion men if they apply to him * * *.

> * * * Neither the law nor [NLRB and court] decisions forbid hiring halls, even hiring halls operated by the unions as long as they are not so operated as to create a closed shop with all of the abuses possible under such an arrangement, including discrimination against employees, prospective employees, members of union minority groups, and operation of a closed union."   S.Rep.No.1827, 81st Cong., 2d Sess., pp. 13, 14.

There being no express ban of hiring halls in any provisions of the Act, those who add one, whether it be the Board or the courts, engage in a legislative act. The Act deals with discrimination either by the employers or unions that encourages or discourages union membership.   As respects § 8(a) (3) we said in Radio Officers, etc., v. National Labor Relations Board, 347 U.S. 17, 42–43, 74 S.Ct. 323, 337, 98 L.Ed. 455:

> "The language of § 8(a) (3) is not ambiguous. The unfair labor practice is for an employer to encourage or discourage membership by means of discrimination. Thus this section does not outlaw all encouragement or discouragement of membership in labor organizations; only such as is accomplished by discrimination is prohibited. Nor does this section outlaw discrimination in employment as such; only such discrimination as encourages or discourages membership in a labor organization is proscribed."

It is the "true purpose" or "real motive" in hiring or firing that constitutes the test. Id., 347 U.S. 43, 74 S.Ct. 337. Some conduct may by its very nature contain the implications of the required intent; the natural foreseeable consequences of certain action may warrant the inference. Id., 347 U.S. 45, 74 S.Ct. 338. And see Republic Aviation Corp. v. National Labor Relations Board, 324 U.S. 793, 65 S.Ct. 982, 89 L.Ed. 1372. The existence of discrimination may at times be inferred by the Board, for "it is permissible to draw on experience in factual inquiries." Radio Officers, etc., v. National Labor Relations Board, supra, 347 U.S. 49, 74 S.Ct. 340.

But surely discrimination cannot be inferred from the face of the instrument when the instrument specifically provides that there will be no discrimination against "casual employees" because of the presence or absence of union membership. The only complaint in the case was by Slater, a union member, who sought to circumvent the hiring-hall agreement. When an employer and the union enforce the agreement against union members, we cannot say without more that either indulges in the kind of discrimination to which the Act is addressed.

It may be that the very existence of the hiring hall encourages union membership. We may assume that it does. The very existence of the union has the same influence. When a union engages in collective bargaining and obtains increased wages and improved working conditions, its prestige doubtless rises and, one may assume, more workers are drawn to it. When a union negotiates collective bargaining agreements that include arbitration clauses and supervises the functioning of those provisions so as to get equitable adjustments of grievances, union membership may also be encouraged. The truth is that the union is a service agency that probably encourages membership whenever it does its job well. But as we said in Radio Officers, etc., v. National Labor Relations Board, supra, the only encouragement or discouragement of union membership banned by the Act is that which is "accomplished by discrimination." 347 U.S. at page 43, 74 S.Ct. at page 337.

Nothing is inferrable from the present hiring-hall provision, except that employer and union alike sought to route "casual employees" through the union hiring hall and required a union member who circumvented it to adhere to it.

It may be that hiring halls need more regulation than the Act presently affords. * * * Perhaps the conditions which the Board attaches to hiring-hall arrangements will in time appeal to the Congress. Yet where Congress has adopted a selective system for dealing with evils, the Board is confined to that system. * * * Where, as here, Congress has aimed its sanctions only at specific discriminatory practices, the Board cannot go farther and establish a broader, more pervasive regulatory scheme.

The present agreement for a union hiring hall has a protective clause in it, as we have said; and there is no evidence that it was in fact used unlawfully. We cannot assume that a union conducts its operations in violation of law or that the parties to this contract did not intend to adhere to its express language. Yet we would have to make those assumptions to agree with the Board that it is reasonable to infer the union will act discriminatorily. * * *

Reversed.

MR. JUSTICE FRANKFURTER took no part in the consideration or decision of this case.

MR. JUSTICE HARLAN, whom MR. JUSTICE STEWART joins, concurring. * * *

While I agree with the opinion of the Court that the Board could not infer from the mere existence of the "hiring hall" clause an intent on the part of employer or union to discriminate in favor of union status, I think it was within the realm of Board expertness to say that the natural and foreseeable effect of this clause is to make employees and job applicants think that union status will be favored. For it is surely scarcely less than a fact of life that a certain number of job applicants will believe that joining the union would increase their chances of hire when the union is exercising the hiring function.

What in my view is wrong with the Board's position in these cases is that a mere showing of foreseeable encouragement of union status is not a sufficient basis for a finding of violation of the statute. It has long been recognized that an employer can make reasonable business decisions, unmotivated by an intent to discourage union membership or protected concerted activities, although the foreseeable effect of these decisions may be to discourage what the act protects. For example, an employer may discharge an employee because he is not performing his work adequately, whether or not the employee happens to be a union organizer. See National Labor Relations Board v. Universal Camera Corp., 2 Cir., 190 F.2d 429. Yet a court could hardly reverse a Board finding that such firing would foreseeably tend to discourage union activity. Again, an employer can properly make the existence or amount of a year-end bonus depend upon the productivity of a unit of the plant, although this will foreseeably tend to discourage the protected activity of striking. Pittsburgh-Des Moines Steel Co. v. National Labor Relations Board, 9 Cir., 284 F.2d 74. A union, too, is privileged to make decisions which are reasonably calculated to further the welfare of all the employees it represents, nonunion as well as union, even though a foreseeable result of the decision may be to encourage union membership.

This Court's interpretation of the relevant statutory provisions has recognized that Congress did not mean to limit the range of either employer or union decision to those possible actions which had *no* foreseeable tendency to encourage or discourage union membership or concerted activities. In general, this Court has assumed that a finding of a violation of §§ 8(a) 3 or 8(b) 2 requires an affirmative showing of a *motivation* of encouraging or discouraging union status

or activity.   See, e. g., National Labor Relations Board v. Jones &
Laughlin Co., 301 U.S. 1, 45–46, 57 S.Ct. 615, 628, 81 L.Ed. 893;
Universal Camera Corp. v. National Labor Relations Board, 340 U.S.
474, 71 S.Ct. 456, 95 L.Ed. 456.   There have, to be sure, been exceptions to this requirement, but they have been narrow ones, usually
analogous to the exceptions made to the requirements for a showing of
discrimination in other contexts.   For example, in Republic Aviation
Corp. v. National Labor Relations Board, 324 U.S. 793, 65 S.Ct. 982,
89 L.Ed. 1372, the Court affirmed a Board decision that a company
"no solicitation" rule was overbroadly applied to prevent solicitation
of union membership on company property during periods when employees were otherwise free to do as they pleased.   A finding of a motivation to discourage union membership was there held unnecessary
because there was no employer showing of a nondiscriminatory purpose for applying the rule to union solicitation during the employees'
free time.   *   *   *

Another field of exceptions to the requirement of a showing of
a purpose to encourage or discourage union activity is found in the
Court's affirmance of the Second Circuit in Gaynor News Co., Inc.,
v. National Labor Relations Board, 347 U.S. 17, 74 S.Ct. 323, 98 L.Ed.
455, a companion case to Radio Officers: If a union or employer is
to be permitted to take action which substantially—though uninten-
tionally—encourages or discourages union activity, the union or employer ends served by the action must not only be of some significance, but they must also be legitimate, or at least not otherwise forbidden by the National Labor Relations Act.   *   *   *

Considered in this light, I do not think we can sustain the Board's
holding that the "hiring hall" clause is forbidden by the Taft-Hartley
Act.   The Board has not found that this clause was without substantial justification in terms of legitimate employer or union purposes.
Cf. Republic Aviation v. National Labor Relations Board, supra;
Gaynor News Co., Inc., v. National Labor Relations Board, supra.
Whether or not such a finding would have been supported by the record is not for us now to decide.   The Board has not, in my view, made
the type of showing of an actual motive of encouraging union membership that is required by Universal Camera v. National Labor Relations Board, supra.   All it has shown is that the clause will tend to
encourage union membership, and that without substantial difficulty
the parties to the agreement could have taken additional steps to isolate the valid employer or union purposes from the discriminatory effects of the clause.   I do not think that these two elements alone can
justify a Board holding of an unfair labor practice unless we are to approve a broad expansion of the power of the Board to supervise nondiscriminatory decisions made by employer or union.   Whether or
not such an expansion would be desirable, it does not seem to me con-

sistent with the balance the labor acts have struck between freedom of choice of management and union ends by the parties to a collective bargaining agreement and the freedom of employees from restraint or coercion in their exercise of rights granted by § 7 of the Act.

MR. JUSTICE CLARK, dissenting in part.   *   *   *

[T]he employer's "true purpose" and "real motive" [are] to be tested by the "natural consequences" and "foreseeable result" of his resort, however justifiably taken, to an institution so closely allied to the closed shop.   I believe, as this Court has recognized, that "the desire of employees to unionize is directly proportional to the advantages *thought to be* obtained   *   *   *." Radio Officers, supra, 347 U.S. at page 46, 74 S.Ct. at page 339. (Emphasis added.)   I therefore ask, "Does the ordinary applicant for casual employment, who walks into the union hall at the direction of his prospective employer, consider his chances of getting dispatched for work diminished because of his non-union status or his default in dues payment?"   Lester Slater testified—and it is uncontradicted—that "He [the applicant] had to be a union member; otherwise he wouldn't be working there;   *   *   *   you got to have your dues paid up to date and so forth."   When asked how he knew this, Slater replied, "I have always knew that."   Such was the sum of his impressions gained from contact with the hall from 1953 or 1954 when he started to 1958 when he ended.   The misunderstanding—if it is that—of this common worker, who had the courage to complain, is, I am sure, representative of many more who were afraid to protest or, worse, were unaware of their right to do so.

Of the gravity of such a situation the Board is the best arbiter and best equipped to find a solution.   It is, after all, "permissible [for the Board] to draw on experience in factual inquiries."   Radio Officers, supra, 347 U.S. at page 49, 74 S.Ct. at page 340.   It has resolved the issue clearly, not only here, but in its 1958 Report which, as I have said, repeated its Mountain Pacific position "that a union to which an employer has so delegated hiring powers will exercise its powers with a view to securing compliance with membership obligations and union rules."   At p. 68.   In view of Slater's experience, for one, the idea is certainly not farfetched.   *   *   *

However, I need not go so far as to presume that the union has set itself upon an illegal course, conditioning referral on the unlawful criterion of union membership in good standing (which inference the majority today says cannot be drawn), to reach the same result.   I need only assume that, by thousands of common workers like Slater, the contract and its conditioning of casual employment upon union referral will work a misunderstanding as to the significance of union affiliation unless the employer's abdication of his role be made less than total and some note of the true function of the hiring hall be posted where all may see and read. The tide of encouragement may not be turned, but it will in part at least be stemmed. As an added dividend, the inherent probability of the free-wheeling operation of the union hiring hall resulting in arbitrary dispatching of job seekers would to some significant extent be diminished.

I would hold that there is not only a reasonable likelihood, but that it must inescapably be concluded under this record, that, without the safeguards at issue, a contract, conditioning employment *solely upon union referral*, encourages membership in the union by that very distinction itself. * * *

Problems for Discussion

1. Which of the opinions in the *Local 357* case most accords with the more recent approach of the Court articulated in such cases as *Great Dane Trailers*, p. 851, supra? Is that more recent decision pertinent on the question of the employer's discretion in hiring or firing individual workers?

2. Longshore employees are referred through the hiring hall of the International Longshoremen's Association to employers which are members of the Pacific Maritime Association. The union has traditionally maintained two halls, one for "regular" longshoremen who work full-time and indefinitely on the docks and the other for "casual" workers; priority in referrals for available work is given to the "regular" job applicants. The union has recently created a third category of workers, consisting of those persons who are normally employed as longshoremen but who are currently unemployed as a result of a strike (either against their own employer or against another employer upon whose business operations their own work depends) sponsored by a labor organization. The union now gives second priority in referrals to this new category of job applicant, in preference to the "casuals." Cole is a "casual" longshore worker who on a number of occasions has been denied a job referral (and thus a job) while "strikers" have been granted work. He has filed unfair labor practice charges against both the union and the PMA. Do these charges have merit? *Pacific Maritime Ass'n*, 172 N.L.R.B. 2055 (1968).

3. The labor contract between the Operating Engineers and the Associated General Contractors of Illinois (AGC) provides that job referrals through the union-operated hiring hall shall be nondiscriminatory and shall be based on length of service in the area with contractors who are members of the AGC. When the jobsite on which one Parker worked was temporarily closed down because of the contractor's financial situation, Parker was laid off; he is not a union member and does not maintain a permanent residence in the area. When the jobsite opens up again, Parker is not recalled, the union informing him that this is because there are others available with longer employment experience with contractors who are parties to the labor agreement. Does the union's refusal to refer violate the Labor Act? See *Robertson v. NLRB*, 597 F.2d 1331 (10th Cir. 1979); *J–M Co.*, 173 N.L.R.B. 1461 (1969).

4. The labor contract between the local Association of General Contractors and Operating Engineers local provides for exclusive hiring
through a "nondiscriminatory" hiring hall. The union incurs administrative expenses in the operation of the hall, and requires that all persons
who wish to be listed for referral and who are not members of the union
must pay a monthly charge of $9.00 to defray the expenses of the union's
services. The union has declined to register one Hender for referral and
has refused to refer him for any job ·openings, claiming that he has consistently refused to tender the $9.00 monthly service fee. Hender has ob-
jected that no union member must pay that fee, but the union has rejoined
that union members already pay, in addition to their initiation fees and
assessments, monthly dues of $10.00 (of which $1.10 is remitted to the International). Would you advise Hender to file charges with the NLRB
against the union local for violation of Section 8(b)(2)? See *Local 825,
Operating Engineers,* 137 N.L.R.B. 1043 (1962).

D. BENEFITS FOR UNION OFFICIALS

NLRB v. MILK DRIVERS AND DAIRY EMPLOYEES, LOCAL 338 (DAIRYLEA COOPERATIVE, INC.)

United States Court of Appeals, Second Circuit, 1976.
531 F.2d 1162.

IRVING R. KAUFMAN, CHIEF JUDGE:

Basic to the National Labor Relations Act is an overriding policy
to insulate employees' positions from their union activities. The
Act's provisions were designed to permit workers to exercise freely
the right to join unions, to be active or passive members, or to abstain
from joining any union at all without imperiling their right to a
livelihood. *Radio Officers' Union v. N.L.R.B.,* 347 U.S. 17, 39–42,
74 S.Ct. 323, 335–337, 98 L.Ed. 455, 476–478 (1954). The issue we
must resolve is whether this clear statutory purpose is contravened
by a clause in a collective bargaining agreement providing that the
union's shop steward shall be deemed the most senior employee in the
plant even if other workers have accumulated far more years of service.

I.

The facts underlying this case have been stipulated and may be
briefly summarized. The Milk Drivers & Dairy Employees Union,
Local 338 (the Union) maintains collective bargaining agreements
with eighteen dairies in the New York metropolitan area. All of its
bargaining agreements have, since 1937, contained provisions afford-

ing the Union's steward "super-seniority" over all other workers in the plant. The steward is the Union's official representative within the plant, and his selection, under the terms of the bargaining agreement, is totally within the unfettered discretion of the Union. He bears initial responsibility for processing workers' complaints and ensuring that employers and workers abide by union rules.

The steward's perquisites are rather more extensive and tangible than his duties. Under the union contract, the steward is automatically *primus inter pares* within the seniority system, which determines not only the order of layoff and recall, but the allocation of numerous and significant on-the-job benefits. The employee deemed most senior may, for example, choose the most lucrative delivery routes as they become vacant. Seniority also controls the assignment of vacation time, work shifts, and days off.

The parties have stipulated to a specific incident which graphically highlights the operation of the super-seniority provision. In December, 1972, a particularly profitable milk delivery route became vacant in the plant of Dairylea Cooperative, Inc. Howard Rosengrandt, the steward, applied for the route, as did Peter Daniels, a driver who had worked more than twenty-four years longer than Rosengrandt. The company was, by the terms of the bargaining agreement, required to assign the route to the applicant with the greatest seniority. Since Rosengrandt, as steward, was considered most senior, he received preferential treatment in winning the unusually remunerative route.

Because of this incident, the Board issued a complaint against the Union and Dairylea, charging that the "super-seniority" clause, and its application to Rosengrandt, contravened the National Labor Relations Act. * * * The Board considered the case en banc and decided that the clause was unlawful. It found that Dairylea had violated §§ 8(a)(1) and (3) of the Act, 29 U.S.C.A. §§ 158(a)(1) and (3), and that the Union had contravened §§ 8(b)(1)(A) and 8(b)(2), 29 U.S.C.A. §§ 158(b)(1)(A) and (2). Accordingly, the Board ordered the Union and Dairylea to refrain from enforcing such clauses in the future, and to reimburse Daniels for the losses he had sustained. Dairylea agreed to comply, and the Union therefore is the sole respondent in this petition by the Board for enforcement of its order.

II.

Section 8(b)(2) of the Act prohibits a labor union from causing an employer to violate § 8(a)(3), which in turn forbids the employer

> by discrimination in regard to * * * any term or condition of employment to encourage or discourage membership in any labor organization.

The Union has not undertaken the futile task of contending there was no discrimination against Daniels. The Union argues, however, that the General Counsel failed to prove that the clause in question encourages membership in the Union. Of course, as the Union recognizes, the phrase "encourage membership", as used in § 8(a)(3), encompasses not only discrimination which induces workers to join a union, but also conduct which encourages employees to be "good" union members, to support and assist the union, or to participate in union activities. Radio Officers' Union v. N.L.R.B., 347 U.S. 17, 39–42, 74 S.Ct. 323, 335–337, 98 L.Ed. 455, 476–478 (1954).

The Board found that the "super-seniority" clause spurred ambitious workers to be "good" union members, within the meaning of *Radio Officers'*. No employee would be appointed by the Union to the lucrative and desirable position of steward, the Board reasoned, unless he first proved himself "a good, enthusiastic unionist. * * *" The Union, responds, however, that there is no evidence in the record demonstrating a relationship between the extent of a worker's union activity and his likelihood of being selected a steward.

The stipulated facts, it is true, contain no specific reference to union policies in choosing stewards. But, the Board is, as is any other trier of fact, accorded the power to draw reasonable inferences from the evidence before it. * * *

The Board's finding of encouragement of union membership in this case was well within these parameters of reasonableness and fairness. The steward is the Union's representative in the plant selected solely by—and within the unlimited discretion of—the Union. He is responsible for reporting violations of the collective bargaining agreement by the employer, and for enforcing the rules of the Union. It is hardly unreasonable for the Board to infer, absent evidence to the contrary, that the Union will, for so sensitive a post, take care not to select someone who has not demonstrated loyalty to the Union.

Of course, union activism is, we may assume, not always the sole determinant of steward effectiveness. Yet, we think the Board was entitled to infer—using its common sense as much as its expertise—that an employee militantly opposed to the Union, or even one merely uninterested in its success, would, *ceteris paribus*, prove far less likely to be selected as union representative than an active union supporter. From this fact, and from the widely disparate treatment accorded stewards and nonstewards, the Board could properly infer sufficient encouragement to trigger the prohibition of § 8(a)(3). See *Radio Officers' Union*, supra, 374 U.S. at 46, 51, 74 S.Ct. at 338, 341, 98 L.Ed. at 480, 483.

The Union, moreover, was accorded ample opportunity to introduce evidence of its steward selection policies to rebut the Board's conclusion. It failed to do so. Indeed, the Union *twice* waived the opportunity for a hearing before an Administrative Law Judge, the second time after the Board had remanded for evidence on this precise question. The Board's finding therefore could hardly be said to have been made in a manner unfair to the Union.

Finally, we note that under §§ 8(a)(3) and 8(b)(2), encouragement of membership is a *sine qua non* of a violation, but does not, without more, establish a violation. The Union will (since there was no evidence of improper motive) prevail if it "come[s] forward with evidence of legitimate and substantial business justifications" for the clause. N.L.R.B. v. Great Dane Trailers, 388 U.S. 26, 34, 87 S.Ct. 1792, 1798, 18 L.Ed.2d 1027, 1035 (1967). The Union contended below—although it apparently abandoned this claim at oral argument before this Court—that the "super-seniority" provisions did have such a justification: they encourage service as a steward, thereby attracting qualified persons to fill the post. But we conclude, as did the Board, that this justification is of doubtful legitimacy.[5]

We need not, however, decide whether this asserted justification should be considered sufficient. If a union finds that it must offer incentives to attract qualified stewards, it may pay a salary to the stewards, or may give them other non-job benefits. The policy of §§ 8(a)(3) and 8(b)(2) is to insulate employees' jobs from their organizational rights. *Radio Officers'*, supra, 347 U.S. at 40, 74 S.Ct. at 335, 98 L.Ed. at 477; N.L.R.B. v. Local 50, supra, at 328. For the union to employ job-related benefits to maintain its own organization would, thus, fly in the face of this statutory purpose. * * *

Enforcement granted.

NOTE: In its decision below in Dairylea Cooperative, Inc., 219 N.L.R.B. 656 (1975), the Board had reached the following conclusions:

" * * * [T]here can be no question but that the super seniority clause ties job rights and benefits to union activities, a dependent relationship essentially at odds with the policy of the Act, which is to insulate the one from the other.

"In reaching the above conclusion, we are aware that it is well established that steward super seniority limited to layoff and recall is proper even though it, too, can be de-

5. The General Counsel did not challenge that portion of the "super-seniority" provisions protecting stewards from layoff because, in his opinion, that preference had a legitimate and substantial justification: a union may find itself powerless to supply any real representation if it is unable to maintain the same steward continuously on the job. Obviously, this justification does not apply to the on-the-job benefits accorded the steward. The validity of the layoff "super-seniority" provisions is, we note, not before us.

scribed as tying to some extent an on-the-job benefit to union status. The lawfulness of such restricted super seniority is, however, based on the ground that it furthers the effective administration of bargaining agreements on the plant level by encouraging the continued presence of the steward on the job. It thereby not only serves a legitimate statutory purpose but also redounds in its effects to the benefit of all unit employees. Thus, super seniority for layoff and recall has a proper aim and such discrimination as it may create is simply an incidental side effect of a more general benefit accorded all employees. It has not, however, been established in this case or elsewhere that super seniority going beyond layoff and recall serves any aim other than the impermissible one of giving union stewards special economic or other on-the-job benefits solely because of their position in the Union. That is not to say, of course, that proper justification may not be forthcoming in some future case involving particular circumstances calling for steward super seniority with respect to terms and conditions of employment other than layoff and recall. Consequently, there is no occasion here for finding super seniority—even that going beyond layoff and recall—to be *per se* unlawful. The issue ultimately is one of justification. However, in view of the inherent tendency of super seniority clauses to discriminate against employees for union-related reasons, and thereby to restrain and coerce employees with respect to the exercise of their rights protected by Section 7 of the Act, we do find that super seniority clauses which are not on their face limited to layoff and recall are presumptively unlawful, and that the burden of rebutting that presumption (i. e., establishing justification) rests on the shoulders of the party asserting their legality."

Problems for Discussion

1. Assuming that the *Local 357* and *Great Dane* cases represent the views of the current Supreme Court, how would that Court decide the *Dairylea* case? Would the outcome in *Dairylea* be different if the charge against the union were to be formulated in terms of breach of the duty of fair representation?

2. Would a superseniority provision such as that in the *Dairylea* case fall within the prohibition of state right-to-work laws such as those described above at pages 1076–80?

3. The collective bargaining agreement between Company and Local Union provides: "The highest seniority preference shall be given to Officers

and Union Stewards in regard to layoffs provided they are capable of performing the available work in their unit." Patricia Jenkins is the recording secretary of Local Union, and pursuant to the agreement she was kept on the job when Anna D'Amico, an employee with two years more seniority at the Company, was laid off. Ms. D'Amico filed charges under Sections 8(b)(1)(A) and (2) of the NLRA. At the hearing before the Administrative Law Judge, the Union introduced in evidence its constitution, which provides that the recording secretary is to maintain, record and manage Union finances, and is also to provide union members with dues books and copies of the Union constitution, by-laws and collective bargaining agreement. In addition to performing these tasks, Ms. Jenkins attended and prepared minutes of meetings of the Local Union's executive board; posted notices of membership meetings; and procured materials needed by the shop stewards in processing grievances. (However, she has never directly participated in the processing of grievances with the Company.) The Union rested its case before the Administrative Law Judge after introducing this evidence, and the General Counsel introduced no further evidence, choosing to rely upon a presumption that the super-seniority provision in the collective agreement was invalid. How should the Judge decide the case? See *Pattern Makers' Ass'n of Detroit v. NLRB,* 622 F.2d 267 (6th Cir. 1980); *D'Amico v. NLRB,* 582 F.2d 820 (3d Cir. 1978).

4. The same collective bargaining agreement also provides that union stewards (who are paid $100 per year by the Union for their services) are to receive a wage differential on the job of five cents per hour. The Company and the Union agreed that this was a rough approximation of the expenses incurred by the stewards for such matters as telephone calls, gasoline and stationery used in the processing of grievances. The Union has also stated that such additional wage payment is designed to provide some added incentive to employees to take on the "headaches" of being a steward. Should the contractual wage differential withstand attack under Sections 8(a)(3) and 8(b)(2)? See *Teamsters Local 20 (Seaway Food Town, Inc.),* 235 N.L.R.B. 1554 (1978).

5. A collective bargaining agreement contains a no-strike clause, which provides among other things that the Union and its officers are to take all reasonable steps to restore normal operations in the event of a work stoppage. A three-day strike recently occurred, in which three shop stewards participated. When the strike was over, the employer imposed one-week suspensions on only those three employees, asserting they were specially culpable, as distinguished from other strikers, because of their specific contractual responsibility not only to refrain from striking but also affirmatively to attempt to end the strike. The Union asks you whether the suspensions are lawful. What is your answer? See *Indiana & Michigan Elec. Co. v. NLRB,* 599 F.2d 227 (7th Cir. 1979).

III. DISCIPLINE OF UNION MEMBERS

A. THE EFFECT OF THE NATIONAL LABOR RELATIONS ACT [1]

NLRB v. ALLIS–CHALMERS MFG. CO.

Supreme Court of the United States, 1967.
388 U.S. 175, 87 S.Ct. 2001, 18 L.Ed.2d 1123.

MR. JUSTICE BRENNAN delivered the opinion of the Court.

* * *

Employees at the West Allis and La Crosse, Wisconsin, plants of respondent Allis-Chalmers Manufacturing Company were represented by locals of the United Automobile Workers. Lawful economic strikes were conducted at both plants in support of new contract demands. In compliance with the UAW constitution, the strikes were called with the approval of the International Union after at least two-thirds of the members of each local voted by secret ballot to strike. Some members of each local crossed the picket lines and worked during the strikes. After the strikes were over, the locals brought proceedings against these members charging them with violation of the International constitution and bylaws. The charges were heard by local trial committees in proceedings at which the charged members were represented by counsel. No claim of unfairness in the proceedings is made. The trials resulted in each charged member being found guilty of "conduct unbecoming a Union-member" and being fined in a sum from $20 to $100. Some of the fined members did not pay the fines and one of the locals obtained a judgment in the amount of the fine against one of its members, Benjamin Natzke, in a test suit brought in the Milwaukee County Court. An appeal from the judgment is pending in the Wisconsin Supreme Court.

Allis-Chalmers filed unfair labor practice charges against the locals alleging violation of § 8(b) (1) (A). [The National Labor Relations Board dismissed the complaint. The Seventh Circuit set

1. See Archer, Allis-Chalmers Recycled: A Current View of a Union's Right to Fine Employees for Crossing a Picket Line, 7 Indiana L.Rev. 498 (1974); Atleson, Union Fines and Picket Lines: The NLRA and Union Disciplinary Power, 17 U.C.L.A.L.Rev. 681 (1970); Craver, The *Boeing* Decision: A Blow to Federalism, Individual Rights and Stare Decisis, 122 U.Pa.L.Rev. 556 (1974); Gould, Some Limitations Upon Union Discipline Under the National Labor Relations Act: The Radiations of *Allis-Chalmers,* 1970 Duke L.J. 1067; Note, Union Power to Discipline Members Who Resign, 86 Harv.L.Rev. 1536 (1973); Silard, Labor Board Regulation of Union Discipline After Allis-Chalmers, Marine Workers, and Scofield, 38 Geo.Wash.L.Rev. 187 (1969).

the order aside, holding that the locals had violated § 8(b) (1) (A). The Supreme Court granted certiorari.]

I.

The panel and the majority *en banc* of the Court of Appeals thought that reversal of the NLRB order would be required under a literal reading of §§ 7 and 8(b) (1) (A); under that reading union members who cross their own picket lines would be regarded as exercising their rights under § 7 to refrain from engaging in a particular concerted activity, and union discipline in the form of fines for such activity would therefore "restrain or coerce" in violation of § 8(b) (1) (A) if the section's proviso is read to sanction no form of discipline other than expulsion from the union. The panel rejected that literal reading. The majority *en banc* adopted it, stating that the panel "mistakenly took the position that such a literal reading was unwarranted in the light of the history and purposes" of the sections, 358 F.2d 659, and holding that "The statutes in question present no ambiguities whatsoever, and therefore do not require recourse to legislative history for clarification." Id., p. 660.

It is highly unrealistic to regard § 8(b) (1), and particularly its words "restrain or coerce," as precisely and unambiguously covering the union conduct involved in this case. On its face court enforcement of fines imposed on members for violation of membership obligations is no more conduct to "restrain or coerce" satisfaction of such obligations than court enforcement of penalties imposed on citizens for violation of their obligations as citizens to pay income taxes, or court awards of damages against a contracting party for nonperformance of a contractual obligation voluntarily undertaken. But even if the inherent imprecision of the words "restrain or coerce" may be overlooked, recourse to legislative history to determine the sense in which Congress used the words is not foreclosed. * * *

National labor policy has been built on the premise that by pooling their economic strength and acting through a labor organization freely chosen by the majority, the employees of an appropriate unit have the most effective means of bargaining for improvements in wages, hours, and working conditions. The policy therefore extinguishes the individual employee's power to order his own relations with his employer and creates a power vested in the chosen representative to act in the interests of all employees. * * *

Integral to this federal labor policy has been the power in the chosen union to protect against erosion its status under that policy through reasonable discipline of members who violate rules and regulations governing membership. That power is particularly vital when the members engage in strikes. The economic strike against the employer is the ultimate weapon in labor's arsenal for achieving agreement upon its terms, and "the power to fine or expel strikebreakers is essential if the union is to be an effective bargaining agent * * *." Provisions in union constitutions and bylaws for fines and expulsion of recalcitrants, including strikebreakers, are therefore commonplace and were commonplace at the time of the TaftHartley amendments.

In addition, the judicial view current at the time § 8(b) (1) (A) was passed was that provisions defining punishable conduct and the procedures for trial and appeal constituted part of the contract between member and union and that "The courts' role is but to enforce the contract." * * *

To say that Congress meant in 1947 by the § 7 amendments and § 8(b) (1) (A) to strip unions of the power to fine members for strikebreaking, however lawful the strike vote, and however fair the disciplinary procedures and penalty, is to say that Congress preceded the Landrum-Griffin amendments with an even more pervasive regulation of the internal affairs of unions. It is also to attribute to Congress an intent at war with the understanding of the union-membership relation which has been at the heart of its effort "to fashion a coherent labor policy" and which has been a predicate underlying action by this Court and the state courts. More importantly, it is to say that Congress limited unions in the powers necessary to the discharge of their role as exclusive statutory bargaining agents by impairing the usefulness of labor's cherished strike weapon. It is no answer that the proviso to § 8(b) (1) (A) preserves to the union the power to expel the offending member. Where the union is strong and membership therefore valuable, to require expulsion of the member visits a far more severe penalty upon the member than a reasonable fine. Where the union is weak, and membership therefore of little value, the union faced with further depletion of its ranks may have no real choice except to condone the member's disobedience. Yet it is just such weak unions for which the power to execute union decisions taken for the benefit of all employees is most critical to effective discharge of its statutory function.

Congressional meaning is of course ordinarily to be discerned in the words Congress uses. But when the literal application of the imprecise words "restrain or coerce" Congress employed in § 8(b) (1) (A) produce the extraordinary results we have mentioned we should determine whether this meaning is confirmed in the legislative history of the section.

II.

The explicit wording of § 8(b) (2), which is concerned with union powers to affect a member's employment, is in sharp contrast with the imprecise words of § 8(b) (1) (A). Section 8(b) (2) limits union power to compel an employer to discharge a terminated member other than for "failure of the employee to tender the periodic dues and initiation fees uniformly required as a condition of acquiring or retaining membership." It is significant that Congress expressly disclaimed in this connection any intention to interfere with union self-government or to regulate a union's internal affairs. The Senate Report stated:

> "The committee did not desire to limit the labor organization with respect to either its selection of membership or expulsion therefrom. But the committee did wish to protect the employee in his job if unreasonably expelled or denied membership. The tests provided by the amendment are based upon facts readily ascertainable and *do not require the employer to inquire into the internal affairs of the union.*" (S.Rep. No. 105, 80th Cong., 1st Sess., 20, I 1947 Leg.Hist. 426.) (Emphasis supplied.)

* * *

What legislative materials there are dealing with § 8(b) (1) (A) contain not a single word referring to the application of its prohibitions to traditional internal union discipline in general, or disciplinary fines in particular. On the contrary there are a number of assurances by its sponsors that the section was not meant to regulate the internal affairs of unions.

* * * The first suggestion that restraint or coercion of employees in the exercise of § 7 rights should be an unfair labor practice appears in the Statement of Supplemental Views to the Senate Report, in which a minority of the Senate Committee, including Senators Ball, Taft, and Smith, concurred. The mischief against which the Statement inveighed was restraint and coercion by unions in *organizational campaigns*. "The committee heard many instances of union coercion of employees such as that brought about by threats of reprisal against employees and their families in the course of organizing campaigns; also direct interference by mass picketing and other violence." S.Rep. No. 105, supra, at 50, I Leg.Hist. 456. * *

Cogent support for an interpretation of the body of § 8(b) (1) as not reaching the imposition of fines and attempts at court enforcement is the proviso to § 8(b) (1). It states that nothing in the section shall "impair the right of a labor organization to prescribe its own rules with respect to the acquisition or retention of membership therein * * *." * * * At the very least it can be said that the proviso preserves the rights of unions to impose fines, as a lesser penalty than expulsion, and to impose fines which carry the explicit or implicit threat of expulsion for nonpayment. Therefore, under the proviso the rule in the UAW constitution governing fines is valid and the fines themselves and expulsion for non-payment would not be an unfair labor practice. Assuming that the proviso cannot also be read to authorize court enforcement of fines, a question we need not reach, the fact remains that to interpret the body of § 8(b) (1) to apply to the imposition and collection of fines would be to impute to Congress a concern with the permissible *means* of enforcement of union fines and to attribute to Congress a narrow and discreet interest in banning court enforcement of such fines. Yet there is not one word of the legislative history evidencing any such congressional concern. And as we have pointed out, a distinction between court enforcement and expulsion would have been anomalous for several reasons. First Congress was operating within the context of the "contract theory" of the union-member relationship which widely prevailed at that time. The efficacy of a contract is precisely its legal enforceability. A lawsuit is and has been the ordinary way by which performance of private money obligations is compelled. Second, as we have noted, such a distinction would visit upon the member of a strong union a potentially more severe punishment than court enforcement of fines, while impairing the bargaining facility of the weak union by requiring it either to condone misconduct or deplete its ranks. * * *

The 1959 Landrum-Griffin amendments, thought to be the first comprehensive regulation by Congress of the conduct of internal union affairs, also negate the reach given § 8(b) (1) (A) by the majority *en banc* below. "To be sure, what Congress did in 1959 does not establish what it meant in 1947. However, as another major step in an evolving pattern of regulation of union conduct, the 1959 Act is a relevant consideration. Courts may properly take into account the later Act when asked to extend the reach of the earlier Act's vague language to the limits which, read literally, the words might permit." National Labor Relations Board v. Drivers, etc., Local Union No. 639, 362 U.S. 274, 291–292, 80 S.Ct. 706, 4 L.Ed.2d 710. In 1959 Congress did seek to protect union members in their relationship to the union by adopting measures to insure the provision of democratic processes in the conduct of union affairs and procedural due process to members subjected to discipline. Even then, some Senators emphasized that "in establishing and enforcing statutory standards great care should be taken not to undermine union self-government or weaken unions in their role as collective-bargaining agents." S.Rep. No. 187, 86th Cong., 1st Sess., 7. The Eighty-sixth Congress was thus plainly of the view that union self-government was not regulated in 1947. Indeed, that Congress expressly recognized that a union member may be "fined, suspended, expelled, or otherwise disciplined," and enacted only procedural requirements to be observed. 73 Stat. 523, 29 U.S.C.A. § 411(a) (5). Moreover,

Congress added a proviso to the guarantee of freedom of speech and assembly disclaiming any intent "to impair the right of a labor organization to adopt and enforce reasonable rules as to the responsibility of every member toward the organization as an institution * * *." 29 U.S.C.A. § 411(a) (2).

* * *

III.

The collective bargaining agreements with the locals incorporate union security clauses. Full union membership is not compelled by the clauses: an employee is required only to become and remain "a member of the union to the extent of paying his monthly dues * * *." The majority *en banc* below nevertheless regarded full membership to be "the result not of individual voluntary choice but of the insertion of [this] union security provision in the contract under which a substantial minority of the employees may have been forced into membership." 358 F.2d, at 660. * * * Whether those prohibitions would apply if the locals had imposed fines on members whose membership was in fact limited to the obligation of paying monthly dues is a question not before us and upon which we intimate no view.

* * *

MR. JUSTICE WHITE, concurring. * * *

MR. JUSTICE BLACK, whom MR. JUSTICE DOUGLAS, MR. JUSTICE HARLAN, and MR. JUSTICE STEWART join, dissenting.

* * * The real reason for the Court's decision is its policy judgment that unions, especially weak ones, need the power to impose fines on strikebreakers and to enforce those fines in court. It is not enough, says the Court, that the unions have the power to expel those members who refuse to participate in a strike or who fail to pay fines imposed on them for such failure to participate; it is essential that weak unions have the choice between expulsion and court-enforced fines, simply because the latter are more effective in the sense of being more punitive. Though the entire mood of Congress in 1947 was to curtail the power of unions, as it had previously curtailed the power of employers, in order to equalize the power of the two, the Court is unwilling to believe that Congress intended to impair "the usefulness of labor's cherished strike weapon." I cannot agree with this conclusion or subscribe to the Court's unarticulated premise that the Court has power to add a new weapon to the union's economic arsenal whenever the Court believes that the union needs that weapon. That is a job for Congress, not this Court.

Though the Court recognizes that a union fine is in fact coercive, it seeks support for its holding—that court-enforced fines are not prohibited by § 8(b) (1) (A)—by reference to the proviso which authorizes a union to prescribe its own rules with respect to the retention of membership. * * * Just because a union might be free, under the proviso, to expel a member for crossing a picket line does not mean that Congress left unions free to threaten their members with fines. Even though a member may later discover that the threatened fine is only enforceable by expulsion, and in that sense a "lesser penalty," the direct threat of a fine, to a member normally unaware of the method the union might resort to for compelling its payment, would often be more coercive than a threat of expulsion.

Even on the assumption that § 8(a) (1) (A) permits a union to fine a member as long as the fine is only enforceable by expulsion, the fundamental error of the Court's opinion is its failure to recognize the practical and theoretical difference between a court-enforced fine, as here, and a fine enforced by expulsion or less drastic intra-union means. As the Court recognizes, expulsion for nonpayment of a fine may, especially in the case of a strong union, be more severe than judicial collection of the fine. But, if the union membership has little value and if the fine is great, then court-enforcement of the fine may be more effective punishment, and that is precisely why the Court desires to provide weak unions with this alternative to expulsion, an alternative which is similar to a criminal court's power to imprison defendants who fail to pay fines. * * *

The Court disposes of this tremendous practical difference between court-enforced and union-enforced fines by suggesting that Congress was not concerned with "the permissible means of enforcement of union fines" and that court-enforcement of fines is a necessary consequence of the "contract theory" of the union-member relationship. * * * At the very least Congress intended to preclude a union's use of certain means to collect fines. It is clear, as the Court recognizes, that Congress in enacting § 8(b)(2) was concerned with insulating an employee's job from his union membership. If the union here had attempted to enforce the payment of the fines by persuading the employer to discharge the nonpaying employees or to withhold the fines from their wages, it would have clearly been guilty of an unfair labor practice under § 8(b)(2). If the union here, operating under a union shop contract, had applied the employees' dues to the satisfaction of the fines and then charged them extra dues, that, under Board decisions, would have been a violation of § 8(b)(1)(A), since it jeopardized the employees' jobs. Yet here the union has resorted to equally effective outside assistance to enforce the payment of its fines, and the Court holds that within the ambit of "internal union discipline." I have already pointed to the impact that $100 per day court-enforced fines may have on an employee's job—they would totally discourage him from working at all—and I fail to see how court enforcement of union fines is any more "internal" than employer enforcement. The undeniable fact is that the union resorts to outside help when it is not strong enough to enforce obedience internally. And even if the union does not resort to outside help but uses threats of physical violence by its officers or other members to compel payment of its fines, I do not doubt that this too would be a violation of § 8(b)(1)(A).

Finally, the Court attempts to justify court-enforcement of fines by comparing it to judicial enforcement of the provisions of an ordinary commercial contract—a comparison which, according to the Court's own authority, is simply "a legal fabrication." The contractual theory of union membership, at least until recently, was a fiction used by the courts to justify judicial intervention into union affairs to protect employees, not to help unions. I cannot believe that Congress intended the effectiveness of § 8(b) (1) (A) to be impaired by such a fiction, or that it was content to rely on the state courts' use of this fiction to protect members from union coercion. Particularly is that so where the "contract" between the union and the employee is the involuntary product of a union shop. * * *

The union here had a union security clause in its contract with Chalmers. That clause made it necessary for all employees, including the ones involved here, to pay dues and fees to the union. But § 8(a)(3) and § 8(b)(2) make it clear that "Congress intended to prevent utilization of union security agreements for any purpose other than to compel payment of union dues and fees." Radio Officers' Union, etc. v. National Labor Relations Board, 347 U.S. 17, 41, 74 S.Ct. 323, 336, 98 L.Ed. 455. If the union uses the union security clause to compel employees to pay dues, characterizes such employees as members, and then uses such membership as a basis for imposing court-enforced fines upon those employees unwilling to participate in a union strike, then the union security clause is being used for a purpose other than "to compel payment of union dues and fees." It is being used to coerce employees to join in union activity in violation of § 8(b)(2).

The Court suggests that this problem is not present here, because the fined employees failed to prove they enjoyed other than full union membership, that their role in the union was not in fact limited to the obligation of paying dues. For several reasons, I am unable to agree with the Court's approach. Few employees forced to become "members" of the union by virtue of the union security clause will be aware of the fact that they must somehow "limit" their membership to avoid the union's court-enforced fines. Even those who are brash enough to attempt to do so may be unfamiliar with how to do it. Must they refrain from doing anything but paying dues, or will signing the routine union pledge still leave them with less than full membership? And finally, it is clear that what restrains the employee from going to work during a union strike is the union's threat that it will fine him and collect those fines from him in court. How many employees in a union shop whose names appear on the union's membership rolls will be willing to ignore that threat in the hope that they will later be able to convince the Labor Board or the state court that they were not full members of the union? By refusing to decide whether § 8(b) (1) (A) prohibits the union from fining an employee who does nothing more than pay union dues as a condition to retaining his job in a union shop, the Court adds coercive impetus to the union's threat of fines. Today's decision makes it highly dangerous for an employee in a union shop to exercise his § 7 right to refrain from participating in a strike called by a union in which he is a member by name only.

* * *

Problem for Discussion

Jones is an employee of the ABC Company which has incorporated a union shop provision in its contract with the Truckers Union, which represents all of the Company's employees. The provision, legal in this state, requires that all employees must—as a condition of continued employment—become a member of the Union. Jones initially protested this membership requirement but has over the years continued to pay the dues required for membership; he has attended no Union meetings and has not otherwise participated in the activities of the Union. In a recent strike during contract negotiations, Jones reported to work through the Union picket lines, in spite of warnings by Union officials that this was contrary to provisions of the Union constitution. At the conclusion of the strike, Union disciplinary proceedings were instituted against Jones, and a $100 fine imposed for strikebreaking. Jones has consulted you to determine whether he must pay the fine and whether there are any steps he may take to overturn the fine (and any similar fines in the future). What advice can you give him?

SCOFIELD v. N L R B

Supreme Court of the United States, 1969.
394 U.S. 423, 89 S.Ct. 1154, 22 L.Ed.2d 385.

MR. JUSTICE WHITE delivered the opinion of the Court.

* * *

[The union has represented production employees of the Wisconsin Motor Corporation since 1937. For the substantial number of workers in the unit who are paid on a piecework or incentive basis, the labor contract sets a minimum hourly "machine rate" (based on the productivity of an average employee working at a reasonable pace) which may be exceeded by a faster worker. Since

1938, the union has implemented among its members a ceiling on the production for which members would accept immediate piecework pay; although members may produce as much as they like each day, they may draw pay only up to the ceiling rate and any balance is "banked" by the company, to be paid out later for days on which the member does not reach the production ceiling. If a member demands immediate payment for work over the ceiling rate during the pay period, the company will comply, but the union assesses a fine of up to $100 for repeated violators. The apparent purpose of the production ceiling is to protect negotiated rest periods for the workers. Both the "machine rate" and the "ceiling rate" have been negotiated between the company and the union, with the union gradually over the years agreeing to increase the margin between the two but not acceding to the company's demands to eliminate the ceiling altogether. The company opens its work records to the union to permit a check on members' compliance with the ceiling, and the ceiling rate has been used in computing piece-rate increases and in settling grievances. In 1961, the union imposed fines of $50 to $100 (and a one-year suspension from union membership) on several employees, and sued in state court to collect the fines. Charges of unfair labor practices were rejected by the trial examiner, the NLRB, the court of appeals, and ultimately by the Supreme Court.]

II.

Based on the legislative history of [Section 8(b)(1)(A)], including its proviso, the Court in NLRB v. Allis-Chalmers Mfg. Co., 388 U.S. 175, 195, 87 S.Ct. 2001, 2014, 18 L.Ed.2d 1123 (1967) * * * essentially accepted the position of the National Labor Relations Board dating from Minneapolis Star and Tribune Co., 109 N.L.R.B. 727 (1954) where the Board also distinguished internal from external enforcement in holding that a union could fine a member for violating a rule against working during a strike but that the same rule could not be enforced by causing the employer to exclude him from the work force or by affecting his seniority without triggering violations of §§ 8(b)(1), 8(b)(2), 8(a)(1), 8(a) (2), and 8(a)(3). These sections form a web, of which § 8(b)(1)(A) is only a strand, preventing the union from inducing the employer to use the emoluments of the job to enforce the union's rules.[2] * * *

2. The Court has held that the "policy of the Act is to insulate employees' jobs from their organizational rights." Radio Officers' Union v. National Labor Relations Board, 347 U.S. 17, 40, 74 S.Ct. 323, 335, 98 L.Ed. 455 (1954). As an employee, he may be a "good, bad, or indifferent" member so long as he meets the financial obligations of the union security contract. Thus the Board has found an unfair labor practice by union and employer where an employee was discharged for violation of a union rule limiting production. Printz Leather Co., 94 N.L.R.B. 1312 (1951). But as a union member, so long as he chooses to remain one, he is subject to union discipline.

Although the Board's construction of the section emphasizes the sanction imposed, rather than the rule itself, and does not involve the Board in judging the fairness or wisdom of particular union rules, it has become clear that if the rule invades or frustrates an overriding policy of the labor laws the rule may not be enforced, even by fine or expulsion, without violating § 8(b)(1). In both *Skura*[3] and *Marine Workers*,[4] the Board was concerned with union rules requiring a member to exhaust union remedies before filing an unfair labor practice charge with the Board. That rule, in the Board's view, frustrated the enforcement scheme established by the statute and the union would commit an unfair labor practice by fining or expelling members who violated the rule.

The *Marine Workers* case came here[5] and the result reached by the Board was sustained, the Court agreeing that the rule in question was contrary to the plain policy of the Act to keep employees completely free from coercion against making complaints to the Board. Frustrating this policy was beyond the legitimate interest of the labor organization, at least where the member's complaint concerned conduct of the employer as well as the union.

Under this dual approach, § 8(b)(1) leaves a union free to enforce a properly adopted rule which reflects a legitimate union interest, impairs no policy Congress has imbedded in the labor laws, and is reasonably enforced against union members who are free to leave the union and escape the rule. This view of the statute must be applied here.

III.

In the case at hand, there is no showing in the record that the fines were unreasonable or the mere fiat of a union leader, or that the membership of petitioners in the union was involuntary. Moreover, the enforcement of the rule was not carried out through means unacceptable in themselves, such as violence or employer discrimination. It was enforced solely through the internal technique of union fines, collected by threat of expulsion or judicial action. The inquiry must therefore focus on the legitimacy of the union interest vindicated by the rule and the extent to which any policy of the Act may be violated by the union-imposed production ceiling.

3. Local 138, International Union of Operating Engineers, 148 N.L.R.B. 679 (1964).

4. Industrial Union of Marine and Shipbuilding Workers of America, 159 N.L.R.B. 1065 (1966).

5. National Labor Relations Board v. Industrial Union of Marine & Shipbuilding Workers, 391 U.S. 418, 88 S. Ct. 1717, 20 L.Ed.2d 706 (1968).

As both the trial examiner and the Court of Appeals noted, union opposition to unlimited piecework pay systems is historic. Union apprehension, not without foundation, is that such systems will drive up employee productivity and in turn create pressures to lower the piecework rate so that at the new, higher level of output employees are earning little more than they did before. The fear is that the competitive pressure generated will endanger workers' health, foment jealousies, and reduce the work force. In addition, the findings of the trial examiner were that the ceiling served as a yardstick for the settlement of job allowance grievances, that it has played an important role in negotiating the minimum hourly rate and that it is the standard for "factoring" the hourly rate raises into the piecework rate. The view of the trial examiner was that "[i]n terms of a union's traditional function of trying to serve the economic interests of the group as a whole, the union has a very real, immediate, and direct interest in it." 145 N.L.R.B., at 1135. * * *

The principal contention of the petitioner is that the rule impedes collective bargaining, a process nurtured in many ways by the Act. But surely this is not the case here. The union has never denied that the ceiling is a bargainable issue. It has never refused to bargain about it as far as this record shows. Indeed, the union has at various times agreed to raise its ceiling in return for an increase in the piece rate, and the ceiling has been regularly used to compute the new piece rate. In light of this bargaining history it can hardly be said that the union rule has removed this issue from the bargaining table. * * *

Nor does the union ceiling itself or compliance with it by union members violate the collective contract. The company and the union have agreed to an incentive pay scale, but they have also established a guaranteed minimum or machine rate considerably below the union ceiling and defined in the contract as the rate of production of an average, efficient worker. The contract therefore leaves in the hands of the employee the option of taking full advantage of his allowances, performing only as an average employee and not reaching even the ceiling rate. * * *

Petitioner purports to characterize the union rule as featherbedding, but it is hard to square this with his collective agreement that an average, efficient employee produces at a "machine" rate substantially below the ceiling. Beyond that, however, Congress has addressed itself specifically to the problem of featherbedding in § 8(b) (6), making it an unfair labor practice "to cause or attempt to cause an employer to pay or deliver or agree to pay or deliver any money or other thing of value, in the nature of an exaction, for services which are not performed or not to be performed * * *." 61 Stat. 142, 29 U.S.C.A. § 158(b) (6). This narrow prohibition was enacted partly because the Congress found it difficult to define with more particularity just where the area between shiftlessness and over-work should lie. Since Congress has addressed itself to the problem specifically and left a broad area for private negotiation, there is no present occasion for the courts to interfere with private decision. Indeed, there is no claim before us that the rule violates § 8(b) (6). If the company wants to require more work of its employees, let it strike a better bargain. The labor laws as presently drawn will not do so for it. * * *

The union rule here left the collective bargaining process unimpaired, breached no collective contract, required no pay for unperformed services, induced no discrimination by the employer against any class of employees, and represents no dereliction by the union of its duty of fair representation. In light of this, and the acceptable manner in which the rule was enforced, vindicating a legitimate union interest, it is impossible to say that it contravened any policy of the Act.

We affirm, holding that the union rule is valid and that its enforcement by reasonable fines does not constitute the restraint or coercion proscribed by § 8(b) (1) (A).

Affirmed.

MR. JUSTICE MARSHALL took no part in the consideration or decision of this case.

[MR. JUSTICE BLACK dissented for reasons set forth in his *Allis-Chalmers* dissent.]

NLRB v. BOEING Co., 412 U.S. 67, 93 S.Ct. 1952, 36 L.Ed.2d 752 (1973). During an 18-day strike, some 143 employees out of 1900 production and maintenance workers crossed the union's picket lines, which resulted in their being fined by the union when the strike was settled and a new labor contract signed. The base weekly income of the employees fined ranged from $95 to $145; they were fined $450 and barred from holding union office for five years. No union member paid in full, and the union sued nine employees in state court to collect the fines and attorneys' fees. The company's claim that the fines were excessive and thus in violation of Section 8(b)(1)(A) was rejected by the NLRB, which concluded that Congress did not give it authority to regulate the size of union fines or establish standards for their reasonableness. A divided Supreme Court agreed.

Justice Rehnquist for the Court conceded that all union fines are "coercive" in some degree but noted that the fines in *Allis-*

Chalmers and *Scofield* were sustained not because they were "reasonable" but rather because Congress did not intend Section 8(b)(1)(A) to outlaw union fines not affecting the employer-employee relationship and not otherwise prohibited by the Act. Were the NLRB to attempt to pass upon the reasonableness of the amount of a fine, it would have to consider the motivation of union leaders and thus "delve into internal union affairs in a manner which we have previously held Congress did not intend." The Court majority rejected the argument that Congress contemplated Board scrutiny of the amount of fines as a way of providing labor expertise and uniformity of decisions. State courts have for many years been enforcing union fines in conventional contract actions, and "state courts applying state law are quite willing to determine whether disciplinary fines are reasonable in amount. Indeed, the expertise required for a determination of reasonableness may well be more evident in a judicial forum that is called upon to assess reasonableness in varying factual contexts than it is in a specialized agency. In assessing the reasonableness of disciplinary fines, for example, state courts are often able to draw on their experience in areas of the law apart from labor relations." And, even assuming uniformity of decisions is thought to be desirable in this area, giving the NLRB authority to determine the reasonableness of fines in an unfair labor practice proceeding will not oust continued state-court jurisdiction to make such a determination in the context of an action by a union to enforce a fine.

In a dissenting opinion, Chief Justice Burger pointed out the irony of the union's supporting state-court jurisdiction to determine reasonable union fines given the long history of union opposition to state-court "intervention" in industrial disputes and consistent union claims of NLRB "expertise." The Board has the experience and sensitivity to devise uniform national rules which draw the line between legitimate union interests and oppressively retributive fines. In another dissenting opinion, Justice Douglas (for a total of three Justices, including the Chief Justice) pointed out that by fining the strikebreakers in excess of their earnings during the strike, the union was in substance effecting their post-strike suspension without pay, which would have clearly been unlawful had the union induced Boeing to take such action. In any event, it is no consolation to tell the union member that an oppressive fine can be contested in a state-court suit, since the individual member is typically unsophisticated and without adequate financial resources; in an NLRB case, the union member is represented without cost by the General Counsel. Moreover, the Board has the expertise in labor-management relations which state judges lack.

Problems for Discussion

1. Under *Allis-Chalmers* and *Scofield,* will the validity of union discipline turn upon whether it "restrains and coerces" union members in the exercise of their statutory rights? Will it turn upon whether the discipline takes the form of affecting only "the acquisition or retention of membership" as opposed to court-enforceable fines or loss of job rights? Does the formula articulated in these two cases comport at all with the language of Section 8(b)(1)(A)?

Evaluate the following proposition: "The text of Section 8(b)(1) (A) is of no greater assistance in deciding specific cases of union coercion than is the text of Section 8(a)(1) in cases of employer coercion. When a union disciplines a member for purposes of strengthening the union in a strike or collective bargaining situation, it is using an economic weapon much as the employer does when pressuring employees by replacement or lockout. The validity of the union discipline is determined in the same manner—by balancing the substantiality of the union's interest against the severity of the impact on significant employee rights. That is essentially a lawmaking function, and the NLRB should be accorded great deference in striking the balance."

2. The Tannery Workers Union represents employees under a collective bargaining agreement with the Smith Leather Company. All Company workers are paid on a piece-work basis. The Union, sensing an economic downturn, unilaterally decides to protect future work by imposing a production ceiling on its members. The Union quotas are not bargained for, nor are they acknowledged in the collective bargaining agreement. In fact, the customary production rate for Company employees substantially exceeds the union quota. Thomas, a member of the Union, exceeds the Union quota and the Union fines him. Has the Union violated Section 8(b)(1)? Would it be relevant whether he had also exceeded the customary production rate?

3. Strawson is a member of the International Molders Union, which is the certified bargaining representative for production employees at the Blackhawk Tanning Company. Strawson, along with several other employees, is unhappy with the policies of the Union, and after some weeks of gathering signed cards requesting a new election she has filed a petition with the NLRB for a decertification election. If these facts are found after a Union disciplinary proceeding instituted against Strawson, what action may the Union take?

(a) May it induce the Blackhawk Company to discharge her?

(b) May it expel her from the Union? See *Tawas Tube Prod. Inc.,* 151 N.L.R.B. 46 (1965); *Price* v. *NLRB,* 373 F.2d 443 (9th Cir. 1967), cert. denied 392 U.S. 904 (1968).

(c) May it impose a fine upon her in the amount of $100? (Does it matter whether nonpayment of the fine will lead to Strawson's expulsion from the Union, or will lead instead to a lawsuit to collect the fine?) See *International Molders Local 125 (Blackhawk Tanning Co.),* 178 N.L.R.B. 208 (1969), enf'd 442 F.2d 92 (7th Cir. 1971).

4. McCloskey is an officer of the Aluminum Workers Union, which represents employees at the Deluxe Canning Company. Several months ago, the Company suspended two employees, each for ten days, because of their alleged violation of Company rules; these employees filed a grievance and the case ultimately went to arbitration. McCloskey gave testimony in support of the Company's case before the arbitrator, and the suspensions were upheld. The Union brought charges against McCloskey, and after a hearing removed him from union office. Has the union violated Section 8(b)(1)(A)?

Would it matter if the union could demonstrate that the testimony given by McCloskey was knowingly false? Compare *Teamsters Local 788 (San Juan Islands Cannery)*, 190 N.L.R.B. 24 (1971), with *United Lodge 66, IAM (Smith-Lee Co.)*, 182 N.L.R.B. 849 (1970).

5. Lombardi is a member of a traveling orchestra and is also a member in good standing of the American Federation of Musicians. At a one-night engagement in Salina, Kansas, Lombardi played alongside a musician who was called in as a last-minute substitute and who was not a member of the Federation (and Lombardi was aware of this fact). Lombardi was charged with violating Federation bylaws prohibiting a member from working alongside a nonmember and, after due proceedings, he was fined $50. Has the union committed an unfair labor practice? Would your analysis be different if Lombardi served that night as the orchestra leader and was thus (while still a member of the Federation) considered an employer? See *Glasser* v. *NLRB*, 395 F.2d 401 (2d Cir. 1968).

6. Is it lawful for a union to discipline (by fine or suspension from membership) a member who, contrary to the union constitution, crosses a union picket line to report for work when there is a collective bargaining agreement in effect and that agreement forbids strikes and picketing by the union during the contract term? See *Glaziers Local 1162 (Tusco Glass, Inc.)*, 177 N.L.R.B. 393 (1969).

NLRB v. GRANITE STATE JOINT BD., TEXTILE WORKERS LOCAL 1029, 409 U.S. 213, 93 S.Ct. 385, 34 L.Ed.2d 422 (1972). After the expiration of the labor contract, the union called a strike pursuant to an earlier strike vote by its members; the membership also voted to subject members who aided the employer during the strike to a fine of $2,000. Six weeks into the strike, two members sent the union letters of resignation from membership, and six months or more later, twenty-nine other members resigned; all of these employees reported for work through the union's picket lines. These individuals were tried in union proceedings, a fine was imposed and suits were filed by the union to collect the fines. The union's actions were held by the Board to violate Section 8(b)(1) and the Supreme Court agreed. The Court noted that in the *Allis-Chalmers* case the union imposed discipline on those enjoying "full union membership," and it observed that "when a member lawfully resigns from the union, its power over him ends." The Court noted that workers are ordinarily free to join or to resign from associations, and that the union had no provisions in its constitution or bylaws which purported to limit the right to resign from membership. The union's power to discipline an employee for crossing a picket line (an employee right under Section 7 of the NLRA) stems from "the union-member contract. When a member lawfully resigns from a union and thereafter engages in conduct which the union rule proscribes, the union commits an unfair labor practice when it seeks enforcement of fines for that conduct. That is to say, when there is a lawful dissolution of a union-member relation, the union has no more control over the former member than it has over the man in the street." The Court also held that the former member did not relinquish these rights by virtue of having voted earlier in support of the strike; the employee should be free to reconsider his position after experiencing the unforeseen hardships of a lengthy strike (barring possibly valid union limitations upon the right to resign).

Problems for Discussion

1. Howard is employed at the Ace Manufacturing Company, which has a collective bargaining agreement with the Machinists Union. Two months ago, the union membership voted overwhelmingly to strike in support of their contract demands, and a strike was called. Howard, however, resigned from membership in the union and crossed the union picket lines to report for work. Charges were filed against him within the union, and the union last week imposed a fine on Howard in an amount equal to the wages paid him during the period he reported for work through the picket line; he was declared barred from union membership until he pays the fine. Has the union violated Section 8(b)(1)? See *Local 1255, IAM* v. *NLRB*, 456 F.2d 1214 (5th Cir. 1972).

2. Hatten was a member of the United Auto Workers and an employee of the General Electric Company. The union began a strike in November when its labor contract terminated, and on January 19 while the strike was ongoing Hatten resigned from the union and reported for work. Union charges were filed against Hatten and he was fined $100. Hatten has filed a charge with the NLRB under Section 8(b)(1)(A), asserting that it was unlawful for the union to fine him for his post-resignation strike-breaking. The union, however, relies upon a provision in its constitution which limits resignations to the ten-day period prior to the end of the union's fiscal year (which coincides with the calendar year); moreover, resignations do not become effective until sixty days after the end of the year. Should the Board find a violation of Section 8(b)(1)? See *UAW, Local 647 (General Elec. Co.)*, 197 N.L.R.B. 608 (1972). Cf. *Local 1384, UAW (Ex-Cell-O Corp.)*, 227 N.L.R.B. 1045 (1977).

Would the issue be materially changed if the union constitution generally allowed resignations at any time but provided that if the union was on strike resignations would be effective only if tendered within the first five days following the strike's commencement?

AMERICAN BROADCASTING COMPANIES, INC. v. WRITERS GUILD OF AMERICA, WEST, INC.

Supreme Court of the United States, 1978.
437 U.S. 411, 98 S.Ct. 2423, 57 L.Ed.2d 313.

Mr. Justice White delivered the opinion of the Court.

[The respondent, Writers Guild of America, West, Inc. (the Guild), represents writers hired by producers of motion pictures and television films. The petitioners—the Association of Motion Picture and Television Producers, Inc., and the three television networks (ABC, CBS, NBC)—had collective bargaining agreements with the Guild, which were to expire in early 1973. In March 1973, the Guild called a strike against the producers and the networks, picketed the various premises, and issued strike rules applicable to its members. These rules forbade such conduct as defeating a strike, crossing a Guild picket line or entering struck premises. A Guild member could not avoid these strike rules by resigning from membership, since Guild rules forbade resignation (until six months after negotiations were completed) once a strike began.

Certain Guild members were employed primarily to perform executive and supervisory functions, as producers, directors or script writers; these functions required a limited amount of writing (which the Guild agreement expressly excluded from its coverage), and these members were referred to as "hyphenates." In their primary and regular duties, which did not include writing, the hyphenates were represented by labor organizations other than the Guild. During the Guild strike, these other labor organizations—then still operating under collective bargaining agreements with no-strike clauses—urged the hyphenates to work, as did the petitioner employers.

Many hyphenates did report to work, performing only their supervisory functions and not performing any writing work covered by the expired Guild agreements (i. e., so-called rank-and-file work). After Guild hearings, these hyphenates were found to have violated union rules and were subjected to various penalties, including expulsion from Guild membership, suspension, and substantial fines (some as high as $10,000 and $50,000).

Unfair labor practice charges under Section 8(b)(1)(B) were filed with the NLRB, and the Administrative Law Judge concluded that the Guild had violated the Act. He found that the hyphenates were supervisors; that among their primary functions was the adjustment of grievances (and in some cases actually engaging in collective bargaining) ; that during the strike the hyphenates were available to deal, and some did deal, with grievances of employees (such as actors and writers) ; that the hyphenates who reported for work during the strike performed only their primary supervisory duties and performed no rank-and-file work; and that it was for this that the Guild subjected them to discipline. The Administrative Law Judge thus concluded that the Guild had, through its strike rules and disciplinary sanctions, coerced and restrained the producers and networks in the selection of representatives for collective bargaining and grievance adjustment. He also concluded that the Supreme Court decision in Florida Power & Light Co. v. International Bhd. of Elec. Workers Local 641, 417 U.S. 790, 94 S.Ct. 2737, 41 L.Ed. 2d 477 (1974) (*FP&L*), was not controlling.

On review of the Administrative Law Judge, the Board adopted his principal findings and conclusions, reasoning that *FP & L*, which involved supervisors who performed rank-and-file bargaining-unit work, did not extend to cases where union discipline was imposed upon supervisors who performed only their ordinary supervisory functions (including the adjustment of grievances). The Board relied upon two of its own decisions rendered subsequent to *FP&L*: Chicago Typog. Union No. 16 (Hammond Publishers, Inc.), 216 N.L. R.B. 903 (1975), and New York Typog. Union No. 6 (Triangle Publications, Inc.), 216 N.L.R.B. 896 (1975). A divided court of appeals denied enforcement of the Board's order, treating the Supreme Court decision in *FP&L* as controlling. The Supreme Court granted certiorari because of the recurring nature of the issue and a conflict within the circuits.]

II

As the Court has set out in greater detail in its comprehensive review of § 8(b)(1)(B) in *FP&L*, the prohibition against restraining or coercing an employer in the selection of his bargaining representative was, until 1968, applied primarily to pressures exerted by the union directly upon the employer to force him into a multiemployer bargaining unit or otherwise to dictate or control the choice of his representative for the purpose of collective bargaining or adjusting grievances in the course of administering an existing contract. In San Francisco-Oakland Mailers' Union No. 18, International Typographical Union (Northwest Publications, Inc.), 172 N.L.R.B. 2173 (1968), however, the Board applied the section to prohibit union discipline of one of its member-supervisors for the manner in which he had performed his supervisory task of grievance adjustment. Although the union "sought the substitution of attitudes rather than persons, and may have exerted its pressures upon the [employer] by indirect rather than direct means," the ultimate fact was that the pressure interfered with the employer's control over his representative. "Realistically, the Employer would have to replace its foreman or face *de facto* nonrepresentation by them." *Oakland Mailers, supra,* at 2173.

The application of the section to indirect coercion of employers through pressure applied to supervisory personnel continued to evolve until the *FP&L* and *Illinois Bell* [6] cases reached the Court of Appeals for the District of Columbia Circuit and then this Court. In each of those cases, the union disciplined supervisor-members who had performed rank-and-file work behind a union picket line during a strike. In a companion case to *Illinois Bell,* [7] upon which *Illinois Bell* explicitly relied, the Board found an infraction of § 8(b)(1)(B), broadly construing its purpose "to assure to the employer that its selected collective-bargaining representatives will be completely faithful to its desires" and holding that this could not be achieved "if the union has an effective method, union disciplinary action, by which it can pressure such representatives to deviate from the interests of the employer." In like fashion, in *FP&L,* the Board held that fining supervisors for doing rank-and-file work during a work stoppage "struck at the loyalty an employer should be able to expect from its representatives for the adjustment of grievances and therefore restrained and coerced employers in their selection of such representatives."

The Court of Appeals overturned both decisions of the Board, holding that although the section could be properly applied to union efforts to discipline supervisors for their performance as collective-bargaining or grievance-adjustment representatives, it could not reasonably be applied to prohibit union discipline of supervisors crossing picket lines to perform bargaining unit work: "[w]hen a supervisor forsakes his supervisory role to do rank-and-file work ordinarily the domain of nonsupervisory employees, he is no longer acting as a management representative and no longer merits any immunity from discipline."

This Court affirmed the judgment of the Court of Appeals:

"The conclusion is thus inescapable that a union's discipline of one of its members who is a supervisory employee can constitute a violation of § 8(b)(1)(B) only when that discipline may adversely affect the supervisor's conduct in per-

6. IBEW, Local 134 v. NLRB, 159 U.S. App.D.C. 242, 487 F.2d 1113, rev'd on r'hrng en banc, 159 U.S.App.D.C. 272, 487 F.2d 1143 (1973), refusing to enforce IBEW, Local 134, 192 N.L.R.B. 85 (1971) (*Illinois Bell*), and IBEW Systems Council U–4, 193 N.L.R.B. 30 (1971) (*FP&L*).

7. Local Union No. 2150, IBEW, and Wisconsin Electric Power Co., 192 N.L.R.B. 77 (1971).

forming the duties of, and acting in his capacity as, grievance
adjustor or collective bargainer on behalf of the employer."
417 U.S., at 804–805, 94 S.Ct., at 2745.

The Court thus rejected the claim that "even if the effect of [union]
discipline did not carry over to the performance of the supervisor's
grievance adjustment or collective bargaining functions," it was
enough to show that the result would be "to deprive the employer of
the full allegiance of, and control over, a representative he has selected for grievance adjustment or collective bargaining purposes." 417
U.S., at 807, 94 S.Ct. at 2746. Assuming without deciding that the
Board's decision in *Oakland Mailers* fell within the outer reaches of
§ 8(b)(1)(B), the Court concluded that the *Illinois Bell* and *FP&L*
decisions did not, because it was "certain that these supervisors were
not engaged in collective bargaining or grievance adjustment, or in
any activities related thereto, when they crossed union picket lines
during an economic strike to engage in rank-and-file struck work."
417 U.S., at 805, 94 S.Ct., at 2745.

Subsequent to *FP&L*, in applying § 8(b)(1)(B) to cases involving union discipline of supervisor-members, the Board directed its
attention, as it understood *FP&L* to require, to the question whether
the discipline may adversely affect the supervisor's conduct in performing his grievance-adjustment or collective-bargaining duties on
behalf of the employer. In Hammond Publishers, supra, and Triangle Publications, supra, the Board held that it was an unfair practice under § 8(b)(1)(B) for a union to discipline a supervisor-member whose regular duties included the adjustment of grievances for
crossing a picket line to perform his regular functions during a strike.
See also Wisconsin River Valley District Council (Skippy Enterprises, Inc.), 218 N.L.R.B. 1063 (1975). These cases rested on the
Board's conclusion that such discipline imposed on the supervisor
would have a "carry-over" effect and would influence the supervisor
in the performance of his adjustment functions after the strike and
hence interfere with and coerce the employer in the choice of his
grievance representative. See Triangle, 216 N.L.R.B., at 897; Hammond, 216 N.L.R.B., at 904. The Triangle decision was not challenged
in the courts, but Hammond was enforced, 176 U.S.App.D.C. 240, 539
F.2d 242 (1976), as was Skippy Enterprises, 532 F.2d 47 (CA7
1976). * * *

IV

We cannot agree with what appears to be the fundamental position of the Court of Appeals and the union that under § 8(b)(1)(B),
as the section was construed in *FP&L*, it is never an unfair practice
for a union to discipline a supervisor-member for working during a
strike, regardless of the work that he may perform behind the picket

line. The opinion in *FP&L* expressly refrained from questioning *Oakland Mailers* or the proposition that an employer could be coerced or restrained within the meaning of § 8(b)(1)(B) not only by picketing or other direct actions aimed at him but also by debilitating discipline imposed on his collective-bargaining or grievance-adjustment representative. Indeed, after focusing on the purposes of the section, the Court in *FP&L* delineated the boundaries of when that "carryover" effect would violate § 8(b)(1)(B): whenever such discipline may adversely affect the supervisor's conduct in his capacity as a grievance adjustor or collective bargainer. In these situations—that is, when such impact might be felt—the employer would be deprived of the full services of his representatives and hence would be restrained and coerced in his selection of those representatives.

* * * The Board addressed those issues here, and if its ultimate factual conclusions in this regard are capable of withstanding judicial review, it seems to us that its construction of the section fairly recognizes and respects the outer boundaries established by *FP&L*, and represents an "acceptable reading of the statutory language and a reasonable implementation of the purposes of the relevant statutory sections * * *" NLRB v. Bridge Workers, 434 U.S. 335, 341, 98 S.Ct. 651, 656, 54 L.Ed.2d 586 (1978).

Respondent objects that this construction of the Act impermissibly intrudes on the union's right to resort to economic sanctions during a strike. However, an employer also has economic rights during a strike, and the statute declares that, in the unrestrained freedom to select a grievance-adjustment and collective-bargaining representative, the employer's rights dominate. Ample leeway is already accorded to a union in permitting it to discipline any member, even a supervisor, for performing struck work—to carry that power over to the case of purely supervisorial work is an inappropiate extension and interference with the employer's prerogative. The Board has so ruled, and as the Court has often observed "[t]he function of striking [the] balance to effectuate national labor policy is often a difficult and delicate responsibility, which the Congress committed primarily to the National Labor Relations Board, subject to limited judicial review." * * *

V

We are also unpersuaded that the Board's findings and conclusions are infirm on any of the grounds submitted. * * *

[A]s to those hyphenates who reported for work, it is strenuously urged that there is no basis for concluding that the discipline imposed upon them would adversely affect the performance of their grievance-adjustment duties either during or after the strike. * * *

[I]t does not strike us as groundless or lacking substantial evidence for the Board to conclude on this record that the discipline imposed would have the necessary adverse effect.[8]   Strike rules were distributed in February; the strikes against the association began on March 4 and terminated June 24; the strikes against the networks began on March 29 and ended on July 12.   Between April 6 and November 8—both during and after the strikes—some 31 hyphenates who had worked during the strikes were charged with violating union rules, 15 hearings had been held prior to the closing of evidence in November 1973, and from June 25 to September 28, very substantial penalties were imposed in 10 cases although nine have already been reduced on appeal.   These penalties were widely publicized at the time of their imposition.   Other charges were pending and remained to be tried when the record was closed in this case.

These penalties were meted out at least in part because the accused hyphenates had complied with the orders of their employers by reporting for work and performing only their normal supervisory functions, including the adjustment of grievances, during the strike. Hyphenates who worked were thus faced not only with threats but with the *actuality* of charges, trial and severe discipline simply because they were working at their normal jobs.   And if this were not enough, they were threatened with a union blacklist that might drive them from the industry.   How long such hyphenates would remain on the job under such pressure was a matter no one, particularly the employer, could predict.

Moreover, after the strike, with the writers back at work, the hyphenates who had worked during the strike still faced charges and trials or were appealing large fines and long suspensions.   At the same time, they were expected to perform their regular supervisory duties and to adjust grievances whenever the occasion demanded, functions requiring them to deal with the same union which was considering the appeal of their personal sanctions.   As to these supervisors, who had felt the union's wrath, not for doing rank-and-file work contrary to union rules, but for performing only their primary supervisory duties during the strike and who were in a continuing controversy with the union, it was not untenable for the Board to conclude that these disciplined hyphenates had a diminished capacity

---

8.   It is suggested that there was insufficient proof that the hyphenates who worked actually engaged in grievance adjustment of any kind during the strike.   But the findings were to the contrary; and, in any event, there is no question that they were authorized to do so and were available for that purpose when and if the occasion arose.   Section 8(b)(1)(B) obviously can be violated by attempting coercively to control the choice of the employer's representative, before, as well as after, the representative has actually dealt with the grievance.

to carry out their grievance-adjustment duties effectively and that the employer was deprived of the full range of services from his supervisors. Such a hyphenate might be tempted to give the union side of a grievance a more favorable slant while the threat of discipline remained, or while his own appeal of a union sanction was pending. At the very least, the employer could not be certain that a fined hyphenate would willingly answer the employer's call to duty during a subsequent work stoppage, particularly if it occurred in the near future. For an employer in these circumstances to insure having satisfactory collective-bargaining and grievance-adjustment services would require a change in his representative.

As the Board has construed the Act from *Oakland Mailers* to *Triangle, Hammond* and the cases now before us, such a likely impact on the employer constitutes sufficient restraint and coercion in connection with the selection of collective-bargaining and grievance-adjustment representatives to violate § 8(b)(1)(B). In *FP&L* the Court declined the invitation to overrule *Oakland Mailers,* and we do so again. Union pressure on supervisors can affect either their willingness to serve as grievance adjustors or collective bargainers, or the manner in which they fulfill these functions; and either effect impermissibly coerces the employer in his choice of representative.

* * * Because we have concluded that the Board's construction of § 8(b)(1)(B) is not an unreasonable reading of its language or inconsistent with its purposes, and because we cannot say that the Board's findings lacked substantial evidence, we must reverse the judgment of the Court of Appeals.

So ordered.

MR. JUSTICE STEWART, with whom MR. JUSTICE BRENNAN, MR. JUSTICE MARSHALL, and MR. JUSTICE STEVENS join, dissenting.

The Court holds today that a labor union locked in a direct economic confrontation with an employer is powerless to impose sanctions on its own members who choose to pledge their loyalty to the adversary. Nothing in § 8(b)(1)(B) or any other provision of the National Labor Relations Act permits such a radical alteration of the natural balance of power between labor and management. I therefore respectfully dissent.

A union's ability to maintain a unified front in its confrontations with management, and to impose disciplinary sanctions on those who "adher[e] to the enemy in time of struggle," are essential to its survival as an effective organization. See Summers, Legal Limitations on Union Discipline, 64 Harv.L.Rev. 1049, 1066 (1951). An employer also has an interest in securing the loyalty of those who represent him in dealings with the union, and that interest is protected by spe-

cific provisions of the Act.[9] Thus, as the Court observed in Florida
Power & Light Co. v. Electrical Workers, 417 U.S. 790, 94 S.Ct. 2737,
41 L.Ed.2d 477, very real concerns are raised on both sides when
supervisory employees with collective bargaining and grievance adjustment responsibilities are also union members. But § 8(b)(1)(B)
is not "any part of the solution to the generalized problem of supervisor-member conflict of loyalties." Id., at 813, 94 S.Ct., at 2749.

That statutory provision was enacted for the primary purpose of
prohibiting a union from exerting direct pressure on an employer to
force him into a multiemployer bargaining unit or to dictate his choice
of representatives for the settlement of employee grievances. S.Rep.
No.105, 80th Cong., 1st Sess., pt. 1, p. 21 (1947). The Court in
Florida Power & Light reserved decision on whether union pressure
expressly aimed at affecting the *manner* in which supervisor-members
performed their collective bargaining or grievance adjustment functions might fall within the "outer limits" of the proscription of §
8(b)(1)(B). 417 U.S., at 805, 94 S.Ct., at 2745. See San Francisco-
Oakland Mailers Union No. 18 (Northwest Publications, Inc.), 172
N.L.R.B. 2173. But it flatly rejected the argument that union discipline aimed at enforcing uniform rules violated § 8(b)(1)(B) simply because it might have the ancillary effect of "depriv[ing] the
employer of the full allegiance of, and control over, a representative
he has selected for grievance adjustment or collective bargaining purposes." 417 U.S., at 807, 94 S.Ct., at 2746.

In the present cases it is entirely clear that the union had no
interest in restraining or coercing the employers in the *selection* of
their bargaining or grievance adjustment representatives, or in affecting the *manner* in which supervisory employees performed those
functions. As the Court notes, * * * the union expressed
no interest at the disciplinary trials in the kind of work that was done
behind its picket lines. Its sole purpose was to enforce the traditional
kinds of rules that every union relies on to maintain its organization
and solidarity in the face of the potential hardship of a strike. Cf.
NLRB v. Allis-Chalmers Mfg. Co., 388 U.S. 175, 181–184, 87 S.Ct.
2001, 2007–2008, 18 L.Ed.2d 1123.

---

9. This interest is protected by § 2(3) of
the National Labor Relations Act,
which excludes "supervisors" as defined in § 2(11) from the definition of
"employees," thereby excluding them
from the coverage of the Act. Thus an
employer may discharge or otherwise
penalize a supervisory employee for
engaging in what would otherwise be
protected concerted activity under the
Act. In addition, § 14(a) of the Act
provides that "no employer * * *
shall be compelled to deem * * *
supervisors as employees for the purpose of any law * * * relating to
collective bargaining." See Florida
Power & Light Co. v. Electrical Workers, 417 U.S. 790, 808–811, 94 S.Ct.
2737, 2746–2748, 41 L.Ed.2d 477.

In reversing the judgment of the Court of Appeals, this Court today forbids a union from disciplining a supervisor-member who crosses its picket line—who clearly gives "aid and comfort to the enemy" during a strike, see Summers, supra, at 1066—solely because that action may have the incidental effect of depriving the employer of the hypothetical grievance adjustment services of that particular supervisor for the duration of the strike. This ruling quite simply gives the employer the superior right to call on the loyalty of *any* supervisor with grievance adjustment responsibilities, whenever the union to which the supervisor belongs calls him out on strike. In short, the Court's decision prevents a union with supervisory members from effectively calling and enforcing a strike.

Nothing in § 8(b)(1)(B) permits such a sweeping limitation on the choice of economic weapons by unions that include supervisory employees among their members. On the contrary, as the Court clearly held in *Florida Power & Light*, supra, an employer's remedy if he does not want to share the loyalty of his supervisors with a union is to insist that his supervisory personnel not belong to a union; or if he does not welcome the consequences of his supervisors' union membership he may legally penalize them for engaging in union activities, * * *, or "resolv[e] such conflicts as arise through the traditional procedures of collective bargaining." *Florida Power & Light*, supra, 417 U.S., at 812–813, 94 S.Ct., at 2749.

The sole function of § 8(b)(1)(B) is to protect an employer from any union coercion of the free choice of his bargaining or grievance adjustment representative. In prohibiting union interference in his choice of representatives for dealings with the union, this statutory provision does not in any way grant him a right to interfere in the union's relationship with its supervisor-members. The statute leaves the balance of power in equipoise. The Court's decision, by contrast, tips it measurably in favor of the employer at the most delicate point of direct confrontation, by completely preventing the union from enlisting the aid of its supervisor-members in a strike effort. It seems to me that the Court's reading of § 8(b)(1)(B) is "fundamentally inconsistent with the structure of the Act and the function of the sections relied upon." American Shipbuilding v. NLRB, 380 U.S. 300, 318, 85 S.Ct. 953, 967, 13 L.Ed.2d 855.

Accordingly, I would affirm the judgment of the Court of Appeals.

_____

Problems for Discussion

1. In the *Florida Power* case, sustaining the union's power to fine supervisor-members for performing "rank and file" work during a strike, the outcome was different from the *Writers Guild* case but the alignment of the Justices was substantially the same. Justice White dissented in

Florida Power, endorsing the NLRB's finding that the union had violated §
8(b)(1)(A); he argued, among other things, that the employer's assignment of rank-and-file work to supervisors was economic pressure designed
to enhance the employer's bargaining position and was thus "part and
parcel of the process of collective bargaining." Assuming that to be true,
does it not follow that Justice White, rather than dissenting in *Florida
Power*, should have joined the majority? And should he have not joined
the dissenters in the *Writers Guild* case and permitted the union to fine
its supervisor-members?

2.   Andrews, Barnard and Crawford are members of the Carpenters
Union and are employed as supervisors by Aurora Industries. During a
recent strike in support of union demands for a new labor contract, the
three supervisors reported for work and have been fined by the union in
substantial amounts. They have asked your advice about whether such
fines may lawfully be imposed under the National Labor Relations Act.
You learn that: (1) Andrews before the strike performed only supervisory
work and did no rank-and-file work; during the strike, his workload did
not change. (2) Barnard normally performs no rank-and-file work, but
during the strike he regularly performed some 35 minutes of rank-and-file
work in what he asserts was roughly a 22-hour day. (3) Crawford before
the strike spent one-half his time in supervisory activities and one-half
his time in rank-and-file activities; during the strike, his workload did
not change. What advice can you give these three workers concerning
the legality of the union fines? Is there any further information you
need in order to give accurate advice? See *Columbia Typog. Union No. 101
(Washington Post Co.)*, 242 N.L.R.B. 1079 (1979).

B.   JUDICIAL SUPERVISION OF UNION DISCIPLINE [10]

Although the Labor Management Reporting and Disclosure Act
does not insulate the member against all forms of unreasonable or arbitrary union discipline, Section 101 of the Act does protect members
in exercising a number of political rights within the union, *e. g.*, by
requiring that they be given equal rights to nominate candidates and
to vote, and that all members be given the right to attend meetings,
to express their views on union business and so forth. In addition,
Section 101(a) (5) of the LMRDA requires that before any union
member may be expelled or disciplined for any reason other than nonpayment of dues he must receive specific written charges, be given a
reasonable time to prepare his defense and be afforded a "full and
fair hearing."

For many years prior to the passage of the LMRDA, state courts
had undertaken to review the disciplinary action of labor unions. In
so doing, state courts have often been guided by very similar principles to those now embodied in Section 101 of the LMRDA, but they

---

10.   For a general discussion see Summers, Legal Limitations on Union Discipline, 64 Harv.L.Rev. 1049 (1951);
and, by the same author, The Law of
Union Discipline: What the Courts
Do in Fact, 70 Yale L.J. 175 (1960).

have also exercised still broader powers of review either by insisting that disciplinary action conform to the provisions of the union constitution and by-laws or by declaring certain types of disciplinary action to be void as contrary to public policy. As a result, bearing in mind that Section 103 of the LMRDA leaves the jurisdiction of state courts undisturbed, the "common law" of union disciplinary action deserves to be considered together with the developing case law under the federal act.

The materials that follow have been divided into three sections. The first section is devoted to the problems that have arisen in interpreting Section 101 of the LMRDA. These problems fall into three general categories: the kind of union action that constitutes "discipline" within the reach of the Act; the kind of member conduct which a union may properly subject to discipline; and the procedures which the union must utilize before imposing discipline. The second section deals with the regulation of union discipline by state courts, through the application of common law principles. As just noted, these principles may go beyond those of the LMRDA in limiting such discipline. The third section takes up the requirement that internal union remedies be exhausted prior to bringing suit to challenge union discipline—a requirement commonly observed by state courts and carried forward in a modified form under the LMRDA.

1. *The Discipline of Union Members under the Labor-Management Reporting and Disclosure Act* [11]

Section 101(a) (5) of the Landrum-Griffin Act requires the union to observe the procedural safeguards of a "full and fair hearing" before a member is "fined, suspended, expelled, or otherwise disciplined" by the union or its officers. Section 609 makes it unlawful for the union "to fine, suspend, expel or otherwise discipline" any member for exercising rights provided him under the Act. What, then, is "discipline" within the meaning of these provisions?

---

11. See Aaron, The Labor-Management Reporting & Disclosure Act of 1959, 73 Harv.L.Rev. 851 (1960); Atleson, A Union Member's Right of Free Speech and Assembly: Institutional Interests and Individual Rights, 51 Minn.L.Rev. 403 (1967); Beaird & Player, Free Speech and the Landrum-Griffin Act, 25 Ala.L.Rev. 577 (1973); Beaird & Player, Union Discipline of its Membership Under Section 101(a) (5) of Landrum-Griffin: What is "Discipline" and How Much Process is Due?, 9 Ga.L.Rev. 383 (1975); Bellace & Berkowitz, The Landrum-Griffin Act—Twenty Years of Federal Protection of Union Members' Rights (1979); Cox, Internal Affairs of Labor Unions Under the Labor Reform Act of 1959, 58 Mich.L.Rev. 819 (1960); Etelson & Smith, Union Discipline Under the Landrum-Griffin Act, 82 Harv.L.Rev. 727 (1969); McLaughlin & Schoomaker, The Landrum-Griffin Act and Union Democracy (1979); Summers, The Law of Union Discipline: What the Courts Do in Fact, 70 Yale L.J. 175 (1960); Summers, Legal Limitations on Union Discipline, 64 Harv.L.Rev. 1049 (1951).

To constitute "discipline," first of all, it is necessary that the alleged sanction be imposed by union officers acting in their official capacities.   As for the nature of the sanction itself, some courts have suggested that "discipline" exists only when the member is injured or deprived in such a way as to affect his rights *qua* union member.   Under this view, no "discipline" would result from the failure of union officials to protest the discharge of a member by an employer or even from a union official's request that the employer suspend a member from work.   See e. g., Allen v. Armored Car Chauffeurs and Guards, Local 820, 185 F.Supp. 492 (D.N.J. 1960).   Other courts, however, have taken a broader view; they would interpret "discipline" under Section 609 to include any union action which harms a member in retaliation for the exercise of his rights under the Act.   The same courts would interpret "discipline" under Section 101(a) (5) to include any action imposing any detriment upon a member because of his conduct as a union member.   See e. g., Scovile v. Watson, 338 F.2d 678 (7th Cir. 1964), cert. denied 380 U. S. 963, 85 S.Ct. 1107, 14 L.Ed.2d 154 (1965); Detroy v. American Guild of Variety Artists, p. 1154 infra.   Which is the preferable reading of the LMRDA?

GRAND LODGE v. KING

United States Court of Appeals, Ninth Circuit, 1964.
335 F.2d 340.

BROWNING, CIRCUIT JUDGE.   Plaintiffs brought suit alleging they were summarily discharged as officers of defendant union because they supported an unsuccessful candidate in a union election.   They sought reinstatement and damages.   The district court denied defendants' motion to dismiss, and this interlocutory appeal under 28 U.S.C.A. § 1292 followed.

The district court concluded that plaintiffs' allegation of summary dismissal stated a claim under section 101(a) (5) of the Labor-Management Reporting and Disclosure Act of 1959 (73 Stat. 522, 29 U.S.C.A. § 411(a) (5)), which provides: "No member of any labor organization may be fined, suspended, expelled, or otherwise disciplined * * * unless such member has been (A) served with written specific charges; (B) given a reasonable time to prepare his defense; (C) afforded a full and fair hearing."

We are satisfied, however, that Congress did not intend section 101(a) (5) to preclude summary removal of a member from union office.   While the Act was being considered by Congress, objection was raised to section 101(a) (5) on the ground that it would permit wrongdoing union officials to remain in control while the time-consuming "due process" requirements of the section were met. As an alternative it was proposed that the union's power of summary discipline be retained, and that notice and hearing be required after, rather than before, disciplinary action. This solution was rejected; instead, the objection to section 101(a) (5) was met by including limiting language in the legislative history. The Conference Report on the Act stated that section 101(a) (5) "applies only to suspension of membership in the union; it does not refer to suspension of a member's status as an officer in the union." Senator Kennedy, as a Senate conferee, advised the Senate that "this provision does not relate to suspension or removal from a union office. Often this step must be taken summarily to prevent dissipation or misappropriation of funds."

In deference to the "patent legislative intent" it has been held with virtual unanimity that section 101(a)(5) does not apply to removal or suspension from union office. We think these decisions are correct. Furthermore, we think it makes no difference what the reason for the summary removal may have been. Congress's primary concern was that section 101(a) (5) should not bar summary removal of union officials suspected of malfeasance, but the means Congress chose to accomplish its purpose was to wholly exclude suspension or removal from union office from the category of union action to which section 101(a) (5) applied.

Plaintiffs also sought to state a claim under sections 101(a) (1), 101(a) (2), and 609 of the Act. We think they have succeeded, and are therefore authorized by section 102 of the Act to bring a civil action in the district court for appropriate relief.

Plaintiffs allege they were discharged because they actively supported a particular candidate for union office by meeting with other members and expressing views favorable to that candidate. Defendants concede that the right to engage in such intra-union political activity is guaranteed to members by sections 101(a) (1) and 101(a) (2) of the Act, but argue that these and other rights protected by Title I of the Act do not extend to members who are also officers of the union. However, sections 101(a) (1) and (2) apply in terms to "every member," and nothing in the statutory language excludes members who are officers.[12] Nor is there any intimation in the legislative history that Congress intended these guarantees of equal political rights and freedom of speech and assembly to be inapplicable to officer-members.[13] Indeed, the general purpose of the Act points

12. This is also true of other sections of Title I. Our conclusion that § 101 (a) (5) is inapplicable to the present case is based upon the conclusion that one removed from office is not "otherwise disciplined" within the meaning of § 101(a) (5), rather than upon a reading of the word "member" in that section as excluding officers. * * *

13. Defendants call attention to the fact that as § 101(a) (4) originally passed the Senate it applied to "members or officers," and the words "or officers" were deleted in conference. S. 1555, 86th Cong., 1st Sess. § 101(a) (4) (1959), 1 Leg.His. LMRDA 520; H.R. 8490, 86th Cong., 1st Sess. § 101(a) (4) (1959), 1 Leg.His. LMRDA 877. Defendants

to the contrary.   The guarantees of sections 101(a) (1) and (2) were adopted to strengthen internal union democracy.   To exclude officer-members from their coverage would deny protection to those best equipped to keep union government vigorously and effectively democratic.   We therefore conclude that sections 101(a) (1) and (2) apply to officer-members such as plaintiffs.

Section 102 (73 Stat. 523, 29 U.S.C.A. § 412) provides that "[a]ny person whose rights secured by the provisions of this title have been infringed by any violation of this title may bring a civil action in a district court of the United States for such relief (including injunctions) as may be appropriate." We think it follows that plaintiffs' complaint for reinstatement and damages was sufficient to withstand dismissal for failure to state a claim upon which relief could be granted.

In any event, section 609 (73 Stat. 541, 29 U.S.C.A. § 529) "makes doubly secure the protection of the members in the exercise of their rights" by making it unlawful for a union "to fine, suspend, expel, or otherwise discipline any of its members for exercising any right to which he is entitled under the provisions of this Act," and by providing explicitly that an action may be brought under section 102 to enforce the specific prohibitions of section 609.

Defendants argue that the words "otherwise discipline" in section 609 must be read as not including removal from union office, since the same words have that restricted meaning in section 101(a) (5). The argument is a plausible one, for it is natural to suppose that within a single statute the same words will be used with the same meaning. But it is also common experience that identical words may be used in the same statute, or even in the same section of a statute, with quite different meanings.   And when they are, it is the duty of the courts to give the words "the meaning which the Legislature intended [they] should have in each instance." Atlantic Cleaners & Dyers, Inc. v. United States, 286 U.S. 427, 433, 52 S.Ct. 607, 609, 76 L.Ed. 1204 (1932).

Sections 101(a) (5) and 609 have wholly different purposes, and the difference is such as to satisfy us that although Congress did not intend the words "otherwise discipline" to include removal from union

argue that this change evidences a congressional understanding that union officers were excluded from the whole of Title I. See Judge Kalodner's opinion in Sheridan v. United Bhd. of Carpenters & Joiners, 306 F.2d 152, 156–157 (3d Cir. 1962).

The language change in § 101(a) (4) was made without comment of any sort. Prior to the change, it was assumed in Senate debate that officer-members were included in § 101(a) (4) (see remarks of Senator Mundt at 105 Cong.Rec. 6478 (1959), 2 Leg.His.

LMRDA 1105). Thus, defendants' argument requires the inference that the Conference Committee drastically narrowed the assumed coverage of § 101 (a) (4) with no explanation whatever. A more reasonable conclusion is that the Conference Committee recognized that the deleted words "or officers" were surplusage since as a practical matter union officers were also union members, and therefore deleted these words to conform § 101(a) (4) in style with other sections of Title I which used only the inclusive word "members."

office in section 101(a) (5), it did intend the words to include such action in section 609.[14]

Section 101(a) (5) guarantees to union members, as one of several independent rights conferred upon them by Title I of the Act, that they shall be accorded procedural due process before being subjected to disciplinary action, for whatever reason. Section 609, on the other hand, has no bearing upon the procedures to be followed in disciplining union members. Section 609 appears in Title VI of the Act, a collection of sections having to do with miscellaneous administrative and enforcement matters; section 609 itself is not a source of additional independent rights, but is an enforcement provision, designed, as we have noted, to effectuate rights conferred in other sections of the Act by making it unlawful to punish members who seek to exercise such rights. Punishment for the exercise of these rights is prohibited by section 609 whether inflicted summarily or after a full panoply of procedural protections.

Congress, through the legislative history materials, imposed a limiting gloss upon the words "otherwise discipline" in section 101(a) (5) to preserve union power to summarily remove officer-members suspected of wrongdoing in order to protect unions from continuing depredations while charges are being investigated and resolved. This object is fully accomplished by reading the words "otherwise discipline" in section 101(a) (5) as not including removal from union office. It would not further this purpose in any way to impose the same restriction upon the same words in section 609, since that section has nothing to do with whether or not discipline is summary. There is nothing in the legislative history to indicate that Congress wished to preserve an unrestricted power in the union to discipline officer-members (the subject matter of section 609, when discipline is imposed because of the exercise of rights under the Act), as distinguished from the power to discipline summarily (the subject matter of section 101(a) (5)). Thus, to construe section 609 to exclude from its coverage dismissal from union office would immunize a most effective weapon of reprisal against officer-members for exercising political rights guaranteed by the Act without serving any apparent legislative purpose; and, as we have noted, the members thus exposed to reprisal

14. " * * * [B]ecause much of the bill was written on the floor of the Senate or House of Representatives and because many sections contain calculated ambiguities or political compromises essential to secure a majority," it is particularly important, in interpreting the Labor-Management Reporting and Disclosure Act of 1959, "to seek out the underlying rationale without placing great emphasis upon close construction of the words." Cox, Internal Affairs of Labor Unions under the Labor Reform Act of 1959, 58 Mich.L.Rev. 819, 852 (1960).

See also Thatcher, Rights of Individual Union Members under Title I and Section 610 of the Landrum-Griffin Act, 52 Geo.L.J. 339, 340 n. 4 (1964); Smith, The Labor-Management Reporting and Disclosure Act of 1959, 46 Va.L.Rev. 195, 197–98 (1960).

would be those whose uninhibited exercise of freedom of speech and assembly is most important to effective democracy in union government.[15] * * *

WAMBLES V. INTERNATIONAL BROTH. OF TEAMSTERS, 488 F.2d 888 (5th Cir. 1974). Prior to December 1971, two of the three plaintiffs were assistant business managers of Local 991 of the Teamsters, and the third plaintiff was bookkeeper. In that month, one of the former, Mosley, with the support of the other two plaintiffs, ran against one Sherman for the office of business manager of the local. When Sherman won the election, he discharged the plaintiffs from their positions. This was done pursuant to clear authorizing provisions of the constitution and bylaws of the International and local unions. The plaintiffs claimed that they were willfully and maliciously discharged in violation of the LMRDA Bill of Rights. The court of appeals affirmed a summary judgment for the defendants (the International, the local, and Sherman), and adopted the district judge's decision, portions of which follow:

> "As a practical matter, the Union president should be able to work with those who will cooperate with his program and carry out his directives. It can be argued that an appointed office holder under the president who has opposed him in the election does not guarantee obstructionist policies while he serves in his position as an appointed Union official and that before the appointed official could be discharged for cause he would have to show an actual conflict of interest. This is a rather charitable view of persons recently involved in political conflict. A more realistic view would be that in a great majority of cases the friction generated in the election campaign would infect and seriously impede the successful candidate's implementation of his program approved by the membership electing him.

> "To extend the protection of labor's 'Bill of Rights', Section 101(a)(1), 29 U.S.C. Sec. 411(a)(1) and 'Free Speech Rights', Section 101(a)(2), 29 U.S.C. Sec. 411(a)(2) to such office holders would, in effect, give such officer a

---

15. It has been suggested that the right of union members to remove their officers is itself essential to the democratic self-government. Sheridan v. United Bhd. of Carpenters & Joiners, 306 F.2d 152, 158–159 (3d Cir. 1962). The power of the member-electorate to turn out elected officials for "serious misconduct" is guaranteed by § 401 (h) of the Act (73 Stat. 532, 29 U.S.C.A. § 481(h)), and is not at issue here. And, as we have said, there is nothing to indicate that Congress believed effective union democracy required that controlling union officials have power to discharge other officers for exercising freedom of speech and assembly in internal union political affairs.

lifetime job except on dismissal for cause. The elected officials necessarily rely on appointed officials to implement policies and plans presumably approved by the Union membership in the election. To tie the President's hands, an elected official, by not allowing him to discharge without cause or for any reason those who must serve under him, would so restrict the elected officers in the discharge of their duties that elections could be meaningless. An appointed official should carry out the approved policies of the Union. His convictions and loyalties should be to the Union and not a personal fiefdom beyond the reach of the membership, here expressed by the appointive powers of its elected officers.

"The dismissed officials worked against the election of the President, one of them ran against him, which means the President was opposed on personal grounds or policy grounds, but in either event, [this] would create an intolerable situation for the elected official in implementing his programs on which he was elected.

"To force the President to cast around for grounds to discharge appointed officials 'for cause' would force the courts into a thicket of subtleties and hypocrisies of charges in an effort to ascertain whether or not the charges were bona fide or merely a cloak for dismissal for other reasons. In fact, it might well serve appointed officials, such as the plaintiff, to oppose any candidate for President that he might think would appoint someone in his place, therefore clouding the issue of 'for cause' with a claim he was exercising his right of free speech.

"Appointed officials certainly have the right to run for office, support or oppose any one of their choosing, promote or oppose any policy or program and not be discharged from membership in the Union or disciplined as a member, but it appears to me to go beyond the intent of the Act to freeze them in a job in which they serve not for a term, but at the pleasure of an elected official with appointive powers set out in the Unions' Constitutions.

"The elected official has the right to the personal loyalty and loyalty to his programs from those working under him."

Problems for Discussion

1. Which view is to be preferred—that of *King* or that of *Wambles*? Would the underlying principles of the King case also protect against removal of a union officer who has organized, and is candidate for president of, a rival union (which is about to file a competing petition for an NLRB representation election)?

2. Does the court's decision in *King* improperly give "substantive" significance to Section 609 in creating rights, and not merely the procedural role contemplated by the court?

3. Assume that the plaintiffs in *King*, rather than being discharged from union office, had been reassigned by their elected superiors (pursuant to union bylaws) to provide service as an official in another location within the union's jurisdiction, specifically in a desert location 170 miles from their homes. Could this reassignment be challenged under the LMRDA? See *Cooke v. Orange Belt Dist. Council of Painters No. 48*, 529 F.2d 815 (9th Cir. 1976).

SALZHANDLER v. CAPUTO

United States Court of Appeals, Second Circuit, 1963.
316 F.2d 445.

LUMBARD, CHIEF JUDGE. Solomon Salzhandler, a member of Local 442, Brotherhood of Painters, Decorators & Paperhangers of America, brought suit in the district court following the decision of a Trial Board of the union's New York District Council No. 9 that he had untruthfully accused Isadore Webman, the president of the local, of the crime of larceny. The Trial Board found that Salzhandler's "unsupported accusations" violated the union's constitution which prohibited "conduct unbecoming a member * * *", "acts detrimental to * * * interests of the Brotherhood", "libeling, slandering * * * fellow members [or] officers of local unions" and "acts and conduct * * * inconsistent with the duties, obligations and fealty of a member."

Salzhandler's complaint alleged that his charges against Webman were an exercise of his rights as a member of the union and that the action of the Trial Board was in violation of the provisions of the LMRDA under which he was entitled to relief. * * *

[Salzhandler was serving as financial secretary of Local 442, an elective office, in November 1960, at which time he reviewed the union's checks for purposes of an audit. He found two checks, in the amounts of $800 and $375, which had been used by Webman and by the local's business agent at two union conventions; he also found two union checks, each in the amount of $6.00, representing a refund of union dues (normally paid to the widow) upon the death of the local's business agent. Salzhandler, in a leaflet distributed to members of the local, charged that the larger checks represented expenses well in excess of those to which Webman was entitled, that there was no indication that any part of those checks was used to reimburse the expenses of the business agent, and that the two $6.00 checks were improperly diverted by Webman to unauthorized purposes. The leaflet referred to Webman as a "petty robber," unworthy of trust, and accused him of having referred to union members as "thieves, scabs, robbers, scabby bosses, bums, pimps, f-bums and jail birds." In December 1960, Webman filed charges against Salzhandler with New York District Council No. 9 of the union, alleging that Salzhandler had violated the union constitution by libeling him, that Salzhandler was guilty of conduct inconsistent with his duties as a member and officer of the union, and that Salzhandler had untruthfully accused him of the crime of larceny. A six-hour hearing was conducted in February 1961 before a five-member Trial Board of the District Council, with evidence being presented by both Webman and Salzhandler (who was represented by a union member who was not a lawyer). In early April 1961, Salzhandler was informed by the Trial Board that he was to be removed from office, that he was no longer to participate in the affairs of any local within the union for five years, and that he was to be barred from union meetings, from speaking on the floor at any meetings and from running for any office in any local or in the District Council. Salzhandler filed intraunion appeals, as so provided in the union constitution, but there was no disposition of those appeals at the time he commenced his action in the federal district court. Salzhandler was also prevented from attending a union meeting; he claimed that Webman assaulted him and used violence in removing him. Salzhandler's action pursuant to Section 102 of the LMRDA sought a nullification of the Trial Board's order, reinstatement as financial secretary, and damages.]

Judge Wham dismissed the complaint holding that the Trial Board's conclusion that the leaflet was libelous was sufficiently supported by the evidence. He went further, however, and made an independent finding that the statements were, in fact, libelous. The court held, as a matter of law, that "The rights accorded members of labor unions under Title I of the Labor-Management Reporting and Disclosure Act of 1959 * * * do not include the right of a union member to libel or slander officers of the union." We do not agree.

The LMRDA of 1959 was designed to protect the rights of union members to discuss freely and criticize the management of their unions and the conduct of their officers. The legislative history and the extensive hearings which preceded the enactment of the statute abundantly evidence the intention of the Congress to prevent union officials from using their disciplinary powers to silence criticism and punish those who dare to question and complain. The statute is clear and explicit. [The court here quoted sections 101(a) (1), 101 (a) (2), 102, and 609 of the LMRDA.]

Appellees argue that just as constitutionally protected speech does not include libelous utterances, Beauharnais v. Illinois, 343 U.S. 250, 266, 72 S.Ct. 725, 96 L.Ed. 919 (1952), the speech protected by the statute likewise does not include libel and slander. The analogy to the First Amendment is not convincing. In Beauharnais, the Supreme Court recognized the possibility that state action might stifle criticism under the guise of punishing libel. However, because it felt that abuses could be prevented by the exercise of judicial authority, 343 U.S. at 263–264, 72 S.Ct. at 733–734, 96 L.Ed. 919, the court sustained a state criminal libel statute. But the union is not a political unit to whose disinterested tribunals an alleged defamer can look for an impartial review of his "crime." It is an economic action group, the success of which depends in large measure on a unity of purpose and sense of solidarity among its members.

The Trial Board in the instant case consisted of union officials, not judges. It was a group to which the delicate problems of truth or falsehood, privilege, and "fair comment" were not familiar. Its procedure is peculiarly unsuited for drawing the fine line between criticism and defamation, yet, were we to adopt the view of the appellees, each charge of libel would be given a trial de novo in the federal court—an impractical result not likely contemplated by Congress, see 105 Cong.Rec. 6026 (daily ed. April 25, 1959) (colloquy between Senator Goldwater and Senator Clark)—and such a Trial Board would be the final arbiter of the extent of the union member's protection under § 101(a)(2).[16]

---

16. See Summers, American Legislation for Union Democracy, 25 Mod.L.Rev. 273, 287:

"The most difficult problem arises when a member is expelled for 'slandering a union officer.' Union debates are characterized by vitriol and calumny, and campaigns for office are salted with overstated accusations. Defining the scope of fair comment in political contests is never easy, and in this context is nearly impossible. To allow the union to decide this issue in the first instance is to invite retaliation and repression and to frustrate one of the principal reasons for protect-

ing this right—to enable members to oust corrupt leadership through the democratic process." [Editor's note— The usual disciplinary procedure provides for a trial board—consisting either of the union's executive board or of members appointed by the President, elected by the members, or selected by lot. A hearing is held after notice to the respondent member and both sides can sometimes use counsel selected from among the membership. The trial board then decides, usually by majority vote, and presents its verdict to the membership which may accept, reject or modify the board's

In a proviso to § 101(a) (2), there are two express exceptions to the broad rule of free expression. One relates to "the responsibility of every member toward the organization as an institution." The other deals with interference with the union's legal and contractual obligations.

While the inclusion of only two exceptions, without more, does not mean that others were intentionally excluded, we believe that the legislative history supports the conclusion that Congress intended only those exceptions which were expressed.[17]

The expression of views by Salzhandler did not come within either exception in the proviso to § 101(a) (2). The leaflet did not interfere in any way with the union's legal or contractual obligations and the union has never claimed that it did. Nor could Salzhandler's charges against Webman be construed as a violation of the "responsibility of every member toward the organization as an institution." Quite the contrary; it would seem clearly in the interest of proper and honest management of union affairs to permit members to question the manner in which the union's officials handle the union's funds and how they treat the union's members. It is that interest which motivated the enactment of the statute and which would be immeasurably frustrated were we to interpret it so as to compel each dissatisfied and questioning member to draw, at the peril of union discipline, the thin and tenuous line between what is libelous and what is not. This is especially so when we consider that the Act was designed largely to curtail such vices as the mismanagement of union funds, criticism of which by union members is always likely to be viewed by union officials as defamatory.

The union argues that there is a public interest in promoting the monolithic character of unions in their dealings with employers. But the Congress weighed this factor and decided that the desirability of protecting the democratic process within the unions outweighs any

recommendations. As a rule, either side may appeal this decision to the international president, executive board, and/or the international union convention.]

17. As initially introduced before the Senate, the freedom of speech section was absolute in form. See 105 Cong. Rec. 5810 (daily ed. April 22, 1959). The section was in fact passed in that form. Id. at 5827. Later the question came to be reconsidered and the free speech section was amended to include the two express exceptions. Id. at 6030 (daily ed. April 25, 1959).

In effect, the section as initially passed took away the power of unions to punish for expressions of views. The subsequent amendment restored that power in only two situations.

We are referred to certain statements made during the debate in the Senate which allegedly indicate that "reasonable restraints" on speech were intended. See: e. g., 105 Cong.Rec. 6022 (daily ed. April 25, 1959) (remarks of Senator Kuchel). We find these statements to be ambiguous and we are not persuaded that exceptions other than those specified were intended.

possible weakening of unions in their dealings with employers which may result from the freer expression of opinions within the unions.

The democratic and free expression of opinion in any group necessarily develops disagreements and divergent opinions. Freedom of expression would be stifled if those in power could claim that any charges against them were libelous and then proceed to discipline those responsible on a finding that the charges were false. That is precisely what Webman and the Trial Board did here when they punished Salzhandler with a five-year ban of silence and stripped him of his office.

So far as union discipline is concerned Salzhandler had a right to speak his mind and spread his opinions regarding the union's officers, regardless of whether his statements were true or false. It was wholly immaterial to Salzhandler's cause of action under the LMRDA whether he spoke truthfully or not, and accordingly Judge Wham's views on whether Salzhandler's statements were true are beside the point. Here Salzhandler's charges against Webman related to the handling of union funds; they concerned the way the union was managed. The Congress has decided that it is in the public interest that unions be democratically governed and toward that end that discussion should be free and untrammeled and that reprisals within the union for the expression of views should be prohibited. It follows that although libelous statements may be made the basis of civil suit between those concerned, the union may not subject a member to any disciplinary action on a finding by its governing board that such statements are libelous. The district court erred in dismissing the complaint.

Accordingly, we reverse the judgment of the district court and direct entry of judgment for the plaintiff which, among other things, should assess damages and enjoin the defendants from carrying out any punishment imposed by the District Council Trial Board.

Problems for Discussion

1. If Caputo were to bring a libel action against Salzhandler in a state court, as the Second Circuit suggests, would the policies of the LMRDA articulated by the federal court limit the ability of the state court to fashion and apply its rules of defamation? If so, is the suggestion of the Second Circuit merely illusory? Cf. *Linn v. Plant Guard Workers Local 114*, 383 U.S. 53, 86 S.Ct. 657, 15 L.Ed.2d 582 (1966).

2. Is any of the following conduct of a union member a lawful basis, under the LMRDA, for suspension or expulsion from the union?

(a) crossing a picket line established by the union allegedly in breach of contract?

(b) urging members to strike during a collective bargaining negotiation despite the union officers' admonitions to continue to work because a tentative agreement has been reached with the employer? See *Falcone v. Dantinne*, 288 F.Supp. 719 (E.D.Pa.1968), rev'd 420 F.2d 1157 (3d Cir. 1969).

(c) urging members not to pay a union assessment which has been held by a trial court to be unlawful? See *Farowitz v. Associated Musicians' Local 802*, 330 F.2d 999 (2d Cir. 1964).

(d) testifying adversely to the union in grievance arbitration?

(e) campaigning on behalf of (and being an officer of) another union competing in an NLRB election? See *Airline Maintenance Lodge 702 v. Loudermilk*, 444 F.2d 719 (5th Cir. 1971).

(f) writing letters to state legislators urging the enactment of a right-to-work law (forbidding an agreement to make union membership a condition of employment)?

(g) refusing to march with union members in a Labor Day parade?

(h) being a member of the Communist Party (or the Ku Klux Klan)?

(i) threatening a union officer, at a heated union meeting, to "step outside to settle this matter"? Compare *Kelsey v. Local 8, Theatrical Stage Employees*, 294 F.Supp. 1368 (E.D.Pa.1968), aff'd 419 F.2d 491 (3d Cir. 1969), cert. denied 397 U.S. 1064 (1970), with *Reyes v. Laborers Local 16*, 327 F.Supp. 978 (D.N.M.1971), aff'd 464 F.2d 595 (10th Cir. 1972), cert. denied 411 U.S. 915 (1973).

INTERNATIONAL BROTHERHOOD OF BOILERMAKERS v. HARDEMAN

Supreme Court of the United States, 1971.
401 U.S. 233, 91 S.Ct. 609, 28 L.Ed.2d 10.

MR. JUSTICE BRENNAN delivered the opinion of the Court.

Section 102 of the Labor-Management Reporting and Disclosure Act (hereafter LMRDA) provides that a union member who charges that his union violated his rights under Title I of the Act may bring a civil action against the union in a district court of the United States for appropriate relief. Respondent was expelled from membership in petitioner union and brought this action under § 102 in the District Court for the Southern District of Alabama. He alleged that in expelling him the petitioner violated § 101(a)(5) of the Act, 73 Stat. 523, 29 U.S.C. § 411(a)(5) which provides: "No member of any labor organization may be fined, suspended, expelled, or otherwise disciplined except for nonpayment of dues by such organization or by any officer thereof unless such member has been (A) served with written specific charges; (B) given a reasonable time to prepare his defense; (C) afforded a full and fair hearing." A jury awarded respondent damages of $152,150. The Court of Appeals for the Fifth Circuit affirmed. 420 F.2d 485 (1969). We granted certiorari limited to the questions whether the subject matter of the suit was preempted because exclusively within the competence of the National Labor Relations Board and, if not preempted, whether the courts below had applied the proper standard of review to the union proceedings, 398 U.S. 926, 90 S.Ct. 1816, 26 L.Ed.2d 88 (1970). We reverse.

The case arises out of events in the early part of October 1960. Respondent, George Hardeman, is a boilermaker. He was then a member of petitioner's Local Lodge 112. On October 3, he went to the union hiring hall to see Herman Wise, business manager of the Local Lodge and the official responsible for referring workmen for jobs. Hardeman had talked to a friend of his, an employer who had promised to ask for him by name for a job in the vicinity. He sought assurance from Wise that he would be referred for the job. When Wise refused to make a definite commitment, Hardeman threatened violence if no work was forthcoming in the next few days.

On October 4, Hardeman returned to the hiring hall and waited for a referral. None was forthcoming. The next day, in his words, he "went to the hall   *   *   *   and waited from the time the hall opened until we had the trouble. I tried to make up my mind what to do, whether to sue the Local or Wise or beat hell out of Wise, and then I made up my mind." When Wise came out of his office to go to a local jobsite, as required by his duties as business manager, Hardeman handed him a copy of a telegram asking for Hardeman by name. As Wise was reading the telegram, Hardeman began punching him in the face.

Hardeman was tried for this conduct on charges of creating dissension and working against the interest and harmony of the Local Lodge, and of threatening and using force to restrain an officer of the Local Lodge from properly discharging the duties of his office. The trial committee found him "guilty as charged," and the Local Lodge sustained the finding and voted his expulsion for an indefinite

period.   Internal union review of this action, instituted by Hardeman, modified neither the verdict nor the penalty.   Five years later,
Hardeman brought this suit alleging that petitioner violated § 101(a)
(5) by denying him a full and fair hearing in the union disciplinary
proceedings.

I

We consider first the union's claim that the subject matter of
this lawsuit is, in the first instance, within the exclusive competence
of the National Labor Relations Board.   *   *   *   We hold that this
claim was not within the exclusive competence of the National Labor
Relations Board.   *   *   *   [T]he critical question in this action is
whether Hardeman was afforded the rights guaranteed him by § 101
(a)(5) of the LMRDA.   If he was denied them, Congress has said
that he is entitled to damages for the consequences of that denial.
Since these questions are irrelevant to the legality of conduct under
the National Labor Relations Act, there is no danger of conflicting
interpretation of its provisions.   And since the law applied is federal
law explicitly made applicable to such circumstances by Congress,
there is no danger that state law may come in through the back door
to regulate conduct that has been removed by Congress from state
control.   Accordingly, this action was within the competence of the
District Court.

II

Two charges were brought against Hardeman in the union disciplinary proceedings.   He was charged with violation of Art. XIII,
§ 1, of the Subordinate Lodge Constitution, which forbids attempting
to create dissension or working against the interest and harmony
of the union, and carries a penalty of expulsion.   He was also charged
with violation of Art. XII, § 1, of the Subordinate Lodge By-Laws,
which forbids the threat or use of force against any officer of the
union in order to prevent him from properly discharging the duties
of his office; violation may be punished "as warranted by the offense."   Hardeman's conviction on both charges was upheld in internal union procedures for review.

The trial judge instructed the jury that "whether or not he
[respondent] was rightfully or wrongfully discharged or expelled is
a pure question of law for me to determine."   He assumed, but did
not decide, that the transcript of the union disciplinary hearing contained evidence adequate to support conviction of violating Art. XII.
He held, however, that there was no evidence at all in the transcript of the union disciplinary proceedings to support the charge of

violating Art. XIII. This holding appears to have been based on the Fifth Circuit's decision in International Brotherhood of Boilermakers v. Braswell, 388 F.2d 193 (CA5 1968). There the Court of Appeals for the Fifth Circuit had reasoned that "penal provisions in union constitutions must be strictly construed," and that as so construed Art. XIII was directed only to "threats to the union as an organization and to the effective carrying out of the union's aims," not to merely personal altercations. 388 F.2d at 199. Since the union tribunal had returned only a general verdict, and since one of the charges was thought to be supported by no evidence whatsoever, the trial judge held that Hardeman had been deprived of the full and fair hearing guaranteed by § 101(a)(5). The Court of Appeals affirmed, simply citing *Braswell.* 420 F.2d 485 (CA5 1969).

We find nothing in either the language or the legislative history of § 101(a)(5) that could justify such a substitution of judicial for union authority to interpret the union's regulations in order to determine the scope of offenses warranting discipline of union members. Section 101(a)(5) began life as a floor amendment to S. 1555, the Kennedy-Ervin Bill, in the 86th Congress. As proposed by Senator McClellan, and as adopted by the Senate on April 22, 1959, the amendment would have forbidden discipline of union members "except for breach of a published written rule of [the union]." 105 Cong.Rec. 6476, 6492–6493. But this language did not long survive. Two days later, a substitute amendment was offered by Senator Kuchel, who explained that further study of the McClellan amendment had raised "some rather vexing questions." Id., at 6720. The Kuchel substitute, adopted the following day, deleted the requirement that charges be based upon a previously published, written union rule; it transformed Senator McClellan's amendment, in relevant part, into the present language of § 101(a)(5). Id., at 6720, 6727. As so amended, S. 1555 passed the Senate on April 25. Id., at 6745. Identical language was adopted by the House, Id., at 15884, 15891, and appears in the statute as finally enacted.

The Congress understood that Senator Kuchel's amendment was intended to make substantive changes in Senator McClellan's proposal. Senator Kennedy had specifically objected to the McClellan amendment because

> "In the case of * * * the * * * official who bribed a judge, unless there were a specific prohibition against bribery of judicial officers written into the constitution of the union, then no union could take disciplinary action against [an] officer or member guilty of bribery.

*   *   *   *   *   *   *   *   *   *

"It seems to me that we can trust union officers to run their affairs better than that." Id., at 6491.

Senator Kuchel described his substitute as merely providing "the usual reasonable constitutional basis" for union disciplinary proceedings: union members were to have "constitutionally reasonable notice and a reasonable hearing." Id., at 6720. After the Kuchel amendment passed the Senate, Senator Goldwater explained it to the House Committee on Labor and Education as follows:

> "[T]he bill of rights in the Senate bill requires that the union member be served with written specific charges prior to any disciplinary proceedings but it does not require that these charges, to be valid, must be based on activity that the union had proscribed prior to the union member having engaged in such activity." Labor-Management Reform Legislation, Hearings before a Joint Subcommittee of the House Committee on Education and Labor, 86th Cong., 1st Sess., pt. 4, p. 1595 (1959).

And Senator McClellan's testimony was to the same effect. Id., pt. 5, pp. 2235–2236, 2251, 2285.

We think that this is sufficient to indicate that § 101(a)(5) was not intended to authorize courts to determine the scope of offenses for which a union may discipline its members.[18] And if a union may discipline its members for offenses not proscribed by written rules at all, it is surely a futile exercise for a court to construe the written rules in order to determine whether particular conduct falls within or without their scope.

Of course, § 101(a)(5)(A) requires that a member subject to discipline be "served with written specific charges." These charges must be, in Senator McClellan's words, "specific enough to inform the accused member of the offense that he has allegedly committed." Where, as here, the union's charges make reference to specific written provisions, § 101(a)(5)(A) obviously empowers the federal courts to examine those provisions and determine whether the union member had been misled or otherwise prejudiced in the presentation of his defense. But it gives courts no warrant to scrutinize the union

---

18. State law, in many circumstances, may go further. See Summers, The Law of Union Discipline: What the Courts Do in Fact, 70 Yale L.J. 175 (1960). But Congress, which preserved state law remedies by § 103 of the LMRDA, 29 U.S.C. § 413, was well aware that even the broad language of Senator McClellan's original proposal was more limited in scope than much state law. See 105 Cong.Rec. 6481–6489 (1959).

regulations in order to determine whether particular conduct may be punished at all.

Respondent does not suggest, and we cannot discern, any possibility of prejudice in the present case. Although the notice of charges with which he was served does not appear as such in the record, the transcript of the union hearing indicates that the notice did not confine itself to a mere statement or citation of the written regulations that Hardeman was said to have violated: the notice appears to have contained a detailed statement of the facts relating to the fight that formed the basis for the disciplinary action. Section 101(a).(5) requires no more.

III

There remains only the question whether the evidence in the union disciplinary proceeding was sufficient to support the finding of guilt. Section 101(a)(5)(C) of the LMRDA guarantees union members a "full and fair" disciplinary hearing, and the parties and the lower federal courts are in full agreement that this guarantee requires the charging party to provide some evidence at the disciplinary hearing to support the charges made. This is the proper standard of judicial review. We have repeatedly held that conviction on charges unsupported by any evidence is a denial of due process * * * ; and we feel that § 101(a)(5)(C) may fairly be said to import a similar requirement into union disciplinary proceedings. Senator Kuchel, who first introduced the provision, characterized it on the Senate floor as requiring the "usual reasonable constitutional basis" for disciplinary action, 105 Cong.Rec. 6720, and any lesser standard would make useless § 101(a)(5)(A)'s requirement of written, specific charges. A stricter standard, on the other hand, would be inconsistent with the apparent congressional intent to allow unions to govern their own affairs, and would require courts to judge the credibility of witnesses on the basis of what would be at best a cold record.

Applying this standard to the present case, we think there is no question that the charges were adequately supported. Respondent was charged with having attacked Wise without warning, and with continuing to beat him for some time. Wise so testified at the disciplinary hearing, and his testimony was fully corroborated by one other witness to the altercation. Even Hardeman, although he claimed he was thereafter held and beaten, admitted having struck the first blow. On such a record there is no question but that the charges were supported by "some evidence."

Reversed.

[The concurring opinion of MR. JUSTICE WHITE and the dissenting opinion of MR. JUSTICE DOUGLAS have been omitted.]

ANDERSON v. UNITED BROTHERHOOD OF CARPENTERS, 47 CCH Lab.Cases par. 18,400 (D.C.Minn.1963). Plaintiff was expelled from defendant union for having attended Communist Party meetings in the 1940's and 1950's and for answering "No" to questions concerning whether he was a Communist or sympathetic to communist philosophy upon his application for union membership in 1948. At his hearing before the union trial committee, plaintiff was allowed to testify and to present witnesses, but he was not allowed to confront or cross-examine his accusers or witnesses against him. After exhausting internal union remedies, plaintiff brought suit for reinstatement under Section 102. *Held,* plaintiff is entitled to immediate reinstatement. The proceedings before the trial committee did not constitute a "full and fair hearing" under Section 101(a) (5) of the LMRDA in view of the absence of confrontation and the right to cross-examine.

SMITH v. GENERAL TRUCK DRIVERS, LOCAL 467, 181 F.Supp. 14 (S.D.Cal.1960). Plaintiff was issued an honorable withdrawal card because he was no longer engaged in the trade or occupation covered by the jurisdiction of the defendant local. In a suit under Section 101 of the Labor-Management Reporting and Disclosure Act for an injunction and damages, *held, inter alia,* that plaintiff was not entitled to be represented by counsel. "The answer to the contention lies in the statement of the fundamental principle that the right to be represented by counsel, guaranteed by the Sixth Amendment to the Constitution of the United States, does not apply to hearings before labor unions. The reason is obvious. All that a union member is entitled to in any controversy between him and the union is a fair hearing. This means only that before any action is taken against him he must be informed of the charges and be given an opportunity to hear them and refute them. * * * This satisfies the constitutional concept as to all administrative proceedings. * * * Except in rare instances of illegality the general concept of due process applicable in criminal prosecutions is not applied to members of a union."

---

2. *Union Discipline under the Common Law*

State courts in actions at common law have affirmed the power of unions to expel, suspend or otherwise discipline their members for a wide variety of reasons. For example, disciplinary action has been upheld against members who have failed to pay initiation fees, dues or assessments; or who have violated union work rules by working in a non-union shop or by accepting less than the union wage. Penalties have likewise been upheld against members for engaging in a wildcat strike or for strike breaking or for aiding or promoting a rival union. Inevitably, however, unions have sought to discipline members in order to promote objectives which have been considered as offensive to public policy, and courts have generally struck down such discipline. Thus, courts have enjoined a union from punishing those who refused to join in an illegal strike, and similar action was taken against the Railroad Trainmen for expelling a member who merely voted for a rival union in an election carried out pursuant to the Railway Labor Act. The case which follows is designed to suggest some of the problems that may arise in seeking to draw a line between proper and improper disciplinary action.

MITCHELL v. INTERNATIONAL ASSOCIATION OF MACHINISTS

District Court of Appeals, California, 1961.
196 Cal.App.2d 796, 16 Cal.Rptr. 813.

Fox, P. J. This appeal is from a judgment denying a petition for a writ of mandate. Petitioners seek reinstatement in respondent union, having been expelled for "conduct unbecoming a member." The conduct involved is their "peaceable, open, public, active, and vigorous campaign and support" for Proposition 18, the "right-to-work" law, in contravention of the expressed official policy of the union. (Respondents will be referred to in the singular.)

Petitioner Mitchell was a member of respondent from 1942 to July 8, 1959, the date of his expulsion. Petitioner Mulgrew was a member from 1953 until his expulsion on July 8, 1959. Both petitioners have been continuously employed by the California Division of Lockheed Aircraft from 1942 and 1953 respectively to the present time. Pursuant to an agreement between respondent union and Lockheed, the former is the exclusive bargaining representative of the company's employees in the bargaining unit described therein. Petitioners are within that bargaining unit. Neither lost his job as a result of the expulsion. The trial court found that the expulsion has not interfered with or threatened interference with petitioners' employment, nor is their opportunity for continued employment with Lockheed uncertain as a result of their expulsion. Lockheed is engaged in interstate commerce and the Taft-Hartley Act applies to it.

Proposition 18 was an initiative measure placed on the 1958 ballot for the general election held in California on November 4.

It sought to alter the state Constitution so that both closed shops and union shops would be prohibited in this state. The proposition was defeated by a majority of the voters. The trial court found that respondent was reasonable and justified in regarding the effect of the initiative measure as a serious threat to its best interests, strength, welfare, and existence.

It was further found that petitioners, as individual citizens and "as union members" supported Proposition 18 in the manner stated above by, among other things, issuing releases to the press, distributing handbills, and making speeches on television and before groups in various parts of the State of California. It was not found that they purported to represent their union. They conducted their campaign although they were aware of the union's opposition to the measure and they were aware of the union's opposition to the measure and the union's recommendation that its members oppose adoption in every possible legal way.

Petitioners were charged with conduct unbecoming a member of the union and tried on January 13, 1959. They were found guilty as charged. Petitioners waived in open court any claims relating to the regularity of the internal union trial or appeal procedure. The trial court affirmed the union's determination that petitioners' acts constituted conduct unbecoming a member and concluded as a matter of law that the expulsions were justified and not in contravention of public policy or petitioners' constitutional rights.

Once again a court is asked to choose between rights which conflict. On the one hand there is a voluntary, private organization that insists it has the right to determine its membership, which includes the right to expel members whom it considers obnoxious so long as the union constitution and by-laws are complied with. On the other hand there is the individual member, insisting that he has the right to express himself on political matters as he will, without interference from his group. Viewing this conflict from a first row seat is the community, certainly not without interest in the outcome of the dispute.

It would seem proper to begin by dispelling two troublesome illusions. The first is that unions are purely voluntary organizations like Republicans, Democrats, Elks, and church groups. A modern labor union, both in structure and in function, bears little resemblance to other voluntary associations. (Summers, Legal Limitations on Union Discipline, 64 Harv.L.Rev. 1049, 1051.) "It is this omnipotent analogy that leads the courts astray." (Williams, The Political Liberties of Labor Union Members, 32 Tex.L.Rev. 826, 829.) Unions can be distinguished from other voluntary organizations in many respects. Most importantly, a large part of their power and authority is derived from government which makes it exclusive bargaining agent. Further, they are not primarily social groups which require homogeneous views in order to retain smooth functioning. They are large, heterogeneous groups, whose members may agree on one thing only—they want improved working conditions and greater economic benefits. The union's power, when considered together with its source, imposes upon it reciprocal responsibilities toward its membership and the public generally that other voluntary organizations do not bear. (James v. Marinship Corp., 25 Cal.2d 721, 731 [155 P.2d 329, 160 A.L.R. 900]; Chavez v. Sargent, 52 Cal.2d 162 [339 P.2d 801]; Betts v. Easley, 161 Kan. 459 [169 P.2d 831, 166 A.L.R. 342].)

Secondly, it cannot be assumed that the only value in membership is job retention. Even though a member may keep his job when expelled, his expulsion causes him to suffer a detriment the apprehension of which would no doubt have a coercive effect on the membership. First of all, it is not clear what his rights would be if he quit his job to seek another, at least in intrastate commerce. Also, he has a financial stake in the strike fund, perhaps a pension fund, and other funds to which he has contributed. Further, he is denied the right to participate in his union "government." Although the union is required by law to represent him impartially (Steele v. Louisville & N. R. Co., 323 U.S. 192 [65 S.Ct. 226, 89 L.Ed. 173]), he has no voice in how that representation is to be conducted. In addition, there are frequently social ramifications for a nonmember working among members that cannot be overlooked. All this is solely for the purpose of demonstrating that there *is* a real conflict which cannot be dismissed by the assertion that since a member is assured by federal legislation that loss of membership for a reason other than nonpayment of dues does not mean loss of job, he is free to do as he wishes.

A review of the case law in and around this area will serve to orient the reader. * * *

Other groups of cases involving the question of the extent of the limitation on personal rights imposed by union membership have been fairly well categorized by the writers. At one extreme there are the "treason" cases in which an individual's acts are patently antagonistic to the continued existence of the union as a collective bargaining agent. Company spies and dual unionists are two examples. (See *Summers,* supra, at p. 1059 et seq. See also Davis v. International Alliance etc. Employees, 60 Cal.App.2d 713 [141 P.2d 486].) Similar cases are those in which members impair adherence to the collective bargaining agreement by violating work rules, working below scale, and engaging in wildcat strikes. (See *Williams,* supra, at p. 831.) The courts lose no time in such cases in upholding union discipline. At the other extreme are cases in which the courts frustrated union attempts to interfere with specific citizenship obligations. The Barbers were enjoined from expelling a member for enforcing Sunday laws against a fellow member (Manning v. Klein, 1 Pa.Super. 210). The Plumbers were prevented from expelling a member who, as a public official, refused to appoint another member as a plumbing inspector (Schneider v. Local Union No. 60, 116 La. 270 [40 So. 700, 114 Am.Ct.Rep. 549, 7 Ann.Cas. 868, 5 L.R.A.,N.S., 891]). Another union was compelled to reinstate a member who testified before the Interstate Commerce Commission against safety devices sought by the union (Abdon v. Wallace, 95 Ind.App. 604 [165 N.E. 68]). Other unions have been ordered to reinstate members who testified against the union in court (Angrisani v. Stearn, 167 Misc. 731 [3 N.Y.S.2d 701]; Thompson v. Grand International Brotherhood of L. E., 41 Tex.Civ.App. 176 [91 S.W. 834]).

Somewhere between these two extremes lies the small group of cases involving political activity by members, obligatory only in the moral sense, which the union as a whole opposes. Spayd v. Ringing Rock Lodge No. 665, 270 Pa. 67 [113 A. 70, 14 A.L.R. 1443], involved an action by a member of the union to compel reinstatement following expulsion for violation of a rule prohibiting any member from using his influence to defeat any action taken by union officials concerned with legislation. Plaintiff was expelled because he signed a petition asking the Legislature to reconsider its adoption of the "full crew law." Using every legal theory available under the circumstances, the court held that the union's action violated plaintiff's property rights, the Constitution, and public policy. Concluding, the opinion states, at page 73, "The right here involved, and the voting franchise, are the only means by which peaceful changes in our laws and institutions may be sought or brought about, and they cannot, with safety to the state, or the whole body of the people, be gathered into the hands of the few for any purpose whatsoever." * * *

In deciding whether a union may, *under these facts,* be permitted to penalize a member for engaging in political activity which the union opposes, certain considerations must be brought to light: (1) the interest of the community and the individual in the latter's membership; (2) the importance to the community of the individual's untrammeled right to express himself on political questions; (3) the interest of the union in excluding obnoxious members; (4) the interest of the union in speaking with one voice; (5) the nature of the political activity and the manner of its conduct. As to the first consideration, the value of membership to the individual has already been demonstrated. And to the extent that industrial democracy is important to the community, its interest is also manifest. (Cox, Law and the National Labor Policy [1960] p. 110.)

With respect to the second, few subjects in the history of western civilization have drawn such a unanimity of support. In a dissenting opinion Mr. Justice Brandeis observed, "The right of a citizen of the United States to take part, for his own or the country's benefit, in the making of federal laws and in the conduct of the Government, necessarily includes the right to speak or write about them; * * * Full and free exercise of this right * * * is ordinarily also his duty; for its exercise is more important to the Nation that it is to himself." (Gilbert v. Minnesota, 254 U.S. 325, 337–338 [41 S.Ct. 125, 65 L.Ed. 287].) * * * Further quotation is unnecessary. Suffice it to say that the unlimited freedom to express political views is the very heart of a democratic body, pumping the lifeblood of ideas without which our system could not survive.

As to the union's interest in excluding obnoxious members, it would be completely unrealistic to assume that unions are composed of like-thinking individuals. It is only when dissident views are expressed in a forum where they have a chance of acceptance that the member becomes "undesirable." But expulsion cannot serve to quiet the individual. It can only serve to intimidate those who remain. While this, too, might be a legitimate objective under some circumstances, the very question to be decided is whether the community ought to tolerate that result in *these* circumstances.

As to the interest of the union in presenting a unified front, this cannot be gainsaid. And where activity of the union is directly designed to attain economic goals, such as the decision to strike or not to strike, or adherence to the collective bargaining agreement, judicial regard for this interest has already been demonstrated. And it is no doubt true that economic and political objectives of unions frequently cannot be treated as completely separate things.[19] * * * But still a distinction should be made in this context. Where purely economic activity is concerned, the community interest is not so deeply involved as it would be if the entire union membership in the nation were limited in its political expression (on matters of legitimate union interest) to the opinions of the majority or the union

19. Archibald Cox, professor of law at Harvard and presently Solicitor General of the United States, says, "It is difficult, if not impossible, to separate the economic and political functions of labor unions. Right-to-work laws affect union organization and collective bargaining. Legislation subjecting unions to the antitrust laws or confining their scope to the employees of a single company would greatly weaken their bargaining power, if it did not destroy them altogether. Although it seems unlikely that the LMRDA will seriously impair the strength of labor organizations, many union leaders hold an opposite view which time may prove correct. Political action in these spheres of union interest is hardly more than incidental to the union's economic activities. A similar link exists even when a union takes political action upon a broader front. The basic philosophy of a President and his party affects appointments to agencies like the National Labor Relations Board, which in turn exerts tremendous influence upon the course of labor relations. Even the tariff impinges on labor negotiations. The bargaining power of the Hatters Union, for example, is affected by the competition of low-cost foreign goods." (Cox, Law and the National Labor Policy [1960] p. 107.)

leadership. If this were the case we would be deprived of an immeasurably important source of political thought. Furthermore, so long as the individual member purports to represent only himself, and not his union, the union's public position is not diluted.[20]

This brings us to the question of the nature of the political doctrine propounded and the manner in which it is advocated. We are not called upon to decide what the result would be if a member was expelled for advocating repeal of the Wagner Act or the abolition of unions. Only the right-to-work law is here involved. The union argues that it may reasonably consider such a law seriously inimical to its interests. This is certainly not an unreasonable position * * * But there is a substantial respectable opinion to the contrary. Cox, supra, at page 110 says, "The member who acts as a strikebreaker may be guilty of treason, but one can believe in right-to-work laws and remain a good trade-unionist." * * * There being such a disparity of opinion as to the long-run effect of voluntary unionism, the question becomes not whether the union is justified in its opinion, but whether the point is sufficiently debatable so that society's interest in the debate, together with the individual's right to speak freely on political matters, outweighs the union's interest in subduing public dissent among union members.

With respect to the manner in which the campaign was conducted, petitioners did speak as union members. But they did not purport to represent their union * * *.

It could not be more apparent where the balance lies. On this point, Cox, supra, page 111, has this to say: "It needs no argument to demonstrate the importance of freedom to pursue personal political activities. It begs the question to say that a man has a right to engage in whatever political activity he wishes but no right to be a union member. The question is whether there will be an excessive loss of freedom if unions are permitted to make political conformity the price of membership. Bearing in mind the size and importance of unions in industry as well as their growing interest in politics, it seems apparent that the total loss would be great indeed if a significant number of large labor organizations adopted the attitude of the International Association of Machinists. It would also work serious changes in our political system if individuals can be insulated from direct political

20. "For many years labor unions were extraordinarily fragile. Dissent created strains which might easily cause disintegration. The risks of dissension were increased by the unions' vulnerability to attacks by employers. Conformity to group decisions was the price of survival. It seems doubtful, however, whether this factor should be given as much weight under modern conditions. Labor unions have achieved strength and stability. The centrifugal forces are counterbalanced by full-time officials, professional staffs, and, often, closely-knit internal organization. Furthermore, disagreement upon political issues, even upon the desirability of a right-to-work law, does not go to the heart of a labor union's functions." (Cox, supra, note 33 at p. 110.)

action by the decisions of organized groups even though the decisions are reached by majority rule." It is therefore clear that, at least where the political activity of the member is not patently in conflict with the union's best interests, the union should not be permitted to use its power over the individual to curb the advocacy of his political views. * * *

Problems for Discussion

1. Consider the grounds for expulsion from union membership set forth in the Problem at page 1136, supra. Under the principles announced in the *Mitchell* case, would these be valid grounds for expulsion at common law?

2. If it were determined that any particular ground for expulsion was valid under the LMRDA, would it follow that the expelled member could not secure reinstatement to membership by an action in a state court? If it were determined that any particular ground for expulsion was valid under Section 8(b)(1)(A) of the Labor Act, would it follow that the expelled member could not secure reinstatement to membership by an action in a state court? For example, assume that a member is expelled for crossing a lawful union picket line or for filing a decertification petition against his own union, and assume that expulsion does not violate the NLRA; can it be held to violate state law and to furnish a basis for reinstatement to membership?

3. Assume that an expelled member has a claim for reinstatement to membership that may be pursued under Section 8(b)(1)(A) of the Labor Act, Section 101(a) of the LMRDA and state common law. What factors should be considered in determining the forum in which to seek relief?

3. *Exhaustion of Internal Union Remedies*

FALSETTI v. LOCAL 2026, UNITED MINE WORKERS

Supreme Court of Pennsylvania, 1960.
400 Pa. 145, 161 A.2d 882.

COHEN, J. This is an appeal from the order of the Court of Common Pleas of Allegheny County dismissing appellant's Bill in Equity on preliminary objections. Appellant's amended complaint alleged that he was a dues-paying member in good standing in appellee Local No. 2026, United Mine Workers of America (Union); that he was employed by appellee Pittsburgh Consolidation Coal Company (Company) with seniority from 1939; that on January 8, 1954, in violation of appellant's seniority rights under the collective bargaining agreement between Union and Company, he was laid off by the Company while at least one, and possibly more, employees with less seniority than he were retained; that appellee Company continues to employ such employee or employees and has rehired others with less seniority than appellant; that appellant's loss of seniority rights came about as a result of an unlawful conspiracy between appellee Company and the named individual appellees (Union officials) under the pretext that appellant was no longer able to fulfill his job obligations;

that after appellant filed the original complaint in this action he was expelled from the Union; that he has demanded to be restored to Union membership, but appellee Union has refused, and that all remedies under the Union constitution and collective bargaining agreement between the Union and the Company have been exhausted and further resort thereto would be futile. In his prayer for relief, appellant asks that the Union be compelled to restore appellant's membership; that the appellee Company be compelled to reinstate appellant in his employment with the same job classification he had before the alleged discharge; that damages be awarded appellant for loss of wages; and that such other and further relief that may be just and equitable be allowed. * * *

Since our holding is that the amended complaint alleges two distinct claims, each will be treated separately to determine whether, under our own rules and under the pleadings now before us, the courts of the Commonwealth may exercise jurisdiction over either claim upon a severance. First, we will consider appellant's claim that he was wrongfully expelled from appellee Union. Appellees contend in this regard that appellant has failed to exhaust his internal remedies within the Union and therefore the issue presented is not "ripe" for adjudication by our courts. * * *

At this late date in the history of labor-management relations, it is but pointing out the obvious to state that autonomous, self-disciplining labor unions are beneficial to the public. The rule of exhaustion of internal remedies, applicable when a dispute arises between an association and a member thereof, evolved by our courts through the years and applicable to all "voluntary" unincorporated associations, serves to promote the desired autonomy and to encourage the establishment of fair procedures for maintaining internal discipline. Although this court has often relied on the contract rationale that a member, by voluntarily joining an association, has bound himself perpetually to abide by its constitution and by-laws, there are today other and more justifiable policy reasons for applying the exhaustion rule. If exhaustion of internal remedies were to be treated simply as a contractual condition, we might often be driven to a mechanical application of the rule in instances where such application would be unjust. And we would be constrained to engraft exceptions onto the rule which would lead to its eventual emasculation.[21]

* * * [W]e find the doctrine of exhaustion of internal remedies to be a necessary and proper incentive for achieving true association democracy.

In intra-association disputes, there are three sets of interests to be considered: (1) the interest of the association as such, (2) the

21. Application of the exhaustion rule does not turn upon the membership status of the party bringing the suit. Applicable to an association member seeking relief within the group, it applies equally to an expelled member who is seeking reinstatement.

interest of the members of the association, and (3) the interest of the courts. There is as well an over-riding *public* interest in promoting well-managed autonomous associations which are able to perform their functions effectively and still provide internally for the fair treatment of individual members who must be disciplined. See Chafee, op. cit. supra. The exhaustion rule is beneficial to the association in that by encouraging intra-association resolution of internal disputes, it permits officials in positions of higher authority within the association to carry out a uniform application of the association's policies. The association, in this manner, is able to prevent its "dirty linen" from being washed in public. Moreover, such a rule often saves the association the unnecessary burden and expense of litigation.

The exhaustion rule is beneficial as well to the vast majority of association members. Since very few members are willing to appeal beyond the association level when they are required to exhaust their internal remedies, the majority of members are benefited for the same reasons as the association in having disputes resolved within the association. The rule, when properly applied, will also tend to improve the machinery of the intra-association appellate system and make it a more responsible and efficient means of settling problems of discipline.

We are fully cognizant of the tremendous burden that premature judicial intervention into internal association-member disputes would place on already overcrowded court dockets. The exhaustion rule reduces litigation by forcing disputes through a private system where they may be settled before reaching the courts. This undoubtedly eliminates a needless waste of judicial time and duplication of litigation. The aggrieved member will quite often obtain satisfaction within the association's hierarchy, thereby terminating the dispute before it ripens into a full-blown legal contest. The rule, in summary, is extremely valuable in encouraging private adjustment, self-correction, and fair internal procedures.

This is not to say, of course, that the interests of the majority should persuade the courts to ignore the rights and interests of an occasional member who, with good cause, has ignored the association's internal procedure. But in holding that a case falls within one of the narrow exceptions to the exhaustion rule, we must be overly careful not to completely undercut it. Such exceptions as there are should be narrowly construed in line with the beneficial purposes of the rule itself. The exceptions are few and should be mentioned at this point.

First and foremost, a person will not be required to take intra-association appeals which cannot in fact yield remedies. If a remedy exists in theory only, it can well be considered illusory. Secondly, there is no need for a member to exhaust his internal remedies where the association officials have, by their own actions, precluded the member from having a fair or effective trial or appeal. See Heasley v.

Operative P. & C. F. I. Assn., 234 Pa. 257, 188 A. 206 (1936); Weiss v. The Musical Protective Union, 189 Pa. 446, 42 A. 118 (1899). This includes those situations in which a member is not given due notice, right of hearing or review (see *e. g.* Labor Management Reporting and Disclosure Act of 1959, Sec. 101(a)(5)), and those where the association's officials are obviously biased or have prejudged the member's case before hearing it. See Blenko v. Schmeltz, 362 Pa. 365, 57 A.2d 99 (1949).[22]

Still another exception to the rule is where to insist that a member exhaust the appellate procedure would be unreasonably burdensome, *e. g.*, if the appellate procedure requires a member to appeal to a national convention which does not convene for several years.[23] See O'Neill v. United Plumbers, 348 Pa. 531, 36 A.2d 325 (1944); Heasley v. Operative P. & C. F. I. Assn., supra. In this regard, for all situations which arise subsequent to the passage of the new "Labor Bill of Rights" contained in the Labor Management Reporting and Disclosure Act of 1959, Sec. 101(a)(4) and to which the Act is applicable a member of a labor organization may be required to exhaust internal remedies *only if* such hearing procedures are "reasonable" and if they are completed within four months.

And finally there are instances where the requirement of exhaustion of remedies would subject a member to an injury that is in a practical sense irreparable. Such a situation would arise where a person expelled from a union and suing for re-admittance would, during the interim of his appeal, be barred from working in a union shop. Our courts are aptly armed, however, to prevent such irreparable injury to plaintiffs without destroying the vitality of the exhaustion rule.[24]

We hasten to emphasize, at this point, that the subject matter of the plaintiff's complaint, the harm complained of, should have little bearing on whether at that instant our courts may exercise jurisdiction. * * *

22. Even though there is a showing of bias at a lower level of the association's appellate system, however, if there is an unbiased tribunal on a higher level in the hierarchy, the policies behind the exhaustion rule require that the member appeal to that higher tribunal.

23. On its face, certainly, the two or three step appellate procedure provided for in the constitution of the International Union is not so burdensome or time-consuming as to justify immediate judicial intervention in an internal dispute.

24. Many associations voluntarily stay the imposition of penalty themselves, but if the association fails to do so, our courts are empowered to issue a temporary injunction staying the imposition of penalty while the member is taking an intra-association appeal. Such injunction must be based upon proof of a potential severe injury to the member and a colorable claim for relief. There need be no fear of dilatory tactics by the plaintiff since the injunction can be expressly conditioned upon his prompt exhaustion of all available internal remedies. The injunction *pendente lite*, of course, should be used but sparingly. See Summers, supra at 1096–97; Comment, 65 Yale L.J. 369, 383–85 (1956).

We are not unaware of the strong emphasis now being accorded the problem of internal union democracy. It is with a view toward the recent important steps taken legislatively to safeguard in the federal courts the rights of individual members against organizational excesses that we today elevate the rule of exhaustion to such a prominent position in our jurisdictional scheme. The Labor Management Reporting and Disclosure Act of 1959, Title I—Bill of Rights of Members of Labor Organizations, is not an attempt by the Congress of the United States to control the internal affairs of labor organizations. Rather, it represents the establishment of certain channels within which union activities which affect membership rights may proceed. * * * Rather than adopt judicial rules that would discourage resort to union processes which now must meet detailed elementary standards of fairness, we will attempt in every way to encourage the steady evolution of internal democracy. A strict adherence to the rule of exhaustion will go far toward placing the initial responsibility where it rightfully belongs—on the association itself. It is only when an issue has become fully "ripe" for adjudication that our courts will enter the picture.

In the instant case, appellant has averred seemingly inconsistent facts. He avers (a) that he has exhausted all remedies within the Union, and (b) that a further resort thereto would be futile. Passing over this inconsistency and treating these allegations as alternative, we find that appellant's own pleadings indicate (1) that he has not exhausted all the remedies afforded him, and (2) that he has not alleged sufficient facts to raise an issue of futility. * * *

[The union constitution] provides an appellate procedure which begins with the local union, proceeds to the sub-district convention if in session, continues to the district executive board and district convention, and then to the International Union. The individual member's appeal as of right, however, apparently ends with the district executive board as stated in Section 3 of Art. III. For purposes of the exhaustion rule, therefore, an appeal to the district executive board can be considered the final step. Appellant has alleged only that he demanded restoration in defendant local union. He does not allege that he took any further steps than making demand of the local union itself. Certainly a mere allegation of exhaustion will not be held sufficient to create a triable issue of fact for the court. Such an allegation is simply a conclusion of the pleader insufficient to support jurisdiction.

An examination of appellant's contention (b) that it would have been futile to proceed further indicates a similar absence of facts which might lead us to believe that appellant's complaint would not be adequately processed through the union appellate procedure. Here again, a mere allegation by the pleader of futility or illusoriness will not satisfy the jurisdictional requirement. Durso v. Philadelphia

Musical Society, 11 D. & C.2d 463, 469–70 (1957), aff'd 392 A.2d 30, 139 A.2d 555 (1958). Appellant's only allegation in the complaint which bears on this issue at all is his averment that "further resort thereto would be futile and useless in view of the past and continued refusal of the defendants to process the plaintiff's grievance." Even were we to assume that appellant took all the necessary steps to have the Union process his discharge grievance, as required by the collective bargaining agreement, it would fly in the face of reason and logic to hold that simply because the Union refused to press appellant's grievance in negotiations with the employer, for any one of several reasons it might deem justifiable, that the appellant has thereby demonstrated that the Union will not provide an effective forum and internal procedure whereby appellant may fairly resolve a subsequent Union-member disciplinary dispute. We conclude, therefore, that aside from the procedural defect of joining this expulsion claim to the discharge claim against the Company and the individual appellees, our courts will not exercise jurisdiction to entertain the expulsion claim until the internal remedies are exhausted. Cf. Strano v. Local Union No. 690, 398 Pa. 97, 156 A.2d 522 (1959).

* * *

DETROY v. AMERICAN GUILD OF VARIETY ARTISTS, 286 F.2d 75 (2d Cir.1961). Plaintiff, who performed with a troupe of trained chimpanzees, alleged that his union had deprived him of rights under Section 101(a) (5) of the Labor Management Reporting and Disclosure Act by placing his name on the "National Unfair List" without providing him with notice or hearing. The union urged that the suit be dismissed, since plaintiff had not exhausted his remedies within the union as required by Section 101(a) (4) of the LMRDA. On appeal from an order by the district court dismissing the complaint, *held*, reversed. Section 101(a) (4) does not impose an absolute duty to exhaust internal remedies but leaves the federal courts to develop their own principles of exhaustion. In the case in issue, the facts on their face revealed a violation of the procedural safeguards required by Section 101(a) (5). Moreover, the nature of plaintiff's employment made it difficult to determine the amount of damages resulting from the union's action so that speedy intervention by the courts would be desirable. Finally, plaintiff's internal remedies were dubious, for the union's constitution did not clearly provide a means of review over decisions to place a member's name on the Unfair List nor had any appropriate remedy been brought to the attention of the plaintiff. "The absence of any of these elements might, in the light of Congressional approval of the exhaustion doctrine, call for a different result. The facts of this case, however, warrant immediate judicial intervention." Compare, Smith v. General Truck Drivers Union, 181 F.Supp. 14 (S.D.Cal.1960) (Section 101(a) (4) "is *unconditional.* * * * as we are not bound by

State law, we decline to read exceptions into the specific language of the federal statute under discussion. * * * ").

IV. UNION ELECTIONS [1]

The election of officers is the heart of union democracy. The policies of any large organization must be formulated and administered by a small group of officials. Their responsiveness to the members depends upon the frequency of elections, a fair opportunity to nominate and vote for candidates, and an honest count of the ballots.

Virtually all unions provide in their constitutions for some method of electing officers. According to a 1959 study, covering the constitutions of seventy unions, sixteen unions provided for a direct election of national officers while the remaining fifty-four selected national officers by the vote of delegates at periodic conventions.[2] Where the convention method is used, of course, much turns upon the method of selecting delegates. Nevertheless, until recently, this matter has been treated only sketchily, if at all, in union constitutions. Thus, the above-mentioned study reported that of fifty-four unions utilizing the convention method in 1959, thirty neglected, in providing for the election of delegates, to include such safeguards as the separation of nomination and election dates and the requirement of notice.[3] Fifteen other unions left the selection of delegates entirely to the locals.[4] Union constitutions have also paid scant attention to the process by which the delegates select national officers at the convention. One observer has concluded:

> "Only rarely do the constitutions provide a reasonable time interval between nominations and elections. There is no method of acquainting the delegates with the program of the candidates running against the incumbents, except through short speeches from the floor. And no special time is reserved for criticism of the incumbent's record and discussion of the platform on which the rival candidates are running".[5]

1. For a detailed discussion of the regulation of union elections by the state courts of New York, see Summers, Judicial Regulation of Union Elections, 70 Yale L.J. 1221 (1961); and for a study of union elections under the Landrum-Griffin Act, see Beaird, Union Officer Election Provisions of the LMRDA of 1959, 51 Va.L.Rev. 1306 (1965); Bellace & Berkowitz, The Landrum-Griffin Act—Twenty Years of Federal Protection of Union Members' Rights (1979); Comment, Union Elections and the LMRDA: Thirteen Years of Use and Abuse, 81 Yale L.J. 407 (1972); Harris, Titles I and IV of the LMRDA: A Resolu-

tion of the Conflict of Remedies, 42 U.Chi.L.Rev. 166 (1974); McLaughlin & Schoomaker, The Landrum-Griffin Act and Union Democracy (1979); Note, Pre-Election Remedies Under the Landrum-Griffin Act, 74 Colum. L.Rev. 1105 (1974); Topol, Union Elections Under the LMRDA, 74 Yale L.J. 1282 (1965).

2. Bromwich, Union Constitutions 24 (1959).

3. Id. at 25.

4. Ibid.

5. Id. at 24.

While direct elections have been used by only a small minority of unions in choosing national officers, they have generally been employed to select local officials. Union experience with direct elections has been distinctly varied. At one extreme is the International Typographical Union, which has maintained a two-party system for many decades.[6] Elaborate election safeguards have been established and 60–80% of the electorate have traditionally participated in elections fought over such issues as the five-day week, bargaining policy, efficient administration and the like. The experience of the ITU is unique among American unions, however, and vigorous elections are encountered less frequently elsewhere. In a study of thirty-four unions published in 1954, one observer found that only 18.8% of all presidential elections and 23.7% of all other elections were even contested.[7] Other studies suggest that while participation in elections has sometimes risen above 50% of the electorate, it has frequently fallen below 10%.[8]

The common law concerning the conduct of labor-union elections has had an uneven development. The member who complains that an election has not been held or that the nominations or voting were not conducted in accordance with the constitution and bylaws cannot maintain an action for damages because he has sustained no measureble loss. The only remedy is a decree in equity ousting the officers or ordering an election, and the complaining member may find that this relief is barred by the old rule that equity acts only for the protection of property.[9] In *Leahigh v. Beyer*,[10] for example, the court refused to interfere with an allegedly improper run-off election in a United Automobile Workers local because "no individual property rights of any of the plaintiffs are in any manner affected or involved in the action of the defendants sought to be relieved against." [11]

In some jurisdictions there is greater hope of relief. Some courts have found the property interest necessary to give jurisdiction in the risk of misappropriation of union funds and have gone on to supervise the conduct of an election as an incident to the protection of the assets.[12] Others have merely given lip service to the rule that equity intervenes only for the protection of property by saying that the right to elect union officers is as much a right of property as the right to union membership. In *Raevsky v. Upholsterer's Int'l Union* [13] the court retained jurisdiction of a bill to

6. Lipset, Trow & Coleman, Union Democracy (1956).

7. Taft, The Structure and Government of Labor Unions 38 (1954)

8. Sayles & Strauss, The Local Union 192 (1953).

9. See, e. g., Stanton v. Harris, 152 Fla. 736, 13 So.2d 17 (1943); State ex rel. Givens v. Superior Court, 233 Ind. 235, 117 N.E.2d 553 (1954); cf. Finley v. Duffy, 88 Ohio App. 159, 94 N.E.2d 466, appeal dismissed, 154 Ohio St. 390, 95 N.E.2d 759 (1950); Way v. Patton, 195 Or. 36, 241 P.2d 895 (1952).

10. 116 N.E.2d 458 (Ohio C.P.1953).

11. Id. at 462.

12. See e. g., Wilson v. Miller, 194 Tenn. 390, 250 S.W.2d 575 (1952).

13. 38 Pa.D. & C. 187 (C.P.1940).

enjoin an international president from interfering with a local election, saying:

> It may well be here that the officers have the authority to distribute jobs, collect dues, make expenditures, control the property of the union, pay out strike benefits, and represent the union with the employer. These we know are typical of trade-union duties, through their agents. These are important powers, which in the hands of leaders seeking economic or personal gain may be abused to the detriment of members of a trade union. Such an abuse of power might interfere with the economic welfare of the members as much as expulsion from the union itself. Moreover, it can be said that the right to have an election within a trade union is a property right which courts have recognized * * *.
>
> The cases cited in defendants' brief are for the most part distinguishable because they concern political associations in which the court was unable to find a property right which had been abrogated. Social clubs, political clubs, and trade unions, though all with the same basis of unincorporation, must be differentiated. Our modern economic life so dictates.[14]

Several Pennsylvania[15] and New Jersey[16] courts have intervened in union elections without considering the basis of jurisdiction.[17]

In states permitting a cause of action, a wide variety of challenges have been entertained. In New York alone, courts have insisted that the names of candidates improperly stricken be restored to the ballot;[18] that candidates receive equal access to the union newspaper and to voting lists;[19] that proper notice of an election or nomination meeting be given;[20] that voters not be intimidated from making nominations;[21] and that the election district be properly drawn.[22] After elections have been held, the New York courts have been willing to examine the qualifications of candidates,[23] to

14. Id. at 195.

15. O'Neil v. United Ass'n of Journeymen Plumbers, 348 Pa. 531, 36 A.2d 325 (1944); Maloney v. UMW, 308 Pa. 251, 162 A. 225 (1932); see O'Hara v. Teamsters, 63 Pa.D. & C. 573 (C.P. 1948).

16. Sibilia v. Western Elec. Employees, 142 N.J.Eq. 77, 59 A.2d 251 (Ct.Err. & App.1948).

17. See also Dusing v. Nuzzo, 177 Misc. 35, 29 N.Y.S.2d 882 (S.Ct.), modified, 263 App.Div. 59, 31 N.Y.S.2d 849 (1941); O'Connell v. O'Leary, 167 Misc. 324, 3 N.Y.S.2d 833 (S.Ct.1938).

18. DiBucci v. Ulrich, 21 Misc.2d 1069, 189 N.Y.S.2d 717 (S.Ct.1959).

19. Contes v. Ross, 125 N.Y.L.J. June 12, 1951, p. 2175 col. 5.

20. Fisher v. Kempter, 25 L.R.R.M. 2189 (N.Y.S.Ct.1949).

21. Alaimo v. Rossiter, S.Ct. Erie Cty., May 23, 1941 cited in Summers, Judicial Regulation of Union Elections, 70 Yale L.J. 1221, 1230, n. 52 (1961).

22. Caliendo v. McFarland, 13 Misc.2d 183, 175 N.Y.S.2d 869 (S.Ct.1958).

23. Litwin v. Novak, 9 A.D.2d 789, 193 N.Y.S.2d 310 (1959).

review challenged ballots [24] and to consider such questions as the improper use of the union newspaper by the incumbent officers.[25]

Despite the willingness of judges in some states to intervene, various obstacles have hindered the courts in playing an effective role to insure democratic union elections. A court lacks authority to do much more than enforce the union's own constitution and bylaws. True, a court may invalidate a constitutional provision which is contrary to public policy, but even this will do little to enforce democratic control, for a court cannot always provide a substitute for the provisions which it invalidates. Ambiguous provisions or gaps in the union constitution can sometimes be resolved or filled in by reference to traditional notions of fair play and democratic principles, and courts have not hesitated to act in this manner in order to improve election procedures.[26] Nevertheless, a court cannot write a union constitution. Without the consent of the union, it cannot prescribe the time, place, and frequency of elections, create machinery for nominations, or define the electorate. In short, in the absence of legislation, the common law may be hard put to supply minimum electoral guarantees if they are missing from a union constitution.

A court is also a clumsy instrument for supervising an election. The judicial process may be suitable for determining the validity of an election which has already been held; but if it is found invalid, or if no election has been held, judges have few facilities for providing an effective remedy. Merely to order an election might turn the authority to conduct the balloting over to the very same officers whose misconduct gave rise to the litigation. The court has no tellers, watchers, or similar officials. It would become mired in the details of the electoral process. Probably it is the consciousness of these weaknesses that has made judges so reluctant to exercise broad supervision over union elections, for few elections seem to have been held under the direction of the courts.[27] One alternative is to conduct an election under the supervision of a master appointed by the court, but this device has actually been employed in only a few instances.[28]

---

24. Carey v. Int. Bhd. of Paper Makers, 123 Misc. 680, 206 N.Y.S. 73 (S.Ct. 1924).

25. Ford v. Curran, 36 L.R.R.M. 2407 (S.Ct.1955).

26. See Irwin v. Possehl, 143 Misc. 855, 257 N.Y.S. 597 (S.Ct.1932); Caliendo v. McFarland, 13 Misc.2d 183, 175 N.Y. S.2d 869 (S.Ct.1958).

27. See Dusing v. Nuzzo, 177 Misc. 35, 29 N.Y.S.2d 882 (S.Ct.), modified, 263

App.Div. 59, 31 N.Y.S.2d 849 (1941); O'Neil v. United Ass'n of Journeymen Plumbers, 348 Pa. 531, 36 A.2d 325 (1944); Wilson v. Miller, 194 Tenn. 390, 250 S.W.2d 575 (1952).

28. See Holdeman v. Interntl. Org. of Masters, 7 A.D.2d 1021, 184 N.Y.S. 2d 698 (1959), aff'd 6 N.Y.2d 869, 188 N.Y.S.2d 987, 160 N.E.2d 119 (1959); Yellin v. Schaeffer, 46 L.R.R.M. 2723 N.Y.S.Ct.1960).

In the face of all these problems, Congress enacted the Labor Management Reporting and Disclosure Act which established comprehensive requirements for the conduct of union elections. Under this statute, local officers must be elected every three years or oftener by a secret ballot.[29] International officers must be elected every five years or oftener by a secret ballot of the members or by a convention of delegates chosen by secret ballot.[30] There are appropriate guarantees of the right to nominate and support candidates, to run for office, to get written notice of the election, and to vote without "improper interference or reprisal of any kind." [31] Every member is guaranteed one vote, a provision which not only invalidates the practice of limiting the vote to a special class of members but which also assures apprentices and even employers a voice in the selection of the officers of any labor organization to which they may belong. The statute assures honest elections by giving each candidate the right to have an observer at the polls and at the counting of the ballots, and by requiring separate publication of the results of the balloting in each local union. The latter requirement is pertinent to international elections. The division of sentiment in a single local is usually well enough known to its members to reveal any serious dishonesty in counting the ballots, provided that the figures are not concealed by lumping them into a single total with the results in other local unions. The Act makes compliance with the union's constitution and bylaws a statutory obligation in order that a federal remedy may be available for violations.[32]

To prevent union officials from gaining improper advantage in union elections Section 401(c) requires the union to distribute any candidate's campaign literature at his expense and to refrain from discrimination between candidates. Section 401(g) prohibits using union funds to promote the candidacy of any person. The administration of the latter provision will require delicate judgments. When a union president visits major locals on union business during the months before an election, he is not unmindful of his political fences. The international representative who goes to another city to handle grievances may be expected to discuss an impending election. The incumbents invariably command more space in the union newspaper than the opposition. Compare Hodgson v. United Mine Workers, 344 F.Supp. 17 (D.D.C.1972), with New Watch-Dog Comm. v. Taxi Drivers Local 3036, 438 F.Supp. 1242 (S.D.N.Y.1977). Legislation can no more wipe out these advantages than it can prevent a President's dramatic move toward world peace from aiding his campaign for re-election. Nevertheless the statute can help to eliminate such grossly unfair tactics as hiring additional organizers to campaign

29. LMRDA § 401(b).

30. LMRDA § 401(a).

31. LMRDA § 401(e).

32. LMRDA § 401(e) and (f).

for the re-election of incumbent officials or using the union treasury to send out election propaganda.

The demand that all candidates be given access to the union's membership list produced sharp debate in Congress because two irreconcilable principles were at stake. Since a candidate seeking to defeat the incumbent would be seriously hampered by the lack of a voting list, access to membership lists became a symbol of truly democratic elections in the eyes of those congressmen who would not count it a loss if labor unions were damaged in the process. On the other hand, the unions attach great importance to the secrecy of their membership lists because employers, rival unions, and subversive organizations have often used the lists for improper purposes. Under present conditions the need for secrecy is probably exaggerated, but one friendly to the labor movement could hardly ignore the strength of the tradition or the force of experience even though he was also driven to acknowledge that the preservation of secrecy diminished the fairness of the election. In the end a compromise was reached which gives a candidate the right to inspect a list of members who are employed under union security contracts, once within thirty days of the election and without copying the list. This limited privilege can hardly be abused.[33]

Enforcement of the election requirements is vested in the Secretary of Labor. A member desiring to challenge an election must first invoke his remedies within the organization. After they are exhausted or if three months elapse without a decision, he may file a complaint with the Secretary who, upon investigation, will either dismiss the complaint or file an action in the federal court to set aside the election. The complaint is to be upheld only if it appears that the violation of the statute "may have affected the outcome of the election."[34] It would be wasteful to set aside an election for violations which could not have affected the result, but obviously proof that the outcome would have been different is not required. If an election is set aside, the Secretary is to conduct a new election.[35]

In three recent decisions, the Supreme Court has addressed procedural questions of significance in the administration of the provisions of the LMRDA concerning post-election attack by the Secretary of Labor.

In HODGSON v. LOCAL 6799, STEELWORKERS, 403 U.S. 333, 91 S. Ct. 1841, 29 L.Ed.2d 510 (1971), internal union appeals were exhausted by an unsuccessful candidate for local union president, who claimed that union facilities had been used to prepare campaign material for the incumbent president who was reelected. In his complaint to the Secretary of Labor, the member asserted not only that impropriety

33. LMRDA § 401(c).

34. LMRDA § 402(c).

35. Ibid.

but also a claim that it was unreasonable for the union to condition eligibility for office upon attendance at one-half of the local's meetings. Although the Secretary of Labor brought an action to challenge the election on both grounds—and the District Court found that Section 401(g) was violated by the use of union facilities to aid the incumbent (and thus ordered a new election)—the Supreme Court held that the Secretary could properly sue only for violations raised by the union member during his internal union appeals. The Court observed: "[T]he primary objective of the exhaustion requirement [in Section 402(a)] is to preserve the vitality of internal union mechanisms for resolving election disputes—mechanisms to decide complaints brought by members of the union themselves. To accept [the Secretary's] contention that a union member, who is aware of the facts underlying an alleged violation, need not first protest this violation to his union before complaining to the Secretary would be needlessly to weaken union self-government. Plainly [the Secretary's] approach slights the interest in protecting union self-regulation and is out of harmony with the congressional purpose reflected in § 402(a)." See Hodgson v. Local 734, Teamsters, 336 F.Supp. 1243 (N.D.Ill.1972): "[I]f the member presented an inartfully drawn protest to the union which can be said to cover several violations, the Secretary may litigate other claims arguably covered by the protest when the union can be charged with knowledge thereof under the heavy duty placed upon it by *Local 6799* to discern all various violations that a member might be asserting. * * * [T]he Secretary is allowed to litigate an alleged § 401 violation relating to and arising from the same series of transactions about which a union member did internally protest but which specific violation the member did not internally protest because of his ignorance of the facts as to the scope of the violations at the time that he filed his protest."

Later, the Court placed certain limitations upon the discretion of the Secretary in deciding not to bring a post-election action under Title IV of the LMRDA and in actually controlling any litigation brought. Although the Secretary asserted that his discretion not to bring an action to set aside a union election was not subject to judicial review, the Court held to the contrary in DUNLOP V. BACHOWSKI, 421 U.S. 560, 95 S.Ct. 1851, 44 L.Ed.2d 377 (1975). While conceding that the Secretary need not sue *whenever* the information before him suggests a suit *might* be successful, and that he may in deciding not to sue exercise his judgment about the probability of success, the Court held that a district court could review such action to assure that it is not arbitrary or capricious. To police this requirement, the Court held that the complainant was entitled to a statement of reasons from the Secretary to support his decision not to sue. Such a statement—setting forth the grounds of decision and the essential facts—would also "promote thought" by the Secretary and would compel him to "cover the relevant points and eschew irrelevancies." Judicial review, however, is to be sharply limited. The court is (except in "the rare case") simply to examine the statement of reasons to see whether on its face it "is so irrational as to constitute the decision arbitrary and capricious." There is to be no trial of any claim by the complainant that the Secretary lacks factual support for concluding that no violation occurred or that any violation did not affect the outcome of the election. Judicial scrutiny would go further only when the Secretary's action is "plainly beyond the bounds of the Act," such as an outright refusal to assume his enforcement responsibilities, or his prosecution of complaints in a constitutionally discriminatory manner.

In a third decision, TRBOVICH v. UNITED MINE WORKERS, 404 U.S. 528, 92 S.Ct. 630, 30 L.Ed.2d 686 (1972), the Court held that once the Secretary commences an action to set aside a union election, affected union members may intervene as parties. Although Section 402 of the LMRDA makes it clear that the only party who may sue to overturn an election already held is the Secretary of Labor—and the legislative history makes it clear that such lawsuits are not to be initiated by aggrieved union members—the Court concluded that it was not inconsistent to permit a union member to intervene in the Secretary's lawsuit. The Court held that Congress gave the Secretary the exclusive right to sue after elections for two reasons: "(1) to protect unions from frivolous litigation and unnecessary judicial interference with their elections, and (2) to centralize in a single proceeding such litigation as might be warranted with respect to a single election." Once the Secretary has screened out frivolous complaints and has consolidated all meritorious complaints in a single proceeding, there is no reason to believe Congress was opposed to participation by union members in the litigation. The Court, however, limited the participation of the intervening members to the presentation of evidence and argument in support of only those grounds for setting aside the union election which are mentioned in the Secretary's complaint; to permit the intervenor to assert additional grounds in the lawsuit "would be to circumvent the screening function assigned by statute to the Secretary" and would be to subject the union to claims determined by the Secretary to lack merit.

Though the foregoing provisions of the Act and Court decisions go far to guarantee free and fair union elections, they leave unsettled a number of important issues of election regulation. One of those issues—the relationship between Title IV and the guarantee of equal rights to vote and to nominate candidates under Section 101(a)—is treated in the following opinion of the Supreme Court.

CALHOON v. HARVEY

Supreme Court of the United States, 1964.
379 U.S. 134, 85 S.Ct. 292, 13 L.Ed.2d 190.

MR. JUSTICE BLACK delivered the opinion of the Court.

This case raises important questions concerning the powers of the Secretary of Labor and federal courts to protect rights of employees guaranteed by the Labor-Management Reporting and Disclosure Act of 1959.

The respondents, three members of District No. 1, National Marine Engineers' Beneficial Association, filed a complaint in Federal District Court against the union, its president and its secretary-treasurer, alleging that certain provisions of the union's bylaws and national constitution violated the Act in that they infringed "the right of members of defendant District No. 1, NMEBA, to nominate candidates in elections of defendant, which right is guaranteed to each member of defendant, and to each plaintiff, by Section 101(a) (1) of the LMRDA * * *." It was alleged that § 102 of Title I of the Act gave the District Court jurisdiction to adjudicate the controversy. The union bylaws complained of deprived a member of the right to nominate anyone for office but himself. The national constitution in turn provided that no member could be eligible for nomination or election to a full-time elective office unless he had been a member of the national union for five years and had served 180 days or more of seatime in each of two of the preceding three years on vessels covered by collective bargaining agreements with the national or its subsidiary bodies. On the basis of these allegations respondents asked that the union be enjoined from preparing for or conducting any election until it revised its system of elections so as to afford each of its members a fair opportunity to nominate any persons "meeting fair and reasonable eligibility requirements for any or all offices to be filled by such election."

The union moved to dismiss the complaint on the grounds that (1) the court lacked jurisdiction over the subject matter, and (2) the complaint failed to state a claim upon which relief could be granted. The District Court dismissed for want of "jurisdiction," holding that the alleged conduct of the union, even if true, failed to show a denial of the equal rights of all members of the union to vote for or nominate candidates guaranteed by § 101(a) (1) of Title I of the Act, so as to give the District Court jurisdiction of the controversy under § 102. The allegations, said the court, showed at most imposition of qualifications of eligibility for nomination and election so restrictive that they might violate § 401(e) of Title IV by denying members a reasonable opportunity to nominate and vote for candidates. The District Court further held that it could not exercise jurisdiction to protect § 401(e) rights because § 402(a) of Title IV provides a rem-

edy, declared by § 403 to be "exclusive," authorizing members to vindicate such rights by challenging elections after they have been held,
and then only by (1) first exhausting all remedies available with the
union, (2) filing a complaint with the Secretary of Labor, who (3)
may, after investigating the violation alleged in the complaint, bring
suit in a United States District Court to attack the validity of the
election. The Court of Appeals reversed, holding that "the complaint
alleged a violation of § 101(a) (1) and that federal jurisdiction existed under § 102." 324 F.2d 486, 487. Because of the importance of
the questions presented and conflicting views in the courts of appeals
and the district courts, we granted certiorari, 375 U.S. 991.

Jurisdiction of the District Court under § 102 of Title I depends
entirely upon whether this complaint showed a violation of rights
guaranteed by § 101(a) (1), for we disagree with the Court of Appeals' holding that jurisdiction under § 102 can be upheld by reliance
in whole or in part on allegations which in substance charge a breach
of Title IV rights. An analysis and understanding of the meaning
of § 101(a) (1) and of the charges of the complaint is therefore essential to a determination of this issue. Respondents charge that the
bylaws and constitutional provisions referred to above infringed their
right guaranteed by § 101(a) (1) to nominate candidates. The result of their allegations here, however, is an attempt to sweep into
the ambit of their right to sue in federal court if they are denied
an equal opportunity to nominate candidates under § 101(a) (1), a
right to sue if they are not allowed to nominate anyone they choose
regardless of his eligibility and qualifications under union restrictions. But Title IV, not Title I, sets standards for eligibility and
qualifications of candidates and officials and provides its own separate and different administrative and judicial procedure for challenging those standards. And the equal-rights language of § 101(a)
(1) would have to be stretched far beyond its normal meaning to hold
that it guarantees members not just a right to "nominate candidates,"
but a right to nominate anyone without regard to valid union rules.
All that § 101(a) (1) guarantees is that

> every member of a labor organization shall have equal rights
> and privileges * * * to nominate candidates, to vote
> in elections or referendums of the labor organizations
> * * * and to participate in the deliberations and vot-
> ing * * * subject to reasonable rules and regulations
> in such organization's constitution and bylaws.

Plainly, this is no more than a command that members and classes
of members shall not be discriminated against in their right to nominate and vote. And Congress carefully prescribed that even this
right against discrimination is "subject to reasonable rules and regulations" by the union. The complaining union members here have
not been discriminated against in any way and have been denied no

privilege or right to vote or nominate which the union has granted to others. They have indeed taken full advantage of the uniform rule limiting nominations by nominating themselves for office. It is true that they were denied their request to be candidates, but that denial was not a discrimination against their right to nominate, since the same qualifications were required equally of all members. Whether the eligibility requirements set by the union's constitution and by-laws were reasonable and valid is a question separate and distinct from whether the right to nominate on an equal basis given by § 101 (a) (1) was violated. The District Court therefore was without juris-diction to grant the relief requested here unless, as the Court of Ap-peals held, the *"combined* effect of the eligibility requirements and the restriction to self-nomination" are to be considered in determining whether § 101 (a) (1) has been violated.

We hold that possible violations of Title IV of the Act regarding eligibility are not relevant in determining whether or not a district court has jurisdiction under § 102 of Title I of the Act. Title IV sets up a statutory scheme governing the election of union officers, fixing the terms during which they hold office, requiring that elections be by secret ballot, regulating the handling of campaign literature, re-quiring a reasonable opportunity for the nomination of candidates, authorizing unions to fix "reasonable qualifications uniformly impos-ed" for candidates, and attempting to guarantee fair union elections in which all the members are allowed to participate. Section 402 of Title IV, as has been pointed out, sets up an exclusive method for protecting Title IV rights, by permitting individual members to file a complaint with the Secretary of Labor challenging the validity of any election because of violations of Title IV. Upon complaint the Secretary investigates and if he finds probable cause to believe that Title IV has been violated, he may file suit in the appropriate district court. It is apparent that Congress decided to utilize the special knowledge and discretion of the Secretary of Labor in order best to serve the public interest. Cf. San Diego Building Trades Council v. Garmon, 359 U.S. 236, 242, 79 S.Ct. 773, 778. In so doing Congress, with one exception not here relevant,[36] decided not to permit individ-uals to block or delay union elections by filing federal court suits for violations of Title IV. Reliance on the discretion of the Secretary is in harmony with the general congressional policy to allow unions great latitude in resolving their own internal controversies, and, where that fails, to utilize the agencies of government most familiar with union problems to aid in bringing about a settlement through discus-sion before resort to the courts. Without setting out the lengthy leg-

---

36. Section 401(c) of the Act permits suits prior to election in the United States District Courts by any bona fide candidate for union office to enforce the rights, guaranteed by that section, to equal treatment in the distribution of campaign literature and access to membership lists. 73 Stat. 532, 29 U.S.C.A. § 481(c).

islative history which preceded the passage of this measure, it is sufficient to say that we are satisfied that the Act itself shows clearly by its structure and language that the disputes here, basically relating as they do to eligibility of candidates for office, fall squarely within Title IV of the Act and are to be resolved by the administrative and judicial procedures set out in that Title.

Accordingly, the judgment of the Court of Appeals is reversed and that of the District Court is affirmed.

It is so ordered.

MR. JUSTICE STEWART, whom MR. JUSTICE HARLAN joins, concurring.

This case marks the first interpretation by this Court of the significant changes wrought by the Labor-Management Reporting and Disclosure Act of 1959 increasing federal supervision of internal union affairs. At issue are subtle questions concerning the interplay between Title I and Title IV of that Act. In part, both seem to deal with the same subject matter: Title I guarantees "equal rights and privileges * * * to nominate candidates"; Title IV provides that "a reasonable opportunity shall be given for the nomination of candidates." Where the two Titles of the legislation differ most substantially is in the remedies they provide. If a Title I right is at issue, the allegedly aggrieved union member has direct, virtually immediate recourse to a federal court to obtain an adjudication of his claim and an injunction if his complaint has merit. 29 U.S.C.A. § 402. Vindication of claims under Title IV may be much more onerous. Federal court suits can be brought only by the Secretary of Labor, and then, only after the election has been held.   * * *

The Court precludes the District Court from asserting jurisdiction over this complaint by focusing on the fact that one of the [restrictions imposed by the union] speaks in terms of eligibility.[37] And since these are "possible violations of Title IV of the Act regarding eligibility" they "are not relevant in determining whether or not a district court has jurisdiction under § 102 of Title I of the Act." By this reasoning, the Court forecloses early adjudication of claims concerning participation in the election process. But there are occasions when eligibility provisions can infringe upon the right to nominate. Had the NMEBA issued a regulation that only Jesse Calhoon was eligible for office, no one could place great store on the right to self-nomination left to the rest of the membership.   * * *

After today, simply by framing its discriminatory rules in terms of eligibility, a union can immunize itself from pre-election attack in

37. An additional restriction applicable solely to the post of president required that all candidates for that office have served the union in some prior official capacity.

a federal court even though it makes deep incursions on the equal right of its members to nominate, to vote, and to participate in the union's internal affairs.   *   *   *

Nonetheless, the Court finds a "general congressional policy" to avoid judicial resolution of internal union disputes. That policy, the Court says, was designed to limit the power of individuals to block and delay elections by seeking injunctive relief. Such an appraisal might have been accurate before the addition of Title I, but it does not explain the emphasis on prompt judicial remedies there provided. In addition to the injunctive relief authorized by § 102 and the savings provisions of § 103, § 101(a) (4) modifies the traditional requirement of exhausting internal remedies before resort to litigation. Even § 403 is not conclusive on the elimination of pre-election remedies. At the least, state court actions may be brought in advance of an election to "enforce the constitution and bylaws." And as to federal courts, it is certainly arguable that recourse through the Secretary of Labor is the exclusive remedy only after the election has been held.[38] By reading Title I rights so narrowly, and by construing Title IV to foreclose absolutely pre-election litigation in the federal courts, the Court sharply reduces meaningful protection for many of the rights which Congress was so assiduous to create.[39] By so simplifying the tangled provisions of the Act, the Court renders it virtually impossible for the aggrieved union member to gain a hearing when it is most necessary—when there is still an opportunity to make the union's rules comport with the requirements of the Act.

My difference with the Court does not reach to the disposition of this particular case. Whether stated in terms of restrictions on the right to nominate, or in terms of limitations on eligibility for union office, I think the rules of a labor organization would operate illegally to curtail the members' equal right to nominate within the meaning of Title I only if those rules effectively distorted the basic democratic process. The line might be a shadowy one in some cases. But I think that in this case the respondents did not allege in their complaint nor demonstrate in their affidavits that this line was cross-

---

38. See Summers, Pre-Emption and the Labor Reform Act—Dual Rights and Remedies, 22 Ohio St.L.J. 119, 138–139 (1961). It would be strange indeed if only state courts were available to enforce the federal law created by the Act during the pre-election period.

39. The Court's reading of federal-court remedies available under Title I and Title IV is particularly restrictive because of the limited powers of the district judge once the balloting has occurred. Under § 401(c), the court is confined to setting the election aside only if "the violation of section 401 may have affected the outcome." For the aggrieved union member, this protection may be totally inadequate. The function of nominating a candidate is not always to gain the office. A faction may be vitally interested in appearing on the ballot merely to show that it is part of the political structure of the union. Under the Court's view, until such a faction approaches majority status, judicial relief in the federal courts will be absent. See Summers, Judicial Regulation of Union Elections, 70 Yale L.J. 1221, 1257 (1961).

ed. I would therefore remand the case to the District Court with directions to dismiss the complaint for failure to state a claim for relief.

MR. JUSTICE DOUGLAS would affirm the judgment of the Court of Appeals for the reasons stated in its opinion as reported in 324 F.2d 486.

_____

Problems for Discussion

1. Which of the two positions in the *Calhoon* case finds support in Section 403 of the LMRDA, which deals with remedies in union election cases?

2. After a union election was conducted, but before the ballots were tallied, one of the ballot boxes mysteriously disappeared for several hours. When the box reappeared and the votes were about to be tallied, several union members instituted an action in a federal court for an injunction to restrain the counting of ballots. The complaint alleged that the ballots in the temporarily missing box were tampered with, and either the ballots validly cast by the plaintiffs were removed from the box before it was returned or a completely new ballot box (with different ballots) was substituted. The plaintiffs base their claim for relief on Section 101(a)(1), asserting that the tampering has effectively deprived them of their right under that Section as members of the union to vote. The union officials named as defendants have moved to dismiss the action as beyond the jurisdiction of the federal district court. Should the motion to dismiss be granted? *Beckman* v. *Local 46, Bridge Workers*, 314 F.2d 848 (7th Cir. 1963).

3. Shortly before an election for the presidency of the United Mine Workers International, membership lists were being used to send to all members copies of the union newspaper known as the Journal. The paper, like all union newspapers, was sent to members on a regular basis and, like all union newspapers, it tended to focus on the constructive activities of incumbent union officials. As the election approached, more coverage than usual—pictorially and textually—was given in the Journal to the activities of the incumbent International president, Tony Boyle; for some five months, no reference was made to the activities of Jock Yablonski, who was running against Boyle. While Yablonski concedes that the Journal's format is not materially different from that of the past, or from that of other union newspapers, he claims that the LMRDA requires the union to cease discriminating by using the Journal as a campaign instrument for Boyle. Claiming that delay until the Secretary of Labor can sue after the election will be an inadequate remedy, Yablonski brings an action in the federal district court (asserting jurisdiction under Sections 401(c) and 501 of the LMRDA) seeking a preliminary injunction against the union requiring the Journal to provide sufficient coverage in future issues for Yablonski's positions and actions, to give Yablonski equal space in the Journal until the election is held, and to print copy supplied by Yablonski for the next two issues. Should the district court

issue such an injunction? Could comparable relief be secured at the suit of the Secretary of Labor after the election in the event Boyle wins? Could the district court in advance of the election grant some other relief to Yablonski that would help him communicate directly with union members? *Yablonski* v. *United Mine Workers of America*, 305 F.Supp. 868 (D.D.C.1970).

LOCAL 3489, UNITED STEELWORKERS OF AMERICA v. USERY

Supreme Court of the United States, 1977.
429 U.S. 305, 97 S.Ct. 611, 50 L.Ed.2d 502.

MR. JUSTICE BRENNAN delivered the opinion of the Court.

The Secretary of Labor brought this action in the District Court for the Southern District of Indiana under § 402(b) of the Labor-Management Reporting and Disclosure Act of 1959 (LMRDA), 29 U.S.C.A. § 482(b), to invalidate the 1970 election of officers of Local 3489, United Steelworkers of America. The Secretary alleged that a provision of the Steelworkers' International Constitution, binding on the Local, that limits eligibility for local union office to members who have attended at least one-half of the regular meetings of the local for three years previous to the election (unless prevented by union activities or working hours), violated § 401(e) of the LMRDA, 29 U.S.C.A. § 481(e). The District Court dismissed the complaint, finding no violation of the Act. The Court of Appeals for the Seventh Circuit reversed. 520 F.2d 516 (1976). We granted certiorari to resolve a conflict between circuits over whether the Steelworkers' constitutional provision violates § 401(e). 424 U.S. 907, 96 S.Ct. 1100, 47 L.Ed.2d 311 (1976). We affirm.

I

At the time of the challenged election, there were approximately 660 members in good standing of Local 3489. The Court of Appeals found that 96.5% of these members were ineligible to hold office, because of failure to satisfy the meeting attendance rule. Of the 23 eligible members, nine were incumbent union officers. The Secretary argues, and the Court of Appeals held, that the failure of 96.5% of the local members to satisfy the meeting attendance requirement, and the rule's effect of requiring potential insurgent candidates to plan their candidacies as early as 18 months in advance of the election when the reasons for their opposition might not have yet emerged,[40] established that the requirement has a substantial anti-

---

40. Regular meetings were held on a monthly basis. Thus, in order to attend half of the meetings in a three-year period, a previously inactive member desiring to run for office would have to begin attending 18 months before the election.

democratic effect on local union elections. Petitioners argue that the rule is reasonable because it serves valid union purposes, imposes no very burdensome obligation on the members, and has not proved to be a device that entrenches a particular clique of incumbent officers in the local.

II

The opinions in three cases decided in 1968 have identified the considerations pertinent to the determination whether the attendance rule violates § 401(e). Wirtz v. Hotel, etc. Employees Union Local 6, 391 U.S. 492, 88 S.Ct. 1743, 20 L.Ed.2d 763 (1968); Wirtz v. Bottle Glass Blowers Assn., 389 U.S. 463, 88 S.Ct. 643, 19 L.Ed.2d 705 (1968); Wirtz v. Local Union No. 125, Laborers Intern'l Union, 389 U.S. 477, 88 S.Ct. 639, 19 L.Ed.2d 716 (1968).

LMRDA does not render unions powerless to restrict candidacies for union office. The injunction in § 401(e) that "every member in good standing shall be eligible to be a candidate and to hold office" is made expressly "subject to * * * reasonable qualifications uniformly imposed." But "Congress plainly did not intend that the authorization * * * of 'reasonable qualifications * * *' should be given a broad reach. The contrary is implicit in the legislative history of the section and its wording * * *." Wirtz v. Hotel Employees, supra, 391 U.S., at 499, 88 S.Ct., at 1748. The basic objective of Title IV of LMRDA is to guarantee "free and democratic" union elections modeled on "political elections in this country" where "the assumption is that voters will exercise common sense and judgment in casting their ballots." Id., at 504, 88 S.Ct., at 1750. Thus, Title IV is not designed merely to protect the right of a union member to run for a particular office in a particular election. " * * * Congress emphatically asserted a vital public interest in assuring free and democratic union elections that transcends the narrower interest of the complaining union member." Wirtz v. Bottle Blowers Assn., supra, 389 U.S., at 475, 88 S.Ct., at 650; Wirtz v. Local 125, Laborers Intern'l Union, 389 U.S., at 483, 88 S.Ct., at 642. The goal was to "protect the rights of rank-and-file members to participate fully in the operation of their union through processes of democratic self-government, and, through the election process, to keep the union leadership responsive to the membership." Wirtz v. Hotel Employees, supra, 391 U.S., at 497, 88 S.Ct., at 1747.

Whether a particular qualification is "reasonable" within the meaning of § 401(e) must therefore "be measured in terms of its consistency with the Act's command to unions to conduct 'free and democratic' union elections." Wirtz v. Hotel Employees, supra, 391 U.S., at 499, 88 S.Ct., at 1748. Congress was not concerned only with corrupt union leadership. Congress chose the goal of "free and democratic" union elections as a preventive measure "to curb the possibility of abuse by benevolent as well as malevolent entrenched leadership." Id., at 503, 88 S.Ct., at 1750. *Hotel Employees* expressly held that that check was seriously impaired by candidacy qualifications which substantially deplete the ranks of those who might run in opposition to incumbents, and therefore held invalid the candidacy limitation there involved that restricted candidacies for certain positions to members who had previously held union office. "Plainly, given the objective of Title IV, a candidacy limitation which renders 93% of union members ineligible for office can hardly be a 'reasonable qualification.'" Id., at 502, 88 S.Ct., at 1749.

III

Applying these principles to this case, we conclude that here too the antidemocratic effects of the meeting attendance rule outweigh the interests urged in its support. Like the by-law in *Hotel Employees*, an attendance requirement that results in the exclusion of 96.5% of the members from candidacy for union office hardly seems to be a "reasonable qualification" consistent with the goal of free and democratic elections. A requirement having that result obviously severely restricts the free choice of the membership in selecting their leaders.

Petitioners argue however that the by-law held violative of § 401(e) in *Hotel Employees* differs significantly from the attendance rule here. Under the *Hotel Employees* by-law no member could assure by his own efforts that he would be eligible for union office, since others controlled the criterion for eligibility. Here, on the other hand, a member can assure himself of eligibility for candidacy by attending some 18 brief meetings over a three-year period. In other words, the union would have its rule treated not as excluding a category of member from eligibility, but simply as mandating a procedure to be followed by any member who wishes to be a candidate.

Even examined from this perspective, however, the rule has a restrictive effect on union democracy. In the absence of a permanent "opposition party" within the union, opposition to the incumbent leadership is likely to emerge in response to particular issues at different times, and member interest in changing union leadership is therefore likely to be at its highest only shortly before elections. Thus it is probable that to require that a member decide upon a potential candidacy at least 18 months in advance of an election when no issues exist to prompt that decision may not foster but discourage candidacies and to that extent impair the general membership's freedom to oust incumbents in favor of new leadership.

Nor are we persuaded by the Union's argument that the Secretary has failed to show an antidemocratic effect because he has not shown that the incumbent leaders of the Union became "entrenched" in their offices as a consequence of the operation of the attendance rule. The reasons why leaderships become entrenched are difficult to isolate. The election of the same officers year after year may be a signal that antidemocratic election rules have prevented an effective challenge to the regime, or might well signal only that the members are satisfied with their stewardship; if elections are uncontested, opposition factions may have been denied access to the ballot, or competing interests may have compromised differences before the election to maintain a front of unity. Conversely, significant turnover in offices may result from an open political process, or from a competition so limited as to offer no real opposition to an entrenched establishment. But Congress did not saddle the courts with the duty to search out and remove improperly entrenched union leaderships. Rather, Congress chose to guarantee union democracy by regulating not the results of a union's electoral procedure, but the procedure itself. Congress decided that if the elections are "free and democratic," the members themselves are able to correct abuse of power by entrenched leadership. Procedures that unduly restrict free choice among candidates are forbidden without regard to their success or failure in maintaining corrupt leadership.

Petitioners next argue that the rule is reasonable within § 401(e) because it encourages attendance at union meetings, and assures more qualified officers by limiting election to those who have demonstrated an interest in union affairs, and are familiar with union problems. But the rule has plainly not served these goals. It has obviously done little to encourage attendance at meetings, which continue to attract only a handful of members.[41] Even as to the more limited goal of encouraging the attendance of potential dissident candidates, very few members, as we have said, are likely to see themselves as such sufficiently far in advance of the election to be spurred to attendance by the rule.

As for assuring the election of knowledgeable and dedicated leaders, the election provisions of LMRDA express a congressional determination that the best means to this end is to leave the choice of leaders to the membership in open democratic elections, unfettered by arbitrary exclusions. Pursuing this goal by excluding the bulk of the membership from eligibility for office, and thus limiting the possibility of dissident candidacies, run directly counter to the basic premise of the statute. We therefore conclude that Congress, in guaranteeing every union member the opportunity to hold office, sub-

41. Attendance at Local 3489's meetings averages 47 out of approximately 660 members. There is no indication in the record that this total represents a significant increase over attendance before the institution of the challenged rule.

ject only to "reasonable qualifications," disabled unions from establishing eligibility qualifications as sharply restrictive of the openness of the union political process as is petitioners' attendance rule. * * *

Affirmed.

MR. JUSTICE POWELL, with whom MR. JUSTICE STEWART and MR. JUSTICE REHNQUIST join, dissenting.

* * * As this holding seems to me to be an unwarranted interference with the right of the union to manage its own internal affairs, I dissent. * * *

The Court * * *, relying heavily on *Hotel Employees*, holds that this rule imposes an unreasonable qualification, violative of § 401(e). *Hotel Employees* involved a "prior office" rule that limited candidates for local union office to members who previously had held elective union office. The Court's opinion in that case emphasized that the effect of the prior office rule was to disqualify 93.1% of the union's membership. In this case, the Government argues that *Hotel Employees* enunciated a *per se* "effects" rule, requiring invalidation of union elections whenever an eligibility rule disqualifies all but a small percentage of the union's membership. Although the Court today does not in terms adopt a *per se* "effects" analysis, it comes close to doing so. The fact that 96.5% of Local 3489's members chose not to comply with its rule was given controlling weight.

In my view, the Court has extended the reach of *Hotel Employees* far beyond the holding and basic rationale of that case. Indeed, the rule there involved was acknowledged to be a sport— "virtually unique in trade union practice." Id., at 505, 88 S.Ct., at 1751. It was a rule deliberately designed, as intimated by the Court's opinion, to entrench union leadership. Id., at 499, 88 S.Ct., at 1748. Moreover, the general effect of the rule in *Hotel Employees* was predictable at the time the rule was adopted. By limiting eligibility to members who held or previously had held elective office, the disqualification of a large proportion of the membership was a purposeful and inevitable effect of the structure of the rule itself. The attendance rule before the Court today has no comparable feature. No member is precluded from establishing eligibility. Nor can the effect of the rule be predicted, as any member who demonstrates the requisite interest in union affairs is eligible to seek office. In short, the only common factor between the prior office rule in *Hotel Employees* and that before the Court today is the similarity in the percentage of ineligible members. But in one case the effect was predetermined for the purpose of perpetuating control of a few insiders, whereas here the effect resulted from the free choice—perhaps the indifference—of the rank and file membership.

* * * [I believe that the union's attendance rule, at least facially, serves] legitimate and meritorious union purposes: (i) encouraging attendance at meetings; (ii) requiring candidates for office to demonstrate a meaningful interest in the union and its affairs; and (iii) assuring that members who seek office have had an opportunity to become informed as to union affairs. One may argue that requiring attendance at 18 of the 36 meetings prior to the election goes beyond what may be necessary to serve these purposes. But this is a "judgment call" best left to the unions themselves absent a stronger showing of potential for abuse than has been made in this case.

The record in this case is instructive. Twenty-three members were eligible to run for office in the 1970 election. These were members who were nominated and who also had complied with the attendance requirement. The record does not show, and indeed no one knows, how many members were eligible under the rule but who were not nominated. Three candidates competed for the office of president, four for the three trustee offices, and six ran unopposed for the remaining offices. Of the 10 officers elected, six were incumbents. Nonincumbents were elected to the offices of vice president, treasurer, recording secretary, and the minor office of guide. There was no history of entrenched leadership and no evidence of restrictive union practices precluding free and democratic elections. Indeed, the record is to the contrary. Five different presidents had been elected during the preceding 10 years, and an estimated 40 changes in officers had occurred in the course of four separate elections. Bernard Frye, who initiated this case by complaint to the Secretary, won the presidency in an election subsequent to 1970 and thereafter lost it.

In the final analysis, respondent, which bears the burden of proving that the rule is "unreasonable," rests its entire case on a facial attack upon the attendance rule itself, an attack supported by a statistical "effects test" that at best is ambiguous and one that could invalidate almost any attendance requirement that served legitimate union purposes. In my view, the respondent has failed to prove that the rule is unreasonable. For these reasons, I would reverse the judgment of the Court of Appeals.

WIRTZ v. LOCAL 153, GLASS BOTTLE BLOWERS ASS'N, 389 U.S. 463, 88 S.Ct. 643, 19 L.Ed.2d 705 (1968). The Secretary of Labor brought suit to void a local union election and direct a new election under his supervision on the basis of a member's complaint that the union violated Section 401(e) by its bylaw requiring as a prerequisite to run for union office that a member have attended at least 75% of the Local's regular meetings in the two years' prior to the election.

The union argued that the case was mooted because the next biennial local union election had already been conducted while the suit was still being appealed. On certiorari, *held,* the decision of the Court of Appeals declaring the Secretary's action moot is reversed. The union "argues that granting the Secretary's relief after a supervening election would terminate the new officers' tenure prematurely on mere suspicion." Congress, however, concluded that there was a substantial risk that officials, once improperly elected, would exert enough influence over subsequent elections to perpetuate themselves or their supporters in office. "The only assurance that the new officers do in fact hold office by reason of a truly fair and democratic vote is to do what the Act requires, rerun the election under the Secretary's supervision." In concluding that it would serve no practical purpose to void an old election after the terms of office conferred therein had been terminated by a new election, the Court of Appeals "seems to view the Act as designed merely to protect the right of a union member to run for a particular office in a particular election. But the Act is not so limited, for Congress emphatically asserted a vital public interest in assuming free and democratic union elections that transcends the narrower interest of the complaining union member."

Problems for Discussion

1. The Steelworkers now require, as a condition of eligibility for office, attendance at one-third of the meetings which the member could have attended in the twenty-four months preceding an election. Will that rule withstand attack under the LMRDA? Is there *any* reasonable rule which a union can lawfully adopt to assure that its candidates for office will be familiar with the operations and affairs of the union? If that union purpose will normally be inadequate to shelter candidacy requirements, will any other purpose suffice?

2. Given the emphasis of the Court in *Steelworkers Local 3489* upon the percentage, pure and simple, of union members disqualified for candidacy, can a union know with any confidence at the time it promulgates requirements for candidates whether those requirements will be valid? How, if at all, might such "guesswork" be eliminated?

3. Plaintiff brought suit in a federal district court for a temporary injunction to prevent the holding of an election scheduled to take place a few days later for the office of District Director in District 20 of the United Steelworkers Union. In his complaint plaintiff alleged that he was president and a member in good standing of Local 1211 of the Steelworkers and that he was qualified under its constitution to be a candidate for the office of District Director of District 20. The complaint further stated that the defendant Steelworkers, by the provisions of its constitution, had chosen to permit the nomination for office of District Director by the vote of local unions within the District, requiring, however, that a person be chosen by five local unions in order to go on the District ballot. The complaint further alleged that the constitution of the union did not establish any

detailed procedure for the conduct of nominations for the office of District Director. However, plaintiff alleged that his name was placed in nomination at meetings in various locals. An immediate *viva voce* vote was taken by the members present at the meetings, and plaintiff was defeated in each of the seven locals in which his name was entered. The evidence further showed that the incumbent was nominated in all thirty-five locals in District 20.

The evidence indicated that the nomination procedures followed at the meeting of Local 1211 were reasonably typical and that what happened there happened in many of the other locals with regard to the election under discussion. Local 1211 had over 11,000 qualified members. In accordance with the Steelworkers' constitution, local members were given at least one week's notice of a nomination meeting. This notice was, however, a posted notice at the union hall. The meeting itself took place in the regular union hall. The union hall used by Local 1211 did not seat over five to six hundred, and only some three hundred members were present in the union hall for the meeting in question. The names of the plaintiff and the incumbent nominee were put forward, and an immediate vote was taken at which the incumbent was the victor. During the hours set for the meeting, one-third of the membership was at work and unable to attend.

Should the district court enjoin the election under Section 101 of the LMRDA? Could a state court enjoin the election? If suit had been brought by the Secretary of Labor after the completion of the election, pursuant to Title IV of the LMRDA, should the district court set the election aside? See *Mamula* v. *United Steelworkers of America*, 198 F.Supp. 652 (W.D. Pa.1961), rev'd 304 F.2d 108 (3d Cir.), cert. denied 371 U.S. 823 (1962).

V. CORRUPTION AND RELATED ABUSES [1]

HIGHWAY TRUCK DRIVERS LOCAL 107 v. COHEN

United States District Court, Eastern District of Pennsylvania, 1960.
182 F.Supp. 608, affirmed 284 F.2d 162 (3d Cir. 1960), cert. denied
365 U.S. 833 (1961).

Opinion of the District Court

CLARY, DISTRICT JUDGE. This is a private suit brought under the recently enacted Labor Management Reporting and Disclosure Act of 1959, Public Law 86–257 (hereinafter referred to as the "Act"), 29 U.S.C.A. § 401 et seq. That Act establishes a fiduciary responsibility on the part of officers of a labor organization [§ 501(a)], and further provided for a suit in a Federal district court to enforce these

---

1. See Clark, The Fiduciary Duties of Union Officials Under Section 501 of the LMRDA, 52 Minn.L.Rev. 437 (1967); Note, The Fiduciary Duty of Union Officers Under the LMRDA: A Guide to the Interpretation of Section 501, 37 N.Y.U.L.Rev. 486 (1962).

responsibilities [§ 501(b)]. The present suit has been brought under § 501(b) to enforce certain of these duties.

The moving parties are nine rank-and-file members of Highway Truck Drivers and Helpers, Local 107, of the International Brotherhood of Teamsters, Chauffeurs, Warehousemen and Helpers of America (hereinafter referred to as "Local 107"), who were given leave by this Court on November 12, 1959 to file a complaint against the defendants, the governing officers of Local 107. The complaint charged the defendants with a continuing mass conspiracy to cheat and defraud the union of large sums of money—the conspiracy alleged to have begun in 1954 and continued to the present time.

The defendants have yet to answer these very serious charges. Having been unsuccessful in first opposing the plaintiffs' petition for leave of this Court to sue,[2] defendants now move to have the complaint dismissed. They are supported in this motion by counsel for Local 107, which has been allowed to intervene as a party defendant. This motion to dismiss is presently before the Court along with the plaintiffs' prayer for a preliminary injunction to prohibit the defendants from using union funds to defray the legal costs and other expenses being incurred by the defendants (and several other members of Local 107) in the defense of civil and criminal actions brought against them in the Courts of Pennyslvania and also the present suit in our own Court. The charges in these cases, in essence, grow out of the alleged activities of the defendants complained of here. The question of the preliminary injunction will be taken up after we resolve the motion to dismiss the complaint. * * *

The defendants' contention that those alleged wrongs which occurred *prior* to the enactment of § 501 can not alone constitute a basis for recovery under that section, must be accepted. Aside from the fact that the plaintiffs have not attempted to meet this contention, the principle that a statute which creates a new substantive right or duty will not, in the absence of clear legislative intent to the contrary, be construed to apply restrospectively, is too well established to admit of argument. * * *

To avoid the effect of this conclusion plaintiffs' attorney has astutely advanced the somewhat novel contention that §§ 157 and 158(a) (3) of Title 29 U.S.C.A. (popularly referred to as the Taft-Hartley Act) create an independent basis for recovery in this action. Since the Taft-Hartley Act became law on June 23, 1947 it would, of course, if applicable here, dispel any problem of retrospective application. However, we are convinced that it is not applicable and that the plaintiffs' argument must fail.

2. § 501(b) specifically provides that "No such proceeding shall be brought except upon leave of the court obtained upon verified application and for good cause shown * * *".

Generally speaking the sections of the Taft-Hartley Act relied upon by the plaintiffs recognize under federal law the right of employees to organize unions and further makes it an unfair labor practice for an employer to discriminate in regard to the hiring or tenure of employment *except* that they may discriminate against an employee for nonpayment of union dues, (i. e., § 158(a) (3) recognizes the right of a union and an employer to enter a union shop agreement whereby a new employee must within 30 days join the union or lose his job.)

From this, plaintiffs argue that the employee under a collective bargaining agreement containing this union shop clause (which clause is contained in a great majority of Local 107's contracts) must pay dues to the union in order to retain his job *as a result of the specific command of federal law*. Having reached this point, they maintain that it necessarily follows that the union and its officers must use the dues money they thus receive by virtue of federal law to further proper union objectives and not for purely private gain. This they argue is a federally created duty concomitant with the federally created right to exact dues. To strengthen this argument plaintiffs' counsel points to a series of Supreme Court cases beginning with Steele v. Louisville & Nashville Railroad Co., 1944, 323 U.S. 192, 65 S.Ct. 226, 89 L.Ed. 173, and Tunstall v. Brotherhood of Locomotive Firemen & Enginemen, 1944, 323 U.S. 210, 65 S.Ct. 235, 89 L.Ed. 187, which they maintain bear out this conclusion. * * *

[T]he Steele case and all of those following it which the plaintiffs have cited, deal with problems arising *directly* out of the union's activity in the process of collective bargaining, (i. e., most of them involved actions to declare discriminatory collective bargaining agreements void). The Steele case, which is the prototype of this line of cases, was decided by the Supreme Court upon an interpretation of the specific language of the Railway Labor Act. They interpreted the word "represent", used in the Act, to mean "represent fairly" and that the Act thus prohibited discrimination *in collective bargaining activity*—the very subject which both the Railway Labor Act and the Taft-Hartley Act purport to regulate. Nowhere in their complaint do the plaintiffs allege that Local 107 has in any way discriminated against them in its collective bargaining activity. On the other hand, the Taft-Hartley Act nowhere attempts to regulate the *use of union funds*. Because of this important distinction, we feel that the holding in this line of cases is not applicable here.

* * * [I]t is important to understand the reach of [the plaintiffs'] argument. If accepted, it would create federal jurisdiction in every suit wherein a single union member alleged that a particular union expenditure was made for a purpose not germane to collective bargaining. It is submitted that such a sweeping expansion of federal jurisdiction is not justified by a proper inter-

pretation of the Taft-Hartley Act or the Railway Labor Act. To say that by enacting these laws Congress intended to open the federal courts to such a vast area of litigation does not appear to us well-founded and, as defendants point out, no such jurisdiction has been recognized in the many years that these Acts have been in existence. It would appear that so long as a union performs its purpose of representing the employee in a fair and reasonable way in its collective bargaining capacity, the fact that they may incidentally spend union moneys for a noncollective bargaining purpose affords no right of action under §§ 157 or 158(a)(3) of the Taft-Hartley Act. If such expenditures should reach the point where they actually interfere with such fair and reasonable representation in collective bargaining, a different question might arise.

     * * * There is a more obvious reason why the plaintiffs' theory is of no avail here. The rights which § 158(a)(3) of the Taft-Hartley Act confer, as well as the corresponding duties imposed by it (whatever we might hold them to be) are rights and duties conferred upon the collective bargaining unit, i. e., *the union*. They are not conferred upon the individual officers of that union. Therefore, the plaintiffs really must argue that a federal law which confers numerous rights upon a *union*, must necessarily impose strict duty upon its *individual officers* not to spend the union's money for noncollective bargaining purposes. This does not follow. The language in the opinions relied upon by the plaintiffs speak [sic] in terms of the "duty of the union". Yet the whole tenor of the plaintiffs' complaint makes it evident that this suit is against the individual officers of Local 107 and not against the union. In their brief in opposition to Local 107's motion to intervene, the plaintiffs specifically state that "The Union itself * * * has no standing as a party litigant" since the plaintiffs appear as trustees ad litem for the union.

     Nor do we view this as a mere technicality which has been corrected by the Court's Order allowing the union to intervene as a party defendant. It is evident that the plaintiffs' claim here is not against the union. The acts complained of were not acts of the union done on its behalf by an acting officer. If anything, they are acts done in flagrant breach of duty. If they were in fact done, they were done for the defendant's own personal gain *at the expense of the union*. In such a suit against private individuals, the Taft-Hartley Act clearly does not confer federal jurisdiction. * * *

     If the only matter before the Court were the motion to dismiss discussed above, the Court might be disposed to grant the motion. However, there is another facet to the case which prevents the dismissal of the action. That facet relates to the motion for a preliminary injunction to prohibit the defendants from using union funds to defray the expense of legal fees in civil and criminal actions which have been brought against them in the Courts of Pennsylvania as well as to defray legal costs of the present action. The charges in those cases, in essence, grow out of alleged misappropriation of funds by the officers, and the plaintiffs maintain that such expenditures are in violation of the fiduciary duties imposed upon officers of a labor union by Section 501(a) of the Act, supra, and that unless such expenditures are enjoined the union will suffer irreparable harm thereby.

Shortly after the effective date of the Act and the institution of suits, criminal and civil, in the local Courts against the defendants, the union at a regular monthly meeting, with few dissenting votes, adopted a resolution authorizing the union to bear "Legal costs of such actions [against the officers] which are in reality not directed at our officers but are directed at us, the members of Local 107, our good contracts, our good wages and our good working conditions."

The question, therefore, which faces us is: Does the expenditure of union funds to pay for legal fees in the defense of both criminal and civil actions brought against the various defendant officers for an alleged conspiracy to cheat and defraud their union of large sums of money constitute a breach of that fiduciary duty imposed upon them by Section 501(a), supra, notwithstanding the purported authorization of such expenditures by a resolution of the union membership passed at a regular union meeting?

At the hearing on the preliminary injunction, it was brought out that within the limit of some four or five weeks after the adoption of the resolution the union, pursuant to the resolution, paid upwards of $25,000 to the attorneys representing the defendants. It is also clear that counsel for the union has advised the officers that such expenditures are proper. We are, therefore, with the payment of those large sums of money already accomplished and threatened further payments about to occur, in a position factually to pass upon the merits of the plaintiffs' contention.[3] * * *

Section 501, with which we are particularly concerned, is entitled "Fiduciary responsibility of officers of labor organizations." This section * * * attempts to define in the broadest terms possible the duty which the new federal law imposes upon a union official. Congress made no attempt to "codify" the law in this area. It appears evident to us that they intended the federal courts to fashion a new federal labor law in this area, in much the same way that the federal courts have fashioned a new substantive law of collective bargaining

---

3. There has been no showing on the part of the defendants, nor was it argued in defendants' brief, that defendants are responsible persons who would be able to reimburse the union for funds expended in their behalf. The sums involved are neither nominal nor minimal and in the circumstances the Court holds that a showing of irreparable harm (assuming the illegality of the payments) has been established.

contracts under § 301(a) of the Taft-Hartley Act, 29 U.S.C.A. § 185 (a). See Textile Workers Union of America v. Lincoln Mills, 1957, 353 U.S. 448, 77 S.Ct. 923, 1 L.Ed.2d 972. In undertaking this task the federal courts will necessarily rely heavily upon the common law of the various states. Where that law is lacking or where it in any way conflicts with the policy expressed in our national labor laws, the latter will of course be our guide.

We turn then to Section 501, not expecting to find a detailed command or prohibition as to the particular act complained of, but rather to find a general guide which, properly developed, will lead us to an answer. We feel that that answer here must be in plaintiffs' favor.

In determining whether or not the expenditures now sought to be enjoined violate the fiduciary responsibility of an officer of a labor organization we must necessarily determine the legal effect of the September 20th Resolution. This goes to the heart of the present problem and appears to be the main ground on which the defendants seek to avoid the injunction.

The plaintiffs assert that the Resolution authorizing such expenditures is encompassed within the express prohibition of § 501(a) against any "general exculpatory resolution". Although not expressly purporting to absolve the defendants of guilt, plaintiffs argue that the Resolution *in effect* does just this. Unfortunately the Act does not define the phrase "general exculpatory resolution".

The defendants take issue with the plaintiffs' interpretation. They maintain that the Resolution should be taken at face value, i. e., as a pledge of the union's faith in their officers and a pledge of financial aid to defend suits which are in reality directed at the union movement. They point to several remarks made in Congress which make it clear that this provision was not intended to restrict in any way the right of the membership to give a grant of authority—which they allege is all that the September 20th Resolution does.

A plain reading of the last sentence in § 501(a) leads me to agree with the defendants, at least in their conclusion. On the other hand, it is not necessary for a resolution to read "The officers are hereby absolved of all responsibility created by the Act" before a court will strike it down as "exculpatory" under § 501(a). Nor must a court accept at face value the stated purpose of a resolution when reason and common sense clearly dictate a different purpose. Nevertheless in my interpretation of § 501(a), the Resolution under discussion is *not* one "purporting to relieve any [officer] of liability for breach of the duties declared by this section * * *."

We must distinguish between a resolution which purports to *authorize* action which is beyond the power of the union to do and for that reason in violation of § 501(a) when done by an officer (such as the present Resolution) and a resolution which purports to *relieve* an officer of liability for breach of the duties declared in § 501(a). At times this distinction may be a fine one. Very often the result will be the same. Nevertheless we feel that such a distinction should be made here unless the "exculpatory" provision is to be read as a mere "catch-all" phrase.[4]

We turn then to the question of whether the September 20th Resolution is valid, i. e., conforms with the law of Pennsylvania and the Federal Labor laws. See International Union of Operating Engineers, A.F.L.-C.I.O. v. Pierce, Tex.Civ.App., 1959, 321 S.W.2d 914, at page 917–918. If it is inconsistent with either, we think it follows that the present expenditures by the defendants violate that provision in § 501 (a) which imposes upon them a strict duty to "expend [union funds] in accordance with its constitution and bylaws and any resolutions of the governing bodies adopted thereunder * * *."—since we read this sentence to authorize only those expenditures made pursuant to a *lawful* bylaw or resolution.

[The Court here concluded that the Resolution was beyond the powers of the Union as set forth in its Constitution and that the Local could not authorize the expenditures in question by a mere majority vote taken at a regular union meeting. Hence, the Resolution was not valid under Pennsylvania law.]

There is a further reason why the present Resolution is no defense here. Aside from its validity under Pennsylvania law, it is inconsistent with the aims and purposes of the Labor Management Reporting and Disclosure Act and violates the spirit of that Act. A stated purpose of the Act is "to *eliminate* * * * improper practices on the part of labor organizations * * * and their officers". (Emphasis added.) To allow a union officer to use the power and wealth of the very union which he is accused of pilfering, to defend himself against such charges, is totally inconsistent with Congress' effort to eliminate the undesirable element which has been uncovered in the labor-management field. To allow even a majority of members in that union to authorize such action when, if the charges made against these defendants are true, it is these very members whom the officers have deceived, would be equally inconsistent with the Act. If some of those members have not been deceived by the defendants, but because of the immediate gains in their income and working conditions which Local 107 has won for them, they are content to accept as officers anyone who produces immediate results, regardless of what other wrongs those officers may commit in so doing, this Court would still not feel constrained to bow to their will in the light of its duty both to those members of Local 107 who place honesty above material gain as well as to the

4. We might point out in this regard that the original Senate version of the Act (i. e., The Kennedy-Ives Bill, S. Rep.No.187, 86th Cong., First Session, 1959) contained a somewhat similar prohibition against any exculpatory resolution and *also* contained a clause prohibiting unions from paying the legal fees or fines of any person indicted or convicted of a violation of the Bill.

millions of others in the labor movement whose cause would be seriously injured by such an attitude.

Although we have not attempted to treat defendants' arguments individually, since we feel they are satisfactorily answered in this opinion, something should be said concerning their argument that the plaintiffs are here asking us to do that which Congress specifically refused to do when it failed to adopt Subsection 107(b) of the original Senate version of the Labor Bill (The Kennedy-Ives Bill), which specifically prohibited "both unions and employers from directly or indirectly paying or advancing the costs of defense, of any of their officers * * * who [are] indicted for * * * any violation of any provision of the Bill." S.Rep.No.187, 86th Cong., First Session, 1959, U.S.Code Cong. and Adm.News 1959, p. 2318. * * * [T]here are reasons why we are not persuaded by their argument here.

First, the language contained in the Kennedy-Ives Bill is much broader than our holding in the present case. It is essential to an understanding of our position in this case that this point be made clear. That section quoted above would foreclose financial aid by the union to an officer in suits under the Act, under *any* circumstances. In our case we have expressly limited our holding *to the facts before us*. In the light of all of these facts we do not feel that the several actions brought against the defendants involve any question of sufficient interest to Local 107 to warrant their expending large sums of union money to pay the legal costs of the defendants in these suits. That Congress refused to foreclose the right of a union under *any* circumstances to lend financial aid to an officer when sued under any section of the Kennedy-Ives Bill is not, we feel, a strong argument for the conclusion that under *no* circumstances could a union be prohibited from lending financial aid to an accused officer.

Second, in none of the cases cited by the defendants to support their argument as to the conclusion to be drawn from the omission of Section 107(b) were there two distinct bills involved. Here the Act finally passed by Congress (with modification) was the Landrum-Griffin House Bill and not the Kennedy-Ives Senate Bill. Strictly speaking, the Conference Committee did not amend the final Bill as to the provision in question, since it was never contained in it to begin with. Had the Kennedy-Ives Bill ultimately been adopted with Section 107(b) deleted, the defendants' argument would be more convincing.

Finally, even assuming that Congress intended to leave a union free to use its funds for the purpose of paying its officers legal expenses in actions brought against them under the new Act, if under the law of Pennsylvania, the state in which the union membership contractual relationship arose, such expenditures are illegal, a union officer could not consistent with his duty to the union (which duties ultimately flow from its Constitution) expend union funds for this purpose. This would follow unless we interpret the omission of this prohibition as creating an affirmative federal right in a union to so spend its funds, which right is intended to supersede any state law to the contrary. We flatly reject such an interpretation of the new Act. * * *

Opinion of the Court of Appeals

PER CURIAM. * * * In contesting the application for preliminary injunction the defendants relied on a resolution of the local purportedly authorizing the expenditures complained of. Judge Clary in a carefully considered opinion held that although the resolution was not within the prohibition of the last sentence of Section 501(a), above quoted, it was nevertheless invalid because it authorized action beyond the powers of the union as derived from its constitution and was inconsistent with the aims and purposes of the Labor Management Reporting and Disclosure Act. He specifically stated that: "This ruling in no way attempts to pass upon the question of whether or not Local 107 may with propriety, by appropriate resolution, reimburse its officers for their legal expenses in the event they are exonerated from any wrongdoing in connection with the handling of union funds involved in the actions presently pending." [182 F.Supp. 622].

Our own examination of the record and the 1959 Act satisfies us that under the facts the district court here has acted in complete accord with the letter and spirit of the Labor Management Reporting and Disclosure Act.

The order of the district court will be affirmed.

HIGHWAY TRUCK DRIVERS LOCAL 107 v. COHEN, 215 F.Supp. 938 (E.D.Pa.1963), affirmed, 334 F.2d 378 (3d Cir.1964). Between the effective date of the LMRDA and the issuance of the injunction in the first *Cohen* case, *supra,* almost $25,000 had been paid out in counsel fees on behalf of defendant officials. After the case returned to the district court for trial, the plaintiffs sought reimbursement on behalf of the union for these expenditures. On July 3, 1961, however, the International union had amended its constitution to authorize payment of all legal expenses on behalf of officers accused in civil or criminal suits provided certain procedures were followed. *Held,* the payments made must be restored to the union. "Defendant urges that while the Local 107 resolution was *ultra vires* when these opinions were written, it has subsequently been validated by an amendment to the constitution of the international union. This view is all right as far as it goes, but it completely disregards the statement in 284 F.2d at page 164 which says that the resolution was 'invalid because it authorized action beyond the powers of the union as derived from its constitution *and was inconsistent with the aims and purposes of the Labor-Management Reporting and Disclosure Act.* * * *' This clearly establishes the Act as the primary basis for prohibiting payment of the defendants' attorney fees. Judge Clary was merely adding another string to his bow in holding the payments to be *ultra vires.* Assuming that string was broken by the constitutional amendment, without any doubt the Act itself is sufficient reason for requiring defendant to repay the money in question. The Act seeks to prevent exploitation of the union by union officers and by an unscrupulous majority. How can the salutary effect of the Act be attained by this court if payment of defendants' legal costs are paid in any case where officers are charged with acts inimical to the union? The union could secure its own legal representation and pay therefor from the union treasury. If defendants and an unprincipled majority of the union members are allowed to mix a defense of the union with a defense of those charged with looting the union, assuming the charges are true, the Act would be emasculated. * * *" On appeal, *held,* the decision of the district court is affirmed. "That abortive attempt to validate the illegal 1959 resolution, could not of course in 1961 legitimize the 1959 payments which have been held to have been wrongful. And the action of the International was just as inconsistent with Section 501 of the Labor Management Act as was the Local's ill conceived resolution."

HOLDEMAN v. SHELDON, 204 F.Supp. 890 (S.D.N.Y.1962), affirmed 311 F.2d 2 (2d Cir.1962). The president of a local union brought action under Section 501 of the LMRDA against two officers of the union for making unauthorized salary payments to two persons who were not union employees. The complaint alleged: (1) that the officers were not authorized by the union constitution to execute the checks in question, and (2) that the money was paid for services never performed. The defendants controverted both allegations. The district court granted plaintiff's motion to enjoin the defendants from using counsel employed by the union under an annual retainer to defend them and also denied the union's motion to intervene and file a common answer with the defendants. "[A] blanket condemnation of intervention in cases of this type is not warranted. However, in the instant case, it seems clear that the union has no interest other than the protection of the two defendants. * * * Counsel for the proposed intervenors earnestly contended during the argument and in briefs that this case would be defended at no extra cost to the union since counsel is paid on an annual retainer. The court does not accept this argument as persuasive. Although cost to the union is a factor, more important is the idea that in a suit of this type a person who is charged with a violation of his fiduciary responsibility to the union should not be given the opportunity to overwhelm his opponent by putting at his disposal the power and resources of the union. The evils which Sec. 501 was designed to cure would often continue unchecked if a union official was to be permitted to use the power of the union to protect himself whenever he is accused of a wrongful act. It could very well be that the officer so charged with the offense is in a position to control the union machinery." On appeal, *held*, the judgment of the district court is affirmed. In a per curiam opinion the court of appeals declared: "We specifically note approval of the court's suggestion that on motions for injunctions of this sort, the district court should, after a preliminary hearing if necessary, determine whether the plaintiff has made a reasonable showing that he is likely to succeed, and whether the conduct of the defendants is in conflict with the interests of the Union. This, in combination with a policy of permitting a union to reimburse a defendant if he is successful in his defense, or perhaps even where his actions were based on a reasonable judgment as to appropriate procedures and do not evidence bad faith, should provide sufficient financial protection of union officials against nuisance suits."

In addition to providing regulations and safeguards pertaining to elections, union discipline and individual rights, the LMRDA contains a number of other provisions designed to eliminate abuses disclosed during the McClellan Committee hearings.[5] Certain of these provisions, requiring the filing of various sorts of information, are founded on the premise that public opinion and democratic processes within the union can curb much abuse if information concerning union activities is systematically collected and made available. Other provisions in the LMRDA, however, operate more directly by simply prohibiting certain types of conduct on the part of union officials.

A. DISCLOSURE OF INFORMATION

Section 201(a) of the LMRDA requires every labor organization to file with the Secretary of Labor information setting forth, *inter alia:* the name and address of the organization; the names of its officers; the initiation fees and dues that it charges; its procedures with regard to membership qualifications, financial audits, selection of officers, discipline of members and officers, etc. Section 201(b) requires the filing of information setting forth the assets and liabilities of the organization (specifying all receipts of any kind), the emoluments, both direct and indirect, received by union officers; loans received by any officer, employee or member; and loans extended by the organization to any business enterprise and other disbursements made. Pursuant to Section 201(c), all the information referred to above must be made avail-

5. For general discussions see Aaron, The Labor-Management Reporting and Disclosure Act of 1959, 73 Harv.L.Rev. 581 (1960); Cox, Internal Affairs of Labor Unions Under the Labor Reform Act of 1959, 58 Mich.L.Rev. 819 (1960).

able to members of the union, and members are also given the right to examine all records and reports on which this information is based.

Since these filing requirements apply to all unions, there is some danger that an overwhelming load of paper work may be imposed upon small unions. Power is conferred upon the Secretary of Labor, however, to alleviate this problem by permitting any union to file simplified reports whenever this procedure will effectuate the purposes of the Act.

Filing requirements are also imposed upon officers and employees (other than clerical or custodial) of labor organizations. Section 202(a) provides that each such person shall file with the Secretary of Labor a report listing all income or other property received by himself, his spouse or minor child from any employers with whom his union deals, either commercially or as a bargaining representative. The effect of this provision is to compel disclosure of transactions which might involve the union official or employee in a conflict of interest.

Finally, Section 203 of the Act requires employers to report every payment or loan (and every agreement to make a payment or loan) to any official, agent or other representative of a labor union. Employers must also report any expenditure designed to interfere with or restrain or coerce employees in the exercise of their right to organize and bargain collectively. In addition, reports must be filed of any agreement with a labor relations consultant or other outside organization [6] whereby the latter undertakes to influence employees in the exercise of their right to organize and bargain collectively. Employers must also disclose any expenditures or agreements with outside consultants or organizations [7] designed to obtain information concerning the activities of employees or of a labor organization in connection with a labor dispute in which that employer is involved (unless the information is needed for use in an arbitration or in a court or administrative proceeding).

Section 209 of the Act imposes a fine of not more than ten thousand dollars or a prison term of not more than one year, or both, on anyone who wilfully violates Title II or who knowingly falsely represents a material fact or fails to disclose such a fact in his required reports or who wilfully conceals or destroys essential records. In addition, Section 210 empowers the Secretary of Labor to bring a civil action in federal district court to enjoin or otherwise remedy past or threatened violations of Title II. Enforcement of the various fil-

6. Section 203(e) exempts the employer from reporting payments to his officers, supervisors, and employees for their regular services.

7. Section 203(b) requires such consultants or organizations to report to the Secretary of Labor within thirty days concerning any arrangement with an employer to enter into any of the activities mentioned above.

ing requirements is facilitated by Section 601 which empowers the Secretary to inspect any records and question such persons as he considers necessary in order to determine whether any individual has violated, or is about to violate, any provision of the LMRDA (other than Title I or amendments made by the LMRDA of other statutes).

B. LIMITATIONS ON UNION OFFICIALS

In Title V of the LMRDA, various limitations are placed directly upon union officials. Of prime importance is Section 501(a) which states that it is the duty of all officers and representatives of a labor organization "taking into account the special problems and functions of a labor organization, to hold its money and property solely for the benefit of the organization and its members and to manage, invest and expend the same in accordance with its constitution and bylaws * * *." Some concern was voiced by union spokesmen that the effect of this provision might be to curtail various expenditures for a variety of economic and social objectives not directly connected with the aims and activities of the union making the donation. A careful reading of the section, however, together with its legislative history, suggests that save, perhaps, in extreme situations such as the *Cohen* case, supra, the law does not limit the purposes for which expenditures may be made so long as the expenditure conforms to the constitution and by-laws of the organization.

Section 501 goes on to make clear that each representative is under a duty not to acquire financial or other interests which conflict with his responsibilities to his union, and the final sentence of subsection (a) declares that no provision in the constitution or by-laws nor any resolution of the governing body of a union which seeks to circumvent the above-mentioned duties shall have legal validity. Section 501(b) provides that any member may sue a representative of his union for violating the duties set forth in Section 501(a) and may receive damages or an accounting or other appropriate relief. As a safeguard against harassing or frivolous suits, prior permission to bring suit must be sought from the court, and in order to satisfy the court the prospective plaintiff must make a showing of good cause. The final safeguard provided by Section 501 is set forth in subsection (c) which declares that any officer or employee of a union who embezzles or steals funds or other properties of his labor organization shall be punished by a fine of ten thousand dollars and/or imprisonment for five years.

Section 504(a) prohibits any person who has been a member of the Communist Party within the past five years or who has been convicted within the past five years of any one of several specified crimes from serving as an officer, representative or employee (other than clerical or custodial) of a labor organization. The constitutionality of section 504(a) was not altogether free from doubt, particularly the disqualification of persons who have been Communist Party members within the past five years. The Supreme Court had ruled that a union may be denied access to the National Labor Relations Board if its officials have not filed an affidavit denying membership or affiliation with the Communist Party. American Communications Assoc. v. Douds, 339 U.S. 382 (1950) (upholding the constitutionality of Section 9(h) of the National Labor Relations Act which has since been repealed). Nevertheless, Section 504(a) imposes a criminal penalty upon union officers violating this provision rather than an administrative restraint upon the union. Relying in part on this distinction, the Supreme Court declared Section 504(a) unconstitutional as a bill of attainder. United States v. Brown, 381 U.S. 437 (1965).

C. TRUSTEESHIPS [8]

Title III of the LMRDA deals with the problem of trusteeships. The constitutions of many international unions authorize the international officers to suspend the normal government of a constituent local union, assume control of its property, and conduct its affairs. Under some constitutions charges must be filed against the local and a hearing must be held before the international intervenes. Others allow the General President to take over a local without a hearing, subject to the approval of the General Executive Board after a hearing. Apparently there are still a few international unions which make no provision for a hearing.

Any thoughtful discussion of trusteeships must recognize their indispensability. Trusteeships provide one device by which international officers can keep the labor movement strong and free from subversion or corruption. Thus, a trusteeship may be imposed to prevent embezzlement or misuse of funds, to restore democracy to an autocratic local, to curb irresponsible strikes or contract violations by local leaders or to revivify a moribund organization.

Unfortunately trusteeships have also been a virulent source of political autocracy and financial corruption, and the abuses which have been perpetrated with the aid of this device are familiar to every student of labor history. There appear to be four chief motivations for the imposition of improper trusteeships.

8. Note, a Fair Hearing Requirement for Union Trusteeships Under the LMRDA, 40 U.Chi.L.Rev. 873 (1973); Beaird, Union Trusteeship Provisions of the Labor-Management Reporting and Disclosure Act of 1959, 2 Ga.L. Rev. 469 (1968).

(1) The opportunity to loot rich local treasuries has been a significant temptation.

(2) The desire to control the policies of a local union may stem from honorable motives but in a good many cases there has been evidence of a desire to use union position for personal advantage.

(3) Other trusteeships have been imposed in order to keep in office men friendly to the international union. The McClellan Committee reported that when a Teamsters' local in Pontiac, Michigan revolted against four officials who had been accused of extortion, the international put the local under the trusteeship of James Hoffa, who then appointed two of the four officials as business agents to run the affairs of the local.

(4) The imposition of a trusteeship may be a method of controlling an international convention. Frequently the trustee appoints the delegates of the local union under his control. Since the General President will name a trustee friendly to himself, the trustee may be expected to follow the president's suggestions in choosing delegates, and the delegates themselves will not be blind to their dependence upon the president's good will. With ten or twenty per cent of the membership in trusteeships the international officers would have a strong bloc of votes.

In order to curb the abuses of trusteeship, section 302 of the LMRDA declares that:

"Trusteeships shall be established and administered by a labor organization over a subordinate body only in accordance with the constitution and by laws of the organization which has assumed trusteeship over the subordinate body and for the purpose of correcting corruption or financial malpractice, assuring the performance of collective bargaining agreements or other duties of a bargaining representative, restoring democratic procedures or otherwise carrying out the legitimate objects of such labor organization."

In addition, section 303 prohibits the counting of any votes from trusteed locals in a convention or election of a national officer unless the delegates from such a local have been chosen by secret ballot in an election in which all local members in good standing were eligible to participate. Moreover, no funds may be transferred from the local to the national union in excess of the normal assessments levied upon other locals which are not in trusteeship. In order to facilitate the enforcement of these provisions, section 301(c) requires that every labor organization which assumes trusteeship must file a report with the Secretary of Labor within thirty days setting forth the reasons for the trusteeship, the means by which it is carried out, the extent of participation by the trusteed local in national conventions and elections, etc. Similar reports must be filed semi-

annually until the trusteeship is removed.   Any member or subordinate body of the union imposing a trusteeship may either sue in
a federal court or request investigation and suit by the Secretary
of Labor in order to enforce the rules set forth in sections 302 and
303.   If suit is brought, a trusteeship established in accord with the
constitution and by-laws of the union shall be presumed valid for
a period of eighteen months from the date of its establishment and
shall not be subject to attack "except upon clear and convincing proof
that the trusteeship was not established or maintained in good faith
for a purpose allowable under section 302."   After eighteen months,
the opposite presumption prevails.

Problem for Discussion

Local 1735 of the Brewery Bottlers Union has functioned as an autonomous local union for more than 75 years.   In 1953, Local 1735 and several
other sister locals became affiliated with the Teamsters.   In 1962, the Executive Board of the Teamsters announced that Local 1735 and seven other locals
would be merged into two large groups, a production local and a delivery
local.   The members of Local 1735 are violently opposed to the merger and
fear that their Local will lose its autonomy and become subject to officials
of the larger group who will simply carry out policies dictated by the International.   The International, however, declares that the "urgent need for today is a unified, powerful and streamlined organization; one that can successfully negotiate with the Industry and police the contracts after they are
signed;   *   *   *   Only this type of merged organization can hope to meet
the growing problems of automation, merger of companies and labor-saving
programs which threaten the job-security of every member of our local unions."   Can the members of Local 1735 prevent the merger under Section
302 of the LMRDA?   See *Brewery Bottlers, Local 1345 v. International
Brotherhood of Teamsters*, 202 F.Supp. 464 (E.D.N.Y.1962).

*

APPENDIX

FIRST NATIONAL MAINTENANCE CORP. v. NLRB

Supreme Court of the United States, 1981.
— U.S. —, 101 S.Ct. 2573, — L.Ed.2d —.

JUSTICE BLACKMUN delivered the opinion of the Court.

Must an employer, under its duty to bargain in good faith "with respect to wages, hours, and other terms and conditions of employment," §§ 8(d) and 8(a)(5) of the National Labor Relations Act, as amended (the Act), 29 U.S.C. §§ 158(d) and 158(a)(5), negotiate with the certified representative of its employees over its decision to close a part of its business? In this case, the National Labor Relations Board (the Board) imposed such a duty on petitioner with respect to its decision to terminate a contract with a customer, and the United States Court of Appeals, although differing over the appropriate rationale, enforced its order.

I

Petitioner, First National Maintenance Corporation (FNM), is a New York corporation engaged in the business of providing housekeeping, cleaning, maintenance, and related services for commercial customers in the New York City area. It supplies each of its customers, at the customer's premises, contracted-for labor force and supervision in return for reimbursement of its labor costs (gross salaries, FICA and FUTA taxes, and insurance) and payment of a set fee. It contracts for and hires personnel separately for each customer, and it does not transfer employees between locations.[1]

During the Spring of 1977, petitioner was performing maintenance work for the Greenpark Care Center, a nursing home in Brooklyn. Its written agreement dated April 28, 1976, with Greenpark specified that Greenpark "shall furnish all tools, equipment [*sic*], materials, and supplies," and would pay petitioner weekly "the sum of five hundred dollars plus the gross weekly payroll and fringe benefits." App. in No. 79–4167 (CA2), pp. 43, 44. Its weekly fee, however, had been reduced to $250 effective November 1, 1976. *Id.*, at 46.

---

1. The record does not show the precise dimension of petitioner's business. See 242 N.L.R.B. 462, 464 (1979). One of the owners testified that petitioner at that time had "between two and four" other nursing homes as customers. *Ibid.* The administrative law judge hypothesized, however: "This is a large Company. For all I know, the 35 men at this particular home were only a small part of its total business in the New York area." *Id.*, at 465.

[Footnote numbers have not been altered—ed.]

The contract prohibited Greenpark from hiring any of petitioner's employees during the term of the contract and for 90 days thereafter. *Id.*, at 44. Petitioner employed approximately 35 workers in its Greenpark operation.

Petitioner's business relationship with Greenpark, seemingly, was not very remunerative or smooth. In March 1977, Greenpark gave petitioner the 30 days' written notice of cancellation specified by the contract, because of "lack of efficiency." *Id.*, at 52. This cancellation did not become effective, for FNM's work continued after the expiration of that 30-day period. Petitioner, however, became aware that it was losing money at Greenpark. On June 30, by telephone, it asked that its weekly fee be restored at the $500 figure and, on July 6, it informed Greenpark in writing that it would discontinue its operations there on August 1 unless the increase were granted. *Id.*, at 47. By telegram on July 25, petitioner gave final notice of termination. *Id.*, at 48.

While FNM was experiencing these difficulties, District 1199, National Union of Hospital and Health Care Employees, Retail, Wholesale and Department Store Union, AFL–CIO (the union), was conducting an organization campaign among petitioner's Greenpark employees. On March 31, 1977, at a Board-conducted election, a majority of the employees selected the union as their bargaining agent. On July 12, the union's vice president, Edward Wecker, wrote petitioner, notifying it of the certification and of the union's right to bargain, and stating: "We look forward to meeting with you or your representative for that purpose. Please advise when it will be convenient." *Id.*, at 49. Petitioner neither responded nor sought to consult with the union.

On July 28, petitioner notified its Greenpark employees that they would be discharged 3 days later. Wecker immediately telephoned petitioner's secretary-treasurer, Leonard Marsh, to request a delay for the purpose of bargaining. Marsh refused the offer to bargain and told Wecker that the termination of the Greenpark operation was purely a matter of money, and final, and that the 30-days' notice provision of the Greenpark contract made staying on beyond August 1 prohibitively expensive. *Id.*, at 79–81, 83, 85–86, 94. Wecker discussed the matter with Greenpark's management that same day, but was unable to obtain a waiver of the notice provision. *Id.*, at 91–93, 98–99. Greenpark also was unwilling itself to hire the FNM employees because of the contract's 90-day limitation on hiring. *Id.*, at 100–101, 106–107. With nothing but perfunctory further discussion, petitioner on July 31 discontinued its Greenpark operation and discharged the employees. *Id.*, at 110–116.

The union filed an unfair labor practice charge against petitioner, alleging violations of the Act's §§ 8(a)(1) and (5). After a hearing held upon the Regional Director's complaint, the administrative law judge made findings in the union's favor. Relying on *Ozark Trailers, Inc.*, 161 N.L.R.B. 561 (1966), he ruled that petitioner had failed to satisfy its duty to bargain concerning both the decision to terminate the Greenpark contract and the effect of that change upon the unit employees. * * * The National Labor Relations Board adopted the administrative law judge's findings without further analysis * * *.

The United States Court of Appeals for the Second Circuit, with one judge dissenting in part, enforced the Board's order, although it adopted an analysis different from that espoused by the Board. 627 F.2d 596 (1980). The Court of Appeals reasoned that no *per se* rule could be formulated to govern an employer's decision to close part of its business. Rather, the court said, § 8(d) creates a *presumption* in favor of mandatory bargaining over such a decision, a presumption that is rebuttable "by showing that the purposes of the statute would not be furthered by imposition of a duty to bargain," for example, by demonstrating that "bargaining over the decision would be futile," or that the decision was due to "emergency financial circumstances," or that the "custom of the industry, shown by the absence of such an obligation from typical collective bargaining agreements, is not to bargain over such decisions." *Id.*, at 601–602.

The Court of Appeal's decision in this case appears to be at odds with decisions of other Courts of Appeals, some of which decline to require bargaining over any management decision involving "a major commitment of capital investment" or a "basic operational change" in the scope or direction of an enterprise, and some of which indicate that bargaining is not mandated unless a violation of § 8(b) (3) (a partial closing motivated by antiunion animus) is involved. The Court of Appeals for the Fifth Circuit has imposed a duty to bargain over partial closing decisions. See *NLRB v. Winn-Dixie Stores, Inc.*, 361 F.2d 512, cert. denied, 385 U.S. 935, 87 S.Ct. 295, 17 L.Ed.2d 215 (1966). The Board itself has not been fully consistent in its rulings applicable to this type of management decision.

Because of the importance of the issue and the continuing disagreement between and among the Board and the Courts of Appeals, we granted certiorari. —— U.S. ——, 101 S.Ct. 854, 66 L.Ed.2d 798 (1981).

II

* * * Although parties are free to bargain about any legal subject, Congress has limited the mandate or duty to bargain to matters of "wages, hours, and other terms and conditions of employment." * * * Congress deliberately left the words "wages, hours, and other terms and conditions of employment" without further defini-

tion, for it did not intend to deprive the Board of the power further to define those terms in light of specific industrial practices.[14]

Nonetheless, in establishing what issues must be submitted to the process of bargaining, Congress had no expectation that the elected union representative would become an equal partner in the running of the business enterprise in which the union's members are employed. Despite the deliberate openendedness of the statutory language, there is an undeniable limit to the subjects about which bargaining must take place:

> "Section 8(a) of the Act, of course, does not immutably fix a list of subjects for mandatory bargaining. . . . But it does establish a limitation against which proposed topics must be measured. In general terms, the limitation includes only issues that settle an aspect of the relationship between the employer and the employees." *Chemical & Alkali Workers v. Pittsburgh Plate Glass Co.*, 404 U.S. 157, 178, 92 S.Ct. 383, 397, 30 L.Ed.2d 341 (1971).

See also *Ford Motor Co. v. NLRB*, 441 U.S. 488, 99 S.Ct. 1842, 60 L.Ed. 2d 420 (1979); *Fibreboard Paper Products Corp. v. NLRB*, 379 U.S. 203, 85 S.Ct. 398, 13 L.Ed.2d 233 (1964); *Teamsters v. Oliver*, 358 U.S. 283, 79 S.Ct. 297, 3 L.Ed.2d 312 (1959).

Some management decisions, such as choice of advertising and promotion, product type and design, and financing arrangements,

---

14. In enacting the Labor Management Relations Act, 1947, Congress rejected a proposal in the House to limit the subjects of bargaining to
"(i) [w]age rates, hours of employment, and work requirements; (ii) procedures and practices relating to discharge, suspension, lay-off, recall, seniority, and discipline, or to promotion, demotion, transfer and assignment within the bargaining unit; (iii) conditions, procedures, and practices governing safety, sanitation, and protection of health at the place of employment; (iv) vacations and leaves of absence; and (v) administrative and procedural provisions relating to the foregoing subjects." H.R. 3020 § 2(11), 80th Cong., 1st Sess. (1947).

The adoption, instead, of the general phrase now part of § 8(d) was clearly meant to preserve future interpretation by the Board. See H.R.Rep. No. 245, 80th Cong., 1st Sess., 71 (1947) (minority report) ("The appropriate scope of collective bargaining cannot be determined by a formula; it will inevitably depend upon the traditions of an industry, the social and political climate at any given time, the needs of employers and employees, and many related factors. What are proper subject matters for collective bargaining should be left in the first instance to employers and trade-unions, and in the second place, to any administrative agency skilled in the field and competent to devote the necessary time to a study of industrial practices and traditions in each industry or area of the country, subject to review by the courts. It cannot and should not be strait-jacketed by legislative enactment."); H.R.Conf.Rep. No. 510, 80th Cong., 1st Sess., 34–35 (1947). U.S. Code Cong.Serv.1947 p. 1135. Specific references in the legislative history to plant closings, however, are inconclusive. See 79 Cong.Rec. 7673, 9682 (1935) (comments of Sen. Walsh and Rep. Griswold).

have only an indirect and attenuated impact on the employment relationship. See *Fibreboard*, 379 U.S., at 223, 85 S.Ct., at 409 (Stewart, J., concurring). Other management decisions, such as the order of succession of layoffs and recalls, production quotas, and work rules, are almost exclusively "an aspect of the relationship" between employer and employee. *Chemical Workers*, 404 U.S., at 178, 92 S.Ct., at 397. The present case concerns a third type of management decision, one that had a direct impact on employment, since jobs were inexorably eliminated by the termination, but had as its focus only the economic profitability of the contract with Greenpark, a concern under these facts wholly apart from the employment relationship. This decision, involving a change in the scope and direction of the enterprise, is akin to the decision whether to be in business at all, "not in [itself] primarily about conditions of employment, though the effect of the decision may be necessarily to terminate employment." *Fibreboard*, 379 U.S., at 223, 85 S.Ct., at 409 (Stewart, J., concurring). Cf. *Textile Workers v. Darlington Co.*, 380 U.S. 263, 268, 85 S.Ct. 994, 998, 13 L.Ed.2d 827 (1965) ("an employer has the absolute right to terminate his entire business for any reason he pleases"). At the same time, this decision touches on a matter of central and pressing concern to the union and its member employees: the possibility of continued employment and the retention of the employees' very jobs. See *Brockway Motor Trucks, Etc. v. NLRB*, 582 F.2d 720, 735–736 (CA3 1978); *Ozark Trailers, Inc.*, 161 N.L.R.B. 561, 566–568 (1966).

Petitioner contends it had no duty to bargain about its decision to terminate its operations at Greenpark. This contention requires that we determine whether the decision itself should be considered part of petitioner's retained freedom to manage its affairs unrelated to employment.[15] The aim of labeling a matter a mandatory subject of bargaining, rather than simply permitting, but not requiring, bargaining, is to "promote the fundamental purpose of the Act by bringing a problem of vital concern to labor and management within the framework established by Congress as most conducive to industrial peace," *Fibreboard*, 379 U.S., at 211, 85 S.Ct., at 403. The concept of mandatory bargaining is premised on the belief that collective discussions backed by the parties' economic weapons will result in decisions that are better for both management and labor and for society as a whole. *Ford Motor Co.*, 441 U.S., at 500–501, 99 S.Ct., at 1851; *Borg-Warner*, 356 U.S., at 350, 78 S.Ct., at 723 (condemning employer's proposal of "ballot" clause as weakening the collective-

15. There is no doubt that petitioner was under a duty to bargain about the results or effects of its decision to stop the work at Greenpark, or that it violated that duty. Petitioner consented to enforcement of the Board's order concerning bargaining over the effects of the closing and has reached agreement with the union on severance pay. App. to No. 79–4167 (CA2), at 21–22.

bargaining process). This will be true, however, only if the subject proposed for discussion is amenable to resolution through the bargaining process. Management must be free from the constraints of the bargaining process [17] to the extent essential for the running of a profitable business. It also must have some degree of certainty beforehand as to when it may proceed to reach decisions without fear of later evaluations labeling its conduct an unfair labor practice. Congress did not explicitly state what issues of mutual concern to union and management it intended to exclude from mandatory bargaining. Nonetheless, in view of an employer's need for unencumbered decision-making, bargaining over management decisions that have a substantial impact on the continued availability of employment should be required only if the benefit, for labor-management relations and the collective bargaining process, outweighs the burden placed on the conduct of the business.

The Court in *Fibreboard* implicitly engaged in this analysis with regard to a decision to subcontract for maintenance work previously done by unit employees. Holding the employer's decision a subject of mandatory bargaining, the Court relied not only on the "literal meaning" of the statutory words, but also reasoned:

> "The Company's decision to contract out the maintenance work did not alter the Company's basic operation. The maintenance work still had to be performed in the plant. No capital investment was contemplated; the Company merely replaced existing employees with those of an independent contractor to do the same work under similar conditions of employment. Therefore, to require the employer to bargain about the matter would not significantly abridge his freedom to manage the business." 379 U.S., at 213, 85 S.Ct., at 404.

The Court also emphasized that a desire to reduce labor costs, which it considered a matter "peculiarly suitable for resolution within the collective bargaining framework," *id.*, at 214, 85 S.Ct., at 404, was at the base of the employer's decision to subcontract:

> "It was induced to contract out the work by assurances from independent contractors that economies could be derived by reducing the work force, decreasing fringe benefits, and eliminating overtime payments. These have long been re-

17. The employer has no obligation to abandon its intentions or to agree with union proposals. On proper subjects, it must meet with the union, provide information necessary to the union's understanding of the problem, and in good faith consider any proposals the union advances. In concluding to reject a union's position as to a mandatory subject, however, it must face the union's possible use of strike power. See generally Fleming, The Obligation to Bargain in Good Faith, 47 Va. L.Rev. 988 (1961).

garded as matters peculiarly suitable for resolution within the collective bargaining framework, and industrial experience demonstrates that collective negotiation has been highly successful in achieving peaceful accommodation of the conflicting interests." *Id.*, at 213–214, 85 S.Ct., at 404.

The prevalence of bargaining over "contracting out" as a matter of industrial practice generally was taken as further proof of the "amenability of such subjects to the collective bargaining process." *Id.*, at 211, 85 S.Ct., at 403.

With this approach in mind, we turn to the specific issue at hand: an economically-motivated decision to shut down part of a business.

III

A

Both union and management regard control of the decision to shut down an operation with the utmost seriousness. As has been noted, however, the Act is not intended to serve either party's individual interest, but to foster in a neutral manner a system in which the conflict between these interests may be resolved. It seems particularly important, therefore, to consider whether requiring bargaining over this sort of decision will advance the neutral purposes of the Act.

[handwritten margin note: Act is to be neutral]

A union's interest in participating in the decision to close a particular facility or part of an employer's operations springs from its legitimate concern over job security. The Court has observed: "The words of [§ 8(d)] * * * plainly cover termination of employment which * * * necessarily results" from closing an operation. *Fibreboard*, 379 U.S., at 210, 85 S.Ct., at 402. The union's practical purpose in participating, however, will be largely uniform: it will seek to delay or halt the closing. No doubt it will be impelled, in seeking these ends, to offer concessions, information, and alternatives that might be helpful to management or forestall or prevent the termination of jobs.[19] It is unlikely, however, that requiring bar-

---

19. We are aware of past instances where unions have aided employers in saving failing businesses by lending technical assistance, reducing wages and benefits or increasing production, and even loaning part of earned wages to forestall closures. See S. Slichter, J. Healy & E. Livernash, The Impact of Collective Bargaining on Management 845–851 (1960); C. Golden & H. Rutenberg, The Dynamics of Industrial Democracy 263–291 (1942). See also *United States Steel Workers*, *Etc. v. U. S. Steel Corp.*, 492 F.Supp. 1 (ND Ohio), aff'd in part and vacated in part, 631 F.2d 1264 (CA6 1980) (union sought to purchase failing plant); 104 Lab.Rel.Rep. 239 (1980) (employee ownership plan instituted to save company); *id.*, at 267–268 (union accepted pay cuts to reduce plant's financial problems). These have come about without the intervention of the Board enforcing a statutory requirement to bargain.

gaining over the decision itself, as well as its effects, will augment this flow of information and suggestions. There is no dispute that the union must be given a significant opportunity to bargain about these matters of job security as part of the "effects" bargaining mandated by § 8(a)(5). See, *e. g., NLRB v. Royal Plating & Polishing Co.*, 350 F.2d 191, 196 (CA3 1965); *NLRB v. Adams Dairy, Inc.*, 350 F.2d 108 (CA8 1965), cert. denied, 382 U.S. 1011, 86 S.Ct. 619, 15 L.Ed.2d 256 (1966). And, under § 8(a)(5), bargaining over the effects of a decision must be conducted in a meaningful manner and at a meaningful time, and the Board may impose sanctions to insure its adequacy. A union, by pursuing such bargaining rights, may achieve valuable concessions from an employer engaged in a partial closing. It also may secure in contract negotiations provisions implementing rights to notice, information, and fair bargaining. See BNA, Basic Patterns in Union Contracts 62–64 (9th ed., 1979).

Moreover, the union's legitimate interest in fair dealing is protected by § 8(a)(3), which prohibits partial closings motivated by anti-union animus, when done to gain an unfair advantage. *Textile Workers v. Darlington Co.*, 380 U.S. 263, 85 S.Ct. 994, 13 L.Ed.2d 827 (1965). Under § 8(a)(3) the Board may inquire into the motivations behind a partial closing. An employer may not simply shut down part of its business and mask its desire to weaken and circumvent the union by labeling its decision "purely economic."

Thus, although the union has a natural concern that a partial closing decision not be hastily or unnecessarily entered into, it has some control over the effects of the decision and indirectly may ensure that the decision itself is deliberately considered. It also has direct protection against a partial closing decision that is motivated by an intent to harm a union.

Management's interest in whether it should discuss a decision of this kind is much more complex and varies with the particular circumstances. If labor costs are an important factor in a failing operation and the decision to close, management will have an incentive to confer voluntarily with the union to seek concessions that may make continuing the business profitable. Cf. U. S. News & World Report, Feb. 9, 1981, p. 74; BNA, Labor Relations Yearbook–1979, p. 5 (UAW agreement with Chrysler Corp. to make concessions on wages and fringe benefits). At other times, management may have great need for speed, flexibility, and secrecy in meeting business opportunities and exigencies. It may face significant tax or securities consequences that hinge on confidentiality, the timing of a plant closing, or a reorganization of the corporate structure. The publicity incident to the normal process of bargaining may injure the possibility of a successful transition or increase the economic damage to the business. The employer also may have no feasible alternative to the closing, and even good-faith bargaining over it may be both futile and cause the employer additional loss.

There is an important difference, also, between permitted bargaining and mandated bargaining. Labeling this type of decision mandatory could afford a union a powerful tool for achieving delay, a power that might be used to thwart management's intentions in a manner unrelated to any feasible solution the union might propose. See Comment, "Partial Terminations"—A Choice between Bargaining Equality and Economic Efficiency, 14 UCLA L.Rev. 1089, 1103–1105 (1967). In addition, many of the cases before the Board have involved, as this one did, not simply a refusal to bargain over the decision, but a refusal to bargain at all, often coupled with other unfair labor practices. See, *e. g.*, *Electrical Products Div. of Midland-Ross Corp. v. NLRB*, 617 F.2d 977 (CA3 1980), cert. denied, —— U.S. ——, 101 S.Ct. 210, 66 L.Ed.2d 91 (1981); *NLRB v. Amoco Chemicals Corp.*, 529 F.2d 427 (CA5 1976); *Royal Typewriter Co. v. NLRB*, 533 F.2d 1030 (CA8 1976); *NLRB v. American Mfg. Co.*, 351 F.2d 74 (CA5 1965) (subcontracting); *Smyth Mfg. Co.*, 247 N.L.R.B. No. 164 (1980). In these cases, the employer's action gave the Board reason to order remedial relief apart from access to the decisionmaking process. It is not clear that a union would be equally dissatisfied if an employer performed all its bargaining obligations apart from the additional remedy sought here.

While evidence of current labor practice is only an indication of what is feasible through collective bargaining, and not a binding guide, see *Chemical Workers*, 404 U.S., at 176, 92 S.Ct., at 396, that evidence supports the apparent imbalance weighing against mandatory bargaining. We note that provisions giving unions a right to participate in the decisionmaking process concerning alteration of the scope of an enterprise appear to be relatively rare. Provisions concerning notice and "effects" bargaining are more prevalent. See II BNA, Collective Bargaining Negotiations and Contracts § 65:201–233 (1981); U. S. Dept. of Labor, Bureau of Labor Statistics, Bull. 2065, Characteristics of Major Collective Bargaining Agreements, January 1, 1978, pp. 96, 100, 101, 102–103 (charting provisions giving interplant transfer and relocation allowances; advance notice of layoffs, shutdowns, and technological changes; and wage-employment guarantees; no separate tables on decision-bargaining, presumably due to rarity). See also U. S. Dept. of Labor, Bull. No. 1425–10, Major Collective Bargaining Agreements, Plant Movement, Transfer, and Relocation Allowances (July 1969).

Further, the presumption analysis adopted by the Court of Appeals seems ill suited to advance harmonious relations between employer and employee. An employer would have difficulty determining beforehand whether it was faced with a situation requiring bargaining or one that involved economic necessity sufficiently compelling to obviate the duty to bargain. If it should decide to risk not bargaining, it might be faced ultimately with harsh remedies forcing it to pay large amounts of backpay to employees who likely would have been discharged regardless of bargaining, or even to consider reopening a failing operation. See, *e. g., Electrical Products Div. of Midland-Ross Corp.*, 239 N.L.R.B. 323 (1978), enf'd. 617 F.2d 977 (CA3 1980), cert. denied, —— U.S. ——, 101 S.Ct. 210, 66 L.Ed.2d 91 (1981). Cf. *Lever Brothers Co. v. International Chemical Workers Union*, 554 F.2d 115 (CA4 1976) (enjoining plant closure and transfer to permit negotiations). Also, labor costs may not be a crucial circumstance in a particular economically-based partial termination. See, *e. g., NLRB v. International Harvester Co.*, 618 F.2d 85 (CA9 1980) (change in marketing structure); *NLRB v. Thompson Transport Co.*, 406 F.2d 698 (CA10 1969) (loss of major customer). And in those cases, the Board's traditional remedies may well be futile. See *ABC Trans-National Transport, Inc. v. NLRB*, 642 F.2d 675 (CA3 1981) (although employer violated its "duty" to bargain about freight terminal closing, court refused to enforce order to bargain). If the employer intended to try to fulfill a court's direction to bargain, it would have difficulty determining exactly at what stage of its deliberations the duty to bargain would arise and what amount of bargaining would suffice before it could implement its decision. Compare *Burns Ford, Inc.*, 182 N.L.R.B. 753 (1970) (one week's notice of layoffs sufficient), and *Hartmann Luggage Co.*, 145 N.L.R.B. 1572 (1964) (entering into executory subcontracting agreement before notifying union not a violation since contract not yet final), with *Royal Plating & Polishing Co.*, 148 N.L.R.B. 545, 555 (1964), enf. denied, 350 F.2d 191 (CA3 1965) (two weeks' notice before final closing of plant inadequate). If an employer engaged in some discussion, but did not yield to the union's demands, the Board might conclude that the employer had engaged in "surface bargaining," a violation of its good faith. See *NLRB v. Reed & Prince Mfg. Co.*, 205 F.2d 131 (CA1), cert. denied, 346 U.S. 887, 74 S.Ct. 139, 98 L.Ed. 391 (1953). A union, too, would have difficulty determining the limits of its prerogatives, whether and when it could use its economic powers to try to alter an employer's decision, or whether, in doing so, it would trigger sanctions from the Board. See, *e. g., International Offset Corp.*, 210 N.L.R.B. 854 (1974) (union's failure to realize that shutdown was imminent, in view of successive advertisements, sales of equipment, and layoffs, held a waiver of right to bargain); *Shell Oil Co.*, 149 N.L.R.B. 305 (1965) (union waived its right to bargain by failing to request meetings when employer announced intent to transfer a few days before implementation).

We conclude that the harm likely to be done to an employer's need to operate freely in deciding whether to shut down part of its business purely for economic reasons outweighs the incremental benefit that might be gained through the union's participation in making the decision;[22] and we hold that the decision itself is *not* part of § 8(d)'s "terms and conditions," over which Congress has mandated bargaining.[23]

---

22. In this opinion we of course intimate no view as to other types of management decisions, such as plant relocations, sales, other kinds of subcontracting, automation, etc., which are to be considered on their particular facts. See, *e. g., International Ladies' Garment Workers Union v. NLRB*, 150 U.S.App.D.C. 71, 463 F.2d 907 (1972) (plant relocation predominantly due to labor costs); *Weltronic Co. v. NLRB*, 419 F.2d 1120 (CA6 1969), cert. denied, 398 U.S. 938, 90 S.Ct. 1841, 26 L.Ed.2d 270 (1970) (decision to move plant three miles); *Dan Dee West Virginia Corp.*, 180 N.L.R.B. 534 (1970) (decision to change method of distribution, under which employee-drivers became independent contractors); *Young Motor Truck Service, Inc.*, 156 N.L.R.B. 661 (1966) (decision to sell major portion of business). See also Schwarz, Plant Relocation or Partial Termination—The Duty to Decision-Bargain, 39 Ford.L.Rev. 81, 100–102 (1970).

23. Despite the contentions of *amicus* AFL–CIO our decision in *Order of Railroad Telegraphers v. Chicago & N. W. R. Co.*, 362 U.S. 330, 80 S.Ct. 761, 4 L.Ed.2d 774 (1960), does not require that we find bargaining over this partial closing decision mandatory. In that case, a union certified as bargaining agent for certain railroad employees requested that the railroad bargain over its decision to close down certain stations thereby eliminating a number of jobs. When the union threatened to strike over the railroad's refusal to bargain on this issue, the railroad sought an injunction in federal court. Construing the scope of bargaining required by § 2, First, of the Railway Labor Act, 45 U.S.C. § 152, the Court held that the union's effort to negotiate was not "an unlawful bargaining demand," 362 U.S., at 341, 80 S.Ct., at 767, and that the District Court was precluded from enjoining the threatened strike by § 4 of the Norris-LaGuardia Act, 29 U.S.C. § 104, which deprives federal courts of "jurisdiction to issue any restraining order or temporary or permanent injunction in any case involving or growing out of any labor dispute to prohibit any person or persons participating or interested in such dispute * * * from * * * [c]easing or refusing to perform any work * * *." Although the Court in part relied on an expansive interpretation of § 2, First, which requires railroads to "exert every reasonable effort to make and maintain agreements concerning rates of pay, rules, and working conditions," and § 13(c) of the Norris-LaGuardia Act, 29 U.S.C. § 113(c), defining "labor dispute" as "any controversy concerning terms or conditions of employment," its decision also rested on the particular aims of the Railway Labor Act and national transportation policy. See 362 U.S., at 336–338, 80 S.Ct., at 764–765. The mandatory scope of bargaining under the Railway Labor Act and the extent of the prohibition against injunctive relief contained in Norris-LaGuardia are not coextensive with the National Labor Relations Act and the Board's jurisdiction over unfair labor practices. See *Chicago & N. W. R. Co. v. Transportation Union*, 402 U.S. 570, 579, n. 11, 91 S.Ct. 1731, 1736, n. 11, 29 L.Ed.2d 187 (1971) ("parallels between the duty to bargain in good faith and duty to exert every reasonable effort, like all parallels between the NLRA and the Railway Labor Act, should be drawn with the utmost care and with full awareness of the differences between the statutory schemes"). Cf. *Boys Market, Inc. v. Retail Clerks*, 398 U.S. 235, 90 S.Ct. 1583, 26 L.Ed.2d 199 (1970); *Buffalo Forge Co. v. United Steelworkers of America*, 428 U.S. 397, 96 S.Ct. 3141, 49 L.Ed.2d 1022 (1976).

B

In order to illustrate the limits of our holding, we turn again to the specific facts of this case. First, we note that when petitioner decided to terminate its Greenpark contract, it had no intention to replace the discharged employees or to move that operation elsewhere. Petitioner's sole purpose was to reduce its economic loss, and the union made no claim of anti-union animus. In addition, petitioner's dispute with Greenpark was solely over the size of the management fee Greenpark was willing to pay. The union had no control or authority over that fee. The most that the union could have offered would have been advice and concessions that Greenpark, the third party upon whom rested the success or failure of the contract, had no duty even to consider. These facts in particular distinguish this case from the subcontracting issue presented in *Fibreboard*. Further, the union was not selected as the bargaining representative or certified until well after petitioner's economic difficulties at Greenpark had begun. We thus are not faced with an employer's abrogation of ongoing negotiations or an existing bargaining agreement. Finally, while petitioner's business enterprise did not involve the investment of large amounts of capital in single locations, we do not believe that the absence of "significant investment or withdrawal of capital," *General Motors Corp., GMC Truck & Coach Div.*, 191 N.L.R.B., at 952, is crucial. The decision to halt work at this specific location represented a significant change in petitioner's operations, a change not unlike opening a new line of business or going out of business entirely.

The judgment of the Court of Appeals, accordingly, is reversed and the case is remanded to that court for further proceedings consistent with this opinion.

It is so ordered.

JUSTICE BRENNAN, with whom JUSTICE MARSHALL joins, dissenting. * * *

As this Court has noted, the words "terms and conditions of employment" plainly cover termination of employment resulting from a management decision to close an operation. *Fibreboard Paper Products Corp. v. NLRB*, 379 U.S. 203, 210, 85 S.Ct. 398, 402, 13 L.Ed.2d 233 (1964). As the Court today admits, the decision to close an operation "touches on a matter of central and pressing concern to the union and its member employees." Moreover, as the Court today further concedes, Congress deliberately left the words "terms and conditions of employment" indefinite, so that the NLRB would be able to give content to those terms in light of changing industrial conditions. In the exercise of its congressionally-delegated authority and accumulated expertise, the Board has determined that an employer's decision to close part of its operations affects the "terms and conditions of employment" within the meaning of the Act, and is thus a mandatory subject for collective bargaining. *Ozark Trailers, Inc.,* 161 N.L.R.B. 561 (1966). Nonetheless, the Court today declines to defer to the Board's decision on this sensitive question of industrial relations, and on the basis of pure speculation reverses the judgment of the Board and of the Court of Appeals. I respectfully dissent.

The Court bases its decision on a balancing test. It states that "bargaining over management decisions that have a substantial impact on the continued availability of employment should be required only if the benefit, for labor-management relations and the collective-bargaining process, outweighs the burden placed on the conduct of the business." I cannot agree with this test, because it takes into account only the interests of *management;* it fails to consider the legitimate employment interests of the workers and their Union. Cf. *Brockway Motor Trucks v. NLRB,* 582 F.2d 720, 734–740 (CA3 1978) (balancing of interests of workers in retaining their jobs against interests of employers in maintaining unhindered control over corporate direction). This one-sided approach hardly serves "to foster in a neutral manner" a system for resolution of these serious, two-sided controversies.

Even if the Court's statement of the test were accurate, I could not join in its application, which is based solely on speculation. Apparently, the Court concludes that the benefit to labor-management relations and the collective-bargaining process from negotiation over partial closings is minimal, but it provides no evidence to that effect. The Court acknowledges that the Union might be able to offer concessions, information, and alternatives that might obviate or forestall the closing, but it then asserts that "[i]t is unlikely, however, that requiring bargaining over the decision * * * will augment this flow of information and suggestions." Recent experience, however, suggests the contrary. Most conspicuous, perhaps, were the negotiations between Chrysler Corporation and the United Auto Workers, which led to significant adjustments in compensation and benefits, contributing to Chrysler's ability to remain afloat. See Wall St. Journal, Oct. 26, 1979, at 3, col. 1. Even where labor costs are not the direct cause of a company's financial difficulties, employee concessions can often enable the company to continue in operation—if the employees have the opportunity to offer such concessions.*

---

* Indeed, in this case, the Court of Appeals found: "On the record, * * * there is sufficient reason to believe that, given the opportunity, the union might have made concessions, by accepting a reduction in wages or benefits (take-backs) or a reduction in the work force, which would in part or in

The Court further presumes that management's need for "speed, flexibility, and secrecy" in making partial closing decisions would be frustrated by a requirement to bargain. In some cases the Court might be correct. In others, however, the decision will be made openly and deliberately, and considerations of "speed, flexibility, and secrecy" will be inapposite. Indeed, in view of management's admitted duty to bargain over the effects of a closing, it is difficult to understand why additional bargaining over the closing itself would necessarily unduly delay or publicize the decision.

I am not in a position to judge whether mandatory bargaining over partial closings *in all cases* is consistent with our national labor policy, and neither is the Court. The primary responsibility to determine the scope of the statutory duty to bargain has been entrusted to the NLRB, which should not be reversed by the courts merely because they might prefer another view of the statute. *Ford Motor Co. v. NLRB*, 441 U.S. 488, 495–497, 99 S.Ct. 1842, 1848–1849, 60 L.Ed. 2d 420 (1979); see *NLRB v. Erie Resistor Corp.*, 373 U.S. 221, 236, 83 S.Ct. 1139, 1149, 10 L.Ed.2d 308 (1963). I therefore agree with the Court of Appeals that employers presumptively have a duty to bargain over a decision to close an operation, and that this presumption can be rebutted by a showing that bargaining would be futile, that the closing was due to emergency financial circumstances, or that, for some other reason, bargaining would not further the purposes of the National Labor Relations Act. 627 F.2d 596, 601 (CA2 1980). I believe that this approach is amply supported by recent decisions of the Board. *E. g., Brooks-Scanlon, Inc.*, 246 N.L.R.B. No. 76, 102 L.R.R.M. 1606 (1979); *Raskin Packing Co.*, 246 N.L.R.B. No. 15, 102 L.R.R.M. 1489 (1979); *M. & M. Transportation Co.*, 239 N.L.R.B. 73 (1978). With respect to the individual facts of this case, however, I would vacate the judgment of the Court of Appeals, and remand to the Board for further examination of the evidence. See *SEC v. Chenery Corp.*, 318 U.S. 80, 94–95, 63 S.Ct. 454, 462, 87 L.Ed. 626 (1943).

---

whole have enabled Greenpark to give FNM an increased management fee. At least, if FNM had bargained over its decision to close, that possibility would have been tested, and management would still have been free to close the Greenpark operation if bargaining did not produce a solution." 627 F.2d 596, 602 (CA2 1980).

INDEX

References are to Pages

INDEX

References are to Pages

LABOR–MANAGEMENT REPORTING AND DISCLOSURE ACT—Cont'd

Discipline of union officials, 1125–1131
Disclosure of information, 1186–1188
Elections, 1159–1176
Exhaustion of union remedies, 1154–1155
Expenditure of funds, 1176–1189
Fiduciary responsibilities, 1176–1189
Qualification for office, 1163–1176
Trusteeships, 1189–1191

LANDRUM–GRIFFIN ACT

See Labor-Management Reporting and Disclosure Act

LOCKOUTS

See also Discrimination
Bargaining lockout, 842–851
Business justification, 841–851
Defensive, 841–842
Multiemployer, 841–842
Offensive, 842–851

MAINTENANCE OF MEMBERSHIP

See Union Security

MANAGERIAL EMPLOYEES, 93–94

MULTIEMPLOYER BARGAINING

Bargaining units, 299–303
Lockouts, 841–842
Union coercion of employer representative, 305–306

NATIONAL EMERGENCY DISPUTES, 489–491

NATIONAL LABOR RELATIONS ACT

See also major headings
Constitutionality, 77–79
History, 69–79
Jurisdiction, see Jurisdiction of NLRB
Procedures, 104–113
See also Judicial Review
Election proceedings, see Election Proceedings
Unfair labor practice proceedings, 104–112

NATIONAL LABOR RELATIONS BOARD

See also major headings
Adjudication, 136–139
Administrative law judge, 107–108
Arbitration awards, deference to, see Jurisdiction of NLRB
Arbitration machinery, deferral to, see Jurisdiction of NLRB
General counsel, 105–113
Judicial review, see Judicial Review
Jurisdiction, see Jurisdiction of NLRB

NATIONAL LABOR RELATIONS BOARD—Cont'd

Procedures,
Election proceedings, see Election Proceedings
Rulemaking, 136–139
Unfair labor practice proceedings, 104–112
Regional office, 105–113
Remedies, see Remedies
Retroactive orders, 136–139, 860–861
Rulemaking, 136–139
Statistics on NLRB caseload, 106–107

NORRIS–LaGUARDIA ACT

See also Antitrust Laws; Injunctions; No-Strike Clause; Strike Injunctions
Arbitration clauses, 559
Collective bargaining agreements, 559, 605–624
History, 55–69
Labor exemption, 39–40, 44–55, 60–69
No-strike clauses, 605–624

NO–STRIKE CLAUSE

Federal Law, 605–624
Implied, 560–563
Injunction, 605–624
Section 301, pp. 560–563, 605–624

ORGANIZATIONAL PICKETING

See Recognition Picketing

PICKETING

See also Concerted Activities; Recognition Picketing; Secondary Boycotts; Strikes
Common law treatment, 17–32, 55–62
Common-situs picketing, 724–732
Constitutional protection, 675–696
Consumer picketing, 749–765
Economic strikes, see Strikes
Expedited election, 704–713
Information-picketing proviso to section 8(b)(7), pp. 707, 715–720
Organizational picketing, see Recognition Picketing
Primary situs and secondary situs, compared, 722–724
Publicity proviso to section 8(b)(4), pp. 749–765
Recognition picketing, see Recognition Picketing
Reserved gate picketing, 738–748
Secondary boycott, see Secondary Boycotts
Unprotected activities, see Concerted Activities
Violence, 18–31, 56, 58, 807–809

†